EXPERIENCING MANAGEMENT

Important Information!

The Evergreen On-line Series in Business Education

Experiencing Management

R. Dennis Middlemist

Colorado State University

www.experiencingmanagement.com

Your four-month subscription serial number
is enclosed.

THOMSON

SOUTH-WESTERN

THOMSON

SOUTH-WESTERN

Don't Throw This Out!
This is your access certificate.

This is your access certificate for Experiencing Management, online modules that are going to be important to your study of this text. The serial number below will allow you to enter the site and take advantage of all the study help available.

Here is how to register:

Go to www.experiencingmanagement.com

Click the "Register" button to enter your serial number.

Enter your serial number exactly as it appears below and select a user ID.

When prompted, select a password.

Record your password and user ID in a secure location.

Once registered you will always select the "Enter" button to access, choosing the "Access Certificate" entrance.

Serial Number: PPNMSOBPP3D2ZP

First Canadian Edition

MANAGEMENT

First Canadian Edition

MANAGEMENT

Chuck Williams
Texas Christian University

Alex Z. Kondra
Athabasca University

Conor Vibert
Acadia University

THOMSON

NELSON

Australia   Canada   Mexico   Singapore   Spain   United Kingdom   United States

THOMSON

NELSON

Management
First Canadian Edition
by Chuck Williams, Alex Z. Kondra,
and Conor Vibert

Editorial Director and Publisher:
Evelyn Veitch

Executive Editor:
Veronica Visentin

Marketing Manager:
Don Thompson

Senior Developmental Editor:
Joanne Sutherland

Permissions Coordinator:
Paula Joiner

Production Editor:
Wendy Yano

Copy Editor/Proofreader:
Wendy Thomas

Indexer:
Elizabeth Bell

Production Coordinator:
Hedy Sellers

Creative Director:
Angela Cluer

Interior Design:
Mike Stratton

Interior Design Modifications:
Tammy Gay

Cover Design:
Peter Papayanakis

Cover Image:
Cover left: Chad Baker/Ryan
McVay/PhotoDisc Green/Getty
Images; Cover right: Jason Reed/
Ryan McVay/PhotoDisc
Green/Getty Images

Compositor:
Susan Calverley

Printer:
Quebecor World Dubuque

**National Library of Canada
Cataloguing in Publication Data**

Williams, Chuck, 1959–
  Management / Chuck Williams,
Alex Z. Kondra, Conor Vibert.—
1st Canadian ed.

Includes bibliographical references
and index.
ISBN-13: 978-0-17-622322-9
ISBN-10: 0-17-622322-3

1. Management—Textbooks.
I. Kondra, Alex II. Vibert, Conor,
1962– III. Title.

HD31.W515 2004   658
C2003-907348-3

CONTENTS

Preface

If you walk down the aisle of the business section in your local bookstore (or surf the "Business" page at Amazon.ca), you'll find hundreds of books that explain precisely what companies need to do to be successful. Unfortunately, these books tend to be faddish, changing every few years. Lately, the best-selling business books have emphasized technology, leadership, and dealing with change, whereas ten years ago the hot topics were reengineering, going global, mergers, and management buyouts.

One thing that hasn't changed, though, and never will, is the importance of good management. Management is getting work done through others. Organizations can't succeed for long without it. Well-managed companies are competitive because their workforces are smarter, better trained, more motivated, and more committed. Furthermore, good management leads to satisfied employees who, in turn, provide better service to customers. Because employees tend to treat customers the same way that their managers treat them, good management can improve customer satisfaction. Finally, companies that practise good management consistently have greater revenues and profits than companies that don't.

In writing the first Canadian edition of *Management*, our goal was to develop a textbook that students would enjoy, that students would refer to for practical, theory-driven advice using Canadian and international examples, and that encourages students to put theory-driven knowledge into practice for themselves. In short, the ideas and concepts you'll learn about in this book can improve the performance of the organization and department where you work, can even help you solve job-related problems, and can improve your own job performance, even if you're not a manager.

So, welcome to *Management*, First Canadian Edition. Please take a few minutes to read the preface and familiarize yourself with the approach (combining theory with specific stories and examples), in *Management*. This is time well spent. After all, besides your instructor, this book will be your primary learning tool.

Approach of the Text

Say "theory" to college students and they assume that you're talking about complex, arcane ideas and terms that have nothing to do with the "real world," but which need to be memorized for a test and then forgotten (at least until the final exam). However, students needn't be wary of theoretical ideas and concepts. Theories are simply good ideas. And good theories are simply good ideas that have been tested through rigorous scientific study and analysis.

Where textbooks go wrong is that they stop at theory and read like dictionaries. Or they focus on theoretical issues related to research rather than practice. However, good management theories (i.e., good ideas) needn't be complex and arcane. In fact, the late Rensis Likert, an organizational psychologist, once said that there is nothing as practical as a good theory.

So, to make sure that you're exposed to good ideas (i.e., good theories), that you can refer to for practical, theory-driven advice, and that encourage you to put theory-driven knowledge into practice for yourselves, each chapter in this book contains many stories and examples that illustrate how managers are using management ideas in their organizations.

To be honest, much of the material in the following chapters is fairly standard, research-based information. You'll find it in most textbooks. Is it important for students to know this information? You bet! Is it likely that students will find this and the thousands of other pieces of theory and research-based facts throughout the book particularly compelling or interesting (and thus easier to learn)? Ah, there's the problem. However, what if we combined theory and research with specific, "real world" stories and examples that illustrated good or poor use of those theories? That is our strategy and we think you will enjoy reading about them.

The stories and examples you'll read in each chapter are relevant and up-to-date. You'll read about the strategic issues facing Sobeys as it grew from a small regional grocery chain to the second largest player in Canada. You'll read about the challenges facing Estelle Metayer in her attempts to establish a European beachhead for her small Competitive Intelligence firm, Competia Inc. You will also follow McDonald's efforts to run a profitable business while addressing the concerns of the animal rights organization, PETA. On average, each chapter has 25 to 30 stories or examples to help you understand how management concepts and theories are being used in the business world.

In short, both research and theory and stories and examples are important for effective learning. Therefore, this book contains hundreds of specific examples and stories to make management theories and ideas more interesting. So, to get more out of this book, read and understand the theories and theoretical ideas. Then read the stories or examples to learn how those ideas should or should not be used in practice. You'll find that both are current and up-to-date.

Acknowledgements

Let's face it; writing a textbook is a long and lonely process. It's surely among the most difficult (and rewarding) projects that we have ever tackled. And, as we sat in front of our computers on opposite sides of the country with a rough outline in front of us, it was easy at times to feel isolated. But, as we found out, a book like this doesn't get done without the help of many other talented people.

First, we'd like to thank the outstanding team from Nelson for the support (and patience) they provided while we developed this book. Pure and simple, everyone at Nelson has been great to work with throughout the entire project. Special thanks go to Joanne Sutherland who was our Senior Developmental Editor and with whom we had the most contact while writing the book. We'd also like to thank our Publisher, Evelyn Veitch, who brought us this wonderful opportunity. Also worthy of thanks are the Executive Editor of the book Veronica Visentin, our Marketing Manager, Don Thompson, our Copy Editor, Wendy Thomas, and our Production Editor, Wendy Yano. Thanks to all of you and here's to many more editions.

We'd like to thank an outstanding set of reviewers whose diligent and thoughtful comments helped shape this First Canadian Edition.

Dr. Beverly Linnell, Southern Alberta Institute of Technology (SAIT)
Robert E. Ankli, University of Guelph
Kristi Harrison, Centennial College
Chris Bovaird, University of Toronto
Jane Haddad, Seneca College
Jeff Young, Mount Saint Vincent University
George Stroppa, Douglas College
Monica Diochon, Saint Francis Xavier University
Judith Koch, Grant MacEwan College
Ed Leach, Dalhousie University
Dr. Colleen A. McKey, McMaster University
Dr. Lewie Callahan, Lethbridge Community College
Brian Harrocks, Algonquin College
Carol Ann Samhaber, Algonquin College
Les Lewchuck, Kwantlen University College
Ron Shay, Kwantlen University College
Kirk Bailey, Ryerson University
Joe Trubic, Ryerson University
Dr. John P. Logan, Ryerson University

The support package for the text was developed with the help of three outstanding colleagues. Special thanks go to Jeff Young of Mount Saint Vincent University for his work on the Test Bank and PowerPoint slides, to Ron Shay of Kwantlen University College for his work on the Study Guide, and to Tyler Chamberlin of the University of Ottawa for his contributions to the Student CD-ROM. Finally, our families deserve the greatest thanks of all for their love, patience, and support. Writing a textbook is an enormous project with incredible stresses and pressures on authors as well as their loved ones. However, throughout this project, our wives, Sonia and Janette, were unwavering in their support of our writing. Colin, Brendan, Jennifer, and Sean also deserve special thanks for their patience and for understanding why Dad was locked away at the computer for all of this time.

Conor Vibert   Alex Z. Kondra
Acadia University   Athabasca University

Text Features

Features of *Management*, First Canadian Edition

Management, First Canadian Edition, offers a wide variety of pedagogical features to help you learn and apply the concepts at hand. Take a few minutes to familiarize yourself with these features. Doing so will help you get more out of the book and your management class.

At the beginning of each chapter, you'll find a numbered **Chapter Outline**.

The outline is broken out into **numbered sections and subsections** and corresponds with the headings and subheadings within the chapter.

The numbered Chapter Outline also corresponds with the numbered **Learning Objectives**. There is one Learning Objective for each of the numbered sections in the chapter, and these are listed both at the beginning of the chapter and at the beginning of each major section.

Each section ends with a **Review** that effectively summarizes the concepts presented in that section of the chapter.

Together, the chapter outline, numbering system, learning objectives, section headings (which mark the beginning of a section), and section reviews (which mark the end of a section) allow you to break the chapter into smaller, self-contained sections that can be read in their entirety over several study sessions.

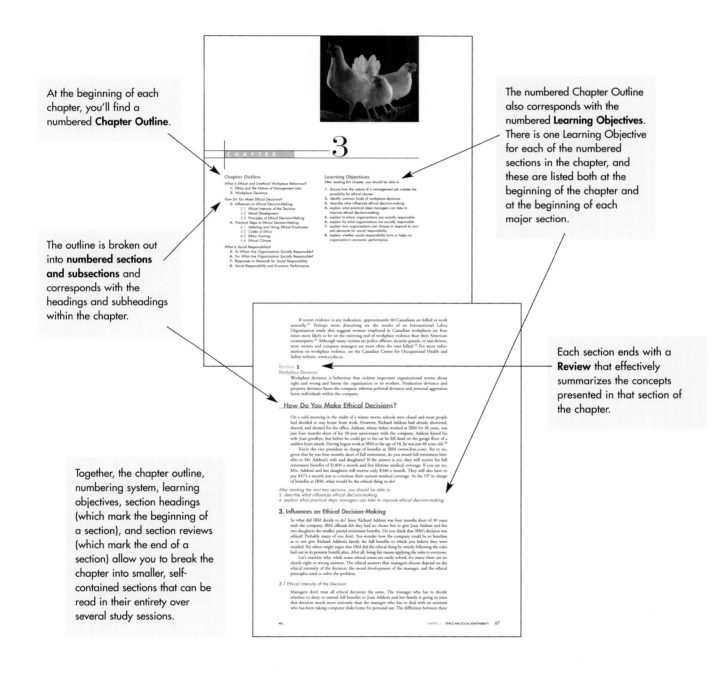

The **What Would You Do?** chapter-opening vignettes set the scene for introducing business problems. In each case a manager faces an interesting problem or situation that is tied to the information presented in the chapter. You are called upon to think like managers and apply what you've learned in order to provide the solutions to unique problems posed by each case.

The **What Really Happened?** end-of-chapter wrap-ups provide information to understand how things turned out, what the real company did and why, and whether it worked. This is a great way for you to compare your own thinking with that of real managers.

Each **What Really Works** section is based on meta-analysis research, which provides the best scientific evidence that management professors and researchers have about what works and what doesn't work in management. An easy-to-understand index known as the "probability of success" is used to indicate how well a management idea or strategy is likely to work in the workplace.

Key terms appear in boldface in the text, with definitions in the margins to make it easy to check your understanding. A complete alphabetical list of key terms appears at the end of each chapter as a study checklist, with page citations for easy reference.

Experiencing Management margin notes direct you to specific modules in the *Experiencing Management* online teaching assistant to reinforce key management concepts.

Located in the margins, **Personal Productivity Tips** are designed to give quick, useful, practical management advice that can make an immediate difference.

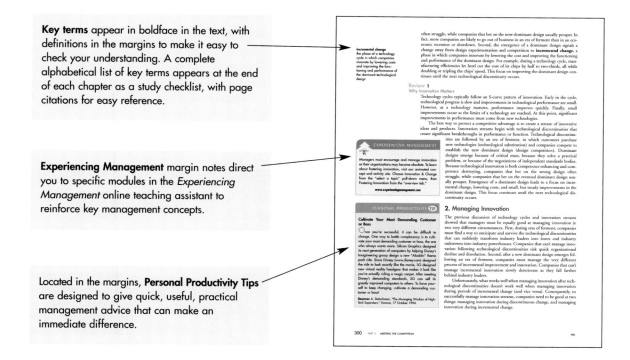

End-of-Chapter Assignments

At the end of each chapter in Management, there are a variety of assignments from which to choose. This gives instructors more choice in selecting just the right assignment for their classes. It also gives you a greater variety of activities, making it less likely that you'll repeat the same kind of assignment chapter after chapter.

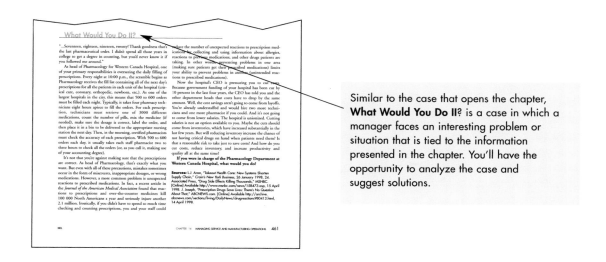

Similar to the case that opens the chapter, **What Would You Do II?** is a case in which a manager faces an interesting problem or situation that is tied to the information presented in the chapter. You'll have the opportunity to analyze the case and suggest solutions.

Each **Critical Thinking Video Case** describes and frames the CBC video clip that accompanies the chapter so you can apply what you've learned to answer the Critical Thinking Questions.

There are two **Management Decisions** in each chapter. Typically, these are somewhat shorter, more focused assignments in which you must decide what to do and then answer several questions to explain your choices.

Develop Your Management Potential assignments are self-directed activities that are designed to help you build skills you can use now. These assignments de-emphasize traditional "book-learning" based on memorization and regurgitation, in order to develop the practical knowledge and skills that help managers perform their jobs better.

Discussion Questions allow you to further apply chapter concepts to other business situations.

Sixteen different **Study Tips** give you many ideas for reviewing key concepts and mastering chapter content.

Critical Thinking Video Case

Nova Scotian Crystal
In Chapter 1, we defined *management* as getting work done through others. In other words, managers don't do the work themselves. Managers help others do their jobs better. By contrast, *leadership* is the process of influencing others to achieve group or organizational goals. Think back to Chapter 1 and the discussion about Nova Scotian Crystal, the company that makes fine crystal in Halifax. In that video you observed how two seemingly opposites, chairman Denis Ryan and president Rod McCallum, use their distinct skills to guide Nova Scotian Crystal through a series of ups and downs in its quest for growth and sustainability.

Denis Ryan and president Rod McCallum are described as being the "odd couple" because they bring different skills and personalities to the company. Nonetheless, both are important to the continued success of the company. While there has been much debate over the differences between management and leadership, in this chapter we discussed the concept of leadership and the differences between leadership and management. There are different traits and skills associated with each role and both can be important to an organization's success. As you watch the video, consider the following critical thinking questions.

Critical Thinking Questions
1. The two Nova Scotian Crystal executives portrayed in the video play different roles. How would you describe their roles?
2. What traits and behaviours do they exhibit? Which of these traits and behaviours are associated with leaders and which are associated with managers?
3. Do they both exhibit leadership and management behaviours and traits? What are these traits and how might they affect the success of the company?

Management Decisions

Subbing for Leaders
Six months ago when you accepted the job as the president of a small marketing agency, you knew that it would be a tough task. You had no idea, however, that it would be nearly impossible. While interviewing, you conducted some basic research and found that even though the company was profitable, it had a bad reputation of not playing fair in the advertising industry. Many people that you talked to voiced their concerns about the firm, saying that its people were sneaky, backstabbing individuals who would stop at nothing to make a buck. Despite their concerns, you accepted the [...] ceptions were somewhat b[...]

Unfortunately, soon aft[...] that many people [...] Initially, George, your as[...] company, seemed like a g[...] even abrasive, but otherwi[...] tions about George's relian[...] to ensure that the marketi[...] enue each quarter. In fact, [...] heard, and the uneasier yo[...]

As you began to watch [...] he was definitely an ende[...] focus was on increasing a [...] eventually for himself), re[...] began to notice that durin[...] rent customers' marketing[...] majority of the talking. An[...]

inconsistent with George's was immediately cut off and publicly scolded. In fact, this morning as you walked past one such meeting, you overheard John, a junior-level marketing agent, propose a new strategy for an important customer. George replied to John in front of the group, saying, "Now you folks see why John is only a junior-level agent after working over 12 years with this firm. Does anyone else have any stupid comments to offer, or can we move on with our meeting?"

As you stood outside the conference room, you realized that something must be done to change the culture, perception, and

---

Management Decisions

Employee of the Month!
As you get back to your desk with your third cup of coffee this morning, your boss stops at your desk in the middle of his morning rounds. He says, "Hey, you've got a degree in management, don't you? Heck, even if you don't, you're probably more up to date on all these new motivational theories and ideas than I am. Here's what I want. We need an employee-of-the-month award for our clerical employees. I want to boost their morale and motivate them to work harder and do their jobs better! So take a couple of weeks and design a basic employee award program, but make sure that it's got an employee-of-the-month award in it. That's the key. Have it on my desk two weeks from Friday." Before you can say yes, he's off to another co-worker's desk, to give her some other assignment that he brainstormed last night. You're not even sure he heard you say, "Sure, Mr. Smith, no problem."

However, what you really wanted to say was, "I don't know, Mr. Smith. I've never seen an employee-of-the-month award motivate anyone." In fact, no one really seemed to care about

being employee-of-the-month in the places you had worked before, even when there was a small amount of cash involved. You think to yourself, "Well, if he wants an employee-of-the-month award, I'll make sure that's in there. But there have got to be better ways to motivate the clerical staff. I'm just going to have to figure out what those are."

Questions
1. What is wrong with many employee-of-the-month award programs? Why wouldn't they be particularly effective at motivating employees?
2. Describe the three most important steps you'd take to motivate the clerical staff in your office. Explain what the steps are, the reasoning behind them, and what they're meant to accomplish. Be specific.

Develop Your Management Potential

Show Me the Noncash Rewards?
"Show me the money! Show me the money!" Lots of managers mistakenly assume that money is the primary motivator for most employees. However, studies regularly show that while money affects people's decisions to take or leave a job, it is not one of the primary motivators once someone has a job.

New managers also assume that they'll have access to the money they need to "really motivate" their workers. This is wrong in two ways. First, most managers are given a pool of money to allocate among all employees as raises. So if they give one employee a large raise, they have less money for other raises. Second, psychological studies show that pay increases must be at least 15 to 20 percent before employees really feel that they've got a substantial increase in pay. In other words, with most annual pay raises between 2 and 4 percent, most managers simply aren't given the money they need to create the wow-what-a-great-raise reaction they want from their employees.

As a result of these factors, more and more managers are turning to noncash rewards to motivate their employees.

Questions
1. Develop a list of 10 creative, noncash rewards that would be effective in motivating employees. If you're not sure what would be effective, think of the things that motivate you and your friends. You also might want to ask two or three managers about the noncash rewards they offer their employees.
2. Describe how you would administer each of these rewards. In other words, explain when and why you would give employees these particular rewards. Be specific.

Discussion Questions

1. Think back on the jobs that you have had. What sorts of things did the companies you worked for do to motivate you? Did they work? Why or why not?
2. Have you ever felt underrewarded in a job? Why did you feel underrewarded? What could have been done to address the perceived inequity?
3. What is the difference between a leader and a manager? Provide specific examples.
4. Provide examples of good leaders. What characteristics make them good leaders?

Study Tip

Your professor and TA are the most valuable resources in your course. If you have questions on the fundamental concepts of motivation and leadership, go to them during office hours. Report back to your study partner or group.

Student Supplements

Study Guide (ISBN 0-17-641490-8)

To go beyond mere memorization and actually apply management principles, the *Management*, First Canadian Edition, *Study Guide* provides students with a wide range of study tools. Each study guide chapter begins with questions that will help students approach the text's What Would You Do? opening case. A pre-test then follows. The purpose of the pre-test is to show students areas where they need the most review. A chapter outline, containing the learning objectives, key term definitions, and major points in the chapter, serves as a useful review tool. After reading the chapter and reviewing the outline, students can test their understanding with multiple-choice, true-false, short-answer, agree-disagree, and critical thinking questions similar to those they might see on the tests. Solutions with text page references appear at the end of each study guide chapter.

Multimedia CD-ROM

The Multimedia CD-ROM, packaged free with every new copy of *Management*, First Canadian Edition, contains a variety of interactive study resources. Among the study tools available on the CD-ROM are practice quizzes that allow students to check their understanding of concepts presented in the text, worksheets based on the text's exhibits, and glossary flashcards and crossword puzzles using the text's key terms and definitions.

Experiencing Management
(www.experiencingmanagement.com)

An access card for the *Experiencing Management* website is packaged free with every new copy of *Management*, First Canadian Edition. Created by R. Dennis Middlemist, this online teaching assistant helps students understand and reinforce management concepts—24 hours a day.

This award-winning, web-based teaching tool is a fully integrated, online instructional system that engagingly and dynamically presents management content and scenarios. Four areas of information (Overview, Key Terms, Exercises, and Animated Scenario) are presented for a variety of key topics.

Experiencing Management margin notes in the text direct the reader to specific modules in the *Experiencing Management* website that will help students learn more about key concepts presented in each chapter.

InfoTrac®
(www.infotrac-college.com)

Packaged free with every new copy of *Management*, First Canadian Edition, is a password for the InfoTrac database by Gale Research. InfoTrac enables students to connect with the real world of management through academic journals, business and popular magazines and newspapers, and a vast array of government publications. InfoTrac can also be a valuable tool for working through the What Would You Do II? at the end of each chapter.

Management, First Canadian Edition, Website

(www.management1e.nelson.com)

The *Management* website contains a wealth of resources for both instructors and students. Here is what's available for students at the *Management* website:

- Learning Objectives from the text
- Lecture notes for each chapter
- Links to the URLs from the book
- Multiple-choice quiz questions for each chapter
- Internet exercises for each chapter
- CBC video clips and cases
- Worksheets based on the illustrations from the text
- Articles about a variety of management topics
- Flashcards of the key terms and definitions from the text
- *Experiencing Management* margin notes from the text

Instructor Supplements

Instructor's Manual (ISBN 0-17-641440-1)

Care has been taken to develop an *Instructor's Manual* that helps professors create interesting and relevant classes. Each chapter of the *Instructor's Manual* opens with a pedagogy grid that details all the pedagogy in the chapter and the companies and teaching points presented. By giving you all the options you have in the chapter and the chapter content addressed by each option, you will be able to decide what you want to emphasize and assign your students. Following the pedagogy grid are lesson plans.

Each type of lesson plan includes pre-class preparation for professor and for students; how to organize the content for the chapter during the class period; a list of possible assignments; and more. A detailed chapter outline (lecture notes) is also provided in the *Instructor's Manual*. The lecture notes include additional examples, teaching notes for key concepts and for feature boxes, and prompts for where to show the video. Solutions for chapter features are included, plus 10 discussion questions per chapter, five group activities per chapter, and Internet activities for each chapter.

Test Bank

Print Test Bank (ISBN 0-17-641445-2)

The Test Bank for *Management*, First Canadian Edition, contains a comprehensive selection of questions from which to choose. Each chapter contains an average of 65 true-false, 70 multiple-choice, 10 short-answer, and 5 critical thinking essay questions. Thorough solutions are provided for each question, including difficulty ratings and page references where solutions appear in the text. A correlation table at the beginning of each test bank chapter makes it easy for instructors to select the appropriate mix of questions for their students.

Computerized Test Bank

A computerized version of the test bank is available on your Instructor Resource CD-ROM (0-17-641429-0). ExamView allows to you create, edit, store, print, and otherwise customize your quizzes, tests, and exams. The system is menu-driven, making it quick and easy to use.

PowerPoint® Slides

A rich set of PowerPoint slides, with teaching notes, will make class preparations easy and interesting. The approximately 30 to 40 slides per chapter cover all key concepts, terms, features, cases, and even some exhibits from the text. Animations and transitions add movement to many of the slides, allowing instructors to show one point at a time and adding a dynamic feel that will hold student interest throughout the presentation. The slides are available on your Instructor Resource CD-ROM (0-17-641429-0).

Instructor Resource CD-ROM (ISBN 0-17-641429-0)

For your convenience, the Instructor Manual, Test Bank, ExamView Software, and PowerPoint presentations are available on a single CD-ROM.

CBC

CBC Videos (ISBN 0-17-641427-4)

Nothing helps students master management concepts like seeing them put into practice in the real world. This video package will add visual impact and current, real-world examples to your lectures. The VHS tape contains seven video segments from different CBC programs that are used as the basis for the Critical Thinking Video Cases in the text.

Turner Learning CNN Video (ISBN 0-324-11791-4)

New video examples from CNN's extensive news-footage library have been selected to go with many of the major topics covered in the text. Clips are short, so you can view and review them easily and quickly.

Management, First Canadian Edition, Website

(www.management1e.nelson.com)

The *Management* website contains a wealth of resources for both instructors and students. Here is what's available for instructors at the *Management* website:

- The full PowerPoint presentation slides
- Files for the full *Instructor's Manual* are also available online. If you don't have your materials on hand, you can download the chapters you need and customize them to suit your lesson plan.
- Solutions to the student Internet Exercises

Meet the Authors

Alex Z. Kondra
Athabasca University

Alex Kondra is an Associate Professor and Chair of the Centre for Organizational Analysis and Marketing, School of Business, Athabasca University in Athabasca, Alberta. He obtained a Ph.D. in Industrial Relations from the University of Alberta in 1995. Previously he was on faculty at the Fred C. Manning School of Business of Acadia University in Wolfville, Nova Scotia. At Athabasca University, he teaches Organization Theory, Managing Change, and Administrative Principles. His current research interests focus on changing organizational and industry structures, organizational ethics and organizational culture. He has published in the journals *Organization Studies, Journal of Labor Research, Journal of Individual Employment Rights,* and the *Journal of Collective Negotiations in the Public Sector.* He also serves as an academic reviewer for numerous academic journals and conferences and has chaired the Organizational Theory division of the Administrative Sciences Association of Canada Conference.

Conor Vibert
Acadia University

Conor Vibert is an Associate Professor of Business Strategy at the Fred C. Manning School of Business of Acadia University in Wolfville, Nova Scotia. He obtained a Ph.D. in Organizational Analysis from the University of Alberta in 1996. At Acadia University, he teaches Business Strategy and Organization Theory; his current research interests focus on the application of the Internet to contemporary business issues. He is the author of *Theorizing on Macro-organizational Behavior: A Handbook of Ideas and Explanations* and *Competitive Intelligence: A Framework for Web-based Analysis and Decision-Making.* Conor has published in *Competitive Intelligence Review, Education and Information Technology*, and the *Journal of Competitive Strategy.* He is also a recipient of the 2002 Outstanding Teacher Award for Acadia's Faculty of Professional Studies as well as a recipient of the 2000 Acadia University President's Award for Innovation.

Chuck Williams

Texas Christian University

Chuck Williams is an Associate Professor of Management and Associate Dean at the M.J. Neeley School of Business at Texas Christian University. He received his B.A. in Psychology from Valparaiso University, and specialized in the areas of Organizational Behavior, Human Resources, and Strategic Management while earning his M.B.A and Ph.D. in Business Administration from Michigan State University. Previously, he taught at Michigan State University and was on the Faculty of Oklahoma State University.

His research interests include employee recruitment and turnover, performance appraisal, and employee training and goal-setting. Chuck has published research in the *Journal of Applied Psychology*, the *Academy of Management Journal*, *Human Resource Management Review*, *Personnel Psychology*, and the *Organizational Research Methods Journal*. He was a member of the *Journal of Management*'s Editorial Board, and serves as a reviewer for numerous other academic journals. He was also the webmaster for the Research Methods Division of the Academy of Management (www.aom.pace.edu/rmd). Chuck is also a co-recipient of the Society for Human Resource Management's Yoder-Heneman Research Award.

Chuck has consulted for a number of organizations, General Motors, IBM, JCPenney, Tandy Corporation, Trism Trucking, Central Bank and Trust, StuartBacon, the City of Fort Worth, the American Cancer Society, and others. He has taught in executive development programs at Oklahoma State University, The University of Oklahoma, and Texas Christian University.

Chuck teaches a number of different courses, but has been privileged to teach his favourite course, Introduction to Management, for nearly 20 years. His teaching philosophy is based on four principles: (1) courses should be engaging and interesting; (2) there's nothing as practical as a good theory; (3) students learn by doing; and (4) students learn when they are challenged. The undergraduate students at TCU's Neeley School of Business named him instructor of the year. He has also been a recipient of TCU's Dean's Teaching Award.

1

Introduction to Management

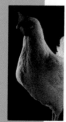

CHAPTER 1

Chapter Outline

Learning Objectives

After reading this chapter, you should be able to

1. describe what management is.
2. explain the three functions of management.
3. describe different kinds of managers.
4. explain the major roles and subroles that managers perform in their jobs.
5. explain what companies look for in managers.
6. discuss the top mistakes that managers make in their jobs.
7. describe the transition that employees go through when they are promoted to management.
8. explain how and why companies can create competitive advantage through people.

Management

What Would You Do?

September is a nice time of year in New Brunswick. Warm days accompanied by cool nights mark a clear change from the heat of the summer, allowing well-rested minds to comfortably drift away from the pleasures of cottages and ocean vacations back to the trials and tribulations of the workplace. Unfortunately for Mario Theriault, vacation time spent with the family at Parlee Beach had not been the break from the workplace that he had hoped for.

A year previously, Mario had founded a small management consulting firm in Moncton. As a former vice president with communications firm GCP Bristol and Fundy Communications, Theriault had been intrigued about the role that the Internet was playing in the private and public sectors. With many others, he had realized that the Internet had fundamentally changed the way information is collected, research is practised, and strategy is devised. As an Acadian with extensive roots in the province, Theriault had also come to understand how many of the large regional employers operated.

Discussions with colleagues throughout Atlantic Canada convinced him of two things. Technological advances, freer trade, the dot-com era, and the subsequent downturn in the economy had hindered most firms' ability

to understand the direction of their own markets and industries let alone the behaviour of competitors. Second, the Internet had become a mixed blessing. Although this new technology offered access to critical information at the touch of a keypad, most of these same institutions were now faced with overcoming the hurdle of information overload at a time when executives needed timely as well as accurate information to make important decisions.

Theriault also realized that an opportunity lay before his eyes. Reducing competitive uncertainty and managing information overload could be costly, labour intensive, and technology-intensive exercises for any organization. He envisioned his firm, Shift Central (www.shiftcentral.com), as a provider of outsourced technologically enhanced research and strategic planning services for the firms operating in Atlantic Canada and major metropolitan areas.

Unfortunately, a number of concerns stood in the way of his vision. To begin, his company was young and small. It had yet to develop an extended track record of success, and the rash of new start-up failures from the dot-com era only served to increase the wariness among established firms of working with new entities.

Further, Shift Central's potential adversaries were mostly large, well known, and well established. They included management consulting firms

such as Deloitte Consulting (Braxton), Accenture, and PricewaterhouseCoopers as well as traditional communications and market research companies such as CCL, Decima Research, Environics, and Cossette Communications.

His final concern was somewhat different. The services that Theriault had in mind would fit under the heading of a burgeoning new discipline termed Competitive Intelligence (CI), which even had its own international professional association, the Society of Competitive Intelligence Professionals (SCIP) (www.scip.org). CI was defined as "a continuous process involving the legal and ethical collection of information, analysis that doesn't avoid unwelcome conclusions, and controlled dissemination of actionable intelligence to decision makers."

Unfortunately, the practice of CI was not always well understood, a number of its tools and processes originate with military intelligence organizations and spy agencies, and it had a language associated with it that was unfamiliar to many business executives. Sadly, the field of CI had also recently been mired in controversy. In a story that was brought to the public's attention by the *New York Times*, it was revealed that "Procter & Gamble had ... engaged in a corporate espionage program against Unilever in its hair care business that included ... searching for material in trash containers and the use of spies who misrepresented themselves as market analysts." Further, *Business 2.0* magazine and others had noted that the president of the company that had performed the acts of espionage on behalf of P&G was also the president of SCIP.

As Theriault looked out his window, he realized that what he sought to offer the market was a narrow but well-defined portfolio of CI services. Unfortunately, labelling Shift Central as a CI service provider could also cost it dearly. To overcome the challenges that lay ahead, he understood that he would have to display leadership to employees; meet the competition; organize Shift Central's people, projects, and processes; and most importantly, make things happen. **If you were the CEO of Shift Central, what would you do?**

Sources: C. Richard, "Shift Central Inc. Launches Its New Competitive Intelligence Position Tool," Shift Central Inc. [Online] Available www.shiftcentral.com. Retrieved 19/09/2002. "Frequently Asked Questions,"

Society of Competitive Intelligence Professionals (2002). [Online] Available www.scip.org. C. Fleisher, "Should the Field Be Called 'Competitive Intelligence' or Something Else?" In C. Fleisher and D. Blenkhorn, eds., *Enduring Issues in Competitive Intelligence.* Westport, CT: Praeger Business. Forthcoming. A. Serwer, "P&G Comes Clean on Spying Operation," *Business 2.0.* August 30, 2001. Available at www.business2.com. K. Alison, "Espionage Update—Competitive Intelligence," *Darwin Magazine,* December 2001. Available at www.darwinmag.com. M. Higgins, "The Renaissance Man," *Atlantic Progress,* 21 January 2002. C. Spence, "Net Monitor for Business," *New Brunswick Telegraph Journal,* June 5, 2002.

The issues facing Mario Theriault and Shift Central are fundamental to any organization: What is management, and what do managers do? Good management is basic to starting a business, growing a business, and maintaining a business once it has achieved some measure of success.

This chapter begins by defining management and discussing the functions of management. Next, we look at what managers do by examining the four kinds of managers and reviewing the various roles that managers play. Third, we investigate what it takes to be a manager by reviewing management skills, what companies look for in their managers, the most serious mistakes managers make, and what it is like to make the tough transition from being a worker to being a manager. We finish this chapter by examining the competitive advantage that companies gain from good management. In other words, we end the chapter by learning how to establish a competitive advantage through people.

What Is Management?

"Over the last decade, almost three quarters of all business and government organizations in Canada used the services of a management consultant."[1] These recipients had many consultants to choose from as over 25 000 Canadian establishments offered management, scientific, and technical services to businesses and the general public.[2] How large is the market for such services? Well, consider that each year, Canadian federal, provincial, and municipal governments alone spend more than $600 million for similar services. Further, it's estimated that Canadian management consultants were paid well over $6 billion in 2001.[3] What private and public entities are really paying for is management advice. Clearly, companies are looking for help with basic management issues, such as how to make things happen, how to beat the competition, how to manage large-scale projects and processes, and how to effectively lead people. This textbook will help you understand some of the basic issues that management consultants help companies resolve (and, unlike the government and business sectors, this won't cost you millions of dollars).

After reading the next two sections, you should be able to
1. *describe what management is.*
2. *explain the three functions of management.*

1. Management Is...

Many of today's managers got their start welding on the factory floor, clearing dishes off tables, helping customers fit a suit, or wiping up a spill in aisle 3. Lots of you will start at the bottom and work your way up, too. There's no better way to get to know your competition, your customers, and your business. But whether you begin your career at the entry level or as a supervisor, your job is not to do the work, but to help others do their work. **Management** is getting work done through others. Pat Carrigan, a former elementary school principal who became a manager at a General Motors car parts plant, said, "I've never made a part in my life, and I don't really have any plans to make one. That's not my job. My job is to create an environment where people who do make them can make them right, can make them right the first time, can make them at a competitive cost, and can do so with some sense of responsibility and pride in what they're doing. I don't have to know how to make a part to do any of those things."[4]

Pat Carrigan's description of managerial responsibilities indicates that managers also have to be concerned with efficiency and effectiveness in the work process. **Efficiency** is getting work done with a minimum of effort, expense, or waste.

But, by itself, efficiency is not enough to ensure success. For years, Chrysler Motor Company (now DaimlerChrysler) (www.daimlerchrysler.ca) watched its sales, market share, and profits shrink, despite being able to make a car for much less than either Ford or General Motors. It wasn't until Chrysler began producing award-winning car designs such as the Dodge Stratus, Chrysler Concorde, Dodge Ram truck, and its completely redesigned, aerodynamic minivans that it began to regain market share and profitability. So, besides being concerned about efficiency, managers must also strive for **effectiveness**, which is accomplishing tasks that help fulfil organizational objectives.

Review 1
Management Is...

Good management is working through others to accomplish tasks that help fulfil organizational objectives as efficiently as possible.

---

management
getting work done through others

efficiency
getting work done with a minimum of effort, expense, or waste

effectiveness
accomplishing tasks that help fulfil organizational objectives

---

PERSONAL PRODUCTIVITY

Do You Know How Efficient Your Business Is?

Many managers fail to keep track of one of the most important outcomes in business: efficiency. With more than 900 self-service and staffed locations throughout Canada alone, managers at United Parcel Service (www.ups.ca) understand why this can be a problem. Long regarded as the most efficient and productive company in the package shipping business, UPS recently concluded that it had become much less efficient in the last few years. One clear indication: It took eight separate phone calls to find a lost package! UPS's solution is to simply let customer service representatives directly contact drivers, thus reducing the process to a much more manageable four steps. If you want to improve how well your company is performing, keep close track of efficiency and productivity.

Sources: R. Frank, "Efficient UPS Tries to Increase Efficiency," *The Wall Street Journal*, 24 May 1995, B1; www.ups.ca.

---

2. Management Functions

Traditionally, a manager's job has been described according to the classical functions of management: planning, organizing, leading, and controlling. **Planning** is determining organizational goals and a means for achieving them. **Organizing** is deciding where decisions will be made, who will do what jobs and tasks, and who will work for whom in the company. **Leading** is inspiring and motivating workers to work hard to achieve organizational goals. **Controlling** is monitoring progress toward goal achievement and taking corrective action when progress isn't being made.

Studies indicate that managers who perform these management functions well are better managers. The more time that chief executive officers (CEOs) spend planning, the more profitable their companies are.[5] Over a 25-year period, one telecommunications firm found that employees with better planning and decision-making skills were more likely to be promoted into management jobs, to be successful as managers, and to be promoted into upper levels of management.[6]

The evidence is clear. Managers serve their companies well when they plan, organize, lead, and control. However, companies with familiar names such as the Bank of Montreal, CN, Air Canada, General Motors, and Zellers are facing tremendous changes and are asking—if not demanding—that managers change the way they perform these functions. According to *Fortune* magazine (www.fortune.com), these changes are

---

planning
determining organizational goals and the means for achieving them

organizing
deciding where decisions will be made, who will do what jobs and tasks, and who will work for whom

leading
inspiring and motivating workers to work hard to achieve organizational goals

controlling
monitoring progress toward goal achievement and taking corrective action when needed

WhatReallyWorks

Meta-Analysis

Some studies show that two drinks a day increase life expectancy by decreasing your chances of having a heart attack. Yet other studies show that two drinks a day will shorten your life expectancy. For years, we've "buttered" our morning toast with margarine instead of butter because it was supposed to be better for our health. However, new studies now show that the trans-fatty acids in margarine may be just as bad for our arteries as butter. Confusing scientific results like these frustrate ordinary people who want to "eat right" and "live right." It also makes many people question just how useful most scientific research really is.

Managers also have trouble figuring out what works, based on the scientific research published in journals such as the *Academy of Management Journal*, the *Academy of Management Review*, the *Strategic Management Journal*, the *Journal of Applied Psychology*, the *Canadian Journal of Administrative Sciences*, and *Administrative Science Quarterly*. It's common for the *Globe and Mail's Report on Business* (www.globeandmail.com) to quote a management research article from one of these journals that says that total quality management is the best thing since sliced bread (without butter or margarine). Then, just six months later the *Report on Business* will quote a different article from the same journal that says that total quality management doesn't work. If management professors and researchers have trouble deciding what works and what doesn't, how can practising managers know?

Thankfully, a research tool called **meta-analysis**, which is a study of studies, is helping management scholars understand how well their research supports management theories. However, meta-analysis is also useful for practising managers, because it shows what works and the conditions under which management techniques may work better or worse in the "real world." Meta-analysis is based on the simple idea that if one study shows that a management technique doesn't work and another study shows that it does, an average of those results is probably the best estimate of how well that management practice works (or doesn't work). For example, medical researchers Richard Peto and Rory Collins averaged all the different results from several hundred studies investigating the relationship between aspirin and heart attacks. Their analysis, based on more than 120 000 patients from numerous studies, showed that aspirin lowered the incidence of heart attacks by an average of 4 percent. Prior to this study, doctors prescribed aspirin as a preventive measure for only 38 percent of heart attack victims. Today, because of the meta-analysis results, doctors prescribe aspirin for 72 percent of heart attack victims.

Fortunately, you don't need a Ph.D. to understand the statistics reported in a meta-analysis. In fact, one primary advantage of meta-analysis over traditional significance tests is that you can convert meta-analysis statistics into intuitive numbers that anyone can easily understand.

Each meta-analysis reported in the "What Really Works?" section of each chapter is accompanied by an easy-to-understand statistic called the probability of success. As its name suggests, the probability of success shows how often a management technique will work.

For example, meta-analyses suggest that the best predictor of a job applicant's on-the-job performance is a test of general mental ability. In other words, smarter people tend to be better workers. The average correlation (one of those often-misunderstood statistics) between scores on general mental ability tests and job performance is .60. However, very few people understand what a correlation of .60 means. What most managers want to know is how often they will hire the right person if they choose job applicants based on general mental ability test scores. Likewise, they want to know how much of a difference a cognitive ability test makes when hiring new workers. The probability of success may be high, but if the difference isn't really that large, is it really worth a manager's time to have job applicants take a general mental ability test?

Well, our user-friendly statistics indicate that it's wise to have job applicants take a general mental ability test. In fact, the probability of success, shown in graphical form below, is 76 percent. This means that an employee hired on the basis of a good score on a general mental ability test stands a 76 percent chance of being a better performer than someone picked at random from the pool of all job applicants. So chances are, you're going to be right much more often than you are wrong if you use a general mental ability test to make hiring decisions.

General Mental Ability

In summary, each "What Really Works?" section in this textbook is based on meta-analysis research, which provides the best scientific evidence that management professors and researchers have about what really works and what really doesn't work in management. An easy-to-understand index known as the "probability of success" will be used to indicate how well a management idea or strategy is likely to work in the workplace. Of course, no idea or technique works every time and in every circumstance. However, the management ideas and strategies discussed in the "What Really Works?" sections of this textbook can usually make a meaningful difference where you work. In today's competitive, fast-changing, global marketplace, few managers can afford to overlook proven management strategies like the ones discussed in "What Really Works?"

Sources: R.J. Grisson, "Probability of the Superior Outcome of One Treatment over Another," *Journal of Applied Psychology* 79 (1994): 314–316. J.E. Hunter & F.L. Schmidt, *Methods of Meta-analysis: Correcting Error and Bias in Research Findings* (Beverly Hills, CA: Sage, 1990).

embodied in the difference between "old" management and "new" management. Old-style managers think of themselves as the "manager" or the "boss." New-style managers think of themselves as sponsors, team leaders, or internal consultants. Old-style managers follow the chain of command (reporting to the boss, who reports to the next boss at a higher managerial level, etc.), while new-style managers work with anyone who can help them accomplish their goals. Old-style managers make decisions by themselves. New-style managers ask others to participate in decisions. Old-style managers keep proprietary company information confidential. New-style managers share that information with others. Old-style managers demand long hours. New-style managers demand results.[7]

Such changes don't make the classical managerial functions obsolete. Indeed, managers are still responsible for performing the functions of management. For example, consider this description of a new-style manager and the people she works with (not the people who work for her, which is "old" management). The managerial functions represented by each action have been inserted in brackets.

> Three years ago Ransom asked her workers at a 100-person manufacturing facility to redesign the plant's operations [planning and organizing]. As she watched, intervening only to answer the occasional question [controlling], a team of hourly workers established training programs, set work rules for absenteeism [controlling], and reorganized the once traditional factory into five customer-focused business units [organizing and leading]. As the workers took over managerial work [decision-making, organizing, and leading], Ransom used her increasing free time to attend to the needs of customers and suppliers [planning and controlling].[8]

As indicated within the brackets, Ransom and the members of her work group still perform the classical management functions. They just do them differently than old-style managers used to.

To reconcile the "new" with the "old," this textbook is organized around these three management functions (see Exhibit 1.1), which have evolved out of the traditional functions:

- Making Things Happen
- Meeting the Competition
- Organizing People, Projects, and Processes

Note that these functions do not replace the classical functions of management; they build on them. For example, two of the three chapters under "Part 2: Making Things Happen" are classical management functions (planning and controlling). Furthermore, two of the four classical functions of management, organizing and leading, remain as part of the "new" management functions and are found under the heading "Organizing People, Projects, and Processes." Finally, a brand new management function, "Meeting the Competition," has been added to reflect the importance of adapting and innovating to remain competitive in today's ever-changing and increasingly global marketplace.

Aside from an emphasis on these new management functions, this book stands out from the crowd for a number of other reasons. The book was written in response to the similarity and dryness of these traditional principles, and its main premise is in keeping management simple, with a focus on what really works for managers, while also presenting management theory through stories and cases rather than lists and lists of topics. It captures the key activities and realities of management (such as risk, decision-making, people, and projects) at all levels without overwhelming the student with theory and research.

Throughout this text, the major sections within a chapter will be numbered using a single digit: 1, 2, 3, and so on. Then the subsections will be consecutively numbered, beginning with the major section number. For example, "2.1" marks the first subsection under the second major section. This numbering system should help you easily see the relationships among topics and follow the topic sequence. It will also help your instructor refer to specific topics during class discussion.

meta-analysis
a study of studies, a statistical approach that provides the best scientific estimate of how well management theories and practices work

EXHIBIT 1.1

MANAGEMENT FUNCTIONS AND ORGANIZATION OF THE TEXTBOOK

Traditional Management Functions	Table of Contents for This Text		
	Part One	**Introduction to Management**	
		Chapter 1	Management
		Chapter 2	Organizational Environments and Cultures
		Chapter 3	Ethics and Social Responsibility
	Part Two	**Making Things Happen**	
Planning		Chapter 4	Planning
		Chapter 5	Managing Information
Controlling		Chapter 6	Decision-Making
		Chapter 7	Control
	Part Three	**Meeting the Competition**	
		Chapter 8	Global Management
		Chapter 9	Organizational Strategy
		Chapter 10	Innovation and Change
		Chapter 11	Organizational Structures and Processes
	Part Four	**Organizing People, Projects, and Processes**	
Organizing		Chapter 12	Managing Teams
		Chapter 13	Managing Human Resource Systems
Leading		Chapter 14	Managing Service and Manufacturing Operations
		Chapter 15	Motivation and Leadership
		Chapter 16	Managing Communication

Now let's take a close look at each of the management functions, which can be categorized as making things happen; meeting the competition; and organizing people, projects, and processes.

2.1 Making Things Happen

Prior to its acquisition by Sears Roebuck, Lands' End (www.landsend.ca) had been, for most of its existence, a small, informally run organization. Exceptional products and the advent of Web-based ordering contributed to the development of a large, loyal base of customers located throughout the United States, Canada, and Europe. Struggling under tremendous growth (pre-acquisition revenues were approximately $3.2 billion a year), the founder of this successful catalogue retailer, Gary Comer, looked outside the company to hire a new CEO to institute modern management methods. Comer hired William End (no relationship to the company name). End quickly introduced the latest management techniques: production teams, performance appraisal systems based on peer reviews (rather than supervisor-based reviews), and over 20 different training courses, such as effective communication. Although some of the techniques worked, others resulted in a large number of lost, late, or undelivered orders. Employees, many of whom had worked at the company since its inception, strongly resisted the changes. Furthermore, confusion resulted because too many changes were made in too little time.

In his zeal to introduce the latest management techniques, End forgot that the most important management function is making things happen. To "make things happen," you must determine what you want to accomplish, plan how to achieve these goals, gather and manage the information needed to make good decisions, and control performance, so that you can take corrective action if performance falls short. In his estimation, company founder Gary Comer took corrective action when he fired William End for his failure to make things happen at Lands' End. In Chapters 4 to 7, you will learn more about how to make things happen. These include planning, managing information, decision-making, and controlling.

Microsoft was not in business 25 years ago. Yet only recently, because of its dominance of the software industry, the *Financial Post* (www.nationalpost.com), *Newsweek*, and the *Report on Business* were abuzz about antitrust action on the part of the U.S. federal government that could have broken Microsoft into several smaller, less dominant companies.[9] Not too long ago, these magazines and newspapers said the same thing about IBM and its dominance of the computer industry. But because of stiff competition from Compaq, Dell, and dozens of other manufacturers of "IBM-compatible" computers, IBM lost more than $10 billion and saw its market share in personal computers drop from 80 percent to 8 percent by the early 1990s. Today, no one worries anymore about IBM dominating the computer industry. What made the difference in the fortunes of these two companies?

With free trade agreements that promote international competition, shorter product development cycles, and barriers to entry falling in most industries, market followers will continue to topple market leaders as companies are exposed to more competition than ever in the next decade. Companies that want to remain market leaders must consider the threat from international competitors, have a well-thought-out competitive strategy, be able to embrace change and foster new product and service ideas, and structure their organizations to quickly adapt to changing customers and competitors. Thus, "meeting the competition" is a critical management function in today's business world. In Chapters 8 to 11, you will learn some management skills for meeting the competition. More specifically, you will enhance your understanding of global management and organizational strategy. You will also learn about how organizations innovate, change, and adapt their structures to their competitive environments.

2.3 Organizing People, Projects, and Processes

Ford Motor Company purchased Jaguar, a British auto maker. Under Ford's guidance, Jaguar's new management laid off one-third of its employees and reorganized its North American operations into three smaller divisions. To emphasize its renewed commitment to customer satisfaction, Jaguar's new vice president of customer care met with Jaguar dealers to talk to them about working harder to please customers. But instead of lecturing the dealers, they lectured him. How could they take care of customers, they said, when Jaguar's management wasn't taking care of them, when all Jaguar's management did was put out recurring fires? The new vice president was surprised and admittedly not prepared for two days of "ranting" from Jaguar dealers.[10]

Like other managers who have tried to "reengineer" their companies, Jaguar's vice president of customer care found out that large-scale changes won't work without simultaneous consideration of people issues and work processes (how the work gets done).[11] Therefore, our next management function is "organizing people, projects, and processes." You will learn about this management function throughout Chapters 12 to 16. Under this heading, you will enhance your understanding of how to manage teams, human resource systems, service and manufacturing operations, and communications. You will also learn about motivating people.

In these litigious times, managers are sued for sexual harassment, wrongful discharge, and discrimination. They are shot at, lampooned in the funny pages (*Dilbert* is the fastest-growing syndicated cartoon strip in years), and, in general, not accorded the respect they once had. In this time of corporate layoffs, many would argue that managers are to be feared and disliked.

How is it, then, in this time of corporate distrust, that Mary Ash, founder of Mary Kay cosmetics (www.marykay.ca), and Yves Landry, former CEO of Chrysler Canada, still garnered the respect and admiration of the people they lead or led? Gloria Mayfield, a former IBMer and a graduate of Harvard's MBA program, says, "I didn't see much recognition at IBM. At Mary Kay, if you do well, you know for a fact you'll get recognition. It's not influenced by politics." Not bad for a company that employs 26 000 independent

For nearly 40 years, Mary Kay Ash was the leader of her own cosmetics empire. She mesmerized and inspired an army of women to sell Mary Kay products door to door. Her charismatic and inspirational leadership was one of the many reasons she was a good manager.

© Fritz Hoffmann/The Image Works

beauty consultants in Canada alone. Mayfield goes on to say that "Mary Kay calls you her daughter and looks you dead in the eye. She makes you feel you can do anything. She's sincerely concerned about your welfare."[12]

At Chrysler Canada, so respected was Landry that Buzz Hargrove, head of the Canadian Auto Workers (www.caw.ca), admitted that Landry "was not offended at all that the union had different ideas about how to do things in the work place. That was unique in dealing with most of the country's business leadership."[13]

No one who has worked for an ordinary manager would ever deny the positive effects that inspirational leaders such as Mary Kay and Yves Landry can bring to their companies. Thus, under our last management function, Organizing People, Projects, and Processes, you will also find the more traditional function of "leading," which you will learn about specifically in Chapters 12 and 15.

Review 2
Management Functions

Managerial jobs have traditionally been described according to the classical functions of management: planning, organizing, leading, and controlling. Although managers still perform these managerial functions, it's also true that companies and the managers who run them have undergone tremendous changes in the last decade. Accordingly, this text incorporates the classical functions of management into broader, updated management functions: making things happen; meeting the competition; and organizing people, projects, and processes.

What Do Managers Do?

Not all managerial jobs are the same. The demands and requirements placed on the chief executive officer of Canadian Tire Corporation are significantly different from those placed on the manager of your local Sobey's or Superstore outlet.

After reading the next two sections, you should be able to
3. *describe different kinds of managers.*
4. *explain the major roles and subroles that managers perform in their jobs.*

3. Kinds of Managers

As shown in Exhibit 1.2, there are four different kinds of managers with different jobs and responsibilities: top managers, middle managers, first-line managers, and team leaders.

3.1 Top Managers

Top managers hold positions such as chief executive officer (CEO) or chief operating officer (COO) and are responsible for the overall direction of the organization. Top managers have the following responsibilities.[14] First, they are responsible for creating a context for change. In fact, it may be suggested that the CEOs of Geac Computer Corp., Fisheries Products International, PanCanadian Energy Corp., and Nortel Networks all left the executive suite within a year's time precisely because they had not moved fast enough to bring about significant changes in their companies.[15] Creating a context for change also includes forming a long-range vision or mission for their companies. As one CEO said, "The CEO has to think about the future more than anyone."

top managers
executives responsible for the overall direction of the organization

---

EXHIBIT 1.2

JOBS AND RESPONSIBILITIES OF FOUR KINDS OF MANAGERS

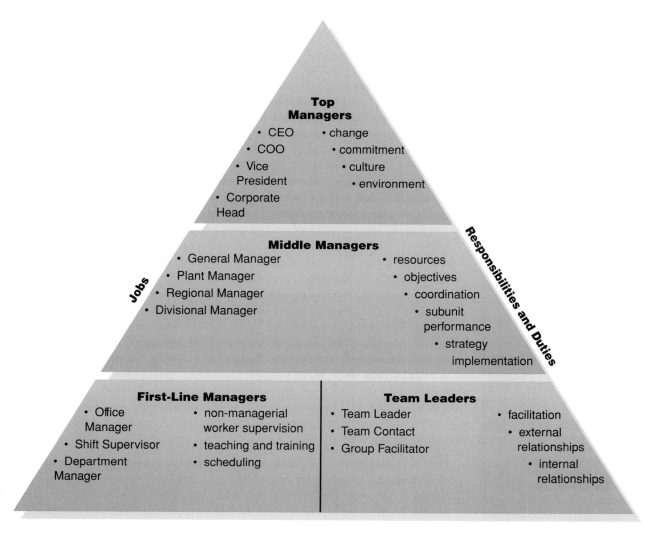

Second, much more than used to be the case, top managers are responsible for helping employees develop a sense of commitment to the business. Stories abound at DaimlerChrysler Canada (www.daimlerchrysler.ca) about Landry's willingness to address the concerns of his employees. One such story has Landry "voluntarily trading in his starched white shirt for a blue collar outfit and [taking] to the shop floor along with Canadian Auto Workers head Buzz Hargrove working on a minivan line and learning from those he regarded as his fellow plant workers."[16] The point of the story is that Landry, supposedly the most important person in the company, felt it necessary to understand the problems of assembly line workers, supposedly some of the least important persons in the company, so he could more effectively deal with their concerns and those of customers.

Third, top managers are responsible for creating a positive organizational culture through language and action. Top managers impart company values, strategies, and lessons through what they do and say to others, both inside and outside the company. One CEO said, "I write memos to the board and our operating committee. I'm sure they get the impression I dash them off, but usually they've been drafted ten or twenty times. The bigger you get, the more your ability to communicate becomes important. So what I write, I write very carefully. I labor over it."[17]

Finally, top managers are responsible for monitoring their business environments. This means that top managers must closely monitor customer needs, competitors' moves, and long-term business, economic, and social trends. How important is this task? Just ask the CEOs of telecommunications companies such as Telus, SaskTel, Bell, or Aliant. Their difficult task has been to try to make sense of chaotic product and service markets that have seen better days.

3.2 Middle Managers

middle managers
managers responsible for setting objectives consistent with top management's goals, and planning and implementing subunit strategies for achieving these objectives

Middle managers hold positions such as plant manager, regional manager, or divisional manager. They are responsible for setting objectives consistent with top management's goals and planning and implementing subunit strategies for achieving these objectives. One specific middle-management responsibility is to plan and allocate resources to meet objectives. Deans at Canadian universities such as Carleton or Dalhousie spend much of their time allocating resources among competing departments and planning for changes in student enrolments. Another major responsibility is to coordinate and link groups, departments, and divisions within a company. Project managers of flight simulators at CAE Electronics (www.cae.com) in Montreal undertake these responsibilities.

A third responsibility of middle management is to monitor and manage the performance of the subunits and individual managers who report to them. For example, one of the first things that Andy Wilson, a Wal-Mart regional vice president, will do when he visits a store in his territory is to find the store manager and then make a walking inspection of the store. On one inspection tour of a new store in his territory, Wilson was disappointed to find that products were not displayed according to headquarters' plans. Furthermore, because department managers had been slow to reorder products, many shelves were empty because replacement supplies had not yet arrived from the Wal-Mart (www.walmart.com) warehouses. Rather than waiting for the next truck shipment, Wilson told the department managers to correct the problem by arranging to transfer out-of-stock products from the nearest Wal-Mart store.[18] Finally, middle managers are also responsible for implementing the changes or strategies generated by top managers.

3.3 First-Line Managers

first-line managers
managers who train and supervise performance of non-managerial employees and who are directly responsible for producing the company's products or services

First-line managers hold positions such as office manager, shift supervisor, or department manager. The primary responsibility of first-line managers is to manage the performance of entry-level employees, who are directly responsible for producing a company's goods and services. Thus, first-line managers are the only managers who don't supervise other managers. For example, as a result of their large bilingual workforces, Montreal and New Brunswick are home to a number of large telemarketing operations. These are the firms whose sales representatives always seem to call you at home during dinner or your favourite TV show. Working as a telemarketing representative can be a high-stress, thankless job. However, it is the job of each shift supervisor to encourage, monitor, and reward the performance of that shift's telemarketing representatives.

First-line managers also spend time teaching entry-level employees how to do their jobs. Because telemarketing work is so stressful, most workers quit after three or four months on the job. In fact, any stay over three months is considered long-term employment. Because employee turnover is so high, telemarketing supervisors are constantly training new employees. This is one of the reasons that supervisors listen in on telemarketing representatives' phone calls: to observe their performance so that they can teach them how to make sales.

First-line managers also make detailed schedules and operating plans based on middle management's intermediate-range plans. In fact, contrary to the long-term plans of top managers (three to five years out), and the intermediate plans of middle managers (six to eighteen months out), first-line managers engage in plans and actions that typically produce results within two weeks.[19]

3.4 Team Leaders

The fourth kind of manager is a team leader. This is a relatively new kind of management job that developed as companies shifted to self-managing teams, which, by definition, have no formal supervisor. In traditional management hierarchies, first-line managers are responsible for the performance of non-managerial employees and have the authority to hire and fire workers, make job assignments, and control resources. By contrast, team leaders have a much different role, because nearly all of the functions performed by first-line managers under traditional hierarchies are now performed by teams in this new structure. Instead of directing individuals' work, **team leaders** facilitate team activities toward goal accomplishment. For example, Hewlett-Packard advertises its team leader positions with an ad that says, "Job seeker must enjoy coaching, working with people, and bringing about improvement through hands-off guidance and leadership."[20] Team leaders who fail to understand this key difference often struggle in their roles.

Team leaders fulfil the following responsibilities.[21] First, team leaders are responsible for facilitating team performance. This doesn't mean team leaders are responsible for team performance. They aren't. The team is. Team leaders help their teams plan and schedule work, learn to solve problems, and work effectively with each other. Eric Doremus, a team leader whose team helped develop the B-2 bomber, said, "My most important task was not trying to figure out everybody's job. It was to help this team feel as if they owned the project by getting them whatever information, financial or otherwise, they needed. I knew that if we could all charge up the hill together, we would be successful."[22]

Second, team leaders are responsible for managing external relationships. Team leaders act as the bridge or liaison between their teams and other teams and other departments and divisions in a company. Third, team leaders are responsible for internal team relationships. Getting along with others is much more important in team structures, because team members can't get work done without the help of their teammates. And when conflicts arise on a six-, seven-, or eight-person team, the entire team suffers. So it is critical for team leaders to know how to help team members resolve conflicts. For example, at XEL Communications Inc. (www.xel.com), a provider of voice and data transmission equipment for Canadian telecommunications service providers, the standard procedure is for a team leader to take the fighting team members to a conference room. The team leader attempts to mediate the disagreement, hearing each side, and encouraging the team members to agree to a practical solution.[23]

team leaders
managers responsible for facilitating team activities toward goal accomplishment

There are four different kinds of managers. Top managers are responsible for creating a context for change, developing attitudes of commitment and ownership, creating a positive organizational culture through words and actions, and monitoring their companies' business environments. Middle managers are responsible for planning and allocating resources, coordinating and linking groups and departments, monitoring and managing the performance of subunits and managers, and implementing the changes or strategies generated by top managers. First-line managers are responsible for managing the performance of non-managerial employees, teaching direct reports how to do their jobs, and making detailed schedules and operating plans based on middle management's intermediate-range plans. Team leaders are responsible for facilitating team performance, managing external relationships, and facilitating internal team relationships.

4. Managerial Roles

So far, we have described managerial work by focusing on the functions of management (making things happen; meeting the competition; organizing people, projects, and processes; and leading) and by examining the four kinds of managerial jobs (top managers, middle managers, first-line managers, and team leaders). Although these are valid and accurate ways of categorizing managerial work, if you followed managers around as they performed their jobs, you would probably not use the terms planning, organizing, leading, and controlling to describe what they do.

In fact, that's exactly the same conclusion that McGill University business professor Henry Mintzberg came to when he followed five North American CEOs around. Mintzberg spent a week "shadowing" each CEO and analyzing their mail, whom they talked to, and what they did. Mintzberg concluded that managers fulfil three major roles while performing their jobs:[24]

1. interpersonal roles

2. informational roles

3. decisional roles

In other words, managers talk to people, gather and give information, and make decisions. Furthermore, as shown in Exhibit 1.3, these three major roles can be subdivided into ten subroles. Let's examine each major role—interpersonal, informational, and decisional—and their ten subroles.

4.1 Interpersonal Roles

More than anything else, management jobs are people-intensive. Estimates vary with the level of management, but most managers spend between two-thirds and four-fifths of their time in face-to-face communication with others.[25] If you're a loner, or if you consider dealing with people to be a "pain," you may not be cut out for management work. In fulfilling the interpersonal role of management, managers perform three interpersonal subroles: figurehead, leader, and liaison.

In the **figurehead role**, managers perform ceremonial duties, like greeting company visitors, making opening remarks when a new facility opens, or representing the company at a community luncheon to support local charities. Each time that Coca-Cola (www.cocacola.com) opens a new bottling plant somewhere around the world, Coke's CEO flies in on the Coke corporate jet for an opening celebration. In the **leader role**, managers motivate and encourage workers to accomplish organizational objectives. Acadia University (www.acadiau.ca) in Wolfville, Nova Scotia, recognizes outstanding innovations from both its faculty and staff members by offering an annual award, called the President's Award for Innovation, the brainchild of former president Kelvin Ogilvie. It is awarded for ideas that increase the use of the laptop computers that are issued to all

figurehead role
the interpersonal role managers play when they perform ceremonial duties

leader role
the interpersonal role managers play when they motivate and encourage workers to accomplish organizational objectives

EXHIBIT 1.3

MINTZBERG'S MANAGERIAL ROLES AND SUBROLES

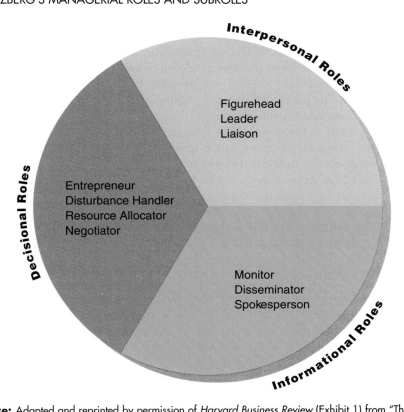

faculty members and students. Successful innovations to date have included real-time business-case-analysis pedagogy, virtual learning environments, and laptop-based sound-recording studios. Finally, in the **liaison role**, managers deal with people outside their units. Studies consistently indicate that managers spend as much time with "outsiders" as they do with their own subordinates and their own bosses.

liaison role
the interpersonal role managers play when they deal with people outside their units

4.2 Informational Roles

While managers spend most of their time in face-to-face contact with others, most of that time is spent obtaining and sharing information. Indeed, Mintzberg found that the managers in his study spent 40 percent of their time giving and getting information from others. In this regard, management can be viewed as processing information, gathering information by scanning the business environment and listening to others in face-to-face conversations, and then sharing that information with people inside and outside the company. Mintzberg described three informational subroles: monitor, disseminator, and spokesperson.

In the **monitor role**, managers scan their environment for information, actively contact others for information, and, because of their personal contacts, receive a great deal of unsolicited information. Besides receiving firsthand information, managers monitor their environment by reading local newspapers and papers such as the *Globe and Mail* or *Financial Post* to keep track of customers, competitors, and technological changes that may affect their businesses. However, electronic monitoring and distribution services such as Canada NewsWire (www.canadanewswire.com) and Rocketinfo (www.rocketnews.com) deliver customized electronic newspapers to managers, including only the stories on topics the managers specify.

monitor role
the informational role managers play when they scan their environment for information

disseminator role
the informational role managers play when they share information with others in their departments or companies

Because of their numerous personal contacts, and because of the access they have to subordinates, managers are often hubs for distribution of critical information. In the **disseminator role**, managers share the information they have collected with their subordinates and others in the company. Although there will never be a complete substitute for face-to-face dissemination of information, a primary method of communication in large companies such as Intel, maker of Pentium processors, and Aliant (www.aliant.ca), an eastern Canadian based provider of telecommunications services and technologies, is e-mail. David Rathbun, a senior vice president at Aliant, estimates that he regularly spends two hours per day writing and responding to his e-mail—in other words, gathering and disseminating information.[26]

spokesperson role
the informational role managers play when they share information with people outside their departments or companies

In contrast to the disseminator role, in which managers distribute information to employees inside the company, in the **spokesperson role**, managers share information with people outside their departments and companies. One of the most common ways in which CEOs serve as spokespeople for their companies is at annual meetings with company shareholders or the board of directors. For example, at McDonald's shareholder meeting, Michael Quinlan, who had been CEO for 11 years, announced that Jack Greenberg would replace him as McDonald's new CEO. Quinlan stayed on as chairperson of McDonald's board of directors.[27]

4.3 Decisional Roles

While managers spend most of their time in face-to-face contact with others, obtaining and sharing information, that time, according to Mintzberg, is not an end in itself. The time spent talking to and obtaining and sharing information with people inside and outside of the company is useful to managers because it helps them make good decisions. According to Mintzberg, managers engage in four decisional subroles: entrepreneur, disturbance handler, resource allocator, and negotiator.

entrepreneur role
the decisional role managers play when they adapt themselves, their subordinates, and their units to incremental change

disturbance handler role
the decisional role managers play when they respond to severe problems that demand immediate action

In the **entrepreneur role**, managers adapt themselves, their subordinates, and their units to incremental change. In the **disturbance handler role**, managers respond to pressures and problems so severe that they demand immediate attention and action. Managers often play the role of disturbance handler when the company board hires a new CEO who is charged with turning around a failing company. When Nortel Networks' (www.nortelnetworks.com) CEO John Roth retired in October 2001, he handed the controls over to his chief financial officer, Frank Dunn,[28] whose role would be nothing short of designated saviour in the face of the collapse of the market for many of the firm's telecommunications products. In an effort to turn around the troubled firm, Dunn proceeded to drastically cut Nortel's workforce, product lines, and research and development expenditures while closing facilities around the world.

In some instances, entrepreneur-style managers will follow disturbance handlers. When GEAC Computer Corp.'s (www.geac.com) 1999 acquisition, enterprise resource planning firm JBA Holdings Plc, began losing approximately $1 million a week during 2000, its newly hired CEO, a turnaround expert or disturbance handler, John Caldwell, took drastic action by laying off 30 percent of its workforce, altering his top management team, and focusing its product offerings. Once the financial crisis was stabilized, Caldwell was in turn let go by GEAC's board of directors and replaced by its chief operating officer, Paul Birch, who then played an entrepreneur role seeking out new but less risky acquisitions to help the Toronto-based firm grow.[29,30]

resource allocator role
the decisional role managers play when they decide who gets what resources

In the **resource allocator role**, managers decide who will get what resources and how many resources they get.

negotiator role
the decisional role managers play when they negotiate schedules, projects, goals, outcomes, resources, and employee raises

In the **negotiator role**, managers negotiate schedules, projects, goals, outcomes, resources, and employee raises. For example, every three years the United Auto Workers labour union renegotiates its labour contract with the "Big Three" auto companies— Ford, DaimlerChrysler, and General Motors.

Managers perform interpersonal, informational, and decisional roles in their jobs. In fulfilling the interpersonal role, managers act as figureheads by performing ceremonial duties, as leaders by motivating and encouraging workers, and as liaisons by dealing with people outside their units. In performing their informational role, managers act as monitors by scanning their environment for information, as disseminators by sharing information with others in the company, and as spokespersons by sharing information with people outside their departments or companies. In fulfilling decisional roles, managers act as entrepreneurs by adapting their units to incremental change, as disturbance handlers by responding to larger problems that demand immediate action, as resource allocators by deciding who will get what resources and how many resources they will get, and as negotiators by bargaining with others about schedules, projects, goals, outcomes, and resources.

What Does It Take to Be a Manager?

I didn't have the slightest idea what my job was. I walked in giggling and laughing because I had been promoted and had no idea what principles or style to be guided by. After the first day I felt like I had run into a brick wall. (Sales Representative 1).

Suddenly, I found myself saying, boy, I can't be responsible for getting all that revenue. I don't have the time. Suddenly you've got to go from [taking care of] yourself and say now I'm the manager, and what does a manager do? It takes a while thinking about it for it to really hit you ... a manager gets things done through other people. That's a very, very hard transition to make.[31] (Sales Representative 2).

The above statements were made by two star sales representatives, who, on the basis of their superior performance, were promoted to the position of sales manager. Their comments clearly indicate that at first they did not feel confident about their ability to do their jobs as managers. Like most new managers, these sales managers were suddenly faced with the realization that the knowledge, skills, and abilities that led to success early in their careers (and which were probably responsible for their promotion into the ranks of management) would not necessarily help them succeed as managers. As sales representatives, they were responsible only for managing their own performance. But as sales managers, they were now directly responsible for supervising all the sales representatives in their sales territories. Furthermore, they were now held directly accountable for whether those sales representatives achieved their sales goals.

If performance in non-managerial jobs doesn't necessarily prepare you for a managerial job, then what does it take to be a manager?

After reading the next three sections, you should be able to
5. *explain what companies look for in managers.*
6. *discuss the top mistakes that managers make in their jobs.*
7. *describe the transition that employees go through when they are promoted to management.*

5. What Companies Look for in Managers

Broadly speaking, when companies look for employees who would be good managers, they look for individuals who have technical skills, human skills, and conceptual skills, and are motivated to manage.[32] Exhibit 1.4 shows the relative importance of these four skills to the jobs of team leaders, first-line managers, middle managers, and top managers.

technical skills
the ability to apply the specialized procedures, techniques, and knowledge required to get the job done

Technical skills are the ability to apply the specialized procedures, techniques, and knowledge required to get the job done. For the sales managers described above, technical skills are the ability to find new sales prospects, develop accurate sales pitches based on customer needs, and close the sale.

Technical skills are most important for lower-level managers, because these managers supervise the workers who produce products or serve customers. Team leaders and first-line managers need technical knowledge and skills to train new employees and help employees solve problems. Technical knowledge and skills are also needed to troubleshoot problems that employees can't handle. Technical skills become less important as managers rise through the managerial ranks, but they are still important. Indeed, Bill Gates, founder and former CEO of Microsoft Corporation, used to spend roughly 40 percent of his time dealing with the technical issues related to development of Microsoft software products.

human skill
the ability to work well with others

Human skill is the ability to work well with others. Managers with "people" skills work effectively within groups, encourage others to express their thoughts and feelings, are sensitive to others' needs and viewpoints, and are good listeners and communicators. Human skills are equally important at all levels of management, from first-line supervisors to CEOs. However, because lower-level managers spend much of their time solving technical problems, upper-level managers may actually spend more time dealing directly with people. On average, first-line managers spend 57 percent of their time with people, middle managers spend 63 percent of their time directly with people, and top managers spend as much as 78 percent of their time dealing with people.[33]

conceptual skill
the ability to see the organization as a whole, how the different parts affect each other, and how the company fits into or is affected by its environment

Conceptual skill is the ability to see the organization as whole, how the different parts of the company affect each other, and how the company fits into or is affected by its external environment, such as the local community, social and economic forces, customers, and competition. Good managers have to be able to recognize, understand, and reconcile multiple complex problems and perspectives. In other words, managers have to

---

EXHIBIT 1.4

RELATIVE IMPORTANCE OF MANAGERIAL SKILLS TO DIFFERENT MANAGERIAL JOBS

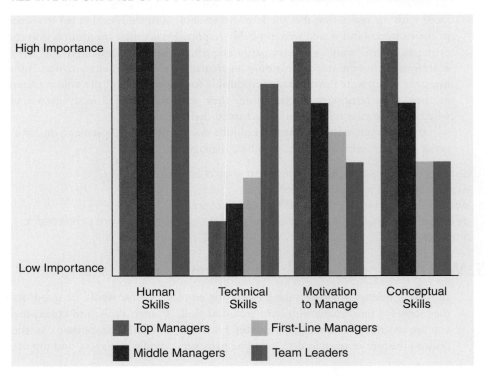

be smart! In fact, intelligence makes so much difference for managerial performance that managers with above-average intelligence typically outperform managers of average intelligence by approximately 48 percent.[34] Clearly, companies need to be careful to promote smart workers into management. Conceptual skill increases in importance as managers rise through the management hierarchy.

However, there is much more to good management than intelligence. For example, making the department genius a manager can be disastrous if that genius lacks technical skills, human skills, or one other factor known as the motivation to manage. **Motivation to manage** is an assessment of how motivated employees are to interact with superiors, participate in competitive situations, behave assertively toward others, tell others what to do, reward good behaviour and punish poor behaviour, perform actions that are highly visible to others, and handle and organize administrative tasks. Implicit in the research of Dr. Barry Wright of St. Francis Xavier University is the need for managers to be extremely motivated when performing certain tasks. He examined the human toll that managers face when charged with organizational downsizing and found that the personal costs include social and organizational isolation, a decline in personal well-being, and decreased family functioning.

Managers typically have a stronger motivation to manage than their subordinates, and managers at higher levels usually have stronger motivation to manage than managers at lower levels. Furthermore, managers with stronger motivation to manage are promoted faster, are rated by their employees as better managers, and earn more money than managers with a weak motivation to manage.[35]

motivation to manage
an assessment of how enthusiastic employees are about managing the work of others

Review 5
What Companies Look for in Managers

Companies do not want one-dimensional managers. They want managers with a balance of skills. They want managers who know their stuff (technical skills), are equally comfortable working with blue-collar and white-collar employees (human skills), are able to assess the complexities of today's competitive marketplace and position their companies for success (conceptual skills), and want to assume positions of leadership and power (motivation to manage). Technical skills are most important for lower-level managers, human skills are equally important at all levels of management, and conceptual skills and motivation to manage increase in importance as managers rise through the managerial ranks.

6. Mistakes Managers Make

Another way to understand what it takes to be a manager is to look at the mistakes managers make. One mistake is to assume too many personal responsibilities. For example, as mayor of Calgary (www.calgary.com), Al Duerr, a husband and father of two children, typically worked 60 to 80 hours a week. On top of this, in 1995 Duerr enrolled in an MBA program at the University of Calgary; he completed it in 2001. Not surprisingly, he decided not to run for re-election that year following more than a decade as mayor. During one hectic 60-day period, Duerr found himself arriving at the office at 8:00 a.m., undertaking mayoral functions until he left for evening classes, and then meeting late in the evening with union officials to resolve a transit strike.[36] Duerr's example suggests that we can learn just as much from what managers shouldn't do as we can from what they should do. Exhibit 1.5 lists the top ten mistakes managers make.

Several studies of North American and British managers have compared "arrivers," managers who made it all the way to the top of their companies, to "derailers," managers who were successful early in their careers but were knocked off the "fast track" by the time they reached middle to upper levels of management.[37] The first result they found was that there were few differences between arrivers and derailers. For the most part, both groups were talented and both groups had weaknesses. But what distinguished derailers from arrivers was that derailers possessed two or more "fatal flaws" with respect to the

EXHIBIT 1.5

TOP TEN MISTAKES THAT MANAGERS MAKE

1. Insensitive to others: abrasive, intimidating, bullying style.
2. Cold, aloof, arrogant.
3. Betrayal of trust.
4. Overly ambitious: thinking of next job, playing politics.
5. Specific performance problems with the business.
6. Overmanaging: unable to delegate or build a team.
7. Unable to staff effectively.
8. Unable to think strategically.
9. Unable to adapt to boss with different style.
10. Overdependent on advocate or mentor.

Source: M.W. McCall, Jr. & M.M. Lombardo, "What Makes a Top Executive?" *Psychology Today*, February 1983, 26–31.

way that they managed people! By contrast, arrivers, who were by no means perfect, usually had no more than one fatal flaw, or they had found ways to minimize the effects of their flaws on the people with whom they work.

The number one mistake made by derailers was that they were insensitive to others by virtue of their abrasive, intimidating, and bullying management style. The authors of one study cited the manager who walked into his subordinate's office and interrupted a meeting by saying, "I need to see you." When the subordinate tried to explain that he wasn't available because he was in the middle of a meeting, the manager barked, "I don't give a damn. I said I wanted to see you now."[38] Not surprisingly, only 25 percent of derailers were rated by others as being good with people, compared to 75 percent of arrivers.

Not being able to build a team is a fatal management mistake. Managers on the diversity council, pictured here, work as a team to ensure that their company has a diverse employee base. Effective diversity managers take care to build strong teams and avoid making a fatal management mistake.

www.comstock.com

The second mistake was that derailers were often cold, aloof, or arrogant. While this sounds like insensitivity to others, this has more to do with derailed managers being so smart, so expert in their areas of knowledge, that they treated others with contempt because they weren't experts, too.

The third and fourth mistakes made by derailers, betraying a trust and being overly ambitious, indicate a lack of concern for co-workers and subordinates. Betraying a trust doesn't mean being dishonest. Instead, it means making others look bad by not doing what you said you would do when you said you would do it. That mistake, in itself, is not fatal, because managers and their workers aren't machines. Tasks go undone in every company every single business day. There's always too much to do and not enough time, people, money, or resources to do it. The fatal betrayal of trust is failing to inform others when things would not be done on time. This failure to admit mistakes, to quickly inform others of the mistakes, to take responsibility for the mistakes, and then to fix the mistakes without blaming others clearly distinguished the behaviour of derailers from arrivers.

The fourth mistake, mentioned above, was being overly political and ambitious. Managers who always have their eye on their next job rarely do more than establish superficial relationships with peers and co-workers. In their haste to gain credit for successes that would be noticed by upper management, they make the fatal mistake of treating people like they don't matter.

The fatal mistakes of being unable to delegate, to build a team, and to staff effectively indicate that many derailed managers were unable to make the most basic transition to managerial work: to quit being hands-on "doers" and get work done through others. Two things go wrong when managers make these mistakes. First, when managers meddle in decisions that their subordinates should be making, when they can't quit being doers, they alienate the people who work for them. Second, because they are trying to do their subordinates' jobs in addition to their own, managers who fail to delegate to their workers will not have enough time to do much of anything well.

For example, before becoming president of Harvard University, Neil Rudenstine's management style had always been to take on more and more work himself. So when he became a university president, and the demands placed on him increased, he responded by working even longer hours, usually 12 to 14 hours a day. While it is the norm for university presidents to put in long hours, Dr. Rudenstine made it even tougher on himself by failing to delegate work to his associates. Figuring out how to solve the shortage of parking spaces on campus or arranging to have contractors fix leaky roofs are not good uses of a university president's time. Indeed, the combination of long hours and his inability to delegate led to mental and physical exhaustion and a physician-mandated leave of absence from his job as Harvard University president.[39]

Review 6
Mistakes Managers Make

Another way to understand what it takes to be a manager is to look at the top mistakes managers make. Five of the most important mistakes made by managers are being abrasive and intimidating; being cold, aloof, or arrogant; betraying trust; being overly ambitious; and failing to build a team and then delegate to that team.

7. The Transition to Management: The First Year

In her book *Becoming a Manager: Master of a New Identity*, Harvard Business School professor Linda Hill followed the development of 19 people in their first year as managers. Two overall themes emerged from Dr. Hill's study. First, becoming a manager produced a profound psychological transition that changed the way these managers viewed themselves and others. Second, the only way to really learn how to manage was to be a manager. As shown in Exhibit 1.6, a good way to appreciate the magnitude of the changes these managers experienced is to describe their thoughts, expectations, and realities as they evolved over the course of their first year in management.

Initially, the managers in Hill's study believed that their job was to exercise formal authority and to manage tasks—basically being the boss, telling others what to do, making decisions, and getting things done. One manager said, "Being the manager means running my own office, using my ideas and thoughts." In fact, most of the new managers were attracted to management positions because they wanted to be "in charge." Surprisingly, the new managers did not believe that their job was to manage people. The only two aspects of people management mentioned by the new managers were hiring and firing.

After six months, most of the new managers had come to the conclusion that their initial expectations about managerial work were wrong. Management wasn't being "the boss." It wasn't just about making decisions and telling others what to do. The first surprise to the new managers was the fast pace and heavy workload involved in being a manager. One manager stated, "This job is much harder than you think. It is 40 to 50 percent more work than being a producer! Who would have ever guessed?" The pace of managerial work was startling, too. Another manager said, "You have eight or nine people looking for your time ... coming into and out of your office all day long."

Informal descriptions like this are consistent with studies that indicate that the average first-line manager spends no more than two minutes on a task before being interrupted by a request from a subordinate, a phone call, or an e-mail. The pace is somewhat less hurried for top managers, who spend an average of approximately nine minutes on a task before having to switch to another. In practice, this means that supervisors may perform thirty different tasks per hour, while top managers perform seven different tasks per hour, with each task typically different from the one that preceded it. A manager described this frenetic level of activity by saying, "The only time you are in control is when you shut your door, and then I feel I am not doing the job I'm supposed to be doing, which is being with the people."

EXHIBIT 1.6

THE TRANSITION TO MANAGEMENT: INITIAL EXPECTATIONS, AFTER SIX MONTHS, AND AFTER A YEAR

MANAGER'S INITIAL EXPECTATIONS	AFTER SIX MONTHS AS A MANAGER	AFTER A YEAR AS A MANAGER
• Be the boss	• Initial expectations were wrong	• No longer "doers"
• Formal authority	• Fast pace	• Communication, listening, and positive reinforcement
• Manage tasks	• Heavy workload	
• Job is not managing people	• Job is to be problem-solver and trouble-shooter for subordinates.	• Job is people development

Source: L.A. Hill, *Becoming a Manager: Mastery of a New Identity* (Boston, MA: Harvard Business School Press, 1992).

The other major surprise after six months on the job was that the managers' expectations about what they should do as managers were very different from their subordinates' expectations. Initially, the managers defined their jobs as helping their subordinates perform their jobs well. For the managers, who still defined themselves as doers rather than managers, assisting their subordinates meant going out on sales calls or handling customer complaints. One manager said, "I like going out with the rep, who may need me to lend him my credibility as manager. I like the challenge, the joy in closing. I go out with the reps and we make the call and talk about the customer; it's fun." But when the managers "assisted" in this way, their subordinates were resentful and viewed their help as interference. What the subordinates wanted in the way of assistance was for their managers to solve problems that they couldn't solve. Once the managers realized this contradiction, they embraced their role as problem-solver and troubleshooter. Thus, they could help without interfering with their subordinates' jobs.

After a year on the job, most of the managers no longer thought of themselves as doers, but managers. In making the transition, they finally realized that people management was the most important part of their jobs. Most of the managers now regretted the rather heavy-handed approach they had used in their early attempts to manage their subordinates. "I wasn't good at managing..., so I was bossy like a first-grade teacher." "Now I see that I started out as a drill sergeant. I was inflexible, just a lot of how-to's." By the end of the year, most of the managers had abandoned their authoritarian approach for one based on communication, listening, and positive reinforcement. One manager explained, "Last night at five I handed out an award in the boardroom just to the individual. It was the first time in his career that he had done [earned] $100 000, and I gave him a piece of glass [a small award] and said I'd heard a rumour that somebody here just crossed over $100 000 and I said congratulations, shook his hand, and walked away. It was not public in the sense that I gathered everybody around. But I knew and he did too."

Finally, after beginning their year as managers in frustration, the managers came to feel comfortable with their subordinates, with the demands of their jobs, and with their emerging managerial styles. While being managers had made them acutely aware of their limitations and their need to develop as people, it also provided them with an unexpected reward of the "thrill" of coaching and developing the people who worked for them. One manager said, "It gives me the best feeling to see somebody do something well after I have helped them. I get excited."

Review **7**

The Transition to Management: The First Year

Managers often begin their jobs by using more formal authority and less people management. However, most managers find that being a manager has little to do with "bossing" their subordinates. After six months on the job, the managers were surprised at the fast pace, the heavy workload, and that "helping" their subordinates was viewed as interference. After a year on the job, most of the managers no longer thought of themselves as doers, but managers who get things done through others. And, because they finally realized that people management was the most important part of their job, most of them had abandoned their authoritarian approach for one based on communication, listening, and positive reinforcement.

Why Management Matters

If you walk down the aisle of the "business" section in your local bookstore, you'll find hundreds of books that explain precisely what companies need to do to be successful. Unfortunately, business books tend to be faddish, changing every few years. Lately, the best-selling business books have emphasized technology, reengineering, and going global, whereas ten years ago the hot topics were joint ventures, mergers, and management buyouts. One thing that hasn't changed, though, is the importance of good people and good management: Companies can't succeed for long without them.

8. Competitive Advantage Through People

In his book, *Competitive Advantage Through People*, Stanford University business professor Jeffrey Pfeffer contends that what separates top companies from their competitors is the way they treat their workforces; in other words, management. Managers in top-performing companies use ideas like employee ownership, incentive pay, employee participation and empowerment, and the other techniques explained in Exhibit 1.7 to develop workforces that are smarter, better trained, more motivated, and more committed than their competitors' workforces. And, as indicated by the phenomenal growth and return on investment earned by the companies in his study, smarter, better trained, and more committed workforces provide superior products and service to customers, who keep buying and who, by telling others about their positive experiences, bring in new customers.

Pfeffer also argues that companies that invest in their people will create long-lasting competitive advantages that are difficult for other companies to duplicate. Indeed, studies clearly demonstrate that sound management practices can produce substantial advantages in three critical areas of organizational performance: sales revenues, profits, and customer satisfaction. For example, a study of nearly 1000 North American firms indicated that companies that use just some of the ideas shown in Exhibit 1.7 had approximately $43 000 more sales per employee and approximately $6000 more profit

---

EXHIBIT 1.7

COMPETITIVE ADVANTAGE THROUGH PEOPLE: MANAGEMENT PRACTICES

1. **Employment Security**—Employment security is the ultimate form of commitment that companies can make to their workers. Employees can innovate and increase company productivity without fearing the loss of their jobs.
2. **Selective Hiring**—If employees are the basis for a company's competitive advantage, and those employees have employment security, then the company needs to aggressively recruit and selectively screen applicants in order to hire the most talented employees available.
3. **Self-Managed Teams and Decentralization**—Self-managed teams are responsible for their own hiring, purchasing, job assignments, and production. Self-managed teams can often produce enormous increases in productivity through increased employee commitment and creativity. Decentralization allows employees who are closest to (and most knowledgeable about) problems, production, and customers to make timely decisions. Decentralization increases employee satisfaction and commitment.
4. **High Wages Contingent on Organizational Performance**—High wages are needed to attract and retain talented workers and to indicate that the organization values its workers. Employees, like company founders, shareholders, and managers, need to share in the financial rewards when the company is successful. Why? Because employees who have a financial stake in their companies are more likely to take a long-run view of the business and think like business owners.
5. **Training and Skill Development**—Like a high-tech company that spends millions of dollars to upgrade computers or research and development labs, a company whose competitive advantage is based on its people must invest in the training and skill development of its people.
6. **Reduction of Status Differences**—These are fancy words that indicate that the company treats everyone, no matter what their job, as equals. There are no reserved parking spaces. Everyone eats in the same cafeteria and has similar benefits. The result: much improved communication as employees focus on problems and solutions rather than how they are less valued than managers.
7. **Sharing Information**—If employees are to make decisions that are good for the long-run health and success of the company, they need to be given information about costs, finances, productivity, development times, and strategies that were previously known only by company managers.

Source: J. Pfeffer, *The Human Equation: Building Profits by Putting People First* (Boston, MA: Harvard Business School Press, 1996).

per employee than companies that didn't.[40] For a 100-person company, these differences amount to $4.3 million more in sales and more than $600 000 extra in annual profit! For a 1000-person company, the difference grows to an additional $43 million in sales and at least $6 million more in annual profit!

Another study found that poorly performing companies that adopted management techniques as simple as setting expectations (setting goals, results, and schedules), coaching (informal, ongoing discussions between managers and subordinates about what is being done well and what could be done better), reviewing (annual, formal discussion about results), and rewarding (adjusting salaries and bonuses based on employee performance and results) were able to improve average return on investment from 5.1 percent to 19.7 percent and increase sales by $150 000 per employee![41] So, in addition to significantly improving the profitability of healthy companies, sound management practices can turn around failing companies.

Research also indicates that managers have an important effect on customer satisfaction. However, many people find this surprising. They don't understand how managers, who are largely responsible for what goes on inside the company, can affect what goes on outside the company. They wonder how managers, who often interact with customers under negative conditions (when customers are angry or dissatisfied), can actually improve customer satisfaction. It turns out that the way managers influence customer satisfaction is through employee satisfaction. When employees are satisfied with their jobs, their bosses, and the companies they work for, they provide much better service to customers.[42] In turn, customers are more satisfied, too.

Review 8
Competitive Advantage Through People

Why does management matter? Well-managed companies are competitive because their workforces are smarter, better trained, more motivated, and more committed. Furthermore, companies that practise good management consistently have greater revenues and profits than companies that don't. Finally, good management matters because good management leads to satisfied employees who, in turn, provide better service to customers. Because employees tend to treat customers the same way that their managers treat them, good management can improve customer satisfaction.

What Really Happened?

At the beginning of this chapter, you read about the challenges facing Mario Theriault and the company he founded, Shift Central. As you'll see below, their response was quite interesting and addressed the basic functions performed by managers. Find out what really happened at Shift Central by reading the following answers to the chapter-opening case "What Would You Do?"

Making Things Happen

Top managers realize that the key to strong performance is making things happen in their company. Mario Theriault's role was to, first, develop an in-house capability to deliver customized information and analysis in a timely manner to geographically dispersed clients, and, second, sell those services. Once an in-house capability was established, Theriault began knocking on doors of regional corporate players. Among his first successes was a contract to provide surveillance services for the e-learning marketplace to a subsidiary of Aliant Inc. Soon other clients followed, including Industry Canada, Université de Moncton, and Emera (formerly Nova Scotia Power).

Meeting the Competition

Along with making things happen, top managers also need to understand the behaviour of competitors, offer products and services that fit the competitive environment, and respond to industry or market changes when necessary. Theriault chose to meet the challenge of the traditional management consulting and communications firms by initially occupying a niche in between. That niche was as a provider of timely and relevant market surveillance research customized by industry and obtained from publicly available websites. This strategy ensured that any research activity undertaken by Shift Central would not cross the line of ethical conduct and that information obsolescence would not be an issue with clients as it was in the case of some traditional marketing research companies. It also laid the groundwork for future partnerships with these larger competitors. Customers' concerns about spying were removed by using public information services; delivering timely information online satisfied customers' requests that information be sent on an ongoing basis rather than at the end of each deliverable cycle. Using language commonly associated with marketing research as opposed to the "government" or "military" intelligence profession increased the user-friendliness of the service.

Leading

In good times or bad, top managers are responsible for the overall direction and performance of their company. In the case of Shift Central, Theriault needed to find a niche for his company. His vision was to integrate technology with research and strategic planning and offer the service to clients using the well-known language of marketing research with the ethical computer-aided practices of CI. Shift Central would present itself as a flexible service provider that could change easily to meet customer needs and help clients make sense of their complex operating environments. Theriault's objectives were fairly straightforward: within two years enhance revenues, broaden the client base, and offer a simpler and easier-to-use set of services. The result was a doubling of revenues, a client base that included Aliant, Emera, Atlantic Canada Opportunities Agency, the Université de Moncton, and Human Resources Development Canada, and services that included information dissemination through "push technology" (in other words, the service provides the client with information, the client doesn't need to access a website), archiving, information tailoring, and strategic planning.

Organizing People, Projects, and Processes

Finally, top managers need to build solid organizations. Given the youth and size of Shift Central, as well as an awareness of his own personal limitations, Theriault focused his efforts on building an in-house culture geared toward growth. Shift Central offered higher salaries, a global vision in a Moncton office, and an awareness that the company was on the cutting edge of innovation. Realizing that his firm's strength would be information and not necessarily technology, Theriault limited in-house software development to building the platform that would support the information offerings provided to clients. These included the information archive, the user interface, the client portal, and the search utility.

The subsequent positioning of Shift Central's offer of Ongoing Insight as the company's branded approach crystallized its growth effort: ongoing for the use of technology and the reference to real-time research; and insight as the determining factor of the professional services industry.

Shift Central's processes were not complicated. For instance, with regard to information tailoring, publicly available news aggregator websites (sites that gather news stories from many different online sources) allowed Shift Central employees to identify relevant information. Once identified, this information was then summarized in a paragraph with a link to the original story. These headlines and links were sent once a day by e-mail to clients and were also archived. Clients accessed this information and the archives from their computers through a customized password-protected portal or website.

Sources: M. Higgins, "The Renaissance Man," *Atlantic Progress*, 21 January 2002. C. Spence, "Net Monitor for Business," *New Brunswick Telegraph Journal*, 5 June 2002.

Key Terms

conceptual skill (18)
controlling (5)
disseminator role (16)
disturbance handler role (16)
effectiveness (5)
efficiency (5)
entrepreneur role (16)
figurehead role (14)
first-line managers (12)

human skill (18)
leader role (14)
leading (5)
liaison role (15)
management (5)
meta-analysis (7)
middle managers (12)
monitor role (15)
motivation to manage (19)

negotiator role (16)
organizing (5)
planning (5)
resource allocator role (16)
spokesperson role (16)
team leaders (13)
technical skills (18)
top managers (11)

What Would You Do II?

It's Sunday morning as you sit on the patio of your 14th-floor condo overlooking Ile des Soeurs, soaking up the sunshine and reading your copy of the *Globe and Mail's Report on Business*. As head of North American futures market trading for your bank's regional headquarters in Montreal, you supervise 20 different traders who, by buying thousands of dollars of futures contracts, can take advantage of price differences between contracts traded around the world. Technically, what they trade doesn't really matter because the traders make their money by buying something for 50 cents in one location and selling it for 50 and 3/8 cents in another. By making volume purchases, that small price difference earns the banks profits.

Most of the people who work for you are professionals. The typical trader in your office was a finance major as an undergraduate and then attended one of the better graduate schools of business in Europe, Canada, or the United States. Traders work long hours and must follow financial news around the world as it happens. Seventy-hour weeks are the norm. Furthermore, futures trading is an aggressive business and is not for the faint of heart. Millions can be won or lost in a very short time. This is why you are concerned about two of your employees, John and Mary. John is extremely talented, one of your best performers, but he is insensitive to others and does not have good interpersonal skills. Because of his capabilities and his sheer intelligence, John is impatient with co-workers who cannot keep up with his trading activity and strategies. Not only have you

begun to get complaints about John from his co-workers, but you're also beginning to get complaints from traders outside the company.

In contrast, Mary is very easy to get along with. Charming is a word that is frequently used to describe her. While a fun person to be around, Mary's job performance is a problem. Frequently, you and other traders have to cover for mistakes she makes or for work she did not get done on time. She has been careful to build alliances with important people in the company. She can often be found at higher-up social gatherings or at lunch with important company clients. However, you fear that her performance is putting you and the company at risk.

Unfortunately, you're not sure how to handle John or Mary. In fact, you have been avoiding them for the past few months, hoping that the problems would just take care of themselves. The issue is complicated because it is difficult to find good traders. Financial firms are in strong competition for trading talent, so it won't be easy to find good replacements.

Suddenly, the wind from the harbour blows the *Report on Business* out of your hand. It sails off the patio and slowly begins its descent, alternately rising and falling with the wind gusting between the high-rise buildings that dominate the downtown skyline. A bad omen? You hope not as you watch the paper float away. **If you were the head of trading at the Canadian bank regional headquarters in Montreal, what would you do?**

Critical Thinking Video Case

Nova Scotian Crystal

The waterfront of Halifax, Nova Scotia, is a wonderful place to be a tourist in the summer. It is also the home of a unique Canadian company. Nova Scotian Crystal makes fine crystal the old-fashioned way. Its scenic location offers tourists the opportunity to both observe how traditional craftsmen produce fine crystal and purchase selections from its retail store. Nova Scotian Crystal is typical of many small firms. Its home market, Halifax, is too small to sustain it over time. To offset this drawback, it also sells directly to customers through a catalogue, a website, and trade shows.

In this video we learn how two seeming opposites, chairman Denis Ryan and president Rod McCallum, use their distinct skills to guide Nova Scotian Crystal through a series of ups and downs in its quest for growth and sustainability. As you watch the video, consider the following critical thinking question.

Critical Thinking Question

The two Nova Scotian Crystal executives portrayed in the video play different decisional and informational roles. What are their roles and how might they affect the success of the company?

Management Decisions

Who Deserves the Promotion?

This week was destined to be a difficult one. After eight years, I had finally achieved a long sought after goal—managing director of a medium-sized public relations firm based in Ottawa. Our firm had experienced steady growth over the last decade due in part to a decision made years ago to focus our resources on helping Canada's provincial and territorial governments promote their positions nationwide. Also tied to this success was a strong sense of teamwork and collegiality among a loyal, committed group of employees. Unfortunately, growth had forced on me an important decision.

Celine, my first boss and long-time mentor, laughed when I asked her what she thought I should do. "You're the one who wanted to be an executive, hotshot. What do *you* think you should do?" she asked with a laugh. "Seriously, I can't make this decision for you. Trust your instincts. But remember, you're going to have to live with the consequences of your decision for a long time."

Celine was right. Whoever I promoted was going to be working with me and supervising one of my units for at least three years. And whoever I didn't promote was going to be disappointed for a long time, too. But who deserved the promotion? Should it go to Mathieu? When I asked him why he wanted the promotion, he said he had earned it by turning in three solid years of performance. Or should it go to Valerie? Valerie's teams had been top producers. When I asked her why she wanted the promotion, she said it was because she was getting burned out in her current job and needed a change. However, she also mentioned that management had been a long-time goal.

Questions

1. Who would you promote, Mathieu or Valerie? Why?
2. In order of importance, name three criteria that companies should use when deciding who to promote. Explain why each is important and why they can help companies make good promotion decisions.

Management Decisions

Eeny Meeny Miny Mo...

You are the regional director of research and development for a mid-sized chemical company. This morning, two project directors called to schedule appointments to see you concerning a memo your office released yesterday informing all staff members of budget cuts for the new fiscal year. Because of factors beyond the company's control—a slowing economy, declining sales, lowered earnings projections, and so forth—company officials have mandated an across-the-board cost reduction of 15 percent in all departments. Unfortunately, this reduction will affect your department the most since research and development costs have averaged 23 percent of the company's total expenditures over the last five years. Despite the fact that every dollar invested in chemical research today will yield two dollars of operating income over six years, only one of the two lead projects your department is working on will be fully funded under the new budget. Both project directors will be campaigning for their spe-cific project, and it will be your decision to choose which one receives full funding and which one does not. As you check your daily calendar for possible meeting times, you recall that both projects are equally viable and are expected to require approximately the same amount of money and resources. In meeting with each project director individually, however, you will need to gather specific information in order to make an unbiased, informed decision.

Questions

1. Assuming the role of decision maker, write the script for the part of the meeting in which you tell your project directors you can fund only one project.
2. Assuming the role of resource allocator, what questions will you likely ask to help you make your decision?

Source: N. Gross, "Measuring the Muscle of R&D Spending," *Business Week*, 11 June 2001.

Develop Your Management Potential

Interview Two Managers

Welcome to the first "Develop Your Management Potential" activity! These assignments have one purpose: to help you develop your present and future capabilities as a manager. What you will be learning through these assignments is not traditional "book-learning" based on memorization and regurgitation, but practical knowledge and skills that help managers perform their jobs better. Lessons from some of the assignments—for example, goal setting—can be used for immediate benefit. Other lessons will obviously take time to accomplish, but you can still benefit now by making specific plans for future improvement.

Step 1: Interview Two Practising Managers

In her book *Becoming a Manager: Master of a New Identity*, Harvard Business School professor Linda Hill conducted exten-sive interviews with 19 people in their first year as managers. To learn firsthand what it's like to be a manager, interview two managers you know, asking them some of the same questions, shown below, that Professor Hill asked her managers. Be sure to interview managers with different levels of experience. Interview one person with at least five years' experience as a manager and then interview another person with no more than two years' experience as a manager. Ask the managers these questions:

1. Briefly describe your current position and responsibilities.
2. What do your subordinates expect from you on the job?
3. What are the major stresses and challenges you face on the job?
4. What, if anything, do you dislike about the job?
5. What do you like best about your job?
6. What are the critical differences between average man-agers and top-performing managers?
7. Think about the skills and knowledge that you need to be effective in your job. What are they and how did you acquire them?
8. What have been your biggest mistakes thus far? Could you have avoided them? If so, how?

Step 2: Prepare to Discuss Your Findings

Prepare to discuss your findings in class or write a report (if assigned by your instructor). What conclusions can you draw from your interview data?

Source: L.A. Hill, *Becoming a Manager: Mastery of a New Identity* (Boston, MA: Harvard Business School Press, 1992).

Discussion Questions

1. Junior hockey is an important part of the social fabric of many smaller Canadian cities and towns. Many of these teams are run as businesses. What is the difference between an efficiently run hockey team and an effectively run team?

2. Three management functions are used to organize this text. Describe each briefly and indicate which of the three would clearly be considered different from the traditional management functions.

3. Take a quick look at the career section of your local newspaper. Find one ad that seeks to attract a solid candidate for a middle manager position. With regard to that company and that particular position, what four major responsibilities might a successful candidate be assigned?

4. Go to the Monster.ca website. Browse the available jobs by company. Identify one job that looks particularly appealing to you. If you were given the task of hiring an individual for this position, which four sets of characteristics would you look for in such a manager?

5. Despite changes over the last decade, most bank branches still have managers. Think of the manager at the branch nearest you. A few tellers and administrators probably report to this individual. From time to time he or she may make mistakes while performing his or her duties. Describe at least three of the five most important mistakes that he or she might make.

Study Tip

Use your textbook more like a notebook and less like a reference book. The margins are a great place for writing questions on content you don't understand, highlighting important concepts, and adding examples to help you remember the material. Writing in your book makes it a more comprehensive resource for management and a better study tool.

2

Chapter Outline

Learning Objectives

After reading this chapter, you should be able to

1. discuss how changing environments affect organizations.
2. describe the four components of the general environment.
3. explain the five components of the specific environment.
4. describe the process that companies use to make sense of their changing environments.
5. explain how organizational cultures are created and how they can help companies be successful.

Organizational Environments and Cultures

What Would You Do?

Starting your own airline seems like a great idea. British billionaire Richard Branson built Virgin Atlantic Airways from nothing into a great success in less than a decade. You think to yourself, "He looks like he's having fun. Why not?" Then, on a trip to Boeing, the U.S. passenger jet manufacturer, someone suggests that you look at Southwest Airlines, which runs the lowest cost, yet most profitable airline in U.S. history and the same airline that Westjet successfully modelled itself on. After taking a Southwest flight, you know that their business model (use only one model of plane, the 737, to simplify maintenance and pilot and flight attendant training and certification; ensure quick turnarounds at the gate to keep planes full and in the air; take most of your reservations on the Internet to reduce costs; fly out of smaller, underused airports with much lower landing fees; maintain a fun culture that treats employees and customers right) will work in Europe. The dominant airlines, including British Airways, Lufthansa, and Air France, are heavily subsidized by their governments, face little competition, and are inefficient. You know that you will be able to undercut their prices and still make a significant profit!

So you start EasyJet by leasing two Boeing 737s that fly from Glasgow and Edinburgh in Scotland to London's Luton airport, the smallest of London's four airports and 50 kilometres (roughly 50 minutes) north of central London. With prices half that of the major carriers, customers race to travel in your planes. However, you aren't the only one with this great idea. Dublin-based RyanAir; Portugal's PGA; U.K.-based British Midland, Debonair, and AirOne; and Richard Branson's Virgin Express are also trying to establish themselves as low-cost airlines in Europe.

The biggest threat, though, comes from the largest airline in Europe, British Airways (BA). BA becomes a direct competitor by starting its own low-cost airline, Go, based in London's Stansted airport. But it just isn't BA, with its huge financial resources, entering the game, it's the way they do it. BA's CEO invites you to tea, ostensibly to discuss the possibility of investing in your company. You are flattered, open up your books to show him the numbers, and let BA closely examine every single part of the company. But it is just a trick. BA didn't want to invest in EasyJet. It wants to put you out of business. And with Go's initial success, £40 million ($96 million) in revenue and 700 000 passengers in its first year alone, you should be worried. Go's managing director says, "I underestimated the huge potential."

With start-up costs, intense competition, and rising fuel prices, you lose £5 million (about $12 million) the first year. As if this weren't enough, London's Luton airport, which is owned and run for profit by Barclay's Bank, tries to raise its landing fees from £1.80 ($4.30) to £7.50 ($18.00) per passenger. With 65 percent of your passengers flying through Luton airport, this increased cost will make it much more difficult to make a profit and keep prices low. And, at this point, you haven't been able to convince the Civil Aviation Authority to regulate these charges (airports are privatized and deregulated in Britain). The best you can do is dig in your heels and stall. You tell the newspapers, "We were not willing to be dragged into negotiations with a gun against our heads, which is what Barclay's was hoping for."

So the question is "Will you make it?" The odds are stacked against you. In the United States, 130 airlines have gone out of business in the last 25 years, most of them new start-ups like EasyJet. The same forces that brought them down could bring EasyJet down too. You know that Southwest Airline's low-cost model worked in the United States, but can it work in Europe when so many other air carriers are following the same model? What do you do about the competition? Also, is there anything you can do to influence the cost of landing fees at Luton airport? If EasyJet continues to grow, dealing with airport authorities will become increasingly important. For example, Swissair used its political and financial leverage to try to prevent you from flying between Geneva, Switzerland, and Barcelona, Spain. How do you deal with potentially uncontrollable industry regulators and gatekeepers? Finally, how do you make sense of all this? Your initial business plan was sound and recognized the fantastic opportunities for low-cost airlines in Europe. But now those opportunities seem to be overwhelmed by a growing number of threats.

If you were the founder and CEO of EasyJet airlines, what would you do?

Sources: D. Appell, "The EasyEmpire Strikes Back: Throwing Down the Gauntlet to Europe's Old-Guard Airlines, the Young Greek Entrepreneur Who Birthed Easyjet Airlines and Easyrentacar Has Been Shaking Up the Continent's Budget Travel Market," *Arthur Frommer's Budget Travel.* [Online] Available www.msnbc.com/news/587392. asp?0dm=C29JL, 22 June 2001. M. Harrison, "Easythis, Easythat, Easyfloat: At Least, That's

How Stelios Haji-Ioannou (That's Stelios to You) Would Like to See the Stock Market Debut of EasyJet, the Cut-Price Airline He Has Shouldered into the Big Time. But Will It Be that Simple?" *The Independent* (London), 11 October 2000, 1B. K. Kemp, "Airlines Net Sky-High Results," *The Sunday Herald,* 11 June 1999, 16. B. Wysocki, Jr., "The Challengers—Headwinds: The Odds Are Against Starting an Airline—And Still They Try—With Tenacity and Little Else, These Two Men Took on Majors' Entrenched System— Getting Past 'The Sniff Test'," *The Wall Street Journal,* 16 April 2001, A1.

Starting a new airline is incredibly difficult. Wherever you look, you see changes and forces beyond your control that threaten your ability to make your new business a success. This chapter examines the internal and external forces that affect companies.

External Environments

<dl>
<dt>external environments</dt>
<dd>all events outside a company that have the potential to influence or affect it</dd>
</dl>

External environments are all the events outside a company that have the potential to influence or affect it. For example, Canada exported more than $10 billion worth of lumber to the United States in 2000. In mid-2002, after many years of threatening to place tariffs on Canadian exports, the United States imposed a 27 percent tariff on softwood lumber. This significantly affected producers in British Columbia, Quebec, Ontario, and Alberta, with exports from Quebec and Ontario falling by more than half. Canadian trade officials and industry groups are expected to appeal to the World Trade Organization (WTO) and under the North American Free Trade Agreement (NAFTA) but resolution of these appeals could take years. In the meantime, the effect on some companies and communities has been devastating. Abitibi-Consolidated planned to indefinitely close three sawmills in Quebec and shut down all 22 of its mills in Quebec and Ontario for up to a month.[1]

<dl>
<dt>environmental change</dt>
<dd>the rate at which a company's general and specific environments change</dd>
</dl>

After reading the next four sections, you should be able to
1. *discuss how changing environments affect organizations.*
2. *describe the four components of the general environment.*
3. *explain the five components of the specific environment.*
4. *describe the process that companies use to make sense of their changing environments.*

<dl>
<dt>stable environment</dt>
<dd>environment in which the rate of change is slow</dd>
</dl>

1. Changing Environments

Let's examine the three basic characteristics of changing external environments: environmental change, environmental complexity and munificence, and uncertainty.

<dl>
<dt>dynamic environment</dt>
<dd>environment in which the rate of change is fast</dd>
</dl>

1.1 Environmental Change

Environmental change is the rate at which a company's general and specific environments change. In **stable environments**, the rate of environmental change is slow. In **dynamic environments**, the rate of environmental change is fast. While it would seem that companies would either be in stable external environments or dynamic external environments, recent research suggests that companies often experience both stable and dynamic external environments. According to **punctuated equilibrium theory**, companies go through long, simple periods of stability (equilibrium), followed by short, complex periods of dynamic, fundamental change (revolutionary periods), finishing with a return to stability (new equilibrium).[2]

<dl>
<dt>punctuated equilibrium theory</dt>
<dd>theory that holds that companies go through long, simple periods of stability (equilibrium), followed by short periods of dynamic, fundamental change (revolution), and ending with a return to stability (new equilibrium)</dd>
</dl>

One example of punctuated equilibrium theory is the Canadian airline industry. Twice in the last 25 years, the Canadian airline industry has experienced revolutionary periods. The first occurred with the advent of airline deregulation that began in 1978 in response to U.S. deregulation. Prior to deregulation, the industry was dominated by the "friendly duopoly" of CP Air and Air Canada that shared over 95 percent of the market, but the federal government controlled where airlines could fly, when they could fly, prices they could charge, and the number of flights they could have on a particular route. Although full deregulation was not seen in Canada until 1988, airlines had more choices to make and many competitors such as Wardair, which was primarily a charter airline, and Pacific Western Airlines, a regional carrier, expanded and new air carriers were started. Competition among the airlines was fierce, and Pacific Western Airlines purchased several smaller airlines, including Wardair. In 1987 it purchased the much larger CP Air to form Canadian Airlines. Canadian Airlines was a truly national carrier, and although somewhat smaller than Air Canada, it was in a position to compete with Air Canada on an even basis. After experiencing substantially increased levels of competition, two companies again dominated the skies, Canadian Airlines and Air Canada, and a period of relative stability was seen. The dominance of these two carriers was first seriously challenged in 1996 with the emergence of WestJet Airlines, which started as a western-based airline. Canadian, too, was a western-based airline. Competition once again increased and a faltering Canadian Airlines was purchased by Air Canada in 2000, leaving only two national carriers, Air Canada and WestJet. Although we are not now in a new position of stability as there is much uncertainty surrounding the airline industry, these two periods of stability followed by revolution illustrate punctuated equilibrium theory well.[3]

1.2 Environmental Complexity and Munificence

Environmental complexity is the number of external factors in the environment that affect organizations. **Simple environments** have few environmental factors, whereas **complex environments** have many environmental factors. For example, the baking industry exists within a relatively simple external environment. Except for more efficient ovens (i.e., technology), bread is baked, wrapped, and delivered fresh to stores each day much as it always has been. Baking bread is a highly competitive, but simple business environment that has experienced few changes.

By contrast, in recent years, cereal companies such as Kellogg's, maker of Kellogg's Corn Flakes, Frosted Flakes, Sugar Pops, and other popular cereals, find themselves in a more complex environment in which three significant changes have occurred. The first significant change has been more competition. Twenty years ago, Kellogg's competed against just a few cereal companies, such as General Mills and Post. Today, Kellogg's competes against those companies, as well as private-label store brands (IGA, President's Choice, Safeway, etc.).

The second important change in the cereal industry has been significant price cuts. For years, Kellogg's made gross profits of 50 percent on a box of cereal. Yet, with profits that high, private-label store brands could still make a profit of $1 per box by slashing the price that consumers paid.

The third significant change has been the entrance of Wal-Mart into the grocery business. Wal-Mart often relies on cheaper private-label store brands, such as its own Sam's Choice soft drinks, produced by Canada's Cott Corporation, and Old Roy dog food. Consumers like these products because they cost substantially less than brand-name products. However, Wal-Mart prefers private-label store brands because, even with their lower prices, the store makes a higher profit on these brands. So when Wal-Mart aggressively expanded into the grocery business in the last few years, Kellogg's saw its market share drop even more as Wal-Mart pushed cheaper private-label cereals. Together, these three changes have made Kellogg's external environment much more complex than it used to be.[4]

environmental complexity
the number of external factors in the environment that affect organizations

simple environment
an environment with few environmental factors

complex environment
an environment with many environmental factors

environmental munificence
degree to which an organization's external environment has an abundance or scarcity of critical organizational resources

Environmental munificence is the degree to which an organization's external environment has an abundance or scarcity of critical organizational resources. For many companies, qualified employees are one of the scarcest resources around. While companies continue to lay off workers in particular industries or jobs, when the economy is good job applicants are hard to find. The reason is simple: Demand for job applicants can exceed the supply. Consequently, employers often have to work very hard to find and attract skilled employees.

Prior to the downturn in the technology sector, for example, qualified employees were in short supply so Cisco Systems started a "Friends" program to help recruit more engineers. When potential job applicants visited Cisco's Internet home page to read about job openings, they would visit the "Friends" page (www.cisco.com/jobs/friends/), where they would electronically submit their résumés. When this happened, an e-mail would automatically be forwarded to a Cisco employee who had volunteered to be a "Friend." That "Friend" would then call the job applicant within 24 hours. The program, which has been an overwhelming success, helped Cisco solve the problem of job applicant scarcity. Cisco's CEO said, "Basically, over 60 percent of our hires are through that program."[5] During the boom in the technology sector, many companies in Ottawa, including Cognos and Mitel, developed employee referral programs to help recruit qualified employees. Employees received up to $5000 for a successful referral.[6]

1.3 Uncertainty

uncertainty
extent to which managers can understand or predict which environmental changes and trends will affect their businesses

Exhibit 2.1 shows that environmental change, complexity, and resources (i.e., munificence) affect environmental **uncertainty**, which is how well managers can understand or predict the external changes and trends affecting their businesses. Starting at the left side of the figure, environmental uncertainty is lowest when there is little complexity and change, and resources are plentiful. In these environments, managers feel confident that they can understand and predict the external forces that affect their business. By contrast, the right side of the figure indicates that environmental uncertainty is highest when there

---

EXHIBIT 2.1

ENVIRONMENTAL CHANGE, COMPLEXITY, AND MUNIFICENCE

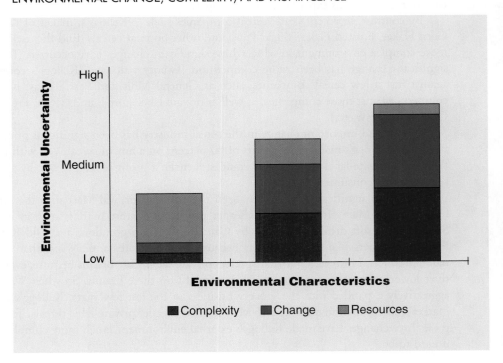

is much complexity and change, and resources are scarce. In these environments, managers may not be at all confident that they can understand and predict the external forces affecting their businesses.

Environmental change, complexity, and munificence are the basic components of external environments. Environmental change is the rate at which conditions or events affecting a business change. Environmental complexity is the number of external factors in an external environment. Environmental munificence is the scarcity or abundance of resources available in the external environment. The greater the rate of environmental change and environmental complexity and the lower the environmental munificence, the less confident managers are that they can understand and predict the trends affecting their businesses. According to punctuated equilibrium theory, companies experience periods of stability followed by short periods of dynamic, fundamental change, followed by a return to periods of stability.

2. General Environment

Exhibit 2.2 shows the two kinds of external environments that influence organizations: the general environment and the specific environment. The **general environment** consists of the economy and the technological, sociocultural, and political/legal trends that

general environment
the economic, technological, sociocultural, and political trends that indirectly affect all organizations

---

EXHIBIT 2.2

GENERAL AND SPECIFIC ENVIRONMENTS

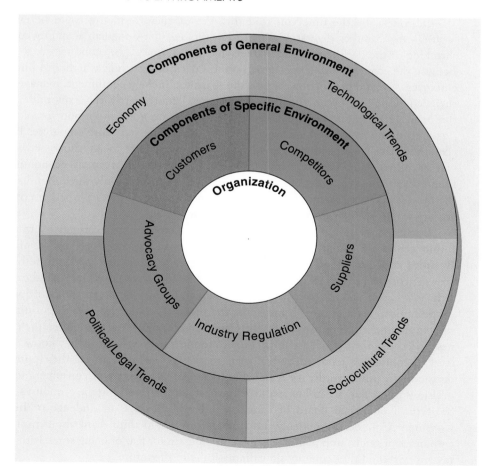

specific environment
the customer, competitor, supplier, industry regulation, and public pressure group trends that are unique to an industry and that directly affect how a company does business

indirectly affect all organizations. Changes in any sector of the general environment eventually affect most organizations. By contrast, each organization has a **specific environment** that is unique to that firm's industry and directly affects the way it conducts day-to-day business. The specific environment, which will be discussed in detail in Section 3 of this chapter, includes customers, competitors, suppliers, industry regulation, and advocacy groups.

Let's take a closer look at the four components of the general environment that indirectly affect all organizations: economy, technological component, sociocultural component, and political/legal component.

2.1 Economy

The current state of a country's economy affects most organizations operating in it. A growing economy means that, in general, more people are working and therefore have relatively more money to spend. More products are being bought and sold than in a static or shrinking economy. While a growing economy doesn't mean that sales of an individual firm are necessarily growing, it does provide an environment favourable to business growth.

For example, in 2003 Canada was in its 12th straight year of economic expansion.[7] While company profits have shrunk from the heady days prior to the terrorist attacks on the World Trade Center, inflation and interest rates remain low and the Canadian economy, while seeing a slowing of growth, is still showing signs of continued strength.[8]

So, according to economic statistics, Canadian businesses exist in a relatively healthy, growing economy. In contrast, Japan, after having suffered from almost a decade of recession, could be finally turning an economic corner. Japanese companies such as Mazda Motors had been reporting regular, if not record, losses. Unemployment, while still low by Canadian standards, had been growing. Now there are signs of an economic turnaround but economists are still unsure as to whether the upturn is sustainable.[9]

Of course, by the time you read this, the Japanese economy could be enjoying healthy growth rather than struggling to recover, and the Canadian economy could be shrinking as the decline in stock markets and the slowing U.S. economy takes its toll. Because the economy influences basic business decisions, such as whether to hire more employees, expand production, or take out loans to purchase equipment, managers scan their economic environments for signs of change. Unfortunately, the economic statistics that managers rely on when making these decisions are notoriously poor predictors of *future* economic activity. A manager who decides to hire ten more employees because economic data suggest future growth could very well have to lay those newly hired workers off when the economic growth does not occur. In fact, a famous economic study found that at the beginning of a business quarter (a period of only three months), even the most accurate economic forecasters could not accurately predict whether economic activity would grow or shrink in that same quarter![10]

business confidence indices
indices that show managers' level of confidence about future business growth

Because economic statistics are such poor predictors, some managers try to predict future economic activity by keeping track of business and consumer confidence. **Business confidence indices** show how confident managers are about future business growth. For example, the Conference Board of Canada (www.conferenceboard.ca) quarterly asks CEOs of approximately 1000 Canadian businesses to express their optimism (or pessimism) about future business sales and prospects. They also survey Canadian consumers about their optimism about the Canadian economy. Managers often prefer business and consumer confidence indices to economic statistics, because they know that the level of confidence reported by real managers and consumers affects their purchasing decisions. In other words, it's reasonable to expect managers and consumers to make decisions today that are in line with their expectations concerning the economy's future. So if the Conference Board of Canada's Index of Business Confidence or Index of Consumer Confidence suddenly drops, managers would think hard about hiring new employees or might stop plans to increase production for fear of being stuck with unsold inventory should the economy slow dramatically in the future.

Technology is the knowledge, tools, and techniques used to transform inputs (raw materials, information, etc.) into outputs (products and services). For example, the knowledge of authors, editors, and artists (technology) and the use of equipment such as computers and printing presses (also technology) transformed paper, ink, and glue (raw material inputs) into this book (the finished product).

Changes in technology can help companies provide better products or produce their products more efficiently. For example, advances in surgical techniques and imaging equipment have made open-heart surgery much faster and safer in recent years. While technological changes can benefit a business, they can also threaten it. For example, CD-ROM technology has allowed publishers of traditional print material, such as books and encyclopedias, to cheaply add videos, sound, and animation to their products. Since the arrival of CD-ROM encyclopedias, sales of the paper version of *Encyclopaedia Britannica* are down by 30 percent. Rather than pay $2250 for Britannica's 32-volume edition, consumers are buying CD-ROM encyclopedias that retail for less than $150.[11] Companies must embrace new technology and use it to improve products and services or decrease costs. If they don't, they will lose out to competitors who do.

technology
knowledge, tools, and techniques used to transform inputs (raw material) into outputs (finished products or services)

PERSONAL PRODUCTIVITY TIP

Computer Skills and Lifetime Earnings

Studies show that workers with basic computer skills earn 15 percent to 30 percent higher lifetime incomes than workers without them. Computers are becoming an integral part of managerial work. What should you do to learn about computers? Subscribe to *PC Magazine*, *PC World*, or *Mac World*. Take applied computer classes about word processing, spreadsheets, relational databases, and the Internet. Learn about File Transfer Protocol, World Wide Web, Telnet, e-mail, Usenet groups, FAQs—if these computer terms sound like a foreign language to you, start learning about computers now, or you may experience less job security and smaller lifetime income.

Source: J. Hearn & D. Lewis, "Keyboarding Course Work and Employment, Earnings, and Educational Attainment," *Journal of Education for Business* 68 (1993): 147.

2.3 Sociocultural Component

The sociocultural component of the general environment refers to the demographic characteristics and general behaviour, attitudes, and beliefs of people in a particular society. Sociocultural changes and trends influence organizations in two important ways.

First, changing demographic characteristics, such as the number of people with particular skills, or the growth or decline in particular population segments (single or married; old or young; men or women; or visible minorities, Aboriginals, or the disabled, etc.) affect how companies run their businesses. For example, women with children are much more likely to work outside the home today than 25 years ago. In 1976, only 39 percent of women with children under 16 years old and 28 percent of women with children under 3 years old worked outside the home. In 2001, those percentages had risen to 70 percent and 62 percent, respectively.[12] Because of these changes, many more companies now offer child care as a benefit to attract and retain scarce, talented workers of both genders. One example: Ontario Hydro, now called Hydro One, provided space and paid the occupancy costs for Hydro Kids, its on-site day care.[13]

Second, sociocultural changes in behaviour, attitudes, and beliefs also affect the demand for a business's products and services. One consequence of the large number of working women is that companies such as Avon and Tupperware now get more of their sales from rush-hour and lunchtime "parties" in workplaces than from "parties" in people's living rooms. Another is the increased sale of cell phones for teenagers. Working parents increasingly use cell phones to keep track of their teenagers during after-school hours.

Many parents have provided teenagers with cell phones to help keep them in touch with their children, partly as a result of an increasing number of women in the workforce.

Photodisc Green/AA032235

2.4 Political/Legal Component

The political/legal component of the general environment includes the legislation, regulation, and court decisions that govern and regulate business behaviour. Throughout the last decade, new legislation and regulations have placed additional responsibilities on companies. Unfortunately, many managers are unaware of these new responsibilities. For example, the Canadian Human Rights Act prohibits discrimination against those who are infected with HIV/AIDS. Discrimination against anyone with HIV/AIDS could result in the company having to pay damages and back pay.

Many managers are also unaware of the potential legal risks associated with traditional managerial decisions such as recruiting, hiring, and firing employees. Indeed, it is increasingly common for businesses and managers to be sued for negligent hiring and supervision, defamation, invasion of privacy, emotional distress, fraud, and misrepresentation during employee recruitment.[14] Likewise, there were few wrongful dismissal cases (i.e., unfairly firing employees) in the past but, for example, it is estimated that about 10 percent of all trials scheduled in Calgary's Court of Queen's Bench involve allegations of wrongful dismissal, and court awards can exceed $100 000 and are increasing in size.[15]

Not everyone agrees that companies face severe legal risks. Indeed, many believe that government should do more to regulate and restrict business behaviour, and that it should be easier for average citizens to sue dishonest or negligent corporations. From a managerial perspective, the best medicine against legal risk is prevention. As a manager, it is your responsibility to educate yourself about the laws and regulations and potential lawsuits that could affect your business. Failure to do so may put you and your company at risk of sizable penalties, fines, or legal charges.

Review 2
General Environment

The general environment consists of economic, technological, sociocultural, and political/legal events and trends that affect all organizations. Because the economy influences basic business decisions, managers often use economic statistics and business confidence indices to predict future economic activity. Changes in technology, which is used to transform inputs into outputs, can be a benefit or a threat to a business. Sociocultural trends, such as changing demographic characteristics, affect how companies run their businesses. Similarly, sociocultural changes in behaviour, attitudes, and beliefs affect the demand for a business's products and services. Court decisions and revised federal and provincial laws have placed much larger political/legal responsibilities on companies. The best way to manage legal responsibilities is to educate managers and employees about laws and regulations and potential lawsuits that could affect a business.

3. Specific Environment

In contrast to general environments that indirectly influence organizations, changes in an organization's specific environment directly affect the way a company conducts its business. If customers decide to use another product, or a competitor cuts prices 10 percent, or a supplier can't deliver raw materials, or federal regulators specify that industry pollutants must be reduced, or environmental groups accuse your company of selling unsafe products, the impact on your business is immediate.

Let's examine how the different aspects of the specific environment affect businesses. These can be broken down into the customer component, competitor component, supplier component, industry regulation component, and advocacy groups.

3.1 Customer Component

Customers purchase products and services. Companies cannot exist without customer support. Therefore, monitoring customers' changing wants and needs is critical to business success.

There are two basic strategies for monitoring customers: reactive and proactive. *Reactive customer monitoring* is identifying and addressing customer trends and problems after they occur. One reactive strategy is to identify customer concerns by listening closely to customer complaints. Not only does listening to complaints help identify problems, but the way in which companies respond to complaints indicates how closely they are attending to customer concerns. For example, companies that respond quickly to customers' letters of complaint are viewed much more favourably than companies that are slow to respond or never respond. In particular, studies have shown that when a company's follow-up letter thanks customers for writing, offers a sincere, specific response to the customer's complaint (i.e., not a form letter, but an explanation of how the problem will be handled), and contains a small gift, coupons, or a refund to make up for the problem, customers will be much more likely to purchase products or services again from that company.[16]

Proactive monitoring of customers means trying to sense events, trends, and problems before they occur (or before customers complain). For example, Cotton Incorporated, the trade group that encourages consumers to purchase cotton clothing ("The look, the feel of cotton…"), publishes a quarterly newsletter called *Lifestyle Monitor* that reports the results of ongoing research. According to Cotton Inc.'s president and CEO, the research is an "early radar detection system" for changes in consumer attitudes and behaviour regarding clothing, appearance, fashion, home furnishings, and other topics.[17] To illustrate, this research indicates that blue jeans continue to be as popular as ever. Eighty-five percent of respondents disagreed with a statement saying, "Jeans are in my past, not in my future." Furthermore, when women were asked whether "a good-looking man looks most sexy in denim jeans and a casual shirt, or a jacket and tie or slacks and a nice sweater?" 53 percent said denim jeans, 25 percent said slacks and a sweater, and 20 percent said a jacket and tie.[18]

3.2 Competitor Component

Competitors are companies in the same industry that sell similar products or services to customers. GM, Ford, and DaimlerChrysler all compete for automobile customers. CBC, CTV, and Global compete for TV viewers' attention. And Tim Hortons, Subway, and McDonald's compete for fast-food customers' dollars. Often, the difference between business success and failure comes down to whether your company is doing a better job of satisfying customer wants and needs than your competitors. Consequently, companies need to keep close track of what their competitors are doing. To do this, managers perform what's called a **competitive analysis**, which is deciding who your competitors are, anticipating competitors' moves, and determining competitors' strengths and weaknesses. Surprisingly, because they tend to focus on only two or three well-known competitors with similar goals and resources, managers often do a poor job of identifying potential competitors.[19]

The second mistake managers make when analyzing the competition is to underestimate potential competitors' capabilities. When this happens, managers don't take the steps they should to continue to improve their products or services. The result can be significant decreases in both market share and profits. For example, with software products such as Internet Phone, it is possible to make free long-distance phone calls on the Internet. To use Internet Phone, you need an Internet service provider (typically $20 to $30 a month) and a computer with a sound card, speakers, and a microphone. The sound quality using Internet Phone is only as good as AM radio (but it's getting better).[20] Yet, despite these limitations, the prospect of free long-distance calls (especially free international calls!) is leading many people and companies to try these products.

competitors
companies in the same industry that sell similar products or services to customers

competitive analysis
a process for monitoring competitors that involves identifying competitors, anticipating their moves, and determining their strengths and weaknesses

PERSONAL PRODUCTIVITY

Improve Your Competitive IQ

Ninety percent of organizations do a poor job of gathering information about competitors. However, by using publicly available information, you can improve your competitive IQ. You can get information from government documents, public speeches, published writings, press releases, court transcripts, industry seminars, trade shows, Canadian embassies (which write economic, demographic, and political studies about foreign countries), and even the competitors' own websites. One example is the Department of Foreign Affairs and International Trade website (www.dfait-maeci.gc.ca), which provides a great deal of information about international trade by industry.

However, because the number of Internet Phone users is still small, phone companies don't yet see Internet Phone as a competitive threat. Indeed, when a phone company manager was asked whether he was worried about the likes of Internet Phone, his response was: "Some people will use it. But it won't really affect our business."[21]

3.3 Supplier Component

suppliers
companies that provide material, human, financial, and informational resources to other companies

Suppliers are companies that provide material, human, financial, and informational resources to other companies. Stelco, Canada's largest steel producer, buys iron ore from suppliers to make steel products. When IBM sells a mainframe computer, it also provides support staff, engineers, and other technical consultants to the company that bought the computer. If you're shopping for desks, chairs, and office supplies, chances are Office Depot will be glad to help your business open a revolving charge account to pay for your purchases.

supplier dependence
degree to which a company relies on a supplier because of the importance of the supplier's product to the company and the difficulty of finding other sources of that product

A key factor influencing the relationship between companies and their suppliers is how dependent they are on each other.[22] **Supplier dependence** is the degree to which a company relies on a supplier because of the importance of the supplier's product to the company and the difficulty of finding other sources of that product. For example, until recently, manufacturers of IBM-compatible personal computers had one primary source for computer processor chips: Intel Corporation, maker of the Pentium chip. Because Intel controls 80 percent of this market, manufacturers such as Compaq Computers had little choice but to buy their chips from Intel. However, two competitors now produce alternatives to the Pentium chip: Cyrix and AMD.[23] Now that they have a choice, computer manufacturers are somewhat less dependent on Intel.

buyer dependence
degree to which a supplier relies on a buyer because of the importance of that buyer to the supplier and the difficulty of selling its products to other buyers

Buyer dependence is the degree to which a supplier relies on a buyer because of the importance of that buyer to the supplier and the difficulty of selling its products to other buyers. For example, because it believed that the clothes sold in its stores were too expensive, Wal-Mart's Canadian division sent letters to its clothing suppliers, demanding a "retroactive, nonnegotiable price rollback of between 4 and 10 percent." So if Wal-Mart had purchased $100 000 of goods from a supplier in the last six months, it expected to receive a refund from the supplier totalling between $4000 and $10 000. The suppliers were furious, but had little choice since Wal-Mart was one of their largest customers.[24]

opportunistic behaviour
transaction in which one party in the relationship benefits at the expense of the other

As Wal-Mart's demand indicates, greater buyer or seller dependence can lead to **opportunistic behaviour**, in which one party benefits at the expense of the other. Opportunistic behaviour between buyers and suppliers will never be completely eliminated. However, many companies believe that both buyers and suppliers can benefit by improving the buyer–supplier relationship. General Motors, for example, which has a long history of adversarial relationships with its suppliers, has recently begun its new "Ambassador Program." The Ambassador Program is designed to improve communication between GM and its suppliers by assigning a GM executive (but not the GM executive who makes purchases from the company) to meet regularly with the supplier to discuss problems or new ideas. In contrast to opportunistic behaviour, buyer–supplier transactions such as GM's Ambassador Program emphasize **relationship behaviour**, which focuses on establishing a mutually beneficial, long-term relationship between buyers and suppliers. Like General Motors, the trend in the last decade is for companies to reduce the number of suppliers they deal with and to improve the relationships they have with remaining suppliers.[25]

relationship behaviour
mutually beneficial, long-term exchanges between buyers and suppliers

3.4 Industry Regulation Component

industry regulation
regulations and rules that govern the business practices and procedures of specific industries, businesses, and professions

In contrast to the political/legal component of the general environment that affects all businesses, the **industry regulation** component consists of regulations and rules that govern the business practices and procedures of specific industries, businesses, and professions. Regulatory agencies and government departments affect businesses by creating and enforcing rules and regulations to protect consumers, workers, or society as a whole.

For example, after many year of debate, the federal government passed the Employment Equity Act, which is enforced by the Canadian Human Rights Commission (www.chrc-ccdp.ca). This act places a responsibility on federally regulated employers to increase the representation of four historically disadvantaged groups (women, Aboriginals, visible minorities, and persons with disabilities). In addition, it also enforces the Canadian Human Rights Act, which places further responsibilities on federally regulated employers. Failure to comply with the Employment Equity Act or the Human Rights Act can lead to fines of as much as $50 000. Not only must one be aware of the acts themselves, employers must constantly monitor regulations under the act and new policies developed by the Canadian Human Rights Commission.

There are almost 100 federal government agencies, departments and regulatory commissions that can affect nearly any kind of business (http://canada.gc.ca/depts/major/depind_e.html). Exhibit 2.3 lists some of the most influential federal agencies and commissions.

However, businesses are not just subject to federal regulations. They must also meet provincial, county, and city regulations, too. Surveys indicate that managers rank keeping up to date with and implementing government regulations as one of the most demanding and frustrating parts of their jobs.

3.5 Advocacy Groups

Advocacy groups are groups of concerned citizens who band together to try to influence the business practices of specific industries, businesses, and professions. The members of a group generally share the same point of view on a particular issue. For example,

advocacy groups
groups of concerned citizens who band together to try to influence the business practices of specific industries, businesses, and professions

---

EXHIBIT 2.3

FEDERAL REGULATORY AGENCIES AND COMMISSIONS

FEDERAL AGENCY	REGULATORY RESPONSIBILITIES
Environmental Assessment Agency www.ceaa-acee.gc.ca	Reduces and controls pollution through research, monitoring, standard setting, and enforcement activities
Canadian Human Rights Commission www.chrc-ccdp.ca	Promotes fair hiring and promotion practices
Canadian Radio-television and Telecommunications Commission (CRTC) www.crtc.gc.ca	Regulates communications by radio, television, wire, satellite, and cable
Bank of Canada www.bank-banque-canada.ca	As the nation's central bank, controls interest rates and money supply, and monitors the Canadian banking system to produce a growing economy with stable prices
Competition Tribunal www.ct-tc.gc.ca	Restricts unfair methods of business competition and misleading advertising
Health Canada www.hc-sc.gc.ca	Protects nation's health by making sure food, drugs, and cosmetics are safe
Canadian Industrial Relations Board www.cirb-ccri.gc.ca	Monitors union elections and stops companies from engaging in unfair labour practices
Canadian Centre for Occupational Health and Safety www.ccohs.ca	Saves lives, prevents injuries, and protects the health of workers

environmental advocacy groups might try to get manufacturers to reduce smokestack pollution emissions. Unlike the industry regulation component of the specific environment, advocacy groups cannot force organizations to change their practices. However, they can use a number of techniques to try to influence companies: public communications, media advocacy, and product boycotts.

The **public communications** approach relies on *voluntary* participation by the news media and the advertising industry to get an advocacy group's message out. For example, the Canadian Cancer Society (www.cancer.ca) undertakes public information campaigns on a variety of issues, including tobacco use and diets, that aims to reduce the rate of cancer in Canada by reducing smoking rates and improving people's eating habits. To accomplish its goals, the Canadian Cancer Society makes heavy use of public service announcements on TV and radio (as part of their community service, TV and radio stations donate this time). It also maintains an extensive website, provides a toll-free number to disseminate cancer information, provides a community services directory, issues news releases, and works in conjunction with other groups to make Canadians more aware of cancer-related issues.

In contrast to the public communications approach, media advocacy is a much more aggressive form of advocacy. A **media advocacy** approach typically involves framing issues as public issues (i.e., affecting everyone); exposing questionable, exploitative, or unethical practices; and forcing media coverage by buying media time or creating controversy that is likely to receive extensive news coverage. Millionaire Phillip Sokolof conducted one of the most famous media advocacy campaigns against McDonald's. Sokolof, who had once suffered a heart attack, took out full-page ads in 20 major newspapers to decry McDonald's "Poisoning of America." The ads stated, "McDonald's, your hamburgers still have too much fat and your french fries are cooked with beef tallow!" The ads also encouraged McDonald's to reduce fat levels in its hamburgers, cook french fries in vegetable oil, and use skim milk rather than 2 percent milk. By buying advertising in 20 major newspapers and picking on a well-known, respected company like McDonald's, Sokolof knew that press coverage would be guaranteed.

A **product boycott** is a tactic in which an advocacy group actively tries to convince consumers to not purchase a company's product or service. For example, when it was learned that Shell Oil was going to dispose of an old oil storage rig by letting it drop to the bottom of the North Sea, Greenpeace, an environmental advocacy group, complained to the press that this posed environmental hazards. Greenpeace members drew attention to this cause by boarding the barge that was taking the oil storage rig to sea. Customers in Denmark, Holland, and Germany boycotted and cut Shell's sales by 30 percent, costing the company millions in revenues and profit.[26]

Review 3
Specific Environment

The specific environment is made up of five components: customers, competitors, suppliers, industry regulators, and advocacy groups. Companies can monitor customers' needs by identifying customer problems after they occur or by anticipating problems before they occur. However, because they tend to focus on well-known competitors, managers often underestimate their competition or do a poor job of identifying future competitors. Since suppliers and buyers are very dependent on each other, that dependence sometimes leads to opportunistic behaviour, in which one benefits at the expense of the other. Regulatory agencies affect businesses by creating rules and then enforcing them, and the number of rules and regulations continues to increase. Advocacy groups cannot regulate organization practices. However, through public communications, media advocacy, and product boycotts, they try to convince companies to change their practices.

public communications
an advocacy group tactic that relies on voluntary participation by the news media and the advertising industry to get an advocacy group's message out

media advocacy
an advocacy group tactic of framing issues as public issues, exposing questionable, exploitative, or unethical practices, and forcing media coverage by buying media time or creating controversy that is likely to receive extensive news coverage

product boycott
an advocacy group tactic of protesting a company's actions by convincing consumers not to purchase its product or service

4. Making Sense of Changing Environments

In Chapter 1, you learned that managers are responsible for making sense of their business environments. However, our just-completed discussions of the general and specific environments indicate that making sense of business environments is not an easy task. Because external environments can be dynamic, confusing, and complex, managers use a three-step process to make sense of the changes in their external environments. The steps are environmental scanning, interpreting environmental factors, and acting on threats and opportunities.

4.1 Environmental Scanning

Environmental scanning is searching the environment for important events or issues that might affect an organization. Managers scan the environment to stay up to date on important factors in their industry. Managers also scan their environments to reduce uncertainty. For example, many mail-order, catalogue, and Internet-based businesses were hurt when they didn't anticipate the Teamsters Union strike against United Parcel Service. Because they relied on UPS to deliver their products to customers, their sales dropped immediately when the strike began. However, some companies, such as Amazon.com, the Internet-based bookseller (www.amazon.com), saw the strike coming. The weekend before the strike was announced, Amazon shifted its shipments to the U.S. Postal Service and Airborne Express.[27]

environmental scanning
searching the environment for important events or issues that might affect an organization

Organizational strategies also affect environmental scanning. In other words, managers pay close attention to trends and events that are directly related to their companies' abilities to compete in the marketplace.[28] And by keeping their eyes and ears open, managers sometimes come across important information by accident. For example, Gary Costley, an employee of Kellogg's, was pulling into the parking lot at work when he noticed a crane on the loading dock of the General Foods' Post cereal plant across the street. He could see that the crane was unloading a special machine made by a German company for manufacturing cereal. This caught his attention, because Kellogg's was having trouble getting a similar machine from a French manufacturer to work. So he went to a store, purchased a camera and film, and stood across the street taking pictures. A Post employee yelled, "Hey, you can't do that." Costley responded, "I'm standing on a public street taking photos. You shouldn't unload your machines in plain sight." The pictures helped convince Kellogg's management to buy the German machines and to not spend any more time or money to make the French machines work.[29]

Finally, environmental scanning is important because it contributes to organizational performance. Environmental scanning helps managers detect environmental changes and problems before they become organizational crises.[30] Furthermore, companies whose CEOs do more environmental scanning have higher profits.[31] CEOs in better-performing firms scan their firms' environments more frequently and scan more key factors in their environments in more depth and detail than do CEOs in poorer-performing firms.[32]

PERSONAL PRODUCTIVITY

Manage by Reading Around

Traditionally, managers have used personal contacts and newspapers to track changes that affect their businesses. However, Intel's chairman, Andy Grove, says that the Internet, America Online, Prodigy, and CompuServe can help uncover trends. Grove conducts electronic keyword searches on news databases. Others track Internet discussion groups for mention of their companies' products or services. Indeed, the public first learned that Intel's Pentium chips could produce wrong answers for basic math computations from an Internet discussion group. So get online, get connected, and do what Andy Grove calls "managing by reading around."

Source: A. Deutschman, "The Managing Wisdom of High-Tech Superstars," *Fortune*, 17 October 1994, 197–206.

4.2 Interpreting Environmental Factors

After scanning, managers determine what environmental events and issues mean to the organization. Typically, managers view environmental events and issues as either threats or opportunities. When managers interpret environmental events as threats, they take steps to protect the company from further harm. For example, in France, the neighbourhood boulangerie, boucherie, fromagerie, patisserie, and poissonnerie (bakery, butcher, cheese, pastry, and fish shops) have begun to go out of business in large numbers. Their existence is now threatened by the Carrefour, huge hypermarkets that are sometimes as large as three football fields. French shoppers load up on cartloads of groceries once a week at the Carrefour to save scarce time and money. One of the best buys is France's traditional loaf of bread, the baguette, which sells for about $1.50 at small bakeries but goes for 60 cents at the hypermarket. So with their businesses in decline, the neighbourhood boulangerie, boucherie, fromagerie, patisserie, and poissonnerie have turned to the French government for help, asking it to enact laws limiting construction of new hypermarkets. They're also asking the French government to prevent hypermarkets from selling products below cost, a practice that hypermarkets say they don't use.[33]

By contrast, when managers interpret environmental events as opportunities, they will consider strategic alternatives for taking advantage of the event to improve company performance. In the snack business, Hostess Frito-Lay saw opportunities in the increasing demand for healthier snacks. By being quick to market with Baked Frito-Lay Potato Crisps, Baked Tostitos, and Rold Gold Fat Free Pretzels, Hostess Frito-Lay captured a large share of the Canadian low-fat snack market.[34]

Environmental factors such as the rise of the Carrefour in France have forced many smaller, specialized food retailers out of business.

AP/Wide World Photos

4.3 Acting on Threats and Opportunities

After scanning for information on environmental events and issues, and interpreting them as threats or opportunities, managers have to decide how to respond to these environmental factors. However, deciding what to do under conditions of uncertainty is difficult. Managers are never completely confident that they have all the information they need, or that they correctly understand the information they have.

Because it is impossible to comprehend all the factors and changes, managers rely on simplified models of external environments called cognitive maps. **Cognitive maps** summarize the perceived relationships between environmental factors and possible organiza-

cognitive maps
graphic depictions of how managers believe environmental factors relate to possible organizational actions

tional actions. For example, the cognitive map shown in Exhibit 2.4 represents a small clothing store owner's interpretation of her business environment. The map shows three kinds of variables. The first, shown as rectangles, are environmental factors such as Wal-Mart or a large mall 20 minutes away. The second, shown in ovals, are potential actions that the store owner might take, such as a low-cost strategy; a good value, good service strategy; or a large selection of the latest fashions strategy. The third, shown as trapezoids, are company strengths, such as low employee turnover, and weaknesses, such as small size.

The arrows on the map indicate whether the manager believes there is a positive or negative relationship between variables. For example, the manager believes that a low-cost strategy wouldn't work, because Wal-Mart and Zellers are nearby. Offering a large selection of the latest fashions would not work either—not with the small size of the store and that large nearby mall. However, this manager believes that a good value, good service strategy would lead to success and profits, because of low employee turnover, knowing customers well, a reasonable selection of clothes at reasonable prices, and a good location.

In the end, managers must complete all three steps—environmental scanning, interpreting environmental factors, and acting on threats and opportunities—to make sense of changing external environments. Environmental scanning helps managers more accurately interpret their environments and take actions that improve company performance. Through scanning, managers keep tabs on what competitors are doing, identify market trends, and stay alert to current events that affect their companies' operations. Armed with the environmental information they have gathered, managers can then take action to minimize the impact of threats and turn opportunities into increased profits.

EXHIBIT 2.4

COGNITIVE MAPS

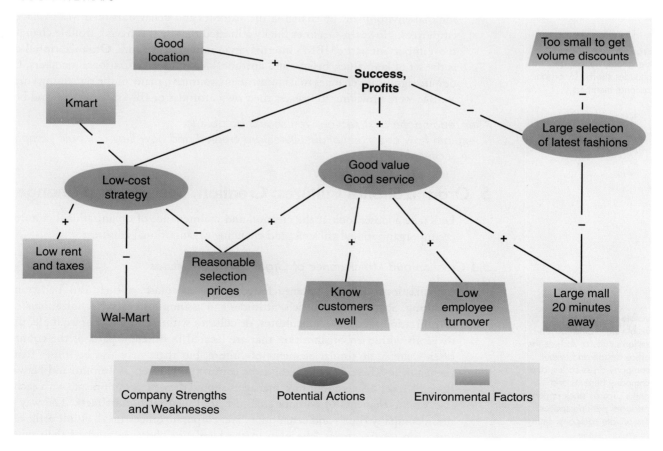

Managers use a three-step process to make sense of external environments: environmental scanning, interpreting information, and action. Managers scan their environments based on their organizational strategies, their need for up-to-date information, and their need to reduce uncertainty. When managers identify environmental events as threats, they take steps to protect the company from harm. When managers identify environmental events as opportunities, they formulate alternatives for taking advantage of them to improve company performance. Using cognitive maps can help managers visually summarize the relationships between environmental factors and the actions they might take to deal with them.

Internal Environments

internal environment
the events and trends inside an organization that affect management, employees, and organizational culture

External environments are external trends and events that have the potential to affect companies. The **internal environment** consists of the trends and events within an organization that affect the management, employees, and organizational culture.

Since its inception, IBM's culture promised lifetime employment to its workers and corporate benevolence to the towns in which IBM plants and offices were located. However, in the early 1990s, as IBM lost market share in the mainframe computer and personal computer businesses, it had to cut costs to minimize financial losses. Manufacturing plants were sold, the long-term research and development budget was cut, and the number of IBM employees was reduced by 40 percent. With such significant changes to the company's internal environment, one might expect that IBMers would have a different attitude about how their company should be run. However, a survey of 1200 top managers indicated that 40 percent did not see "the need for change." In fact, many IBMers were angry at new CEO Louis Gerstner for introducing "unnecessary" changes.[35]

organizational culture
the values, beliefs, and attitudes shared by organizational members

Clearly, CEO Gerstner was doing many things that he hoped would change IBM's internal environment by changing the attitudes and behaviours of IBM's managers and employees. However, Gerstner finally admitted that he was having trouble changing the most important part of IBM's internal environment: its culture. **Organizational culture** is the set of key values, beliefs, and attitudes shared by organizational members. Clearly, despite significant changes to its internal environment, many of the remaining employees at IBM were unwilling to reassess their own attitudes or IBM's core values and beliefs.

After reading the next section, you should be able to
5. *explain how organizational cultures are created and how they can help companies be successful.*

5. Organizational Cultures: Creation, Success, and Change

Let's take a closer look at the creation and maintenance of organizational cultures, successful organizational cultures, and changing organizational cultures.

5.1 Creation and Maintenance of Organizational Cultures

Organizational culture, often referred to as corporate culture, can be strong and enduring. Shared values, beliefs, attitudes and assumptions drive organizational culture. Organizations also have subcultures, or cultures within cultures. For example, different divisions within an organization that are located in different parts of the country will often share some similar elements of culture, but there may also be things that make them a little different. Within the same company, managers in Toronto and Hawaii may have different beliefs about how managers should dress or communicate with each other.

visible artifacts
visible signs of an organization's culture, such as the office design and layout, company dress codes, and company benefits and perks such as stock options, personal parking spaces, or the private company dining room

Visible elements of corporate culture are called **visible artifacts**. The way people dress, company rituals and ceremonies, and corporate offices are all visible artifacts. IBM was once referred to as "the men in the blue suits" because most of their employees dressed in dark blue suits and employees' dress reflected the uniformity and strength of IBM's organizational culture. In addition to dress, language and forms of communication can indicate the level of formality expected within a workplace. The way language is used in the workplace can also tell you a lot about an organization. How do co-workers address each other? How do you address your boss? Is it by first name or is it Ms. Smith? Is communication formal and usually written or is it informal and usually in person? What sort of job titles are used? The answers to these questions can speak loudly about organizational culture. For example, Wal-Mart calls employees "associates" to indicate their importance in the success of the organization while at W. L. Gore, the maker of GoreTex fabric, there are no job titles and anybody can talk to anybody.[36] Each of these patterns of behaviour forms part of the corporate culture and tells us something about the organization.

A primary source of organizational culture is the company founder. Founders such as Thomas J. Watson (IBM), Frank Stronach (Magna), Bill Gates (Microsoft), or John Forzani (Forzani) create organizations in their own images that they imprint with their beliefs, attitudes, and values. Microsoft employees share founder Bill Gates's intensity for staying ahead of software competitors. Says a Microsoft vice-president, "No matter how good your product, you are only 18 months away from failure."[37]

While company founders are instrumental in the creation of organizational cultures, founders retire, die, or choose to leave their companies. For example, neither Michael Cowpland, founder of Corel Corporation, nor Mitch Kapor, founder of Lotus software, which created Lotus 1-2-3, one of the first and most successful spreadsheet programs, is still with the companies they created. Yet they both still work in the computer industry. So when the founders are gone, how are the founders' values, attitudes, and beliefs sustained in the organizational culture? Answer: stories and heroes.

Organizational members tell **stories** to make sense of organizational events and changes, and to emphasize culturally consistent assumptions, decisions, and actions.[38] For example, Mark McCormack, author of *What They Don't Teach You at Harvard Business School*, tells a story that made the rounds at Ford Motor Company.

> Many years ago the Ford Motor Company went through a period in which the numbers people literally took over the company and were closing plants left and right in order to cut costs. They had already succeeded in shutting down plants in Massachusetts and Texas and seemed to be relishing their newfound power.
>
> Robert McNamara, who was president of Ford at the time, called a meeting of his top executives to discuss a recommendation he had received for the closing of yet another plant. Everyone was against it, but the predictions from the accountants were so glum that no one was willing to speak up.
>
> Finally, a salty Ford veteran by the name of Charlie Beacham said, "Why don't we close down all the plants and then we'll really start to save money?"
>
> Everyone cracked up. The decision was made to postpone any more closings for a while, and the bean counters went back to working for the company rather than running it.[39]

In fact, Charlie Beacham's humorous comment, and the retelling of it in story form at Ford, was consistent with founder Henry Ford's belief that costs should not be cut for the sake of cutting costs (and making more profit), but to make cars more affordable for customers.[40]

A second way in which organizational culture is sustained is by creating and celebrating heroes. By definition, **organizational heroes** are organizational people admired for their qualities and achievements within the organization. For example, when Jack Welch became the CEO at General Electric Corporation, he tried to change the then-conservative corporate culture by encouraging managers and employees to be creative

organizational stories
stories told by organizational members to make sense of organizational events and changes, and to emphasize culturally consistent assumptions, decisions, and actions

organizational heroes
people celebrated for their qualities and achievements within an organization

organizational rituals
routine activities that emphasize the organization's culture

organizational ceremonies
planned activities or events that emphasize culturally consistent assumptions, decisions, and actions

organizational symbols
something that represents another thing

and innovative and to take risks. After a $30-million project failed, Welch rewarded the project manager with a bonus and a promotion. The members of the project team were rewarded with bonuses and videocassette recorders. Welch was not celebrating their failure. He was celebrating their willingness to take risks. In other words, he treated the manager and the project team as heroes for other GE employees to emulate.[41]

A third way in which organizational culture is sustained is through **rituals, ceremonies**, and **symbols**. Wal-Mart is famous for having all its employees gather before the store opens and sing the national anthem and perform the company cheer.[42] Annual employee awards ceremonies can reinforce company values, and company picnics are examples of organizational ceremonies that provide opportunities for organizations to transmit and maintain its culture. One can consider physical artifacts such as buildings, logos, stories, slogans, rituals, and ceremonies to be organizational symbols that represent organizational values.[43]

5.2 Successful Organizational Cultures

Preliminary research shows that organizational culture is related to organizational success. As shown in Exhibit 2.5, cultures based on adaptability, involvement, a clear mission, and consistency can help companies achieve higher sales growth, return on assets, profits, quality, and employee satisfaction.[44] Weak corporate cultures can leave companies without vision leading to unfocused strategies and unmotivated employees. On the other hand, a strong corporate culture can stifle change or create conflict when organizations merge.

Adaptability is the ability to notice and respond to changes in the organization's environment. Previously, we discussed the difficulty that CEO Louis Gerstner was having trying to turn around IBM. Frustrated with his inability to change IBM culture,

EXHIBIT 2.5

SUCCESSFUL ORGANIZATIONAL CULTURES

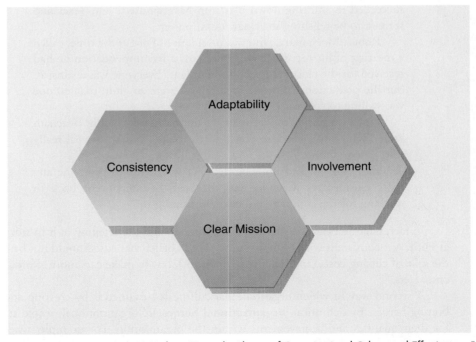

Source: D.R. Denison & A. K. Mishra, "Toward a Theory of Organizational Culture and Effectiveness," *Organization Science* 6 (1995): 204–223.

Gerstner eventually decreed that the core IBM beliefs set forth by founder Thomas J. Watson, Sr. (excellence, customer satisfaction, and respect for the individual) were to be replaced with the eight new goals shown in Exhibit 2.6. Instead of responding to his attempts to improve the company, many IBMers were shocked because Thomas J. Watson, Jr., who succeeded his father as IBM's CEO, once stated that IBM's success was dependent on its ability to change everything "except those basic beliefs."[45]

In cultures that promote higher levels of employee involvement in decision-making, employees feel a greater sense of ownership and responsibility. For example, at Hewlett-Packard, each "business," such as laser printers, calculators, or personal computers, makes its own decisions. So when the video products division was deciding which computer chips to use in its products, it chose not to use H-P's own computer chips because they were too expensive. Instead, they purchased integrated circuits for half the price from one of the H-P computer chip division's competitors. Because involvement and participation are so central to H-P's culture, no one (even in the H-P computer chip division) questioned this decision.[46]

A company's **vision** is its purpose or reason for existing. In organizational cultures in which there is a clear organizational vision, the organization's strategic purpose and direction are apparent to everyone in the company. And, when managers are uncertain about their business environments, the vision helps guide the discussions, decisions, and behaviour of the people in the company. For example, at Ford Motor Company, the advertising slogan is "Quality is Job 1." However, this isn't just an ad slogan; this is a succinct, but powerful statement of Ford's strategic purpose and direction. Since "Job 1" is auto industry terminology for the first car rolling off an assembly line in a new model year, "Quality is Job 1" sends the message that every car, even the very first of the year, must meet Ford's high standards for quality. Most importantly, however, this slogan helps Ford employees make everyday decisions. Whether they're installing seats, testing new safety features, or designing a new interior, Ford employees know that when given the choice between quality work and acceptable work, or quality and cutting expenses, the answer is clear: "Quality is Job 1."[47]

Finally, in consistent organizational cultures, the company actively defines and teaches organizational values, beliefs, and attitudes. Consistent organizational cultures are also called strong cultures, because the core beliefs are widely shared and strongly held.

company vision
a company's purpose or reason for existence

EXHIBIT 2.6

IBM'S NEW CULTURAL PRINCIPLES

1. The marketplace is the driving force behind everything we do.
2. At our core, we are a technology company with an overriding commitment to quality.
3. Our primary measures of success are customer satisfaction and shareholder value.
4. We operate as an entrepreneurial organization with a minimum of bureaucracy and a never-ending focus on productivity.
5. We never lose sight of our strategic vision.
6. We think and act with a sense of urgency.
7. Outstanding, dedicated people make it all happen, particularly when they work together as a team.
8. We are sensitive to the needs of all employees and to the communities in which we operate.

Source: L. Hays, "Gerstner Is Struggling as He Tries to Change Ingrained IBM Culture," *The Wall Street Journal*, 13 May 1994, A1.

At the beginning of this section, we learned about the problems that CEO Louis Gerstner was having trying to change IBM's culture. However, managers can and do change organizational cultures. Indeed, thanks to Gerstner's prodding, IBM has returned to solid profitability by becoming more customer-oriented, faster at decision-making, and quicker to apply the new technologies invented by its legendary research and development labs.[48] As IBM's experience demonstrates, changing organizational culture just takes patience, vigilance, and a focus on changing the parts of an organizational culture that managers can control: behaviour and symbolic artifacts.

One way of changing a corporate culture is to use behavioural addition or behavioural substitution to establish new patterns of behaviour among managers and employees.[49] **Behavioural addition** is the process of having managers and employees perform a new behaviour, while **behavioural substitution** is having managers and employees perform a new behaviour in place of another behaviour. The key in both instances is to choose behaviours that are central to and symbolic of the "old" culture you're changing and the "new" culture that you want to create. For example, Claudette MacKay-Lassonde, CEO of Enghouse Systems Ltd. (a small software company located in Markham, Ontario), wanted to transform Enghouse's culture. Despite having a good product line, Enghouse suffered a $3.2-million loss in 1994 and the threat of bankruptcy became a reality. MacKay-Lassonde implemented a strategic planning process, restructured the company, and tightened financial controls. Three years later Enghouse turned a profit. She says, "The reality is that a turnaround means a culture change."[50] Sometimes organizations change their name and/or logo to help reinforce cultural change.

The second way in which managers can begin to change corporate culture is to change visible artifacts of their old culture, such as the office design and layout, company dress codes, and who benefits (or doesn't) from company benefits and perks such as stock options, personal parking spaces, or the private company dining room. At Petro-Canada, once a Crown corporation, corporate jets were eliminated and senior executives had to purchase their own golf-club memberships. Even their Calgary headquarters, dubbed "Red Square" and a symbol of federal government intrusion in the private sector, was sold and only half of it leased back. Change was in the air, and the company eventually sold its large Canadian art collection, gave up its most expensive office space, and closed the executive dining room.[51]

Corporate cultures are very difficult to change. Consequently, there is no guarantee that behavioural substitution, behavioural addition, or changing visible cultural artifacts will change a company's organizational culture. However, these methods are some of the best tools that managers have for changing culture, because they send the clear message to managers and employees that "the accepted way of doing things" has changed.

Review 5
Organizational Cultures: Creation, Success, and Change

Organizational culture is the set of key values, beliefs, and attitudes shared by organizational members. Organizational cultures are often created by company founders and then sustained through the telling of organizational stories and the celebration of organizational heroes. Adaptable cultures that promote employee involvement, that make clear the organization's strategic purpose and direction, and that actively define and teach organizational values and beliefs can help companies achieve higher sales growth, return on assets, profits, quality, and employee satisfaction. Behavioural substitution, behavioural addition, and changing visible artifacts are ways in which managers can begin to change their organizational cultures.

behavioural addition
the process of having managers and employees perform new behaviours that are central to and symbolic of the new organizational culture that a company wants to create

behavioural substitution
the process of having managers and employees perform new behaviours central to the "new" organizational culture in place of behaviours that were central to the "old" organizational culture

What Really Happened?

Many people believe that managers have total control over their organizations. If management wants something done, it happens. Yet, as you learned in the case of EasyJet, managers cannot control all external factors. However, a lack of control isn't necessarily a bad thing. Companies can succeed by scanning their business environments for events and trends, interpreting what those changes mean, and then acting to adapt to those changes. Read the following to find out what really happened to EasyJet as it tried to make sense of the changes in its external environment.

So the question is "Will you make it?" The odds are stacked against you. In the United States, 130 airlines have gone out of business in the last 25 years, most of them new start-ups like EasyJet. The same forces that brought them down could bring EasyJet down too.

Many people mistakenly believe that the answer to the question "Will your company make it?" is a function of whether a company has sufficient funds, strong management capability, and a sound strategy. While clearly important, you can't answer this question without taking a look at external environments, meaning the forces and events outside a company that have the potential to influence or affect it. Organizations are influenced by two kinds of external environments: the general environment, which consists of economic, technological, sociocultural, and political/legal events and trends, and the specific environment, which consists of customers, competitors, suppliers, industry regulators, and advocacy groups.

At this point in its young life, EasyJet faces challenges in the economic, supplier, competitor, and industry components of its environment (the latter two are discussed below). EasyJet faces a slowing economy with rising jet prices. However, unlike most airlines, it has not used financial hedging to protect itself from suddenly rising prices (hedging is a method of shielding companies from the risk associated with changing prices). Increasing fuel prices will make it much more difficult to keep prices low. With regard to suppliers, EasyJet decided early on to not use travel agents to book tickets. In fact, some of its first ads said, "Cut out travel agents. Book direct." When EasyJet first flew from London to Athens, travel agents took the company to court to force it to sell tickets through them. Founder Stelios Haji-Ioannou, who is originally from Greece, then put out another ad that promised a free ticket to anyone who came to court to support EasyJet. Nearly 1000 people showed up for the free tickets, including some travel agents! Today, as from the start, EasyJet books all its tickets to reduce costs and avoid paying commissions to travel agents. In fact, nearly 90 percent of its tickets are purchased via its www.easyjet.com website. Travel agents don't make a dime in commissions and EasyJet keeps its prices low. Says Stelios with a smile, "We have a very simple relationship with travel agents. We hate them and they hate us."

You know that Southwest Airline's low-cost model worked in the United States, but can it work in Europe when so many other air carriers are following the same model? What do you do about the competition?

In the United States, Southwest Airlines is the only major, low-cost airline that flies coast to coast (there are five regional low-cost airlines). However, in Europe, EasyJet faces competition from Dublin-based RyanAir; Portugal's PGA; U.K.-based British Midland, Debonair, and AirOne airlines; and Richard Branson's Virgin Express. One of the first things that EasyJet or any other company needs to do is conduct a competitive analysis. That is, decide who their competitors are, anticipate their moves, and then determine their strengths and weaknesses. Surprisingly, because they tend to focus on only two or three well-known competitors with similar goals and resources, managers often do a poor job of identifying potential competitors. Managers also need to be sure to not underestimate competitors' capabilities. When this happens, managers don't take the steps they should to continue to improve their products or services. The result can be significant decreases in both market share and profits. Fortunately, neither of these mistakes has been made at EasyJet.

More than any of its competitors, EasyJet has used technology to keep prices low. By offering only online promotions, by discounting purchases made on the Web, and by charging extra for phone bookings, more than 90 percent of its customers, the highest rate in the industry, book tickets on the Web. And if it can get 100 percent of its customers to buy online, it will save nearly 30 percent per ticket compared to its competitors. Moreover, as EasyJet expands throughout Europe, it translates its website into new languages for each new market. That's much cheaper than having to hire another set of staffers who are fluent in new languages.

And while the computer system is highly complex to allow EasyJet to fill as many seats as possible, its ticketing rules are extremely simple. The earlier you purchase, the cheaper your ticket. And because of its price promise, EasyJet won't undercut customers who buy early by selling empty seats for cheap on the day of departure. Still, with its low cost and yield management software, it flies its jets 84 percent full, much higher than the industry average of 70 percent.

So can EasyJet beat or meet the competition? Thus far, the answer is yes. When British Airway's low-cost airline, Go, was started, Stelios got even by getting tickets for Go's inaugural flight. He and his management team showed up in EasyJet's trademark colour orange to hand out coupons promising free flights. Journalists on hand ignored Go's CEO and interviewed Stelios. Go still exists, but BA sold it because of huge losses. Moreover, Stelios has outlasted Bob Ayling, the BA CEO who tricked him into believing that BA wanted to invest in EasyJet. Said Stelios, "If you'd asked anyone at the time if I would survive longer than the boss of the World's Favourite Airline [British Airlines' motto], they would have laughed at you. Outlasting a BA chief executive shows that I've got staying power."

Also, is there anything you can do to influence the cost of landing fees at Luton airport? If EasyJet continues to grow, dealing with airport authorities will become increasingly important. For example, Swissair used its political and financial leverage to try to prevent EasyJet from flying between Geneva, Switzerland, and Barcelona, Spain. How do you deal with potentially uncontrollable industry regulators and gatekeepers?

The industry regulation component of the specific environment consists of regulations and rules that govern the business practices and procedures of particular industries, businesses, and professions. Regulatory agencies affect businesses by creating and enforcing rules and regulations that are supposed to protect consumers, workers, or society as a whole. However, surveys indicate that managers rank implementing and complying with industry regulation as one of the most demanding and frustrating parts of their jobs. This is certainly true for Stelios and EasyJet. In fact, Stelios is so frustrated with Barclays Bank, Luton Airport's owner, for tripling landing fees that he cut his Barclays credit card in half on television and is threatening to reduce the number of EasyJet flights out of the airport. He said, "It would not be realistic to try to uproot the company from Luton, but what we are trying to do is make it more immune by growing our operations out of Liverpool and Geneva and by establishing a base at Amsterdam." He went on to say, "Don't discount the possibility of us developing a third UK hub—it could be Cardiff or Newcastle or Glasgow. Next time there is a

Barclays-style problem, we want to make sure it affects as small a part of the business as possible."

Finally, how do you make sense of all this? Your initial business plan was sound and recognized the fantastic opportunities for low-cost airlines in Europe. But now those opportunities seem to be overwhelmed by a growing number of threats.

Managers use a three-step process to make sense of external environments. First, they scan their environments based on their organizational strategies, their need for up-to-date information, or their need to reduce uncertainty. Second, when they identify environmental events as threats, they take steps to protect their companies from harm. And third, when they identify environmental events as opportunities, they formulate strategies to improve company performance.

Stelios realized that the same principles used to start and run EasyJet could also be used in other industries. For instance, Stelios and his management team observed that the Internet cafés in the cities to which EasyJet flew were very expensive, were run by nerds, and were quickly failing. With more tourists travelling and nearly all business people needing access to e-mail wherever they are, they figured they had another made-to-order business. The result? EasyEverything Internet Cafés, seating anywhere from 200 to 800 people, are open 24 hours a day in 24 cities in 10 countries. Users pay a dollar, a pound, 10 francs, or 200 pesetas to buy anywhere from 20 minutes to 4 hours of high-speed Internet access. You get more minutes for your money when demand is low, meaning the café is empty, and fewer minutes when it is bustling with customer activity. Customers get high-speed access, flat screen monitors, Web cams, and access to cheap Internet phone calls. With 2.2 million customers and $6.8 million a month in revenues, business is booming. In fact, 18 percent of revenues comes from ads displayed on computer monitors. Critics claimed the

cafés would fail outside Europe, but after six months, the monster EasyEverything in New York—it seats 800 people—is profitable. Additional stores are planned for San Francisco, Miami, Boston, and New York.

Likewise, Stelios has now started EasyRentacar in 14 locations. Like EasyJet and EasyEverything Internet Cafés, prices can be as much as two-thirds less than competitors provided you reserve early. For instance, prices start at about $21 a day and top out at $84 if you rent the last car in the lot, a price that is still cheaper than competitors. Stelios says, "There is no reason why hiring a car should be so expensive. By offering just one model [the Mercedes A-Class] and trading only on the Internet, we can bring down costs."

Maurice Kelly, the chief executive who runs the EasyEverything Cafés, says, "He [Stelios] looks at old industries and smashes them to pieces. Why do car rentals have to offer lots of models? Why do airlines have to issue tickets?" Say Stelios, "What I want to achieve is to have a family of companies linked by a common brand but each developing its own identity."

Sources: D. Appell, "The EasyEmpire Strikes Back: Throwing Down the Gauntlet to Europe's Old-Guard Airlines, the Young Greek Entrepreneur Who Birthed Easyjet Airlines and Easyrentacar Has Been Shaking Up the Continent's Budget Travel Market," *Arthur Frommer's Budget Travel.* [Online] Available, http://stocks.msnbc.com/news/587392.asp, 22 June 2001. M. Fletcher, "High Flyer on Easy Street: King of Cut-Price Air Travel Takes off to Conquer New Online Territory," *Mail on Sunday,* 26 March 2000, 16. M. Harrison, "Easythis, Easythat, Easyfloat: At Least, That's How Stelios Haji-Ioannou (That's Stelios to You) Would Like to See the Stock Market Debut of Easyjet, the Cut-Price Airline He Has Shouldered into the Big Time. But Will It Be That Simple?" *The Independent* (London), 11 October 2000, 1B. K. Kemp, "Airlines Net Sky-High Results," *The Sunday Herald,* 11 June 1999, 16. R. Morais, "Proving Papa Wrong," *Forbes,* 9 July 2001. B. Wysocki, Jr., "The Challengers—Headwinds: The Odds Are Against Starting an Airline—And Still They Try—With Tenacity and Little Else, These Two Men Took on Majors' Entrenched System—Getting Past 'The Sniff Test'," *The Wall Street Journal,* 16 April 2001, A1.

Key Terms

advocacy groups (43)
behavioural addition (52)
behavioural substitution (52)
business confidence indices (38)
buyer dependence (42)
cognitive maps (46)
company vision (51)
competitive analysis (41)
competitors (41)
complex environment (35)
dynamic environment (34)
environmental change (34)
environmental complexity (35)

environmental munificence (36)
environmental scanning (45)
external environments (34)
general environment (37)
industry regulation (42)
internal environment (48)
media advocacy (44)
opportunistic behaviour (42)
organizational ceremonies (50)
organizational culture (48)
organizational heroes (49)
organizational rituals (50)
organizational stories (49)

organizational symbols (50)
product boycott (44)
public communications (44)
punctuated equilibrium theory (34)
relationship behaviour (42)
simple environment (35)
specific environment (38)
stable environment (34)
supplier dependence (42)
suppliers (42)
technology (39)
uncertainty (36)
visible artifacts (48)

What Would You Do II?

Ford versus Firestone

It is 8:30 a.m. on Monday. You have just received a phone call informing you that another Ford Explorer has been involved in a fatal roll-over accident. Two of the passengers were killed and the other two are seriously injured. Original equipment Firestone tires are suspected to be the cause of the accident. A police officer on the scene states that the tread of the left rear tire tore off "like a banana peel," which caused the vehicle to lose control and roll over four to five times before coming to a stop.

As president and CEO of Ford Motor Company, you have known about problems with Firestone tires on Ford Explorers in the Middle East and in South America since late 1998, however, only recently have problems begun to appear in North America. To date, there have been 88 deaths and over 1400 accidents connected to Ford Explorers equipped with Firestone tires. Additionally, since 1992, more than 100 suits have been filed by injured motorists or their families against Ford and Firestone. Many questions remain to be answered. Are the Firestone tires defective and are they dangerous? Are the problems related to owner abuse or misuse? Does the Explorer have an inherent design flaw that makes it more susceptible to a loss of control or roll-over? It may take weeks or months to dig through the data needed to answer these questions; however, after this morning's phone call, you know that a decision must be made. Ford Motor Company must push Firestone to recall the affected tires.

Your staff has prepared the associated cost and logistic problems connected with such a recall. A recall of this magnitude will involve over 6.5 million tires initially and possibly up to 13 million long-term. Completing the recall could take up to 18 months to complete and will undoubtedly affect the year-end earnings for the company. Additionally, up to three assembly plants will have to be idled for up to one month so that stockpiled tires can be shipped to aid in recall efforts. Early cost figures for shutting down the three plants for one month have been estimated at $150 million, which doesn't include the cost of temporary unemployment for the laid-off workers or the costs associated with the loss of productivity and decreased sales.

To further compound the problem, Bridgestone, the parent company of Firestone, alleges that Ford Motor Company advised Explorer owners to lower inflation pressures (from 30 psi to 26 psi) in order to reduce the possibility of roll-over and to improve ride characteristics. This decrease in pressure, according to Bridgestone officials, increased the probability of excessive heat damage and subsequent tread separation within the tires. Engineers with Ford have refuted the claim saying that other brands of tires used on Ford Explorers have exhibited no damage when operated at the lower pressure. The problem, at this point, is not to determine who is at fault, but to determine how this problem can be resolved in a manner that will maintain the level of consumer confidence and trust that Ford Motor Company has developed with the American public over the years. An additional constraint in this issue is the potential of damaging the close-knit relationship that Ford has developed with Firestone for over 95 years. To complicate matters further, Martha Firestone Ford, the mother of William Clay Ford, Ford's current chairman, is a Firestone heiress. Her father was a chief executive with Firestone in its infancy. Therefore, more than just a name is at stake. How are you going to ensure that the public maintains its level of trust and respect for your company as you initiate a recall to replace all of the 13 million potentially defective tires installed on your company's vehicles? What, if anything, could you do to satisfy both your customers and maintain your relationship with Firestone, one of your long-term suppliers? **If you were the president and CEO of Ford Motor Company, what would you do?**

Sources: J. Greenwald, "Firestone's Tire Crisis," *Time*, 21 August 2000, 64–65. M. Lavelle, "Where the Rubber Meets the Road," *U.S.*

News & World Report, 4 September 2000, 43. A. Taylor, "Jac Nasser's Biggest Test," *Fortune*, 18 September 2000, 123–128. D. Eisenberg, "Is This Vehicle Safe?," *Time*, 2 October 2000, 59. T. Aeppel, "Ford Intends to Replace Millions of Tires," *The Wall Street Journal*, 23 May 2001. B. Garfield, "Nasser Spot Lacks Star Quality, But Gets Tire Message Across," *Advertising Age*, 28 August 2000. J. Nasser, "A Letter from Ford CEO Nasser To Bridgestone/Firestone CEO Lampe," *The Wall Street Journal*, 23 May 2001. J. Lampe, "Letter from Firestone to Ford, Ending Business Relationship," *The Wall Street Journal*, 21 May 2001. M. Geyelin, "Firestone Quits as Tire Supplier to Ford," *The Wall Street Journal*, 22 May 2001. B. Clark, "Ford vs. Firestone," *Newsweek*, 18 September 2000.

Management Decisions

Culture Shock

As a vice president of a medium-sized software technology company located in Ottawa, you have been involved in several acquisitions of smaller firms over the last few years, each having resulted in increased growth and profitability for your firm. Recently, your company has been discussing plans to acquire a small, relatively new, computer-networking services company located in California's Silicon Valley. Your firm is interested in this acquisition because it has the skills, equipment, and knowledge desperately needed but currently lacking in your firm. Additionally, some of your current clients are located in and around the Silicon Valley.

The firm being considered has a solid reputation and a growing number of customers located in Canada. If this acquisition occurs, it will serve to broaden the services currently provided by your firm, increase your firm's presence nationwide, and strengthen your firm's core competencies by alleviating the need to outsource certain activities. Investment capital has already been garnered to facilitate the acquisition.

Tomorrow morning, you and several other top executives will decide whether to go ahead with the proposed acquisition. Unfortunately, one item makes you uncomfortable with this plan. In comparing the two companies, you have found that your firm's corporate culture differs dramatically from that of the firm being considered. Although some of your colleagues denounce this as being an insignificant problem and one that can be easily solved, you consider it to be one of high importance.

Your firm is larger and more bureaucratic, is formal in structure, and utilizes centralized decision-making techniques. Typically before key decisions are made, an extensive amount of time is spent involving group discussions and developing con-

sensus before any action is taken. Additionally, there is a clear chain of command within your firm, and individuals have distinct job descriptions and duties. On the other hand, the proposed company's structure and culture appear to be very informal. The organizational hierarchy is relatively flat, with key decisions being made at all levels. Employees have no clear responsibilities or duties and are empowered to "take the ball and run with it." The firm's founder claims that it is their unique culture that has resulted in the firm's rapid growth in market share, profitability, and innovativeness.

Your main fear regarding the proposed acquisition is that the new company's culture will be too different to effectively mesh the two companies together. Further, it is your belief that the employees of the new company will feel trapped and constrained by your firm's formalized structure. As you look over the acquisition proposal, the projections and possibilities are certainly appealing. If the acquisition becomes a success, your firm could stand to become the largest, most powerful communications firm in the industry. Tomorrow morning, you and four others will vote to move ahead or abandon the proposed acquisition.

Questions

1. How will you vote and why?
2. If you vote to pursue the acquisition, what changes might you recommend to ensure that the acquisition and subsequent transition succeed?
3. If you vote to abandon the acquisition, what changes might you propose that (if accepted by the group) would change your mind regarding pursuing the acquisition?

Source: M. Roger, "How Culture Affects Mergers and Acquisitions," *Industrial Management*, September 2000 Vol. 42, No. 5: 22–26.

Cultural Change: Evolution or Revolution?

Tandem Computer makes "fault tolerant" computers guaranteed to keep working during power outages, natural disasters, and catastrophic computer glitches that would easily shut down standard computers. Since 1974, Tandem has sold its computers at high prices and high profit margins to stock exchanges, phone companies, banks, airlines, and other companies whose businesses are dependent on uninterrupted computer service. Tandem computers are used in 75 percent of all ATM transactions, 66 percent of all credit card transactions, and 70 percent of electronic interchange networks (data sharing between companies).

Jimmy Treybig, Tandem's CEO, founded the company with $1.5 million in venture capital money from Thomas Perkins, who chairs Tandem's board of directors. That $1.5-million investment grew into a company with $3.1 billion in annual revenues. During its 20-year run of success, Treybig developed a patriarchal culture at Tandem. Once a week, at every Tandem facility, there was a "beer bust." Attendance wasn't mandatory, but most people wanted to attend. The point: not to promote drinking, but to get to know each other better and encourage informal communication, which is often lacking in corporate environments. Treybig's stated management philosophy was that

(1) all people are good;
(2) workers, management, and company are all the same thing;
(3) every single person in the company must understand the essence of the business;
(4) every employee must benefit from the company's success;
(5) you must create an environment where all the above can happen. (Ward, 1995)

One symbol of this philosophy was that Tandem's sales representatives had one of the most generous compensation plans in the industry, earning $150 000 to $600 000 a year. In all, CEO Treybig was well liked and ran the company like an extended family.

Unfortunately, the party ended a few years ago. Customers began refusing to pay premium prices for Tandem's computers, especially since they used Tandem's proprietary software, Guardian, which was not compatible with other kinds of computers. In just three years, profits, which had been running between $150 million and $300 million annually, dropped to a loss of more than $750 million. Customers wanted Tandem to produce computers that run UNIX, an "open" operating system that runs on different kinds of computers, unlike Guardian, which runs only on Tandem computers.

The company's struggles have not only affected profits, but have also begun to affect Tandem's organizational culture. Said CEO Treybig, "Nothing is as fun as it used to be. My wife says I never use the word 'fun' anymore. In the 1980s you could just do a good job and make money. But nowadays, you have to be the best. I mean, every day you have to really worry about being successful. The bar for success is higher. It takes fun out of it" (Ward, 1995).

Questions

1. At critical times like this, CEOs have two basic choices: evolutionary change or revolutionary change. Explain which would be the best choice for returning Tandem to profitability. Why?
2. Either approach will affect Tandem's family-like culture. Depending on which you chose, explain three ways in which a company like Tandem could incrementally change its culture or change its culture in a revolutionary way.

Sources: R. Karpinski, "Tandem Slates Web Server Product Line," *Interactive Age*, 10 April 1995, 24. T.J. Peters & N.K. Austin, *A Passion for Excellence* (New York: Random House, 1985). E. Ramstad & L. Gomes, "Compaq to Acquire Tandem Computers," *The Wall Street Journal*, 24 June 1997, A3. J.E. Rigdon, "Cruel World: Cannibalism Is a Virtue in Computer Business, Tandem's CEO Learns," *The Wall Street Journal*, 24 August 1994, A1. J. Ward, "The Thrill Is Gone," *Financial World*, 11 April 1995, 32. A.L. Wilkins & N.J. Bristow, "For Successful Organization Culture, Honor Your Past," *Academy of Management Executive* 1 (1987): 221–229.

Develop Your Management Potential

Dealing with the Press

In this age of 24-hour cable news channels, tabloid news shows, and aggressive local and national news reporters intent on exposing corporate wrong-doing, one of the most important skills for a manager to learn is how to deal effectively with the press. Test your ability to deal effectively with the press by putting yourself in the following situation. To make the situation more realistic, read the scenario and then give yourself two minutes to write a response to each question.

Fatty Restaurant Food Contributes to Heart Attacks

Today, in the nation's capital, a public-interest group held a press conference to release the results of a study that found that the food sold in most Chinese restaurants is high in fat. The group claims that the most popular Chinese dishes, such as orange chicken, pork fried rice, and Hunan beef, contain nearly as much fat as the food you get from fast-food chains such as McDonald's, Wendy's, and Burger King. (Much of it is fried or is covered with heavy sauces.) Furthermore, the group says that customers who hope to keep their cholesterol and blood pressure low by eating Chinese food are just fooling themselves.

A TV reporter from Channel 5 called your Szechuan-style Chinese restaurant, Szechuan, to get your response to this study. When she and the camera crew arrived, she asked you the following questions. (To simulate these conditions, give yourself only two minutes to write a response to each question.)

1. "A new study released today claims that food sold in Chinese restaurants is on average nearly as fattening as that sold at fast-food restaurants. How healthy is the food that you serve at Szechuan's?"

2. "Get the camera in close here [camera closes in to get the shot] because I want the audience at home to see that you don't provide any information on your menu about calories, calories from fat, or cholesterol. Without this information [camera pulls back to get a picture of you and the reporter], how can your customers know that the food that you serve is healthy for them?"

3. "These new studies were based on lunches and dinners sampled from Chinese restaurants across the country. A local company, Huntington Labs, has agreed to test foods from local restaurants so that we can provide accurate information to our viewers. Would you agree to let us sample the main dishes in your restaurant to test the level of calories, calories from fat, and cholesterol? Furthermore, can we take the cameras into your restaurant, so that we can get your customers' reactions to these studies?"

Discussion Questions

1. Universities and colleges have elements of culture that are shared and some elements that are unique to each university or college. Thinking of your university or college, what elements of its culture are shared with other universities or colleges and which are unique?

2. Punctuated equilibrium theory states that industries go through alternating periods of stability and change. Identify an industry that has been relatively stable which is now being transformed by a change in the external environment. What caused the change and what are the likely consequences of the change?

3. Uncertainty refers to how well managers can understand or predict the external changes and trends affecting their businesses. Name an organization that faces a low level of uncertainty and explain why it has a low level of uncertainty. Name an organization that faces a high level of uncertainty and explain why it has a high level of uncertainty. What could it do to reduce the level of uncertainty it faces?

4. Advocacy groups are groups of concerned citizens who band together to try to influence the business practices of specific industries, businesses, and professions. Identify an advocacy group and provide examples of activities they undertake to communicate their position. Do you think their activities are effective? Why or why not?

5. Give an example of an attempted product boycott. Which group(s) initiated the boycott and why? Was the boycott effective? Why or why not? How did the company that was boycotted respond and was the response effective?

Create your own diagram of the business environment and compare it to the example in the chapter. Read a selection of business press articles and list the factors at play in each of the articles you read. Visit the Management website at www.management1e.nelson.com or use your Student CD-ROM for a wealth of review and mastery activities.

3

CHAPTER

Chapter Outline

Learning Objectives

After reading this chapter, you should be able to

1. discuss how the nature of a management job creates the possibility for ethical abuses.
2. identify common kinds of workplace deviance.
3. describe what influences ethical decision-making.
4. explain what practical steps managers can take to improve ethical decision-making.
5. explain to whom organizations are socially responsible.
6. explain for what organizations are socially responsible.
7. explain how organizations can choose to respond to societal demands for social responsibility.
8. explain whether social responsibility hurts or helps an organization's economic performance.

© Corel

three

Ethics and Social Responsibility

What Would You Do?

McDonald's Restaurant, Calgary Trail, Edmonton: "Welcome to McDonald's. May I take your order, please?" "Yes, I'd like an Egg McMuffin, hash browns, a small orange juice, and a large coffee." More than 5 million times a day, someone in the United States or Canada purchases an Egg McMuffin at a McDonald's. In fact, McDonald's (www.mcdonalds.ca) 14 000 Canadian and U.S. restaurants buy approximately 2 billion of the 80 billion eggs produced each year in these two countries.

Customers go to McDonald's for its quick service and good prices. But that doesn't matter to PETA, People for the Ethical Treatment of Animals, an advocacy group run by vegetarian activists who care only about advancing the rights of animals worldwide. For the last few years, PETA (www.peta.org) has been running a "McCruelty to Go" publicity campaign against McDonald's. Through 400 demonstrations in 23 countries, including Canada, numerous magazine and billboard ads, and its www.mccruelty.com website, PETA has pressured McDonald's to require the farmers from whom it gets its food products to treat animals more "humanely." How powerful is PETA? In Canada alone, it has forced Burger King, Wendy's, and Canada Safeway Ltd. to alter controversial aspects of their business practices. Indeed, Safeway also found

itself the subject of a PETA website, www.shameway. com. PETA wants McDonald's to buy eggs only from suppliers that don't debeak hens (cutting off a chicken's beak reduces damage from chicken fighting), that give egg-laying hens 465 square centimetres of living space (most egg-laying hens are kept in small cages no larger than half a piece of letter-size paper, which, according to PETA, prevent them from standing up, stretching their legs and wings, or moving around), and that don't withhold food to increase molting and thus egg production (forced molting, meaning the shedding of feathers, is a process in which birds are rested from egg production and food is temporarily withheld. This restores hens' ability to lay eggs).

Of course, not everyone agrees with PETA's views and recommendations. Egg farmers say that they go to great lengths to treat their hens well and keep them in good health. Jerry Armstrong, who owns an egg ranch with 1 million hens, said, "We're always concerned with our birds' welfare. If they're not happy and contented, they won't lay eggs and we're out of the egg business." The egg industry says that hens are kept in cages to decrease costs, which matters to consumers, but also to improve sanitation and bird health. If McDonald's adopts PETA's recommendations to double the size of hens' cages, they would have to pay an extra 25 or 30 cents for a dozen eggs. And with too

many egg producers in an overly crowded market, increased costs of any kind, but especially those that would require producers to double the size of their production facilities, could lead to huge costs and losses. Jerry Armstrong claims, "These rules would put me out of business."

What is the ethical thing to do in this situation? Should McDonald's give in to PETA's demands, or should it ignore them? Given that protests are not a new thing for McDonald's, how does it decide how serious an issue this is and the lengths to which it should go to address these issues, if any? If McDonald's seriously considers PETA's demands, how does it decide whose interests take precedence? Is it more socially responsible to require its egg suppliers to change their practices if changing them leads to financial losses and puts some suppliers out of business? Which comes first, the chickens or the egg producers? No matter what McDonald's decides, someone or some group will be very unhappy.

If you were making this decision for McDonald's, what would you do?

Sources: "Egg Production Information," American Egg Board. [Online] Available www.aeb.org/eii/production.html, 29 June 2001. "Did You Know...?" Canadian Egg Marketing Agency. [Online] Available www.canadaegg.ca, 10 October 2002. A. Butler, "PETA Celebrates Meat-Out at...Burger King!" PETA News Releases. [Online] Available www.peta-online.org, 19 March 2002. B.G. Friedrich, "PETA to Praise Onetime

Target Wendy's at Shareholder Meeting." PETA News Releases. [Online] Available www.peta-online.org, 1 May 2002. "B.C. SPCA Plans to Launch Line of Certified Chickens Eggs," *Canadian Press Newswire*, 2 April 2002. D. Campbell, "Chicken Run:

McDonald's Takes a Cue from the Hit Film and Demands Better Conditions for Hens Used to Supply Eggs for Its McMuffins," *The Guardian*, 8 September 2000. T. Perry, "Egg Producers Are McMiffed: Industry Balks at McDonald's Tough Rules on Hen Treatment," *Los Angeles*

Times, 7 September 2000, C1. D. Wetzel, "McDonald's to Require Its Egg Suppliers to Improve Conditions for Hens," *Chicago Tribune*, 24 August 2001.

McDonald's dilemma about the treatment of chickens is an example of the tough decisions that managers face regarding ethics and social responsibility. Unfortunately, one of the "real world" aspects of these decisions is that no matter what you decide, someone or some group will be unhappy with the decision. Managers don't have the luxury of choosing theoretically optimal, win-win solutions that are obviously correct to everyone involved. In practice, solutions to ethics and social responsibility problems aren't optimal. Often, they are "make-do" or "do the least harm" kinds of solutions. Clear rights and wrongs rarely reveal themselves to managers charged with "doing the right thing." The business world is much messier than that.

What Is Ethical and Unethical Workplace Behaviour?

ethics
the set of moral principles or values that defines right and wrong for a person or group

Ethics is the set of moral principles or values that defines right and wrong for a person or group. In light of highly publicized cases such as Enron, Worldcom, Tyco, and Adelphia, it is not surprising that several studies have produced distressing results about the state of ethics in today's business world. In a broad survey of 2300 workers, 75 percent indicated that they had seen unethical behaviour at work, such as deceptive sales practices, unsafe working conditions, environmental breaches, and mishandling of confidential or proprietary information within the last year.[1] A similar survey of 2293 workers found that less than half (47 percent) felt that the senior leaders in their companies were ethical.[2] Furthermore, 60 percent of workers felt substantially pressured to commit unethical or illegal acts at work. Only 6 percent reported feeling little pressure to commit such acts.[3] Finally, in a study of 1324 randomly selected workers, managers, and executives across many industries, 48 percent of respondents admitted to committing an unethical or illegal act in the past year! These acts included cheating on an expense account, discriminating against co-workers, forging signatures, paying or accepting kickbacks, and "looking the other way" when environmental laws were broken.[4] Winn Swenson, director for integrity management services at KPMG, said, "Corporations need to recognize that the problem is out there."[5]

However, these studies also contained good news. When people are convinced that they work in an ethical work environment, they are six times more likely to stay with that company than if they believe that they work in an unethical environment.[6] In short, a lot of work needs to be done to make workplaces more ethical, but, and this is very important, managers and employees want this to happen.

After reading the next two sections, you should be able to
1. *discuss how the nature of a management job creates the possibility for ethical abuses.*
2. *identify common kinds of workplace deviance.*

1. Ethics and the Nature of Management Jobs

ethical behaviour
behaviour that conforms to a society's accepted principles of right and wrong

Ethical behaviour follows accepted principles of right and wrong. Probably the most famous recent example of unethical corporate behaviour involves the American energy trading company Enron (www.enron.com). By using a complex web of "off-balance-sheet" partnerships and active efforts to avoid paying corporate taxes, its senior executive managed to overstate its earnings by over $600 million. These actions led to the eventual bankruptcy of the company as well as the loss of billions of dollars in future pension income for employees and in shareholders' investments. On the other hand, Wal-Mart (www.walmart.com) has very strict guidelines concerning its employees' ethical behaviour. Any employee who accepts anything of value (dinner, free tickets to a sports event, a round of golf, etc.) from a company that Wal-Mart does business with will immediately be dismissed. Wal-Mart employees aren't even permitted to allow representatives from other companies to buy them a cup of coffee. Furthermore, to encourage employees to behave ethically, all of Wal-Mart's suppliers and vendors are required to do business with Wal-Mart employees in "glass rooms," visible to anyone who walks through the lobby at company headquarters. Finally, the walls in each of these glass rooms are covered with posters that say, "Any item received [from a supplier or vendor] will be returned to sender at their expense."[7]

Unethical management behaviour occurs when managers personally violate accepted principles of right and wrong. The authority and power inherent in some management positions can tempt managers to engage in unethical practices. In the case of Tyco, its CEO Dennis Kozlowski was accused of failing to pay over $1 million in sales taxes on sales of artwork after his efforts to hide the transactions were discovered. Since managers often control company resources, there is a risk that some managers will cross over the line from legitimate use of company resources to personal use of those resources. For example, treating a client to dinner is a common and legitimate business practice in many companies. But what about treating a client to a ski trip? Taking the company jet to attend a business meeting in Winnipeg is legitimate. But how about using the jet to come home to Toronto by way of Calgary and the skiing wonders of Lake Louise? Two large U.S. companies recently gained notoriety for questionable uses of company resources. Human resources can be misused as well. For example, using employees to do personal chores, such as picking up the manager's dry cleaning, is unethical behaviour.

Handling information is another area in which managers must be careful to behave ethically. Information is a key part of management work. Managers collect it, analyze it, act on it, and disseminate it. However, they are also expected to deal in truthful information and, when necessary, to keep confidential information confidential. Leaking company secrets to competitors, "doctoring" the numbers, wrongfully withholding information, or lying are some possible misuses of the information entrusted to managers. For example, in Hong Kong, "Ba dan" literally means white sheet. At Bausch & Lomb's (www.bauschandlomb.com) Hong Kong division, managers used the term "Ba dan" to refer to the fake sales numbers they sent to company headquarters each month. To maintain its status as Bausch & Lomb's top international division, Hong Kong managers would fake the sales numbers for its Southeast Asian customers. Then, to make the fake numbers look like real sales, it would ship its product (glasses and contact lenses) to a phony customer warehouse.[8] Bausch & Lomb used company auditors plus its internal security department, which was run by ex-Secret Service agents and police officers, to set up "sting" operations to catch the employees who were running the "Ba dan" scam in Hong Kong.

A third area in which managers must be careful to engage in ethical behaviour is the way in which they influence the behaviour of others, especially those they supervise. Managerial work gives managers significant power to influence others. If managers tell employees to perform unethical acts (or face punishment), such as "faking the numbers to get results," they are abusing their managerial power. This is sometimes called the "move it or lose it" syndrome. "Move it or lose it" managers tell employees, "Do it. You're paid to do it. If you can't do it, we'll find somebody who can."[9]

Not all unethical managerial influence is intentional, however. Sometimes managers unintentionally influence employees to act unethically by creating policies that inadvertently reward employees for unethical acts. For example, in an attempt to make its automotive repair shops more profitable, Sears restructured its incentive system. It paid mechanics and shop managers a commission depending on the number of batteries, shock absorbers, oil changes, or tune-ups they sold per work shift. However, this pay system put the workers' best interests (higher pay) directly in conflict with the interests of customers (honest repair work). What management was trying to accomplish was greater productivity, but instead, employees started selling unneeded parts and repair work. This practice became so widespread that many customers and government regulators accused Sears of cheating customers by selling unnecessary parts and repairs. Sears management has since ended the incentive program.[10]

Setting goals is another way that managers influence the behaviour of their employees. If managers set unrealistic goals, the pressure to perform and to achieve these goals can influence employees to engage in unethical business behaviours. For example, at Bausch & Lomb, there was tremendous pressure to achieve double-digit increases in revenues each year. Said a former company president, "Once you signed up for your target number, you were expected to reach it," no excuses accepted. As a result, Bausch & Lomb has changed its compensation and reward systems to reward managers and employees for long-term rather than short-term performance.

Review 1
Ethics and the Nature of Management Jobs

Ethics is the set of moral principles or values that define right and wrong. Ethical behaviour occurs when managers follow those principles and values. Because they set the standard for others in the workplace, managers can model ethical behaviour by using resources for company and not personal business. Furthermore, managers can encourage ethical behaviour by handling information in a confidential and honest fashion, by not using their authority to influence others to engage in unethical behaviour, by not creating policies that unintentionally reward employees for unethical behaviour, and by setting reasonable rather than unreasonable goals.

Unfortunately, as will become apparent throughout this chapter, the issue of appropriate behaviour is not a simple one. Managers are often responsible for addressing behaviours or potential behaviours that are ethical or unethical. These unfortunately need to be distinguished from legal and illegal behaviours. In the following paragraphs you will read about employee theft or "shrinkage," which is not only a criminal offence in Canada but is also unethical. But also keep in mind the situation of an employee lying to a customer about a boss being out of town when that individual is actually in the office. Although dishonest, morally wrong, and from the point of view of the recipient of the message, unethical, this act is not a criminal act and hence not illegal. These examples illustrate the dilemma that many managers face when seeking to respond to controversial behaviour and the need for organizations to develop solid codes of conduct to help decision makers. Before addressing this issue, let us first discuss the concern of workplace deviance.

2. Workplace Deviance

Depending on which study you look at, one-third to three-quarters of all employees admit that they have stolen from their employers or committed computer fraud, embezzled funds, vandalized company property, sabotaged company projects, or been "sick" from work when they really weren't sick. Experts estimate that unethical behaviours like these, which researchers call "workplace deviance," may cost companies as much as

$400 billion U.S. a year.[11] Further, one survey estimates that 20 percent of Canadian workers know when deviant behaviour is occurring in their workplace. Indeed, in Canada alone, the same survey places the cost at $23 000 per company per year.[12]

More specifically, **workplace deviance** is unethical behaviour that violates organizational norms about right and wrong. Exhibit 3.1 shows that workplace deviance can be categorized by how deviant the behaviour is, from minor to serious, and by the target of the deviant behaviour, either the organization or particular people in the workplace.[13] One kind of workplace deviance, called **production deviance**, hurts the quality and quantity of work produced. Examples include leaving early, taking excessively long work breaks, purposely working slower, or intentionally wasting resources.

Property deviance is unethical behaviour aimed at company property. Examples include sabotaging, stealing, or damaging equipment or products, or overcharging for services and then pocketing the difference. While it's certainly scary to think about, Boeing, the passenger jet manufacturer, has had instances of product sabotage. In a number of instances during routine product testing, the manufacturer has found wires cut in its 737 jets. Each 737 has 57 600 km of wiring. No one has ever been caught for cutting the wires. A spokesperson for EasyJet (www.easyjet.com), a London-based airline, recently said, "This incident is very disturbing, and we are demanding a full investigation into how it could have happened. We need a guarantee from Boeing that these

workplace deviance
unethical behaviour that violates organizational norms about right and wrong

production deviance
unethical behaviour that hurts the quality of work produced

property deviance
unethical behaviour aimed at the organization's property

EXHIBIT 3.1

TYPES OF WORKPLACE DEVIANCE

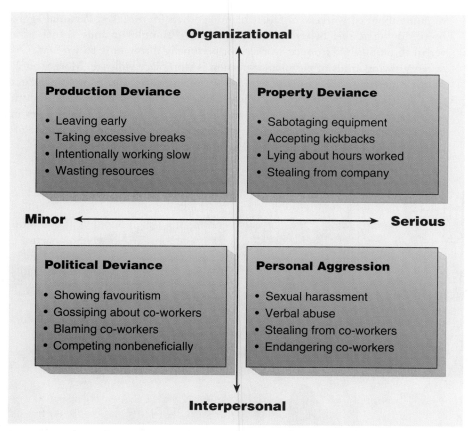

Source: Academy of Management, PO Box 3020, Briar Cliff Manor, NY 10510-8020. "A Typology of Deviant Workplace Behaviors," (Figure), S.L. Robinson & R.J. Bennett. *Academy of Management Journal*, 1995, Vol. 38. Reproduced by permission of the publisher via Copyright Clearance Center.

planes are 100 percent free of any further problems. Like all airlines, we rely on the manufacturer delivering a safe product."[14] Sometimes, however, property deviance occurs with company property, rather than company products. An employee planted a software bomb in the centralized file server that contained one company's key programs and data. The code destroyed the programs and data that ran the machines in the company's manufacturing plant. The company lost $10 million as a result, including $2 million in reprogramming costs. Eighty employees had to be laid off because of lost business resulting from the incident.[15]

shrinkage
employee theft of company merchandise

Another common form of property deviance called **shrinkage** is the theft of company merchandise by employees. One industry in particular, retail, tracks losses of this nature fairly intensely. One estimate places shrinkage costs for traditional Canadian retailers at more than $3 million a day and more than $3 billion for the entire industry or 1.8 percent of annual sales.[16] These shrinkage costs represent 33 percent of all corporate losses in the retail sector attributed to criminal activity of one type or another. Further, the Retail Council of Canada (www.retailcouncil.org) estimates the average loss for an employee theft at over $600. Not surprisingly, some firms have been hit harder than others. Recent figures suggest companies such as Chapters Inc. and Shoppers Drug Mart have faced shrinkage losses in the order of 2.1 percent and 1.5 percent of annual sales.[17] In the case of Shoppers Drug Mart, that works out to more than $6 million annually. Researchers have also attempted to profile the typical dishonest employee. Such an individual will work for a company an average of nine months and steal approximately $1500 worth of goods or services.[18]

While workplace and production deviance harm companies, political deviance and personal aggression are unethical behaviours that hurt particular people within companies. **Political deviance** is using one's influence to harm others in the company. Examples include making decisions based on favouritism rather than performance, spreading rumours about co-workers, or falsely blaming others for mistakes. **Personal aggression** is hostile or aggressive behaviour toward others. Examples include sexual harassment, verbal abuse, stealing from co-workers, or personally threatening co-workers. One of the fastest growing kinds of personal aggression is workplace violence. More than 2 million North Americans are victims of workplace violence each year. A prominent example is the OC Transpo case in Ottawa, where a worker, who had been teased for stuttering, returned to the work site with a gun and killed four co-workers.[19] In another infamous case, Concordia University engineering professor Valery Fabrikant killed three of his academic colleagues at the institution's downtown campus.[20]

political deviance
using one's influence to harm others in the company

personal aggression
hostile or aggressive behaviour toward others

Although violence is on the decline, workplace violence is not. Police are pictured outside a Navistar Engine plant where a man shot and killed five co-workers and injured four others before turning the gun on himself.

AP/Wide World Photos

If recent evidence is any indication, approximately 60 Canadians are killed at work annually.[21] Perhaps more disturbing are the results of an International Labor Organization study that suggests women employed in Canadian workplaces are four times more likely to be on the receiving end of workplace violence than their American counterparts.[22] Although many victims are police officers, security guards, or taxi drivers, store owners and company managers are most often the ones killed.[23] For more information on workplace violence, see the Canadian Centre for Occupational Health and Safety website, www.ccohs.ca.

Review 2
Workplace Deviance

Workplace deviance is behaviour that violates important organizational norms about right and wrong and harms the organization or its workers. Production deviance and property deviance harm the company, whereas political deviance and personal aggression harm individuals within the company.

How Do You Make Ethical Decisions?

On a cold morning in the midst of a winter storm, schools were closed and most people had decided to stay home from work. However, Richard Addessi had already showered, shaved, and dressed for the office. Addessi, whose father worked at IBM for 36 years, was just four months short of his 30-year anniversary with the company. Addessi kissed his wife Joan goodbye, but before he could get to his car he fell dead on the garage floor of a sudden heart attack. Having begun work at IBM at the age of 18, he was just 48 years old.[24]

You're the vice president in charge of benefits at IBM (www.ibm.com). Yes or no, given that he was four months short of full retirement, do you award full retirement benefits to Mr. Addessi's wife and daughters? If the answer is yes, they will receive his full retirement benefits of $1800 a month and free lifetime medical coverage. If you say no, Mrs. Addessi and her daughters will receive only $340 a month. They will also have to pay $473 a month just to continue their current medical coverage. As the VP in charge of benefits at IBM, what would be the ethical thing to do?

After reading the next two sections, you should be able to
3. describe what influences ethical decision-making.
4. explain what practical steps managers can take to improve ethical decision-making.

3. Influences on Ethical Decision-Making

So what did IBM decide to do? Since Richard Addessi was four months short of 30 years with the company, IBM officials felt they had no choice but to give Joan Addessi and her two daughters the smaller, partial retirement benefits. Do you think that IBM's decision was ethical? Probably many of you don't. You wonder how the company could be so heartless as to not give Richard Addessi's family the full benefits to which you believe they were entitled. Yet others might argue that IBM did the ethical thing by strictly following the rules laid out in its pension benefit plan. After all, being fair means applying the rules to everyone.

Let's examine why, while some ethical issues are easily solved, for many there are no clearly right or wrong answers. The ethical answers that managers choose depend on the ethical intensity of the decision, the moral development of the manager, and the ethical principles used to solve the problem.

3.1 Ethical Intensity of the Decision

Managers don't treat all ethical decisions the same. The manager who has to decide whether to deny or extend full benefits to Joan Addessi and her family is going to treat that decision much more seriously than the manager who has to deal with an assistant who has been taking computer disks home for personal use. The difference between these

ethical intensity
the degree of concern people have about an ethical issue

decisions is one of **ethical intensity**, which is how concerned people are about an ethical issue. When addressing issues of high ethical intensity, managers are more aware of the impact their decisions have on others. They are more likely to view the decision as an ethical or moral decision rather than an economic decision. They are also more likely to worry about doing the "right thing."

Ethical intensity depends on six factors:[25]

- magnitude of consequences
- social consensus
- probability of effect
- temporal immediacy
- proximity of effect
- concentration of effect

magnitude of consequences
the total harm or benefit derived from an ethical decision

social consensus
agreement on whether behaviour is bad or good

probability of effect
the chance that something will happen and then result in harm to others

temporal immediacy
the time between an act and the consequences the act produces

proximity of effect
the social, psychological, cultural, or physical distance between a decision maker and those affected by his or her decisions

concentration of effect
the total harm or benefit that an act produces on the average person

Magnitude of consequences is the total harm or benefit derived from an ethical decision. The more people who are harmed, or the greater the harm to those people, the larger the consequences. **Social consensus** is agreement on whether behaviour is bad or good. For example, other than the act of self-defence, most people agree that killing is wrong. However, people strongly disagree about whether abortions or the death penalty are wrong. **Probability of effect** is the chance that something will happen and then result in harm to others.

Temporal immediacy is the time between an act and the consequences the act produces. Temporal immediacy is stronger if a manager has to lay off workers next week as opposed to three months from now. **Proximity of effect** is the social, psychological, cultural, or physical distance of a decision maker to those affected by his or her decisions. In the previous example, proximity of effect would be greater for the manager who works with employees who are to be laid off than it would be for a staff person who works where no layoffs are occurring. Finally, whereas the magnitude of consequences is the total effect across all people, **concentration of effect** is how much an act affects the average person. Cheating 10 investors out of $10 000 apiece is a greater concentration of effect than cheating 100 investors out of $1000 apiece.

Many people will likely feel IBM was wrong to deny full benefits to Joan Addessi. Why? Because IBM's decision met five of the six characteristics of ethical intensity. The difference in benefits ($23 000 per year) is likely to have serious consequences on the family. The decision is certain to affect them. It will affect them immediately. We can closely identify with Joan Addessi and her daughters (as opposed to IBM's faceless, nameless corporate identity). And the decision will have a concentrated effect on the family with regard to their monthly benefits ($1800 and free medical coverage if you award full benefits versus $340 a month and medical care coverage that costs $473 per month if you don't).

The exception, as we will discuss below, is social consensus. Not everyone will agree that IBM's decision was unethical. The judgment also depends on your level of moral development and which ethical principles you use.

3.2 Moral Development

A friend has given you the latest version of Microsoft Word. She stuffed the computer disks in your backpack with a note saying that you should install it on your computer and get it back to her in a couple of days. You're tempted. You have papers to write, notes to take, presentations to plan. Besides, all of your friends have the same version of Microsoft Word. They didn't pay for it either. Copying the software to your hard drive without buying your own copy clearly violates copyright laws. But no one would find out. Even if they do, Microsoft isn't going to come after you. Microsoft goes after the big fish, companies that illegally copy and distribute software to their workers. Your computer has booted up, and you've got your mouse in one hand and the installation disk in the other. What are you going to do?[26]

In part, according to Lawrence Kohlberg, the decision will be based on your level of moral development. Kohlberg identified three phases of moral development, with two stages in each phase (see Exhibit 3.2).[27] At the **preconventional level of moral development**, people decide based on selfish reasons. For example, if you were in Stage 1, the punishment and obedience stage, your primary concern would be not to get in trouble. So you wouldn't copy the software. Yet, in Stage 2, the instrumental exchange stage, you make decisions that advance your wants and needs. So you copy the software.

People at the **conventional level of moral development** make decisions that conform to societal expectations. In Stage 3, the good boy–nice girl stage, you normally do what the other "good boys" and "nice girls" are doing. If everyone else is illegally copying software, you will, too. In the law and order stage, Stage 4, you do whatever the law permits, so you wouldn't copy the software.

People at the **post conventional level of moral development** always use internalized ethical principles to solve ethical dilemmas. In Stage 5, the legal contract stage, you would refuse to copy the software because, as a whole, society is better off when the rights of others—in this case, the rights of software authors and manufacturers—are not violated. In Stage 6, the universal principle stage, you might or might not copy the software, depending on your principles of right and wrong. Moreover, you will stick to your principles even if your decision conflicts with the law (Stage 4) or what others believe is best for society (Stage 5). For example, someone with socialist or communist beliefs would always choose to copy the software, because they view goods and services as owned by society rather than by individuals and corporations. (For information about the dos, don'ts, and legal issues concerning software piracy, see the Software Publisher's Association website [www.spa.org].)

Kohlberg originally predicted that people would progress sequentially from earlier stages to later stages. We now know that one's level of moral maturity can change, depending on individual and situational factors. As people age, become more educated, or deal with dilemmas high in ethical intensity, they are more likely to make ethical decisions using a higher level of moral maturity.

preconventional level of moral development
first level of moral development in which people make decisions based on selfish reasons

conventional level of moral development
second level of moral development in which people make decisions that conform to societal expectations

post conventional level of moral development
third level of moral development in which people make decisions based on internalized principles

---

PERSONAL PRODUCTIVITY

The "Sleep Test"

Professors use fancy words like "utilitarian benefits" to describe ethical decision-making. However, practising managers refer to something much simpler, the "sleep test." "If I do this, can I sleep at night?" "Can I look at myself in the mirror in the morning?" "The bottom line is what you're comfortable with. I want … to be able to both meet my house payments, and have some dignity left." In short, if you're asked to do something that just "feels" wrong, sleep on it. If it still feels wrong in the morning, don't do it.

Sources: J.L. Badaracco, Jr. & A.P. Webb, "Business Ethics: A View from the Trenches," *California Management Review* 37 (1995): 8–28.

EXHIBIT 3.2

KOHLBERG'S STAGES OF MORAL DEVELOPMENT

PRECONVENTIONAL LEVEL
    Stage 1: Punishment and Obedience
    Stage 2: Instrumental Exchange
CONVENTIONAL LEVEL
    Stage 3: Good Boy–Nice Girl
    Stage 4: Law and Order
POST CONVENTIONAL LEVEL
    Stage 5: Legal Contract
    Stage 6: Universal Principle

Source: W. Davidson III & D. Worrell, "Influencing Managers to Change Unpopular Corporate Behavior Through Boycotts and Divestitures," *Business & Society* 34 (1995): 171–196.

principle of long-term self-interest
ethical principle that holds that you should never take any action that is not in your or your organization's long-term self-interest

principle of personal virtue
ethical principle that holds that you should never do anything that is not honest, open, and truthful, and which you would not be glad to see reported in the newspapers or on TV

principle of religious injunctions
ethical principle that holds that you should never take any action that is not kind and that does not build a sense of community; a sense of everyone working together for a commonly accepted goal

principle of government requirements
ethical principle that holds that you should never take any action that violates the law, for the law represents the minimal moral standard

principle of utilitarian benefits
ethical principle that holds that you should never take any action that does not result in greater good for society. Instead, do whatever creates the greatest good for the greatest number

principle of individual rights
ethical principle that holds that you should never take any action that infringes on others' agreed-on rights

principle of distributive justice
ethical principle that holds that you should never take any action that harms the least among us: the poor, the uneducated, the unemployed

Besides an issue's ethical intensity and a manager's level of moral maturity, the particular ethical principles that managers use will also affect how they solve ethical dilemmas. Unfortunately, there is no one "ideal principle" by which to make ethical business decisions.

According to Professor Larue Hosmer, a number of different ethical principles can be used to make business decisions: long-term self-interest, personal virtue, religious injunctions, government requirements, utilitarian benefits, individual rights, and distributive justice.[28] What these ethical principles have in common is that they encourage managers and employees to take others' interests into account when making ethical decisions. At the same time, however, these principles can lead to very different ethical actions. This is illustrated by using these principles to decide whether to award full benefits to Joan Addessi and her children.

According to the **principle of long-term self-interest**, you should never take any action that is not in your or your organization's long-term self-interest. While it sounds as if the principle of self-interest promotes selfishness, it doesn't. What we do to maximize our long-term interests (save more, spend less, exercise every day, watch what we eat) is often very different from what we do to maximize short-term interests (max out our credit cards, be a couch potato, eat whatever we want). At any single time, IBM has nearly 1000 employees who are just months away from retirement. Thus, because of the costs involved, it serves IBM's long-term interest to pay full benefits only after employees have put in their 30 years.

The **principle of personal virtue** holds that you should never do anything that is not honest, open, and truthful, and which you would not be glad to see reported in the newspapers or on TV. Using the principle of personal virtue, IBM should have quietly awarded Joan Addessi her husband's full benefits. Had it done so, it could have avoided the publication of an embarrassing newspaper article on this topic.

The **principle of religious injunctions** holds that you should never take an action that is unkind or that harms a sense of community, such as the positive feelings that come from working together to accomplish a commonly accepted goal. Using the principle of religious injunctions, IBM would have been concerned foremost with compassion and kindness. Thus, it would have awarded full benefits to Joan Addessi.

According to the **principle of government requirements**, the law represents the minimal moral standards of society, so you should never take any action that violates the law.

The **principle of utilitarian benefits** states that you should never take any action that does not result in greater good for society. In short, you should do whatever creates the greatest good for the greatest number. At first, this principle suggests that IBM should award full benefits to Joan Addessi. However, if IBM did this with any regularity, the costs would be enormous, profits would shrink, and IBM's stock price would drop, harming countless shareholders, many of whom rely on IBM stock dividends for retirement income. So, in this case, the principle does not lead to a clear choice.

The **principle of individual rights** holds that you should never take any action that infringes on others' agreed-on rights. Using the principle of individual rights, IBM would deny Joan Addessi full benefits. If it carefully followed the rules specified in its pension plan, and if it permitted Mrs. Addessi due process, meaning the right to appeal the decision, then IBM would not be violating Mrs. Addessi's rights. In fact, it could be argued that providing full benefits to Mrs. Addessi would violate the rights of employees who had to wait 30 years to receive full benefits.

Finally, the **principle of distributive justice** is that you should never take any action that harms the least among us in some way. This principle is designed to protect the poor, the uneducated, and the unemployed. While Joan Addessi could probably find a job, it's unlikely, after 20 years as a stay-at-home mom, that she could easily find one that would support herself and her daughters in the manner to which they were accustomed. Using the principle of distributive justice, IBM would award her full benefits.

As stated at the beginning of this chapter, one of the "real world" aspects of ethical decisions is that no matter what you decide, someone or some group will be unhappy with the decision. This corollary is also true: No matter how you decide, someone or some group will be unhappy. Consequently, despite the fact that all of these different ethical principles encourage managers to balance others' needs against their own, they can also lead to very different ethical actions. So, even when managers strive to be ethical, there are often no clear answers when it comes to doing "the" right thing.

PERSONAL PRODUCTIVITY TIP

Could You Tell Your Parents or the Public?

Besides the sleep test, managers also judge the ethics of what they're doing by trying to anticipate how others would view their actions. One manager said, "Ummm... This is going to sound trite. But if you can comfortably tell your parents, I think you are probably doing the right thing." Or "Can you tell your grandfather about it and be proud?" Practising managers were also aware of the importance of how their choices were viewed by the general public. Said one manager, "If you wouldn't share it with 'CBC News' cameras, don't do it."

Sources: J.L. Badaracco, Jr. & A.P. Webb, "Business Ethics: A View from the Trenches," *California Management Review* 37 (1995): 8–28.

Review 3
Influences on Ethical Decision-Making

Three factors influence ethical decisions: the ethical intensity of the decision, the moral development of the manager, and the ethical principles used to solve the problem. Ethical intensity is strong when decisions have large, certain, immediate consequences, and when we are physically or psychologically close to those affected by the decision. There are three phases of moral maturity and two steps within each phase. At the preconventional level, decisions are made for selfish reasons. At the conventional level, decisions conform to societal expectations. At the post conventional level, internalized principles are used to make ethical decisions. Finally, managers can use a number of different principles when making ethical decisions: self-interest, personal virtue, religious injunctions, government requirements, utilitarian benefits, individual rights, and distributive justice.

EXPERIENCING MANAGEMENT

A variety of approaches can be used to foster ethical and socially responsible behaviours. Interact with four of these approaches at our animated concept and activity site. Choose Ethics & Social Responsibility from the "select a topic" pull-down menu, then Fostering Social Responsibility from the "overview tab."

www.experiencingmanagement.com

4. Practical Steps to Ethical Decision-Making

Let's examine how managers can encourage more ethical decision-making in their organizations. They can do this by carefully selecting and hiring new employees, establishing a specific code of ethics, training employees to make ethical decisions, and creating an ethical climate.

4.1 Selecting and Hiring Ethical Employees

As an employer, you can increase your chances of hiring honest people if you give job applicants integrity tests. **Overt integrity tests** estimate employee honesty by directly asking job applicants what they think or feel about theft or about punishment of unethical behaviours.[29] For example, an employer might ask an applicant, "Do you think you would ever consider buying something from somebody if you knew the person had stolen the item?" or "Don't most people steal from their companies?" Surprisingly, because they believe that the world is basically dishonest and that dishonest behaviour is normal, unethical people will usually answer yes to such questions.[30]

Personality-based integrity tests indirectly estimate employee honesty by measuring psychological traits such as dependability and conscientiousness. For example, prison inmates serving time for white-collar crimes (counterfeiting, embezzlement, and fraud) scored much lower than a comparison group of middle-level managers on scales measuring reliability, dependability, honesty, and being conscientious and rule-abiding.[31] These results show that companies can selectively hire and promote people who will be more ethical.[32]

For more on integrity testing, see the "What Really Works" feature in this chapter.

overt integrity test
written test that estimates employee honesty by directly asking job applicants what they think or feel about theft or about punishment of unethical behaviours

personality-based integrity test
written test that indirectly estimates employee honesty by measuring psychological traits such as dependability and conscientiousness

WhatReallyWorks

Integrity Tests

In some cases and in some countries, unethical employee behaviour can lead to multimillion-dollar fines for corporations. Moreover, workplace deviance, such as stealing, fraud, and vandalism, can cost companies an estimated $200 billion a year. One way to reduce workplace deviance and the chance of a large fine for unethical employee behaviour is to use overt and personality-based integrity tests to screen job applicants.

One hundred eighty-one studies, with a combined total of 576 460 study participants, have examined how well job performance and various kinds of workplace deviance are predicted by integrity tests. Not only do these studies show that integrity tests can help companies reduce workplace deviance, but they have the added bonus of helping companies hire workers who are better performers in their jobs.

Workplace Deviance (Counterproductive Behaviours)

Compared to job applicants who score poorly, there is an 82 percent chance that job applicants who score well on overt integrity tests will participate in less illegal activity, unethical behaviour, drug abuse, or workplace violence.

Overt Integrity Tests & Workplace Deviance

Personality-based integrity tests also do a good job of predicting who will engage in workplace deviance. Compared to job applicants who score poorly, there is a 68 percent chance that job applicants who score well on personality-based integrity tests will participate in less illegal activity, unethical behaviour, excessive absences, drug abuse, or workplace violence.

Personality-Based Integrity Tests & Workplace Deviance

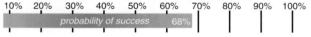

Job Performance

Integrity tests not only reduce unethical behaviour and workplace deviance, but they also help companies hire better performers. Compared to employees who score poorly, there is a 69 percent chance that employees who score well on overt integrity tests will be better performers.

Overt Integrity Tests & Job Performance

The figures are nearly identical for personality-based integrity tests. Compared to those who score poorly, there is a 70 percent chance that employees who score well on personality-based integrity tests will be better at their jobs.

Personality-Based Integrity Tests & Job Performance

Theft

While integrity tests can help companies decrease most kinds of workplace deviance and increase employees' job performance, they have a smaller effect on a specific kind of workplace deviance: theft. Compared to employees who score poorly, there is a 57 percent chance that employees who score well on overt integrity tests will be less likely to steal. No theft data were available to assess personality-based integrity tests.

Overt Integrity Tests & Theft

Source: D.S. Ones, C. Viswesvaran, & F.L. Schmidt, "Comprehensive Meta-Analysis of Integrity Test Validities: Findings and Implications for Personnel Selection and Theories of Job Performance," *Journal of Applied Psychology* 78 (1993): 679–703.

4.2 Codes of Ethics

As shown in Exhibit 3.3, Shell Canada (www.shell.ca) has had in place a set of business principles and code of ethics for over 30 years.[33]

Today, nine out of ten large corporations have an ethics code in place.[34] However, two things must happen if those codes are to encourage ethical decision-making and behaviour. First, companies must communicate the codes to others both within and outside the company. An excellent example of a well-communicated code of ethics can be found at Nortel Networks' Internet site (www.nortelnetworks.com). Anyone inside or outside the company can quickly and easily obtain detailed information about the company's core values, specific ethical business practices, and much more.

Second, in addition to general guidelines and ethics codes such as "Do unto others as you would have others do unto you," management must also develop practical ethical standards and procedures specific to the company's line of business. Visitors to Nortel

Networks' Internet site can instantly access references to 36 specific ethics codes, ranging from bribes and kickbacks to expense vouchers and illegal copying of software. For example, most business people believe that it is wrong to take bribes or other gifts from a company that wants your business. Therefore, one of Nortel Network's ethical guidelines is "Under no circumstances is it acceptable to offer, give, solicit, or receive any form of bribe, kickback, or inducement. This principle applies to Nortel Networks transactions everywhere in the world, even where the practice is widely considered 'a way of doing business.'" Specific codes of ethics such as these make it much easier for employees to decide what they should do when they want to do the "right thing."

4.3 Ethics Training

The first objective of ethics training is to develop employee awareness about ethics.[35] This means helping employees recognize what issues are ethical issues, and then avoid the rationalization of unethical behaviour: "This isn't really illegal or immoral" or "No one will ever find out."

EXHIBIT 3.3

SHELL CANADA'S STATEMENT OF GENERAL BUSINESS PRINCIPLES

Shell's Statement of General Business Principles sets out the company's objectives and its responsibilities to various stakeholders—shareholders, customers, employees, those individuals or organizations with whom it does business and society in general. The code of ethics covers

- Business integrity (including conflict of interest; gifts, entertainment, and bribery; the integrity of the company's financial information; protection and use of property; business controls; confidential information; insider trading; and timely disclosure).
- Health, safety, and the environment.
- Competition law.
- Political activities.

The conduct required by this code means that all employees will

- Act with honesty and integrity and be open in dealings with all stakeholders;
- Treat others with fairness, dignity, and respect to create and protect a trusting environment free from harassment and discrimination; and
- Strive for excellence and professionalism, taking pride in what they do individually and as part of a team.

Although the code of ethics provides some specific examples of ethical conduct, employees are cautioned that the examples are not exhaustive and that they must use their best judgment in the application of Shell's Business Principles and Code of Ethics. They are also encouraged to consult with their supervisor. In assessing whether a situation might contravene the principles or code, employees should consider whether

- The conduct is legal.
- The conduct violates Shell's policies or procedures.
- The conduct is within Shell's authorized system of business controls.
- The results of the conduct would be fair in both the short and long term.
- The conduct would meet Shell's responsibilities to its stakeholders.
- The disclosure of such conduct, internally, would not be of concern.
- The public would consider the conduct to be honest and ethical.

Source: Courtesy Shell Canada Limited. Available www.shell.ca, 21 October 2002.

The second objective for ethics training programs is to achieve credibility with employees. Not surprisingly, employees can be highly suspicious of management's reasons for offering ethics training. At one telecommunications company, employees initially assumed that management instituted the program to get employees to "rat" on each other. So they labelled the program "1-800-SNITCH."[36] One of the ways in which companies mistakenly hurt the credibility of their ethics programs is by having outside instructors and consultants conduct the classes. Employees often complain that outside instructors and consultants are teaching theory that has nothing to do with their jobs and the "real world." Seeking to regain credibility with its workers, this company avoided this problem by having supervisors conduct 30-minute "tailgate" sessions in which they could literally begin the training by talking to their workers from atop a truck tailgate rather than a classroom.

The third objective of ethics training is to teach employees a practical model of ethical decision-making. A basic model should help them think about the consequences their choices will have on others and consider how they will choose between different solutions. Exhibit 3.4 presents a basic model of ethical decision-making.

4.4 Ethical Climate

In study after study in which researchers have asked, "What is the most important influence on your ethical behaviour at work?" the answer comes back, "My manager." The first step in establishing an ethical climate is for managers to act ethically themselves. Managers who decline to accept lavish gifts from company suppliers; who use the company phone, fax, and copier only for business and not personal use; or who keep their

---

EXHIBIT 3.4

A BASIC MODEL OF ETHICAL DECISION-MAKING

1. Identify the problem.
   What makes it an ethical problem? Think about rights, obligations, fairness, relationships, and integrity. How would you define the problem if you stood on the other side of the fence?

2. Identify the constituents.
   Who has been hurt? Who could be hurt? Who could be helped? Are they willing players, or are they victims? Can you negotiate with them?

3. Diagnose the situation.
   How did it happen in the first place? What could have prevented it? Is it going to get worse or better? Can the damage now be undone?

4. Analyze your options.
   Imagine the range of possibilities. Limit yourself to the two or three most manageable. What are the likely outcomes of each? What are the likely costs? Look to the company mission statement or code of ethics for guidance.

5. Make your choice.
   What is your intention in making this decision? How does it compare with the probable results? Can you discuss the problem with the affected parties before you act? Could you disclose without qualm your decision to your boss, the CEO, the board of directors, your family, or society as a whole?

6. Act.
   Do what you have to do. Don't be afraid to admit errors. Be as bold in confronting a problem as you were in causing it.

Source: L.A. Berger, "Train All Employees to Solve Ethical Dilemmas," *Best's Review-Life-Health Insurance Edition* 95 (1995): 70–80.

promises to employees, suppliers, and customers encourage others to believe that ethical behaviour is normal and acceptable. Although transgressions such as these may appear to be obvious to many readers, thousands of former Enron and Tyco employees may have reason to suspect that a number of their former senior managers did not take the idea of an ethical work climate very seriously.

A second step in establishing an ethical climate is for top management to be active in the company ethics program. Shell Canada believes that its reputation and credibility are based on its total commitment to ethical business practices.[37] Top management must play an active leadership role in the establishment of an ethical climate. For example, Harold Lemieux is the "custodian" of Shell Canada's business principles and code of ethics at Shell Canada Limited. However Lemieux, who is the vice president, general counsel, and secretary of the company, assumes this role on behalf of the entire senior management team. The team also includes (at the time of writing) the president and chief executive officer, Tim Faithfull, and the vice presidents of Shell's three major business units. As a member of the Royal Dutch/Shell Group of companies, Shell Canada shares one of the world's most recognizable emblems. Faithfull sends an annual letter of assurance to the group's London office stating that Shell Canada Limited has conducted its business ethically and in accordance with its business principles. "We established a set of business principles and code of ethics almost 30 years ago and today, perhaps more than ever, these standards for ethical behaviour are our best safeguard against wrongdoing," Faithfull says. "By knowing and following these standards, we protect our own individual reputation and the reputation of the company. We actively encourage openness at all levels through an annual employee survey, which includes questions about the ethical standards of the individual work groups. We have also created an ombuds position to whom employees can take their concerns in complete confidence."

A third step is to put in place a reporting system that encourages managers and employees to report potential ethics violations. **Whistle blowing**—that is, reporting others' ethics violations, is a difficult step for most people to take and occasionally results in unwanted public visibility for the whistle blower. One example of a high-profile Canadian case involved accusations by the former chief financial officer of Livent Inc. of accounting audit irregularities of Livent's books by the accounting firm Deloitte & Touche.[38]

Potential whistle blowers often fear that they will be punished rather than the ethics violators.[39] Managers who have been interviewed about whistle blowing have said, "In every organization, someone's been screwed for standing up." "If anything, I figured that by taking a strong stand I might get myself in trouble. People might look at me as a 'goody two shoes.' Someone might try to force me out." Today, some companies, like Northrup Gruman, a defence contractor, have made it easier to report possible violations by establishing anonymous toll-free corporate ethics hot lines. However, the factor that does the most to discourage whistle blowers is lack of company action on their complaints.[40] Thus, the final step in developing an ethical climate is for management to fairly and consistently punish those who violate the company's code of ethics.

whistle blowing
reporting others' ethics violations to management or legal authorities

Review 4
Practical Steps to Ethical Decision-Making

Employers can increase the chances of hiring more ethical employees by administering overt integrity tests and personality-based integrity tests to all job applicants. Most large companies now have corporate codes of ethics. But for those codes to affect ethical decision-making, they must be known both inside and outside the organization. In addition to offering general rules, ethics codes must also offer specific, practical advice. Ethics training seeks to make employees aware of ethical issues, to make ethics a serious, credible factor in organizational decisions, and to teach employees a practical model of ethical decision-making. The most important factors in creating an ethical business climate are the personal examples set by company managers, involvement of management in the company ethics program, a reporting system that encourages whistle blowers to report potential ethics violations, and fair but consistent punishment of violators.

What Is Social Responsibility?

social responsibility
a business's obligation to pursue policies, make decisions, and take actions that benefit society.

Social responsibility is a business's obligation to pursue policies, make decisions, and take actions that benefit society.[41] Unfortunately, because there are strong disagreements over to whom and for what in society organizations are responsible, it can be difficult for managers to know what is or will be perceived as socially responsible corporate behaviour. One example involves many Canadian retail organizations such as London Drugs, Pharmaprix, and Shoppers Drug Mart that are struggling with the issue of selling tobacco products alongside other store offerings intended to promote and preserve good health. If you are reading this while sitting in a Canadian university lecture hall, you are probably concerned about tuition hikes. A challenge for almost all Canadian university administrators is deciding where to draw the line with tuition levels given the financial constraints imposed on academic institutions because of government funding cutbacks. At what point does education no longer remain affordable for the masses? Another example, Gillette Corporation's (www.gillette.com) use of rats and rabbits for product testing continues to draw protests from PETA (People for the Ethical Treatment of Animals (www.peta-online.org/) and from elementary school teachers who encourage their students to write directly to Gillette. In one such letter, a 13-year-old wrote, "Would you like it if someone put acids in your eyes and shoved cleaning materials down your throat?" In response to complaints, Gillette now spends about a million dollars a year on alternatives to animal testing. However, Gillette argues that eliminating animal testing altogether would be socially irresponsible, because it is critical to producing a safe product for its customers. Furthermore, if a product liability lawsuit were to be filed against the company, its best legal defence would be the scientific testing it performs on rats and rabbits.[42]

EXPERIENCING MANAGEMENT

Organizations are expected to benefit in many ways beyond simply providing jobs. To learn more about social responsibilities of organizations, visit our animated concept and activity site. Choose Ethics & Social Responsibility from the "select a topic" pulldown menu, then Social Responsibility from the "overview tab."

www.experiencingmanagement.com

After reading the next four sections, you should be able to explain
5. *to whom organizations are socially responsible.*
6. *for what organizations are socially responsible.*
7. *how organizations can choose to respond to societal demands for social responsibility.*
8. *whether social responsibility hurts or helps an organization's economic performance.*

5. To Whom Are Organizations Socially Responsible?

There are two perspectives on to whom organizations are socially responsible: the shareholder model and the stakeholder model. According to Nobel prize-winning economist Milton Friedman, the only social responsibility that organizations have is to satisfy their owners, that is, company shareholders. This view—called the **shareholder model**—holds that the only social responsibility that businesses have is to maximize profits. By maximizing profit, the firm maximizes shareholder wealth and satisfaction. More specifically, as profits rise, the company stock owned by company shareholders generally increases in value. For example, the year after Microsoft (www.microsoft.com) released its Windows 95 operating software, company earnings increased by 45 percent over the previous year. During this time, Microsoft's stock rebounded from a low of $58.25 to $90, increasing the wealth of Microsoft shareholders by 54.5 percent.

shareholder model
view of social responsibility that holds that an organization's overriding goal should be profit maximization for the benefit of shareholders

Friedman argues that it is socially irresponsible for companies to divert their time, money, and attention from maximizing profits to social causes and charitable organizations. The first problem he sees is that organizations cannot act effectively as moral agents for all company shareholders. While shareholders are likely to agree on investment issues concerning a company, it's highly unlikely that they possess common views on what social causes a company should or should not support. For example, after 25 years of support, one large telecommunications provider announced that it would no longer provide cash grants to Planned Parenthood. A company spokesperson said that "eighty percent of the decision to stop funding Planned Parenthood was based on its ever-increasing political nature, and its increasing attention to a very divisive issue [abortion]."[43] Rather than act as moral agents, Friedman argues that companies should maximize profits for shareholders. Shareholders can then use their time and increased wealth to contribute to the social causes, charities, or institutions they want, rather than those that companies want.

The second major problem, according to Friedman, is that the time, money, and attention diverted to social causes undermine market efficiency. In competitive markets, companies compete for raw materials, talented workers, customers, and investment funds. Spending money on social causes means there is less money to purchase quality materials or to hire talented workers who can produce a valuable product at a good price. If customers find the product less desirable, sales and profits will fall. If profits fall, stock prices will decrease and the company will have difficulty attracting investment funds that could be used to fund long-term growth. In the end, Friedman argues, diverting the firm's money, time, and resources to social causes hurts customers, suppliers, employees, and shareholders.

By contrast, under the **stakeholder model**, management's most important responsibility is long-term survival (not just maximizing profits), which is achieved by satisfying the interests of multiple corporate stakeholders (not just shareholders). **Stakeholders** are people or groups with a legitimate interest in a company.[44] Since stakeholders are interested in and affected by the organization's actions, they have a "stake" in what those actions are. Consequently, stakeholder groups may try to influence the firm to act in their own interests. Exhibit 3.5 shows the various stakeholder groups that the organization must satisfy to ensure long-term survival.

stakeholder model
theory of corporate responsibility that holds that management's most important responsibility, long-term survival, is achieved by satisfying the interests of multiple corporate stakeholders

stakeholders
persons or groups with a "stake" or legitimate interest in a company's actions

EXHIBIT 3.5

STAKEHOLDER MODEL OF CORPORATE SOCIAL RESPONSIBILITY

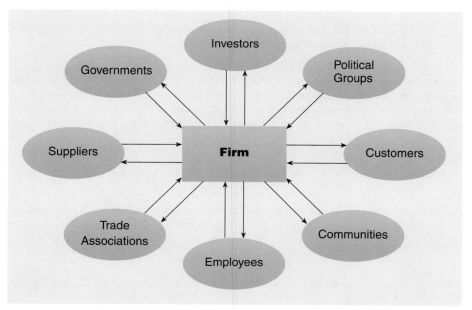

Source: Academy of Management Review by T. Donaldson & L.E. Preston. Copyright 1995 by Academy of Management. Reproduced with permission of the publisher via Copyright Clearance Center.

primary stakeholder
any group on which an organization relies for its long-term survival

Being responsible to multiple stakeholders raises two basic questions. First, how does a company identify organizational stakeholders? Second, how does a company balance the needs of different stakeholders? Distinguishing between primary and secondary stakeholders can answer these questions.[45]

Some stakeholders are more important to the firm's survival than others. **Primary stakeholders** are groups, such as shareholders, employees, customers, suppliers, governments, and local communities, on which the organization depends for long-term survival. So when managers are struggling to balance the needs of different stakeholders, the stakeholder model suggests that the needs of primary stakeholders take precedence over the needs of secondary stakeholders. However, contrary to the shareholder model, no primary stakeholder group is more or less important than another, since all are critical to the firm's success and survival. So managers must try to satisfy the needs of all primary stakeholders. The issues important to primary stakeholders are noted below in Exhibit 3.6. For example, responding to concerns from car manufacturers, consumers, environmental groups, and proposed government legislation, Irving Oil Ltd. of Saint John, New Brunswick, "became the first gasoline refiner in the country to get a thumbs-up from the Canadian Vehicle Manufacturers Association for its new 'green' gas."[46] Irving Oil (www.irvingoil.com) reduced the sulphur content in its gas to 150 parts per million (ppm) down from the Canadian average of 360 ppm and an Ontario average of 560 ppm. Despite significant refinery upgrading costs, this and other improvements positioned the company as the first in Canada to offer consumers cleaner-burning fuel that does not clog the sophisticated pollution control devices in newer vehicles.[47]

secondary stakeholder
any group that can influence or be influenced by the company and can affect public perceptions about its socially responsible behaviour

Secondary stakeholders, such as the media and special interest groups, can influence or be influenced by the company. Yet in contrast to primary stakeholders, they do not engage in regular transactions with the company and are not critical to its long-term survival. Consequently, meeting the needs of primary stakeholders is usually more important than meeting the needs of secondary stakeholders. While not critical to long-term survival, secondary stakeholders are still important, because they can affect public perceptions

---

EXHIBIT 3.6

ISSUES IMPORTANT TO PRIMARY STAKEHOLDERS

COMPANY
Company history, industry background, organization structure, economic performance, competitive environment, mission or purpose, corporate codes, stakeholder and social-issues management systems.

EMPLOYEES
Benefits, compensation and rewards, training and development, career planning, employee assistance programs, health promotion, absenteeism and turnover, leaves of absence, relationships with unions, dismissal and appeal, termination, layoffs, retirement and termination counselling, employment equity and discrimination, women in management and on the board, day care and family accommodation, employee communication, occupational health and safety, and part-time, temporary, or contract employees.

SHAREHOLDERS
Shareholder communications and complaints, shareholder advocacy, shareholder rights, and other shareholder issues.

CUSTOMERS
Customer communications, product safety, customer complaints, special customer services, and other customer issues.

SUPPLIERS
Relative power, general policy, and other supplier issues.

PUBLIC STAKEHOLDERS
Public health, safety, and protection, conservation of energy and materials, environmental assessment of capital projects, other environmental issues, public policy involvement, community relations, social investment and donations.

Source: M.B.E. Clarkson, "A Stakeholder Framework for Analyzing and Evaluating Corporate Social Performance," *Academy of Management Review* 20 (1995): 92–117.

and opinions about socially responsible behaviour. For instance, many Canadians wore fur coats up until the early 1980s. However, soon after that, public perceptions about the treatment of animals and the fur industry in general had turned negative as a result of environmental groups publicizing the cruel manner by which many animals were being trapped in the wilderness, clubbed on ice floes, or raised on farms. Consequently, many stores stopped selling furs.

So to whom are organizations socially responsible? Many, especially economists and financial analysts, continue to argue that organizations are responsible only to shareholders. However, many top managers have increasingly come to believe that they and their companies must be socially responsible to their stakeholders.[48] Surveys show that as many as 80 percent of top-level managers believe that it is unethical to focus just on shareholders. So while there is not complete agreement, a majority of opinion makers would make the case that companies must be socially responsible to their stakeholders.

EXPERIENCING MANAGEMENT

Different stakeholders have differing interests in the organization's social responsibilities. To interact with stakeholder issues, visit our animated concept and activity site. Choose Ethics & Social Responsibility from the "select a topic" pull-down menu, then Responsibility to Stakeholders from the "overview tab."

www.experiencingmanagement.com

Review 5
To Whom Are Organizations Socially Responsible?

Social responsibility is a business's obligation to benefit society. Who are organizations socially responsible to? According to the shareholder model, the only social responsibility that organizations have is to maximize shareholder wealth by maximizing company profits. According to the stakeholder model, companies must satisfy the needs and interests of many corporate stakeholders, not just shareholders. However, the needs of primary stakeholders, on which the organization relies for its existence, take precedence over those of secondary stakeholders.

6. For What Are Organizations Socially Responsible?

If organizations are to be socially responsible to stakeholders, just what are they to be socially responsible for? As illustrated in Exhibit 3.7, companies can best benefit their stakeholders by fulfilling their economic, legal, ethical, and discretionary responsibilities.[49]

Environmentalists from Rainforest Relief and Wetlands Rainforest Action Group hold up a banner outside a Home Depot store. Protesters convinced the company to quit selling wood and wood products from threatened old-growth forests.

AP/Wide World Photos

Exhibit 3.7 indicates that economic and legal responsibilities play a larger part in a company's social responsibility than do ethical and discretionary responsibilities. However, the relative importance of economic, legal, ethical, and discretionary responsibilities depends on the expectations that society has toward corporate social responsibility at a particular point in time.[50] A century ago, society expected businesses to meet their economic and legal responsibilities and little else. Today, however, when society judges whether businesses are socially responsible, ethical and discretionary responsibilities are considerably more important than they used to be.

Historically, economic responsibility, making a profit by producing a product or service valued by society, has been a business's most basic social responsibility. Organizations that don't meet their financial and economic expectations come under tremendous pressure. For example, company boards are very, very quick these days to fire CEOs. Typically, all it takes is two or three bad quarters in a row. William Rollnick, who became acting chairman of Mattel after the company fired CEO Jill Barad, said, "There's zero forgiveness. You screw up and you're dead." Indeed, at least 38 of the largest 200 firms in North America have got rid of their CEOs between 2000 and 2003.[51]

Historically, **economic responsibility**, making a profit by producing a product or service valued by society, has been a business's most basic social responsibility. Organizations that don't meet their financial and economic expectations come under tremendous pressure. **Legal responsibility** is the expectation that companies will obey a society's laws and regulations as they try to meet their economic responsibilities.

Ethical responsibility is society's expectation that organizations will not violate accepted principles of right and wrong when conducting their business. Because different stakeholders may disagree about what is or is not ethical, meeting ethical responsibilities is more difficult than meeting economic or legal responsibilities. **Discretionary responsibilities** pertain to the social roles that businesses play in society beyond their economic, legal, and ethical responsibilities. For example, MasterCard and its cardholders have teamed up with Canadian organizations such as the Juvenile Diabetes Research Foundation (www.jdrf.org), the Ontario Soccer Association (www.soccer.on.ca), and Scouts Canada (www.scouts.ca), to support research, minor soccer, and the scouting movement respectively.[52] Every time someone uses a MasterCard credit card to make a

economic responsibility
the expectation that a company will make a profit by producing a valued product or service

legal responsibility
the expectation that a company will obey society's laws and regulations

ethical responsibility
the expectation that a company will not violate accepted principles of right and wrong when conducting its business

discretionary responsibilities
the expectation that a company will voluntarily serve a social role beyond its economic, legal, and ethical responsibilities

EXHIBIT 3.7

SOCIAL RESPONSIBILITIES

Total Social Responsibilities

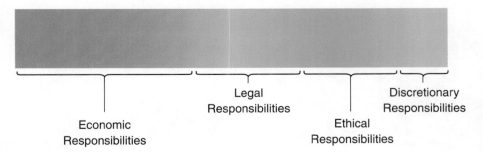

Economic Responsibilities | Legal Responsibilities | Ethical Responsibilities | Discretionary Responsibilities

Source: Academy of Management Review by A.B. Carroll. Copyright 1979 by Academy of Management. Reproduced with permission of the publisher via Copyright Clearance Center.

purchase, MasterCard donates a small percentage of the purchase to the designated affinity partners. While the amounts per transaction may be small, the thousands of purchases made yearly by affinity cardholders (3000 in the case of Scouts Canada[53]) can prove to be extremely valuable to any organization over time. Discretionary responsibilities are voluntary. Companies will not be considered unethical if they don't perform them. However, today, corporate stakeholders expect companies to do much more than in the past to meet their discretionary responsibilities.

Companies can best benefit their stakeholders by fulfilling their economic, legal, ethical, and discretionary responsibilities. Being profitable, or meeting one's economic responsibility, is a business's most basic social responsibility. Legal responsibility consists of following a society's laws and regulations. Ethical responsibility means not violating accepted principles of right and wrong when doing business. Discretionary responsibilities are social responsibilities beyond basic economic, legal, and ethical responsibilities.

7. Responses to Demands for Social Responsibility

Social responsiveness is the strategy chosen by a company to respond to stakeholders' economic, legal, ethical, or discretionary expectations concerning social responsibility. A social responsibility problem exists whenever company actions do not meet stakeholder expectations. One model of social responsiveness, shown in Exhibit 3.8, identifies four strategies for responding to social responsibility problems: reactive, defensive, accommodative, and proactive. These strategies differ in the extent to which the company is willing to act to meet or exceed society's expectations.

A company using a **reactive strategy** will do less than society expects. It may deny responsibility for a problem or "fight all the way" any suggestions that the company should solve a problem. For example, *Consumer Reports* magazine (www.consumerreports.org) came out with a report showing that the Suzuki Samurai would tip over when drivers changed lanes or went around corners at normal speeds. The Samurai, a four-wheel-drive vehicle, was easy to tip over because it was a lightweight vehicle with a high centre of gravity and a narrow wheelbase. Rather than admit this safety problem, Suzuki Corporation immediately embarked on a multimillion-dollar television advertising campaign to dispute *Consumer Reports'* findings.[54]

By contrast, a company using a **defensive strategy** would admit responsibility for a problem, but would do the least required to meet societal expectations. For example, when the sudden and unpredictable tread separation problems associated with Firestone ATX tires first became public knowledge, Firestone's response was to deny that there were problems (a reactive strategy). However seven months later, when public fury over the problem grew intense, Firestone recalled 6.5 million of the 15-inch ATX tires. However, Firestone angered lawmakers by refusing to recall all the tires recommended by the U.S. National Highway Traffic Safety Administration (www.nhtsa.gov) (a defensive strategy).[55] Firestone also frustrated and angered consumers at that time by proposing a "phased rollout," in which it would first replace tires in southern and western states—where higher temperatures seemed to be related to the problems. Steven Fink, president of Lexicon Communications, a crisis management consulting firm, criticized Firestone's response: "After they announced the recall, they were not prepared to deal with it. They were telling consumers they will have to wait up to a year to get tires."[56] In fact, Firestone's crisis management firm was so frustrated with the company's refusal to admit the problem and quickly act to restore consumer confidence (by immediately apologizing and quickly recalling and replacing all tires) that it quit.[57]

social responsiveness
the strategy chosen by a company to respond to stakeholders' economic, legal, ethical, or discretionary expectations concerning social responsibility

reactive strategy
a social responsiveness strategy where a company chooses to do less than society expects and to deny responsibility for problems

defensive strategy
a social responsiveness strategy where a company chooses to admit responsibility for a problem but do the least required to meet societal expectations

EXHIBIT 3.8

SOCIAL RESPONSIVENESS

Reactive	**Defensive**	**Accommodative**	**Proactive**
Fight all the way	Do only what is required	Be progressive	Lead the industry

Withdrawal	Public Relations Approach	Legal Approach	Bargaining	Problem Solving

DO NOTHING ← → DO MUCH

Source: Academy of Management Review by A.B. Carroll. Copyright 1979 by Academy of Management. Reproduced with permission of the publisher via Copyright Clearance Center.

accommodative strategy
a social responsiveness strategy where a company chooses to accept responsibility for a problem and do all that society expects to solve problems

A company using an **accommodative strategy** would accept responsibility for a problem and take a progressive approach by doing all that was expected to solve the problem. For example, in 1997 Noranda (www.noranda.com) was faced with the difficult task of having to close two mines in Quebec prior to opening a new mine two years later. A creative employment and benefits package constructed by Noranda and a number of government agencies allowed 70 employees to upgrade their skills and further their education while waiting for the new mine to re-open.[58] In contrast to Suzuki, Nissan Motors took an accommodative strategy when it voluntarily recalled 33 000 minivans sold in North America that were prone to catch fire when the engine's fan belt broke. Nissan spent approximately $70 million Cdn to fix the vans, installing a brand-new heavy-duty cooling system with warning lights in each vehicle. However, it also reimbursed customers for 900 vans that were beyond repair. Then it destroyed the 900 vans, so that they could not be resold to unsuspecting used-car buyers. To maintain customers' goodwill, Nissan also made other major repairs on the vans, such as air conditioning or transmission repairs, for free.[59]

proactive strategy
a social responsiveness strategy where a company anticipates responsibility for a problem before it occurs and would do more than society expects to address the problem

Finally, a company using a **proactive strategy** would anticipate responsibility for a problem before it occurred, do more than expected to address the problem, and lead the industry in its approach. For example, Andrew Benedek, founder and CEO of Zenon Environmental Inc. (www.zenonenv.com), understood that much of the world's population has limited access to clean drinking water. Using cell membrane technology, his company developed water filtration products used in 40 countries that purify water without the use of harmful chemicals. His firm also "donated a micro filtration-based water purification plant to the Temagami First Bear Nation in Bear Island Ontario" which in turn "reduced high incidence of giardiasis or 'beaver fever.'"[60]

Review 7
Responses to Demands for Social Responsibility

Social responsiveness is a company response to stakeholders' demands for socially responsible behaviour. There are four social responsiveness strategies. When a company uses a reactive strategy, it denies responsibility for a problem. When it uses a defensive strategy, it takes responsibility for a problem, but does the minimum required to solve it. When a company uses an accommodative strategy, it accepts responsibility for problems and does all that society expects to solve them. Finally, when a company uses a proactive strategy, it does much more than expected to solve social responsibility problems.

This recycled waste paper in Toronto is ready for shipment to a processing plant. Recycling is one example of social responsibility being profitable.

8. Social Responsibility and Economic Performance

One question that managers often ask is "Does it pay to be socially responsible?" While this is an understandable question, asking whether social responsibility pays is a bit like asking if giving to your favourite charity will help you get a better-paying job. The obvious answer is no. There is not an inherent relationship between social responsibility and economic performance. Yet a number of ethical or socially responsible investment vehicles are available to Canadians. These include mutual funds such as the Meritas Fund, Manulife's Canadian Balance Ethics fund, and 12 funds from Ethical Funds Inc.[61] Not surprisingly, many investors do "put their money where their mouths are." In Canada alone, one recent estimate suggests Canadians support socially responsible investments to the tune of almost $50 billion or 3 percent of the Canadian mutual fund market.[62] Further, between 1998 and 2000, social investment assets grew at more than twice the rate of the Canadian mutual fund industry as a whole.[63] Supporters of corporate social responsibility also claim a positive relationship. For example, in Canada, the Jantzi Social Index (www.mjra-jsi.com), claims to have outperformed the TSE 60 in its first year of operation.[64] On the other hand, critics have plenty of facts to support their claim that social responsibility hurts economic performance. For example, another study of 42 socially responsible mutual funds found that the socially responsible companies under-performed the Standard and Poor's 500 by 8 percent.[65]

When it comes to social responsibility and economic performance, the first reality is that it can sometimes cost a company significantly if it chooses to be socially responsible. During the 1980s, American multinational corporations were under intense public pressure to withdraw their operations from South Africa. Political activists argued that if businesses withdrew from South Africa, the white-controlled government would be hurt economically. Thus it would be more difficult for it to maintain its system of apartheid against black South Africans. Many companies chose to pull their businesses out of South Africa. Yet when they did, they paid a steep price, selling corporate land, buildings, and equipment at a fraction of their value. Furthermore, within days of announcing that they were leaving South Africa, their company stock price dropped an average of 5.5 percent.[66] Here, socially responsible behaviour not only harmed the company financially, but harmed its shareholders financially, too. Nonetheless, hundreds of top managers still felt it was the right thing to do. In Canada one might argue that Petro-Canada (www.petrocanada.ca) gave up potentially large future revenues when it chose to forfeit its undersea mineral rights in the vicinity of the Queen Charlotte Islands off the coast of British Columbia in order to help preserve the wildlife eco-system.[67]

The second reality of social responsibility and economic performance is that sometimes it does pay to be socially responsible. Zenon Environmental Inc.'s water purification technology based on cell membranes was responsible for $125 million in revenues in 2001.[68] Another good example is Ben & Jerry's Homemade Ice Cream. Ben & Jerry's started in 1978 when founders Ben Cohen and Jerry Greenfield mailed away for a $5 course on how to make ice cream. Today, Ben & Jerry's is as well known for its super premium ice cream as it is for its reputation as a socially responsible company. Ben & Jerry's donates 7.5 percent of its pretax profits to social causes: to charitable groups supporting AIDS patients, the homeless, and the environment.[69] The company buys brownies from a bakery that employs homeless workers and blueberries from Native North American Indian tribes. Moreover, customers buy Ben & Jerry's ice cream because it tastes great and because they want to support a socially responsible company. As Ben Cohen says, "We see ourselves as somewhat of a social service agency and somewhat of an ice cream company."[70]

The third reality of social responsibility and economic performance is that while socially responsible behaviour may be "the right thing to do," it does not guarantee profitability. Socially responsible companies experience the same ups and downs in economic performance that traditional businesses do. For example, after a year in which neither market share nor profits grew and the company's stock dropped 72 percent in value, Ben Cohen announced that he was stepping aside as Ben & Jerry's CEO. A "professional manager" who is now charged with turning around the company's financial performance replaced him. Ben & Jerry's is now owned by Unilever, a multinational consumer products company.

However, while Ben & Jerry's struggled, a Vancouver-based mining company, BHP Billiton Diamonds (www.bhpbilliton.com), has prospered while going the extra mile for its employees who are located at its remote Ekati Diamond mine in the Northwest Territories.[71] The firm hires locally, offers residences to its workers who live elsewhere in the North, sources its supplies as much as possible locally, has developed a well-received adult education program for its workers, and offers its employees a diamond purchase plan. While at work, employees benefit from a free 24-hour dining room as well as sporting facilities and private rooms. Edmonton-based power utility Epcor is another example of a profitable company giving back to its community.[72] In instances where an employee volunteers 50 hours or more per year, the company contributes $150 to that charity or community group.

In the end, if company management chooses a proactive or accommodative strategy toward social responsibility (rather than a defensive or reactive strategy), it should do so because it wants to benefit society and its corporate stakeholders, not because it expects a better financial return.

Review 8
Social Responsibility and Economic Performance

Does it pay to be socially responsible? Sometimes it costs and sometimes it pays. Overall, there is no clear relationship between social responsibility and economic performance. Consequently, managers should not expect an economic return from socially responsible corporate activities. If your company chooses to practise a proactive or accommodative social responsibility strategy, it should do so to better society and not to improve its financial performance.

What Really Happened?

Contrary to popular belief, a clear choice between right and wrong rarely reveals itself to managers charged with "doing the right thing." The business world is much messier than that. Plus, in practice, solutions to ethics and social responsibility problems aren't optimal. Often, they are "make do" or "do the least harm" kinds of solutions. Let's find out what really happened at McDonald's as it struggled with the real-world tradeoffs between PETA's demands that its egg suppliers treat animals humanely and the business demands associated with supplying those eggs.

What is the ethical thing to do in this situation?

Ethical behaviour follows accepted standards of right and wrong. However, it's difficult to judge what's ethical in this instance, because at this point there are no accepted ethical standards when it comes to the egg industry. Industry standards are different in the United States, Canada, and Europe. For example, caging hens is illegal in the United Kingdom and several European countries but is accepted practice in the United States and in Canada. And while PETA maintains that being kept in small cages mistreats egg-laying hens, the egg industry believes that using small cages is economical, prevents the spread of disease, maintains sanitation, and, when combined with an automatic feeding system, provides the ability to deliver a balanced diet of proteins, fats, carbohydrates, vitamins, and minerals.

Should McDonald's give in to PETA's demands or should it ignore them? Given that protests are not a new thing for McDonald's, how does it decide how serious an issue this is and the lengths to which it should go to address these issues, if any?

How serious are PETA's demands and how seriously should McDonald's take them? Ethical intensity is how concerned or how serious people are about an ethical issue. When addressing issues of high ethical intensity, managers are more aware of the impact their decisions have on others. They are more likely to view the decision as an ethical or moral decision rather than an economic decision. They are also more likely to worry about doing the "right thing." Ethical intensity is strong when decisions have large, certain, immediate consequences, and when we are physically or psychologically close to those affected by the decision.

In the last few years, McDonald's has enlisted the help of a team of university and professional experts to form the McDonald's Animal Advisory Council. The council's role is to provide McDonald's with information, advice, and expertise and to make recommendations to McDonald's and its suppliers regarding animal welfare problems and progress. Because of its work with this council, McDonald's upper management viewed the treatment of hens as an "ethically intense" issue rather than an economic decision.

Furthermore, McDonald's developed a set of Animal Welfare Guiding Principles for itself and its suppliers to follow. Those principles were to provide customers with safe food (safety); to treat animals with care and respect (quality assurance); to make sure that animals are free from cruelty, abuse, and neglect (animal treatment); to work with suppliers to monitor and improve animal welfare practices (partnership); to lead the industry by working with scientific experts and suppliers to improve animal welfare practice (leadership); to measure how its corporate purchasing leads to improved animal welfare (performance measurement); and to communicate its animal welfare programs, plans, and progress (communication).

So what did McDonald's decide? Because of its animal welfare council and guidelines, McDonald's decided that it would no longer purchase eggs from suppliers that debeaked chickens, kept them in overly small cages, and withheld food to increase molting and thus egg production. Bob Langert, who heads up animal welfare and environmental programs for McDonald's, said, "We think we're moving the needle on an important issue. When it comes to social responsibility, McDonald's plans to be a leader."

If McDonald's seriously considers PETA's demands, how does it decide whose interests take precedence?

There are two views on this issue. The shareholder model says that McDonald's should only concern itself with what its shareholders think of animal welfare programs. And if McDonald's can convince its shareholders that the costs are low and the benefits are high, then the shareholders would probably approve, because it will help the company be more profitable. By contrast, the stakeholder model says that companies must satisfy the needs and interests of multiple corporate stakeholders. The problem for McDonald's is that as the world's largest restaurant, it has to try to balance the needs of many different stakeholder groups.

So if McDonald's is supposed to satisfy the needs of multiple stakeholders, and the stakeholders disagree, how does it decide whose wishes take precedence? The stakeholder model argues that the needs of primary stakeholders (customers, employees, suppliers, shareholders, etc.) on which the organization relies for its existence take precedence over those of secondary stakeholders (the press, advocacy groups). But what if primary stakeholders disagree?

In this case, McDonald's was lucky enough to be reconsidering its views on animal welfare and treatment at exactly the same time that the egg producer's industry association was addressing the same issues. Committee chair and professor Jeff Armstrong said, "When McDonald's went looking for a way to address their concerns about laying operations, they were excited to find we had what they needed." The key, according to Bob Krouse, a member of that committee was that "egg producers knew they needed to have a production based on science, not just experience or common practices." Armstrong said, "The guidelines are based on the best available science. That means we validated certain practices and counselled against others based on objective studies and not just emotion or status quo." The guidelines, which are near completion, increased cage sizes from 432 to 529 square centimetres, more than the 465 square centimetres recommended by McDonald's. However, contrary to McDonald's, the guidelines permit forced molting under specific conditions, something that McDonald's does not permit.

Is it more socially responsible to require its egg suppliers to change their practices if changing them leads to financial losses and puts some of them out of business? Which comes first, the chickens or the egg producers?

Social responsibility is a business's obligation to pursue policies, make decisions, and take actions that benefit society. Unfortunately, there is little agreement on what does or does not benefit society. Being profitable, or meeting one's economic responsibility, is a business's most basic social responsibility. However, companies also have legal (comply with the law), ethical (do the right thing), and discretionary (do more than what's expected) responsibilities to fulfil.

Again, this means that corporate efforts to behave in a socially responsible manner often require tradeoffs. In this instance, McDonald's felt that the negative fallout to its business from not pushing animal welfare practices would be greater than the increased costs of requiring its suppliers to decrease the number of hens per cage. In short, somebody has to pay for corporate responsibility. Armstrong said, "Producers' margins are slim. Ultimately, farmers can incorporate practices that are more animal friendly—but somebody needs to pay for them." The key question for egg producers is will McDonald's back up its commitment to animal welfare practices by paying them an additional 20 to 30 cents Cdn per dozen to cover the increased costs of following its animal welfare practices (larger cages, no forced molting, and no debeaking)? Tom Miner, a food consultant, believes that McDonald's will cover those costs. He said, "They have the best kind of relationship with the farmers and it's a major advantage in the market. Setting a good example in North America will help McDonald's establish sound supply chains with farmers in new markets abroad." McDonald's spokesperson Walt Riker said, "We are doing this because we feel the social responsibility to enhance animal welfare. As to the costs, we don't have the details yet and will work on this with our suppliers."

Sources: "Eggs Over Easy Thanks to Egg Producers," Ag Answers. [Online] Available www.agriculture.purdue.edu/aganswers/2000/8-29%20_Eggs_Over_Easy.html, 29 June 2001. "Egg Production Information," American Egg Board. [Online] Available, www.aeb.org/eii/production.html, 29 June 2001. "McDonald's Animal Welfare Council," McDonald's. [Online] Available, www.mcdonalds.com/countries/usa/community/welfare/index.html, 29 June 2001. "McDonald's Animal Welfare Guiding Principles," McDonald's. [Online] Available www.mcdonalds.com/corporate/social/animalwelfare/index.html, 29 June 2001. D. Campbell, "Chicken Run: McDonald's Takes a Cue from the Hit Film and Demands Better Conditions for Hens Used to Supply Eggs for Its Mcmuffins," *The Guardian*, 8 September 2000. T. Perry, "Egg Producers Are McMiffed Industry Balks at McDonald's Tough Rules on Hen Treatment," *Los Angeles Times*, 7 September 2000, C1. D. Wetzel, "McDonalds to Require Its Egg Suppliers to Improve Conditions for Hens," *Chicago Tribune*, 24 August 2001.

Key Terms

accommodative strategy (82)
concentration of effect (68)
conventional level of moral
   development (69)
defensive strategy (81)
discretionary responsibilities (80)
economic responsibility (80)
ethical behaviour (62)
ethical intensity (68)
ethical responsibility (80)
ethics (62)
legal responsibility (80)
magnitude of consequences (68)
overt integrity test (71)
personal aggression (66)
personality-based integrity test (71)

political deviance (66)
post conventional level of moral
   development (69)
preconventional level of moral
   development (69)
primary stakeholder (78)
principle of distributive justice (70)
principle of government requirements (70)
principle of individual rights (70)
principle of long-term self-interest (70)
principle of personal virtue (70)
principle of religious injunctions (70)
principle of utilitarian benefits (70)
proactive strategy (82)
probability of effect (68)
production deviance (65)

property deviance (65)
proximity of effect (68)
reactive strategy (81)
secondary stakeholder (78)
shareholder model (76)
shrinkage (66)
social consensus (68)
social responsibility (76)
social responsiveness (81)
stakeholder model (77)
stakeholders (77)
temporal immediacy (68)
whistle blowing (75)
workplace deviance (65)

November 2002 was a special month for Dr. Nancy Olivieri. After six long years of struggle, Olivieri won a settlement from the University of Toronto and Hospital for Sick Children ending a highly public battle that began with her involvement in clinical drug trials of a major pharmaceutical company. Little did she know in 1996 that her name would soon be on everyone's lips in Canadian medical and academic circles and published frequently in national newspapers such as the *Globe and Mail* and the *National Post*. Her struggles would be documented in the *New England Journal of Medicine* and would serve as a basis for a re-examination of many medical institutions' relationships with private-sector stakeholders.

Olivieri is a clinical haematologist. In 1996 she was studying thalassemia and sickle cell disease, inherited blood diseases that are also two of the world's most common single gene disorders that affect one in seven people around the world. The Online Bulletin of the Canadian Association of University Teachers described the case as follows. In 1995,

> Dr. Olivieri made what she describes as a "very big mistake" in her effort to arrange funding for her study of a promising new drug. She signed a confidential agreement with Apotex, Inc., a Canadian pharmaceutical company. In return for partly financing a study of the drug, deferiprone, Apotex received rights to potential sales from the drug, and Dr. Olivieri agreed that data from the study would be the company's property. Corporate interests and research ethics began to clash when Dr. Olivieri's study suggested the drug may be harmful.
>
> Dr. Olivieri's interest in deferiprone was the potential it offered in the treatment of…thalassemia. The only available treatment requires patients to receive monthly transfusions of red blood cells. But this treatment causes life-threatening complications. The iron-rich red blood cells accumulate in the body, damaging the heart and liver.
>
> To get rid of the iron, patients are hooked up to a pump that slowly injects the drug deferoxamine for a 12-hour period every day for the rest of their lives. The new drug, deferiprone, would be administered in pill form—eliminating the often unbearable standard treatment. With the work financed by the Medical Research Council of Canada, Dr. Olivieri and her team had some of the compound produced and tested it on 21 of her patients. Over the next three years test results showed a steady decline in iron levels in her study group. The revolutionary findings were published in the *New England Journal of Medicine* in April of 1995.
>
> But, as with any new findings in drug research, a lot more work was needed to prove that deferiprone was safe and effective with long-term use. The researchers started planning a much larger study with Apotex, in conjunction with the Medical Research Council of Canada and the U.S. National Institutes of Health. It was at this stage Dr. Olivieri signed the ill-fated agreement with the Apotex firm.
>
> In the fall of 1995, liver biopsies in some of the Toronto patients showed dangerous levels of iron overload throwing the researchers into a panic. Toxic levels can compromise liver function and lead to scarring and life-threatening cirrhosis.
>
> Dr. Olivieri immediately stopped giving the drug to those patients most at risk but, at the time, was convinced the study should continue in those in whom the drug appeared useful. The researchers thought the drug treatment could be appropriate for some of the patients. The only way to find out for sure was to keep the study on track and carefully monitor the patients.
>
> When Dr. Olivieri approached Apotex with her negative findings and a request to change the patient consent form to include the contraindications, the company disagreed that the patients were at risk. Apotex opposed changing the consent form.
>
> But when Dr. Olivieri went ahead anyway, drafted a new consent form, and forwarded it to Apotex in May, 1996, the company's response was to fire her as principal investigator of the Toronto studies and as chair of the international study's steering committee. The study at the Hospital for Sick Children was halted, and Apotex confiscated the drugs from the hospital's pharmacy.
>
> Dr. Olivieri was also repeatedly threatened with legal action if she divulged the findings to her patients. She spoke out anyway, believing that the health care of her patients was paramount. Dr. Olivieri also believed she would be supported by the Hospital. But her request for legal assistance from the institution was denied on the grounds that she had not obtained the administration's approval for her deal with Apotex.
>
> [When] the controversy became public in 1998, the hospital removed Dr. Olivieri as the director of one of its programs, publicly questioned her conduct and ordered that she and four researchers who defended her to not speak publicly about what had happened.

As noted earlier, the Olivieri case was kept alive for four more years. Its coverage placed ethics in the media spotlight at a time when many individuals were more interested in the stratospheric rise of share prices than the conduct of organizations and their employees. Most importantly, the case caused many people to stop and think about responses to a number of questions. **What issues did the case raise? How might the problem have been avoided? What were the implications of the "Olivieri affair"?**

Sources: Allison Lawlor, "Sick Kids' Olivieri Wins Settlement," *The Globe and Mail*, 12 November 2002. [Online] Available www.globeandmail.com. "CAUT Brokers Settlement in Olivieri Case," CAUT Bulletin Online, February 1999. [Online] Available www.caut.ca. "Research Ethics vs Corporate Interests: Investigator's Disclosure Fuels Ethics Debate," CAUT Bulletin Online 45, no. 7 (September 1998). With Permission of CAUT (Canadian Association of University Teachers).

Critical Thinking Video Case

E-Mail Alert

E-mail is great for cutting costs, easing the flow of communications between customers and clients, and transferring knowledge within companies, right? Perhaps yes, but unfortunately, its use by employees also poses a major risk for many companies these days. The reason is that sometimes employees say things in e-mail that really should not be said. Unfortunately, once typed in, e-mail content is often very difficult to erase and usually does not disappear simply by deleting it.

In this video, you will learn that the use of e-mail by company employees is now considered an important risk to be managed by many companies. It is also big business for accounting firms such as KPMG Forensics and law firms such as McMillan Binch. It has also spawned a new form of operation that processes electronic evidence. One example is Minnesota-based Kroll Ontrack, a company that specializes in finding e-mail indiscretions. As you watch the video, consider the following critical thinking question.

Critical Thinking Question

Assume the role of Chief Information Officer for a mid-sized company. You are concerned that most of your employees from time to time may be using the company's e-mail system for personal correspondence. You are concerned about what the system is being used for, how often it is being used for these purposes, and by whom it is being used. You are contemplating hiring an electronic evidence processing company such as Kroll Ontrack to look into this issue. Before doing do so, however, you feel it necessary to reflect on the ethics of a typical employee's use of the company e-mail system for personal use. How might the principles of ethical decision-making noted in this chapter apply in this instance?

Management Decisions

To Lie or to Tell the Truth?

Ethical dilemmas in the workplace occur often. Some are completely obvious, while others are subtle. Suppose you are the purchasing agent for a large corporation. A supplier has approached you regarding a recently submitted bid and has stated that if you choose his company as the winning bidder, he will provide you and your spouse with round-trip airfare tickets to Hawaii. His company's bid is 25 percent higher than the lowest bid. Accepting his offer would clearly be an unethical response, since it provides you, the purchasing agent, with a gain (airline tickets for you and your spouse) and costs your company money by accepting the proposal from the supplier with the highest price. Additionally, since your company has a policy forbidding cash, gifts, and other entitlements from suppliers and vendors, you would most likely lose your job if anyone found out. Therefore, the only ethical choice is to refuse the supplier's offer and award the contract to the vendor with the best product and the best price.

Now look at a scenario that has less obvious challenges. Assume that you have recently been hired as an entry-level manager for a small marketing agency and your supervisor, Ms. Johnson, tells you that she is running behind on an advertising proposal for a client. Ms. Johnson states that the client will be dropping in this afternoon to discuss the proposal. She has asked that you intercept the client and tell him that she was called out of town for an emergency business meeting and to inform him that she will contact him when she returns from her trip. Delaying the client will buy Ms. Johnson the necessary time to finalize the client's proposal and allow her to appear more professional when she presents the proposal to him. In this dilemma, the gain is more time for Ms. Johnson to complete her assignment and the cost is that the client is delayed and deceived. There appears to be no personal gain for you.

Questions

1. Describe what you would do in the preceding scenario: accept the order from Ms. Johnson or refuse to cover for her.
2. Suppose a colleague tells you that your predecessor was fired for refusing to accommodate Ms. Johnson and her continual demands for unethical behaviour and unethical responses. Would that change your decision in question 1? Why or why not?
3. If you had to choose a principle of ethical decision-making to support your decision to this scenario, which principle would you choose and why?

Management Decisions

Speeding Tickets or a Poor Credit Record?

Who is the poorer risk for an insurance company: someone who has been caught speeding numerous times or someone who has a bad credit record? Logically, it should be the speeder, because everyone knows that "speed kills," that speeders are in more accidents themselves, and that speeders cause other drivers to have accidents. In fact, government studies confirm that speed is one of the major causes of fatal car accidents. Everyone knows this to be true!

Surprisingly, however, the speeder is less likely to file benefit claims with an insurance company than someone with a poor credit record. Why? It is not exactly clear. However, insurance executives suspect that people who are good with their money are reliable and conscientious about driving (except for speeding). On the other hand, they speculate that people with poor credit records may be more likely to file false claims.

Regardless of the reasons, auto insurers have found that adding a request for credit information to a standard auto insurance application helps them do a better job of screening good insurance risks, that is, identifying people who will pay their premiums each month and those who will file claims for insurance benefits. "The data is absolutely overwhelming," says one insurance industry executive. "There is a very strong correlation between serious financial instability and future loss."

Critics charge that insurers who use credit records when deciding whether to offer insurance coverage are simply discriminating against the poor and minorities. Studies show that credit problems are inversely related to one's level of income. Others simply doubt that credit records are accurate predictors of insurance risk.

Questions

1. Is it unethical or socially irresponsible for auto insurers to use credit records to screen applicants for auto insurance? Explain.
2. There is often disagreement about what companies should be socially responsible for. Explain what an insurance company's economic, legal, ethical, and discretionary responsibilities should be.

Sources: J. Barks, "Credit Reports Aid Underwriters, But Is It Worth the Controversy?", *Bests Review/Property-Casualty Insurance* 96 (1 August 1995): 44. K. Hoke, "Big Insurers Divide on Linking Auto Premiums to Credit History," *Business First-Columbus*, 8 January 1996. G. Sanders, "Arizona Probing Insurers on Redlining, Credit Checks," *Best Review / Property-Casualty Insurance* 95 (1 January 1995): 12. L. Scism, "Turned Down: A Bad Credit Record Can Get You Rejected for Auto Insurance," *The Wall Street Journal*, 11 November 1995.

Develop Your Management Potential

"It is only the farmer who faithfully plants seeds in the Spring, who reaps a harvest in the Autumn."
B.C. Forbes, Founder of *Forbes* Magazine

The purpose of these assignments is to develop your present and future capabilities as a manager. Since stakeholders increasingly expect companies to do more to fulfil their discretionary responsibilities, chances are you and your company will be expected to support your community in some significant way. To begin learning about community needs and corporate social responsibility, visit a local charity or nonprofit organization of your choosing, perhaps a hospital, the Red Cross, a soup kitchen, or a homeless shelter. Talk to the people who work or volunteer there. Gather the information you need to answer the following questions.

Questions

1. What is the organization's mission?
2. Whom does the organization serve and how does it serve them?
3. What percentage of the organization's donations is used for administrative purposes? What percentage is used to directly benefit those served by the organization? What is the ratio of volunteers to paid workers?
4. What job or task does the "typical" volunteer perform for the organization? How much time per week does the typical volunteer give to the organization? For what jobs do they need more volunteers?
5. How does the business community support the organization?
6. Why are you interested in the activities of this organization?

Discussion Questions

1. Canadian Tire is one of the most Canadian and best-known retailers—for example, everyone knows immediately what is meant by "Canadian Tire money." As with all large organizations, managers may from time to time be faced with dealing with worker behaviour that fits under the heading of "workplace deviance." Think of a typical Canadian Tire store. What four categories of deviant behaviour might a typical manager need to be wary of as he or she leads the day-to-day operations? In this instance, what does deviant behaviour refer to?

2. Times are tough for CEOs. Recent evidence suggests that boards of directors are far less tolerant of wayward managers. Higher turnover rates means that more new faces are being found in the executive suite. For a newly hired CEO, what four steps might he or she take to encourage more ethical decision-making?

3. Picture yourself being offered a high-profile challenge. You have been asked to take over the reins of Worldcom (now known as MCI), reinvent the top management team, and create a work environment that will be the envy of the industry. What are the four most important factors that you should consider as you attempt to create an ethical business climate?

4. Food banks are a necessary but unfortunate part of many towns and cities. Newly graduated from the University of Alberta's undergraduate Business program, you have taken on the responsibility of managing one of Edmonton's food banks. Among your most important responsibilities is to ensure that your organization can respond to the needs of the unfortunate on a day-to-day basis. Unfortunately, as the administrator you also have to manage other issues. Recently, you have been feeling overwhelmed by the different tasks and have decided to start ranking issues. Before doing this, however, you recognize that the needs and requests of some stakeholders may be more important than others. If you were to categorize the various stakeholders, which would be considered primary and which would be categorized as secondary? In this instance, what would be the difference between a primary stakeholder and a secondary stakeholder?

5. As manager of the food bank, you are also given the task of ensuring that the organization behaves in a socially responsible manner. Which four areas of corporate social responsibility would be most relevant to the food bank's stakeholders? Briefly describe each.

Study Tip

Think back over the last year. In your own life can you recall any instances when you were forced to make an ethical decision? Reflecting on the decision, are there any principles of ethical decision-making that might apply to the case in question? Try to summarize your ideas in one paragraph.

2 PART

Making Things Happen

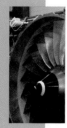

CHAPTER 4

Chapter Outline

Learning Objectives

After reading this chapter, you should be able to

1. discuss the costs and benefits of planning.
2. describe how to make a plan that works.
3. discuss how companies can use plans at all management levels, from top to bottom.
4. describe the different kinds of special-purpose plans that companies use to plan for change, contingencies, and product development.

Planning

What Would You Do?

WestJet Airlines (www.westjet.ca) began operating a no-frills air service in 1996 with three airplanes while its main competitors, Air Canada (www.aircanada.ca/) and Canadian Airlines, had a combined fleet that approached 300. Tiny by comparison to the "friendly duopoly" of Canadian and Air Canada, WestJet concentrated on short-haul routes in western Canada and originally serviced only five cities. It focused on the self-described VFR market: visiting friends and relatives. These were travellers who were less concerned with comfort and convenience but were interested in low-cost airfares. WestJet modelled itself on the very successful U.S.-based Southwest Airlines, one of the few consistently profitable airlines in North America. After starting with a few destinations and a small fleet, it embarked on a model of slow and cautious growth. By the end of 2002, WestJet had turned a profit for 22 consecutive fiscal quarters, a great accomplishment given that the U.S. industry lost $16.5 billion in 2001 and was expected to lose almost half as much again in 2002. Air Canada, WestJet's main Canadian competitor, lost money in 2000 and 2001 and the prospects did not look much better for 2002.

Air Canada had controlled approximately 90 percent of the domestic market

after it purchased and merged with Canadian Airlines in early 2000. By the first quarter of 2001, the airline had slipped and held only 73 percent of the market while WestJet's share climbed to 14 percent. When WestJet made its first public share offering in mid-1999, a share cost $10. Three years later that share was worth about $100. In comparison, Air Canada's shares were worth about $6 in mid-1999, about the same as at the end of 2002. Air Canada's CEO, Robert Milton, acknowledged that WestJet was hurting them on western routes. "In just four years, short-haul routes in the west have become the most unprofitable in our system," he said in early 2001. Ticket prices were a major problem for Air Canada as in most cases Air Canada's ticket prices were significantly higher than WestJet's. Travellers who wanted to fly on short notice or not stay over a Saturday night could pay up to six times more to fly on Air Canada than on WestJet. Air Canada had also relied heavily on business travellers who were willing to pay premium prices, but in the wake of the bursting of the dot-com bubble and the terrorist attacks on the World Trade Center in New York, this market was in significant decline. WestJet was able to keep ticket prices low because it had a cost structure that was 40 percent lower than Air Canada's. There were several factors that contributed to its lower

cost structure. One key item was that WestJet operated only one type of aircraft, the Boeing 737. Having only one type of airplane allowed the company to save on the cost of mechanics' and pilots' training and spare part inventories. It also has a non-unionized, flexible workforce that is motivated by profit sharing. On the other hand, Air Canada has a unionized workforce with rigid work rules and strong unions. Another factor is that, as opposed to Air Canada, WestJet does not offer food service on its flights. All these factors lead to significant cost savings.

In 2002 WestJet started to service Hamilton, Ontario, a lower-cost alternative to Toronto, its first foray into central Canada. There were also plans in the works to move into the Maritimes. Up to this point, Air Canada had a virtual stranglehold on central Canada and the Maritimes and these markets were essential to Air Canada's bottom line. Now its key markets were being threatened. A further indication of trouble ahead was the fact that WestJet seemed to be constantly increasing the size of its fleet even faster that it had originally planned. It had already placed firm orders for 30 new aircraft and had options to purchase a further 40. The new airplanes were very fuel-efficient and would need less maintenance, which could cut WestJet's operating costs even further. It seemed like it would not take long for WestJet to grow to almost the same size as Canadian Airlines, just prior to its purchase by Air Canada, and compete directly with Air Canada as Canada's second national carrier. Grey skies were clearly ahead for Air Canada.

If you were the CEO of Air Canada, what would you do?

Sources: "Air Canada's Boss Worried about Competition from Discount Carriers," *Canadian Press Newswire*, 23 February 2001. "No Need for US Airlines to Fly in Canada for Competition, Says Collenette," *Canadian Press Newswire*, 18 January 2001. "Air Canada Reports Market Share Drop to 73%," *Canadian Press Newswire*, 25 April 2001. Peter Fitzpatrick, "WestJet Spends $1b Expanding Its Fleet: Company Adding 30 Planes in Bid to Grab Bigger Market," *Financial Post* 2, no. 105, C1, C9. Gillian Livingston, "Air Canada CEO Says Discount Market Vital as Business Market Declines," *Canadian Press Newswire*, 1 August 2002. Peter Verburg, "Reach for the Bottom," *Canadian Business* 73, no. 4, 42–48; http://c0dsp.westjet.com/internet/sky/about/index.jsp.

As Air Canada's troubles show, creating and executing a plan is one of the most important tasks a manager has. This chapter begins by examining the costs and benefits of planning. Next, you will learn how to make a plan that works. Then you will look at the different kinds of plans that are used from the top to the bottom in most companies. Finally, you will investigate the different kinds of special-purpose plans that managers use today.

Planning

planning
choosing a goal and developing a strategy to achieve that goal

Planning is choosing a goal and developing a method or strategy to achieve that goal. You may have heard of Forzani's, but you may not know that their parent company, The Forzani Group Ltd. (www.forzanigroup.com), also owns Sport Chek and Sport Experts, among other sports retail chains. In many ways they are seen as one of the darlings of the Canadian retail sector. From the spring of 2001 to the spring of 2002, Forzani's share price went from around $4 to $25. Its stock posted the best performance in the TSE's merchandising sector in 2001, an outstanding increase of 259 percent.[1] Even in the wake of the bear market of 2002, Forzani's has been able to keep its share price close to $20, a remarkable accomplishment given today's stock market. Things were not always so rosy. In 1996, a year after a large acquisition, the company was not in good financial health. Something had to be done.

The Forzani Group hired several new senior managers who brought the experience needed to the company. A plan for recovery was quickly formed. Unprofitable stores were closed and staff were cut. They focused on their core businesses of Forzani's, Sport Chek, and Sport Experts; increased advertising budgets; and successfully developed a strategy of being price leaders.[2] The turnaround came quickly. Despite being price leaders, they maintained healthy profit margins and have become a retail success.

After reading the next two sections, you should be able to
1. discuss the costs and benefits of planning.
2. describe how to make a plan that works.

1. Costs and Benefits of Planning

Are you one of those naturally organized people who always makes a daily to-do list, who always writes everything down so you won't forget, and who never misses a deadline because you keep track of everything with your handy time-management notebook or your Palm PC? Or are you one of those flexible, creative, go-with-the-flow people who dislikes planning and organizing because it restricts your freedom, energy, and performance? Some people are natural planners. They love it and can see only the benefits of planning. However, others dislike planning and can see only its disadvantages. It turns out that both views are correct.

Planning has advantages and disadvantages. Let's learn about the benefits of planning and the pitfalls of planning.

1.1 Benefits of Planning

Planning has several important benefits: intensified effort, persistence, direction, and creation of task strategies.[3] First, managers and employees put forth greater effort when following a plan. Take two workers. Instruct one to "do his or her best" to increase production, and instruct the other to achieve a 2 percent increase in production each month. Research shows that the one with the specific plan will work harder.[4] When Mike Weir started to play golf at the age of ten, he would often play 36 holes a day throughout the summer to improve his game. His mother often sent his meals to the golf course where he would be practising putting and chipping on the practice green—after playing

CP (David J. Phillip)

Mike Weir plans his schedule and workout cycles so he will be in peak form for golf's major tournaments, a factor in his success, he believes.

his 36 holes. After winning his first professional golf tournament in 1999, he set a long-term goal of continuous improvement and started to plan his schedule and workout cycles so he would be in peak form for golf's major tournaments (the Master, U.S. Open, British Open, the PGA Championship). His hard work and planning seem to have paid off. In 2003, he became the first Canadian male to win a major golf championship and only the second left-handed golfer to win a major.[5]

Second, planning leads to persistence, that is, working hard for long periods. In fact, planning encourages persistence even when there may be little chance of short-term success.[6] Mary Kay Ash overcame numerous professional and personal obstacles before founding Mary Kay Cosmetics. For example, after 11 years as head of sales for a company (which she won't name), she was replaced by her assistant, a man whom she had spent the previous nine months training. Then, despite her proven track record and years of experience, the company paid him twice what they had been paying her. Frustrated, she quit to start her own company, only to have her 45-year-old husband suddenly die of a heart attack a month prior to the company's startup. Today, because of her persistence and hard work, Mary Kay Cosmetics has 750 000 sales representatives worldwide and is the leading cosmetics company in the United States, with over $3.8 billion in annual sales.[7]

The third benefit of planning is direction. Plans encourage managers and employees to direct their persistent efforts toward activities that help accomplish their goals and away from activities that don't. For example, a large insurance company wanted to improve the way its managers gave employees performance evaluation feedback. To help managers improve, company trainers taught them 43 effective performance feedback behaviours. Examples included "I will give my subordinate a clear understanding of the results I expect him or her to achieve," or "During the performance appraisal interview, I will be very supportive, stressing good points before discussing needed improvement." However, during training, managers were instructed to choose just 12 behaviours (out of

---

PERSONAL PRODUCTIVITY TIP

"Fail Forward" to Learn from Failure

Failing forward means learning something when you fail. To fail forward, experiment by trying several different things. You'll learn what works and what doesn't. When things fail, gather a group with different backgrounds to analyze what went wrong. Identify the failure as soon as possible. This gives you more time to analyze the problem and figure out how to fix it. Don't blame anyone. Be glad that someone brought the failure to your attention. Thomas Edison failed 10 000 times before inventing light bulb filaments. Abraham Lincoln lost 12 times before finally being elected to office. You can fail forward by learning from your failures, too.

Source: Harvard Management Update, "Learn by 'Failing Forward,'" *The Globe and Mail*, 31 October 2000, B17.

the 43) on which they wanted to make the most improvement. When subordinates rated their managers on the 43 effective feedback behaviours, it became clear that no matter which 12 behaviours different managers chose, they only improved on the 12 behaviours for which they had set improvement goals. Plans direct behaviour toward activities that lead to goal accomplishment and away from those that don't.

The fourth benefit of planning is that it encourages the development of task strategies. After selecting a goal, it's natural to ask, "How can it be achieved?" For example, Telus (www.telus.com) a provider of data, Internet protocol, and voice and wireless communications located in Burnaby, B.C., received an unfavourable ruling from the Canadian Radio-television and Telecommunications Commission that would reduce its operating income by about $45 million in 2002 and by $75 million in subsequent years. Coupled with an earlier ruling, Telus found itself in a position where it would see a substantial decline in revenue; its share price had slid to less than $6. In March 2001 share prices had peaked at $40. It set a goal to cut $300 million in annual costs. To reach this goal, Telus offered severance and early retirement packages to 11 000 employees, rationalized product offerings, and focused on its core business. By the end of 2002 the restructuring was nearly complete and share prices in early 2003 rose to over $20.[8] As this example shows, not only does planning encourage people to work hard for extended periods and to engage in behaviours directly related to goal accomplishment, but it also encourages them to think of better ways to do their jobs.

Finally, perhaps the most compelling benefit of planning is that it has been proven to work for both companies and individuals. On average, companies with plans have larger profits and grow much faster than companies that don't.[9] The same holds true for individual managers and employees. There is no better way to improve the performance of the people who work in a company than to have them set goals and develop strategies for achieving those goals. For more on the benefits of planning, see the "What Really Works?" feature in this chapter.

1.2 Planning Pitfalls

Despite the significant benefits associated with planning, planning is not a cure-all. Plans won't fix all organizational problems. In fact, many management authors and consultants believe that planning can harm companies in several ways.[10]

The first pitfall of planning is that it can impede change and prevent or slow needed adaptation. Sometimes companies become so committed to achieving the goals set forth in their plans or they become so intent on following the strategies and tactics spelled out in them, that they fail to see that their plans aren't working or that their goals need to change.

The second pitfall of planning is that it can create a false sense of certainty. Planners sometimes feel that they know exactly what the future holds for their competitors, their suppliers, and their companies. However, all plans are based on assumptions. "The price of gasoline will increase by 4 percent per year." "Exports will continue to rise." For plans to work, the assumptions on which they are based must hold true. If the assumptions turn out to be false, then plans based on them are likely to fail. For example, as cell phones became cheaper and more reliable, Nokia, a Finland-based manufacturer of cell phones, experienced tremendous growth in its business. So when sales suddenly dropped by 25 percent, Nokia was caught off guard. Officially, company management blamed "logistical hiccups." However, *The Wall Street Journal* concluded that "Nokia didn't see it coming and didn't know how to handle it [the drop in sales]."[11] Because Nokia assumed that its cellular phone sales would continue to grow, it bought parts at high prices and did a poor job of controlling its costs. When the assumption (i.e., continued growth) underlying its production plans turned out to be false, the result was a 30 percent decline in operating profits. Jorma Ollila, Nokia's CEO, said the problems were "driven by economic uncertainty, the ongoing technology transition, and less aggressive marketing by the operators [companies that sell mobile phone services]."[12]

The third pitfall of planning is the detachment of planners. In theory, strategic planners and top-level managers are supposed to focus on the big picture and not concern themselves with the details of implementation, that is, carrying out the plan. According to McGill management professor Henry Mintzberg, detachment leads planners to plan for things they don't understand.[13] Plans are not meant to be abstract theories. They are meant to be guidelines for action. Consequently, planners need to be familiar with the daily details of their businesses if they are to produce plans that can work.

For example, if you doubt that the "details" are important to good execution of a plan, imagine that you're about to have coronary bypass surgery to replace four clogged arteries. Rather than having an experienced cardiologist perform your surgery, you're going under the knife of a first-year medical intern. The intern is a fully qualified M.D. who clearly understands the theory and the plan behind bypass surgery, but has never performed such an operation. As you lie on the operating table, who is the last person you'd like to see as the anesthesia kicks in, the first-year intern who knows the plan but has never done a bypass, or the experienced cardiologist who has followed the plan hundreds of times? Planning works better when the people developing the plan are not detached from the process of executing the plan.

Review 1
Costs and Benefits of Planning

Planning is choosing a goal and developing a method to achieve that goal. Planning is one of the best ways to improve organizational and individual performance. It encourages people to work harder (intensified effort), to work hard for extended periods (persistence), to engage in behaviours directly related to goal accomplishment (directed behaviour), and to think of better ways to do their jobs (task strategies). But most important, companies that plan have larger profits and faster growth than companies that don't plan. However, planning also has three potential pitfalls. Companies that are overly committed to their plans may be slow to adapt to changes in their environment. Planning is based on assumptions about the future, and when those assumptions are wrong, plans are likely to fail. Finally, planning can fail when planners are detached from the implementation of plans.

2. How to Make a Plan that Works

Planning is a double-edged sword. If done right, planning brings about tremendous increases in individual and organizational performance. At Pixar Animation Studios (www.pixar.com), the plan is to produce one movie a year. Pixar, which makes digitally animated movies, produced only three movies, *Toy Story*, *A Bug's Life*, and *Toy Story 2*, in five years. So while making one movie a year is nothing for traditional movie studios, making a movie a year has been a significant, long-term goal for Pixar. To achieve this goal, Pixar has implemented a plan to hire more people (550 people now work at Pixar, up from 400), added new divisions to develop new movies (story creation) and to manage movie development (shot by shot), increased its computer capabilities (with a several hundredfold increase in computer power and storage), and moved into a new headquarters that fosters collaboration and creativity (compared to the four different locations in which people previously worked). The plan in place includes four new movies: *Monsters, Inc.* (released in summer 2001), *Finding Nemo*, and two that haven't been announced yet, by 2005. However, if planning is done wrong, it can have just the opposite effect and harm individual and organizational performance. Pixar's first three films, *Toy Story*, *A Bug's Life*, and *Toy Story 2*, were critical and box-office successes. The risk from Pixar's plan is that increasing the frequency of its films may lead to poorer quality. Paul Dergarabedian, president of a box-office tracking company, said, "The more movies you have, the greater the chance you'll falter once in awhile." Indeed, CEO Steve Jobs said that while Pixar's "priority is still to make films that are really great, not every one of our films will succeed."[14]

In this section, you will learn how to make a plan that works.

As depicted in Exhibit 4.1, planning consists of setting goals, developing commitment to goals, developing effective action plans, tracking progress, and maintaining flexibility.

2.1 Setting Goals

Since planning is choosing a goal and developing a method or strategy to achieve that goal, the first step in planning is to set goals. To direct behaviour and increase effort, goals need to be specific and challenging.[15] For example, deciding to "increase sales this year" won't direct and energize workers as much as deciding to "increase Manitoba sales by 4 percent in the next six months." Likewise, choosing to "drop a few pounds" won't motivate you as much as choosing to "lose 15 pounds." Specific, challenging goals provide a target for which to aim and a standard against which to measure success.

One way of writing effective goals for yourself, your job, or your company is to use the S.M.A.R.T. guidelines. **S.M.A.R.T. goals** are Specific, Measurable, Attainable, Results-oriented, and Time-bounded.[16] Let's see how a heating, ventilation, and air-conditioning (HVAC) company might use S.M.A.R.T. goals in its business.

The HVAC business is cyclical. It's extremely busy at the beginning of summer, when homeowners find that their air conditioning isn't working, and at the beginning of winter, when furnaces and heat pumps need repair. During these times, most HVAC companies have more business than they can handle. But at other times of year, business can be very slow. So a specific goal would be to increase sales by 50 percent during the fall and spring, when business is slower. This goal could be measured by keeping track of the number of annual maintenance contracts sold to customers. This goal of increasing sales during the off seasons is attainable, because maintenance contracts typically include spring tune-ups (air-conditioning systems) and fall tune-ups (furnace or heating systems). Moreover, a 50 percent increase in sales during the slow seasons is results-oriented. Since customers want their furnaces and air conditioners to work the first time it gets cold (or hot) each year, they are likely to buy service contracts that ensure their equipment is in working order. Tune-up work can then be scheduled during the slow seasons, increasing sales at those times. Finally, this goal can be made time-bounded by asking the staff to push sales of maintenance contracts before Labour Day, the traditional end of summer, when people start thinking about the cold days ahead, and in March, when winter-weary people start longing for hot days in air-conditioned comfort. The result would be more work during the slow fall and spring seasons.

S.M.A.R.T. goals
goals that are specific, measurable, attainable, results-oriented, and time-bounded

PERSONAL PRODUCTIVITY **TIP**

Planning to Procrastinate?

Are you a great planner, but have trouble getting started or keeping on task? Some signs of a great planner are a compulsion to organize files, long to-do lists, always getting up to get coffee, desk cleaning, and so forth. Here's the clincher. Do you use the computer—that supposedly productivity-enhancing machine—to play solitaire or surf the Internet? Congratulations, you're an official member of the procrastinators' club! If you want your membership to expire, try putting yourself on a schedule or breaking big projects into bite-sized tasks. But not all procrastination is bad. Some plans work out better when you've had longer to mull them over.

Source: H. Lancaster, "Managing Your Career: Mend Procrastinating Ways before Your Job Stalls Out," *The Wall Street Journal Interactive Edition*, 7 May 1996.

EXHIBIT 4.1

HOW TO MAKE A PLAN THAT WORKS

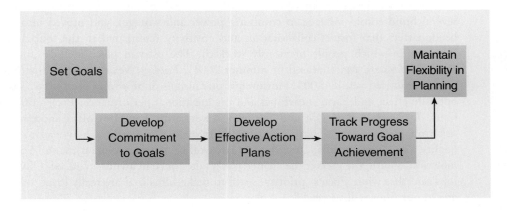

Just because a company sets a goal doesn't mean that people will try to accomplish it. If workers don't care about a goal, then the goal won't encourage them to work harder or smarter. Thus, the second step in planning is to develop commitment to goals.

Goal commitment is the determination to achieve a goal. Commitment to achieve a goal is not automatic. Managers and workers must choose to commit themselves to a goal. For example, Professor Edwin Locke, the foremost expert on how, why, and when goals work, told a story about an overweight friend. After not seeing him for years, Locke ran into his friend, who had finally lost 35 kilograms. Because of the change, he nearly walked by without recognizing him. Locke said, "So I asked him how he did it, knowing how hard it was for most people to lose so much weight." His friend responded, "Actually, it was quite simple. I simply decided that I really wanted to do it."[17] Said in another way, goal commitment is really wanting to achieve a goal.

So how can managers bring about goal commitment? The most popular approach is to set goals participatively. Rather than assigning goals to workers ("Johnson, you've got 'til Tuesday of next week to redesign the flex capacitor so it gives us 10 percent more output"), managers and employees choose goals together. The goals are more likely to be realistic and attainable if employees participate in setting them. Also, people are more likely to strive for a goal they feel they have a reasonable chance of attaining. For example, would you be more likely to stick to an exercise program that required one-half hour per day or one that required three hours per day?

Another technique for gaining commitment to a goal is to make the goal public. For example, college students who publicly communicated their semester grade goals ("This semester, I'm shooting for a 3.5") to significant others (usually a parent or sibling) were much more committed to achieving their grades. More importantly, students who told others about their goals earned grades that were nearly a half-grade higher than students who did not tell others about their grade goals.[18] So, one way to increase commitment to goals is to "go public" by having individuals or work units tell others about their goals. For example, work units could post their goals on a bulletin board for all to see.

Another way to increase goal commitment is to obtain top management's support. Top management can show support for a plan or program by providing funds, speaking publicly about the plan, or participating in the plan itself. When General Electric (GE) announced its new "six sigma" program in which it planned to improve quality by reducing the number of product or service errors to just 3.4 defects or errors per million, top management put an incredible amount of support behind the program. Every employee went through two weeks of intense training in statistical process control. At the end of training, they were expected to demonstrate what they had learned by completing two on-the-job projects that would increase quality or decrease costs. Statistical tools, formulas, guidelines, readings, and employee discussions were made available on the GE intranet to support six sigma efforts. Furthermore, 4500 six sigma project leaders, known internally at GE as "black belts" because of their advanced six sigma training, experience, and expertise, worked full-time throughout the company, managing various improvement projects. Finally, GE shared feedback on six sigma progress by tracking and measuring the results of six sigma projects worldwide. The results thus far indicate an internal savings of more than $3 billion a year. None of this would have happened without complete support from GE's top management, which invested $750 million and four years' time to make the program a success and to institutionalize it in GE's culture.[19]

goal commitment
the determination to achieve a goal

PERSONAL PRODUCTIVITY

Are You an Owl or an Early Bird?

What time do you wake up on Saturday morning? Are you up and out of bed by 7:00 a.m., or are you up just in time to make it to the table for lunch? The term *morningness* describes a preference for morning activities. Studies show that morningness affects performance. Students with morning orientations get much better grades in 8:00 a.m. classes than do students with evening orientations (3.27 versus 2.78). So, to do a better job of achieving your goals, plan to do your most challenging work when you're at your peak energy levels and your routine work when your energy is low.

Source: J.P. Guthrie, R.A. Ash, and V. Bendapudi, "Additional Evidence for a Measure of Morning," *Journal of Applied Psychology* 80 (1995): 186–190.

action plan
the specific steps, people, and resources needed to accomplish a goal

The third step in planning is to develop effective action plans. An **action plan** lists the specific steps, people, resources, and time period for accomplishing a goal. For example, USAir announced a "Management Action Program" to significantly reduce costs and increase revenues. This program (i.e., plan) had three steps:

1. Cut all unprofitable routes.

2. Use technology to cut costs and increase efficiency.

3. Outsource any task that can be done better and more cheaply by someone else.

In step one, the company cut flights to money-losing destinations, such as Austin, Texas; San Antonio, Texas; Cincinnati, Ohio; and Albuquerque, New Mexico. Today, USAir flies only 90 percent of the routes it once did. But the routes it flies are profitable. Peter Haak, USAir's assistant vice president for schedules, said, "We took seats out of the air, but we grew the revenue—a $211-million [U.S.] change in one quarter. That's really news." In step two, USAir installed an expensive computer-run, yield-management system called Excalibur to monitor how its prices compared to its competitors' prices. Excalibur helps USAir determine when to cut prices to stay competitive. Consequently, despite cutting prices, revenues are actually increasing, because USAir's jets now fly with fewer empty seats than previously. In step three, outsourcing, USAir is saving money by having outside companies handle cargo ($22.5 million saved), purchasing ($138 million saved), and crew scheduling ($60 million saved).[20] The only thing missing from USAir's plan was a specific goal and time period for accomplishing its cost savings. For example, Telus's CEO set a goal of cutting $300 million in annual operating costs.[21]

2.4 Tracking Progress

proximal goals
short-term goals or subgoals

distal goals
long-term or primary goals

The fourth step in planning is to track progress toward goal achievement. There are two accepted methods of tracking progress. The first is to set proximal goals and distal goals. **Proximal goals** are short-term goals or subgoals, whereas **distal goals** are long-term or primary goals.[22] The idea behind setting proximal goals is that they may be more motivating and rewarding than waiting to achieve far-off distal goals. When profits dropped 48 percent at Office Depot, new CEO Bruce Nelson put new plans into place. In the short term, his goal was to clean up the company's balance sheet by increasing cash flows and reducing debt. This was accomplished by closing 70 poorly performing stores, reducing the number of items carried in each store, hiring "mystery shoppers" to pose as shoppers to measure customer service, and then adding new signs and lighting to make things easier to find. However, Nelson has three different goals for Office Depot in the long term. First, put most of the company's money into international growth, where it thinks it can make the largest return. Second, partner with Microsoft to put new "Business Solution Centers" into each store to advise small business owners how to incorporate technology into their companies. Third, redo the store format, which is based on a typical department store layout, to a circular design with lower shelves to make it easier for customers to find and use products. Nelson said, "Right now customers can't tell the difference between Office Depot, Office Max, and Staples. I want to change the in-store experience so that the customer will remember their experience at Office Depot."[23]

The second method of tracking progress is to gather and provide performance feedback. Regular, frequent performance feedback allows workers and managers to track their progress toward goal achievement and make adjustments in effort, direction, and strategies.[24] For example, Exhibit 4.2 shows the result of providing feedback on safety behaviour to the makeup and wrapping workers in a large bakery company. The company had a worker safety record that was two and a half times worse than the industry average. During the baseline period, workers in the wrapping department, who measure and mix ingredients, roll the bread dough, and place it into baking pans, performed their jobs safely about 70 percent of the time. The baseline safety record for workers in the makeup department, who bag and seal baked bread and assemble, pack, and tape cardboard cartons for shipping, was a bit better at 78 percent.

Yet after the company gave workers 30 minutes of safety training, set a goal of 90 percent safe behaviour, and then provided daily feedback (such as a chart similar to Exhibit 4.2), performance improved dramatically. During the intervention period, the percentage of safely performed behaviours rose to an average of 95.8 percent for wrapping workers and 99.3 percent for workers in the makeup department, and never fell below 83 percent. Thus, the combination of training, a challenging goal, and feedback led to a dramatic increase in performance.

However, the importance of feedback alone can be seen in the reversal stage, when the company quit posting daily feedback on safe behaviour. Without daily feedback, the percentage of safely performed behaviour returned to baseline levels, 70.8 percent for the wrapping department and 72.3 percent for the makeup department. For planning to be effective, workers need a specific, challenging goal and regular feedback to track their progress.

EXHIBIT 4.2

EFFECTS OF GOAL-SETTING, TRAINING, AND FEEDBACK ON SAFE BEHAVIOUR IN A BREAD FACTORY

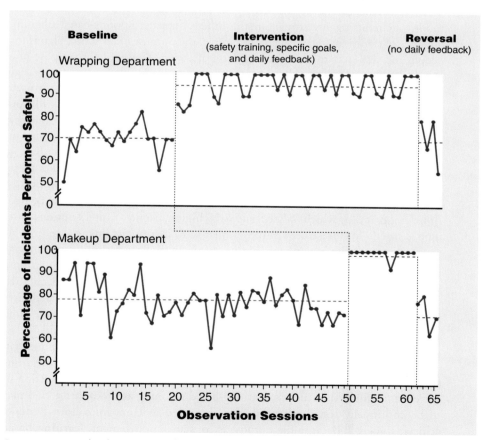

Source: Reprinted with permission of the Journal of Applied Psychology. "A Behavioral Approach to Occupational Safety: Pinpointing and Reinforcing Safe Performance in a Food Manufacturing Plant." Komaki, J., Barwick, K.D., and Scott, L.R., *Journal of Applied Psychology*, 1978, V63. Reproduced with permission of the publisher. Copyright © 1978 by the American Psychological Association.

Because action plans are sometimes poorly conceived and goals sometimes turn out to not be achievable, the last step in developing an effective plan is to maintain flexibility. Claren Wooten and his partner started Metamorphosis Studios to build custom websites for companies. However, most of their customers got sticker shock and walked away because they couldn't believe that it would cost $4500 to $9000 to produce a website (more like $40 000 to $75 000 today). They wanted a sophisticated website, but not at that price. So rather than continue to struggle as a custom maker and designer of websites, Metamorphosis Studios morphed into an online store that allowed small businesses to buy predesigned, customizable websites. Wooten said that this "enabled us to reduce our price to only a couple of hundred dollars without sacrificing quality. No one had really taken that approach before—and we would never have thought to take it had we not listened to our small-business customers."[25] Today, Metamorphosis Studios has become Network Solutions (www.networksolutions.com), a one-stop Internet solution for building your own website, sending out personalized e-mail (for marketing), purchasing the domain name (e.g., mycompany.com) you want, and many other services at reasonable prices for small businesses. So when plans fail, it is far better to scrap the plan and start over than it is to ride the failing plan into the ground.

An even more desirable strategy is to build flexibility into planning from the start. One method of maintaining flexibility while planning is to adopt an options-based approach.[26] The goal of **options-based planning** is to keep options open by making small, simultaneous investments in many options or plans. Then when one or a few of these plans emerge as likely winners, you invest even more in these plans while discontinuing or reducing investment in the others. In part, options-based planning is the opposite of traditional planning. For example, the purpose of an action plan is to commit people and resources to a particular course of action. However, the purpose of options-based planning is to leave those commitments open. Holding options open gives you choices, and choices give you flexibility. Options-based planning is especially useful when uncertainty is high and you don't know how things will change or what will work in the future. Because uncertainty runs very strongly in high-tech industries, it makes sense to take an options-based planning approach to invest in many different companies and many different technologies. In the last few years, Intel has done just that, investing $12.3 billion in 350 new technology companies. Leslie Vadasz, who makes these investments for Intel, knows that some will fail, some will succeed, and if he's lucky, a few will be "megawinners," such as Red Hat Software, the leading Linux software company, and Broadcast.com, for which Yahoo! paid $7.5 billion. Some of Intel's options-based planning is strictly for investment purposes, that is, to increase its financial return. However, many of its options investments are in companies whose technologies can strengthen Intel's core business, computer chips. For example, Intel invested in Primarion because its technology reduces electrical interference in computer chips that occurs when the wires in the chip are closer together. This happens when more integrated circuits are packed into chips to make them faster. If Primarion's technology pays off, Intel's chips should be able to run even faster, giving it a competitive advantage. Said Vadasz, "You judge your return on how you met your strategic goals, and count the money later."[27]

Another method of maintaining flexibility while planning is to take a learning-based approach. In contrast to traditional planning, which assumes that initial action plans are correct and will lead to success, learning-based planning assumes that action plans need to be continually tested, changed, and improved as companies learn better ways of achieving goals.[28] Because the purpose is constant improvement, **learning-based planning** not only encourages flexibility in action plans, but it also encourages frequent reassessment and revision of organizational goals.

For example, Knight-Ridder Corporation, which owns the second-largest newspaper chain in the United States, created project "25/43" to reverse the sharp decline in newspaper readership among people between the ages of 25 and 43. In contrast to traditional

options-based planning
maintaining planning flexibility by making small, simultaneous investments in many alternative plans

learning-based planning
learning better ways of achieving goals by continually testing, changing, and improving plans and strategies

newspapers, where editors and reporters decide on the newspaper's content and design, the first step in Knight-Ridder's learning-based planning was to ask readers what they wanted in their newspaper. The second step was to test those ideas and keep the ones that readers liked. Suggested changes included columns on environmental tips, shopping, parenting, high-tech, and fitness. Readers also insisted on shorter articles, the use of colour, and better layouts and indexes, which made it easier to find what they were looking for. As the third and final step, which is the key to learning-based planning, Knight-Ridder now regularly questions, experiments, and tests the changes it makes. Knight-Ridder's vice president of news said,

Tupperware removed its products from Target stores after less than a year due to poor sales and the feeling that in-store sales were threatening its traditional home parties.

Routinely now, our papers go to focus groups when they are going to try something new. Many of our editors have established a 25/43 goal, which means they conduct research, involve task forces from their newsrooms and other departments, assess the strengths and weaknesses of their papers, propose changes, and test some of these changes in the marketplace. It sounds so simple, but it is not the way the newspaper business tended to operate.[29]

Review 2
How to Make a Plan that Works

There are five steps to making a plan that works: (1) Set S.M.A.R.T. goals—goals that are Specific, Measurable, Attainable, Results-oriented, and Time-bounded. (2) Develop commitment to the goal from the people who contribute to goal achievement. Managers can increase workers' goal commitment by encouraging worker participation in goal setting, making goals public, and getting top management to show their support for workers' goals. (3) Develop action plans for goal accomplishment. (4) Track progress toward goal achievement by setting both proximal and distal goals and by providing workers with regular performance feedback. (5) Maintain flexibility. Keeping options open through options-based planning and seeking continuous improvement through learning-based planning help organizations maintain flexibility as they plan.

Kinds of Plans

You may have heard of Waste Management International, the largest garbage and recycling company in North America. But you're probably not familiar with United Waste Systems, a small garbage company only 3.6 percent the size of Waste Management. Yet, despite its smaller size, United Waste makes more profit per dollar of revenue than does Waste Management (a 24 percent operating margin versus 18 percent for Waste Management).[30]

What makes United Waste Systems more profitable than Waste Management? It has instituted successful planning processes at each level of the company. Beginning at the top, the company has a clear mission. Says CEO Bradley Jacobs, "We are not in medical waste. We are not in hazardous waste. We are not in incineration." What the company is in are rural areas, where, unlike giant Waste Management, it has little competition in the trash-pickup business. But once the trash is picked up, it's got to be delivered to a dump. Since competitors pay cities upwards of $68 per ton to empty their garbage trucks at municipally owned dumps, United's middle managers are in charge of a plan to find, buy, and run company-owned dump sites. Why? Because this lowers United's dumping costs to just $45 a ton. Finally, at lower levels, company managers and employees focus on plans to lower costs and increase productivity. For example in one small town, United has a one-truck, two-person crew pick up trash for the entire town on Wednesdays, Thursdays, and Fridays. The same route used to be covered by two trucks and two crews from another waste hauler.

After reading the next two sections, you should be able to
3. *discuss how companies can use plans at all management levels, from top to bottom.*
4. *describe the different kinds of special-purpose plans that companies use to plan for change, contingencies, and product development.*

3. Planning from Top to Bottom

Planning works best when the goals and action plans at the bottom and middle of the organization support the goals and action plans at the top of the organization. In other words, planning works best when everybody pulls in the same direction. Exhibit 4.3 illustrates this planning continuity, beginning at the top with a clear definition of the company vision and ending at the bottom with the execution of operational plans.

Let's see how top managers create the organizational vision and mission; how middle managers develop tactical plans and use management by objectives to motivate employee efforts toward the overall vision and mission; and how first-level managers use operational, single-use, and standing plans to implement the tactical plans in the following sections: starting at the top, bending in the middle, and finishing at the bottom.

3.1 Starting at the Top

As shown in Exhibit 4.4, top management is responsible for developing long-term **strategic plans** that make clear how the company will serve customers and position itself against competitors in the next two to five years. (The strategic planning and management process is reviewed in its entirety in Chapter 9.) Strategic planning begins with the creation of an organizational vision and an organizational mission.

A **vision** is a statement of a company's purpose or reason for existing.[31] Vision statements should be brief—no more than two sentences. They should also be inspirational, clear, and consistent with widely shared company beliefs and values. For example, Mountain Equipment Co-op (www.mec.ca), Canada's largest retail cooperative by membership, has a vision to be "an innovative, thriving co-operative that inspires excellence in products and services, passion for wilderness experiences, leadership for a just world, and action for a healthy planet." Mountain Equipment Co-op's vision is clear and inspirational and guides the company in its business practices. For example, MEC, as it is more commonly known, does not sell motorized vehicles and ensures that its new stores are built in an environmentally friendly way. When building a new store in Winnipeg, it used salvaged materials at considerable expense to reduce the environmental impact of the new store.[32] Its website even hosts an equipment swap so that members don't have to buy new equipment and consume even more of the earth's resources. All these activities

strategic plans
overall company plans that clarify how the company will serve customers and position itself against competitors over the next two to five years

vision
inspirational statement of an organization's enduring purpose

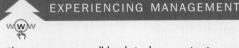

EXHIBIT 4.3

PLANNING FROM TOP TO BOTTOM

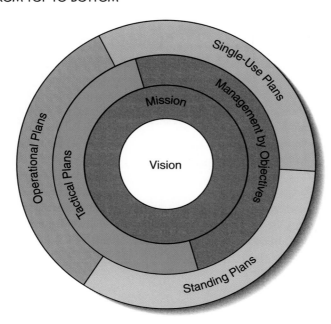

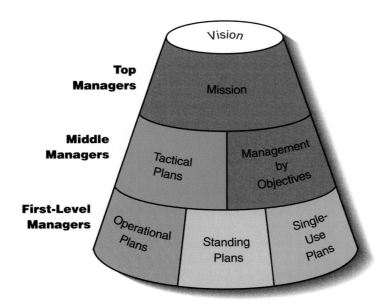

are intended to provide for a "healthy planet."[33] Other examples of organizational visions are Walt Disney Corporation's "to make people happy" and Schlage Lock Company's "to make the world more secure."[34]

The **mission**, which flows from the vision, is a more specific goal that unifies company-wide efforts, stretches and challenges the organization, and possesses a finish line and a timeframe. For example, in 1961, President John F. Kennedy established an organizational mission for NASA with this simple statement: "Achieving the goal, before this decade is out, of landing a man on the moon and returning him safely to earth."[35] NASA achieved this goal on 20 July 1969, when astronaut Neil Armstrong walked on the moon.

mission
statement of a company's overall goal that unifies company-wide efforts toward its vision, stretches and challenges the organization, and possesses a finish line and a timeframe

EXHIBIT 4.4

TIMELINES FOR STRATEGIC, TACTICAL, AND OPERATIONAL PLANS

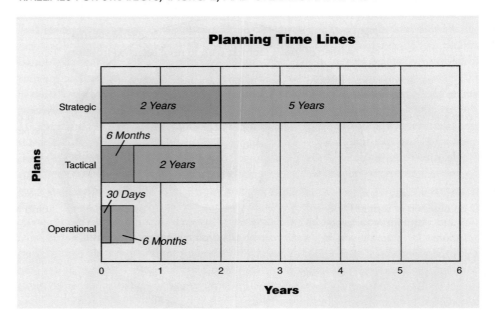

Once a mission has been accomplished, a new one should be chosen. Again, however, the new mission must grow out of the organization's vision, which does not change over time. For example, NASA's vision statement is "As explorers, pioneers, and innovators, we boldly expand frontiers in air and space to inspire and serve America, and to benefit the quality of life on earth." NASA used this vision to develop the three-part mission statement shown in Exhibit 4.5. Notice that for each mission statement, NASA has created specific, challenging goals to be accomplished from 1998 to 2002, from 2003 to 2009, and from 2010 to 2023, and beyond.

Companies can set missions in four ways.[36] One is **targeting**, setting a clear, specific target and "aiming" for it. For example, Medtronic, one of the world's leading medical technology companies, provides products and solutions for people with chronic disease. Medtronic's mission is "to contribute to human welfare by the development of biomedical devices that restore health, relieve pain, and extend life." Medtronic makes sure all its employees aim for this mission through its regularly held medallion ceremonies, where all new hires are awarded a medallion with a "rising man" on it who represents the company mission, and are asked by the CEO to "put this medallion at your workplace and remember why you're here: not just to make money for yourself or the company, but to help restore people to full life and health."[37] Medtronic CEO and chairman William George describes a medallion ceremony that occurred in Switzerland:

> After the ceremony, the European team arranged for four patients and their physicians to tell their stories. One of them was a big Swiss farmer suffering from the tremors of Parkinson's disease. His physician asked him to demonstrate how he had lost his tremor. Then he asked him to shut the device off and immediately the tremors returned. As he turned the device back on, the tremors stopped immediately and a loud gasp went up from the employees in the audience. In that instant our 150 new Swiss employees "got it": they knew why the quality of their pacemakers, defibrillators, and stimulators had to be perfect and what they were working for.[38]

targeting
mission stated as a clear specific company goal

A second type of mission is the **common-enemy mission**, in which the company vows to defeat one of its corporate rivals. Pepsi's aspirations of beating Coke, Burger King's desire to defeat McDonald's, or Avis's hopes ("We're number two. We try harder.") to catch Hertz Rental Cars are all examples of common-enemy missions. At one point, when Honda was making only motorcycles, its mission was "We will crush, squash, and slaughter Yamaha." A third type of mission is the **role-model mission**. Here, rather than focusing on defeating specific competitors, as in the common-enemy mission, the company emulates the characteristics and practices of a successful company. For example, according to Ted Larkin, the airline analyst for HSBC securities, "WestJet makes no secret of emulating Southwest [airlines]." [39] A fourth type of mission is the **internal-transformation mission**, in which the company aims to achieve dramatic changes to remain competitive in its markets. For example, at the beginning of the chapter, you learned that Air Canada was in serious competitive and financial trouble. A new direction would clearly be needed to improve its bottom line and halt the erosion of its market share.

Before leaving this section, you should know that there is disagreement among academics and business people regarding the differences between organizational visions and missions. Some say that a vision is a statement of a company's purpose or reason for existing, while others would say that's a mission statement. The bottom line is that developing a statement of purpose and then linking long-term and short-term goals to that statement is critical to success. Studies consistently show that companies with more comprehensive vision/mission statements do better financially than those with ambiguous visions/missions or none at all. [40]

3.2 Bending in the Middle

Middle management is responsible for developing and carrying out tactical plans to accomplish the organization's mission. **Tactical plans** specify how a company will use resources, budgets, and people to accomplish specific goals within its mission. Whereas strategic plans and objectives are used to focus company efforts over the next two to five years, tactical plans and objectives are used to direct behaviour, efforts, and attention over the next six months to two years. For example, after three years of losses, Disneyland Paris managed to earn a profit in its fourth year of operation by making specific changes in its tactical plans that were not helping the company accomplish its mission "to make people happy." Management redesigned special package deals (for tickets, hotel, and food), because it realized that most families wanted to spend only two or three days at the park instead of five days or longer, which was the original tactical plan. Likewise, to increase attendance, Disney cut admission prices by 20 percent and hotel and food prices by 10 percent. Finally, management realized that it had miscalculated by "Europeanizing" park rides and shows. It turned out that European visitors wanted an "American experience." So instead of sit-down restaurants with waiters and servers, the emphasis is now on fast food and self-service. Rather than fine food and fine wines, restaurants serve hamburgers, brownies, stuffed potatoes, and carbonated beverages in disposable paper cups. [41] Today, Disneyland Paris is the number one tourist destination in Europe. [42]

Management by objectives (see the feature "What Really Works? Management by Objectives") is a management technique often used to develop and carry out tactical plans. **Management by objectives**, or **MBO**, is a four-step process in which managers and their employees (1) discuss possible goals, (2) participatively select goals that are challenging, attainable, and consistent with the company's overall goals, (3) jointly develop tactical plans that lead to accomplishment of tactical goals and objectives, and (4) meet regularly to review progress toward accomplishment of those goals. Lee Iacocca, the former CEO who brought Chrysler Corporation back from the verge of bankruptcy,

common-enemy mission
company goal of defeating a corporate rival

role-model mission
company goal of imitating the characteristics and practices of a successful company

internal-transformation mission
company goal of remaining competitive by making dramatic changes in the company

tactical plans
plans created and implemented by middle managers that specify how the company will use resources, budgets, and people over the next six months to two years to accomplish specific goals within its mission

> ### EXPERIENCING MANAGEMENT
>
> Management by objectives is a common planning technique. To interact with a model of this technique visit our animated concept and activity site. Choose Planning & Strategic Processes from the "select a topic" pull-down menu, then Management by Objectives from the "overview tab."
>
> **www.experiencingmanagement.com**

management by objectives (MBO)
a four-step process in which managers and employees discuss and select goals, develop tactical plans, and meet regularly to review progress toward goal accomplishment

EXHIBIT 4.5

NASA'S MISSION AND STRATEGIC GOALS

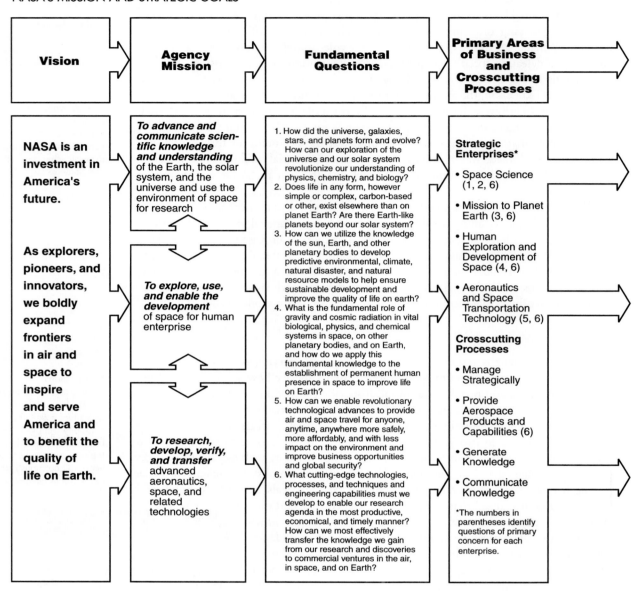

credits MBO (though he called it a "quarterly review system") for his 30 years of extraordinary success as a manager. Iacocca said, "Over the years, I've regularly asked my key people—and I've had them ask their key people, and so on down the line—a few basic questions: 'What are your objectives for the next ninety days? What are your plans, your priorities, your hopes? And how do you intend to go about achieving them?'"[43]

When done right, MBO is an extremely effective method of tactical planning. However, MBO is not without disadvantages.[44] Some MBO programs involve excessive paperwork, requiring managers to file annual statements of plans and objectives, plus quarterly or semiannual written reviews assessing goal progress. However, electronic and Web-based management systems and software, such as WebMBO (www.webmbo.com), which automates the MBO process, are making it easier for managers and employees to set goals, link them to the organization's strategic direction, and continuously track and evaluate their progress.[45] Another difficulty is that managers are frequently reluctant to give employees feedback about their performance. A third disadvantage is that managers

EXHIBIT 4.5

NASA'S MISSION AND STRATEGIC GOALS *CONT'D*

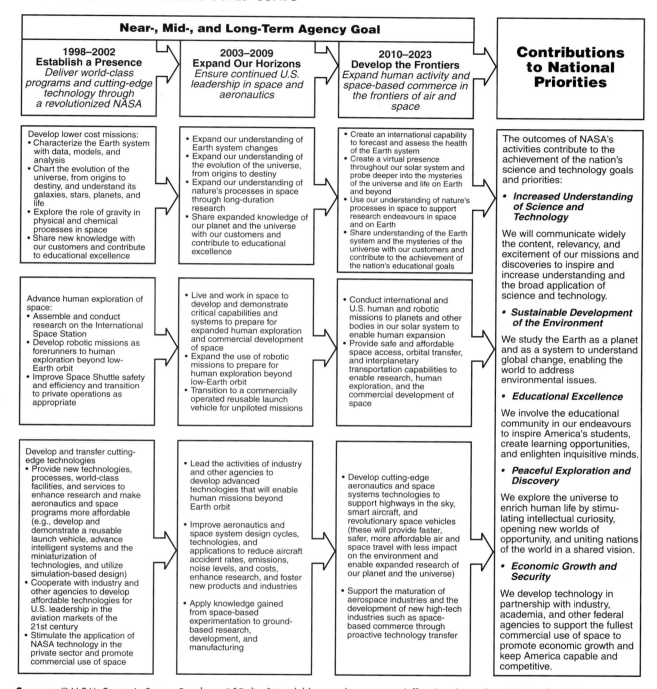

Source: "NASA's Strategic System Roadmap," [Online] Available www.hq.nasa.gov/office/nsp/maps.htm, 24 March, 1998.

and employees sometimes have difficulty agreeing on goals. And when employees are forced to accept goals that they don't want, goal commitment and employee effort suffer. Last, because MBO focuses on quantitative, easily measured goals, employees may neglect important unmeasured parts of their jobs. In other words, if your job performance is judged only by whether you reduce costs by 3 percent or raise revenues by 5 percent, then you are unlikely to give high priority to the unmeasured, but still important parts of your job, like mentoring new employees or sharing new knowledge and skills with co-workers.

WhatReallyWorks

Management by Objectives

For years, both managers and management researchers have wondered how much of a difference planning made in organizational performance, or whether it really made any difference at all. While proponents argued that planning encouraged workers to work hard, to persist in their efforts, to engage in behaviours directly related to goal accomplishment, and to develop better strategies for achieving goals, opponents argued that planning impeded organizational change and adaptation, created the illusion of managerial control, and artificially separated thinkers and doers.

Now, however, the results from 70 different organizations strongly support the effectiveness of management by objectives (i.e., short-term planning).

Management by Objectives (MBO)

Management by objectives is a process in which managers and subordinates at all levels in a company sit down together to jointly set goals, to share information and discuss strategies that could lead to goal achievement, and to regularly meet to review progress toward accomplishing those goals. Thus, MBO is based on goals, participation, and feedback. On average, companies that effectively use MBO will out-produce those that don't use MBO by an incredible 44.6 percent! And in companies where top management is committed to MBO, that is, where objective setting begins at the top, the average increase in performance is an even more astounding 56.5 percent. By contrast, when top management does not participate in or support MBO, the average increase in productivity drops to 6.1 percent. In all, though, there is a 97 percent chance that companies that use MBO will outperform those that don't! Thus, MBO can make a very big difference to the companies that use it.

MBO

Source: R. Rodgers & J.E. Hunter, "Impact of Management by Objectives on Organizational Productivity," *Journal of Applied Psychology* 76 (1991): 322–336.

3.3 Finishing at the Bottom

operational plans
day-to-day plans, developed and implemented by lower-level managers, for producing or delivering the organization's products and services over a 30-day to 6-month period

Lower-level managers are responsible for developing and carrying out **operational plans**, which are the day-to-day plans for producing or delivering the organization's products and services. Operational plans direct the behaviour, efforts, and priorities of operative employees for periods ranging from 30 days to six months. There are three kinds of operational plans: single-use plans, standing plans, and budgets.

single-use plans
plans that cover unique, one-time-only events

Single-use plans deal with unique, one-time-only events. For example, Canadian Pacific Ltd., a huge Calgary-based conglomerate perhaps best known as the owner of CP Rail, broke up into five separate companies, each now traded on the Toronto Stock Exchange. The company felt that its full value was not being realized and that shareholders would benefit from the ability of each of the five divisions (railways, coal, hotels, shipping, and energy) to develop independent strategies. The decision proved to be very successful. A year after the breakup, the sum of Canadian Pacific Ltd.'s parts was worth about 30 percent more, during a period when the largest 60 public firms in Canada had fallen in value by 14 percent.[46]

standing plans
plans used repeatedly to handle frequently recurring events

Unlike single-use plans that are created, carried out, and then never used again, **standing plans** save managers time, because they are created once and then used repeatedly to handle frequently recurring events. If you encounter a problem that you've seen before, someone in your company has probably written a standing plan that explains how to address it. There are three kinds of standing plans: policies, procedures, and rules and regulations.

policy
standing plan that indicates the general course of action that should be taken in response to a particular event or situation

Policies indicate the general course of action that company managers should take in response to a particular event or situation. A well-written policy will also specify why the policy exists and what outcome the policy is intended to produce. For example, most Canadian employers have an employment equity policy. The Canadian Imperial Bank of Commerce (www.cibc.com) has its employment equity policy posted on its careers page. It states that the "CIBC is an equal opportunity employer. It is the Company's policy to recruit and select applicants for employment solely on the basis of their qualifications, with emphasis on selecting the best-qualified person for the job. CIBC does not discriminate against applicants based on race, colour, religion, sex, national origin, disability or any other status or condition protected by applicable federal, [provincial] or local law."[47] Companies have these policies in place partly in response to federal and provincial law but also due to a growing recognition among companies that it is in their best interest to have a diversified workforce and that it is a socially responsible thing to do. This policy is intended to provide guidance to managers as they handle many human resource functions.

Procedures are more specific than policies, because they indicate the series of steps that should be taken in response to a particular event. For example, when the Canadian Human Rights Commission (www.chrc-ccdp.ca) receives a complaint from an individual who claims to have been discriminated against, it follows very specific procedures. A complaints officer assesses the application to see if it meets certain criteria and in most cases sends the complaint on to mediation. If this fails, then an investigator is assigned and given the nature of the investigator's report, the complaint may go on to conciliation.[48]

Rules and regulations are even more specific than procedures, because they specify what must happen or not happen. They describe precisely how a particular action should be performed. For instance, rules and regulations forbid many managers from writing job reference letters for employees who have worked at their firms. Companies insist on such rules because a negative reference letter may prompt a former employee to sue for defamation of character.[49]

Another area in which companies are struggling to create effective rules and regulations is the Internet. For example, several years ago, a study by Nielsen Media Research found that of the 54 million "hits" to Penthouse Magazine's website during a two-month period, the most came from workers at IBM, Apple, Hewlett-Packard, and AT&T.[50] As a result of behaviours like these, more than 75 percent of major U.S. companies now block or monitor workers' Web use, while 38 percent review employees' e-mail. Tim Carney, founder of a network security firm, said, "If you're going to supply a company car, you can dictate they won't drag-race it. The same thing holds with Internet access."[51] The *New York Times* fired 22 employees for inappropriate use of e-mail, Xerox fired 40 people, and Dow Chemical fired 50 and disciplined 200 others for e-mailing and accessing pornographic material at work. In fact, one out of four companies has fired someone for inappropriate workplace use of the Internet. Why do companies need to take these steps? Because, says Roland Cloutier, at Brac Solutions, a network security firm, "you have Joe Schmoe going to some porno dot-com site while a female counterpart walks behind him, and it's a potential lawsuit."[52]

Budgets are the third kind of operational plan. **Budgeting** is quantitative planning, because it forces managers to decide how to allocate available money to best accomplish company goals. According to Jan King, author of *Business Plans to Game Plans*, "Money sends a clear message about your priorities. Budgets act as a language for communicating your goals to others."

procedure
standing plan that indicates the specific steps that should be taken in response to a particular event

rules and regulations
standing plans that describe how a particular action should be performed, or what must happen or not happen in response to a particular event

> ### EXPERIENCING MANAGEMENT
>
> Budgeting is a specific planning device that is also important in Control (see Chapter 6). To learn more about budgets, visit our animated concept and activity site. Choose Organizational Control from the "select a topic" pull-down menu, then Financial and Human Controls from the "overview tab." Budgeting is presented as one type of financial control.
>
> **www.experiencingmanagement.com**

budgeting
quantitative planning through which managers decide how to allocate available money to best accomplish company goals

Review 3
Planning from Top to Bottom

Proper planning requires that the goals at the bottom and middle of the organization support the objectives at the top of the organization. Top management develops strategic plans that indicate how a company will serve customers and position itself against competitors over a two- to five-year period. Strategic planning starts with the creation of an organizational vision and mission. There are four kinds of organization missions: targeting, common enemy, role model, and internal transformation. Middle managers use techniques such as management by objectives to develop tactical plans that direct behaviour, efforts, and priorities over the next six months to two years. Finally, lower-level managers develop operational plans that guide daily activities in producing or delivering an organization's products and services. Operational plans typically span periods ranging from 30 days to six months. There are three kinds of operational plans: single-use plans, standing plans (policies, procedures, and rules and regulations), and budgets.

4. Special-Purpose Plans

You wouldn't use a hammer to flip your pancakes. You wouldn't hire a Ph.D. in archeology to install a new hard drive in your computer. And you wouldn't light an acetylene torch to make popcorn. Everyone knows that a big part of getting a job done right is to hire people who know what they're doing. Or, if you're brave enough to try to fix something on your own, the secret to getting something done right is to use the right tools.

Plans are like tools and technicians. If you use the wrong one, your plan will fail. But if you use them for what they were intended, they'll serve you well. Let's examine how companies use special-purpose plans when they're planning for change, planning for contingencies, and planning for product development.

4.1 Planning for Change

People are creatures of habit. It's extremely difficult to get them to change. Therefore, managers and employees are more comfortable trying to achieve small incremental improvements than overhauling the way they do business. They know that if they work a little harder, plan a bit smarter, and don't catch any unlucky breaks, they should be able to hit 3 percent, 4 percent, or 5 percent improvement goals year after year.

However, sometimes doing more of the same won't improve business performance sufficiently to achieve the company's mission. When this is the case, companies use stretch goals. **Stretch goals**, by definition, are extremely ambitious goals that you don't know how to reach.[53] The purpose of stretch goals is to achieve extraordinary improvements in company performance. Stretch goals are so demanding that they force managers and workers to throw away old comfortable solutions and adopt radical, never-used solutions. Steve Kerr, former dean of the University of Southern California's Business School, who is now Morgan Stanley's "Chief Learning Officer," illustrates the idea of stretch goals with this story:

> You give a team an orange and say that each person must handle the orange—you can throw it to each other, do anything you want—but the orange has to end up in the hands of the person who started it. The group throws the orange back and forth, and you time it. The first time we did it, it took nine seconds. When asked to improve, they stood a little closer, threw it a little faster, and got it down to seven seconds. Then we said, "Many groups do this in less than a second, and it's possible to do it in less than half a second." In the third trial, the team did it in less than a second, by simply stacking up their hands. The guy with the orange dropped it, it went swoosh through everybody's hands, and he caught it at the bottom—that was it. It was a neat example of the power of a stretch goal.[54]

In 1991 Richmond Savings, a credit union located in Richmond, B.C., developed an ambitious ten-year business plan that set itself a goal of having 100 000 members and $2.8 billion in assets. In order to do this it undertook an ambitious marketing campaign using a fictitious bank known as Humungous Bank. The idea was to target consumers who were tired of the poor service at the largest six Canadian banks by poking fun at them. Richmond Savings wanted to highlight its responsiveness to the needs of its cus-

stretch goals
extremely ambitious goals that, initially, employees don't know how to accomplish

tomers, needs that it thought were not being met elsewhere. The ad campaign was credited with increasing membership by 55 percent to 80 000 and increasing the asset base to $2.8 billion. Richmond Savings has now merged with Pacific Coast Savings, headquartered in Victoria, B.C.[55] The two credit unions formed Coast Capital Savings and bought a third company, Surrey Metro Savings. Coast Capital now has assets of $6.1 billion and 300 000 members, making it the largest in the country. Clearly Richmond Savings' stretch goals paid off.

Since the first reaction to most stretch goals is "You've got to be kidding," Kerr recommends setting "achievable" stretch goals. However, knowing what is too easy (and thus not a stretch goal) and what is too difficult (and thus not achievable) is difficult. One way companies choose a stretch goal of just the right difficulty is by benchmarking. **Benchmarking** is the process of identifying outstanding practices, processes, and standards in other companies and adapting them to your company.[56] For example, one of the biggest hassles associated with most hospital stays is the amount of paperwork and time it takes to complete the admissions process. If you were a hospital administrator, who would you benchmark to learn how to streamline your slow, cumbersome admissions process? What business or company would know how to handle admissions-like situations and paperwork faster than your hospital? Well, many hospitals actually benchmark their admissions processes against Marriott Hotels. Think about it. Both admit people to rooms, typically for no more than a couple of nights, but longer if necessary. Both collect basic information, such as your name, address, phone number, and how payment will be made (a credit card for the hotel and a medical insurance card for the hospital). And both try to determine your preferences upon admission (smoking or nonsmoking room, the kind of room you desire, food preferences, etc.). The processes are nearly identical. Consequently, benchmarking helps employees realize that they can achieve extraordinary levels of performance; after all, it's being done at another company—in this case, Marriott.

Based on General Electric's experience, Kerr strongly recommends that companies not punish managers and workers when they fail to achieve stretch goals. Since the purpose of stretch goals is to achieve extraordinary improvements in performance, it is a mistake for companies to measure progress by assessing whether new levels of performance meet or fall short of the stretch goal. For example, Kerr would likely argue that it was wrong for DaimlerChrysler's board of directors to cut top management's annual bonuses by 18 percent because DaimlerChrysler failed to achieve stretch goals for improvements in car quality. Because of the inherent difficulty of stretch goals, companies need to assess progress by comparing new levels of performance to old levels. For example, though DaimlerChrysler's board punished top management by reducing its annual bonus, the punishment wasn't because quality didn't improve. DaimlerChrysler spokesperson Steve Harris said, "We just didn't reach the tough stretch goals we set," noting that DaimlerChrysler had made double-digit percentage improvements in quality in the last year.[57] What do you think? Did DaimlerChrysler managers fail because they didn't achieve their stretch goal? Or did they succeed because they achieved double-digit improvements in quality?

4.2 Planning for Contingencies

When senior managers from Duke Energy Corp., an electric utility company, met for a two-day meeting, their job was to confront three different scenarios about the future that might affect their business. In the first scenario, called the "economic treadmill," they assumed that economic growth would slow to just 1 percent a year. In this scenario, energy prices would drop, making it difficult for Duke to pay the significant debt it had accumulated in the last few years to build new electric plants. In the "market.com" scenario, the Internet would lead to fully deregulated market trading of electricity and gas, giving industrial and home buyers an advantage over energy producers and sellers. Finally, the "flawed competition" scenario assumes that deregulation will be uneven and inconsistent from place to place, producing volatile swings in energy demand, supply,

benchmarking
the process of identifying outstanding practices, processes, and standards in other companies and adapting them to your company

and prices. Why is Duke considering these different planning scenarios? Because with $13.5 billion in debt to pay off, even small changes in growth, energy costs, or deregulation could affect the profitability of the company by tens of millions of dollars.[58]

scenario planning
the process of developing plans to deal with several possible future events and trends that might affect the business

Scenario planning is the process of developing plans to deal with events and trends that might affect a business in the future. It helps managers answer "what if" questions and prepare responses should those "what if" scenarios actually occur. You probably do scenario planning often in your own life. Your plans could go something like this: "If I get the scholarship I applied for, I won't work this term. If I don't get it, I'll apply to work in the library."

Scenario planning was first used extensively in World War II when teams of Allied military strategists created scenarios by assuming the role of enemy battle planners. Their job was to devise alternative strategies that enemy forces might use to attack Allied troops and to figure out the best way to defend against each strategy.[59] By anticipating possible enemy strategies and planning actions to counter each one, Allied commanders could be ready no matter which strategy the enemy actually employed.

Scenario planning can be broken down into these steps:[60]

1. *Define the scope of the scenario.* The scope might include a time frame, assumptions about the product, and a geographic area in which the scenario is to take place. For example, a hospital might create a scenario like this:

   > Ten years from now, most hospital care (the product) will be short-term or outpatient treatment, and rather than just treating local community residents, our hospital will serve a wider geographic area, as doctors use the Internet and teleconferencing to offer medical analysis and treatment to patients who currently live too far away to be treated by hospital staff.

2. *Identify the major stakeholders (customers, suppliers, competitors, government, etc.) and the roles you expect them to play in the scenario.*

3. *Identify basic political, economic, societal, technological, competitive, and legal trends that you expect to occur in the scenario.*

4. *Identify key uncertainties and the likely outcomes associated with them.* One of the key uncertainties is how hospitals will change if they primarily provide short-term and outpatient care. Will they become much smaller? If so, will they need fewer doctors, nurses, and staffers? Will this make it easier or more difficult for hospitals to be more efficient? Another set of uncertainties would be the legal questions surrounding "distant" care. Traditionally, medical care requires doctors to have face-to-face visits with their patients. However, with technology allowing doctors to recommend treatment without traditional face-to-face visits, would patients be more likely to sue if something went wrong? Would hospitals and doctors then deal with the threat of lawsuits by requiring patients to sign waivers in order to gain access to "distant" care?

5. *Using Steps 1 through 4, put together your initial scenarios.* A common technique is to write scenarios that use different combinations of key uncertainties. Another is to create best-case and worst-case scenarios.

6. *Check for consistency and plausibility of facts and assumptions in each scenario.* The key here is to make sure that the scenario holds together as a whole. There shouldn't be any obviously inconsistent facts. For example, if the scenario states that the use of "distant" care will increase, it wouldn't make sense to also write that hospitals would be spending less money on technology when, in fact, they'd probably be spending much more. Before being used, each scenario should be read and checked by a number of people within an organization and industry.

7. *Write the final scenarios and conduct a series of planning sessions for management teams to develop contingency plans for each scenario.*

8. *Develop measures or signposts for each scenario that allow managers to know when the events predicted in this scenario are occurring.* Once scenarios have been created, signposts or measures serve as triggers to let managers know when their business environments have changed (i.e., various scenarios) and when they should implement action plans to address those changes. For example, at Solutia, a chemical company, managers put together four different short-term outcomes for each scenario, with each set of outcomes containing short-term signposts that allow the company to abandon or embrace different scenarios or strategies in days. These signposts proved effective when Solutia was deciding whether to resell another company's chemical, one used in computer chip production. At first, said Mitch Pulwer, Solutia's chief scenario strategist, "We thought that because of our expertise, we'd have a wonderful new business opportunity here." But when one of the key signposts, prices for chip memory, dropped significantly, Solutia decided against the project within days.[61]

4.3 Planning for Product Development

Drip, drip, drip. Time to replace that leaky faucet? Just a few years ago, your only choice would have been chrome, not pretty, but functional. However, that changed when Moen, which manufactures plumbing fixtures, decided it was in the home decorating business, selling "jewelry for the bathroom and the kitchen." President Jeff Svoboda calls this Moen's "9 to 5" strategy, meaning that if customers had a choice of new styles, they would buy a new Moen faucet every five years instead of every nine years (www.moen.com). The only problem was that Moen averaged only one new product line per year. Today, though, Moen's 50 design engineers work on three to fifteen new faucet product lines per year. The speed-up was accomplished by using "ProjectNet," an online collaboration site where Moen's designers share product plans and designs with suppliers all over the world. When a supplier makes changes, those changes are then saved in a master Web file for later use, cutting development time by one-third. Likewise, Moen has used its website to even allow customers to design and customize their kitchens, bathrooms, and faucets. So with more products being developed at a faster pace, Moen's sales are up dramatically in the last few years, moving it from third in the industry to a tie for first.[62]

Product development is an increasingly important competitive tool. Like Moen, companies that are the first to market with new products or newly redesigned products that customers want can quickly increase market share, earn higher profits, and stay ahead of competitors who are forced to play catch-up.

The first step in effective product-development planning is to create an aggregate project plan.[63] Because very few companies can survive by relying on just one product, companies develop **aggregate product plans** to manage and monitor all new products in development at any one time. Aggregate product plans should indicate the resources (funds, equipment, facilities, materials, and employees) being used for each product and that product's place within the company's mission and strategic plan.

aggregate product plans
plans developed to manage and monitor all new products in development at any one time

More than anything else, aggregate product plans help companies avoid the classic mistake of having too many products in development at any one time. For example, in one subsidiary of an American firm, a product-development staff of 40 people was responsible for almost 140 projects. Not surprisingly, the subsidiary's managing director complained that "nothing is getting done as well as we would like." And when asked if all 140 projects were equally important to the company, he replied, "We have no method of weighing the merits of one against another."[64] By contrast, after creating an aggregate product plan, a large manufacturer of scientific instruments and laboratory equipment reduced the number of products it planned to develop by nearly two-thirds. After topping out at a high of 30 products, it now has a much more manageable group of 11 products, all of which are consistent with the company's long-term strategic goals.

Besides keeping the overall set of products in balance and limited to a reasonable number, the second step is effective management of the product-development process itself. Four factors lead to a better, faster product-development process: cross-functional teams, internal and external communication, overlapping development phases, and frequent testing of product prototypes.[65]

Cross-functional teams, which are made up of individuals from different functional backgrounds (e.g., manufacturing, engineering, marketing), make better product-development decisions. The diversity of functional backgrounds means that cross-functional teams have a greater amount and variety of information, knowledge, and experience available as they develop new products. At food manufacturer Sara Lee, cross-functional teams test and bring new food products to market. Paul Bernthal, senior vice president of Research and Development, said, "One of our core competencies is the diverse background of our R&D group. Our staff has backgrounds in culinary arts, food science, meat science, grain science, animal science, package engineering, and chemical engineering, with varying degrees, including B.S., M.S., M.B.A. and Ph.D." He continued, "As a development company, cross-functional teams help bring us to market more quickly. And with all of us under one roof, there is a greater understanding of each group's functions."[66] According to Sandy Glatter, director of Bakery Research and Development, when Sara Lee was testing its new microwave calzone products (a calzone is pizza dough with meat, cheeses, or veggies baked in the middle), "We utilized our meat products group and combined their expertise with the bakery side to enter a category that we were not competing in—hand-held sandwiches." Then, "We leveraged our refrigerated folks to help determine the types of meats that should go inside and truly differentiate our product, making Calzone Creations live up to the Sara Lee name."[67]

Frequent internal and external communication is the second critical factor in the product-development process. Like cross-functional teams, frequent internal communication between product-development team members increases the amount of relevant information used to make decisions. It also builds group cohesion and reduces mistakes and misunderstandings that are commonplace in the product-development process. External communication with outsiders, such as customers and suppliers, broadens development team members' perspectives by helping them see their product and its uses through others' eyes. While communication with outsiders is typically beneficial, development teams may want to give more weight to what customers and suppliers do with new products (during product testing) than what they say they will do. For example, surveys and focus groups of fast-food restaurant customers usually result in the same conclusion: customers say they want healthier, low-fat food on the menu. However, Taco Bell's Border Lights, McDonald's McLean, Kentucky Fried Chicken's skinless chicken, and Pizza Hut's low-cal pizza all flopped and have been removed from restaurant menus. Not surprisingly, a National Restaurant Association study found a large difference between what people say they will eat (fruit, vegetables, etc.) and what they really eat (cheeseburgers and french fries).[68]

Overlapping development phases is the third critical factor when planning the product-development process. In contrast to a sequential design process, where each step (product plans and specs, product testing, product roll-out) must be completed before beginning the next step, overlapping development means multiple product-development steps and phases are started and completed at the same time. Exhibit 4.6 shows the development time line used by Silicon Graphics Incorporated (SGI) to develop one of its new "supercomputer" computer servers. The white rectangles indicate traditional planning processes. Here, SGI created the block diagram (the general plan) and the system specifications (the details behind the plan) that it wanted in its new computer. Notice, however, that product testing, indicated by the grey (computer software simulations) and black rectangles (prototype hardware testing), began long before SGI had completed its plans and detailed product specifications. The primary advantage of overlapping development is that it speeds up product development and makes the entire process much

EXHIBIT 4.6

SILICON GRAPHICS: OVERLAPPING PRODUCT-DEVELOPMENT PHASES FOR A NEW "SUPERCOMPUTER" SERVER

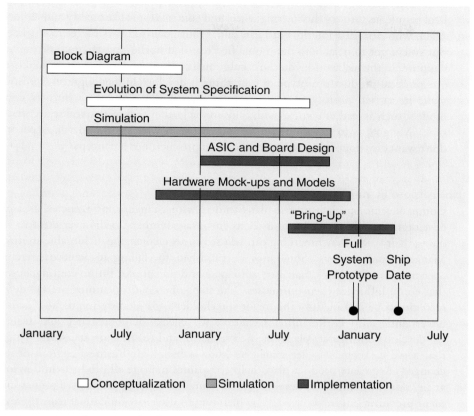

Source: Copyright © 1995, by The Regents of the University of California. Reprinted from the *California Management Review*, Vol. 38, no. 1. By permission of The Regents.

more flexible. In fact, SGI began software simulation testing just four months after product development began. And by having customers participate in product testing at an early stage, SGI had the flexibility to incorporate their feedback (and any last-minute changes in computer technology—which always occur at a rapid pace).[69]

The last critical component in the product-development process is frequent testing of product prototypes. A **product prototype** is a full-scale, working model that is being tested for design, function, and reliability. A good product plan or blueprint is essential. Very few new products succeed without them. But planning is no substitute for the hands-on learning that comes from frequent testing of product prototypes. At Lear Corporation, which designs and makes automotive interiors for companies such as General Motors, designers, engineers, and sculptors used to make initial design prototypes with 3D clay models of seats and doors. These days, however, with advanced CAD (computer-aided design) software, prototyping is as much "virtual" as it is "hands-on." In fact, Lear has constructed a special "reality centre" with a screen stretching 6 metres wide and 2.5 metres tall to view computerized prototypes. As the lights come down and the computerized 3D design is projected onto the screen, it feels as if you're actually sitting in a new car. Glance to the right and you view the centre console and controls. Turn to your right and view the passenger seat. Make the computer "glance" over your "right shoulder" and you can see what the back seat looks like, too.[70] Normally, it takes Lear three years to completely design the interior of a new car, but with its CAD-based virtual-reality prototypes, it has been able to cut that development time in half.

product prototype
a full-scale, working model of a final product that is being tested for design, function, and reliability

Prototype testing works best as a "hands-on" process. It begins by testing a prototype, making changes in the product based on what you learned, testing the new version of the prototype, and then making changes again, and so on. While Lear now makes many of these tests and changes on computers, it realized that there are limitations to completely relying on computer-based design prototypes. Leather seats have to be sat on. Real people need to try the steering wheel and controls for functionality and logic. Steven Allen, who designed interiors at Lear, said, "Our goal is always to get to market faster. But you've got to be able to put a qualified rear end in the seat. If you don't understand sculpture in the real world, you can't sculpt on a computer." So Lear always makes at least one physical product prototype of everything it develops in its design centre. In fact, to make its virtual prototypes more realistic, Lear builds "mistakes" into its computer models, such as leather textures with folds in the leather that mimic real seats. Steve Allen said, "My goal is to destroy the difference between what's real and what's perceived. I don't want any doubt that you're looking at a product, not a concept."[71]

Review 4
Special-Purpose Plans

Companies use special-purpose plans to deal with change, contingencies, and product development. Stretch goals are used to encourage workers to discover creative ways of doing their work. Benchmarking can be used to set challenging, achievable stretch goals. Managers and workers should not be punished for failing to achieve stretch goals. Scenario planning helps managers anticipate and prepare for future contingency factors that could influence their businesses. The steps of scenario planning are (1) define the scenario scope, (2) identify the major stakeholders, (3) identify trends, (4) identify key uncertainties, (5) create initial scenarios, (6) check for consistency and plausibility, (7) develop contingency plans for each scenario, and (8) develop measures or signposts that serve as triggers to let managers know when their business environments have changed. Aggregate product plans help companies manage all products in development at any one time and avoid developing too many low-priority products. Product-development processes can be accelerated by planning to use cross-functional teams, promoting internal and external communication, using overlapping development phases, and frequently testing product prototypes.

What Really Happened?

Air Canada faced a serious problem at the beginning of the chapter. It had already lost market share in western Canada, and now WestJet was slowly marching eastward into markets that Air Canada dominated. WestJet had a significantly lower cost structure and its growth seemed to be unstoppable. By contrast, Air Canada was stuck with a much higher cost structure and a stagnant or even shrinking market share.

Given the current circumstances and constraints, what would improve Air Canada's competitive position? How could they possibly stop the continuous erosion of their market?

Planning is one of the best ways to improve organizational and individual performance. It encourages people to work harder (intensified effort), to work hard for extended periods (persistence), to engage in behaviours directly related to goal accomplishment (directed behaviour), and to think of better ways to do their jobs (task strategies). But most important, companies that plan have larger profits and faster growth than companies that don't plan. For Air Canada to have a successful plan, it needed to set specific goals, develop commitment to goals, develop action plans, track progress, and maintain flexibility. Air Canada's foremost goals were to keep WestJet from continuing to take away its market share and to reverse its financial losses.

There is a danger for decision makers, however, when it becomes widely believed that there is only one way to solve a problem. When top management sits around a table and quickly decides that layoffs are the answer without considering any other options, this danger is called "groupthink" or "satisficing." Yet, regardless of the label you attach to it, premature definition of the problem ("We've got too many employees.") and limited consideration of alternative solutions ("We've got no choice. We have to start layoffs.") will almost always produce poor decisions and poor results. Air Canada had

already laid off a substantial number of workers but the losses continued. It had to address the three major cost items that were keeping ticket prices high: labour costs, service levels, and using multiple types of aircraft.

What alternatives were available that directly addressed the different cost structures?

The first step in decision-making is defining the problem, that is, figuring out what's going wrong. The traditional way to do that is to look for gaps between desired states and existing states. If you remember from the beginning of the chapter, the higher cost structure was the result of the three main factors: labour costs, service levels and use of multiple types of aircraft. Clearly Air Canada had to focus on these issues.

How could Air Canada address these key cost issues?

Air Canada took a bold and risky move. It launched two new no-frills airlines called Tango, launched in October 2001, and Zip, launched in September 2002. It was hoped these two airlines would mimic the success of WestJet and Southwest Airlines. Zip is based in Calgary and is focused on the western Canadian short-haul market. It started with six planes and hopes to grow to twenty. It is intended that this service would complement longer-haul Air Canada flights and provide "seamless" service connecting to these flights. Tango, on the other hand, is intended to compete directly with Air Canada. It focuses on the medium and long-haul market and is also expected to grow to 20 aircraft. Both are intended to be low-cost, no-frills carriers. Each airline is intended to fly only one type of aircraft in order to cut costs. Tango will fly Boeing 737s while Zip will fly Airbus A320s.

The move is by no means guaranteed to resurrect Air Canada's fortunes. Other large international airlines such as British Airways have launched low-cost subsidiaries and have generally failed in the attempt as the low-cost

subsidiaries found it very difficult to disentangle themselves from the parent airline's high cost structure. There is also the problem that Air Canada could cannibalize higher-paying passengers from itself to its lower-cost airlines thereby reducing its overall revenue and possibly even profits. Also, attempts to reduce labour costs, while somewhat successful, have been fraught with troubles. Many of the unions at Air Canada resisted the launch of Tango and Zip and claimed that all employees of Tango and Zip should work under the same conditions as at Air Canada, resulting in no savings in labour costs. Air Canada wanted to pay employees at Tango less while at Zip they wanted to merge three employee groups that have direct contact with customers into a single bargaining group (reservation agents, passenger agents, and flight attendants) to increase workforce flexibility and also pay lower wages. At the time of writing, the labour problems at Tango seemed to have been settled with the unions agreeing to reduced wages while limiting Tango to 20 planes in order to protect Air Canada jobs. In September 2002 Air Canada reached an agreement with two of its largest unions over the operation of Zip and a third union has put its Canadian Industrial Relations Board complaint on hold. Zip was not able to combine work groups but the agreements lowered wages and introduced more flexible work rules while limiting ZIP to 20 planes. Despite the rocky start, Air Canada turned a profit in the second and third quarters of 2002, something they attributed at least in part to the launch of Tango. It was also the first international North American carrier to turn a quarterly profit since the terrorist attacks on the World Trade Center. Whether these changes have been sufficient to change the long-term fortunes of Air Canada is not known yet and Air Canada has been hit hard by the Iraqi conflict, SARS, and a weakening economy. They lost money in the last quarter of 2002 and were forced to seek bankruptcy protection in April 2003.

They are now seeking concessions from unions and creditors. Only time will tell if this strategy will return them to fiscal health.

Sources: Joel Baglole, "Airlines in Turmoil: Air Canada Files for Protection from Creditors," *The Wall Street Journal*, 2 April 2003, A2. Frances Fiorino, "Air Canada Adds 'Zip' to Low-Fare Market," *Aviation Week and Space Technology* 156, no. 17. Peter Fitzpatrick, "Air Canada to Slash 6,000 Jobs, Cut Fleet in Bid to Save $500m: 'Industry in Freefall'," *Financial Post*, 25 September 2001, B1, B4. Peter Fitzpatrick, "Leaner Air Canada Back in the Black," *Financial Post*, 2 August 2002, FP6. Perry Flint, "Interview: Zip President and CEO Steve Smith," *Air Transport World* 39, no. 6 (June 2002): 68. C.C. Miller, "Strategic Planning and Firm Performance: A Synthesis of More Than Two Decades of Research," *Academy of Management Review* 37 (1994): 1649–1665. Kevin Restivo, "Air Canada Unions Won't Acquiesce to Pay Cuts: Want Books Opened First," *National Post*, 5 May 2003, FP 1. Allan Swift, "Air Canada's Tango Brand Doing Better Than Expected Says CEO," *Canadian Press Newswire*, 2 May 2002. Allan Swift, "Air Canada Reports $125 Million Q3 Earning," *Canadian Press Newswire*, 25 October 2002. Peter Verburg, "Emergency Exit," *Canadian Business* 75, no. 19 (14 October 2002): 16.

Key Terms

action plan (100)	mission (105)	S.M.A.R.T. goals (98)
aggregate product plans (115)	operational plans (110)	scenario planning (114)
benchmarking (113)	options-based planning (102)	single-use plans (110)
budgeting (111)	planning (94)	standing plans (110)
common-enemy mission (107)	policy (110)	strategic plans (104)
distal goals (100)	procedure (111)	stretch goals (112)
goal commitment (99)	product prototype (117)	tactical plans (107)
internal-transformation mission (107)	proximal goals (100)	targeting (106)
learning-based planning (102)	role-model mission (107)	vision (104)
management by objectives (107)	rules and regulations (111)	

What Would You Do II?

Tupperware, We're Still Here!

Mention the term "brand recognition" and people will immediately think about brand names such as Coca-Cola, McDonald's, and Tupperware. That's right, Tupperware, the name your mum believed in and trusted for years, still exists. Only a few consumers have trouble visualizing the "Super Crisp-It," the plastic device that magically keeps a head of lettuce grocery-fresh for weeks at a time.

However, many consumers today are unaware of where to go to buy Tupperware's products. For over 50 years, Tupperware products have been sold only through commissioned sales representatives. These sales representatives have been demonstrating Tupperware products in customers' homes through their famed Tupperware parties. At a typical party, the hostess invites many friends who delight in the preparation of a microwave-cooked meal and who are fascinated by the unique timesaving abilities provided by the Tupperware products. As an incentive for offering the use of her home, the hostess keeps many of the demonstrated items. In-home demonstrations and direct selling by product representatives have been the only avenues available for customers to purchase Tupperware products in the past.

Unfortunately, since a majority of women are working today, in addition to raising a family and maintaining a household, Tupperware parties are beginning to lose their edge nationwide. Most families cannot afford the precious time needed to offer or attend a Tupperware demonstration, even though many of the products can be demonstrated during one's lunch hour.

Increased competition has also begun to cut into Tupperware's ability to promote their products. Many manufacturers, such as Glad, Rubbermaid, and Sterilite, are producing food storage containers and utensils that compete directly with Tupperware's products. Additionally, these competing products are found in most local retail shops, further affecting Tupperware's sales. Direct selling has seen an increase in competition as well. Tupperware and others, such as Avon, Mary Kay, and Kirby, initially dominated the direct-selling market. Now many other products are sold in a similar format, including Pampered Chef and Home Interiors, who utilize a party format similar to Tupperware's.

In spite of increased competition and a resulting decrease in Tupperware demonstrations, Tupperware has flourished in other parts of the world. Currently, Tupperware products are available in over 100 countries, which provided $1.7 billion of revenue last year, an 8 percent increase over the previous fiscal year.

Despite the apparent success, as president of Tupperware, you believe that more can be done to improve sales and build product awareness. You need a plan to make your products more accessible to consumers and promote continued brand awareness. What kind of strategy will work? And what should your goals be? After all, you need a success.

If you were the president of Tupperware, what would you do?

Sources: "Tupperware Corp.: Target Venture Paves Way for Products' Retail Debut," *The Wall Street Journal*, 18 July 2001 http://interactive. wsj.com. S. Kapellusch, "Mall Kiosks Raise Tupperware Image," *Arizona Republic*, 3 November 1999. Tupperware website, www.tupperware.com, Annual Report, 29 July 2001.

Critical Thinking Video Case

Gun Registry

Planning is choosing a goal and developing a method or strategy to achieve that goal. In 1995, the Canadian government announced a plan to implement a national gun registry. In 2000 it passed Bill C-68, which created a central registry for every firearm in Canada; it was intended that all firearms be registered by December 31, 2002. The registry would be available to police forces across the country in the hopes that it would help them prevent crime. When the program was announced, the federal government said that the net cost to taxpayers would be $2 million to set up the registry, as the bulk of the costs for the registry was to be covered by registration fees.

By 2002, the auditor general had determined that the full taxpayer cost would be closer to $1 billion, and gun owners were having difficulty registering their firearms. As a result, the gov-ernment was forced to extend the registration deadline to June 30, 2003. This massive cost overrun and administrative mis-management is now being used by critics of the bill as a reason to scrap the project. Even some people who support the bill are having second thoughts, given the huge cost increases and problems associated with the program. Clearly there were problems with the implementation of the program.

Critical Thinking Questions

1. If you were in charge of the gun registry program, what sort of goals would you set for the program?
2. What would be the key elements of your action plan?
3. What proximal and distal goals would you set?
4. What do you think was the cause of the problems in this case?

Management Decisions

What's Your Policy?

Ah, what's this, a Post-it note from the boss attached to a couple of newspaper articles? The first story is about a McDonald's manager who used the company voice-mail system to record "intimate exchanges" with a co-worker. For reasons that were not made clear in the article, McDonald's later played the tape for his wife. The manager sued, claiming that his voice-mail messages were private and protected because they could be accessed only by someone who possessed his voice-mail security password. McDonald's countered by claiming that since the voice-mail system was owned, run, and maintained by the company, nothing contained on the voice-mail system could be construed as personal or private.

The second news story is about Irene Wechselberg, a university librarian who works in the rare books department. Like most people, a large percentage of the e-mails that she sends and receives on her university e-mail account are business-related. However, some are personal. When Irene went on medical leave, her supervisor asked for her e-mail password so that the library staff could keep up with her responsibilities. (No doubt, Irene subscribed to several professional listserv groups that kept her informed on issues related to rare books.) When she refused, calling the request an "invasion of privacy," the university redirected all her e-mail to her supervisor's computer. The campus is now in an uproar over this issue. The article quoted Daniel Tsang, a biographer and host of a campus radio show, as saying, "Just because the university owns the public buildings, does that mean the state has the right to install cameras in the bathroom?"

Oh, here's a second Post-it note from the boss. "ASAP, write a policy that makes clear to all employees the appropriate and inappropriate uses of e-mail. Without a clear policy, we're leaving ourselves exposed to problems, controversies, and potential lawsuits. Have a draft in my e-mail account by 9:00 a.m. Monday."

Questions

1. Before writing a rough draft of the e-mail policy, specify, in writing, the purpose of the policy and its desired outcomes.
2. Write a rough draft of the new e-mail policy for your company. Be as specific as possible about appropriate and inappropriate uses of e-mail. Keep the policy short, no more than a page. Since it will be used to guide the actions of everyone in the company, make it easy to read and understand (no techno-speak).

Sources: M. Miller, "Should Email Be Private? UC, Employees Tangle over Rights of University to Access Computers of Staff on Leave," *Los Angeles Times*, 12 November 1995. D.H. Seifman & C.W. Trepanier, "Email and Voicemail Systems," *Employee Relations Law Journal*, 1 December 1995. D. Young, "Office Email: There's No Right of Privacy," *Chicago Tribune*, 8 April 1996.

Management Decisions

Cell Phone Dilemma

You've just finished watching a CTV news item on Newfoundland's recent ban on using hand-held cell phones while driving, something that has happened in over 30 countries. You agree that talking on a cell phone while driving, along with other activities such as eating or searching for a radio station, is a distraction and can increase the probability of having an accident.

As you think about the implications the ban may have on individuals and companies, you begin to realize that most of your employees currently use cell phones on the job, many while driving. Suddenly, you find yourself subconsciously practising scenario planning. Questions immediately pop into your head, such as would your company be held liable if an employee injures or kills someone while talking on a company-issued cell phone while driving? Should you develop a policy regarding safe cell phone use while driving? As a manufacturer, your company certainly has plenty of other safety policies in place, so perhaps one concerning cell phones is needed. You decide to investigate the matter further before drafting a cell phone safety proposal.

In doing some basic research, you discover a case involving an investment broker who, while using a company-provided cell phone, ran a red light and killed the driver of a motorcycle. The family of the motorcycle rider sued the broker's employer, claiming that the employer encouraged the broker to use his cell phone after hours to maintain contact with clients. Although the investment-banking firm did not admit fault, it decided to avoid a jury trial by settling the suit for $750 000. Now you believe you have the ammunition needed to draft an operational plan about cell phone safety.

Questions

1. Do you need a policy, a set of procedures, or rules and regulations? Or maybe all three?
2. As the manager in question, draft the appropriate operational plan(s) for this situation.

Sources: S. Shellenbarger, "Should Employers Set Limits on Cellphone Use in Vehicles?," *The Wall Street Journal*, 18 July 2001, B1. "Survey Shows About 3 Percent of Drivers Are Using Cellphones at Any Time," *The Wall Street Journal*, B1. 24 July 2001, www.wsj.com, www.ctv.ca/servlet/ArticleNews/story/CTVNews/1049066881078_88//, accessed 20 May, 2003.

Develop Your Management Potential

What Do You Want To Be When You Grow Up?

What do you want to be when you grow up? Still not sure? Ask around. You're not alone. Chances are, your friends and relatives aren't certain either. Sure, they may have jobs and careers, but what you're likely to find out is that, professionally, many of them don't want to be where they are today. One reason this occurs is that people's interests change. Burnout is another reason that people change their minds about what they want to be when they grow up. For example, a former lawyer, Michael Stone, said, "I hated it." So he and a partner created a licensing agency that helps companies obtain licences to sell products bearing the names and logos of corporations such as Coca-Cola and Harley-Davidson. Another reason some people are unhappy with their current jobs or careers is that they were never in the right one to begin with. For example, lawyer Marsha Cohen said that it took the results of a personality test for her to realize why she disliked her jobs in large organizations. The reason? She was an introvert. Today, she runs her own small practice in international business and is much happier.

Getting the job and career you want is not easy. It takes time, effort, and persistence. Moreover, in today's ever-more-mobile society, it's common for people to have three to five fairly different career paths over the course of their working lives. No matter what you decide to be "when you grow up," your career-planning process will be easier (and more effective!) if you take the time to develop a personal career plan.

Write a personal career plan by answering the following questions. (Hint: Type it up. Treat this seriously. If you do it effectively, this plan could guide your career decisions for the next five to seven years.)

Questions

1. Describe your strengths and weaknesses. Don't just rely on your opinions of your abilities. Ask your parents, relatives, friends, and employers what they think, too. Encourage them to be honest and then be prepared to hear some things that you may not want to hear. Remember, though, this information can help you pick the right job or career.

2. Write an advertisement for the job you want to have five years from now. Be specific. Describe the company, title, responsibilities, required education, required experience, salary, and benefits that you desire. If you're not sure where to begin, model the advertisement for your ideal job after the employment ads appearing in the Sunday job listings.

3. Create a detailed plan to obtain this job. In the short term, what classes do you need to take? Do you need to change your major? Do you need to get a business major or minor or maybe a minor in a foreign language? What kind of summer work experience will move you closer to getting the job you want five years from now? What job do you need to get right out of college in order to get the work experience you need? At the very least, you should have a specific plan for each of the five years in your career plan. Don't worry too much about locking in your fourth- and fifth-year plans. Those are likely to change anyway. The value in planning is that it forces you to think about what you want and what steps you can take now to help achieve those goals.

4. Decide when you will monitor and evaluate the progress you're making with your plan. Career experts suggest that every six months is about right. How about your birthday and six months after your birthday? Others prefer January 1 and July 4, the beginning and middle of the calendar year. Whatever dates you choose, write them in your schedule. Furthermore, right now, before you forget, set five specific, challenging goals that you need to accomplish in the next six months in order to accomplish your career plans.

Sources: "20 Hot Job Tracks," *U.S. News & World Report*, 30 October 1995, 98–104. C. Boivie, "Planning for the Future . . . Your Future," *Journal of Systems Management* 44 (1993): 25–27. J. Connelly, "How to Choose Your Next Career," *Fortune*, 6 February 1995, 145–146. P. Sherrid, "A 12-Hour Test of My Personality," *U.S. News & World Report*, 31 October 1994, 109.

Discussion Questions

1. What activities can managers undertake to enhance goal commitment? What activities will detract from goal commitment?
2. Is there a difference between a company's vision and its mission? Give examples.
3. What is the difference between a policy and a procedure? Give examples.
4. How could you use management by objective to complete (a) this course, (b) this semester, (c) your diploma/degree?

Study Tip

Try to explain the key concepts of this chapter to a friend or family member who is not taking the class with you. This will help you identify areas where you need to review—and how much.

CHAPTER 5

Chapter Outline

Learning Objectives

After reading this chapter, you should be able to

1. explain the strategic importance of information.
2. describe the characteristics of useful information.
3. explain the basics of capturing, storing, processing, and protecting information.
4. describe how companies can share and access information and knowledge.

five

Managing Information

What Would You Do?

It's hard to imagine a more successful company than Dell Computers over the last 15 years. It was started in Michael Dell's dorm room at the University of Texas at Austin in the mid-1980s, and a $1000 investment at Dell's inception would have been worth more than $100 000 after just six years. In recent years, Dell Computers (www.dell.com) has grown so fast and been so profitable that sales jumped from $3.4 to $12.3 billion (U.S.) per year while profits leapt from $140 to $944 billion (U.S.). Furthermore, Dell's share of the PC market has doubled, and it continues to grow twice as fast as any of its competitors.

Dell achieved that growth by selling faster, more powerful, more expensive personal computers to more experienced buyers who were willing to pay a premium for a better personal computer. Dell's chief financial officer said, "Increasingly, we find that we don't need a discount. We are winning on quality and service." Likewise, catering to experienced buyers made sense for Dell because they needed less hand-holding and were thus less expensive to serve than new computer users.

However, the PC business has changed substantially in the last few years. As *Fortune* magazine described it, "Making PCs has been, is, and will continue to be a nasty business. It's a business in which competitors cut prices literally every week, where the product you make is obsolete just months after you make it, where customers choose between your boxes and essentially similar boxes made by a slew of rivals." If you're slow to sell a PC with a 16x speed CD-ROM because it's priced too high, you're certainly not going to be able to sell it when the technology races ahead two months later and your competitor sells the same PC with a 32x speed CD-ROM for 10 percent less than your machine. In other words, in the new PC business, computer components age quickly and can quickly lose their market value, if not their entire value in less than a year. With prices dropping below $1500 a machine (most people can remember when the average price of a PC was $7000!), and with those machines having basically the same components, will customers necessarily care any more about buying from Dell?

Thus, while Dell's initial strategy of "building a better box" worked great in the past, as prices on PCs drop like a rock, it's unlikely to work as well in the future. But this won't be the first time that Dell and his company have had to make major adjustments. Five years ago, when the company grew so fast it was spiralling out of control, Michael Dell brought in experienced top managers to manage the growth and the company's day-to-day operations, leaving him to focus on strategic issues and direction.

With PC prices dropping so quickly and technological advances moving so fast, the key is no longer just building a better PC, but quickly building a PC with the latest technological components at an aggressive price. However, doesn't that mean that Dell and its memory, hard drive, chip, and motherboard suppliers will have to work more closely (i.e., share more information) than they ever have before? How can that be done? And if Dell and its suppliers can figure out how to do that, won't that mean that its competitors can do the same thing? Why invest in an information system if it gives you only a temporary competitive advantage? If your competitors can buy the same inventory and customer tracking software that you have, you're only temporarily ahead of the game. Finally, in such a fast-moving, competitive environment, if information is the key, how is Dell to make sense of all the information it generates from customers, uses within the company, and then shares with its suppliers? Having lots of data doesn't do you any good unless you know how to figure out what they mean. So what should Dell do with all that information once it gets its hands on it?

If you were in charge at Dell Computers, what would you do?

Sources: C. Lydgate, "Cutting Out the Middle Man," *Asian Business*, 1 May 1998, 12. Dell 2001 Annual Report. Available www.dell.com. 02/01/2002. G. McWilliams, "Dell's New Push: Cheaper Laptops Built to Order," *The Wall Street Journal*, 17 June 1999, B1. G. McWilliams, "Boss Talk: Dell to Detroit: Get into Gear Online! PC Whiz Advises Auto Makers Web Is Best Venue to Handle Suppliers, Serve Customers," *The Wall Street Journal*, 1 December 1999, B1. G. McWilliams, "How Dell Fine Tunes Its PC Pricing to Gain Edge in a Slow Market: Working with Suppliers, It Quickly Passes Changes in Costs to Customers, Three Prices for One Product," *The Wall Street Journal*, 8 June 2001, A1. A. Serwer, L. Smith, & P. de Llosa, "Michael Dell Rocks: Actually, He's Plain Vanilla," *Fortune*, 11 May 1998, 58.

A generation ago, computer hardware and software had little to do with managing business information. Rather than storing information on hard drives, managers stored it in filing cabinets. Instead of uploading daily sales and inventory levels by satellite to corporate headquarters, they mailed hard-copy summaries to headquarters at the end of each month. Instead of word processing, there was the electric typewriter. Instead of spreadsheets, there were adding machines. Managers didn't communicate by e-mail; they communicated by sticky notes. Phone messages weren't left on voice-mail; assistants and co-workers wrote them down. Workers didn't use desktop or laptop computers as a daily tool to get work done; they scheduled limited access time to run batch jobs on the mainframe computer (and prayed that the batch job computer code they wrote would work—it often didn't).

Today, a generation later, computer hardware and software are an integral part of managing business information. In large part, this is due to something called **Moore's law**. Gordon Moore is one of the founders of Intel Corporation (www.intel.com), which makes 80 percent of the integrated processors used in personal computers. In 1966, Moore predicted that every 18 months, the cost of computing would drop by 50 percent as computer-processing power doubled.[1] As shown in Exhibit 5.1, Moore was right. Every few years, computer power, as measured by the number of transistors per computer chip, has more than doubled. Consequently, the computer sitting in your lap or your

Moore's law
prediction that every 18 months, the cost of computing will drop by 50 percent as computer-processing power doubles

---

EXHIBIT 5.1

MOORE'S LAW

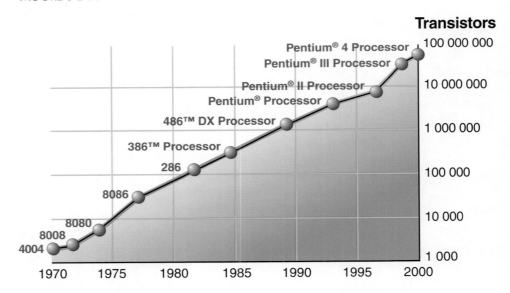

Source: Reprinted by permission of Intel Corporation, copyright Intel Corporation 2003.

desk is not only smaller, but also much cheaper and more powerful than the large mainframe computers used by Fortune 500 companies in the early 1990s. In fact, if car manufacturers had achieved the same power increases and cost decreases attained by computer manufacturers, a fully outfitted Lexus or Mercedes sedan would cost less than $1500!

Why Information Matters

Raw data are facts and figures. For example, 11, $363, 128, and 6100 are some data used the day this section of the chapter was written. However, facts and figures aren't particularly useful unless they have meaning. For example, you probably can't guess what these four pieces of raw data represent, can you? And if you can't, these data are useless. That's why researchers make the distinction between raw data and information. While raw data consist of facts and figures, **information** is useful data that can influence someone's choices and behaviour. So what did those four pieces of data mean? Well, 11 stands for channel 11, the local Global affiliate on which the author of this chapter watched part of the men's Canadian Open golf tournament; $363 is how much it would cost him to rent a minivan for a week of skiing over spring break; 128 is for the 128 megabytes of memory needed by the laptop computer this chapter was written on (prices are low right now—a good time to act); and 6100 means that it's time to get the car's oil changed.

After reading the next two sections, you should be able to
1. *explain the strategic importance of information.*
2. *describe the characteristics of useful information.*

1. Strategic Importance of Information

If you ask most top managers whether they thought real estate (i.e., office space, factory space, etc.) was critical to their businesses, most would say no. By contrast, Charles Woznick, CEO of Facility Information Systems (www.fisinc.com), said, "If you talk to somebody who manufactures automobiles, they can tell you what each of 40 000 parts costs down to the penny, and how many they will need to make cars this year."[2] However, according to Woznick, top managers should be paying attention to their real estate costs and gathering critical information to manage it. Using FIS's software, companies and government agencies operating in Canada and abroad can determine how much vacant space they have, which workers are sitting at which desks, even if those desks are in New York, Toronto, or Edmonton, and whether they can move workers into the spaces they have or need to rent or build new space. Paul Savastano, director of information technology, said, "You can say I have this many workstations nationwide, how many are vacant, and where they are. If I can find 100 workstations in the appropriate city or combination of buildings, I can save the company several million dollars over the term of a new lease."[3]

In today's hypercompetitive business environments, information, whether it's about real estate, product inventory, pricing, or costs, is as important as capital (i.e., money) for business success. It takes money to get businesses started, but businesses can't survive and grow without the right information. Information has strategic importance for organizations, because it can be used to obtain first-mover advantage and to sustain a competitive advantage once it has been created.

raw data
facts and figures

information
useful data that can influence people's choices and behaviour

1.1 First-Mover Advantage

first-mover advantage
the strategic advantage that companies earn by being the first in an industry to use new information technology to substantially lower costs or to differentiate a product or service from competitors

First-mover advantage is the strategic advantage that companies earn by being the first in an industry to use new information technology to substantially lower costs or to differentiate a product or service from competitors. For example, cable TV companies have taken a surprising lead over telephone companies in providing high-speed Internet access to people's homes. As this is written, 1.8 million Canadian homes have high-speed cable modems, compared to just 1.15 million that have high-speed digital subscriber lines (DSL) from phone companies.[4] These figures suggest that of the 75 percent of the Canadian population that has Internet access in the home, almost half have a broadband connection. Cable companies outflanked the phone companies initially by spending billions over four years to rewire their systems, replacing copper coaxial lines with 750 mHz digital lines that feed high-speed cable modems and digital TV cable channels alike (to compete with satellite TV, such as BellExpressvu or StarChoice). By contrast, the phone companies, having run into unexpected technical difficulties and high expenses, had until recently moved at a slower pace in bringing high-speed DSL service to people's homes. A recent poll, however, suggests that DSL providers are now moving more quickly to close the gap, having gone from 29 percent of Canadian households with broadband in 2000 to a current figure of just under 40 percent.[5]

In all, first-mover advantages can be sizable. On average, first movers earn 30 percent market share, compared to 19 percent for companies that follow.[6] For example, banks that were early adopters of ATM technology were able to increase both market share and profits by 26 percent over non-adopters of ATM technology.[7] Likewise, over 70 percent of today's market leaders started as first movers.[8]

1.2 Sustaining a Competitive Advantage

Sustaining a competitive advantage through information technology is not easy to do. For example, smaller banks with fewer ABMs eventually caught up with larger banks by forming ABM networks such as Plus and Cirrus. Because these networks allow ABM machines to process transactions on most bank cards (as long as you're willing to pay a small fee), it didn't matter whether a bank had two or 2000 ABM machines. Furthermore, because new information technology always costs more when it is new, first-mover strategies are typically much more expensive than adopting technology after it has been established (and prices have fallen). This means that companies that establish first-mover advantage and then lose it can lose substantial amounts of money and market share. In many instances, this can put the company that had first-mover advantage out of business, such as failed Web companies such as Pets.com and Webvan (a defunct Internet grocery store).[9]

According to the resource-based view of information technology shown in Exhibit 5.2, companies need to address three critical issues in order to sustain a competitive advantage through information technology. First, does the information technology create value for the firm by lowering costs or providing a better product or service? If an information technology doesn't add value, investing in it would put a firm at a competitive disadvantage to companies that choose information technologies that do add value.

Second, is the information technology the same or different across competing firms? If all the firms have access to the same information technology and use it in the same way, no firm has an advantage over another (i.e., competitive parity).

Third, is the firm's use of information technology difficult for another company to create or buy? If so, a firm has established a sustainable competitive advantage over competitors through information technology. If not, the competitive advantage is just temporary, and competitors should eventually be able to duplicate the advantages the leading firm has gained from information technology. You'll learn more about sustainable competitive advantage and its sources in Chapter 9.

In short, the key to sustaining a competitive advantage is not faster computers, more memory, and larger hard drives. The key is using information technology to continuously improve and support the core functions of a business. For instance, every time someone goes through the register, Wal-Mart (www.walmart.com) collects "market-basket data" to better figure out what products customers are likely to purchase together. Because of these data, stored in the second-largest database in the world (only the U.S. government's is larger), Wal-Mart knows that bananas are the most common item in shoppers' grocery carts. However, because these data indicated that people tend to buy bananas and cereal

EXHIBIT 5.2

USING INFORMATION TECHNOLOGY TO SUSTAIN A COMPETITIVE ADVANTAGE

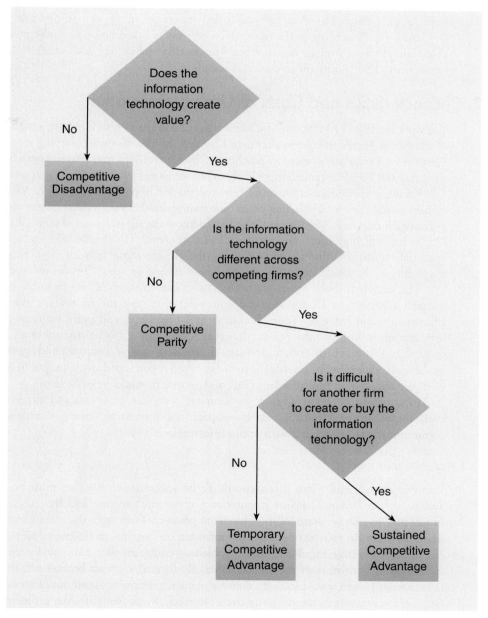

Source: Adapted from F.J. Mata, W.L. Fuerst, & J.B. Barney, "Information Technology and Sustained Competitive Advantage: A Resource-Based Analysis," *MIS Quarterly*, December 1995, 487–505. Copyright © 1995 by the Management Information Systems Research Center (MISRC) of the University of Minnesota.

at the same time, it now places bananas near the cereal aisle, in addition to the fruits and vegetables aisle. Likewise, Kleenex can be found in the paper goods aisle, but also near cold medicine.[10] Measuring spoons are in the housewares aisle, but also next to the Crisco shortening. Every chance it gets, Wal-Mart digs farther into this database to improve sales by making it easier for customers to find and buy what they want. Companies such as Wal-Mart that achieve first-mover advantage with information technology and then sustain it with continued investment create a moving target that competitors have difficulty hitting.

Review 1
Strategic Importance of Information

The first company to use new information technology to substantially lower costs or differentiate products or services often gains first-mover advantage, higher profits, and larger market share. However, creating a first-mover advantage can be difficult, expensive, and risky. According to the resource-based view of information technology, sustainable competitive advantage occurs when information technology adds value, is different across firms, and is difficult to create or acquire.

2. Characteristics and Costs of Useful Information

You work for Toyota Motor, and you know that the company's goal is to have a higher share of the North American auto market than DaimlerChrysler. If you were trying to convince Chrysler or Dodge car owners to purchase a Toyota, wouldn't you like to know how old their cars are? People are much more likely to buy a new car when their car nears seven years old. Knowing this information could help you market Toyotas to Chrysler or Dodge car owners just as they were thinking about purchasing another one instead of just after they purchased a new one. Wouldn't you also like to know the repair record of their Chrysler or Dodge car and how much those repairs had cost them? This would allow you to send potential customers information comparing the average repair bills for Toyota cars they might buy to the actual repair bills they had been paying on their Chrysler or Dodge cars.

The answer to both questions is obviously "Yes!" Yes, you'd like to know how old people's Chrysler or Dodge cars are and what they pay for repairs for those cars. Information can influence people's choices and behaviour, and you'd want to use this information to improve the chance that they would buy a Toyota instead of a Chrysler or Dodge. While this information would be fantastic to have, more than likely it would be difficult, expensive, or impossible to obtain. And if you somehow managed to get hold of it, the data would probably be so out of date that it would be of little use.

Information is useful when it is accurate, complete, relevant, and timely. However, there can be significant costs—acquisition, processing, storage, retrieval, and communication—associated with useful information.

2.1 Accurate Information

Information is useful when it is accurate. To be accurate, information must be reliable and valid. For instance, airline maintenance crews can't service and fix passenger jets unless they receive accurate information from plane crews or from the plane's own information system. In fact, at one time, the information systems on Boeing's 747 passenger jets indicated a large number of false problems—problems that didn't really exist.[11] If, for example, a member of the crew accidentally flipped a circuit breaker off, the 747's information system would indicate that the plane needed to be taken out of service to be fixed. However, simply resetting the circuit breaker switch would fix the problem. Since maintenance costs represent 20 percent of the cost of running an airline, inaccurate information can lead to expensive mistakes.

Wal-Mart's information collection is second only to the Pentagon. Knowing what people are likely to purchase together helps the company place products throughout the store. Any parent who has purchased a toy whose batteries weren't included would appreciate having some placed in the toy aisle.

© Susan Van Etten

2.2 Complete Information

Information is useful when it is complete. To be complete, the amount of information must be sufficient to identify the problem and begin to identify potential solutions. Aircraft manufacturers recognized the importance of providing flight crews and maintenance personnel with more information about how their jets were running. Consequently, new-generation planes, such as Boeing's 777, contain 600 computer sensors that airlines can use to fix problems and schedule maintenance. United Airlines (www.ual.com), an Air Canada Star Alliance partner, feeds this information into a system called AMIS, Aircraft Maintenance Information System. In turn, ground crews use laptop computers to run diagnostic tests on information gleaned from AMIS, while flight crews use computer monitors to access hundreds of colour graphs that continuously monitor and display the plane's performance.[12]

2.3 Relevant Information

Information is useful when it is relevant. Information is relevant when it pertains to the problem, so that decision makers can use it to define the problem and begin to identify potential solutions. The U.S. Federal Aviation Administration (FAA) classifies maintenance problems on planes into three categories.[13] Once a priority-one problem has been identified, it must be fixed after the plane lands or before it is allowed to take off. Anything that could lead to engine failure would be a priority-one problem. A priority-two problem does not require immediate action. The FAA (www.faa.gov) allows planes with priority-two problems to take off, fly, and land for a specified time period. But the plane must be fixed within this timeframe, or the FAA will ground the plane. Priority-three problems are minor maintenance problems, such as broken refrigerators or video monitors that airlines can fix at their own discretion. Since the new information systems, like United's AMIS system, provide information on all three kinds of problems, flight crews and maintenance crews are much more likely to have the relevant information they need to make good decisions. Although the FAA is a U.S. government regulator, its classifications and decisions matter to most of the world's major airlines, airplane manufacturers, and air transport authorities, including those located in Canada such as Air Canada, WestJet, and Bombardier. Failure to adhere to FAA safety rules can result in foreign carriers being barred from travel to American destinations and American carriers being barred from travel to unsafe destinations.

2.4 Timely Information

Finally, information is useful when it is timely. To be timely, the information must be available when needed to define a problem or begin to identify possible solutions. If you've ever thought, "I wish I'd known that ahead of time," you understand the importance of timely information and the opportunity cost of not having it. For the airlines, the information that can now be obtained on plane performance is not only more accurate, more complete, and more relevant, but also more timely. In fact, United Airline's maintenance crews track the performance and problems of their planes while they're en route to their destinations. For example, if you're 25 000 feet over upper New York State on the way back to New York City from your business trip to Toronto, United's ground crews are tracking the performance of your plane on their computer workstations. And because problems can be identified while planes are in the air, ground crews now have several hours to gather the tools, parts, and mechanical expertise needed to begin repairs as soon as the plane stops at the passenger gate. The timeliness of this information greatly increases the chances of keeping planes in service and on time.[14]

2.5 Acquisition Costs

acquisition cost
the cost of obtaining data that you don't have

Acquisition cost is the cost of obtaining data that you don't have. For example, Acxiom Inc. (www.acxiom.com) gathers and processes data for direct-mail marketing companies. Competitors offering similar services for the Canadian market include Equifax Canada Inc. (www.equifax.com) and InfoUSA.com. If you've received an unsolicited, "preapproved" credit card application recently (and who hasn't?), chances are one of these three companies helped the credit card company gather information about you. Where does a firm such as Acxiom get that information? The first place it turns is to companies that sell consumer credit reports at a wholesale cost of $1 each. Acxiom also obtains information from retailers. Each time you use your credit card, retailers' checkout scanners gather information about your spending habits and product preferences. Many retailers sell this information to companies such as Acxiom that use it for market research. So why pay for this information? Because acquiring it can help credit card companies do a better job of identifying who will mail back a signed credit card application and who will rip the credit card application in half and toss it in the wastebasket.[15]

2.6 Processing Costs

processing cost
the cost of turning raw data into usable information

Processing cost is the cost of turning raw data into usable information. As the chief technology officer of one large North American insurance company said, "We have massive amounts of data. But whether we have massive amounts of information is another question."[16] Often, companies already have the data they want, but it's not in the form or combination that they need it to be in. When one large U.S. insurer wanted to build a better customer database, it realized that it had good information on more than 10 million households, information that could help it do a better job of targeting its insurance, money market, and real estate services to those customers. However, the processing costs were enormous, because the raw data had to be processed from 15 different computer systems that stored the data in incompatible formats.

2.7 Storage Costs

Storage cost is the cost of physically or electronically archiving information for later use and retrieval. One of the reasons that credit card companies hire companies such as Equifax Canada or Acxiom to help them identify good customer prospects is that they maintain databases of extremely useful information. For instance, in Acxiom's database one can find the following information on about 195 million North Americans: age, estimated income, home ownership, cars owned, occupation, children, number of credit cards, and so on. All of that information is stored in Acxiom's "data warehouse" at its corporate headquarters. Acxiom uses 16 mainframes and 600 000 computer tapes to process and store all that information. In all, Acxiom has 350 terabytes (a terabyte is the equivalent of 500 million pages of single-spaced text) of information in storage in its data warehouse. And it intends to store even more. Axciom's CEO said, "Our customers today are saying, 'Save everything, because we might find a use for this information a year from now.'"[17]

storage cost
the cost of physically or electronically archiving information for later use and retrieval

2.8 Retrieval Costs

Retrieval cost is the cost of accessing already-stored and processed information. One of the most common misunderstandings about information is that it is easy and cheap to retrieve once the company has it. Not so. First, you have to find the information. Then, you've got to convince whoever has it to share it with you. Then the information has to be processed into a form that is useful for you. By the time you get the information you need, it may not be timely anymore.

For example, R.R. Donnelley & Sons (www.rrdonnelley.com), which is headquartered in Chicago, is the largest printer of phone books in the world and has offices in Montreal, Toronto, Ottawa, and Calgary, as well as around the world. Donnelley designed software that would make it easier to convert electronic information into the metal printing plates that are used to print each page of the phone book. When the software didn't work the way it was supposed to, the printers who used the software to make the metal printing plates called the software designers to get the information they needed to fix the problem. An assistant then forwarded the request for information. However, it often took several weeks (sometimes months!) for the software designers to provide the information that fixed the problem.[18] Because phone book information is "perishable" (people move, numbers change, new numbers are added), the printers not only lost production time, but they also frequently had to start over in order to print the most up-to-date information in the phone book. In theory, retrieval should be quick and easy. In practice, it often isn't.

retrieval cost
the cost of accessing already-stored and processed information

2.9 Communication Costs

Communication cost is the cost of transmitting information from one place to another. For example, the most important information that an electric utility company collects each month is the information from the electric meter attached to the side of your house. Traditionally, electric companies have employed meter readers to walk from house to house to gather information that would then be entered into company computers. However, meter readers are losing their jobs to radio networks that work by placing a small transceiver in your electric meter. Every five minutes, the transceiver uses radio waves to transmit data indicating how much electricity was used at your house. The data are transmitted to a nearby electric pole that holds a small computer. The small computer forwards the information to a somewhat larger computer within a 400-metre range, which then sends the information to a base-station computer that is no more than 14 kilometres away. The base-station computer completes the communication process by forwarding the information via phone lines or microwave towers to company headquarters. The cost: less than $1.50 per month for each household.[19]

communication cost
the cost of transmitting information from one place to another

Raw data are facts and figures. Raw data don't become information until they are in a form that can affect decisions and behaviour. For information to be useful, it has to be reliable and valid (accurate), of sufficient quantity (complete), pertinent to the problems you're facing (relevant), and available when you need it (timely). Useful information does not come cheaply. The five costs of obtaining good information are the costs of acquiring, processing, storing, retrieving, and communicating information.

Getting and Sharing Information

In 1907, Metropolitan Life Insurance built a huge office building in for its brand-new, state-of-the-art information technology system. What was the system that represented such a breakthrough in information management? The advanced system was card files. That's right, the same card file systems that every library in Canada and the United States used before computers. Metropolitan Life's information "technology" consisted of 20 000 separate file drawers that sat in hundreds of file cabinets more than 4.5 metres tall. This filing system held 20 million insurance applications, 700 000 accounting books, and 500 000 death certificates. Metropolitan Life employed 61 workers who did nothing but sort, file, and climb ladders to pull files as needed.[20]

Less than a century later, the cost, inefficiency, and ineffectiveness of using this system that was previously state of the art would put a contemporary insurance company out of business within months. Today, if storms, fire, or accidents damage policyholders' property, insurance companies write cheques on the spot to cover the losses. When policyholders buy a car, they call their insurance agent from the car dealership to activate their insurance before driving off in their new car. And now, insurance companies are marketing their products and services to customers directly from the Internet.

Wow! From card files to Internet files in 95 years. The rate of change in information technology is spectacular.

After reading the next two sections, you should be able to
3. explain the basics of capturing, processing, and protecting information.
4. describe how companies can share and access information and knowledge.

3. Capturing, Processing, and Protecting Information

In many instances, when you go to your local pharmacy to pick up a prescription, the pharmacist reviews an electronic file that shows all the medications you're now taking. That same system automatically checks to make sure that your new prescription won't create adverse side effects by interacting with the other medications you take. When you pay for your prescription, the point-of-sale information system determines whether you've written any bad cheques lately (to the pharmacy or other stores), records your payment, and then checks with the computer of the pharmaceutical company that makes your prescription drugs to see if it's time to reorder. Finally, the system protects your information to make sure that your data are readily available to only you, your physician, and your pharmacist.

In this section, you will learn about the information technologies that companies use for capturing information, processing information, and protecting information.

3.1 Capturing Information

There are two basic methods of capturing information: manual and electronic. Manual capture of information is a labour-intensive process by which data are recorded and entered by hand into a data storage device. For example, when you applied for a driver's licence, you probably recorded personal information about yourself by filling out a form.

Then, after passing your driver's test, someone typed your handwritten information into the department of motor vehicles' computer database so that local and provincial police could access it from their patrol cars when they pulled you over for speeding. (Isn't information great?) The problem with manual capture of information is that it is slow, expensive, and often inaccurate.

Consequently, companies are relying more on electronic capture, in which data are electronically recorded and entered into electronic storage devices. For example, scientists are now using a software program called WinWedge 32 to capture research data electronically. By connecting their scientific instruments (scales, thermometers, etc.) directly to the computer, WinWedge 32 can automatically record the data from these instruments into a computer spreadsheet (such as Lotus 1-2-3 or Microsoft Excel). For researchers, this software allows data to be quickly dumped directly into a computer database with no hand-entry errors.[21]

Bar codes and document scanners are the most common methods of electronically capturing data. **Bar codes** represent numerical data by varying the thickness and pattern of vertical bars. The primary advantage that bar codes offer is that the data they represent can be read and recorded in an instant with a hand-held or pen-type scanner. One pass of the scanner (okay, sometimes several) and "Beep!" The information has been captured. Bar codes were invented in 1952 and were first used to track parts inventory in factories in 1961. In 1967, railroad companies began using bar codes for tracking railroad cars. In 1973, the grocery business adopted the Universal Product Code, which required product manufacturers to place bar codes on their products or product labels. However, it took nearly two decades for bar code scanners to become standard equipment in most retail and grocery stores. Once adopted, bar codes cut checkout times in half, reduced data entry errors by 75 percent, and saved stores money because stockers didn't have to go through the labour-intensive process of placing a price tag on each item in the store.[22]

Because they are inexpensive and easy to use, **electronic scanners**, which convert printed text and pictures into digital images, have become an increasingly popular method of electronically capturing data. However, text that has been digitized cannot be searched or edited like the regular text in your word-processing software. Therefore, companies can use **optical character recognition** software to scan and convert original or digitized documents into ASCII text (American Standard Code for Information Interchange). ASCII text can be searched, read, and edited in standard word-processing, e-mail, desktop publishing, database management, and spreadsheet software. Once data have been captured, they have to be stored before they are accessed and shared. Exhibit 5.3 describes the advantages and disadvantages of different kinds of data storage media.

3.2 Processing Information

Processing information means transforming raw data into meaningful information that can be applied to business decision-making. Evaluating sales data to determine the best- and worst-selling products, examining repair records to determine product reliability, or monitoring the cost of long-distance phone calls are all examples of processing raw data into meaningful information. And, with automated, electronic capture of data, increased processing power, and cheaper and more plentiful ways to store data, managers no longer worry about getting data. Instead, they scratch their heads about how to use the overwhelming amount of data that pours into their businesses every day. Furthermore, most managers know little about statistics and have neither the time nor the inclination to learn how to use them to analyze data.

One promising tool to help managers dig out from under the avalanche of data is data mining. **Data mining** is the process of discovering unknown patterns and relationships in large amounts of data.[23] Data mining works by using complex algorithms such as neural networks, rule induction, and decision trees. If you don't know what those are, that's okay. With data mining, you don't have to. Most managers only need to know that data mining looks for patterns that are already in the data but are too complex for them to spot on their

bar code
a visual pattern that represents numerical data by varying the thickness and pattern of vertical bars

electronic scanner
an electronic device that converts printed text and pictures into digital images

optical character recognition
software to convert digitized documents into ASCII text (American Standard Code for Information Interchange) that can be searched, read, and edited by word processing and other kinds of software

processing information
transforming raw data into meaningful information

data mining
the process of discovering unknown patterns and relationships in large amounts of data

EXHIBIT 5.3

ADVANTAGES AND DISADVANTAGES OF DIFFERENT KINDS OF DATA STORAGE DEVICES

DATA STORAGE MEDIUM	ADVANTAGES	DISADVANTAGES
1. Paper	• Most common form of data storage	• Expensive • Takes tremendous space • Manual search processes • Only one person can access at a time
2. Microfilm—picture of the data is stored on a small photographic slide	• Reel of microfilm can store hundreds of pages of data • Inexpensive and cheaper than paper • Requires little storage space • Good for storing infrequently accessed data	• Only one person can access at a time • Access only available where microfilm is stored • Slow searches
3. CDs—hold 650 megabytes of data	• Inexpensive • Easy • Nearly all computers have CD drives	• Need CD-burner to put data on CD • Easily lost or misplaced
4. DVDs—hold 4.7 gigabytes of data	• Becoming less expensive • Easy • DVD drives can read CDs	• Need special DVD-burner to put data on DVD • Easily lost or misplaced • Not all computers have DVD drives; CD drives cannot read DVDs
5. Data Storage Tapes—magnetic tapes used to archive data for long-term storage	• Holds huge amounts of data • Not much larger than floppy disks • Portable, used to transport large files	• Requires special tape device for accessing and recording data • Easily lost or misplaced
6. Hard Drives—magnetic disks that read and write (store) data	• Primary storage for data used most often in performing jobs • Fastest data retrieval • Holds huge amounts of data • Cheap storage	• Only one person can access at a time, unless drive is networked • Access only available where drive is located, unless accessed via network or Internet • Unreliability—drives can crash
7. RAID—redundant array inexpensive disk system	• Uses a series of small disk drives together to act as a large disk drive (i.e., combining 10 20-gig hard drives to act as a 200-gig hard drive) • More reliable since data are duplicated across small drives • If one disk fails, backup data are immediately retrieved from another drive in the series • Good for mission-critical data	• More expensive • Typically must be networked to justify additional cost

own. For example, IBM has provided 25 National Basketball Association teams with data mining software called Advanced Scout. Advanced Scout allows basketball coaches to ask "What if?" questions such as "What if I start a certain lineup or run certain plays?" "When should we go for more three-pointers?" and "Does this strategy lead to victory?" Dr. Inderpal Bhandari, a computer scientist at IBM, said, "The beauty of Advanced Scout is that it requires little computer training or data analysis background. It was written with the coach in mind."[24] As well, Advanced Scout is easy to use. It asks users simple questions and makes suggestions that may help them find what they're looking for.

Data mining typically splits a data set in half, finds patterns in one half, and then tests the validity of those patterns by trying to find them again in the second half of the data set. The data typically come from a **data warehouse** that stores huge amounts of data that have been prepared for data mining analysis by being cleaned of errors and redundancy.

The data in a data warehouse can then be analyzed using two kinds of data mining. **Supervised data mining** usually begins with the user telling the data mining software to look and test for specific patterns and relationships in a data set. For instance, a grocery store manager might instruct the data mining software to determine if coupons placed in the Sunday paper increase or decrease profits. By contrast, with **unsupervised data mining**, the user simply tells the data mining software to uncover whatever patterns and relationships it can find in a data set. For example, Dr. John Nearhos is the general manager of the professional review division at Australia's Health Insurance Commission, which processes 300 million health insurance claims and makes $11 billion of payments each year. Dr. Nearhos gave IBM 10 data tapes with a total of three gigabytes of information and asked the company to use its data mining software to find anything that might help the commission cut costs. Three days later, the software had uncovered an illegal billing practice that was costing the commission millions of dollars that it shouldn't have to pay. Dr. Nearhos said, "I don't know if we would have ever made the connection on our own. I was able to make a call and put a stop to it that day. Data mining targets the problem areas for us and we can do the rest."[25]

Unsupervised data mining is particularly good at identifying association or affinity patterns, sequence patterns, and predictive patterns. It can also identify what data mining "techies" call data clusters.[26] **Association or affinity patterns** occur when two or more database elements tend to occur together in a significant way. Earlier in the chapter, you learned how Wal-Mart discovered that people tend to buy the following items at the same time: bananas and cereal, Kleenex and cold medicine, and Crisco and measuring spoons. These items are an example of an association or affinity pattern. **Sequence patterns** occur when two or more database elements occur together in a significant pattern, but with one of the elements preceding the other. For example, by analyzing website registration and car purchasing behaviour, a car company such as Acura might find out that people who first register on the www.acura.ca website are then more likely to purchase an Acura car. Or a credit card company may find people who have been denied a request to raise their credit card limit are more likely to change credit card companies in the next few months.

By contrast, predictive patterns are just the opposite of association or affinity patterns. While association or affinity patterns look for database elements that seem to go together, **predictive patterns** help identify database elements that are different. For example, mortgage companies can make more accurate lending decisions by studying a database that contains people who make their mortgage payments each month and those who don't, and then asking the data mining software to look for differences between the two. If reliable differences are found, those differences can then be used when approving or denying mortgage applications.

Data clusters are the last kind of pattern found by data mining. **Data clusters** occur when three or more database elements occur together (i.e., cluster) in a significant way. For example, after analyzing several years' worth of repair and warranty claims, Ford might find that, compared to cars built in its Oakville plant, the cars it builds in Atlanta (first element) are more likely to have problems with over-tightened fan belts (second element) that break (third element) and result in overheated engines (fourth element), ruined radiators (fifth element), and payments for tow trucks (sixth element), which are paid for by Ford's three-year, 60 000-kilometre warranty.

data warehouse
stores huge amounts of data that have been prepared for data mining analysis by being cleaned of errors and redundancy

supervised data mining
user tells the data mining software to look and test for specific patterns and relationships in a data set

unsupervised data mining
user simply tells the data mining software to uncover whatever patterns and relationships it can find in a data set

association or affinity patterns
when two or more database elements tend to occur together in a significant way

sequence patterns
when two or more database elements occur together in a significant pattern, but one of the elements precedes the other

predictive patterns
help identify database elements that are different

data clusters
when three or more database elements occur together (i.e., cluster) in a significant way

protecting information
the process of insuring that data are reliably and consistently retrievable in a usable format for authorized users, but no one else

firewall
hardware or software device that sits between the computers in an internal organizational network and outside networks, such as the Internet

virus
a program or piece of code that attaches itself to other programs on your computer and can trigger anything from a harmless flashing message to the reformatting of your hard drive to the system-wide network shutdown

Traditionally, data mining has been very expensive and very complex. Today, however, with services and analysis provided by companies such as Digimine.com, data mining is much more affordable and within reach of most companies' budgets. And, if it follows the path of most technology, it will become even easier and cheaper to use in the future.

3.3 Protecting Information

Protecting information is the process of insuring that data are reliably and consistently retrievable in a usable format for authorized users, but no one else. For instance, when you place an order online, your personal information and credit card information are encrypted using SSL (Secure Sockets Layer) encryption technology before being sent over the Internet, making it virtually impossible for your information to be stolen or intercepted while being transferred to the vendor. Your credit card information is always stored in encrypted form in a database that is away from the website database so it isn't connected to the Internet and is therefore safe from hackers.

Many companies find it necessary to protect information because of the numerous security threats to data and data security listed in Exhibit 5.4. From denial-of-service Web server attacks that can bring down some of the busiest and best-run sites on the Internet (e.g., Yahoo.com), to e-mail viruses that spread quickly and result in data loss and business disruption, to keystroke monitoring in which every mouse and keystroke you make is unknowingly monitored, stored, and sent to unauthorized users, there are many ways for people inside and outside of companies to steal or destroy company data.

As shown in the right-hand column of Exhibit 5.4, there are numerous steps to properly securing data and data networks. Some of the most important are using firewalls, antivirus software for PCs and e-mail servers, data encryption, and virtual private networks.[27]

If you have an Internet service provider such as Microsoft Network (MSN), Sympatico, or AOL Canada, any time you make a dial-up connection, there's literally nothing between your personal computer and the Internet. Data files and website information are downloaded directly to your PC. By contrast, **firewalls** are hardware or software devices that sit between the computers in an internal organizational network and outside networks, such as the Internet. Firewalls filter and check incoming and outgoing data. They prevent company insiders from accessing unauthorized sites or from sending confidential company information to people outside the company. Firewalls also prevent outsiders from identifying and gaining access to company computers and data. Indeed, if a firewall is working properly, the computers behind the company firewall cannot be seen or accessed by outsiders.

A **virus** is a program or piece of code that attaches itself to other programs on your computer and can trigger anything from a harmless flashing message to the reformatting of your hard drive to the system-wide network shutdown.[28] Antivirus software for personal computers scans e-mail, downloaded files, and computer hard drives and memory to detect and stop computer viruses from doing damage. However, it is effective only to the extent that users of individual computers have and use up-to-date versions of antivirus software. With new viruses appearing all the time, users should update their antivirus software at least once a month. By contrast, antivirus software for e-mail servers automatically scans e-mail attachments, such as Microsoft Word documents, graphics, or text files, which contain viruses as they come across the company e-mail server. The e-mail server is simply a computer on which all e-mail resides before being sent to everyone's personal computer. Think of e-mail servers as airports and e-mail as airplanes. Before heading off to their next destination, airplanes have to land at airports.

EXHIBIT 5.4

SECURITY THREATS TO DATA AND DATA NETWORKS

SECURITY PROBLEM	SOURCE	AFFECTS	SEVERITY	THE THREAT	THE SOLUTION
Denial-of-service Web server attacks and corporate network attacks	Internet hackers	All servers	High	Loss of data, disruption of service, and theft of service.	Implement firewall, password control, server-side review, threat monitoring, and bug fixes.
Unauthorized access to PCs	Local area network, Internet	All users, especially digital subscriber line and cable Internet users	High	Hackers take over PCs. Privacy can be invaded. Corporate users' systems are exposed to other machines on the network.	Close ports and firewall, disable file and print sharing, and use strong passwords.
Viruses, worms, Trojan horses	E-mail, downloaded and distributed software	All users	Moderate to high	Monitor activities and cause data loss, file deletion, and compromise security.	Use antivirus software and firewalls, and control Internet access.
Malicious scripts and applets	Rogue Web pages	All users	Mild, overestimated	Invade privacy, intercept passwords, and damage files or file system.	Disable browser script support, and use security and blocking software.
E-mail snooping	Hackers on your network and the Internet	All users	Moderate to high	People read your e-mail from intermediate servers or packets, or they physically access your machine.	Encrypt message, ensure strong password protection, and limit physical access to machines.
Keystroke monitoring	Trojan horses, people with direct access to PCs	All users	High	Records everything typed at the keyboard and intercepts keystrokes before password masking or encryption occurs.	Use antivirus software to catch Trojan horses, control Internet access to transmission, and implement system monitoring and physical access control.
Referrers	Websites you visit	Individual users	Mild	Send e-mail notification of your Web activity.	Use ad blockers and security packages.
Spam	E-mail	All users and corporations	Mild	Clogs e-mail servers and inboxes with junk mail. HTML-based spam may be used for profiling and identifying users.	Filter known spam sources and senders, block Internet access by HTML messages.
Cookies	Websites you visit	Individual users	Mild to moderate	Trace Web usage and permit the creation of personalized Web pages that track behaviour and interest profiles.	Use cookie managers to control and edit cookies, and use ad blockers.

Source: "Protect & Defend," B. Machrone, *PC Magazine*, 27 June 2000, 168–181.

Similarly, before being sent to individual users' personal computers, e-mail has to first be sent to the company e-mail server. At this point the antivirus software for e-mail servers can scan for viruses and prevent infected files from being sent to others, even if individual personal computers lack antivirus software. So while antivirus software for personal computers prevents individual computers from being infected, antivirus software for e-mail servers adds another layer of protection by preventing infected files from multiplying and being sent to others.

Another way of protecting information is to encrypt sensitive data. **Data encryption** transforms data into complex, scrambled digital codes that can be unencrypted only by authorized users who possess unique decryption keys. One method of data encryption is to use products such as PGP Desktop Security (www.pgp.com) to encrypt the files stored on personal computers. This is especially important with laptop computers, which are easily stolen. For example, the CEO of Qualcomm (www.qualcomm.com), a maker of chips and technologies used in mobile phones and wireless communication, had his laptop computer stolen after providing a presentation at a journalism conference. The stolen laptop contained megabytes of confidential corporate information, including several years of financial and strategic data.[29]

The Internet works by cutting data into smaller packets that are numbered and reassembled in order after being transported from one location to another. Imagine a high-speed video of a finished, 1000-piece jigsaw puzzle, with all the pieces numbered for easy assembly, which is quickly taken apart, moved from one place to another, and then quickly reassembled. The Internet does the same thing with software, text, data, or graphic files as it moves data files from one place to another. Unfortunately, since Internet data are not encrypted, "packet sniffer" software easily allows hackers to read everything you send or receive. For most of us, this is not a high-security risk. Hackers are not especially interested in what millions of ordinary people are doing on the Internet. However, there is a security risk for people away from their offices (e.g., sales people, business travellers, telecommuters who work at home) who interact with their company networks via the Internet. For them, packet sniffing can represent a substantial risk and an easy target for hackers. Previously, the only practical solution was to have employees dial in to secure company phone lines for direct access to the company network. Of course, with international and long-distance phone calls, the costs quickly add up. However, **virtual private networks** (VPN) solve this problem by encrypting Internet data at both ends of the transmission process. Instead of making long-distance calls, employees dial an Internet service provider, such as MSN or AOL, that provides local service all over the world. Unlike typical Internet connections in which Internet data packets are unencrypted, the virtual private network encrypts the data sent by employees outside the company network, decrypts the data when they arrive within the company computer network, and does the same when data are sent back to the computer outside the network.

Review 3
Capturing, Processing, and Protecting Information

Electronic data capture (bar codes, scanners, optical character recognition, and devices that record data straight into structured data sets) is much faster, easier, and cheaper than manual data capture. Processing information means transforming raw data into meaningful information that can be applied to business decision-making. Data mining helps managers with this transformation by discovering unknown patterns and relationships in data. Supervised data mining looks for patterns specified by managers, while unsupervised data mining looks for four general kinds of data patterns: association/affinity patterns, sequence patterns, predictive patterns, and data clusters. Protecting information insures that data are reliably and consistently retrievable in a usable format for authorized users, but no one else. Firewalls, antivirus software for PCs and e-mail servers, data encryption, and virtual private networks are some of the best ways to protect information.

data encryption
transforms data into complex, scrambled digital codes that can be unencrypted only by authorized users who possess unique decryption keys

virtual private network
encrypts Internet data at both ends of the transmission process

4. Accessing and Sharing Information and Knowledge

Imagine a situation in which the only way customers could contact your company would be to fax a company in Switzerland, which would then fax the customer faxes to you. A company would have to be crazy to do that, right? Well, that's exactly the situation that Ingersoll-Rand (www.irco.com), a $5-billion manufacturing company, put itself in with its international customers. For example, Sermatec (www.sermatec.com), which sells Ingersoll-Rand air compressors in Santiago, Chile, would fax its order for more air compressors to Ingersoll-Rand's international trading company in Switzerland, which would then fax the order to factories in North America. Sermatec's general manager said, "It would take up to two weeks just to get confirmation that I'd placed an order." With no direct contact and no way to discover order status, distributors might as well have put a message in a bottle and dropped it in the ocean with the hope that Ingersoll-Rand would someday get the message and respond.

It didn't take long for Ingersoll-Rand's manager of global business systems to realize that "we had to make a change, and we had to make it quickly." So the company installed a $1.5-million (U.S.) system that lets customers make orders and check on pricing, inventory, and the status of previous orders from their own office computers. With instant access to this information, Sermatec increased its sales. Now when a customer calls about the price and availability of an Ingersoll-Rand part or product, Sermatec logs onto the system to provide an immediate answer. Moreover, Ingersoll-Rand has reduced product delivery times to distributors like Sermatec from well over a month to three days.[30]

Today, information technologies are letting companies communicate, share, and provide data access to workers, managers, and customers in ways that were unthinkable just a few years ago. After reading this section, you should be able to explain how companies use information technology to improve communication, internal access, and external access, and to share knowledge and expertise.

PERSONAL PRODUCTIVITY TIP

Privacy Through Public Key Encryption

One of the biggest fears about computers is privacy. However, you can use a system called "public key encryption" to protect your files. First, give copies of your "public key" to anyone who sends you files or e-mail. Have them use the public key, which is actually a piece of software, to encrypt files before sending them to you. The only way to decrypt the files is with a companion "private key" that you keep to yourself. If you want to learn more or want to begin encrypting your own files, download a free program called Pretty Good Privacy from http://web.mit.edu/pgp.

Source: D. Clark, "E-Commerce (A Special Report): The Lessons We've Learned—Privacy: You Have No Secrets—It's the Dark Side of E-Commerce: You Leave a Trail of Personal Information Wherever You Go," *The Wall Street Journal*, 23 October 2000, R32.

4.1 Communication

E-mail, voice messaging, and conferencing systems are changing how managers, workers, and customers communicate and work with each other. E-mail, the transmission of messages via computers, is the fastest growing form of communication in organizations. At 9 cents per message, e-mail is the cheapest way to send a message and is substantially faster, usually appearing in the receiver's electronic mailbox within minutes, sometimes seconds.[31] Because of its similarity to regular mail (which devoted e-mail users call "snail mail"), e-mail is easy to learn and use.

Of course, the ease and simplicity of e-mail create their own disadvantages: too much e-mail! Patricia Baldwin, director of business simplification for Sun Microsystems (http://www.sun.com), makers of Unix-based computers and the Java software language, gets more than 250 e-mails a day. Of those 250 messages, no more than 20 have any significant impact on her job.[32] Unfortunately, the volume of e-mail that Patricia receives is not unusual.

Voice messaging, or "voice-mail," is a telephone answering system that records audio messages. Surveys indicate that 89 percent of respondents believe that voice messaging is critical to business communication, 78 percent believe that it improves productivity, and 58 percent would rather leave a message on a voice messaging system than with a receptionist.[33] Voice messaging systems are easy to use and cut costs because workers don't have to spend their time recording and forwarding messages. However, handling voice messages can take a considerable amount of time. By contrast, because people read six times faster than they can listen, 30 e-mail messages can usually be handled in 10 to 15 minutes.[34] As well, some companies have found that customers prefer to talk to "real" people, even if only to leave a message. Winguth, Dohahue & Co., a North American executive search firm, scrapped its $28 000 voice messaging system. Owner Ed Winguth said, "At first clients said it was terrific that we were in the 21st century. But soon customers started saying it was too cold and annoying. These were CEOs and VPs calling in. Our repeat customers really got annoyed."[35]

Unlike e-mail and voice-mail, which permit users only to leave messages, **conferencing systems** allow two or more users in different locations to see and talk to each other as if they were working side by side in the same room. There are three kinds of conferencing systems: document conferencing, application sharing, and video conferencing.[36] The key similarity across all three is that time and space don't matter when it comes to getting work done. No matter where people are, conferencing systems allow them to work together.

Document conferencing, also called "white boarding," allows two or more people to use computers to simultaneously view and make comments about a document. **Application sharing** takes document conferencing several steps further by allowing two or more people in different locations to actually make changes in a document by sharing control of the software application running on one computer. Here's how it works. A lawyer in Halifax and her client, a business person in Calgary, are making the final changes on a contract for the business person's company. Step one: The lawyer and the business person talk on the phone while they work. Step two: Both use a second phone line or a company network to connect their computers as they talk. Step three: The lawyer opens the contract in word-processing software and then starts the application sharing software. (Several companies make this software: Netscape's Conference, www.netscape.com, and Microsoft's NetMeeting, www.microsoft.com/windows/netmeeting/.) Seconds later, the first page of the contract appears on the lawyer's computer in Halifax, and a few seconds after that, it appears on the business person's computer in Calgary. Now both can make changes to the document. For example, the lawyer could change $5000 to $50 000 on the first page while the business person is correcting a misspelling on page 20.[37] As the changes are being made, the computers communicate the changes over the phone line or network, so that both parties can work on identical versions of the file at all times.

There are numerous advantages to application sharing. Companies save an enormous amount of money and time by eliminating or reducing travel. Rather than holding a meeting to talk about proposed changes and then making them, the changes are made instantly. Therefore, there are no follow-up notes, e-mails, or faxes to make sure that agreed-on changes actually get made. Beyond the initial cost of the software, the only expense is for long-distance phone calls. Even that can be eliminated if both parties have fast enough systems to use the Internet to transmit their phone calls. Unlike videoconferencing, which is discussed next, document sharing runs well over standard phone lines. Thus, most companies and business people can use it now without having to invest funds for additional equipment.

Desktop videoconferencing allows two or more people in different locations to use video cameras and computer monitors to see and hear each other and to share documents. Unlike application sharing, desktop videoconferencing does not work well over regular phone lines. For adequate transmission of audio and video, participants need access to a high-speed network or high-speed connection to the Internet. All participants also need to place an audio microphone and a small inexpensive video camera on top of their personal computers. As shown in Exhibit 5.5, a participant in a desktop videoconference sees (and hears) live pictures of other participants. Also, like document sharing,

conferencing system
communications system that lets two or more users in different locations see and talk to each other as if they were in the same room

document conferencing
communications system that allows two or more people in different locations to simultaneously view and make comments about a document

application sharing
communications system that allows two or more people in different locations to make changes in a document by sharing control of the software application running on one computer

desktop videoconferencing
communications system that allows two or more people in different locations to use video cameras and computer monitors to see and hear each other and share documents

Desktop videoconferencing allows people in different locations to see and hear each other and to share documents.

© Jose Luis Pelaez, Inc./CORBIS/MAGMA

EXHIBIT 5.5

CHARACTERISTICS OF BEST-SELLING EXECUTIVE INFORMATION SYSTEMS

EASE OF USE

- Few commands to learn. Simply drag-and-drop or point-and-click to create charts and tables or get the information you need.
- Important views saved. Need to see weekly sales by store every Monday? Save that "view" of the data, and it will automatically be updated with new data every week.
- 3-D charts to display data. Column, square, pie, ring, line, area, scatter, bar, cube, etc.
- Geographic dimensions. Different geographic areas are automatically colour-coded for easy understanding.

ANALYSIS OF INFORMATION

- Sales tracking. Track sales performance by product, region, account, and channel.
- Easy-to-understand displays. Information is displayed in tabular and graphical charts.
- Time periods. Data can be analyzed by current year, prior year, year to date, quarter to date, and month to date.

IDENTIFICATION OF PROBLEMS AND EXCEPTIONS

- Compare to standards. Compares actual company performance (actual expenses versus planned expenses, or actual sales by sales quotas).
- Trigger exceptions. Allows users to set triggers (5 percent over budget, 3 percent under sales quota), which then highlights negative exceptions in red and positive exceptions in green.
- Drill down. Once exceptions have been identified, users can drill down for more information to determine why the exception is occurring.
- Detect and alert newspaper. When things go wrong, the EIS delivers a "newspaper" via e-mail to alert managers to problems. The newspaper offers an intuitive interface for easily navigating and further analyzing the alert content.
- Detect and alert robots. Detect and alert robots keep an extra "eye" out for events and problems. Want to keep an eye out for news about one of your competitors? Use a news robot to track stories on Dow Jones News Retrieval. Robots can also be used to track stock quotes, internal databases, and e-mail messages.

Sources: "Business Intelligence: Overview: Enterprise Services from Pilot Software," Accrue Software. [Online] Available www.pilotsw.com/Products/Accrue_Pilot_Suite/business_intelligence.html, 9 February 2002. Comshare home page. [Online] Available www.comshare.com, February 2002.

participants can see the files they are sharing. While desktop videoconferencing is more expensive and harder to make work than application sharing, companies with high-speed networks should have few problems taking advantage of this technology.

4.2 Internal Access and Sharing

Two kinds of information technology are used by executives, managers, and workers inside the company to access and share information: executive information systems and intranets. An **executive information system (EIS)** uses internal and external sources of data to provide managers and executives the information they need to monitor and analyze organizational performance.[38] For example, with the click of a mouse, senior and middle managers at United Cigar Stores can pull up graphs and charts of weekly and monthly sales on their computers to see if they're on target. If they're not, they can "drill down" for more information to help them figure out whether the problem is at the divisional, regional, or district level. The managers can look at charts and graphs of data for each of the company's 476 stores. Data can even be cross-referenced, looking at how, for example, various products (cigars, pipe tobacco, or cigarettes) sell in particular stores (hotel shops versus malls) or areas (Vancouver, Toronto, etc.).[39]

executive information system (EIS)
data processing system that uses internal and external data sources to provide the information needed to monitor and analyze organizational performance

Since most managers are not computer experts, EISs must be easy to use and must provide information that managers want and need. Consequently, most EIS programs use touch screens, "point and click" commands, and easy-to-understand displays, such as colour graphs, charts, and written summaries so that little learning or computer experience is required. In addition, basic commands such as find, compare, and show allow managers to easily and quickly get the information they need to make good decisions. Exhibit 5.5 describes the capabilities of two of the best-selling products that companies use for EIS programs.

Intranets are private company networks that allow employees to easily access, share, and publish information using Internet software. Intranet websites are just like external websites, but the firewall separating the internal company network from the Internet only permits authorized internal access.[40] At Boeing (www.boeing.com), employees can access messages from top company leaders, information bulletins, and the doctor and hospital directory wherever they live. Boeing's intranet also helps its engineers work together to design planes wherever they're located. Intranets are exploding in popularity. In 1995, the Business Research Group estimated that only 11 percent of midsize to large companies were using intranets.[41] Today, more than 80 percent have their own intranets.[42] The reasons for this phenomenal growth, as shown in Exhibit 5.6, are many. First, executive information systems can cost as much as several hundred thousand dollars to install for a small group of managers. In comparison, intranets, which can be used by everyone in the company, are inexpensive. Much of the software required to set up an intranet is either **freeware** (no cost) or **shareware** (try before you buy, usually less expensive than commercial software).

intranets
private company networks that allow employees to easily access, share, and publish information using Internet software

freeware
computer software that is free to whoever wants it

shareware
computer software that you can try before you buy, but if you keep it beyond the trial period, usually 30 days, you must buy it

EXHIBIT 5.6

WHY 80 PERCENT OF COMPANIES NOW USE INTRANETS

1. Intranets are inexpensive.
2. Intranets increase efficiencies and reduce costs.
3. Intranets are intuitive and easy to use (Web-based).
4. Intranets work across all computer systems and platforms (Web-based).
5. Intranets can be built on top of existing computer networks.
6. Intranets work with software programs that easily convert electronic documents to HTML files for intranet use.

Second, intranets reduce costs, increase efficiencies, and save organizations money. General Electric (www.ge.com) expects to save $1.6 billion (U.S.) this year from using its intranet to purchase office supplies, handle reimbursement forms, and displace the millions of paper-based forms its 340 000 employees use each year.[43] With 1000 internal websites and more than 2 million pages of information, Microsoft probably has one of the most advanced and used intranets in the world, with one-third of its 30 000 employees using it every day. In fact, MSWeb, Microsoft's intranet, is so advanced, that nearly all company paperwork, forms, and paper documents have been moved onto it.[44]

Third, using Intranets is intuitive and easy. Point your cursor over a word or symbol that you're interested in. If the cursor turns from an arrow into a hand, indicating that the word or symbol is a link to further information, then click it. Presto! The information you want appears on the screen. That's all there is to it. As a result, companies are rushing to put as much information as they can on their Intranets. Indeed, a study of 323 companies in 10 different industries found that 23 percent of company intranets contained information on company benefits; 18 percent have information about savings plans, profit sharing, or company stock plans; 70 percent have information about jobs; 6 percent allow managers to conduct performance appraisals online; 24 percent are used for training; and 57 percent are used for corporate communications.[45]

Fourth, it doesn't matter if the people in marketing use the Macintosh operating system, the finance folks use Windows, and the information systems people use Unix systems—everyone can easily access information if it's available on the company intranet.[46] Intranets work across all kinds of computers and computer operating systems.

Fifth, if you already have a computer network in place, chances are your company already has the computer equipment and expertise to quickly and easily roll out an intranet.

Sixth, while it's not seamless, many software programs easily convert electronic documents from proprietary word processing (WordPerfect, Microsoft Word, etc.), spreadsheet (Lotus 1-2-3, Microsoft Excel), or graphics (Lotus Freelance or Microsoft PowerPoint) formats to the hypertext markup language (HTML) used to display text and graphics on the Internet and intranets. Indeed, many HTML software editors are now as easy to use as word processors. So when employees have information that others in the company want access to, HTML editors make it easy to publish information on the company intranet for all to see. Boeing's intranet contains everything from corporate-policy material to maintenance manuals, and Boeing encourages its employees to publish any information that others might find useful.[47]

4.3 External Access and Sharing

Historically, companies have been unable or reluctant to let outside groups have access to corporate information. However, three information technologies—electronic data interchange, extranets, and the Internet—are making it easier to share company data with external groups such as suppliers and customers. They're also reducing costs, increasing productivity, improving customer service, and speeding communications. As a result, managers are scrambling to find ways to use them in their own companies.

Electronic data interchange, or **EDI**, is the direct electronic transmission of purchase and ordering information from one company's computer system to another company's computer system. For example, when a Wal-Mart checkout clerk drags a CD across the checkout scanner, Wal-Mart's computerized inventory system automatically reorders another copy of that CD through the direct EDI connection that its computer has with the manufacturing and shipping computer at the company that published the CD, say Atlantic Records. No one at Wal-Mart or Atlantic Records fills out paperwork. No one makes phone calls. There are no delays to wait to find out whether Atlantic has the CD in stock. The transaction takes place instantly and automatically.

electronic data interchange (EDI)
the direct electronic transmission of purchase and ordering information from one company's computer system to another company's computer system

EDI saves companies money by eliminating step after step of manual information processing. One study found that EDI could save manufacturing companies $25 per transaction, retail companies $32 per transaction, and wholesalers $15 per transaction.[48] Of course, those are just averages. Some companies save more. R.J. Reynolds, which deals with more than 1400 suppliers and tens of thousands of orders per year, said that EDI reduced the cost of orders from between $105 and $175 to just $1.30![49] And when you consider that 70 percent of the data output from one company, such as a purchase order, ends up as data input at another company, such as a sales invoice or shipping order, EDI also reduces data entry errors. Finally, EDI reduces order and delivery times. Hotel and motel chains such as Marriott and Hilton have found that EDI has reduced the average time for food and beverage orders to their kitchens by half, from six days to three days.[50]

extranet
allows companies to exchange information and conduct transactions with outsiders by providing them direct, Web-based access to authorized parts of a company's intranet or information system

While EDI directly transmits information from one company's computer system to another's, an **extranet**, by contrast, allows companies to exchange information and conduct transactions with outsiders by providing them direct, Web-based access to authorized parts of a company's intranet or information system. Typically, user names and passwords are required to access an extranet.[51] For example, to make sure that its distribution trucks don't waste money by running half empty (or produce late deliveries to customers because it waited to ship until its trucks were full), General Mills (www.generalmills.com) uses an extranet to provide Web-based access to its trucking database to 20 other companies that ship their products over similar distribution routes. When other companies are ready to ship products, they log on to General Mills' trucking database, check the availability, and then enter the shipping load, place, and pickup time. Thus, by sharing shipping capacity on its trucks, General Mills' trucks run fully loaded all the time. In several test areas, General Mills saved 7 percent on shipping costs, or nearly $2 million (U.S.) in the first year. Cost savings will be even larger when the program is expanded company-wide.[52]

Similar to the way in which extranets are used to handle transactions with suppliers and distributors, companies are reducing paperwork and manual information processing by using the Internet to electronically automate transactions with customers. The **Internet** is a global network of networks that allows users to send and retrieve data from anywhere in the world. Companies such as Air Canada (www.aircanada.com), United Airlines (www.ual.com), and American Airlines (www.aa.com), as well as independent travel sites such as Microsoft Expedia (www.expedia.ca), have Internet sites where customers can purchase tickets without calling a ticket agent or the airline's toll-free number. However, most airlines have further automated the ticketing process by eliminating tickets altogether. Simply buy an e-ticket via the Internet and then show the airport ticket agent your driver's licence or passport. The ticket agent then checks the database, confirms your e-ticket, issues you your boarding pass, and you're on your way. Together, Internet purchases and ticketless travel have the potential to fully automate the purchase of airline tickets. By eliminating the recording, printing, handling, and mailing costs of tickets and the commission that would have been paid to travel agents, the airlines save an estimated $35 to $50 per ticket.[53]

Internet
a global network of networks that allows users to send and retrieve data from anywhere in the world

So, in the end, why should companies try to connect Internet sites for customers to company intranets, EDIs, and extranets? Because companies that use information technologies in these ways achieve increases in productivity 2.7 times larger than those that don't.[54]

4.4 Sharing Knowledge and Expertise

At the beginning of the chapter, we distinguished between raw data, which consists of facts and figures, and information, which consists of useful data that influence someone's choices and behaviour. One more important distinction needs to be made, namely, that data and information are not the same as knowledge. **Knowledge** is the understanding that one gains from information. Importantly, knowledge does not reside in information. Knowledge resides in people. That's why companies hire consultants or why family doctors refer patients to specialists. Unfortunately, it can be quite expensive to employ con-

knowledge
the understanding that one gains from information

sultants, specialists, and experts. So companies have begun using two information technologies, decision-support systems and expert systems, to capture and share the knowledge of consultants, specialists, and experts with other managers and workers.

Unlike executive information systems that speed up and simplify the acquisition of information, **decision support systems (DSS)** help managers understand problems and potential solutions by acquiring and analyzing information with sophisticated models and tools.[55] DSS programs have been developed to help managers pick the shortest and most efficient routes for delivery trucks, to pick the best combination of stocks for investors, and to schedule the flow of inventory through complex manufacturing facilities.

It's important to understand that DSS programs don't replace managerial decision-making; they improve it by furthering managers' and workers' understanding of the problems they face and the solutions that might work. For example, Apache Medical Systems [now owned by Cerner Corporation (www.cerner.com)] makes a DSS for emergency room physicians that is sold throughout Canada.[56] Apache's DSS collects data on 17 different physiological signs, such as blood pressure, respiratory rates, temperature, white blood counts, etc. Then, using a database containing the medical records of more than 400 000 people (with 100 diseases) who received treatment at more than 200 different emergency rooms, Apache's DSS gives a diagnosis and then rates the chances of a patient's survival using various treatment procedures. For a patient with heart problems, the Apache DSS would create a graph showing the likelihood (from zero to 100 percent) of surviving five more years, depending on whether the patient had coronary bypass surgery, an angioplasty, or drug treatment.

Apache's DSS also helps physicians analyze the impact of different decision options by using "What if?" scenarios. The ability to analyze "What if" scenarios is a key capability of all DSS systems. What if we continue with our current strategy, would that work? What if we tried something else? Apache's DSS helps physicians pose and answer "What if?" questions by processing the latest information regarding a patient's health status three times a day and then printing out an unbiased, statistically based estimate of whether a given treatment is working. For example, if a nurse receives two printouts, one in the morning, and then another in the afternoon, indicating that a patient's chances of survival have dropped from 75 percent to 55 percent, the nurse has a very good reason to contact the doctor to reconsider treatment options. Apache is not only helping doctors save lives, but it is also giving doctors the confidence to move patients out of intensive care earlier. With intensive care costs in the United States running about $2500 a day, Apache helped one major U.S. medical centre save $2.5 million (U.S.) a year in unnecessary treatments.[57]

Expert systems are created by capturing the specialized knowledge and decision rules used by experts and experienced decision makers. They permit nonexpert employees to draw on this expert knowledge base to make decisions. For example, when two companies draw up a contract, it usually takes at least two lawyers, one for each company. However, at one major North American telecommunications service provider, company purchasing agents are drafting long-term, multimillion-dollar contracts without using lawyers. Instead, they use an expert system designed and created by company lawyers to automate the creation of company contracts.[58]

Most expert systems work by using a collection of "if-then" rules to sort through information and recommend a course of action. For example, let's say that you're using your American Express card to help your spouse celebrate a promotion. You buy dinner and then some movie tickets. After the movie, you and your spouse stroll by a travel office that displays a Lake Louise poster in its window. Thirty minutes later, caught up in the moment, you find yourselves at the Pearson airport ticket counter trying to purchase last-minute tickets to Lake Louise. But there's just one problem. American Express didn't approve your purchase. In fact, the ticket counter agent is on the phone with an American Express (www.americanexpress.com) customer service agent. So what put a temporary halt to your weekend escape to Lake Louise? An expert system that American

decision support system (DSS)
an information system that helps managers to understand specific kinds of problems and potential solutions and to analyze the impact of different decision options using "what if" scenarios

expert system
information system that contains the specialized knowledge and decision rules used by experts and experienced decision makers, so that nonexperts can draw on this knowledge base to make decisions

Express calls "Authorizer's Assistant." The first "if-then" rule that prevented your purchase was the rule "if a purchase is much larger than the cardholder's regular spending habits, then deny approval of the purchase." This rule is built into American Express's transaction-processing system that handles thousands of purchase requests per second. Now that the American Express customer service agent is on the line, he or she is prompted by the Authorizer's Assistant to ask the ticket counter agent to examine your identification. You hand over your driver's licence and another credit card to prove you're you. Then the ticket agent asks for your address, phone number, social insurance number, and your mother's maiden name, and relays the information to American Express. Finally, your ticket purchase is approved. Why? Because you met the last series of "if-then" rules. If the purchaser can provide proof of identity and if the purchaser can provide personal information that isn't common knowledge, then approve the purchase.

Review 4
Accessing and Sharing Information and Knowledge

E-mail, voice messaging, and conferencing systems are changing how we communicate and work with each other. E-mail is cheap, fast, and easy to use. Though also easy to use, voice messages take more time to process than e-mail. Application sharing and document and videoconferencing let people in different locations work as if they were together in the same room. Executive information systems and intranets facilitate internal sharing and access to company information. Electronic data interchange and the Internet allow external groups, such as suppliers and customers, to easily access company information. Both decrease costs by reducing or eliminating data entry, data errors, and paperwork, and by speeding up communication. Organizations use decision support systems and expert systems to capture and share specialized knowledge with nonexpert employees.

What Really Happened?

At the beginning of the chapter, you learned about the phenomenal success that Dell Computers achieved in the first decade and a half of its existence. In fact, *Fortune* magazine speculated that Dell might be the company of the decade. With its incredible early success, you might be surprised to learn that Dell has completely changed its strategy. On the other hand, it might not surprise you to know that Dell's completely different strategy revolves around the strategic use of information technology. Let's find out what really happened at Dell Computers as it used information technology to deal with the fierce competition and incredibly fast pace of the personal computer industry.

With PC prices dropping so quickly and technological advances moving so fast, the key is no longer just building a better PC, but quickly building a PC with the latest technological components at an aggressive price. However, doesn't that mean that Dell and its memory, hard drive, chip, and motherboard suppliers will have to work more closely (i.e., share more information) than they ever have before? How can that be done?

Historically, companies have been unable or reluctant to let outside groups have access to corporate information. However, information technologies such as electronic data interchange, extranets, and the Internet are not only making it easier to share comp any data with external groups such as suppliers and customers, they're also reducing costs, raising productivity, improving customer service, and speeding communications.

Indeed, Michael Dell says that "one of the big changes that is brought about by information technology is that the cost of connections and linkages has gone down dramatically. So if you've got an operation that builds a component, the cost to communicate with that operation in an information sense, if it is done electronically, goes to zero. That means you can build a linkage between a components supplier and a manufacturer and make it very, very efficient." For example, Dell has direct information connections with its main suppliers of computer components (chips, hard drives, memory, etc.). It provides continuous updates to those suppliers on its costs (for selling a PC to you and me), and in return receives continuous updates from its suppliers. Dell has even set up Internet portals (think of Yahoo.com) to enable suppliers to check on inventories, customer purchases, and so forth. In short, Dell took most of the information that it received from customers or generated internally and shared it with suppliers. Sharing all this information is the equivalent of an early warning system that lets Dell and its suppliers know when prices are rising or falling, or what computer components are in or out of demand. The result is that Dell and its suppliers are closer to the PC market and its changes than any of its competitors.

And if Dell and its suppliers can figure out how to do that, won't that mean that its competitors can do the same thing? Why invest in an information system if it only gives you a temporary competitive advantage? If your competitors can buy the same inventory and customer tracking software that you have, you're only temporarily ahead of the game.

Why invest in an information system if it gives you only a temporary competitive advantage? Well, one reason to do so is to keep from falling behind your competition. But when most companies invest in information technology, they're hoping to create a first-mover advantage by being the first in an industry to use new information technology to substantially lower costs or to differentiate a product or service from competitors. However, creating a first-mover advantage can be difficult, expensive, and risky. Sometimes it fails. But it can succeed, if information technology adds value, is different across firms, and is difficult for other firms to create or acquire. Furthermore, faster computers, more memory, and larger hard drives are not the key to sustaining a competitive advantage that you created through information technology. The key is using information technology to continuously improve and support the core functions of a business. This is precisely what Dell Computers has done.

At Dell, because of the instantaneous, direct flow of information from customers (who buy PCs from the Dell website or its 1-800 phone line) to suppliers, Dell has no finished goods inventory. In other words, it doesn't have two-month-old hard drives sitting around its factories waiting to be installed in your newly ordered PC. In fact, the hard drive installed in a Dell PC is probably no more than a week old, and the hard drive manufacturer doesn't send it to Dell's factory until you order it. This ensures that Dell PCs have only the latest and newest technological components. And, since prices tend to fall as technologies mature, this also ensures that Dell pays the lowest costs for those components. In fact, because you pay for that PC before Dell orders its components and before Dell has to pay its suppliers, it has your cash for eight free days before booking the profit on your order. This also allows Dell to cut PC prices much faster than its competitors. A company spokesperson said, "Our flexibility allows us to be [priced] different even within a day." The results from this approach have been nothing short of amazing. Dell's market share has grown from 6 percent of the PC market five years ago to 25 percent today. Competitors, such as Micron Electronics, which had been in the PC business for nearly two decades, find it difficult to compete. In fact, Micron has left the PC business altogether.

So why should companies seek first-mover advantage? Because, on average, first movers earn 30 percent market share compared to 19 percent for companies that follow. Moreover, over 70 percent of today's market leaders, like Dell Computers, started as first movers.

Finally, in such a fast-moving, competitive environment, if information is the key, how is Dell to make sense of all of the information it generates from customers, uses within the company, and then shares with its suppliers? Having lots of data doesn't do you any good unless you know how to figure out what they mean. So what should Dell do with all that information once it gets its hands on it?

Processing information means transforming raw data into meaningful information that can be applied to business decision-making. Unfortunately, with automated, electronic capture of data, increased processing power, and cheaper and more plentiful ways to store data, managers have more data than they could ever imagine. The key is not getting data, but figuring out how to turn the overwhelming amount of data that pours into their businesses into meaningful information that can improve decision-making. One promising tool to help managers dig out from under the avalanche of data is data mining. Data mining is the process of discovering unknown patterns and relationships in large amounts of data. Most managers need only to know that data mining looks for patterns that are already in the data but are too complex for them to spot on their own.

Most PC manufacturers have access to much of the same data that Dell Computers does. Dell, however, uses and analyzes those data differently. Most PC makers determine computer prices by making sales estimates about how many PCs would sell in a particular quarter. Then, moving backward from the sales estimates, they determine sales prices and then what they're willing to pay for computer components such as hard drives and memory chips. Factory production, in turn, is also based on those sales estimates. But woe to the company that gets the sales estimates wrong. Build too many computers and you're going to lose millions of dollars trying to sell older, more expensive, technologically out-of-date computers. By contrast, Dell doesn't estimate sales at all. Instead, because it relies on actual sales before ordering PC parts, and not sales estimates, it completely removes the possibility of getting sales estimates wrong. This allows Dell to carry almost no inventory in its factories, and thus almost no inventory costs. Over the last seven years, Dell has used the information available from its "build-to-order" system to shrink inventory levels from 31 days of on-hand inventory down to just seven days of inventory.

Sources: C. Lydgate, "Cutting Out the Middle Man," *Asian Business*, 1 May 1998, 12. G. McWilliams, "Dell's New Push: Cheaper Laptops Built to Order," *The Wall Street Journal*, 17 June 1999, B1. G. McWilliams, "Boss Talk: Dell to Detroit: Get into Gear Online! PC Whiz Advises Auto Makers Web Is Best Venue to Handle Suppliers, Serve Customers," *The Wall Street Journal*, 1 December 1999, B1. G. McWilliams, "How Dell Fine Tunes Its PC Pricing to Gain Edge in a Slow Market: Working with Suppliers, It Quickly Passes Changes in Costs to Customers, Three Prices for One Product," *The Wall Street Journal*, 8 June 2001, A1. A. Serwer, L. Smith, & P. de Llosa, "Michael Dell Rocks: Actually, He's Plain Vanilla," *Fortune*, May 1998, 58.

Key Terms

acquisition cost (134)
application sharing (144)
association/affinity patterns (139)
bar code (137)
communication cost (135)
conferencing system (144)
data clusters (139)
data encryption (142)
data mining (137)
data warehouse (139)
decision support system (DSS) (149)
desktop videoconferencing (144)
document conferencing (144)
electronic data interchange (EDI) (147)

electronic scanner (137)
executive information system (EIS) (146)
expert system (149)
extranet (148)
firewall (140)
first-mover advantage (130)
freeware (146)
information (129)
Internet (148)
intranets (146)
knowledge (148)
Moore's law (128)
optical character recognition (137)
predictive patterns (139)

processing cost (134)
processing information (137)
protecting information (140)
raw data (129)
retrieval cost (135)
sequence patterns (139)
shareware (146)
storage cost (135)
supervised data mining (139)
unsupervised data mining (139)
virtual private network (142)
virus (140)

What Would You Do II?

It was November 2002 and David Austin was a little nervous. He and his colleagues in the Toronto and Dartmouth offices of The Decision Point (www.thedecisionpoint.com) were keenly anticipating the official launch of their e-business venture. For two years, Austin had teamed up with stakeholders based in Ontario and Nova Scotia to develop an online product that he felt could revolutionize the process by which small businesses survive and grow.

Fortunately Austin was also no fool and recognized the risks inherent in any new business start-up. A lot had changed in the past 24 months. He had been witness to the tail end of the dot-com boom and the transformation of a vibrant economy to one where sentiments were cautious at best. As CEO he had been among the fortunate few to have been on the receiving end of capital funding through a joint venture as well as sound advice from business incubation, investment and mentoring specialist InNOVAcorp (www.innovacorp.ns.ca) of Dartmouth and its CEO Ross McCurdy.

After much discussion and a lot of research and hard work, The Decision Point was being rolled out as a one-stop online business guidance service whose aim was to help small and medium-sized businesses make good decisions for growth and success. Along with customized guidance, users of the portal would have online access to the best practices of effective business guidance, access to peers, experts and mentors, and avenues for creating new business opportunities.

Specific features of the site included a business problem wizard, business intelligence resources, an assessment centre, and a supplier directory. The business problem wizard offered step-by-step approaches to problem solving using interactive decision-making tools, business guides by topic area, calculators, and pre-formatted spreadsheets. The business intelligence function provided access to timely information such as current market data and reports, industry benchmark studies, and regulatory information using a "previewing" business intelligence function. The assessment centre feature offered Web-based diagnostics and business benchmarks for users to assess their own readiness in motivation, leadership, and other characteristics.

The business model underlying The Decision Point was fairly simple. Users would be attracted to the site through their membership in geographic, industry, or professional partner associations such as ITANS—the Information Technology Industry Alliance of Nova Scotia. The task for Austin and his team was thus to identify and attract associations. Why would associations want to partner with The Decision Point? A number of reasons included added exposure to potential new members, increased revenue opportunities, improved credibility through association with The Decision Point, and benefits for individual members through access to the website. These same associations would also benefit the online service provider by bringing opportunities to put services on the website such as an interactive mentoring service, access to a professional association's training literature, a database of marketing contacts for a specific industry as well as providing an opportunity for individual members to join the site.

How would the online service make money? The primary means of revenue generation was expected to be fees from site sponsorship or advertisements. Two other sources of revenue included fees from organizations seeking to offer enhanced supplier listing information to users of the site and fees from users wishing to make use of the mentoring program.

The next few months would be exciting. As part of the marketing effort, Austin had agreed to speak to a Toronto-based industry association. The requested topic was the major information-related decisions that his team had to make while developing The Decision Point portal. As he sat down to write his speech, a number of concerns jumped to mind. Should The Decision Point's technology platform have been developed in-house or contracted out? How would his team members in Toronto and Halifax communicate and collaborate in the most effective manner? How would client information be captured, stored, processed, and protected? How would site users get the information they need in the quickest manner? **If you were David Austin, what would you do?**

Sources: www.thedecisionpoint.com; correspondence with David Austin, Ross McCurdy, and Lorne Ferguson of The Decision Point.

Critical Thinking Video Case

E-Mail Alert

In Chapter 3, you learned from watching the video that the use of company e-mail systems by employees is increasingly posing a major risk for many companies. Despite cutting costs, easing the flow of communications between customers and clients, and transferring knowledge within companies, e-mail indiscretions by employees can sink corporate ships. The reason is that sometimes employees say things in e-mail that really should not be said. Unfortunately, once typed in, e-mail content is often very difficult to erase and usually does not disappear simply by deleting it.

In this video, you will see how assessing and checking the use of e-mail by company employees has become big business for accounting firms such as KPMG Forensics and law firms such as McMillan Binch. It has also spawned a growing number of firms that specialize in processing electronic evidence. One example is Minnesota-based Kroll Ontrack, a company that specializes in finding e-mail indiscretions. As you watch the video, consider the following critical thinking question.

Critical Thinking Question

E-mails are difficult to delete. If your role in a company was to look for employee e-mail indiscretions, where might you look?

Management Decisions

Lease or Buy?

It has been over four years since your company last upgraded any of its computers or peripherals. Unfortunately, system outages and hardware malfunctions are beginning to disrupt worker performance. You are the chief information officer (CIO) of a medium-sized accounting and consulting firm, and maintaining an operational and efficient computer system is one of your main priorities. Over the last year, you have reported the need for newer computers and have presented several proposals toward upgrading the system in phases. Unfortunately, every time you broached the subject, the owner's response was "if it isn't broken, don't fix it." Now he is singing a different tune. Because of a recent system glitch, the company lost one of its biggest and oldest clients. As a result, the owner now agrees that the entire system needs to be upgraded immediately. In fact, just yesterday, he told you "to spare no expense, just buy it and have it up and running as soon as possible. We can't afford to lose another client because of our dilapidated information system."

You want to purchase machines from a name-brand, quality computer manufacturer. The previous machines, also produced by a well-known manufacturer, have only recently begun to exhibit hardware malfunctions. Therefore, due to advances in technology and improvements in quality, you reasonably expect that the new system will have a useful life of at least four years, possibly more. You have been on the phone all morning contacting vendors and requesting price quotes. All the vendors you spoke to have similar purchase plans and most have lease arrangements. After analyzing the differences between leasing and purchasing, you have identified the advantages and disadvantages associated with each.

Although purchasing the computer system will result in a higher monthly payment compared to leasing, the units will belong to the company when paid off, a clear advantage. Additionally, the entire cost of purchasing and maintaining the computer system will be tax deductible, an element the owner will certainly approve of. The main disadvantage associated with purchasing the computer system includes having to pay for computer-related maintenance and repairs once the warranty period expires. An extended policy can be purchased to provide technical support and repairs after the warranty period; however, the monthly fee for this type of service is rather expensive. A second disadvantage associated with purchasing the computer system, one that you will soon face, is determining what to do with the old computer system. It was once common for many businesses to donate old computers to local school districts after an upgrade; however, due to recent technology initiatives within the local school system, most public schools in your area have better computers than your firm currently does. Therefore, disposing of the obsolete machines will be somewhat difficult.

The advantages of leasing a computer system include a smaller monthly payment; free 24-hour technical support and repair services; and the ability to upgrade to newer, faster machines when the lease period expires, approximately 24 months from now.

Disposing of old computers is not a problem under the lease option since leased computers can be traded in on new computers when the lease expires. One of the biggest disadvantages of leasing a computer system is that it is very similar to renting. At the end of the lease period, you have two choices. Either pay a huge balloon payment and keep the two-year-old (outdated) computer system, or renew the lease and upgrade the system again. Given the owner's previous track record, you feel it will be difficult to convince the owner to upgrade the system again after only 24 months. You yourself doubt the need for replacing computers every two years since the majority of employees are currently using less than 20 percent of their computer's processing power at any given time. Additionally, after discussing the leasing option with several accountants within the firm, one accountant informed you that certain computer leases, specifically operational leases, are not tax deductible and cannot be depreciated.

As you jot down the minimum system requirements on your legal pad, you ask yourself, should we buy or lease?

Questions

1. Acting as the CIO mentioned above, which method would you recommend to the owner and why?
2. Go online to a well-known computer manufacturer such as Dell computers at www.dell.ca or Gateway computers at www.gateway.com and compare their purchase/lease options. Reevaluate your recommendation. Did your decision change after viewing the two options? Why or why not?
3. Use the Internet Resources listed below to further your information-gathering. Once you have done all your research, review your decision again. Did it change after more extensive research? Why or why not?

Additional Internet Resources

- Evaluate various machines by consulting several nonmarketing controlled (i.e., independent) sources of information. *Consumer Reports* (www.consumerreports.org) is an example. You may also wish to consult computer magazines such as *PC World* (www.pcworld.com), *PC Magazine* (www.pcmag.com), and *Computer World* (www.computerworld.com). They regularly review hardware and software systems and may provide you with a more detailed analysis of the systems you are considering than you can find anywhere else.
- Consider checking shopping bots—any script or program such as MySimon.com and cnet.com that is designed to perform automated actions on behalf of the owner, usually without the owner's direct intervention—and comparing features and prices. Other good price comparison tools are PriceScan.com and Bizrate.com. Streetprices.com is also a good resource for price shopping.
- If you're thinking of trying to get a deal, review auction sites. A popular site that specializes in electronics is www.ubid.ca. Also try www.pcbuyer.com. PCCost (www.pccost.com) claims it sells computers and peripherals at cost, so check it out.
- And don't forget to check offers at retailers such as Best Buy (www.bestbuy.com). Even office supply retailers such as Office Depot (www.techdepot.com) and Staples (www.staples.com) may have what you're looking for. At the very least, you will have something to compare your hot Internet deal to!

Management Decisions

Hack Attack

As you clear off your desk, getting ready to leave for the night, the phone rings. The voice on the other end of the line is Sue, your company's network administrator. She informs you that a hacker has just broken into the company's e-commerce site. One of the databases entered by the intruder contains personal customer data, including names, addresses, and credit card information. You immediately ask questions, attempting to determine the potential damage caused by this attack. According to Sue, approximately 3.3 million customer files, both past and present, could have been compromised. Upon noticing the intrusion, Sue immediately closed down the network and ordered her staff to get on the phone with the software company's technical support to begin repairing the breach. She informs you that she and her staff will do everything to repair the network and get it back online as soon as possible, but she asks about the information that might have been compromised. Should we tell someone? As the chief information officer (CIO) of Egghead.com, an Internet-based retailer, you assure her that you will notify the proper constituencies.

As you hang up the phone, you begin to calculate the different options of attempting to resolve this current problem. Attempted hacking is not new to your firm. Research shows that most well-known sites face up to five or six attempted intrusions on any given day. Unfortunately, this is the first successful attempt on Egghead.com's site. The fact that they were able to not only get in, but also enter a secure database is disturbing. Currently, Egghead.com has no policy and procedures manual to turn to when a network compromise has occurred. Questions begin to race through your mind. Do you risk notifying all your customers, suppliers, and other stakeholders? Doing so might diminish customer confidence and result in decreased sales. Do you notify the press? Doing so would most likely advertise to would-be hackers that your site has serious security issues. You think to yourself, "We might as well put up a billboard saying, 'We're open, hack away.'"

Questions

1. As the CIO of Egghead.com, would you alert all affected parties and inform them of the breach, or keep the information internal? What is the rationale behind your decision?
2. What policies and procedures could be implemented to keep this problem from recurring?

Source: M. Hicks, "Telling Customers the Bad News—When and How to Get the Word Out That Your Security's Been Breached," *eWeek*, 19 February 2001.

Develop Your Management Potential

Web Privacy Policy

With the advent of the Internet and its explosive growth, the need to protect an individual's privacy has increased dramatically in recent years. Many Internet websites require that personal information such as name, address, phone number(s), social insurance numbers, and credit card information be submitted before allowing a consumer to conduct any type of e-commerce transactions. Most Web-based companies have policies stating the extent to which this information will be used, the length of time the information will be kept, and what will happen to the information if the company folds. However, with the recent crash of many dot-coms, the industry has discovered that a significant portion of these policies are not worth the paper that they are printed on. For instance, Toysmart.com, a recent casualty of the dot-com bust, recently sought to gain approval from a bankruptcy court to auction off their database despite promising to never do so in their Web privacy policy. As more and more dot-coms fail, the opportunity to sell customer information, possibly the only tangible asset that an Internet-based firm owns, will most likely rise. One example of the detrimental effects of sensitive information being publicly released was recently observed when pharmaceutical company Eli Lilly accidentally released the e-mail addresses of more than 600 people currently taking Prozac, a common antidepressant medication. In order to combat the problems caused by the release of sensitive and confidential information, privacy advocates are pushing for more stringent legislation to protect consumers and their personal information. In order to appease legislators and to promote self-regulation as opposed to government regulation, one industry body is proposing several recommendations for Internet-based businesses to adopt in constructing or strengthening their privacy policies. These recommendations are as follows:

1. The word "never" should be taken literally. If a firm promises to never sell customer information, it should abide by its promise. Additionally, this promise should survive and remain true even if the firm's assets are parcelled out as a result of bankruptcy hearings.
2. Consumers should be given a choice. If a firm decides to sell confidential customer information, customers should

be given a choice before that information is released. Although this rule is currently being enforced through current legislation, the current privacy laws require the customer to "opt out" if they wish their information not be released. This places the burden on the consumer to contact the retailer and inform them of their wish to keep their personal information private. Privacy advocates want the rule to be changed so that consumers must "opt in," thereby placing the burden on retailers by requiring them to obtain the consumer's approval before information can be released.

3. Companies should restrict the type of information disclosed. Should a company sell information, they should limit the information disclosed to only names and addresses, typical of information found on most mailing lists. This would require companies to maintain separate databases, one for information that can be sold or disclosed, and the other, a secure database that contains more private information such as age, ethnicity, income, social insurance number, credit information, and so forth.

As a manager charged with constructing a privacy policy for your firm, you are instructed to visit a well-known company website and inspect its Web-privacy policy. As you read the policy, compare its policy with the information proposed above. What elements of its policy could be improved and what elements would you include in developing your own firm's Web-privacy policy? Using the information presented above and another firm's Web-privacy policy as a guide, draft a Web-privacy policy for your firm.

Sources: "Web Form Can Be Used by Consumers to Protect Privacy," *The Wall Street Journal*, 25 May 2001. P. Davidson, "Capitol Hill Support Brews for Internet Privacy Laws," *USA Today*, 12 July 2001. H. Green, "Your Right to Privacy: Going...Going...," *Business Week*, 23 April 2001.

Discussion Questions

1. What is the difference between raw data and useful information?

2. Two years into your position with a major multinational consulting firm, your boss has approached you with an interesting assignment. She has asked you to find out as much as you can about a competitor's new product launch. You are excited about the prospect of pursuing this challenge but you also realize that not all the information you will need will be found in-house. Prior to accepting the assignment, you would like to discuss with her the five costs of obtaining information. What are they? Describe each briefly.

3. Sitting at home one night, an interesting thought pops into your mind. It is that you have extreme good fortune to have joined a small firm upon graduation and stuck with it for a few years while it grew and prospered. Personally you have gained from this experience—a healthy bi-weekly paycheque, numerous promotions, and interesting work. Unfortunately, with growth has also come challenges. One challenge is that your company now faces the need to store large amounts of data for long periods of time. You have been asked to give a presentation in the morning on the kinds of data storage devices available for use by your organization. What are your options in this regard?

4. A good friend of yours has just been offered a position as head of marketing of a small manufacturing company. Oddly, within his portfolio of responsibilities is the I.T. function for his company. Admittedly, he has a few things to learn to get up to speed with this function. He invites you to join him for coffee to share any insight you might be able to offer him given your stature as a business student. In particular, he is interested in learning how his company can protect information and why it is important to do so. What can you tell him?

5. As a favour to a parent, you have agreed to take the daughter of a business client out for coffee. Although you dreaded the occasion, once underway you found yourself fascinated by the curiosity of this 20-year-old. It soon became apparent that you both shared a common interest—information technology. Unfortunately, your actual experiences far outweighed those of your new friend. Of particular interest to her was the function of an intranet and the reasons behind their popularity with companies. What might you tell her?

Imagine you are the professor, and you are making up a test for Chapter 5. What are the main topics and key concepts that students should know? If you work with a study group, exchange practice tests. Work on them individually, then "grade" them collectively. This way you can discuss trouble spots and answer each other's questions.

CHAPTER 6

Chapter Outline

Learning Objectives

After reading this chapter, you should be able to

1. explain the steps to rational decision-making.
2. discuss the limits to rational decision-making.
3. describe how individual decision-making can be improved.
4. explain how group decisions and group decision-making techniques can improve decision-making.

CP (Jonathan Hayward)

Decision-Making

What Would You Do?

Most people who pull up to the gas station for a fill-up are hoping for cheaper prices. But as head of research for British Petroleum Amoco (BP Amoco), you'd rather watch prices rise, which you certainly couldn't do with oil below $22 a barrel (down from $36 a barrel). Indeed, with gas and oil prices at their lowest level in 20 years, consumers are having a great time, driving as far and as long as they like, buying tank-sized, gas-guzzling sport utility vehicles. While consumers love the low price of gasoline, you hate it. Because of the low prices, oil company profits have disappeared, causing oil company stock prices to drop by a third compared to the previous year. Following the stock drops were the inevitable employee layoffs to cut costs. And no matter what anybody says, laying people off is never "just business." Your top finance executive insisted that the layoffs were necessary to restore profits. Still, you took no joy in the cuts, as you watched many long-time friends and associates leave the company. On top of that, company-wide budget cuts mean that you've got significantly less money in the oil exploration budget used to drill test wells and hopefully discover the next big reserve that will produce millions of barrels of crude oil for BP Amoco for years to come.

Ironically, these cuts come just as you were preparing to persuade top manage-ment to significantly increase its oil explo-ration budget for deepwater drilling. Most people know about land-based drilling, in which test wells are drilled 90 to 900 metres deep for oil, and offshore drilling, in which platform-based oil derricks sit in water less than 300 metres deep to drill 300 to 1500 metres below the bottom of the sea floor in offshore locations such as the Hibernia oilfields off the coast of Newfoundland or the North Sea off the coast of Scotland. However, in deepwater drilling, oil companies either submerse an oil-drilling rig to the ocean floor or use a drill ship, the more popular option, to drill for oil in water as much as 3000 metres deep. Drill ships use global positioning systems and sophisticated computer-controlled thrusters and propellers to monitor and maintain their precise loca-tion on the water surface above the drilling site, never floating more than two or three metres away from the desired drilling loca-tion, even in storms and rough waters.

The key difficulty is that deepwater drilling is incredibly expensive. The drill ships used in deepwater drilling range in cost from $600 million to $1.8 billion, depending on their size, and can cost as much as $300 000 per day to lease. Furthermore, drilling a deepwater well typically costs $75 million, compared to about $1.5 million for an onshore well. Beyond that, near freezing temperatures can congeal oil, sand, and other materials into a clog as hard as a diamond that costs $300 000 a day to dig out. Yet, despite these costs, if you can uncover a major oilfield, the numbers you've run seem to indicate that oil retrieved from deepwater drilling sites may cost from one-third to one-half less than the oil flowing from land-based oil wells. Of course, that's what you hope. You can never be sure until production begins.

Well, any way you look at it, you're convinced that deepwater drilling is a good bet, but how can you demonstrate that to top management, especially con-sidering the risks involved and the tough economic conditions? In part, it will depend on how risk averse top managers are. Are they willing to spend huge sums of money to potentially put BP Amoco in front of its competitors for years to come, or are they risk averse, wanting to sit back and see whether other oil companies have success with deepwater drilling first? Finally, it may come down to something as simple as how the problem is defined. Is the problem cutting costs to restore prof-itability, or is the problem investing com-pany funds in smartly calculated risks that might pay off in huge increases in oil rev-enue? In the end, though, you don't want to just convince upper management to do what you want; you want to be right, too.

If you were in charge of oil explo-ration for BP Amoco, what would you do?

NEL

Sources: J. Biers, "Drilling's Leviathans Stumble to Sea: New Generation Rigs, Ships Born in Rough Waters," *Houston Chronicle*, 17 October 1999, Business 6. D. Fisher, "How Sir John Browne Turned BP Amoco into the Hottest Prospect in the Oil Patch," *Forbes*, 2 April 2001, 110. D. Ivanovich, "The New 2000 Millennium—World May Learn to Wean Itself from Oil: The Search for Crude Deepens, As Does the Concern over Its Future," *Houston Chronicle*, 24 October 1999, 1. S. Liesman & A. Sullivan, "Mystery Man: Exxon Mobil Merger Positions an Enigma at Oil Giant's Helm: Hardly a Household Name, Mr. Raymond Fostered a Revolution Quietly Playing Everyman at Valdez," *The Wall Street Journal*, 1 December 1999. Staff Reports, "Giant in the Gulf: BP Amoco's Massive Oil Drilling Platform Has Begun Pumping with 5 Wells in Gulf," *The New Orleans Times Picayune*, 3 December 1999, C1. K. Williams, "Transocean at Standoff on Drill Ship," *Houston Chronicle*, 10 June 2001, Business 2.

EXPERIENCING MANAGEMENT

There are many different models of rational decision-making, but most of them contain common steps. To view an alternative decision-making model, visit our animated concept and activity site. Choose Decision-Making from the "select a topic" pull-down menu, then Decision-Making Process from the "overview tab."

www.experiencingmanagement.com

decision-making
the process of choosing a solution from available alternatives

rational decision-making
a systematic process of defining problems, evaluating alternatives, and choosing optimal solutions

Even inexperienced managers know that decision-making and problem-solving are central parts of their jobs. Figure out what the problem is. Generate potential solutions. Pick the best solution. Make it work. Experienced managers, however, know how hard it really is to make good decisions and solve problems. One seasoned manager said, "I think the biggest surprises are the problems. Maybe I had never seen it before. Maybe I was protected by my management when I was in sales. Maybe I had delusions of grandeur, I don't know. I just know how disillusioning and frustrating it is to be hit with problems and conflicts all day and not be able to solve them very cleanly."[1] Undoubtedly, the manager in charge of oil exploration at BP Amoco feels the same frustration and uncertainty about deepwater drilling. Deepwater drilling holds fantastic potential that might, just might, pay off. However, deepwater drilling is incredibly expensive. And unlike its iffy payoffs, there's no uncertainty about its high costs. Any way you look at it, it's a tough decision for BP Amoco to make.

Decision-making is the process of choosing a solution from available alternatives.[2] We begin the chapter by reviewing **rational decision-making**, a systematic process in which managers define problems, evaluate alternatives, and choose optimal solutions that provide maximum benefits to their organizations. We discuss the steps of rational decision-making as well as its limitations. In the second part of the chapter, we look at how

BP Amoco had to deal with uncertainty while deciding whether to undertake deep-water drilling.

© Reuters NewMedia Inc./CORBIS/MAGMA

managers can improve their decisions. Here we discuss methods for improving rational decision-making and how managers can use groups and group decision techniques to improve decisions.

What Is Rational Decision-Making?

Imagine that you've been away on business. On your first day back at the office, you sort through your phone messages and find this voice-mail from the boss:

> You're a computer jock, aren't you? Well, you know more about this stuff than anyone else in the office. Here's what I need from you. You've got three weeks to get it done. I want you to prepare a presentation and write a report that details the problems we've been having with our computers. It should also summarize our current and future computer needs. Talk to everyone. Find out what they need and want. Be sure to consider upgrade options. I don't want to spend a ton of money to improve our systems only to have them be obsolete in two years. Finally, come up with at least five plans or options for getting us where we need to be. Hey, almost forgot, you're probably going to have to do some educating here. Most of us in management don't speak "computer geek." Heck, half of the dinosaurs we've got in upper management think computers are $1500 paper weights—don't repeat that, okay? So be sure to explain in everyday language how we can decide which plans or options are best. Have a rough draft on my desk in three weeks.

When your boss delegated this "computer problem," what he really wanted from you is a rational decision. In other words, you need to define and analyze the problem, and explore alternatives. Furthermore, the solution has to be "optimal," since the department is going to live with the computer equipment you recommend for the next three years.

After reading the next two sections, you should be able to
1. explain the steps to rational decision-making.
2. discuss the limits to rational decision-making.

1. Steps to Rational Decision-Making

Exhibit 6.1 shows the six steps of the rational decision-making process.

The steps in rational decision making are defining the problem, identifying decision criteria, weighting the criteria, generating alternative courses of action, evaluating each alternative, and computing the optimal decision.

1.1 Define the Problem

The first step in decision-making is identifying and defining the problem. A **problem** exists when there is a gap between a desired state—what managers want—and an existing state—the situation that the managers are facing. For example, despite being the largest and most popular e-tailing site on the Web with, by far, the highest customer satisfaction ratings, Amazon.com has not been profitable in its first five years. In its fifth year, 20 million customers bought $4.2 billion of books, electronics, video, and music. However, the company lost $2.1 billion making those sales![3]

The existence of a gap between an existing state and a desired state is no guarantee that managers will make decisions to solve problems. Three things must occur for this to happen.[4] First, managers have to be aware of the gap. They have to know there is a

problem
a gap between a desired state and an existing state

EXHIBIT 6.1

STEPS OF THE RATIONAL DECISION-MAKING PROCESS

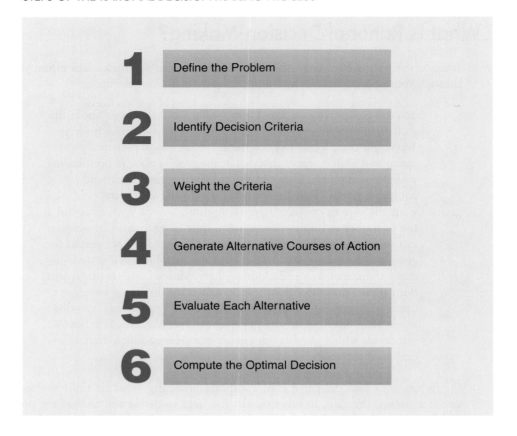

1 Define the Problem

2 Identify Decision Criteria

3 Weight the Criteria

4 Generate Alternative Courses of Action

5 Evaluate Each Alternative

6 Compute the Optimal Decision

problem before they can begin solving it. For example, after noticing that people were spending more money on their pets, a new dog food company created an expensive, high-quality dog food. To emphasize the quality of the product, the dog food was sold in cans and bags with gold labels, red letters, and detailed information about product benefits and nutrients. However, the product didn't sell very well, and the company was out of business in less than a year. Company founders didn't understand why. When they asked a manager at a competing dog food company what their biggest mistake had been, the answer was "Simple. You didn't have a picture of a dog on the package."[5] This problem would have been easy to solve, if management had only been aware of it.

Being aware of the gap between a desired state and an existing state isn't enough to begin the decision-making process. Managers also have to be motivated to reduce the gap. Finally, it's not enough to be aware of a problem and be motivated to solve it. Managers must also have the knowledge, skills, abilities, and resources to fix the problem. Amazon.com is now going "full out" to reverse the gap between its oversized expenses and its undersized revenues. It has a new accounting system that uses product and shipping costs, the frequency with which products are returned, and 47 other factors to show how much money Amazon makes or loses on each product it sells. For example, this program (which Amazon built internally using 800 000 equations) indicated that, given the difference between retail and wholesale prices, Amazon should have been making a profit on a $15 pack of Polaroid instant film. However, after factoring in all its costs, from inventory to packing to billing to shipping, Amazon lost $1.50 each time it sold this product. Since Amazon lost money on this item, the computer then suggested several options to make it profitable: "consider bundling with other items" (to reduce shipping costs), "find another merchant to handle and ship the film," "press vendor for lower costs," or "raise prices."[6] After making many changes, Amazon showed its second quarterly profit at the end of 2002.[7]

1.2 Identify Decision Criteria

Decision criteria are the standards used to guide judgments and decisions. Typically, the more criteria that a potential solution meets, the better that solution should be.

Let's return to the employee who was given the responsibility for making a rational decision about the office computer setup. What general kinds of factors would be important when purchasing computers for the office? Reliability, price, warranty, on-site service, and compatibility with existing software, printers, and computers would all be important, wouldn't they? However, you can't buy computer equipment without considering the technical details. So what kinds of specific factors would you want the office computer to have? Well, with technology changing so quickly, you'll probably want to buy computers with as much capability as you can afford. At the minimum, according to *PC Magazine*, you'll probably want a 64-bit 1.5-gigahertz Pentium 4 or Athlon chip, with 256 megs of memory, a 40-gig hard drive, a DVD drive holding 8 gigabytes of data, a 100 megabit per second network card for high-speed Internet connections, and a 19-inch monitor—all for a price of $3000 or less![8] These general and specific factors represent the criteria that could guide the purchase of computer equipment.

1.3 Weight the Criteria

After identifying decision criteria, the next step is deciding which criteria are more or less important. For example, despite *PC Magazine*'s advice, a 19-inch monitor and a DVD-ROM drive aren't that important for business computers. In most cases, a lower-cost 17-inch monitor would suffice for office work (word processing, e-mail, and spreadsheets). And, as long as someone on the office network has a DVD-ROM drive that can be accessed from any other computer on the network, then most office computers don't have to have a DVD-ROM drive. A CD-ROM drive in each computer will do. On the other hand, a 1.5-gigahertz Pentium or Athlon computer chip, 256 megabytes of memory, high-speed network/Internet connections, and at least a 40-gigabyte hard drive are "must-haves" for today's desktop corporate computers. (These specifications may be outdated by the time you read this.)

While there are numerous mathematical models for weighting decision criteria, all require the decision maker to provide an initial ranking of the decision criteria. Some use **absolute comparisons**, in which each criterion is compared to a standard or ranked on its own merits. For example, *Consumer's Digest* uses a 12-point checklist when it rates and recommends new cars. Six points address the car's performance (starting and acceleration, fuel economy, handling and steering, shifting/transmission, ride quality, and braking), and six address the car's design (overall design, interior ergonomics, seating, accessories and amenities, cargo space, and fit and finish).[9]

Exhibit 6.2 shows the absolute weights that someone buying a car might use. Because these weights are absolute, each criterion is judged on its own importance, using a five-point scale, with "5" representing "critically important" and "1" representing "completely unimportant." In this instance, fuel economy, seating, and cargo space were rated most important, while shifting/transmission, accessories, and amenities were rated least important.

EXHIBIT 6.2

ABSOLUTE WEIGHTING OF DECISION CRITERIA FOR A CAR PURCHASE

5 critically important
4 important
3 somewhat important
2 not very important
1 completely unimportant

PERFORMANCE CHARACTERISTICS

1. starting and acceleration	1	2	3	**4**	5
2. fuel economy	1	2	3	4	**5**
3. handling and steering	1	2	**3**	4	5
4. shifting/transmission	1	**2**	3	4	5
5. ride quality	1	2	**3**	4	5
6. braking	1	2	3	**4**	5

DESIGN CHARACTERISTICS

1. overall design	1	2	3	**4**	5
2. interior ergonomics	1	2	**3**	4	5
3. seating	1	2	3	4	**5**
4. accessories and amenities	**1**	2	3	4	5
5. cargo space	1	2	3	4	**5**
6. fit and finish	1	2	**3**	4	5

relative comparisons
a process in which each decision criterion is compared directly to every other criterion

Another method is **relative comparisons**, in which each criterion is compared directly to every other criterion.[10] For example, moving down the first column of Exhibit 6.3, we see that starting/acceleration has been rated less important (–1) than fuel economy; more important (+1) than handling and steering, shifting/transmission, and

EXHIBIT 6.3

RELATIVE COMPARISON FOR CAR PERFORMANCE CHARACTERISTICS

CAR PERFORMANCE CHARACTERISTICS	STARTING/ ACCELERATION	FUEL ECONOMY	HANDLING AND STEERING	SHIFTING/ TRANSMISSION	RIDE QUALITY	BRAKING
starting/ acceleration		+1	–1	–1	–1	0
fuel economy	–1		–1	–1	–1	–1
handling and steering	+1	+1		0	0	+1
shifting/ transmission	+1	+1	0		0	0
ride quality	+1	+1	0	0		0
braking	0	+1	–1	0	0	
Total weight	+2	+5	–3	–2	–2	0

ride quality; but just as important as braking (0). Total weights, which are obtained by summing the scores in each column, indicate that fuel economy and starting/acceleration are the most important factors to this car buyer, while handling and steering, shifting/transmission, and ride quality are the least important.

1.4 Generate Alternative Courses of Action

After identifying and weighting the criteria that will guide the decision-making process, the next step is to identify possible courses of action that could solve the problem. In general, at this step, the idea is to generate as many alternatives as possible. For instance, let's assume that your high-tech manufacturing company wants to reduce costs by moving its headquarters out of Toronto. Why? Because real estate costs are astronomical, congested roadways lead to long commuting times, and housing costs make it difficult to attract talented employees from other parts of the country. Not surprisingly, the location of your new headquarters would have to meet the following criteria: high quality of life (easy commutes), low operating costs, low corporate tax rates, a highly educated workforce, low cost of labour, and a low cost of living (low real estate costs). After meeting with your staff, you generate a list of alternative locations: Calgary, Edmonton, Halifax, Ottawa, Regina, Saskatoon, St. John, and Winnipeg.

1.5 Evaluate Each Alternative

The next step is to systematically evaluate each alternative against each criterion. Because of the amount of information that must be collected, this step can take much longer and be much more difficult than other steps in the decision-making process. For example, in order to evaluate the quality of locations, one has to find information from such organizations as Statistics Canada (www.statcan.ca). In addition, KPMG has done extensive work on such things as tax rates, operating costs, and cost of labour (www.competitive alternatives.com). Their data were based on the cost averages for the last ten years and looked at more than 30 000 cost items.

Once the necessary information has been gathered, it is used to evaluate each alternative against each criterion. Exhibit 6.4 shows how each of the eight cities fared on each criterion (higher scores are better). For example, Ottawa has some of the highest costs in all categories (housing, labour, and operating), while Halifax has the lowest labour costs.

EXHIBIT 6.4

CRITERIA RATINGS USED TO EVALUATE THE BEST COMPANY LOCATIONS

	COMMUTING DISTANCE	OPERATING COSTS	TAX RATES	EDUCATION LEVEL	LABOUR COSTS	HOUSING COSTS
Calgary	3	2	7	7	2	2
Edmonton	2	3	6	3	6	3
Halifax	6	4	3	7	8	4
Regina	8	7	5	4	4	7
Ottawa	1	1	8	8	1	1
Saskatoon	7	6	4	5	5	5
Saint John	3	8	1	1	7	8
Winnipeg	5	5	2	3	3	6

Sources: www.statcan.ca, www.competitivealternatives.com.

The final step in the decision-making process is to compute the optimal decision by determining each alternative's value. This is done by multiplying the rating for each criterion (Step 5) by the weight for that criterion (Step 3), and then summing those scores for each alternative course of action that you generated (Step 4). For example, your company rated the six criteria in the following manner: commuting time (15 percent), operating costs (25 percent), tax rates (15 percent), education level (10 percent), labour costs (15 percent), and housing costs (20 percent). Those weights are then multiplied by the ratings in each category. For example, Regina's optimal value of 6.10 (i.e., weighted average) is determined using the following calculation:

$$(.15 \times 8) + (.25 \times 7) + (.15 \times 5) + (.10 \times 4) + (.15 \times 4) + (.15 \times 7) = 6.10$$

Exhibit 6.5 shows that Regina is clearly the best location for your company, no doubt because of its extremely short commuting distances, low housing cost, and low labour costs. By contrast, Ottawa is the worst location by virtue of its high commuting distances and high labour, housing, and operating costs.

Review 1
Steps to Rational Decision-Making

Rational decision-making is a six-step process in which managers define problems, evaluate alternatives, and compute optimal solutions. The first step is identifying and defining the problem. Problems exist where there is a gap between desired and existing states. Managers won't begin the decision-making process unless they are aware of the gap, are motivated to reduce it, and possess the necessary resources to fix it. The second step is defining the decision criteria that are used when judging alternatives. In Step 3, an absolute or relative comparison process is used to rate the importance of decision criteria. Step 4 involves generating as many possible courses of action (i.e., solutions) as possible. Potential solutions are assessed in Step 5 by systematically gathering information and evaluating each alternative against each criterion. In Step 6, criterion ratings and weights are used to compute the optimal value for each alternative course of action. Rational managers then choose the alternative with the highest optimal value.

2. Limits to Rational Decision-Making

In general, managers who diligently complete all six steps of the rational decision-making model will make better decisions than those who don't. So, when they can, managers should try to follow the steps in the rational decision-making model, especially for big decisions with long-range consequences.

EXHIBIT 6.5

CITIES RANKED BY SELECTION CRITERIA

VALUES

1.	Regina	6.10
2.	Saskatoon	5.40
3.	Saint John	5.35
4.	Halifax	5.05
5.	Winnipeg	4.25
6.	Edmonton	3.75
7.	Calgary	3.40
8.	Ottawa	2.75

However, it's highly doubtful that rational decision-making can help managers choose optimal solutions that provide maximum benefits to their organizations. The terms "optimal" and "maximum" suggest that rational decision-making leads to perfect or near-perfect decisions. Of course, for managers to make perfect decisions, they have to operate in perfect worlds with no real-world constraints. For example, in an optimal world, the manager who was given three weeks to define, analyze, and fix computer problems in the office would have followed *PC Magazine*'s advice to buy all employees the "perfect personal computer" (i.e., 1-gigahertz chip, 256 megabytes of memory, etc.). And in arriving at that decision, our manager would not have been constrained by price ("$5000 per computer? Sure, no problem.") or time ("Need six more months to decide? Sure, take as long as you need."). Furthermore, without any constraints, our manager could identify and weight an extensive list of decision criteria, generate a complete list of possible solutions, and then test and evaluate each computer against each decision criterion. Finally, our manager would have to have the necessary experience and knowledge with computers to easily make sense of all these sophisticated tests and information.

Of course, it never works like that in the real world. Managers face time and money constraints. They often don't have time to make extensive lists of decision criteria. And they often don't have the resources to test all possible solutions against all possible criteria.

Let's see how bounded rationality, risk and risky decisions, and common decision-making mistakes make it difficult for managers to make completely rational, optimal decisions.

2.1 Bounded Rationality

The rational decision-making model describes the way decisions should be made. In other words, decision makers wanting to make optimal decisions should not have to face time and costs constraints. They should have unlimited resources and time to generate and test all alternative solutions against all decision criteria. And they should be willing to recommend any decision that produces optimal benefits for the company, even if that decision would harm their own jobs or departments. Of course, very few managers actually make rational decisions the way they should. The way in which managers actually make decisions is more accurately described as "bounded (or limited) rationality."

Bounded rationality means that managers try to take a rational approach to decision-making, but are restricted by real-world constraints, incomplete and imperfect information, and their own limited decision-making capabilities. More specifically, as shown in Exhibit 6.6, at least four problems prevent managers from making rational decisions.[11] First, as described above, limited resources often prevent managers from making rational decisions. Managers only have so much time, so much money, and so many people, machines, or offices to devote to a specific problem. When resources increase or decrease, managers change their decisions. For example, when the economy slowed down, Jiffy-Tite, an auto parts manufacturer, cut back on capital spending for expensive new product testing equipment. CEO Jeff Zillig said, "We had planned on the worst . . . and cut the spending budget for testing equipment in half to $100 000." Less than a year later, however, finances improved, so Zillig said, "We're going back to our original budget." Therefore, Jiffy-Tite bought the new testing equipment.[12] Because of limited resources, there is almost always a difference between what managers would like to do (i.e., rational decision-making) and what they can do (i.e., bounded rationality).

Second, attention problems limit the information that a decision maker can pay attention to at any one time. Often, attention problems stem from **information overload**, or too much information. For example, since *PC Magazine* uses 24 specific decision criteria to describe the "perfect PC," and since it typically tests approximately 50 computers every time it conducts a review, our rational decision maker would have to process 1200 different pieces of information. This is simply too much information for one person to make sense of. Even 10 decision criteria and 10 computers would be too much.

bounded rationality
decision-making process restricted in the real world by limited resources, incomplete and imperfect information, and managers' limited decision-making capabilities

information overload
situation in which decision makers have too much information to attend to

EXHIBIT 6.6

PROBLEMS ASSOCIATED WITH BOUNDED RATIONALITY

Third, memory problems make it difficult to recall or retrieve stored information. Managers forget important facts and details. Companies don't always keep the best records. Since the new computer equipment has to be compatible with the old computer equipment, our manager's first task would be to find out what equipment the company already owns. However, if detailed records have not been kept, and if employees don't know the configuration of their computers ("Does it have an Athlon, or a Pentium chip? What speed is the chip, 1-, 1.3-, or 1.5-gigahertz?"), then each computer will have to be manually inspected to gather this information. Furthermore, information retrieval is not free. It costs time and money.

Fourth, expertise problems make it difficult for decision makers to organize, summarize, and fully comprehend all the information that is available for making the decision. Realistically, even though our manager is a self-professed computer "geek," he or she probably doesn't have the required experience or knowledge to make sense of all the test results and determine which computer is the "perfect PC." The difficulty of this task is illustrated by the fact that *PC Magazine* employs 30 full-time staffers in two research labs stuffed with hundreds of thousands of dollars of equipment to make such decisions. No one, not even managers, can possess expert knowledge about everything.

In theory, fully rational decision makers **maximize** decisions by choosing the optimal solution. However, limited resources, along with attention, memory, and expertise problems, make it nearly impossible for managers to maximize decisions. Consequently, most managers don't maximize—they "satisfice." Whereas maximizing is choosing the best alternative, **satisficing** is choosing a "good enough" alternative. With 24 decision criteria, 50 alternative computers to choose from, two computer labs with hundreds of thousands of dollars of equipment, and unlimited time and money, our manager could test all alternatives against all decision criteria and choose the "perfect PC." However, our manager's limited time, money, and expertise mean that only a few alternatives will be assessed against a few decision criteria. In practice, our manager will visit two or three computer or electronic stores, read a couple of recent computer reviews,

maximizing
choosing the best alternative

satisficing
choosing a "good enough" alternative

and then get three or four bids from local computer stores that sell complete computer systems at competitive prices. The decision will be complete when our manager finds a "good enough" computer that meets a few decision criteria, most likely low price, a 1.5-gigahertz chip, a 40-gigabyte hard drive, and 256 megabytes of memory.

2.2 Risk and Decision-Making under Risky Conditions

Step 5 of the rational decision-making model assumes that managers can gaze into their crystal balls and accurately predict how well a potential solution will fix a problem. Furthermore, it assumes that managers make decisions under **conditions of certainty**, with complete information and knowledge of all possible outcomes. It's like knowing who won the Stanley Cup the last 10 times and then travelling 10 years back in time with $1000 in your pocket. Because you already know who won, deciding which team to bet on is easy. You're a guaranteed winner.

Of course, if decision-making were this easy, companies wouldn't need very many managers. In most situations, managers make decisions under **conditions of risk**, with a very real possibility of losing (making the wrong decision). Thus, risk and risky conditions make it difficult for managers to make completely rational, optimal decisions.

Furthermore, risk has a significant effect on how decision makers define and solve problems. Consider this problem from Max Bazerman's book *Judgment in Managerial Decision Making*:

> A large car manufacturer has recently been hit with a number of economic difficulties, and it appears as if three plants need to be closed and 6,000 employees laid off. The vice president of production has been exploring alternative ways to avoid this crisis. She has developed two plans:
>
> Plan A: This plan will save one of three plants and 2,000 jobs.
>
> Plan B: This plan has a one-third probability of saving all three plants and 6,000 jobs, but has a two-thirds probability of saving no plants and no jobs.

Did you choose Plan A? According to Bazerman, 80 percent of people given these choices choose Plan A rather than Plan B. What would you have done if you were faced with the following choices to the same problem?

> Plan C: This plan will result in the loss of two of the three plants and 4,000 jobs.
>
> Plan D: This plan has a two-thirds probability of resulting in the loss of all three plants and all 6,000 jobs, but has a one-third probability of losing no plants and no jobs.

This time, did you choose Plan D? Again, according to Bazerman, 80 percent choose Plan D. However, if you look closely at both sets of choices, you can see that Plans A and C both save 2000 jobs, and Plans B and D both provide a two-thirds chance of losing all 6000 jobs. So why would 80 percent of decision makers choose Plan A in the first context, while only 20 percent chose its equivalent, Plan C, in the second? Likewise, why would 20 percent of decision makers choose Plan B in the first context, while 80 percent chose its equivalent, Plan D, in the second?

conditions of certainty
conditions in which decision makers have complete information and knowledge of all possible outcomes

conditions of risk
conditions in which decision makers face a very real possibility of making the wrong decisions

positive frame
couching a problem in terms of a gain, thus influencing decisions makers toward becoming risk-averse

The critical difference is how the problem is framed. A **positive frame** is the presentation of a problem in terms of a gain. When you begin with the belief that 6000 people will lose their jobs, Plan A's ability to keep 2000 jobs is clearly a gain. When faced with the prospect of a gain, decision makers tend to become risk-averse. In gambling terms, it's like quitting while you're ahead. You don't want to risk losing what you've already won. And in this situation, you start with 6000 lost jobs, but Plan A helps you win 2000 back. So most decision makers don't want to put that gain at risk.

negative frame
couching a problem in terms of a loss, thus influencing decisions makers toward becoming risk-seeking

By contrast, a **negative frame**, such as that shown in Plan D, is the presentation of a problem in terms of a loss. With nothing left to lose (i.e., there's already a two-thirds chance of losing all 6000 jobs), most decision makers become risk-seeking. In other words, if it's your last night in Las Vegas, and you've lost $900 of the $1000 you brought to town, why not put your last $100 in a $100 slot machine? You only get one chance, but if it pays off, you'll get all your money back and more. And if you lose, it doesn't really matter, you were going to lose that money anyway. In sum, risk not only affects how decision makers define problems, but it also affects the solutions they choose to fix those problems.

conditions of uncertainty
conditions in which decision makers don't know the odds of winning or losing

Managers also make decisions under **conditions of uncertainty**. How is uncertainty different from risk? With risk, a gambler knows there is a 1 in 52 chance of drawing a particular card, say, the ace of spades. But with uncertainty, you don't know how many cards there are, and you don't know how many aces of spades are in the deck or whether the deck even has an ace of spades. So under conditions of uncertainty, you can lose, but you don't even know the odds of winning or losing.[13]

risk propensity
a person's tendency to take or avoid risk

Very few people are willing to bet years of their lives and their own money under conditions of uncertainty. After all, why make the bet if you have no idea what your odds of success are? However, people differ in their willingness to embrace risks. For example, would you be willing to bungee jump off a bridge? Some, including at least one author of this book, wouldn't do it for all the money in the world. However, others would do it in a heartbeat. **Risk propensity** is a person's tendency to take or avoid risks. And it usually takes an individual with a high risk propensity to be willing to take risks under conditions of uncertainty. One such person is Bill Gross, founder and CEO of Idealab, an Internet business incubator that started the Internet companies eToys, Citysearch, Netzero, CarsDirect, Cooking.com, FreePC, Tickets.com, and GoTo.com. Idealab generates ideas for new businesses (mostly from Bill Gross), specs out the business plans and the business models, hires the managers to run the new businesses, gets the company websites running, gets venture capital funding to get the businesses running, and then takes the companies public with an initial public offering of stock. For the first few years, as the Internet took off, Idealab and its companies were wildly successful. But as dot-coms turned into dot-bombs, Gross and Idealab burned through $1.2 billion in funding in eight months! Even then, as eToys went bankrupt, CarsDirect blew through $300 million, and Gross's companies' stock prices fell 90 percent in value, Gross was undeterred. Idealab, he proclaimed, would bounce back with "several multibillion-dollar ideas." GoTo.com, whose stock had fallen from $120 to $15, "could be a $100 stock if they show profitability." Only someone like Gross, who started all these companies and managed to nurse Idealab through all those failures, could be comfortable in the face of such uncertainties.[14]

2.3 Common Decision-Making Mistakes

Another reason that managers have difficulty making rational decisions is that, like all decision makers, they are susceptible to the common mistakes shown in Exhibit 6.7: over-reliance on intuition, availability bias, representative bias, and anchoring and adjustment bias.[15]

EXHIBIT 6.7

COMMON DECISION-MAKING MISTAKES

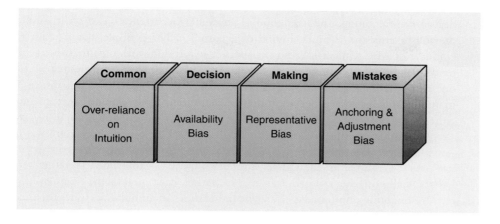

Have you ever had an "Aha!" experience, in which the solution to a problem you've been working on jumps into your head when you weren't thinking about it? If so, you've experienced intuition. While it's widely believed that scientists and business people use only logical, analytical, research-based methods, it's actually quite common for intuition to play a large role in the decisions and discoveries of both professions. For example, physicist Albert Einstein, discoverer of the law of relativity, claimed, "I did not arrive at my understanding of the fundamental laws of the universe through my rational mind." Robert Pittman, CEO of Time Warner Enterprises, who helped create MTV and Nickelodeon's "Nick at Nite," said, "Research is not policy making. People make policy. Research just answers some questions. At the end of the day, it's a gut decision."[16]

Intuition works best for experienced decision makers who can quickly analyze patterns of problems that they've seen before. Unfortunately, over-reliance on intuition can lead even experienced decision makers to become overconfident, careless, and inconsistent. For example, nine radiologists participated in a study in which they examined 96 cases of possible stomach ulcers. Their task was to determine the likelihood that the ulcers were malignant. One week after initially reviewing these cases, the radiologists were shown the same cases again, but in a different order. Amazingly, these highly trained professionals, who knew that the purpose of the research was to study their diagnostic skills, arrived at different conclusions (malignant versus benign) for nearly one out of four patients in the second week of the study.[17] Put another way, if all 96 patients actually had cancer, 22 of the 96 would have been wrongly diagnosed as disease-free in the second week of the study.

The second common mistake occurs because decision makers have an availability bias when judging the frequency, probability, or causes of an event. The **availability bias** is the tendency of decision makers to give preference to recent information, vivid images that evoke emotions, and specific acts and behaviours that they personally observed. For example, in the last decade, there has been a steady significant decline in the total number of crimes committed in the United States. In particular, murders are down by 42 percent nationwide. However, during this same period, Americans actually increased their spending on security-related items from $60 to $83 billion a year. What accounts for this discrepancy? Television and the availability bias. Jason Knott, editor of *Security Sales* magazine, said, "The best advertising a security company has is the local television news." And, according to the Center for Media & Public Affairs, network news has increased its coverage of murders by 700 percent during the same period.[18] So, despite

availability bias
unrecognized tendency of decision makers to give preference to recent information, vivid images that evoke emotions, and specific acts and behaviours that they personally observed

the fact that most people are actually much safer today than they were 10 years ago, they continue to purchase car alarms and home security systems because their minds are filled with the vivid images of murders that are televised to their homes via the local news.

The third common decision-making mistake is the **representative bias**, in which decision makers judge the likelihood of an event's occurrence based on its similarity to previous events and their likelihood of occurrence. For example, if a manager hired a graduate of ABC University, and that person just didn't work out, that manager might tend to avoid hiring any other ABC graduates. In other words, in the manager's mind, one ABC graduate represents all ABC graduates. If one didn't succeed in the job, the manager's unconscious expectation may be that others likely wouldn't succeed in the job either.

As another example, consider this riddle:

> A father and son are en route to a baseball game when their car stalls on the railroad tracks. The father can't restart the car. An oncoming train hits the car. The father dies. An ambulance rushes the boy to a nearby hospital. In the emergency room, the surgeon takes one look and says: "I can't operate on this child; he's my son."[19]

Researchers have found that it's common for people to invent strange scenarios—some involving extraterrestrials—to explain how this scenario could happen. However, since most surgeons are male, the representative bias prevents most people from considering the simple explanation that the surgeon is the boy's mother.

The fourth common decision-making mistake is the **anchoring and adjustment bias**, in which judgment (good-bad, large-small, yes-no, etc.) is "anchored" by an initial value. Once the anchor is "dropped," two things happen: (1) all subsequent experiences are judged by their similarity to the anchor, and (2) all possible decision alternatives tend to cluster around the anchor. For example, if you were accidentally bumped up from coach to first-class seating the first time you flew to Europe on business, the fine food, free drinks, attentive service, and fully reclining seats would make every subsequent trans-Atlantic trip in coach seating seem miserable. Likewise, when negotiating salaries or selling prices, the first number discussed tends to serve as the anchor for the entire negotiation. For example, in house shopping, the "listing price" stated by the house seller is typically the anchor value for negotiations. Consequently, buyers and sellers tend to judge whether they got a "good deal" by how close the selling price was to the listing price.

Review 2
Limits to Rational Decision-Making

The rational decision-making model describes how decisions should be made in an ideal world without limits. However, bounded rationality recognizes that in the real world, managers' decision-making processes are restricted by limited resources, incomplete and imperfect information, and managers' limited decision-making capabilities. These limitations often prevent managers from being rational decision makers. So do common decision-making mistakes, such as over-reliance on intuition and the availability, representative, and anchoring and adjustment biases. The rational decision-making model assumes that decisions are made under conditions of certainty. However, most managerial decisions are made under conditions of risk, where there is limited information and knowledge and a very real chance of making a bad decision. Risk also affects how decision makers define and solve problems. Positive frames encourage decision makers to be risk averse, whereas negative frames encourage them to be risk-seeking. Finally, managers also make decisions under conditions of uncertainty, in which the odds of winning or losing are unknown. It takes a high risk propensity to be willing to take risks under conditions of uncertainty.

---

representative bias
unrecognized tendency of decision makers to judge the likelihood of an event's occurrence based on its similarity to previous events

anchoring and adjustment bias
unrecognized tendency of decision makers to use an initial value or experience as a basis of comparison throughout the decision process

Improving Decision-Making

What's the biggest decision you've ever made? Was it choosing where to go to college? Was it choosing a major? Or was it a personal decision, such as deciding whether to get married, where to live, or which car or house to buy? Considering the lasting effect that decisions like these have on our lives, wouldn't it be great if we could learn how to make them better? Managers struggle with decisions, too. They wring their hands over who to hire or promote, or when and how somebody should be fired. They fret about which suppliers the company should do business with. They lose sleep over who should get how much for pay raises or how to change the company strategy to respond to aggressive competitors. And, considering the lasting effect that these decisions have on themselves and their companies, managers also want to learn how to make better decisions.

After reading the next two sections, you should be able to
3. describe how individual decision-making can be improved.
4. explain how group decisions and group decision-making techniques can improve decision-making.

3. Improving Individual Decision-Making

In theory, rational decision-making leads to optimal decisions. However, in practice, we know that real-world constraints, common decision-making mistakes, and risky situations make fully rational decisions difficult to achieve. Consequently, in the business world, managers are much more likely to satisfice and make "good enough" decisions than they are to maximize and make "optimal" decisions.

Managers can make better decisions by using decision rules, multivariable testing, and decision softwear, and by avoiding a common post-decision-making error called escalation of commitment.

3.1 Decision Rules

A **decision rule** is a set of criteria that alternative solutions must meet to be acceptable to the decision maker.[20] If an alternative doesn't meet the criteria in the decision rule, it is rejected. Nearly every kind of business uses basic decision rules. In restaurants, the general pricing decision rule is to price food at three times its cost, beer at four times its cost, and hard liquor at six times its cost. In clothing stores, the rule is to sell clothing for 60 percent over wholesale, and then reduce that price by 20 percent every two weeks until the clothing has been sold. Decision rules improve decision-making because they are easy to understand and simple to follow. Managers who don't have the time or resources to use the complete rational decision-making model can use simpler decision rules instead.

There are two general kinds of decision rules: the dictionary rule and the threshold rule. In much the same way that a dictionary sorts words by their first letter and then their second letter, and so forth, the **dictionary rule** encourages decision makers to rank their criteria in order of importance and then assess alternative solutions against these criteria in rank order. Specifically, alternatives that meet the most important criterion must then meet the second most important criterion, and so on. For example, the first house a friend and his wife owned had a living room and a family room. They found that the living room went basically unused, except when they had guests. So as their family grew and they started shopping for a larger house, the first thing they told the realtor was "Don't show us any houses with two living areas. We want a house with one large living room." Second, because they had three children, "It would be great to have four bedrooms." They were willing to look at any houses that met those criteria.

Sometimes decision makers need to make yes/no or accept/reject decisions. Should a bank accept or reject a mortgage application? Should MasterCard approve or deny a jeweller's request to charge your card $3500 for a jewellery purchase? When these kinds of decisions must be made, companies often use the **minimum threshold rule**, which

decision rule
set of criteria that alternative solutions must meet to be acceptable to the decision maker

dictionary rule
decision rule that requires decision makers to rank criteria in order of importance and then test alternative solutions against those criteria in rank order, so that alternatives that meet the most important criterion must then meet the second most important criterion, and so on

minimum threshold rule
decision rule that requires alternative solutions to meet all the established minimum decision criteria

requires an alternative to pass all the established minimum decision criteria. For example, one of the most common problems seen in emergency rooms is injured ankles. However, only 15 percent of ankle x-rays taken indicate fractures. In other words, doctors are ordering expensive x-rays much more than they need to. Recently, clinical research has resulted in the development of the "Ottawa rule," which states that physicians should send patients with ankle injuries for confirmatory x-rays only if there is (1) pain near the ankle joint, and (2) bone tenderness, and (3) an inability to bear weight on the ankle. All three criteria must be met before sending patients to have their ankles x-rayed. Studies showed that physicians using the Ottawa rule correctly ordered x-rays for 100 percent of the patients who fractured their ankles. Also, the Ottawa rule helped reduce the overall number of ankle x-rays by 34 percent.[21]

3.2 Multivariable Testing

multivariable testing (MVT)
a systematic approach of experimentation used to analyze and evaluate potential solutions

In practice, analyzing alternatives is one of the weakest steps in the decision-making process. Much of the "analysis" that gets done is based on guesswork ("We think that Plan E has a 90 percent chance of working") rather than on actual tests of possible solutions. Because it is based on data from small experiments rather than guesswork, **multivariable testing (MVT)** helps managers take a much more systematic approach to analyzing and evaluating potential solutions. Dwight Glover, CEO of Evans Clay, a small manufacturing company, said, "What I like about [MVT] is it provides data instead of opinions. It involves employees throughout the organization. You are using the brainpower that you have."[22]

Multivariable testing improves decision-making in a number of important ways. First, instead of letting arguments determine what the best solution is ("I really like that plan that manufacturing came up with because ... "), MVT encourages managers to conduct small-scale experiments and let the data decide. Says MVT consultant and trainer Charles Holland, "The power of experimental design is not only its efficiency with data, but that it forces a team to make decisions based on facts. Hierarchy, politics, or emotions are refuted with data."[23] For example, the marketing team of a mail-order catalogue company wanted to improve sales. Rather than debating what might or might not increase sales, the team came up with 12 ideas that might work, such as adding more expensive white fibrefill in pillows, adding a price grid for easy reference on each page, or printing the background of the catalogue with white ink (instead of just using the natural colour of the paper for the catalogue background). Instead of arguing about what might work, the marketing team tested all 12 ideas separately by printing up 16 different catalogue inserts for one mailing.[24]

Second, traditional scientific experimentation typically relies on controlled testing, in which all potential influences, except the ones you want to test, are controlled. This sounds simple enough, but the 12 ideas that the marketing team came up with to improve mail-order catalogue sales would require 4096 different experiments to test all possible combinations of those 12 variables (i.e., ideas). The advantage of MVT is that it saves time and money by using a mathematical shortcut so that just a few quick tests can get you 70 percent of the information that you'd get if you tested all possible combinations of variables. Rather than running 4096 possible combinations of ideas that would improve catalogue sales, the marketing team only had to use 16 different tests for their 12 ideas. After mailing out 386 000 catalogues, they found that 7 of the 12 ideas made a difference. For instance, it turns out that the more expensive white fibrefill in pillows made no difference in sales. The company saved $450 000 by switching back to cheaper, grey fibrefill. However, the price grid on each page allowed more photo space to feature items, resulting in an increase of $750 000 in sales. In all, by quickly testing all meaningful combinations of their 12 ideas in one printing of the catalogue, MVT earned the company more than a million dollars in increased sales and lower costs.[25]

Exhibit 6.8 shows a simple multivariable testing experiment that a small amusement park might use to increase park attendance on Tuesdays, typically the slowest day in the park. On the first Tuesday, Test 1, no changes are made. The park earns a profit of $4000. On the next Tuesday, Test 2, the park runs a 2-for-1 admission special and gives everyone who enters the park a coupon for a free hot dog and a Coke between 11:00 a.m. and 1:00 p.m. The park earns just $2000, losing money on all the free lunches it gave away to all those people who were admitted for free. On the next Tuesday, Test 3, parking is free and everyone who enters the park gets a free lunch coupon. The park makes $9000. Finally, on the fourth Tuesday, the park again offers 2-for-1 admission, but this time with free parking. Profits this time are $5000. What's the answer? It's obvious: Offer free parking and free lunch on Tuesdays.

MVT can be used in all kinds of businesses for many kinds of decisions. However, managers and employees will need to be trained how to design simple experiments and how to gather and analyze basic statistical data. Nonetheless, despite its cost, MVT allows managers to test and evaluate potential solutions before committing large amounts of money to their use. So instead of arguing about what you "think" the best solution might be, use MVT to test alternative solutions.

3.3 Staying Rational: Decision Software

Most decision makers satisfice, accepting the first "good enough" solution that comes to mind. Furthermore, because of time pressures and situational limitations, intuitive, unstructured decision-making is the norm rather than the exception. Together, these factors make it nearly impossible for managers and business people to "stay rational" and maximize decisions.

Computer software, however, may do for decision-making what it did for the nasty tasks of balancing your chequebook and doing your taxes—make it simpler, faster, and easier. If you've got a computer, you probably use Quicken (or a similar program) to balance your chequebook and stick to a budget. Likewise, if you do your own taxes, you probably use QuickTax (www.intuit.com/canada/quicktax/) or TAXWHIZ (or a similar program) to figure out how much money you owe the government (or, if you're lucky, how much they owe you). Millions of people swear by these programs. According to Walter Mossberg, who writes the Personal Technology column for *The Wall Street Journal*, one such program, DecideRight, "does a far better job of organizing your options in a decision, and then ranking them by criteria you choose, than the traditional yellow legal pad with columns labeled 'pro' and 'con'—the method used by millions."[26]

Here's how it works. DecideRight starts with its QuickBuild tool, which, in an interview-like style, walks decision makers through the decision-making process. Step 1, label the decision. "What bank should we choose for the business?" Step 2, enter the decision

---

EXHIBIT 6.8

MULTIVARIABLE TESTING TO INCREASE AMUSEMENT PARK ATTENDANCE ON TUESDAYS

TEST	2-FOR-1	FREE LUNCH	FREE PARKING	PROFITS
Test 1				$4000
Test 2	X	X		$2000
Test 3		X	X	$9000
Test 4	X		X	$5000

criteria. "Location, hours, fees, and so forth." Step 3, enter the options you're considering. "Bank One, Credit Union Two, Treasury Branch Three, and so on." Step 4, weight the decision criteria. For example, click on "location" and then drag and drop it on the high-, medium-, or low-importance button on your screen. Step 5, rate each option against each decision criterion. Again, all you do is drag and drop. If Central Bank & Trust is just right around the corner from your business, click on "Central Bank & Trust" and then drag and drop it onto the "excellent" button on your screen for location. Step 6, the ranking of alternatives is performed automatically. There's no math involved (unless you choose this option).

Not only does DecideRight automatically rank alternatives, it also generates a report with charts and tables that explains why and how the decision was made. The report even explains why one alternative was chosen over another. Decision-making software such as DecideRight is no guarantee of good decisions. After all, Quicken can't guarantee that you'll always have money in the bank, and TAXWHIZ can't guarantee a tax refund. But to the extent that decision software tools such as DecideRight (www.performancesolutionstech.com), iDecide (www.definitivesoftware.com), and ExpertChoice (www.expertchoice.com) encourage managers to work through the steps of the rational decision-making model, it should help them make better decisions.[27]

3.4 After the Decision: Avoiding Escalation of Commitment

In Section 2.3, you learned about the common mistakes that occur when managers are in the process of making decisions: over-reliance on intuition, availability bias, representative bias, and the anchoring and adjustment bias. However, individuals and organizations often make a serious post-decision mistake called "escalation of commitment." **Escalation of commitment** is the tendency for a person who has already made a decision to more strongly support that original decision despite negative information that clearly indicates it was wrong.[28] For example, one of the reasons that Montgomery Ward's closed after more than a century in business is that it sat on $911 million in on-hand cash and never opened a new store—not one—between 1941 and 1957. Ward's chairman at the time, Sewell Avery, had created a chart that showed that every world war since the time of Napoleon had been followed by a major economic depression. After World War II ended in 1945, Sewell declared, "Who am I to argue with history? Why build $14-per-foot buildings when we soon can do it for $3 per foot?" So, as post-war Americans moved in mass from the cities to the suburbs, Ward's sat back and watched Sears and JCPenney build hundreds of new stores in suburbs and malls.

Montgomery Ward's tried to catch up by building similar stores in the 1970s and 1980s, but unlike Sears and Penney's, it never had enough stores in enough good locations to survive. Avery's obviously wrong decision to not build any new stores, which he stuck to for 16 years, eventually led to Ward's closing half a century later.[29]

Besides committing to a failing course of action, like Ward's chairman Sewell Avery, escalation of commitment often involves an increased commitment of resources (i.e., time, money, and people) to try to save the failed effort or decision. The problems associated with B.C. Ferry Corp.'s ill-fated launch of three PacifiCat ferries illustrates this problem well. Then B.C. premier Glen Clark announced in June 1994 that B.C. Ferry Corp. would build three high-speed ferries. The intent was to create shipbuilding jobs and to provide new and faster ferries. The first ferry was intended to be launched in April 1997 at a cost of $70 million. In April of 1995 a marine engineer warned B.C. Ferries that the project was economically unfeasible, it could endanger the public, and there could be difficulties building the ships because shipyard workers had to learn new and difficult shipbuilding techniques. B.C. Ferries ignored these warnings and proceeded anyway. The first ferry was not launched until June 1998 and because of technical difficulties did not see service until July 1999, two years late. The total cost had risen to $210 million and the entire project looked like it would cost $400 million. This despite the fact the Glen Clark bragged that "it's budgeted right down to the toilet paper."[30]

---

escalation of commitment
the tendency for a person who has already made a decision to more strongly support that original decision despite negative information that clearly indicates it was wrong

After it was finally put in service, the new ferry was immediately plagued by more technical difficulties, operating costs were higher than expected, and there were serious concerns raised about public safety due to the speed and size of the wake created. Given the operational problems, cost overruns, and public safety issues seen with the first ferry, the Liberal opposition urged the government to stop building the next two ferries. By this time the level of commitment had gone too far. The project was completed at a cost of $454 million, although one columnist estimated the total cost as closer to $1 billion. The three ferries were finally pulled from service and sold for $19.2 million, a fraction of their cost.[31] Professor Barry Staw, a leading researcher on escalation of commitment, said, "Typically the leader is defensive and doesn't want to hear that he might be wrong. Then comes a social process in which other people's careers get staked to his course of action—even if it's wrong, they think they have to defend it or they'll lose their jobs. It's like propping up a defunct government."[32]

While nothing is failsafe, here are a few suggestions for avoiding the traps associated with escalation of commitment. To minimize escalation of commitment from the start, organizations should require frequent, detailed progress reports to make managers compare actual and planned spending, performance, and progress. If there are differences, they should explain why.[33] A second way to minimize escalation from the start is to hire an independent auditor to provide an objective assessment. Independent auditors have no psychological or financial investment in the decisions or projects they audit and are generally not directly affected by internal company politics. Their job is to provide a fresh set of eyes and to communicate a third-party perspective. And, if a project is failing, seriously behind schedule, or over cost, auditors should also be asked to suggest alternative courses of action to continued funding or investment in the project. Furthermore, the presence of an auditor is often enough to encourage managers to be more realistic about the progress or success of their decisions.[34]

Finally, several things can be done to minimize the damage and cost if escalation of commitment does occur. One of the most effective is to change managers. Like independent auditors, new managers with a fresh perspective are much more likely to discontinue decisions resulting in huge cost overruns or unproductive returns. For example, B.C. Ferry Corp. did not shut down its PacifiCat service and decide to sell the ferries until a new premier was in place and significant turnover of senior management at B.C. Ferries had occurred, including the firing of the entire board of directors of B.C. Ferries.[35] A second way to deal with escalation of commitment is to label the decision as an "experiment." Calling a failed decision or project an "experiment" indicates that failure was a possibility, that the project was designed to help the company learn something, and that there was no permanent commitment to the decision. This gets the company off the hook, permits managers associated with the failed decision to save face, and in general makes it easier to stop or shut down a failed decision or project.[36] For example, after the Priceline WebHouse Club lost $545 million selling gasoline and groceries using Priceline's "name your price" strategy, Priceline.com announced that it was shutting down the Priceline WebHouse Club.[37] Jay Walker, Priceline founder, said this about the closing:[38]

- "In scale and scope the WebHouse Club was a business opportunity with great potential but with real risks." [Translation: "We weren't sure it would work."]
- "We specifically structured the WebHouse Club as a separate company from Priceline.com so that private investors, not Priceline.com shareholders, would bear that risk." [Translation: "Because we weren't sure it would work, we kept it separate from the main business, Priceline.com."]
- "All of us here at WebHouse Club are terribly disappointed, but I am proud of what we accomplished since we commenced operations." [Translation: "We tried our best, but we're hemorrhaging money, so we're going to close this down."]
- "In light of the weakness of the current capital market environment, the WebHouse Club executive team has reluctantly concluded that it was unlikely to be able to raise

the additional capital the WebHouse Club would need next year to achieve the necessary scale and our goal of profitability. Accordingly, we have determined that the prudent course of action is to wind down our operations on an orderly basis while fully satisfying all of the WebHouse Club's obligations to customers, employees, and suppliers." [Translation: "We didn't have enough money to keep absorbing these tremendous losses. WebHouse is no more."]

Review 3
Improving Individual Decision-Making

Decision rules are a relatively simple method of improving decision-making. The dictionary rule helps decision makers choose among multiple alternative solutions, whereas the threshold rule helps decision makers make yes/no or accept/reject decisions. Managers use multivariable testing to do a better job of analyzing and evaluating potential solutions. The basic idea is to experimentally test several potential solutions at the same time and let data, rather than beliefs, guide decision-making. While most decision makers "satisfice," accepting the first "good enough" solution that comes to mind, decision software (such as DecideRight, which prompts managers to identify and weight decision criteria, generate alternative solutions, and then rank those solutions by their decision weights) can help them be better decision makers by working through the steps of the rational decision-making model. Escalation of commitment occurs when someone continues to strongly support a decision with funding and resources despite negative information that shows the decision was wrong. The damage and costs associated with escalation of commitment can be minimized by asking managers to make detailed progress reports comparing actual and planned spending and progress, hiring independent auditors, replacing managers who made the original decisions with new managers, and being willing to label the failed decision an "experiment," thus making it easier to end support for that decision.

4. Using Groups to Improve Decision-Making

Using teams, task forces, or groups is a common method that companies choose for solving complex problems. For example, Celestica Inc., with headquarters in Toronto, used a group process to implement a widespread redesign of work practices in order to increase productivity. A steering committee was formed that had senior managers from all functional areas. A central design team and a resource team were also put together, and they in turn formed 21 design teams, one for each of the functions being redesigned. Further sub-teams were formed to complete detailed implementation plans. Despite the fact that Celestica was already a successful and profitable company, these undertakings managed to double the company's productivity.[39]

When done properly, as at Celestica, group decision-making can lead to much better decisions than individual decision-making. In fact, numerous studies show that groups consistently outperform individuals on complex tasks.

Let's explore the advantages and pitfalls of group decision-making and see how the following group decision-making methods—structured conflict, the nominal group technique, the Delphi technique, the stepladder technique, and electronic brainstorming—can be used to improve decision-making.

EXPERIENCING MANAGEMENT

There are both advantages and disadvantages to group decision-making, and managers must know what action to take when group decision-making is a possibility. Examine some ideas about group decision-making at our animated concept and activity site. Choose Decision-Making from the "select a topic" pull-down menu, then Decision-Making Process from the "overview tab."

www.experiencingmanagement.com

4.1 Advantages and Pitfalls of Group Decision-Making

Groups can do a much better job than individuals in two important steps of the decision-making process: defining the problem and generating alternative solutions. Four reasons explain why.

First, because group members usually possess different knowledge, skills, abilities, and experiences, groups will be able to view problems from several perspectives. Being able to view problems from several perspectives, in turn, can help groups perform better on complex tasks and make better decisions than individuals.[40] In fact, groups made up of members with a greater diversity of knowledge, skills, abilities, and experiences will typically outperform groups with less diversity on those dimensions. For example, companies with more women in top management had better financial performance during initial public offerings, that is, the very first time a company publicly sells stock to investors (IPOs). Companies with top management groups composed of 10 percent females had IPO stock prices 4.6 percent higher than companies with no women in top management jobs. And when women held half the top management positions in a company, IPO stock prices were 23 percent higher. Company performance and stock prices were higher after the initial public offering, too. Professor Theresa Welbourne, who conducted the study, said, "When you have diversity in top management, you have people looking at data differently, and that brings better decision making overall."[41]

Second, groups can find and access much more information than can individuals. For example, Clough, Harbour & Associates, an engineering consulting firm, uses a hiring team for interviewing potential employees. The company's director of human resources said, "We think we make better hiring decisions when we get a number of people involved. It's like working a crossword puzzle. If you get four people together, their chances of solving the puzzle are greater than if the four work separately."[42]

Third, the increased knowledge and information available to groups make it easier for them to generate more alternative solutions. Studies show that generating lots of alternative solutions is a critical part of improving the quality of decisions. Fourth, if groups are involved in the decision-making process, group members will be more committed to making chosen solutions work.

Although groups can do a better job of defining problems and generating alternative solutions, group decision-making is subject to some pitfalls that can quickly erase these gains. One possible pitfall is groupthink. **Groupthink** occurs in highly cohesive groups when group members feel intense pressure to agree with each other, so that the group can approve a proposed solution.[43] Because groupthink leads to consideration of a limited number of solutions and because it restricts discussion of any considered solutions, it usually results in poor decisions. Groupthink is most likely to occur under the following conditions:

groupthink
a barrier to good decision-making caused by pressure within the group for members to agree with each other

- The group is insulated from others with different perspectives.
- The group leader begins by expressing strong preference for a particular decision.
- There is no established procedure for systematically defining problems and exploring alternatives.
- Group members have similar backgrounds and experiences.[44]

NASA's decision to launch the ill-fated space shuttle Challenger is an example of groupthink. Despite cold weather conditions that would normally have postponed a launch, NASA placed heavy pressure on Morton Thiokol (maker of the o-rings) and other engineering firms involved in the launch decision to give their approval to launch. After being told twice that a launch was not recommended, NASA administrators pressured Morton Thiokol one last time for an okay. Because of the pressure and time constraints, Thiokol reversed its decision. Tragically, as Thiokol had originally feared, the o-rings failed, and the shuttle exploded, killing all aboard.[45]

A second potential problem with group decision-making is that it takes considerable time. It takes time to reconcile schedules (so that group members can meet). Furthermore, it's a rare group that consistently holds productive task-oriented meetings to effectively work through the decision process. Some of the most common complaints about meetings (and thus decision-making) are that the

PERSONAL PRODUCTIVITY

Want to Help? Shhhhhh, Chew Your Nails

Managers sometimes impede group decision-making by beginning the process by saying what they think should be done. Group members tend to place more importance on what their leaders say than on what other members say. This can impair group decision-making by leading to premature acceptance of alternatives and decision criteria. So the best thing to do as a manager is to keep quiet. Do what this manager did when group members said, "Why don't you just tell us what to do so we can move on?" Her response? "I sat on my hands. Chewed on my fingernails."

Source: S. Sherman, "Secrets of HP's 'Muddled' Team," *Fortune*, 18 March 1996, 116–120.

meeting's purpose is unclear, meeting participants are unprepared, critical people are absent or late, conversation doesn't stay focused on the problem, and no one follows up on the decisions that were made.

A third possible pitfall is that sometimes just one or two people, perhaps the boss or a strong-willed, vocal group member, dominate group discussion, restricting consideration of different problem definitions and alternative solutions. Another possible problem is that, unlike their own decisions and actions, group members often don't feel accountable for the decisions made and actions taken by the group.

While these pitfalls can lead to poor decision-making, this doesn't mean that managers should avoid using groups to make decisions. When done properly, group decision-making can lead to much better decisions. The pitfalls of group decision-making are not inevitable. Most of them can be overcome through good management; Chapter 12 discusses more aspects of managing teams. Let's see how structured conflict, the nominal group technique, the Delphi technique, the stepladder technique, and electronic brainstorming help managers improve group decision-making.

4.2 Structured Conflict

Most people view conflict negatively. However, the right kind of conflict can lead to much better group decision-making. **C-type conflict**, or "**cognitive conflict**," focuses on problem- and issue-related differences of opinion.[46] In c-type conflict, group members disagree because their different experiences and expertise lead them to different views of the problem and its potential solutions. However, c-type conflict is also characterized by a willingness to examine, compare, and reconcile those differences to produce the best possible solution. Alteon WebSystems, now a division of Nortel Networks, makes critical use of c-type conflict. Top manager Dominic Orr described Alteon's c-type conflict this way:

> There's no silent disagreement, and no getting personal, and definitely no "let's take it offline" mentality. Our goal is to make each major decision in a single meeting. People arrive with a proposal or a solution—and with the facts to support it. After an idea is presented, we open the floor to objective, and often withering, critiques. And if the idea collapses under scrutiny, we move on to another: no hard feelings. We're judging the idea, not the person. At the same time, we don't really try to regulate emotions. Passionate conflict means that we're getting somewhere, not that the discussion is out of control. But one person does act as referee—by asking basic questions like "Is this good for the customer?" or "Does it keep our time-to-market advantage intact?" By focusing relentlessly on the facts, we're able to see the strengths and weaknesses of an idea clearly and quickly.[47]

By contrast, **a-type conflict**, meaning "**affective conflict**," refers to the emotional reactions that can occur when disagreements become personal rather than professional. A-type conflict often results in hostility, anger, resentment, distrust, cynicism, and apathy. Unlike c-type conflict, a-type conflict undermines team effectiveness by preventing teams from engaging in the activities characteristic of c-type conflict that are critical to team effectiveness. Examples of a-type conflict phrases are "your idea," "our idea," "my department," "you don't know what you are talking about," or "you don't understand our situation." Rather than focusing on issues and ideas, these statements focus on individuals.[48]

Devil's advocacy and dialectical inquiry are two methods that introduce structured c-type conflict into the group decision-making process. **Devil's advocacy** creates c-type conflict by assigning an individual or a subgroup the role of critic. The following five steps establish a devil's advocacy program:

1. Generate a potential solution.

2. Assign a devil's advocate to criticize and question the solution.

3. Present the critique of the potential solution to key decision makers.

4. Gather additional relevant information.

5. Decide whether to use, change, or not use the originally proposed solution.[49]

Dialectical inquiry creates c-type conflict by forcing decision makers to state the assumptions of a proposed solution (a thesis) and to then generate a solution that is the opposite (antithesis) of the proposed solution. The following are the five steps of the dialectical inquiry process:

1. Generate a potential solution.

2. Identify the assumptions underlying the potential solution.

3. Generate a conflicting counterproposal based on the opposite assumptions.

4. Have advocates of each position present their arguments and engage in a debate in front of key decision makers.

5. Decide whether to use, change, or not use the originally proposed solution.[50]

When properly used, both the devil's advocacy and dialectical inquiry approaches introduce c-type conflict into the decision-making process. Further, contrary to the common belief that conflict is bad, studies show that these methods lead to less a-type conflict, improved decision quality, and greater acceptance of decisions once they have been made.[51] See the "What Really Works" feature for more information on both techniques.

dialectical inquiry
a decision-making method in which decision makers state the assumptions of a proposed solution (a thesis) and generate a solution that is the opposite (antithesis) of that solution

4.3 Nominal Group Technique

"Nominal" means "in name only." Accordingly, the **nominal group technique** received its name because it begins with "quiet time," in which group members independently write down as many problem definitions and alternative solutions as possible. In other words, the nominal group technique begins by having group members act as individuals. After the "quiet time," the group leader asks each group member to share one idea at a time with the group. As they are read aloud, ideas are posted on flipcharts or wallboards for all to see. This step continues until all ideas have been shared. The next step involves a discussion of the advantages and disadvantages of these ideas. The nominal group technique closes with a second "quiet time," in which group members independently rank the ideas presented. Group members then read their rankings aloud, and the idea with the highest average rank is selected.[52]

The nominal group technique improves group decision-making by decreasing a-type conflict. However, in doing so, it also restricts c-type conflict. Consequently, the nominal group technique typically produces poorer-quality decisions than do the devil's advocacy or dialectical inquiry approaches. Nonetheless, more than 80 studies have found that nominal groups produce better-quality ideas than traditional group decisions.[53]

nominal group technique
decision-making method that begins and ends by having group members quietly write down and evaluate ideas to be shared with the group

4.4 Delphi Technique

The **Delphi technique** is a decision-making method in which a panel of experts responds to questions and to each other until reaching agreement on an issue. The first step is to assemble a panel of experts. However, unlike other approaches to group decision-making, it isn't necessary to bring the panel together in one place. Since the Delphi technique does not require the experts to leave their offices or disrupt their schedules, they are more likely to participate in the process. For example, two colleagues were asked to conduct a Delphi technique assessment of the "10 most important steps for small businesses." With the help of the dean of a nearby business school and a former mayor of the city, they assembled a panel of local top-level managers and CEOs.

Delphi technique
a decision-making method in which a panel of experts responds to questions and to each other until reaching agreement on an issue

The second step is to create a questionnaire consisting of a series of open-ended questions for the experts. For example, the panel was asked to answer these questions: "What is the most common mistake made by small-business persons?" "Right now, what do you think is the biggest threat to the survival of most small businesses?" "If you had one piece of advice to give to the owner of a small business, what would it be?"

In Step 3, panel members' written responses are analyzed, summarized, and fed back to the panel for reactions until panel members reach agreement. In the Delphi study described above, it took about a month to get the panel members' written responses to the first three questions. Then their written responses were summarized and typed into a brief report (no more than two pages). The summary was sent to the panel members and were asked to explain why they agreed or disagreed with these conclusions from the first round of questions. Asking why they agreed or disagreed is important, because it helps uncover panel members' unstated assumptions and beliefs. Again, this process of summarizing panel feedback and obtaining reactions to that feedback continues until panel members reach agreement. For this study, it took just one more round for panel members' views to reach a consensus. In all, it took approximately three and a half months to complete this Delphi study.

WhatReallyWorks

Devil's Advocacy and Dialectical Inquiry

Ninety percent of the decisions managers face are well-structured problems that recur frequently under conditions of certainty. For example, showing up at an airline ticket counter without your ticket is a well-structured problem. It happens every day (recurs frequently), and it's easy to determine if you have your ticket or not (conditions of certainty).

Well-structured problems are solved with programmed decisions, in which a policy, procedure, or rule clearly specifies how to solve the problem. Thus, there's no mystery about what to do when someone shows up without a ticket. After you present identification to prove who you are, and after you pay a transaction fee (around $120), the airline gives you another ticket.

In some sense, programmed decisions really aren't decisions, because anyone with any experience knows what to do. There's no thought involved. What keeps managers up at night is the other 10 percent of problems. Ill-structured problems that are novel (no one's seen them before) and exist under conditions of uncertainty are solved with nonprogrammed decisions. Nonprogrammed decisions do not involve standard methods of resolution. Every time managers make a nonprogrammed decision, they have to figure out a new way of handling a new problem. That's what makes them so tough.

Both the devil's advocacy and dialectical inquiry approaches to decision-making can be used to improve nonprogrammed decision-making. Both approaches work because they force decision makers to identify and criticize the assumptions underlying the nonprogrammed decisions that they hope will solve ill-structured problems.

Devil's Advocacy
There is a 58 percent chance that decision makers who use the devil's-advocacy approach to criticize and question their solutions will produce better-quality decisions than decisions based on the advice of experts.

Dialectical Inquiry
There is a 55 percent chance that decision makers who use the dialectical-inquiry approach to criticize and question their solutions will produce better-quality decisions than decisions based on the advice of experts.

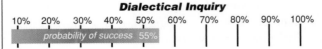

Note that each technique has been compared to decisions obtained by following experts' advice. So, while these probabilities of success, 58 percent and 55 percent, seem small, they very likely understate the effects of both techniques. In other words, the probabilities of success would have been much larger if both techniques had been compared to unstructured decision-making processes.

Source: C.R. Schwenk, "Effects of Devil's Advocacy and Dialectical Inquiry on Decision Making: A Meta-Analysis," *Organizational Behavior and Human Decision Performance* 47 (1990): 161–176.

The Delphi technique is not an approach that managers should use for common decisions. Because it is a time-consuming, labour-intensive, and expensive process, the Delphi technique is best reserved for important long-term issues and problems. Nonetheless, the judgments and conclusions obtained from it are typically better than those you would get from one expert.

4.5 Stepladder Technique

The **stepladder technique** improves group decision-making by making sure that each group member's contributions are independent, are considered, and are discussed. As shown in Exhibit 6.9, the stepladder technique begins with discussion between two group members, each of whom presents to the other their thoughts, ideas, and recommendations before jointly making a tentative decision. At each step, as other group members are added to the discussion one at a time, like a stepladder, the existing group members take the time to listen to each new member's thoughts, ideas, and recommendations. The group then shares the ideas and suggestions that it had already considered, discusses the new and old ideas, and then makes a tentative decision. This process (new member's ideas are heard, group shares previous ideas and suggestions, discussion is held, tentative group decision is made) continues until each group member's ideas have been discussed.

For the stepladder technique to work, group members must have enough time to consider the problem or decision on their own, to present their ideas to the group, and to thoroughly discuss all ideas and alternatives with the group at each step. Rushing through each step destroys the advantages of this technique. Also, groups must make sure that subsequent group members are completely unaware of previous discussions and suggestions. This will ensure that each member who joins the group brings truly independent thoughts and suggestions, thus greatly increasing the chances of making better decisions.

stepladder technique
when group members are added to a group discussion one at a time (i.e., like a stepladder), the existing group members first take the time to listen to each new member's thoughts, ideas, and recommendations, and then the group, in turn, shares the ideas and suggestions that it had already considered, discusses the new and old ideas, and then makes a decision

EXHIBIT 6.9

STEPLADDER TECHNIQUE FOR GROUP DECISION-MAKING

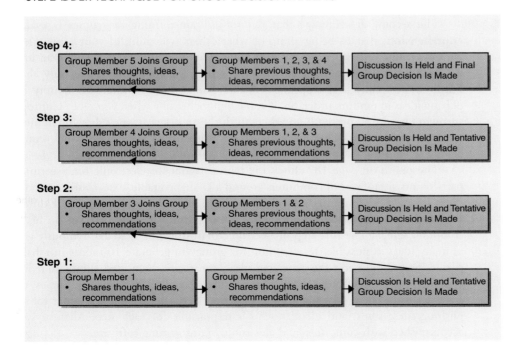

One study found that compared to traditional groups in which all group members are present for the entire discussion, groups using the stepladder technique produced significantly better decisions. Moreover, the stepladder groups performed better than the best individual member of their group 56 percent of the time, while traditional groups outperformed the best individual member of their group only 13 percent of the time.[54] Besides better performance, groups using the stepladder technique also generated more ideas and were more satisfied with the decision-making process.

4.6 Electronic Brainstorming

brainstorming
a decision-making method in which group members build on each other's ideas to generate as many alternative solutions as possible

Brainstorming, in which group members build on others' ideas, is a technique for generating a large number of alternative solutions. Brainstorming has four rules:

1. The more ideas, the better.

2. All ideas are acceptable, no matter how wild or crazy they might be.

3. Other group members' ideas should be used to come up with even more ideas.

4. Criticism or evaluation of ideas is not allowed.

electronic brainstorming
a decision-making method in which group members use computers to build on each other's ideas and generate many alternative solutions

While brainstorming is great fun and can help managers generate a large number of alternative solutions, it does have a number of disadvantages. Fortunately, **electronic brainstorming**, in which group members use computers to communicate and generate alternative solutions, overcomes the disadvantages associated with face-to-face brainstorming.[55] Tom Corcoran, vice president of group insurance at Canada Life, is a big advocate of electronic brainstorming and regularly uses the brainstorming facilities at Queen's University Executive Decision Centre, one of the first of its kind to be made accessible to the public. He brings employees together to deal with such issues as product development and strategic planning. He feels it avoids big debates and allows the discussion to converge, rather than having long debates.[56]

production blocking
a disadvantage of face-to-face brainstorming in which a group member must wait to share an idea because another member is presenting an idea

The first disadvantage that electronic brainstorming overcomes is **production blocking**, which occurs when you have an idea, but you have to wait to share it because someone else is already describing an idea to the group. This short delay may make you forget your idea or decide that it really wasn't worth sharing. But with electronic brainstorming, production blocking doesn't happen. With all group members seated at computers, everyone can type in their ideas whenever they occur. There's no "waiting your turn" to be heard by the group.

evaluation apprehension
fear of what others will think of your ideas

The second disadvantage that electronic brainstorming overcomes is **evaluation apprehension**, that is, being afraid of what others will think of your ideas. However, with electronic brainstorming, all ideas are anonymous. When you type in an idea and hit the "Enter" key to share it with the group, group members see only the idea. Furthermore, many brainstorming software programs also protect anonymity by displaying ideas in random order. So, if you laugh maniacally when you type "Cut top management's pay by 50 percent!" and then hit the "Enter" key, it won't show up immediately on everyone's screen. This makes it doubly difficult to determine which comments belong to whom.

The photo on page 187 shows the typical layout for electronic brainstorming. All participants sit in front of computers around a U-shaped table. This configuration allows them to see their computer screens, each other, and a large main screen. Exhibit 6.10 shows what the typical electronic brainstorming group member will see on his or her computer screen. The first step in electronic brainstorming is to anonymously generate as many ideas as possible. It's common for groups to generate 100 ideas in a half-hour period. Step 2 is to edit the generated ideas, categorize them, and eliminate redundancies. Step 3 is to rank-order the categorized ideas based on their quality. Step 4, the last step, has three parts: generate a series of action steps, decide the best order for accomplishing these steps, and identify who is responsible for each step. All four steps are accomplished with computers and electronic brainstorming software.[57]

Courtesy of the Queen's University Executive Decision Centre

Queen's Executive Decision Centre has an electronic brainstorming facility.

Studies show that electronic brainstorming is much more productive than face-to-face brainstorming. Compared to regular four-person brainstorming groups, the same-sized electronic brainstorming groups produce 25 percent to 50 percent more ideas. Compared to regular 12-person brainstorming groups, the same-sized electronic brainstorming groups produce 200 percent more ideas! In fact, because production blocking (i.e., waiting your turn) is not a problem for electronic brainstorming, the number and quality of ideas generally increases with group size.[58]

Even though it works much better than traditional brainstorming, electronic brainstorming has disadvantages, too. An obvious problem is the expense of computers, networks, software, etc. As these costs continue to drop, however, electronic brainstorming will become cheaper.

Another problem is that the anonymity of ideas may bother people who are used to having their ideas accepted by virtue of their position (i.e., the boss). On the other hand, one CEO said, "Because the process is anonymous, the sky's the limit in terms of what you can say, and as a result it is more thought-provoking. As a CEO, you'll probably discover things you might not want to hear but need to be aware of."[59]

EXHIBIT 6.10

WHAT YOU SEE ON THE COMPUTER DURING ELECTRONIC BRAINSTORMING

Source: "GroupSystems Tour Stop 2: Generating a List of Ideas," Ventana website. [Online] Available www.ventana.com/html/vc_tour_stop_2_categorizer.html, 12 January 1999.

A third disadvantage is that outgoing individuals who are more comfortable expressing themselves verbally may find it difficult to express themselves in writing. Finally, the most obvious problem is that participants have to be able to type. Those who can't type, or who type slowly, may be easily frustrated and find themselves at a disadvantage to experienced typists. For example, one meeting facilitator was tipped off that an especially fast typist was pretending to be more than one person. Said the facilitator, "He'd type 'Oh, I agree' and then 'Ditto, ditto' or 'What a great idea,' all in quick succession, using different variations of uppercase and lowercase letters and punctuation. He tried to make it seem like a lot of people were concurring, but it was just him." Eventually, the person sitting next to him got suspicious and began watching his screen.[60]

Review 4
Using Groups to Improve Decision-Making

When groups view problems from several perspectives, use more information, have a diversity of knowledge and experience, and become committed to solutions they help choose, they can produce better solutions than individual decision makers. However, group decisions suffer from these disadvantages: groupthink, slowness, discussions dominated by just a few individuals, and unfelt responsibility for decisions. Group decisions work best when group members encourage c-type conflict. However, group decisions don't work as well when groups become mired in a-type conflict. The devil's-advocacy and dialectical-inquiry approaches improve group decisions because they bring structured c-type conflict into the decision-making process. By contrast, the nominal group technique and the Delphi technique both improve decision-making by reducing a-type conflict through limited interactions between group members. The stepladder technique improves group decision-making by adding each group member's independent contributions to the discussion one at a time. Finally, because it overcomes the problems of production blocking and evaluation apprehension, electronic brainstorming is a more effective method of generating alternatives than face-to-face brainstorming.

What Really Happened?

The cleanliness of the rational decision-making model (defining the problem, defining and weighting decision criteria, generating and evaluating alternative courses of action, and computing the optimal decision) rarely matches up with the messiness of real-world decision-making. Indeed, at the beginning of this chapter, you heard one manager say, "I just know how disillusioning and frustrating it is to be hit with problems and conflicts all day and not be able to solve them very cleanly." BP Amoco was faced with a messy, tough decision about whether to invest millions in deepwater drilling. Let's find out what really happened at BP Amoco as it struggled with this difficult decision.

Any way that you look at it, you're convinced that deepwater drilling is a good bet, but how can you demonstrate that to top management, especially considering the risks involved and the tough economic conditions?

The rational decision-making model assumes that managers can gaze into crystal balls and accurately predict whether a potential solution will fix a problem. The model also assumes that managers make decisions under conditions of certainty, with complete information and knowledge of all possible outcomes and their likelihood. Under those assumptions, it should be easy to demonstrate to top management that investing in deepwater drilling is the right thing to do. In fact, under conditions of certainty (you know precisely whether various alternatives will work), it should be self-evident.

This was certainly, no pun intended, not the case when BP Amoco was trying to decide whether to invest millions, if not billions, of dollars in deepwater drilling. Indeed, deepwater drilling was unproven at the time, and the risks were great. When an onshore well comes up dry, it costs the company only $1.5 million. By contrast, when a deepwater well comes up dry, it costs the company $75 million! In short, like most big decisions, BP Amoco was making a multimillion-dollar choice under conditions of uncertainty, not knowing the precise odds of winning or losing.

Today, however, BP Amoco is using technology to increase its chances of hitting a wet (i.e., oil producing) deepwater well. Before spending $75 million on a new deepwater well, it has teams of geologists, engineers, and drillers work together in a room called the "hive" to view and analyze 3D images of rock and shale formations at the bottom of the sea. It used to take months to analyze enough information to have a reasonable certainty of hitting a wet deepwater well, but thanks to teamwork and improvements in technology, today it takes BP Amoco only one day to decide whether to spend $75 million on a new deepwater well.

In part, it will depend on how averse to risk top managers are. Are they willing to spend huge sums of money to potentially put BP Amoco in front of its competitors for years to come, or are they averse to risk, wanting to sit back and see whether other oil companies have success with deepwater drilling first?

Risk propensity is a person's tendency to take or avoid risks. Managers differ greatly with regard to risk propensity. Some people have a high risk propensity and are willing to bet years of their lives and lots of money under conditions of uncertainty. However, others with a low risk propensity say to themselves, "Why take a chance if you don't know what your odds of success are?"

At BP Amoco, CEO Sir John Browne developed a high risk propensity early in his career when he worked in Prudhoe Bay, Alaska, the site of BP's huge 14-million-barrel oilfield. However, Browne learned an important lesson: building the pipeline to carry the crude oil 1300 kilometres to the sea to be picked up by oil tankers increased the cost of the oil by a factor of 10. Fortunately, he said, "the price of oil went up by a factor of five." After that, when he became chief financial officer of BP's Sohio division, he concluded that BP's Alaskan oilfields would never yield a meaningful profit. So, when BP geologist Jack Golden started to talk about his new ideas on deepwater exploration, Browne was interested, but knew that the economics of this even more expensive drilling would have to be right for BP to make a profit. Still, he decided to gamble and took Sohio's entire $75-million exploration budget and diverted it to deepwater drilling. He said, "The key was to take a position in advance of the then-fashionable theory. It wasn't a 'bet-the-company' strategy, but it was clear that if it didn't work, our position in North America would be limited to Alaska." However, Browne hedged his bet by investing the $75 million to purchase a share in two deepwater projects that Shell Oil had just begun.

When Shell's deepwater wells paid off, Brown and BP invested millions more in deepwater drilling and went farther out into the Gulf of Mexico in search of bigger fields. Again, this increased BP's risk, but by going farther out, the company could purchase 23 square kilometre tracts of underwater land for only $225 000, compared to $30 million closer to shore. So the higher cost and risk associated with drilling farther from shore was greatly reduced by the much lower cost of purchasing underwater land for drilling. If Sir John Browne's bets on deepwater drilling pay off (two huge oilfields have been found thus far), BP should surpass Shell Oil as the second-largest oil company in the world and might even knock ExxonMobil from its number one position.

Interestingly, ExxonMobil's drilling strategy, which stems from its risk-averse CEO, Lee Raymond, is to let other oil companies move into a potential oil-producing location first. Once large oilfields have been found, Exxon then moves in with its resources. Using this strategy, Exxon's oilfield production has fallen 8 percent over the last few years. By contrast, thanks to the risk propensity of CEO John Browne, BP Amoco's oilfield production has increased by 10 percent over the same time and is expected to increase by another 6 percent over the next two years. The key issue, discussed next, is whether those additional reserves will improve company performance.

Finally, it may come down to something as simple as how the problem is defined. Is the problem cutting costs to restore profitability, or is the problem investing company funds in smartly calculated risks that might pay off in huge increases in oil revenue? In the end, though, you don't want to just convince upper management to do what you want; you want to be right, too.

The first step in decision-making is defining the problem, that is, figuring out what's going wrong. Typically, this means looking for gaps between desired states and existing states. When crude oil prices dropped, the gap on which everyone in the oil industry was focused was profits, which, for most oil companies, had turned into losses because of the low prices.

One way to define that gap is to conclude that costs are too high. For example, ExxonMobil has focused on keeping costs down, cutting 7000 employees over the last seven years. In fact, Exxon's earnings were up 27 percent during that time, largely because its operating expenses have not increased. However, another way to define the profit gap is to conclude that revenues are too low. This is why BP Amoco has focused on finding large, offshore deepwater oilfields to greatly increase the oil and gas available to sell.

As mentioned above, BP's oil production is up 10 percent in the last few years and is expected to climb another 6 percent over the next two years. However, because BP was an early player, it was much cheaper to acquire oil rights through deepwater drilling (i.e., $225 000 for a 23-square kilometre tract of deepwater land, compared to $30 million to acquire typical offshore sites). In fact, BP owns as much as 40 percent of the deepwater oil reserves in the Gulf of Mexico. Jack Golden, who heads BP's exploration unit, said, "We managed to come from nowhere over the course of the decade." Furthermore, despite costing as much as $1.5 billion to develop a deepwater oilfield, the low cost of acquisition and BP's technology make deepwater oilfields much less expensive than land-based oilfields. BP can produce a barrel of deepwater oil for about $7 to $9 a barrel. So even if oil drops below $22 a barrel, as it did several years ago, BP will still make close to $15 a barrel. Said Jack Golden, deepwater oil "improves the financial characteristics of the whole business."

Sources: J. Biers, "Drilling's Leviathans Stumble to Sea: New Generation Rigs, Ships Born in Rough Waters," *Houston Chronicle*, 17 October 1999, Business 6. D. Fisher, "How Sir John Browne Turned BP Amoco into the Hottest Prospect in the Oil Patch," *Forbes*, 2 April 2001, 110. D. Ivanovich, "The New 2000 Millennium—World May Learn to Wean Itself from Oil: The Search for Crude Deepens, As Does the Concern over Its Future," *Houston Chronicle*, 24 October 1999, 1. S. Liesman & A. Sullivan, "Mystery Man—Exxon Mobil Merger Positions an Enigma at Oil Giant's Helm: Hardly a Household Name, Mr. Raymond Fostered a Revolution Quietly Playing Everyman at Valdez," *The Wall Street Journal*, 1 December 1999. "petroleum production" Encyclopædia Britannica Online. search.eb.com/bol/topic?artcl=110684&seq_nbr=1&page=n&isctn=6 [Accessed 18 August 2001]. D. Soils, "Oil Discovery Called Largest Ever in Gulf: BP Amoco, Mobil Share in Billion Barrel Find," *Dallas Morning News*, 16 July 1999, 1D. Staff Reports, "Giant in the Gulf: BP Amoco's Massive Oil Drilling Platform Has Begun Pumping with 5 Wells in Gulf," *The New Orleans Times Picayune*, 3 December 1999, C1. K. Williams, "Transocean at Standoff on Drill Ship," *Houston Chronicle*, 10 June 2001, Business 2.

Key Terms

absolute comparisons (165)
anchoring and adjustment bias (174)
a-type conflict (affective conflict) (182)
availability bias (173)
bounded rationality (169)
brainstorming (186)
conditions of certainty (171)
conditions of risk (171)
conditions of uncertainty (172)
c-type conflict (cognitive conflict) (182)
decision criteria (165)
decision-making (162)
decision rule (175)

Delphi technique (183)
devil's advocacy (182)
dialectical inquiry (183)
dictionary rule (175)
electronic brainstorming (186)
escalation of commitment (178)
evaluation apprehension (186)
groupthink (181)
information overload (169)
maximizing (170)
minimum threshold rule (175)
multivariable testing (MVT) (176)
negative frame (172)

nominal group technique (183)
positive frame (172)
problem (163)
production blocking (186)
rational decision-making (162)
relative comparisons (166)
representative bias (174)
risk propensity (172)
satisficing (170)
stepladder technique (185)

What Do You Say?

As the director of human resources for a large, publicly traded manufacturing firm, you are privy to all types of corporate information regarding employee issues. Just yesterday, you attended a meeting with the CEO, president, vice president, and other top-level executives to discuss a proposed merger with a large competing firm. As a result of the merger, slated to be announced in approximately three weeks, a total of 8 percent of the employees at your firm will be laid off in an effort to combine overlapping jobs and reduce costs. At this same meeting, you were given a tentative list of the affected employees. All members present at the meeting were instructed to not mention a word of the proposed merger or layoff until it has been released by the corporate office. Early release of the confidential information could result in widespread panic among the firm's employees, drastically reduce the company's stock price, and possibly violate the securities trading laws that control how investment information regarding mergers, acquisitions, and tender offers are to be released to the public. If an employee or investor receives information regarding the proposed merger before it is publicly released and uses that information to make investment decisions, that person and the individual who leaked the information may be prosecuted for practising insider trading. Therefore, keeping this information private is extremely important.

This morning, as you were walking across the parking lot, Jim, an employee of the firm and a long-time friend of your family, approached you for some advice. He and his wife have been married for less than a year and are looking to purchase a home. Jim tells you that the bank will be calling your office soon to verify his employment and salary information as part of the prequalification process. Jim also asks you for your personal opinion regarding the amount that he should provide as a down payment on the home. He tells you that as a first-time home buyer, he can qualify for the loan by providing only 3 percent of the total purchase price as a down payment. However, he and his wife have amassed a significant nest egg in the last six months, and, as a result, are able to put approximately 10 percent down on the home. Additionally, Jim tells you that he and his wife, Maggie, recently learned that she is pregnant and will deliver in approximately seven months.

Suddenly, you have a sinking feeling in your stomach. Yesterday, as you briefly glanced over the list of employees to be cut, you noticed that Jim was one of the affected employees. In order to buy some time, you tell Jim that you are late for an important meeting but that you will call him as soon as you are free to discuss his home-buying dilemma. As you turn to walk toward your office, Jim comments, "I'll wait for your call before making my decision. Maggie and I really trust your advice and experience." As you reach your office door, you think to yourself, I can't tell him that he is about to lose his job. Nor can I honestly tell him to invest his savings into a home, knowing that he has a baby on the way and will soon have no job. You sink into your executive leather high-back chair, and you ponder how you will decide what information to give Jim and his wife without jeopardizing the company's interest and your personal friendship. **As the director of human resources for this firm, choose a decision-making process and determine what information you can honestly and professionally provide to Jim.**

Source: J. Seglin, "When an Employee About to Be Axed Asks for Advice," *Fortune*, 23 July 2001.

Critical Thinking Video Case

Nunavut and Kyoto

In 2002, the Canadian government signed the Kyoto Accord, which committed Canada to reduce greenhouse gas emissions to 6 percent below 1990 levels by 2012. It is believed that rising global temperatures, called global warming, are a result of increasing carbon dioxide in the atmosphere that results from human activity. As you will see in the video, this has warmed the arctic regions of Canada, perhaps the region most sensitive to rising global temperatures. These rising temperatures risk altering the Inuit way of life. Because of this, many residents of Nunavut welcome the implementation of the Kyoto Accord because they hope that it will stop climate change and allow them to preserve their traditional way of life. Not surprisingly, the premier of Nunavut, Paul Okalik, pushed particularly hard for its implementation.

On the other hand, there are others in Nunavut who see the Kyoto Accord as a threat to Nunavut's economic future, for this is an area where unemployment is traditionally very high. Nunavut is rich in natural resources, most of which remain untapped, and there is a significant group of Inuit who would like to develop these resources in order to generate employment and tax revenues. Unfortunately, the development of Nunavut's natural resources would significantly increase the region's production of greenhouse gases. This leaves the government with difficult choices.

Critical Thinking Questions

1. Define the problem the government of Nunavut faces.
2. What are the decision criteria that should be used to make decisions in this case?
3. What role does bounded rationality play in the decision-making process?

Management Decisions

Sugar-Free Kool-Aid: Let's Brainstorm!

What comes to mind when you think of Kool-Aid? Summer? Pool parties and picnics? Third grade? Kool-pops that you made, poured into moulds, and froze in the freezer? Was one of these flavours your favourite: Black Cherry, Cherry, Grape, Incrediberry, Kickin'-Kiwi-Lime, Lemonade, Lemon-Lime, Man-o-Mangoberry, Oh-Yeah Orange-Pineapple, Orange, Pina-Pineapple, Pink Lemonade, Pink Swimmingo, Purplesaurus Rex, Raspberry, Rock-a-dile Red, Slammin' Strawberry-Kiwi, Strawberry, Strawberry-Raspberry, Tropical Punch, or Watermelon-Cherry?

When most people think of Kool-Aid, they think of kids. Just over a decade ago, Kool-Aid sales started to decline. In part, this was due to long-term demographic changes. Families were simply having fewer children. Since the makers of Kool-Aid obviously couldn't do anything to change demographic trends, the next best thing was to encourage groups other than kids, such as teens and adults, to drink more Kool-Aid. With the explosion in popularity of diet drinks, the answer seemed simple: Sugar-Free Kool-Aid. However, Kool-Aid's management knew that it would still have a tough time convincing teens and adults to make Sugar-Free Kool-Aid their drink of choice. So, to figure out how they might do this, Kool-Aid sponsored a contest for MBA students at the top business schools in the nation.

MBA student teams submitted their ideas, and the teams with the most promising proposals were flown to New York to make formal presentations. Unfortunately, their suggestions were not very creative. Kool-Aid management was extremely disappointed with the results.

The purpose of this in-class management-decision activity is to correct that problem by using brainstorming to generate as many ideas as possible for selling Sugar-Free Kool-Aid to teens and adults. Keep in mind the following rules of brainstorming:

- The more ideas, the better.
- All ideas are acceptable, no matter how wild or crazy they might be.
- Other group members' ideas should be used to come up with even more ideas.
- Criticism or evaluation of ideas is not allowed.

Remember, creativity requires playfulness. Make this fun! Be wild and crazy! And, most important, don't criticize others' ideas. No moaning, groaning, or commenting allowed (or aloud). The first step in brainstorming is to generate as many different ideas as possible. Evaluation comes later.

Question

1. Think of as many ways as possible to get teens and adults to buy and use Sugar-Free Kool-Aid.

Management Decisions

Cafeteria or Gym?

Due to a record-breaking year, your company posted profits of 24 percent above analysts' expectations. In an attempt to retain qualified employees and to continue to provide an atmosphere of innovation and creativity, a decision was made to allot $1 million of retained earnings toward improving employee incentives. Upon announcing the program, a memo was circulated describing the rationale behind this decision. The memo encouraged employees to submit proposals for ideas regarding the type of incentives to spend money on. A minimum threshold rule was imposed on all proposals to be submitted. In order to be considered, the proposal must provide a tangible return for the organization through an increase in productivity, aesthetic beauty, functionality, morale, or profitability. Additionally, the proposal must benefit a majority of stakeholders within the company.

A total of 36 ideas were submitted. After analyzing each of the proposals, determining their feasibility, and weighing them against the minimum threshold rule, 10 ideas were chosen to be further reviewed, discussed, and ranked. Several meetings were held discussing the pros and cons of each proposal, and a second memo was circulated asking all employees to rank the proposals from least to most desired. The results showed that the two proposals favoured most by employees appear to be the construction of a cafeteria and the construction of a gymnasium/workout centre. Both ideas received an equal ranking of importance. You have been chosen to decide which proposal should be implemented.

The cafeteria, as described in the proposal, would include both working and nonworking areas for employees. The working areas would have, in addition to the normal tables and chairs, erasable marker boards, flipcharts, networked computer workstations and projection devices, telephones, and teleconferencing equipment. The nonworking area, separated by a glass partition, would house the normal tables and chairs, along with a big-screen television and a CD-jukebox. The cafeteria would serve a daily special in addition to "on-demand" items, such as hamburgers, hot dogs, salads, burritos, and other common food items. Food would be provided at a reduced price for all employees. Additionally, employees who regularly take clients and representatives out for business lunches would be allowed to charge their meals to their expense account, thus providing a savings for the company through reduced meal expenses.

Proponents of this plan claim that innovativeness, creativity, and profitability would be increased because most employees (whether they realize it or not) would be inclined to discuss work-related matters during their lunch hour. By assembling diverse groups of employees in a common area, these discussions could evolve into new projects or the improvement of existing ones. Having technology-enhanced components available in the working area would provide employees with the tools necessary to perform further research of their ideas during active discussions. The ideas could then be presented and discussed on markerboards or through the computer's LCD projector. Proponents also stated that the cafeteria could improve employee morale since having an on-site cafeteria would reduce the hassle of fighting traffic and crowds during the lunch-time rush and would increase productivity by ensuring that employees do not spend more than their allotted time during lunch.

The proposed gymnasium/workout centre would include a half-court basketball area with goal, two racquetball courts, and a complete workout area, containing items such as Stairmasters, rowing machines, stationary bikes, Nautilus equipment, locker rooms, showers, and hot tubs. Proponents of this plan state that employee morale and productivity would be enhanced as studies show that exercise helps eliminate stress and boosts energy levels. Proponents further claim that the increased productivity would, in time, translate into increased profits for the firm. In addition, healthier employees would reduce health insurance costs over the long run. To avoid congestion, time slots for the use of the workout centre would be available by reservation. In order not to affect work time, employees would be encouraged to use the workout centre before work, during their lunch break, or after work.

Questions

1. If you were the manager in question, which proposal would you choose to implement and why?
2. Looking back at the proposal not chosen, did you fall prey to one of the common decision-making mistakes (intuition, availability bias, representative bias, or anchoring and adjustment bias) in not choosing this proposal? Explain.

Source: M. Schrage, "I'll Have the Pasta Primavera, With a Side of Strategy," *Fortune,* 8 January 2001.

Making Better Decisions

Modern research shows that managers who make the best decisions don't overanalyze things by relying on rational decision-making models, nor do they oversimplify them by relying solely on their intuition. Instead, many managers utilize a concept referred to as "recognitional decision-making." Recognitional decision-making leads to quicker decisions than rational decision-making because it integrates the use of memory in connection with the context of a situation in order to develop an immediate feel of the current situation. Recurrences from previous experiences help provide sample solutions to current problems. Managers then subconsciously combine these recurrences with their intuition and imagination to help develop potential solutions for the current dilemma. Once a manager has a potential solution(s) in mind, he or she then begins to practise a mental game to see how the situation will play out. This approach is often compared to the strategies used by professional chess players when analyzing their next move. Professional chess players calculate each possible move and the subsequent move(s) of their opponents in their heads. By analyzing the opponent's expected move, chess players narrow their options for moves until one results in the best possible option (or least negative consequence), given the current situation. Unfortunately, making good decisions, like becoming a master chess player, requires a lot of experience and practice. Managers and potential managers can improve their decision-making skills by practising the following activities:

First, define your decision criteria for a given situation. For example, if when making decisions under the pressure of a deadline, you often underestimate the length of time it takes to accomplish a task, you should begin by dissecting the situation to see if certain patterns exist. By knowing the components of the decision and by determining which components give you the most trouble, chances are that you can determine the best approach to simplify your choices should this type of decision recur. To reinforce your decision-making ability, intentionally place yourself into situations where these commonalities exist. Doing so will provide further experience and help strengthen your decision-making ability.

Second, obtain feedback regarding current and previous decisions you have made. For example, if part of your job involves scheduling tasks, you can obtain feedback concerning your decisions by logging the expected time to complete a task and comparing that to the actual time taken. Analyzing the factors that contributed to the difference will help you recall them in the future, thus increasing your accuracy. Keep in mind that in most cases, feedback will not occur on its own; it has to be collected.

Third, practise decision-making by reading case studies of actual problems and placing yourself in the shoes of the decision maker. This textbook reinforces this approach by offering two "What Would You Do?" case scenarios for each chapter. The scenarios build on information presented in the text and discuss current problems of real-world situations. By comparing your answer to the "What Really Happened" answer, you can determine your decision-making ability and see if you understood and retained the information from the chapter.

Fourth, practise decision-making under conditions of uncertainty. Recall some previous decisions that you have made. Was uncertainty present, and if so, how did you handle it? What steps did you take, or could you have taken, that would have helped reduce the uncertainty or ambiguity involved?

Lastly, improve recognitional decision-making by using the expertise of others. If you respect and admire others for their ability to make quick, competent decisions, approach those people and ask them how they were able to arrive at their decisions. Also, ask what clues directed them to the solution that they chose.

Making decisions is a skill not unlike many other skills you have learned. The more you practise, the better decisions you will make. As your skill progresses, you'll notice that you now quickly and effortlessly make decisions that previously caused you grief. Additionally, you will be able to recognize patterns and recall potential solutions due to your increased decision-making experience.

Exercise

Recall a tough decision involving conditions of uncertainty that you recently made. Some examples include finding a roommate, buying a car, or picking your classes for next semester. The decision you select for this exercise should be one that you felt could have been improved. Analyze that decision using the five activities discussed above. After you analyze the decision, determine what steps you might take in the future to improve your decision-making ability, should this type of situation arise again.

Source: G. Klein & K. Weick, "Decisions: Making the Right Ones. Learning from the Wrong Ones," *Across the Board*, June 2000.

Discussion Questions

1. What are the costs and benefits of planning? Give examples of situations when planning has been either advantageous or disadvantageous.
2. If you were buying a new car, what decision criteria would you rely on and why?
3. What is the relationship among bounded rationality, satisficing, and information overload? Give examples where bounded rationality, satisficing and information overload have affected decisions you have made.
4. Define and give examples of common decision-making mistakes (intuition, availability bias, representative bias, or anchoring and adjustment bias).

Study Tip

Find a study partner and have him or her quiz you using the end-of-chapter materials and the quizzes on your Management CD-ROM. Instead of giving the simple answer, try to give the rationale also.

7

CHAPTER

Chapter Outline

Learning Objectives

After reading this chapter, you should be able to

1. describe the basic control process.

2. answer the question: Is control necessary or possible?

3. discuss the various methods that managers can use to maintain control.

4. describe the behaviours, processes, and outcomes that managers are choosing to control in today's organizations.

seven

Control

What Would You Do?

Howmet Aluminum Castings (www. alcoa.com/howmet) is well known as a producer of titanium and superalloy parts primarily for industrial gas turbines and airplanes. It employs approximately 11 000 people and has manufacturing plants across North America and Europe. About 85 percent of Howmet's aerospace business is in commercial aircraft, and it supplies both the U.S. Airforce and Airbus but one of its largest customers is Boeing Aerospace (www.boeing.com). In 1999 Howmet Aluminum opened a new state-of-the-art manufacturing plant in Laval, Quebec. Opening a new manufacturing plant is difficult at the best of times as there are many challenges in getting a new plant up and running and trying to have it turn a profit. It usually takes time to get all the problems worked out of a production line and in the case of Howmet, they were required to build parts to highly exacting specifications.

The problem of trying to get a new plant to turn a profit is made even more difficult when the decision to build a new plant is based on faulty assumptions and forecasting. When a company plans on building a new plant, extensive forecasting is usually undertaken in order to see whether there is sufficient demand for the increased production of the proposed plant. If it is forecasted that the plant can

turn a profit, the company will likely build it. In Howmet's case, it relied heavily on selling aircraft parts to aircraft manufacturers and airlines for maintaining their planes, and Howmet had planned to have about 60 percent of Laval's sales come from aircraft components. The worldwide commercial airline fleet had grown substantially since 1996, and when the opening of the plant was announced in 1998, Howmet believed that aircraft parts sales were strong and growing despite the downturn in the demand for new aircraft—even after a few years, new aircraft need to have many parts replaced as the result of significant wear and tear during normal use. Based on forecasts made from information gathered from many third parties and using its own computer models to simulate demand, Howmet believed that the demand for spare parts would grow 9 percent in 2000, and the industry would continue to have an annual growth rate of 8 percent.

Unfortunately, the sales forecasts were wrong, and by the time the plant was opened in 2000 the market for replacement parts was actually in decline. As noted above, new aircraft production had already been in decline but after the terrorist attack on the World Trade Center, the problem was even worse. Boeing, North America's largest airline producer, saw its orders cut in half in

2002. With Boeing being its largest customer, this was not good news for Howmet. The plant had originally planned on producing high volumes to reach its breakeven point but this was no longer feasible because of greatly lessened demand.

The general manager of Howmet Aluminum Castings' new production plant, Sylvain Poissant, was quoted as saying: "The future of the plant is uncertain." The company had already been laying off workers at many of its U.S. plants and had closed its plant in Los Angeles because of the downturn in Boeing's aircraft manufacturing. Alcoa, Howmet's parent company and the world's biggest aluminum maker, was in a similar situation and had just laid off 6500 staff the previous year.

Howmet had forecasted the level of production that would be needed for the plant to turn a profit. Without the growth in the market, it appeared it would be very difficult for the plant to turn a profit with the current cost of production. The company now knew that growth in sales was not likely and it would have to cut costs rather than increase production to meet overhead costs. Something had to be done to reduce production costs or the company would have to close the plant. The pressure on the management team was immense. "In today's market, it's incredibly important that Laval operate profitably," the president of Howmet was quoted as saying.

If you were the manager of Howmet's production plant in Laval, what would you do to cut costs to overcome the shortage in sales?

Sources: Larry Adams, "Howmet Inspects Critical Parts in a Nondestructive Way," *Quality* 39, no. 10 (October 2000): 36.

Amanda Bronstad, "Aluminum Plant to Be Scrapped," *Los Angeles Business Journal* 23, no. 45 (5 November 2001): 10. "Howmet Cuts at U.S. Plants," *Foundry Management and Technology* 130, no. 2 (February 2002): 11. Darrell Hassler, "Alcoa to Fire 6,500 Staff, Close Plants: Sales Down 13%," *National Post*, 20 November 2001, FP11. Carol Matlack and Stanley Holmes, "Look Out Boeing Airbus Is Grabbing Share, but Can It Make Money This Way?," *Business Week*, 28 October 2002, 50; Anthony L. Velocci, "Full Potential of Six Sigma Eludes Most Companies Exclusive Survey Reveals How Many Contractors Are

Underutilizing This Process-Improvement Methodology," *Aviation Week and Space Technology* 157, no. 14 (30 September 2002): 56. Anthony L. Velocci, "Casting Plant Demonstrates Power of Focusing on Quality," *Aviation Week and Space Technology* 157, no. 14 (30 September 2002): 61. Anthony L. Velocci, "Commercial Aircraft Downturn Unlikely to Affect Parts Demand," *Aviation Week and Space Technology* 149, no. 13 (28 September 1998): 66; www.howmet.com/home.nsf/pages/About+Howmet.

---

control
a regulatory process of establishing standards to achieve organizational goals, comparing actual performance against the standards, and taking corrective action, when necessary

Control is a regulatory process of establishing standards that will achieve organizational goals, comparing actual performance to those standards, and then, if necessary, taking corrective action to restore performance to those standards.

Control is achieved when behaviour and work procedures conform to standards, and company goals are accomplished.[1] For example, after the World Trade Center attack, control at airport security became even tighter as authorities tried to guarantee the goal of personal safety by making sure security procedures were followed. However, control is not just an after-the-fact process. Preventive measures, such as having passengers or Olympic stadium ticket holders pass through metal detectors, are also a form of control. In fact, we should remember that control is the last step in the first function of management, making things happen. To review, making things happen is a function of planning what you want to accomplish (Chapter 4), gathering and managing the information needed to make good decisions (Chapter 5), deciding how to achieve those plans (Chapter 6), and controlling behaviour and processes through preventive or corrective action (Chapter 7).

We begin this chapter by examining the basic control process used in organizations. Then we examine whether control is always necessary or possible (it isn't). In the third part of the chapter, we go beyond the basics to an in-depth examination of the different methods that companies use to achieve control. We finish the chapter by taking a look at the things that companies choose to control (i.e., finances, product quality, customer retention, etc.).

Basics of Control

If you wanted to control traffic speeds in your town, how would you do it? Well, most municipalities put in speed bumps, lower speed limits, put up traffic lights, or write more speeding tickets. However, the city of Culemborg in the Netherlands is planning to use sheep to slow down speeding cars on its neighbourhood streets. Why sheep? One of the city council members, who had observed the driving patterns on country roads in rural England, said, "After all, it's impossible to speed past the sheep [in the middle of the road] if you drive in the Yorkshire Dales." When animal rights groups complained that this was a bad idea, the city responded by erecting a special kind of fence to prevent the sheep from wandering onto busier, high-speed roads where they would clearly be endangered. However, Culemborg's city leaders were apparently not familiar with the tradition of some Yorkshire locals who "accidentally" hit sheep, hoping to make off with a free supply of lamb chops.[2] The city plans to release five or six sheep at first. If motorists actually do slow down, as many as 100 sheep may eventually be released onto city streets.

After reading the next two sections, you should be able to
1. describe the basic control process.
2. answer the question: Is control necessary or possible?

1. The Control Process

The basic control process involves standards; comparison to standards; corrective action; dynamic process; and feedback, concurrent, and feedforward control.

EXPERIENCING MANAGEMENT

Learn more about the three basic control methods and their relationship to inputs, transformation, and output processes at our animated concept and activity site. Choose Organizational Control from the "select a topic" pull-down menu, then Types of Control from the "overview tab."

www.experiencingmanagement.com

1.1 Standards

The control process begins when managers set goals, such as satisfying 90 percent of customers, or increasing sales by 5 percent. Companies then specify the performance standards that must be met to accomplish those goals. **Standards** are a basis of comparison for measuring the extent to which organizational performance is satisfactory or unsatisfactory. For example, many pizzerias use 30 minutes as the standard for delivery times. Since anything longer than that is viewed as unsatisfactory, they'll typically reduce their prices if they can't deliver a hot pizza to you in 30 minutes or less.

So how do managers set standards? How do they decide which levels of performance are satisfactory and which are unsatisfactory? The first criterion for a good standard is that it must enable goal achievement. If you're meeting the standard, but still not achieving company goals, then the standard may have to be changed. Companies also determine standards by listening to customers or observing competitors. When study after study indicated that customers preferred Burger King's menu to its own, McDonald's finally decided to introduce the Big Xtra, a burger with lettuce, tomato, mayonnaise, and ketchup that is clearly a knockoff of Burger King's Whopper (though McDonald's management denies that this is so).[3]

Standards can also be determined by benchmarking other companies. **Benchmarking** is the process of determining how well other companies (though typically not competitors) perform business functions or tasks. In other words, benchmarking is the process of determining other companies' standards. So the first step in setting standards is to determine what to benchmark. Companies can benchmark anything, from cycle time (how fast) to quality (how well). The next step is to identify the companies against which to benchmark your standards. Since this can require a significant commitment on the part of the benchmarked company, it can take time to identify and get agreement from them to be benchmarked. The last step is to collect data to determine other companies' performance standards. For example, countless companies have visited MBNA, the credit card company that has moved aggressively into the Canadian market in recent years.[4] They have come to learn how to respond quickly, if not immediately, to customer requests. Indeed, visitors learn that MBNA answers its phones by the second ring 98.5 percent of the time, and that it takes no more than 30 minutes to approve (or deny) customer requests for higher credit limits.[5] Another method for setting standards is to look to external standard-setting processes. For example, this can be done by implementing the ISO 9000 series of standards, which is discussed in more detail in Chapter 14.

1.2 Comparison to Standards

The next step in the control process is to compare actual performance to performance standards. While this sounds straightforward, the quality of the comparison largely depends on the measurement and information systems a company uses to keep track of performance. The better the system, the easier it is for companies to track their progress and identify problems that need to be fixed.

standards
a basis of comparison when measuring the extent to which various kinds of organizational performances are satisfactory or unsatisfactory

benchmarking
the process of identifying outstanding practices, processes, and standards in other companies and adapting them to your company

For example, because it is so difficult to gather detailed information about how customers are treated when they interact with employees, retail stores and restaurants spend millions a year to hire "secret shoppers," who visit their stores or restaurants to determine whether their employees provide helpful customer service. In fact, the "secret shoppers" aren't shoppers at all. They're hired consultants who, acting like customers, make detailed observations of the service provided (or not) by employees. For instance, on visiting a grocery store, a "secret shopper" gave a bagboy positive points for hustle, but negative points for wearing his hat backwards. More negative points are tallied when the store clerk in the produce department fails to greet the "secret shopper," when a service counter employee is chewing gum, and when a cashier enters an incorrect price code for an item that the scanner couldn't pick up.[6] Companies such as Calgary-based Service Intelligence Inc. (www.serviceintelligence.com) specialize in providing secret shoppers to the retail and service sectors. In 2002, McDonald's signed the company on to help it improve its customer service, and Service Intelligence has been sending secret shoppers to locations all over North America.[7]

1.3 Corrective Action

The next step in the control process is to identify performance deviations, analyze those deviations, and then develop and implement programs to correct them. This is similar to the planning process discussed in Chapter 4: Regular, frequent performance feedback allows workers and managers to track their performance and make adjustments in effort, direction, and strategies.

1.4 Dynamic Process

As shown in Exhibit 7.1, control is a continuous, dynamic process. It begins with actual performance and measures of that performance. Managers then compare performance to the pre-established standards. If they identify deviations from standard performance, they analyze the deviations and develop corrective programs. Then implementing the programs (hopefully) achieves the desired performance. To maintain performance levels at standard, managers must repeat the entire process again and again in an endless feedback loop. So control is not a one-time achievement or result. It continues over time (a dynamic process) and requires daily, weekly, and monthly attention from managers.

For example, at Pepsi, when the weekly Nielsen numbers come in, indicating the popularity of the television shows on which Pepsi bought commercial time, 70 people immediately begin analyzing and questioning the numbers to see if Pepsi got the audiences it wanted for its advertising dollar. If it didn't, the company may cancel its advertising on shows that didn't measure up and purchase advertising time on shows that appear to hold more promise.[8]

Sure, it's a cliché, but it's just as true in business as it is in sports: If you take your eye off the ball, you're going to strike out. Control is an ongoing, dynamic process.

1.5 Feedback, Concurrent, and Feedforward Control

feedback control
a mechanism for gathering information about performance deficiencies after they occur

There are three basic control methods: feedback control, concurrent control, and feedforward control.[9] **Feedback control** is a mechanism for gathering information about performance deficiencies after they occur. This information is then used to correct or prevent performance deficiencies. Study after study has clearly shown that feedback

EXHIBIT 7.1

CYBERNETIC CONTROL PROCESS

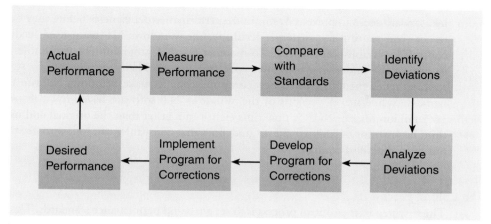

Source: H. Koontz & R.W. Bradspies, "Managing Through Feedforward Control: A Future Directed View," *Business Horizons*, June 1972, 25–36.

improves both individual and organizational performance. In most instances, any feedback is better than no feedback. However, if there is a downside to feedback, it is that it sometimes occurs too late. Sometimes it comes after big mistakes have been made.

For example, while everyone knows about Microsoft's (www.microsoft.com) current success with its Windows operating system, relatively few know that Microsoft's first try at writing operating software for networked computers and file servers was a bust. This program—the early version of Windows NT ("NT" stands for "new technology")—was huge and painfully slow. Unfortunately, the Windows NT development team did not become aware of these problems until the product was shipped and customers began complaining. Why hadn't the team gotten any early indication (i.e., feedback) of these problems? Because, unlike most of their customers who were running slower computers with little computer memory, the NT development team used fast, state-of-the-art computers with nearly four times more memory.[10] So Windows NT ran great for them, but terribly for regular users.

Concurrent control is a mechanism for gathering information about performance deficiencies as they occur. Thus, it is an improvement over feedback, because it attempts to eliminate or shorten the delay between performance and feedback about the performance. Because it had not been aware of the slow speed (and other problems) in the initial version of Windows NT, the NT development team abandoned its reliance on late-coming customer feedback and quickly adopted a development model based on concurrent control and feedforward control (discussed below).

For example, rather than waiting for customer complaints to come to them, the NT development team developed concurrent controls by establishing systematic, ongoing relationships between the team engineers and NT customers. When there was a problem, they heard about it immediately. Furthermore, NT programmers took turns answering the help line that NT customers called for technical support. They travelled to companies using NT, so that they could talk to customers directly and find out how they were using NT and where its performance fell short. Microsoft sent thousands of test copies of redesigned NT software to officially approved beta-testers who, through regular phone calls and e-mails, told the development team what they liked and didn't like.

concurrent control
a mechanism for gathering information about performance deficiencies as they occur, eliminating or shortening the delay between performance and feedback

feedforward control
a mechanism for monitoring performance inputs rather than outputs to prevent or minimize performance deficiencies before they occur

Feedforward control is a mechanism for gathering information about performance deficiencies before they occur. In contrast to feedback and concurrent control, which provide feedback on the basis of outcomes and results, feedforward control provides information about performance deficiencies by monitoring inputs, not outputs. Thus, feedforward seeks to prevent or minimize performance deficiencies before they occur. So rather than waiting for customer feedback, the Windows NT team used feedforward controls by establishing a special 16-member team of programmers whose sole job was to inspect the underlying computer code (the input). Then, literally step by step, they rewrote, redesigned, or created new computer code to make Windows NT run faster. It worked. While newer versions of the Windows NT software have grown from 6.1 to 16.5 million lines of code, it now runs eight times faster than the original and uses one-third less memory. Exhibit 7.2 lists guidelines that companies can follow to get the most out of feedforward control.

Review 1
The Control Process

The first step in the control process is to set goals and performance standards. The second is to compare actual performance to performance standards. The better a company's information and measurement systems, the easier it is to make these comparisons. The last step is to identify and correct performance deviations. However, control is a continuous, dynamic process, not a one-time achievement or result. Control requires frequent managerial attention. The three basic control methods are feedback control (after-the-fact performance information), concurrent control (simultaneous performance information), and feedforward control (preventive performance information).

2. Is Control Necessary or Possible?

control loss
situation in which behaviour and work procedures do not conform to standards

Control is achieved when behaviour and work procedures conform to standards, and goals are accomplished. By contrast, **control loss** occurs when behaviour and work procedures do not conform to standards.[11] Control loss usually prevents goal achievement. For example, several years ago, the Fidelity Investment Magellan Fund, which is the world's largest and, historically, one of the best-performing stock mutual funds, made a $3.6-billion mistake. When the accountants were closing the books in December, they accidentally recorded a $1.8-billion loss as a gain, thus overstating end-of-year returns by $3.6 billion. Fortunately, because it was a simple error and because it was quickly corrected, no one lost any money. However, this highly publicized mistake, which came just six months after a similar well-publicized error, did damage Fidelity's reputation with investors and the financial community.[12]

EXHIBIT 7.2

GUIDELINES FOR USING FEEDFORWARD CONTROL

1. Thorough planning and analysis are required.
2. Careful discrimination must be applied in selecting input variables.
3. The feedforward system must be kept dynamic.
4. A model of the control system should be developed.
5. Data on input variables must be regularly collected.
6. Data on input variables must be regularly assessed.
7. Feedforward control requires action.

Source: H. Koontz & R.W. Bradspies, "Managing Through Feedforward Control: A Future Directed View," *Business Horizons*, June 1972, 25–36.

When control losses occur, managers need to find out what they could have done, if anything, to prevent these mistakes from occurring. In Fidelity's case, there was a simple solution: Be sure to show the end-of-year summary statement to the fund manager before releasing it to mutual fund shareholders and the public. Any fund manager would easily catch a mistake of that size.

In general, when control loss occurs, managers need to consider three alternatives: Is more control necessary? Is more control possible? What do you do when control isn't possible?

2.1 Is More Control Necessary?

Two factors can help managers determine whether more (or different) control is necessary: the degree of dependence and resource flows.[13] **Degree of dependence** is the extent to which a company needs a particular resource to accomplish its goals. The more important a resource is for meeting organizational standards and goals, the more necessary it is to control that resource.

Note, however, that resources are more than just raw materials. A **resource** is anything that can be used to fulfil a need or solve a problem. Thus, resources can include employee skills, space, intellectual capability, capital ($), specialized know-how, a cohesive corporate culture, etc. Basically, critical resources, whatever form they take, make it easier for managers and employees to carry out the work processes that conform to standards and lead to goal accomplishment.

The second factor that determines whether more control is necessary is resource flow. **Resource flow** is the extent to which companies have easy access to critical resources. For example, the production of chlorofluorocarbons (CFCs) has been illegal in North America since 1996. CFCs are used in air conditioners and refrigerators as a coolant.[14] This created a problem for auto and appliance repair companies: where were they going to get CFCs for their customers? The lack of ready supplies led to soaring CFC prices and cross-border smuggling as U.S. companies wanted to tap into large Canadian stockpiles. In response to the growing demand, companies such as Halozone, operating in Mississauga, Ontario, created a system to extract and recycle CFCs, leading to an increased supply.[15]

When companies are reliant on critical resources, they often attempt to increase resource flows by creating or obtaining some form of control over them. If a company has control of critical resources, it is much easier for them to manage their business. For example, gas retailer Petro-Canada (www.petro-canada.ca) also drills for oil and refines it. This makes their retail gasoline business less subject to outside influences. Independent gasoline retailers such as Canadian Tire and Superstore have to purchase their gasoline supplies from other companies, leaving them at risk.

degree of dependence
the extent to which a company needs a particular resource to accomplish its goals

resource
anything that can be used to fulfil a need or solve a problem

resource flow
the extent to which companies have access to critical resources

---

PERSONAL PRODUCTIVITY TIP

Gain Control—Lower Your Expectations

Control loss occurs when performance falls short of standards. When this happens, the automatic response is to put in more hours and do everything possible to meet the standard. But remember: One way to maintain control is to change goals. This may seem like an admission of failure. But in many cases, it's just being realistic. You can't excel at everything. Disappointed because you're five kilograms over your high school weight? Celebrate that it's *only* five kilograms and not ten. Bummed because you didn't get that raise? Be glad you've still got your job. Selectively lower your expectations and regain control.

2.2 Is More Control Possible?

Degree of dependence and resource flows can help determine whether control is needed. However, the cost of control and cybernetic feasibility help determine whether control is possible. First, to determine whether more control is possible (or worthwhile), managers need to carefully assess the costs, benefits, and unintended consequences of control, because sometimes the costs of control exceed its benefits. For example, one of the reasons that the number of U.S. pharmaceutical companies producing major vaccines has dropped significantly is that the cost of controlling legal risk (through liability insurance and in-house legal staffs) is just too high.[16] Indeed, the threat of lawsuits has led 47 percent of companies to drop one or more products, has encouraged 25 percent of companies to drop research and development programs, and has stopped 39 percent of companies from bringing new products to market.[17] Before choosing to implement control, managers should be confident that the benefits exceed the costs.

An often-overlooked factor in determining the cost of control is the set of unintended consequences that sometimes accompanies increased control. Control systems help companies, managers, and workers accomplish their goals, but at the same time that they help solve some problems, they can create others. For example, Delta Airlines wanted to reduce its costs from 14.7 cents per seat-mile to 11.3 cents per seat-mile. In many respects, Delta succeeded, lowering its costs and returning to solid profitability. However, in some places, the cost-cutting was so deep that Delta's performance suffered in other key areas. For example, Delta used to keep one mechanic at each gate to fix minor problems between flights. Yet, after cost-cutting, it assigned only one mechanic to every three or four gates. Because the mechanic could repair only one plane at a time, the unintended consequence was that many flights were delayed. At the time, this caused Delta to fall to last among domestic airlines in on-time arrivals.[18]

The second factor that helps managers determine whether control is possible is cybernetic feasibility. **Cybernetic feasibility** is the extent to which it is possible to implement each step in the control process: clear standards of performance, comparison of performance to standards, and corrective action. If one or more steps cannot be implemented, then maintaining effective control may be difficult or impossible.

2.3 Quasi-Control: When Control Isn't Possible

If control is necessary, but not possible because of costs or cybernetic infeasibility, managers can use two **quasi-control** options: reducing dependence or restructuring dependence. **Reducing dependence** involves an explicit choice to abandon or change organizational goals by reducing dependence on critical resources. Companies are likely to choose to reduce dependence under the same conditions that they would choose control. The difference, however, is that companies choose to reduce dependence when control is not possible, that is, when the cost is too high or cybernetic feasibility is near zero.

For example, over the last 20 years, PepsiCo (www.pepsi.com) operated three distinct businesses: soft drinks (Pepsi, Mountain Dew, etc.), fast-food restaurants (Pizza Hut, Taco Bell, and Kentucky Fried Chicken), and snack foods (Frito-Lay). Each business was a resource that Pepsi used to earn profits. However, in the last decade, no matter what it tried, Pepsi found that it couldn't be successful in all three businesses at the same time. Increasingly, money invested in the restaurants was needed to fight Coca-Cola in the soft drink business. So, rather than continue to depend on three different resources, Pepsi reduced its dependence by deciding to focus on just two. Consequently, it sold its restaurants for more than $16.5 billion and reinvested the proceeds in its soft drink and snack food businesses.[19]

Instead of reducing dependence when control is not possible, companies can choose to **restructure dependence**—exchange dependence on one critical resource for dependence on another. One area in which companies are exchanging resources is to substitute private planes for commercial air travel. Surprisingly, travelling by private plane has a number of advantages over travelling via commercial airlines. To start, compared to last-minute business class tickets, which are much more expensive now than just a few years ago and approximately three to five times the cost of coach class tickets, corporate planes can be cheaper to fly. Tim Quinn, who owns a construction company, saw his monthly air-travel expenses drop almost in half, from $18 000 to $9000, even after making the monthly payments for his company plane. Furthermore, private planes can fly into more airports.[20]

There are three advantages to restructuring dependence. First, like private planes, the new critical resource may be more controllable. Second, even better, the new critical resource may not require any control at all. Third, the company does not have to change its goals.

cybernetic feasibility
the extent to which it is possible to implement each step in the control process

quasi-control
reducing dependence or restructuring dependence when control is necessary but not possible

reducing dependence
abandoning or changing organizational goals to reduce dependence on critical resources

restructuring dependence
exchanging dependence on one critical resource for dependence on another

Is Control Necessary or Possible?

Exhibit 7.3 summarizes the questions that managers should answer to determine if control is necessary or possible. First, if the degree of dependence on a critical resource is high, or if resource flows are poor, managers will want to initiate greater control over critical resources. However, if resource flows and the degree of dependence are low, managers do not need to do anything to increase control. Next, if cybernetics (i.e., the basic control process) is feasible, managers should determine if the cost of control is acceptable. If it is, then managers should choose to regulate or control the degree of dependence on critical resources. However, if cybernetics is not feasible, the next step is deciding whether goals can be changed. If goals are fixed and unchangeable, managers should restructure their dependence on critical resources by exchanging dependence on one critical resource for dependence on another. On the other hand, if goals can be changed, managers should reduce dependence on critical resources by abandoning or changing key goals.

EXPERIENCING MANAGEMENT

Various financial and human control techniques are presented at our animated concept and activity site. Some controls are closely related to the Planning Process (see Chapter 4). Choose Organizational Control from the "select a topic" pull-down menu, then Financial and Human Controls from the "overview tab."

www.experiencingmanagement.com

How and What to Control

Have you developed a taste for gourmet coffee? With gourmet coffee seemingly everywhere, chances are you have or someone in your office has. However, the popularity of specialty coffees and coffee shops has created a problem in many offices: the long coffee

---

EXHIBIT 7.3

IS CONTROL NECESSARY OR POSSIBLE?

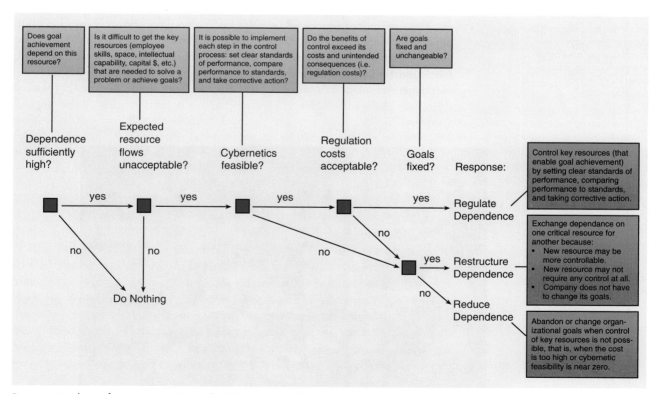

Source: Academy of Management Review by S.G. Green and M.A. Welsh. Copyright 1988 by Academy of Management. Reproduced with permission of the publisher via Copyright Clearance Center.

break. Instead of wandering down the hall to brew a fresh pot of regular coffee and chat with co-workers during a 15-minute coffee break, workers are now running out of their offices to find the nearest gourmet coffee shop. One department manager declared coffee shops off-limits after finding five department staffers missing well beyond their regular coffee breaks.[21]

The question for aspiring managers is how would you handle this situation? Should you declare coffee shops off-limits? Should you simply discuss it with employees and rely on them to exercise their own judgment? Should you closely watch for potential violators and then punish them? And then there is the question of whether long coffee breaks are something that managers should even try to control. Paul Ivers, who works for Lotus Development Corporation, believes that there's nothing wrong with trips to the coffee shop. He said, "It's not good to be doing something straight for nine to ten hours." Likewise, Carol Raymer, who is a manager at a courier company (and gets six to eight cups a day from the coffee shop in her office building!), said, "You talk to customers and issues come up. It's a good networking place."

After reading the next two sections, you should be able to
3. discuss the various methods that managers can use to maintain control.
4. describe the behaviours, processes, and outcomes that managers are choosing to control in today's organizations.

3. Control Methods

There are five different methods that managers can use to achieve control in their organizations: bureaucratic control, objective control, normative control, concertive control, and self-control.

3.1 Bureaucratic Control

bureaucratic control
use of hierarchical authority to influence employee behaviour by rewarding or punishing employees for compliance or noncompliance with organizational policies, rules, and procedures

When most people think of managerial control, what they have in mind is bureaucratic control. **Bureaucratic control** is top-down control, in which managers try to influence employee behaviour by rewarding or punishing employees for compliance or noncompliance with organizational policies, rules, and procedures. However, most employees would argue that bureaucratic managers emphasize punishment for noncompliance much more than rewards for compliance. For example, in the Sejen Electronics TV manufacturing plant in Zhuhai, China, Kim Jin Sun, the manager who runs the plant,

Coffee breaks provide an opportunity for employees to informally interact with each other and customers. Long coffee breaks may also reduce productivity.

© CORBIS/MAGMA

found several workers napping during their breaks. Consequently, she punished all 100 of her workers by making them kneel before her. When asked why she intimidated the workers this way, she responded, "It was the best way to make them understand that they had done wrong. Kneeling down in Korea isn't considered as shameful as in China. I didn't mean to demean them as human beings. It was just a management strategy I had to resort to."[22]

Ironically, bureaucratic management and control were created to prevent just this type of managerial behaviour. By encouraging managers to apply well-thought-out rules, policies, and procedures in an impartial, consistent manner to everyone in the organization, bureaucratic control is supposed to make companies more efficient, effective, and fair. Perversely, it frequently has just the opposite effect. Managers who use bureaucratic control often put following the rules above all else.

Another characteristic of bureaucratically controlled companies is that due to their rule- and policy-driven decision-making, they are highly resistant to change and slow to respond to customers and competitors. Even Max Weber, the German philosopher who is largely credited with popularizing bureaucratic ideals in the late 19th century, referred to bureaucracy as the "iron cage." He said, "Once fully established, bureaucracy is among those social structures which are the hardest to destroy."[23]

3.2 Objective Control

In many companies, bureaucratic control has evolved into **objective control**, which is the use of observable measures of employee behaviour or outputs to assess performance and influence behaviour. Objective control differs from bureaucratic control in that managers focus on the observation or measurement of worker behaviour or outputs rather than policies and rules.

Behaviour control is the regulation of the behaviours and actions that workers perform on the job. The basic assumption of behaviour control is that if you do the right things (i.e., the right behaviours) every day, then those things should lead to goal achievement. However, behaviour control is still management-based, which means that managers are responsible for monitoring, rewarding, and punishing workers for exhibiting desired or undesired behaviours. When Alan Greenberg, the CEO of Bear Stearns, a Wall Street investment company, wrote the following memo to his firm's managing partners, he was enacting behavioural control about the importance of always being available.

> Bear Stearns is moving forward at an accelerated rate and everyone is contributing. It is absolutely essential for us to be able to talk to our [the firm's] partners at all times. All of us are entitled to eat lunch, play golf and go on vacation. But you must leave word with your secretary or associates where you can be reached at all times. Decisions have to be made and your input can be important!
>
> I conducted a study of the 200 firms that have disappeared from Wall Street over the last few years, and I discovered that 62.349 percent went out of business because the important people did not leave word where they went when they left their desk if even for 10 minutes.
>
> That idiocy will not occur here![24]

Instead of measuring what managers and workers do, **output control** measures the results of their efforts. Whereas behaviour control regulates, guides, and measures how workers behave on the job, output control gives managers and workers the freedom to behave as they see fit as long as it leads to the accomplishment of pre-specified, measurable results. Output control is often coupled with rewards and incentives. However, three things must occur for output control and rewards to lead to improved business results.

objective control
use of observable measures of worker behaviour or outputs to assess performance and influence behaviour

behaviour control
regulation of the behaviours and actions that workers perform on the job

output control
regulation of worker results or outputs through rewards and incentives

First, output control measures must be reliable, fair, and accurate. Second, employees and managers must believe that they can produce the desired results. Third, the rewards or incentives tied to outcome control measures must truly be dependent on achieving established standards of performance. For example, it seems that each year *The Globe and Mail* or *Canadian Business* runs a story about some CEO who racked up another multimillion-dollar bonus. Nonetheless, this is not always the case. Hank Swartout, CEO of Precision Drilling, Canada's largest oilfield services company, received no bonus in 2002 after receiving a $2.2-million bonus in 2001. His bonus is tied to a strict formula based on company earnings and return on capital. Because company performance was poor, he received no bonus in 2002.[25] So for output control to work with rewards, the rewards must truly be at risk if performance doesn't measure up.

3.3 Normative Control

Rather than monitoring rules, behaviour, or outputs, another way to control what goes on in organizations is to shape the beliefs and values of the people who work there through normative control. With **normative controls**, a company's widely shared values and beliefs guide workers' behaviour and decisions. For example, at Mountain Equipment Co-op (MEC), an outdoor equipment retailer based in Vancouver, one value permeates the entire workforce from top to bottom: environmental responsibility.[26] MEC (www.mec.ca) builds environmentally friendly buildings and used salvage materials when building a new store in Winnipeg. It also monitors the safety and environmental practices of its suppliers and prints its catalogue on recycled paper.

Normative controls are created in two ways. First, companies that use normative controls are very careful about whom they hire. While many companies screen potential applicants on the basis of their abilities, normatively controlled companies are just as likely to screen potential applicants based on their attitudes and values. For example, the president of MEC, Peter Robinson, was a park ranger in British Columbia, indicating his interest in the environment began before his stint as president of MEC. Second, with

normative control
regulation of workers' behaviour and decisions through widely shared organizational values and beliefs

Mountain Equipment Co-op's store in Winnipeg is partly built from salvaged materials, an example of its environmental responsibility.

Courtesy of Mountain Equipment Co-op

normative controls, managers and employees learn what they should and should not do by observing experienced employees and by listening to the stories they tell about the company.

3.4 Concertive Control

Whereas normative controls are based on the strongly held, widely shared beliefs throughout a company, **concertive controls** are based on beliefs that are shaped and negotiated by work groups.[27] So while normative controls are driven by strong organizational cultures, concertive controls usually arise when companies give autonomous work groups complete responsibility for task completion. **Autonomous work groups** are groups that operate without managers and are completely responsible for controlling work group processes, outputs, and behaviour. These groups do their own hiring, firing, worker discipline, work schedules, materials ordering, budget making and meeting, and decision-making.

Concertive control is not established overnight. Autonomous work groups evolve through two phases as they develop concertive control. In phase one, autonomous work group members learn to work with each other, supervise each other's work, and develop the values and beliefs that will guide and control their behaviour. And because they develop these values and beliefs themselves, work group members feel strongly about following them.

For example, a member of an autonomous team at ISE Electronics, a small manufacturer of electronic boards, said, "I feel bad, believe it or not. Last Friday, we missed a shipment. I feel like *I* missed the shipment since I'm the last person that sees what goes to ship. But Friday we missed the shipment by two boards and it shouldn't have been missed. But it was and I felt bad because it's me, it's a reflection on me, too, for not getting the boards out the door."[28]

The second phase in the development of concertive control is the emergence and formalization of objective rules to guide and control behaviour. The beliefs and values developed in phase one usually develop into more objective rules as new members join teams. The clearer those rules, the easier it becomes for new members to figure out how and how not to behave.

For example, a team member at ISE Electronics described how the team dealt with members showing up late to work: "Well, we had some disciplinary thing, you know. We had a few certain people who didn't show up on time and made a habit of coming in late. So the team got together and kinda set some guidelines and we told them, you know, 'If you come in late the third time and you don't wanna do anything to correct it, you're gone.' That was a team decision that this was a guideline that we were gonna follow."[29] Again, the key difference in concertive control is that the teams and not management enforced these rules.

3.5 Self-Control

Self-control, also known as **self-management**, is a control system in which managers and workers control their own behaviour.[30] However, self-control is not anarchy in which everyone gets to do whatever they want. In self-control or self-management, leaders and managers provide workers with clear boundaries within which they may guide and control their own goals and behaviours.[31] Leaders and managers also contribute to self-control by teaching others the skills they need to maximize and monitor their own work effectiveness. In turn, individuals who manage and lead themselves establish self-control by setting their own goals, monitoring their own progress, rewarding or

concertive control
regulation of workers' behaviour and decisions through work group values and beliefs

autonomous work groups
groups that operate without managers and are completely responsible for controlling work group processes, outputs, and behaviour

---

PERSONAL PRODUCTIVITY

Learn to Say No!

Control is not just setting standards and identifying performance discrepancies. A key issue in control is deciding what to control and what to ignore. We can't do everything, and that means that sometimes we have to say no when we're asked to participate. Here are four tips for saying no. First, listen to show interest and understanding. Second, say no immediately to avoid raising false expectations concerning your involvement. Three, explain why you can't, so that the reasons for your refusal are understood. Fourth, offer alternatives to your participation. "I can't, but you should contact Mary Smith. Mary knows how to do this."

Sources: V.M. Parachin, "Overcoming Work Addiction: Twelve Ways to Slow Down and Take Care of Yourself," *Vibrant Life*, 13 March 1996, 10.

---

self-control (self-management)
control system in which managers and workers control their own behaviour by setting their own goals, monitoring their own progress, and rewarding themselves for goal achievement

punishing themselves for achieving or for not achieving their self-set goals, and constructing positive thought patterns that remind them of the importance of their goals and their ability to accomplish them.[32]

One technique for reminding yourself of your goals is daily affirmation, in which you write down or speak your goals aloud to yourself several times a day. Skeptics contend that daily affirmations are nothing more than positive thinking. However, an affirmation is just a simple way to help control what you think about and how you spend your time. Basically, it's a technique to prevent (i.e., control) yourself from getting sidetracked on unimportant thoughts and activities.

Scott Adams, who illustrates the cartoon strip "Dilbert," was skeptical that affirmations would work, but he gave them a try. His first affirmations were to see the price of a company's stock rise and to impress a particular woman. Both happened. Then when he was getting ready to take the GMAT test to get into an MBA program, every day he wrote that he wanted a score of 94. His score was 94. When he began affirming, "I will be the best cartoonist on the planet," "Dilbert" ballooned in popularity. Where it once appeared in only 100 newspapers, it now appears in more than 1100. What's he affirming now? "I will win a Pulitzer Prize."[33] Okay, start writing, "I will get an 'A' in Management. I will get an 'A' in Management...."

Review 3
Control Methods

There are five methods of control: bureaucratic, objective, normative, concertive, and self-control (self-management). Bureaucratic and objective controls are top-down, management- and measurement-based. Normative and concertive controls represent shared forms of control, because they evolve from companywide or team-based beliefs and values. Self-control, or self-management, is a control system in which managers largely, but not completely, turn control over to the individuals themselves.

Bureaucratic control is based on organizational policies, rules, and procedures. Objective controls are based on reliable measures of behaviour or outputs. Normative control is based on strong corporate beliefs and careful hiring practices. Concertive control is based on the development of values, beliefs, and rules in autonomous work groups. Self-control is based on individuals' setting their own goals, monitoring themselves, and rewarding or punishing themselves with respect to goal achievement.

We end this section by noting that there are more or less appropriate circumstances for using each of these control methods. Examine Exhibit 7.4 to find out when each of these five control methods should be used.

4. What to Control

In the second part of this chapter we asked, "Is control necessary or possible?" In part three we asked, "How should control be obtained?" In this fourth and final section, we ask the equally important question "What should managers control?" The way their managers answer this question has critical implications for most businesses. After reading this section, you should be able to explain the balanced scorecard approach to control, and how companies can achieve balanced control of company performance by choosing to control economic value added, customer defections, quality, and waste and pollution.

4.1 The Balanced Scorecard

In most companies, performance is measured using standard financial and accounting measures, such as return on capital, return on assets, return on investments, cash flow, net income, net margins, etc. That's why employees at Americas Marketing and Refining (AM&R), the largest division of Mobil Oil Corporation (now Exxon Mobil), were not looking forward to their quarterly meeting with their tough division vice president. On most of these traditional measures, division performance had been poor, and lower-level employees and managers expected to be blasted for their poor performance. In the past, poor financial performance usually led to firings and layoffs. So no one wanted to go to the meeting.

EXHIBIT 7.4

BUREAUCRATIC CONTROL

- When it is necessary to standardize operating procedures
- When it is necessary to establish limits

BEHAVIOUR CONTROL

- When it is easier to measure what workers do on the job than what they accomplish on the job
- When "cause-effect" relationships are clear, that is, when companies know which behaviours will lead to success and which won't
- When good measures of worker behaviour can be created

OUTPUT CONTROL

- When it is easier to measure what workers accomplish on the job than what they do on the job
- When good measures of worker output can be created
- When it is possible to set clear goals and standards for worker output
- When "cause-effect" relationships are unclear

NORMATIVE CONTROL

- When organizational culture, values, and beliefs are strong
- When it is difficult to create good measures of worker behaviour
- When it is difficult to create good measures of worker output

CONCERTIVE CONTROL

- When responsibility for task accomplishment is given to autonomous work groups
- When management wants workers to take "ownership" of their behaviour and outputs
- When management desires a strong form of worker-based control

SELF-CONTROL

- When workers are intrinsically motivated to do their jobs well
- When it is difficult to create good measures of worker behaviour
- When it is difficult to create good measures of worker output
- When workers have or are taught self-control and self-leadership skills

Sources: L.J. Kirsch, "The Management of Complex Tasks in Organizations: Controlling the Systems Development Process," *Organization Science 7* (1996): 1–21. S.A. Snell, "Control Theory in Strategic Human Resource Management: The Mediating Effect of Administrative Information," *Academy of Management Journal 35* (1992): 292–327.

However, this time it was different. After opening the meeting with a discussion of the poor financial results, the meeting turned positive. Market share had improved. Operating expenses were down. And employees, as measured by a recent attitudinal survey, were satisfied with their jobs and their bosses. The VP declared, "In all the areas we could control, we moved the needle in the right direction." The employees, who expected to be handed their heads, were shocked by the praise. Greg Berry, the division's manager of business and performance analysis, said, "It was a total departure from the past. Here was a Mobil executive saying, 'Hey, we didn't make any money, but I feel good about where the business is going.'"[34]

The **balanced scorecard** encourages managers to look beyond traditional financial measures to four different perspectives on company performance. How do customers see us (the customer perspective)? What must we excel at (the internal perspective)? Can we continue to improve and create value (the innovation and learning perspective)? How do we look to shareholders (the financial perspective)?[35]

balanced scorecard measurement of organizational performance in four equally important areas: finances, customers, internal operations, and innovation and learning

The balanced scorecard has several advantages over traditional control processes that rely solely on financial measures. First, it forces managers at each level of the company to set specific goals and measure performance in each of the four areas. For example, Mobil Oil's AM&R division uses 23 different measures in its balanced scorecard. Of those 23, only five are standard financial measures of performance.

Exhibit 7.5 shows the balanced scorecard used by a large semiconductor company. This company does measure its performance in traditional financial terms—cash flows, quarterly sales growth, and increased market share and return on equity. But it also measures the percentage of sales from new products and on-time deliveries (customer perspective), unit costs and whether the company met the projected schedule for new product introductions (internal business perspective), and how long it takes to develop the next generation of new products and how well it rolls out new products compared to its competition (innovation and learning perspective).

The second major advantage of the balanced scorecard approach to control is that it minimizes the chances of **suboptimization**, where performance improves in one area, but only at the expense of decreased performance in others. For example, at Mobil Oil's AM&R division, everyone in the plant now measures performance based on the balanced scorecard. When the division's executive team meets, all managers must bring their copy

suboptimization
performance improvement in one part of an organization but only at the expense of decreased performance in another part

---

EXHIBIT 7.5

EXAMPLE OF A BALANCED SCORECARD

FINANCIAL PERSPECTIVE		CUSTOMER PERSPECTIVE	
GOALS	**MEASURES**	**GOALS**	**MEASURES**
Survive	Cash flow	New Products	Percent of sales from new products
Succeed	Quarterly sales growth and operating income by division		Percent of sales from proprietary products
Prosper	Increased market share and ROE (return on equity)	Responsive supply Preferred customer Customer partnership	On-time delivery Share of key accounts' purchases Number of cooperative engineering efforts

INTERNAL BUSINESS PERSPECTIVE		INNOVATION AND LEARNING PERSPECTIVE	
GOALS	**MEASURES**	**GOALS**	**MEASURES**
Technology capability	Manufacturing geometry vs. competition	Technology leadership	Time to develop next generation product
Manufacturing excellence	Cycle time, Unit cost	Product focus	Percent of products equalling 80 percent sales
Design productivity	Silicon efficiency, Engineering efficiency	Time to market	New product introduction vs. competition

Source: Adapted and reprinted by permission of Harvard Business Review. From "The Balanced Scorecard: Measures that Drive Performance" by R.S. Kaplan and D.P. Norton, January–February 1992, copyright © 1992 by the Harvard Business School Publishing Corporation; all rights reserved.

of the balanced scorecard to explain how their actions will affect finances, customers, internal business, and innovation and learning. AM&R's vice president said, "It's the basis of every conversation. When I go out in the field and talk with a guy running a coker on the midnight shift at one of our refineries, he can tell me what he's doing to impact the scorecard."[36]

Let's examine some of the ways in which companies are controlling the four basic parts of the balanced scorecard: the financial perspective (economic value added), the customer perspective (customer defections), the internal perspective (total quality management), and the innovation and learning perspective (waste and pollution).

4.2 The Financial Perspective: Controlling Economic Value Added

The traditional approach to controlling financial performance focuses on measures such as analysis of financial ratios, cash flow, capital budgets, balance sheets, and income statements. For years, management textbooks have recommended that managers use these measures to monitor and control the financial performance of their companies. In reality, though, most managers don't (but should) have a good understanding of accounting measures.[37] (If you struggle with these, you might find help in the following books: *Accounting the Easy Way* by Peter J. Eisen, *Accounting for Dummies* and *How to Read a Financial Report: Wringing Vital Signs Out of the Numbers*, both by John A. Tracy.) Furthermore, the complexity and sheer amount of information contained in these measures can shut down the brains and glaze over the eyes of even the most experienced managers.[38]

On the other hand, the balanced scorecard focuses on one simple question when it comes to finances: How do we look to shareholders? One of the best ways to answer that question is through something called economic value added.

Conceptually, **economic value added (EVA)** is fairly easy for managers and workers to understand. It is the amount by which profits (after expenses) exceed the cost of capital in a given year. It is based on the simple idea that it takes capital to run a business, and capital comes at a cost. While most people think of capital as cash, capital is more likely to be found in a business in the form of computers, manufacturing plants, employees, raw materials, etc. And just like the interest that a homeowner pays on a mortgage or that a college student pays on a student loan, there is a cost to that capital.

The most common costs of capital are the interest paid on long-term bank loans used to buy all those resources, the interest paid to bondholders (who lend organizations their money), and the dividends (cash payments) and growth in stock value that accrue to shareholders. EVA is positive when company profits (revenues minus expenses minus taxes) exceed the cost of capital in a given year. In other words, if a business is to truly grow, its revenues must be large enough to cover both short-term costs (annual expenses and taxes) and long-term costs (the cost of borrowing capital from bondholders and shareholders). If you're a bit confused, Robert Goizueta, the former CEO of Coca-Cola, explained it this way: "You borrow money at a certain rate and invest it at a higher rate and pocket the difference. It is simple. It is the essence of banking."[39]

So why is EVA so important? First and most important, since it includes the cost of capital, it shows whether a business, division, department, or profit centre is really paying for itself. Second, because EVA can easily be determined for subsets of a company, such as divisions, regional offices, manufacturing plants, and sometimes even departments, it makes managers at all levels pay much closer attention to how they run their segment of the business. For example, at Coke, when the managers of the fountain business realized that they weren't even covering the cost of capital (i.e., a negative EVA), they looked for ways to do more with less capital. They determined that instead of delivering Coke concentrate in thousands of small 20-gallon steel containers, they could save money by delivering it to restaurants in huge tanker trucks.[40] In other words, EVA motivates all managers to think like small business owners who must scramble to contain costs and generate enough business to meet their bills each month.

economic value added (EVA)
the amount by which company profits (revenues minus expenses minus taxes) exceed the cost of capital

Finally, unlike many kinds of financial controls, EVA doesn't specify what should or should not be done to improve performance. Thus, it encourages managers and workers to be creative as they try to find ways to improve EVA performance.

Exhibit 7.6 shows the capital, return on capital, and cost of capital, for some major companies. Remember that EVA is the amount by which profits (after expenses) exceed the cost of capital in a given year. So the more that return on capital exceeds the cost of capital, the better a company is using investors' money.

4.3 The Customer Perspective: Controlling Customer Defections

The second aspect of organizational performance that the balanced scorecard helps managers monitor is customers. It does so by forcing managers to address the question "How do customers see us?" Unfortunately, most companies try to answer this question through customer satisfaction surveys that are often misleadingly positive. Most customers are reluctant to talk about their problems, because they don't know who to complain to, or they don't think that complaining will do any good. Indeed, a study by the Strategic Planning Institute indicated that 96 percent of unhappy customers never complain to anyone in the company and nine out ten of the people who didn't complain never did business with the company again.[41] Another reason that customer satisfaction surveys can be misleading is that sometimes even very satisfied customers will leave to do business with competitors. Dave Nichol, founder of the President's Choice brand and former president of Loblaws, explained why: "Customer loyalty is the absence of something better."[42] So even if customers are pleased, they may go elsewhere if they believe they can get a better product or service.

customer defections
performance assessment in which companies identify which customers are leaving and measure the rate at which they are leaving

Rather than poring over customer satisfaction surveys from current customers, studies indicate that companies may do a better job of answering the question "How do customers see us?" by closely monitoring **customer defections**, that is, by identifying which customers are leaving the company and measuring the rate at which they are leaving. In contrast to customer satisfaction surveys, customer defections and retention have a much greater effect on profits.

EXHIBIT 7.6

LEADING COMPANIES, AS MEASURED BY ECONOMIC VALUE ADDED

MVA RANKING IN 2000	MVA RANKING IN 1999	COMPANY	MARKET VALUE ADDED ($MILLIONS)	ECONOMIC VALUE ADDED ($MILLIONS)
1	2	General Electric	$753 460	$5248
2	1	Microsoft	$583 383	$8694
3	3	Cisco Systems	$566 824	$ 273
4	5	Intel	$422 748	$7042
5	21	Pfizer	$391 476	$2929
6	12	Merck	$290 022	$5173
7	23	EMC	$287 856	$1002
8	8	Oracle	$271 327	$ 907
9	19	American International Group	$266 973	($ 178)
10	4	Wal-Mart Stores	$266 175	$2292

Source: G. Colvin, "America's Best and Worst Wealth Creators: The Real Champions Aren't Always Who You Think. Here's an Eye-Opening Look at Which Companies Produce and Destroy the Most Money for Investors—Plus a New Tool for Spotting Future Winners," *Fortune*, 18 December 2000, 207.

For example, very few managers realize that it costs five times as much to obtain a new customer as it does to keep a current one. In fact, the cost of replacing old customers with new ones is so great that most companies could double their profits by increasing the rate of customer retention by just 5 to 10 percent per year.[43] And, if a company can keep a customer for life, the benefits are even larger. For Taco Bell, keeping a customer is worth $16 500 in lifetime sales. For a Cadillac dealer, the value is $498 000. For a grocery store, it can approach $300 000.[44]

Beyond the clear benefits to the bottom line, the second reason to study customer defections is that customers who have defected to other companies are much more likely than current customers to tell you what you are doing wrong. Perhaps the best way to tap into this source of good feedback is to have top-level managers from various departments talk directly to customers who have left. Some might argue that it's a waste of valuable executive time to have upper-level managers make these calls, but there's no faster way to get the people in charge to realize what needs to be done than to hear it directly from customers who decided that their company's performance was lacking.

Finally, companies that understand why customers leave can not only take steps to fix ongoing problems, but can also identify which customers are likely to leave and make changes to prevent them from leaving. For example, a large bank discovered that departing customers would send signals that they were getting ready to leave. A small business that made regular overnight deposits would make them less frequently. Or a customer with a personal bank account who withdrew money each Friday might withdraw money only once or twice a month. Since these changes usually occurred before customers left, the bank used its computers to create a daily "retention alert" that would identify customers whose regular interaction patterns had changed. Then, each of those customers would receive a personal phone call from bank account managers to determine what could be done to solve their problems and keep their business.[45]

4.4 The Internal Perspective: Controlling Quality

The third part of the balanced scorecard, the internal perspective, consists of the processes, decisions, and actions that managers and workers make within the organization. So, in contrast to the financial perspective of EVA and the outward-looking customer perspective, the internal perspective asks the question "What must we excel at?" For McDonald's, the answer would be quick, low-cost food. For an Internet service provider, the answer would be reliability—when your modem dials, the network should be up and running and you should be able to connect without getting a busy signal. Yet no matter what area a company chooses, the key is to excel in that area. Consequently, the internal perspective of the balanced scorecard usually leads managers to a focus on quality.

Quality is typically defined and measured in three ways: excellence, value, and conformance to expectations.[46] When the company defines its quality goal as *excellence*, then managers must try to produce a product or service of unsurpassed performance and features. For example, by almost any count, Singapore International Airlines (SIA) is "the best" airline in the world. It has been named so eight of the last nine years by readers of *Conde Nast Traveler* magazine.[47] Even SIA's competitors recognize its excellence. *Air Transport World*, the magazine read by those who work in the airline industry, stated, "SIA aimed to be the best and most successful airline in the world."[48] SIA was the first airline to introduce a choice of meals, and complementary drinks and earphones in coach class in the 1970s. Today, it continues to innovate, introducing the first worldwide video, news, telephone, and fax service on any airline. This system offers 22 video channels with movies, news, and documentaries, 12 audio channels, and 10 different Nintendo games.

Value is the customer perception that the product quality is excellent for the price offered. At a higher price, for example, customers may perceive the product to be less of a value. When a company emphasizes value as its quality goal, managers must simultaneously control excellence, price, durability, or other features of a product or service that

value
customer perception that the product quality is excellent for the price offered

customers strongly associate with value. One company that has put value at the core of everything it does is Lands' End, the catalogue company that sells quality clothing and accessories at reasonable prices. In its advertising, Lands' End said, "Value is more than price. Value is the combination of product quality, world class customer service and a fair price." Lands' End puts its commitment to value into practice through its eight principles of doing business, which are shown in Exhibit 7.7.

When a company defines its quality goal as conformance to specifications, employees must base decisions and actions on whether services and products measure up to standard specifications. In contrast to excellence and value-based definitions of quality that can be somewhat ambiguous, measuring whether products and services are "in spec" is relatively easy. Furthermore, while conformance to specifications is usually associated with manufacturing, it can be used equally well to control quality in nonmanufacturing jobs. Exhibit 7.8 shows a quality checklist that a cook or restaurant owner would use to ensure quality when buying fresh fish.

The way in which a company defines quality affects the methods and measures that workers use to control quality. Accordingly, Exhibit 7.9 shows the advantages and disadvantages associated with the excellence, value, and conformance to specification definitions of quality.

EXHIBIT 7.7

THE LANDS' END PRINCIPLES OF DOING BUSINESS

Principle 1. We do everything we can to make our products better. We improve material, and add back features and construction details that others have taken out over the years. We never reduce the quality of a product to make it cheaper.

Principle 2. We price our products fairly and honestly. We do not, have not, and will not participate in the common retailing practice of inflating mark-ups to set up a future phony "sale."

Principle 3. We accept any return for any reason, at any time. Our products are guaranteed. No fine print. No arguments. We mean exactly what we say: GUARANTEED. PERIOD.

Principle 4. We ship faster than anyone we know of. We ship items in stock the day after we receive the order. At the height of the last Christmas season the longest time an order was in the house was 36 hours, excepting monograms which took another 12 hours.

Principle 5. We believe that what is best for our customer is best for all of us. Everyone here understands that concept. Our sales and service people are trained to know our products, and to be friendly and helpful. They are urged to take all the time necessary to take care of you. We even pay for your call, for whatever reason you call.

Principle 6. We are able to sell at lower prices because we have eliminated middlemen because we don't buy branded merchandise with high protected mark-ups; and because we have placed our contracts with manufacturers who have proven that they are cost conscious and efficient.

Principle 7. We are able to sell at lower prices because we operate efficiently. Our people are hard-working, intelligent, and share in the success of the company.

Principle 8. We are able to sell at lower prices because we support no fancy emporiums with their high overhead. Our main location is in the middle of a 40-acre cornfield in rural Wisconsin.

Source: "The Lands' End Principles of Doing Business," Lands' End website. [Online] Available www.landsend.com/cd/fp/help/0,2471,1_26215_26859_26906_,00.html?sid=0999527403537, 3 September 2001.

EXHIBIT 7.8

CONFORMANCE TO SPECIFICATIONS CHECKLIST FOR BUYING FRESH FISH

QUALITY CHECKLIST FOR BUYING FRESH FISH

FRESH WHOLE FISH	ACCEPTABLE	NOT ACCEPTABLE
Eyes	clear, bright, bulging, black pupils	dull, sunken, cloudy, grey pupils
Gills	bright red, free of slime, clear mucus	brown to greyish, thick, yellow mucus
Flesh	firm and elastic to touch, tight to the bone	soft and flabby, separating from the bone
Smell	inoffensive, slight ocean smell	ammonia, putrid smell
Skin	opalescent sheen, scales adhere tightly to skin	dull or faded colour, scales missing, or easily removed
Belly Cavity	no viscera or blood visible, lining intact, no bone protruding	incomplete evisceration, cuts or protruding bones, off-odour

Sources: "A Closer Look: Buy It Fresh, Keep It Fresh," *Consumer Reports Online.* [Online] www.seagrant.sunysb.edu/SeafoodTechnology/SeafoodMedia/CR02-2001/CR-SeafoodII020101.htm, 3 September 2001. Philipps, "Turn to Pros for Fish Buying Tips," *Cincinnati Post*, 2 September 2000, 3C. "How to Purchase: Buying Fish," *AboutSeaFood* website. [Online] www.aboutseafood.com/faqs/purchase1.html, 3 September 2001.

EXHIBIT 7.9

ADVANTAGES AND DISADVANTAGES OF DIFFERENT MEASURES OF QUALITY

QUALITY AS EXCELLENCE

ADVANTAGES	DISADVANTAGES
Promotes clear organizational vision.	Provides little practical guidance for managers.
Being/providing the "best" motivates and inspires managers and employees.	Excellence is ambiguous. What is it? Who defines it?
Appeals to customers, who "know excellence when they see it."	Difficult to measure and control.

QUALITY AS VALUE

ADVANTAGES	DISADVANTAGES
Customers recognize differences in value.	Can be difficult to determine what factors influence whether a product/service is seen as having value.
Easier to measure and compare whether products/services differ in value.	Controlling the balance between excellence and cost (i.e., affordable excellence) can be difficult.

QUALITY AS CONFORMANCE TO SPECIFICATIONS

ADVANTAGES	DISADVANTAGES
If specifications can be written, conformance to specifications is usually measurable.	Many products/services cannot be easily evaluated in terms of conformance to specifications.
Should lead to increased efficiency.	Promotes standardization, so may hurt performance when adapting to changes is more important.
Promotes consistency in quality.	May be less appropriate for services, which are dependent on a high degree of human contact.

Source: *Academy of Management Review* by C.A. Reeves and D.A. Bednar. Copyright 1994 by Academy of Management Review. Reproduced with permission of the publisher via Copyright Clearance Center.

The last part of the balance scorecard, the innovation and learning perspective, addresses the question "Can we continue to improve and create value?" Thus, the innovation and learning perspective is concerned with new product development, continuous improvement in ongoing products and services (discussed in Chapter 14), and relearning and redesigning the processes by which products and services are created (discussed in Chapter 10). Since all three categories are discussed in more detail elsewhere in the text, this section reviews an increasingly important topic, waste and pollution minimization, that is affected by all three of these issues.

As shown in Exhibit 7.10, there are four levels of waste minimization, with waste prevention and reduction producing the greatest minimization of waste and waste disposal producing the smallest minimization of waste.[49] The top level is *waste prevention and reduction*, in which the goals are to prevent waste and pollution before they occur, or to reduce them when they do occur. There are three strategies for waste prevention and reduction.

1. *Good housekeeping*—regularly scheduled preventive maintenance for offices, plants, and equipment. Making sure to quickly fix leaky valves, or making sure machines are running properly so they don't use more fuel than necessary are examples of good housekeeping.

EXHIBIT 7.10

FOUR LEVELS OF WASTE MINIMIZATION

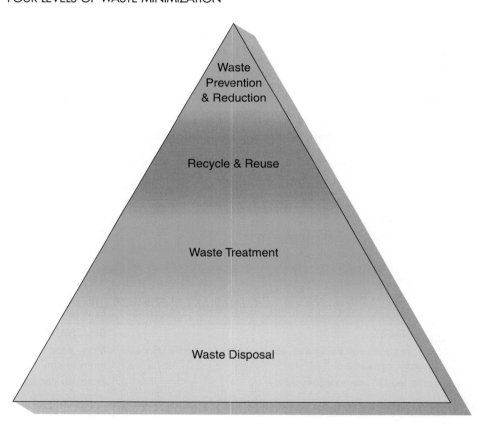

Source: D.R. May & B.L. Flannery, "Cutting Waste with Employee Involvement Teams," *Business Horizons*, September-October 1995, 25–38. Reprinted with permission from Business Horizons, September–October 1995. Copyright 1995 by The Trustees at Indiana University, Kelley School of Business.

2. *Material/product substitution*—replacing toxic or hazardous materials with less harmful materials. For example, Maytag redesigned its dishwashers, substituting a molded polypropylene tub and door liner for the porcelain enamel steel tub it had used for years. Not only was the new material cheaper and lighter, but it also eliminated the paint residue and metal sludge that were by-products of the old porcelain enamel steel tub.[50]

3. *Process modification*—changing steps or procedures to eliminate or reduce waste. For example, Coors found ways to make its beer bottles thinner. The results were annual savings of $3 million and a 17-million-kilogram reduction in the amount of glass used each year to bottle Coors beer.[51]

The second level of waste minimization is *recycle and reuse*. At this level, wastes are reduced by reusing materials as long as possible, or by collecting materials for on- or off-site recycling. For example, Red Spot Paint and Varnish Company, which makes specialized protective coatings for the plastics used in automobiles, was using almost 4000 litres of cleaning solvents in its factory every day. However, through simple trial and error, the company found out that it could reuse the solvents until they contained 15 percent solids (sort of like reusing soapy water until it gets too dirty to clean anymore). This simple change reduced solvent use by 90 percent to just 400 litres a day.[52]

The third level of waste minimization is *waste treatment*, where companies use biological, chemical, or other processes to turn potentially harmful waste into harmless compounds or useful by-products. For example, one of the processes in the manufacture of steel sheets is called "pickling." Pickling is simply bathing the steel in an acid solution to clean impurities and oxides (that would rust) from the surface of the steel sheet. Getting rid of the "pickle juice" has always been a problem. Not only is the juice an acid, but it also contains ferric chloride and other metals that prevent steel makers from dumping it into local water supplies. Fortunately, Magnetics International has found a safe, profitable way to treat the pickle juice. It sprays the juice into a 30-metre high chamber at 650 degrees Celsius. The iron chloride in the juice reacts with oxygen at that temperature to form pure iron oxide, which can be transformed into a useful magnetic powder. Inland Steel is now using this process to transform pickle juice into 25 000 tons of magnetic powder that can be reused in electric motors, stereo speakers, and refrigerator gaskets.[53]

The fourth and last level of waste minimization is *waste disposal*. Wastes that cannot be prevented, reduced, recycled, reused, or treated should be safely disposed of in environmentally secure landfills that prevent leakage and damage to soil and underground water supplies. Contrary to common belief, all businesses, not just manufacturing firms, have waste-disposal problems. For example, although the fluorescent lights used in most businesses are environmentally friendly because they last longer and use less electricity, burned-out fluorescent bulbs contain mercury, a hazardous waste.[54]

Review 4
What to Control

Deciding what to control is just as important as deciding whether to control or how to control. In most companies, performance is measured using financial measures alone. However, the balanced scorecard encourages managers to measure and control company performance from four perspectives: financial, customers, internal operations, and innovation and learning. One way to measure financial performance is through economic value added (EVA). Unlike traditional financial measures, EVA helps managers assess whether they are performing well enough to pay the cost of the capital needed to run the business. Instead of using customer satisfaction surveys to measure customer performance, companies should pay attention to customer defectors, who are more likely to speak up about what the company is doing wrong. Performance of internal operations is often measured in terms of quality, which is defined in three ways: excellence, value, and conformance to expectations.[55] Minimization of waste has become an important part of innovation and learning in companies. The four levels of waste minimization are waste prevention and reduction, recycle and reuse, waste treatment, and waste disposal.

What Really Happened?

At the beginning of this chapter you learned that Howmet Aluminum was faced with a downturn in the aircraft manufacturing industry just as it opened a new plant in Laval, Quebec. Without the ability to meet its original production targets that would allow it to break even, the plant was faced with the possibility that it would have to be closed down. Given the need to cut the cost of production, the company had to develop a strategy to tackle the problem. Cost control is a classic problem in any type of industry. What did it do to address cost issues?

One of the best places to start is to figure out what you are good at and what can differentiate you from your competitors. What sort of standards do you want to set? What are the relevant benchmarks?
Control is a process of establishing standards that will achieve organizational goals, comparing actual performance to those standards, and then, if necessary, taking corrective action to restore performance to those standards. While they had already been focusing on continuous improvement for a number of years, one of the things that Howmet wanted to do was to focus on customer satisfaction. A basic assumption in the control process is that it's possible to measure performance but the question remains: What should be measured? Indeed, many would argue that in a manufacturing environment a company should focus on the product rather than the customer, but Howmet felt that focusing on customer satisfaction would, in turn, lead to improved production processes and reduce costs. The company looked at the plant's performance concentrating on those factors that they felt were most important to the customers and used them as standards. Previously there had been a mismatch between how the company and its customers measured its performance. Customers focused on things such as on-time delivery and rework. If this is how customers measured Howmet's performance, it seemed natural that this is how Howmet should measure itself too.

Companies can investigate what existing programs are available for the improvement of production processes. This is exactly what Howmet did.
One of the things that a company can do is implement improvement processes that have been successfully implemented elsewhere. One of the programs that was looked at and implemented was the Six Sigma system. The Six Sigma system is an analytically based program aimed at the elimination of defects and variability in any process. Of course, reducing defects and variability would translate into lower costs because it would reduce scrap rates and the number of parts that had to be reworked. Although this system is becoming common in the aerospace industry, the main problem with it is that it often has little direct impact on the customer. Six Sigma processes that are too internally focused are not likely to do well. Howmet coupled its Six Sigma implementation with a clear cultural shift that focused on the needs of the customer. The company also implemented a number of other programs that would improve customer service.

The Six Sigma process has five basic steps. The first is to define the problem not just as the final product but on the processes associated with creating the product or service. The second is to measure the key elements of your production process, benchmark those measures, and set your standards. Third is to gauge how well your company is doing when compared to your predetermined standards. The fourth step is to improve all processes for which you have set standards. The last step is to control key variables, maintain consistency, and measure your progress.

One of the things the company did changed its entire production process—it moved from metal fabrication and forging to investment casting. Although it is difficult to convince a customer to change the fundamental nature by which their parts are to be produced, there are substantial savings associated with the process. This process provides savings in the form of reduced tooling, inventory floor space, inventory costs, and manu-

facturing costs as it reduces the overall number of parts that need to be produced. In one case the number of parts in a military transport refuelling door were reduced from 80 to four. Hard to believe but this change reduced the cost of the part by 60 percent! Howmet's quality and on-time delivery, coupled with cost competitiveness, are winning them new converts to the investment casting system.

Would the focus on customer service translate into improved profits?
The success of the program was phenomenal. The plant substantially reduced customer lead time, rework, work in progress, and scrap material while doubling the plant's productivity. With these improvements and an improvement in quality, the plant had cut in half the amount of sales needed to break even. Although there is pressure to continue to perform well, the plant seems to have secured a permanent place in the company. Howmet went on to win the "Superior Performance Award" from Boeing for its on-time performance in supplying titanium casting for its F-22 military aircraft program. A managing partner at the consulting firm of PricewaterhouseCoopers was quoted as saying, "In terms of setting the right goals, keeping their eye on the ball and continuous process improvements, Howmet is a model for how it should be done in any industry." Without this substantial improvement in performance, the Laval plant would likely have been shut down. The combination of a Six Sigma program, a cultural change focusing on customer service, and a general interest in continuous improvement allowed the Laval plant to cut its costs substantially, providing it with a powerful competitive advantage and a new lease on life. As a consequence of its hard work in the implementation of the Six Sigma program and continuous improvement, Howmet's Laval plant became the first of its 18 casting plants to become AS 9100 certified— this was the first industry-wide certification program associated with the ISO 9100 certification process, a quality assurance

program. This certification was particularly critical to the Laval plant as Boeing now requires its suppliers to have AS 9100 certification. All in all, this was a very successful change for Howmet and especially for the Laval plant.

Sources: "The ABCs of Six Sigma," *Aviation Week and Space Technology* 157, no. 14 (30 September 2002): 56. "Best-Managed United in Ability to Embrace Change," *Aviation Week and Space Technology* 157, no. 14 (30 September 2002): 56. Subir Chowdhury, "Working Toward Six-Sigma Success," *Manufacturing Engineering* 127, no. 1 (July 2001): 14. Derek Coppinger, "The New AS9100 Lifts Off," *Quality* 40, no. 9 (September 2001): 56. "Howmet Castings," *Foundry Management and Technology* 129, no. 3 (March 2001): 11. Anthony L. Velocci, "Full Potential of Six Sigma Eludes Most Companies Exclusive Survey Reveals How Many Contractors Are Underutilizing This Process-Improvement Methodology," *Aviation Week and Space Technology* 157, no. 14 (30 September 2002): 56. Anthony L. Velocci, "Casting Plant Demonstrates Power of Focusing on Quality," *Aviation Week and Space Technology* 157, no. 14 (30 September 2002): 61.

Key Terms

autonomous work groups (209)
balanced scorecard (211)
behaviour control (207)
benchmarking (199)
bureaucratic control (206)
concertive control (209)
concurrent control (201)
control (198)
control loss (202)

customer defections (214)
cybernetic feasibility (204)
degree of dependence (203)
economic value added (EVA) (213)
feedback control (200)
feedforward control (202)
normative control (208)
objective control (207)
output control (207)

quasi-control (204)
reducing dependence (204)
resource (203)
resource flow (203)
restructuring dependence (204)
self-control (self-management) (209)
standards (199)
suboptimization (212)
value (215)

What Would You Do II?

"Spit Happens"

As the owner of a fast-food franchise, you have plenty of problems to worry about. Problems you face on a daily basis include meeting or exceeding minimum profitability requirements imposed by the franchisor, constantly battling employee turnover (typically exceeding 200 percent at times), employee scheduling, employee morale, customer satisfaction . . . the list goes on and on. Selecting and retaining qualified people has always been difficult because you cannot afford to pay much more than minimum wage and there aren't many opportunities for advancement within your company. In addition, the majority of your employees are young, immature, and either currently in school or fresh out of school.

Despite the negative aspects of the fast-food industry, you are happy with your restaurant's success and are considering expanding by opening another store across town. As you peruse today's newspaper, you read an article that could have detrimental effects on you and your restaurant. The article discusses police becoming the victims of disgruntled teens working at fast-food establishments. Some uniformed police officers have reported instances when their food was tampered with. For instance, one policeman claimed that a fast-food employee spit in his hamburger. The officer could tell by the look on the boy's face that he was up to something, and the policeman opened the bun to inspect the burger. A crime lab confirmed that the slimy substance found inside the hamburger was, indeed, saliva. The employee was immediately fired and the officer was given an undisclosed cash settlement by the restaurant owner.

Unfortunately, spit isn't the only thing that officers have ingested. The article explained that one officer became violently ill after eating at a fast-food restaurant. Tests later confirmed that the food the officer ingested was tainted with urine and an oven cleanser. As a result, the officer has filed a $20.5-million civil suit against Burger King, the franchisee, and two of its employees. As you begin to digest the information from the article, you wonder if this situation could happen to you and your business. Many police officers frequent your establishment, and you like the security that they provide while dining. You are also aware that you cannot constantly watch your employees 24 hours a day, seven days a week. In order to control your employees' output, what standards could you set, and once you set them how will you measure them? How will you ensure that your employees do not intentionally harm your customers? Additionally, which method of control would work the best in your situation (bureaucratic, objective, or concertive)? **If you were the manager of a fast-food restaurant, what would you do?**

Source: J. Ordonez, "Spit Happens: Police in Uniform Are Leery of Fast-Food Places," *The Wall Street Journal*, 23 May 2001.

Critical Thinking Video Case

Gun Registry

Control is a regulatory process of establishing standards that will achieve organizational goals, comparing actual performance to those standards, and then, if necessary, taking corrective action to restore performance to those standards. Control processes can be very important to the success or failure of a project. A project with poor or no proper control processes risks running over budget and/or a failure to meet goals. In Chapter 4 you learned about the problems associated with Bill C-68, Canada's national gun registry, which required that all firearms be registered by December 31, 2002. When the program was announced, the federal government said that the net cost to taxpayers to set up the registry would be $2 million, as the bulk of the costs for the registry were to be covered by registration fees. The registration was to be handled by the Canadian Firearms Centre.

By 2002, the auditor general had determined that the full taxpayer cost would be closer to $1 billion, and gun owners were having difficulty registering their firearms. The government was even forced to extend the registration deadline to June 30, 2003. Failure to control costs and the inability of gun owners to register their guns has, at least temporarily, reopened the debate over the usefulness of Bill C-68.

Critical Thinking Questions

1. What sort of control processes should have been implemented at the start of the program?
2. What sort of standards should be set for a project of this nature?
3. What should a balanced scorecard for the Canadian Firearms Centre look like?

Management Decisions

Controlling Employee Health Costs

In Canada, an increasing portion of health care costs are falling to employers in the form of increased costs for group insurance policies. The trend is only expected to get worse as Canada's population ages. For example, Canadians spent 13 percent more on prescription drugs in 2002 than they did in 2001. Not surprisingly, companies are doing everything they can to cut medical costs.

In the last decade, more companies have turned to wellness programs, which have roots in preventive medicine. Instead of reducing the costs of current medical treatments, or encouraging doctors and hospitals to use lower-cost treatments, wellness programs try to reduce costs by preventing employees from getting sick in the first place. Since nearly 70 percent of all illnesses are preventable, wellness programs encourage employees to exercise more, quit smoking, eat a low-fat diet, and manage stress in hopes that these lifestyle changes will help them lose weight, lower cholesterol, lower blood pressure, and reduce the incidence of strokes, heart attacks, cancer, diabetes, and other illnesses. Furthermore, studies show that wellness programs work. Low-risk employees who exercise regularly, quit smoking, eat right, and manage their stress average $300 a year in health claims compared to over $2400 a year on average for high-risk employees who don't practise these preventive guidelines. For example, it was found that obese employees who claim short-term disability benefits average $13 000 per claim versus an average of $5800 per claim. Indeed, of the 48 studies on work-site wellness programs in the last decade, only one failed to show a cost savings for the company.

Ironically, while studies show that wellness programs do exactly what they're supposed to when employees join them, they also show that it's very difficult to get most employees to actually join

and continue to participate in wellness programs. David Anderson, vice president of operations at StayWell Health Management Systems, said, "One of the real problems [confronting] wellness programs is that the healthier employees are the ones more interested in getting involved." Of course, this does little to reduce costs, since these employees are already healthier than most.

Questions

1. Explain how you could use bureaucratic control ideas to encourage more employees, especially those who really need it, to participate in wellness programs.
2. Explain how you could use self-control ideas to encourage more employees, especially those who really need it, to participate in wellness programs.
3. Explain how you could use objective control ideas to encourage more employees, especially those who really need it, to participate in wellness programs.

Sources: John W. Gainsford, Annie Lam, & Ana Fradkin, "Costs of Obesity for Employers and Employees: A Canadian Analysis," *Canadian Healthcare Manager* 6, no. 5 (August-September, 1999): Insert 3. Larry Jackson & Cyprian McFarlane, "Trending Upwards: Why Major Canadian Group Insurers Are Projecting Increases in Employer-Sponsored Health Plan Costs," *Canadian Healthcare Manager* 8, no. 4 (August 2001): 41. L. Litvan, "Preventive Medicine," *Nation's Business*, 1 September 1995, 32. Celia Milne, "Controlling Drug Costs," *Medical Post* 39, no. 17 (29 April 2003): 30. M. Parent, "How to Launch a Corporate Fitness Program," *Boston Business Journal*, 28 June 1996, 39. L. Postman, "Employers Banking on Worker Wellness," *Indianapolis Business Journal*, 10 June 1996, 25. M.A. Robbins, "Giving Workers Healthy Incentives," *Trustee*, 1 February 1996, 30. D. Stokols, K.R. Pelletier, & J.E. Fielding, "Integration of Medical Care and Worksite Health Promotion," *The Journal of the American Medical Association*, 12 April 1995. "Wellness Programs Pay Dividends," *Business & Health*, 1 March 1995, 23.

Preventing Piracy

Point, click, and pirate. Software piracy, which includes the unauthorized copying, use, or distribution of software, costs the computer industry approximately $18 billion each year in lost licensing revenue. Software piracy is a problem in the United States and Canada. In Canada it is estimated that in 2002 38 percent of business applications didn't have proper licences, compared with 25 percent in the United States. It is estimated that illegal software cost the Canadian economy $289 million in 2001. However, it appears to be worse in other parts of the world such as South America and Asia. According to a recent study by the Business Software Alliance (BSA), six out of ten computers operating in Mexico contain pirated software. Unfortunately, the numbers are just as dreary in China and elsewhere across the globe. As the director of piracy for Microsoft, you feel as though your job is a never-ending battle. In order to crack down on piracy in North America, you and your staff have begun discussions aimed at coming up with solutions to the piracy problem. Piracy occurs in both private homes and in businesses, yet a recent study by the Software & Information Industry Association (SIIA) suggests that one-quarter of piracy committed in the United States occurs in high-tech companies.

One factor that leads to piracy among businesses today is expansion. Most businesses start out by purchasing legal copies of software for their firms. As a firm grows, however, some businesses choose to purchase additional computers and copy their existing software onto the new machines. For example, Microsoft allows companies to sign volume agreements that allow for unlimited copying of their software with the expectation that the company will pay for each copy made. Some firms unintentionally do not keep accurate records and end up underpaying Micsrosoft. Another common act of piracy involves "soft-loading." Soft-loading occurs when a firm purchases one legal copy of software and installs it on the local area network (LAN). By installing the software on the server, one copy can support hundreds of machines through a network connection.

Although the SIIA and the BSA conduct routine audits in large companies looking for piracy violations, you and your staff want to step up efforts to identify companies engaging in piracy. Some of the computer manufacturers to which you supply software have notified you recently that there has been an increase in the number of "naked" computer system orders. A computer system is "naked" when it is ordered without any operating system software. Although there are several reasons for ordering a naked system (for example, perhaps a company wants to use a competitor's operating software, such as Linux), you suspect that companies are beginning to pirate operating software in addition to application software. Software piracy not only costs your company money through a loss of revenue, but is also a violation of copyright law, and is therefore illegal.

Questions

1. What policies or plans could you implement that might help control or diminish piracy of your operating system software within American businesses?

2. How vigorously will you pursue offenders once you identify them? Remember, there is a cost to control.

Sources: R. Buckman, "Microsoft Offers Prizes to Identify Orders of PCs Without Windows," *The Wall Street Journal*, 2 May 2001. B. Kruger, "High-Tech Firms Get Piracy Alert," *Electronic News*, 7 February 2000. J. Stevenson, "Piracy Plague," *Business Mexico*, November 2000. Z. Thomas, "High Tech's Dirty Little Software Piracy Secret," *Electronic Business*, November 2000. F. Gallegos, "Software Piracy: Some Facts, Figures, and Issues," *Information System Security*, Winter 2000. Andrew Whal, "Rumors of War," *Canadian Business* 75, no. 17 (16 September 2002): 67.

Learning from Failure

"There is the greatest practical benefit of making a few failures early in life." —T.H. Huxley

No one wants to fail. Everyone wants to succeed. However, some business people believe that failure can have enormous value. At Microsoft, founder and former CEO Bill Gates encouraged his managers to hire people who have made mistakes in their jobs or careers. A Microsoft vice president said, "We look for somebody who learns, adapts, and is active in the process of learning from mistakes. We always ask, what was a major failure you had? What did you learn from it?" Another reason that failure is viewed positively is that it is often a sign of risk taking and experimentation, both of which are in short supply in many companies. John Kotter, a Harvard Business School professor, says, "I can imagine a group of executives 20 years ago discussing a candidate for a top job and saying, 'This guy had a big failure when he was 32.' Everyone else would say, 'Yep, yep, that's a bad sign.' I can imagine that same group considering a candidate today and saying, 'What worries me about this guy is that he's never failed.'" Jack Matson, who teaches a class at the University of Michigan called Failure 101, says, "If you are doing something innovative, you are going to trip and fumble. So the more failing you do faster, the quicker you can get to success."

One of the most common mistakes that occurs after failure is the *attribution error*. An *attribution* is to assign blame or credit. When we succeed, we take credit for the success by owning up to our strategies, how we behaved, and how hard we worked. However, when we fail, we ignore our strategies, or how we behaved, or how hard we worked (or didn't). Instead, when we fail, we assign the blame to other people, or to the circumstances, or to bad luck. In other words, the basic attribution error is that success is our fault but failure isn't. The disappointment we feel when we fail often prevents us from learning from our failures.

What this means is that attribution errors disrupt the control process. The three basic steps of control are to set goals and performance standards, to compare actual performance to performance standards, and to identify and correct performance deviations. When we put all the blame on external forces rather than our own actions, we stop ourselves from identifying and correcting performance deviations. Furthermore, by not learning from our mistakes, we make it even more likely that we will fail again.

Your task in this Developing Your Management Potential is to begin the process of learning from failure. This is not an easy thing to do. When *Fortune* magazine writer Patricia Sellers wrote an article called "So You Fail," she found most of the people she contacted reluctant to talk about their failures. She wrote,

> Compiling this story required months of pleading and letter writing to dozens of people who failed and came back. "If it weren't for the 'F' word, I'd talk," lamented one senior executive who got fired twice, reformed his know-it-all management style, and considered bragging about his current hot streak. Others cringed at hearing the word "failure" in the same breath as "your career."

Questions

1. Identify and describe a point in your life when you failed. Don't write about simple or silly mistakes. The difference between a failure and a mistake is how badly you felt afterwards. Years afterwards, a real failure still makes you cringe when you think about it. What was the situation? What were your goals? And how did it turn out?

2. Describe your initial reaction to the failure. Were you shocked, surprised, angry, or depressed? Initially, who or what did you blame for the failure? Explain.

3. One purpose of control is to identify and correct performance deviations. With that in mind, describe three mistakes that you made that contributed to your failure. Now that you've had time to think about it, what would you have done differently to prevent these mistakes? Finally, summarize what you learned from your mistakes that will increase your chances of success the next time around.

Sources: S. Caulkin, "If You Want to Stay a Winner, Learn from Your Mistakes," *The Observer*, 3 March 1996, 7. J. Hyatt, "Failure 101," *Inc.*, January 1989, 18. B. McMenamin, "The Virtue of Making Mistakes," *Forbes*, 9 May 1994, 192–194. P. Sellers, "So You Fail," *Fortune*, 1 May 1995, 48–66. P. Sellers, "Where Failures Get Fixed," *Fortune*, 1 May 1995, 64. B. Weiner, I. Freize, A. Kukla, L. Reed, S. Rest, & R.M. Rosenbaum, "Perceiving the Causes of Success and Failure," in *Attribution: Perceiving the Causes of Behavior*, eds. E. Jones, D. Kanouse, H. Kelley, R. Nesbitt, S. Valins, and B. Weiner (Morristown, N.J.: General Learning Press, 1971): 45–61.

Discussion Questions

1. What sort of strategies could a company use to reduce customer defections? Why do they work?
2. There are five different methods that managers (managerial control) can use to achieve control in their organizations. What are they and when would they be most appropriate to use? Give examples.
3. What kinds of organizations have a great deal of control over their resource flows? Which have little control and why? How can organizations increase control over their resource flows?
4. There are three basic control methods: feedback control, concurrent control, and feedforward control. Define each and give examples of when they might be most appropriate to use.

Study Tip

The list of key terms on page 221 can be a valuable study aid. Write down the definition of each term on a separate piece of paper and without consulting the margin terms in the chapter. Cement your understanding by also writing an example if possible.

3

Meeting the Competition

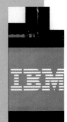

CHAPTER 8

Chapter Outline

Learning Objectives

After reading this chapter, you should be able to

1. describe the impact of global business on Canada.
2. discuss the trade rules and agreements that govern global trade.
3. explain why companies choose to standardize or adapt their business procedures.
4. explain the different ways that companies can organize to do business globally.
5. explain how to find a favourable business climate.
6. discuss the importance of identifying and adapting to cultural differences.
7. explain how to successfully prepare workers for international assignments.

eight

Global Management

What Would You Do?

The first Wal-Mart opened in Rogers, Arkansas, in 1962. Four decades later, headquartered in Bentonville, Arkansas, with 1657 stores, 1016 Wal-Mart Supercenters (Wal-Marts that have grocery stores), 486 Sam's Stores, 962 000 employees, and $186.8 billion (U.S.) in annual sales, Wal-Mart is clearly the dominant retailer in the United States and Canada. Guided by founder Sam Walton's passion for customer satisfaction and a focused mission of "Every Day Low Prices," Wal-Mart was named "Retailer of the Century" by *Discount Store News*, was recognized by *Fortune* magazine as one of the "Most Admired Companies " and one of the "100 Best Companies To Work For," and was ranked by the *Financial Times* on its "Most Respected in the World" list.

Despite these enormous domestic achievements, Wal-Mart has stumbled in its efforts outside North America. In fact, Wal-Mart's international performance has been so bad that Toby Radford, an industry analyst, called Wal-Mart's international strategy "rudderless." For example, when Wal-Mart first entered Mexico, it was so set in its ways that it filled its Mexican stores with ice skates, riding lawn mowers, fishing tackle, and clay pigeons for skeet shooting, none of which—to anyone's surprise—were very popular items. And when Mexican store managers managed to sell all these items

at heavy discounts, Wal-Mart's computerized inventory system compounded the mistake by automatically reordering all these "sold out" items.

Although in North America Wal-Mart clearly outnumbers and outmuscles its competitors, internationally Wal-Mart is just another kid on the block. In fact, the dominant player around the world is not Wal-Mart, but a French-based company called Carrefour. Carrefour, the world's second-largest retailer (Wal-Mart is the largest), is the top retailer in France, Spain, Portugal, and Greece and is number two in Italy. Wal-Mart has no stores in those countries. Furthermore, Carrefour is well established in Latin America and Asia and has 22 stores in nine major cities in China, the largest growth market in the world. In addition to being well ahead of Wal-Mart in key countries around the world, Carrefour is very careful about the new markets it enters, usually taking a year to investigate before making new commitments. But once that commitment is made, Carrefour is quickly up and running. To start, nearly every Carrefour store in the world has the same basic layout, with wide aisles and signature white tiles. While the stores look the same, the food in each Carrefour store is different since 90 percent of the foods come from local suppliers. Carrefour's chairman and CEO says, "You have to adapt your food and other products to the local culture." In

short, according to Jamie Vasquez, an industry analyst, "Carrefour is the world's most success international retailer. Wal-Mart has no track record outside of North America."

Of course, your boss, Wal-Mart's CEO, doesn't really care what Jamie Vasquez thinks. In fact, he says it's your job as head of Wal-Mart International to prove Vasquez wrong, to begin making Wal-Mart the world's most successful retailer. The question is how. Initial successes came easily in Canada, but not in Mexico. So which countries should Wal-Mart enter? At some time, Wal-Mart and Carrefour are likely to cross paths. And while Carrefour is now the leading international retailer, just how fierce a competitor will Carrefour be in the long run when lined up against Wal-Mart's experience and deep pockets? In other words, what kind of competition is Wal-Mart likely to find when it crosses swords directly with Carrefour? Also, what impact will free trade agreements in North America (NAFTA), Europe (the Maastricht Treaty), Asia (APEC and ASEAN), and South America (FTAA) likely have on Wal-Mart's international expansion? Finally, should Wal-Mart focus on global consistency, doing around the world what it does in Canada and the United States, or like Carrefour, should it adapt what it sells throughout the world? **If you were head of Wal-Mart International, what would you do?**

Sources: W. Boston & A. Zimmerman, "Wal-Mart Girds for Major German Expansion—U.S. Retail Giant to Stress Internal Growth in Push to Add 50 New Stores," *The Wall Street Journal*, 20 July 2000, A21. Business Brief, "Wal-Mart Stores, Inc.: Retailer Expects to Open Six New Stores in China," *The Wall Street Journal*, 4 June 1988, B10. Business Brief, "Wal-Mart Stores Inc.: New Supermarkets Expected to Add 27,000 British Jobs," *The Wall Street Journal*, 11 January 2000. J. Friedland & L. Lee, "Foreign Aisles: The Wal-Mart Way Sometimes Gets Lost in Translation Overseas—Chain Changes Some Tactics to Meet Local Tastes; Competitors Are Tough—But Brazil's 'Market Is Ripe'," *The Wall Street Journal*, 8 October 1997, A1. M. Jordan, "Wal-Mart Gets Aggressive about Brazil—New Neighborhood Store Is Latest Step to Seize Bigger Market Share," *The Wall Street Journal*, 25 May 2001, A8. L. Lee & C. Rohwedder, "Wal-Mart to Acquire German Retailer, Moving into Europe for the First Time," *The Wall Street Journal*, 19 December 1997, A2. D. Luhnow, "Crossover Success: How NAFTA Helped Wal-Mart Reshape the Mexican Market—Lower Tariffs, Retail Muscle Translate into Big Sales; Middlemen Are Squeezed—'Like Shopping in the U.S.'," *The Wall Street Journal*, 31 August 2001, A1. F. McCarthy, "Chimera Wal-Mart Struggles Abroad," *Economist*, 18 May 2000. R. Tomlinson, "Who's Afraid of Wal-Mart? Not Carrefour. The World's Second-Largest Retailer Is Bounding Ahead of the Bentonville Behemoth in Most Markets Outside North America. But Can the French Titan Hold Its Lead?" *Fortune*, 26 June 2000, 186. "Fortune: Wal-Mart on Top," cnnmoney, [Online] Available http://money.cnn.com/2003/03/30/news/companies/fortune_500/ (accessed 22 August 2003).

Wal-Mart's international expansion is an example of the key issue in global business: How can you be sure that the way you run your business in one country is the right way to run that business in another? This chapter discusses how organizations make those decisions. We will start by examining global business in two ways: first, by exploring its impact on Canadian businesses, and second, by reviewing the basic rules and agreements that govern global trade. Next, we will examine how and when companies go global by examining the tradeoff between consistency and adaptation and by discussing how to organize a global company. Finally, we will look at how companies decide where to expand globally. Here, we will examine how to find the best business climate, how to adapt to cultural differences, and how to better prepare employees for international assignments.

What Is Global Business?

global business
the buying and selling of goods and services by people from different countries

Business is the buying and selling of goods or services. Buying this textbook was a business transaction. So was selling your first car. So was getting paid for babysitting or for mowing lawns. **Global business** is the buying and selling of goods and services by people from different countries. The Timex watch the author of this chapter wears was purchased at a Zellers in Nova Scotia. But since it was made in the Philippines, I participated in global business when I wrote Zellers a cheque. Zellers, in turn, paid Timex, which then paid the company that employs the Filipino managers and workers who made the watch. Of course, there is more to global business than buying imported products at Zellers.

After reading the next two sections, you should be able to
1. *describe the impact of global business on Canada.*
2. *discuss the trade rules and agreements that govern global trade.*

1. Impact of Global Business

foreign direct investment (FDI)
a method of investment in which a company builds a new business or buys an existing business in a foreign country

Foreign direct investment (FDI) is a method of investment in which a company builds a new business or buys an existing business in a foreign country. Kao Corporation, maker of Japanese laundry detergent and body soaps and shampoos, made a foreign direct investment when it purchased Andrew Jergens Company, which makes hair- and skin-care products.

The United States is an especially large investor in Canada. Exhibit 8.1 shows which countries have the largest foreign direct investment in the Canada. Recent figures[1] suggest that the United States accounts for 72 percent of FDI in Canada, while the European Union countries account for about 19 percent. Approximately 5 percent of FDI in Canada originates with Japan, while the next largest contributor is Latin America with 2 percent. All other countries account for 2 percent of the total foreign direct investment in Canada. Which areas of the Canadian economy have benefited the most from these investments? Over the decade of the 90s, the big winners were companies operating in the petroleum and natural gas sector, insurers, chemical producers, electronic equipment manufacturers, computer service providers, and motor vehicle manufacturers. In what areas has FDI been growing the most? Three areas in particular stand out: railway transportation, electronic equipment manufacturers and computer service providers, and financing intermediaries.

However, foreign direct investment in Canada is just half the picture. Canadian companies also have made large foreign direct investments in businesses throughout the world.[2] Exhibit 8.2 shows that Canadian companies have made their largest foreign direct investments, $134 billion, in the United States, followed by the European Union

REGIONAL DISTRIBUTION OF INWARD FDI, 1999

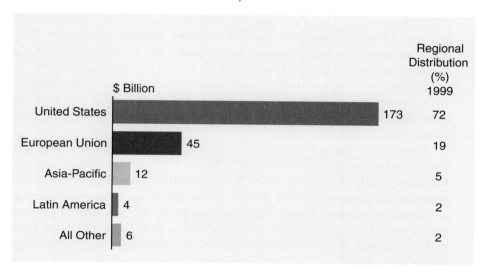

Source: Document: Trends in Canada's Inward FDI Oct. 2000 prepared by Strategic Investment Analysis, Micro-Economic Policy Analysis Branch, Industry Canada. <http://strategis.ic.gc.ca/sc_ecnmy/mera/engdoc/11.html>

REGIONAL DISTRIBUTION OF OUTWARD FDI, 1999

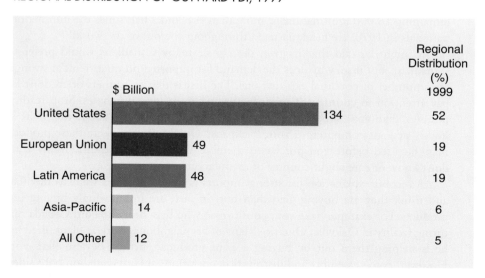

Source: Document: Trends in Canada's Inward FDI Oct. 2000 prepared by Strategic Investment Analysis, Micro-Economic Policy Analysis Branch, Industry Canada. <http://strategis.ic.gc.ca/sc_ecnmy/mera/engdoc/11.html>

and Latin America. Up until recently, the United States was the destination for just over 52 percent of Canadian investment abroad while the latter regions accounted for 19 percent of FDI outflow. Despite the liberalization of the Chinese economy and the great size of the Japanese marketplace, these two regions accounted for only 6 percent of all Canadian outward-bound FDI. Into what industries did Canadian money flow? Just over 20 percent or $42 billion was invested in the foreign banking sector. At the same time, 14 percent of all outflowing FDI was made up of non-ferrous metals and primary metal products while 11 percent was invested in foreign insurance operations.

Overall, foreign direct investment throughout the world has more than doubled in the last decade. So whether foreign companies invest in Canada or Canadian companies invest abroad, foreign direct investment is an increasingly important and common method of conducting global business.

North American companies face stiff competition in the world market, especially in high-tech industries. One survey suggests many North Americans consider this a serious problem. However, data from the U.S. National Science Board show that North American companies lead Japan, Germany, France, the United Kingdom, China, and South Korea in global high-technology market share. Furthermore, the North American share of the global high-technology markets has increased, not decreased, since 1980. By 1995, North American high-tech companies were market leaders in four out of the seven global high-technology industries: aircraft, scientific instruments, computers and office equipment, and pharmaceuticals.[3]

Despite these gains, U.S. and Canadian companies are not alone in their quest for a share of global markets. The economies of France, Germany, Italy, Japan, and the United Kingdom, which were decimated by World War II, are now part of a group of seven countries that account for more than 70 percent of the **world gross national product** (Canada and the United States are the other two members). This is roughly the same portion of world GNP controlled by the United States alone following World War II. Add to these countries the economy of China and it is easy to see how the playing field is increasingly crowded.

Another sign of increased competition in world markets is the number of multinational corporations and where those multinational corporations are headquartered. **Multinational corporations** are corporations that own businesses in two or more countries. In 1970, more than half the world's 7000 multinational corporations were headquartered in just two countries, the United States and Britain. Today, there are more than 35 000 multinational companies.[4] Roughly 17 000 of the multinationals are headquartered in four countries: Switzerland, Germany, Japan, and the United States. The remaining 18 000 multinationals, more than two and a half times the number of multinationals in 1970, are headquartered throughout the rest of the world!

It might be said that if given the choice many Canadians would prefer to "buy Canadian," but if so, why does the demand for imported products remain strong? There are a number of potential explanations. The first is that consumers often don't know or pay attention to **country of manufacture** when making purchases. Stop reading for a minute. Take your shoes off. Where were they made? What about the VCR in your house, or your computer, or your backpack? Did you learn where these products were manufactured before you purchased them? Chances are you didn't. Many consumers don't know or care about country of manufacture.

A second explanation for strong imports is that consumers want to buy Canadian and think they are buying Canadian but, in fact, are unknowingly buying imported products. For example, take your cousin Fred who lives near the Ford Canada manufacturing facility in Oakville, Ontario. Many of his neighbours work at plant. Fred feels that he is helping them out by buying a Ford product. Further, he also likes Ford cars. However, Ford's assembly and distribution operations are integrated on both sides of the border. The chances are that his new purchase may be an import as opposed to one manufactured in Oakville. Cousin Fred may have confused the country of manufacture,

world gross national product
the value of all the goods and services produced annually worldwide

multinational corporation
corporation that owns businesses in two or more countries

country of manufacture
country where product is made and assembled

where the product is made, with the **country of origin**, which is the company's home country, which for Ford Canada is Canada. However, this is an easy mistake to make in today's global marketplace.

country of origin
the home country for a company, where its headquarters is located

The third explanation for the continued increases in sales of imported products is that consumers know that many products they purchase are imported, but they just don't care. For example, until recently, Japan had closed its markets to foreign-grown apples, claiming that imported apples contained insects that would infest Japanese orchards. With no foreign competition, Japanese apples were expensive, about $7 for a bag of six "bargain" apples, and about $8.50 for a flawless, gourmet apple. The president of the Aomori Apple Association said, "This is Japanese culture. Japanese don't want apples with scratches or uneven colour, even if they taste fine." However, Japan is now allowing apples to be imported from "approved" apple orchards in North America. If the president of the Aomori Apple Association is wrong, Japanese consumers will buy North American apples because they cost about a third less. Early indications are that value will win out. Sadako Watanabe, a Japanese grandmother, said, "If they taste good, I'll keep buying them."[5]

Review 1
Impact of Global Business

Contrary to common opinion, Canadian companies are competitive in world markets, and consumers are less concerned with patriotism than value. In the last decade, foreign direct investment has doubled, making world markets much more competitive than they used to be. Yet despite this competition, Canadian companies (and American companies, and German companies, and Japanese companies, and ...) continue to expand to meet the demands of consumer-driven world markets.

2. Trade Rules and Agreements

The rules governing global trade are many and complex and have changed tremendously in the last few years. In the next two sections, we'll look at trade barriers and trade agreements.

2.1 Trade Barriers

Although most consumers don't especially care where the products they buy come from, national governments have preferred that consumers buy domestically made products in hopes that such purchases would increase the number of domestic businesses and workers. However, governments have done much more than hope that you buy from domestic companies. For most of this century, governments have actively used **trade barriers** to make it much more difficult or expensive (or sometimes impossible) for their citizens to buy imported goods. For example, the U.S. government placed a 27 percent excise tax on Canadian softwood lumber. By establishing this tax, the U.S. government engaged in **protectionism**, which is the use of trade barriers to protect local companies and their workers from foreign competition.[6]

Governments have used two general kinds of trade barriers: tariff and nontariff barriers. A **tariff** is a direct tax on imported goods. Like the U.S. excise tax on Canadian softwood lumber, tariffs increase the cost of imported goods relative to domestic goods. **Nontariff barriers** are nontax methods of increasing the cost or reducing the volume of imported goods. There are five types of nontariff barriers: quotas, voluntary export restraints, government standards, government subsidies, and customs valuation/classification. Because there are so many different kinds of nontariff barriers, they can be an even more potent method of shielding domestic industries from foreign competition.

Quotas are specific limits on the number or volume of imported products. Canada sets quotas for the importation of a number of products, including textiles, apparel, and fabrics, and agricultural products, especially dairy, poultry, and milk.

trade barriers
government-imposed regulations that increase the cost and restrict the number of imported goods

protectionism
a government's use of trade barriers to shield domestic companies and their workers from foreign competition

tariff
a direct tax on imported goods

nontariff barriers
nontax methods of increasing the cost or reducing the volume of imported goods

quota
limit on the number or volume of imported products

voluntary export restraints
voluntarily imposed limits
on the number or volume of
products exported to a particular country

Voluntary export restraints are similar to quotas in that there is a limit on how much of a product can be imported annually. The difference is that the exporting country rather than the importing country imposes the limit. However, the "voluntary" offer to limit imports usually occurs because of the implicit threat of forced trade quotas by the importing country. For example, the European Union holds yearly "monitoring talks" with Japanese auto manufacturers to discuss limits on the number of imported Japanese cars. When the sales of European-made cars fell significantly, the Japanese "voluntarily" agreed to cut their exports by 100 000 cars.[7] However, according to the World Trade Organization (see the discussion on the General Agreement on Trade and Tariffs following), countries should have phased out voluntary export restraints after 1999.[8]

In theory, government standards are specified for imports to protect the health and safety of citizens. In reality, government standards are often used to restrict or ban imported goods. For example, China is the only nation in the world that requires North American-grown grain to be 100 percent fungus free. Although preventing the importation of a fungus-infected agricultural product sounds reasonable enough, having a very small percentage of fungus is normal for harvested wheat. Since there is no chance that the fungus will spread once wheat has been harvested, and since China is the only nation to insist on this standard, the Chinese government is actually using this government standard to protect the economic health of its wheat farmers, rather than the physical health of its consumers.[9]

subsidies
government loans, grants,
and tax deferments given to
domestic companies to
protect them from foreign
competition

Many nations also use **subsidies**, such as long-term, low-interest loans, cash grants, and tax deferments, to develop and protect companies in special industries. European governments have invested billions of dollars to develop a commercial airplane manufacturing industry to support Airbus Industries (www.airbus.com), a manufacturer of commercial airplanes. Japan has historically supported domestic rice producers. The Canadian government has provided subsidies for many firms, including some of those operating in the auto industry; Bombardier, a manufacturer of trains and airplanes, has received subsidies from the Canadian government. Not surprisingly, businesses complain about unfair trade practices when other companies receive government subsidies. For example, efforts by the Government of Canada to enhance economic growth by supporting specific companies in certain regions of the country through agencies such as the Atlantic Canada Opportunities Agency (ACOA) have been criticized for offering an unfair advantage to some companies at the expense of others. Boeing Corporation (www.boeing.com), the world's largest manufacturer of commercial airplanes, frequently complains to U.S. government officials about the millions of dollars in direct government subsidies that Airbus receives each year from European governments.[10]

The last nontariff barrier is customs classification. As products are imported into a country, they are examined by customs agents, who must decide into which thousands of categories they should classify a product. Classification is important, because the category assigned by customs agents can affect the size of the tariff and consideration of import quotas.

2.2 Trade Agreements

Thanks to the trade barriers described above, buying imported goods has often been much more expensive and difficult than buying domestic goods. However, the regulations governing global trade were transformed in the 1990s. The most significant change was that 124 countries agreed to adopt the **General Agreement on Tariffs and Trade (GATT)**.

**General Agreement on
Tariffs and Trade (GATT)**
worldwide trade agreement
that will reduce and eliminate tariffs, limit government subsidies, and protect
intellectual property

Through tremendous decreases in tariff and nontariff barriers, GATT will make it much easier and cheaper for consumers in all countries to buy foreign products. First, by the year 2005, GATT will cut average tariffs worldwide by 40 percent. Second, GATT will eliminate tariffs in ten specific industries: beer, alcohol, construction equipment, farm machinery, furniture, medical equipment, paper, pharmaceuticals, steel, and toys. Third, GATT puts stricter limits on government subsidies. For example, GATT places

In Kuala Lumpur, a city hall worker spreads millions of pirated DVDs, software, and CDs on the floor before destroying them. Malaysia has been escalating its crackdown on pirated software.

limits on how much national governments can subsidize company research in electronic and high-technology industries. Fourth, GATT protects intellectual property such as trademarks, patents, and copyright. Protection of intellectual property has been an increasingly important issue in global trade because of widespread product piracy. For example, Chinese bootleggers were selling illegal copies of Disney's *The Lion King* and *Mulan* videos even before Disney could get its official copies to stores in North America.[11] Product piracy like this costs companies billions in lost revenue each year. Finally, trade disputes between countries will be fully settled by arbitration panels from the World Trade Organization. For more information about GATT and the World Trade Association (WTO), go to the WTO website at www.wto.org.

The second major development in the historic move toward reduction of trade barriers has been the creation of **regional trading zones**, in which tariff and nontariff barriers are reduced or eliminated for countries within the trading zone. The largest and most important trading zones are in Europe (the Maastricht Treaty), North America (the North American Free Trade Agreement, NAFTA), South America (the Free Trade Area of the Americas, FTAA), and Asia (ASEAN, Association of South East Nations, and APEC, Asia-Pacific Economic Cooperation). The map in Exhibit 8.3 shows the extent to which free trade agreements govern global trade.

In 1992, the countries of Belgium, France, Germany, Italy, Luxembourg, the Netherlands, Denmark, Ireland, United Kingdom, Greece, Portugal, and Spain implemented the **Maastricht Treaty of Europe**. The purpose of this treaty was to transform their 12 different economies and 12 currencies into one common economic market, called the European Union, and one common currency, the euro. Austria, Finland, and Sweden are now members, too.[12]

regional trading zones
areas in which tariff and nontariff barriers on trade between countries are reduced or eliminated

Maastricht Treaty of Europe
regional trade agreement between most European countries

EXPERIENCING MANAGEMENT

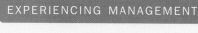

You may learn more about international trade agreements and their provisions by visiting our animated concept and activity site. Choose International Management from the "select a topic" pull-down menu, then International Trade Agreements from the "overview tab."

www.experiencingmanagement.com

EXHIBIT 8.3

GLOBAL MAP OF REGIONAL AGREEMENTS

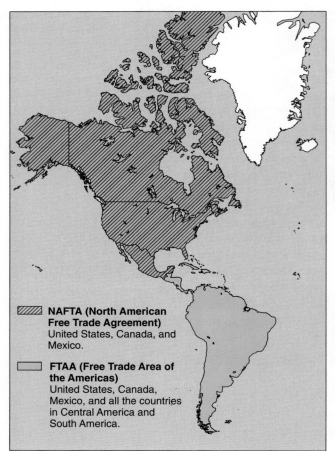

NAFTA (North American Free Trade Agreement) United States, Canada, and Mexico.

FTAA (Free Trade Area of the Americas) United States, Canada, Mexico, and all the countries in Central America and South America.

Maastricht Treaty of Europe Austria, Belgium, Denmark, Finland, France, Germany, Greece, Italy, Ireland, Luxembourg, The Netherlands, Portugal, Spain, Sweden, and the United Kingdom.

ASEAN Brunei Darussalam, Cambodia, Indonesia, Laos, Malaysia, Myanmar, the Philippines, Singapore, Thailand, and Vietnam.

APEC Australia, Canada, Chile, China, Hong Kong, Japan, Korea, Mexico, New Zealand, Papua New Guinea, Peru, Russia, the United States, and all members of ASEAN except Cambodia, Laos, and Myanmar.

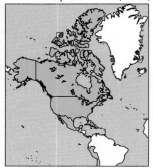

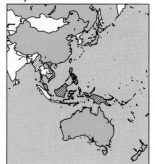

Prior to the treaty, trucks carrying products were stopped and inspected by customs agents at each border. Furthermore, since the required paperwork, tariffs, and government product specifications could be radically different in each country, companies often had to file 12 different sets of paperwork, pay 12 different tariffs, and produce 12 different versions of their basic product to meet various government specifications.

Likewise, open business travel, which we take for granted in Canada as we travel from province to province, was complicated by inspections at each border crossing. For example, if you lived in Germany, but worked across the border in Luxembourg, your car was stopped and your passport was inspected twice a day, every day, as you travelled to and from work. Also, every business transaction required a currency exchange, for example, from German deutsche marks to Italian lira, or from French francs to British pounds. Imagine all of this happening to millions of trucks, cars, and business people, and you can begin to appreciate the difficulty and cost of conducting business across Europe before the Maastricht Treaty.

For more information about the European Union, go to http://europa.eu.int. For more about Europe's new currency, the euro, which has replaced the currencies of 11 countries (Austria, Belgium, Finland, France, Germany, Ireland, Italy, Luxembourg, Netherlands, Portugal, and Spain), see http://europa.eu.int/euro/entry.html.

NAFTA, the **North American Free Trade Agreement** between Canada, the United States, and Mexico, went into effect January 1, 1994. More than any other regional trade agreement, NAFTA liberalizes trade between countries so that businesses can plan

North American Free Trade Agreement (NAFTA) regional trade agreement between Canada, the United States, and Mexico

for one market, North America, rather than for three separate markets, Canada, the United States, and Mexico. One of NAFTA's most important achievements was to eliminate most product tariffs. On January 1, 1994, product tariffs were eliminated on the first and largest group of products traded among the three countries. The result? Overall, both Canadian and Mexican exports to the United States doubled after NAFTA went into effect.[13] In fact, trade between Mexico and the United States is so strong that more than 2500 eighteen-wheeler trucks full of U.S. and Mexican products cross the border at Laredo, Texas, each day.[14] Cross-border traffic is heavy between the United States and Canada, too. Canadian Pacific, one of Canada's largest railroad companies, saw an immediate 10 percent increase in its north-south shipments after NAFTA went into effect.

The second set of NAFTA product tariffs was eliminated in 1998, with the third and final set being eliminated in 2003. Importantly, NAFTA also prevents Canada, the United States, and Mexico from increasing existing tariffs or introducing new tariffs. For more information about NAFTA, see www.sice.oas.org/trade/nafta/naftatce.asp.

The goal of **FTAA, Free Trade Area of the Americas**, is to establish a free trade zone similar to NAFTA throughout the western hemisphere. If created, FTAA would be the largest trading zone in the world, consisting of 850 million people in 36 countries in both North and South America. Similar to NAFTA, FTAA pledges to support trade "without barriers, without subsidies, without unfair practices, and with an increasing stream of productive investments."[15] Negotiations may take a decade. However, leaders from each of the 36 countries have agreed to finish FTAA negotiations by 2005. For more information about FTAA, see www.ftaa-alca.org.

ASEAN, the **Association of Southeast Asian Nations**, and **APEC, Asia-Pacific Economic Cooperation**, are the two largest and most important regional trading groups in Asia. ASEAN is a trade agreement between Brunei Darussalam, Cambodia, Indonesia, Laos, Malaysia, Myanmar, the Philippines, Singaore, Thailand, and Vietnam that, together, form a market of more than 330 million people. APEC is a broader agreement between Australia, Canada, Chile, China, Hong Kong, Japan, Mexico, New Zealand, Papua New Guinea, Peru, Russia, South Korea, the United States, and all members of ASEAN except Cambodia, Laos, and Myanmar. APEC countries began reducing trade barriers in the year 2000, though it will take until 2020 for all trade barrier reductions to be completely phased in. For more information about ASEAN, see www.aseansec.org. For more information about APEC, see www.apecsec.org.sg/.

Review 2
Trade Rules and Agreements

Tariffs and nontariff trade barriers, such as quotas, voluntary export restraints, government standards, government subsidies, and customs classifications, have made buying foreign goods much harder or expensive than buying domestically produced products. However, worldwide trade agreements, such as GATT, along with regional trading agreements such as the Maastricht Treaty of Europe, NAFTA, FTAA, ASEAN, and APEC, substantially reduced tariff and nontariff barriers to international trade. Companies have responded by investing in growing markets in Asia, Eastern Europe, and Latin America. Consumers have responded by purchasing products based on value, rather than geography.

How to Go Global

Once a company has decided that it will go global, it must decide how to go global. For example, if you decide to sell in Singapore, should you try to find a local business partner who speaks the language, knows the laws, and understands the customs and norms of Singapore's culture, or should you simply export your products from your home country? What do you do if you are also entering Eastern Europe, perhaps starting in Hungary? Should you use the same approach in Hungary that you used in Singapore?

Free Trade Area of the Americas (FTAA)
regional trade agreement that, when signed, will create a regional trading zone encompassing 36 countries in North and South America

Association of Southeast Asian Nations (ASEAN)
regional trade agreement between Brunei Darussalam, Cambodia, Indonesia, Laos, Malaysia, Myanmar, the Philippines, Singaore, Thailand, and Vietnam

Asia-Pacific Economic Cooperation (APEC)
regional trade agreement between Australia, Canada, Chile, China, Hong Kong, Japan, Mexico, New Zealand, Papua New Guinea, Peru, Russia, South Korea, the United States, and all members of ASEAN except Cambodia, Laos, and Myanmar

After reading the next two sections, you should be able to
3. *explain why companies choose to standardize or adapt their business procedures.*
4. *explain the different ways that companies can organize to do business globally.*

3. Consistency or Adaptation?

In this section, we return to a key issue in the chapter: How can you be sure that the way you run your business in one country is the right way to run that business in another? In other words, how can you strike the right balance between global consistency and local adaptation?

Global consistency means that when a multinational company has offices, manufacturing plants, and distribution facilities in different countries, it will run those offices, plants, and facilities based on the same rules, guidelines, policies, and procedures. Managers at company headquarters value global consistency, because it simplifies decisions. For example, IBM's international sales used to be organized by country. Under this system, if a multinational company with offices in ten different countries wanted to purchase IBM personal computers, it would deal with ten different IBM offices and would likely get different prices and levels of service from each one. Today, multinational customers have to deal with IBM's central sales office only. Once a deal has been cut, they can expect similar prices and service in each location.[16]

Local adaptation is a company policy to modify its standard operating procedures to adapt to differences in foreign customers, governments, and regulatory agencies. Surprisingly, even aspects of the U.S. market need to be paid close attention to by Canadian firms seeking to pursue export opportunities. For instance, Tilano Fresco is a Canadian manufacturer and distributor of decorative tile-making kits. To understand the local business practices of potential customers operating in the Atlanta, Georgia, area of the United States, it needed to work hand in hand with Canadian consular representatives. The result was placement of its products in over 400 stores in just under a year.[17] Local adaptation is typically more important to local managers who are charged with making the international business successful in their countries. In his book *Blunders in International Business*, David Ricks describes an ill-fated advertising theme used by Sumitomo Corporation of Japan (www.sumitomo.com), to introduce a new kind of steel pipe to the North American market. Following the advice of a Japanese advertising agency, the steel was named "Sumitomo High Toughness" and was advertised in full-page advertisements with nearly full-page letters as SHT, the steel "made to match its name." Sumitomo could probably have prevented this mistake if they had given some control of their advertising to local managers who understood the culture and language.

Multinational companies struggle to find the correct balance between global consistency and local adaptation. If they lean too much toward global consistency, they run the risk of using management procedures poorly suited to particular countries' markets, cultures, and employees. However, if companies focus too much on local adaptation, they run the risk of losing the cost efficiencies and productivity that result from using standardized rules and procedures throughout the world.

Review 3
Consistency or Adaptation?

Global business requires a balance between global consistency and local adaptation. Global consistency means using the same rules, guidelines, policies, and procedures in each foreign location. Managers at company headquarters like global consistency, because it simplifies decisions. Local adaptation means adapting standard procedures to differences in foreign markets. Local managers prefer a policy of local adaptation, because it gives them more control. Not all businesses need the same combinations of global consistency and local adaptation. Some thrive by emphasizing global consistency and ignoring local adaptation. Others succeed by ignoring global consistency and emphasizing local adaptation.

4. Forms for Global Business

Besides determining whether to adapt organizational policies and procedures, a company must also determine how to organize itself for successful entry into foreign markets. Historically, companies have generally followed the phase model of globalization.

This means that companies made the transition from a domestic company to a global company in sequential phases, through exporting, cooperative contracts, strategic alliances, wholly owned affiliates[18], and global new ventures.[19]

4.1 Exporting

When companies produce products in their home countries and sell those products to customers in foreign countries, they are **exporting**. For example, Canadian wine producers are active in their efforts to export wine around the world. Recently, Canadian companies such as Andres Wine, Colio Estate, Vineland, Hillebrand Estates, and Creekside Estate Winery presented their wines to an invited group of high-end restaurants and hotel chains in Stockholm, Sweden. After an initial introduction of these products at the Canadian Embassy and a follow-up by European-based agents, at least one of the Canadian company's products have been listed with the Swedish alcohol retail monopoly.[20] Another example can be found in India. Few people realize that India is the second-largest exporter of computer software in the world (North American software companies are first). In fact, when the Japanese subsidiary of Digital Equipment Corporation (now part of Compaq) needed software that automatically translated English words into Japanese characters, they hired Indian rather than Japanese software engineers, because they were cheaper and, according to DEC, more talented.[21]

exporting
selling domestically produced products to customers in foreign countries

Indian movie star Amitabh Bachchan, right, welcomes participants to the popular television program *Kuan Banega Crorepati? (Who Wants to Be a Millionaire?)* in Bombay, India. The Indian version of the successful American program has high ratings, with millions of Indian viewers glued to their television sets from Monday to Thursday.

AP/Wide World Photos

Exporting has many advantages as a form of global business. It makes the company less dependent on sales in its home market and provides a greater degree of control over research, design, and production decisions. While advantageous in a number of ways, exporting also has its disadvantages.

The primary disadvantage is that many exported goods are subject to tariff and nontariff barriers that can substantially increase their final cost to consumers. A second disadvantage of exporting is that transportation costs can significantly increase the price of an exported product. For example, a 22-kilogram box of Nicaraguan sweet onions costs about $24, but shipping those onions to North America costs $7, adding more than 29 percent to the price.[22] Another disadvantage of exporting is that companies that export are dependent on foreign importers for distribution of their products. For example, if the foreign importer makes a mistake on the paperwork that accompanies a shipment of imported goods, those goods can be returned to the foreign manufacturer at the manufacturer's expense.

4.2 Cooperative Contracts

cooperative contract
an agreement in which a foreign business owner pays a company a fee for the right to conduct that business in his or her country

When an organization decides to expand its business globally, but does not want to make large financial commitments to do so, it will sign a **cooperative contract** with a foreign business owner, who pays the company a fee for the right to conduct that business in his or her country. There are two kinds of cooperative contracts: licensing and franchising.

licensing
agreement in which a domestic company, the licensor, receives royalty payments for allowing another company, the licensee, to produce its product, sell its service, or use its brand name in a specified foreign market

Under a **licensing** agreement, a domestic company, the licensor, receives royalty payments for allowing another company, the licensee, to produce its product, sell its service, or use its brand name in a particular foreign market.

One of the most important advantages of licensing is that it allows companies to earn additional profits without investing more money. As foreign sales increase, the royalties paid to the licensor by the foreign licensee increase. Moreover, the licensee, not the licensor, invests in production equipment and facilities to produce the licensed product. Licensing also helps companies avoid tariff and nontariff barriers. Since the licensee manufactures the product within the foreign country, tariff and nontariff barriers don't apply. For example, Arctic Beverages is licensed to bottle and distribute Pepsi-Cola in northern Manitoba and parts of Saskatchewan. Because it bottles Pepsi in Canada, tariff and nontariff barriers do not affect the price or supply of these products.

The biggest disadvantage associated with licensing is that the licensor gives up control over the quality of the product or service sold by the foreign licensee. Other than specific restrictions in the licensing agreement, the licensee controls the entire business, from production to marketing to final sales. Many licensors include inspection clauses in their licence contracts, but closely monitoring product or service quality from thousands of kilometres away can be difficult. An additional disadvantage is that licensees can eventually become competitors, especially when a licensing agreement includes access to important technology or proprietary business knowledge.

franchise
a collection of networked firms in which the manufacturer or marketer of a product or service, the franchisor, licenses the entire business to another person or organization, the franchisee

A **franchise** is a collection of networked firms in which the manufacturer or marketer of a product or service, the franchisor, licenses the entire business to another person or organization, the franchisee. For the price of an initial franchise fee plus royalties, franchisors provide franchisees training, help with marketing and advertising, and give an exclusive right to conduct business in a particular location. Most franchise fees run between $7000 and $50 000. Atlantic Canada success story Greco Pizza (www.greco.ca) is currently accepting franchise applications for its expansion into Quebec. Its website suggests you would need a minimum of $30 000 to be eligible for serious consideration as a franchisee.

Overall, franchising is a fast way to enter foreign markets. During the 1980s, North American franchisors increased their global franchises by an astronomical 79 percent, for a total of almost 40 000 global franchise units! Because it gives the franchisor additional cash flows from franchisee fees and royalties, franchising can be a good strategy when a company's domestic sales have slowed. For example, in the last decade, McDonald's (www.mcdonalds.com) has nearly doubled its number of overseas stores. Pizza Hut (www.pizzahut.com) plans to open at least 300 new stores in Asia by the year 2004, while KFC (www.kfc.com), plans to build more than 1100 new stores in Asia during the same period.[23]

Despite its many advantages, franchisors face a loss of control when they sell businesses to franchisees who are thousands of kilometres away. Although there are successful exceptions, franchising success may be somewhat culture-bound. In other words, because most global franchisors begin by franchising their businesses in similar countries or regions (Canada is by far the first choice for American companies taking their first step into global franchising), and because 65 percent of franchisors make absolutely no change in their business for overseas franchisees, that success may not generalize to cultures with different lifestyles, values, preferences, and technological infrastructures. Because of this, simple things taken for granted in one's own country can trip up the most successful businesses when they franchise overseas. For example, in Eastern Europe, less than half the households have working phones. Greco Pizza (www.greco.ca) might find it difficult to franchise its pizza delivery business under those circumstances.

4.3 Strategic Alliances

Companies forming **strategic alliances** combine key resources, costs, risks, technology, and people. The most common strategic alliance is a **joint venture**, which occurs when two existing companies collaborate to form a third company. The two founding companies remain intact and unchanged, except that, together, they now own the newly created joint venture.

One of the oldest, most successful global joint ventures is Fuji-Xerox, which is a joint venture between Fuji Photo Film of Japan and Xerox Corporation, based in North America, which makes copiers and automated office systems. More than 35 years after its creation, Fuji-Xerox employs nearly 30 000 employees and has close to $7 billion (U.S.) in revenues. Fuji-Xerox is largely responsible for copier sales in Asia, whereas Xerox is responsible for North American sales. Rank Xerox, which is a Xerox subsidiary, is responsible for sales in Europe.[24]

One of the advantages of global joint ventures is that, like licensing and franchising, they help companies avoid tariff and nontariff barriers to entry. Another advantage is that companies participating in a joint venture bear only part of the costs and the risks of that business. Many companies find this attractive, because of how expensive it is to enter foreign markets or develop new products.

Global joint ventures can be especially advantageous to smaller, local partners that link up with larger, more experienced foreign firms that can bring advanced technology, management, and business skills to the joint venture. After the Berlin Wall fell, General Motors (www.gm.com), the world's largest auto manufacturer, committed to a joint venture with German Automobil Werke Eisenach, an automobile manufacturer in Eisenach, Germany (formerly East Germany). Together, General Motors and GEW-Eisenach built a brand-new factory that allowed General Motors to introduce the most up-to-date manufacturing machines, teamwork-based assembly, and just-in-time inventory systems, none of which had been used in the antiquated factory that GEW-Eisenach used to manufacture East German cars.[25]

Global joint ventures are not without problems, though. Because companies share costs and risk with their joint venture partners, they must also share their profits. Setting up global joint ventures is also complex, often requiring detailed contracts that specify the obligations of each party. Toshiba (www.toshiba.com), which participated in its first global joint ventures in the early 1900s by making light bulb filaments with General Electric (www.ge.com), treats joint ventures like a marriage of two companies and views the contract as a prenuptial agreement.[26] In other words, the joint venture contract specifies how much each company will invest, what its rights and responsibilities are,

strategic alliance
agreement in which companies combine key resources, costs, risk, technology, and people

joint venture
a strategic alliance in which two existing companies collaborate to form a third, independent company

and what it is entitled to if the joint venture does not work out. These steps are important, because it is estimated that the rate of failure for global joint ventures is as high as 33 percent to 50 percent.[27] Global joint ventures can also be difficult to manage, because they represent a merging of four cultures: the country and the organizational cultures of the first partner, and the country and the organizational cultures of the second partner.

4.4 Wholly Owned Affiliates (Build or Buy)

wholly owned affiliates
foreign office, facilities, and manufacturing plants that are 100 percent owned by the parent company

Approximately one-third of multinational companies enter foreign markets through **wholly owned affiliates**. Unlike licensing, franchising, or joint ventures, wholly owned affiliates are 100 percent owned by the parent company. For example, Honda Canada, located in the Greater Toronto Area of Ontario, is 100 percent owned by Honda Motors of Japan. The Ford Motor Company of Canada, in Oakville, Ontario, is 100 percent owned by the Ford Motor Company in Detroit, Michigan.

The primary advantage of wholly owned businesses is that they give parent companies all the profits and complete control over foreign facilities. The biggest disadvantage is the expense of building new operations or buying existing businesses. While the payoff can be enormous if wholly owned affiliates succeed, the losses can be immense if they fail. For example, when Volkswagen (www.volkswagen.com) spent over a quarter of a billion dollars (U.S.) to purchase and modernize an American auto manufacturing plant from Chrysler, everyone, including the state of Pennsylvania that lured Volkswagen to Pennsylvania with a $63-million (U.S.) tax break, thought Volkswagen would be wildly successful. However, nearly a decade later, Volkswagen sales had dropped and the plant, which was running at only 40 percent of capacity, was losing $120 million (U.S.) a year. Twenty-five hundred workers lost their jobs when Volkswagen closed the plant for good.[28]

4.5 Global New Ventures

It used to be that companies slowly evolved from being small and selling in their home markets to being large and selling to foreign markets. Furthermore, as companies went global, they usually followed the phase model of globalization. However, three trends have combined to allow companies to skip the phase model when going global. First, quick, reliable air travel can transport people to nearly any point in the world within one day. Second, low-cost communication technologies, such as the Internet, e-mail, teleconferencing, and phone conferencing, make it easier to communicate with global customers, suppliers, managers, and employees. Third, there is now a critical mass of business people with extensive personal experience in all aspects of global business.[29] This combination of events has made it possible to start companies that are global from inception. With sales, employees, and financing in different countries, **global new ventures** are new companies founded with an active global strategy.[30]

global new ventures
new companies with sales, employees, and financing in different countries that are founded with an active global strategy

While there are several different kinds of global new ventures, they share two common factors. First, the company founders successfully develop and communicate the company's global vision. Second, rather than going global one country at a time, new global ventures bring a product or service to market in several foreign markets at the same time. National GYP-Chipper, based in Texas, manufactures and sells a $10 000 machine that crushes scrap gypsum (drywall) into a recyclable powder.[31] It is cheaper and faster for building contractors to grind up used or leftover drywall board into a recyclable powder than it is to pay to have it hauled to the dump. Because National Gyp-Chipper feared that potential overseas competitors would copy its machine, it established licensing contracts with companies in Canada, Britain, and Japan and was seeking other relationships in Europe and the Middle East. By entering so many markets so quickly, National Gyp-Chipper hoped to get ahead of and deter any copycat competitors.

The phase model of globalization says that as companies move from a domestic to a global orientation, they use these organizational forms in sequence: exporting, cooperative contracts (licensing and franchising), strategic alliances, and wholly owned affiliates. Yet not all companies follow the phase model. For example, global new ventures are global from their inception.

Where To Go Global

Deciding where to go global is just as important as deciding how your company will go global.

After reading the next three sections, you should be able to
5. explain how to find a favourable business climate.
6. discuss the importance of identifying and adapting to cultural differences.
7. explain how to successfully prepare workers for international assignments.

5. Finding the Best Business Climate

When deciding where to go global, companies try to find countries or regions with promising business climates. An attractive global business climate positions the company for easy access to growing markets, is an effective but cost-efficient place to build an office or manufacturing site, and minimizes the political risk to the company.

5.1 Positioning for Growing Markets

The most important factor in an attractive business climate is access to a growing market. Two factors help companies determine the growth potential of foreign markets: purchasing power and foreign competitors. **Purchasing power** is measured by comparing the relative cost of a standard set of goods and services in different countries. For instance, a Coke costs $1.50 in Tokyo. But because a Coke costs about $1.40 in Canada while only about 70 cents in the United States, the average Canadian would have similar purchasing power to a Japanese while an American would have more purchasing power. Purchasing power is surprisingly strong in countries such as Mexico, India, and China, which have low average levels of income. This is because consumers still have money to spend after paying for basic living expenses, such as food, shelter, and transportation, which are very inexpensive in those countries. Because basic living expenses are so small, purchasing power is strong, and millions of Chinese, Mexican, and Indian consumers increasingly have extra money to spend on what they want, in addition to what they need.

Consequently, countries with high levels of purchasing power are good choices for companies looking for attractive global markets. Coke has found that the per capita consumption of Coca-Cola—how many Cokes a person drinks per year—rises directly with purchasing power. In Eastern Europe, as countries began to embrace capitalism after the fall of communism, per capita consumption of Coke increased from 20 to 31 Cokes in just two years. Today, the average has tripled to 93 drinks per year.[32]

The second part of assessing growing global markets is to analyze the degree of global competition, which is determined by the number and quality of companies that already compete in foreign markets. Canadians who have shopped from time to time in the United States will recognize the name JCPenney (www.jcpenney.com). Before JCPenney began developing stores in foreign markets, it sent a small team of experienced retailers to scout its global competition. In East Berlin, the team found display windows with nothing more than one dusty shirt on display. In Istanbul, they found retail stores with plumbing supplies next to the women's lingerie and clothing. Because its top-selling stores were right on the U.S.–Mexican border, Penney's managers didn't even have to leave the United

purchasing power
a comparison of the relative cost of a standard set of goods and services in different countries

States to assess its competition in Mexico. Studies confirmed that 60 percent of the sales in these U.S. stores came from Mexicans who crossed the border to shop.[33] Because its foreign competitors were weak in marketing, customer service, and product distribution, JCPenney followed through on its plan to expand into global markets.

5.2 Choosing an Office/Manufacturing Location

Companies do not have to establish an office or manufacturing location in each country they enter. They can license, franchise, or export to foreign markets, or they can serve a larger region from one country. Thus, the criteria for choosing an office/manufacturing location are different from the criteria for entering a foreign market.

Rather than focusing on costs alone, companies should consider both qualitative and quantitative factors. Two key qualitative factors are work force quality and company strategy. Work force quality is important because it is often difficult to find workers with the specific skills, abilities, and experience that a company needs to run its business. Work force quality was the most important consideration when Lands' End (www.landsend.com), an American mail-order catalogue company used by many Canadians, built a communications centre in Oakham, England. Lands' End's project manager for the Oakham location said, "We operate a service business over the phone. We need polite operators with neutral accents, so quality of labour was one through five on our list of priorities."[34]

Quantitative factors, such as the kind of facility being built, tariff and nontariff barriers, exchange rates, and transportation and labour costs, should also be considered when choosing an office/manufacturing location. Exhibit 8.4 shows *Fortune* magazine's rankings for the world's top cities for global business. This information is a good starting point if your company is trying to decide where to put an international office or manufacturing plant.

5.3 Minimizing Political Risk

When managers think about political risk in global business, they envision burning factories and riots in the streets. Although political events such as these receive dramatic and extended coverage from the press, the political risks that most companies face usually will not be covered as breaking stories on CTV Newsnet (www.ctv.ca), or CBC Newsworld (www.cbc.ca/newsworld/). However, the negative consequences of ordinary political risk can be just as devastating to companies that fail to identify and minimize those risks.

When conducting global business, companies should attempt to identify two types of political risk: political uncertainty and policy uncertainty.[35] **Political uncertainty** is associated with the risk of major changes in political regimes that can result from war, revolution, death of political leaders, social unrest, or other influential events. **Policy uncertainty** refers to the risk associated with changes in laws and government policies that directly affect the way foreign companies conduct business. This is the most common form of political risk in global business and perhaps the most frustrating. For example, the busiest McDonald's in the world used to be in a prime location in Wangfujing, China—that is, until the Chinese government broke McDonald's 20-year lease after only two years, telling McDonald's that it would have to build a brand-new store just blocks away from the original location. The Chinese government broke McDonald's lease so that a Hong Kong billionaire could develop the location. Ironically, after agreeing to let him build on the site, the Chinese government retracted that permission, too.[36]

Several strategies can be used to minimize or adapt to the political risk inherent to global business. An *avoidance strategy* is used when the political risks associated with a foreign country or region are viewed as too great. If firms are already invested in high-risk areas, they may divest or sell their businesses. If they have not yet invested, they will likely postpone their investment until the risk shrinks.

political uncertainty
the risk of major changes in political regimes that can result from war, revolution, death of political leaders, social unrest, or other influential events

policy uncertainty
the risk associated with changes in laws and government policies that directly affect the way foreign companies conduct business

EXHIBIT 8.4

WORLD'S BEST CITIES FOR BUSINESS

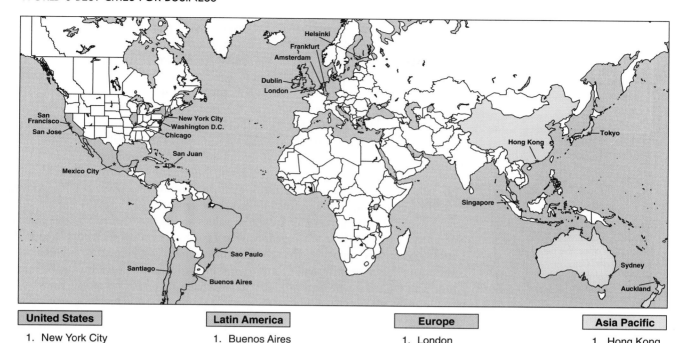

United States	Latin America	Europe	Asia Pacific
1. New York City	1. Buenos Aires	1. London	1. Hong Kong
2. San Francisco	2. San Juan	2. Frankfurt	2. Sydney
3. Chicago	3. Mexico City	3. Helsinki	3. Singapore
4. Washington D.C. area	4. Sao Paulo	4. Amsterdam	4. Auckland
5. San Jose	5. Santiago	5. Dublin	5. Tokyo

Source: M. Borden, "The Best Cities for Business: Big, Established, Monied Metropolises—With a Tech Twist—Top FORTUNE's Annual Ranking at the Turn of the Century," *Fortune*, 27 November 2000, 218. C. Murphy, "Winners of the World," *Fortune*, 27 November 2000, 232.

Control is an active strategy to prevent or reduce political risks. Firms using a control strategy will lobby foreign governments or international trade agencies to change laws, regulations, or trade barriers that hurt their business in that country.

Another method for dealing with political risk is *cooperation*, which makes use of joint ventures and collaborative contracts, such as franchising and licensing. Although cooperation does not eliminate the political risk of doing business in a country, it does limit the risk associated with foreign ownership of a business. For example, a German company forming a joint venture with a Chinese company to do business in China may structure the joint venture contract so that the Chinese company owns 51 percent or more of the joint venture. Doing so qualifies the newly formed joint venture as a Chinese company and exempts it from Chinese laws that apply to foreign-owned businesses.[37]

Review 5
Finding the Best Business Climate

The first step in deciding where to take your company global is finding an attractive business climate. Be sure to look for a growing market where consumers have strong purchasing power and foreign competitors are weak. When locating an office or manufacturing facility, consider both qualitative and quantitative factors. In assessing political risk, be sure to examine political uncertainty and policy uncertainty. If the location you choose has considerable political risk, you can avoid it, try to control the risk, or use a cooperation strategy.

EXPERIENCING MANAGEMENT

You may learn more about international cultures and their effect on managerial behaviour by interacting with cultural concepts at our animated concept and activity site. Choose International Management from the "select a topic" pull-down menu, then Cultural Differences from the "overview tab."

www.experiencingmanagement.com

6. Becoming Aware of Cultural Differences

Some of the more interesting and amusing aspects of global business are the unexpected confrontations that people have with cultural differences, "the way they do things over there." For example, as part of a class assignment in global business, a North American high school class and a high school class in Valle, Spain, agreed to form a global "joint venture." The two classes agreed that the North American students would buy Spanish products from the Spanish high school students and resell them at a profit to other North American students. Likewise, the Spanish students would purchase North American products from the American students and then resell them at a profit to their Spanish friends. Now, what to buy from each other? The American students decided to buy giant beach towels showing teenaged Spanish lovers. One of the towels showed a boy helping his girlfriend remove her shirt. Another showed him unzipping her jeans. In Spain's culture, which is much more relaxed about sexuality than North American culture, no one gives these towels a second thought. Of course, despite protestations of censorship, the North American high school teacher vetoed the towels as too suggestive.[38]

national culture
the set of shared values and beliefs that affect the perceptions, decisions, and behaviour of the people from a particular country

National culture is the set of shared values and beliefs that affects the perceptions, decisions, and behaviour of the people from a particular country. The first step in dealing with culture is to recognize that there are meaningful differences in national cultures. Psychologist Geert Hofstede (http://geert-hofstede.international-business-center.com/index.shtml) has spent the last 20 years studying cultural differences in 53 different countries. His research shows that there are five consistent differences across national cultures: power distance, individualism, short-term versus long-term orientation, masculinity, and uncertainty avoidance.[39]

A veiled Muslim woman travels past a large billboard advertising a film that catalogues the plight of a middle-class Cairo family as it tries to come to terms with the pregnancy of its teenage daughter. The film captures the prevailing mood of contemporary urban Egypt struggling to balance tradition and modernity, religion, and science.

AP/Wide World Photos

Power distance is the extent to which people in a country accept that power is distributed unequally in society and organizations. In countries where power distance is weak, such as Denmark and Sweden, employees don't like their organizations or their bosses to have power over them or to tell them what to do. They want to have a say in decisions that affect them. As shown in Exhibit 8.5, Russia and China, with scores of 95 and 80, are much stronger in power distance than Germany (35), the Netherlands (38), and the United States (40). Canada's rating is 39; the world average is 55.

Individualism is the degree to which societies believe that individuals should be self-sufficient. In individualistic societies, employees put loyalty to themselves first, and loyalty to their company and work group second. The United States (91), the Netherlands (80), France (71), and Germany (67) are the strongest in individualism, while West Africa (20), China (20), and Indonesia (14) are the weakest. Like many other English-speaking countries such as Britain, New Zealand, and Australia, Canada ranks individualism highly—at 80, it's the highest ranking of all the dimensions.

Masculinity and *femininity* capture the difference between highly assertive and highly nurturing cultures. Masculine cultures emphasize assertiveness, competition, material success, and achievement, whereas feminine cultures emphasize the importance of relationships, modesty, caring for the weak, and quality of life. Japan (95), Germany (66), and the United States (62) have the most masculine orientations, while the Netherlands (14) has the most feminine orientation. Canada ranks it at about 47.

The cultural difference of *uncertainty avoidance* is the degree to which people in a country are uncomfortable with unstructured, ambiguous, unpredictable situations. In countries with strong uncertainty avoidance, such as Greece and Portugal, people are aggressive, emotional, and seek security (rather than uncertainty). Japan (92), France (86), West Africa (90), and Russia (90) are strongest in uncertainty avoidance, while Hong Kong (29) is the weakest. Canada's ranking is about 42.

EXHIBIT 8.5

HOFSTEDE'S FIVE CULTURAL DIMENSIONS

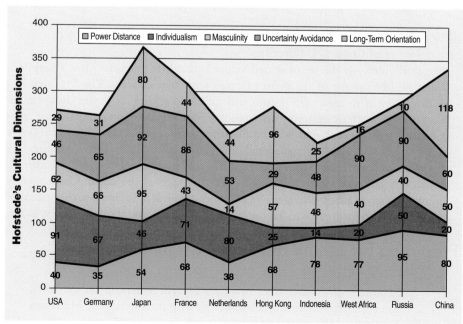

Source: Geert H. Hofstede, "Cultural Constraints in Management Theories," *Academy of Management Executive 7*, no. 1 (1993): 81–94.

Short-term/long-term orientation addresses whether cultures are oriented to the present and seek immediate gratification, or to the future and defer gratification. Not surprisingly, countries with short-term orientations are consumer driven, whereas countries with long-term orientations are savings driven. China (118) and Hong Kong (96) have very strong long-term orientations, while West Africa (16), Indonesia (25), the United States (29), and Germany (31) have very strong short-term orientations. Canada gives it the lowest ranking of all the dimensions, at 23.

Cultural differences affect perceptions, understanding, and behaviour. Recognizing cultural differences is critical to succeeding in global business. However, Hofstede said we should recognize that these cultural differences are based on averages—the average level of uncertainty avoidance in Portugal, or the average level of power distance in Argentina, etc. Hofstede said, "If you are going to spend time with a Japanese colleague, you shouldn't assume that overall cultural statements about Japanese society automatically apply to this person."[40]

After becoming aware of cultural differences, the second step is deciding how to adapt your company to those cultural differences. Unfortunately, studies investigating the effects of cultural differences on management practice point more to difficulties than to easy solutions. One problem is that different cultures will probably perceive management policies and practices differently. For example, blue-collar workers in France and Argentina, all of whom performed the same factory jobs for the same multinational company, perceived the company's corporate-wide safety policy differently.[41] French workers perceived that safety wasn't very important to the company, but Argentine workers thought that it was. The fact that something as simple as a safety policy can be perceived differently across cultures shows just how difficult it can be to standardize management practices across different countries and cultures.

Another difficulty is that cultural values are changing, albeit slowly, in many parts of the world. The fall of communism in Eastern Europe and the former Soviet Republic and the broad economic reforms in China have combined to produce sweeping changes on two continents. Thanks to increased global trade resulting from GATT and other regional free trade agreements, major economic transformations are also under way in India, Mexico, Central America, and South America. The difficulty that companies face when trying to adapt management practices to cultural differences is that they may be adapting the way they run their businesses based on outdated and incorrect assumptions about a country's culture.

Review 6
Becoming Aware of Cultural Differences

National culture is the set of shared values and beliefs that affect the perceptions, decisions, and behaviour of the people from a particular country. The first step in dealing with culture is to recognize meaningful differences, such as power distance, individualism, short-term/long-term orientation, masculinity, and uncertainty avoidance. Cultural differences should be carefully interpreted, because they are based on averages, not individuals. Adapting managerial practices to cultural differences is difficult, because policies and practices can be perceived differently in different cultures. Another difficulty is that cultural values may be changing in many parts of the world. Consequently, when companies try to adapt management practices to cultural differences, they need to be sure that those changes are not based on outdated assumptions about a country's culture.

7. Preparing for an International Assignment

Around a conference table in a large [North American] office tower, three [North American] executives sat with their new boss, Mr. Akiro Kusumoto, the newly appointed head of a Japanese firm's [North

American] subsidiary, and two of his Japanese lieutenants. The meeting was called to discuss ideas for reducing operating costs. Mr. Kusumoto began by outlining his company's aspiration for its long-term continental presence. He then turned to the budgetary matter. One Japanese manager politely offered one suggestion, and a [North American] then proposed another. After gingerly discussing the alternatives for quite some time, the then exasperated [North American] blurted out: "Look, that idea is just not going to have much impact. Look at the numbers!" In the face of such bluntness, uncommon and unacceptable in Japan, Mr. Kusumoto fell silent. He leaned back, drew air between his teeth, and felt a deep longing to return East. He realized his life in this country would be filled with many such jarring encounters, and lamented his posting to a land of such rudeness.[42]

Mr. Kusumoto is a Japanese **expatriate**, someone who lives outside his or her native country. The cultural shock that he was experiencing is common. The difficulty of adjusting to language, cultural, and social differences is the primary reason that so many expatriates fail in overseas assignments. For example, it is estimated that 10 percent to 45 percent of North American expatriates sent abroad by their companies will return home before they have successfully completed their international assignments.[43] Of those who do complete their international assignments, as many as 30 percent to 50 percent are judged by their companies to be no better than marginally effective.[44] Since the average cost of sending an employee on an international assignment can run between $280 000 and $1.7 million, failure in those assignments can be extraordinarily expensive.[45]

expatriate
someone who lives outside his or her native country

However, the chances for a successful international assignment can be increased through language and cross-cultural training; and considering spouse, family, and dual-career issues.

7.1 Language and Cross-Cultural Training

The purpose of pre-departure language and cross-cultural training is to reduce the uncertainty that expatriates feel, the misunderstandings that take place between expatriates and natives, and the inappropriate behaviours that expatriates unknowingly commit when they travel to a foreign country. Indeed, simple things like using a phone, finding a public toilet, asking for directions, knowing how much things cost, exchanging greetings, or ordering in a restaurant can become tremendously complex when expatriates don't know a foreign language or a country's customs and cultures. In his book *Blunders in International Business*, David Ricks tells the story of a North American couple in Asia. After a walk with their dog, the couple had dinner at a local restaurant. Since the waiters and waitresses did not speak English, they ordered by pointing to items on the menu. Because their dog was hungry, they pointed to the dog and to the kitchen. The waiter had trouble understanding, but finally took the dog to the kitchen. The couple assumed that this meant the dog could not be fed in the dining room, but was going to be fed in the kitchen. Unfortunately, to the couple's dismay, the waiter and the chef returned later to proudly show them how well they had cooked the poodle.

Expatriates who receive pre-departure language and cross-cultural training make faster adjustments to foreign cultures and perform better on their international assignments (and are better at ordering in foreign restaurants).[46] Unfortunately, only a third of the managers who go on international assignments receive any kind of pre-departure training. This is somewhat surprising given the failure rates for expatriates and the high cost of those failures. It is also surprising because, with the exception of some language courses, pre-departure training is not particularly expensive or difficult to provide.

WhatReallyWorks

Cross-Cultural Training

Most expatriates will tell you that cross-cultural training helped them adjust to foreign cultures. However, anecdotal data are not as convincing as systematic studies. Twenty-one studies, with a combined total of 1611 participants, have examined whether cross-cultural training affects the self-development, perceptions, relationships, adjustment, and job performance of expatriates. Overall, they show that cross-cultural training works extremely well in most instances.

Self-Development

When you first live in another country, you must learn how to make decisions that you took for granted in your home country: how to get to work, how to get to the grocery, how to pay your bills, and so on. If you've generally been confident about yourself and your abilities, an overseas assignment can challenge that sense of self. However, cross-cultural training helps expatriates deal with these and other challenges. Expatriates who receive cross-cultural training are 79 percent more likely to report healthy psychological well-being and self-development than those who don't receive training.

Psychological Well-Being & Self Development

Fostering Relationships

One of the most important parts of an overseas assignment is establishing and maintaining relationships with host nationals. If you're in Brazil, you need to make friends with Brazilians. However, many expatriates make the mistake of making friends only with expatriates from their home country. In effect, they become social isolates in a foreign country. They work and live there, but as much as they can, they speak their native language, eat their native foods, and socialize with other expatriates from their home country. Cross-cultural training makes a big difference in whether expatriates establish relationships with host nationals. Expatriates who receive cross-cultural training are 74 percent more likely to have established such relationships.

Fostering Relationships with Native Citizens

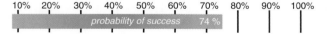

Accurate Perceptions of Culture

Another thing that distinguishes successful from unsuccessful expatriates is that they understand the cultural norms and practices of the host country. For example, many Americans do not understand pictures that many of them may have seen of Japanese troops turning their backs to American military commanders on V-J day, the day that Japan surrendered to the United States in World War II. Americans viewed this as a lack of respect, when in fact in Japan, turning one's back in this way is a sign of respect. Cross-cultural training makes a big difference in the accuracy of perceptions concerning host country norms and practices. Expatriates who receive cross-cultural training are 74 percent more likely to have accurate perceptions.

Accurate Cultural Perceptions

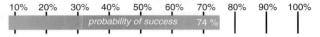

Rapid Adjustment

New employees are most likely to quit in the first six months, because this initial period requires the most adjustment: learning new names, new faces, new procedures, and new information. It's tough. Of course, expatriates have a much tougher time making a successful adjustment, because besides learning new names, faces, procedures, and information, expatriates are learning new languages, new foods, new customs, and often new lifestyles. Expatriates who receive cross-cultural training are 74 percent more likely to make a rapid adjustment to a foreign country.

Rapid Adjustment to Foreign Cultures and Countries

Job Performance

It's good that cross-cultural training improves self-development, fosters relationships, improves the accuracy of perceptions, and helps expatriates make rapid adjustments to foreign cultures. However, from an organizational standpoint, the ultimate test of cross-cultural training is whether it improves expatriates' job performance. The evidence shows that cross-cultural training makes a significant difference in expatriates' job performance. This is not quite as big a difference as for the other factors. However, it is estimated that cross-cultural training for 100 managers could bring about $500 000 worth of benefits to a company, nearly $5600 per manager. This is an outstanding return on investment, especially when you consider the high rate of failure for expatriates. Expatriates who have received cross-cultural training are 71 percent more likely to have better on-the-job performance than those who did not receive cross-cultural training.

On-the-Job Performance

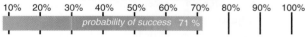

Source: S.P. Deshpande & C. Viswesvaran, "Is Cross-Cultural Training of Expatriate Managers Effective: A Meta-Analysis," *International Journal of Intercultural Relations* 16, no. 3 (1992): 295–310.

For example, a Canadian electronics manufacturer prepared workers for assignments in South Korea by using a combination of documentary training, cultural simulations, and field experiences. Documentary training focuses on identifying the critical specific differences between various cultures. Trainees learned that Canadian subordinates will normally look their bosses in the eye, whereas Korean subordinates avoid eye contact unless their bosses ask them questions. Trainees also learned about other Canadian–South Korean differences, such as how to greet business people, how to behave toward South Korean women or elders, and how to respect privacy.

After learning critical specific differences in documentary training, trainees participated in a cultural simulation, in which they had the opportunity to practise adapting to cultural differences. For example, the trainees participated in a simulated cocktail party in which company managers who had spent time in South Korea posed as South Korean business people and their spouses. Trainees practised South Korean greetings, introductions, and communication styles, and then received feedback on their performance.

PERSONAL PRODUCTIVITY TIP

Money and International Travel

Credit cards, such as Visa, MasterCard, and American Express, are accepted worldwide and offer the best exchange rates. Traveller's cheques are replaceable if lost or stolen. Carry enough local currency to pay for food, transportation, and lodging your first day in a country. If you need more, you can exchange local currency at hotels, post offices, or for-profit currency exchange stores. However, because of the 2 percent to 10 percent exchange fees, many travellers now use ABM machines to withdraw cash directly from their personal bank accounts. ABMs are widely available (see www.mastercard.com/cardholderservices/atm/ for the Cirrus network), and they offer exchange rates as good as credit cards.

7.2 Consideration of Spouse, Family, and Dual-Career Issues

The evidence clearly shows that how well an expatriate's spouse and family adjust to the foreign culture is the most important factor in determining the success or failure of an international assignment.[47] Unfortunately, despite its importance, there has been little systematic research on what does and does not help expatriates' families successfully adapt. However, a number of companies have found that adaptability screening and intercultural training for families can lead to more successful overseas adjustment.

Adaptability screening is used to assess how well managers and their families are likely to adjust to foreign cultures. For example, one large North American multinational has developed an "Overseas Assignment Inventory" to assess the spouse and family's open-mindedness, respect for others' beliefs, sense of humour, and marital communication. But adaptability screening is not just companies assessing employees; it can also mean that employees screen international assignments for desirability. Since more employees are becoming aware of the costs of international assignments (spouses having to give up or change jobs, children having to change schools, having to learn a new language, etc.), some companies are willing to pay for a pre-assignment trip for the employee and his or her spouse to investigate the country before accepting the international assignment.[48]

Language and cross-cultural training for families is just as important as language and cross-cultural training for expatriates. In fact, it may be more important, because unlike expatriates, whose professional jobs often shield them from the full force of a country's culture, spouses and children are often fully immersed in foreign neighbourhoods and schools. Households must be run, shopping must be done, and bills must be paid. Likewise, children and their parents must deal with different cultural beliefs and practices about discipline, alcohol, dating, and other issues. Language and cross-cultural training can help reduce uncertainty about how to act and decrease misunderstandings between expatriates, their families, and locals.

Review 7
Preparing for an International Assignment

Many expatriates return prematurely from international assignments because of poor performance. However, this is much less likely to happen if employees receive language and cross-cultural training, such as documentary training, cultural simulations, or field experiences, before going on assignment. Adjustment of expatriates' spouses and families, which is the most important determinant of success in international assignments, can be improved through adaptability screening and intercultural training.

What Really Happened?

At the beginning of the chapter, you learned that it took Wal-Mart only four decades to become the dominant retailer in the United States. However, you also learned that Wal-Mart's success in the United States did not automatically translate to other countries. Despite its initial missteps, Wal-Mart continued to invest in international markets. Let's find out what really happened to see if Wal-Mart became more successful in other places around the world.

Initial successes came easily in Canada, but not in Mexico. So which countries should Wal-Mart enter?

An attractive global-business climate positions a company for easy access to growing markets, chooses effective but cost-efficient places to build offices or manufacturing sites, and minimizes the political risk to the company. In particular, it's important to look for a growing market where consumers have strong purchasing power and foreign competitors are weak. So on the basis of these criteria, which countries did Wal-Mart enter?

Besides Mexico (see the discussion on NAFTA and free trade agreements below), Wal-Mart chose to enter Germany, Britain, and Brazil (see the next question for a discussion of Brazil). While Germany's general retail markets are competitive, competition is very weak in food retailing. In general, German supermarkets don't have cheaper store brands (like Wal-Mart Cola), do a poor job of managing and reordering inventory, and, unlike Wal-Mart, struggle to keep costs low. Wal-Mart entered Germany by buying two German retailers, Wertkauf GmbH and Spar Handels AG, both of which have hypermarket stores (retail and groceries combined). Wal-Mart is still losing money in Germany, but expects profits soon. Now that Wal-Mart is in charge of these stores, Manfred Siwek, a German shopper, said, "It's much better than before. Prices are lower, and the service is friendlier."

And, for similar reasons (e.g., lack of strong competition), Wal-Mart has also expanded aggressively into the United Kingdom, paying $10.84 billion (U.S.) to acquire ASDA Group PLC and its 229 stores. Furthermore, it has cut prices to U.S. levels, which are typically much lower than in the United Kingdom. Wal-Mart also says it will add 27 000 ASDA jobs over the next five years because of extremely strong sales growth in existing stores and construction of new ASDA stores.

While Carrefour is now the leading international retailer, just how fierce a competitor will Carrefour be in the long run when lined up against Wal-Mart's experience and deep pockets? In other words, what kind of competition is Wal-Mart likely to find when it crosses swords directly with Carrefour?

The most important factor in an attractive international business climate is access to a growing market. Two factors help companies determine the growth potential of foreign markets: purchasing power and foreign competitors. Purchasing power is measured by comparing the relative cost of a standard set of goods and services in different countries. The greater the purchasing power in a country, the better the potential business climate, but only if there isn't strong business competition, too. Therefore, the second part of assessing growing global markets is to analyze the degree of global competition, which is determined by the number and quality of companies that already compete in particular foreign markets.

While Wal-Mart's incredible success in the United States gives it the resources and deep pockets that it will need to be successful internationally, Carrefour is its fiercest competitor, period. (Carrefour is currently the largest *international* retailer in the world. Wal-Mart is the largest retailer in the world due to its domestic U.S. sales, not its relatively small international sales.) For example, in Brazil, customers see little difference between the standard goods and prices offered at Wal-Mart and Carrefour. Because Carrefour

has so many stores in South America (and Brazil), its purchasing power with suppliers is as good as, if not better than, Wal-Mart's. Therefore, in Brazil Wal-Mart finds it difficult to gain business by cutting prices. In fact, just hours after Wal-Mart distributes fliers advertising bargains, Carrefour offers the same products for just a few cents less. And because it has been in international markets for years, if not decades, before Wal-Mart, its large number of stores gives Carrefour the capability to match Wal-Mart's prices worldwide. Finally, Carrefour is better at some things. Carrefour's CEO said, "They [Wal-Mart] learn from us in fresh food and merchandising," the latter meaning the attractive display of retail items.

What impact, if any, are free trade agreements likely to have on Wal-Mart's international expansion?

In addition to GATT, the General Agreement on Tariffs and Trade, the second major development in the historic move toward reduction of trade barriers has been the creation of regional trading zones, in which tariff and nontariff barriers are reduced or eliminated for countries within the trading zone.

Today, Wal-Mart has 520 stores, $9 billion (U.S.) in revenues, and $1.1 billion (U.S.) in profits in Mexico. It's fair to say that it wouldn't have achieved this success in Mexico without the advantages of free trade provided by NAFTA. Here's why.

Before NAFTA, in the early 1990s, Wal-Mart had to use expensive middlemen to distribute goods to its stores. Furthermore, it sometimes took months for deliveries to clear customs at the border. Paperwork for imports into Mexico was torturous and burdensome. And Mexican officials often pressured Wal-Mart managers for bribes. All of this is different with NAFTA. Take the example of Act II popcorn, a product that Wal-Mart buys from ConAgra, a company in the United States. Wal-Mart has ConAgra pack the popcorn in Spanish-labelled packages and then ships the popcorn to a Wal-

Mart distribution centre on the Mexican border where it is picked up and taken across the border by a Mexican trucking company hired by Wal-Mart. The next day, the popcorn is on the shelf at Sam's and Wal-Mart stores for the same price that the popcorn costs in the United States. By contrast, Wal-Mart's competitors are still forced to buy Act II popcorn through more expensive Mexican distributors. Or take the example of 29-inch Sony Wegas flat-screen TVs from Japan, which, thanks to a 23 percent tariff (since it was imported from Japan), Wal-Mart sold for $1600 (U.S.) each. However, because of NAFTA, Sony built a new Wegas factory in Mexico, which allows it to ship the TVs duty free anywhere in the United States, Canada, or Mexico. With shipping costs now next to nothing and the 23 percent tariff eliminated, today Wal-Mart sells the 29-inch, flat-screen TVs for $600 (U.S.), or approximately what they sell for in the United States.

Finally, should Wal-Mart focus on global consistency, doing around the world what it does in Canada and the United States, or should it adapt what it sells throughout the world (like Carrefour)?

Global consistency means that when a multinational company has offices, manufacturing plants, and distribution facilities in different countries, it will run those offices, plants, and facilities based on the same rules, guidelines, policies, and procedures. Managers at company headquarters value global consistency, because it simplifies decisions. Local adaptation is a company policy to modify its standard operating procedures to adapt to differences in foreign customers, governments, and regulatory agencies. Local adaptation is typically more important to local managers who are charged with making the international business successful in their countries. Multinational companies struggle to find the correct balance between global consistency and local adaptation. If companies focus too much on local adaptation, they run the risk of losing the cost efficiencies and productivity that result from using standardized rules and procedures throughout the world. If they lean too much toward global consistency, they run the risk of using management procedures poorly suited to particular countries' markets, cultures, and employees.

Early on, Wal-Mart focused too little on local adaptation and too much on global consistency. This was evident in the way in which it ordered store items that its Canadian and U.S. customers would want, but not necessarily what its international customers would want. For example, recall that when Wal-Mart first entered Mexico, it filled its stores with ice skates, riding lawn mowers, fishing tackle, and clay pigeons for skeet shooting. And when Mexican store managers managed to sell all of these items at heavy discounts, Wal-Mart's computerized inventory system compounded the mistake by automatically reordering all of these "sold out" items. Wal-Mart made the same mistake in South America, ordering live trout, cordless tools, and leaf blowers, none of which South Americans use. But Wal-Mart learned to listen to local managers. Consequently, sushi, soccer balls, and feijoada (a mix of beef, pork, and black beans) are now available in its South American stores.

However, because of its vast purchasing power around the world, Wal-Mart hasn't given up completely on global consistency. Why? Franciso Martinez, chief financial officer of Comercial Mexicana SA, Wal-Mart's key rival in Mexico, says, "I buy 20 000 plastic toys, and Wal-Mart buys 20 million. Who do you think gets them cheaper?" So, to systematically take advantage of this purchasing power, Wal-Mart has formed a new global sourcing team of 100 people to buy common global products such as laundry detergent. The risk, of course, is that the global sourcing team may overlook local tastes and preferences. However, if these standard products are accepted by the locals, they'll be much, much cheaper than anything Wal-Mart's competition, even Carrefour, which is one-third Wal-Mart's size, has to offer. For instance, one person on the global sourcing team could buy Tide detergent from Procter & Gamble for all of Wal-Mart's 4000 stores around the world. Jay Allen, a Wal-Mart spokesperson, said, "There are economies of scale all the way around. We want to make sure we're getting the best deal. Global sourcing is a big opportunity for us. [But] we're not there yet."

Sources: W. Boston & A. Zimmerman, "Wal-Mart Girds for Major German Expansion—U.S. Retail Giant to Stress Internal Growth in Push to Add 50 New Stores," *The Wall Street Journal*, 20 July 2000, A21. "Wal-Mart Stores, Inc.: Retailer Expects to Open Six New Stores in China," *The Wall Street Journal*, 4 June 1988, B10. "Wal-Mart Stores Inc.: New Supermarkets Expected to Add 27,000 British Jobs," *The Wall Street Journal*, 11 January 2000. J. Friedland & L. Lee, "Foreign Aisles: The Wal-Mart Way Sometimes Gets Lost in Translation Overseas—Chain Changes Some Tactics to Meet Local Tastes; Competitors Are Tough—But Brazil's 'Market Is Ripe'," *The Wall Street Journal*, 8 October 1997, A1. M. Jordan, "Wal-Mart Gets Aggressive about Brazil—New Neighborhood Store Is Latest Step to Seize Bigger Market Share," *The Wall Street Journal*, 25 May 2001, A8. L. Lee & C. Rohwedder, "Wal-Mart to Acquire German Retailer, Moving into Europe for the First Time," *The Wall Street Journal*, 19 December 1997, A2. D. Luhnow, "Crossover Success: How NAFTA Helped Wal-Mart Reshape the Mexican Market—Lower Tariffs, Retail Muscle Translate into Big Sales; Middlemen Are Squeezed—'Like Shopping in the U.S.'," *The Wall Street Journal*, 31 August 2001, A1. F. McCarthy, "Chimera Wal-Mart Struggles Abroad," *Economist*, 18 May 2000. R. Tomlinson, "Who's Afraid of Wal-Mart? Not Carrefour. The World's Second-Largest Retailer Is Bounding Ahead of the Bentonville Behemoth in Most Markets Outside North America. But Can the French Titan Hold Its Lead?" *Fortune*, 26 June 2000, 186.

Key Terms

Asia-Pacific Economic Cooperation (APEC) (237)

Association of Southeast Asian Nations (ASEAN) (237)

cooperative contract (240)

country of manufacture (232)

country of origin (233)

expatriate (249)

exporting (239)

foreign direct investment (FDI) (230)

franchise (240)

Free Trade Area of the Americas (FTAA) (237)

General Agreement on Tariffs and Trade (GATT) (233)

global business (230)

global new ventures (242)

joint venture (241)

licensing (240)

Maastricht Treaty of Europe (235)

multinational corporation (232)

North American Free Trade Agreement (NAFTA) (236)

national culture (246)

nontariff barriers (233)

policy uncertainty (244)

political uncertainty (244)

protectionism (233)

purchasing power (243)

quota (233)

regional trading zones (235)

strategic alliance (241)

subsidies (234)

tariff (233)

trade barriers (233)

voluntary export restraints (234)

wholly owned affiliates (242)

world gross national product (232)

What Would You Do II?

It is December 2001 in Montreal and snow is in the air and on the ground. Peeking out her window, Estelle Metayer grimaces. She has a 4:00 p.m. appointment in the West Island, and if this day is not different from any other snowy day, Decarie Blvd. will be backed up. Soon, the thoughts of the weather and the short drive give way to reflection upon the past year and the opportunities that lay ahead.

The firm that Metayer founded, Competia (www.competia.com), was entering its fourth year of operation and on track for revenues of a million dollars. In its brief history, this provider of strategic planning and competitive intelligence-related consulting and training services had grown from a one-person outfit to one with seven full-time employees and dozens of freelance relationships around the world. Pleased with its success, Metayer realized, however, that Competia was just skimming the surface of a worldwide market estimated to be in the tens of billions of dollars (U.S.). She also knew that Competia was well positioned to grow.

Metayer and her team had developed a well-integrated package of services that was enticing to senior executives and analysts seeking to make sense of the complexities and uncertainties of the marketplace, as well as the behaviour of customers and competitors. Its four revenue-generating service areas were Competia Online Magazine, an online virtual community, portal, and magazine; Competia Academy, its training arm; Competia Symposium, a series of annual networking conferences; and Competia Consulting, which focused on helping clients develop inhouse strategic planning and intelligence functions.

Thirty percent of its clients were in Europe, 40 percent were in North America, and 30 percent were elsewhere throughout the world. More importantly, however, most of these clients were, or were employed by, Fortune 500 companies. Metayer was especially pleased with the performance of her units in North America. Symposia had been successfully delivered in Quebec City, Ottawa,

and Cape Cod, and an upcoming event was slated for Amsterdam. On the training front, aside from private engagements, Competia events could now be found open to the public on a regular basis in London, New York, Montreal, Toronto, and Calgary. Important for the long-term success of Competia was the complementary nature of each of the offerings. Client attendance at one event often carried over to another. Most importantly, Metayer believed that client awareness of Competia consulting, training, or symposium services would lead to an increased subscriber base for Competia.com, the firm's flagship product, and vice versa.

Competia.com had quickly grown to 125 000 subscribers located around the world. Corporate rates aside, the $109 (U.S.) annual subscription rate made the bundle of services attached to this product affordable to most individual subscribers. For this fee they were offered access to a network of 600 competitive intelligence (CI) professionals to whom they could turn for advice, an online magazine, an online library with over 1000 articles, a catalogue of online industry-specific bookmarks, and a constantly updated database of news and articles on CI and strategic planning.

Despite these successes, Metayer realized that her company had not yet begun to tap the potential of the European market. Over the holidays, her mind would be busy thinking through a number of issues. In particular three stood out. Which organizational options were available to Competia for expanding its presence in the European market? Which factors would be the most important in determining the best European business climate for Competia? **What should Competia do and why?**

Sources: H. Baril, "Unfazed by Risky Future: Comfortable Job Was Not Enough," *The Gazette* (Montreal), 4 January 2002. J. Lee Siew Ming, "High Flying Aptitude: Aviatrix Spreads Wings after Going Solo in the Corporate Field of Competitive Intelligence," *The Gazette* (Montreal), 18 June 2001. J. Block & J. Blossom, "Competia International Symposium," *The Information Advisor* 14, no. 6 (June 2002). Fact Sheet, Competia Academy. [Online] Available www.competia.com, December 2002.

Critical Thinking Video Case

China Toys

How do managers conduct business in foreign markets that are homes to different nationalities, religions, and cultures? The answer is not simple. This chapter offers a few clues. Along with physically being on the ground, managers need to understand trade practices and government regulations, be able to identify potential customers, suppliers, and agents, and be capable of dealing with individuals whose mannerisms and understanding of the world may be completely different from their own.

In this video, you will learn that finding new products for established markets is not always an easy task. The video follows the efforts of Luc Jalbert, a Moncton-based entrepreneur who has identified China as a source for innovative new product offerings. Along with scouting new product prospects at an extremely large trade show in Hong Kong, Jalbert also takes time to visit a manufacturing facility to check up on production of a different imported product. Coupled with this, our Canadian entrepreneur also finds time to look for clones of his star product, a battery Anysizer, and stop in at his trading partner's office to discuss strategy for dealing with a client whose shipments of goods are of poor quality. As you watch the video, consider the following critical thinking question.

Critical Thinking Question

How might insights from Hofstede's research on national cultures help Jalbert succeed in his quests?

Management Decisions

When in China, Negotiate Like the Chinese Do?

You are the chief executive officer of a medium-sized machine manufacturing company in Mississauga, Ontario. Twelve months ago, one of your best customers referred a Chinese manufacturer to you for business. Since then, a delegation of Chinese managers has twice visited your Ontario factory. You, your sales manager, and your plant manager took a ten-day trip to China to visit the Chinese company and to investigate shipping, banking, and customs procedures. After months of preparation, you are ready to begin formal negotiations. In ten days, representatives from your company will meet in Hong Kong with representatives from the Chinese company to negotiate a contract specifying the size, price, and delivery date of what you believe will be the largest overseas shipment your company has ever made.

You're concerned, however, because no one on your team has any experience negotiating with the Chinese, who are patient and skilled negotiators. As you were considering your options, some questions occurred to you.

Questions

1. Should you, the CEO, attend and be part of the negotiations?
2. North Americans and Chinese typically have very different negotiating styles. Since the Chinese are unlikely to adopt a North American style of negotiating, would negotiations go better if your team was prepared to negotiate "Chinese-style"?
3. Your sales manager feels that you should hire a Hong Kong consultant with extensive experience dealing with the Chinese to negotiate for your company. You can see the merit in this, but you also know that "guanxi," or personal relationships, is one of the most important parts of doing business in China. If you hired a Hong Kong consultant to do the negotiations, would you damage the "guanxi" that it has taken you six months to establish?

Sources: S. Lubman, "Round and Round: To Survive Your Business Negotiations, You'll Need Patience, Skill—and Perhaps an Extra Coat," *The Wall Street Journal*, 10 December 1993, R3. I. Matthee, "Accountant Opens Trade Doors: Firm Helps Businesses Gain Access to China," *Seattle Post-Intelligencer*, 3 October 1997, E1. M.A. Sabo & S. Leith, "What West Michigan Wants: A Payoff on the Business Gamble and the Costly Foothold," *The Grand Rapids Press*, 21 June 1998, D1. S.E. Weiss, "Negotiating with 'Romans'— Part 1," *Sloan Management Review*, Winter 1994, 51–61. T. Yeung & L.L. Yeung, "Negotiations in the People's Republic of China: Results of a Survey of Small Businesses in Hong Kong," *Journal of Small Business Management*, 1 January 1995, 70.

Management Decisions

Hearts at Home and Going Native

In the last five years, your company has considerably improved the way in which it prepares employees for international assignments. Except in emergencies, employees are typically given four to five months' notice before being sent abroad. Employees, their spouses, and their families are carefully screened and selected. Moreover, all employees and their families receive two months of extensive language and cultural training before beginning an international assignment. Although these steps have greatly improved the success and performance of your company's expatriates, you're still running into two serious problems.

Problem number one is the expatriate who "goes native." Expatriates who go native are strongly committed to doing what is right for the foreign office, even at the expense of ignoring parent company policy. For example, Gary, a manager who had spent half his 15 years with a company on three different overseas assignments, stated, "My first commitment is to the unit here [in France]. In fact, half the time I feel as if corporate is a competitor I must fight rather than a benevolent parent I can look to for support." While he had only six months remaining on his French assignment, Gary had already asked the home office for an extended stay.

Problem number two is the expatriate whose heart is still at home. Consider Earl, who, after two decades with the parent company, was promoted to managing director of European headquarters. This was Earl's first international assignment.

Consequently, his allegiance was first and foremost to the parent company rather than the European office. In fact, when his two years as managing director are up, he is going straight back home.

Expatriates who go native make it very difficult for companies to achieve global consistency in their operations. Expatriates whose hearts are at home ignore the importance of local adaptation. As one senior manager put it, "How can we get expatriate managers who are committed to the local overseas operation during their international assignments, but who remain loyal to the parent firm?"

Questions

1. What steps would you take to reduce the chances that an expatriate would go native?
2. What steps would you take to reduce the chances that an expatriate would leave his or her heart at home?
3. What steps could be taken to encourage expatriates to develop a dual allegiance to the parent company and the overseas operation?

Sources: J.S. Black, "Serving Two Masters: Managing the Dual Allegiance of Expatriate Employees," *Sloan Management Review,* Summer 1992, 61–71. H.B. Gregersen, "Commitments to a Parent Company and a Local Work Unit during Repatriation," *Personnel Psychology* 45 (1992): 29–54. J. Kaufman, "In China, John Aliberti Gets VIP Treatment; At Home, Grass Grows in the Patio," *The Wall Street Journal,* 19 November 1996, A1.

Develop Your Management Potential

Are You Nationminded or Worldminded?

There are three parts to this assignment:

Step 1: Complete the questionnaire shown below.

Step 2: Determine your score.

Step 3: Develop a plan to increase your global managerial potential.

Step 1

Use the six-point rating scale to complete the questionnaire shown below.

Rating Scale

6	Strongly Agree	3	Mildly Disagree
5	Agree	2	Disagree
4	Mildly Agree	1	Strongly Disagree

_____ 1. Our country should have the right to prohibit certain racial and religious groups from establishing residency here.

_____ 2. Immigrants should not be permitted to come into our country if they compete with our own workers.

_____ 3. It would be a dangerous procedure if every person in the world had equal rights which were guaranteed by an international charter.

_____ 4. All prices for exported food and manufactured goods should be set by an international trade committee.

_____ 5. Our country is probably no better than many others.

_____ 6. Race prejudice may be a good thing for us because it keeps many undesirable foreigners from coming into this country.

_____ 7. It would be a mistake for us to encourage certain racial groups to become well educated because they might use their knowledge against us.

_____ 8. We should be willing to fight for our country without questioning whether it is right or wrong.

_____ 9. Foreigners are particularly obnoxious because of their religious beliefs.

_____10. Immigration should be controlled by a global organization rather than by each country on its own.

_____11. We ought to have a world government to guarantee the welfare of all nations irrespective of the rights of any one.

_____12. Our country should not cooperate in any global trade agreements which attempt to better world economic conditions at our expense.

_____13. It would be better to be a citizen of the world than of any particular country.

_____14. Our responsibility to people of other races ought to be as great as our responsibility to people of our own race.

_____15. A global committee on education should have full control over what is taught in all countries about history and politics.

_____16. Our country should refuse to cooperate in a total disarmament program even if some other nations agree to it.

_____17. It would be dangerous for our country to make international agreements with nations whose religious beliefs are antagonistic to ours.

_____18. Any healthy individual, regardless of race or religion, should be allowed to live wherever he or she wants to in the world.

_____19. Our country should not participate in any global organization which requires that we give up any of our national rights or freedom of action.

_____20. If necessary, we ought to be willing to lower our standard of living to cooperate with other countries in getting an equal standard for every person in the world.

_____21. We should strive for loyalty to our country before we can afford to consider world brotherhood.

_____22. Some races ought to be considered naturally less intelligent than ours.

_____23. Our schools should teach the history of the whole world rather than of our own country.

_____24. A global police force ought to be the only group in the world allowed to have armaments.

_____25. It would be dangerous for us to guarantee by international agreement that every person in the world should have complete religious freedom.

_____26. Our country should permit the immigration of foreign peoples even if it lowers our standard of living.

_____27. All national governments ought to be abolished and replaced by one central world government.

_____28. It would not be wise for us to agree that working conditions in all countries should be subject to international control.

_____29. Patriotism should be a primary aim of education so our children will believe our country is the best in the world.

_____30. It would be a good idea if all the races were to intermarry until there was only one race in the world.

_____31. We should teach our children to uphold the welfare of all people everywhere even though it may be against the best interests of our own country.

_____32. War should never be justifiable even if it is the only way to protect our national rights and honour.

Step 2

Determine your score by entering your response to each survey item below, as follows. In blanks that say regular scoring, simply enter your response for that item. If your response was a 4, place a 4 in the regular scoring blank. In blanks that say reverse scoring, subtract your response from 6 and enter the result. So if your response was a 4, place a 2 (6 − 4 = 2) in the reverse scoring blank.

1. reverse score _____	17. reverse score _____
2. reverse score _____	18. regular score _____
3. reverse score _____	19. reverse score _____
4. regular score _____	20. regular score _____
5. regular score _____	21. reverse score _____
6. reverse score _____	22. reverse score _____
7. reverse score _____	23. regular score _____
8. reverse score _____	24. regular score _____
9. reverse score _____	25. reverse score _____
10. regular score _____	26. regular score _____
11. regular score _____	27. regular score _____
12. reverse score _____	28. reverse score _____
13. regular score _____	29. reverse score _____
14. regular score _____	30. regular score _____
15. regular score _____	31. regular score _____
16. reverse score _____	32. regular score _____

Total your scores from items 1–16 _____
Total your scores from items 17–32 _____
Add together to compute total score _____
Higher scores show greater worldmindedness.

Step 3

Develop a plan to increase your global managerial potential.

People don't change from being nationminded to worldminded overnight. Below you'll find the outlines of a plan to increase your worldmindedness. You need to fill in the details to make it work. This plan is based on foreign languages, living overseas, global news and television, and your openness to the different cultural experiences available right where you live!

3A. Language. How many languages do you speak fluently? Develop a plan to become fluent in another language. Specify the courses you would need to take to become conversationally fluent. A minimum of two years is recommended. Even better is minoring in a language! What courses would you have to take to complete a minor?

3B. *Living overseas.* Develop a plan to study overseas. List the facts for two different overseas study programs available at your university or another university. Be sure to specify how long the program lasts, whether you would receive language training, where you would live, the activities in which you would participate, and any other important details.

3C. *Global news and television.* Another way to increase your worldmindedness is to increase the diversity of your news sources. Most Canadians get their news from local TV and radio, or from the major networks, CBC, CTV, and Global. Luckily, you don't have to leave the country to gain access to foreign news sources. Furthermore, you don't have to speak a foreign language. Many foreign newspapers and television and radio shows are presented in English. List the foreign newspapers and television and radio shows available to you where you live. Hint: Check your university library, CNN, CBC, and the Internet. Be sure to indicate where you can find the newspapers, the day and time the shows are on, and whether the newspapers or TV shows are in English or a foreign language.

3D. *Local cultural experiences.* Many students wrongly assume that they have to travel overseas to gain exposure to foreign cultures. Fortunately, many Canadian cities and universities are rich in such experiences. Ethnic neighbourhoods, restaurants, festivals, foreign films, and art displays, along with other Canadians who continue to live and celebrate their heritage, present ample opportunities to sample and learn about foreign cultures right here in our own backyards. Specify a plan of foreign restaurants, ethnic neighbourhoods, and cultural events that you could attend this year.

Sources: R.W. Boater, "Study Abroad: Impact on Student Worldmindedness," *Journal of Teaching in International Business* 2, no. 2 (1990):17–13. R.W. Boater, "Worldminded Attitude Change in a Study Abroad Program: Contact and Content Issues," *Journal of Teaching in International Business* 3, no. 4 (1992): 59–68. H. Lancaster, "Learning to Manage in a Global Workplace (You're on Your Own)," *The Wall Street Journal*, 2 June 1998, B1. D.L. Sampson & H.P. Smith, "A Scale to Measure Worldminded Attitudes," *Journal of Social Psychology* 45, 1957, 99–106.

Discussion Questions

1. Explain what is meant by trade barriers and identify two general kinds of trade barriers used by government.
2. IBM, Microsoft, Sony, and Nokia are examples of companies that operate and sell products around the world. How they sell their products and services often differs from country to country. Yet surprisingly, they often standardize their basic business procedures regardless of location. Why do they do this?
3. Briefly explain the phase model of globalization and list its stages in the appropriate order.
4. Convi Ltd. is a small Nova Scotia exporter of apple products including jams, sauces, and dried fruit. Recently, its CEO has been considering the potential of Sweden as a market for its products. Faced with limited human resources, she has asked your firm to prepare a consulting report to determine the growth potential of this market. How will you and your colleagues assess this new market opportunity for her?
5. Japan is an important market for Canadian firms that sell mineral sands products. You work in the Montreal offices of one of these firms. A request has come from your firm's Tokyo office asking for another employee to be hired to aid in the sales effort in Asia. The immediate reaction of a number of your colleagues is to question the need for a new body and to wonder aloud about what is so different about selling in Japan. Sympathising with your colleague in Japan, you suggest that he might prepare a brief presentation regarding the differences in national culture for his trip to Montreal in the upcoming weeks. You agree to help him and offer to send by e-mail a brief discussion of the five dimensions that one might use to differentiate one national culture from another. What will you put in the e-mail message?

Study Tip

Take advantage of all the review opportunities on the *Management* website at www.management1e.nelson.com. Write up a list of questions you have about concepts you don't understand and visit your professor or TA during office hours.

Chapter Outline

Learning Objectives

After reading this chapter, you should be able to

1. explain the components of sustainable competitive advantage and why it is important.
2. describe the steps involved in the strategy-making process.
3. explain the different kinds of corporate-level strategies.
4. describe the different kinds of industry-level strategies.
5. explain the components and kinds of firm-level strategies.

nine

Organizational Strategy

What Would You Do?

Sobeys Inc.: Up until a few years ago, few Canadians outside of Atlantic Canada had heard the name. Then in 1998, this $3-billion regional grocery retailer and food-service company bought the Oshawa Group Limited, an $8-billion company. This acquisition made Sobeys one of only two national food distributors with retail and food-service presence in all 10 provinces and the territories. Sobeys is now a public company (TSX:SBY) whose stock is controlled by Empire Company Limited (TSX:EMP.A), which owns 64.5 percent of the outstanding shares.

Its history is typical of many companies that started small and then grew slowly over time. It took root in 1907, when J.W. Sobey opened a meat delivery business in Stellarton, Nova Scotia. By 1947, the Sobeys chain had opened its first modern supermarket in Nova Scotia, followed two years later by the very first all-cash, self-serve supermarket. After 80 years in business, in 1987, Sobeys achieved sales of over $1 billion for the first time. That same year, the first Sobeys store in Ontario opened in Guelph. Expansion continued through the early 1990s in Ontario and Quebec, where Sobeys stores had been a fixture in the Gaspé region since the mid-1960s.

The year 1998 was a turning point in more ways than one. Along with the prominence and market reach associated with being a national player, Sobeys faced the daunting task of addressing, over a relatively short period of time, a number of integration and optimization opportunities resulting from the Oshawa Group acquisition that would ultimately determine its long-term success. These challenges would require the focus of Sobeys' management team in the period immediately following the acquisition. They began with the varied group of stores (called banners) falling under the headings of Sobeys and the Oshawa Group; the great variety made consumer brand identification difficult at best. Inherited from Oshawa Group were Garden Market IGA, IGA Extra, Price Chopper, Marché Bonichoix, Les Marchés Tradition, and Knechtel banners. From Sobeys were banners such as Lo-Food, Foodland, Sobeys, Needs, Green Gables, Kwik-Way, Riteway, and Clover Farm and Lawtons, the latter a pharmacy chain.

Not surprisingly, the acquisition had also affected Sobeys' operating cash flow, leaving it below that of its two major Canadian competitors, Metro and Loblaws. If this was not enough, Sobeys experienced IT-related problems. Prior to the acquisition, Sobeys recognized the need for improved understanding of its cost structure. In response to this concern, it began implementation of company-wide management information software released by a company called SAP. In the fall of 2000, the SAP program, which had been installed at 15 percent of the stores, crashed, leading to an abandonment of its national rollout. The result was a large financial write-down that had an impact on the company's credibility with many Canadian securities analysts.

Although Sobeys is now the national leader measured by the number of stores operated, its major competitor, Loblaws, was by far the market share leader at 30 percent of the market. With only 12 percent of the market, Sobeys would also have to pay attention to the aspirations and behaviour of Safeway and Metro, whose market shares were 7.4 percent and 6.5 percent respectively. Unfortunately, aside from internally generated slow growth, Sobeys prospects for another quick jump in Canadian market share were not that bright. Potential acquisition candidates were few and far between. The major candidates included A&P Canada, Safeway Canada, and Overwaitea. Only Overwaitea, situated in western Canada, was rumoured to be for sale but unfortunately, its asking price was high.

Along with cost, IT, and market share concerns, Sobeys also had a portfolio of stores that, competitively speaking, were not necessarily optimal in size and operation. On average, the size of the stores in Sobeys overall portfolio were small, averaging only 12 000 square feet. In comparison, its corporate-owned (as opposed to franchise) stores and those of many of its competitors ranged from 40 000 to 55 000 square feet. This suggested a need for ongoing investment to increase the size of the stores. Further, of the stores acquired from the Oshawa Group, most were underperforming and suffering from a lack of capital investment for years. Unfortunately, the physical shortcomings of many of these stores also had dire consequences for merchandising operations.

While Sobeys addressed these operational concerns throughout the late 90s and early in the new century, it soon faced worries of a different nature. Commencing in early 2001, a poor economy, coupled with a recession in the United States, served to slow consumer spending south of the border. This along with rising unemployment, a discouraging job outlook, and weak holiday retail sales left many consumers pessimistic. The question for the Sobeys senior management team was whether these effects would cross into Canada and result in a similar phenomenon of same-store sales reductions and missed sales estimates. In early 2002, a new force emerged on the grocery scene in the form of entrants such as Wal-Mart. The result was a series of price wars as established retailers sought to protect their market shares from erosion. Finally, the continued downturn in the stock market had a negative impact on personal spending habits. Budget-conscious shoppers were looking for all the bargains they could get. Lower-priced no-name or private-label items continued to appeal to customers in some food segments.

With these challenges in mind, if you were the CEO of Sobeys, what would you do?

Sources: Bill McEwan, remarks to the St. John's Board of Trade, December 4, 2002, St. John's, Newfoundland. Christina Veiders, "Investors Cautious Following Share Price Slides," *Supermarket News*, 13 January 2003. Elliot Zwiebach, "Sobeys Meets Half Year Goals in 2nd Quarter," *Supermarket News* 16 December 2002. Elliot Zwiebach, "Sobeys Goes National," *Supermarket News*, 4 February 2002. Building Sustainable Worth, A presentation to CIBC World Markets, 15 January 2003.

In Chapter 4, you learned that strategic plans are overall company plans that clarify how a company intends to serve customers and position itself against competitors over the next two to five years. Picking the wrong strategic plan can have devastating consequences. This chapter begins with an in-depth look at how managers create and use strategies to obtain a sustainable competitive advantage. Then you will learn the three steps of the strategy-making process. Next, you will learn about corporate-level strategies that help managers answer the question: What business or businesses should we be in? You will then examine the industry-level competitive strategies that help managers determine how to compete successfully within a particular line of business. The chapter finishes with a review of the firm-level strategies of direct competition and entrepreneurship.

Basics of Organizational Strategy

Strategy is a term used frequently when discussing the behaviour of corporations. Unfortunately it occasionally suffers from overuse and often the term is not well understood. Even when conceived by the brightest of minds, strategies often fail. The reasons for this are that strategies are carried out within competitive environments, are designed by humans and thus subject to our own inherent frailties, can occur at different levels and take different forms. Efforts to improve the effectiveness of strategies will most often include planning. Planning helps to reduce uncertainty, thus increasing the probability that an implemented strategy will be successful. Planning, as you may recall, was the subject of Chapter 4. Strategy is the subject of this chapter.

After reading the next two sections, you should be able to
1. *explain the components of sustainable competitive advantage and why it is important.*
2. *describe the steps involved in the strategy-making process.*

1. Sustainable Competitive Advantage

An organization's **resources** are the assets, capabilities, processes, information, and knowledge that the organization controls. Firms use their resources to improve organizational effectiveness and efficiency. Resources are critical to organizational strategy because they can help companies create and sustain an advantage over competitors.[1]

Organizations can achieve a **competitive advantage** by using their resources to provide greater value for customers than competitors can. A competitive advantage becomes a **sustainable competitive advantage** when other companies cannot duplicate the value a firm is providing to customers. Importantly, sustainable competitive advantage is not the same as a long-lasting competitive advantage, though companies obviously want a competitive advantage to last a long time. Instead, a competitive advantage is sustained if that advantage still exists after competitors have tried unsuccessfully to duplicate the advantage and have, for the moment, stopped trying to duplicate it.

Four conditions must be met if a firm's resources are to be used to achieve a sustainable competitive advantage. The resources must be valuable, rare, imperfectly imitable, and nonsubstitutable.

Valuable resources allow companies to improve their efficiency and effectiveness. Unfortunately, changes in customer demand and preferences, competitors' actions, and technology can make once-valuable resources much less valuable. For sustained competitive advantage, valuable resources must also be rare resources. Think about it. How can a company sustain a competitive advantage if all of its competitors have similar resources and capabilities? Consequently, **rare resources**, resources that are not controlled or possessed by many competing firms, are necessary to sustain a competitive advantage. For sustained competitive advantage, other firms must be unable to imitate or find substitutes for those valuable, rare resources. **Imperfectly imitable resources** are impossible or extremely costly or difficult to duplicate. Finally, valuable, rare, imperfectly imitable resources can produce sustainable competitive advantage only if they are also **nonsubstitutable resources**, meaning that no other resources can replace them and produce similar value or competitive advantage.

Review 1
Sustainable Competitive Advantage

Firms can use their resources to create and sustain a competitive advantage, that is, to provide greater value for customers than competitors can. A competitive advantage becomes sustainable when other companies cannot duplicate the benefits it provides and have, for now, stopped trying. To provide a sustainable competitive advantage, the firm's resources must be valuable (capable of improving efficiency and effectiveness), rare (not possessed by many competing firms), imperfectly imitable (extremely costly or difficult to duplicate), and nonsubstitutable (competitors cannot substitute other resources to produce similar value).

2. Strategy-Making Process

Companies use a strategy-making process to create strategies that produce sustainable competitive advantage.[2] Exhibit 9.1 displays the three steps of the strategy-making process.

The three steps of the strategy-making process are listed below. Let's examine each of these steps in more detail: assessing the need for strategic change, situational analysis, and choosing strategic alternatives.

---

resources
the assets, capabilities, processes, information, and knowledge that an organization uses to improve its effectiveness and efficiency and to create and sustain an advantage over competitors

competitive advantage
providing greater value for customers than competitors can

sustainable competitive advantage
a competitive advantage that other companies have tried unsuccessfully to duplicate and have, for the moment, stopped trying to duplicate

valuable resource
a resource that allows companies to improve efficiency and effectiveness

rare resource
a resource that is not controlled or possessed by many competing firms

imperfectly imitable resource
a resource that is impossible or extremely costly or difficult for other firms to duplicate

nonsubstitutable resource
a resource, without equivalent substitutes or replacements, that produces value or competitive advantage

EXHIBIT 9.1

THREE STEPS OF THE STRATEGY-MAKING PROCESS

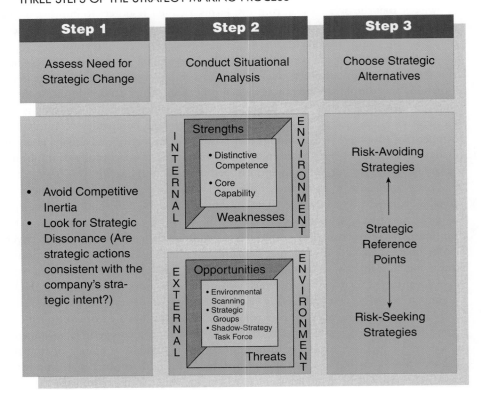

Step 1	Step 2	Step 3
Assess Need for Strategic Change	Conduct Situational Analysis	Choose Strategic Alternatives

Step 1
- Avoid Competitive Inertia
- Look for Strategic Dissonance (Are strategic actions consistent with the company's strategic intent?)

Step 2

INTERNAL ENVIRONMENT

Strengths
- Distinctive Competence
- Core Capability

Weaknesses

EXTERNAL ENVIRONMENT

Opportunities
- Environmental Scanning
- Strategic Groups
- Shadow-Strategy Task Force

Threats

Step 3

Risk-Avoiding Strategies

↑

Strategic Reference Points

↓

Risk-Seeking Strategies

Sobeys is an Atlantic Canadian success story. Originating as a small operation in Stellarton, Nova Scotia, it has grown to be the second largest grocery chain in the country.

Brian Pieters Photography

WhatReallyWorks

Strategy-Making for Firms, Big *and* Small

The strategy-making process (assessing the need for strategic change, conducting a situational analysis, and choosing strategic alternatives) is the method by which companies create strategies that produce sustainable competitive advantage. For years, it had been thought that strategy-making was something that only large firms could do well. It was believed that small firms did not have the time, knowledge, or staff to do a good job of strategy-making. However, two meta-analyses indicate that strategy-making can improve the profits, sales growth, and return on investment of both big and small firms.

Strategy-Making for Big Firms

There is a 72 percent chance that big companies that engage in the strategy-making process will be more profitable than big companies that don't. However, strategy-making not only improves profits, but also helps companies grow. Specifically, there is a 75 percent chance that big companies that engage in the strategy-making process will have greater sales and earnings growth than big companies that don't. Thus, in practical terms, the strategy-making process can make a significant difference in a big company's profits and growth.

Strategic Planning & Profits for Big Companies

Strategic Planning & Growth for Big Companies

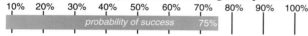

Strategy-Making for Small Firms

However, strategy-making can also improve the performance of small firms. There is a 61 percent chance that small firms that engage in the strategy-making process will have more sales growth than small firms that don't. Likewise, there is a 62 percent chance that small firms that engage in the strategy-making process will have a larger return on investment than small companies that don't. Thus, in practical terms, the strategy-making process can make a significant difference in a small company's profits and growth, too.

Strategic Planning & Sales Growth for Small Companies

Strategic Planning & Return on Investment for Small Companies

Sources: S. Hart & C. Banbury, "How Strategy-Making Processes Can Make a Difference," *Strategic Management Journal* 15 (1994): 251–269. C.C. Miller & L.B. Cardinal, "Strategic Planning and Firm Performance: A Synthesis of More Than Two Decades of Research," *Academy of Management Journal* 37 (1994): 1649–1665. C.R. Schwenk, "Effects of Formal Strategic Planning on Financial Performance in Small Firms: A Meta-Analysis," *Entrepreneurship Theory and Practice*, Spring 1993, 53–64.

2.1 Assessing the Need for Strategic Change

The external business environment is much more turbulent than it used to be. With customers' needs constantly growing and changing, and with competitors working harder, faster, and smarter to meet those needs, the first step in strategy-making is determining the need for strategic change. In other words, the company needs to determine whether or not it needs to change its strategy to sustain a competitive advantage.[3]

It might seem that determining the need for strategic change would be easy to do, but in reality, it's not. There's a great deal of uncertainty in strategic business environments. Furthermore, top-level managers are often slow to recognize the need for strategic change, especially at successful companies that have created and sustained competitive advantages. Because they are acutely aware of the strategies that made their companies successful, they continue to rely on them, even as the competition changes. In other words, success often leads to **competitive inertia**—a reluctance to change strategies or competitive practices that have been successful in the past.

For example, just a few years ago, no one in the cable TV industry believed that direct broadcast satellite dishes would threaten their business. With huge satellite dishes costing over $1000, why would the millions of Canadians who already had

competitive inertia
a reluctance to change strategies or competitive practices that have been successful in the past

cable TV in their homes pay more than $1500 to install an unsightly ten-foot-diameter satellite dish in their yard to get the same number of channels that they could get from their local cable company for an installation fee of less than $100 and a moderate monthly charge? Managers of cable TV companies would laugh that "DBS" (direct broadcast satellite) really stood for "Don't Be Stupid." However, now that satellite dishes are smaller (two feet in diameter), cost less than $200, and offer 200 channels compared to the 60 or fewer channels available on most cable systems, no one who manages a cable company is laughing anymore. Indeed, the number of subscribers to satellite TV service providers such as Bell ExpressVu and Star Choice is predicted to increase dramatically in the next few years.[4]

So, besides being aware of the dangers of competitive inertia, what can managers do to improve the speed and accuracy with which they determine the need for strategic change? One method is to actively look for signs of strategic dissonance. **Strategic dissonance** is a discrepancy between upper management's intended strategy and the strategy actually implemented by the lower levels of management. Upper management sets overall company strategy, but middle and lower-level managers must carry out the strategy. Middle and lower-level managers are held directly responsible for meeting customers' needs and responding to competitors' actions. While strategic dissonance can indicate that these managers are not doing what they should to carry out company strategy, it can also mean that the intended strategy is out of date and needs to be changed.

2.2 Situational Analysis

A situational analysis can also help managers determine the need for strategic change. A **situational analysis**, also called a **SWOT analysis** for *strengths, weaknesses, opportunities,* and *threats,* is an assessment of the strengths and weaknesses in an organization's internal environment and the opportunities and threats in its external environment.[5] Ideally a SWOT analysis helps a company determine how to increase internal strengths and minimize internal weaknesses while simultaneously maximizing external opportunities and minimizing external threats. However, a basic situational analysis of Apple Computer (www.apple.com) shows this is not always easy to do. One of Apple's strengths used to be that its computers were much easier to learn and use than others on the market. Indeed, millions of customers were willing to pay much more for an Apple because this was so. However, there have been key changes in Apple's external environment. One of the most important was the introduction of Microsoft's Windows 95 (followed by Windows 98) software, which made IBM-compatible computers much easier to use. Consequently, Apple's strength, coupled with the much higher prices that Apple charged for its computers, eventually became a tremendous weakness. The result: Apple's share of the personal computer market plummeted from 16 percent to 4 percent in less than three years.[6]

As Apple's experience shows, competitive advantages can erode over time if internal strengths eventually become weaknesses. Consequently, an analysis of an organization's internal environment, that is, a company's strengths and weaknesses, begins with an assessment of distinctive competencies and core capabilities. A **distinctive competence** is something that a company can make, do, or perform better than its competitors. For example, *Consumer Reports* magazine (www.consumerreports.org) consistently ranks Toyota cars number one in quality and reliability.

While distinctive competencies are tangible—for example, a product or service is faster, cheaper, or better—the core capabilities that produce distinctive competencies are not. **Core capabilities** are the less visible, internal decision-making routines, problem-solving processes, and organizational cultures that determine how efficiently inputs can be turned into outputs.[7] Distinctive competencies cannot be sustained for long without superior core capabilities.

strategic dissonance
a discrepancy between upper management's intended strategy and the strategy actually implemented by lower levels of management

situational (SWOT) analysis
an assessment of the strengths and weaknesses in an organization's internal environment and the opportunities and threats in its external environment

EXPERIENCING MANAGEMENT

Gain additional insight about situational analysis at our animated concept and activity site. Choose Planning & Strategic Processes from the "select a topic" pull-down menu, then Strategic Situational Analysis from the "overview tab."

www.experiencingmanagement.com

distinctive competence
what a company can make, do, or perform better than competitors

core capabilities
the internal decision-making routines, problem-solving processes, and organizational cultures that determine how efficiently inputs can be turned into outputs

After examining internal strengths and weaknesses, the second part of a situational analysis is to look outside the company and assess the opportunities and threats in the external environment. In Chapter 2, you learned that environmental scanning is searching the environment for important events or issues that might affect the organization. With environmental scanning, managers usually scan the environment to stay up to date on important factors in their environment, such as pricing trends and changes in technology in the industry. However, in a situational analysis, managers use environmental scanning to identify specific opportunities and threats that can either improve or harm the company's ability to sustain its competitive advantage. Identification of strategic groups and formation of shadow-strategy task forces are two ways to do this.

Strategic groups are not "actual" groups, but are selected for study by managers. A strategic group is a group of other companies within an industry that top managers choose for comparing, evaluating, and benchmarking their company's strategic threats and opportunities.[8] Typically, managers include companies as part of their strategic group if they compete directly with those companies for customers or if those companies use strategies similar to theirs. For example, it's likely that the managers at CanWest Global, the largest Canadian newspaper publisher (over 30 daily newspapers, including the *National Post*, the *Montreal Gazette*, the *Calgary Herald*, and the *Ottawa Citizen*), assess strategic threats and opportunities by comparing themselves to a strategic group consisting of the other major newspaper companies. This would probably include Quebecor Inc. through its Sun Media subsidiary (the *Toronto Sun*, the *Calgary Sun*, the *Ottawa Sun*, and many other newspapers), BellGlobe Media (the *Globe and Mail*), and Torstar Corporation (the *Toronto Star*). Indeed, CanWest links its newspapers together online through the Canada.com website (www.canada.com) while the Sun Media papers may be found by browsing the Canoe.ca site (www.canoe.ca). By contrast, given that millions of Canadians read CanWest publications, it's unlikely that its management worries much about student newspapers such as the *McGill Daily* or Acadia University's *The Atheneum*. The *McGill Daily* is a fine paper, but with a total circulation of less than 5000, mostly within the McGill University community, managers at CanWest would probably not include it in their strategic group.

In fact, when scanning the environment for strategic threats and opportunities, managers tend to categorize the different companies in their industries into core and secondary strategic groups.[9] The first kind of strategic group consists of **core firms**, that is, central companies in a strategic group. CanWest's core firms would be Quebecor Media and BellGlobe Media. When most managers scan their environments for strategic threats and opportunities, they do so by primarily scanning the strategic actions of core firms. **Secondary firms** are firms that use related but somewhat different strategies from core firms. For CanWest, this might be Torstar, which publishes the *Toronto Star* and other daily newspapers. However, Torstar is somewhat different, in that it is also a book publisher with little presence in the television market; CanWest, BellGlobe Media, and Quebecor Media all own and operate television stations. Managers are aware of the potential threats and opportunities posed by secondary firms. However, they spend more time assessing the threats and opportunities associated with core firms.

Because top managers tend to limit their attention to the core firms in their strategic group, some companies have started using shadow-strategy task forces to more aggressively scan their environments for strategic threats and opportunities. The goal of a **shadow-strategy task force** is to actively seek out its own company's weaknesses and then, thinking like a competitor, determine how other companies could exploit them for competitive advantage.[10] Furthermore, to make sure that the task force challenges conventional thinking, its members should be independent-minded, come from a variety of company functions and levels, and have the access and authority to question the company's current strategic actions and intent. An interesting example relates to a manufacturer of pharmaceutical drugs, agricultural chemicals, plastics, pigments, and additives that had a large operation in Canada—Ciba-Geigy. Its industrial chemicals division

strategic group
a group of companies within an industry that top managers choose to compare, evaluate, and benchmark strategic threats and opportunities

core firms
the central companies in a strategic group

secondary firms
the firms in a strategic group that follow related but somewhat different strategies than do the core firms

shadow-strategy task force
a committee within the company that analyzes the company's own weaknesses to determine how competitors could exploit them for competitive advantage

made dyes used in carpet manufacturing. One of the difficulties in this business is ensuring colour consistency, that is, making sure that the dark grey carpet manufactured today looks the same colour as the dark grey carpet manufactured next week. Ciba-Geigy's shadow-strategy task force determined that if its competitors could find ways to consistently, precisely, and cheaply match colour carpet dyes (so that carpet colours looked the same regardless of when and where they were manufactured), Ciba-Geigy would be at a considerable competitive disadvantage. After the shadow-strategy task force challenged top management with its conclusions, the company went about developing distinctive competencies in dye research and manufacturing, which allowed it to make dyes with scientific preciseness.[11]

In short, there are two basic parts to a situational analysis. The first is to examine internal strengths and weaknesses by focusing on distinctive competencies and core capabilities. The second is to examine external opportunities and threats by focusing on environmental scanning, strategic groups, and shadow-strategy task forces.

2.3 Choosing Strategic Alternatives

After determining the need for strategic change and conducting a situational analysis, the last step in the strategy-making process is to choose strategic alternatives that will help the company create or maintain a sustainable competitive advantage. According to Strategic Reference Point Theory, managers choose between two basic alternative strategies. They can choose a conservative, risk-avoiding strategy that aims to protect an existing competitive advantage. Or they can choose an aggressive, risk-seeking strategy that aims to extend or create a sustainable competitive advantage.

The choice to be risk-seeking or risk-avoiding typically depends on whether top management views the company as falling above or below strategic reference points. **Strategic reference points** are the targets that managers use to measure whether their firms have developed the core competencies that they need to achieve a sustainable competitive advantage. For example, if a hotel chain decided to compete by providing superior quality and service, then top management would track the success of this strategy through customer surveys or published hotel ratings, such as those provided by the prestigious Mobil Travel Guide (http://exxonmobiltravel.com). By contrast, if a hotel chain decided to compete on price, it would regularly conduct market surveys that checked the prices of other hotels. The competitors' prices are the hotel managers' strategic reference points against which to compare their own pricing strategy. If competitors can consistently underprice them, then the managers need to determine whether their staff and resources have the core competencies to compete on price.

As shown in Exhibit 9.2, when companies are performing above or better than their strategic reference points, top management will typically be satisfied with company strategy. Ironically, this satisfaction tends to make top management conservative and risk-averse. After all, since the company already has a sustainable competitive advantage, the worst thing that could happen would be to lose it. Consequently, new issues or changes in the company's external environments are viewed as threats. But when companies are performing below or worse than their strategic reference points, top management will typically be dissatisfied with company strategy. However, in this instance, managers are much more likely to choose a daring, risk-taking strategy. After all, if the current strategy is producing substandard results, what does the company have to lose by switching to risky new strategies in the hopes that it can create a sustainable competitive advantage? Consequently, for companies in this situation, new issues or changes in external environments are viewed as opportunities for potential gain.

However, Strategic Reference Point Theory is not deterministic. Managers are not predestined to choose risk-averse or risk-seeking strategies for their companies. Indeed, one of the most important points in Strategic Reference Point Theory is that managers can influence the strategies chosen at their companies by actively changing and adjusting the strategic reference points they use to judge strategic performance. To illustrate, if a

strategic reference points
the strategic targets managers use to measure whether a firm has developed the core competencies it needs to achieve a sustainable competitive advantage

EXHIBIT 9.2

STRATEGIC REFERENCE POINTS

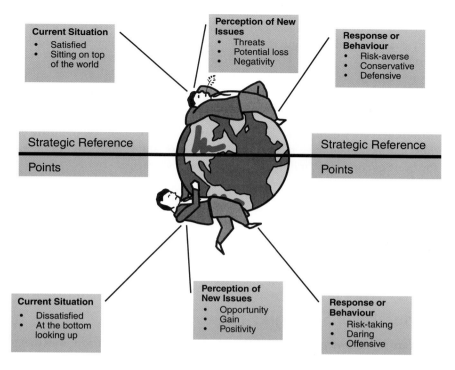

Current Situation
- Satisfied
- Sitting on top of the world

Perception of New Issues
- Threats
- Potential loss
- Negativity

Response or Behaviour
- Risk-averse
- Conservative
- Defensive

Strategic Reference Points

Strategic Reference Points

Current Situation
- Dissatisfied
- At the bottom looking up

Perception of New Issues
- Opportunity
- Gain
- Positivity

Response or Behaviour
- Risk-taking
- Daring
- Offensive

Source: A. Fiegenbaum, S. Hart, & D. Schendel, "Strategic Reference Point Theory," *Strategic Management Journal* 17 (1996): 219–235.

company has become complacent after consistently surpassing its strategic reference points, then top management can change the company's strategic risk orientation from risk-averse to risk-taking by raising the standards of performance (i.e., strategic reference points).

So even when (perhaps especially when) companies have achieved a sustainable competitive advantage, top managers may adjust or change strategic reference points to challenge themselves and their employees to develop new core competencies for the future. In the long run, effective organizations will frequently revise their strategic reference points to better focus managers' attention on the new challenges and opportunities that occur in their ever-changing business environments.

Review 2
Strategy-Making Process

The first step in strategy-making is determining whether a strategy needs to be changed in order to sustain a competitive advantage. Because uncertainty and competitive inertia make this difficult to determine, managers can improve the speed and accuracy of this step by looking for differences between top management's intended strategy and the strategy actually implemented by lower-level managers (i.e., strategic dissonance). The second step is to conduct a situational analysis that examines internal strengths and weaknesses (distinctive competencies and core capabilities), as well as external threats and opportunities (environmental scanning, strategic groups, and shadow-strategy task

PERSONAL PRODUCTIVITY

To Which Party Do You Belong?

One of the most difficult steps in strategy-making is getting top managers to recognize the need for strategic change. Professor Gary Hamel advises senior executives to answer two questions. First, over time, have they become more or less willing to challenge conventional thinking about their business? Second, have they become more or less curious about the changes taking place outside their industry? Ralph Waldo Emerson wrote, "There are always two parties, the party of the past and the party of the future; the establishment and the movement." Hamel, paraphrasing Emerson, asks top managers, "To which party do you belong? The past or the future?"

Source: G. Hamel, "Strategy as Revolution," *Harvard Business Review*, July-August 1996, 69–82.

forces). In the third step of strategy-making, Strategic Reference Point Theory suggests that when companies are performing better than their strategic reference points, top management will typically choose a risk-averse strategy. When performance is below strategic reference points, risk-seeking strategies are more likely to be chosen. Importantly, however, managers can influence the choice of strategic alternatives by actively changing and adjusting the strategic reference points they use to judge strategic performance.

Corporate-, Industry-, and Firm-Level Strategies

What business are we in? How should we compete in this industry? Who are our competitors and how should we respond to them? These simple but powerful questions are at the heart of corporate-, industry-, and firm-level strategies.

After reading the next three sections, you should be able to
3. explain the different kinds of corporate-level strategies.
4. describe the different kinds of industry-level strategies.
5. explain the components and kinds of firm-level strategies.

Exhibit 9.3 provides an overview of the various corporate-, industry-, and firm-level strategies that you'll learn about in these sections.

3. Corporate-Level Strategies

corporate-level strategy
the overall organizational strategy that addresses the question "What business or businesses are we in or should we be in?"

Corporate-level strategy is the overall organizational strategy that addresses the question "What business or businesses are we in or should we be in?"

Let's learn more about how companies decide which businesses they should be in by examining the two major approaches to corporate-level strategy: portfolio strategy and grand strategies.

3.1 Portfolio Strategy[12]

diversification
a strategy for reducing risk by buying a variety of items (stocks or, in the case of a corporation, types of businesses), so that the failure of one stock or one business does not doom the entire portfolio

One of the standard strategies for stock market investors is **diversification**: buy stocks in a variety of companies in different industries. The purpose of this strategy is to reduce risk in the overall stock portfolio (i.e., the entire collection of stocks). The basic idea is simple: If you invest in ten companies in ten different industries, you won't lose your entire investment if one company performs poorly. Furthermore, because they're in different industries, one company's losses are likely to be offset by another company's gains. Portfolio strategy is based on these same ideas.

portfolio strategy
corporate-level strategy that minimizes risk by diversifying investment among various businesses or product lines

Portfolio strategy is a corporate-level strategy that minimizes risk by diversifying investment among various businesses or product lines. Like an investor who invests in a variety of stocks, portfolio strategy guides the strategic decisions of corporations that compete in a variety of businesses. For example, it could be used to guide the strategy of a company such as 3M, which makes 50 000 products for 16 different industries. Similarly, it could be used by Johnson & Johnson, which has 190 divisions making health care products for the pharmaceuticals, diagnostics, consumers, and health care professionals markets. And, just as investors consider the mix of stocks in their stock portfolio when deciding which stocks to buy or sell, portfolio strategy provides the following guidelines to help managers acquire companies that fit well with the rest of their corporate portfolio and sell those that don't.

First, the more businesses in which a corporation competes, the smaller its overall chances of failing. Think of a corporation as a stool and its businesses as the legs of the stool. The more legs or businesses added to the stool, the less likely it is to tip over. Using this analogy, portfolio strategy reduces 3M's risk of failing, because the corporation's sur-

EXHIBIT 9.3

CORPORATE-, BUSINESS-, AND FIRM-LEVEL STRATEGIES

CORPORATE-LEVEL STRATEGIES

PORTFOLIO STRATEGY
- Acquisitions, unrelated diversification, related diversification, single businesses
- Boston Consulting Group Matrix
  - Stars
  - Question marks
  - Cash cows
  - Dogs

GRAND STRATEGIES
- Growth
- Stability
- Retrenchment/recovery

INDUSTRY-LEVEL STRATEGIES

FIVE INDUSTRY FORCES
- Character of rivalry
- Threat of new entrants
- Threat of substitute products or services
- Bargaining power of suppliers
- Bargaining power of buyers

POSITIONING STRATEGIES
- Cost leadership
- Differentiation
- Focus

ADAPTIVE STRATEGIES
- Defenders
- Prospectors
- Analyzers
- Reactors

FIRM-LEVEL STRATEGIES

DIRECT COMPETITION
- Market commonality
- Resource similarity

STRATEGIC MOVES OF DIRECT COMPETITION
- Attack
- Response

ENTREPRENEURIAL ORIENTATION
- Autonomy
- Innovativeness
- Risk-taking
- Proactiveness
- Competitive aggressiveness

---

vival depends on essentially 16 different businesses. Because the emphasis is on adding "legs to the stool," managers who use portfolio strategy are often on the lookout for **acquisitions**, that is, other companies to buy.

Second, beyond adding new businesses to the corporate portfolio, portfolio strategy can reduce risk even more through **unrelated diversification**—creating or acquiring companies in completely unrelated businesses. If the businesses are unrelated, then losses in one business or industry will have minimal effect on the performance of other companies in the corporate portfolio. One of the best examples of unrelated diversification is Samsung Corporation of Korea (www.samsung.com). Samsung has eight businesses in electronics, four companies in its machinery business group, five companies in chemicals, five companies in finance and insurance, and sixteen other companies in businesses ranging from automobiles to hotels to entertainment. Because most internally grown businesses tend to be related to existing products or services, acquiring new businesses is the preferred method of unrelated diversification.

Third, investing the profits and cash flows from mature, slow-growth businesses into newer, faster-growing businesses can reduce long-term risk. The best-known portfolio strategy for guiding investment in a corporation's businesses is the Boston Consulting Group (BCG) matrix. The **BCG matrix** is a portfolio strategy that managers use to cat-

acquisition
purchase of a company by another company

unrelated diversification
creating or acquiring companies in completely unrelated businesses

BCG matrix
a portfolio strategy, developed by the Boston Consulting Group, that managers use to categorize the corporation's businesses by growth rate and relative market share, helping them decide how to invest corporate funds

egorize their corporation's businesses by growth rate and relative market share, helping them decide how to invest corporate funds. The matrix, shown in Exhibit 9.4, separates businesses into four categories, based on how fast the market is growing (high growth or low growth) and the size of the business's share of that market (small or large). **Stars** are companies that have a large share of a fast-growing market. To take advantage of a star's fast-growing market and its strength in that market (large share), the corporation must invest substantially in it. However, the investment is usually worthwhile, because many stars produce sizable future profits. **Question marks** are companies that have a small share of a fast-growing market. If the corporation invests in these companies, they may eventually become stars, but their relative weakness in the market (small share) makes investing in question marks more risky than investing in stars. **Cash cows** are companies that have a large share of a slow-growing market. Companies in this situation are often highly profitable, hence the name "cash cow." Finally, **dogs** are companies that have a small share of a slow-growing market. As the name "dogs" suggests, having a small share of a slow-growth market is often not profitable.

Since the idea is to redirect investment from slow-growing to fast-growing companies, the Boston Consulting Group matrix (www.bcg.com) starts by recommending that, while they last, the substantial cash flows from cash cows should be reinvested in stars to help them grow even faster and obtain even more market share. Using this strategy, current profits help produce future profits. Cash flows should also be directed to some question marks. Though riskier than stars, question marks have great potential because of their fast-growing market. However, managers must decide which question marks are most likely to turn into stars and therefore warrant further investment, and which ones are too risky and should be sold. Finally, because dogs lose money, the corporation should "find them new owners" or "take them to the pound." In other words, dogs should be sold to other companies, or should be closed down and liquidated for their assets.

While the BCG matrix and other forms of portfolio strategy are relatively popular among managers, portfolio strategy has some drawbacks. The most significant is that the evidence does not support the usefulness of acquiring unrelated businesses. As shown in Exhibit 9.5, there is a U-shaped relationship between diversification and risk. The left side of the curve shows that single businesses with no diversification are extremely risky (if the single business fails, the entire business fails). So, in part, the portfolio strategy of diversifying is correct—competing in a variety of different businesses can lower risk. However, portfolio strategy is partly wrong, too—the right side of the curve shows that conglomerates composed of completely unrelated businesses are even riskier than single, undiversified businesses.

The second set of problems with portfolio strategy has to do with the dysfunctional consequences that occur when companies are categorized as stars, cash cows, question marks, or dogs. Contrary to expectations, the BCG matrix often yields incorrect judgments about a company's future potential. This is because it relies on past performance (i.e., previous market share and previous market growth), which is a notoriously poor predictor of future company performance.

Furthermore, using the BCG matrix can also weaken the strongest performer in the corporate portfolio, the cash cow. As funds are redirected from cash cows to stars, corporate managers essentially take away the resources needed to take advantage of the cash cow's new business opportunities. The result is that the cash cow becomes less aggressive in seeking new business or in defending its present business. Finally, labelling a top performer as a cash cow can harm employee morale. Instead of working for themselves, cash cow employees realize that they have inferior status because their successes are now being used to fund the growth of stars and question marks.

EXHIBIT 9.4

BOSTON CONSULTING GROUP MATRIX

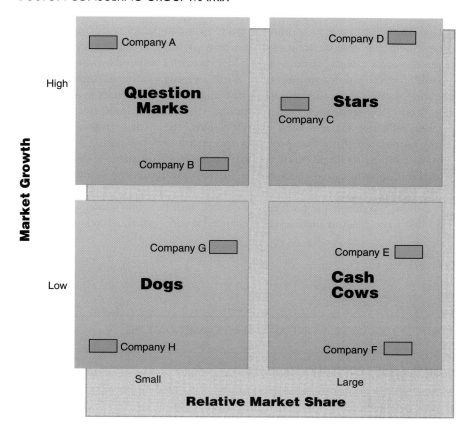

EXHIBIT 9.5

U-SHAPED RELATIONSHIP BETWEEN DIVERSIFICATION AND RISK

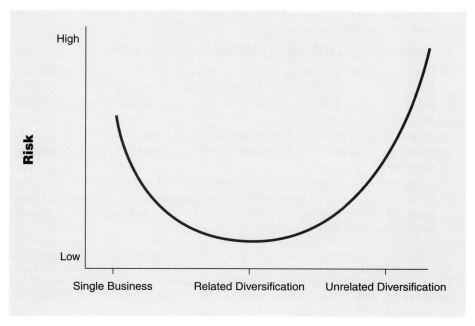

Source: "Psst...The Merger Mavins Still Have It Wrong." (Figure) M. Lubatkin and P.J. Lane, *Academy of Management Executive*, 1996. Vol. 10.

related diversification creating or acquiring companies that share similar products, manufacturing, marketing, technology, or cultures

So, what kind of portfolio strategy does the best job of helping managers decide which companies to buy or sell? The U-shaped curve in Exhibit 9.5 indicates that the best approach is probably **related diversification**, in which the different business units share similar products, manufacturing, marketing, technology, or cultures. The key to related diversification is to acquire or create new companies with core capabilities that complement the core capabilities of businesses already in the corporate portfolio. We began this section with the example of 3M (www.3m.com) and how its 50 000 products are sold in over 16 different industries. While seemingly different, most of 3M's product divisions are based in some fashion on its distinctive competencies in adhesives and tape (e.g., wet or dry sandpaper, Post-it notes, Scotchgard fabric protector, transdermal skin patches, reflective material used in traffic signs, etc.). Furthermore, divisions share a strong corporate culture that promotes and encourages risk-taking and innovation. In sum, in contrast to single, undiversified businesses or unrelated diversification, related diversification reduces risk, because the different businesses can work as a team, relying on each other for needed experience, expertise, and support.

Exhibit 9.6 details the problems associated with portfolio strategy and recommends ways that managers can increase their chances of success through related diversification.

EXHIBIT 9.6

PORTFOLIO STRATEGY: PROBLEMS AND RECOMMENDATIONS

PROBLEMS WITH PORTFOLIO STRATEGY

- Unrelated diversification does not reduce risk.
- Uses present performance to predict future performance.
- Assessments of a business's growth potential are often inaccurate.
- Cash cows fail to aggressively pursue opportunities and defend themselves from threats.
- Being labelled a "cash cow" can hurt employee morale.
- Companies often overpay to acquire stars.
- Acquiring firms often treat acquired stars as "conquered foes." Key stars' managers, who once controlled their own destinies, often leave because they are now treated as relatively unimportant middle managers.

RECOMMENDATIONS FOR MAKING PORTFOLIO STRATEGY WORK

- Don't be so quick to sell dogs or question marks. Instead, management should commit to the markets in which it competes by strengthening core capabilities.
- Put your "eggs in similar (not different) baskets," by acquiring companies in related businesses.
- Acquire companies with complementary core capabilities.
- Encourage collaboration and cooperation between related firms and businesses within the company.
- "Date before you marry." Work with a business before deciding to acquire it.
- When in doubt, don't acquire new businesses. Mergers and acquisitions are inherently risky and difficult to make work. Acquire only firms that can help create or extend a sustainable competitive advantage.

Sources: M. Lubatkin, "Value-Creating Mergers: Fact or Folklore?" *Academy of Management Executive* 2 (1988): 295–302. M. Lubatkin & S. Chatterjee, "Extending Modern Portfolio Theory into the Domain of Corporate Diversification: Does It Apply?" *Academy of Management Journal* 37 (1994): 109–136. M.H. Lubatkin & P.J. Lane, "Psst...The Merger Mavens Still Have It Wrong!" *Academy of Management Executive* 10 (1996): 21–39.

A **grand strategy** is a broad strategic plan used to help an organization achieve its strategic goals.[13] Grand strategies guide the strategic alternatives that managers of individual businesses or subunits may use. There are three kinds of grand strategies: growth, stability, and retrenchment/recovery.

The purpose of a **growth strategy** is to increase profits, revenues, market share, or the number of places (stores, offices, locations) in which the company does business. Companies can grow in several ways. They can grow externally by merging with or acquiring other companies. In recent years, some of the largest mergers and acquisitions have involved well-known corporate actors such as Chapters acquiring Indigo, Sobeys' purchasing of assets of the Oshawa Group, Air Canada merging with Canadian Airlines, and Loblaws' takeover of Provigo.

Another way to grow is internally, directly expanding the company's existing business or creating and growing new businesses. Reuters (www.reuters.com), a British news agency, has grown over the last decade by creating new businesses. Reuters' CEO said, "Acquisitions are about buying market share. Our challenge is to create markets. There is a difference. Creating markets is something two out of three times you fail to do. But the third time, if you create it and you're the first, it can grow rapidly." Proof of that rapid growth can be found in Reuters' rising sales, which have increased by a factor of 9 in the last 12 years. In the next 12 years, Reuters expects to achieve similar growth by expanding many of its new businesses on the Internet. For now, Reuters is the leading news provider on the Internet, with its news reports available at 900 different websites. However, Reuters' Reality Online division also designs transaction-based websites for stock brokerage companies that allow customers to research, buy, and sell investments via the World Wide Web.[14]

The purpose of a **stability strategy** is to continue doing what the company has been doing, but just do it better. Consequently, companies following a stability strategy try to improve the way in which they sell the same products or services to the same customers. For example, Danzas Corporation (www.danzas.com), an international air and sea freight company with 13 offices in Canada, is pursuing a stability strategy. Danzas, using what it calls its "core carriers strategy," has decided to limit the number of customers it serves and the number of air hubs and seaports where it will handle freight. The reason? To improve the quality of service it provides to its four core customers, Hapag-Lloyd, DSR-Senator Lines, Cho Yang, and Mediterranean Shipping Company, each of which has a long-term contract with the company.[15] Companies often choose a stability strategy when their external environment doesn't change much, or after they have struggled with periods of explosive growth.

The purpose of a **retrenchment strategy** is to turn around very poor company performance by shrinking the size or scope of the business. The first step of a typical retrenchment strategy might include significant cost reductions, layoffs of employees, closing of poorly performing stores, offices, or manufacturing plants, or closing or selling entire lines of products or services.[16]

After cutting costs and reducing a business's size or scope, the second step in a retrenchment strategy is recovery. **Recovery** consists of the strategic actions that a company takes to return to a growth strategy. This two-step process of cutting and recovery is analogous to pruning roses. Prior to each growing season, roses should be cut back to two-thirds of their normal size. However, pruning doesn't damage the roses; it makes them stronger and more likely to produce beautiful, fragrant flowers. The retrenchment-and-recovery process is similar. Cost reductions, layoffs, and plant closings are sometimes necessary to restoring companies to "good health." But like pruning, those cuts are intended to allow companies to eventually return to growth strategies (i.e., recovery). For example, to restore its profitability, Canadian label and business form maker Moore Corporation

grand strategy
a board corporate-level strategic plan used to achieve strategic goals and guide the strategic alternatives that managers of individual businesses or subunits may use

growth strategy
strategy that focuses on increasing profits, revenues, market share, or the number of places in which the company does business

stability strategy
strategy that focuses on improving the way in which the company sells the same products or services to the same customers

retrenchment strategy
strategy that focuses on turning around very poor company performance by shrinking the size or scope of the business

recovery
the strategic actions taken after retrenchment to return to a growth strategy

(www.moore.com) cut 4000 jobs and reduced annual expenses by over $100 million during 2001.[17] The effect in 2002 was a return to profitability in the second and third quarters.[18,19] So when company performance drops significantly, a strategy of retrenchment and recovery may help companies return to a successful growth strategy.

Review 3
Corporate-Level Strategies

Corporate-level strategies, such as portfolio strategy and grand strategies, help managers determine what businesses they should be in. Portfolio strategy focuses on lowering business risk by being in multiple, unrelated businesses and by investing the cash flows from slow-growth businesses into faster-growing businesses. One portfolio strategy, the BCG matrix, suggests that cash flows from cash cows should be reinvested in stars and in carefully chosen question marks. Dogs should be sold or liquidated. However, portfolio strategy has several problems. Acquiring unrelated businesses actually increases risk rather than lowering it. The BCG matrix is often wrong when predicting companies' (e.g., dogs, cash cows) future potential. And redirecting cash flows can seriously weaken cash cows. The most successful way to use the portfolio approach to corporate strategy is to reduce risk through related diversification.

The three kinds of grand strategies are growth, stability, and retrenchment/recovery. Companies can grow externally by merging with or acquiring other companies, or they can grow internally through direct expansion or creating new businesses. Companies choose a stability strategy—selling the same products or services to the same customers—when their external environment changes very little or after they have dealt with periods of explosive growth. Retrenchment strategy, shrinking the size or scope of a business, is used to turn around poor performance. If retrenchment works, it is often followed by a recovery strategy that focuses on increasing the business again.

4. Industry-Level Strategies

industry-level strategy
corporate strategy that addresses the question "How should we compete in this industry?"

Industry-level strategy is a corporate strategy that addresses the question "How should we compete in this industry?" For example, the strategy of most nursing homes has been to provide medical care for elderly people who were no longer able to physically take care of themselves. However, in recent years, nursing homes have had to compete with assisted-living facilities. Assisted-living facilities don't offer the medical support available at most nursing homes. Although they provide assistance with things such as bathing and dressing, they have a different goal: to help residents be independent and active for as long as possible. Consequently, assisted-living facilities are much more livable than traditional nursing homes.

Let's find out more about industry-level strategies by discussing five industry forces, positioning strategies, and adaptive strategies.

4.1 Five Industry Forces

According to Harvard professor Michael Porter, five industry forces—character of rivalry, threat of new entrants, threat of substitute products or services, bargaining power of suppliers, and the bargaining power of buyers—determine an industry's overall attractiveness and potential for long-term profitability. The stronger these forces, the less attractive the industry becomes to corporate investors, because it is more difficult for companies to be profitable. Let's examine how these industry forces are bringing changes to several kinds of industries.

character of the rivalry
a measure of the intensity of competitive behaviour between companies in an industry

Character of the rivalry is a measure of the intensity of competitive behaviour between companies in an industry. Is the competition among firms aggressive and cutthroat, or do competitors focus more on serving customers than attacking each other? Both industry attractiveness and profitability decrease when rivalry is cutthroat. For example, selling cars is a highly competitive business. Pick up a local newspaper on

Friday, Saturday, or Sunday morning, and you'll find dozens of pages of car advertising ("Anniversary Sale-A-Bration," "Ford March Savings!" and "$99 Down, You Choose!"). In fact, competition is so intense that if it weren't for used car sales, repair work, and replacement parts, many auto dealers would actually lose money.

The **threat of new entrants** is a measure of the degree to which barriers to entry make it easy or difficult for new companies to get started in an industry. If it is easy for new companies to get started in the industry, competition will increase and prices and profits will fall. However, if there are sufficient barriers to entry, such as large capital requirements to buy expensive equipment or plant facilities or the need for specialized knowledge, competition will be weaker and prices and profits will generally be higher. For example, anyone wanting to start a new car dealership would have to give a large sum of money to one of the major auto manufacturers (e.g., GM, Ford) to become an official dealer. Then, on top of that, they would have to spend millions more to purchase sufficient land and construct buildings to showcase cars, hold dealership offices, and house repair bays and parts inventory. Not surprisingly, the number of new auto dealerships has steadily declined over the last two decades. However, the Internet has now made it possible for Internet sites such as Autobytel (www.autobytel.com) to bypass these barriers to entry, increase competition, and drive down auto prices for American (and until recently, Canadian) consumers.

So how does Internet-based auto-buying work? Well, on Autobytel's free website, customers indicate when and what they plan to buy. Autobytel then contacts a participating local car dealer who phones the customer (within 48 hours) with a low, no-haggle price for the car model the customer wants. One Autobytel customer said, "When he [car salesman] quoted me a price, I nearly fell over—[it was] nearly $7000 (U.S.) less than what we were quoted earlier in the week at the dealership down the road." Another said, "I filled out your query and was contacted by the same dealership I had haggled with before. They found a vehicle, quoted a price (which was $1500 [U.S.] less than the one we had agreed to two weeks prior), and we reached a financing plan in 20 minutes."[20] Autobytel earns money by charging dealers an annual fee of $2500 (U.S.), and $500 to $1500 (U.S.) a month per car brand (e.g., Ford, Chevy). In return, dealers receive exclusive territories, low costs (by not having to advertise in local papers or on local radio and TV stations), and customers who are much more likely to buy.[21] As for the threat to car dealers who are not aligned with these Internet car-selling sites, it's likely to grow. Today, 16 percent of car buyers buy online, but within several years, it's estimated that more than half of all car buyers will purchase their cars this way.[22]

Digital Vision/dv609094

Intel is one of many suppliers of chips to the consumer electronics industry, so it has less bargaining power in that industry than in personal computers, where it is the dominant supplier.

threat of substitute products or services
a measure of the ease with which customers can find substitutes for an industry's products or services

The **threat of substitute products or services** is a measure of the ease with which customers can find substitutes for an industry's products or services. If customers can easily find substitute products or services, the competition will be greater and profits will be lower. If there are few or no substitutes, competition will be weaker and profits will be higher. Generic medicines are some of the best-known examples of substitute products. Under U.S. patent law, a company that develops a drug has exclusive rights to produce and market that drug for 20 years. During this time, if the drug sells well, prices and profits are generally high. However, at the end of 20 years, after the patent has expired, any pharmaceutical company can manufacture and sell the same drug. When this happens, drug prices drop substantially, and the company that developed the drug typically sees its revenues drop sharply. For example, Capoten, a heart drug sold by Bristol-Myers Squibb, sold for 80 cents a pill while under patent, and just 4 cents a pill as a generic brand when produced by Bristol-Myers Squibb's competitors.[23]

bargaining power of suppliers
a measure of the influence that suppliers of parts, materials, and services to firms in an industry have on the prices of these inputs

Bargaining power of suppliers is a measure of the influence that suppliers of parts, materials, and services to firms in an industry have on the prices of these inputs. If an industry has numerous suppliers from whom to buy parts, materials, and services, companies will be able to bargain with suppliers to keep prices low. On the other hand, if there are few suppliers, or if a company is dependent on a supplier with specialized skills and knowledge, suppliers will have the bargaining power to dictate price levels.

bargaining power of buyers
a measure of the influence that customers have on a firm's prices

Bargaining power of buyers is a measure of the influence that customers have on the firm's prices. If a company is dependent on just a few high-volume buyers, those buyers will typically have enough bargaining power to dictate prices. By contrast, if a company sells a popular product or service to multiple buyers, the company has more power to set prices.

4.2 Positioning Strategies

After analyzing industry forces, the next step in industry-level strategy is to effectively protect your company from the negative effects of industry-wide competition and to create a sustainable competitive advantage. According to Michael Porter, there are three positioning strategies: cost leadership, differentiation, and focus.

cost leadership
the positioning strategy of producing a product or service of acceptable quality at consistently lower production costs than competitors can, so that the firm can offer the products or service at the lowest price in the industry

Cost leadership means producing a product or service of acceptable quality at consistently lower production costs than competitors, so that the firm can offer the product or service at the lowest price in the industry. Cost leadership protects companies from industry forces by deterring new entrants, who will have to match low costs and prices. Cost leadership also forces down the prices of substitute products and services, attracts bargain-seeking buyers, and increases bargaining power with suppliers, who have to keep their prices low if they want to do business with the cost leader.

differentiation
the positioning strategy of providing a product or service that is sufficiently different from competitors' offerings that customers are willing to pay a premium price for it

Differentiation means making your product or service sufficiently different from competitors' offerings that customers are willing to pay a premium price for the extra value or performance that it provides. Differentiation protects companies from industry forces by reducing the threat of substitute products. It also protects companies by making it easier to retain customers and more difficult for new entrants trying to attract new customers. Anyone who has been to the movies lately should recognize that the major theatre companies are using differentiation to steal customers from each other. For example, some Empire Theatres located throughout Atlantic Canada have party facilities and video game rooms to broaden their appeal to families.

focus strategy
the positioning strategy of using cost leadership or differentiation to produce a specialized product or service for a limited, specially targeted group of customers in a particular geographic region or market segment

A **focus strategy** means that a company uses either cost leadership or differentiation to produce a specialized product or service for a limited, specially targeted group of customers in a particular geographic region or market segment. Focus strategies typically work in market niches that competitors have overlooked or have difficulty serving. BMC Software (www.bmc.com), with offices in Calgary, Mississauga, Montreal, and Ottawa, is an example of a firm pursuing a focus strategy. It provides e-business systems management software with an emphasis on ensuring availability of information, on performance, and on recovery of information technology resources for both mainframe and distributed systems.

Adaptive strategies are another set of industry-level strategies. While the aim of positioning strategies is to minimize the effects of industry competition and build a sustainable competitive advantage, the purpose of adaptive strategies is to choose an industry-level strategy that is best suited to changes in the organization's external environment. There are four kinds of adaptive strategies: defenders, analyzers, prospectors, and reactors.[24]

Defenders seek moderate, steady growth by offering a limited range of products and services to a well-defined set of customers. In other words, defenders aggressively "defend" their current strategic position by doing the best job they can to hold on to customers in a particular market segment.

Prospectors seek fast growth by searching for new market opportunities, encouraging risk-taking, and being the first to bring innovative new products to market. Prospectors are analogous to gold miners who "prospect" for gold nuggets (i.e., new products) in hopes that it will lead them to a mine that has a rich deposit of gold (i.e., fast growth). Regnery Publishing (www.regnery.com), a small book publisher, is using a prospector strategy to achieve fast growth. Regnery grows by publishing controversial books. It published Detective Mark Fuhrman's best-seller, *Murder in Brentwood*. Fuhrman is the controversial LAPD detective who, in O.J. Simpson's murder trial, allegedly lied about his use of racial slurs. Concerning the risks that Regnery takes with its prospector strategy, Phyllis Gran, president of Penguin Putnam, a large publisher, said, "We wouldn't do the Fuhrman book because I don't think any of our editors would want to sponsor it."[25]

Analyzers are a blend of the defender and prospector strategies. Analyzers seek moderate, steady growth and limited opportunities for fast growth. Analyzers are rarely first to market with new products or services. Instead, they try to simultaneously minimize risk and maximize profits by following or imitating the proven successes of prospectors. For example, while 75 percent of personal computers are made by the 20 largest PC manufacturers (Compaq, Dell, IBM, Gateway, etc.), the remaining 25 percent are made by 100 000 small manufacturers, most of whom use an analyzer strategy. Rather than trying to design new computer products (a prospector strategy), smaller manufacturers may typically make computers with the same options and configurations as the large PC manufacturers offer. However, they may also distinguish themselves by offering personal service. Instead of impersonal websites and 24-hour phone support, small manufacturers can frequently send service technicians to customers' homes to make repairs. Likewise, when customers call with questions, they can often talk directly to the technicians who manufactured their computers.[26]

Finally, unlike defenders, prospectors, or analyzers, **reactors** do not follow a consistent strategy. Furthermore, rather than anticipating and preparing for external opportunities and threats, reactors tend to "react" to changes in their external environment after they occur. Not surprisingly, reactors tend to be poorer performers than defenders, prospectors, or analyzers.

defenders
an adaptive strategy aimed at defending strategic positions by seeking moderate, steady growth and by offering a limited range of high-quality products and services to a well-defined set of customers

prospectors
an adaptive strategy that seeks fast growth by searching for new market opportunities, encouraging risk-taking, and being the first to bring innovative new products to market

analyzers
an adaptive strategy that seeks to minimize risk and maximize profits by following on imitating the proven successes of prospectors

reactors
an adaptive strategy of not following a consistent strategy, but instead reacting to changes in the external environment after they occur

Review **4**
Industry-Level Strategies

Industry-level strategies focus on how companies choose to compete in their industry. Five industry forces determine an industry's overall attractiveness to corporate investors and potential for long-term profitability. Together, a high level of new entrants, substitute products or services, bargaining power of suppliers, bargaining power of buyers, and rivalry between competitors combine to increase competition and decrease profits. Three positioning strategies can help companies protect themselves from the negative effects of industry-wide competition. Under a cost leadership strategy, firms try to keep production costs low, so that they can sell products at prices lower than competitors'.

Differentiation is a strategy aimed at making a product or service sufficiently different from those of competitors that it can command a premium price. Using a focus strategy, firms seek to produce a specialized product or service for a limited, specially targeted group of customers. The four adaptive strategies help companies adapt to changes in the external environment. Defenders want to "defend" their current strategic positions. Prospectors look for new market opportunities by bringing innovative new products to market. Analyzers minimize risk by following the proven successes of prospectors. Reactors do not follow a consistent strategy, but instead react to changes in their external environment after they occur.

5. Firm-Level Strategies

Firm-level strategy addresses the question "How should we compete against a particular firm?" For example, over the last two decades, McDonald's (www.mcdonalds.com) has dominated its nearest rival, Burger King, in sales, profits, market share, and growth. Consequently, McDonald's is twice Burger King's size. However, over the last few years, Burger King (www.burgerking.com) has become the attacker and McDonald's the nervous follower. Burger King started its attack by heavily advertising that its Whopper sandwich was bigger than McDonald's Big Mac. McDonald's responded by creating larger, more expensive Deluxe sandwiches such as the Arch Deluxe hamburger. When it did, Burger King's sales (not McDonald's) increased by 11 percent. To keep weight and health-conscious customers coming in, Burger King created a grilled chicken sandwich. Several years later, McDonald's did the same. Then Burger King attacked McDonald's stranglehold on the fast-food breakfast business, introducing its own croissant and biscuit breakfast sandwiches and selling them for 27 to 34 cents less than McDonald's better-known Egg McMuffin and Sausage McMuffin sandwiches. Moreover, Burger King was able to lower prices on items across its entire menu at the same time that McDonald's food prices increased.[27]

All told, Burger King's aggressive attacks have worked. Burger King's sales are increasing while McDonald's are decreasing. Indeed, an internal McDonald's memo indicated that price cuts might be needed because of an "overt competitive attack by BK."[28]

Let's find out more about firm-level competition between companies by reading about direct competition, strategic moves of direct competition, and entrepreneurship: a firm-level strategy.

5.1 Direct Competition

While Porter's five industry forces indicate the overall level of competition in an industry, most companies do not compete directly with all the firms in their industry. For example, McDonald's and Olive Garden are both in the restaurant business, but no one would characterize them as competitors. McDonald's offers low-cost, convenient fast food in a "seat yourself" restaurant, while Olive Garden offers mid-priced, sit-down dinners complete with servers and a bar.

Instead of "competing" with the industry, most firms compete directly with just a few companies. **Direct competition** is the rivalry between two companies offering similar products and services that acknowledge each other as rivals and take offensive and defensive positions as they act and react to each other's strategic actions.[29] Two factors determine the extent to which firms will be in direct competition with each other: market commonality and resource similarity. **Market commonality** is the degree to which two companies have overlapping products, services, or customers in multiple markets. The more markets in which there is product, service, or customer overlap, the more intense the direct competition between the two companies. **Resource similarity** is the extent to which a competitor has similar amounts and kinds of resources, that is, similar assets, capabilities, processes, information, and knowledge used to create and sustain an advantage over competitors. From a competitive standpoint, resource similarity means that the strategic actions your company takes can probably be matched by your direct competitors.

Exhibit 9.7 shows how market commonality and resource similarity interact to determine when and where companies are in direct competition.[30] The overlapping area (between the triangle and the rectangle or between the differently coloured rectangles) in each quadrant depicts market commonality. The larger the overlap, the greater the market commonality. Shapes depict resource similarity, with rectangles representing one set of competitive resources and triangles representing another. Quadrant I shows two companies in direct competition, because they have similar resources at their disposal and a high degree of market commonality as they try to sell similar products and services to similar customers. McDonald's and Burger King would clearly fit here as direct competitors.

In Quadrant II, the overlapping parts of the triangle and rectangle show two companies going after similar customers with some similar products or services, but doing so with different competitive resources. McDonald's and Wendy's restaurants would fit here. Wendy's is after the same lunchtime and dinner crowds that McDonald's is. However, it is less of a direct competitor to McDonald's than Burger King is, because Wendy's hamburgers, fries, and shakes are more expensive. A representative from Wendy's said, "We believe you win customers by consistently offering a better product at a strong, everyday value." As well, Wendy's is now competing less with McDonald's as it expands its Tim Hortons chain of coffee shops that also serve doughnuts, baked goods, bagels, soups, deli sandwiches, cookies, and soft drinks.[31]

In Quadrant III, the very small overlap shows two companies with different competitive resources and little market commonality. McDonald's and Subway fit here. Although both are in the fast-food business, there's almost no overlap in products and

---

EXHIBIT 9.7

A FRAMEWORK OF DIRECT COMPETITION

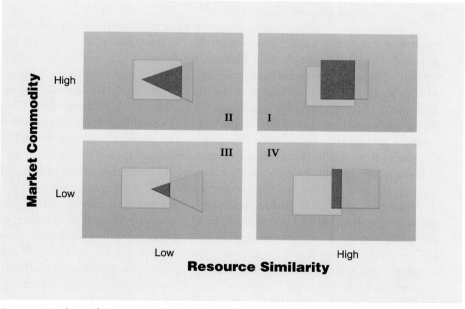

Source: Academy of Management Review by M. Chen. Copyright 1996 by Academy of Management. Reproduced with permission of the publisher via Copyright Clearance Center.

customers. For example, Subway (www.subway.com) sells submarine sandwiches, a food type not available at McDonald's. Furthermore, Subway customers aren't likely to eat at McDonald's.

Finally, in Quadrant IV, the small shaded overlap between the two rectangles shows two companies competing with similar resources but with little market commonality. Surprisingly, McDonald's and Burger King fit here too. However, the major difference from Quadrant I is that Quadrant IV represents direct competition between McDonald's and Burger King in Japan, not Canada or the United States. Both sell burgers and fries in Japan (i.e., similar products). However, unlike the North American market, market commonality is low, because of Burger King's small size and because few Japanese fast-food customers have ever heard of it. Jun Fujita, an assistant manager at a Tokyo McDonald's, said, "We don't see them as a threat at all. Who has ever heard of Burger King?"[32] This example also illustrates the point that even between direct competitors, competition in each market (e.g., geographic regions, particular products or services) is unique. Furthermore, direct competitors have different strengths and weaknesses in different markets. For example, although Burger King has been gaining on McDonald's in North America, McDonald's is clearly dominant in Japan. McDonald's has been in Japan for 25 years and has over 2000 restaurants. By contrast, Burger King hopes to open 200 restaurants in Japan over the next five years.

5.2 Strategic Moves of Direct Competition

While corporate-level strategies help managers decide what business to be in and business-level strategies help them determine how to compete within an industry, firm-level strategies help managers determine when, where, and what strategic actions should be taken against a direct competitor. There are two basic strategic moves in direct competition between firms: attacks and responses.

An **attack** is a competitive move designed to reduce a rival's market share or profits. For example, with its Pampers and Luv's brands, Procter & Gamble (www.pg.com) is the largest maker of disposable baby diapers. However, Procter & Gamble's market share is being attacked by Paragon Trade Brands (www.paragontradebrands.com). Paragon, which manufactures the cheaper, private-label diapers that grocery and discount stores in Canada and the United States sell under their own store brand names, now has a 16 percent share of the disposable-diaper market.[33]

A **response** is a countermove, prompted by a rival's attack, designed to defend or improve a company's market share or profit. For example, in an extremely aggressive response, Procter & Gamble sued Paragon for damages and lost profits, alleging that Paragon violated the patents it has for putting elastic in diapers to prevent leaking around a baby's legs. To those unfamiliar with the diaper business, "elastic around the legs" may not sound like an especially important thing. However, Andrew Urban, a diaper-technology consultant, called this design "one of the most important advances in diapers" since the invention of tight-fitting hourglass-shaped diapers.[34] Consequently, Procter & Gamble's intent was to force Paragon to stop making diapers with elastic in the legs or to make it pay a royalty for each diaper. Either would have greatly reduced Paragon's profitability. Luckily, for Paragon, the two parties settled the lawsuit.

Attacks and responses can include smaller, more tactical moves, such as price cuts, specially advertised sales or promotions, or improvements in service. However, they can also include resource-intensive strategic moves, such as expanding service and production facilities, introducing new products or services within the firm's existing business, or entering a completely new line of business for the first time. Of these, market entries and exits are probably the most important kinds of attacks and responses. Entering a new market is a clear offensive signal to an attacking or responding firm that your company is committed to gaining or defending market share and profits at their expense. By contrast, exiting a market is an equally clear defensive signal that your company is

attack
a competitive move designed to reduce a rival's market share or profits

response
a competitive countermove, prompted by a rival's attack, to defend or improve a company's market share or profit

retreating.[35] For example, because its core computer business is struggling, Apple Computers has decided that it can no longer afford to make and sell its Newton "palm" computers, which can be used to take handwritten notes and to store calendars, lists of contacts, phone numbers, etc. Apple's exit from the palm computer market is ironic for two reasons. First, the Apple Newton was one of the first palm computers introduced to the market. Second, Apple's exit comes at a time when demand for palm computers is projected to increase dramatically over the next few years.[36]

Exhibit 9.8 shows that market commonality and resource similarity determine the likelihood of an attack or response, that is, whether a company is likely to attack a direct competitor or to strike back with a strong response when attacked. When market commonality is strong and companies have overlapping products, services, or customers in multiple markets, there is less motivation to attack and more motivation to respond to an attack. The reason for this is straightforward: when firms are direct competitors in a large number of markets, there is much more at stake.

While market commonality affects the likelihood of an attack or a response to an attack, resource similarity largely affects response capability, that is, how quickly and forcefully a company can respond to an attack. When resource similarity is strong, the responding firm will generally be able to match the strategic moves of the attacking firm. Consequently, firms are less likely to attack firms with similar levels of resources, because they're unlikely to gain any sustained advantage when the responding firm strikes back. On the other hand, if one firm is substantially stronger than another (i.e., low resource similarity), a competitive attack is more likely to produce sustained competitive advantage.

In general, the greater the number of moves (i.e., attacks) a company initiates against direct competitors, and the greater a firm's tendency to respond when attacked, the better its performance. More specifically, attackers and early responders (companies that are quick to launch a retaliatory attack) tend to gain market share and profits at the expense of late responders. This is not to suggest that a "full-attack" strategy always works best. In fact, attacks can provoke harsh retaliatory responses. Consequently, when deciding when, where, and what strategic actions to take against a direct competitor, managers should always consider the possibility of retaliation.

PERSONAL PRODUCTIVITY TIP

Competitive Intelligence, Shopping the Competition

One of the best ways to keep abreast of the need for strategic change is to "shop the competition." Every time the Wal-Mart CEO visits a local Wal-Mart store, he also visits a nearby competitor. When FedEx wants to benchmark its delivery services against the competition, it has FedEx employees, posing as customers, mail identical packages with identical destinations at FedEx and UPS offices. Likewise, when Burger King wants to study the efficiency of its drive-through windows, it sends researchers through the drive-through windows at Burger King, McDonald's, and Wendy's. Curious about what your competitors are up to? Go shopping.

Source: J. Kass, "Business Intelligence Operatives Organize Information: Group Helps Companies Stay Ahead, Advising Them on Knowing Their Customers, Competitors, and Industry," *Los Angeles Times*, 11 April 1995.

EXHIBIT 9.8

LIKELIHOOD OF ATTACKS AND RESPONSES IN DIRECT COMPETITION

Competitor Analysis	Interfirm Rivalry: Action and Response
Strong Market Commonality ——→	Less Likelihood of an Attack
Weak Market Commonality ——→	Greater Likelihood of an Attack
High Resource Similarity ——→	Greater Likelihood of a Response
Low Resource Similarity ——→	Less Likelihood of a Response

Source: M. Chen, "Competitor Analysis and Interfirm Rivalry: Toward a Theoretical Integration," *Academy of Management Review* 21 (1996): 100–134.

Firm-level strategy addresses how one company should compete against another. Furthermore, of the various kinds of attacks and responses used in direct competition, market entry is perhaps the most forceful attack or response, because it sends the clear signal that the company is committed to gaining or defending market share and profits at a direct competitor's expense.

Since **entrepreneurship** is the process of entering new or established markets with new goods or services, entrepreneurship is also a firm-level strategy. In fact, the basic strategic act of entrepreneurship is new entry—creating a new business from a brand-new startup firm or from an existing firm.

While the goal of an entrepreneurial strategy is new entry, the process of carrying out an entrepreneurial strategy depends on the ability of the company's founders or existing managers to foster an entrepreneurial orientation. An **entrepreneurial orientation** is the set of processes, practices, and decision-making activities that lead to new entry. Five key dimensions characterize an entrepreneurial orientation: autonomy, innovativeness, risk-taking, proactiveness, and competitive aggressiveness.[37] Without these, an entrepreneurial strategy is unlikely to succeed.

1. *Autonomy*. If a firm wants to successfully develop new products or services to enter new markets, it must foster creativity among employees. To be creative, employees need the freedom and control to develop a new idea into a new product or service opportunity without interference from others. In other words, they need autonomy. For example, when IBM was developing its first personal computer in the early 1980s, it created a dozen design teams, gave them complete freedom to design what they wanted, and sent them to different locations away from IBM's regular offices. In fact, the winning team worked out of an old rundown manufacturing plant. Furthermore, to prevent interference or influence from IBM's existing business, almost no one in the company knew these teams existed.

2. *Innovativeness*. Entrepreneurial firms also foster innovativeness by supporting new ideas, experimentation, and creative processes that might produce new products, services, or technological processes. One example is Great Plains Software, which makes accounting software for small companies. Recently it was acquired by Microsoft. Prior to this, along with 63 other firms also producing accounting software, the obvious question was how to make the company's accounting software stand out in a crowded market. The answer was to provide extensive phone support to customers who purchased the software. The innovation was to charge for that support, something that no software company had dared try. In fact, Great Plains found that customers were more than willing to pay a fixed amount for unlimited support, because Great Plains was not only helping them learn to use its software, but was also helping them set up their accounts and ledgers correctly. Indeed a major selling point was its promise to customers who paid a fixed annual fee for support, to have their own personal support representative call back within 30 minutes of a support request.[38]

3. *Risk-taking*. Entrepreneurial firms are also willing to take some risks, by making large resource commitments that may result in costly failure.[39] Another way to conceptualize risk-taking is to think of it as managers' preferences for bold rather than cautious acts.

4. *Proactiveness*. Entrepreneurial firms have the ability to anticipate future problems, needs, or changes by developing new products or services that may not be related to their current business, by introducing new products or services before the competition does, and by dropping products or services that are declining (and likely to be replaced by new products or services).[40] Internet Security Systems (ISS) (www.iss.net) anticipated the security risks associated with corporate e-mail, Internet access, and company intranets by developing software that helps companies protect company data and computer systems. For example, ISS's software scans company password databases, looking for 25 000 easy-to-crack account passwords, such as "Spot,"

entrepreneurship
the process of entering new or established markets with new goods or services

entrepreneurial orientation
the set of processes, practices, and decision-making activities that lead to new entry, characterized by five dimensions: autonomy, innovativeness, risk-taking, proactiveness, and competitive aggressiveness

"Steelers," and "Startrek." When it finds them, users must then submit a more secure password. In all, ISS's software can shut down over 200 computer hacker tricks that compromise corporate computer security. Christopher Klaus, the company founder, said, "We make sure all the windows are closed and the doors are locked."[41]

5. *Competitive aggressiveness.* Because new entrants are more likely to fail than are existing firms, they must be aggressive if they want to succeed. A new firm often must be willing to use unconventional methods to directly challenge competitors for their customers and market share.

Review 5
Firm-Level Strategies

Firm-level strategies are concerned with direct competition between firms. Market commonality and resource similarity determine whether firms are in direct competition and thus likely to attack each other or respond to each other's attacks. In general, the more markets in which there is product, service, or customer overlap, and the greater the resource similarity between two firms, the more intense the direct competition between them. When firms are direct competitors in a large number of markets, attacks are less likely, because responding firms are highly motivated to quickly and forcefully defend their profits and market share. By contrast, resource similarity affects response capability, meaning how quickly and forcefully a company responds to an attack. When resource similarity is strong, attacks are much less likely to produce a sustained advantage, because the responding firm is capable of striking back with equal force. Market entries and exits are the most important kinds of attacks and responses.

Entering a new market is a clear offensive signal, while exiting a market is a clear signal that a company is retreating. In general, attackers and early responders gain market share and profits at the expense of late responders. However, attacks must be carefully planned and carried out, because they can provoke harsh retaliatory responses. Firm-level strategy addresses how one company should compete against another. Of the various kinds of attacks and responses used in direct competition, market entry is perhaps the most forceful attack or response, because it sends the clear signal that the company is committed to gaining or defending market share and profits at a direct competitor's expense. Finally, the basic strategic act of entrepreneurship is new entry. To carry out an entrepreneurial strategy, a company must create an entrepreneurial orientation by encouraging autonomy, innovativeness, risk-taking, proactiveness, and competitive aggressiveness.

What Really Happened?

At the beginning of this chapter, you learned that Sobeys Inc. had recently vaulted itself onto the national retail stage by acquiring assets of the Oshawa Group Limited. The company faced numerous post-acquisition challenges as it sought to integrate the two companies. Let's find out what strategy Sobeys followed to succeed.

In a nutshell, as a result of the acquisition and subsequent strategic moves, Sobeys positioned itself in the market by focusing its product lines, improving its store network, and removing costs from its structure. It did so by undertaking a number of actions. These are described below in specific order.

First, it focused its effort on the retail grocery market—in short, selling food. In doing so, it chose to not put too much emphasis on its non-food product lines. To support focused product offerings, it clearly identified its customers and their needs. In 2001, it conducted a market overview that identified 1784 distinct food marketing areas in Canada. The study indicated Sobeys was operating in 902 areas, and it was No. 1 in 610 areas. In each community it sought out its competitive position, the maturity of the market, and opportunities for greenfield (land or locations for new facilities) development. The result of this effort was an organization better structured to understand local markets, execute plans, and overcome marketing challenges.

Second, in 2002, Sobeys chose to sell off its highly successful SERCA food-service business. The buyer was Sysco Corp. of Houston, Texas.

Third, it strengthened its top management team, appointing Bill McEwan to the position of CEO in 2000. McEwan brought his experiences with Coca-Cola and A&P to the table and in turn bolstered the senior leadership team.

Fourth, Sobeys addressed the problem of non-optimal physical store layouts by allocating approximately $450 million a year (or $1.8 billion over four years) to retail development for new stores and existing store expansion.

Fifth, it tackled the issue of costs head on through a comprehensive cost management program. Measures to do so included banner rationalization, a national procurement strategy, a streamlining of its administration, expansion of its private-label lines, and efforts to develop a culture that emphasized cost containment.

Sobeys chose to streamline the number of corporate and franchised banners from 12 down to five or six primary banners. After the streamlining, Sobeys operated 1331 stores in Canada's 10 provinces and one of its two territories, including 466 corporate stores and 865 franchised stores. Of the corporate stores (at the time of writing), 281 were supermarkets, 65 were drug stores, and 120 were convenience stores.

Sobeys also developed national procurement and merchandising strategies. It dealt with the merchandising challenges through a new national program featuring regional execution. The program called C.O.R.E.—Consumer Opportunity Realization Engagement—entailed securing longer contracts with a smaller number of key vendors, "designed to leverage selling opportunities, not just procurement opportunities." Instead of several one-year purchasing agreements with single vendors, each with its own sales targets, the C.O.R.E. program focused on signing a single contract with each vendor and a single sales target for all of that vendor's products. As a further step, it entered into an alliance with Sysco, the largest North American food-service distributor, to optimize sourcing and procurement as well as increase efficiencies in the area of distribution and logistics.

Finally, the company decided to create a balance of national, regional, and private-label products to satisfy consumer demand for choice. By the end of 2003 its goal was to expand the private-label category to more than 3500 product offerings through the addition of another 126 items.

Overall, what was the impact of this focus strategy at the time of writing? From 1998 through to the end of its 2002 fiscal year, Sobeys' revenues increased from $2.75 billion to over $10 billion while its share price jumped from $17.88 to $44.25. Its operating earnings also increased over this period from $37.4 million to $141.7 million.

Sources: Bill McEwan, remarks to the St. John's Board of Trade, 4 December 2002, St. John's Newfoundland. Christina Veiders, "Investors Cautious Following Share Price Slides," *Supermarket News*, 13 January 2003. Elliot Zwiebach, "Sobeys Meets Half Year Goals in 2nd Quarter," *Supermarket News*, 16 December 2002. Elliot Zwiebach, "Sobeys Goes National," *Supermarket News*, 4 February 2002, 1. Building Sustainable Worth. A presentation to CIBC World Markets, January 15, 2003.

Key Terms

acquisition (271)
analyzers (279)
attack (282)
bargaining power of buyers (278)
bargaining power of suppliers (278)
BCG matrix (272)
cash cow (272)
character of the rivalry (276)
competitive advantage (263)
competitive inertia (265)
core capabilities (266)
core firms (267)
corporate-level strategy (270)
cost leadership (278)
defenders (279)
differentiation (278)
direct competition (280)
distinctive competence (266)
diversification (270)

dog (272)
entrepreneurial orientation (284)
entrepreneurship (284)
firm-level strategy (280)
focus strategy (278)
grand strategy (275)
growth strategy (275)
imperfectly imitable resource (263)
industry-level strategy (276)
market commonality (280)
nonsubstitutable resource (263)
portfolio strategy (270)
prospectors (279)
question mark (272)
rare resource (263)
reactors (279)
recovery (275)
related diversification (274)
resources (263)

resource similarity (280)
response (282)
retrenchment strategy (275)
secondary firms (267)
shadow-strategy task force (267)
situational (SWOT) analysis (266)
stability strategy (275)
star (272)
strategic dissonance (266)
strategic group (267)
strategic reference points (268)
sustainable competitive advantage (263)
threat of new entrants (277)
threat of substitute products or services (278)
unrelated diversification (271)
valuable resource (263)

What Would You Do II?

It's 9:00 Sunday night in Vancouver, and your local grocery store is packed with parents filling shopping carts with the milk, bread, and cereal they need to get their kids going on Monday morning. Waiting in the checkout line (of course, only one checkout lane is open), you smile when you notice that half the carts are filled with Kimberly-Clark products, particularly disposable diapers and wipes. The diaper business is a good one. From birth to potty training, which typically lasts about three years, the average child uses 6000 disposable diapers. At a cost of about $30 a week, the total cost comes to about $4700 per child. Even better, the market has grown to the point where disposable diapers now cover over 90 percent of North American babies' bottoms.

Yes, it's a good business to be in, but it's a cutthroat business. Your company, Kimberly-Clark, has been battling with market leader Procter & Gamble (P&G) for nearly three decades. It began when P&G introduced Pampers, the first disposable diaper, in 1961. Seven years later, Kimberly-Clark produced its first disposable, Kimbies. In the 1970s, P&G innovated by adding tape closures to Pampers to replace the safety pins that parents used to keep disposable diapers on babies. P&G also introduced sizes for toddlers and premature infants. These aggressive moves killed Kimbies' sales, forcing Kimberly-Clark to pull Kimbies from the market. However, in 1978, Kimberly-Clark introduced Huggies, diapers with elastic around the legs to prevent leakage. Then, in 1983, Kimberly-Clark added refas-

tenable tape closures to Huggies. Now parents could unfasten the diaper to see if it was dirty and then refasten it for continued use if it wasn't. The result: P&G's profits and market share dropped significantly. However, three years later, P&G responded with Pampers Ultras, ultra-absorbent diapers that were half the thickness of regular disposable diapers. A year later, Kimberly-Clark followed with Huggies SuperTrim.

Attack, response, and attack: The battle continues today. But instead of a domestic battle, it has become a battle for global dominance of the diaper market. Right now, the fiercest scuffles are in Europe. When Kimberly-Clark introduced its diapers in Europe, P&G responded with a deep price cut. P&G's move forced Kimberly-Clark to match the lower prices, costing Kimberly-Clark over $80 million (U.S.) in lost profits. Another factor complicating Kimberly-Clark's move into Europe is that most European grocery stores are small and have much more limited shelf space. Consequently, stores only carry a small selection of well-known brands, like P&G's Pampers, and are reluctant to add new brands that might not sell as well. Because of these difficulties, Kimberly-Clark doesn't expect its European diaper business to break even for several years.

Slam! The carry-out assistant finishes putting the groceries in your car and closes the trunk. As you pull out of the parking lot, you wonder what the company needs to do to create a sustained competitive advantage against P&G. Since the company has a variety of business units (trucking, beauty/barbershops, a regional airline, cigarette papers, pulp and paper mills that process a variety of raw materials used in Kimberly-Clark products) in addition to diapers, there's no shortage of strategic alternatives. What kind of corporate-level strategy should the company pursue? Should it be growth, stability, or retrenchment/recovery? Also, what kind of diversification strategy should Kimberly-Clark employ? Likewise, what kind of industry-level strategy should the company follow: cost-leadership, differentiation, or focus? Or might an adaptive strategy be better? But which one: defender, prospector, analyzer, or reactor? Finally, given the brutal competition with P&G, how aggressive should Kimberly-Clark be in its firm-level competition? How quick should it be to attack and respond to P&G? And, if

Kimberly-Clark chooses to attack or respond to P&G, how should it do so?

If you were in charge of the strategy-making process at Kimberly-Clark, what would you do?

Sources: D. Decwikiel-Kane, "Oh, How Diapers Have Changed/The Disposable Changed Diapers for Babies," *Greensboro News & Record*, 4 November 1996. B. Deener, "Continental Divide: Kimberly-Clark Faces Tough Competition in Europe from Rival P&G," *The Dallas Morning News*, 16 July 1995. B. Deener, "Kimberly-Clark Plans to Acquire Scott Paper," *The Dallas Morning News*, 18 July 1995. G. Lazarus, "Procter Wipes Up Towelette Brands," *Chicago Tribune*, 24 May 1996. R. Lenzner & C. Shook, "The Battle of the Bottoms," *Forbes*, 24 March 1997, 98–104. R. Narisetti, "P&G to Embark on an Overhaul of Diaper Lines," *The Wall Street Journal Europe*, 10 June 1996.

Critical Thinking Video Case

Scenario Planning

How do managers make sense of complex, uncertain future business environments? Management theory offers a number of frameworks to help in this regard. One important analytical tool in widespread use is scenario planning. An alternative to traditional forecasting, it is a tool for imagining developed by the Shell Oil company in the early 1970s that helps executives stay ahead of surprises.

In this video, you will learn that scenario planning is a critical analytical tool for many companies operating in unstable and uncertain markets. For instance, scenario development and analysis helped the Royal Bank of Canada manage over $40 billion of loans to the Canadian oil industry. Finning International Inc., a Vancouver-based distributor of industrial equipment,

employs a consultant to throw scenarios at it on an ongoing basis to keep it alert and in tune with its global market. Further, helping companies understand potential scenarios is an increasingly important service for organizations such as the Canadian Energy Research Institute, the Global Business Network, and software developer Envision Sustainability Tools. As you watch the video, consider the following critical thinking question.

Critical Thinking Question

How might the industry forces, adaptive strategies, and positioning strategies discussed under the heading of Industry Level Strategies be used by corporate scenario planners to reduce uncertainty for a particular company or organization?

How About a "Cuppa?"

In Great Britain, when someone asks, "How about a cuppa?" they're asking if you want a cup of tea. And with an average of 3.6 "cuppas" a day per person, Great Britain, which has a population approximately twice the size of Canada's, consumes an amazing 10 percent of the world's tea each year—more than North America and Europe put together. In Great Britain, people of all ages and economic levels drink tea, bringing annual sales to more than $1.05 million per year. Indeed, the British drink so much tea that market researchers estimate that tea accounts for 42 percent of all liquid intake in Great Britain.

Yet even in tea-crazed Britain, tea is not as popular as it once was. Tea still outsells coffee and soft drinks combined, but tea sales are no longer growing. By contrast, coffee sales, especially among young professionals, are increasing approximately 4 percent per year. Mark Beales, a coffee marketing manager at Nestlé Foods, said, "It's seen to be more sophisticated than tea now. Out-of-home consumption is being driven by the increasing number of quality café bars, which improves the perception of coffee and makes it more widely available." With sales of soft drinks increasing, too, especially among children and teens, the long-term prospects for tea don't look promising.

Questions

1. Using Michael Porter's Industry Forces model, explain how each of the five forces will affect the tea industry's overall attractiveness and potential for long-term profitability.

2. If you worked for one of the leading tea companies in Britain (tea bags account for 83 percent of all tea sold by these companies), what industry-level strategy would you recommend to the company? Would it be focus, cost-leadership, differentiation, defender, prospector, analyzer, reactor, or a combination of these strategies? Explain which you recommend, why you recommend it, and how the company should use that strategy to gain competitive advantage.

Sources: E. Beck, "New 3-D Tea Bag Rattles Some Tea Cups in the U.K.," *The Wall Street Journal Interactive Edition*, 24 March 1997. L. Bray, "Boiling Points: Life Is Not an Easy Ride for Tea and Coffee Manufacturers These Days, with Innovation in Other Beverage Categories Increasing All the Time," *Grocer*, 16 November 1996, 45–46. N. Clayton, "Workforce Is Showing Bags of Innovation," *The Times of London*, 2 October 1994. R. Mulholland, "Storm Brewing in Britain's Teacups," *Agence France-Presse*, 24 February 1996. R. Turcsik, "A Bounty of Teas," *Supermarket News*, 13 November 1995, 42–43.

Management Decisions

Absolutely, Positively Overnight

It begins at 11:00 each night. Every 90 seconds an orange, blue, and white FedEx cargo plane lands at the Memphis airport. By 1:00 a.m., all the planes have arrived. As FedEx workers scurry between planes, loading and unloading packages and cargo containers, activity is everywhere. The scene is not unlike a busy colony of ants lucky enough to find itself underneath a park picnic table. Before the planes return to the runway several hours later, stuffed to the cockpit with packages guaranteed to be delivered to their final destinations "absolutely, positively overnight," FedEx's 9000 Memphis workers will have sorted 1 million packages in less than four hours. However, the daily numbers for the entire company are even more impressive: 637 cargo planes and 43 500 vans delivering 4.5 million packages in 211 countries, including Canada.

Thanks to the increasing pace of the business world (and the human tendency to want immediate gratification, despite determined procrastination), FedEx has had unparalleled growth over the last two decades. Revenues have grown from zero, when FedEx invented the overnight delivery business a quarter century ago, to more than $14 billion a year. But can FedEx achieve the same explosive growth in the next 25 years that it had in its first 25? Unlike 1973, when founder and CEO Fred Smith started the company, FedEx faces numerous competitors, as well as technology (e.g., faxes and the Internet) that no one had even imagined a quarter century ago.

Questions

1. Conduct a situational analysis for FedEx. What are its internal strengths (i.e., core competencies) and weaknesses? What strategic opportunities and threats does it face?

2. Assume that CEO Fred Smith has made you head of FedEx's shadow-strategy task force. Thinking like a competitor, actively determine FedEx's weaknesses and how a competitor could exploit them for competitive advantage.

Sources: D.A. Blackmon, "FedEx Plans to Establish a Marketplace in Cyber Space–Shipper Aims to Deliver the Goods as it Moves into Internet Commerce," *The Wall Street Journal*, 9 October 1996. D.A. Blackmon, "Federal Express Sees Strong 4Q, Backs Yr View above $3/Shr," *Dow Jones News Service*, 31 March 1997. D.A. Blackmon, "Federal Express Plans 3-Day Service to Challenge UPS," *The Wall Street Journal*, 2 April 1997. "Dietzgen's New Same-Day Satellite Document Delivery Service for Architectural and Engineering Blueprints Takes Direct Aim at Overnight Courier Business," *Business Wire*, 21 March 1997. T. Lappin, "FedEx: The Airline of the Internet," *Wired Magazine*, December 1996.

Strategic Planning, Protean Careers, and Psychological Success

For most of the 20th century, planning for a career has been as simple as planning for your next job. This is because most 20th-century careers have been linear—a progressive series of upward job promotions in the same field. For example, college graduates might begin a marketing career by starting as sales representatives. Then, over time, as they acquired knowledge and experience, they could expect to be promoted to marketing jobs with more authority and responsibility, perhaps sales manager or account manager. Eventually, they would retire, having spent their entire career in marketing-related jobs.

Today, however, careers are much more likely to be protean than linear. The term "protean" comes from the mythical Greek god Proteus, who would change shapes to keep others from finding him and obtaining his knowledge about all things past, present, and future. So, by contrast to linear careers in which the next job was simply a step up from one's previous job, protean career paths change frequently. If the ladder is the appropriate symbol for linear careers, then a parachute is the best symbol for protean careers, as people jump from one set of jobs to a completely different set of jobs. Instead of a job path that heads straight up the same career ladder, the job path in protean careers zigs and zags as "career jumpers" land their job parachutes far away from their original targets.

Of course, this creates a problem. How do you plan for a protean career when it's highly likely that what you do in your current job will be completely unrelated to what you do in your next job or the job after that? Fortunately, there is something you can do to plan for a protean career.

Since there's no way to know when a significant job change may present itself, career experts recommend that you focus on psychological success rather than that next job or promotion. A common reaction to this advice is that the "experts" have got it backwards. It's widely believed that you can't achieve career success, happiness, or wealth without keeping an eye on that next promotion. The "experts" have two responses. First, several decades of research clearly indicate that there's only a tiny positive relationship between money (which, for most of us, comes from getting promoted) and happiness. In fact, only 2 percent of the differences between happy and miserable people stem from money. Second, many business people don't achieve real success until they let go of their "careerist" goals (i.e., promotion after promotion) and focus on enjoying and excelling at their jobs. Ironically, after this occurs, promotions and other career opportunities tend to take care of themselves. In other words, over the long run, that is, from a strategic perspective, it makes more sense to worry about whether you enjoy what you're doing than when and where that next promotion will come from and how much more money you'll earn when you get it.

Begin your plan for a protean career by answering the following questions.

Questions

1. Of all the jobs you've had, which made you feel the best about yourself as a person? What did you enjoy most about this job? Be specific. Now, of all the jobs you've had, which made you feel the worst about yourself as a person? What was the worst part of this job? Finally, describe three significant differences between your best and worst jobs.

2. What do you do in your free time? Do you have any hobbies or interests in which you become readily absorbed? Describe your favourite outside interest or hobby. List three reasons why this activity or interest is so much fun for you.

Sources: K.R. Brousseau, M.J. Driver, K. Eneroth, & R. Larsson, "Career Pandemonium: Realigning Organizations and Individuals," *Academy of Management Executive*, November 1996, 52–66. D.T. Hall, "Protean Careers of the 21st Century," *Academy of Management Executive*, November 1996, 8–16. D. Seligman, "Does Money Buy Happiness?" *Forbes*, 21 April 1997, 394–396.

Discussion Questions

1. Sony and Sanyo are two well-known manufacturers of DVD players and other home entertainment products. Every few months, they place on vendor shelves new versions of their products that are priced and appear quite similar to each other. If one puts an innovative product on the market, the other soon has its own version on the shelves. Evidently, when referring to DVD players, neither firm possesses a sustainable competitive advantage relative to the other. In this light, differentiate competitive advantage from sustainable competitive advantage.

2. With thousands of Canadians flying on its planes daily, Air Canada is a company of interest to many of us. Along with other competitors in the global aviation industry, it faces a number of interesting challenges, including the existence of powerful unions, a decreasing customer base, an aging fleet of airplanes, costly government regulations and taxes, unstable fuel prices, and a business model designed for a different operating environment. Solutions to these challenges are not simple. A form of analysis may, however, clarify needed steps forward. In this light, identify the roles and basic components of a situational analysis.

3. Briefly explain what the BCG matrix is, and what its basic recommendations are.

4. When one thinks of business in Canada, industries such as lumber, oil and gas, wheat, automobiles, pharmaceuticals, financial services, aeronautics, and fish products often come to mind. Despite being distinct from one another, each can be described in terms of a number of generic forces. Choose one particular industry and list the five industry forces that determine overall levels of competition in that industry. Next, identify what happens to competition as these forces increase in strength.

5. Canadian Pacific and CN compete in the North American transportation industry. These two rail carriers face two major challenges: competition from other railroaders and the trucking industry and changes to their overall operating environments due to altered macroeconomic forces, new regulations, new technologies, or stakeholder pressures. In order to respond to these pressures, both CN and Canadian Pacific will need to implement specific strategies. Differentiate between the position strategies and the adaptive strategies available to these two important players.

Study Tip

Pick up a recent copy of *The Globe and Mail Report on Business* and read several articles. List the strategy issues facing the companies you read about.

CHAPTER 10

Chapter Outline

Learning Objectives

After reading this chapter, you should be able to

1. explain why innovation matters to companies.
2. discuss the different methods that managers can use to effectively manage innovation in their organizations.
3. discuss why change occurs and why it matters.
4. discuss the different methods that managers can use to better manage change as it occurs.

CP (Fabian Bimmer)

ten

Innovation and Change

What Would You Do?

IBM Headquarters. Not in your brief-case. Not in the glove compartment. Not in your coat pocket. Darn! Where did you put those antacids? Ah, there they are on the floor. Better get them while the light is still red. Ugh, cherry, nasty. But the stress is killing your stomach. Every time you think about lunch and your management consultant's advice, your stomach turns. Her message was direct: If IBM (www.ibm.com) doesn't change, it will join a long list of once-large corporate dinosaurs that have shrunk in size and profitability or, even worse, gone out of business.

Her words painted a frightening picture. "Sears, General Motors, and U.S. Steel. For decades, these companies dominated their industries. You name it: clothing, furniture, tools, appliances, lawn mowers, car batteries, in the store or by catalogue. Sears sold it all and dominated retailing. General Motors sold six out of every ten cars made in the United States. Sixty percent! In fact, GM was so large and contributed so much to the U.S. economy that its domination of the auto industry was expressed in the well-known phrase 'What's good for General Motors is good for the country.' U.S. Steel so dominated the steel industry that

it was larger than its next three competitors combined. Then," she warned, "their businesses changed but they didn't." She explained, "Wal-Mart, not Sears, now dominates retailing. JCPenney's catalogue sales now dwarf Sears' catalogue sales. In the auto industry, GM's market share dropped nearly in half, from just over 60 percent to barely over 30 percent. Who has that 30 percent now? Toyota, Honda, Ford, and Chrysler, that's who. And, in steel, mini-mills, like those run by Nucor Corporation, cut U.S. Steel's business in half as easily as a hot knife cuts through warm butter. Cut in half in less than a decade. The mini-mills were cheaper, faster, and easily out-innovated slow-moving U.S. Steel. And the same thing will happen to you. If you don't change, IBM will be the next giant to fall."

Unfortunately, you know she's right. IBM has to change. IBM (short for International Business Machines) once dominated sales of office equipment, first with typewriters, then mainframe computers, and then personal computers. Today, however, typewriters, replaced by computers, are a dead business. Mainframe sales, which accounted for half of IBM's revenues, are off by one-third. And in personal computers, where it once had more than 70 percent of the market, IBM now has a 7 percent market share

behind Gateway, Compaq, and Dell Computers, none of which were even in business when IBM began selling personal computers.

But how do you quickly and effectively change a company like IBM? Should the change be slow and gradual or quick and revolutionary? IBM has a long history and a strong culture. So any changes that you try to make will probably be resisted. How can you identify and manage that resistance so IBM can make the changes that it needs to make? In the fast-paced environment of computers, it takes IBM much too long to develop and bring new products to market. How can you speed up that process?

If you were at IBM, what would you do?

Sources: A. Goldstein, "Big Blue Pulls Ahead of the Pack," *Dallas Morning News*, 14 February 1999, 1H. L. Hays, "Another Top IBM Executive Quits Amid Reorganization by Gerstner," *The Wall Street Journal Europe*, 10 January 1995. "IBM's Finances: Now Comes the Hard Part," *Infoperspectives* 18 (1 April 1997). D.Q. Mills, "The Decline and Rise of IBM," *Sloan Management Review* 37 (1 June 1996). R. Narisetti, "How IBM Turned Around Its Ailing PC Division," *The Wall Street Journal*, 12 March 1998, B1. S. Sherman, "Is He Too Cautious to Save IBM?" *Fortune*, 3 October 1994. B. Ziegler, "IBM's Research Cutbacks Now Seem to Be Brilliant," *The Wall Street Journal*, 6 October 1997.

organizational innovation
the successful implementation of creative ideas in organizations

creativity
the production of novel and useful ideas

organizational change
a difference in the form, quality, or condition of an organization over time

We begin this chapter by reviewing the issues associated with **organizational innovation** and **creativity**. You will learn why innovation matters and how to manage innovation to create and sustain a competitive advantage.

In the second half of this chapter, you will learn about **organizational change** and why changes occur. You will also learn about the risk of not changing, the different kinds of change, and the ways in which companies can manage change.

Organizational Innovation

Do you remember the first time, probably as a child, that you saw a blimp floating overhead? It moved slowly, was clearly visible for kilometres, and held your attention as it got closer, passed overhead, and then floated away. Interestingly, the things that make blimps fascinating to kids also make them great for advertising (e.g., slow, visible, holds attention). Company names are clearly displayed on the side of their blimps at sporting events that are attended by thousands and seen by millions on TV. Blimps are so commonplace that major sporting events such as the Grey Cup, the Superbowl, and the World Series would seem incomplete without traditional overhead camera shots from the blimp.

Today, however, the "Lightship," an innovative new blimp made by the American Blimp Company (www.americanblimp.com), is revolutionizing the blimp business and the advertising revenues that go with it. Lightships have several advantages over traditional blimps. To start, they're much smaller and cheaper. A typical, full-size blimp costs about $420 000 a month to operate. Most of that cost is for the 24 people who work in the blimp's ground and flight crews. Because American Blimp's Lightships are smaller, it takes only 14 people to staff the ground and flight crews. Consequently, monthly costs run around $280 000, one-third less than full-size blimps. Another advantage is that Lightships are lighted from the inside. So when it gets dark, the company name and logo on the side of the blimp are still visible! This is critical since most sporting events take place at night to maximize the size of their TV audience.[1]

Organizational innovation, like American Blimp's new Lightships, is the successful implementation of creative ideas in an organization.[2] This chapter focuses largely on innovation with regard to changes in technology or design. Innovation can of course take other forms. Innovation can refer to changes in an organization as a whole. It can refer to specific products. It can also refer to business processes. These latter three innovation types are addressed indirectly in this chapter.

After reading the next two sections, you should be able to
1. *explain why innovation matters to companies.*
2. *discuss the different methods that managers can use to effectively manage innovation in their organizations.*

1. Why Innovation Matters

We can only guess what changes technological innovations will bring in the next 20 years. Maybe we'll be listening to compact chips rather than compact discs. Maybe cars won't need tune-ups. Maybe we'll use the Internet to have cookies delivered hot to our homes like pizza. And maybe TVs will be voice-activated, so it doesn't matter if you lose the remote (just don't lose your voice). Who knows? The only thing we do know about the next 20 years is that innovation will continue to change our lives. The

Government of Canada agrees. It has developed a national innovation strategy[3] and has committed millions of dollars to ensuring that innovation is supported throughout the private and educational sectors. Through two programs, it supports innovative behaviour by Canadians. One program, Achieving Excellence: Investing in People, Knowledge and Opportunity, recognizes the need to consider knowledge as a strategic national asset and has introduced a variety of programs to meet its goals. It focuses on how to strengthen our science and research capacity and on how to ensure that this knowledge contributes to building an innovative economy that benefits all Canadians. Industry Canada is the department implementing this program. The other program, Knowledge Matters: Skills and Learning for Canadians, recognizes that a country's greatest resource in the knowledge society is its people. It looks at what can be done to strengthen learning in Canada, to develop people's talent, and to provide opportunity for all to contribute to and benefit from the new economy. Human Resources Development Canada is the department responsible for implementing this program. Programs such as these help to foster innovation. But what does this term innovation mean? Let's begin our discussion of innovation by learning about technology cycles, and innovation streams.

1.1 Technology Cycles

In Chapter 2, you learned that technology is the knowledge, tools, and techniques used to transform inputs (raw materials, information, etc.) into outputs (products and services). A **technology cycle** begins with the "birth" of a new technology and ends when that technology reaches its limits and "dies" as it is replaced by a newer, substantially better technology.[4] For example, technology cycles occurred when air conditioning supplanted fans and when Henry Ford's Model T replaced horse-drawn carriages.

From Gutenberg's invention of the printing press in the 1400s to the rapid advance of the Internet in the last few years, studies of hundreds of technological innovations have shown that nearly all technology cycles follow the typical **S-curve pattern of innovation** shown in Exhibit 10.1.[5] Early in a technology cycle, there is still much to learn and progress is slow, as depicted by point A on the S-curve. The flat slope indicates that increased effort (i.e., money, research and development) brings only small improvements in technological performance. Intel's technology cycles have followed this pattern. Intel spends billions to develop new computer chips and to build new production facilities to produce them. Intel has found that the technology cycle for its integrated circuits (that power personal computers) is about three years. In each three-year cycle, Intel introduces a new chip, improves the chip by making it a little bit faster each year, and then replaces that chip at the end of the cycle with a brand-new chip that is substantially faster than the old chip. But at first, those billions typically produce only small improvements in performance. For instance, as shown in Exhibit 10.2, Intel's first 60 megahertz (MHz) Pentium processors ran at a speed of 51 based on the iComp Index.[6] (The iComp Index is a benchmark test for measuring relative computer speed. For example, a computer with an iComp score of 200 is twice as fast as a computer with an iComp score of 100.) Yet, six months later, Intel's new 75 MHz Pentium was only slightly faster, with an iComp speed of 67.

Fortunately, as the technology matures, researchers figure out how to get better performance from the new technology. This is represented by point B of the S-curve in Exhibit 10.1. The steeper slope indicates that small amounts of effort will result in significant increases in performance. Again, Intel's technology cycles have followed this

technology cycle
cycle that begins with the "birth" of a new technology and ends when that technology reaches its limits and is replaced by a newer, substantially better technology

S-curve pattern of innovation
a pattern of technological innovation characterized by slow initial progress, then rapid progress, and then again by slow progress as a technology matures and reaches its limits

EXHIBIT 10.1

S-CURVES AND TECHNOLOGICAL INNOVATION

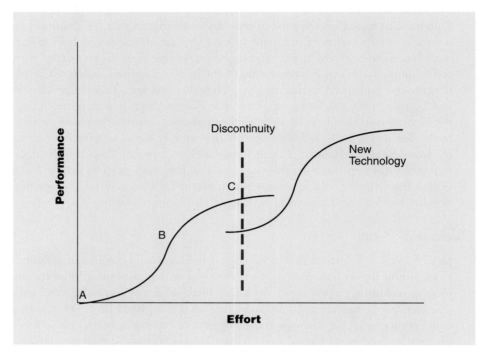

Source: R.N. Foster, *Innovation: The Attacker's Advantage* (New York: Summit, 1986)

pattern. In fact, after six months to a year with a new chip design, Intel's engineering and production people have typically figured out how to make the new chips much faster than they were initially. For example, as shown in Exhibit 10.2, Intel soon rolled out 100 MHz, 120 MHz, 133 MHz, 150 MHz, and 166 MHz Pentium chips that were 76 percent, 117 percent, 124 percent, 149 percent, and 178 percent faster than its original 60 MHz speed.

At point C, the flat slope again indicates that further efforts to develop this particular technology will result in only small increases in performance. More importantly, however, point C indicates that the performance limits of that particular technology are being reached. In other words, additional significant improvements in performance are highly unlikely. For example, Exhibit 10.2 shows that with iComp speeds of 127 and 142, Intel's (www.intel.com) 166 MHz and 200 MHz Pentiums were 2.49 and 2.78 times faster than its original 60 MHz Pentiums. Yet, despite these impressive gains in performance, Intel was unable to make its Pentium chips run any faster, because the basic Pentium design had reached its limits.

After a technology has reached its limits at the top of the S-curve, significant improvements in performance usually come from radical new designs or new performance-enhancing materials. In Exhibit 10.1, that new technology is represented by the second S-curve. The changeover or discontinuity between the new and old technologies is represented by the dotted line. At first, the new and old technologies will likely coexist. Eventually, however, the new technology will replace the old technology. When that happens, the old technology cycle will be complete and a new one will have started. The changeover between Intel's Pentium processors, the old technology, and its Pentium II processors, the new technology (these chips are significantly different technologies despite their similar names), took approximately a year. Exhibit 10.2 shows this

EXHIBIT 10.2

ICOMP INDEX 2.0 COMPARING THE RELATIVE PERFORMANCE OF DIFFERENT MICROPROCESSORS

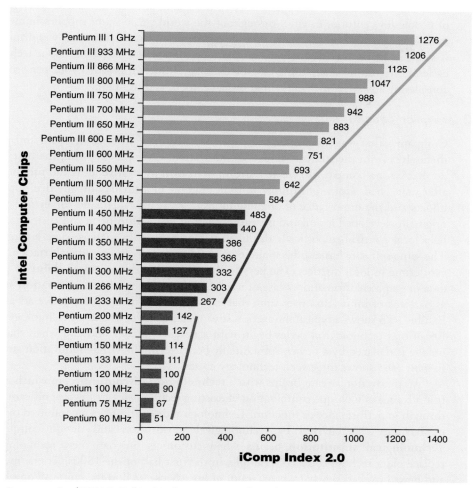

Sources: "Intel iCOMP (Full List)," Ideas International. [Online] Available www.ideasinternational.com/ benchmark/intel/icomp.html, 13 October 2001. "Benchmark Resources: iCOMP Index3.0," Intel. [Online] Available http://developer.intel.com/procs/perf/icomp/inex.htm, 13 October 2001.

changeover or discontinuity between the two technologies. With an iComp speed of 267, the first Pentium II (233 MHz) was 88 percent faster than the last and fastest 200 MHz Pentium processor. And because their design and performance are significantly different (and faster) than Pentium II chips, Intel's new Pentium III chips represent the beginning of yet another S-curve technology cycle in integrated circuits.

While the evolution of Intel's Pentium chips has been used to illustrate the idea of S-curves and technology cycles, it's important to note that technology cycles and technological innovation don't necessarily mean "high technology." Remember, technology is simply the knowledge, tools, and techniques used to transform inputs (raw materials, information, etc.) into outputs (products and services). So a technology cycle occurs whenever there are major advances or changes in the knowledge, tools, and techniques of a field or discipline. For example, one of the most important technology cycles in the history of civilization occurred in 1859, when 1300 miles of central sewer line were constructed throughout London to carry human waste to the sea more than 11 miles away. This extensive sewer system replaced the widespread practice of directly dumping raw sewage into streets, where people walked through it and where it drained into public wells that supplied drinking water. Though the relationship wasn't known at the time, preventing waste runoff from contaminating water supplies stopped the spread of cholera that had killed millions of people for centuries in cities throughout the world.[7] Safe water supplies immediately translated into better health and longer life expectancies. Indeed, the water you drink today is safe thanks to this "technology" breakthrough. So when you think about technology cycles, don't automatically think "high technology." Instead, broaden your perspective by considering advances or changes in knowledge, tools, and techniques.

1.2 Innovation Streams

Companies that want to sustain a competitive advantage must understand and protect themselves from the strategic threats of innovation. Over the long run, the best way to do that is for a company to create a stream of its own innovative ideas and products year after year. Focus Corp. of Edmonton is an example of a small company that appears to understand the importance of ongoing innovation. It has taken land surveying software originally developed for oil and gas exploration in northern Alberta and customized it to help local government officials throughout North America manage civic emergencies. The same software has also been altered to help law enforcement officials track and prevent crime in local districts. The keys to this success are the software's ability to present data in graphical form and its ease of use.[8] Consequently, we define **innovation streams** as patterns of innovation over time that can create sustainable competitive advantage.[9] Exhibit 10.3 shows a typical innovation stream consisting of a series of technology cycles. Recall that technological cycles begin with a new technology and end when that technology is replaced by a newer, substantially better technology. The innovation stream in Exhibit 10.3 shows three such technology cycles.

An innovation stream begins with a **technological discontinuity**, in which a scientific advance or a unique combination of existing technologies creates a significant breakthrough in performance or function. Technological discontinuities are followed by an **era of ferment** characterized by technological substitution and design competition. **Technological substitution** occurs when customers purchase new technologies to replace older technologies. For example, in the first half of the 1800s, letters, messages, and news travelled slowly by boat, train, or horseback, such as the famous Pony Express that, using a large number of fresh riders and fresh horses, could deliver mail from one part of the continent to another in 10 days.[10] However, between 1840 and 1860, many businesses began using the telegraph, because it allowed messages and news to be sent cross-country (or even around the world) in minutes rather than days, weeks, or months.[11] Indeed, telegraph companies were so successful that the Pony Express went out of business almost immediately after the completion of the transcontinental telegraph, which linked telegraph systems from coast to coast.

An era of ferment is also characterized by **design competition** in which the old technology and several different new technologies compete to establish a new technological standard or dominant design. Because of large investments in old technology, and because the new and old technologies are often incompatible with each other, companies and consumers are reluctant to switch to a different technology during design competition. Indeed, the telegraph was so widely used as a means of communication in the late 1800s that, at first, almost no one understood why telephones would be a better way to communicate. In his book *Interactive Excellence: Defining and Developing New Standards for the Twenty-First Century*, Edwin Schlossberg wrote, "People could not imagine why they would want or need to talk immediately to someone who was across town or, even more absurdly, in another town."[12] Also, during design competition, the changeover from older to newer technologies is often slowed by the fact that older technology usually improves significantly in response to the competitive threat from the new technologies.

innovation streams
patterns of innovation over time that can create sustainable competitive advantage

technological discontinuity
scientific advance or unique combination of existing technologies that creates a significant breakthrough in performance or function

era of ferment
phase of a technology cycle characterized by technological substitution and design competition

technological substitution
purchase of new technologies to replace older ones

design competition
competition between old and new technologies to establish a new technological standard or dominant design

EXHIBIT 10.3

INNOVATION STREAMS: TECHNOLOGY CYCLES OVER TIME

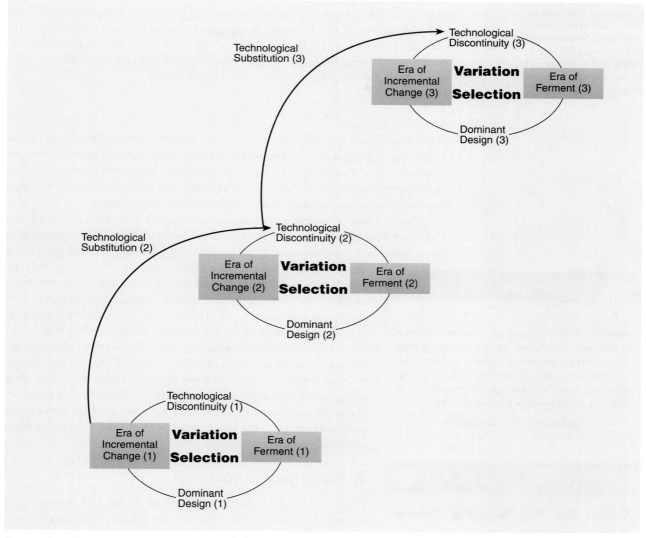

Source: From *Managing Strategic Innovation and Change: A Collection of Readings* by Michael L. Tushman & Philip C. Anderson, copyright © 1997 by Oxford University Press, Inc. Used by permission of Oxford University Press, Inc.

An era of ferment is followed by the emergence of a **dominant design**, which becomes the accepted market standard for technology.[13] Dominant designs emerge in several ways. One is critical mass, meaning that a particular technology can become the dominant design simply because most people use it. Since millions more people bought VCRs that used VHS tapes, VHS tapes beat out Sony's Beta format to become the dominant design for VCRs. Likewise, a design can become dominant if it solves a practical problem. For example, the QWERTY keyboard (look at the top left line of letters on a keyboard) became the dominant design for typewriters, because it slowed typists who, by typing too fast, caused mechanical typewriter keys to jam.

Yet, no matter how they occur, the emergence of a dominant design is a key event in an innovation stream. First, emergence of a dominant design indicates that there are winners and losers. Technological innovation is both competence enhancing and competence destroying. Companies that bet on the wrong design or on the old technology

dominant design
a new technological design or process that becomes the accepted market standard

often struggle, while companies that bet on the now-dominant design usually prosper. In fact, more companies are likely to go out of business in an era of ferment than in an economic recession or slowdown. Second, the emergence of a dominant design signals a change away from design experimentation and competition to **incremental change**, a phase in which companies innovate by lowering the cost and improving the functioning and performance of the dominant design. For example, during a technology cycle, manufacturing efficiencies let Intel cut the cost of its chips by half to two-thirds, all while doubling or tripling the chips' speed. This focus on improving the dominant design continues until the next technological discontinuity occurs.

incremental change
the phase of a technology cycle in which companies innovate by lowering costs and improving the functioning and performance of the dominant technological design

Review 1
Why Innovation Matters

Technology cycles typically follow an S-curve pattern of innovation. Early in the cycle, technological progress is slow and improvements in technological performance are small. However, as a technology matures, performance improves quickly. Finally, small improvements occur as the limits of a technology are reached. At this point, significant improvements in performance must come from new technologies.

The best way to protect a competitive advantage is to create a stream of innovative ideas and products. Innovation streams begin with technological discontinuities that create significant breakthroughs in performance or function. Technological discontinuities are followed by an era of ferment, in which customers purchase new technologies (technological substitution) and companies compete to establish the new dominant design (design competition). Dominant designs emerge because of critical mass, because they solve a practical problem, or because of the negotiations of independent standards bodies. Because technological innovation is both competence enhancing and competence destroying, companies that bet on the wrong design often struggle, while companies that bet on the eventual dominant design usually prosper. Emergence of a dominant design leads to a focus on incremental change, lowering costs, and small, but steady improvements in the dominant design. This focus continues until the next technological discontinuity occurs.

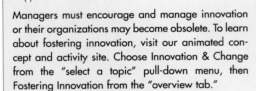

PERSONAL PRODUCTIVITY (TIP)

Cultivate Your Most Demanding Customer or Boss

Once you're successful, it can be difficult to change. One way to battle complacency is to cultivate your most demanding customer or boss, the one who always wants more. Silicon Graphics designed its next generation of computers by helping Disney's Imagineering group design a new "Aladdin" theme park ride. Since Disney (www.disney.com) designed the ride to look exactly like the movie, SG designed new virtual reality headgear that makes it look like you're actually riding a magic carpet. After meeting Disney's demanding standards, SG can sell its greatly improved computers to others. To force yourself to keep changing, cultivate a demanding customer or boss!

Source: A. Deitschman, "The Managing Wisdom of High-Tech Superstars," *Fortune*, 17 October 1994.

2. Managing Innovation

The previous discussion of technology cycles and innovation streams showed that managers must be equally good at managing innovation in two very different circumstances. First, during eras of ferment, companies must find a way to anticipate and survive the technological discontinuities that can suddenly transform industry leaders into losers and industry unknowns into industry powerhouses. Companies that can't manage innovation following technological discontinuities risk quick organizational decline and dissolution. Second, after a new dominant design emerges following an era of ferment, companies must manage the very different process of incremental improvement and innovation. Companies that can't manage incremental innovation slowly deteriorate as they fall farther behind industry leaders.

Unfortunately, what works well when managing innovation after technological discontinuities doesn't work well when managing innovation during periods of incremental change (and vice versa). Consequently, to successfully manage innovation streams, companies need to be good at two things: managing innovation during discontinuous change, and managing innovation during incremental change.

2.1 Managing Innovation During Discontinuous Change

A study of 72 product development projects (i.e., innovation) in 36 computer companies across North America, Europe, and Asia found that companies that succeeded in periods of discontinuous change (in which a technological discontinuity created a significant breakthrough in performance or function) typically followed an experiential approach to innovation.[14] The experiential approach to innovation assumes that innovation is occurring within a highly uncertain environment, and that the key to fast product innovation is to use intuition, flexible options, and hands-on experience to reduce uncertainty and accelerate learning and understanding. There are five parts to the **experiential approach to innovation**: design iterations, testing, milestones, multifunctional teams, and powerful leaders.[15]

An "iteration" is a repetition. So a **design iteration** is a cycle of repetition in which a company tests a prototype of a new product or service, improves on the design, and then builds and tests the improved product or service prototype. As you learned in Chapter 4, a product prototype is a full-scale working model that is being tested for design, function, and reliability. **Testing** is a systematic comparison of different product designs or design iterations. Companies that want to create a new dominant design following a technological discontinuity quickly build, test, improve, and retest a series of different product prototypes.

For example, it took a number of design iterations for Starbucks and its suppliers to successfully create a paper coffee cup that would keep coffee hot but not burn customers' hands. To prevent customers from burning themselves, Starbucks had either stacked two paper cups together or used cardboard sleeves that slid over the outside of the cup. However, customers complained that sleeves fell off or prevented cups from fitting into cup holders and that using two cups was wasteful. As a result, Starbucks and its suppliers worked for three years to come up with a paper cup that was light, cheap, environment friendly, and heat insulating. Prototypes ranged from a layered cup that folded and wrapped one long piece of paper into three layers of paper, to a Japanese-designed cup coated with a special plastic. Testing was both practical, using human hands to pick up different cups filled with steaming coffee, and scientific, using an infrared temperature gauge to test cups' external temperatures. The breakthrough cup design, now being tested in Starbucks stores, sandwiches a thin air layer between an inner polyethylene liner and outer layer of brown recycled paper.[16]

By trying a number of very different designs, or by making successive improvements and changes in the same design, frequent design iterations reduce uncertainty and improve understanding. Simply put, the more prototypes you build, the more likely you are to learn what works and what doesn't. Plus, building a number of prototypes also means that designers and engineers are less likely to "fall in love" with a particular prototype. Instead, they'll be more concerned with improving the product or technology as much as they can. Testing speeds up and improves the innovation process, too. Testing two very different design prototypes against each other, or testing the new design iteration against the previous iteration, quickly makes product design strengths and weaknesses apparent. Likewise, testing uncovers errors early in the design process when they are easiest to correct. Finally, testing accelerates learning and understanding by forcing engineers and product designers to examine hard data about product performance. An example of an innovation involving a number of different design iterations originates with Pro Mac Manufacturing Ltd., of Courtney, British Columbia. An added bonus of its innovation is that it will inevitably save lives. So what is it? The company has developed a blast-proof excavator for removing land mines from war zones.[17]

experiential approach to innovation
an approach to innovation that assumes a highly uncertain environment, and uses intuition, flexible options, and hands-on experience to reduce uncertainty and accelerate learning and understanding

design iteration
a cycle of repetition in which a company tests a prototype of a new product or service, improves on that design, and then builds and tests the improved prototype

testing
systematic comparison of different product designs or design iterations

milestones
formal project review points used to assess progress and performance

multifunctional teams
work teams composed of people from different departments

Milestones are formal project review points used to assess progress and performance. For example, a company that has put itself on a 12-month schedule to complete a project might schedule milestones at the 3-month, 6-month, and 9-month points on the schedule. By making people regularly assess what they're doing, how well they're performing, and whether they need to take corrective action, milestones provide structure to the general chaos that follows technological discontinuities. Milestones also shorten the innovation process by creating a sense of urgency that keeps everyone on task. For example, when one electrical utility was building its first nuclear power facility, the company's construction manager passed out 2000 desk calendars to company employees, construction contractors, vendors, and suppliers, so that everyone involved in the project was aware of the construction timeline. Contractors that regularly missed deadlines were replaced.[18] Finally, milestones are beneficial for innovation, because meeting regular milestones builds momentum by giving people a sense of accomplishment.

Multifunctional teams are work teams composed of people from different departments. Multifunctional teams accelerate learning and understanding by mixing and integrating technical, marketing, and manufacturing activities. By involving all key departments in development from the start, multifunctional teams speed innovation through early identification of problems that would typically not have been identified until much later.

Powerful leaders provide the vision, discipline, and motivation to keep the innovation process focused, on time, and on target. Powerful leaders are able to get resources when they are needed, are typically more experienced, have high status in the company,

Multifunctional work teams are a key part of generating new ideas. When Kellogg's realized that it was experiencing a dearth of new ideas and products, it implemented multifunctional work teams. In their first month, the teams generated 65 new product ideas, including the now-popular prepackaged Rice Krispie Treat.

© Jeff Sciortino

and are held directly responsible for product success or failure. On average, powerful leaders can get innovation-related projects done nine months faster than leaders with little power or influence.

2.2 Managing Innovation During Incremental Change

While the experiential approach is used to manage innovation during periods of discontinuous change, a compression approach can be used during periods of incremental change, in which the focus is on systematically improving the performance and lowering the cost of the dominant technological design. A **compression approach to innovation** assumes that innovation is a predictable process, that incremental innovation can be planned using a series of steps, and that compressing the time it takes to complete those steps can speed up innovation. There are five parts to the compression approach to innovation: planning, supplier involvement, shortening the time of individual steps, overlapping steps, and multifunctional teams.[19]

In Chapter 4, planning was defined as choosing a goal and a method or strategy to achieve that goal. When planning for incremental innovation, the goal is to squeeze or compress development time as much as possible, and the general strategy is to create a series of planned steps to accomplish that goal. Planning for incremental innovation helps avoid unnecessary steps. In addition, planning allows developers to sequence steps in the right order to avoid wasted time and shorten the delays between steps. Planning also reduces misunderstandings and decreases coordination problems regarding when and how things are to be done.

Most planning for incremental innovation is based on the idea of generational change. **Generational change** occurs when incremental improvements are made to a dominant technological design such that the improved version of the technology is fully backward compatible with the older version.[20] So unlike technological discontinuities that result in the replacement of older technologies, generational change allows the old and newer versions of the same technological design to coexist in the marketplace. For example, Sony (www.sony.com) used the idea of generational change to extend the life of its Sony Walkman products. After inventing the Walkman tape player in 1978, Sony introduced 250 different kinds of Walkmans over the next decade. However, there were few significant changes in the basic Walkman over that time. In fact, 85 percent of the new models simply represented small improvements such as adding AM/FM stereo radio, auto reverse, Dolby sound, water resistance, TV audio band, digital tuning, and enhanced bass. Together, these generational changes have helped Sony maintain above-average profits and a 50 percent share of this market.[21]

Because the compression approach assumes that innovation can follow a series of preplanned steps, one of the ways to shorten development time is supplier involvement. Delegating some of the preplanned steps in the innovation process to outside suppliers reduces the amount of work that internal development teams must do. As well, suppliers provide an alternative source of ideas and expertise that can lead to better designs. Supplier involvement also takes advantage of distinctive competencies by allowing both the development team and the suppliers to do what they do best. In general, the earlier suppliers are involved, the quicker they are to catch and prevent future problems, such as unrealistic designs or mismatched product specifications.

Another way to shorten development time is to simply shorten the time of individual steps in the innovation process. One of the most common ways to do that is through computer-aided design (CAD). CAD speeds up the design process by allowing designers and engineers to make and test design changes using computer models. In many steps of the design process, Ford (www.ford.com) found that CAD models and computer simulations can replace physical testing of expensive automobile prototypes. And since computer-based CAD systems store design specifications and characteristics in computer files (the same way that a personal computer stores word processing files), CAD speeds innovation by making it easy to access and reuse previous designs. At Ford, product designers and

compression approach to innovation
an approach to innovation that assumes that incremental innovation can be planned using a series of steps, and that compressing those steps can speed innovation

generational change
change based on incremental improvements to a dominant technological design such that the improved technology is fully backward compatible with the older technology

engineers use desktop and laptop computers to access a design knowledge base containing standard parts, standard design guides (that walk designers through the process of creating new parts), and detailed performance and testing information. The design knowledge base is accessible to any computer connected to Ford's company network. Finally, CAD systems improve communication and organization by making sure that all design team members work with the latest design iteration. If the engineers in charge of engine design change the size of an engine from four to six cylinders, those changes are automatically registered in what Ford calls the "common total vehicle data model." So when the designers in charge of the car's suspension system log on, they'll find that the engine has been changed and can make the necessary changes to the car's suspension system.[22]

In a sequential design process, each step must be completed before the next step begins. But sometimes multiple development steps can be performed at the same time. Overlapping steps shorten the development process by reducing the delays or waiting time between steps. By using overlapping rather than sequential steps, most car companies have reduced the time it takes to develop a brand-new car from five years to three years. However, they still develop new models sequentially. First they design and build, say, a four-door sedan. Then, after perfecting the design and manufacture of the sedan, two or three years later they introduce the two-door coupe. A couple of years after that, they introduce the station wagon version of the same model.

Review 2
Managing Innovation

To successfully manage innovation streams, companies must manage the sources of innovation and learn to manage innovation during both discontinuous and incremental change. Since innovation begins with creativity, companies can manage the sources of innovation by supporting a creative work environment, in which creative thoughts and ideas are welcomed, valued, and encouraged. Creative work environments provide challenging work; offer organizational, supervisory, and work group encouragement; allow significant freedom; and remove organizational impediments to creativity.

Companies that succeed in periods of discontinuous change typically follow an experiential approach to innovation. The experiential approach assumes that intuition, flexible options, and hands-on experience can reduce uncertainty and accelerate learning and understanding. This approach involves frequent design iterations, frequent testing, regular milestones, creation of multifunctional teams, and use of powerful leaders to guide the innovation process.

A compression approach to innovation works best during periods of incremental change. This approach assumes that innovation can be planned using a series of steps, and that compressing the time it takes to complete those steps can speed up innovation. The five parts to the compression approach are planning (generational change), supplier involvement, shortening the time of individual steps (computer-aided design), overlapping steps, and multifunctional teams.

Organizational Change

"Ding-dong. Avon calling." When people think of Avon, they think of their local "Avon Lady." In North America alone, Avon (www.avon.com) has more than 450 000 Avon Ladies who, using the company's distinctive one-on-one marketing approach, have been selling Avon products directly to customers for decades. Now, however, Avon management is testing the idea of selling Avon products through Avon retail stores. This strategy has been successful overseas, particularly in Malaysia, where 145 Avon stores now account for half of Avon's Malaysian sales. The company is also testing a direct-mail catalogue. Early results indicate that catalogue customers spend twice as much per order as customers who place orders through Avon Ladies. While these changes look promising, they are also risky, because they're likely to cut into the sales and earnings of Avon's North American sales force, which accounts for almost all of their North American sales! Avon hopes to keep its Avon Ladies happy by giving them franchising opportunities with its new Avon stores. Or it may try to refer store customers to them for additional sales. However, when Avon has tried to make changes before, its Avon Ladies have responded angrily. For example, when management tried to cut costs by eliminating sales representative discounts on a limited number of Avon products, 25 000 Avon Ladies quit their jobs in protest.[23]

Why would a company like Avon consider such drastic changes in the way it does business? And with the strong resistance it expects from its sales force, how can it implement these changes successfully?

After reading the next two sections, you should be able to
3. *discuss why change occurs and why it matters.*
4. *discuss the different methods that managers can use to better manage change as it occurs.*

3. Why Change Occurs and Why It Matters

Businesses operate in a constantly changing environment. Recognizing and adapting to internal and external changes can mean the difference between continued success and going out of business.

Let's learn about change forces and resistance forces, and organizational decline: the risk of not changing.[24]

3.1 Change Forces and Resistance Forces

According to social psychologist Kurt Lewin, change is a function of the forces that promote change and the opposing forces that slow or resist change.[25] **Change forces** lead to differences in the form, quality, or condition of an organization over time. By contrast, **resistance forces** support the status quo, that is, the existing state of conditions in organizations.

Exhibit 10.4 illustrates how the relative strengths of resistance and change forces interact to bring about different levels of change. Change can be nonexistent, sporadic, continuous, or discontinuous, depending on whether change forces are stronger or

change forces
forces that produce differences in the form, quality, or condition of an organization over time

resistance forces
forces that support the existing state of conditions in organizations

HOW CHANGE AND RESISTANCE FORCES CREATE CHANGE

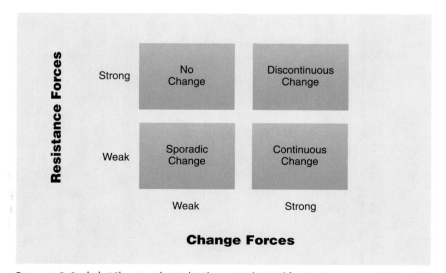

Source: P. Strebel, "Choosing the Right Change Path," *California Management Review*, Winter 1994, 29–51.

weaker than resistance forces. At one extreme, when resistance forces are strong and change forces are weak, there is no change. When resistance and change forces are both weak, chance events can lead to sporadic change that occurs in random patterns or for accidental reasons.

When change forces are strong and resistance forces are weak, continuous change occurs, as organizations are forced to adapt to ongoing change forces. If both change and resistance forces are strong, and the resistance forces can no longer hold back the change forces, sudden discontinuous change can occur. Discontinuous change is similar to an arm-wrestling match between two 250-pound men. Both men are strong, but after a while, one is likely to lose his grip or tire. When that happens, the match will end seconds later, as the winner suddenly overpowers the loser.

3.2 Organizational Decline: The Risk of Not Changing

Organizational decline occurs when companies don't anticipate, recognize, neutralize, or adapt to the internal or external pressures that threaten their survival.[26] In other words, decline occurs when organizations don't recognize the need for change. GM's loss of market share in the automobile industry (from 60 percent to 30 percent) is an example of organizational decline. There are five stages of organizational decline: blinded, inaction, faulty action, crisis, and dissolution.[27]

GM's concerns are well known. Yet few organizational declines have been as dramatic as that of Nortel Networks. One estimate suggests that in early 2000, 75 percent of North America's Internet traffic was carried by Nortel equipment. Over 90 000 individuals were employed by Nortel, most of them in high-paying jobs, much of this the result of a multi-year corporate acquisition spree that cost well over $28 billion. Throughout the world, the Nortel insignia could be found on 24 production facilities. Its 2000 revenues alone were greater than $40 billion, a double-digit increase from the year before and the year before that.[28] At its pinnacle during the summer of 2000, the price of Nortel's shares had peaked at $124.50 while the company stock value was almost

Following the recent downturn in the telecommunications sector, Nortel Networks was faced with the difficult task of drastically reducing its workforce and manufacturing facilities while continuing to offer state-of-the-art products and services.

Erik S. Lesser/Getty Images

$400 billion. Nortel's impact on many Canadians was enormous. During the same period, Nortel's value was equal to 36 percent of the value of the entire TSE 300, an index fund that held 300 major stocks traded on the Toronto Stock Exchange. Few Canadian pension or mutual funds did not contain some Nortel stocks in their holdings.[29]

Unfortunately, just as Nortel was experiencing success building the information highway, so too were its competitors. In the fall of 2000 cracks began to appear in the mirage of continuous industry growth. In many case, large, small, and medium-sized telecommunication service providers throughout North America and Europe soon discovered that the large debts acquired to purchase state-of-the-art telecommunications equipment from companies such as Nortel were not being offset by revenue increases from customers seeking to take advantage of their new gear. Just as Nortel competed with other equipment manufacturers to create new technologies so too did large numbers of telecommunication service providers compete to lay Internet pipe into the home, and across cities, countries, and oceans. The result was too many service providers saddled with too much debt and Internet capacity selling services to too few customers, many of whom were simply not buying.

Nortel Networks' senior management team appeared blinded through much of 2000 by a hazy cloud of optimism and rosy sales forecasts. In the *blinded stage*, decline begins because key managers don't recognize the internal or external changes that will harm their organizations. This "blindness" may be due to a simple lack of awareness about changes. It may stem from an inability to understand the significance of changes. Or it may simply come from the overconfidence that can develop when companies have been successful. In this case, success may have been the villain. While Nortel executives were forecasting future industry growth in the double digits during the early fall of 2000, a prominent New York based analyst, Paul Sagawa, was predicting a dramatic fall in telecommunication carrier spending throughout 2001.[30]

Nortel Networks' reaction to these signals could best be described for a long time as "inaction." Up until October of 2001, it still employed 55 000 people with many of its facilities still in operation and its CEO, John Roth, still the architect of its growth. In the *inaction stage*, as organizational performance problems become more visible, management may recognize the need to change but still take no action. The managers may be waiting to see if the problems will correct themselves. Or they may find it difficult to change previous practices and policies that once led to success. Another possible reason is that they wrongly assume that they can make changes to correct problems, so they don't feel the problems are urgent. It is here where Nortel Networks sat in 2003. With employment levels near 35 000 and with its product lines reorganized, the jury is out as to whether its actions will be labelled in the future as "faulty actions," or whether this is the stage where Nortel halts and turns around its decline.

In the *faulty action stage*, due to rising costs and decreasing profits and market share, management will announce "belt-tightening" plans designed to cut costs, increase efficiency, and restore profits. In other words, rather than recognizing the need for fundamental changes, managers assume that if they just run a "tighter ship," company performance will return to previous levels.

In the *crisis stage*, bankruptcy or dissolution (i.e., breaking up and selling the different parts of the company) is likely to occur unless the company completely reorganizes the way it does business. At this point, however, companies typically lack the resources needed to fully change how they run their businesses. Cutbacks and layoffs will have reduced the level of talent among employees. Furthermore, talented managers who were savvy enough to see the crisis coming will have begun taking jobs with other companies (often with competitors). Because of rising costs and lower sales, cash is tight. And lenders and suppliers are unlikely to extend further loans or credit to ease the cash crunch.

In the *dissolution stage*, after failing to make the changes needed to sustain the organization, the company is dissolved through bankruptcy proceedings or by selling assets in order to pay suppliers, banks, and creditors. At this point, a new CEO may be brought in to oversee the closing of stores, offices, and manufacturing facilities; the final layoff of managers and employees; and the sale of assets to pay bills and loans.

Finally, because decline is reversible at each of the first four stages, not all companies in decline reach final dissolution. For example, after nearly a decade in decline, GM has cut costs, stabilized its market share, and had several consecutive years of small profits.

Review 3
Why Change Occurs and Why It Matters

Change is a function of the relative strength of the change forces and resistance forces that occur inside and outside of organizations. Change can be nonexistent, sporadic, continuous, or discontinuous, depending on whether change forces are stronger or weaker than resistance forces. The five-stage process of organizational decline begins when organizations don't recognize the need for change. In the blinded stage, managers don't recognize the changes that threaten their organization's survival. In the inaction stage, management recognizes the need to change, but doesn't act, hoping that the problems will correct themselves. In the faulty action stage, management focuses on cost cutting and efficiency rather than facing up to fundamental changes needed to insure survival. In the crisis stage, failure is likely unless fundamental reorganization occurs. Finally, in the dissolution stage, the company is dissolved through bankruptcy proceedings, by selling assets to pay creditors, or through the closing of stores, offices, and facilities. However, if companies recognize the need to change early enough, dissolution may be avoided.

4. Managing Change

resistance to change
opposition to change resulting from self-interest, misunderstanding and distrust, or a general intolerance for change

Resistance to change is caused by self-interest, misunderstanding and distrust, and a general intolerance for change.[31] People resist change out of self-interest, because they fear that change will cost or deprive them of something they value. For example, resistance might stem from a fear that the changes will result in a loss of pay, power, responsibility, or even perhaps one's job. People also resist change because of misunderstanding and distrust, that is, they don't understand the change or the reasons for it, or they distrust the people, typically management, behind the change. Ironically, when this occurs, some of the strongest resisters may support the changes in public, nodding and smiling their agreement, but then ignore the changes in private and just do their jobs as they always have.

Resistance may also come from a generally low tolerance for change. Some people are simply less capable of handling change than others. People with a *low tolerance for change* are threatened by the uncertainty associated with change and worry that they won't be able to learn the new skills and behaviours needed to successfully negotiate change in their companies.

Because resistance to change is inevitable, successful change efforts require careful management. So, in this section you will learn about managing resistance to change, change tools and techniques, managing conversations to promote change, and what not to do when leading change.

4.1 Managing Resistance to Change

unfreezing
getting the people affected by change to believe that change is needed

change intervention
the process used to get workers and managers to change their behaviour and work practices

refreezing
supporting and reinforcing the new changes so they "stick"

According to Kurt Lewin, managing organizational change is a basic process of unfreezing, change intervention, and refreezing. **Unfreezing** is getting the people affected by change to believe that change is needed. During the **change intervention** itself, workers and managers change their behaviour and work practices. **Refreezing** is supporting and reinforcing the new changes so they "stick."

Resistance to change is an example of frozen behaviour. Given the choice between changing and not changing, most people would rather not change. Because resistance to change is natural and inevitable, managers need to unfreeze resistance to change to create successful change programs. The following methods can be used to manage resistance to change: education and communication, participation, negotiation, top management support, and coercion.

When resistance to change is based on insufficient, incorrect, or misleading information, managers should *educate* employees about the need for change and *communicate* change-related information to them. Managers must also supply the information and funding or other support employees need to make changes.

Another way to reduce resistance to change is to have those affected by the change *participate in planning and implementing the change process.* Employees who participate have a better understanding of change and the need for it. Furthermore, employee concerns about change can be addressed as they occur if employees participate in the planning and implementation process. For example, in 1996, when Acadia University incorporated IBM laptops into its educational program, its administrators realized that a challenge lay before them. Its faculty members were unionized. Tenure and promotion decisions were based primarily on publication record as opposed to teaching effectiveness. There were few if any other universities to learn from. Classroom pedagogy for fully wired classroom settings was virtually nonexistent. Future bandwidth and server usage needs were at best educated guesses given the continual improvements to Internet-related technologies and applications such as videostreaming, file swapping software, and MP3 technology. Finally, an in-house capacity to service a campus of 4200 laptops was yet to be fully developed and tested. So how was the laptop program implemented given these concerns? To begin, implementation committees were formed and staffed by volunteers. The laptops were phased in over four years with pilot initiatives occurring in the first year. Standard technologies and laptops were adopted. A User Support Centre (USC) was established to support the operation and maintenance of laptop technologies both in the classroom and beyond. The Acadia Institute for Teaching Technology (AITT) was formed to support faculty efforts to develop technology-related pedagogy. Funding and student support for faculty-initiated projects to improve teaching were made available on an annual basis for development each summer. Finally, the union agreements were altered to recognize the importance of teaching and innovation in promotion and tenure.[32]

Employees are less likely to resist change if they are allowed to *discuss and agree on who will do what after change occurs.* For example, construction projects are notoriously hard to manage. It's difficult to get clients, architects, contractors, and subcontractors to agree on things such as prices, materials, schedules, or who should be held responsible for unexpected changes and expenses. Often, lawsuits have to be filed to force reluctant parties to fulfil their responsibilities. Resistance to change also decreases when change efforts receive *significant managerial support.* Top managers must do more than talk about the importance of change. They must provide the training, resources, and autonomy needed to make change happen.

Finally, use of formal power and authority to force others to change is called **coercion**. Because of the intense negative reactions it can create (e.g., fear, stress, resentment, sabotage of company products), coercion should be used only when a crisis exists or when all other attempts to reduce resistance to change have failed. Exhibit 10.5 summarizes some additional suggestions for what managers can do when employees resist change.

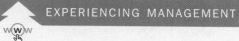

EXPERIENCING MANAGEMENT

A common model of change involves unfreezing old methods, changing and refreezing the new methods. To learn more about this management model of change, visit our animated concept and activity site. Choose Innovation & Change from the "select a topic" pull-down menu then Managing Change from the "overview tab."

www.experiencingmanagement.com

EXPERIENCING MANAGEMENT

Four general approaches for overcoming resistance to change and their advantages and disadvantages are presented at our animated concept and activity site. Choose Innovation & Change from the "select a topic" pull-down menu, then Overcoming Resistance from the "overview tab."

www.experiencingmanagement.com

coercion
use of formal power and authority to force others to change

EXHIBIT 10.5

WHAT TO DO WHEN EMPLOYEES RESIST CHANGE

UNFREEZING

- Share Reasons: Share the reason for change with employees.
- Empathize: Be empathetic to the difficulties that change will create for managers and employees.
- Communicate: Communicate the details simply, clearly, extensively, verbally, and in writing.

CHANGE

- Benefits: Explain the benefits, "What's in it for them."
- Champion: Identify a highly respected manager to manage the change effort.
- Input: Allow the people who will be affected by change to express their needs and offer their input.
- Timing: Don't begin change at a bad time, for example, during the busiest part of the year or month.
- Security: If possible, maintain employees' job security to minimize fear of change.
- Training: Offer training to ensure that employees are both confident and competent to handle new requirements.
- Pace: Change at a manageable pace. Don't rush.

REFREEZING

- Top Management Support: Send consistent messages and free resources
- Publicize Success: Let others know when and where change is working.
- Employee Services: Offer counselling or other services to help employees deal with the stress of change.

Source: G.J. Iskat & J. Liebowitz, "What to Do When Employees Resist Change," *Supervision,* 1 August 1996.

4.2 Change Tools and Techniques

If your boss came to you and said, "All right, genius, you wanted it. You're in charge of turning around the division," how would you start? Where would you begin? How would you encourage change-resistant managers to change? What would you do to include others in the change process? How would you get the change process off to a quick start? Finally, what long-term approach would you use to promote long-term effectiveness and performance? Results-driven change, the General Electric Workout, transition management teams, and organizational development are different change tools and techniques that can be used to address these issues.

One of the reasons that organizational change efforts fail is that they are activity oriented, meaning that they primarily focus on changing company procedures, management philosophy, or employee behaviour. Typically, there is much buildup and preparation as consultants are brought in, presentations are made, books are read, and employees and managers are trained. There's a tremendous emphasis on "doing things the new way." But for all the focus on activities, on "doing," there's almost no focus on results, on seeing if all this activity has actually made a difference.

results-driven change
change created quickly by focusing on the measurement and improvement of results

By contrast, **results-driven change** supplants the sole emphasis on activity with a laser-like focus on quickly measuring and improving results.[33] Another advantage of results-driven change is that managers introduce changes in procedures, philosophy, or behaviour only if they are likely to improve measured performance. In other words, managers actually test to see if changes make a difference.

A third advantage of results-driven change is that quick, visible improvements motivate employees to continue to make additional changes to improve measured performance. Are these ideas used throughout the corporate world? It appears so. Indeed, consultants have introduce the results-driven change programs in such important institutions as Bell Canada, Pfizer Canada, the Industrial Accident Prevention Association of Ontario, DuPont Canada, and Pitney Bowes Canada.[34] For example, at one company, a team used cross-training to reduce the number of job categories from 120 to 32. Another, encouraged by the success of 90 other problem-solving teams, trained machine operators to enter production data directly into the computer on the factory floor, eliminating the 7600 hours of staff work that it used to take to enter those data from paper records. Consequently, unlike most change efforts, the quick successes associated with results-driven change were particularly effective at reducing resistance to change. Exhibit 10.6 describes the basic steps of results-driven change.

The **General Electric Workout** is a special kind of results-driven change. It is a three-day meeting that brings together managers and employees from different levels and parts of an organization to quickly generate and act on solutions to specific business problems.[35] On the first morning of a workout, the boss discusses the agenda and targets specific business problems that the group is to try to solve. Then the boss leaves, and an outside facilitator breaks the group, typically 30 to 40 people, into five or six teams and helps them spend the next day and a half discussing and debating solutions. On day three, in what GE calls a "town meeting," the teams present specific solutions to their boss, who has been gone since day one. As each team spokesperson makes specific suggestions, the boss has only three options: agree on the spot, say no, or ask for more information so that a decision can be made by a specific agreed-on date. Prior to its merger with TransCanada Pipelines Ltd., Calgary-based Nova Gas Transmission Ltd. used a GE Workout to help improve the operating conditions of its gas plant maintenance workers operating throughout Alberta.

Amand Lauzon is a GE boss who sweated his way through a town meeting. To encourage him to say yes, his workers set up the meeting room so that he couldn't make eye contact with his boss. He said, "I was wringing wet within half an hour. They had 108 proposals, I had about a minute to say yes or no to each one, and I couldn't make eye contact with my boss without turning around, which would show everyone in the room that I was chicken."[36] In the end, Lauzon agreed to all but eight suggestions. Furthermore, once those decisions were made, no one at GE was allowed to overrule them.

While the GE Workout clearly speeds up change, it may fragment change, as different managers approve different suggestions in different town meetings across a company. By contrast, a transition management team provides a way to coordinate change throughout an organization. A **transition management team (TMT)** is a team of 8 to 12 people whose full-time job is to manage and coordinate a company's change process.[37] Exhibit 10.7 outlines the primary responsibilities of the TMT. One member of the TMT

General Electric Workout
a three-day meeting in which managers and employees from different levels and parts of an organization quickly generate and act on solutions to specific business problems

transition management team (TMT)
a team of 8 to 12 people whose full-time job is to completely manage and coordinate a company's change process

EXHIBIT 10.6

RESULTS-DRIVEN CHANGE PROGRAMS

1. Create measurable, short-term goals to improve performance.
2. Use action steps only if they are likely to improve measured performance.
3. Management should stress the importance of immediate improvements.
4. Consultants and staffers should help managers and employees achieve quick improvements in performance.
5. Managers and employees should test action steps to see if they actually yield improvements. Action steps that don't should be discarded.
6. It takes few resources to get results-driven change started.

Source: R.H. Schaffer & H.A. Thomson, J.D., "Successful Change Programs Begin with Results," *Harvard Business Review on Change* (Boston: Harvard Business School Publishing, 1998), 189–213.

is assigned the task of anticipating and managing the emotions and behaviours related to resistance to change. Despite their importance, many companies overlook the impact that negative emotions and resistant behaviours can have on the change process. Also, TMTs report to the CEO every day, decide which change projects are approved and funded, select and evaluate the people in charge of different change projects, and make sure that different change projects complement one another. For example, entertainment company Viacom used a TMT to handle the changes that occurred when it acquired two much larger companies, Paramount Communications (TV and films) and Blockbuster Entertainment. The TMT reported directly to the CEO and included managers from Viacom, Paramount, and Blockbuster. Furthermore, Viacom's TMT was charged with eliminating duplication in television production, distribution and sales, and overhead and administrative costs in order to cut $280 million in expenses.[38]

Organizational development is a philosophy and collection of planned change interventions designed to improve an organization's long-term health and performance. Organizational development takes a long-range approach to change; assumes that top management support is necessary for change to succeed; creates change by educating workers and managers to change ideas, beliefs, and behaviours so problems can be solved in new ways; and emphasizes employee participation in diagnosing, solving, and evaluating problems.[39] As shown in Exhibit 10.8, organizational development interventions begin with recognition of a problem. Then the company designates a change agent to be formally in charge of guiding the change effort. This person can be someone from the company or a professional consultant. The **change agent** clarifies the problem, gathers information, works with decision makers to create and implement an action plan, helps to evaluate the plan's effectiveness, implements the plan throughout the company, and then leaves only after making sure the change intervention will continue to work.

Organizational development interventions are aimed at changing large systems, small groups, or people.[40] More specifically, the purpose of *large system interventions* is to change the character and performance of an organization, business unit, or department. The purpose of a *small group intervention* is to assess how a group functions and help it work more effectively toward the accomplishment of its goals. The purpose of a *person-focused intervention* is to help people become aware of their attitudes and behaviours and acquire new skills and knowledge to increase interpersonal effectiveness. Exhibit 10.9 describes the most frequently used organizational development interventions for large systems, small groups, and people.

organizational development
a philosophy and collection of planned change interventions designed to improve an organization's long-term health and performance

change agent
the person formally in charge of guiding a change effort

EXHIBIT 10.7

THE PRIMARY RESPONSIBILITIES OF TRANSITION MANAGEMENT TEAMS

1. Establish context for change and provide guidance.
2. Stimulate conversation.
3. Provide appropriate resources.
4. Coordinate and align projects.
5. Ensure congruence of messages, activities, policies, and behaviours.
6. Provide opportunities for joint creation.
7. Anticipate, identify, and address people problems.
8. Prepare the critical mass.

Source: J.D. Duck, "Managing Change: The Art of Balancing," *Harvard Business Review on Change* (Boston: Harvard Business School Publishing, 1998), 55–81.

EXHIBIT 10.8

GENERAL STEPS FOR ORGANIZATIONAL DEVELOPMENT INTERVENTIONS

1.	Entry	A problem is discovered and the need for change becomes apparent. Search begins for someone to deal with the problem and facilitate change.
2.	Start-up	A change agent enters the picture and works to clarify the problem and gain commitment to a change effort.
3.	Assessment and Feedback	The change agent gathers information about the problem and provides feedback about it to decision makers and those affected by it.
4.	Action Planning	The change agent works with decision makers to develop an action plan.
5.	Intervention	The action plan, or organizational development intervention, is carried out.
6.	Evaluation	The change agent helps decision makers assess the effectiveness of the intervention.
7.	Adoption	Organizational members accept ownership and responsibility for the change, which is then carried out through the entire organization.
8.	Separation	The change agent leaves the organization after first ensuring that the change intervention will continue to work.

Source: W.J. Rothwell, R. Sullivan, & G.M. McLean, *Practicing Organizational Development: A Guide For Consultants* (San Diego: Pfeiffer & Company, 1995).

EXHIBIT 10.9

DIFFERENT KINDS OF ORGANIZATIONAL DEVELOPMENT INTERVENTIONS

LARGE SYSTEM INTERVENTIONS

Sociotechnical Systems	An intervention designed to improve how well employees use and adjust to the work technology used in an organization.
Survey Feedback	An intervention that uses surveys to collect information from organizational members, reports the results of that survey to organizational members, and then uses those results to develop action plans for improvement.

SMALL GROUP INTERVENTIONS

Team Building	An intervention designed to increase the cohesion and cooperation of work group members.
Unit Goal Setting	An intervention designed to help a work group establish short- and long-term goals.

PERSON-FOCUSED INTERVENTIONS

Counselling/Coaching	An intervention designed so that a formal helper or coach listens to managers or employees and advises them how to deal with work or interpersonal problems.
Training	An intervention designed to provide individuals the knowledge, skills, or attitudes they need to become more effective at their jobs.

Source: W.J. Rothwell, R. Sullivan, & G.M. McLean, *Practicing Organizational Development: A Guide for Consultants* (San Diego: Pfeiffer & Company, 1995).

WhatReallyWorks

Change the Work Setting or Change the People? Do Both!

Let's assume that you believe that your company needs to change. Congratulations! Just recognizing the need for change puts you ahead of 80 percent of the companies in your industry. But now that you've recognized the need for change, how do you make change happen? Should you focus on changing the work setting or the behaviour of the people who work in that setting? It's a classic chicken or egg type of question. Which would you do?

A recent meta-analysis based on 52 studies and a combined total of 29 611 study participants indicated that it's probably best to do both!

Changing the Work Setting

An organizational work setting has four parts: organizing arrangements (control and reward systems, organizational structure), social factors (people, culture, patterns of interaction), technology (how inputs are transformed into outputs), and the physical setting (the actual physical space in which people work).

Overall, there is a 55 percent chance that organizational change efforts will successfully bring changes to a company's work setting. While the odds are still 55-45 in your favour, this is undoubtedly a much lower probability of success than you've seen with the management techniques discussed in other chapters. This simply reflects how strong resistance to change is in most companies.

Probability of Success

Changing the People

Changing people means changing individual work behaviour. The idea is powerful. Change the decisions people make.

Change the activities they perform. Change the information they share with others. And change the initiatives they take on their own. Change these individual behaviours and collectively you change the entire company. Overall, there is a 57 percent chance that organizational change efforts will successfully change people's individual work behaviour. If you're wondering why the odds aren't higher, consider how difficult it is to simply change personal behaviour. It's incredibly difficult to quit smoking, change diet, or maintain a daily exercise program. Not surprisingly, changing personal behaviour at work is also difficult. Thus, viewed in this context, a 57 percent chance of success is a notable achievement.

Probability of Success

Changing Individual Behaviour and Organizational Performance

The point of changing individual behaviour is to improve organizational performance (i.e., higher profits, market share, and productivity, and lower costs). Overall, there is a 76 percent chance that changes in individual behaviour will produce changes in organizational outcomes. So if you want to improve your company's profits, market share, or productivity, focus on changing the way that your people behave at work.

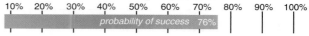

Probability of Success

Source: P.J. Robertson, D.R. Roberts, & J.I. Porras, "Dynamics of Planned Organizational Change: Assessing Empirical Support for a Theoretical Model," *Academy of Management Journal* 36 (1993): 619–634.

4.3 Managing Conversations to Promote Change

Think about where you have worked. How well and often did managers, especially top management, talk to you and other employees? Was it one-way, top-down communication, or did management listen and respond to the ideas of lower-level managers and employees? How did people from different parts of the company talk to each other? Did they try to understand each other, or did they talk past each other by using terms and ideas particular to their jobs or departments?

organizational dialogue
the process by which people in an organization learn to talk effectively and constructively with each other

Organizational dialogue is the process by which people in an organization learn to talk effectively and constructively with each other.[41] Unfortunately, in most companies, the quality of organizational dialogue isn't very good. But when change forces are strong and managers and workers are stressed, organizational dialogue can be nonexistent. Consequently, the way managers and workers talk (or don't talk) to each other can be a significant barrier to successful change efforts.

According to this line of thinking, talk is not cheap. Conversations shape attitudes, intentions, and actions. What is said or not said really matters. So when organizational dialogue breaks down, change efforts break down, too. From this perspective, managing change is akin to managing the conversations that make up organizational dialogue.

When change efforts work, change begins with initiative conversations. These are followed by conversations about understanding, performance, and closure.[42] **Initiative conversations** start the change process by discussing what should or needs to be done to bring about change. **Conversations for understanding** generate a deeper understanding of why change is needed, what problems have been occurring, and what might be done to solve those problems. **Conversations for performance** refer to action plans, in which managers and workers make specific requests and promise specific results. Finally, **conversations for closure** end the change process by indicating that the work is done and the change process is complete.

4.4 What Not to Do When Leading Change

So far, you've learned about the basic change process (unfreezing, change, refreezing), managing resistance to change, the four kinds of change tools and techniques (results-driven change, the GE Workout, transition management teams, and organizational development), and using conversations to promote change. However, John Kotter of the Harvard Business School argues that knowing what not to do is just as important as knowing what to do when it comes to achieving successful organizational change.[43]

Exhibit 10.10 shows the most common errors that managers make when they lead change. The first two errors occur during the unfreezing phase, in which managers try to get the people affected by change to believe that change is really needed. The first and potentially most serious of these errors is *not establishing a great enough sense of urgency*. Indeed, Kotter estimates that more than half of all change efforts fail because the people affected by change are just not convinced that change is necessary. However, people will feel a greater sense of urgency about change if a leader in the company makes a public, candid assessment of the company's problems and weaknesses.

initiative conversations
conversations that start the change process by discussing what should or needs to be done to bring about change

conversations for understanding
conversations that generate a deeper understanding of why change is needed, what problems have been occurring, and what might be done to solve those problems

conversations for performance
conversations about action plans, in which managers and workers make specific requests and promise specific results

conversations for closure
conversations that end the change process by indicating that the work is done and the change process is complete

---

EXHIBIT 10.10

ERRORS MANAGERS MAKE WHEN LEADING CHANGE

UNFREEZING
1. Not establishing a great enough sense of urgency.
2. Not creating a powerful enough guiding coalition.

CHANGE
3. Lacking a vision.
4. Undercommunicating the vision by a factor of ten.
5. Not removing obstacles to the new vision.
6. Not systematically planning for and creating short-term wins.

REFREEZING
7. Declaring victory too soon.
8. Not anchoring changes in the corporation's culture.

Source: J.P. Kotter, "Leading Change: Why Transformation Efforts Fail," *Harvard Business Review* 73, no. 2 (March-April 1995): 59.

The second mistake that occurs in the unfreezing process is *not creating a powerful enough coalition*. Change often starts with one or two people, but in order to build enough momentum to change an entire department, division, or company, change has to be supported by a critical and growing group of people. Besides top management, Kotter recommends that key employees, managers, board members, customers, and even union leaders be members of a core change coalition, which guides and supports organizational change. Furthermore, it's important to strengthen this group's resolve by periodically bringing its members together for off-site retreats. At Merck, a leading pharmaceutical firm, CEO Raymond Gilmartin uses off-site retreats to break down barriers and build confidence. He said, "What goes on during the breaks and during the dinners or lunches is often just as important" as what is discussed in the meetings. Likewise, to encourage an openness to change, former IBM CEO Lou Gerstner took his top 40 managers to an off-site retreat every six weeks. The purpose? To get IBM's managers to challenge their thinking and to learn to view IBM's business from different perspectives.[44]

The next four errors that managers make occur during the change phase, in which a change intervention is used to try to get workers and managers to change their behaviour and work practices.

Lacking a vision for change is a significant error at this point. As you learned in Chapter 4, a vision is a statement of a company's purpose or reason for existing. A vision for change makes clear where a company or department is headed and why the change is occurring. Change efforts that lack vision tend to be confused, chaotic, and contradictory. By contrast, change efforts guided by visions are clear, easy to understand, and can be effectively explained in five minutes or less.

Undercommunicating the vision by a factor of ten is another mistake in the change phase. According to Kotter, companies mistakenly hold just one meeting to announce the vision. Or, if the new vision receives heavy emphasis in executive speeches or company newsletters, senior management then undercuts the vision by behaving in ways contrary to it. Successful communication of the vision requires that top managers link everything the company does to the new vision and that they "walk the talk" by behaving in ways consistent with the vision. Furthermore, even companies that begin change with a clear vision sometimes make the mistake of *not removing obstacles to the new vision*. Insisting on change, but then failing to redesign jobs, pay plans, and technology to support the new way of doing things leaves formidable barriers to change in place.

Similar to results-driven change, another error in the change phase is *not systematically planning for and creating short-term wins*. Most people don't have the discipline and patience to wait two years to see if the new change effort works. Change is threatening and uncomfortable, so for people to continue to support it, they need to see an immediate payoff. Kotter recommends that managers create short-term wins by actively picking people and projects that are likely to work extremely well early in the change process.

The last two errors that managers make occur during the refreezing phase, when attempts are made to support and reinforce changes so they "stick."

Declaring victory too soon is a tempting mistake in the refreezing phase. Managers typically declare victory right after the first large-scale success in the change process. Ironically, declaring success too early has the same effect as draining the gasoline out of a car. It stops change efforts dead in their tracks. With success declared, supporters of the change process stop pushing to make change happen. After all, why "push" when success has been achieved? Rather than declaring victory, managers should use the momentum from short-term wins to push for even bigger or faster changes. This maintains urgency and prevents change supporters from slacking off before the changes are frozen into the company's culture.

The last mistake that managers make is *not anchoring changes in the corporation's culture*. An *organization's culture* is the set of key values, beliefs, and attitudes shared by organizational members that determines the "accepted way of doing things" in a company. As you learned in Chapter 2, cultures are extremely difficult and slow to change. Kotter said that two things help anchor changes in a corporation's culture. The first is directly showing people that the changes have actually improved performance. The second is to make sure that the people who get promoted fit the new culture. If they don't, it's a clear sign that the changes were only temporary.

Review 4
Managing Change

The basic change process is unfreezing, change, and refreezing. Resistance to change, which stems from self-interest, misunderstanding and distrust, and a general intolerance for change, can be managed through education and communication, participation, negotiation, coercion, and top management support. When change efforts work, change begins with initiative conversations and is followed by conversations about understanding, performance, and closure. But when conversations break down, change efforts break down, too. Change conversations can break down in five ways: nothing happens, unclear conditions of satisfaction, agreement isn't action, lack of rigour, and omitting closure.

Managers can use a number of change techniques. Results-driven change and the GE Workout reduce resistance to change by getting change efforts off to a fast start. Transition management teams, which manage a company's change process, coordinate change efforts throughout an organization. Organizational development is a collection of planned change interventions (large system, small group, person-focused) guided by a change agent that are designed to improve an organization's long-term health and performance. Finally, knowing what not to do is as important as knowing what to do to achieve successful change. Managers should avoid these errors when leading change: not establishing urgency, not creating a guiding coalition, lacking a vision, undercommunicating the vision, not removing obstacles to the vision, not creating short-term wins, declaring victory too soon, and not anchoring changes in the corporation's culture.

What Really Happened?

In the opening case, you learned about the financial difficulties that IBM (www.ibm.com) experienced as a result of its inability to change or to bring innovative products to market. Read the answers to the opening case to find out how IBM is addressing these problems.

But how do you quickly and effectively change a company like IBM? Should the change be slow and gradual or quick and revolutionary?

It's never easy to change a company, especially one as large as IBM (revenues over $80 billion [U.S.] and more than 200 000 employees). However, in less than five years, then-CEO Lou Gerstner and his management team managed to bring change to IBM and return it to solid profitability.

Organizational change is a function of the relative strength of the change forces and resistance forces that occur inside and outside of organizations. Change can be nonexistent, sporadic, continuous, or discontinuous, depending on whether change forces are stronger or weaker than resistance forces. Many analysts and experts were frustrated by what they saw as Gerstner's steady, continuous approach to changing IBM. They criticized Gerstner and IBM for being "incrementalists" and for not changing the basic way IBM does business. Essentially, they wanted Gerstner to greatly increase the change forces within IBM, for example, changing the management structure, changing the reward systems, and so forth. And Gerstner did some of these things. Today, 75 percent of an IBM manager's bonus is tied to overall company profitability compared to just 25 percent before Gerstner arrived. With so much more money riding on the company's success, IBM managers have been quicker to change.

However, most of Gerstner's efforts were aimed at weakening resistance forces that promoted and protected the status quo in all organizations. And at IBM, the greatest deterrent to change was its guarantee of lifetime employment. As long as you were a good performer, you'd have a job of some kind at IBM, even if your division or job no longer existed. This guarantee was supposed to demonstrate IBM's commitment to its workforce and, in turn, gain workers' loyalty. In practice, however, IBM managers guaranteed jobs to all employees, regardless of job performance. Not surprisingly, in annual attitude surveys IBM's best performers complained that company management was too soft on poor performers who, in their view, should have been fired. So, in a move that many would describe as revolutionary for IBM, Gerstner began a program of layoffs that would eventually cut IBM's workforce in half, from just over 400 000 employees to approximately 200 000 today. And with layoffs occurring, IBMers who previously had every reason to resist change (i.e., lifetime job guarantee) began listening to what needed to be done to stem IBM's losses and restore profitability. Said Gerstner, "Transforming IBM is not something we can do in one or two years. The better we are at fixing some of the short-term things, the more time we have to deal with the long-term issues. You can't really start addressing the long-term issues unless you've got a stabilization."

IBM has a long history and a strong culture. So any changes that you try to make will probably be resisted. How can you identify and manage that resistance so IBM can make the changes that it needs to make?

The basic change process is one of unfreezing, change, and then refreezing. Unfreezing is getting the people affected by change to believe that change is needed. During the change intervention itself, workers and managers change their behaviour and work practices. Refreezing is supporting and reinforcing the new changes so they "stick." This basic change process of unfreezing, change, and refreezing works best by first reducing resistance to change.

Gerstner managed resistance to change by focusing on participation and by selectively using coercion. Participation reduces resistance to change by having those affected by change participate in the planning and implementation of the change process. Whereas the "old IBM" was incredibly slow to make decisions, Gerstner tried to force IBMers to quickly act on decisions. He did this by making snap, on-the-spot decisions and then granting full authority to particular individuals to make those decisions happen. For example, Gerstner began eight reengineering projects in areas such as hardware development and production processes, and then made sure that each project was "owned" by a manager who was fully responsible for it.

Coercion is the use of formal power and authority to force others to change. Because of the negative reactions it can create, coercion should be used only when a crisis exists or when other change techniques have failed. When IBM needed to downsize its workforce in France, it offered French workers this deal: You can save your jobs if you replace your guaranteed annual bonus with a compensation package that ties your earnings to company performance.

In the fast-paced environment of computers, it takes IBM much too long to develop and bring new products to market. How can you speed up that process?

IBM has never had problems coming up with new ideas. For example, IBM invented computer hard drives and memory, two of the key components of modern computers. IBM's mistake, however, was that it has been slow to bring its new inventions and new product ideas to market. Until recently, IBM seems not to have understood that technology cycles follow an S-curve pattern of innovation. Early in the cycle, technological progress is slow and improvements in technological performance are small. However, as a technology matures, performance improves quickly. Finally, small improvements occur as the limits of a technology are reached. At this point, significant improvements in performance must come from new technologies. It's at this last point that IBM has been consistently outgunned by competitors such as Intel and Microsoft who have been much quicker to introduce new technologies.

Over the long run, the best way for a company to protect its competitive advantage is to create a stream of innovative ideas and products. To do this well, the company must learn how to manage the sources of innovation, how to manage innovation during discontinuous change, and how to manage innovation during incremental change. In the last few years, IBM has made significant strides in these areas by doing a much better job of bringing new technologies to market. A former IBM researcher said, "The difference that the Gerstner regime introduced was, it wasn't enough anymore to just move ideas into the product world. What was important for us in Research was to understand what the market wanted."

For example, IBM has a new program called "First of a Kind," in which new research projects are shared with IBM customers who use them to solve real-world problems. One of the more successful "First of a Kind" products was IBM's voice-dictation software. After developing the software, IBM shared it with radiologists in New York and Boston hospitals. When reading x-rays, these doctors usually dictated their findings onto audio tapes that were later transcribed and placed in patients' files. Now, however, the doctors simply dictate their notes directly to a computer that, using IBM's software, instantly converts them to written files. IBM now sells this software worldwide.

Sources: A. Goldstein, "Big Blue Pulls Ahead of the Pack," *Dallas Morning News*, 14 February 1999, 1H. L. Hays, "Another Top IBM Executive Quits Amid Reorganization by Gerstner," *The Wall Street Journal Europe*, 10 January 1995. "IBM's Finances: Now Comes the Hard Part," *Infoperspectives* 18 (1 April 1997). D.Q. Mills, "The Decline and Rise of IBM," *Sloan Management Review* 37 (1 June 1996). R. Narisetti, "How IBM Turned Around Its Ailing PC Division," *The Wall Street Journal*, 12 March 1998, B1. S. Sherman, "Is He Too Cautious to Save IBM?" *Fortune*, 3 October 1994. B. Ziegler, "IBM's Research Cutbacks Now Seem to Be Brilliant," *The Wall Street Journal*, 6 October 1997.

Key Terms

change agent (312)
change forces (305)
change intervention (308)
coercion (309)
compression approach to innovation (303)
conversations for closure (315)
conversations for performance (315)
conversations for understanding (315)
creativity (294)
design competition (298)
design iteration (301)
dominant design (299)

era of ferment (298)
experiential approach to innovation (301)
General Electric Workout (311)
generational change (303)
incremental change (300)
initiative conversations (315)
innovation streams (298)
milestones (302)
multifunctional teams (302)
organization decline (306)
organizational change (294)
organizational development (312)

organizational dialogue (314)
organizational innovation (294)
refreezing (308)
resistance forces (305)
resistance to change (308)
results-driven change (310)
S-curve pattern of innovation (295)
technological discontinuity (298)
technological substitution (298)
technology cycle (295)
testing (301)
transition management team (TMT) (311)
unfreezing (308)

What Would You Do II?

It is 2000. As you look over your calendar, your hands automatically begin to rub your temples. The annual Toy Fair is right around the corner, and newspapers and magazines around the world are publishing their lists of the most successful toys of last year and their predictions of what will be hot next year. Unfortunately, you pretty much know that none of your company's products will be on any of them. Founded nearly 70 years ago by your grandfather, Lego (www.lego.com) has a long history in the toy industry, but it can't seem to keep up with today's kids' (or even yesterday's kids') thirst for so-called interactive toys. Technically, Lego is interactive, but nowadays that means battery-operated, software-driven, and done-for-you rather than do-it-yourself. Today's children grow up in an entertainment-saturated environment, and open-ended, self-guided play is fading into a nostalgic memory.

The Lego name was created in 1934 by Ole Kirk Christiansen, a Danish toymaker who introduced the first plastic Lego brick in 1949. His son Godtfred Kirk Christiansen then designed an entire system of play around the bricks in the mid-1950s. Since these revolutionary moments, the only real innovation at Lego was the introduction of themed sets, like towns, farms, and space stations, which didn't start until the 1970s. The formula for making the plastic bricks hasn't even changed since then! My, how time flies, you think to yourself.

The only thing brighter and more enduring than Lego's vividly coloured blocks is the company's core value of inspiring and nurturing creativity and play. One extension of this is the fact that you refuse to produce any toy that resembles a 20th-century weapon. Holding onto such admirable values, however, doesn't seem to be helping the company succeed. Your company hasn't had a toy in the list of top 20 North American sellers in the last seven years, and this year doesn't look to be any different. And one could argue that the themed Lego sets already signal a departure from open-ended play. After all, some sets have pages and pages of instructions on how to build the set "right."

Lego is the seventh most powerful worldwide brand among families, behind such giants as Coca-Cola and Disney (you know because you closely follow the research), but Lego hasn't changed the way kids play, let alone the way they learn, for a long time. Can Lego be that kind of leader again, and if so, how? Will you have to change your company values and management, or just your products? What are the risks of not changing?

As Kirk Kjeld Kristiansen (his name was misspelled on his birth certificate), CEO of Lego, what would you do?

Sources: "Bestsellers," *U.S. News & World Report,* 19 February 2001, 66. C. Fishman, "Why Can't Lego Click?" *Fast Company,* September 2001, www.fastcompany.com/online/50/lego.html. S. Jarvis, "New Lego Creation Marketing Up a Storm," *Marketing News,* 9 October 2001, www.marketingpower.com. N. Montfort, "Some Creativity Required," *Technology Review,* July 2000, 110. F. Witsil, "Toy Stores Have Tough Time Keeping Lego-Made Bionicles in Stock," *Tampa Tribune,* 21 October 2001, www.wsj.com.

Critical Thinking Video Case

Scenario Planning

In this video first presented in Chapter 9, you learned that scenario planning has become an important tool for managers seeking to make sense of complex, uncertain future business environments. An alternative to traditional forecasting, it is a tool for imagining developed by the Shell Oil company in the early 1970s that helps executives stay ahead of surprises.

In this video, you will learn that scenario planning is a critical analytical tool for many companies seeking to survive and prosper in unstable and uncertain foreign and domestic markets. For instance, scenario development and analysis help the Royal Bank of Canada manage over $40 billion of loans to the Canadian oil industry. Finning International Inc., a Vancouver-based distributor of industrial equipment, employs a consultant to throw scenarios at it on an ongoing basis to keep it alert and in tune with its global market. So influential is the use of this technique at Finning that it acquired a British-based heavy equipment rental company as the result of insight gleaned from its use. As you watch the video, consider the following critical thinking question.

Critical Thinking Question

How might scenario planning be used by executives worried about the onset of organizational decline in their companies?

Management Decisions

Heads, You Change. Tails, You Change

You are the general manager of a medium-sized appliance manufacturing facility in Mississauga, Ontario. You've just received a phone call that you have been expecting for some time now. Your boss just informed you that if your plant doesn't show markedly better results (in productivity, profitability, etc.) within six months, it will be closed down and relocated to Ciudad Juarez, an industrial Mexican city across the border from El Paso, Texas. Of course, this news is no surprise to you. Your plant is one of only a few left producing appliances in Canada. Due to lower wages, closer proximity to suppliers, and favourable tax treatments, a few Canadian factories have closed their Canadian doors and reopened as Maquiladoras within Mexico's borders. If your plant follows the same road, most of the production workers will lose their jobs. The supervisory, middle, and top-level management positions, however, will be transferred to the new location.

Moving your managers would be a challenge. Even the carrot of job security may not be enough to overcome resistance. Many of your management staff have lived in or around Mississauga their whole lives, have close family ties to the area, or have children who are entrenched in their schools and social lives. The alternative—turning the plant around in six months—is no more attractive. This would require all employees to rethink how work is done and to re-engineer work processes, in short to change the very way they all think about working at your company.

The typical employee at your plant is like Tom, your assistant and best friend, who would probably be very resistant to any kind of change. Tom eats the same kind of sandwich everyday. He is never receptive to new ideas or radical change. And he has worked at the plant since he returned to Mississauga after university.

You really don't want to move to Mexico, and you'd like to keep the 500 production jobs at your plant in Mississauga. But there are so many ways to implement change. Which one would be best-suited to your situation?

Questions

1. Jot down the pros and cons of each change tool and technique presented in the chapter and determine what seems to fit this situation the best. Which one(s) did you choose and why?
2. You are going to have to internally promote whatever option you chose. Outline change conversations that you might have with the typical employee, say Tom, for example. How can you avoid breakdowns in change initiatives during your conversations?
3. If your change initiatives fail to bring the plant into corporate expectations, you will have to handle the equally tough situation of convincing managers to follow the company to Mexico. How will you do this? What can you do as their supervisor to calm their fears and minimize their resistance to this type of change?

Management Decisions

Freedom Not to Worry about Products and Profits?

What a great opportunity! Head of company research and development for a Fortune 100 high-tech company. This is the job you've been wanting for years. And what better time to get it? Thanks to the innovative products and technology produced by your R&D labs, profits are strong and market share is growing. There's only one downside. Its success has attracted numerous competitors and dozens of new start-up companies, all intent on taking a substantial chunk of your customers and profits. If the company doesn't maintain its stream of innovative products, it's sure to lose its competitive advantage to one of these hungry competitors. This morning, when you met with the CEO, you were given one directive: "Find a way to increase the level of innovation we get from our R&D labs. How you do it is up to you. Just make it happen." Your reply was quick and confident, "You can count on me." But as you were leaving the office, you really weren't sure just how to improve on the company's already fine record of innovation.

In general, there are two lines of thought about how to get the most out of R&D labs. The first is to focus on basic research and give researchers the freedom they need to pursue the ideas that intrigue them. This is the model that Bell Labs followed for over 60 years. During that time, Bell Labs researchers came up with more than 25 000 patents, more than one per day, as they invented motion pictures with sound, long-distance transmission of TV signals, stereo recording, transistors, solar power cells, lasers, communications satellites, and cellular phones. Not surprisingly, seven Bell Labs scientists won Nobel Prizes for science during that time, more than any other lab in the world. Under the basic research model, leading scientists study what they want and never have to worry about profits. Furthermore, they have "signatory authority," meaning that they control their own research budgets and have the ability (within that budget) to purchase whatever equipment they need to conduct their research.

The second line of thought is that innovation can be improved by holding researchers accountable for developing marketable ideas that can be turned into practical products. For example, at ICL PLC, the British computer company owned by Fujitsu of Japan, researchers are expected to maintain close contact with customers. When ICL PLC developed a new computer system for Cathay Pacific Airlines, management told the researchers to "get out of their Jesus sandals and into business suits....we're going to transfer you (to Asia) along with the technology." In general, moves like this are designed to make researchers aware of three questions: What can the company do with your idea/technology/product? How big is the market for it? And how much money can the company make from it?

Questions

1. Both approaches have tradeoffs. After reviewing the chapter discussion concerning innovation streams and technology cycles, describe two important advantages and two serious disadvantages for the "basic research" model described above.

2. Describe two important advantages and two serious disadvantages for the "profits and products" model described above.

3. If you were running this company's R & D lab, which would you choose, the "basic research" model or the "profits and products" model? Explain your choice and the reasons for it.

Sources: S. Ascarelli, "European Telecom R&D Labs Adjusting: Scientists Must Think in Terms of Profit and Loss," *The Wall Street Journal*, 15 March 1996. L. Hooper, "Technology (A Special Report): Genius: The Creative Edge: Nurturing High-Tech Talent Requires a Delicate Balancing Act; But the Payoff Can Be Huge," *The Wall Street Journal*, 24 May 1993. J. Keller, "Technology (A Special Report): Finding and Feeding: Ignoring the Bottom Line: NEC's U.S. Research Lab Has a Theory: The Freedom Not to Worry about Products May Lead to the Best Products of All," *The Wall Street Journal*, 24 May 1993. G. Naik, "Corporate Research: How Much Is It Worth? Top Labs Shift Research Goals to Fast Payoffs," *The Wall Street Journal*, 22 May 1995. B. Ziegler & G. Naik, "Bell Labs Faces Mundane Future under Breakup Plan," *The Wall Street Journal*, 22 September 1995.

Develop Your Management Potential

A Personal Force Field Analysis

In the "What Really Works" section of this chapter, you learned that when people change their behaviour in the workplace, there is a 76 percent chance that organizational profits, market share, and productivity can be improved. However, you also learned that organization-wide change efforts have only a 57 percent chance of successfully changing people's work behaviour. So changing people's behaviour works great. The hard part is figuring out how to get them to change their behaviour. This "Develop Your Management Potential" assignment reviews how you can use a personal force field analysis to change your behaviour at work.

At the beginning of this chapter, you learned that organizational change is a function of change forces and resistance forces. Change forces lead to differences in the form, quality, or condition of an organization over time. Resistance forces support the status quo, that is, the existing state of conditions in organizations. One of the ways that managers prepare for specific organizational change is to carefully conduct an organizational force field analysis by listing the change and resistance forces that support and oppose that change. For example, Exhibit 10.11 lists the resistance forces and change forces that oppose and support the possibility of changing a company's corporate headquarters from Toronto to Calgary.

Listing resistance and change forces is also a useful way to conduct a personal force field analysis. The first step of a personal force field analysis is to clearly describe how or what behaviour you intend to change. For example, if you're always late with your expense reports, you might write, "I will turn in my expense reports within three days of returning from a business trip." In Chapter 4, you learned that to be effective, goals need to be S.M.A.R.T.: specific, measurable, attainable, realistic, and timely. Descriptions of the behaviours you intend to change should follow the S.M.A.R.T. guidelines, too.

The second step of a personal force field analysis is to list and describe resistance forces, that is, the reasons that make it difficult for you to change your behaviour. Since resistance to change is caused by self-interest, misunderstanding and distrust, and a general intolerance for change, be sure to assess whether these factors are making it difficult for you to change your behaviour. For example, are you turning your expense reports in late because turning them in on time will cost or deprive you of something of value (i.e., self-interest)? Probably not, because if you turned the expense reports in on time, you'd get your money back sooner.

EXHIBIT 10.11

RESISTANCE AND CHANGE FORCES

POSSIBLE CHANGE: MOVING CORPORATE HEADQUARTERS FROM TORONTO TO CALGARY

RESISTANCE FORCES
- Many employees may not want or be able to move.
- Large expense of making the move, buying or building a new headquarters, and selling old headquarters.
- Negative publicity from local press generated by just considering the move.
- Toronto city officials may offer incentives to encourage firm to stay.

CHANGE FORCES
- Much lower cost of living and no provincial sales tax will make it easier to attract and retain a talented workforce.
- Lower real estate and energy costs will significantly lower the cost of maintaining corporate headquarters.
- Significant customer base has developed in the western regions of the country.
- Calgary city officials may offer incentives to encourage firm to move.

Are you turning in your expense reports late because you misunderstand or distrust the reasons for turning in your expense report on time or distrust the people who review the expenses? Well, we might be on to something here. Misunderstanding probably isn't the problem. What's to misunderstand about an expense report? You fill it out, turn it in, and get reimbursed. In this case, it's more likely that your resistance stems from distrust of the people who review the reports. Perhaps, in the past, you felt that you weren't fairly reimbursed. If so, why turn in your expense report on time when you don't expect to get back all the money you're owed?

Finally, are you turning in your expense reports late because you have a low tolerance for change? In this case, however, a low tolerance for change probably has more to do with habitual behaviour than with any uncertainty associated with the change process.

The final step of a personal force field analysis is to list the change forces, that is, the reasons prompting you to consider changing your behaviour. At this step, it can be useful to separate your reasons by category, such as personal or organizational benefits, or personal or organizational consequences (i.e., the negative consequences associated with not changing your behaviour). For example, turning in your expense report on time gets you your money faster, a personal benefit; helps the organization stay current with its expenses, an organizational benefit; and helps you avoid getting yelled at by your boss for being late with the expense report, which is a personal negative consequence.

Now use these steps to conduct a personal force field analysis.

Questions
1. Clearly describe how or what behaviour you intend to change. Be sure your description is S.M.A.R.T.: specific, measurable, attainable, realistic, and timely.
2. List and describe the resistance forces that make it difficult for you to change this behaviour. Do these reasons have anything to do with
   - Self-interest? Will the change cost or deprive you of something you value?
   - Misunderstanding and distrust? Do you not understand the change or the reasons for it? Do you distrust the people behind the change? In other words, is someone other than yourself pressuring you to make this change?
   - A general intolerance for change? Are you simply less capable of handling change than others? Are you worried that you won't be able to learn the new skills and behaviours needed to successfully negotiate this behaviour change?
3. List and describe the change forces that are leading you to consider changing your behaviour. Separate your reasons into personal or organizational benefits, or personal or organizational consequences (i.e., the negative consequences associated with not changing your behaviour).

Discussion Questions

1. Define innovation streams and list the basic phases in the process.

2. The personal computer (PC) industry is an interesting one to watch these days. Overall, sales in the industry are down as are sales for all major manufacturers with the exception of Dell. Dell is bucking industry trends and has actually increased its sales and market share. One firm particularly hard hit by reduced PC sales is Gateway Inc. In this context, explain what is meant by organizational decline and list its five stages.

3. Identify and briefly explain the three steps involved in the process of managing organizational change according to Kurt Lewin.

4. For many undergraduates, a sign of success upon completion of a degree is a job with a world-class organization. Especially difficult to capture are positions with some of the world's leading consulting firms such as McKinsey and Co. and Bain and Co. These companies are famous for the rigour of their interview process. As graduation approaches, you set your eyes on one of these cherished positions and are a granted an interview. As you begin your preparation for your encounter, a number of questions swirl through your mind. One of them is "What are the tools and techniques available to you as a change agent when seeking to foster change in an organization?"

Study Tip

On a separate sheet, write the titles of the exhibits in this chapter. Then, with your book closed, try to reproduce the diagrams exactly as they are in the text. Write a short description of what the diagram depicts, and then open your book to check your work.

11

Chapter Outline

Learning Objectives

After reading this chapter, you should be able to

1. describe the departmentalization approach to organizational structure.

2. explain organizational authority.

3. discuss the different methods for job design.

4. explain the methods that companies are using to redesign internal organizational processes (i.e., intraorganizational processes).

5. describe the methods that companies are using to redesign external organizational processes (i.e., interorganizational processes).

eleven

Organizational Structures and Processes

What Would You Do?

Exide Technologies Headquarters. "Geez, I can't believe we can't figure this out! In 1898, didn't we supply the batteries for a submarine? In 1901, weren't the first transcontinental telephone and telegraph services powered by Exide batteries? In 1934, whom did Commander Byrd look to when he needed power to establish a military base on Antarctica? In 1969, didn't we build the batteries for NASA's Apollo space missions and its first lunar landing? And in 1991, during Operation Desert Storm, didn't we make tank and ordinance batteries for the U.S. Army? If we're good enough to make products that have been critical to so many historical events, then why can't we figure out how to organize this company?"

Certainly, designing the right organizational structure should be easier than designing new products, but as CEO of Exide Technologies, it doesn't seem that way to you. Your management consultants assure you that Exide's difficulties in choosing the right organizational structure put it in good company. The more global a company, they say—and Exide is in 89 countries including Canada—the more difficult it is figuring out who should have responsibility for what and who should report to whom. For example, under the "Ford 2000" plan, Ford tried to consolidate its functional departments, such as new car development, which had separate departments in Europe (Merkenich, Germany) and North America (Detroit, Michigan) into one global department. Unfortunately, results were mixed. While Ford initially saved $5 billion (U.S.) after reorganizing, it also saw its market share slip significantly in Europe, from 13 percent to 8.8 percent, over the same time.

Likewise, Procter & Gamble's "Organization 2005" plan was designed to take employees who had been organized by geographical markets (e.g., North America, South America, Europe, Mid-East, Asia) into five global business units (GBU), such as the "beauty-care GBU" or the "food and beverage GBU." After the changes, food and beverage managers, most of whom were located in North America, reported to the GBU president in Caracas, Venezuela. Laundry and household employees, most of whom were also located in North America, reported to their GBU president in Brussels, Belgium. Besides separating managers from subordinates, "Organization 2005" also created personal upheaval for P&G managers, half of whom were assigned new jobs. Furthermore, 1000 managers and employees were transferred from various points across Europe to Geneva, Switzerland. Similar numbers of people were moved to other locations. Following the changes, 25 percent of P&G's marketing managers left the company, and market share and financial performance dropped significantly.

Unfortunately, with its geographical structure Exide has found itself in situations eerily similar to Ford and P&G. First, despite being the world's largest producer of industrial and automotive batteries, financial losses are increasing, the company share price is dropping, and the company's debt load is soaring. Second, like Ford and P&G, Exide, although headquartered in Princeton, New Jersey, is organized geographically, with "country managers" in charge of Exide operations in each country. Unfortunately, this has led to competition as company managers try to steal business from each other. For instance, Mark Stevenson, the company's managing director for Britain, argued with the country manager for Germany who was upset that the British unit sold batteries in Austria for 10 percent to 15 percent less. Third, the geographical organization encouraged country managers to build their own fiefdoms, adding offices and manufacturing plants, whether needed or not. In short, said Mark Stevenson, the managing director for Britain, country managers "acted like barons."

Which organizational structure should Exide use? Should it stay with a geographical structure, but tinker with it to fix the problems? What would be the advantages or disadvantages of that approach? Or should it use a product structure—what P&G called "global business units"—to standardize what it does around the world?

What would be the advantages or disadvantages of this approach? When will Exide know when it has found the right organizational structure?

If you were the CEO at Exide Technologies, what would you do?

Sources: E. Nelson, "Rallying the Troops at P&G—New CEO Lafley Aims to End Upheaval by Revamping Program of Globalization," *The Wall Street Journal*, 31 August 2000, B1. "Exide Technologies Announces Restructuring: Focuses on Global Customer Business Units," Exide Technologies. [Online] Available www.exide.com/ 11 November 2001. J. Lublin, "Division Problem, Place Vs. Product: It's Tough to Choose a Management Model—Exide Tore Up System Based on Countries for One Centered on Battery Lines—Rolling over European Fiefs," *The Wall Street Journal*, 27 June 2001, A1. R. Simison, "Ford Hopes Its New Focus Will Be a Global Bestseller—Escort's Replacement Offers Improvements for Same Price," *The Wall Street Journal*, 8 October 1998, B10. "The History of Exide Technologies," Exide Technologies. [Online] Available www.exide.com/ 11 November 2001.

No one builds a house without first looking at the design. Put a window there. Take out a wall here. Soon you've got the design you want. Only then do you start building. These days, the design of a company is just as important as the design of a house. As the Exide Technologies case shows, if you don't have the right design, the company's performance can quickly fall apart like a house of cards.

In the first half of the chapter, you will learn about the traditional vertical and horizontal approaches to **organizational structure**, including departmentalization, organizational authority, and job design. In the second half of the chapter, you will learn how companies are using reengineering, empowerment, and behaviour informality to redesign their internal **organizational processes**. The chapter ends with a discussion about the ways in which companies are redesigning their external processes, that is, how they are changing to improve their interactions with those outside the company. In that discussion, you will explore the basics of modular, virtual, and boundaryless organizations.

organizational structure
the vertical and horizontal configuration of departments, authority, and jobs within a company

organizational process
the collection of activities that transforms inputs into outputs that customers value

Designing Organizational Structures

Reynolds Wrap is a name you may recognize. It is the brand name of the aluminum foil that you may use to keep leftovers fresh in your fridge. It is also a product of Reynolds Metals, an integrated manufacturer, distributor, and marketer of processed and unprocessed aluminum products. Prior to its merger with ALCOA (www.alcoa.com), Reynolds had been organized geographically, with separate regional operations around the world. One day, it announced that it was restructuring. Jeremiah Sheehan, Reynolds' chairman and CEO at the time, said that "as part of our Portfolio Review process, we have streamlined our business focus and assessed new organization structures appropriate for managing our businesses in the future. As a result, we are reorganizing the structure of the company into six worldwide, market-focused businesses...."[1] So instead of having geographic divisions, Reynolds will now use a product structure, with separate divisions focusing on aluminum cans, building and construction, consumer products, infrastructure, packaging, and transportation.

Why would a large company like Reynolds, with 29 000 employees and $4.8 billion (U.S.) in annual revenues, completely restructure its global organizational design? What did it expect to gain as a result of this massive change?

After reading the next three sections, you should be able to
1. *describe the departmentalization approach to organizational structure.*
2. *explain organizational authority.*
3. *discuss the different methods for job design.*

1. Departmentalization

Traditionally, organizational structures have been based on some form of departmentalization. **Departmentalization** is a method of subdividing work and workers into separate organizational units that take responsibility for completing particular tasks.[2] For example, the Sony Corporation has separate departments or divisions for electronics, music, movies, television, games, and theatres.[3] Likewise, Bayer, a German-based company, has separate departments or divisions for health care, agriculture, polymers, chemicals, and photography.[4] Why is the idea of departmentalization important? Well, consider the impact on employees. In most instances, responsibility for attaining corporate goals and objects is shared. Often a boss or manager is also shared as are important resources. Further, departments often form the basis of distinct corporate subcultures and environments where collaboration occurs.[5]

Traditionally, organizational structures have been created by departmentalizing work according to five methods: functional departmentalization, product departmentalization, customer departmentalization, geographic departmentalization, and matrix departmentalization.

departmentalization
subdividing work and workers into separate organizational units responsible for completing particular tasks

1.1 Functional Departmentalization

The most common organizational structure is functional departmentalization. Companies tend to use this structure when they are small or just starting out. **Functional departmentalization** organizes work and workers into separate units responsible for particular business functions or areas of expertise. For example, a common set of functions would consist of accounting, sales, marketing, production, and human resources departments. However, not all functionally departmentalized companies have the same functions. For example, Exhibit 11.1 shows functional structures for an insurance company and an advertising agency. The light-coloured boxes indicate that both companies have sales, accounting, human resources, and information systems departments. The darker boxes are different for each company. As would be expected, the insurance company has separate departments for life, auto, home, and health insurance. By contrast, the advertising agency has departments for artwork, creative work, print advertising, and radio advertising. So the kind of functional departments in a functional structure depends, in part, on the business or industry a company is in. Functional departmentalization has some advantages. First, it allows work to be done by highly qualified specialists. Second, it lowers costs by reducing duplication. Third, with everyone in the same department having similar work experience or training, communication and coordination are less problematic for departmental managers. However, functional departmentalization has a number of disadvantages, too. To start, cross-department coordination can be difficult. Managers and employees are often more interested in doing what's right for their function than in doing what's right for the entire organization. As companies grow, functional departmentalization may also lead to slower decision-making and produce managers and workers with narrow experience and expertise.

functional departmentalization
organizing work and workers into separate units responsible for particular business functions or areas of expertise

EXPERIENCING MANAGEMENT

You may learn more about departmentalization approaches and their advantages and disadvantages by interacting with this concept at our animated concept and activity site. Choose Organizational Design from the "select a topic" pull-down menu, then Departmentalization from the "overview tab."

www.experiencingmanagement.com

1.2 Product Departmentalization

Product departmentalization organizes work and workers into separate units responsible for producing particular products or services. Exhibit 11.2 shows the product departmentalization structure used by the General Electric Corporation. GE is organized along 12 different product lines: aircraft engines, appliances, capital services, lighting,

product departmentalization
organizing work and workers into separate units responsible for producing particular products or services

EXHIBIT 11.1

FUNCTIONAL DEPARTMENTALIZATION

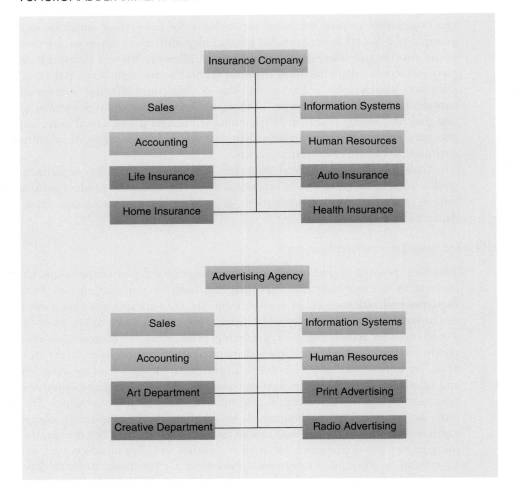

medical systems, NBC television, plastics, power systems, electrical distribution and control, information services, industrial control systems, and transportation systems. One of the advantages of product departmentalization is that, like functional departmentalization, it allows managers and workers to specialize in one area of expertise. However, unlike the narrow expertise and experiences in functional departmentalization, managers and workers develop a broader set of experiences and expertise related to an entire product line. Likewise, product departmentalization makes it easier for top managers to assess work-unit performance. For example, because of their clear separation, it is a relatively straightforward process for GE's top managers to evaluate the performance of their 12 different product divisions. For instance, GE's Aircraft Engines product division outperformed GE's Power Systems product division. Both had similar revenues, $10.78 billion (U.S.) for Aircraft Engines and $11.85 (U.S.) billion for Power Systems, but Aircraft Engines had a profit of $2.46 billion (U.S.), while Power Systems had a profit of $2.19 billion (U.S.).[6] Finally, because managers and workers are responsible for the entire product line rather than for separate functional departments, decision-making should be faster because there are fewer conflicts (compared to functional departmentalization). The primary disadvantage of product departmentalization is duplication as this often results in higher costs. A second disadvantage is that it can be difficult to achieve coordination across the different product departments.

EXHIBIT 11.2

PRODUCT DEPARTMENTALIZATION: GENERAL ELECTRIC CORPORATION

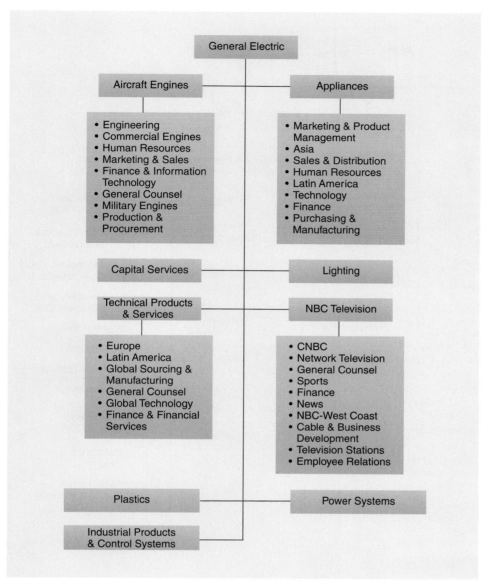

Source: GE Annual Report. [Online] Available www.ge.com/, 3 November 2001.

1.3 Customer Departmentalization

Customer departmentalization organizes work and workers into separate units responsible for particular kinds of customers. For example, Exhibit 11.3 shows that American Express (www.americanexpress.com) is organized into departments that cater to consumers (Cards: credit and charge cards), travellers (Travel: travellers' cheques, airline tickets, vacations, and worldwide travel offices), investors (Financial Services: advisors, mutual and money market funds, etc.), shoppers (Shopping: catalogue, gift, and online shopping), and businesspeople (Business Services: business travel, corporate cards, and financing, accounting, planning, and lending for small businesses). The primary advantage to customer departmentalization is that it focuses the organization on customer needs rather than on products or business functions. Furthermore, creating separate

customer departmentalization
organizing work and workers into separate units responsible for particular kinds of customers

EXHIBIT 11.3

CUSTOMER DEPARTMENTALIZATION: AMERICAN EXPRESS CORPORATION

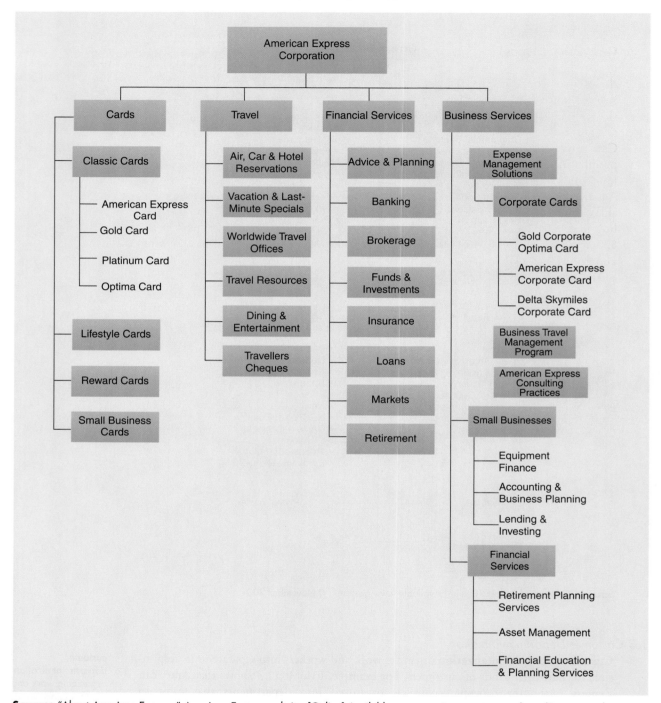

Source: "About American Express," American Express website. [Online] Available www.americanexpress.com/corp/?aexp_nav=hp_corp, 11 January 1999.

departments to serve specific kinds of customers allows companies to specialize and adapt their products and services to customer needs and problems. The primary disadvantage of customer departmentalization is that, like product departmentalization, it leads to duplication of resources. Furthermore, like product departmentalization, it can be difficult to achieve coordination across different customer departments. Finally, the emphasis on meeting customers' needs may lead workers to make decisions that please customers but hurt the business.

1.4 Geographic Departmentalization

Geographic departmentalization organizes work and workers into separate units responsible for doing business in particular geographical areas. For example, Exhibit 11.4 shows the geographic departmentalization used by Coca-Cola Enterprises (CCE) (www.cokecce.com), the largest bottler and distributor of Coca-Cola products in the world. (The Coca-Cola Company develops and advertises soft drinks. CCE, which is a separate company with its own stock, buys the soft drink concentrate from the Coca-Cola Company, combines it with other ingredients, and then distributes the final product in cans, bottles, or fountain containers.) As shown in Exhibit 11.4, CCE has four regional groups: Central North America, Eastern North America, Western North America, and Europe. Exhibit 11.4 shows that each of these four regions would be a sizable company by itself. For example, the European group serves a population of 137 million people in Belgium, France, Great Britain, and the Netherlands, sells more than 825 million cases of soft drinks a year, employs more than 7907 people, and runs 28 bottling facilities.

The primary advantage of geographic departmentalization is that it helps companies respond to the demands of different markets. This can be especially important when selling in different countries. For example, CCE's geographic divisions sell products suited to the taste preferences in different countries. CCE bottles and distributes the

geographic departmentalization organizing work and workers into separate units responsible for doing business in particular geographical areas

EXHIBIT 11.4

GEOGRAPHIC DEPARTMENTALIZATION COCA-COLA ENTERPRISES

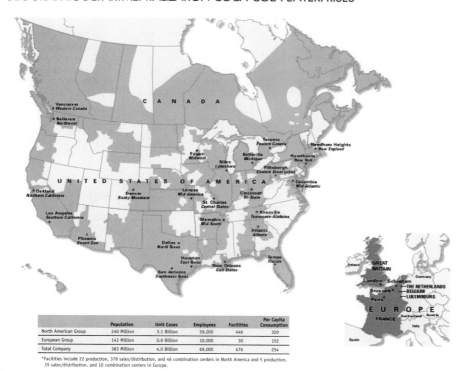

	Population	Unit Cases	Employees	Facilities	Per Capita Consumption
North American Group	240 Million	3.1 Billion	59,000	446	320
European Group	143 Million	0.9 Billion	10,000	30	152
Total Company	383 Million	4.0 Billion	69,000	476	254

*Facilities include 22 production, 378 sales/distribution, and 46 combination centers in North America and 5 production, 15 sales/distribution, and 10 combination centers in Europe.

Source: Territories. Coca-Cola Enterprises. [Online] Available www.cokecce.com, 4 November 2001.

following products in Europe but not in the United States: Aquarius, Bonaqua, Buxton Mineral Water, Coca-Cola light, Cresta flavours, Finley, Kia-Ora, Kinley, Lilt, Oasis, and Roses. Another advantage is that geographic departmentalization can reduce costs by locating unique organizational resources closer to customers. The primary disadvantage of geographic departmentalization is that it can lead to duplication of resources. Also, even more so than with the other forms of departmentalization, it can be especially difficult to coordinate departments that are literally thousands of kilometres from each other and whose managers have very limited contact with each other.

1.5 Matrix Departmentalization

matrix departmentalization
a hybrid organizational structure in which two or more forms of departmentalization, most often product and functional, are used together

Matrix departmentalization is a hybrid structure in which two or more forms of departmentalization are used together. In Canada, CAE Inc. (www.cae.com) makes extensive use of a matrix structure to build flight simulators. The most common matrix combines product and functional forms of departmentalization. Exhibit 11.5 shows the matrix structure used by Pharmacia & Upjohn, a pharmaceutical company. Across the top of Exhibit 11.5, you can see that the company uses a functional structure (research, development, manufacturing, and marketing) within each of its three largest geographic markets, the United States, Europe, and Japan. However, down the left side of the exhibit, notice that the company is using a product structure to research and develop

---

EXHIBIT 11.5

MATRIX DEPARTMENTALIZATION: PHARMACIA & UPJOHN

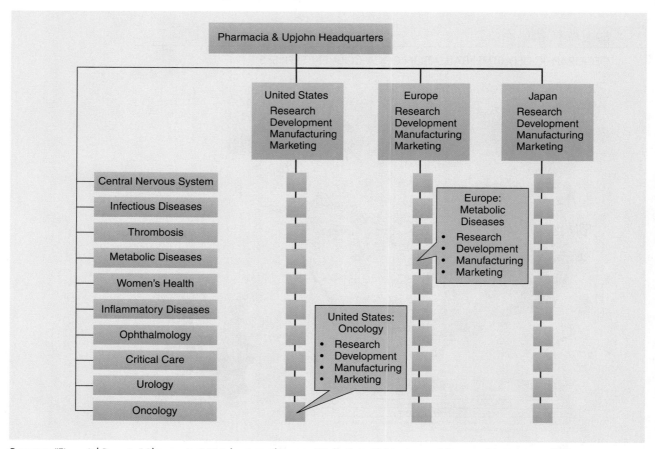

Source: "Financial Reports," Pharmacia & Upjohn Annual Report. [Online] Available www.upjohn.com, 11 January 1999.

drugs for the central nervous system, infectious diseases, metabolic and inflammatory diseases, as well as thrombosis, women's health, ophthalmology, critical care, urology, and oncology.

The boxes in the exhibit represent the matrix structure, created by the combination of the functional/geographic and product structures. For example, in Europe, the Metabolic Diseases group has four functional departments: Research, Development, Manufacturing, and Marketing. In the United States, the Oncology group has the same set of functional departments.

Several things distinguish matrix departmentalization from the other traditional forms of departmentalization.[7] First, most employees report to two bosses, a functional boss and a project or product boss. Second, by virtue of the function-by-project design, matrix structures lead to much more cross-functional interaction than other forms of departmentalization. In fact, while matrix workers are members of only one functional department (based on their work experience and expertise), it is common for them to be members of several ongoing project groups. Third, because of the high level of cross-functional interaction, matrix departmentalization requires significant coordination between functional and project managers. In particular, these managers have the complex job of tracking and managing the multiple project and functional demands on employees' time.

The primary advantage of matrix departmentalization is that it allows companies to efficiently manage large, complex tasks such as researching, developing, and marketing pharmaceuticals. Efficiency comes from avoiding duplication. Another advantage is the ability to carry out large, complex tasks. Because of the ability to quickly pull in expert help from all the functional areas of the company, matrix project managers have a much more diverse set of expertise and experience at their disposal than do managers in the other forms of departmentalization. The primary disadvantage of matrix departmentalization is the high level of coordination required to manage the complexity involved with running large, ongoing projects at various levels of completion. Matrix structures are notorious for confusion and conflict between project bosses, or between project and functional bosses. Disagreements or misunderstandings about project schedules, budgets, available resources, and the availability of employees with particular functional expertise are common. Another disadvantage is that matrix structures require much more management skill than the other forms of departmentalization.

Review 1
Departmentalization

There are five traditional departmental structures: functional, product, customer, geographic, and matrix. Functional departmentalization is based on the different business functions or expertise used to run a business. Product departmentalization is organized according to the different products or services a company sells. Customer departmentalization focuses its divisions on the different kinds of customers that companies have. Geographic departmentalization is based on the different geographical areas or markets in which the company does business. Matrix departmentalization is a hybrid form that combines two or more forms of departmentalization, the most common being the product and functional forms. There is no "best" departmental structure. Each structure has advantages and disadvantages.

2. Organizational Authority

The second part of traditional organizational structures is authority. **Authority** is the right to give commands, take action, and make decisions to achieve organizational objectives.[8]

Traditionally, organizational authority has been characterized by the following dimensions:[9] chain of command, line versus staff authority, delegation of authority, and degree of centralization.

authority
the right to give commands, take action, and make decisions to achieve organizational objectives

chain of command
the vertical line of authority that clarifies who reports to whom throughout the organization

unity of command
a management principle that workers should report to just one boss

span of control
the number of people reporting to a specific supervisor

The **chain of command** is the vertical line of authority that clarifies who reports to whom throughout the organization. People higher in the chain of command have the right, if they so choose, to give commands, take action, and make decisions concerning activities occurring anywhere below them in the chain. One of the key assumptions underlying the chain of command is **unity of command**, which means that workers should report to just one boss.[10] In practical terms, this means that only one person can be in charge at a time. Matrix organizations, in which employees have two bosses, automatically violate this principle. This is one of the primary reasons that matrix organizations are difficult to manage. The purpose of unity of command is to prevent the confusion that might arise when an employee receives conflicting commands from two different bosses. For example, someone walks into an emergency room, describing symptoms similar to a heart attack. The first person in charge, most likely a nurse, makes the initial assessment, assigns the patient to a treatment room, and gets the necessary doctors, nurses, and equipment to begin evaluation and treatment. Then the emergency room physician, who is higher than the nurse in the chain of command, takes charge and begins the process of determining whether the patient is really having a heart attack by conducting an examination, ordering tests, and taking the patient's medical history. If the physician calls in a cardiologist for consultation, the cardiologist becomes the person in charge and makes the final treatment decision. Despite the number of people involved in the process, it's clear who is in charge at each point because the emergency room follows the principle of unity of command.

A second key assumption is the idea termed "**span of control**" or the number of individuals who report to any one supervisor. It is probably not surprising to learn that the fewer the individuals being supervised by any one manager, the easier it is to control the behaviour of subordinates. The reason is quite simple—more time will be available to spend with each subordinate. Is there a magic number when considering how many individuals should report to any one supervisor? The research suggests six or seven.

EXPERIENCING MANAGEMENT

WWW

Learn more about principles of coordination at our animated concept and activity site. Choose Organizational Design from the "select a topic" pull-down menu, then Principles of Coordination from the "overview tab."

www.experiencingmanagement.com

At first glance, many emergency rooms appear chaotic. However, a well-understood command structure passing from nurse to emergency room physician to specialist ensures patients receive the best available care.

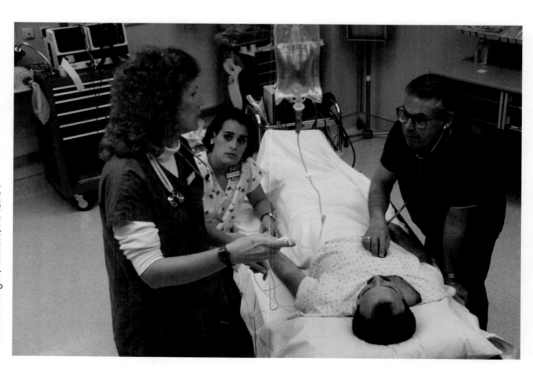

© Warren Morgan/CORBIS/MAGMA

A second dimension of authority is the distinction between line and staff authority. **Line authority** is the right to command immediate subordinates in the chain of command. This person can issue orders to that division manager and expect them to be carried out.

Staff authority is the right to advise but not command others who are not subordinates in the chain of command. The terms "line" and "staff" are also used to describe different functions within the organization. A **line function** is an activity that contributes directly to creating or selling the company's products. A **staff function** is one that does not contribute directly to creating or selling the company's products, but instead supports line activities. Typical staff functions within an organization are accounting, human resources, and legal services.

2.3 Delegation of Authority

Managers can exercise their authority directly by completing the tasks themselves, or they can choose to pass on some of their authority to subordinates. **Delegation of authority** is the assignment of direct authority and responsibility to a subordinate to complete tasks for which the manager is normally responsible.

When a manager delegates work, three transfers occur, as illustrated in Exhibit 11.6. First, the manager transfers full responsibility for the assignment to the subordinate. Many managers find giving up full responsibility somewhat difficult. Indeed, most managers have way too much to do. So, from a practical perspective, they can't assume new responsibilities that come with change and growth until they fully delegate old ones. Another problem is that managers often fear that the task won't be done as well if they don't do it themselves. Sometimes managers delegate "full responsibility" only to later interfere with how the employee is performing the task. "Why are you doing it that way? That's not the way I do it." In short, delegating full responsibility means that the employee—not the manager—is now completely responsible for task completion. Second, delegation transfers to the subordinate full authority over the budget, resources, and personnel needed to do the job. To do the job effectively, subordinates must have the same tools and information at their disposal that managers had when they were responsible for the same task. In other words, for delegation to work, delegated authority must be commensurate with delegated responsibility.

The third transfer that occurs with delegation is the transfer of accountability. The subordinate now has the authority and responsibility to do the job, and is then accountable for getting the job done. In other words, managers give subordinates their managerial authority and responsibility in exchange for results. Exhibit 11.7 gives some tips on how to be an effective delegator.

2.4 Degree of Centralization

Centralization of authority is the location of most authority at the upper levels of the organization. In a centralized organization, managers make most decisions, even the relatively small ones. **Decentralization** is the location of a significant amount of authority in the lower levels of the organization. An organization is decentralized if it has a high degree of delegation at all levels. In a decentralized organization, workers closest to problems are authorized to make the decisions necessary to solve the problems on their own.

Decentralization has a number of advantages. It develops employee capabilities throughout the company and leads to faster decision-making and more satisfied customers and employees. Furthermore, a study of 1000 large companies found that companies with a high degree of decentralization outperformed those with a low degree of decentralization with regard to return on assets (6.9 percent versus 4.7 percent), return

line authority
the right to command immediate subordinates in the chain of command

staff authority
the right to advise but not command others who are not subordinates in the chain of command

line function
an activity that contributes directly to creating or selling the company's products

staff function
an activity that does not contribute directly to creating or selling the company's products, but instead supports line activities

delegation of authority
the assignment of direct authority and responsibility to a subordinate to complete tasks for which the manager is normally responsible

 EXPERIENCING MANAGEMENT

Delegation affects the authority, responsibility, and accountability of employees. Learn how these three concepts are related at our animated concept and activity site. Choose Organizational Design from the "select a topic" pull-down menu, then Delegation from the "overview tab."

www.experiencingmanagement.com

centralization of authority
the location of most authority at the upper levels of the organization

decentralization
the location of a significant amount of authority in the lower levels of the organization

EXHIBIT 11.6

DELEGATION: RESPONSIBILITY, AUTHORITY, AND ACCOUNTABILITY

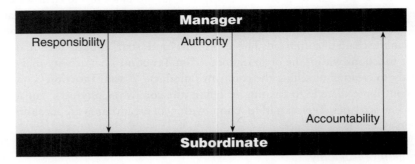

Source: Pringle, *Managing Organizations: Functions and Behaviors*, 1st Edition, © 1988. Reprinted by permission of Pearson Education, Inc., Upper Saddle River, NJ.

---

standardization
solving problems by consistently applying the same rules, procedures, and processes

on investment (14.6 percent versus 9 percent), return on equity (22.8 percent versus 16.6 percent), and return on sales (10.3 percent versus 6.3 percent). Ironically, however, the same study found that few large companies are actually decentralized. Specifically, only 31 percent of employees in these 1000 companies were responsible for recommending improvements to management. Overall, just 10 percent of employees received the training and information needed to support a truly decentralized approach to management.[11]

With results like these, the key question is no longer whether companies should decentralize, but where they should decentralize. One rule of thumb is to stay centralized where standardization is important and to decentralize where standardization is unimportant. **Standardization** is solving problems by consistently applying the same rules, procedures, and processes.

EXHIBIT 11.7

HOW TO BE A MORE EFFECTIVE DELEGATOR

1. Trust your staff to do a good job. Recognize that others have the talent and ability to complete projects.
2. Avoid seeking perfection. Establish a standard of quality and provide a time frame for reaching it.
3. Give effective job instructions. Make sure employees have enough information to complete the job successfully.
4. Know your true interests. Delegation is difficult for some people who actually prefer doing the work themselves rather than managing it.
5. Follow up on progress. Build in checkpoints to help identify potential problems.
6. Praise the efforts of your staff.
7. Don't wait to the last minute to delegate. Avoid crisis management by routinely delegating work.
8. Ask questions, expect answers, and assist employees to help them complete the work assignments as expected.
9. Provide the resources you would expect if you were doing an assignment yourself.
10. Delegate to the lowest possible level to make the best possible use of organizational resources, energy, and knowledge.

Source: S.B. Wilson, "Are You an Effective Delegator?" *Female Executive*, 1 November 1994, 19.

Organizational authority is determined by the chain of command, line versus staff authority, delegation, and the degree of centralization in a company. The chain of command vertically connects every job in the company to higher levels of management and makes clear who reports to whom. Managers have line authority to command employees below them in the chain of command, but have only staff or advisory authority over employees not below them in the chain of command. Managers delegate authority by transferring to subordinates the authority and responsibility needed to do a task, and, in exchange, subordinates become accountable for task completion. In centralized companies, most authority to make decisions lies with managers in the upper levels of the company. In decentralized companies, much of the authority is delegated to the workers closest to problems, who can then make the decisions necessary for solving the problems themselves. Centralization works best for tasks that require standardized decision-making. When standardization isn't important, decentralization can lead to faster decisions, greater employee and customer satisfaction, and significantly better financial performance.

3. Job Design

Imagine that McDonald's (www.mcdonalds.com) decided to pay $50 000 a year to its drive-through window cashiers. Fifty thousand dollars for saying "Welcome to McDonald's. May I have your order please?" Would you take the job? Sure you would. Work a couple of years. Make a hundred grand. Why not? However, let's assume that to get this outrageous salary, you have to be a full-time drive-through McDonald's window cashier for the next 10 years. Would you still take the job? Just imagine, 40 to 60 times an hour you repeat the same basic process:

1. "Welcome to McDonald's. May I have your order please?"

2. Listen to the order. Repeat it for accuracy. State the total cost. "Please drive to the second window."

3. Take the money. Make change.

4. Give customers drinks, straws, and napkins.

5. Give customers food.

6. "Thank you for coming to McDonald's."

Could you stand to do the same simple tasks an average of 50 times per hour, 400 times per day, 2000 times per week, or 8000 times per month? Few can. It's rare for fast-food workers to stay on the job more than six months. Indeed, McDonald's and other fast-food restaurants have well over 100 percent employee turnover each year.[12]

In this next section, you will learn about **job design**—the number, kind, and variety of tasks that individual workers perform in doing their jobs. You will learn about job specialization, job rotation, enlargement, and enrichment.

job design
the number, kind, and variety of tasks that individual workers perform in doing their jobs

3.1 Job Specialization

Job specialization is a job composed of a small part of a larger task or process. Specialized jobs are characterized by simple, easy-to-learn steps, low variety, and high repetition, like the McDonald's drive-through window job described above. One of the clear disadvantages of specialized jobs is that, being so easy to learn, they quickly become boring. This, in turn, can lead to low job satisfaction and high absenteeism and employee turnover, all of which are very costly to organizations. Why, then, do companies continue to create and use specialized jobs? The primary reason is that specialized jobs are very economical. Once a job has been specialized, it takes little time to learn and master. Consequently, when experienced workers quit or are absent, the company loses little productivity when replacing them with a new employee.

job specialization
a job composed of a small part of a larger task or process

Because of the efficiency of specialized jobs, companies are often reluctant to eliminate them. Consequently, job redesign efforts have focused on modifying jobs to keep the benefits of specialized jobs, but to reduce their obvious costs and disadvantages. Three methods, job rotation, job enlargement, and job enrichment, have been used to try to improve specialized jobs.[13]

In factory work, or even some office jobs, many workers perform the same task all day long. For example, if you attach side mirrors in an auto factory, you probably complete this task 45 to 60 times an hour. If you work as the cashier at a grocery store, you check out a different customer every two to three minutes. And if you work as an office receptionist, you may answer and direct phone calls up to 200 times an hour.

Job rotation attempts to overcome the disadvantages of job specialization by periodically moving workers from one specialized job to another to give them more variety and the opportunity to use different skills. For example, the office receptionist who does nothing but answer phones could be systematically rotated to a different job, such as typing, filing, or data entry, every day or two. Because employees simply switch from one specialized job to another, job rotation allows companies to retain the economic benefits of specialized work. However, the greater variety of tasks makes the work less boring and more satisfying for workers. A slightly different example of job rotation can be found in academic institutions. In many departments, the role of academic head is not one that is fought over. Preferring to focus on teaching and research, many scholars shy away from administrative duties whenever possible. As a result, some academic units work on the basis of a voluntary rotation of department heads where an individual assumes the duty for a year and then passes the responsibilities on to a colleague who, after a year, passes the role on to another colleague, and so on. The Management Department of Saint Mary's University in Halifax uses this type of job rotation.

Another way to counter the disadvantages of specialization is to enlarge the job. **Job enlargement** is increasing the number of different tasks that a worker performs within one particular job. So, instead of having to perform just one task, workers with enlarged jobs would be given several tasks to perform. For example, an enlarged "mirror attacher" job might include attaching the mirror, checking to see that the mirror's power adjustment controls work, and then cleaning the mirror's surface. While job enlargement

job rotation
periodically moving workers from one specialized job to another to give them more variety and the opportunity to use different skills

job enlargement
increasing the number of different tasks that a worker performs within one particular job

Specialized jobs are found in most companies. Interestingly, companies are increasingly using job rotation to add variety to the tasks faced by workers such as this assembly line worker. Job rotation also allows workers to add to their repertoire of skills and retain other skills.

© CORBIS/MAGMA

increases variety, many workers report feeling more stress when their jobs are enlarged. Consequently, many workers view enlarged jobs as simply "more work," especially if they are not given additional time to complete the additional tasks.

Job enrichment attempts to overcome the deficiencies in specialized work by increasing the number of tasks and by giving workers the authority and control to make meaningful decisions about their work.[14]

job enrichment
increasing the number of tasks in a particular job and giving workers the authority and control to make meaningful decisions about their work

Review 3
Job Design

Companies use specialized jobs because they are economical and easy to learn and don't require highly paid workers. However, specialized jobs aren't motivating or particularly satisfying for employees. Companies have used job rotation, job enlargement, and job enrichment to make specialized jobs more interesting and motivating. With job rotation, workers move from one specialized job to another. Job enlargement simply increases the number of different tasks within a particular job. Job enrichment increases the number of tasks in a job and gives workers authority and control over their work.

Designing Organizational Processes

Nearly 40 years ago, Tom Burns and G.M. Stalker described how two kinds of organizational designs, mechanistic and organic, are appropriate for different kinds of organizational environments.[15] **Mechanistic organizations** are characterized by specialized jobs and responsibilities; precisely defined, unchanging roles; and a rigid chain of command based on centralized authority and vertical communication. This type of organization works best in stable, unchanging business environments. By contrast, **organic organizations** are characterized by broadly defined jobs and responsibility; loosely defined, frequently changing roles; and decentralized authority and horizontal communication based on task knowledge. This type of organization works best in dynamic, changing business environments.

The key difference between these approaches is that while mechanistic organizational designs focus on organizational structure, organic organizational designs are concerned with organizational processes, the collection of activities that transform inputs into outputs valued by customers.

After reading the next two sections, you should be able to
4. explain the methods that companies are using to redesign internal organizational processes (i.e., intraorganizational processes).
5. describe the methods that companies are using to redesign external organizational processes (i.e., interorganizational processes).

mechanistic organization
organization characterized by specialized jobs and responsibilities; precisely defined, unchanging roles; and a rigid chain of command based on centralized authority and vertical communication

organic organization
organization characterized by broadly defined jobs and responsibility; loosely defined, frequently changing roles; and decentralized authority and horizontal communication based on task knowledge

4. Intraorganizational Processes

An **intraorganizational process** is the collection of activities that take place within an organization to transform inputs into outputs that customers value. The steps involved in an automobile insurance claim are a good example of an intraorganizational process:

1. Document the loss (i.e., the accident).
2. Assign an appraiser to determine the dollar amount of damage.
3. Make an appointment to inspect the vehicle.
4. Inspect the vehicle.
5. Write an appraisal and get the repair shop to agree to the damage estimate.
6. Pay for the repair work.
7. Return the repaired car to the customer.

Let's take a look at how companies are using reengineering, empowerment, and behavioural informality.

intraorganizational process
the collection of activities that take place within an organization to transform inputs into outputs that customers value

reengineering
fundamental rethinking and radical redesign of business processes to achieve dramatic improvements in critical measures of performance, such as cost, quality, service, and speed

In their best-selling book *Reengineering the Corporation*, Michael Hammer and James Champy defined **reengineering** as "the *fundamental* rethinking and *radical* redesign of business *processes* to achieve *dramatic* improvements in critical, contemporary measures of performance, such as cost, quality, service and speed."[16] Hammer and Champy further explained the four key words shown in italics in this definition. The first key word is "fundamental." When reengineering organizational designs, managers must ask themselves, "Why do we do what we do?" and "Why do we do it the way we do?" The usual answer is "Because that's the way we've always done it." The second key word is "radical." Reengineering is about significant change, about starting over by throwing out the old ways of getting work done. The third key word is "processes." Hammer and Champy noted that "most business people are not process oriented; they are focused on tasks, on jobs, on people, on structures, but not on processes." The fourth key word is "dramatic." Reengineering is about achieving "quantum" improvements in company performance.

An example from IBM's credit operation illustrates how work can be reengineered.[17] "IBM Credit" loans businesses money to buy IBM computers. Previously, the loan process would begin when an IBM salesperson called needing credit approval for a customer's purchase. The first department involved in the process would take the credit information over the phone from the salesperson and record it on the credit form. Then, the credit form was sent to a separate credit checking department, and then to a separate pricing department (where the interest rate was determined), and so on. In all, it would take five departments six days to approve or deny the customer's loan. Of course, this delay cost IBM business. Some customers got their loans elsewhere. Others, frustrated by the wait, simply cancelled their orders.

Finally, two IBM managers decided to walk a loan straight through to each of the five departments involved in the process. At each step, they asked the workers to stop what they were doing to immediately process their loan application. They were shocked by what they found. From start to stop the entire process took just 90 minutes! It turns out that the average time of six days was created by delays that occurred in handing off the work from one department to another. The solution: IBM redesigned the process so that one person, not five in five separate departments, handled the entire loan approval process alone without any handoffs. The results were "dramatic." Reengineering the credit process reduced approval time from six days to four hours and allowed "IBM Credit" to increase the number of loans it handled by a factor of 100!

A second example involves the Acadia University (www.acadiau.ca) bookstore. Previously, books were ordered by professors for each course and the books would be stored on the shelves. Students needing textbooks would march into the store, find the books they needed on the shelves, walk to the cash, pay, and then leave. Early in each semester, lineups would be long and tempers short. Shelf space was also limited but for the most part stocked with textbooks that were going to be sold one way or another. Shelf space for higher profit non-academic book items was limited with the result that sales of this nature were stagnant and had been for years. To alter this, Acadia developed an online ordering system for students. With a connection to the Internet, students could order all their textbooks from the convenience of their rooms. The orders were filled and packed for pickup or delivery by university football players for a small fee. Putting the student ordering system on the Web allowed the bookstore to increase revenue possibilities by taking books off valuable shelf space. (They were stored in a room adjoining the bookstore.) Cash register mistakes were drastically reduced and lineups were cut dramatically. The bookstore was also able to collect valuable data about the products it sold and the buying habits of its main clients—students.

Reengineering changes an organization's orientation from vertical to horizontal. Instead of "taking orders" from upper management, lower- and middle-level managers and workers "take orders" from a customer who is at the beginning and end of each process. Instead of running independent functional departments, managers and workers in different departments take ownership of cross-functional processes. Instead of simplifying work so that it becomes increasingly specialized, reengineering complicates work by giving workers increased autonomy and responsibility for complete processes.

In essence, reengineering changes work by changing **task interdependence**, the extent to which collective action is required to complete an entire piece of work. As shown in Exhibit 11.8, there are three kinds of task interdependence.[18] In **pooled interdependence**, each job or department independently contributes to the whole. In **sequential interdependence**, work must be performed in succession, as one group's or job's outputs become the inputs for the next group or job. Finally, in **reciprocal interdependence**, different jobs or groups work together in a back-and-forth manner to

EXHIBIT 11.8

REENGINEERING AND TASK INTERDEPENDENCE

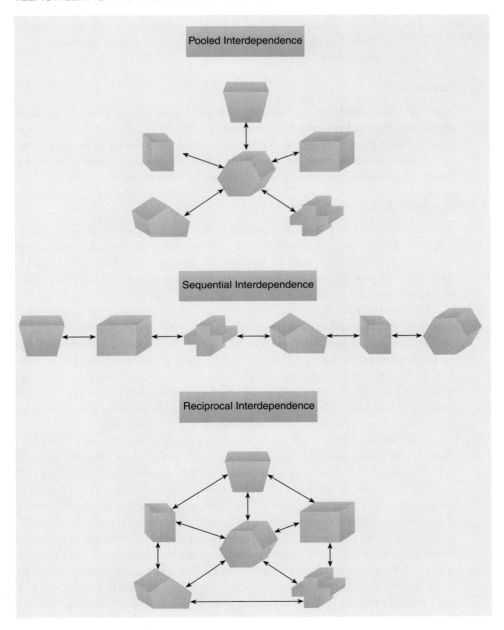

Pooled Interdependence

Sequential Interdependence

Reciprocal Interdependence

Singles, Not Home Runs

Reengineering, the radical redesign of business processes, can dramatically improve business performance. However, when you swing for home runs, you strike out a lot (i.e., the 70 percent failure rate of reengineering projects). Dana Corporation, a maker of car parts, swings for singles, not home runs, by focusing on daily continuous improvement. Every day, teams are encouraged to question how things are done. Employees submit two ideas (in writing) each month for improving manufacturing processes. And when small improvements occur, company management celebrates with a free barbecue and soft drinks for all. Swing for singles every day, and you're much more likely to get a hit.

Source: T. Petzinger, Jr., "Manager Keeps Reinventing His Plant's Production Line," *The Wall Street Journal Interactive Edition*, 19 September 1997.

complete the process. By reducing the handoffs between different jobs or groups, reengineering decreases sequential interdependence. Likewise, reengineering decreases pooled interdependence by redesigning work so that formerly independent jobs or departments now work together to complete processes. Finally, reengineering increases reciprocal interdependence by making groups or individuals responsible for larger, more complete processes in which several steps may be accomplished at the same time.

As an organizational design tool, reengineering promises big rewards. However, it has come under severe criticism, too. The most serious complaint is that, since it allows a few workers to do the work formerly done by many, reengineering is simply a corporate code word for cost cutting and worker layoffs. Likewise, for that reason, detractors claim that reengineering hurts morale and performance. For example, despite reducing ordering times from three weeks to three days, Levi Strauss (www.levistrauss.com) ended an $850-million (U.S.) reengineering project because of the fear and turmoil it created in its workforce. One of the low points occurred when Levi management, encouraged by its reengineering consultants, told 4000 workers that they would have to "reapply for their jobs" as the company shifted from its traditional vertical structure to a process-based form of organizing."[19]

4.2 Empowerment

Another way of redesigning intraorganizational processes is through empowerment. **Empowering workers** means permanently passing decision-making authority and responsibility from managers to workers. However, for workers to be fully empowered, companies must give them the information and resources they need to make and carry out good decisions, and then reward them for taking individual initiative.[20]

4.3 Behavioural Informality

How would you describe the atmosphere in the office in which you last worked? Was it a formal, by-the-book, follow-the-rules, address-each-other-by-last-names atmosphere? Or was it more informal, with an emphasis on results rather than rules, casual business dress rather than suits, and first names rather than last names and titles? Or was it somewhere in between?

Behavioural informality (or formality) is a third influence on intraorganizational processes. **Behavioural informality** refers to workplace situations characterized by spontaneity, casualness, and interpersonal familiarity. By contrast, **behavioural formality** refers to workplace situations characterized by routine and regimen, specific rules about how to behave, and impersonal detachment. Exhibit 11.9 shows that behavioural formality and informality are characterized by four factors: language usage, conversational turntaking and topic selection, emotional and proxemic gestures, and physical and contextual cues. Let's examine each in more detail.[21]

Compared to formal work atmospheres, the language in informal workplaces is often slurred ("Whatcha doin'?"), elliptical ("Coffee?" rather than "Would you like some coffee?"), and filled with slang terms and vivid descriptions. People use first names and perhaps nicknames to address each other, rather than Mr., Ms., Dr., or formal titles. As an example, next time you are in a Tim Hortons coffee shop, watch the interaction of the employees behind the counter. For the most part, the interaction is informal. When it comes to conversations in informal workplaces, people jump right in when they have something to say (i.e., unregulated turntaking), conversations shift from topic to topic, many of which are unrelated to business, and joking and laughter are common. From joy to disappointment, people show much more emotion in informal workplaces. In addition, relaxed expressions, such as putting your feet on your desk, or congregating in hall-

empowering workers
permanently passing decision-making authority and responsibility from managers to workers by giving them the information and resources they need to make and carry out good decisions

behavioural informality
workplace atmosphere characterized by spontaneity, casualness, and interpersonal familiarity

behavioural formality
workplace atmosphere characterized by routine and regimen, specific rules about how to behave, and interpersonal detachment

EXHIBIT 11.9

DIFFERENCES BETWEEN FORMAL AND INFORMAL WORKPLACES

FORMAL	INFORMAL
Language Usage	
Fully articulated speech ("What are you doing?")	Phonological slurring ("Whatcha doin'?")
Grammatically complete phrasing ("Would you like some coffee?")	Use of elliptical expressions ("Coffee?")
Use of formal word choices ("Would you care to dine?")	Use of colloquial and slang expressions ("Wanna grab a bite to eat?")
Use of honorifics ("Ms.," "Sir," "Dr.")	Use of the vivid present ("So I come down the stairs, and she says...")
Elimination of "I" and "you" ("It is requested that...")	First name, in-group names ("Mac," "Bud")
Conversational Turntaking and Topic Selection	
Turntaking well regulated	Turntaking relatively unregulated
Few interruptions or overlaps	Many interruptions or overlaps
Few changes of topic	Many shifts of topic possible
Seriousness of topic	Joking or conversational levity possible
Emotional and Proxemic Gestures	
Sober facial demeanour	Greater latitude of emotional expression
Much interpersonal distance	Small interpersonal distance
No touching, postural attention	Touching, postural relaxation allowed
Physical and Contextual Cues	
Formal clothing, shoes, etc.	Informal clothing, shoes, etc.
Central focus of attention possible	Decentralized, multiple centres of attention
Symmetric arrangement of chairs/furniture	Asymmetric arrangement of chairs/furniture
Artifacts related to official status	Informal trappings: flowers, art, food, soft furniture
Hushed atmosphere, little background noise	Background noise acceptable

Source: Acadamy of Management Review by D.A. Morland. Copyright 1995 by Academy of Management. Reproduced with permission of the publisher via Copyright Clearance Center.

ways for impromptu discussions, are more common, too. With regard to physical and contextual cues, informal workplaces deemphasize differences in hierarchical status or rank to encourage more frequent interaction between organizational members. Consequently, to make their organizations feel less formal, many companies have eliminated what used to be considered "management perks," things such as executive dining rooms, reserved parking spaces, and large corner offices separated from most workers because they were located on a higher floor of the company building (the higher the floor, the greater one's status).

Casual dress policies and open office systems are two of the most popular methods for increasing behavioural informality. While casual dress increases behavioural informality by having managers and workers at all levels dress in a more relaxed manner, open office systems such as those found in some Nortel Networks facilities increase

open office systems
offices in which the physical barriers that separate workers have been removed in order to increase communication and interaction

shared spaces
spaces used by and open to all employees

private spaces
spaces used by and open to just one employee

behavioural informality by significantly increasing the level of communication and interaction among employees. By definition, **open office systems** try to increase interaction by removing physical barriers that separate workers. One characteristic of open office systems is that they have much more shared space than private space. **Shared spaces** are used by and open to all employees. Cubicles with low-to-the-ground partitions, offices with no doors or with glass walls, collections of comfortable furniture that encourage people to congregate, and common areas with tables and chairs that encourage people to meet, work, or eat together are examples of shared space. **Private spaces**, such as a private office with a door, are used by and open to just one employee. Before Steelcase (www.steelcase.com), a leading office furniture manufacturer, switched to open systems, 80 percent of its executive office space was private space used for individual offices, whereas 20 percent was shared space. However, after switching to open offices, 80 percent is shared space and 20 percent is private space. After the change, CEO Jim Hackett went from a private, 700-square-foot office to a 48-square-foot enclosure that sits out in the open of a 22 000-square-foot environment that workers have dubbed "The Leadership Community."[22]

The advantage of this much-shared space in open offices is that it dramatically increases the amount of unplanned, spontaneous, and chance communication among employees.[23] People are much more likely to plan meetings and work together when numerous "collaboration spaces" with conference tables, white boards, and computers are readily available. With no office walls, with inviting common areas, and with different departments mixed together in large open spaces, spontaneous communication occurs more often. Also, open office systems increase chance communication by making it much more likely that people from different departments or areas will run into each other. However, not all companies are enthusiastic about open offices. Microsoft gives employees private offices so they can concentrate on their work.

Review 4
Intraorganizational Processes

Today, companies are using reengineering, empowerment, and behavioural informality to change their intraorganizational processes. Through fundamental rethinking and radical redesign of business processes, reengineering changes an organization's orientation from vertical to horizontal. Reengineering changes work processes by decreasing sequential and pooled interdependence, and by increasing reciprocal interdependence. Reengineering promises dramatic increases in productivity and customer satisfaction, but has been criticized as simply an excuse to cut costs and lay off workers. Empowering workers means taking decision-making authority and responsibility from managers and giving it to workers. Empowered workers develop feelings of competence and self-determination and believe their work to have meaning and impact. Workplaces characterized by behavioural informality are spontaneous and casual. The formality or informality of a workplace depends on four factors: language usage, conversational turn taking and topic selection, emotional and proxemic gestures, and physical and contextual cues. Casual dress policies and open office systems are two of the most popular methods for increasing behavioural informality.

5. Interorganizational Processes

What do "Voodoo Lounge," "$100 million," and an "interorganizational process" have in common? "Voodoo Lounge" is the name of a Rolling Stones tour. "$100 million" is the profit the Stones earned from the Voodoo Lounge tour.[24] And an "interorganizational process" is the method the Stones' business manager used to organize the tour.

An **interorganizational process** is a collection of activities that occur among companies to transform inputs into outputs that customers value. In other words, many companies work together to create a product or service that keeps customers happy. For example, in the interorganizational process used to manage the Voodoo Lounge tour, the Stones did one thing, play music. Everything else in the tour—recording, transportation, marketing, and construction—was farmed out to other companies.

In this section, you'll explore interorganizational processes by learning about modular organizations, virtual organizations, and boundaryless organizations.[25]

5.1 Modular Organizations

Except for the core business activities that they can perform better, faster, and cheaper than others, **modular organizations** outsource all remaining business activities to outside companies, suppliers, specialists, or consultants. The term "modular" is used because the business activities purchased from outside companies can be added and dropped as needed, much like adding pieces to a three-dimensional puzzle. Exhibit 11.10 depicts a modular organization in which the company has chosen to keep training, human resources, sales, research and development, information technology, product design, customer service, and manufacturing as core business activities. However, it has chosen to outsource noncore activities of product distribution, Web page design, advertising, payroll, accounting, and packaging.

interorganizational process
a collection of activities that take place among companies to transform inputs into outputs that customers value

modular organization
an organization that outsources noncore business activities to outside companies, suppliers, specialists, or consultants

EXHIBIT 11.10

MODULAR ORGANIZATION

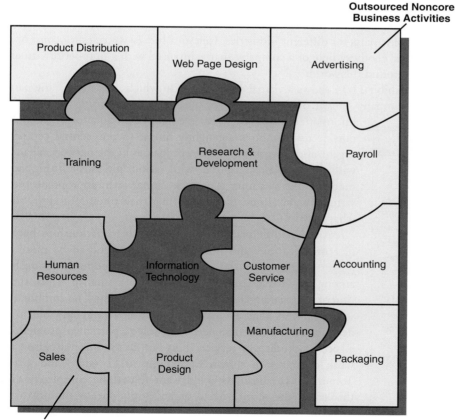

Modular organizations have several advantages. First, because modular organizations pay for outsourced labour, expertise, or manufacturing capabilities only when needed, they can cost significantly less to run than traditional organizations. For example, of the "big three" auto makers in the United States, DaimlerChrysler, which outsources 70 percent of its parts manufacturing to suppliers, has by far the lowest costs.[26] Second, outsourcing allows both modular companies, and the companies to whom they outsource, to focus on the core activities they do best. However, to obtain these advantages, modular organizations need to work closely with reliable partners, that is, vendors and suppliers that they can trust.

However, modular organizations have disadvantages, too. The primary disadvantage is the loss of control that occurs when key business activities are outsourced to other companies. Also, companies may reduce their competitive advantage in two ways if they mistakenly outsource a core business activity. First, competitive and technological change may produce a situation in which the noncore business activities a company has outsourced suddenly become the basis for competitive advantage. Second, related to that point, companies to whom work is outsourced can sometimes become competitors.

5.2 Virtual Organizations

virtual organization
an organization that is part of a network in which many companies share skills, costs, capabilities, markets, and customers to collectively solve customer problems or provide specific products or services

By contrast to modular organizations in which the interorganizational process revolves around a central company, a **virtual organization** is part of a network in which many companies share skills, costs, capabilities, markets, and customers with each other. For example, Puma (www.puma.com), the athletic shoe company, is a virtual organization. Puma takes care of strategy and marketing in Herzogenaurach, Germany. A small network of firms in Asia handles the purchasing and distribution of the materials used to make Puma shoes. Separate companies in China, Taiwan, Indonesia, and Korea manufacture Puma shoes. Separate sales and distribution networks operate in Africa, Asia, Australia, Europe, North America, and South America. In all, 80 different companies throughout the world help make and sell Puma shoes.[27] As a contract manufacturer of electronic parts for different industries, Celestica Inc. (www.celestica.com) of Toronto is another good example of a company that is involved with a number of virtual organizations around the world.

Exhibit 11.11 shows a virtual organization in which, for "today," the parts of a virtual company consist of product design, purchasing, advertising, manufacturing, and information technology. However, unlike modular organizations, in which outside organizations are tightly linked to one central company, virtual organizations work with some companies in the network alliance, but not with all. So, whereas a puzzle with various pieces is a fitting metaphor for modular organizations, a potluck dinner is an appropriate metaphor for virtual organizations. Everyone brings their finest food dish, but eats only what they want.

Another difference is that the working relationships between modular organizations and outside companies tend to be more stable and longer lasting than the shorter, often temporary relationships found among the virtual companies in a network alliance. Thus, the composition of a virtual organization is always changing. The combination of network partners that a virtual corporation has at any one time simply depends on the expertise needed to solve a particular problem or provide a specific product or service. This is why the businessperson in the network organization shown in Exhibit 11.11 said, "Today, I'll have..." Tomorrow, the business could want something completely different. In this sense, the term "virtual organization" means the organization that exists "at the moment."

PERSONAL PRODUCTIVITY (TIP)

Hot Desks and Big Savings?

With "hot desks," workers no longer have permanent offices or desks. Using central storage for personal belongings, networks that permit access to work files from any computer, and phone systems that forward permanent phone numbers to any phone, workers are simply assigned to the next empty desk when they arrive for work. Because you sit next to somebody different each day, "hot desks" improve communication. And, in offices where people spend time with customers or working from home, overall office space can be reduced by 30 percent to 45 percent. Would you be willing to give up your desk to achieve these savings?

Source: G. Gordon, "The Hot Desk Shuffle," *The Scotsman*, 15 June 2000, 10.

EXHIBIT 11.11

VIRTUAL ORGANIZATION

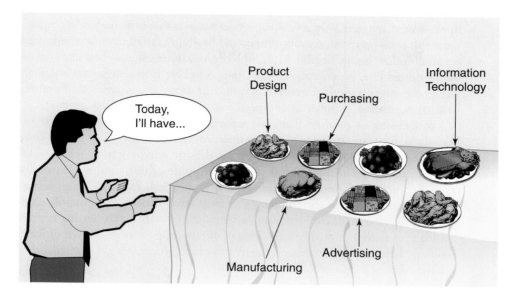

Virtual organizations have a number of advantages. They let companies share costs. And, because members can quickly combine their efforts to meet customers' needs, they are fast and flexible. Finally, because each company in the network alliance is the "best" at what it does, in theory, virtual organizations should provide better products and services in all respects.

Like modular organizations, a disadvantage of virtual organizations is that once work has been outsourced, it can be difficult to control the quality of work done by network partners. However, the greatest disadvantage is that it requires tremendous managerial skills to make a network of independent organizations work well together, especially since their relationships tend to be shorter and task or project based. However, virtual organizations are using two methods to solve this problem. The first is to use a broker whose job is to create and assemble the knowledge, skills, and resources from different companies for outside parties, such as customers.[28] The second way to make networks of virtual organizations more manageable is to use a virtual organization agreement that, somewhat like a contract, specifies the schedules, responsibilities, costs, and payouts to participating organizations.[29]

5.3 Boundaryless Organizations

General Electric (www.ge.com) CEO Jack Welch coined the term "boundaryless organization" in an annual letter to GE shareholders. Welch wrote, "Our dream is a boundaryless company, a company where we knock down the walls that separate us from each other on the inside and from our constituencies on the outside." Why was Welch, arguably one of the most effective CEOs ever, so concerned with boundaries? Steve Kerr, GE's Vice President of Leadership Development, explained: "Boundaries determine how an organization operates. There are vertical boundaries like floors and ceilings that separate levels of the organization; there are inside walls that separate departments from each other; and there are outside walls that separate the firm from its environment, from its customers, outside regulators, suppliers, and other constituencies."[30] Thus, a **boundaryless organization** would break down the vertical, horizontal, external, and geographic boundaries in organizations.[31]

boundaryless organization
a speedy, responsive, and flexible organization in which vertical, horizontal, external, and geographic boundaries are removed or minimized

Exhibit 11.12 shows how a boundaryless organization might work. First, notice that inside the company, in the internal environment, there are no vertical or horizontal relationships. Now, this doesn't mean that there are literally no bosses in boundaryless organizations. It also doesn't mean that lower-level managers and workers aren't responsible to upper-level managers. They are. What it does mean is that in boundaryless organizations the emphasis is on speed, responsiveness, and flexibility rather than to whom you report. Second, notice that in Exhibit 11.12, the organization's external boundary, represented by the dotted line, is permeable. Again, the point here is to remove the boundary separating the organization's internal environment from its external environment (i.e., industry regulation, suppliers, customers, competitors, and advocacy groups).

By focusing on results rather than reporting relationships, one of the advantages of boundaryless organizations is that they make much better use of employee knowledge, skills, and abilities. Instead of asking what department or job is "responsible" for a problem, the question that gets asked is "Who inside or outside the company can best solve this problem?" Another advantage is that they lead to much closer relationships with the components of the company's external environment. For example, one of the ways that GE has made external boundaries more permeable is by putting key managers "on loan" to outside companies. So, instead of reporting to work at a GE office in a GE building, these "on loan" managers report to work at offices that are permanently located in customers' or suppliers' offices or buildings.

EXHIBIT 11.12

BOUNDARYLESS ORGANIZATION

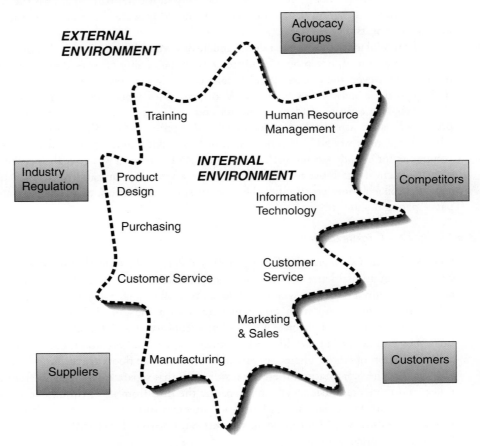

Source: Adapted from G.G. Dess, A.M.A. Rasheed, K.J. McLaughlin, & R.L. Priem, "The New Corporate Architecture," *Academy of Management Executive* 9 (1995): 7–18.

However, boundaryless organizations have significant disadvantages as well. To start, managers and employees often find the transition to boundaryless organizations threatening. Managers and workers who are used to the clear accountability and reporting relationships of vertical hierarchies often struggle with the new emphasis on speed and flexibility. However, the biggest disadvantage to boundaryless organizations is that there is no clear way to achieve them. The suggested methods read like a list of ingredients: create interdivisional committees, establish communication flows, create mutually beneficial relationships with suppliers and customers, build trust with employees, etc. Unfortunately, there is little advice on how best to combine and "cook" them.[32]

Review 5
Interorganizational Processes

Organizations are using modular, virtual, and boundaryless organizations to change interorganizational processes. Because modular organizations outsource all noncore activities to other businesses, they are less expensive to run than traditional companies. However, modular organizations require extremely close relationships with suppliers, may result in a loss of control, and could create new competitors if the wrong business activities are outsourced. Virtual organizations participate in a network in which they share skills, costs, capabilities, markets, and customers. As customer problems, products, or services change, the combination of virtual organizations that work together changes. Virtual organizations reduce costs, respond quickly, and, if they can successfully coordinate their efforts, can produce outstanding products and service. By breaking down internal and external boundaries, boundaryless organizations try to increase organizational speed, flexibility, and responsiveness. However, boundaryless organizations are threatening to managers and workers and are difficult to create.

What Really Happened?

At the beginning of the chapter, you learned that Exide Technologies was having difficulty selecting the correct organizational structure for its business. However, you also learned that such problems weren't unique, that Ford Motor Company's "Ford 2000" plan and that Procter & Gamble's "Organization 2005" plan both intended to establish the correct organizational structure for their companies, but created just as many problems as they solved. Let's find out what really happened at Exide to see if it avoided similar problems when it chose a new organizational structure.

Which organizational structure should Exide use? Should it stay with a geographical structure, but tinker with it to fix the problems? What would be the advantages or disadvantages of that approach?

Geographic departmentalization organizes work and workers into separate units responsible for doing business in particular geographical areas. At Exide, this organizing was done by country. For example, Europe, France, Germany, Spain, and Britain all had their own country managers who were responsible for selling and manufacturing Exide batteries. The primary advantage of geographic departmentalization is that it helps companies respond to the demands of different markets. This can be especially important when selling in different countries. However, it wasn't all that important for Exide, whose country managers often sold identical products in regions throughout the world. This was why Mark Stevenson, Exide's country manager for Britain, was able to sell the same batteries in Austria as Exide's country manager for Germany. Indeed, while there were some differences from country to country, those differences were much less important than the larger differences in products across regions, such as Europe, North America, Asia, and South America. Another advantage of geographic departmentalization is that it can reduce costs by locating unique organizational resources closer to customers.

The primary disadvantage of geographic departmentalization is that it can lead to duplication of resources. This was especially problematic for Exide. Most of Exide's 89 countries had a country manager, production plants, marketing budgets, human resource departments, and so forth. And, despite the duplication that was apparent to everyone, country managers were reluctant to see the problem in their own backyards. For example, Albrecht Leuschner, country manager for Germany's six Exide factories, said, "My region was in good shape. [By changing,] I was afraid we would destroy structure and that would damage the [German] business."

Also, even more so than with the other forms of departmentalization, it can be especially difficult to coordinate geographic departments that are literally thousands of kilometres from each other or whose managers have very limited contact with each other. In fact, because of its country-based system, Exide had created a geographic structure that encouraged its country managers to maximize their country's profits, even at the expense of Exide's other country managers. For example, with 10 country organizations in Europe alone, the temptation to undercut each other's prices was too tempting. Chairman Robert Lutz said, "[They were] driven to maximize their own results—even if it was at the price of their next-door neighbour, who also was Exide. The guys were poking each other in the eye."

Or should it use a product structure—what P&G called "global business units"—to standardize what it does around the world? What would be the advantages or disadvantages of this approach?

Product departmentalization organizes work and workers into separate units responsible for producing particular products or services. One advantage of product departmentalization is that, like functional departmentalization, it allows managers and workers to specialize in one area of expertise. However, unlike the narrow expertise and experiences in functional departmentalization, managers and workers develop a broader set of experiences and expertise related to an entire product line. Likewise, product departmentalization makes it easier for top managers to assess work-unit performance. Finally, because managers and workers are responsible for the entire product line rather than for separate functional departments, decision-making should be faster because there are fewer conflicts.

The primary disadvantage of product departmentalization is duplication. A second disadvantage is that it can be difficult to achieve coordination across the different product departments.

After dumping its country-based geographic structure, Exide implemented a product structure around global business units based on its two core product lines, industrial applications and transportation. Industrial applications included (a) network-power batteries for telecommunications systems, fuel-cell load levelling, electric utilities, railroads, photovoltaic (solar-power related), and uninterruptible power supply (UPS) markets, and (b) motive-power batteries for a broad range of equipment uses, including lift trucks, mining vehicles, and commercial vehicles. Transportation uses included (c) automotive, heavy-duty truck, agricultural, marine, and other batteries; and (d) new technologies developed for hybrid vehicles and new 42-volt automotive applications.

However, just like Ford and Procter & Gamble, Exide seemed to overlook the effect a switch from country management to a product structure would have on its managers. For instance, after the change, most of its country managers were demoted to the job of local coordinator, which was a huge step down for people used to running their own areas. When Chairman Lutz announced, "We don't have 100 percent consensus yet. . . . But I'm going to make a decision, and we are going to go to a global business unit structure," his decision was greeted with immediate dissatisfaction. When Lutz asked a forlorn Eduardo Garnica, Exide's country manager in Spain, "Why don't you give it a try?" Garnica responded, "No, I'm out of here," and soon quit his job with the company. At dinner that same evening, Giovani Mele, Exide's country manager for Italy, told two other country managers, "Being a country manager is my life. It's something I've worked for my whole life. I don't see how I'll have a role going forward." Furthermore, after Exide reduced his role, it moved his job from Italy to Frankfurt, Germany. His family, which refused to leave Italy, has remained in Naples.

When will Exide know when it has found the right organizational structure?

Ironically, Exide's new global business unit structure (i.e., product structure) lasted only six weeks. Albrecht Leuschner from Germany was one of the few country managers promoted to head a global business unit. He said, "For six weeks, I was emperor of the world." But then Exide bought GNB Technologies, another international manufacturer of batteries. Because Exide did not want to lose Mitchell Bregman, president of GNB's industrial-battery division, it changed its organizational structure once again to provide him a role with significant responsibilities. Said Chairman Robert

Lutz, "If we had been rigid about our organizational framework, we would have broken up GNB."

Lutz's solution was to choose an organizational structure that swung back to a focus on geography. But instead of returning to a country-based structure, Exide's six new global business units (i.e., product structures) were rearranged into five global divisions, North America, South America, Europe, Asia, and Africa. However, this organizational structure was in place for less than a year before the company replaced it with three "global power groups," which returned the company full circle to a strict product structure. The Global Network Power Group, based in Lombard, Illinois, provides unique product and service solutions to the communications and data, industrial and security, and government segments of the network-power market, including stationary hybrid electric-power generation applications. Mitchell S. Bregman, who was with GNB Technologies, has been named president. The Global Motive Power Group, based in Manchester, England, provides unique, total energy management solutions to the original-equipment and aftermarket segments of the material handling, access equipment, and electric-powered vehicle markets. Last, the Global Transportation Business Group, based in Atlanta, Georgia, provides unique products and services to both the original-equipment and aftermarket segments of the automotive, heavy truck, agriculture, construction, and marine markets. This division will

also lead Exide's efforts in developing system solutions for emerging 42-volt and hybrid energy management applications.

According to Chairman Lutz, the latest reorganization is "definitely working far better than what we had." But when will Exide know that it has the right structure? In general, companies know they have the right structure when responsibilities are clear to those in and out of the company, when problems are quickly solved, when efficiencies increase, and when people in the company become comfortable in their roles. But, as Exide's experiences shows, finding a proper organizational structure can be difficult. In fact, President Craig Mulhauser said, "Come back a year from now and we will look different. We were searching for the Holy Grail. But there isn't one."

Sources: E. Nelson, "Rallying the Troops at P&G—New CEO Lafley Aims to End Upheaval by Revamping Program of Globalization," *The Wall Street Journal*, 31 August 2000, B1. "Exide Technologies Announces Restructuring: Focuses on Global Customer Business Units," Exide Technologies. [Online] Available www.exide.com/news/pressrelease/general/20011017_exide_restructuring.html, 11 November 2001. J. Lublin, "Division Problem, Place Vs. Product: It's Tough to Choose a Management Model—Exide Tore Up System Based on Countries for One Centered on Battery Lines—Rolling over European Fiefs," *The Wall Street Journal*, 27 June 2001, A1. R. Simison, "Ford Hopes Its New Focus Will Be a Global Bestseller—Escort's Replacement Offers Improvements for Same Price," *The Wall Street Journal*, 8 October 1998, B10. "The History of Exide Technologies," Exide Technologies. [Online] Available www.exide.com/about/history.html, 11 November 2001.

Key Terms

authority (335)
behavioural formality (344)
behavioural informality (344)
boundaryless organization (349)
centralization of authority (337)
chain of command (336)
customer departmentalization (331)
decentralization (337)
delegation of authority (337)
departmentalization (329)
empowering workers (344)
functional departmentalization (329)
geographic departmentalization (333)
interorganizational process (347)
intraorganizational process (341)

job design (339)
job enlargement (340)
job enrichment (341)
job rotation (340)
job specialization (339)
line authority (337)
line function (337)
matrix departmentalization (334)
mechanistic organization (341)
modular organization (347)
open office systems (346)
organic organization (341)
organizational process (328)
organizational structure (328)
pooled interdependence (343)

private spaces (346)
product departmentalization (329)
reciprocal interdependence (343)
reengineering (342)
sequential interdependence (343)
shared spaces (346)
span of control (336)
staff authority (337)
staff function (337)
standardization (338)
task interdependence (343)
unity of command (336)
virtual organization (348)

What Would You Do II?

"Welcome to McDonalds. Can I take your order please?" "Yeah, I'll have a McChicken Value Meal. Oh, and super-size the drinks and fries. That'll be all. Thanks." A decade ago, most drive-through orders were for beef sandwiches, like a Big Mac or a double-cheeseburger. However, today, health-conscious consumers are just as likely to eat chicken. In fact, more than 11 million tonnes of chicken are produced throughout North America each year.

Because of the huge rise in demand for chicken, well over a quarter of a million people now work in poultry-processing factories, more than double the number in 1980. Furthermore, since poultry-processing jobs are a fast-growing job category, hourly wages have almost doubled for work that requires no skill, experience, or training. However, the basic steps of processing poultry, scalding, eviscerating, de-boning, dripping (for removing blood and bodily fluids), removing feet, and removing giblets make this an inherently gruesome job. In addition, due to intensified competition and increased demand, the job has got even worse, as companies have increased the number of chickens they process from around 50 per minute, which was the standard in 1985, to the maximum government-allowed amount of 91 chickens per minute today. The resulting pace is frantic and stressful. Chicken skin, guts, parts, and feathers literally fly as workers struggle to keep up.

With one out of four experiencing job-related injuries, poultry workers suffer one of the highest rates of job injury. Workers wielding sharp knives and scissors frequently cut themselves or others. And since poultry processing involves rapid and repetitive motions, uncomfortable body postures, forceful movements, and no control over the pace of work, repetitive stress injuries, such as carpal tunnel syndrome, are common.

Repetitive stress injuries make up one-quarter of all work-related injuries. Of those, two-thirds involve back injuries, while one-third include upper extremities such as fingers, hands, wrists, elbows, necks, and shoulders. Symptoms can include shooting, searing pain in the joints and tendons or an inability to grasp and control ordinary objects.

If the gore, injuries, and frantic pace weren't tough enough, some companies automatically fire workers if they leave the manufacturing line for any reason, including going to the bathroom. With work shifts often lasting 10 to 12 hours (until the last chicken is processed), and with breaks infrequent and short (one company has been known to allow its workers only three breaks per week), employees often struggle to make it to the end of their shifts. In some instances, employees who have been unable to get their supervisor's attention (the plants are large and very loud) have wet themselves rather than lose their jobs by leaving the line to go to the bathroom.

Not surprisingly, people don't last very long in these jobs. Since most quit within three to six months, the average annual rate of employee turnover is 100 percent or more. However, companies feel there is little they can do to improve working conditions. Poultry processing is a highly competitive business. Consequently, some companies have been more concerned with cutting costs, speeding production, and improving productivity than with improving working conditions. Unfortunately, the tough working conditions aren't necessarily perceived as a problem when unemployment is high. There are always enough job applicants to replace those who leave. But today, with unemployment at record lows, poultry companies are having a much more difficult time attracting and keeping workers. But how do you redesign poultry-processing jobs to make them more tolerable (they're never going to be great jobs), to reduce the number of repetitive stress injuries, and still address the competitive issues of cost, production, and productivity?

If you were in charge of a poultry-processing plant, what would you do?

Sources: M. Cooper, "The Heartlands Raw Deal: How Meatpacking Is Creating a New Immigrant Underclass," *The Nation*, 3 February 1997, 11. F. Greve, "OSHA Demands Bathroom Freedom," *The Des Moines Register*, 24 August 1997, 18. T. Horwitz, "9 to Nowhere: These Six Growth Jobs Are Dull, Dead-End, Sometimes Dangerous: They Show How 90s Trends Can Make Work Grimmer for Unskilled Workers—Blues on the Chicken Line," *The Wall Street Journal*, 1 December 1994. "Just the Facts: The Role of the Meat Industry in the U.S. Economy," American Meat Institute website. [Online] Available www.meatami.org/FactBK01. HTM, 14 September 1997. C.E. Morris & L. Mancini, "No Pain, No Gain," *Chiltons Food Engineering*, 1 May 1996, 53. "Preventing Repetitive Stress Injuries," U.S. Department of Labor, OSHA website. [Online] Available www.osha-slc.gov/ergo/prsi.html, 10 December 1996.

Management Decisions

Outsource or Not?

As you gaze out the windshield of your car while stopped at a red light, you think back on how simple life used to be. Several years ago when you started your small manufacturing company, life was tough, but it wasn't as hectic as it is today. You started your company, which builds partially assembled furniture and components, on a shoestring with only a few employees. Even though everyone worked 15-hour days, six or seven days a week, things still seemed easier back then. Now that your firm has grown and is finally turning a healthy profit, your average workday has dropped to around 10 hours per day. Because of sustained growth, you have distanced yourself from the physical production of the product. Instead, you now spend your time wandering around the factory, looking for ways to streamline the production process, speed up delivery time, improve quality, and solve any other logistical or systems problems that crop up.

One area that is in need of immediate attention is the customer service department. It seems that customer service issues and questions quadrupled overnight. In the beginning, you and your spouse used to take turns returning the occasional customer complaint, question, or request for additional information. When the volume of customer service requests began to consume a large portion of both your work routines, you hired a full-time customer service representative to take over. Today, the company has four full-time customer service reps on staff and is still experiencing long periods of delays and complaints because customers can't get through in a timely basis.

Of course, one easy solution is to outsource the customer service function to an outside agency. An external agency that specializes in customer service is likely better prepared to handle the ever-increasing number of customer service calls and could possibly do so for the same cost you are paying now. Outsourcing is not new to you. During the enormous growth cycle your company has experienced over the last two years, you have outsourced a number of functions within the firm, including accounting, personnel, payroll, and maintenance. You thought those were easy decisions because each required only a little time

each month to perform. In addition, the cost to you of staffing and performing those functions internally significantly outweighed any benefits received. Since you made your decision to outsource those areas, you have been delighted with the service that you receive and have not had to micromanage the providers' results.

Unfortunately, you believe customer service is different. It is a daily activity—sometimes a 24/7 activity—not to mention that it requires specific and detailed knowledge of the 115 products you produce. Your customer service reps are not only well-versed in your product lines, but they are also able to decipher the sometimes-incomprehensible instructions that accompany your products, a critical part of resolving many customer-related issues. You take pride in the fact that two of the four customer service reps have been with you from the start and are good at defusing potentially bad situations. These two individuals can usually turn a disgruntled customer into a happy one and do it without giving away the store. You're afraid that if you outsource the CS department, you'll lose that ability and jeopardize the loyalty of these two employees. On the other hand, you see your market share declining as frustrated customers flock to the competition. You've got to decide.

Questions

1. What factors would you consider before determining whether to outsource the customer service department or not? What advantages and disadvantages are there to outsourcing activities?
2. What would you do? Why?
3. If you choose to outsource the customer service department, how could you control the performance of the outsourcing agency?

Sources: S. Bothe, "Outsourcing for Small and Mid-Sized Businesses," *The CPA Journal*, May 2001. J. Bowles, "Build or Outsource?," *Customer Interface*, June 2001. E. Garaventa & T. Tellefsen, "Outsourcing: The Hidden Costs," *Review of Business*, Spring 2001.

Plush Management Perks: Partaking or Pruning?

"They do, too!" "They do not!" "You don't know what you're talking about." "See, it's attitudes like yours that prove my point!"

Ah, nothing like watching your top two executives argue during lunch to raise your blood pressure. You knew that Sam, the VP of Sales, was going to get mad when Catherine, the VP of Human Resources, suggested getting rid of executive perks (the private dining room, company cars, first-class air travel, etc.). It took Sam 25 years to become a vice president and nobody, including Sam, wants to see his or her perks and rewards reduced. However, you didn't think it was possible for someone to get that mad that fast. Given the way Sam's face instantly turned beet red when Catherine suggested that the reserved parking spaces be eliminated, it's a good thing she caught him between bites or he might have choked on his shrimp salad.

Well, with executive perks topping the agenda for the annual executive retreat next weekend, Sam and Catherine's argument has given you something to think about. Is Catherine right? Do all executive perks need to be eliminated? Or is Sam right? Do the executive perks need to be left alone? After all, even Catherine got defensive when Sam asked her how happy she'd be if the company closed its on-site daycare. When she responded, "They wouldn't dare do that," Sam barked, "That's exactly the way I feel about your recommendations!"

Well, you need to get your thoughts sorted out. A good place to start is with the list of executive perks currently being offered by the company:

- company cars
- reserved parking spaces
- company cellular phones
- personal financial counselling
- personal liability insurance
- executive dining room
- first-class air travel
- spouse travel on extended business trips
- signing bonuses
- stock options
- country club memberships
- large, expensively furnished private offices
- home security systems
- home computer/office equipment

Questions

1. Of the perks listed above, choose three that your managers are most likely to desire. In other words, which three executive perks would your managers scream the most about if you took them away? Explain why for each of the three perks.

2. Of the perks listed above, which three probably create the most resentment among your workforce (i.e., non-managers)? In other words, which three executive perks anger your workforce the most? Explain why for each of the three perks.

3. Choose the option (a, b, or c) that is likely to benefit the company most in the long run:
   a. eliminate all executive perks
   b. retain all executive perks
   c. selectively eliminate perks

   Explain the reasoning behind your choice. If you choose option c, specify the perks you kept and why you kept them.

Sources: M. Budman, "The Persistence of Perks," *Across the Board*, 1 February 1994. L. Fleeson, "In Today's Efficient, Egalitarian Offices, Plush Perks Are Passe," *The News Tribune*, 10 July 1994. S. Lohr, "Cubicle or Cavern? Egalitarian Work Space Duels with Need for Privacy Among Brainy Folks in High-Tech Firms," *Rocky Mountain News*, 7 September 1997. T. Schellhardt, "Executive Pay (A Special Report)—Passing of Perks: Company Cars, Country Club Memberships, Executive Dining Rooms; Where Have All the Goodies Gone?" *The Wall Street Journal*, 13 April 1994.

Develop Your Management Potential

"Work" in Someone Else's Shoes

Why is learning to see things from someone else's perspective one of the most difficult things to do in today's workplace? Sometimes, the inability to see things as others see them has to do with the people involved. Inexperience, ignorance, and self-ishness can all play a role. However, in most organizations, the inability to see things from someone else's perspective results from the jobs themselves, not the people who do them. Because jobs limit who we talk to, what we talk about, what we think about, and what we care about at work, it should not be a surprise that people who perform different jobs have very different views about each other and the workplace.

For example, in the airline industry the pilots who fly the planes and the ground crews who unload, load, and refuel them may have little appreciation for each other. The ground crews may feel that the pilots treat them like second-class citizens. The pilots may not understand why the ground crews aren't doing more to get their planes out of the gates and in the air as fast as possible. To improve understanding and help them see things from each other's perspective, one company created a program in which the captains and ground crews learn a lot about each other's jobs. For example, the pilots bring the ground crews into their cockpits and show them the detailed processes they are required to follow to get planes ready for departure. The pilots, on the other hand, gain appreciation and understanding by actually working as members of a ground crew. After several days of demanding ground crew work, one pilot said:

> I remember one time when I was working the ramp [as a member of a ground crew]. I was dead tired. I had flown that morning and had a couple of legs in, so I got out of my uniform and jumped into my ramp clothes. That afternoon was very hot. It was in the 30's, I was tired and hungry and hadn't had a break. Then I saw this pilot sitting up there in the cockpit eating his frozen yogurt. I said to myself, "Man, I'd like to be up there now." Then I caught myself. I'm up there every day. Now, I know that pilot has been up since 3:00 in the morning. I know that he's been flying an airplane since 6:00 a.m. I know it's 3:00 in the afternoon and he hasn't had a chance to get off and have a meal yet today. I know all that, and yet, the yogurt still looks really good to me. Then I thought, "How can a ramp agent [on the ground crew] who works his butt off for two or three years, working double shifts two or three times a week, understand this?" It hit me that there's a big gap in understanding here.

The misunderstandings between pilots and ground crews are not unique. All organizations experience them. Nurses and doctors, teachers and students, and managers and employees all have difficulty seeing things from each other's perspective. However, as this program shows, you can minimize differences and build understanding by "working" in someone else's shoes.

Questions

1. Describe the job-related differences or tensions where you work. Who is involved? What jobs do they do? Explain why the job-related differences or tensions exist.
2. Since the best way to see things from someone else's perspective is to "work" in his or her shoes, see if you can spend a day, a morning, or even two hours performing one of these jobs. If that's not possible, spend some time carefully observing the jobs and then interview several people who perform them. Describe your boss's reaction to this request. Was he or she supportive or not? Why?
3. Answer the following questions after you have worked the job or conducted your interviews. What most surprised you about this job? What was easiest? What was hardest? Explain. Now that you've had the chance to see things as others see them, what do you think would happen, good or bad, from letting other people in your organization work in someone else's shoes? Explain.

Sources: K. Freiberg & J. Freiberg, *Nuts! Southwest Airlines' Crazy Recipe for Business and Personal Success* (Austin, TX: Bard Press, 1996).

Discussion Questions

1. Manulife, Shell Canada, CAE Inc., Emera, Loblaws, and CN are all important Canadian companies. None operate in the same industry and all offer different products. In each instance, designers have numerous options to choose from when seeking to build effective organizational structures. Which five traditional approaches to organizational structure are available to these designers and which one is best for use by each company?

2. Explain what standardization means and how this concept is relevant to the degree of centralization.

3. IBM, Aliant, Petro Canada, Pfizer, and McGraw-Hill are all well-known companies that experienced large-scale internal change during the last decade. Change efforts of this nature are massive and leave few areas of a company untouched. A number of methods are available to change consultants seeking to redesign internal organizational processes. Identify these methods and briefly describe each.

4. Over the course of your degree program, you have decided to enter into the co-op program for your university. Your first posting is with a small apple exporter in the Annapolis Valley of Nova Scotia. One slow day at work, you were glancing through your textbook with the intention of obtaining a few ideas that might help this company. Your boss noticed your diligence and was curious about the terms "modular," "virtual," and "boundaryless" organization. In the context of the apple industry, how might you define these terms?

Study Tip

Take advantage of all the review opportunities on the *Management* website at www.management1e.nelson.com. Write up a list of questions you have about concepts you don't understand and visit your professor or TA during office hours.

4 PART

Organizing People, Projects, and Processes

CHAPTER 12

Chapter Outline

Learning Objectives

After reading this chapter, you should be able to

1. explain the good and bad of using teams.
2. recognize and understand the different kinds of teams.
3. understand the general characteristics of work teams.
4. explain how to enhance work team effectiveness.

Photodisc Green/BU004693

twelve

Managing Teams

What Would You Do?

Cigna's Customer Service Centre is a busy place. Each day, thousands of calls come in from policyholders with billing questions, claims, or an interest in buying more insurance. Your job, as the manager of the Customer Service Division, is to run an efficient operation and maintain a high level of customer service. You know that customers often judge a company by how they are treated when they call with a problem or question. Therefore, you want to make sure that their needs are met in a polite and expedient manner.

Unfortunately, system bottlenecks are slowing down response times. The centre's three main functions are customer service (including claims), accounting, and new business development. Each is a separate department with its own staff and hierarchy. Unfortunately, this creates complications and communication barriers when employees try to deal with customers. For example, when a policyholder calls with a billing question, the customer service representative has to put the caller on hold, contact the accounting department to retrieve the pertinent information, and then communicate the answer to the customer. This causes delays and frustrates your staff and customers.

You have given this problem a lot of thought. What you have tentatively decided to do may strike some people as radical, but the more you think about it, the more you are convinced that it is the right decision. You are thinking about eliminating the separate departments and replacing them with a number of "customer representative" teams. The teams would be made up of one or more members from each of the departments. Each team would be assigned to service a specific group of Cigna customers from one geographic region. Under this structure, when a customer calls, the customer would be connected to the team assigned to handle all of that customer's business. A handful of support personnel would be needed to handle specific functions, such as underwriting, but would not be needed for most routine calls.

You see several benefits to this plan, especially reduced call times, lower costs, and increased customer and employee satisfaction. A few things worry you, however. Some employees may not fit into a team environment. What if these employees quit their jobs, or complain a lot and make everybody's life miserable? There will also be fewer jobs open at the supervisor level. And the last thing that you want to do is to create the impression that there is no opportunity for top performers to move up in the firm. You also know that despite the outward promise of teamwork, it is difficult to know whether teams will actually work until you try it. What if productivity doesn't go up, and employee morale suffers rather than improves? Will work teams actually improve customer service? Will you be putting your own job on the line? That's a scary thought, particularly with two kids in university.

In the background, you can hear your customer service representatives fielding phone calls, and you know that some of your customers will be on hold longer than they like. A decision has to be made soon.

If you were the head of Cigna's Customer Service Centre, what would you do?

Sources: M. Brown, "National Winner: Cigna Services UK," *Management Today*, June 1994, 95. J.R. Caron, S.L. Jarvenpaa, & D.B. Stoddard, "Business Reengineering at CIGNA Corporation: Experiences and Lessons Learned from the First Five Years," *MIS Quarterly* 18, no. 3 (1994): 233. S.E. Gross, *Compensation for Teams* (New York: American Management Association, 1995). T. Hoffman, "Re-engineering Pays Off at Cigna," *Computerworld*, August 1993, 70. "International Healthcare News," *Business Conference and Management Reports*, 1 December 1995, 6.

Like Cigna, a growing number of Canadian organizations are significantly improving their effectiveness by establishing work teams. Nonetheless, teams really haven't been in place at most companies for more than 10 to 15 years, if that long. In other words, teams are a relatively new phenomenon in companies, and there's still much for organizations to learn about managing them.

We begin this chapter by reviewing the advantages and disadvantages of teams and exploring when companies should use them over more traditional approaches. Next, we discuss the different types of work teams and the characteristics common to all teams. The chapter ends by focusing on the practical steps to managing teams—team goals and priorities and organizing, training, and compensating teams.

Why Work Teams?

work team
a small number of people with complementary skills who hold themselves mutually accountable for pursuing a common purpose, achieving performance goals, and improving interdependent work processes

Work teams consist of a small number of people with complementary skills who hold themselves mutually accountable for pursuing a common purpose, achieving performance goals, and improving interdependent work processes.[1]

When compared with 116 other refineries, Imperial Oil's refinery in Dartmouth, Nova Scotia, used to perform in the bottom 25 percent of the group. Managers worried that the plant would be shut down. After making lists of things that needed to be done, they finally hit on a new solution: teams. The refinery shifted to a team arrangement and formed groups of 40 to 50 workers who took responsibility for entire processes within the plant such as fraction and catalytic conversion (the breaking down of crude oil in to more useful products). As teams took responsibility for processes in the plant, a layer of supervision was eliminated. In less than a year, they found ways to reduce staffing by 46 percent and identified a number of other cost savings. Overall costs fell by 30 percent and the refinery was approaching the top 25 percent. The work teams were clearly a success.[2]

The success that Imperial Oil's Dartmouth refinery experienced with teams is not uncommon. In many industries, teams are growing in importance because they help organizations respond to specific problems and challenges. While work teams are not the answer for every situation or organization, if the right teams are used properly and in the right settings, teams can dramatically improve company performance over more traditional management approaches and instill a sense of vitality in the workplace that is otherwise difficult to achieve.

After reading the next two sections, you should be able to
1. explain the good and bad of using teams.
2. recognize and understand the different kinds of teams.

1. The Good and Bad of Using Teams

Let's begin our discussion of teams by learning about the advantages of teams, the disadvantages of teams, and when to use teams.

1.1 The Advantages of Teams

Companies are making greater use of teams because teams have been shown to increase customer satisfaction, product and service quality, speed and efficiency in product development, and employee job satisfaction.[3] Teams help businesses increase *customer satisfaction* in several ways. One way is to create work teams that are trained to meet the needs of specific customer groups. Businesses also create problem-solving teams and employee-involvement teams to study ways to improve overall customer satisfaction and make recommendations for improvements. Teams like these typically meet on a weekly or monthly basis. The Published Image, a small publishing company, increased customer satisfaction when it switched from a traditional management hierarchy to separate work teams with their own clients and their own sales, editorial, and production workers. Client Peter Herlihy said, "We [now] have one group of people who know all facets of our job, and we can contact any of them during the process."[4]

Teams also help firms improve *product and service quality* in several ways.[5] Here, in contrast to traditional organizational structures where management is responsible for organizational outcomes and performance, one of the primary advantages is that teams take direct responsibility for the quality of the products and service they produce. At Texas Instruments, production teams are directly responsible for resolving quality issues, and even visit suppliers when necessary to track down quality problems.[6] At Whole Foods, a supermarket chain that sells groceries and health foods, the ten teams that manage each store are not only responsible for store quality and performance, but they are also directly accountable, since the size of their team bonus depends on it.[7] And making teams directly responsible for service and production quality pays off. A survey by *Industry Week* indicates that 42 percent of the companies that use teams report revenues of more than $350 000 per employee compared to only 25 percent of the companies that don't use teams.[8]

A third reason that teams are increasingly popular is *the need for speed and efficiency when designing and manufacturing products.*[9] Traditional product design proceeds sequentially, meaning that one department has to finish its work on the design of a product before the next department can start. Unfortunately, this is not only slow, but it also encourages departments to work in isolation from one another.[10] For example, with sequential design processes, it's common for different departments, such as manufacturing, to work for months on their part of the product design only to have it rejected by another department, such as marketing, which was never consulted as the work was being done. *Overlapping development phases* is a faster and better way to design products and is often made possible through the use of teams. With overlapping development phases, teams of employees, consisting of members from the different functional areas in a firm (i.e., engineering, manufacturing, and marketing), work on the product design at the same time. Because each of the different functional areas is involved in the design process from the start, the company can avoid most of the delays and frustration associated with sequential development.

Another reason for using teams is that teamwork often leads to increased job satisfaction.[11] One reason that teamwork can be more satisfying than traditional work is that it gives workers a chance to improve their skills. This is often accomplished through **cross training**, in which team members are taught how to do all or most of the jobs performed by the other team members. The advantage for the organization is that cross training allows teams to function normally when one member is absent or a team member quits or is transferred. The advantage for workers is that cross training broadens their skills and makes them more capable while also making their work more varied and interesting. Village Food Markets, located on Vancouver Island, cross trains its employees to improve service and make employees' work more interesting.[12] Employees will stock shelves, run cash registers, or deliver to customers' homes, depending on the need at any given time.

PERSONAL PRODUCTIVITY

Learn to Celebrate Success

When athletes celebrate success, they share high fives, low fives, torso bumps, and bash bumps (forearm to forearm). There is impromptu dancing, spiking, stuffing, and jumping into the stands. The emotions are palpable, and fans and athletes share the celebration. Celebration and emotions are also important for work teams. Next time your team does something well or exceeds a goal, start a celebration. Order a pizza, print some T-shirts, or plan a team outing. The energy and emotions that you and your teammates share by celebrating will drive you to higher levels of success.

Source: Donald J. Bodwell, "Combined File Print Out of High Performance Team: Celebration," *High Performance Teams.* [Online] Available http://rampages.onramp.net/ ~bodwell/combined. htm, 22 January 2002.

cross training
training team members how to do all or most of the jobs performed by the other team members

Participation in work teams also increases job satisfaction by providing team members unique opportunities that would otherwise not be available to them. At Chaparral Steel, employee work teams routinely visit customers' production facilities to discuss quality-related issues. Team members often gain job satisfaction from unique leadership responsibilities that would typically not be available in traditional organizations. For example, at Colgate-Palmolive work teams are responsible for determining their own work assignments, scheduling overtime, making out vacation schedules, performing preventive equipment maintenance, and ensuring quality control. For each work team, the position of team leader rotates, giving different team members the opportunity to build leadership skills.[13]

Teams share many of the advantages of group decision-making discussed in Chapter 4. For instance, because team members possess different knowledge, skills, abilities, and experiences, teams will be able to view problems from multiple perspectives. This diversity of viewpoints increases the odds that team decisions will solve the underlying causes of problems rather than simply address the symptoms. The increased knowledge and information available to teams also make it easier for them to generate more alternative solutions, which is a critical part of improving the quality of decisions. Finally, because teams members are involved in decision-making processes, they should be more committed to making those decisions work. In short, teams can do a much better job than individuals in two important steps of the decision-making process: defining the problem and generating alternative solutions.

1.2 The Disadvantages of Teams

Although teams can significantly increase customer satisfaction, product and service quality, speed and efficiency in product development, and employee job satisfaction, using teams does not guarantee these positive outcomes. In fact, if you've ever participated in team projects in your classes, you're probably already aware of some of the problems inherent in work teams. So despite all of their promise, teams and teamwork are also prone to these significant disadvantages: initially high turnover, social loafing, and legal risk.

The first disadvantage of work teams is *initially high turnover*. Teams aren't for everyone, and some workers will balk at the responsibility, effort, and learning required in team settings. When General Electric's Salisbury plant switched to teams, the turnover rate, which was near zero, jumped to 14 percent. Plant manager Roger Gasaway said of teams and teamwork, "It's not all wonderful stuff."[14]

Social loafing is another disadvantage of work teams. **Social loafing** occurs when workers withhold their efforts and fail to perform their share of the work. A 19th-century German scientist named Ringleman first documented social loafing when he found that one person pulling on a rope by himself or herself exerted an average of 63 kg of force on the rope. In groups of three, the average force dropped to 53 kg. In groups of eight, the average dropped to just 31 kg. Ringleman concluded that the larger the team, the smaller the individual effort. In fact, social loafing is more likely to occur in larger groups where it can be difficult to identify and monitor the efforts of individual team members.[15] In other words, social loafers count on being able to blend into the background so that their lack of effort isn't easily spotted. Because of team-based class projects, most students already know about social loafers or "slackers," who contribute poor, little, or no work whatsoever. Not surprisingly, research with 250 student teams clearly shows that the most talented students are typically the least satisfied with teamwork because of having to carry "slackers" and having to do a disproportionate share of their team's work.[16]

Finally, teams share many of the disadvantages of group decision-making discussed in Chapter 4. This includes *groupthink*, in which, in highly cohesive groups, group members feel intense pressure not to disagree with each other so that the group can approve a solution that has

social loafing
behaviour in which team members withhold their efforts and fail to perform their share of the work

EXPERIENCING MANAGEMENT

Cement your understanding of the social loafing concept by interacting with the concept and related materials at our animated concept and activity site. Choose Teams from the "select a topic" pull-down menu, then Social Loafing from the "overview tab."

www.experiencingmanagement.com

been proposed. Because groupthink restricts discussion and leads to consideration of a limited number of alternative solutions, it usually results in poor decisions. Also, team decision-making takes considerable time. Furthermore, it's the rare team that consistently holds productive task-oriented meetings to effectively work through the decision process. Another possible pitfall is that sometimes just one or two people dominate team discussions, restricting consideration of different problem definitions and alternative solutions. Last, team members may not feel accountable for the decisions and actions taken by the "team."

1.3 When to Use Teams

The two previous subsections make clear that teams come with significant advantages *and* disadvantages. Therefore, the question is not whether to use teams, but when and where to use teams for maximum benefit and minimum cost. Doug Johnson, associate director at the Center for the Study of Work Teams, said, "Teams are a means to an end, not an end in themselves. You have to ask yourself questions first. Does the work require interdependence? Will the team philosophy fit company strategy? Will management make a long-term commitment to this process?"[17] Exhibit 12.1 provides some additional guidelines on when to use or not use teams.[18]

First, teams should be used where there is a clear, engaging reason or purpose for using them. Too many companies use teams because they're popular or because they assume that teams can fix all problems but forming teams does not guarantee improved performance. But teams are much more likely to succeed if they know why they exist and what they are supposed to accomplish.

Second, teams should be used when the job can't be done unless people work together. This typically means that teams are required when tasks are complex, require multiple perspectives, or require repeated interaction with others to complete. For example, contrary to stories of legendary programmers who write software programs by themselves, Microsoft uses teams to write computer code because of the enormous complexity of today's software. Most software simply has too many options and features for one person (or even one team) to complete it all. Likewise, Microsoft uses teams because writing good software requires repeated interaction with others. Microsoft ensures this interaction by having its teams "check in" their computer code every few days. The different pieces of code written by the different teams are then compiled to create an updated working build or prototype of the software. Then, beginning the next day, all

---

EXHIBIT 12.1

WHEN TO USE OR NOT USE TEAMS

USE TEAMS WHEN...	DON'T USE TEAMS WHEN...
1. There is a clear, engaging reason or purpose.	1. There isn't a clear, engaging reason or purpose.
2. The job can't be done unless people work together.	2. The job can be done by people working independently.
3. Rewards can be provided for teamwork and team performance.	3. Rewards are provided for individual effort and performance.
4. Ample resources are available.	4. The necessary resources are not available.
5. Teams will have clear authority to manage and change how work gets done.	5. Management will continue to monitor and influence how work gets done.

Source: R. Wageman, "Critical Success Factors for Creating Superb Self-Managing Teams," *Organizational Dynamics* 26, no. 1 (1997): 49–61.

---

the teams and team members begin testing and debugging the new build. Over and over again, the computer code is compiled, then sent back to the teams to be tested and improved, and then compiled and tested again.[19]

However, if tasks are simple and don't require multiple perspectives or repeated interaction with others, teams should not be used. For instance, production levels dropped by 23 percent when Levi Strauss introduced teams in its factories. Levi's mistake was assuming that teams were appropriate for garment work, where workers performed single, specialized tasks, like sewing zippers or belt loops. Because this kind of work does not require interaction with others, Levi's unwittingly pitted the faster workers against the slower workers in each team. Arguments, infighting, insults, and threats were common between faster workers and the slower workers who held back team performance. One seamstress even had to physically restrain an angry co-worker who was about to throw a chair at a faster worker who constantly nagged her about her slow pace.[20]

Third, teams should be used when rewards can be provided for teamwork and team performance. Team rewards that depend on team performance rather than individual performance are the key to rewarding team behaviours and efforts. You'll read more about team rewards later in the chapter, but for now it's enough to know that if the level of rewards (individual vs. team) is not matched to the level of performance (individual vs. team), groups won't work. As discussed above, this was the case with Levi's, where a team structure was superimposed on individual jobs that didn't require interaction between workers. After the switch to teams, faster workers placed tremendous pressure on slower workers to increase their production speed. And since pay was determined by team performance, top individual performers saw their pay drop by several dollars an hour, while slower workers saw their pay increase by several dollars an hour, all while overall productivity dropped in the plant.[21]

Fourth, teams should be used when ample resources are available. The resources that teams need include training (discussed later in the chapter), sufficient time and a place or method to work together, job-specific tools, and consistent information and feedback concerning team work processes and job performance. Susan Cohen, a professor at the University of Southern California's Center for Effective Organizations, said, "People keep doing it [teams] because it is popular, a fad, a thing to do. But then they find that they run into problems because these things do require considerable care and feeding. Companies have to invest some resources in making them succeed."[22] At Levi's, team members complained that there were few resources, such as training, to support the transition from independent, individual-based work to team-based work. They also complained about not being given enough time to learn how to run the new machines to which they were assigned on the team system.

Another key problem with resources is management resistance. Managers who have been in charge are often reluctant to help teams or turn over resources to them. At Levi's, when team members would ask supervisors for assistance, a common reaction was that they should handle problems and make decisions for themselves.[23]

Finally, teams should be used when they have clear authority to manage and change how the work gets done. This means that teams—not managers—decide what problem to tackle next, when to schedule time for maintenance or training, or how to solve customer problems. Research clearly shows that teams with the authority to manage their own work strongly outperform teams that don't.[24] Unfortunately, managers can undermine teams' authority by closely monitoring their work, asking teams to change their decisions, or directly ignoring or overruling team decisions. Jeffrey Pfeffer, a Stanford professor and management consultant/author, said, "The fact is, the people doing the work know better how to do it. Get the managers out of the way and you will do better."[25]

Review 1
The Good and Bad of Using Teams

In many industries, teams are growing in importance because they help organizations respond to specific problems and challenges. Teams have been shown to increase customer satisfaction (specific customer teams), product and service quality (direct responsibility), speed and efficiency in product development (overlapping development phases), and employee job satisfaction (cross training, unique opportunities, and leadership responsibilities). While teams can produce significant improvements in these areas, using teams does not guarantee these positive outcomes. Teams and teamwork have the disadvantages of initially high turnover, social loafing (especially in large groups), and groupthink. Teams also share many of the advantages (multiple perspectives, generation of more alternatives, and more commitment) and disadvantages (groupthink, time, poorly run meetings, domination by a few team members, and weak accountability) of group decision-making. Finally, teams should be used for a clear purpose, when the work requires that people work together, when rewards can be provided for both teamwork and team performance, when ample resources can be provided, and when teams can be given clear authority over their work.

2. Kinds of Teams

Workers at the Honeywell plant in Scarborough, Ontario, used to have dull and routine jobs until the plant turned to teams as part of its reorganization. Its 320 workers were placed into 35 teams and given control of different parts of the production process, including quality control of the products they were making. As a result of these changes, they were able to eliminate most of its quality control inspectors, all the jobs assigned to rework, and one-third of the managers. The plant now has 40 percent fewer workers and productivity has almost doubled.[26]

Let's start by looking at autonomy, the key dimension, and special kinds of teams.

EXPERIENCING MANAGEMENT

You may learn more about types of teams and their relationship to the organization by interacting with team concepts at our animated concept and activity site. Choose Teams from the "select a topic" pull-down menu, then Types of Teams from the "overview tab."

www.experiencingmanagement.com

2.1 Autonomy, the Key Dimension

Teams can be classified in a number of ways, such as whether they are permanent or temporary, or functional or cross-functional. However, studies indicate that the amount of autonomy possessed by a team is the key dimension that makes teams different from each another.[27] *Autonomy* is the degree to which workers have the discretion, freedom, and independence to decide how and when to accomplish their jobs.

Exhibit 12.2 displays an autonomy continuum that shows how five kinds of teams differ in their autonomy. Moving left to right at the top of Exhibit 12.2, notice that traditional work groups and employee involvement groups have the lowest levels of autonomy, followed by semi-autonomous work groups, which have a higher level of autonomy, and then self-managing teams and self-designing teams, which have the highest levels of autonomy. Moving from top to bottom along the left side of Exhibit 12.2, note that the number of responsibilities given to each kind of team increases directly with that team's autonomy. Let's review each of these teams and their autonomy and responsibilities in more detail.

The smallest amount of autonomy is found in **traditional work groups**, where two or more people work together to achieve a shared goal. In these groups, workers do not have direct responsibility or control over their work, but are responsible for doing the work or "executing the task." Workers report to managers, who are responsible for their performance and have the authority to hire and fire them, make job assignments, and control resources. For instance, take the situation of an experienced worker who blatantly refuses to do his share of the work, saying, "I've done my time. Let the younger employees do the work." In a team with high autonomy, the responsibility of getting this employee to put forth his fair share of effort would belong to his teammates. But in traditional work groups, the responsibility of telling this employee that his "sitting days are over" belongs to the boss or supervisor. In fact, the supervisor in this situation calmly

traditional work group
group composed of two or more people who work together to achieve a shared goal

EXHIBIT 12.2

TEAM AUTONOMY CONTINUUM

LOW TEAM AUTONOMY ← → HIGH TEAM AUTONOMY

RESPONSIBILITIES	TRADITIONAL WORK GROUPS	EMPLOYEE INVOLVEMENT GROUPS	SEMI-AUTONOMOUS WORK GROUPS	SELF-MANAGING TEAMS	SELF-DESIGNING TEAMS
Execute Task	√	√	√	√	√
Give Advice/ Make Suggestions		√	√	√	√
Information			√	√	√
Major Production/ Service Tasks:					
Make Decisions			√	√	√
Solve Problems			√	√	√
All Production/ Service Tasks:					
Make Decisions				√	√
Solve Problems				√	√
Control Design:					
Team					√
Tasks					√
Membership					√

Sources: R.D. Banker, J.M. Field, R.G. Schroeder, & K.K. Sinha, "Impact of Work Teams on Manufacturing Performance: A Longitudinal Field Study," *Academy of Management Journal* 39 (1996): 867–890. J.R. Hackman, "The Psychology of Self-Management in Organizations," in *Psychology and Work: Productivity, Change, and Employment*, eds. M.S. Pallak & R. Perloff (Washington, D.C.: American Psychological Association), 85–136.

confronted this employee and told him, "We need your talent, [and] your knowledge of these machines. But if you won't work, you'll have to go elsewhere." Within days, the employee's behaviour improved.[28]

Employee involvement teams, which have somewhat more autonomy, meet on company time on a weekly or monthly basis to provide advice or make suggestions to management concerning specific issues, such as plant safety, customer relations, or product quality.[29] And while they offer advice and suggestions, they do not have the authority to make decisions. Membership on these teams is often voluntary, but members may be selected because of their expertise. The idea behind employee involvement teams is that the people closest to the problem or situation are best able to recommend solutions.

Semi-autonomous work groups not only provide advice and suggestions to management, but they also have the authority to make decisions and solve problems related to the major tasks required to produce a product or service. Semi-autonomous groups regularly receive information about budgets, work quality, and performance, as well as competitors' products. Furthermore, members of semi-autonomous work groups are typically cross trained in a number of different skills and tasks. In short, semi-autonomous work groups give employees the autonomy to make decisions that are typically made by supervisors and managers.

However, that authority is not complete. Managers still play a role, though much reduced compared to traditional work groups, in supporting the work of semi-autonomous work groups. At the Ritz-Carlton, Kansas City, where semi-autonomous work groups were implemented, long-time manager Sandi Shartzer, director of house-

employee involvement team
team that provides advice or makes suggestions to management concerning specific issues

semi-autonomous work group
group that has the authority to make decisions and solve problems related to the major tasks of producing a product or service

keeping, said, "I had attendants who for 22 years had been told where to go, what to do. Now they're being told to do it on their own. Sure, the staff still runs to me occasionally, but they're learning to 'own' their own responsibility. I even had one worker tell me today that she's setting goals for herself." Hotel manager Bob Schrader reinforced Shartzer's view of the Ritz's semi-autonomous work groups. Schrader said, "My role is to be out on the floor, not sit in my office and look at paperwork. I attend team meetings and try to get people comfortable about approaching me on issues, but then a lot of my job is directing people back to their teams for solutions. A lot of what I should be doing now is asking questions instead of dictating methods."[30]

Self-managing teams are different from semi-autonomous work groups in that team members manage and control all the major tasks directly related to production of a product or service without first getting approval from management. This includes managing and controlling the acquisition of materials, making a product or providing a service, and ensuring timely delivery. For example, when Ford was bringing out its new version of the Ford Escort, "product specialist" Tom Arnold was part of a self-managing team consisting of engineers, car designers, and auto suppliers. Compared to the limited authority he had before, Arnold said, "I've had so many freedoms, it's unbelievable. I never had this experience until I got here. This [self-managing team] has been fantastic."

Self-designing teams have all the characteristics of self-managing teams, but they can also control and change the design of the teams themselves, the tasks they do and how they do them, and who belongs to the teams. At Saturn, a division of General Motors, self-designing teams of about ten people each build Saturn cars. Each team determines work schedules, vacation time, and even how assembly jobs are to be performed. Furthermore, the teams determine team membership by conducting the hiring interviews.[31]

2.2 Special Kinds of Teams

There are a number of other kinds of teams that can't be easily categorized with regard to autonomy. In other words, depending on how these teams are designed, they can be either low- or high-autonomy teams. Nonetheless, companies are increasingly using these teams. These special kinds of teams are cross-functional teams, virtual teams, and project teams.

Cross-functional teams are purposively composed of employees from different functional areas of the organization.[32] Because their members have different functional backgrounds, education, and experience, cross-functional teams usually attack problems from several perspectives and generate more ideas and alternative solutions, all of which are especially important when trying to innovate or do creative problem solving.[33] Cross-functional teams can be used almost anywhere in an organization and are often used in conjunction with matrix and product organizational structures. They can also be used with either part-time or temporary team assignments, or they can be used with full-time, long-term teams.

Virtual teams are groups of geographically and/or organizationally dispersed co-workers who use a combination of telecommunications and information technologies to accomplish an organizational task.[34] In other words, members of virtual teams rarely meet face to face. The idea of virtual teams is relatively new and has been made possible by advances in communications and technology, such as e-mail, the World Wide Web, videoconferencing, and other products. Virtual teams can be employee involvement teams, self-managing teams, or nearly any kind of team discussed in this chapter. Virtual teams are often (but not necessarily) temporary teams that are set up to accomplish a specific task.[35]

Because the team members don't meet in a physical location, one of the unique qualities of virtual teams is that it is much easier to include other key stakeholders, such as suppliers and customers. The development of the Boeing 777 was largely a virtual team effort. Boeing developed the 777 through the combined efforts of 238 design teams. The

self-managing team
team that manages and controls all the major tasks of producing a product or service

self-designing team
team that has the characteristics of self-managing teams but that also controls team design, work tasks, and team membership

cross-functional team
team composed of employees from different functional areas of the organization

virtual team
team composed of geographically and/or organizationally dispersed co-workers who use telecommunications and information technologies to accomplish an organizational task

project team
team created to complete specific, one-time projects or tasks within a limited time

238 teams used a network of 1700 individual computer systems. Virtual project teams worked on the 777 in each location and used computer technology to communicate with each other, including airlines that had purchased the 777 and suppliers who provided key expertise and parts.[36]

The principal advantage of virtual teams is that they are very flexible. Employees can work with each other, regardless of physical location, time zone, or organizational affiliation.[37] In addition, virtual teams have certain efficiency advantages over traditional team structures. Because the teammates do not meet face to face, the time commitment involved in participating in a virtual team is typically not as great as for a traditional team. Moreover, employees can fulfil the responsibilities of their virtual team membership from the comfort of their own offices, without the travel time or downtime typically required by "real" face-to-face meetings.[38]

A drawback of virtual teams is that the team members must learn to express themselves in new contexts. For example, the give-and-take that naturally occurs in face-to-face meetings is more difficult to achieve through videoconferencing or other methods of virtual teaming. In addition, several studies have shown that physical proximity enhances information processing.[39] Virtual teams have to devise ways to overcome these shortcomings.

Project teams are created to complete specific, one-time projects or tasks within a limited time.[40] Project teams are often used to develop new products (e.g., Ford's Team Taurus), to significantly improve existing products (e.g., Ford's Team Escort), to roll out new information systems, or to build new factories or offices. The project team is typically led by a project manager, who has the overall responsibility for planning, staffing, and managing the team.

Because project tasks are often unique, project teams are often staffed by employees from different functional areas and may also include members from the company's suppliers or customers.

One advantage of project teams is that drawing employees from different functional areas can reduce or eliminate communication barriers. In turn, free-flowing communication encourages cooperation among separate departments and typically speeds up the design process. Another advantage of project teams is their flexibility. When projects are finished, project team members either move on to the next project or return to their functional units. For example, publication of this book required designers, editors, page makeup artists, and Web designers, among others. When the task was finished, these people applied their skills to other text assignments. Because of this flexibility, project teams are often used with the matrix organizational designs discussed in Chapter 11.

Review 2
Kinds of Teams

Companies use different kinds of teams to make themselves more competitive. Autonomy is the key dimension that makes teams different. Traditional work groups (that execute tasks) and employee involvement groups (that make suggestions) have the lowest levels of autonomy. Semi-autonomous work groups (that control major, direct tasks) have more autonomy, followed by self-managing teams (that control all direct tasks) and self-designing teams (that control membership and how tasks are done), which have the highest levels of autonomy. Cross-functional, virtual, and project teams are common, but not easily categorized with regard to autonomy. Cross-functional teams combine employees from different functional areas to help teams attack problems from several perspectives and generate more ideas and solutions. Virtual teams use telecommunications and information technologies to bring co-workers "together," regardless of physical location or time zone. Virtual teams reduce travel and work time, but communication may suffer since team members don't work face-to-face. Finally, project teams are used for specific, one-time projects or tasks that must be completed within a limited time. Project teams reduce communication barriers and promote flexibility, as teams and team members are reassigned to their departments or new projects as old projects are completed.

Managing Work Teams

Operations manager: Why did I ever let you talk me into teams? They're nothing but trouble. I have to spend all my time in training and meetings, and we're behind on our production schedule.

Human resources manager: Hey, you were the one who wanted to try teams, remember? We went to visit that car company and you fell in love with their program.

Operations manager: I know, but obviously there's something wrong here. Maybe the car people were giving us a song and dance.

HR manager: I don't know about that. Maybe we ought to look at ourselves. What is it we're doing that's causing the problem?[41]

"Why did I ever let you talk me into teams?" Lots of managers have this reaction after making the move to teams. However, many don't realize that this reaction is normal, both for them and for workers. In fact, such a reaction is characteristic of the storming stage of team development. Managers who are familiar with these stages and with the other important characteristics of teams will be better prepared to manage the predictable changes that occur when companies make the switch to team-based structures.

After reading the next two sections, you should be able to
3. understand the general characteristics of work teams.
4. explain how to enhance work team effectiveness.

3. Work Team Characteristics

Understanding the characteristics of work teams is a requirement for making teams an effective part of an organization.

Therefore, in this section you'll learn about team norms, team cohesiveness, team size, team conflict, and stages of team development.

3.1 Team Norms

Over time, teams develop **norms**, informally agreed-on standards that regulate team behaviour.[42] Norms are valuable because they let team members know what is expected of them. Studies indicate that norms are one of the most powerful influences on work behaviour. Team norms are often associated with positive outcomes, such as stronger organizational commitment, more trust in management, and stronger job and organizational satisfaction.[43] In general, effective work teams develop norms about the quality and timeliness of job performance, absenteeism, safety, and honest expression of ideas and opinions. The power of norms also comes from the fact that they regulate the everyday kinds of behaviours that allow teams to function effectively. For example, when General Motors changed its Oshawa plant from a traditional production line to one that used a team-based approach, the various teams quickly established and accepted a standard production pace, or team norm.[44]

However, norms can also influence team behaviour in negative ways. For example, most people would agree that "damaging organizational property," "saying or doing something to hurt someone at work," "purposively doing one's work badly, incorrectly,

norms
informally agreed-on standards that regulate team behaviour

or slowly," "griping about co-workers," "deliberately bending or breaking rules," or "doing something to harm the company or your boss" are negative behaviours. However, a study of workers from 34 teams in 20 different organizations found that teams with negative norms strongly influenced their team members to engage in these negative behaviours. In fact, the longer they were a member of a team with negative norms, and the more frequently they interacted with their teammates, the more likely individual team members were to perform negative behaviours. Since team norms typically develop early in the life of a team, these results indicate how important it is for teams to establish positive norms from the outset.[45]

3.2 Team Cohesiveness

cohesiveness
the extent to which team members are attracted to a team and motivated to remain in it

Cohesiveness is another important characteristic of work teams. **Cohesiveness** is the extent to which team members are attracted to a team and motivated to remain in it.[46]

The level of cohesiveness that exists in a group is important for several reasons. To start, cohesive groups have a better chance of retaining their members. As a result, cohesive groups typically experience lower turnover.[47] In addition, team cohesiveness promotes cooperative behaviour, generosity, and a willingness on the part of team members to assist each other.[48] When team cohesiveness is high, team members are more motivated to contribute to the team, because they want to gain the approval of other team members. As a result of these reasons and others, studies have clearly established that cohesive teams are consistently better performing teams.[49] Furthermore, cohesive teams quickly achieve high levels of performance. By contrast, it takes teams low in cohesion much longer to reach the same levels of performance.[50]

What can be done to promote team cohesiveness? First, make sure that all team members are present at team meetings and activities. Team cohesiveness suffers when members are allowed to withdraw from the team and miss team meetings and events.[51] Second, create additional opportunities for teammates to work together by rearranging work schedules and creating common workspaces. When task interdependence is high and team members have lots of chances to work together, team cohesiveness tends to increase.[52] Third, engaging in nonwork activities as a team can help build cohesion. At

Participation in nonwork activities, such as sports and recreation, helps build team cohesiveness.

© PhotoDisc, Inc.

Cambridge Technology Partners, where teams put in extraordinarily long hours coding computer software, the software teams maintained cohesion by doing "fun stuff" together. Team leader Tammy Urban said, "We went on team outings at least once a week. We'd play darts, shoot pool. Teams work best when you get to know each other outside of work—what people's interests are, who they are. Personal connections go a long way when you're developing complex applications in our kind of time frames."[53] Finally, companies build team cohesiveness by making employees feel that they are part of a "special" organization. For example, all the new hires at Disney World in Orlando are required to take a course entitled "Traditions One," in which they learn the traditions and history of the Walt Disney Company (including the names of the seven dwarfs!). The purpose of Traditions One is to instil a sense of pride in working for Disney.

3.3 Team Size

There appears to be a curvilinear relationship between team size and performance. In other words, very small or very large teams may not perform as well as moderately sized teams. For most teams, the right size is somewhere between six and nine members.[54] This size is conducive to high team cohesion, which has a positive effect on team performance as discussed above. Teams of this size are small enough for the team members to get to

WhatReallyWorks

Cohesion and Team Performance

Have you ever worked in a really cohesive group where everyone really liked and enjoyed each other and was glad to be part of the group? It's great. By contrast, have you ever worked in a group where everyone really disliked each other and was unhappy to be a part of the group? It's terrible. Anyone who has had either of these experiences can appreciate how important group cohesion is and the effect it can have on team performance. Indeed, 46 studies based on 1279 groups confirm that cohesion does matter.

Team Performance
On average, there is a 66 percent chance that cohesive teams will outperform less cohesive teams.

Probability of Success

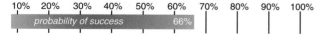

Team Performance with Interdependent Tasks
Teams work best for interdependent tasks that require people to work together to get the job done. When teams perform interdependent tasks, there is a 73 percent chance that cohesive teams will outperform less cohesive teams.

Probability of Success

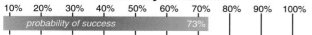

Team Performance with Independent Tasks
Teams are generally not suited for independent tasks in which people can accomplish the job by themselves. When teams perform independent tasks, there is only a 60 percent chance that cohesive teams will outperform less cohesive teams.

Probability of Success

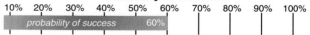

Some caution is warranted in interpreting these results. For example, there is always the possibility that a team could become so cohesive that its team goals become more important than organizational goals. Also, teams sometimes unite around negative goals and norms that are harmful rather than helpful to organizations. However, there is also room for even more optimism about cohesive teams. Teams that are cohesive and committed to the goals they are asked to achieve should have an even higher probability of success than the numbers shown here.

Source: S.M. Gully, D.S. Devine, & D.J. Whitney, "A Meta-analysis of Cohesion and Performance: Effects of Level of Analysis and Task Interdependence," *Small Group Research* 26, no. 4 (1995): 497–520.

know each other, and for each member to have an opportunity to contribute in a meaningful way to the success of the team. However, they're also large enough to take advantage of team members' diverse skills, knowledge, and perspectives. It is also easier to instil a sense of responsibility and mutual accountability in teams of this size.[55]

By contrast, when teams get too large, team members find it difficult to get to know one another and may splinter into smaller subgroups. When this occurs, subgroups sometimes argue and disagree, weakening overall team cohesion. As teams grow, there is a greater chance of *minority domination*, where just a few team members dominate team discussions. Even if minority domination doesn't occur, there still isn't as much time in larger groups for all team members to share their input. And when team members feel that their contributions are unimportant or not needed, the result is less involvement, effort, and accountability to the team.[56] Large teams also face logistical problems, such as finding an appropriate time or place to meet. Finally, the incidence of social loafing, discussed earlier in the chapter, is much higher in large teams. All these factors indicate how large teams can have a negative impact on team performance.

While teams should not be too large, it's also important that they not be too small. Teams with just a few people may lack the diversity of skills and knowledge found in larger teams. Also, teams that are too small are unlikely to gain the advantages of team decision-making (i.e., multiple perspectives, generating more ideas and alternative solutions, and stronger commitment) found in larger teams.

What signs indicate that a team's size needs to be changed? If decisions are taking too long, if it is difficult for the team to make decisions or take action, if the team is dominated by a few members, or if the commitment or efforts of team members are weak, chances are the team is too big. However, if a team is having difficulty coming up with ideas or generating solutions, or if the team does not have the expertise to address a specific problem, chances are the team is too small.

3.4 Team Conflict

Conflict and disagreement are inevitable in most teams. But this shouldn't surprise anyone. From time to time, people who work together are going to disagree about what and how things get done. What causes conflict in teams? While almost anything can lead to conflict—casual remarks that unintentionally offend a team member or fighting over scarce resources—the primary cause of team conflict is disagreement over team goals and priorities.[57] Other common causes of team conflict include disagreements over task-related issues, interpersonal incompatibilities, and simple fatigue.

While most people view conflict negatively, the key to dealing with team conflict is not avoiding conflict, but making sure that teams experience the right kind of conflict. In Chapter 6, you learned about *c-type conflict*, or cognitive conflict, which focuses on problem-related differences of opinion, and *a-type conflict*, or affective conflict, which refers to the emotional reactions that can occur when disagreements become personal rather than professional.[58] Cognitive conflict is strongly associated with improvements in team performance, while affective conflict is strongly associated with decreases in team performance.[59] Why does this happen? With cognitive conflict, team members disagree because their different experiences and expertise lead them to different views of the problem and solutions. Indeed, managers who participated on teams that emphasized cognitive conflict described their teammates as "smart," "team players," and "best in the business." They described their teams as "open," "fun," and "productive." One manager summed up the positive attitude that team members had about cognitive conflict by saying, "We scream a lot, then laugh, and then resolve the issue."[60] Thus, cognitive conflict is also characterized by a willingness to examine, compare, and reconcile differences to produce the best possible solution.

By contrast, affective conflict often results in hostility, anger, resentment, distrust, cynicism, and apathy. Managers who participated on teams that emphasized affective conflict described their teammates as "manipulative," "secretive," "burned out," and "political."[61] Not surprisingly, affective conflict can make people uncomfortable and cause them to withdraw and decrease their commitment to a team.[62] Affective conflict also lowers the satisfaction of team members, may lead to personal hostility between co-workers, and can decrease team cohesiveness.[63] So, unlike cognitive conflict, affective conflict undermines team effectiveness by preventing teams from engaging in the kinds of activities that are critical to team effectiveness.

So what can managers do to manage team conflict? First, managers need to realize that emphasizing cognitive conflict alone won't be enough. Studies show that cognitive and affective conflicts often occur together in the same teams! Therefore, sincere attempts to reach agreement on a difficult issue can quickly deteriorate from cognitive to affective conflict if the discussion turns personal and tempers and emotions flare. So while cognitive conflict is clearly the better approach to take, efforts to engage in cognitive conflict should be approached with caution.

Can teams disagree and still get along? Fortunately, they can. In an attempt to study this issue, researchers examined team conflict in 12 high-tech companies. In 4 of the 12 companies, work teams used cognitive conflict to address work problems but did so in a way that minimized the occurrence of affective conflict. Exhibit 12.3 shows what steps these teams took to be able to have a "good fight."[64]

3.5 Stages of Team Development

As teams develop and grow, they pass through four stages of development. As shown in Exhibit 12.4, those stages are forming, storming, norming, and performing.[65] While not every team passes through each of these stages, teams that do tend to be better performers.[66] This holds true even for teams composed of seasoned executives. However, after a period of time, if not managed well, performance may start to deteriorate as teams begin a process of decline, in which they progress through the stages of de-norming, de-storming, and de-forming.[67]

Forming is the initial stage of team development. This is the getting-acquainted stage, where team members first meet each other, form initial impressions, and try to get a sense of what it will be like to be part of the team. Some of the first team norms will be established during this stage, as team members begin to find out what behaviours will and won't be accepted by the team. Team leaders should allow enough time for team members to get to know each other during this stage and should set early ground rules and begin to set up a preliminary team structure.

> **EXPERIENCING MANAGEMENT**
>
> Reinforce your understanding of the stages of team development by interacting with this concept at our animated concept and activity site. Choose Teams from the "select a topic" pull-down menu, then Stages of Development from the "overview tab."
>
> **www.experiencingmanagement.com**

forming
the first state of team development in which team members meet each other, form initial impressions, and begin to establish team norms

---

EXHIBIT 12.3

HOW TEAMS CAN HAVE A GOOD FIGHT

1. Work with more, rather than less, information.
2. Develop several alternatives to enrich debate.
3. Establish common goals.
4. Inject humour into the workplace.
5. Maintain a balance of power.
6. Resolve issues without forcing a consensus.

Source: K.M. Eisenhardt, J.L. Kahwajy, & L.J. Bourgeois III, "How Management Teams Can Have a Good Fight," *Harvard Business Review* 75, no. 4 (July/August 1997): 77–87.

EXHIBIT 12.4

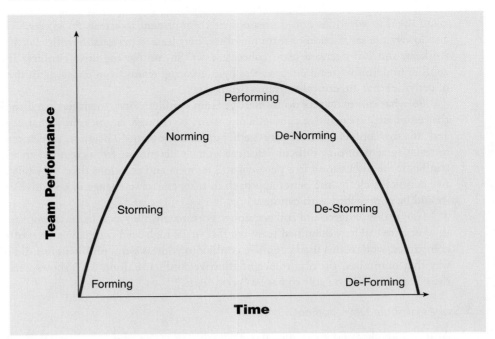

Sources: J.F. McGrew, J.G. Bilotta, & J.M. Deeney, "Software Team Formation and Decay: Extending the Standard Model for Small Groups," *Small Group Research* 30, no. 2 (1999): 209–234. B.W. Tuckman, "Development Sequence in Small Groups," *Psychological Bulletin* 63, no. 6 (1965): 384–399.

storming
the second stage of team development, characterized by conflict and disagreement, in which team members disagree over what the team should do and how it should do it

norming
the third stage of team development, in which team members begin to settle into their roles, group cohesion grows, and positive team norms develop

performing
the fourth stage of team development, in which performance improves because the team has matured into an effective, fully functioning team

Conflicts and disagreements often characterize the second stage of team development, **storming**. As team members begin working together, different personalities and work styles may clash. Team members become more assertive at this stage and more willing to state opinions. This is also the stage when team members jockey for position and try to establish a favourable role for themselves in the team. In addition, team members are likely to disagree about what the group should do and how it should do it. Team performance is still relatively low, given that team cohesion is weak and team members are still reluctant to support each other. Since teams that get stuck in the storming stage are almost always ineffective, it is important for team leaders to focus the team on team goals and on improving team performance. Team members need to be particularly patient and tolerant with each other in this stage.

During **norming**, the third stage of team development, team members begin to settle into their roles as team members. Positive team norms will have developed by this stage, and teammates should know what to expect from each other. Petty differences should also have been resolved, friendships will have developed, and group cohesion will be relatively strong. At this point, team members will have accepted team goals, will be operating as a unit, and, as indicated by the increase in performance, will be working together effectively. This stage can be very short and is often characterized by someone in the team saying, "I think things are finally coming together." However, teams may also cycle back and forth between storming and norming several times before finally settling into norming.

In the last stage of team development, **performing**, performance improves because the team has finally matured into an effective, fully functioning team. At this point, members should be fully committed to the team and think of themselves as "members of a team" and not just "employees." Team members often become intensely loyal to one another at this stage and feel mutual accountability for team successes and failures. Trivial disagreements, which can take time and energy away from the work of the team, should be rare. At this stage, teams get a lot of work done, and it is fun to be a team member.

However, after a period of time, if not managed well, performance may begin to decline, as teams progress through the stages of de-norming, de-storming, and de-forming.[68] Indeed, John Puckett, manufacturing vice president for circuit board maker XEL Communications, said, "The books all say you start in this state of chaos and march through these various stages, and you end up in this state of ultimate self-direction, where everything is going just great. They never tell you it can go back in the other direction, sometimes just as quickly."[69]

In **de-norming**, which is a reversal of the norming stage, team performance begins to decline as the size, scope, goal, or members of the team change. With new members joining the group, older members may become defensive as established ways of doing things are questioned and challenged. Expression of ideas and opinions becomes less open. New members change team norms by actively rejecting or passively neglecting previously established team roles and behaviours.

In **de-storming**, which is a reversal of the storming phase, the team's comfort level decreases. Team cohesion weakens as more group members resist conforming to team norms and quit participating in team activities. Angry emotions flare as the group explodes in conflict and moves into the final stage of de-forming.

In **de-forming**, which is a reversal of the forming stage, team members position themselves to gain control of pieces of the team. Team members begin to avoid each other and isolate themselves from team leaders. Team performance rapidly declines as the team quits caring about even minimal requirements of team performance.

If teams are actively managed, decline is not inevitable. However, managers need to recognize that the forces at work in the de-norming, de-storming, and de-forming stages represent a powerful, disruptive, and real threat to teams that have finally made it to the performing stage. Getting to the performing stage is half the battle. Staying there is the second half.

Review 3
Work Team Characteristics

The most important characteristics of work teams are team norms, cohesiveness, size, conflict, and development. Norms let team members know what is expected of them and can influence team behaviour in positive and negative ways. Positive team norms are associated with organizational commitment, trust, and job satisfaction. Team cohesiveness helps teams retain members, promotes cooperative behaviour, increases motivation, and facilitates team performance. Attending team meetings and activities, creating opportunities to work together, and engaging in nonwork activities can increase cohesiveness. Team size has a curvilinear relationship with team performance, such that very small or very large teams do not perform as well as moderately sized teams of six to nine members. Teams of this size are cohesive and small enough for team members to get to know each other and contribute in a meaningful way, but are large enough to take advantage of team members' diverse skills, knowledge, and perspectives. Conflict and disagreement are inevitable in most teams. The key to dealing with team conflict is to maximize cognitive conflict, which focuses on issue-related differences, and minimize affective conflict, the emotional reactions that occur when disagreements become personal rather than professional. As teams develop and grow, they pass through four stages of development: forming, storming, norming, and performing. However, after a period of time, if not managed well, performance may decline, as teams progress through the stages of de-norming, de-storming, and de-forming.

de-norming
a reversal of the norming stage, in which team performance begins to decline as the size, scope, goal, or members of the team change

de-storming
a reversal of the storming phase, in which the team's comfort level decreases, team cohesion weakens, and angry emotions and conflict may flare

de-forming
a reversal of the forming stage, in which team members position themselves to control pieces of the team, avoid each other, and isolate themselves from team leaders

4. Enhancing Work Team Effectiveness

Making teams work is a challenging and difficult process. However, companies can increase the likelihood that teams will succeed by carefully setting team goals and priorities, selecting people for teamwork, training the team, and addressing team compensation and recognition.[70]

4.1 Setting Team Goals and Priorities

In Chapter 4 you learned that specific, measurable, attainable, results-oriented, and time-bounded (i.e., S.M.A.R.T.) goals are one of the most effective means for improving individual job performance. Fortunately, team goals also improve team performance. In fact, team goals lead to much higher team performance 93 percent of the time.[71] For example, Nucor Steel sets specific, challenging goals for each of its production teams, which consist of first-line supervisors and production and maintenance workers. Each day these teams are challenged to produce a specific number of tons of high-quality steel.[72] Teams that meet their goals earn daily bonuses that can double their base salaries.

Why is the setting of specific, challenging team goals so critical to team success? One reason is that increasing a team's performance is inherently more complex than just increasing one individual's job performance. For instance, consider that for any team there are likely to be at least four different kinds of goals: each member's goal for the team, each member's goal for himself or herself on the team, the team's goal for each member, and the team's goal for itself.[73] In other words, without a specific, challenging goal for the team itself (the last of the four goals listed), these other goals may encourage team members to head off in 12 different directions at once. Consequently, setting a specific, challenging goal *for the team* clarifies team priorities by providing a clear focus and purpose.

Specific, challenging team goals also regulate how hard team members work. In particular, challenging team goals greatly reduce the incidence of social loafing. When faced with difficult goals, team members simply expect everyone to contribute. Consequently, they are much more likely to notice and complain if a teammate isn't doing his or her share. In fact, when teammates know each other well, when team goals are specific, when team communication is good, and when teams are rewarded for team performance (discussed below), there is only a 1 in 16 chance that teammates will be social loafers.[74]

What can companies and teams do to ensure that team goals lead to superior team performance? One increasingly popular approach is to give teams stretch goals. *Stretch goals* are extremely ambitious goals that workers don't know how to reach.[75] The purpose of stretch goals is to achieve extraordinary improvements in performance by forcing managers and workers to throw away old comfortable solutions and adopt radical, never-used solutions. For instance, when Allied Signal bought the Budd Company's wheel and brake division, Allied managers challenged Budd's product development team to cut the development time for new car brake systems in half. The team succeeded, cutting development time from 36 to 18 months.[76]

Four things must occur for stretch goals to effectively motivate teams.[77] First, teams must have a high degree of autonomy or control over how they achieve their goals. Second, teams must be empowered with control resources, such as budgets, workspaces, computers, or whatever they need to do their jobs. Steve Kerr, General Electric's "Chief Learning Officer," said, "We have a moral obligation to try to give people the tools to meet tough goals. I think it's totally wrong if you don't give employees the tools to succeed, then punish them when they fail."[78]

structural accommodation
the ability to change organizational structures, policies, and practices

Third, teams need structural accommodation. **Structural accommodation** means giving teams the ability to change organizational structures, policies, and practices if it helps them meet their stretch goals. When Hewlett-Packard imposed tough goals on its customer service teams, one of the unintended consequences was a big increase in work stress from being called to customer sites on weekends and at all hours of the night. As a result, overworked customer service engineers began quitting their jobs, making it unlikely that the teams could achieve their stretch goals. HP responded by giving teams the ability to "reinvent work" in a way that would meet the stretch goals, but reduce worker stress. The teams decided to throw out existing policies on employee work hours and simply asked who would be willing to work Fridays through Mondays and who would be willing to work Tuesdays through Fridays. Stress dropped immediately, and employees stopped quitting their jobs.[79]

Finally, teams need bureaucratic immunity. **Bureaucratic immunity** means that teams no longer have to go through the frustratingly slow process of multilevel reviews and signoffs to get management approval before making changes. Once granted bureaucratic immunity, teams are immune from the influence of various organizational groups and are only accountable to top management. Therefore teams can act quickly and even experiment with little fear of failure. KI Pembroke, a small Canadian filing-cabinet manufacturer, operates with 11 self-directed work teams with 10 members each. These teams have complete control over the area they are responsible for, whether health and safety, scheduling, or cost control. With no middle managers, each team must report to senior management, thereby providing them with bureaucratic immunity.[80]

bureaucratic immunity
the ability to make changes without first getting approval from managers or other parts of an organization

4.2 Selecting People for Teamwork

University of Southern California Professor Edward Lawler said, "People are very naive about how easy it is to create a team. Teams are the Ferraris of work design. They're high performance but high maintenance and expensive."[81] It's almost impossible to make effective work teams without carefully selecting people who are suited for teamwork or for working on a particular team. A preference for teamwork, team elevation, and team diversity can help companies choose the right team members.[82]

Are you more comfortable working alone or with others? If you strongly prefer to work alone, you may not be well suited for teamwork. Indeed, studies show that job satisfaction is higher in teams when team members prefer working with others.[83] An indirect way to measure someone's *preference for teamwork* is to assess the person's degree of individualism or collectivism. **Individualism-collectivism** is the degree to which a person believes that people should be self-sufficient and that loyalty to one's self is more important than loyalty to one's team or company.[84] *Individualists*, who put their welfare and interests first, generally prefer independent tasks in which they work alone. On the other hand, *collectivists*, who put group or team interests ahead of self-interests, generally prefer interdependent tasks in which they work with others. Collectivists would also rather cooperate than compete and are fearful of disappointing team members or of being ostracized from teams. Given these differences, it makes sense to select team members who are collectivists rather than individualists. Indeed, many companies use individualism-collectivism as an initial screening device for team members. However, as discussed below, individualists may be appropriate if team diversity is desired. To determine your preference for teamwork, take the Team Player Inventory shown in Exhibit 12.5.

individualism-collectivism
the degree to which a person believes that people should be self-sufficient and that loyalty to one's self is more important than loyalty to one's team or company

Team level is the average level of ability, experience, personality, or any other factor on a team. For example, a high level of team experience means that a team has particularly experienced team members. This does not mean that every member of the team has considerable experience, but that enough team members do to significantly raise the average level of experience on the team. Team level is used to guide selection of teammates when teams need a particular set of skills or capabilities to do their jobs well. For instance, in retail sales jobs, teams with high average levels of conscientiousness, agreeableness, and openness to experience have much higher sales than teams with low average levels on these dimensions.[85]

team level
the average level of ability, experience, personality, or any other factor on a team

While team level represents the average level or capability on a team, **team diversity** represents the variances or differences in ability, experience, personality, or any other factor on a team. For example, teams with strong team diversity on job experience would have a mix of team members, ranging from seasoned veterans to people with three or four

team diversity
the variances or differences in ability, experience, personality, or any other factor on a team

EXHIBIT 12.5

THE TEAM PLAYER INVENTORY

	STRONGLY DISAGREE	1	2	3	4	5	STRONGLY AGREE
1. I enjoy working on team/group projects.		1	2	3	4	5	
2. Team/group project work easily allows others to not "pull their weight."		1	2	3	4	5	
3. Work that is done as a team/group is better than the work done individually.		1	2	3	4	5	
4. I do my best work alone rather than in a team/group.		1	2	3	4	5	
5. Team/group work is overrated in terms of the actual results produced.		1	2	3	4	5	
6. Working in a team/group gets me to think more creatively.		1	2	3	4	5	
7. Team/groups are used too often, when individual work would be more effective.		1	2	3	4	5	
8. My own work is enhanced when I am in a team/group situation.		1	2	3	4	5	
9. My experiences working in team/group situations have been primarily negative.		1	2	3	4	5	
10. More solutions/ideas are generated when working in a team/group situation than when working alone.		1	2	3	4	5	

Reverse score items 2, 4, 5, 7, and 9. Then add the scores for items 1–10.

Higher scores indicate a preference for teamwork, while lower total scores indicate a preference for individual work.

Source: T.J.B. Kline, "The Team Player Inventory: Reliability and Validity of a Measure of Predisposition toward Organizational Team-Working Environments," *Journal for Specialists in Group Work* 24, no. 1 (1999): 102–112.

years of experience to rookies with little or no experience. Team diversity is used to guide selection of teammates when teams are asked to complete a wide range of different tasks or when tasks are particularly complex.

Delta Dental Plan used the principle of team diversity to select the team members who service its largest account. Tom Raffio, senior vice president, explained that the company wanted a team of people whose strengths complemented each other. The first step was to administer personality inventories to potential team members. Raffio said, "We were looking for a combination of introverts and extroverts, people who reflect on things and people who close on things, and people who could process claims efficiently on a daily basis, as well as those who could keep in mind the long-term vision of the company." The next step was to make sure there was a mixture of language capabilities on the team: English, French, and Spanish. Finally, the company wanted a mix of experience, including seasoned employees who understood the company culture and new employees who brought outside ideas and perspectives. Accordingly, team members were recruited from both inside and outside the company.[86]

4.3 Team Training

Organizations that create work teams often underestimate the amount of training required to make teams effective. This mistake occurs frequently in successful organizations, where managers assume that if employees can work effectively on their own, they can work effectively in teams. However, companies that successfully use teams provide thousands of hours of training to make sure that teams work. When General Motors successfully changed its Oshawa plant to a team environment, it invested extensively in training in teamwork and problem-solving skills.[87]

The most common type of training provided to members of work teams is training in interpersonal skills. **Interpersonal skills**, such as listening, communicating, questioning, and providing feedback, enable people to have effective working relationships with others. When Super Sack, a maker of heavy-duty plastic bags for the food and phar-

interpersonal skills
skills, such as listening, communicating, questioning, and providing feedback, that enable people to have effective working relationships with others

Teams can be useful but their effectiveness is often dependent on adequate training. The most common type of training provided to members of work teams is training in interpersonal skills, enabling them to have effective working relationships with others.

maceutical industries, first used teams, it failed. David Kellenberger, Super Sack's vice president of manufacturing, said, "One of our greatest mistakes at the beginning was our failure to recognize how important training was. You need to make a huge commitment of time and resources for training people in communication, goal-setting, and general team-building skills to make a successful transition [to teams]...."[88] Experiences like these are why Wilson Sporting Goods provides all of its first-year team members 26 hours of training on team interaction skills and how to run meetings.[89]

Because of their autonomy and responsibility, many companies give teams training in decision-making and problem-solving skills to help them do a better job of cutting costs and improving quality and customer service. Stacy Myers, a consultant who helps companies implement teams, said, "When we help companies move to teams, we also require that employees take basic quality and business knowledge classes as well. Teams must know how their work affects the company, and how their success will be measured."[90] Many organizations also teach teams conflict resolution skills. Coldwater Machine Company formed teams but waited several months to provide conflict resolution training. Ken Meyer, Coldwater's coordinator of work groups, said, "People are starting to encounter differences right now, so we're starting conflict resolution training. We think work group members will appreciate the training more now that they're in particular situations and see the relevance."[91]

Firms must also provide team members the technical training they need to do their jobs, particularly if they are expected to perform all the different jobs on the team (i.e., cross training). Before teams were created at Milwaukee Mutual Insurance, separate employees performed the tasks of rating, underwriting, and processing insurance policies. However, after extensive cross training, each team member can now do all three jobs.[92] Cross training is less appropriate for teams of highly skilled workers. For instance, it is unlikely that a group of engineers, computer programmers, and systems analysts would be cross-trained for each other's jobs.

Finally, companies need to provide training for team leaders, who often feel unprepared for their new duties. Exhibit 12.6 shows the top ten problems reported by new team leaders. These range from confusion about their new roles as team leaders (compared to their old jobs as managers or employees) to not knowing where to go for help when their teams have problems. The solution is extensive training for team leaders.

4.4 Team Compensation and Recognition

Compensating teams correctly is very difficult. For instance, one survey found that only 37 percent of companies were satisfied with their team compensation plans and even fewer, just 10 percent, reported being "very positive."[93] One of the problems, according to Monty Mohrman of the Center for Effective Organizations, is that "there is a very strong set of beliefs in most organizations that people should be paid for how well they do. So when people first get put into team-based organizations, they really balk at being paid for how well the team does. It sounds illogical to them. It sounds like their individuality and their sense of self-worth are being threatened."[94] Consequently, companies need to carefully choose a team compensation plan and then fully explain how teams will be rewarded. One basic requirement is that the level of rewards (individual vs. team) must match the level of performance (individual vs. team) for team compensation to work.

There are three methods of compensating employees for team participation and accomplishments. The first is called skill-based pay. **Skill-based pay** programs pay employees for learning additional skills or knowledge.[95] These programs encourage employees to acquire the additional skills they will need to perform several jobs within a team. For example, at XEL Communications, the number of skills each employee has mastered determines his or her individual pay. An employee who takes a class in advanced soldering (XEL makes circuit boards) followed by on-the-job training will earn thirty cents more per hour. Passing a written test or satisfactorily performing a skill or job for a supervisor or trainer certifies mastery of new skills and results in increased pay.[96]

The second approach to compensating employees for team participation is through **gainsharing** programs, in which companies share the financial value of performance gains, such as productivity, cost savings, or quality, with their workers.[97] The first month

skill-based pay
compensation system that pays employees for learning additional skills or knowledge

gainsharing
compensation system in which companies share the financial value of performance gains, such as productivity, cost savings, or quality, with their workers

---

EXHIBIT 12.6

TOP TEN PROBLEMS REPORTED BY TEAM LEADERS

1. Confusion about their new roles and about what they should be doing differently.
2. Feeling they've lost control.
3. Not knowing what it means to coach or empower.
4. Having personal doubts about whether the team concept will really work.
5. Uncertainty about how to deal with employees' doubts about the team concept.
6. Confusion about when a team is ready for more responsibility.
7. Confusion about how to share responsibility and accountability with the team.
8. Concern about promotional opportunities, especially about whether the "team leader" title carries any prestige.
9. Uncertainty about the strategic aspects of the leader's role as teams mature.
10. Not knowing where to turn for help with team problems, since few if any of their organization's leaders have led teams.

Source: B. Filipczak, M. Hequet, C. Lee, M. Picard, & D. Stamps, "More Trouble with Teams," *Training*, October 1996, 21.

that gainsharing was used at Rogan Corporation, a maker of plastic handles and knobs, employee teams saved the company $35 136 earning an additional $17 568 for themselves. They earned slightly more the second month. Since its inception, gainsharing has added 16 percent to 22 percent to the salaries of Rogan's employees, typically $4500 to $7500 per employee per year. But the company has benefited as well. Before gainsharing, employees produced an average of 95 000 knobs per employee each year. But after gainsharing, employees produced at more than twice that rate, turning out an average of 206 000 knobs per employee per year.[98]

Nonfinancial rewards are another way to reward teams for their performance. These awards, which can range from vacation trips to T-shirts, plaques, and coffee mugs, are especially effective when coupled with management recognition.[99] At Motorola, each year several thousand teams enter a companywide competition in which work teams review their past accomplishments and discuss their future goals. The final 24 teams make presentations to a panel of top managers at company headquarters. Becoming a finalist is quite prestigious and gives those employees unique exposure to Motorola's top managers. Likewise, NCR has a "Great Performance Award" that recognizes its top teams.[100]

Which team plan should your company use? In general, skill-based pay is most effective for self-managing and self-directing teams performing complex tasks. In these situations, the more each team member knows and can do, the better the whole team performs. By contrast, gainsharing works best in relatively stable environments where employees can focus on improving the productivity, cost savings, or quality of their current work system.

Finally, given the level of dissatisfaction with most team compensation systems, what compensation plans would today's managers like to use with the teams in their companies? Forty percent of managers would directly link merit pay increases to team performance, but allow adjustments within teams for differences in individual performance. By contrast, 13.7 percent would link merit-based increases directly to team performance, but would give each team member an equal share of the team's merit-based reward. Nineteen percent would use gainsharing plans based on quality, delivery, productivity, or cost reduction, and then provide equal payouts to all teams and team members. Fourteen and a half percent would use gainsharing, but would vary the team gainsharing award, depending on how much money the team saved the company. Payouts would still be equally distributed within teams. Finally, 12.2 percent of managers would opt for plantwide profit-sharing plans tied to overall company or division performance. In this case, there would be no payout distinctions between or within teams.[101]

Review 4
Enhancing Work Team Effectiveness

Companies can make teams more effective by setting team goals and managing how work team members are selected, trained, and compensated. Team goals provide a clear focus and purpose, reduce the incidence of social loafing, and lead to higher team performance 93 percent of the time. Extremely difficult stretch goals can be used to motivate teams as long as teams have autonomy, control over resources, structural accommodation, and bureaucratic immunity. Not everyone is suited for teamwork. When selecting team members, companies should select people who have a preference for teamwork (individualism-collectivism) and should consider the importance of team level (average ability on a team) and team diversity (different abilities on a team). Organizations that successfully use teams provide thousands of hours of training to make sure that teams work. The most common types of team training are for interpersonal decision-making and problem-solving skills, conflict resolution, technical training to help team members learn several jobs (i.e., cross training), and training for team leaders. There are three methods of compensating employees for team participation and accomplishments: skill-based pay, gainsharing, and nonfinancial rewards.

What Really Happened?

In the opening case, you learned that Cigna's Customer Service Centre was struggling and the company was considering the use of teams to address its problems. After considering the costs and benefits, Cigna replaced the traditional departments in its Customer Service Centre with employee work teams. Read the answers to the opening case to find out how well teams worked at Cigna's Customer Service Centre.

A few things worry you, however. Some employees may not fit into a team environment. What if these employees quit their jobs, or complain a lot and make everybody's life miserable?

One of the clear disadvantages of work teams is initially high turnover. Teams aren't for everyone, and some workers will balk at the responsibility, effort, and learning required in team settings. As you read in the chapter, turnover jumped when GE began implementing teams in its factories. The same thing happened at Cigna, as roughly 25 percent of its customer service representatives left after Cigna switched to teams. Most of those who left just felt that they wouldn't fit well in a team environment. According to William Faris, Assistant Vice President of Compensation Design and Education at the time the switch to teams was made, "It was a recognition thing. They felt they wouldn't be as important as they were before." Chances are the workers who left were individualists, that is, people who put their welfare and interests first. Individualists generally prefer independent tasks in which they work alone. By contrast, the employees who stayed at Cigna to work in teams were more likely to have been collectivists, people who put group or team interests ahead of self-interests. Collectivists generally like team work because they prefer interdependent tasks in which they work with others.

There will also be fewer jobs open at the supervisor level. And the last thing that you want to do is to create the impression that there is no opportunity for top performers to move up in the firm.

Did Cigna's employees believe that self-managed teams would lead to fewer chances for promotion? Some employees genuinely feared that with supervisory jobs being eliminated (due to self-managed teams), there would be less room for advancement. In reality, though, because the teams required a substantial amount of support, Cigna did not reduce the number of upper-level jobs available for promotion. It was difficult, however, to get employees to see it that way.

Despite the outward promise of teamwork, it is difficult to know whether teams will actually work until you try it. What if productivity doesn't go up, and employee morale suffers rather than improves?

While teams are clearly not appropriate for all tasks or all companies, this was not the case at Cigna, where the teams thrived after implementation. The first sign that teamwork was succeeding at Cigna was that employees started liking their jobs. While employee turnover initially jumped to 25 percent soon after the change to teams, it dropped dramatically to just 5 percent within two years. In other words, 95 percent of Cigna's team members were choosing to stay in their jobs and with the company. Productivity increased dramatically as well. Costs dropped 30 percent. Quality rose by 50 percent. The amount of time it took to complete standard tasks, such as delivering price quotes to customers (such as large companies seeking insurance coverage) dropped from 17 days to 3 days, as empowered teams eliminated seven authorization steps and reduced the number of handoffs between departments from 14 to 3. Staff who processed only 35 to 40 claims a day before teams were able to process 75 to 90 claims a day once they became members of self-managed teams.

Will work teams actually improve customer service?

One of the keys to making teams work is to set a specific, challenging goal. Teams work 93 percent of the time when this is done. Accordingly, Cigna made clear that the singular goal of its teams was to "satisfy the customer with one contact," in other words, take care of customers' concerns and problems in one phone call. The teams exceeded this goal, as customer satisfaction rose by more than 50 percent after the implementation of teams. And customer satisfaction levels, measured by periodic surveys, remain high.

Will you be putting your own job on the line? That's a scary thought, particularly with two kids in college.

Could the move to teams have put your job on the line? Most definitely. When teams are appropriate, they can produce incredible improvements in productivity, quality, and employee and customer satisfaction. But when teams aren't appropriate, they can fail miserably. For instance, production levels dropped by 23 percent when Levi Strauss introduced teams in its factories. Levi's mistake was assuming that teams were appropriate for garment work, where workers performed single, specialized tasks, like sewing zippers or belt loops. Because this kind of work does not require interaction with others, teams failed miserably at Levi's.

So the question is not whether to use teams, but when and where to use teams for maximum benefit and minimum cost. In short, teams should be used for a clear purpose, when the work requires that people work together, when rewards can be provided for both teamwork and team performance, when ample resources can be provided, and when teams can be given clear authority over their work.

Sources: M. Brown, "National Winner: Cigna Services UK," *Management Today*, June 1994, 95. J.R. Caron, S.L. Jarvenpaa, & D.B. Stoddard, "Business Reengineering at CIGNA Corporation: Experiences and Lessons Learned from the First Five Years," *MIS Quarterly* 18, no. 3 (1994): 233. S.E. Gross, *Compensation for Teams* (New York: American Management Association, 1995). T. Hoffman, "Re-engineering Pays Off at Cigna," *Computerworld*, August 1993, 70. "International Healthcare News," *Business Conference and Management Reports*, 1 December 1995, 6.

Key Terms

bureaucratic immunity (379)
cohesiveness (372)
cross-functional team (369)
cross training (363)
de-forming (377)
de-norming (377)
de-storming (377)
employee involvement team (368)
forming (375)
gainsharing (382)

individualism-collectivism (379)
interpersonal skills (380)
norming (376)
norms (371)
performing (376)
project team (370)
self-designing team (369)
self-managing team (369)
semi-autonomous work group (368)
skill-based pay (382)

social loafing (364)
storming (376)
structural accommodation (378)
team diversity (379)
team level (379)
traditional work group (367)
virtual team (369)
work team (362)

What Would You Do II?

Jack Murdock, the CEO of Goldstar Trailers, rubbed his eyes and looked up from his computer screen to collect his thoughts. Ten months ago, he had led an effort to organize his employees into self-managing work teams. The employees seemed to like the new structure, and early on he got good feedback. But lately, he was sensing that no real progress was being made. Productivity in the plant was up slightly, but nothing like he had hoped for. In addition, turnover in the plant was, not down like the books and videos on teamwork promised. Rubbing his eyes again, Jack turned his office chair toward the window. Gazing outside, he ran through in his mind one more time why he had insisted on teamwork.

Goldstar manufactures three types of horse trailers: a gooseneck, a hitch trailer, and a slant load. Before the creation of work teams, the employees worked in separate departments: metalwork, assembly, painting, and design. Although the company made good trailers, Jack had worried about his employees. They just didn't seem to be excited about their jobs. He had also worried about a decline in quality. One phone call from a dealer had been particularly disturbing. The dealer said that he had sold nine Goldstar trailers since the first of the year, and five had already come back for repairs. Jack remembered that the call had sent chills down his back.

The idea to implement self-managing work teams came from a book that Jack had read. In fact, Jack reorganized the manufacturing process based on the ideas in the book. The departments were eliminated, and each employee was assigned to a process team. A separate team was set up for each type of trailer that the company made. Jack remembered asking his employees what to call the new teams. He had wanted to call them Team A, Team B, and Team C. The employees would have none of that. They decided to call themselves the Gooseneck Team, the Hitch Trailer Team, and the Slant Load Team, which corresponded to the trailers that each team would be making. Privately, Jack was pleased. He wanted the teams to closely identify with the trailers they made.

The way the new structure worked, each team manufactured only the trailer that corresponded to its name. However, employees on each team were cross-trained in the areas of metalwork, assembly, painting, and in some cases, design. Each team had a team leader, and the teams were responsible for their own hiring, budgeting, purchasing, inventory control, and inspection. The teams had weekly meetings to talk about quality improvements, inventory control, absenteeism, and product design. The idea was to get each team member fully involved in making a better product. He also hoped that the employees would gain a sense of pride in "their" trailers. In fact, a small metal plate containing the names of the team members was welded to the inside wall of the trailer just for this purpose.

Although this all sounded good, it hadn't worked, at least not yet. The overall performance of the plant had not improved, and Jack was hearing more and more complaints. Jack remembered thinking a hundred times over the past ten months, "Are we doing something wrong, or is teamwork a bad idea?" One way or another, Jack knew that he had to find an answer to that question.

A truck on the road outside of Jack's window blew its horn at another vehicle and snapped Jack out of his daydream. He turned back to his computer screen and reread the e-mail message that he had just received from the leader of the Gooseneck Team. The message read as follows:

Dear Jack,

We are all behind you on this teamwork thing, but we have got to get better organized. The team meetings are a good idea, but most of the time we just drink coffee and talk about sports. What, specifically, would you like us to accomplish? Also, our team has outperformed the other two teams for the past two months, but that hasn't affected our take-home pay. We have appreciated your letters, but letters of congratulations only go so far. Jack,

I don't mean to be critical. Your dad hired me and I am committed to Goldstar Trailers. But teamwork has to be more than an idea. We need your help and support. Think it over and let me know what you decide. I need to go to my people with some concrete ideas.

Bill Waters
Team Leader, Gooseneck Team

Jack turned his chair and looked outside his window again. He asked himself aloud, "What should I do?"

If you were CEO of Goldstar Trailers, what would you do?

Sources: P. Berman, "The Wabash Way," *Forbes*, 6 April 1998, 78–81. M. Krantz, "Wabash Keeps Work Flowing on Innovative Truck Trailers," *Investor's Business Daily*, 6 May 1994, A4. R.L. Rose, "Hard Driving: A Productivity Push at Wabash National Puts Firm on a Roll—Workers Are Strongly Urged to Improve Their Skills; Teams Offer Many Ideas: But Paternalism Irks Some," *The Wall Street Journal*, 7 September 1995, A1.

Management Decisions

A Team Leader's Worst Nightmare

"Okay, Ted, tell me one more time what happened." Ted Knight, a new employee just assigned to the Hard Disk Assembly Team, is sitting in your office on a Friday afternoon, and you can't believe what you're hearing.

Each member of the Hard Disk Assembly Team is responsible for assembling and testing hard disks that go into PCs. As a way of creating healthy competition among the team's six members, you've been recording each member's production output each day and posting it near the team's work area. At the end of each week, the team member who has assembled the most hard disks without a quality failure receives a $50 bonus.

You always thought that the competition had worked well. Several different team members had won the $50 bonus, production numbers were inching up, and no one had complained about the availability of extra cash. But Ted's story was making you heartsick. Ted joined the Hard Disk Assembly Team three weeks ago. His first two weeks were primarily training. But this week, Ted had a workstation of his own on the factory floor. Ted is a quick learner, which is one of the reasons you hired him. According to Ted, two of his teammates cornered him in a quiet corner of the snack room during his afternoon break. They told him that under no circumstances was he to assemble more than 30 hard disks during a single day. One of the employees, whom Ted was not willing to identify, told him, "We all work at a comfortable pace around here. If you assemble more than 30 hard disks a day, the team leader will expect us all to." Ted went on to say that the second employee told him, "And by the way, no one gets to win the weekly production award until they've been around for a while. If you are leading toward the end of the week, I'll let you know so you can slow down some."

You took a deep breath and looked Ted straight in the eye. "Ted, thanks for letting me know what's going on. I honestly had no idea that anything like this was happening. Give me the weekend, and on Monday morning I'll let you know what I am going to do."

Questions

1. If you were the team leader, what would you do? Would you call a team meeting and deal directly with this problem, or would you try a more subtle approach?

2. What about Ted? If you go to Ted's teammates and reveal what he told you, will he ever be accepted as a member of the team? Also, what about the weekly production award? Should you cancel it, allow it to continue as is, or change it in some way?

Sources: J. George, "Extrinsic and Intrinsic Origins of Perceived Social Loafing in Organizations," *Academy of Management Journal* 35 (1992): 191–202. R.E. Kidwell, Jr. & N. Bennett, "Employee Propensity to Withhold Effort: A Conceptual Model to Intersect Three Avenues Research," *Academy of Management Review* 18, no. 3 (1993): 429–456. P.W. Mulvey, J.F. Veiga, & P.M. Elsass, "When Teammates Raise a White Flag," *Academy of Management Executive* 10, no. 1 (1996): 40–49.

Management Decisions

You Thought That Awarding Bonuses Would Be Easy. Think Again.

You've just reread the fifth e-mail message this month about the new team bonus plan. None of them has been positive. Two years ago, you switched your Credit Card Customer Service Centre to a team-based design. Prior to the switch, your employees had been assigned to traditional functional areas. But hoping to increase customer service and decrease costs, you eliminated the traditional departments and put your employees into teams. Now you have five teams to service your credit card customers. The teams are as follows:

Team 1   Handles routine requests for personal accounts
Team 2   Handles routine requests for corporate accounts
Team 3   Investigates requests for credit line increases
Team 4   Sells credit card protection insurance
Team 5   Investigates disputed charges

After you created work teams, your employees complained about the lack of team incentives. Basically, you were still paying employees an individually based merit increase plus a cost-of-living adjustment. Six months ago you decided to give team incentives a try. You challenged each team to increase its productivity by 5 percent per month. According to the new plan, teams that increased productivity by that amount would receive a $500 bonus to split among its team members.

But it hasn't worked. Here's the problem. Teams 1, 2, and 3 have won the bonus for each of the six months that the bonus has been in existence. Teams 4 and 5 have never won the bonus. You're getting the same complaint from every member of Teams 4 and 5 that you talk to. What they keep telling you is that it is easier for Teams 1, 2, and 3 to increase their productivity than it is for them. Teams 1 and 2 handle hundreds of routine calls

every day. To increase productivity, all they have to do is move more quickly through their calls. Team 3 investigates requests for credit line increases. Because interest rates have been going down, they have gotten numerous requests and have been able to approve the majority of them. So these teams have been steadily increasing their productivity and have been awarded the $500 bonus each month.

However, according to members of Teams 4 and 5, it is not as easy for them to increase their productivity. Team 4 sells credit card protection insurance, which is a tough product to sell. Team 5 investigates disputed charges. It can sometimes take weeks to get to the bottom of a disputed charge. It is not a process that is easily rushed. As a result, despite their efforts, Teams 4 and 5 have never won the award. Instead, they continue to complain that the bonus program just isn't fair.

As you look up from your desk, a group of employees from Team 4 is waiting to see you. They had called earlier in the day and asked if they could stop by to talk about the bonus program. You are really tiring of this. You thought that awarding bonuses would be easy. What should you tell them?

Questions

1. Is the bonus compensation program fair? If not, would you scrap the program or revise it in some way?
2. Was the implementation of the bonus compensation plan handled appropriately in the first place? What could have been done initially to create a more equitable plan?

Sources: "AT&T Universal Card Services," *Business America* 113, no. 22 (1992): 12–13. S.E. Gross, *Compensation for Teams* (New York: American Management Association, 1995). P.A. Murphy, "It's No Longer Just Teleservices," *Credit Card Management* 11, no. 1 (1998): 115–119.

Develop Your Management Potential

A Quick Check of Your Team Skills

To be part of an effective team, you have to be a good team member. However, sometimes it's hard to objectively judge our contributions in a team or group effort. Think about one of your most important team experiences. Were you an effective team member? Take the following test to find out. After you take the test, answer the questions below to begin thinking about how you can improve.

Instructions:

Step 1: Answer the following questions the way that you think other members of your team would if they were describing your actions.

Step 2: Total your score for each section. Then transfer all totals to the "Quick Check of My Team Skills" section at the conclusion of the exercise.

Scale:

1 = Almost never
2 = Seldom
3 = Sometimes
4 = Usually
5 = Almost always

I. Honour team values and agreements.

As a team member, I   *Your score:*
a. Show appreciation for other team members' ideas. _____
b. Help other team members cope with change. _____
c. Encourage others to use their strengths. _____
d. Help the team develop a productive relationship with other teams. _____
e. Willingly assume a leadership role when needed. _____
Total: _____

II. Promote team development.

As a team member, I   *Your score:*
a. Volunteer for all types of tasks, including the hard ones. _____
b. Help orient and train new team members. _____
c. Help organize and run effective meetings. _____
d. Help examine how we are doing as a team and make any necessary changes in the way we work together. _____
e. Help identify milestones and mini-successes to celebrate. _____
Total: _____

III. Help make team decisions.

As a team member, I   *Your score:*
a. Analyze what a decision entails. _____
b. Ensure that the team selects and includes the appropriate people in the decision process. _____
c. Clearly state my concerns. _____
d. Search for common ground when team members have different views. _____
e. Actively support the team's decisions. _____
Total: _____

IV. Coordinate and carry out team tasks.

As a team member, I   *Your score:*
a. Help identify the information, skills, and resources necessary to accomplish team tasks. _____
b. Help formulate and agree on a plan to meet performance goals. _____
c. Stay abreast of what is happening in other parts of the organization and bring that information to the team. _____
d. Find innovative ways to meet the needs of the team and of others in the organization. _____
e. Maintain a win-win outlook in all dealings with other teams. _____
Total: _____

V. Handle difficult issues with the team.

As a team member, I   *Your score:*
a. Bring team issues and problems to the team's attention. _____
b. Encourage others on the team to state their views. _____
c. Help build trust among team members by speaking openly about the team's problems. _____
d. Give specific, constructive, and timely feedback to others. _____
e. Admit when I've made a mistake. _____
Total: _____

A Quick Check of My Team Skills

Category	Total Score
Honour team values and agreements.	_____
Promote team development.	_____
Help make team decisions.	_____
Coordinate and carry out team tasks.	_____
Handle difficult issues with the team.	_____

Interpreting Scores

- A score of 20 or above in any activity indicates an area of strength.
- A score of 19 or below in any activity indicates an area that needs more attention.

Question

1. Looking at your scores, what areas are strengths? How can you maintain these strengths? What areas are weaknesses? What steps can you take to turn these areas into strengths?

Source: Michael A. West, ed., *Handbook of Work Group Psychology* (Chichester, England: Wiley, 1996).

Discussion Questions

1. Teams have both positive and negative aspects. When working in groups in your courses at college/university, what was good about working in groups? What was bad about working in groups? What could be done to improve group work processes?
2. In what sort of work environments would you think teams would work well? When wouldn't they work well?

3. What strategies might a manager use to overcome the problem of social loafing?
4. Why might employees resist the formation of teams? Why might managers resist the formation of teams?

Study Tip

Make up a crossword puzzle using the key terms in this chapter. Writing the clues will help you remember the definition and the context of each concept. Make photocopies for exam time and for your study group.

CHAPTER 13

Learning Objectives
After reading this chapter, you should be able to

1. describe the basic steps involved in human resource planning.
2. explain how different employment laws affect human resource practice.
3. explain how companies use recruiting to find qualified job applicants.
4. describe the selection techniques and procedures that companies use when deciding which applicants should receive job offers.
5. describe how to determine training needs and select the appropriate training methods.
6. discuss how to use performance appraisal to give meaningful performance feedback.
7. describe basic compensation strategies and how they affect human resource practice.
8. discuss the four kinds of employee separations: termination, downsizing, retirements, and turnover.

CP (Jeff McIntosh)

thirteen

Managing Human Resource Systems

What Would You Do?

In 1999, Shell Canada, Chevron Canada, and Western Oil Sands announced the formation of a new company, Albian Sands Energy Inc., that would build and operate the mine portion of their Athabasca Oil Sands Project (AOSP). The company would spend $1.8 billion over the next few years to build the Muskeg River Mine, 75 kilometres north of Fort McMurray, an hour's drive away. The AOSP is the world's third largest integrated oil sands operations and the first to be built in over 25 years. When complete, the AOSP will supply 10 percent of Canada's crude oil needs. Long-term growth opportunities could bring that number up to 25 percent. It is intended that the Albian Sands will supply the AOSP with 1.65 billion barrels of bitumen over the next 30 years. The bitumen is extracted at the Muskeg River Mine, then piped to AOSP's newly built Scotford Upgrader east of Edmonton. A new pipeline has also been built by yet another company, Terasen, and Shell has modified its refinery to handle its share of the synthetic crude oil to be produced.

Fort McMurray is an isolated oil town located about 450 kilometres north of Edmonton and is well known for its oil sands. There is believed to be three trillion barrels of oil in the Alberta oil sand deposits, far more than the 260 billion barrels of known oil reserves in Saudi Arabia. There is only one problem: how do you get the oil out of the sand? Over a 14-year period (1996 to 2010), it is expected that more than $40 billion will be invested in new oil sands projects. Some say there will be as much as $86 billion invested over 63 different projects. Despite the fact that there seems to be no shortage of new investments in this booming town, the problem really is how to find people to work in Fort McMurray. People have come from all over Canada to find work in the city, where approximately a third of the population is believed to be from the East Coast. The oil sands companies regularly participate in job fairs across Canada. Carey Murphy, a refinery worker, was recruited by Syncrude Canada Ltd., another oil sands producer, from St. John, New Brunswick. He initially didn't want to go to Fort McMurray but the company offered to fly him and his wife to Fort McMurray, no strings attached, just to talk to him. After discussing the pay and the perks, he finally came around and made the move: "For someone who wants big things out of life, this is the place to come."

The tremendous level of investment has not come without its costs. In 1960 Fort McMurray had a population of about 1000. By 2002 it had hit 46 000 and it is estimated that the population will grow to 70 000 by 2010. Up to 12 000 more people live in temporary work camps. One-third of those living in the community work directly for the oil sands industry. The average family income is now over $80 000 and the average starter home costs $230 000. The vacancy rate for rental property is essentially zero—there is nowhere to rent—and if you can find a one-bedroom apartment it can cost over $1000 a month. A house can cost $3000 a month. Even after 1400 new houses were built in 2001, the vacancy rate did not budge. The population is growing at a pace of 20 percent per year and the city appears to be bursting at the seams but it seems that the oil producers are constantly looking for skilled workers—trades such welders, pipefitters, metal workers, and electricians are in high demand—a problem exacerbated by the fact that Canada is generally suffering from a lack of skilled workers.

Even unskilled workers are hard to find. Fast food restaurants are forced to pay $11 an hour for new hires and have even offered perks such as health club memberships—benefits fast food employees can only dream of in other parts of the country. Restaurants and other businesses have been forced to close their doors for lack of staff. If you can find workers, you have trouble holding on to them. Although in the past oil companies tried not to compete with each other for local workers, given the current circumstances competition for workers is fierce and the shortage of workers, and the associated rising cost of labour, has put many oil sands projects over budget—some more than $1 billion over budget.

From the beginning, Albian Sands wanted to hire high-quality team players. Given the shortage of skilled workers in Fort McMurray and across Canada, the competition for the workers already there, the isolation of both Fort McMurray and the Albian Sands plant site, the human resource challenges were immense.

Albian Sands will have 600 permanent employees and you need to hire them all over the next year. **If you were a human resource manager for Albian Sands, what would you do to hire and retain a qualified workforce?**

Sources: "A Distinct Society in the Tar Sands," *The Globe and Mail*, 23 February 1998, A2. "In Oil-Rich Fort McMurray, Service Jobs Go Begging," *Financial Post*, 1 June 2000, C6. Brian Bergman, "Alberta Bound: A Booming Economy Is Drawing Workers from across Canada," *Maclean's*, 2 February 2001, 14. Claudia Cattaneo, "Oilsands Battleground for Skilled Workers," *Financial Post*, 19 August 2002, FP1, FP4. Roy Cook, "Canada's Energy Eldorado," *Edmonton Journal*, 2 May 2002, E1. Jeff Holubitsky and Will Hilliard, "From Boom Town to Home Town," *The St. John's Telegram*, 7 February 2001, 5. Katherine May, "Tradespeople Exchange Blue Collars for Gold Ones," *Southam News*, 5 October 2002. Pat Roche, "Oilsands Klondike: Multi-Billion-Dollar Investments Could Boost Oilsands Output to Nearly 2.5 Million Bbls a Day by 2010," *New Technology Magazine 7*, no. 5 (July/August 2001): 24–26. Marilyn Scales, "The Truly Great Canadian Oilsands: Albian Sands Joins Ranks of Oil Sands Producers," *Canadian Mining Journal* 123, no. 7 (October 2002): 10–17. Chris Varcoe, "Oilsands Boom: Bridge to Nowhere Finally Goes Somewhere," *Victoria Times Colonist*, 23 December 2001, D6.

human resource management
the process of finding, developing, and keeping the right people to form a qualified workforce

Unfortunately, "personnel problems" like those at Albian are all too common. For example, when Erler Industries, a small industrial painting and finishing company, signed a contract for a large amount of work with Dell Computer, it grew from 6 to 175 people almost overnight to meet the increased workload. Co-owner Linda Erler said, "We were so desperate for employees that if we could see the whites of your eyes and it looked as if blood was running through your veins, [you were offered a job]." Linda explained that this approach didn't always translate into successful hiring, like the time that a group of new hires all came to work with "whiskey in their soda cans." And even though new employees could earn bonuses if they stayed for just 30 days, she said, "we had tremendous turnover. Everyone had to be replaced five or six times before we found a person who really wanted to work."[1]

The experiences of Albian and Erler Industries indicate that **human resource management**, the process of finding, developing, and keeping the right people to form a qualified workforce, remains one of the most difficult and important of all management tasks. This chapter is organized around the four parts of the human resource management process shown in Exhibit 13.1: determining human resource needs and attracting, developing, and keeping a qualified workforce.

Accordingly, the chapter begins by reviewing how human resource planning determines human resource needs, such as the kind and number of employees a company requires to meet its strategic plans and objectives. Next, we explore how companies use recruiting and selection techniques to attract and hire qualified employees to fulfil those needs. The third part of the chapter reviews how training and performance appraisal can develop the knowledge, skills, and abilities of the workforce. The chapter concludes with a review of compensation and employee separation, that is, how companies can keep their best workers through effective compensation practices, and how they can manage the separation process when employees do leave the organization.

Determining Human Resource Needs

Should we hire more workers? What should we pay our current employees to slow employee turnover? What kinds of training do our new employees need to be prepared to do a good job, and what's the best way to deliver that training? In other words, what are our human resource needs and what's the best way to address them?

Managers often treat these questions as separate issues. However, the human resource process illustrated in Exhibit 13.1 shows that attracting (recruiting and selecting), developing (training and appraising performance), and keeping or losing employees (compensating and separating) are interdependent issues. You can't solve one problem without considering its impact on the others. More specifically, Exhibit 13.1 indicates that human resource needs affect how the company uses recruiting and selection to attract employees. In turn, the kind and number of employees hired influence the orientation, training, performance appraisal, and compensation strategies the company uses, which then affect who stays and who leaves. Finally, as indicated by the feedback loop, the process comes full circle, as the number and kind of employees who leave the company affect its human resource needs and planning.

EXHIBIT 13.1

THE HUMAN RESOURCE MANAGEMENT PROCESS

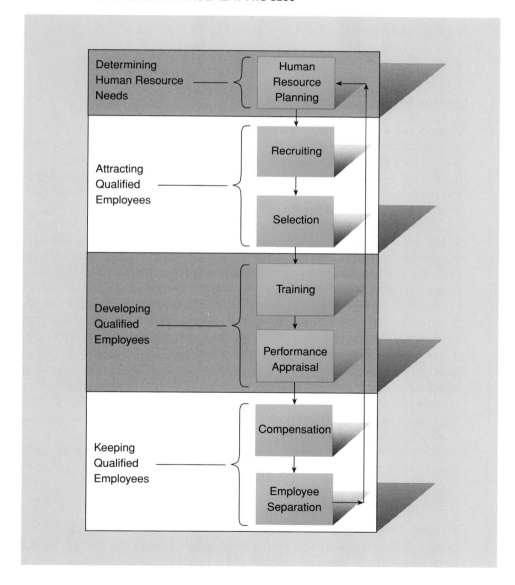

You can see how the HR process works by examining what high-tech companies had to do to deal with the acute shortage of qualified workers in Canada prior to the downturn in the technology sector. For instance, because of the shortage, a number of Canadian software companies had been very aggressive in their recruitment. Many companies in Ottawa, including Cognos and Mitel, developed employee referral programs to help recruit qualified employees. Employees received up to $5000 for a successful referral.[2] During this period they also had to actively compete with U.S. companies, some of whom were offering phenomenal benefits, such as four-star restaurant-quality food in company cafeterias; pool and ping pong tables for recreation; massage therapists; free soft drinks, juice, popcorn, and snacks; dry-cleaning drop-off and pickup; car detailers; dog walkers; and special staffers to run personal errands.[3] Finally, some high-tech companies dealt with the demand for workers by doing less recruiting, hoping instead that retraining current workers would be an effective way to reduce recruiting needs. It is predicted that there will again be a shortage of information technology workers in the near future.[4] Ideally companies should be developing strategies to deal with the shortage now so that they will be prepared when it happens.

Fortunately, there are steps that companies can take to begin to address the expected employee shortfalls in the high-tech industry.

After reading the next two sections, you should be able to
1. *describe the basic steps involved in human resource planning.*
2. *explain how different employment laws affect human resource practice.*

1. Human Resource Planning

human resource planning (HRP)
using an organization's goals and strategy to forecast the organization's human resource needs in attracting, developing, and keeping a qualified workforce

Human resource planning (HRP) is the process of using an organization's goals and strategy to forecast the organization's human resource needs in attracting, developing, and keeping a qualified workforce.[5] Companies that don't use HRP or that do HRP poorly may end up with either a surplus of employees and have to lay off some to correct the surplus, or a shortage of employees that leads to increased overtime costs and an inability to meet demand for the company's product or service.

The HRP process begins with a consideration of the organization's mission, strategy, and objectives. Therefore, HRP is directly related to and should be considered part of an organization's strategic planning process.[6] Dell Computer makes sure that the HRP process is tied to its mission and strategy by splitting its HR function into two departments. "HR Operations" has a service centre that takes care of all "transactional" activities for Dell employees, such as benefits and compensation. HR Operations rarely has direct contact with Dell's business units. Its job is to serve Dell's individual employees. By contrast, the HR staffers in Dell's "HR Management" department report directly to the vice president of HR and the vice president of a Dell business unit (e.g., procurement, higher education sales). The HR staffers then attend that business unit's staff meetings, help to develop that unit's leadership team, and then create a specific HR strategy for that part of Dell's business.[7] Dell's HR Management team also helps business units identify personnel needs, assess training needs, and determine the best organizational structure for reporting relationships (i.e., the organizational chart).

Let's explore human resource planning by examining how to forecast demand and supply and to use human resource information systems.

1.1 Forecasting Demand and Supply

workforce forecasting
the process of predicting the number and kind of workers with specific skills and abilities that an organization will need in the future

Workforce forecasting is the process of predicting the number and kind of workers with specific skills and abilities that an organization will need in the future.[8] There are two kinds of workforce forecasts, internal and external forecasts, and three kinds of forecasting methods, direct managerial input, best guess, and statistical/historical ratios.

Internal forecasts are projections about factors within the organization that affect the supply and demand for human resources. These factors include the financial performance of the organization, productivity, the organization's mission, changes in technology or the way the work is performed, and the termination, promotion, transfer, retirement, resignation, and death of current employees. For example, Telus Corporation, which recently merged with B.C. Telecom and provides local service in both British Columbia and Alberta, recently offered 11 000 employees early retirement and voluntary departure packages as part of plan to increase its workforce productivity.[9] *External forecasts* are projections about factors outside the organization that affect the supply and demand for human resources. These factors include the labour supply for specific types of workers, the economy (unemployment rate), labour unions, demographics of the labour force (i.e., proportion of labour force in various age groups), geographic movement of the labour force, strength of competitors, and growth in particular businesses and markets. For example, Nortel has eliminated more than 50 000 jobs worldwide as it struggles with downturn in demand for its products.[10] Exhibit 13.2 provides a more complete list of factors that influence internal and external forecasts.

Three kinds of forecasting methods—direct managerial input, best guess, and statistical/historical ratios—are often used to predict the number and kind of workers with specific skills and abilities that an organization will need in the future.[11] The most common forecasting method, *direct managerial input*, is based on straightforward projections of cash flows, expenses, or financial measures, such as return on capital. While financial indicators are relatively quick to calculate and can help managers determine how many workers they might need, they don't help managers decide which critical skills new employees should possess.

The *best guess* forecasting method is based on managers' assessment of current head count, plus a best guess of how internal factors and external factors would affect that head count. Summing these together produces the total projection.

Finally, the *statistical/historical ratios* forecasting method uses statistical methods, such as multiple regression, in combination with historical data, to predict the number and kind of workers a company should hire. For example, a manager might run a regression analysis using data from the last two years. In that regression equation, the number of employees that need to be hired is the dependent (predicted) variable, and the number of

---

EXHIBIT 13.2

INTERNAL AND EXTERNAL FACTORS THAT INFLUENCE WORKFORCE FORECASTING

INTERNAL FACTORS
- New positions
- New equipment and technology
- Eliminated positions
- Terminations
- Retirements
- Resignations
- Turnover
- Transfers
- Deaths
- Promotions
- Organization's mission
- Productivity of current employees
- Skills/education of current employees

EXTERNAL FACTORS
- Demographics of labour supply
- Geographic population shifts
- Shift from manufacturing- to service- to information-based economy
- General economic conditions
- Unemployment rate
- Labour unions
- Availability of applicants with specific skills and education
- Technological advances
- Strength and number of competitors
- Growth in particular businesses and markets

items manufactured, number of clients, or average increase in sales, etc., are the independent (predictor) variables. The regression analysis produces a simple equation that indicates how many more employees should be added for each increase in the independent variables, such as items manufactured or increased sales. This approach takes advantage of existing data and can be much more accurate than best guess predictions, but only if a company's internal and external environments have not changed significantly.

Dell also uses statistical/historical ratios to help predict its workforce needs. Andy Esparza, vice president of staffing for Dell's companywide staffing function, said, "One of the things this [HR planning process] maps into is a set of key job openings that we can use to start forecasting and sourcing people in advance." More specifically, Dell's Web-based HR planning process allows managers to play "what if?" with workforce predictions. Kathleen Woodhouse, an HR manager who supports Dell's preferred accounts division, said, "Managers use our intranet to complete HR functions, like appraisals; our appraisal system also feeds into the financial system so they can play with figures if they need to."[12]

1.2 Human Resource Information Systems

human resource information systems (HRIS)
computerized systems for gathering, analyzing, storing, and disseminating information related to the HRM process

Human resource information systems (HRIS) are computerized systems for gathering, analyzing, storing, and disseminating information related to attracting, developing, and keeping a qualified workforce.[13] Exhibit 13.3 shows some of the data that are commonly used in HR information systems, such as personal and educational data, company employment history, performance appraisal information, work history, and promotions.

EXHIBIT 13.3

COMMON DATA CATEGORIES IN HUMAN RESOURCE INFORMATION SYSTEMS

PERSONAL DATA
- Name
- Address/Telephone Number
- Employee Identification Number
- Social Insurance Number
- Medical Plan/Coverage
- Retirement/Investment Plan

EDUCATIONAL DATA
- High School Diploma
- College Diplomas/University Degrees
- Special Courses/Training

COMPANY EMPLOYMENT HISTORY
- Previous Job Assignments
- Current Position
- Date of Initial Employment
- Seniority Date
- Salary/Pay History
- Current Salary/Pay
- Fringe Benefit Package
- Last Pay Raise

PERFORMANCE APPRAISAL
- Date of Last Performance Appraisal
- Productivity Measures
- Disciplinary Action
- Tardiness
- Absenteeism
- Last Performance Rating
- Quality Measures

WORK HISTORY
- Previous Employers
- Previous Positions
- Duties in Previous Positions
- Supervisory Experience

PROMOTION DATA
- Geographic Preferences
- Personal Interests
- Awards
- Job Preferences
- Special Skills/Knowledge
- Foreign Language(s)

Human resource information systems can be used for transaction processing, employee self-service, and decision support. *Transaction processing* is a centralized computer system, often a mainframe, that records the thousands of routine daily transactions involved in running a business. For HRIS systems, transaction processing usually involves employee payroll cheques, taxes, and benefit deductions. HRISs can also reduce administrative costs by preparing certain routine reports that are required of many companies.

While human resource information systems are typically used to give managers and HR staffers access to human resource data, the flip side of today's Web-based HRISs is that they can also give employees immediate, 24-hour *self-service* access to personal data, such as benefits and retirement packages. With secure, Web-based systems, employees need to enter only a user name and password to access and change their medical insurance plan, fill out time sheets, or check on the status of medical or childcare reimbursements.[14] For example, Ontario Power Generation, one of North America's largest power generators with 11 500 employees, recently implemented a Web-based system that allows employees to change their personal information and check the status of their pension plans.[15] According to benefits coordinator Priscilla Craven, the primary advantage of self-service systems is that "you no longer need to call a person when an office is open to get a form or make an enrolment choice." And with access available 24 hours a day, companies have also begun eliminating restricted "open enrolment" periods, in which employees have to make (and then not change) all their benefit decisions for the entire year at one time.[16] With Web-based systems, employees can make changes whenever they want.

Human resource information systems are not only useful for gathering and storing information, but they also help managers by serving as decision support systems for critical human resource decisions.[17] In Chapter 5, you learned that *decision support systems* (DSS) help managers understand problems and potential solutions by acquiring and analyzing information with sophisticated models and tools. For instance, an HRIS can help managers make human resource decisions from the moment that job applicants submit resumés to the company. Those resumés are scanned, turned into text via optical character recognition software, and then fed into the HRIS, where they are analyzed for the quality of the writing and for key words that match the organization's job database. John Reese, founder of Interactive Search, an Internet recruiting site, said, "Whatever the media—paper, e-mail, the Web or fax—we can scan a resumé into a database, re-format it according to our specifications, and then make it available to the hiring manager or HR manager anywhere in a company, anywhere in the world. An applicant can send in an application on Thursday and have an interview by Monday."[18]

An HRIS can even be used to do pre-employment testing or background screening. Elaine Daily, marketing director for Qwiz, Inc., which sells computerized employment tests to companies, said, "We can do remote testing through a website or through software installed on a PC. This saves the company from having to bring in a candidate to headquarters before deciding whether the person is technically competent."[19]

HRISs can also be used effectively to screen internal applicants on particular qualifications, to match the qualifications of external applicants against those of internal applicants, to compare salaries within and between departments, and to review and change employees' salaries instantaneously without lengthy paperwork. In short, today's HRISs can help managers make any number of critical human resource decisions.

Review 1
Human Resource Planning

Human resource planning (HRP) uses organizational goals and strategies to determine what needs to be done to attract, develop, and keep a qualified workforce. Workforce forecasts are used to predict the number and kind of workers with specific skills and abilities that an organization needs. Workforce forecasts consider both internal and external factors that affect the supply and demand for workers and can be formulated using three kinds of forecasting methods: direct managerial input, best guess, and statistical/historical ratios.

Computerized human resource information systems improve human resource planning by gathering, analyzing, storing, and disseminating information (personal, educational, work history, performance, and promotions) related to human resource management activities. Human resource information systems can be used for transaction processing (payroll cheques and routine reports), employee self-service (24-hour Web access allowing instant changes to benefit and retirement packages), and decision support for human resource decisions (analyzing resumés, background screening, and pre-employment testing).

2. Employment Legislation

One of the most challenging aspects of managing human resources is complying with legislation that regulates the employment relationship. There are two reasons for this. The first is that there is a lot of legislation that an employer has to comply with. The second is that legislation and how it is enforced changes often. The combination of these two factors means that human resource management can be a difficult task. Further complicating matters is that the employment relationship is regulated by both the federal and provincial governments. The federal government has jurisdiction over federally regulated industries. These include such industries as banking, airlines, shipping, and telecommunications. Together these industries account for less than 10 percent of the Canadian workforce. Most employers and employees fall under provincial jurisdiction. This means that most companies that operate in more than one province would have to comply with legislation in each province. Many Canadian companies also operate in the United States, where similar laws exist.

Federal and provincial governments all pass human rights laws that affect employment as well as occupational health and safety laws (www.ccohs.ca/oshanswers/information/govt.html) and laws that set minimum standards for such things as vacation pay, parental leave, wages, and hours of work. In addition, the federal government has imposed pay equity and employment equity on federally regulated employers and imposed a federal contractors program (www.pwgsc.gc.ca/sos/corporate/pns/pn50-e.html), which all companies that have at least 100 employees and wish to bid on contracts over $200 000 must comply with. Some provinces also have pay equity and employment equity legislation.

Let's explore employment legislation by reviewing federal and provincial employment laws, employment discrimination, and sexual harassment.

2.1 Federal and Provincial Employment Laws

Exhibit 13.4 lists the major federal employment laws as well as the websites where you can find more detailed information on federal law. It should be remembered that for each of the federal acts listed in Exhibit 13.4, each of the provinces has similar acts that cover workers under provincial jurisdiction (90 percent of the workforce). Human rights laws

---

EXHIBIT 13.4

SUMMARY OF MAJOR FEDERAL EMPLOYMENT LAWS

CANADA LABOUR CODE—PART III http://laws.justice.gc.ca/en/L-2/index.html	Minimum wage, parental leave, hours of work, vacation entitlements.
CANADA LABOUR CODE—PART II http://laws.justice.gc.ca/en/L-2/index.html	Occupational health and safety.
CANADA LABOUR CODE—PART I http://laws.justice.gc.ca/en/L-2/index.html	Guarantees the right to form and join unions.
CANADIAN HUMAN RIGHTS ACT http://laws.justice.gc.ca/en/H-6/index.html	Prohibits discrimination on the basis of race, origin, gender, religion, etc.

are some of the most challenging laws, as it can be difficult to ensure that you do not breach them. Although all human rights laws are not the same across all provinces and the federal government, they are quite similar. Exhibit 13.5 shows the prohibited grounds for discrimination across the various Canadian jurisdictions. The general result

EXHIBIT 13.5

PROHIBITED GROUNDS OF DISCRIMINATION IN EMPLOYMENT IN CANADA

JURISDICTION	FED.	ALTA.	B.C.	MAN.	N.B.	NFLD.	N.S.	ONT.	P.E.I.	QUE.	SASK.	N.W.T.	Y.T.
Dependence on Alcohol/Drugs	•												
Race	•	•	•	•	•	•	•	•	•	•	•	•	•
National/Ethnic Origin	•			•		•	•	•	•	•			•
Colour	•	•	•	•	•	•	•	•	•	•	•	•	•
Nationality/Citizenship				•			•				•	•	
Religion	•	•	•	•	•	•	•			•	•	•	•
Age	•	•	(18+)	(45–65)	•	(19+)	(19–65)	•	(18–65)	•	•	(18–65)	•
Sex	•	•	•	•	•	•	•	•	•	•	•	•	•
Pregnancy/Childbirth*	•	•					•			•			•
Marital Status	•	•	•	•	•	•	•	•		•	•	•	•
Criminal Conviction	•	•	•				•			•		•	•
Mental Disability	•	•	•	•	•	•	•	•	•	•	•	•	•
Physical Disability	•	•	•	•	•	•	•	•	•	•	•	•	•
Ancestry		•	•		•		•			•	•		•
Political Beliefs			•	•		•			•	•			•
Family Status	•	•		•			•				•	•	
Sexual Orientation	•		•	•	•	•	•	•		•	•		•
Harassment**	•				•	•	•			•			•
Civil Status										•			
Language										•			
Source of Income		•		•			•				•		
Social Origin						•							
Social Conditions										•			
Creed		•				•		•	•		•	•	•
Place of Residence												•	
Place of Origin	•	•			•		•				•	•	

* In Alberta, discrimination on the basis of pregnancy is deemed to be discrimination on the basis of sex. In Ontario, Manitoba, Nova Scotia, and the Yukon, discrimination on the basis of pregnancy is included in discrimination on the basis of sex.

** Harassment is banned on all proscribed grounds of discrimination except in New Brunswick and Nova Scotia, where it only refers to sexual harassment.

Source: Reproduced with permission from *The Canadian Master Labour Guide,* 12th ed., published by and copyright CCH Canadian Limited, Don Mills, ON, 1998, p. 339.

of this body of law, which is still evolving through human rights commission and court decisions, is that employers may not discriminate in employment decisions on the basis of gender, age, religion, colour, national origin, race, or disability. The intent is to make these factors irrelevant in employment decisions. Stated another way, employment decisions should be based on factors that are "job related," "reasonably necessary," or a "business necessity" for successful job performance. The only time that gender, age, religion, etc. can be used to make employment decisions is when they are considered a bona fide occupational qualification or requirement (BFOQ or BFOR). For example, a Baptist church hiring a new minister can reasonably specify that being a Baptist rather than a Catholic or Presbyterian is a BFOQ for Baptist ministers. However, it's unlikely that a church could specify race or national origin as a BFOQ. In general, the courts and the human rights commissions take a hard look when a business claims that gender, age, religion, colour, national origin, race, or disability are BFOQs.

It is important to understand, however, that these laws don't just apply to selection decisions (i.e., hiring and promotion), but rather to the entire HRM process. Thus, these laws cover all training and development activities, performance appraisals, terminations, and compensation decisions.

The Canadian Human Rights Act is administered and enforced by the Canadian Human Rights Commission (CHRC) (www.chrc-ccdp.ca) which also provides useful guidelines for employers. Each province has its own human rights commission to administer its human rights legislation. Links can be found to them on provincial government sites (http://canada.gc.ca/othergov/prov_e.html) and on the CHRC website. Employers who use factors such as gender, age, race, or religion, among others, to make employment-related decisions when those factors are unrelated to an applicant's or employee's ability to perform a job may face charges of discrimination from provincial or federal human rights commissions. The Canada Labour Code is administered by the Canada Industrial Relations Board (www.cirb-ccri.gc.ca) and the Department of Human Resources Development (www.hrdc-drhc.gc.ca). As with human rights laws, each province has commissions and boards to administer provincial employment legislation.

Federal and provincial labour laws regulate the interaction between management and labour unions that represent groups of employees. These laws guarantee employees the right to form and join unions of their own choosing. Labour unions can have a significant impact on the terms and conditions of employment by constraining an employer's ability to set pay levels, discipline employees, and set shift assignments, among other things. Federal and provincial occupational health and safety laws require that employers provide employees with a place of employment that is free from recognized hazards that are causing or are likely to cause death or serious physical harm. Occupational health and safety laws set health and safety standards for employers and the departments conduct inspections to determine whether those standards are being met. Employers who do not meet occupational health and safety standards may be fined. At the federal level, these laws are administered by the Canada Industrial Relations Board and there are corresponding commissions and boards to administer provincial legislation.

2.2 Employment Discrimination

reliability
the degree to which a measure (test) is free from random error and is consistent

validity
the degree to which a measure (selection technique) is shown to accurately predict what it is expected to measure (job performance)

Federal and provincial human rights commissions have investigatory, enforcement, and informational responsibilities. Therefore, they investigate charges of discrimination, enforce the provisions of these laws, and publish guidelines that organizations can use to ensure they are in compliance with the law. One of the key issues that must be dealt with is ensuring that all hiring, promotion, or other employment decisions are based on bona fide occupational requirements. This is best done by ensuring the reliability and validity of all selection techniques and qualifications required for a job. The **reliability** of a selection technique refers to the degree to which the test is free from random measurement error and provides consistent results. **Validity** of selection techniques refers to the degree to which a selection technique accurately predicts future job performance. Required qualifications must reflect the actual needs of the job. Failure to ensure the reliability and validity of selection techniques or employment qualifications can lead to charges of discrimination.[20]

In addition to the above-mentioned laws, all employers regulated by the federal government must also comply with the Employment Equity Act. The act compels federally regulated employers to remove employment barriers against persons in designated groups, make reasonable accommodation for designated groups, and set goals for the hiring of designated groups, where they are under-represented in an employer's workforce. Under the law, the designated groups are women, Aboriginals, persons with disabilities, and visible minorities. The goal of the legislation is to have an employer's workforce mirror the workforce at large by matching the appropriate pool of qualified workers (e.g., accountants) with the employer's workforce. For example, if 35 percent of accountants are female, an employer would be expected to have, over time, approximately 35 percent female accountants.[21] Employers can be fined up to $50 000 for failure to comply with the legislation.

2.3 Sexual Harassment

Sexual harassment is a form of discrimination in which unwelcome sexual advances, requests for sexual favours, or other verbal or physical conduct of a sexual nature occur. From a legal perspective, there are two kinds of sexual harassment, quid pro quo and hostile work environment.[22]

sexual harassment
form of discrimination in which unwelcome sexual advances, requests for sexual favours, or other verbal or physical conduct of a sexual nature occur while performing one's job

Many managers mistakenly believe in the stereotype of sexual harassment shown in this photo. However, sexual harassment can also occur between people of the same sex, and men are often the victims. It is also assumed that sexual harassment can occur only between co-workers but sexual harassers can include agents of employers and nonemployees such as customers.

Photodisc Green/SO001588

quid pro quo sexual harassment
form of sexual harassment in which employment outcomes, such as hiring, promotion, or simply keeping one's job, depend on whether an individual submits to sexual harassment

hostile work environment
form of sexual harassment in which unwelcome and demeaning sexually related behaviour creates an intimidating and offensive work environment

Quid pro quo sexual harassment occurs when employment outcomes, such as hiring, promotion, or simply keeping one's job, depend on whether an individual submits to being sexually harassed. For example, in a quid pro quo sexual harassment lawsuit against Prudential Insurance, a female employee alleged that she was repeatedly propositioned for sexual favours by her boss, and that when she refused, he said that "she would not amount to anything in this business without his help."[23] By contrast, a **hostile work environment** occurs when unwelcome and demeaning sexually related behaviour creates an intimidating, hostile, and offensive work environment. One example of a hostile work environment was a Sears manager who would ask his female subordinates to step into his office to look at close-up photos of women's breasts and bottoms that he had taken while on vacation at a beach.[24] Inappropriate sexual comments or jokes about women in front of female workers and the displaying of pornographic material on company property are also prime examples of a hostile work environment.

What common mistakes do managers make when it comes to sexual harassment laws?[25] First, many assume that the victim and harasser must be of the opposite sex and only women can be victims. According to human rights commissions, this assumption is incorrect. Sexual harassment can occur between people of the same sex and men are often the victims of sexual harassment.[26] Second, it is assumed that sexual harassment can occur only between co-workers or between supervisors and subordinates. Not so. Sexual harassers can also include agents of employers, such as consultants, and can even include nonemployees such as customers.[27] The key is not employee status but whether the harassment takes place while conducting company business. Third, it is often assumed that only people who have themselves been harassed can file complaints or lawsuits. In fact, especially in hostile work environments, anyone affected by offensive conduct can file a complaint.

Finally, what should companies do to make sure that sexual harassment laws are followed and not violated?[28] First, respond immediately when sexual harassment is reported. A quick response encourages victims of sexual harassment to report problems to management rather than to lawyers or the human rights commission. Furthermore, a quick and fair investigation may serve as a deterrent to future harassment. Next, take the time to write a clear, understandable sexual harassment policy that is strongly worded, gives specific examples of what constitutes sexual harassment, spells outs sanctions and punishments, and is widely publicized within the company. This lets potential harassers and victims know what will not be tolerated and how the firm will deal with harassment should it occur.

Next, clear reporting procedures that indicate how, where, and to whom incidents of sexual harassment can be reported should also be established. The best procedures ensure a quick response, that impartial parties will handle the complaint, and that the privacy of the accused and accusers will be protected. For example, the Canadian Armed Forces set up a 1-800 hotline to report cases of sexual harassment.[29]

Review 2
Employment Legislation

Human resource management is regulated by both the federal and provincial governments. Each jurisdiction has passed human rights legislation that is administered and enforced by a human rights commission. In general, these laws indicate that gender, age, religion, colour, national origin, race, disability, and pregnancy may not be considered in employment decisions unless these factors reasonably qualify as a BFOQ. In addition the federal government under the Employment Equity Act requires federally regulated employers to set goals to match designated groups with workforce availability.

The two kinds of sexual harassment are quid pro quo and hostile work environment. Managers often wrongly assume that the victim and harasser must be of the opposite sex, that sexual harassment can only occur between co-workers or between supervisors and their employees, that all victims are female, and that only people who have themselves been harassed can file complaints. To make sure that sexual harassment laws are followed, companies should respond immediately when harassment is reported, write a clear, understandable sexual harassment policy, establish clear reporting procedures, and be aware of and follow provincial or federal laws concerning sexual harassment.

Finding Qualified Workers

Finding qualified workers can be very difficult. For example, Fort McMurray, Alberta, has gone through a number of cycles of labour shortages. Recently, both Shell Canada and Suncor saw huge cost overruns due to a shortage of qualified workers. One of Suncor's projects had a cost overrun of almost 50 percent, which amounted to $1.25 billion.[30] Meanwhile many jobs in the service industry go unfilled, leaving the service sector with significant staffing shortages.[31]

As these examples illustrate, finding qualified workers in today's tight labour market is an increasingly difficult task. However, finding qualified applicants is just the first step. Selecting which applicants to hire is the second. CEO John Chambers of Cisco Systems, the leading designer and manufacturer of high-tech equipment that serves as the backbone of the Internet, said, "Cisco has an overall goal of getting the top 10 percent to 15 percent of people in our industry. Our philosophy is very simple—if you get the best people in the industry to fit into your culture and you motivate them properly, then you're going to be an industry leader."[32]

After reading the next two sections, you should be able to
3. explain how companies use recruiting to find qualified job applicants.
4. describe the selection techniques and procedures that companies use when deciding which applicants should receive job offers.

3. Recruiting

Recruiting is the process of developing a pool of qualified job applicants. Let's examine job analysis and recruiting, internal recruiting, and external recruiting.

3.1 Job Analysis and Recruiting

Job analysis is a "purposeful, systematic process for collecting information on the important work-related aspects of a job."[33] Typically, a job analysis collects four kinds of information:

- work activities, such as what workers do and how, when, and why they do it,
- the tools and equipment used to do the job,
- the context in which the job is performed, such as the actual working conditions or schedule, and
- the personnel requirements for performing the job, meaning the knowledge, skills, and abilities needed to do a job well.[34]

Job analysis information can be collected by having job incumbents and/or supervisors complete questionnaires about their jobs, by direct observation, by interviews, or by filming employees as they perform their jobs.

Job descriptions and job specifications are two of the most important results of a job analysis. A **job description** is a written description of the basic tasks, duties, and responsibilities required of an employee holding a particular job. **Job specifications**, which are often included as a separate section of a job description, are a summary of the qualifications needed to successfully perform the job.

Because a job analysis clearly specifies what a job entails, as well as the knowledge, skills, and ability that are needed to do a job well, companies must complete a job analysis *before* beginning to recruit job applicants. Exhibit 13.6 shows that job analysis, job descriptions, and job specifications are the foundation on which all critical human

recruiting
the process of developing a pool of qualified job applicants

job analysis
a purposeful, systematic process for collecting information on the important work-related aspects of a job

job description
a written description of the basic tasks, duties, and responsibilities required of an employee holding a particular job

job specifications
a written summary of the qualifications needed to successfully perform a particular job

resource activities are built. They are used during recruiting and selection to match applicant qualifications with the requirements of the job. They are used throughout the staffing process to ensure that selection devices and the decisions based on these devices are job related. For example, the questions asked in an interview should be based on the most important work activities identified by a job analysis. Likewise, during performance appraisals, employees should be evaluated in areas that a job analysis has identified as the most important in a job.

Job analyses, job descriptions, and job specifications also help companies meet the legal requirement that their human resource decisions be job related. To be judged *job related*, recruitment, selection, training, performance appraisals, and employee separations must be valid and be directly related to the important aspects of the job, as identified by a careful job analysis. For example, the Canadian Human Rights Commission has taken the position that except in limited circumstances pre-employment testing for drugs and alcohol is prohibited.[35]

3.2 Internal Recruiting

internal recruiting
the process of developing a pool of qualified job applicants from people who already work in the company

Internal recruiting is the process of developing a pool of qualified job applicants from people who already work in the company. Internal recruiting, sometimes called "promotion from within," improves employee commitment, morale, and motivation. Recruiting current employees also reduces recruitment start-up time and costs and, because employees are already familiar with the company's culture and procedures, generally increases workers' chances of success in new jobs. Job posting and career paths are two methods of internal recruiting.

EXHIBIT 13.6

IMPORTANCE OF JOB ANALYSIS TO HUMAN RESOURCE MANAGEMENT

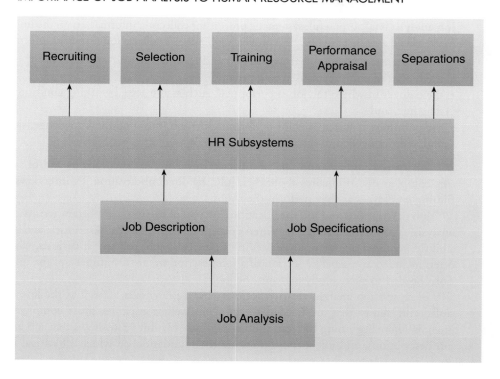

Job posting is a procedure for advertising job openings within the company to existing employees. A job description and requirements are typically posted on a bulletin board, in a company newsletter, or in an internal computerized job bank that is accessible only to employees. Job posting helps organizations discover hidden talent, allows employees to take responsibility for career planning, and makes it easier for companies to retain talented workers who are dissatisfied in their current jobs and would otherwise leave the company.[36] Baxter Health Care calls its job posting program the "Inside Advantage Program." Baxter employees can access this program via an automated telephone prompting system.[37]

A *career path* is a planned sequence of jobs through which employees may advance within an organization. For example, a person who starts as a sales representative may then move up to sales manager, and then to district or regional sales manager. Career paths help employees focus on long-term goals and development while also helping companies do succession or replacement planning. For instance, one of the disadvantages of internal recruitment is that it sets off a domino effect of job changes. When an internal employee changes jobs within a company, this person fills one job opening but automatically creates another. Career paths help companies deal with these changes by quickly identifying possible replacements as job openings ricochet through an organization. Coca-Cola deals with this problem by making sure that all of its managers are developing replacements at least two levels below their current position. Ian Pinto, senior HR manager for Coca-Cola of India, said, "This enables us to cut the costs associated with scrambling for replacements when people leave, or are moved up or sideways."[38]

3.3 External Recruiting

External recruiting is the process of developing a pool of qualified job applicants from outside the company. External recruitment methods include advertising (newspapers, magazines, direct mail, radio, or television), employee referrals (asking current employees to recommend possible job applicants), walk-ins (people who apply on their own), outside organizations (universities, technical/trade schools, professional societies), employment services (federal, provincial or private employment agencies, temporary agencies, and professional search firms), special events (career conferences or job fairs), and Internet job sites.

Which external recruiting method should you use? Studies show that employee referrals, walk-ins, newspaper advertisements, and federal employment agencies tend to be used most frequently for office/clerical and production/service employees. By contrast, newspaper advertisements and college/university recruiting are used most frequently for professional/technical employees. However, in the last few years the biggest changes in external recruiting have come as a result of the Internet. For example, Cisco Systems no longer runs newspaper help-wanted ads. Instead, it takes out simple newspaper ads that direct recruits to its website (www.cisco.com/jobs), where they can see hundreds of job descriptions, learn in detail about Cisco's highly competitive benefits, and submit an online resumé.[39] In addition to extensive job information on corporate websites, some companies have begun subscribing to Internet job sites such as The Monster Board (www.monster.ca) and CareerBuilder (www.careerbuilder.com). For just $3000 to $4000 per month, companies can advertise up to 100 job openings and reach millions of job applicants worldwide at a fraction of newspaper advertising.[40] One advantage of online recruiting is the ability to reach large numbers of people. For example, Computer Sciences Corporation listed 200 jobs on its website and received over 8000 resumés.[41]

external recruiting
the process of developing a pool of qualified job applicants from outside the company

---

PERSONAL PRODUCTIVITY

Formatting an Electronic Resumé for Maximum "Searchability"

Many employers use keyword searches to electronically prescreen resumés. To make sure that your resumé is identified in a keyword search, put your most important information, keywords, objectives, experience, and achievements in the top half of page 1. Your keyword list should include technical knowledge, action words (implementation), personal qualities, software capabilities, and general skills. State clear, specific objectives. Instead of listing previous jobs, specifically describe what you did and accomplished. Finally, use basic fonts like Arial and avoid formatting, such as bold or underlining. Instead, save your resumé as a basic .txt file for easy cutting and pasting into online resumé forms.

Source: H. Oiff, "Can Employers Find You? How to Format an E-Resume for Max Searchability," Career Builder. [Online] Available www.careerbuilder.com/subcat/rcl/grcl030105.html, 5 February 2002.

CHAPTER 13 MANAGING HUMAN RESOURCE SYSTEMS **405**

Despite its promise, there are some disadvantages to Internet recruiting. The main drawback (which some companies consider a plus) is that Internet recruiting is unlikely to reach recruits who don't use or have access to the Internet. And, since it is so easy for applicants to apply, companies may receive hundreds, if not thousands, of applications from unqualified applicants, which increases the importance of proper screening and selection. Furthermore, if the proper security precautions aren't taken, there is also the danger of violating employee/applicant privacy.[42] Still, despite these disadvantages, companies are expected to make even more use of the Internet for external recruiting. It's predicted that 20 percent of all external job recruiting will be done via the Internet by 2005.

Review 3
Recruiting

Recruiting is the process of finding qualified job applicants. The first step in recruiting is to conduct a job analysis to collect information about the important work-related aspects of the job. The job analysis is then used to write a job description of basic tasks, duties, and responsibilities and to write job specifications indicating the knowledge, skills, and abilities needed to perform the job. Job analyses, descriptions, and specifications help companies meet the legal requirement that their human resource decisions be job related. Internal recruiting, finding qualified job applicants from inside the company, can be done through job posting and career paths. External recruiting, finding qualified job applicants from outside the company, is done through advertising, employee referrals, walk-ins, outside organizations, employment services, special events, and Internet job sites. The Internet is a particularly promising method of external recruiting because of its low cost, wide reach, and ability to communicate and receive unlimited information.

4. Selection

Once the recruitment process has produced a pool of qualified applicants, the selection process is used to determine which applicants have the best chance of performing well on the job. Tom Blangiardo, president of Basic Education and Training Associations (BETA Group), uses a fairly typical selection process to hire telemarketers to sell the company's educational videos. "For every ad we place, we get about 100 applicants. I interview everyone over the phone, because the way you come across on the phone is very important here. I evaluate voice tone, friendliness, and persuasiveness." Around 30 to 40 candidates are then chosen for group interviews. Managers explain BETA Group's philosophy and benefits and show the candidates examples of the videos they'll be selling. After the group interviews, 9 candidates are typically eliminated, 6 receive job offers, and 15 go on to individual interviews with human resource director John Brown. During the individual interview, candidates are asked to role-play a sales call. Another 7 applicants are lost at this stage. The 10 to 15 survivors are hired and put through a one-week orientation program that includes product and technology training, practice taking live calls, and more role playing. "We put people on the hot seat to see how they behave," says Kara O'Connor, BETA Group's employee training manager. After 30 to 60 days, about half of these survivors leave because it's either too intense for them, or they're just not selling enough.[43]

selection
the process of gathering information about job applicants to decide who should be offered a job

validation
the process of determining how well a selection test or procedure predicts future job performance. The better or more accurate the prediction of future job performance, the more valid a test is said to be.

As this example illustrates, **selection** is the process of gathering information about job applicants to decide who should be offered a job. To make sure that selection decisions are accurate and legally defensible, all selection procedures should be validated. **Validation** is the process of determining how well a selection test or procedure predicts future job performance. The better or more accurate the prediction of future job performance, the more valid a test is said to be. See the "What Really Works" section of this chapter for more on the validity of common selection tests and procedures.

Let's examine common selection procedures, such as application forms and resumés, references and background checks, selection tests, and interviews.

The first selection devices that most job applicants encounter when they seek a job are application forms and resumés. Both contain similar information about job applicants, such as name, address, job and educational history. While an organization's application form often asks for information already provided by the resumé, most organizations prefer to collect this information in their own format for entry into a human resource information system.

Employment-related laws apply to application forms, as they do all selection devices. Application forms may ask applicants about only valid, job-related information. However, application forms commonly ask applicants to report non-job-related information, such as marital status, maiden name, age, or date of high school graduation. Exhibit 13.7 presents a list of the kinds of information that companies may not request in application forms, during job interviews, or in any other part of the selection process. Attorney Tiberio Trimmer said, "Your objective is to hire someone qualified to perform the requirements of the job. Not asking things that are peripheral to the work itself helps you to stay on the right side of the law."[44] Consequently, most companies should closely examine their application forms for compliance with provincial and federal human rights legislation.

EXHIBIT 13.7

A GUIDE TO SCREENING AND SELECTION IN EMPLOYMENT

SUBJECT	AVOID ASKING	PREFERRED QUESTION	COMMENT
Name	about name change: whether it was changed by court order, marriage or other reason; maiden name.	Ask after selection if needed to check on previously held jobs or educational credentials.	
Address	for addresses outside Canada.	Ask place and duration of current or recent address.	
Age	for birth certificates, baptismal records, or about age in general.	Ask applicants if they are eligible to work under Canadian laws regarding age restrictions.	If precise age is required for benefits plans or other legitimate purposes, it can be determined after selection.
Sex	males or females to fill in different applications; about pregnancy, child-bearing plans, or childcare arrangements.	Can ask applicant if the attendance requirements can be met.	During interview or after selection, the applicant, for purposes of courtesy, may be asked which of Mr., Mrs., Miss, Ms. is preferred.
Marital Status	whether applicant is single, married, divorced, engaged, separated, widowed, or living common-law.	If transfer or travel is part of the job, the applicant can be asked if he or she can meet these requirements. Ask whether there are any circumstance that might prevent completion of a minimum service commitment.	Information on dependants can be determined after selection, if necessary.
Family Status	number of children or dependants; about child-care arrangements.	Ask if the applicant would be able to work the required hours and where applicable, overtime.	Contacts for emergencies and/or details on dependants can be determined after selection.
National or Ethnic Origin	about birthplace, nationality of ancestors, spouse, or other relatives; whether born in Canada; for proof of Canadian citizenship.	Since those who are entitled to work in Canada must be citizens, permanent residents, or holders of valid work permits, applicants can be asked if they are legally entitled to work in Canada.	Documentation of eligibility to work (papers, visas, etc.) can be requested after selection.

EXHIBIT 13.7

A GUIDE TO SCREENING AND SELECTION IN EMPLOYMENT CONT'D

SUBJECT	AVOID ASKING	PREFERRED QUESTION	COMMENT
Military Service	about military service in other countries.	Inquiry about Canadian military service is permitted where employment preference is given to veterans by law.	
Language	mother tongue; where language skills obtained.	Ask if applicant understands, reads, writes, or speaks languages required for the job.	Testing or scoring applicants for language proficiency is not permitted unless job-related.
Race or Colour	any inquiry into race or colour, including colour of eyes, skin, or hair.		
Photographs	for photo to be attached to applications sent to interviewer before interview.		Photos for security passes or company files can be taken after selection.
Religion	about religious affiliation, church membership, frequency of church attendance; if applicant will work a specific religious holiday; for references from clergy or religious leader.	Explain the required work shift, asking if such a schedule poses problems for the applicant.	Reasonable accommodation of an employee's religious beliefs is the employer's duty.
Height and Weight	No inquiry unless there is evidence they are genuine occupational requirements.		
Disability	for listing of all disabilities, limitations, or health problems; whether applicant drinks or uses drugs; whether applicant has ever received psychiatric care or been hospitalized for emotional problems; whether applicant has received workers' compensation.	Ask if applicant has any condition that could affect ability to do the job. Ask if the applicant has any condition that should be considered in selection.	A disability is only relevant to job ability if it threatens the safety or property of others; prevents the applicant from carrying out safe and adequate job performance even when reasonable efforts are made to accommodate the disability.
Medical Information	if currently under physician's care; name of family doctor; if receiving counselling or therapy.		Medical exams should be conducted after selection and only if an employee's condition is related to job duties.
Pardoned Conviction	whether an applicant has a criminal record.		
Sexual Orientation	any inquiry about the applicant's sexual orientation.		Contacts for emergencies and/or details on dependants can be determined after selection.
References			The same restrictions that apply to questions asked of applicants apply when asking for employment references.

Source: "A Guide to Screening and Selection in Employment," Canadian Human Rights Commission. Copyright © 2001 Canadian Human Rights Commission.

Resumés also pose problems for companies, but in a different way. Studies show as many as one out of every three job applicants falsifies some information on his or her resumé. The items most frequently falsified are job responsibilities, job titles, previous salary, and the length of employment on previous jobs. Other frequently falsified information includes educational background, academic degrees, and university majors and minors.[45] Therefore, managers should verify the information collected via resumés and application forms by comparing it with additional information collected during interviews and other stages of the selection process. Another way to check resumé information is to hire a private firm to do it. Costs vary but can often be as low as $75 per person. Cynthia Myers, who runs a company that verifies resumé information, said that companies can discourage false resumés by including this warning in their application forms and recruiting literature: "All information on this form is checked by a national agency that specializes in checking credentials. If any false claims are uncovered, that applicant will no longer be considered for a position."[46]

4.2 References and Background Checks

Nearly all companies ask applicants to provide **employment references**, such as previous employers or co-workers, that they can contact to learn more about job candidates. **Background checks** are used to verify the truthfulness and accuracy of information that applicants provide about themselves and to uncover negative, job-related background information not provided by applicants. Background checks are conducted by contacting "educational institutions, prior employers, court records, police and governmental agencies and other informational sources, either by telephone, mail, remote computer access or through in-person investigations."[47]

Unfortunately, previous employers are increasingly reluctant to provide references or background check information for fear of being sued by previous employees for defamation. If former employers provide unsubstantiated information to potential employers that damages applicants' chances of being hired, applicants can (and do) sue for defamation. As a result, many employers are reluctant to provide information about previous employees. Many provide only dates of employment, positions held, and date of separation.

With previous employers generally unwilling to give full, candid references, companies don't get full, candid references and background information. What can companies do? Dig deeper for more information. Ask references to provide references. Next, ask in writing before checking references or running a background check.

Always document all reference and background checks, who was called, and what information was obtained. And to reduce the success of negligent hiring lawsuits, it's particularly important to document which companies and people refused to share reference check and background information. Finally, consider hiring private investigators to conduct background checks. A background check might have saved Sunbeam Corp. a lot of embarrassment. Albert "Chainsaw Al" Dunlap was appointed CEO in 1996 and was known as a successful business executive who even wrote a best-selling memoir about his experiences. He manipulated Sunbeam's earnings and helped drive the company into bankruptcy. What was not known by Sunbeam's board of directors was that he had been fired twice before for similar behaviour, a fact that he had left off his resumé and that might have been revealed by private investigators.[48]

employment references
sources such as previous employers or co-workers who can provide job-related information about job candidates

background checks
procedures used to verify the truthfulness and accuracy of information that applicants provide about themselves and to uncover negative, job-related background information not provided by applicants

PERSONAL PRODUCTIVITY

Using a Reference Release Form

Employment references are often reluctant to talk. Encourage them to share information by having applicants sign a reference release form like this.

I have applied for employment with [company name] and have listed you as a reference. Please provide answers to the following questions and return this form to [company contact] in the enclosed envelope. By this authorization, I hereby release you from any liability or action based upon the content of your answers. Thank you for your cooperation and assistance.
Sincerely yours,
[candidate signature]
[date]

And when references talk, listen carefully to how they answer the questions (e.g., hesitancy, damning with faint praise).

Source: B. Weinstein, "Tips for Getting References to Talk," *Career.WSJ.Com.* [Online] Available www.careerjournal.com/jobhunting/resumes/19980909-weinstein.html

4.3 Selection Tests

Why do some people do well on jobs while other people do poorly? If only you could know before deciding who to hire! Selection tests give organizational decision makers a chance to know who will likely do well in a job and who won't. The basic idea behind selection testing is to have applicants take a test that measures something directly or indirectly related to doing well on the job. The selection tests discussed here are specific ability tests, cognitive ability tests, biographical data, personality tests, work sample tests, and assessment centres.

specific ability tests (aptitude tests)
tests that measure the extent to which an applicant possesses the particular kind of ability needed to do a job well

cognitive ability tests
tests that measure the extent to which applicants have abilities in perceptual speed, verbal comprehension, numerical aptitude, general reasoning, and spatial aptitude

biographical data (biodata)
extensive surveys that ask applicants questions about their personal backgrounds and life experiences

personality tests
tests that measure the extent to which applicants possess different kinds of job-related personality dimensions

work sample tests
tests that require applicants to perform tasks that are actually done on the job

Specific ability tests are tests that measure the extent to which an applicant possesses the particular kind of ability needed to do a job well. Specific ability tests are also called **aptitude tests**, because they measure aptitude for doing a particular task well. For example, if you were to take the GMAT to get into a graduate business program, you've taken the aptly named Graduate Management Admission Test, which is one predictor of how well students will do in graduate business school (i.e., scholastic performance). Specific ability tests also exist for mechanical, clerical, sales, and physical work. For example, clerical workers have to be good at accurately reading and scanning numbers as they type or enter data.

Cognitive ability tests measure the extent to which applicants have abilities in perceptual speed, verbal comprehension, numerical aptitude, general reasoning, and spatial aptitude. In other words, these tests indicate how quickly and how well people understand words, numbers, logic, and spatial dimensions. While specific ability tests predict job performance in only particular types of jobs, cognitive ability tests accurately predict job performance in almost all kinds of jobs.[49] Why is this so? Because people with strong cognitive or mental abilities are usually good at learning new things, processing complex information, and solving problems and making decisions, and these abilities are important in almost all jobs to some extent. And not only do cognitive ability tests predict job performance well in almost all kinds of jobs, but they are almost always the best predictors of job performance. Consequently, if you were allowed to use just one selection test, a cognitive ability test would be the one to use. (In practice, though, companies use a battery of different tests, because this leads to much more accurate selection decisions.)

Biographical data, or **biodata**, are extensive surveys that ask applicants questions about their personal backgrounds and life experiences. The basic idea behind biodata is that past behaviour (personal background and life experience) is the best predictor of future behaviour. For example, the Canadian life insurance industry has used biodata since 1942 in the selection of applicants.[50]

Most biodata questionnaires have over 100 items that gather information about habits and attitudes, health, interpersonal relations, money, what it was like growing up in your family (parents, siblings, childhood years, teen years), personal habits, current home (spouse, children), hobbies, education and training, values, preferences, and work.[51] In general, biodata are very good predictors of future job performance, especially in entry-level jobs.

You may have noticed that some of the information requested in biodata surveys also appears in Exhibit 13.7 as topics employers should avoid in application blanks, interviews, or other parts of the selection process. This information can be requested in biodata questionnaires provided that companies can demonstrate that the information is job related (i.e., valid) and does not result in discrimination against protected groups of job applicants. Although legal in Canada, biodata surveys should be very carefully validated and tested before using them to make selection decisions; the onus remains on employers to validate any questions that might violate human rights legislation.[52]

Personality is the relatively stable set of behaviours, attitudes, and emotions displayed over time that makes people different from each other. **Personality tests** measure the extent to which applicants possess different kinds of job-related personality dimensions. Research indicates that five major personality dimensions (the Big 5)—extroversion, emotional stability, agreeableness, conscientiousness, and openness to experience—are related to work behaviour.[53] Of these, only conscientiousness, the degree to which someone is organized, hardworking, responsible, persevering, thorough, and achievement oriented, predicts job performance across a wide variety of jobs. Conscientiousness works especially well in combination with cognitive ability tests, allowing companies to select applicants who are organized, hard-working, responsible, and smart!

Work sample tests, also called *performance* tests, require applicants to perform tasks that are actually done on the job. So unlike specific ability, cognitive ability, biographical data, and personality tests, which are indirect predictors of job performance, work sample tests directly measure job applicants' capability to do the job. Work sample tests generally do a very good job of predicting future job performance; however, they can be expensive to administer and can be used for only one kind of job. For example, at an auto dealership, a work sample test for mechanics could not be used as a selection test for sales representatives.

Assessment centres use a series of job-specific simulations that are graded by several trained observers to determine the extent to which applicants can perform managerial work. So unlike the previously described selection tests commonly used for specific jobs or entry-level jobs, assessment centres are most often used to select applicants who have high potential to be good managers. Assessment centres often last two to five days and require participants to complete a number of tests and exercises that simulate managerial work.

Are tests perfect predictors of job performance? No, they aren't. Some people who do well on selection tests will do poorly in their jobs. Likewise, some people who do poorly on selection tests (and should have been hired, but weren't) would have been very good performers. However, valid tests will minimize these selection errors (hiring people who should not have been hired, and not hiring people who should have been hired) while maximizing correct selection decisions (hiring people who should have been hired, and not hiring people who should not have been hired). In short, tests increase the chances that you'll hire the right person for the job, that is, someone who turns out to be a good performer. So while tests aren't perfect, almost nothing predicts future job performance as well as the selection tests discussed here. For more on how well selection tests increase the odds of hiring the right person for the job, see the "What Really Works" section of this chapter.

4.4 Interviews

In **interviews**, company representatives ask job applicants job-related questions to determine whether they are qualified for the job. Interviews are probably the most frequently used and relied-on selection device. There are several basic kinds of interviews: unstructured, structured, and semi-structured.

In *unstructured interviews*, interviewers are free to ask applicants anything they want, and studies show that they do. For instance, because interviewers often disagree about which questions should be asked during interviews, different interviewers tend to ask applicants very different questions.[54] Furthermore, individual interviewers even seem to have a tough time asking the same questions from one interview to the next. This high level of inconsistency lowers the validity of unstructured interviews as a selection device, because it becomes difficult to compare applicant responses. As a result, unstructured interviews do about half as well as structured interviews in accurately predicting which job applicants should be hired.

By contrast, with **structured interviews**, standardized interview questions are prepared ahead of time, so that all applicants are asked the same job-related questions. Four kinds of questions are typically asked in structured interviews:

- *situational questions*, which ask applicants how they would respond in a hypothetical situation (e.g., "What would you do if...?").
- *behavioural questions*, which ask applicants what they did in previous jobs that were similar to the job for which they are applying (e.g., "In your previous jobs, tell me about...").
- *background questions*, which ask applicants about their work experience, education, and other qualifications (e.g., "Tell me about the training you received at...").
- *job-knowledge questions*, which ask applicants to demonstrate their job knowledge (e.g., for nurses, "Give me an example of a time when one of your patients had a severe reaction to a medication. How did you handle it?").[55]

The primary advantage of structured interviews is that asking all applicants the same questions makes comparing applicants a much easier process. Structuring interviews also ensures that interviewers ask only for important, job-related information. These

assessment centres
a series of managerial simulations, graded by trained observers, that are used to determine applicants' capability for managerial work

interviews
selection tool in which company representatives ask job applicants job-related questions to determine whether they are qualified for the job

structured interviews
interviews in which all applicants are asked the same set of standardized questions, usually including situational, behavioural, background, and job-knowledge questions

Preparing for Structured Interviews

Structured interviews assume that past performance predicts future performance. Therefore, structured interview questions often begin with "Tell me about a time when...." or "Give me an example of...." Use the P-A-R (Problem-Action-Result) technique to prepare for structured interviews. Go through the job description and your resumé line by line to think up examples and stories. Then write, edit, and rehearse them in the P-A-R format. And for variety, use the R-A-P approach, too. Start by describing your results. Then describe your actions. Finish by describing the problem you solved. You're less likely to be stumped by questions if you prepare in this way.

Source: A. Hirsh, "Tricky Questions Reign in Behavioral Interviews," *National Business Employment Weekly* (posted on Careers.WSJ. com). [Online] Available www.careerjournal.com/jobhunting/interviewing/19990420-hirsch. html

advantages not only improve the accuracy, usefulness, and validity of the interview, but also reduce the chances that interviewers will ask questions about topics that violate employment laws (go back to Exhibit 13.7 for a list of these topics).

Semi-structured interviews lie somewhere in between structured and unstructured interviews. A major part of the semi-structured interview (perhaps as much as 80 percent) is based on structured questions. However, some time is set aside for unstructured interviewing to allow interviewers to probe into ambiguous or missing information uncovered during the structured portion of the interview.

How well do interviews predict future job performance? Contrary to what you've probably heard, recent evidence indicates that even unstructured interviews do a fairly good job. However, when conducted properly, structured interviews can lead to much more accurate hiring decisions than unstructured interviews. In some cases, the validity of structured interviews can rival that of cognitive ability tests. But even more important, since interviews are especially good at assessing applicants' interpersonal skills, they work especially well together with cognitive ability tests. The combination (i.e., smart people who work well with others) leads to even better selection decisions than using either alone. Exhibit 13.8 provides a set of guidelines for conducting effective structured employment interviews.

EXHIBIT 13.8

GUIDELINES FOR CONDUCTING EFFECTIVE STRUCTURED INTERVIEWS

PLANNING THE INTERVIEW

- Identify and define the knowledge, skills, abilities, and other (KSAO) characteristics needed for successful job performance.
- For each essential KSAO, develop key behavioural questions that will elicit examples of past accomplishments, activities, and performance.
- For each KSAO, develop a list of things to look for in applicants' responses to key questions.

CONDUCTING THE INTERVIEW

- Create a relaxed, nonstressful interview atmosphere.
- Review applicants' application blanks, resumés, and other information.
- Allocate enough time to complete the interview without interruption.
- Put the applicant at ease; don't jump right into heavy questioning.
- Tell the applicant what to expect. Explain the interview process.
- Obtain job-related information from the applicant by asking those questions prepared for each KSAO.
- Describe the job and the organization to applicants. Applicants need adequate information to make a selection decision about the organization.

AFTER THE INTERVIEW

- Immediately after the interview, review your notes and make sure they are complete.
- Evaluate applicants on each essential KSAO.
- Determine each applicant's probability of success and make a hiring decision.

Source: B.M. Farrell, "The Art and Science of Employment Interviews," *Personnel Journal* 65 (1986): 91–94.

WhatReallyWorks

Using Selection Tests to Hire Good Workers

Hiring new employees always seems like a gamble. When you speak the words "We'd like to offer you a job," you never know how it's going to turn out. However, the selection tests discussed in this chapter and reviewed in this section go a long way toward helping employers take the gambling aspect out of the hiring process. Indeed, more than 1000 studies based on over 100 000 study participants strongly indicate that selection tests can give employers a much better than average (50–50) chance of hiring the right workers. In fact, if you had odds like these working for you in Las Vegas, you'd make so much money the casinos wouldn't let you in the door.

Cognitive Ability Tests

There is a 76 percent chance that workers who did well on cognitive ability tests will be much better performers in their jobs than employees who did not do well on such tests.

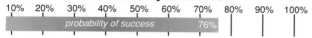

Work Sample Tests

There is a 77 percent chance that workers who did well on work sample tests will be much better performers in their jobs than employees who did not do well on such tests.

Assessment Centres

There is a 69 percent chance that workers who did well on assessment centre exercises will be much better managers than employees who did not do well on such exercises.

Structured Interviews

There is a 76 percent chance that workers who did well in structured interviews will be much better performers in their jobs than employees who did not do well in structured interviews.

Cognitive Ability + Work Sample Tests

When deciding who to hire, most companies use a number of tests together to make even more accurate selection decisions. There is an 82 percent chance that workers who did well on a combination of cognitive ability tests and work sample tests will be much better performers in their jobs than employees who did not do well on both tests.

Cognitive Ability + Integrity Tests

There is an 83 percent chance that workers who did well on a combination of cognitive ability tests and integrity tests (see Chapter 3 for a discussion of integrity tests) will be much better performers in their jobs than employees who did not do well on both tests.

Cognitive Ability + Structured Interviews

There is an 82 percent chance that workers who did well on a combination of cognitive ability tests and structured interviews will be much better performers in their jobs than employees who did not do well on both tests.

Source: F.L. Schmidt & J.E. Hunter, "The Validity and Utility of Selection Methods in Personnel Psychology: Practical and Theoretical Implications of 85 Years of Research Findings," *Psychological Bulletin* 124, no. 2 (1998): 262–274.

Review 4
Selection

Selection is the process of gathering information about job applicants to decide who should be offered a job. Accurate selection procedures are valid, are legally defendable, and improve organizational performance. Application forms and resumés are the most common selection devices. Because many application forms request illegal, non-job-related information, and because as many as one-third of job applicants falsify information on resumés, these procedures can sometimes be of little value when making hiring decisions. References and background checks can also be problematic, given that previous employers are reluctant to provide such information for fear of being sued for defamation. Unfortunately, the lack of this information puts other employers at risk of negligent hiring lawsuits. Selection tests generally do the best job of predicting applicants' future job performance. In general, cognitive ability tests, work sample tests, biographical data, and assessment centres are the most valid tests, followed by personality tests and specific ability tests, which are still good predictors. Selection tests aren't perfect predictors of job performance, but almost nothing predicts future job performance as well as selection tests. The three kinds of job interviews are unstructured, structured, and semi-structured interviews. Of these, structured interviews work best, because they ensure that all applicants are consistently asked the same situational, behavioural, background, or job-knowledge questions.

Developing Qualified Workers

Harmon Industries, which makes signalling and communications equipment for the railway and transit industries, has a new training centre where its employees learn engineering, safety, teamwork, time management, and other workplace skills. Ron Breshears, Harmon's vice president of human resources and safety, said, "Training is an investment, not a cost. Once you see that, you see that you get a good return on your investment."[56] At Sprint, the telecommunications company, 50 000 out of 62 000 employees received training last year. Sprint's University of Excellence has 400 employees, who provide classroom and on-the-job training in 20 cities. Said Brad Harsha, assistant vice president of Sprint's University of Excellence, "Our philosophy is that Sprint supports continuous learning. Our training doesn't stop with orientation to the company. It's a lifelong learning commitment."[57]

Why are Harmon Industries and Sprint spending so much time and money to train their workers? Because, according to the American Society for Training and Development, an investment in training increases productivity by an average of 17 percent, reduces employee turnover, and makes companies more profitable; Toronto Dominion Bank estimates that it gets a 15 percent return from its extensive training programs.[58]

However, giving employees the knowledge and skills they need to improve their performance is just the first step in developing employees. The second step is giving employees formal feedback about their actual job performance. For example, at his last performance appraisal, Thomas Loarie, CEO of KeraVision, a company that invented a patented vision correction procedure, learned that he needed to be more realistic about his sales plans and that he needed to hold his subordinates more accountable for their work. Gilbert Amelio, Apple Computer's former CEO, said, "CEOs really want the feedback about how we're doing and what we can be doing to improve what's going on."[59] So, in today's competitive business environment, even CEOs understand the importance of formal performance feedback.

After reading the next two sections, you should be able to
5. *describe how to determine training needs and select the appropriate training methods.*
6. *discuss how to use performance appraisal to give meaningful performance feedback.*

5. Training

Training means providing opportunities for employees to develop the job-specific skills, experience, and knowledge they need to do their jobs or improve their performance. On average, Canadian firms spent $859 per employee on training in 2000.[60]

To make sure those training dollars are well spent, companies need to evaluate their procedures of determining training needs, training methods, and evaluating training.

5.1 Determining Training Needs

Needs assessment is the process of identifying and prioritizing the learning needs of employees. Needs assessments can be conducted by identifying performance deficiencies, listening to customer complaints, surveying employees and managers, or formally testing employees' skills and knowledge.

Needs assessment usually begins with a job analysis to determine the knowledge and skill levels required to perform a job successfully. For example, Exhibit 13.9 shows that the job of customer service representative requires strong listening, reading, and writing skills, but only moderate capabilities in locating information, applied technology, and teamwork. Following the job analysis, employees are tested and their skill levels are compared to the requirements for the job. The greater the difference between an employee's skill levels and those required by the job, the greater the need for training. Exhibit 13.9 shows the current skill levels in each area for one individual. Based on the needs assessment, this employee needs some training in listening and locating information.

Note that training should never be conducted without first performing a needs assessment. Sometimes, training isn't needed at all, or it isn't needed for all employees. Since the needs assessment shown in Exhibit 13.9 indicates that the customer service representative has reading, applied technology, and teamwork skills that

training
developing the skills, experience, and knowledge employees need to perform their jobs or improve their performance

needs assessment
the process of identifying and prioritizing the learning needs of employees

EXHIBIT 13.9

NEEDS ASSESSMENT FOR A CUSTOMER SERVICE REPRESENTATIVE JOB

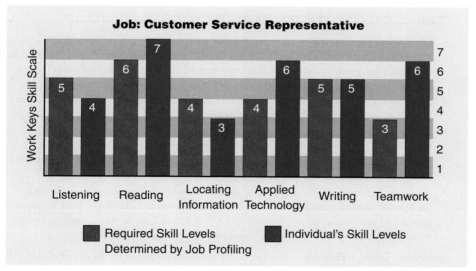

Source: "Work Keys in Action," Introduction to Work Keys. [Online] Available www.act.org/workkeys/, 31 May 1999.

exceed those required for the job, it would be a waste of time and money to send this employee for training in these skills. Unfortunately, however, many organizations simply require all employees to attend training, whether they need to or not. The result is that employees who are not interested or don't need the training may react negatively during or after training. Likewise, employees who should be sent for training but aren't may also react negatively. Consequently, a needs assessment is an important tool for deciding who should or should not attend training. Just like hiring decisions, the selection of training participants should be based on job-related information.

5.2 Training Methods

Assume that you're a training director for a bank and that you're in charge of making sure that all bank employees know what to do in case of a robbery.[61] Exhibit 13.10 lists a number of training methods you could use: films and videos, lectures, planned readings,

---

EXHIBIT 13.10

TRAINING OBJECTIVE AND METHODS

TRAINING OBJECTIVE: IMPART INFORMATION OR KNOWLEDGE

- *Films and Videos*: Films and videos share information, illustrate problems and solutions, and do a good job of holding trainees' attention.
- *Lecture*: Instructors make oral presentations to trainees.
- *Planned Readings*: Trainees read about concepts or ideas before attending training.

TRAINING OBJECTIVE: DEVELOP ANALYTICAL AND PROBLEM-SOLVING SKILLS

- *Case Studies*: Cases are analyzed and discussed in small groups. The cases present a specific problem or decision and trainees develop methods for solving the problem or making the decision.
- *Coaching and Mentoring*: Coaching and mentoring of trainees by managers involves informal advice, suggestions, and guidance. This method is helpful for reinforcing other kinds of training and for trainees who benefit from support and personal encouragement.
- *Group Discussions*: Small groups of trainees actively discuss specific topics. Instructor may perform the role of discussion leader.

TRAINING OBJECTIVE: PRACTISE, LEARN, OR CHANGE JOB BEHAVIOURS

- *On-the-Job Training (OJT)*: New employees are assigned to experienced employees. The trainee is expected to learn by watching the experienced employee perform the job, and eventually by working alongside the experienced employee. Gradually, the trainee is left on his/her own to perform the job.
- *Role Playing*: Trainees assume job-related roles and practise new behaviours by acting out what they would do in job-related situations.
- *Simulations and Games*: Experiential exercises that place trainees in realistic job-related situations and give them the opportunity to experience a job-related condition in a relatively low-cost setting. The trainee benefits from "hands-on experience" before actually performing the job where mistakes may be more costly.
- *Vestibule Training*: Procedures and equipment similar to those used in the actual job are set up in a special area called a vestibule. The trainee is then taught how to perform the job at his/her own pace without disrupting the actual flow of work, making costly mistakes, or exposing the trainee and others to dangerous conditions.

TRAINING OBJECTIVE: IMPART INFORMATION OR KNOWLEDGE; DEVELOP ANALYTICAL AND PROBLEM-SOLVING SKILLS; PRACTISE, LEARN, OR CHANGE JOB BEHAVIOURS

- *Computer-Based Learning*: Interactive videos, software, CD-ROMs, personal computers, teleconferencing, and the Internet may be combined to present multimedia-based training.

Source: A. Fowler, "How to Decide on Training Methods," *People Management* 25, no. 1 (1995): 36.

case studies, coaching and mentoring, group discussions, on-the-job training, role playing, simulations and games, vestibule training, and computer-based learning. Which method would be best?

To choose the best method, you should consider a number of factors, such as the number of people to be trained, the cost of training, and the objectives of the training. For instance, if the training objective is to impart information or knowledge to trainees, you should use films and videos, lectures, and planned readings. In our robbery training example, trainees would hear, see, or read about what to do in case of a robbery.

If developing analytical and problem-solving skills is the objective, use case studies, group discussions, and coaching and mentoring. In our example, trainees would read about a real robbery, discuss what to do, and then talk to people who had been through robberies before.

If practising, learning, or changing job behaviours is the objective, use on-the-job training, role playing, simulations and games, and vestibule training. In our example, trainees would learn about robbery situations on the job, pretend that they were in a robbery situation, or participate in a highly realistic mock robbery. If training is supposed to meet more than one of these objectives, your best choice may be to combine one of the previous methods with computer-based training.

5.3 Evaluating Training

After selecting a training method and conducting the training, the last step is to evaluate the training. Training can be evaluated in four ways: on *reactions*, how satisfied trainees were with the program; on *learning*, how much employees improved their knowledge or

In on-the-job training, new employees learn by watching and working alongside experienced employees. Gradually, the trainee does more and more of the job on his or her own.

PhotoDisc Inc.

skills; on *behaviour*, how much employees actually changed their on-the-job behaviour because of training; or on *results*, how much training improved job performance, such as increased sales or quality, or decreased costs.[62]

Review 5
Training

Training is used to give employees the job-specific skills, experience, and knowledge they need to do their jobs or improve their job performance. To make sure training dollars are well spent, companies need to determine specific training needs, select appropriate training methods, and then evaluate the training. Needs assessments can be conducted by identifying performance deficiencies, listening to customer complaints, surveying employees and managers, or formally testing employees' skills and knowledge. Selection of an appropriate training method depends on a number of factors, such as the number of people to be trained, the cost of training, and the objectives of the training. If the objective is to impart information or knowledge, films and videos, lectures, and planned readings should be used. If developing analytical and problem-solving skills is the objective, case studies, group discussions, and coaching and mentoring should be used. If practising, learning, or changing job behaviours is the objective, on-the-job training, role playing, simulations and games, and vestibule training would be used. If training is supposed to meet more than one of these objectives, it may be best to combine one of the previous methods with computer-based training. Training can be evaluated on reactions, learning, behaviour, or results.

6. Performance Appraisal

performance appraisal
the process of assessing how well employees are doing their jobs

Performance appraisal is the process of assessing how well employees are doing their jobs. Most employees and managers intensely dislike the performance appraisal process. One manager said, "I hate annual performance reviews. I hated them when I used to get them, and I hate them now that I give them. If I had to choose between performance reviews and paper cuts, I'd take paper cuts every time. I'd even take razor burns and the sound of fingernails on a blackboard."[63] Unfortunately, attitudes like this are all too common. One study found that seven out of ten employees are dissatisfied with the performance appraisal process in their companies.[64] In another study, unhappiness with performance appraisal systems were cited as their number one human resource management issue with 34 percent of companies planning to make changes to improve their systems.[65]

Because they are used for so many important purposes, companies with poor performance appraisal systems face tremendous problems. For example, performance appraisals are used as a basis for compensation, promotion, and training decisions. In human resource planning, performance appraisals are used for career planning and for making termination decisions.[66] And because of their key role in so many organizational decisions, performance appraisals are also central to many of the lawsuits that employees (or former employees) file against employers.

Let's explore how companies can avoid some of these problems with performance appraisals by accurately measuring job performance, and sharing performance feedback.

6.1 Accurately Measuring Job Performance

Workers often have strong doubts about the accuracy of their performance appraisals. And they may be right. For example, it's widely known that assessors are prone to rater errors when rating worker performance. Three of the most common rater errors are central tendency, halo, and leniency. *Central tendency* error occurs when assessors rate all workers as average or in the middle of the scale. *Halo error* occurs when assessors rate all workers as performing at the same level (good, bad, or average) in all parts of their jobs.

Leniency error occurs when assessors rate all workers as performing particularly well. One of the reasons that managers make these errors is they often don't spend enough time gathering or reviewing performance data. Winston Connor, the former vice president of human resources at Huntsman Chemical, said, "Most of the time, it's just a ritual that managers go through. They pull out last year's review, update it and do it quickly."[67]

What can be done to minimize rater errors and improve the accuracy with which job performance is measured? In general, two approaches have been used: improving performance appraisal measures themselves and training performance raters to be more accurate.

One of the ways in which companies try to improve performance appraisal measures is to use as many objective performance measures as possible. **Objective performance measures** are measures of performance that are easily and directly counted or quantified. Common objective performance measures include output, scrap, waste, sales, customer complaints, or rejection rates.

But when objective performance measures aren't available, and frequently they aren't, subjective performance measures have to be used instead. **Subjective performance measures** require that someone judge or assess a worker's performance. The most common kind of subjective performance appraisal measure is the trait rating scale shown in Exhibit 13.11. **Trait rating scales** ask raters to indicate the extent to which a worker possesses a particular trait or characteristic, such as reliability or honesty. However, trait rating scales, also called *graphic rating scales*, are typically inaccurate measures of performance. To start, managers are notoriously poor judges of employee traits. Second, traits are not related to job performance in any meaningful way.

objective performance measures
measures of job performance that are easily and directly counted or quantified

subjective performance measures
measures of job performance that require someone to judge or assess a worker's performance

trait rating scales
a rating scale that indicates the extent to which a worker possesses particular traits or characteristics

---

EXHIBIT 13.11

SUBJECTIVE PERFORMANCE APPRAISAL SCALES

TRAIT RATING SCALE

	STRONGLY DISAGREE	1	2	3	4	5	STRONGLY AGREE
1. Employee is a hard worker.		1	2	3	4	5	
2. Employee is reliable.		1	2	3	4	5	
3. Employee is trustworthy.		1	2	3	4	5	

BEHAVIOURAL OBSERVATION SCALE

DIMENSION: CUSTOMER SERVICE	ALMOST NEVER	1	2	3	4	5	ALMOST ALWAYS
1. Greets customers with a smile and a "hello."		1	2	3	4	5	
2. Calls other stores to help customers find merchandise that is not in stock.		1	2	3	4	5	
3. Promptly handles customer concerns and complaints.		1	2	3	4	5	

DIMENSION: MONEY HANDLING	ALMOST NEVER	1	2	3	4	5	ALMOST ALWAYS
1. Accurately makes change from customer transactions.		1	2	3	4	5	
2. Accounts balance at the end of the day, no shortages or surpluses.		1	2	3	4	5	
3. Accurately records transactions in computer system.		1	2	3	4	5	

behavioural observation scales (BOS)
rating scales that indicate the frequency with which workers perform specific behaviours that are representative of the job dimensions critical to successful job performance

So instead of using trait rating scales, subjective performance should be measured using behavioural observation scales. **Behavioural observation scales (BOS)** ask raters to rate the frequency with which workers perform specific behaviours representative of the job dimensions that are critical to successful job performance. Exhibit 13.11 shows a BOS for two important job dimensions for a retail salesperson: customer service and handling money. Notice that each dimension lists several specific behaviours characteristic of a worker who excels in that dimension of job performance. (Normally, the scale would list 7 to 12 items, not 3 as shown in the table.)

Not only do BOSs work well for rating critical dimensions of performance, but studies also show that managers strongly prefer BOSs for giving performance feedback; accurately differentiating between poor, average, and good workers; identifying training needs; and accurately measuring performance. And in response to the statement "If I were defending a company, this rating format would be an asset to my case," lawyers strongly preferred BOSs over other kinds of subjective performance appraisal scales.[68]

rater training
training performance appraisal raters in how to avoid rating errors and increase rating accuracy

The second approach to improving the measurement of workers' job performance appraisal is rater training. **Rater training** is the process of training performance raters how to avoid rating errors (i.e., central tendency, halo, and leniency) and how to increase rating accuracy. In rater training designed to minimize rating errors, trainees view videotapes of managers observing an employee performing some aspect of a job. Following each video, trainees are asked how they would have rated the worker's performance and how the manager on the tape would have rated it. Each videotape, however, is an example of the different kinds of rating errors. So trainees have a chance to actually observe rating errors being made (by the manager in the videotape) and then discuss how to avoid those errors.

Another common form of rater training stresses rater accuracy (rather than minimizing errors). Here, raters closely examine the key dimensions of job performance (e.g., customer service and handling money for the retail salesperson in our example) and discuss specific behaviours representative of each dimension. Trainees may then be asked to role-play examples of these behaviours or to watch videos containing behavioural examples of each dimension of job performance. Both kinds of rater training are effective.[69]

6.2 Sharing Performance Feedback

After gathering accurate performance data, the next step is to share performance feedback with employees. Unfortunately, even when performance appraisal ratings are accurate, the appraisal process often breaks down at the feedback stage. Employees become defensive and dislike hearing any negative assessments of their work, no matter how small. Managers become defensive, too, and dislike giving appraisal feedback as much as employees dislike receiving it. One manager said, "I myself don't go as far as those who say performance reviews are inherently destructive and ought to be abolished, but I agree that the typical annual-review process does nothing but harm. It creates divisions. It undermines morale. It makes people angry, jealous, and cynical. It unleashes a whole lot of negative energy, and the organization gets nothing in return."[70]

So what can be done to overcome the inherent difficulties in performance appraisal feedback sessions? Since performance appraisal ratings have traditionally been the judgments of just one person, the boss, one approach is to use **360-degree feedback**. In this approach, feedback comes from four sources: the boss, subordinates, peers and co-workers, and the employees themselves. The data, which are obtained anonymously (except for the boss), are then compiled into a feedback report comparing the employee's self-ratings to those of the boss, subordinates, and peers and co-workers. Usually, a consultant or human resource specialist discusses the results with the employee. The advantage of 360-degree programs is that negative feedback ("You don't listen") is often more credible if heard from several people. For example, one boss who received 360-degree feedback thought he was a great writer, so he regularly criticized and corrected his sub-

360-degree feedback
a performance appraisal process in which feedback is obtained from the boss, subordinates, peers and co-workers, and the employees themselves

ordinates' reports. Though the subordinates never discussed it among themselves, they all complained about his writing in the 360-degree feedback and mentioned that he should quit rewriting their reports. After receiving the feedback, he apologized and stopped.[71]

A word of caution, though. About half the companies using 360-degree feedback for performance appraisal now use the feedback only for developmental purposes. They found that sometimes with raises and promotions on the line, peers and subordinates would distort ratings to harm competitors or help people they liked, and that sometimes people would give high ratings in order to get high ratings from others. On the other hand, studies clearly show that ratees prefer to receive feedback from several raters, so 360-degree feedback is likely to continue to grow in popularity.[72] A recent study of large Canadian firms found that 43 percent of them used 360-degree feedback in their performance appraisal process.[73]

Herbert Meyer, who has been studying performance appraisal feedback for more than 30 years, made the following specific recommendations for sharing performance feedback with employees.[74] First, managers should separate developmental feedback, which is designed to improve future performance, from administrative feedback, which is used as a reward for past performance, such as for raises. When managers give developmental feedback, they're acting as coaches, but when they give administrative feedback, they're acting as judges. These roles, coaches and judges, are clearly incompatible. As coaches, managers are encouraging, pointing out opportunities for growth and improvement, and employees are typically open and receptive to feedback. But as judges, managers are evaluative, and employees are typically defensive and closed to feedback. Jean Gatz, a training expert, said, "Most of us don't like to sit down and hear where we're lacking and where we need to improve. It's like sitting down with your mom and dad and they're telling you, 'We know what's best.'"[75]

Second, Meyer suggests that performance appraisal feedback sessions be based on self-appraisals, in which employees carefully assess their own strengths, weaknesses, successes, and failures in writing. Because employees play an active role in the review of their performance, managers can be coaches rather than judges. Also, because the focus is on future goals and development, both employees and managers are likely to be more satisfied with the process and more committed to future plans and changes. See Exhibit 13.12 for the list of topics that Meyer recommends for discussion in performance appraisal feedback sessions.

One concern about self-appraisals is that employees will be overly positive when evaluating their performance. However, when the focus is on development and not administrative assessment, studies show that self-appraisals lead to more candid self-assessments than traditional supervisory reviews.[76]

EXHIBIT 13.12

WHAT TO DISCUSS IN A PERFORMANCE APPRAISAL FEEDBACK SESSION

1. Overall progress—an analysis of accomplishments and shortcomings.
2. Problems encountered in meeting job requirements.
3. Opportunities to improve performance.
4. Long-range plans, opportunities—for the job and for the individual's career.
5. General discussion of possible plans and goals for the coming year.

Source: H.H. Meyer, "A Solution to the Performance Appraisal Feedback Enigma," *Academy of Management Executive* 5, no. 1 (1991): 68–76

Third, Meyer suggests eliminating the "grading" aspect of performance appraisal, in which employees are ranked on a 1–5 scale or are scored as below average, average, above average, or exceptional. He says that "assigning a numerical or adjectival grade, such as 'satisfactory,' 'excellent,' 'adequate,' 'outstanding,' or 'poor,' to overall performance or specific performance tends to obstruct rather than facilitate constructive discussion. It treats a mature person like a schoolchild. The administrative action taken, such as the amount of salary increase or a promotion, will communicate an overall appraisal better than will a grade."[77]

Review 6
Performance Appraisal

Most employees and managers intensely dislike the performance appraisal process. However, some of the problems associated with appraisals can be avoided by accurately measuring job performance and effectively sharing performance feedback with employees. Managers are prone to three kinds of rating errors: central tendency, halo, and leniency error. One way to minimize rating errors is to use better appraisal measures, such as objective measures of performance or behavioural observation scales. Another method is to directly train performance raters to minimize errors and more accurately rate the important dimensions of job performance.

After gathering accurate performance data, the next step is to share performance feedback with employees. One way to overcome the inherent difficulties in performance appraisal feedback is to provide 360-degree feedback, in which feedback is obtained from four sources: the boss, subordinates, peers and co-workers, and the employees themselves. Feedback tends to be more credible if heard from several sources. Traditional performance appraisal feedback sessions can be improved by separating developmental and administrative feedback, by basing feedback discussions on employee self-appraisals, and by eliminating the "grading" aspect.

Keeping Qualified Workers

Retaining qualified workers is a major challenge for today's employers. The best employees always have options, and during boom times it seems that everyone has options. Think back to Chapter 2 when we discussed how difficult it was for software firms to obtain qualified employees. Although we often associate employee retention problems with skilled workers, given a hot enough economy even unskilled workers have options. The president of Calgary's Chamber of Commerce was quoted as saying, "We are having trouble holding onto delivery people, finding trained sales people—or even untrained sales people that you train to go forward—because of the growth and the number of new companies that are starting up".[78] Employees are not simply looking for better wages but also quality of working life. Issues such as length of holidays and flexible workdays can help companies retain their employees. And with acute labour shortages in many industries occurring countrywide, nearly all employers now understand the effect that compensation has on their ability to keep qualified workers.

After reading the next two sections, you should be able to
7. describe basic compensation strategies and how they affect human resource practice.
8. discuss the four kinds of employee separations: termination, downsizing, retirements, and turnover.

7. Compensation

compensation
the financial and nonfinancial rewards that organizations give employees in exchange for their work

Compensation includes both the financial and nonfinancial rewards that organizations give employees in exchange for their work.

Let's learn more about compensation by examining the compensation decisions and employment benefits.

There are four basic kinds of compensation decisions: pay level, pay variability, pay structure, and employment benefits. We'll discuss employment benefits in the next subsection.[79]

Pay-level decisions are decisions about whether to pay workers at a level that is below, above, or at current market wages. Companies use job evaluation to set their pay structures. **Job evaluation** determines the worth of each job by determining the market value of the knowledge, skills, and requirements needed to perform it. After conducting a job evaluation, most companies try to pay the "going rate," meaning the current market wage.

Some companies choose to pay above-average wages to attract and keep employees. Above-market wages can attract a larger, more qualified pool of job applicants, increase the rate of job acceptance, decrease the time it takes to fill positions, and increase how long employees stay.[80] Some government agencies and departments that typically pay well below market wages find that it can take months and sometimes years to fill job openings, as applicants go to the private sector for much more money.[81] Service industries, which typically also pay low wages, can have a great deal of difficulty obtaining and retaining employees. For example, a bagel franchise in Banff, a town that finds it notoriously difficult to retain employees, that had 12 employees hired 60 people in one year, an incredible turnover rate of 500 percent![82]

Pay-variability decisions are decisions concerning the extent to which employees' pay varies with individual and organizational performance. Linking pay to organizational performance is intended to increase employee motivation, effort, and job performance. Piecework, sales commission, profit sharing, employee stock ownership plans, and stock options are common pay-variability options. For instance, under **piecework** pay plans, employees are paid a set rate for each item produced up to some standard (e.g., $0.35 per item produced for output up to 100 units per day). Once productivity exceeds the standard, employees are paid a set amount for each unit of output over the standard (e.g., $0.45 for each unit above 100 units). Sales **commission** is another kind of pay variability, in which salespeople are paid a percentage of the purchase price of items they sell. The more they sell, the more they earn.

Because pay plans such as piecework and commissions are based on individual performance, they can reduce the incentive that people have to work together. Therefore, companies also use group incentives and organizational incentives, such as profit sharing, employee stock ownership plans, and stock options, to encourage teamwork and cooperation.

Profit sharing is the payment of a portion of the organization's profits to employees over and above their regular compensation. The more profitable the company, the more profit is shared. In 1998, DaimlerChrysler's assembly workers received about $10 500 each in profit sharing cheques. Ford's assembly workers received about $9200 each. However, General Motors, the least profitable of the three North American auto companies, was able to pay its assembly workers profit sharing cheques of only $300 each.[83]

Employee stock ownership plans (ESOPs) compensate employees by awarding them shares of the company stock in addition to their regular compensation. Castek Software Factory, a Toronto-based software developer, has had an ESOP since 1995. The CFO, Fay Wu, credits this plan for substantially reducing the firm's level of employee turnover, which in the software industry can be quite high.[84]

Stock options give employees the right to purchase shares of stock at a set price. It works like this. If you are awarded the right (or option) to 100 shares of stock valued at $5 a share and the stock price rises to $15 a share, you can exercise your options and make $1000 (100 shares which have increased $10 in value, from $5 to $15). Of course, as company profits and share values increase, stock options become even more valuable to employees.

Pay-structure decisions are concerned with internal pay distributions, meaning the extent to which people in the company receive very different levels of pay.[85] With *hierarchical pay structures*, there are big differences from one pay level to another. The

job evaluation
a process that determines the worth of each job in a company by evaluating the market value of the knowledge, skills, and requirements needed to perform it

piecework
a compensation system in which employees are paid a set rate for each item they produce

commission
a compensation system in which employees earn a percentage of each sale they make

profit sharing
a compensation system in which a percentage of company profits is paid to employees in addition to their regular compensation

employee stock ownership plans (ESOPs)
a compensation system that awards employees shares of company stock in addition to their regular compensation

stock options
a compensation system that gives employees the right to purchase shares of stock at a set price, even if the value of the stock increases above that price

largest pay levels are for people near the top of the pay distribution. The basic idea behind hierarchical pay structures is that large differences in pay between jobs or organizational levels should motivate people to work harder to obtain those higher-paying jobs.

By contrast, with *compressed pay structures*, there are typically fewer pay levels and smaller differences in pay between pay levels. Pay is less dispersed and more similar across jobs in the company. The basic idea behind compressed pay structures is that similar pay levels should lead to higher levels of cooperation, feelings of fairness and a common purpose, and better group and team performance.

So should companies choose hierarchical or compressed pay structures? The evidence isn't straightforward, but studies seem to indicate that there are significant problems with the hierarchical approach. The most damaging is that there appears to be little link between organizational performance and the pay of top managers.[86] Furthermore, studies of professional athletes indicate that hierarchical pay structures (e.g., paying superstars 40 to 50 times more than the lowest-paid athlete on the team) hurt the performance of teams and individual players.[87] For now, the key seems to be that hierarchical pay structures work best for independent work, where it's easy to determine the contributions of individual performers and where little coordination with others is needed to get the job done. In other words, hierarchical pay structures work best when clear links can be drawn between individual performance and individual rewards. By contrast, compressed pay structures, that is, paying everyone similar amounts of money, seem to work best for interdependent work, in which employees must work with each other. But some companies are pursuing a middle ground, in which they try to balance hierarchical and compressed pay structures by giving ordinary workers the chance to earn more through ESOPs, stock options, and profit sharing.

7.2 Employment Benefits

employment benefits
a method of rewarding employees that includes virtually any kind of compensation other than wages or salaries

Employment benefits include virtually any kind of compensation other than direct wages paid to employees.[88] Three employee benefits are mandated by law: Canada Pension Plan, worker's compensation, and employment insurance. However, to attract and retain a good workforce, most organizations offer a wide variety of benefits, including retirement plans and pensions, paid holidays, paid vacations, sick leave, health insurance, life insurance, dental care, eye care, daycare facilities, paid personal days, legal assistance, physical fitness facilities, educational assistance, and discounts on company products and services. In 1996 KPMG estimated that benefits cost Canadian organizations about 46 percent of an employer's payroll costs, up from 34.1 percent in 1991, indicating that they are a key element in compensation packages.[89]

Managers should understand that benefits are not likely to improve employee motivation and performance. However, benefits do affect job satisfaction, employee decisions about staying or leaving the company, and the company's attractiveness to job applicants.[90] One way in which organizations make their benefit plans more attractive to employees is through **cafeteria benefit plans** or **flexible benefit plans**, which allow employees to choose which benefits they receive, up to a certain dollar value.[91] Many cafeteria or flexible benefit plans start with a core of benefits, such as health insurance and life insurance that are available to all employees. Then employees are allowed to select other benefits that best fit their needs, up to a predetermined dollar amount. Some organizations provide several packages of benefits from which employees may choose. Each package is of equivalent value; however, the mix of benefits differs. For example, older employees may prefer more benefit dollars spent on retirement plans, while younger employees may prefer additional vacation days.

cafeteria benefit plans (flexible benefit plans)
plans that allow employees to choose which benefits they receive, up to a certain dollar value

The drawback to flexible benefit plans has been the high cost of administering these programs. However, with advances in information processing technology and HRISs, the cost of administering benefits has begun to drop in recent years.

Compensation includes both the financial and nonfinancial rewards that organizations give employees in exchange for their work. There are four basic kinds of compensation decisions: pay level, pay variability, pay structure, and employment benefits. Pay-level decisions determine whether workers will receive wages below, above, or at current market levels. Pay-variability decisions concern the extent to which pay varies with individual and organizational performance. Piecework, sales commission, profit sharing, employee stock ownership plans, and stock options are common pay-variability options. Pay-structure decisions concern the extent to which people in the company receive very different levels of pay. Hierarchical pay structures work best for independent work, while compressed pay structures work best for interdependent work.

Employee benefits include virtually any kind of compensation other than direct wages paid to employees. Flexible or cafeteria benefit plans, which offer employees a wide variety of benefits, improve job satisfaction, increase the chances that employees will stay with companies, and make organizations more attractive to job applicants. The cost of administering benefits has begun to drop in recent years.

8. Employee Separations

Employee separation is a broad term covering the loss of an employee for any reason. *Involuntary separation* occurs when employers decide to terminate or lay off employees. *Voluntary separation* occurs when employees decide to quit or retire. Because employee separations affect recruiting, selection, training, and compensation, organizations should forecast the number of employees they expect to lose through terminations, layoffs, turnover, or retirements when doing human resource planning.

employee separation
the voluntary or involuntary loss of an employee

Let's explore employee separation by examining terminating employees, downsizing, retirement, and employee turnover.

8.1 Terminating Employees

Hopefully, the words "You're fired!" have never been directed at you. Lots of people hear them. Getting fired is a terrible thing, but many managers make it even worse by bungling the firing process, needlessly provoking the people who were fired, and unintentionally inviting lawsuits. For example, one worker found out he had been fired after a restaurant told him that his company credit card was no longer active. A manager found out that she had been fired when she came back from lunch and found a note on her desk chair. And workers at a high-tech company know that they've been fired when their security codes no longer open their office doors or the front door to their office buildings.[92] How would you feel if you had been fired in one of these ways? While firing is never pleasant (and managers hate firings nearly as much as employees do), there are several things managers can do to minimize the problems inherent in firing employees.

First, in most firing situations, firing should not be the first option. Instead, employees should be given a chance to change their behaviour. So when problems arise, employees should have ample warning and must be specifically informed as to the nature and seriousness of the trouble they're in. After being notified, they should be given sufficient time to change. If the problems continue, they should again be counselled about their job performance, what could be done to improve it, and the possible consequences if things don't change (e.g., written reprimand, suspension without pay, or firing). Sometimes, this is enough to solve the problem. Outplacement specialist Laurence Stybel tells the story about a large hospital that was getting ready to fire its director of radiology because of his bad attitude and increasing rudeness to co-workers. Rather than fire him, hospital management put him on probation and hired a consultant to counsel him about working with others. Within weeks, his attitude and behaviour changed, and the hospital avoided firing him and the expense of replacing him (which could have included a lawsuit).[93] However, after several rounds of warnings and discussions, if the problem isn't corrected, the employee may be terminated.[94]

Second, employees should be fired for a good reason, which is referred to as just cause. Employers used to hire and fire employees under the legal principle of "termination at will," which allowed them to fire employees for a good reason, a bad reason, or no reason at all. However, as employees began contesting their firings in court, the principle of wrongful dismissal emerged. **Wrongful dismissal** is a legal doctrine that requires employers to have a job-related reason to terminate employees. In other words, just like other major human resource decisions, termination decisions should be made on the basis of job-related factors, such as violating company rules or consistently poor performance. Managers should record the job-related reasons for the termination, document specific instances of rule violations or continued poor performance, and keep notes and documents from the counselling sessions held with employees.[95] If an employer does not have just cause for terminating an employee, the employer must compensate the employee in lieu of the notice period to which they would normally be entitled. The minimum entitlement under provincial and federal laws varies and employees can obtain up to two years' pay under common law, depending on the circumstances.

Third, companies need to pay attention to reactions of remaining employees after someone has been fired. Jenai Lane of Respect, Inc., a maker of jewellery and accessories, believes it is important to consider the employees who remain after someone is terminated. After she fires someone, she holds an "emergency pow-wow" and encourages employees to speak their minds. "It takes a little prodding, but it's good to get people's feelings out in the open."[96] However, managers should be careful not to criticize the employee who has just been fired, as this could lead to a wrongful dismissal or defamation lawsuit.

8.2 Downsizing

Downsizing is the planned elimination of jobs in a company. Whether it's because of cost cutting, declining market share, or overaggressive hiring and growth, downsizing is a common strategy.[97] In a recent study it was found that two-thirds of U.S. companies that downsize will downsize a second time within a year. For example, Applied Materials, based in California's Silicon Valley, let 1500 workers go the first time it downsized, followed by another 2000 workers less than three months later.[98] In Canada, Nortel and Air Canada have gone through repeated rounds of downsizing.

Does downsizing work? In theory, downsizing is supposed to lead to higher productivity and profits, better stock performance, and increased organizational flexibility. However, numerous studies demonstrate that it doesn't. For instance, a 15-year study of downsizing found that downsizing 10 percent of a company's workforce only produces a 1.5 percent decrease in costs, that firms that downsized increased their stock price by 4.7 percent over three years compared to 34.3 percent for firms that didn't, and that profitability and productivity were generally not improved by downsizing.[99] These results make it clear that the best strategy is to conduct effective human resource planning and avoid downsizing altogether. Indeed, downsizing should always be used as a measure of last resort and there are a number of alternative strategies such as reducing hours, job sharing, leaves of absence and employee buy-outs.[100]

However, if companies do find themselves in financial or strategic situations where downsizing is required for survival, they should train managers how to break the news to downsized employees, have senior managers explain in detail why downsizing is necessary, and time the announcement so employees hear it from the company and not from other sources, such as TV or newspaper reports.[101] Finally, companies should do everything they can to help downsized employees find other jobs. One of the best ways to do this is to use **outplacement services** that provide employment-counselling services for

wrongful dismissal
a legal doctrine that requires employers to have a job-related reason to terminate employees

downsizing
the planned elimination of jobs in a company

outplacement services
employment-counselling serviced offered to employees who are losing their jobs because of downsizing

employees faced with downsizing. Outplacement services often include advice and training in preparing resumés and getting ready for job interviews, and even identifying job opportunities in other companies.

When Victoria's JDS Uniphase decided that it needed to downsize, it went to great lengths to find each laid-off employee a new job. It put together a 112-page directory of employees' biographical sketches and mailed it to 400 employers. They offered added incentives to employees to remain until the last day that JDS wanted them to work, and most stayed on. They also offered employees job hunting training such as resumé writing, job search techniques, and where to find "hidden jobs." Other training was also made available such as computer skills. Job fairs were organized and speakers were brought in to provide information to employees about a number of helpful issues.[102] Extensive outplacement programs not only help laid-off employees, but also help the company maintain a positive image in the community affected by downsizing. Steps such as these also help employees remain productive during their final days at the company.

8.3 Retirement

Early retirement incentive programs (ERIPs) offer financial benefits to employees to encourage them to retire early. Companies use ERIPs to reduce the number of employees in the organization, to lower costs by eliminating positions after employees retire, to lower costs by replacing high-paid retirees with lower-paid, less-experienced employees, or to create openings and job opportunities for people inside the company. For example, in 2001 DaimlerChrysler agreed on a $90-million retirement package with the Canadian Auto Workers, the union that represents the majority of its employees. It was hoped that this package would reduce the need for layoffs by up to 60 percent. Each package was worth about $52 500, which included a one-time payment of $26 000 and a credit of $16 000 toward the purchase of a Chrysler vehicle.

The biggest problem with most ERIPs is accurately predicting who and how many will accept early retirement. The company will likely lose good as well as poor performers, and sometimes more workers than they expect. For example, Ameritech Corporation, the largest telephone company in the Midwest U.S., offered an ERIP consisting of a $7500 educational assistance program to retrain workers, financial planning counselling, and outplacement advice and guidance. Since most pension benefits are based on a formula including years of service and employee age, the core of Ameritech's program was the "three-plus-three enhancement," which added three years to the employees' age and three years to their years of service to help them qualify for greater retirement benefits. Ameritech carefully identified the number of employees near retirement age and estimated that 5000 to 6000 of its 48 000 employees would take advantage of the program. Instead, nearly 22 000 employees accepted the ERIP offer and applied for early retirement![103]

8.4 Employee Turnover

Employee turnover is the loss of employees who voluntarily choose to leave the company. In general, most companies try to keep the rate of employee turnover low to reduce recruiting, hiring, training, and replacement costs. However, not all kinds of employee turnover are bad for organizations. In fact, some turnover can actually be good. For instance, **functional turnover** is the loss of poor-performing employees who choose to leave the organization.[104] Functional turnover gives the organization a chance to replace poor performers with better replacements. In fact, one study found that simply replacing poor-performing leavers with average replacements would increase the revenues produced by retail salespeople in an upscale department store by $173 000 per person per year.[105] By contrast, **dysfunctional turnover**, the loss of high performers who choose to leave, is a costly loss to the organization.

early retirement incentive programs (ERIPs)
programs that offer financial benefits to employees to encourage them to retire early

employee turnover
loss of employees who voluntarily choose to leave the company

functional turnover
loss of poor-performing employees who voluntarily choose to leave a company

dysfunctional turnover
loss of high-performing employees who voluntarily choose to leave a company

Employee turnover should be carefully analyzed to determine exactly who is choosing to leave the organization, good or poor performers. If the company is losing too many high performers, managers should determine the reasons and find ways to reduce the loss of valuable employees. The company may have to raise salary levels, offer enhanced benefits, or improve working conditions to retain skilled workers. One of the best ways to influence functional and dysfunctional turnover is to link pay directly to performance. A study of four sales forces found that when pay was strongly linked to performance via sales commissions and bonuses, poor performers were much more likely to leave (i.e., functional turnover). By contrast, poor performers were much more likely to stay when paid large, guaranteed monthly salaries and small sales commissions and bonuses.[106]

Review 8
Employee Separations

Employee separation is the loss of an employee, which can occur voluntarily or involuntarily. Before firing or terminating employees, managers should give employees a chance to improve. If firing becomes necessary, it should be done because of job-related factors, such as violating company rules or consistently poor performance. Downsizing is supposed to lead to higher productivity and profits, better stock performance, and increased organizational flexibility, but studies show that it doesn't. The best strategy is to downsize only as a last resort. Companies that do downsize should offer outplacement services to help employees find other jobs. Companies use early retirement incentive programs to reduce the number of employees in the organization, lower costs, and create openings and job opportunities for people inside the company. The biggest problem with ERIPs is accurately predicting who and how many will accept early retirement. Companies generally try to keep the rate of employee turnover low to reduce costs. However, functional turnover can be good for organizations, because it offers the chance to replace poor performers with better replacements. Managers should analyze employee turnover to determine who is resigning and take steps to reduce the loss of good performers.

What Really Happened?

Remember the daunting task that Albian Sands Energy Inc. was facing at the beginning of the chapter? It was just about to embark on a massive project north of Fort McMurray and had to hire more than 600 permanent staff. Given the cutthroat nature of the labour market and the fact the company really wanted to hire and retain good employees, this was a genuinely challenging task.

How do you go about recruiting qualified applicants?

Finding qualified workers in today's job market is an increasingly difficult task. Successful selection decisions begin by using recruiting to develop a pool of qualified job applicants. Clearly as this was an entirely new company and project, it had to rely exclusively on external recruiting. Part of what Albian did was take a long-term view. Many of the employees are required to have a Grade 12 or post-secondary education, so one thing it did was to participate in a number of stay-in-school programs. Over time this would increase the number of local people available for immediate employment but it would also increase the number of people eligible for training in the skilled trades. The company also worked with local trade and professional schools to increase the number of people being trained. Clearly, it wanted to have a long-term influence on the demographics of the labour supply. It also wanted to hire as many local people as possible in the hopes of increasing retention rates. The Aboriginal population in the area is three times the national average, so working with those communities was a priority. These communities have a permanent attachment to the area so housing is not as big an issue as it is for someone who has to move to Fort McMurray from a great distance.

In order to attract applications, Albian undertook a "Recruitment Road Show" and hit all major cities across Canada. It used extensive advertising before its arrival and made presentations to large audiences at local hotels. Although it used many standard advertising strategies, it also used the Internet. On Albian Sand's website (www.albiansands.ca), employment opportunities are quite clearly advertised. Employment opportunities were also listed on the website of its parent companies. It also tapped into industry-based websites such as InfoMine.com, which has an extensive careers section geared toward the mining industry. The company also used government-sponsored employment services with Internet listings.

Once you have found employees, hiring and keeping them becomes the next task. Albian Sands faced tremendous competition, and with the huge amount of investment coming to the area it knew the task would be a challenge. What did Albian Sands do to entice workers to come work for the company and to stay with it?

Albian Sands did a number of things to attract and retain individuals. During its recruitment drive, Albian discussed the challenges of moving to Fort McMurray to ensure those who came were aware of them and were prepared for them. This was done to reduce the likelihood of people quitting because they found the transition to Fort McMurray too difficult. Remember, compensation includes both the financial and nonfinancial rewards that employers give employees in exchange for their work. Things like benefit plans and hours of work can influence workers' choices. Albian Sands, although offering competitive salaries, came up with more incentives in the hope that it would give the company an edge. It developed a rewards package, which included four areas: pay, benefits, learning and development, and work environment. It also offered a full benefits package and competitive salaries. As well, the company gives team members the opportunity to earn up to 15 percent above the base salary on an annual basis. Three months of pay was offered as a signing bonus. The mine was over an hour from Fort McMurray, so the company provided a travel allowance and free buses to and from work and, in order to cut down on employees' commuting time, instituted longer work days, so that people had to work fewer days. One employee on 12-hour shifts said he didn't mind the long days as it meant he really only had to work six months of the year. He compensates for the long days by travelling the world the other half of the year. The company also provided educational opportunities for employees and their families and four weeks of holiday to start.

It also looked beyond the immediate workforce and got involved with projects that benefited the community. It donated money to purchase a CT scanner for the hospital and two 4X4 vehicles to provide health services to local communities. Albian Sands employees have also contributed to the community through participation in nonprofit organizations and community participation events such as "Adopt a Highway." These sorts of activities can contribute to the overall quality of life and help retain people.

Albian has been quite successful. How has its activities paid off?

According to its communications advisor, the company feels that its recruiting and selection drive has been quite successful. It received 17 000 resumés in 2001 and hired 382 people for the permanent workforce. Being creative and having an eye toward high-quality employees seems to have paid off.

Sources: Brian Burton, "Local Residents Find Plenty of Work at the Mines," *Edmonton Journal*, 2 May 2002, E13. Claudia Cattaneo, "Oilsands Battleground for Skilled Workers," *Financial Post*, 19 August 2002, FP1, FP4. Marilyn Scales, "The Truly Great Canadian Oilsands: Albian Sands Joins Ranks of Oil Sands Producers," *Canadian Mining Journal* 123, no. 7 (October 2002): 10–17. "What's New—Latest News," Albian Sands [Online] Available www.albiansands.ca/albiansands/whatsnew/frame.htm, Accessed 8 September 2003.

Key Terms

assessment centres (411)

background checks (409)

behavioural observation scales (BOS) (420)

biographical data (biodata) (410)

cafeteria benefit plans (flexible benefit plans) (424)

cognitive ability tests (410)

commission (423)

compensation (422)

downsizing (426)

dysfunctional turnover (427)

early retirement incentive programs (ERIPs) (427)

employee separation (425)

employee stock ownership plans (ESOPs) (423)

employee turnover (427)

employment benefits (424)

employment references (409)

external recruiting (405)

functional turnover (427)

hostile work environment (402)

human resource information systems (HRIS) (396)

human resource management (392)

human resource planning (HRP) (394)

internal recruiting (404)

interviews (411)

job analysis (403)

job description (403)

job evaluation (423)

job specifications (403)

needs assessment (415)

objective performance measures (419)

outplacement services (426)

performance appraisal (418)

personality tests (410)

piecework (423)

profit sharing (423)

quid pro quo sexual harassment (402)

rater training (420)

recruiting (403)

reliability (400)

selection (406)

sexual harassment (401)

specific ability tests (aptitude tests) (410)

stock options (423)

structured interviews (411)

subjective performance measures (419)

360-degree feedback (420)

training (415)

trait rating scales (419)

validation (406)

validity (400)

workforce forecasting (394)

work sample tests (410)

wrongful dismissal (426)

What Would You Do II?

A Bumpy Ride for Ford

Evaluating employees is something you have grappled with for years, even before you became the CEO of Ford Motor Company. Particularly difficult has been measuring and evaluating the performance of your senior and middle-level managers in a fair and equitable way, while ensuring that managers are motivated and actually performing to preset standards. The system formerly used at Ford produced overly inflated evaluations, as managers were not informed of their deficiencies, nor given constructive feedback on how to improve their performance. This system proved problematic when economic factors created a need to downsize the managerial pool. Based on the old system's inadequacies, good-performing managers were just as likely to be laid off as poor-performing managers.

After several trial and error attempts, you thought you had come up with the perfect system. This system, modelled after one used at General Electric, is a top-down system in which managers are assembled into groups of 30 or 50 and are assigned a ranking based on their peers. Within this group, the managers are ranked according to the bell-curve, a statistical phenomenon used to approximate a "normal-distribution" from a random sample. Within the employee ranking system at Ford, once the 18 000 managers have been assigned to their specific groups, higher-level managers rank the employees, placing them into

one of three categories. For this year's performance evaluations, you have mandated that the top 10 percent get an "A," the middle 80 percent a "B," and the bottom 10 percent a "C." Those employees ranked "B" or better will be rewarded with bonuses, salary increases, and stock options. For those who receive a "C," there will be no pay raise, and, if managers receive a "C" ranking for a second consecutive year, they will either be demoted or terminated. Under this system, those who receive a "C" ranking in the first year will be teamed up with a coach or mentor who will assist them in improving their deficiencies, thereby potentially improving their subsequent evaluations.

After months of discussion and weighing the pros and cons, this performance evaluation system was put in place. It is now in its second year, and you have just received word of a class-action age-discrimination lawsuit filed by 30 middle-aged white Ford managers. They claim that Ford is using this system to weed out older, higher-paid white managers. According to the lawsuit, Ford is so intent on pursuing racial and ethnic diversity, that older white males are disproportionately ranked in the bottom 10 percent. Further, the lawsuit contends that many managers are unfairly evaluated when ranked with their peers. Lawyers for the disgruntled managers claim that a few managers from a highly talented pool will be ranked at the bottom, whereas mediocre managers from an average pool may receive a

"B" ranking. One manager in particular claims that there is no way that the performance evaluation method is fair since 9 out of the 12 managers who ranked him had no idea who he was or what his skills and abilities were. Another claims that when he does his job correctly, there are no problems. However, when there are no problems, he is not visible and, therefore, is assumed to not be performing. This manager claims that the performance evaluation system leads to politicking in order to stay visible and be perceived by higher-level managers as a performer.

Given the debacle with Firestone tires and the Ford Explorer, stalled sales in an uncertain economy, and reduced revenue from your financial service arm (0 percent financing doesn't make the company any money), you certainly don't need any more rough roads, especially not internally. It's clear that you'll have to respond quickly and thoughtfully. You wonder how it is that GE

hasn't had similar problems with its system. How can such a simple, random, bell-curve evaluation system be discriminatory? Maybe it's not the appraisal system that is the problem; maybe the company needs better procedures to deal with employee separation. But for the moment, the issue is about performance appraisals. You've got to evaluate managers somehow. Can you modify the year-old evaluation program, or do you have to start over from scratch?

If you were the CEO of Ford Motor Company, what would you do?

Sources: D. Kiley and D. Jones, "Ford Alters Worker Evaluation Process," *USA Today*, 11 July 2001. D. Jones, "More Firms Cut Workers Ranked at Bottom to Make Way for Talent," *USA Today*, 30 May 2001. C. Hymowitz, "Ranking Systems Gain Popularity but Have Many Staffers Riled," *The Wall Street Journal*, 15 May 2001.

Critical Thinking Video Case

Work–Life Balance

Human resource management is the process of finding, developing, and keeping the right people to form a qualified workforce. Many companies claim that their human resources are their most valuable resources yet some companies fail to recognize that many people have trouble balancing their work commitments with family commitments. Companies tend to overemphasize an employee's paycheque as a major motivator while overlooking quality of working life.

According to the video, a quarter of all employees work more than 50 hours a week, stress levels are rising, and life satisfaction is down. Companies that recognize the need for work–life balance and implement policies to support this balance have a significant competitive advantage when recruiting employees. Companies that do not provide work–life balance have a more

difficult time recruiting employees—remember that the best recruits always have many options. In addition to having a harder time recruiting good employees, companies suffer additional consequences such as increased absenteeism, increased disability claims, high turnover, and increased drug-plan costs. As you watch the video, consider the following critical thinking questions.

Critical Thinking Questions

1. From an employer's point of view, what are the benefits of providing employees with a good work–life balance and how can you help employees achieve it?
2. If you were being interviewed for a job, what sort of policies would you like to see an employer offer?

Management Decisions

A Behavioural Interview for Your Professor?

Interviews are by far the most frequently used selection procedure. In fact, it's rare for people to be hired without first being interviewed. But as you learned in the chapter, most managers conduct unstructured interviews, in which they are free to ask applicants anything they want, and studies show that they do. Indeed, studies show that because interviewers often disagree about which questions should be asked during interviews, different interviewers tend to ask applicants very different questions. However, individual interviewers even seem to have a tough time asking the same questions from one interview to the next. This high level of inconsistency lowers the validity of interviews as a selection device, because it becomes difficult to compare applicant responses. As a result, unstructured interviews do about half as well as structured interviews in accurately predicting which job applicants should be hired.

By contrast, with structured interviews, standardized interview questions are prepared ahead of time, so that all applicants may be asked the same job-related questions. The primary advantage of structured interviews is that asking all applicants the same questions makes comparing applicants a much easier process. Also, structuring interviews ensures that interviewers will ask for only important, job-related information. These advantages significantly improve the accuracy, usefulness, and validity of interviews as a selection procedure. Since you're likely to use interviewing more than any other selection procedure, the purpose of this assignment is to give you some experience creating questions for structured interviews.

You'll be writing questions for the job of college professor, a job with which all of you should be familiar (having observed each of your instructors for an average of 40 hours per college class). Your job is to write 12 questions that you would ask applicants who wanted to teach at your university. Remember, four kinds of questions are typically asked in structured interviews. You'll be writing three questions for each of the four kinds of questions shown below.

- *Situational questions* ask applicants how they would respond in a hypothetical situation (e.g., "What would you do if...?").
- *Behavioural questions* ask applicants what they did in previous jobs that were similar to the job for which they are applying (e.g., "In your previous jobs, can you tell me about...?").
- *Background questions* ask applicants about their work experience, education, and other qualifications (e.g., "Tell me about the training you received at...").
- *Job-knowledge questions* ask applicants to demonstrate their job knowledge (e.g., for nurses, "Give me an example of a time in which one of your patients had a severe reaction to a medication. How did you handle it?").

Always ask open-ended questions, not closed-ended questions that can be answered with a "yes" or a "no." The point of the interview is to get applicants to talk about themselves, so that you can make a good hiring decision. Also, make sure your questions are job related. Finally, remember that if you were actually using this interview to hire college instructors, every person interviewing for the job would be asked these 12 questions. So try to pick questions that would help you differentiate good instructors from bad instructors. For example, asking candidates where they received their Ph.D., which is a research degree, would probably not help you determine which candidates are most qualified to teach.

Assignment

Write three questions of each type (situational, behavioural, background, and job-knowledge) that you would like to ask someone who wanted to teach at your university.

Management Decisions

Job Analysis

Job analysis is a foundation for many of the HRM subsystems. Even though you may never have to actually conduct a job analysis and write job descriptions, you should be familiar with the process to better understand how to use this information in selection decisions. Pick a relatively simple job that you can observe without interrupting the employee. You should observe this job at least twice at different times (e.g., once in the morning and once in the afternoon) for approximately 30 minutes each time. The goal is to observe a representative performance of this job.

Copy or recreate the form below and use it to perform a job analysis of this job. Remember, your goal is to identify the most important activities, responsibilities, and duties, as well as any special equipment or tools that are used or any significant customer/client/co-worker contact. If you are working in teams, have two or three team members observe the same job. When you've finished, write a job description and job specifications for this job.

On the job analysis form below, the column headings stand for I = Importance of the activity, T = Time spent performing the activity (e.g., percentage of each day on average), and D = Difficulty of this activity. Use the following rating scales for these factors:

Importance of Activity
1 Very Unimportant
2 Slightly Unimportant
3 Slightly Important
4 Fairly Important
5 Very Important

Time Spent on Average
1 0–19% of each day
2 20–39% of each day
3 40–59% of each day
4 60–79% of each day
5 80–100% of each day

Difficulty of Activity
1 Extremely Easy
2 Fairly Easy
3 Average Difficulty
4 Above Average Difficulty
5 High Difficulty

After rating each activity, add the scores in each column and the total score. These scores can be used to compare relative values of different jobs to the company. If you are working in teams, average the scores from your group members to come up with a total for the job.

Activity	*I*	*T*	*D*	*I+T+D*
_____	__	__	__	_____
_____	__	__	__	_____
_____	__	__	__	_____
_____	__	__	__	_____
_____	__	__	__	_____
_____	__	__	__	_____
_____	__	__	__	_____
_____	__	__	__	_____
_____	__	__	__	_____
_____	__	__	__	_____
_____	__	__	__	_____
_____	__	__	__	_____
_____	__	__	__	_____
_____	__	__	__	_____

TOTAL _____

Job Description:

Job Specifications:

Develop Your Management Potential

360-Degree Feedback

While most performance appraisal ratings have traditionally come from just one person, the boss, 360-degree feedback is obtained from four sources: the boss, subordinates, peers and co-workers, and the employees themselves. In this assignment, you will be gathering 360-degree feedback from people whom you work with or from a team or group that you're a member of for a class.

Here are some guidelines for obtaining your 360-degree feedback:

- *Carefully select respondents.* One of the keys to good 360-degree feedback is getting feedback from the right people. In general, the people you ask for feedback should interact with you on a regular basis and have the chance to regularly observe your behaviour. Also be sure to get a representative sample of opinions from a similar number of co-workers and subordinates (assuming you have some).
- *Get a large enough number of responses.* Except for the boss, you should have a minimum of three respondents to give you feedback in each category (peers and subordinates). Five or six respondents per category is even better.
- *Ensure confidentiality.* Respondents are much more likely to be honest if they know that their comments are confidential and anonymous. So when you ask respondents for feedback, have them return their comments to someone other than yourself. Have this person, we'll call the person your feedback facilitator, remove the names and any other information that would identify who made particular comments.
- *Explain how the 360-degree feedback will be used.* In this case, explain that the feedback is for a class assignment, that the results will be used for your own personal growth and development, and that the feedback they give you will not affect your grade or formal assessment at work.
- *Ask them to make their feedback as specific as possible.* For instance, writing "bad attitude" isn't very good feedback.

360-Degree Feedback Form

As part of a class assignment, I, _____, am collecting feedback from you about my performance. What you say or write will not affect my grade. The purpose of this assignment is for me to receive honest feedback from the people I work with in order to identify the things I'm doing well and the things upon which I need to improve. So please be honest and direct in your evaluation.

When you have completed this feedback form, please return it to _____. S/he has been selected as my feedback facilitator and is responsible for ensuring that your confidentiality and anonymity are maintained. After all feedback forms have been returned to _____, s/he will make sure that your particular responses cannot be identified. Only then will the feedback be shared with me.

Please provide the following feedback.

Continue doing...
Describe 3 things that _____ is doing that are a positive part of his/her performance and that you want him/her to continue doing.

1.

2.

3.

Start doing...
Describe 3 things that _____ needs to start doing that would significantly improve his/her performance.

1.

2.

3.

Please make your feedback as specific and behavioural as possible. For instance, writing "needs to adjust attitude" isn't very good feedback. However, writing "needs to begin listening to others' suggestions" is much better feedback because the group member now knows exactly what behaviour should change. So please be specific. Also please write more than one sentence per comment. This will help feedback recipients better understand your comments.

However, writing "won't listen to others' suggestions" is much better feedback, because it would let you know how to improve your behaviour. Have your respondents use the feedback form shown below to provide your feedback.

Here's what you need to turn in for this assignment:

1. The names and relationships (boss, peers, subordinates, classmates, teammates) of those you've asked for feedback.
2. The name of the person you've asked to be your feedback facilitator.
3. Copies of all written feedback that was returned to you.
4. A one-page summary of the written feedback.
5. A one-page plan in which you describe specific goals and action plans for responding to the feedback you received.

Discussion Questions

1. What role does job analysis play in recruiting and selection?
2. What type of recruiting strategies can be undertaken to attract workers when qualified workers are in short supply?
3. What are the advantages and disadvantages of internal recruiting? What are the advantages and disadvantages of external recruiting?
4. What are the advantages of having employees access personal information from a company's human resource information system? Are there any disadvantages?
5. What are the advantages and disadvantages of 360-degree feedback?

Study Tip

Use the chapter outline on page 390 as a study tool. After reading the whole chapter, return to the list and write a summary for each learning objective. Check your work by reading the actual review paragraphs on pages 397, 402, 406, 413, 418, 422, 425, and 428.

14

Chapter Outline

Learning Objectives

After reading this chapter, you should be able to

1. discuss the kinds of productivity and their importance in managing operations.
2. explain the role that quality plays in managing operations.
3. explain the essentials of managing a service business.
4. describe the different kinds of manufacturing operations.
5. describe why and how companies should manage inventory levels.

CP (Kevin Frayer)

Managing Service and Manufacturing Operations

What Would You Do?

It's 6:00 a.m. on Friday morning. Phone calls from unhappy *Newsday* (www.newsday.com) subscribers are already rolling into the circulation department. *Newsday* is the leading newspaper on Long Island, and the eighth-largest newspaper in the United States. Callers are complaining, "I just went out in the cold to get my newspaper from the driveway, and it doesn't have all the sports scores!" "I wanted to read about the Rangers–Maple Leafs hockey game, and all you've got is the score through the second period! Who cares about that? I want to know who won the game and why!"

Newspapers like *Newsday* get complaints like this every time a sports game runs late. In fact, newspapers get complaints whenever a late-breaking story of any kind doesn't appear in the morning edition of the newspaper. When subscribers trudge out to their mailboxes for the newspaper or people pick one up at a newsstand on their way to work, they want it to include the latest news stories and updates. However, to get out a daily paper, news stories usually have to be finalized and filed between 9:00 and 11:00 p.m. the night before the paper ends up in readers' hands. It's a limitation that all newspapers face. At some point, you've got to quit covering new stories

and go with the stories you've got. After all, if you waited for all the late stories to come in, you wouldn't be able to get the paper printed and delivered in time for the morning rush hour, which begins when commuters start their morning around 5:30 a.m.

However, the problem for *Newsday* is that it competes in one of the most competitive newspaper markets in the United States. To understand *Newsday*'s predicament, imagine that it is a competitor in the Toronto market. Think of *Newsday* in relation to the *Toronto Sun*. If the *Toronto Sun* doesn't run the latest sports scores and stories, readers may turn to the *Globe and Mail*, the *National Post*, or the *Toronto Star* instead. Even worse, in this age of instant news, potential newspaper readers may decide that they don't need to buy an edition of the *Toronto Sun* at all. With 24-hour TV news channels such as CBC Newsworld and CTV Newsnet, 24-hour TV sports and sports news channels such as TSN or RDSI, and instantly updated websites for news (www.canoe.ca, www.cbc.ca, www.canada.com, www.bbc.co.uk) and sports (www.tsn.ca; www.rds.ca), why pay for a newspaper? Especially if it doesn't have the news you want. This is the situation *Newsday* faces, only it has even more competitors, which include the likes of the *New York Times*, the *New York Post*, and CNN.

The production of a daily newspaper begins when section editors (e.g., sports, lifestyle, politics) and writers decide what stories to cover and approximately how long those stories should be. Writers then conduct their interviews, check their facts, and write the stories. Layout editors manage the overall look and layout on each page, arranging the advertisements, pictures, and the amount of copy space for articles. Copy editors then edit the stories, double-check facts, rearrange paragraphs, and make sure that stories fit in the allotted layout space. Once pages are completed or "closed," they're sent to the printers, who pull the advertisements, pictures, headlines, and stories together to form each page. When all pages have been "assembled," press operators run the giant printing presses that churn out hundreds of thousands of newspapers per day. Additional machines cut, fold, and bind the newspapers into bundles, which are then loaded onto trucks that drive out to delivery points to drop off the bundles to the carriers, who deliver individual copies of newspapers to subscribers' doorsteps, driveways, and mailboxes.

Given the production process described above, how can *Newsday* change its writing, editing, production, printing, and delivery processes to include as many late-breaking stories as possible but still deliver newspapers by 5:30 each morning? In other words, how can *Newsday* become more productive during each 24-hour news cycle? While productivity is important to companies, quality is what matters to customers. What can *Newsday* do to improve quality for customers while increasing productivity for itself? As it makes these changes, what should *Newsday*'s goals be with respect to this production process? Should it focus on speed or flexibility? Finally, if you think of news stories as unfinished inventory, what techniques for managing inventory might *Newsday* use to address these problems?

If you were the publishing editor in charge of *Newsday*, what would you do?

Sources: F. Ahrens, "The Washington Post: One Day in the Life," *The Washington Post*, 11 February 1998. G.B. Knecht, "Newsday Changes Playbook to Offer Later Sports Scores," *The Wall Street Journal Interactive Edition*, 12 March 1997.

The problems that *Newsday* faces in publishing a daily paper are not unique to the newspaper business. Airlines, auto manufacturers, hospitals, restaurants, and many other kinds of businesses also struggle to find ways to efficiently produce quality products and services and then deliver them in a timely manner.

In this chapter, you will learn about **operations management**—managing the daily production of goods and services. You will begin by learning about the basics of operations management: productivity and quality. Next, you will read about managing operations, beginning with service operations, turning next to manufacturing operations, and finishing with an examination of the types, measures, costs, and methods for managing inventory.

operations management
managing the daily production of goods and services

Managing for Productivity and Quality

Brothers Hank and Bucky Kashiwa started Volant, Inc., a manufacturer of skis and snowboards. Combining Hank's experience as an Olympic and professional skier and Bucky's Ph.D. in fluid mechanics, the Kashiwas designed a less expensive, more stable, easier-to-turn ski. In contrast to standard skis made of a composite of several materials layered atop each other, the top and sides of Volant skis were made from a single sheet of steel. Ski shops and customers loved the skis, and sales soared. However, despite their superior design and performance, Volant's skis literally started falling apart on the slopes soon after skiers started using them. The company finally fixed this problem, but because of other problems with quality control in its manufacturing facility, it still had to throw away more than 40 percent of the skis it was producing! This led to sky-high costs and an inability to ship product orders on time. So, even though sales were taking off, productivity and quality levels were so bad that Volant was losing money on every pair of skis it sold.[1]

The Kashiwas eventually solved Volant's problems by hiring a manufacturing consultant, who taught company managers and employees how to improve the quality of their products and the productivity of their factory. Today, Volant skis don't fall apart on the slopes, the company ships orders early, and Volant is profitable for the first time in its history.

EXPERIENCING MANAGEMENT

Learn more about productivity and quality indicators by interacting with them at our animated concept and activity site. Choose Operations Management from the "select a topic" pull-down menu, then Operations Management Objectives from the "overview tab."

www.experiencingmanagement.com

After reading the next two sections, you should be able to
1. discuss the kinds of productivity and their importance in managing operations.
2. explain the role that quality plays in managing operations.

1. Productivity

productivity
a measure of performance that indicates how many inputs it takes to produce or create an output

At their core, organizations are production systems. Companies combine inputs, such as labour, raw materials, capital, and knowledge, to produce outputs in the form of finished products or services. **Productivity** is a measure of performance that indicates how many inputs it takes to produce or create an output.

$$Productivity = \frac{Outputs}{Inputs}$$

The fewer inputs it takes to create an output (or the greater the output from one input), the higher the productivity. For example, a car's gas consumption is a common measure of productivity. A car that gets 25 kilometres (output) per litre (input) is more productive and fuel efficient than a car that gets 12 kilometres per litre.

Let's examine why productivity matters and kinds of productivity.

1.1 Why Productivity Matters

Why does productivity matter? For companies, higher productivity, that is, doing more with less, results in lower costs. In turn, lower costs can lead to lower prices, higher market share, and higher profits. For countries, productivity matters because it produces a higher standard of living. One way productivity leads to a higher standard of living is through increased wages. When companies can do more with less, they can raise employee wages without increasing prices or sacrificing normal profits. For example, because a Motorola (www.motorola.com) plant makes 200 percent more pagers now with only 22 percent more employees, it can give those employees better benefits and wages and still make good profits. Being able to offer higher wages also helps the company by attracting and retaining good workers.

Rising income stemming from increased productivity creates numerous other benefits. For example, during the productive 1980s, charitable giving increased 5.1 percent per year, compared to an average of 3.5 percent per year during the previous 25 years.

Another way that productivity increases the standard of living is by making products more affordable. For example, while inflation has pushed the average cost of a car to more than $20 000, increases in productivity have actually made cars cheaper. In 1960, the average family needed 26 weeks of income to pay for the average car. Today, the average family needs only 23 weeks of income—and today's car is loaded with accessories, such as airbags, power steering and brakes, power windows, cruise control, stereo/CD players, and air conditioning, features that weren't even available in 1960.[2] So, in terms of real purchasing power, productivity gains have actually made the $20 000 car of today cheaper than the $2000 car of 1960.

1.2 Kinds of Productivity

Two common measures of productivity are partial productivity and multifactor productivity. **Partial productivity** indicates how much of a particular kind of input it takes to produce an output.

$$Partial\ Productivity = \frac{Outputs}{Single\ Kind\ of\ Input}$$

Labour is one kind of input that is frequently used when determining partial productivity. Labour productivity typically indicates the cost or number of hours of labour it takes to produce an output. In other words, the smaller the cost of the labour to produce a unit of output, or the less time it takes to produce a unit of output, the higher the labour productivity. For example, the automobile industry often measures labour productivity by determining the average number of hours of labour it takes to completely assemble a car. The three most productive auto manufacturers can assemble a car with 31 or fewer hours of labour. Nissan (www.nissan.com) assembles a car in only 27 hours of labour. Toyota (www.toyota.com) does it in 29 hours, and Honda (www.honda.com) assembles a car in 31 hours. By comparison, Nissan, Toyota, and Honda have much

PERSONAL PRODUCTIVITY TIP

Tracking Your Personal Productivity

Are you productive at work, or are you a time waster? Chances are, you'd be shocked at how much time you really waste. The first step to improved personal productivity is to keep a detailed time log of daily activities, including your time wasters. Keeping time logs can be tedious, but today, computer shareware makes them easier. To download time log software, go to CNet's Download.com, www.download.com, and search for the keyword "time log." You'll find a number of software titles that can help you track your time and improve your personal productivity. Most are free to try but then available for a fee.

Source: S. Vaught, "Time Savers Are Lifesaver for Harried Workers," *Los Angeles Times*, 1 April 2001, W1.

partial productivity
a measure of performance that indicates how much of a particular kind of input it takes to produce an output

higher labour productivity than Ford, which needs 38 hours of labour to assemble a car, or Chrysler, which needs 43 hours, or General Motors, which needs 46.[3] In terms of labour costs, this means that Nissan pays $1332 less for labour per car than does Ford. In turn, Ford pays $507 less for labour per car than does General Motors.[4]

Partial productivity assesses how efficiently companies use only one input, such as labour, when creating outputs. **Multifactor productivity** is an overall measure of productivity that assesses how efficiently companies use all the inputs it takes to make outputs. More specifically, multifactor productivity indicates how much labour, capital, materials, and energy it takes to produce an output.[5]

multifactor productivity
an overall measure of performance that indicates how much labour, capital, materials, and energy it takes to produce an output

$$\text{Multifactor Productivity} = \frac{\text{Outputs}}{\text{Labour + Capital + Materials + Energy}}$$

Exhibit 14.1 shows the trends in multifactor productivity across a number of different U.S. industries since 1987. With a six-fold increase (from the starting point scaled at 100 in 1987 to a productivity level of 631 in 1999), the growth in multifactor productivity in the electronics components and accessories industry far exceeded the productivity growth in the railroad, cement, beverage, and paint products industries, as well as most other industries tracked. On the other hand, multifactor productivity growth in Canada's business sector in 2002 of 1.9 percent was six times the pace of growth compared to 0.3 percent in 2001. Only productivity growth of 2.3 percent in both 1999 and 2000 was better. For most of the 1980s and 1990s Canadian multi-factor productivity growth trailed that of the United States. Only in 2001 was this trend reversed, with Canadian performance ahead of that in the United States.[6]

EXHIBIT 14.1

MULTIFACTOR PRODUCTIVITY GROWTH ACROSS INDUSTRIES

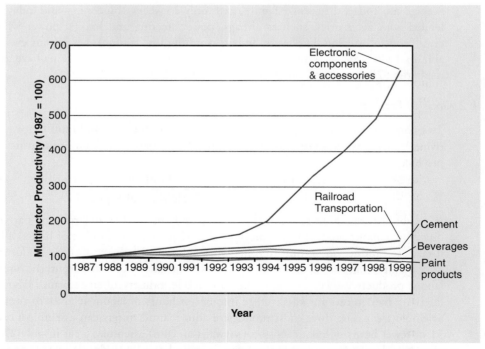

Source: "Industry Multifactor Productivity Indexes (1987=100)," Bureau of Labor Statistics. [Online] Available ftp://ftp.bls.gov/put/special.requests/opt/dipts/indmfp2.txt, 21 February 2002.

Should managers use multiple or partial productivity measures? In general, they should use both. Multifactor productivity indicates a company's overall level of productivity relative to its competitors. In the end, that's what counts most. However, multifactor productivity measures don't indicate the specific contributions that labour, capital, materials, or energy make to overall productivity. To analyze the contributions of these individual components, managers need to use partial productivity measures.

Review 1
Productivity

At their core, companies are production systems that combine inputs, such as labour, raw materials, capital, and knowledge, to produce outputs, such as finished products or services. Productivity is a measure of how many inputs it takes to produce or create an output. The greater the output from one input, or the fewer inputs it takes to create an output, the higher the productivity. Partial productivity measures how much of a single kind of input, such as labour, is needed to produce an output. Multifactor productivity is an overall measure of productivity that indicates how much labour, capital, materials, and energy are needed to produce an output. Increased productivity helps companies lower costs, which can lead to lower prices, higher market share, and higher profits. Increased productivity helps countries by leading to higher wages, lower product prices, and a higher standard of living.

2. Quality

With the average car costing more than $20 000, car buyers want to make sure that they're getting good quality for their money. Fortunately, as indicated by the number of problems per 100 cars (PP100), today's cars are of much higher quality than earlier models. In 1981, Japanese cars averaged 240 PP100. GM (www.gm.com) averaged 670, Ford (www.ford.com), averaged 740, and Chrysler (www.daimlerchrysler.com) averaged 870 PP100! In other words, as measured by PP100, the quality of American cars was three to four times worse than Japanese cars. However, by 1992, U.S. car makers had made great strides, reducing the number of problems to 155 PP100. Japanese vehicles had improved, too, averaging just 125 PP100. By 1997, overall car quality had improved so much that the average number of problems for all kinds of cars was just 100 PP100. In fact, after three months of ownership, half of new car buyers report no problems whatsoever with their cars![7]

The American Society for Quality gives two meanings for **quality**. First, it can mean a product or service free of deficiencies, such as the number of problems per 100 cars. Consumer products that are not free of deficiencies are often not too difficult to spot. They are frequently recalled from the market by government regulators in Canada and the United States. Listings of such products may be found on the websites of the CBC consumer show *Marketplace*, www.cbc.ca, and the U.S. Consumer Product Safety Commission, www.cpsc.gov. Second, quality can mean the characteristics of a product or service that satisfy customer needs.[8] In this sense, today's cars are of higher quality because of the additional standard features (power brakes and steering, stereo/CD player, power windows and locks, rear defrosters, cruise control, etc.) they have compared to 20 years ago.

In this part of the chapter, you will learn about quality-related product characteristics, quality-related service characteristics, ISO 9000, and total quality management.

2.1 Quality-Related Product Characteristics

Quality products usually possess three characteristics: reliability, serviceability, and durability.[9] A breakdown occurs when a product quits working or doesn't do what it was designed to do. The longer it takes for a product to break down, or the longer the time between breakdowns, the more reliable the product. Consequently, many companies define product reliability by the average time between breakdowns.

quality
a product or service free of deficiencies, or the characteristics of product or service that satisfy customer needs

Serviceability refers to how easy or difficult it is to fix a product. The easier it is to maintain a working product or fix a broken product, the more serviceable that product is. For example, Ford redesigned its cars to make them easier for mechanics to fix and owners to maintain. On the Ford Escort and Mercury Tracer, if a bulb burns out in the dashboard, the entire instrument cluster (gauges and speedometer) can be accessed by removing a few simple screws. This process now takes minutes instead of hours. Likewise, a two-piece bracket now holds the car's alternator in a spot that is easy for mechanics to reach. Before, mechanics had to empty and remove the car's radiator to reach the alternator.[10]

A product breakdown assumes that a product can be repaired. However, some products don't break down—they fail. Product failure means these products can't be repaired. They can only be replaced. Thus, durability is a quality characteristic that applies to products that can't be repaired. Durability is defined as the mean time to failure. For example, most household light bulbs have an estimated time to failure of between 750 and 1000 hours. By contrast, the durability of fluorescent light bulbs is as long as 10 000 hours.[11]

2.2 Quality-Related Service Characteristics

Reliability, serviceability, and durability characterize high-quality products. However, services and products are different. With services, there's no point in assessing durability. Unlike products, services don't last. Services are consumed the minute they're performed. For example, once a lawn service has mowed your lawn, the job is done until the mowers come back next week to do it again. Likewise, services don't have serviceability. You can't maintain or fix a service. If a service wasn't performed correctly, all you can do is perform the service again. Finally, the quality of service interactions often depends on how the service provider interacts with the customer. Was the service provider friendly, rude, or helpful? Consequently, five characteristics—reliability, tangibles, responsiveness, assurance, and empathy—typically distinguish a quality service.[12]

Service reliability is the ability to consistently perform a service well. Studies clearly show that reliability matters more to customers than anything else when buying services. Also, while services themselves are not tangible (you can't see or touch them), services are provided in tangible places. Thus, tangibles refer to the appearance of the offices, equipment, and personnel involved with the delivery of a service. Responsiveness is the promptness and willingness with which service providers give good service. Assurance is the confidence that service providers are knowledgeable, courteous, and can be trusted. Empathy is the extent to which service providers give individual attention and care to customers' concerns and problems.

Newark International Airport (www.panynj.gov/aviation/ewrframe.HTM) is a good example of quality service. Many Canadians may recognize it as Air Canada (www.aircanada.com) flies into and out of this airport. If you're thinking to yourself, "Newark Airport and quality?" you're not alone. In the past, Newark was known for dirty terminals, auto theft, and delayed departures and arrivals. However, in the last few years, Newark has improved the quality of the services it provides to the airlines and passengers that use it.[13] For example, with respect to reliability, both flight delays and auto thefts have been greatly reduced. As a result, passenger traffic has increased 32 percent in the last six years.

With respect to tangibles, Newark is much cleaner than it used to be. Standards were set and enforced for the cleanliness of the parking lots and the terminals. Airport manager Benjamin Decosta said, "My philosophy is that if the place appears to be well managed, people looking to break the rules will go elsewhere."

As part of improved responsiveness, Decosta holds monthly meetings with Newark's airlines, giving them a say on things ranging from snow removal to police staffing. Decosta even asks the airlines how he should spend the airport's money.

To improve assurance, Decosta launched a customer-service training program to instill a "customer-first orientation." The mission, now embossed on all airport employees' caps, is "to be the best by putting the customer first."

Decosta also found ways to improve empathy in the airport's service. Continental Airlines had long sought space in a building used by airport management. This building overlooked Newark's tarmac, where planes sit before heading to and from the runways. From this location, Continental could direct its own ground traffic and more easily prevent ground delays, such as a jumbo jet sitting at a gate where its size prevents other planes from getting to and from their terminals. Previously, this request had been denied, because airport managers would have to give up the great view in their cafeteria. Decosta quickly approved the change after taking charge of the airport, deeming Continental's needs much more important than his managers'.[14]

2.3 ISO 9000

ISO, pronounced ice-o, comes from the Greek word *isos*, meaning equal, similar, alike, or identical. Thus, **ISO 9000** is a series of five international standards, from ISO 9000 to ISO 9004, for achieving consistency in quality management and quality assurance in companies throughout the world. The ISO 9000 standards were created by the International Organization for Standards (www.iso.org), which is an international agency that helps set standards for 91 countries. The purpose of this agency is to develop and publish standards that facilitate the international exchange of goods and services.[15]

The ISO 9000 standards publications are general and can be used for manufacturing any kind of product or delivering any kind of service. Importantly, the ISO 9000 standards don't describe how to make a better quality car, computer, or widget. Instead, they describe how companies can extensively document (and thus standardize) the steps they take to create and improve the quality of their products.

Why should companies go to the trouble to achieve ISO 9000 certification? Because, increasingly, their customers want them to. Indeed, DuPont, General Electric, Eastman Kodak, British Telecom, and Philips Electronics are some of the Fortune 500 companies that are telling their suppliers to achieve ISO 9000 certification. John Yates, GE's general manager of global sourcing, said, "There is absolutely no negotiation. If you want to work with us, you have to get it."[16] Are these companies listening? If Toronto-based electronics manufacturing service company Celestica Inc. is a good example, then yes, they are listening. Among the many services that it offers, Celestica manufactures products for other companies on a contract basis. An April 2003 glance at its website, www.celestica.com, suggests that fully 36 of its 38 global manufacturing facilities are ISO 9000 compliant with two others meeting ISO 9002 standards.

Typically, "getting" ISO 9000 means having your company certified for ISO 9000 registration by an accredited third party. The process is similar to having a certified accountant indicate that a company's financial accounts are up-to-date and accurate. But in this case, the certification is for quality, not accounting procedures. To become certified, a process that can take months to prepare for, companies must show that they are following their own procedures for improving production, updating design plans and specifications, keeping machinery in top condition, educating and training workers, and satisfactorily dealing with customer complaints.[17]

Once a company has been certified as ISO 9000 compliant, the accredited third party will issue an ISO 9000 certificate that the company can use in its advertising and publications. This is the quality equivalent of the "Good Housekeeping Seal of Approval." However, ISO 9000 certification is not guaranteed. Accredited third parties typically conduct periodic audits to make sure quality procedures continue to be followed. Companies that don't follow their quality systems have their certifications suspended or cancelled.

ISO 9000
a series of five international standards, from ISO 9000 to ISO 9004, for achieving consistency in quality management and quality assurance in companies throughout the world

In Canada, the National Quality Institute (www.nqi.ca) recognizes exceptional quality-related performance by private- and public-sector organizations. It offers the *Canada Awards for Excellence* to Canadian companies who meet the criteria for demonstrating outstanding achievement across major functions of the organization. Recent award winners have included the Cardiac Care Network of Ontario, Diversicare Canada Management Services Co., Dana Canada Inc., and the Gleneagle Elementary School of West Vancouver.[18]

2.4 Total Quality Management

Total quality management (TQM) is an integrated organization-wide strategy for improving product and service quality. TQM is not a specific tool or technique. Rather, TQM is a philosophy or overall approach to management that is characterized by three principles: customer focus and satisfaction, continuous improvement, and teamwork.[19]

Contrary to most economists, accountants, and financiers, who argue that companies exist to earn profits for shareholders, TQM suggests that customer focus and customer satisfaction should be a company's primary goals. **Customer focus** means the entire organization, from top to bottom, should be focused on meeting customers' needs. **Customer satisfaction** is an organizational goal to make products or deliver services that meet or exceed customers' expectations. And at companies where TQM is taken seriously, such as Cisco Systems (www.ciscosystems.com), a leading provider of the routers used to run the Internet, paycheques depend on keeping customers satisfied. For example, Cisco surveys clients each year about 60 different performance criteria. CEO John Chambers said, "If a manager improves his [customer satisfaction] scores, he can get a fair amount [of a financial bonus]. But if the scores go down, we'll take money out of the manager's pocket."[20] Not surprisingly, this emphasis on quality increased the number of completely satisfied Cisco customers from 81 percent to 85 percent in just one year.

Continuous improvement is an ongoing commitment to increase product and service quality by constantly assessing and improving the processes and procedures used to create those products and services. How do companies know whether they're achieving continuous improvement? Besides higher customer satisfaction, continuous improvement is usually associated with a reduction in variation. **Variation** is a deviation in the form, condition, or appearance of a product from the quality standard for that product. The less a product varies from the quality standard, or the more consistently a company's products meet a quality standard, the higher the quality.

The third principle of TQM is teamwork. **Teamwork** means collaboration between managers and nonmanagers, across business functions, and between the company and its customers and suppliers. In short, quality improves when everyone in the company is given the incentive to work together and the responsibility and authority to make improvements and solve problems. For example, Johnson Controls (www.johnsoncontrols.com) manufactures and sells auto parts in Canada and throughout the world. At one of its factories, 230 workers provided 631 suggestions last year for improving how the plant is run. In particular, one employee, Jason Moncer, came up with 30 different suggestions. Moncer, who said, "I go on sprees," is now trying to figure out how best to organize the metal parts that are used to make car seats.[21]

Together, customer focus and satisfaction, continuous improvement, and teamwork mutually reinforce each other to improve quality throughout a company. Customer-focused continuous improvement is necessary to increase customer satisfaction. However, continuous improvement depends on teamwork from different functional and hierarchical parts of the company.

total quality management (TQM)
an integrated, principle-based, organization-wide strategy for improving product and service quality

customer focus
an organizational goal to concentrate on meeting customers' needs at all levels of the organization

customer satisfaction
an organizational goal to provide products or services that meet or exceed customers' expectations

continuous improvement
an organization's ongoing commitment to constantly assess and improve the processes and procedures used to create products and services

variation
a deviation in the form, condition, or appearance of a product from the quality standard for that product

teamwork
collaboration between managers and nonmanagers, across business functions, and between the companies, customers, and suppliers

EXPERIENCING MANAGEMENT

Learn more about the three principles of TQM at our animated concept and activity site. Choose Operations Management from the "select a topic" pull-down menu, then Total Quality Management from the "overview tab."

www.experiencingmanagement.com

Quality can mean a product or service free of deficiencies or the characteristics of a product or service that satisfy customer needs. Quality products usually possess three characteristics: reliability, serviceability, and durability. Quality service means reliability, tangibles, responsiveness, assurance, and empathy. ISO 9000 is a series of five international standards for achieving consistency in quality management and quality assurance. The ISO 9000 standards can be used for any product or service, because they ensure that companies carefully document the steps they take to create and improve quality. ISO 9000 certification is awarded following a quality audit from an accredited third party. Total quality management (TQM) is an integrated organization-wide strategy for improving product and service quality. TQM is based on three mutually reinforcing principles: customer focus and satisfaction, continuous improvement, and teamwork.

Managing Operations

At the start of this chapter, you learned that operations management means managing the daily production of goods and services. Then you learned that to manage production, you must oversee the factors that affect productivity and quality. In this half of the chapter, you will learn about managing operations in service and manufacturing businesses. The chapter ends with a discussion of inventory management, a key factor in a company's profitability.

After reading the next three sections, you should be able to
3. *explain the essentials of managing a service business.*
4. *describe the different kinds of manufacturing operations.*
5. *describe why and how companies should manage inventory levels.*

3. Service Operations

Imagine that your trusty five-year-old VCR breaks down as you try to record your favourite TV show. You've got two choices. You can run to Wal-Mart or Zellers and spend about $120 to purchase a new VCR. Or you can spend somewhere between $50 and $100 (you hope) to have it fixed at a repair shop. With either choice, you end up with the same thing, a working VCR. However, the first choice, getting a new VCR, involves buying a physical product (a "good"), while the second, dealing with a repair shop, involves buying a service.

Services are different from goods in several ways. First, goods are produced or made, but services are performed. In other words, services are almost always labour intensive. Someone typically has to perform the service for you. A repair shop could give you the parts needed to repair your old VCR, but without the technician to perform the repairs, you're still going to have a broken VCR. Second, goods are tangible, but services are intangible. You can touch and see that new VCR from Zellers (www. hbc.com/zellers). But you can't touch or see the service provided by the technician who fixed your old VCR. All you can "see" is that the VCR works. Third, services are perishable and unstorable. If you don't use them when they're available, they're wasted. For example, if your VCR repair shop is backlogged on repair jobs, you'll just have to wait until next week to get your VCR repaired. You can't store an unused service and use it when you like. By contrast, you can purchase a good, such as motor oil, and store it until you're ready to use it.

Because services are different from goods, managing a service operation is different from managing a manufacturing or production operation. Let's look at the service-profit chain, and service recovery and empowerment.

3.1 The Service-Profit Chain

One of the key assumptions in the service business is that success depends on how well employees, that is, service providers, deliver their services to customers. However, the concept of the service-profit chain, depicted in Exhibit 14.2, suggests that in service businesses, success begins with how well management treats service employees.[22]

The first step in the service-profit chain is internal service quality, meaning the quality of treatment that employees receive from a company's internal service providers, such as management, payroll and benefits, and human resources.

EXHIBIT 14.2

SERVICE-PROFIT CHAIN

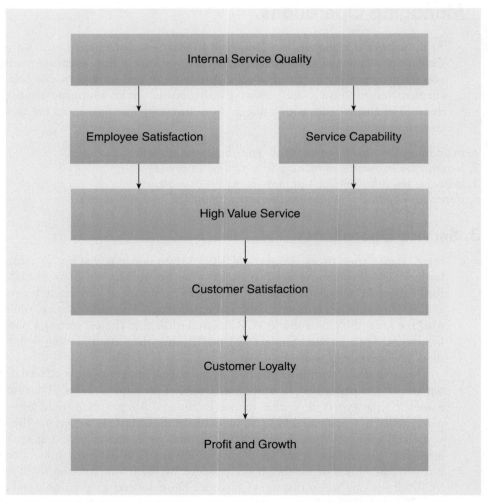

Sources: R. Hallowell, L.A. Schlesinger, & J. Zornitsky, "Internal Service Quality, Customer and Job Satisfaction: Linkages and Implications for Management," *Human Resource Planning* 19 (1996): 20–31. J.L. Heskett, T.O. Jones, G.W. Loveman, W.E. Sasser, Jr., & L.A. Schlesinger, "Putting the Service-Profit Chain to Work," , March-April 1994, 164–174.

As depicted in Exhibit 14.2, good internal service leads to employee satisfaction and service capability. Employee satisfaction occurs when companies treat employees in a way that meets or exceeds their expectations. In other words, the better employees are treated, the more satisfied they are, and the more likely they are to give high-value service to satisfy customers.

Service capability is an employee's perception of his or her ability to serve customers well. When an organization serves its employees in ways that help them to do their jobs well, employees, in turn, are more likely to believe that they can and ought to provide high-value service to customers.

Finally, according to the service-profit chain shown in Exhibit 14.2, high-value service leads to customer satisfaction and customer loyalty, which, in turn, lead to long-term profits and growth. What's the link between customer satisfaction and loyalty and profits? To start, the average business keeps only 70 percent to 90 percent of its existing customers each year. No big deal, you say? Just replace leaving customers with new customers. Well, there's one significant problem with that solution. It costs five times as much to find a new customer as it does to keep an existing customer. Also, new customers typically buy only 20 percent as much as established customers. In fact, keeping existing customers is so cost-effective that most businesses could double their profits by simply keeping 5 percent more customers per year![23]

3.2 Service Recovery and Empowerment

Many service businesses organize themselves like manufacturing companies. Tasks and jobs are simplified and separated, creating a clear division of labour. Equipment and technology are substituted for people whenever possible. Strict guidelines and rules take the place of employee authority and discretion. This production-line approach to running a service business is still widely used today in businesses that sell a high-volume, low-cost service in which there is a brief, simple transaction between customers and service providers.[24]

While the production-line model excels at efficiency and low costs, it doesn't work well when mistakes are made and customers have become dissatisfied with the service they've received. When this occurs, service businesses must switch from the process of service delivery to the process of **service recovery**, that is, restoring customer satisfaction to strongly dissatisfied customers.[25] Sometimes, service recovery requires service employees to not only fix whatever mistake was made, but also perform "heroic" service acts that "delight" highly dissatisfied customers by far surpassing their expectations of fair treatment. For example, at Delta Hotels (www.deltahotels.com), if a guest tells a member of the housecleaning staff that there were no towels in the room, that guest will not only receive fresh towels as quickly as possible, but may also receive a complimentary fruit basket. Likewise, if guests complain that they were mistakenly given a room reserved for smokers, the front desk will transfer them to a nonsmoking room and may also arrange for a free night's stay to make up for the inconvenience.[26] In both instances, Delta Hotel's service employees fixed the original problem and then performed service recovery by surpassing guests' expectations with an additional act meant to make up for the poor service.

Unfortunately, when mistakes occur under a production-line system, service employees typically don't have the discretion to resolve customer complaints. Customers who want service employees to correct or make up for poor service are frequently told, "I'm not allowed to do that," "I'm just following company rules," or "I'm sorry, only managers are allowed to make changes of any kind." In other words, the production-line system prevents them from engaging in acts of service recovery meant to turn dissatisfied customers back into satisfied customers. The result is frustration for customers and service employees and lost customers for the company.

service recovery
restoring customer satisfaction to strongly dissatisfied customers

Because production-line systems make it difficult for service employees to do service recovery, many companies are now empowering their service employees.[27] In Chapter 10, you learned that empowering workers means permanently passing decision-making authority and responsibility from managers to workers. With respect to service recovery, empowering workers means giving service employees the authority and responsibility to make decisions that immediately solve customer problems.[28] For example, at Marriott Hotels (www.marriott.com), doormen like Tony Prsyszlak are now empowered to check in guests if lines are long or solve other problems that guests mention to him. Says Prsyszlak, "I'm a bellman, a doorman, a front-desk clerk, and a concierge all rolled into one. I have more responsibilities. I feel better about my job, and the guest gets better service."[29] In short, the purpose of empowering service employees is zero customer defections, that is, to turn dissatisfied customers back into satisfied customers who continue to do business with the company.

Empowering service workers does entail some costs. Exhibit 14.3 describes some costs and benefits of empowering service workers to act in ways that they believe will accomplish service recovery. The savings to the company of retaining customers usually exceed the costs of empowering workers.

Review 3
Service Operations

Services are different from goods. Goods are produced, tangible, and storable. Services are performed, intangible, and perishable. Likewise, managing service operations is different from managing production operations. The service-profit chain indicates that success begins with internal service quality, meaning how well management treats service employees. Internal service quality leads to employee satisfaction and service capability, which, in turn, lead to high-value service to customers, customer satisfaction, customer loyalty, and long-term profits and growth. Many service businesses are organized like manufacturers. While this "production-line" approach is efficient and inexpensive, its

---

EXHIBIT 14.3

COSTS AND BENEFITS OF EMPOWERING SERVICE WORKERS FOR SERVICE RECOVERY

BENEFITS

1. Quicker responses to customer complaints and problems.
2. Employees feel better about their jobs and themselves.
3. Employee interaction with customers will be warm and enthusiastic.
4. Employees are more likely to offer ideas for improving service or preventing problems.

COSTS OF EMPOWERING SERVICE WORKERS

1. Increased cost of selection to find service workers who are capable of solving problems and dealing with upset customers.
2. Increased cost to train service workers how to solve different kinds of problems.
3. Higher wages to attract and keep talented service workers.
4. A focus on service recovery may lead to less emphasis on service reliability, doing it right the first time. Ultimately, this could lead to slower delivery of services.
5. In their quest to please customers, empowered service workers may cost the company money by being too eager to provide "giveaways" to make up for poor or slow service.
6. Empowered service workers may unintentionally treat customers unfairly by occasionally being overly generous to make up for poor or slow service.

Source: D.E. Bowen & E.E. Lawler III, "The Empowerment of Service Workers: What, Why, How, and When," *Sloan Management Review* 33 (Spring 1992):31–39.

strict rules and guidelines make it difficult for service workers to perform service recovery, restoring customer satisfaction to strongly dissatisfied customers. To resolve this problem, some companies are empowering service employees to perform service recovery by giving them the authority and responsibility to immediately solve customer problems. The hope is that empowered service recovery will prevent customer defections.

4. Manufacturing Operations

Let's play word association. What do the words "Chicken and Stars," "Chicken Noodle," "Cream of Mushroom," and "Cream of Tomato" make you think of? Well, soup, of course! And, chances are, you thought of Campbell's soup (www. campbellsoup.com), the world's best-selling soup brand. In fact, Campbell's soup can be found in over 90 percent of North American households. While Campbell's effective "hmmm-mmmm good" advertisements bring to mind images of home cooking, Campbell's obviously doesn't make its soups in small kitchens. It makes them in large factories. One measures 1.4 million square feet and produces 4.9 million cans of soup per day! It alone can make over 200 different kinds of soup, as well as SpaghettiOs, pork and beans, and different kinds of gravy.

Like the Campbell's soup manufacturing plant described above, all manufacturing operations produce physical goods. But not all manufacturing operations are the same. Even those that produce food are often quite different.

Let's learn how various manufacturing operations differ in the amount of processing in manufacturing operations and in the flexibility of manufacturing operations.

4.1 Amount of Processing in Manufacturing Operations

Manufacturing operations can be classified according to the amount of processing or assembly that occurs after receiving an order from customers. The highest degree of processing occurs in **make-to-order operations**. A make-to-order operation does not start processing or assembling products until it receives a customer order. In fact, some make-to-order operations may not even order parts until that customer order is received. Not surprisingly, these practices permit make-to-order operations to produce or assemble highly specialized or customized products for customers.

make-to-order operation
manufacturing operation that does not start processing or assembling products until a customer order is received

For example, Dell Computer (www.dell.com) has one of the most advanced make-to-order operations in the computer business. Dell has no finished-goods inventory—it does not build a computer until someone buys it. Because Dell doesn't order parts from suppliers until machines are purchased, its computers always have the latest, most advanced computer components. No one who buys a Dell computer gets stuck with old technology. Also, because prices of computer components tend to fall, Dell's make-to-order operation can pass on price cuts to customers. As well, Dell can customize all its orders, big and small. For example, it took Dell just six weeks to make and ship 2000 personal computers and 4000 network servers for Wal-Mart. Furthermore, Dell preloaded each of these 6000 machines with proprietary software that Wal-Mart uses in its stores and offices.[30]

A moderate degree of processing occurs in **assemble-to-order operations**. A company using an assemble-to-order operation divides its manufacturing or assembly process into separate parts or modules. They order parts and assemble modules ahead of customer orders. Then, on the basis of actual customer orders or on research forecasting what customers will want, those modules are then combined to create semi-customized products. For example, when a customer orders a new car, Ford may have already ordered the basic parts or modules it needs from suppliers. In other words, on the basis of sales forecasts, Ford may already have ordered enough tires, air-conditioning compressors, brake systems, and seats from suppliers to accommodate nearly all customer orders on a

assemble-to-order operation
manufacturing operation that divides manufacturing processes into separate parts or modules that are combined to create semi-customized products

© PhotoDisc, Inc.

particular day. However, special orders from customers and car dealers are then used to determine the final assembly checklist for particular cars as they move down the assembly line.

The lowest degree of processing occurs in make-to-stock operations. A company using a **make-to-stock operation** starts ordering parts and assembling finished products before receiving customer orders. These standardized products are typically purchased by consumers at retail stores or directly from the manufacturer. Because parts are ordered and products are assembled before customers order the products, make-to-stock operations are highly dependent on the accuracy of sales forecasts. If sales forecasts are incorrect, make-to-stock operations may end up building too many or too few products, or they may make products with the wrong features or lacking the features that customers want.

These disadvantages led Wilkerson Corporation (www.wilkersoncorp.com), a manufacturer of pneumatic devices such as air compressors, with distributors throughout Canada, to switch to a make-to-order assembly operation. Under its old make-to-stock system, Wilkerson would make large batches of its best-selling products and store them on shelves that reached all the way to the ceiling of its manufacturing plant. Storing unsold inventory was not only expensive (costs ran as high as 30 percent of sales), but it also sometimes took 6 to 18 months to sell off the unsold finished inventory. And because the company was spending all its time producing large batches of its best-selling products, it was frequently unable to make special, customized products for customers

make-to-stock operation
manufacturing operation that orders parts and assembles standardized products before receiving customer orders

who required them. With a product catalogue of more than 50 000 items, it was almost impossible under the make-to-stock system for Wilkerson to have all its products in stock and ready for delivery.[31]

4.2 Flexibility of Manufacturing Operations

A second way to categorize manufacturing operations is by **manufacturing flexibility**, meaning the degree to which manufacturing operations can easily and quickly change the number, kind, and characteristics of products they produce. Flexibility allows companies to respond more quickly to changes in the marketplace (i.e., competitors and customers) and to reduce the lead time between ordering and final delivery of products. However, there is often a tradeoff between flexibility and cost, with the most flexible manufacturing operations frequently having higher costs per unit and the least flexible operations having lower costs per unit.[32] As shown in Exhibit 14.4, the least to most flexible manufacturing operations are continuous-flow production, line-flow production, batch production, job shops, and project manufacturing.

Most production processes generate finished products at a discrete rate. A product is completed, and then, perhaps a few seconds, minutes, or hours later, another is completed, and so on. For instance, if you stood at the end of an automobile assembly line, it would appear as if nothing much was happening for 55 seconds of every minute. However, in that last 5 seconds, a new car would be started and driven off the assembly line, ready for its new owner. By contrast, in **continuous-flow production**, products are produced at a continuous, rather than discrete, rate, in which production of the final product never stops. It's sort of like a water hose that is never turned off. The water (or product) just keeps on flowing. In other words, the product is always and continuously being produced. Liquid chemicals and petroleum products are examples of continuous-flow production. If you're still struggling with this concept (and it can be confusing), think of PlayDoh. Continuous-flow production is similar to squeezing PlayDoh into a toy press and watching the various shapes ooze out of the "PlayDoh Machine." But with continuous-flow production, the PlayDoh machine would never quit oozing or producing rectangle- or triangle-shaped PlayDoh. Because of their complexity, continuous-flow production processes are the most standardized and least flexible manufacturing operations.

Line-flow production processes are preestablished, occur in a serial or linear manner, and are dedicated to making one type of product. In this way, the 10 different steps required to make product X can be completed in a separate manufacturing process (with separate machines, parts, treatments, locations, and workers) from the 12 different steps required to make product Y. Line-flow production processes are inflexible, because they are typically dedicated to the manufacture of one kind of product. Breweries are often built in this fashion with processes or steps that are serial, meaning they must occur in a particular order. For example, in some companies, after empty bottles are sterilized,

manufacturing flexibility degree to which manufacturing operations can easily and quickly change the number, kind, and characteristics of products they produce

continuous-flow production manufacturing operation that produces goods at a continuous, rather than a discrete, rate

line-flow production manufacturing processes that are preestablished, occur in a serial or linear manner, and are dedicated to making one type of product

---

EXHIBIT 14.4

FLEXIBILITY OF MANUFACTURING OPERATIONS

| Continuous-Flow Production | Line-Flow Production | Batch Production | Job Shops | Project Manufacturing |

Least Flexible ← → **Most Flexible**

they are filled with beer using a special dispenser that distributes the beer down the inside walls of the bottle. This fills the bottle from the bottom up and displaces the air that was in the bottle. The bottles are then crowned or capped, checked for under-filling and missing caps, labelled, inspected a final time for fill levels and missing labels, and then placed in cases that are shrink-wrapped on pallets and put on trucks for delivery.[33]

batch production
manufacturing operation that produces goods in large batches in standard lot sizes

The next most flexible manufacturing operation is **batch production**, which involves the manufacture of large batches of different products in standard lot sizes. Consequently, a worker in a batch production operation will perform the same manufacturing process on 100 copies of product X, followed by 200 copies of product Y, and then 50 copies of product Q. Furthermore, these "batches" move through each manufacturing department or process in identical order. So, if the paint department follows chemical treatment, and chemical treatment is now processing a batch of 50 copies of product Q, then the paint department's next task will be to paint 50 copies of product Q. One example of the use of batch production would be found in the creation of Mega Bloks (www.megabloks.com), child toys developed in Montreal that compete directly with Lego. Popular Mega Blok kits such as Alien Agency D.N.A. Lab or Dragons Man O' War each have hundreds of pieces, many of them identical. If we multiply these kits by the tens of thousands, it is easy to see the need for this style of production.

job shops
manufacturing operations that handle customer orders or small batch jobs

The next most flexible manufacturing operation is called a job shop. **Job shops** are typically small manufacturing operations that handle special manufacturing processes or jobs. By contrast to batch production, which handles large batches of different products, job shops typically handle very small batches, some as small as one product or process per "batch." Basically, each "job" in a job shop is different, and once a job is done, the job shop moves on to a completely different job or manufacturing process for, most likely, a different customer. For example, some job shops specialize in assembling products for other firms. One in particular has 12 full-time employees who assemble everything from strobe-light electronics, laser light-show equipment, personal air-monitoring devices, speed-boat steering wheels, and automated chemical dispensers to hand-held bar-code readers.[34]

project manufacturing
manufacturing operations designed to produce large, expensive, specialized products

The most flexible manufacturing operation is project manufacturing. **Project manufacturing** is an operation designed to produce large, expensive, specialized products such as custom homes, defence weapons such as aircraft carriers and submarines, and aerospace products such as passenger planes and the space shuttle. Project manufacturing is highly flexible, because each project is usually significantly different from the one before it, even if the projects produce the same type of product, such as a submarine. Because of each project's size and expense and high degree of customization, project manufacturing can take an extremely long time to complete.

For example, during the last few decades CAE Inc. (www.cae.com) has built itself a strong position in the power plant simulator niche. CAE manufactures simulators that are duplicates of the control rooms of major coal, hydro-electric, and nuclear generation facilities. Its products can be found in electrical utilities throughout North America and around the world. Challenging to CAE and its engineers is a quirky feature of North American nuclear generation facilities. No two are the same, so every time CAE develops a simulator for this market, it has to start from scratch in its planning and project development.

Review 4
Manufacturing Operations

Manufacturing operations produce physical goods. Manufacturing operations can be classified according to the amount of processing or assembly that occurs after receiving an order from customers. Make-to-order operations have the highest degree of processing, in which assembly doesn't begin until products are ordered. The next-highest degree of processing occurs in assemble-to-order operations, in which preassembled modules are combined after orders are received to produce semi-customized products. The lowest degree of processing occurs in make-to-stock operations, in which, on the basis of sales forecasts, standard parts are ordered and assembled before orders occur.

Manufacturing operations can also be classified by flexibility, the degree to which the number, kind, and characteristics of products can easily and quickly be changed. Flexibility allows companies to respond quickly to competitors and customers and to reduce order lead times, but can also lead to higher unit costs. The least to most flexible manufacturing operations are continuous-flow production, line-flow production, batch production, job shops, and project manufacturing.

5. Inventory

In February 1998, Ford shut down one of its North American assembly plants for two weeks. The plant, which assembles Ford Escorts and Mercury Tracers, laid off 3500 workers during that time. According to Jim Bright, a Ford spokesperson, the plant was closed to "maintain dealer inventories at reasonable levels." Said Bright, "We have a 117-day supply on Escort and a 103-day supply on Tracer and that's higher than we'd like to have, which is ideally about a 72-day supply."[35]

Inventory is the amount and number of raw materials, parts, and finished products that a company has in its possession. Ford made the mistake of having too much inventory on hand and had to close its factories to let existing sales draw down inventory levels to an acceptable and affordable level.

In this section, you will learn about types of inventory, measuring inventory, costs of maintaining an inventory, and managing inventory.

5.1 Types of Inventory

Exhibit 14.5 shows the four kinds of inventory a manufacturer stores: raw materials, component parts, work-in-process, and finished goods. The flow of inventory through a manufacturing plant begins when the purchasing department buys raw materials from vendors. **Raw material inventories** are the basic inputs in the manufacturing process. For example, to begin making a car, automobile manufacturers purchase raw materials such as steel, iron, aluminum, copper, rubber, and unprocessed plastic.

Next, raw materials are fabricated or processed into **component parts inventories**, meaning the basic parts used in manufacturing a product. For example, in an automobile plant, steel is fabricated or processed into a car's body panels, and steel and iron are melted and shaped into engine parts such as pistons or engine blocks. Component parts inventories are sometimes purchased directly from vendors.

The component parts are then assembled to make unfinished **work-in-process inventories**, which are also known as partially finished goods. This process is also called initial assembly. For example, steel body panels are welded to each other and to the frame of the car to make a "unibody," which comprises the unpainted interior frame and exterior structure of the car. Likewise, pistons, camshafts, and other engine parts are inserted into the engine block to create a working engine.

Next, all the work-in-process inventories are assembled to create **finished goods inventories**, which are the final outputs of the manufacturing process. This process is also called final assembly. So, for a car, the engine, wheels, brake system, suspension, interior, and electrical system are assembled into a car's painted unibody to make the working automobile, which is the factory's finished product. In the last step in the process, the finished goods are sent to field warehouses or distribution centres or wholesalers, and then to retailers for final sale to consumers.

inventory
the amount and number of raw materials, parts, and finished products that a company has in its possession

raw material inventories
the basic inputs in a manufacturing process

component parts inventories
the basic parts used in manufacturing that are fabricated from raw materials

work-in-process inventories
partially finished goods consisting of assembled component parts

finished goods inventories
the final outputs of manufacturing operations

PERSONAL PRODUCTIVITY

Buy High and Sell Low?

Conventional wisdom in investing says to "buy low and sell high." However, with inventory levels, you should *buy high*, because sellers are more likely to cut prices when they have excess inventory. For example, since 72 days of inventory is the norm in the auto industry, car manufacturers will usually cut car prices when they have 90 or more days of inventory. Likewise, you should *sell low*, because when inventories are low, buyers will typically pay more to obtain hard-to-get items. So, to make your hard-earned money go further, remember to *buy high and sell low*.

EXHIBIT 14.5

TYPES OF INVENTORY

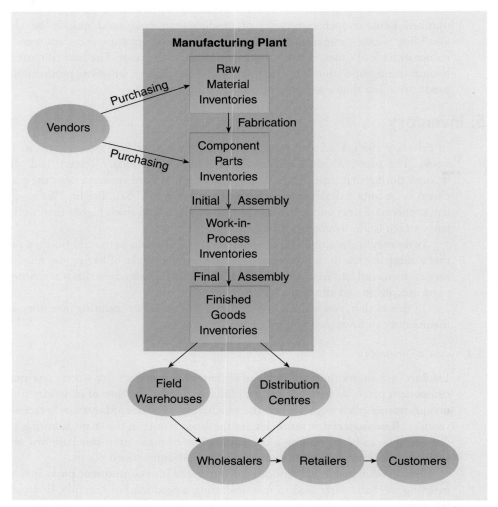

Source: Adapted from *Operations Management* by Markland/Vickery. © 1998. Reprinted with permission of South-Western, a division of Thomson Learning: www.thomsonrights.com. Fax 800-730-2215.

5.2 Measuring Inventory

As you'll learn below, uncontrolled inventory can lead to huge costs for a manufacturing operation. Consequently, managers need good measures of inventory to prevent inventory costs from becoming too large. Three basic measures of inventory are average aggregate inventory, weeks of supply, and inventory turnover.

If you've ever worked in a retail store and have had to "take inventory," you probably weren't too excited about the process of counting every item in the store and storeroom. It's an extensive process. Fortunately, "taking inventory" is somewhat easier today because of bar codes that mark items and computers that can count and track them. However, if you took inventory at the beginning of the month, the inventory count would likely be different from the count at the end of the month. Similar differences in inventory count might occur if inventory was taken on a Friday rather than a Monday. Because of day-to-day differences in inventories, companies often measure **average aggregate inventory**, which is the average overall inventory during a particular time period. Average aggregate inventory for a month can be determined by simply averaging

average aggregate inventory
average overall inventory during a particular time period

A line of New York gamers waits on an escalator for their chance to purchase an Xbox game console before the Christmas 2001 season. But at stores like this, Xbox consoles sold out within the first few hours of being released and stocked on store shelves.

AP/Wide World Photos

the inventory counts at the end of each business day for that month. One way companies know whether they're carrying too much or too little inventory is to compare their average aggregate inventory to the industry average for aggregate inventory. For example, in the automobile industry, 60 to 65 days of inventory is the industry average.

Inventory is also measured by weeks of supply, meaning the number of weeks it would take for a company to run out of its current supply of inventory. In general, there is an acceptable number of weeks of inventory for a particular kind of business. Too few weeks of inventory on the one hand, and a company risks a **stockout**—running out of inventory. Too many weeks of inventory on the other hand, and the business incurs high costs (discussed below). For example, companies that make linerboard used for corrugated cardboard boxes typically have too much inventory when they have more than six weeks' supply on hand and about the right amount of inventory when the level drops to four weeks' supply.[36] Likewise, 3Com (www.3com.com), which makes computer modems and network cards, aims for a four- to six-week supply of network cards, a six- to eight-week supply of modems, and a five- to seven-week supply of network hubs and switches. Anything more than that results in excess inventory, which can be reduced only through price cuts or by temporarily stopping production.[37]

Another common inventory measure, **inventory turnover**, is the number of times per year that a company sells or "turns over" its average inventory. For example, if a company keeps an average of 100 finished widgets in inventory each month, and it sold 1000 widgets this year, then it "turned" its inventory 10 times this year.

stockout
situation in which a company runs out of finished product

inventory turnover
the number of times per year that a company sells or "turns over" its average inventory

EXPERIENCING MANAGEMENT

Reinforce your understanding of inventory management concepts by interacting with them at our animated concept and activity site. Choose Operations Management from the "select a topic" pull-down menu, then Inventory Management from the "overview tab."

www.experiencingmanagement.com

In general, the higher the number of inventory "turns," the better. In practice, a high turnover means that a company can continue its daily operations with just a small amount of inventory on hand. For example, let's take two companies, A and B, which, over the course of a year, have identical inventory levels (520 000 widget parts and raw materials). If company A turns its inventories 26 times a year, it would completely replenish its inventory every two weeks and have an average inventory of 20 000 widget parts and raw materials. By contrast, if company B turned its inventories only two times a year, it would completely replenish its inventory every 26 weeks and have an average inventory of 260 000 widget parts and raw materials. So by turning its inventory more often, company A has 92 percent less inventory on hand at any one time than company B.

Across all kinds of manufacturing plants, the average number of inventory turns is approximately seven per year. However, food manufacturing plants, which have an obvious need for fresh ingredients, average 25 inventory turns per year, while auto and truck makers, which aggressively manage their inventories, can average inventory turns as high as 52 per year![38]

5.3 Costs of Maintaining an Inventory

ordering cost
the costs associated with ordering inventory, including the cost of data entry, phone calls, obtaining bids, correcting mistakes, and determining when and how much inventory to order

Maintaining an inventory incurs four kinds of costs: ordering, setup, holding, and stockout. **Ordering cost** is not the cost of the inventory itself, but the costs associated with ordering the inventory. It includes the costs of completing paperwork, manually entering data into a computer, making phone calls, getting competing bids, correcting mistakes, and simply determining when and how much new inventory should be reordered. For example, ordering costs are relatively high in the restaurant business, because 80 percent of food service orders (in which restaurants reorder food supplies) are processed manually. However, it's estimated that the North American food industry could save more than $9 billion if all restaurants converted to electronic data interchange (see Chapter 5), in which purchase and ordering information from one company's computer system is automatically relayed to another company's computer system. In fact, a number of restaurants and food service trade groups have formed an interest group called Efficient Foodservice Response to encourage restaurants and food suppliers to use EDI and other methods of electronic commerce.[39]

setup cost
the costs of downtime and lost efficiency that occur when changing or adjusting a machine to produce a different kind of inventory

Setup cost is the cost of changing or adjusting a machine so it can produce a different kind of inventory.[40] For example, 3M (www.3m.com) uses the same production machinery to make several kinds of industrial tape. However, different adjustments have to be made to the machines for each kind of tape. There are two kinds of setup costs, downtime and lost efficiency. *Downtime* occurs anytime a machine is not being used to process inventory. So if it takes five hours to switch a machine from processing one kind of inventory to another, then five hours of downtime have occurred. Downtime is costly, because companies earn an economic return only when machines are actively turning raw materials into parts or parts into finished products. The second setup cost is *lost efficiency*. Typically, after a switchover, it takes some time to recalibrate a machine to its optimal settings. It may take several days of fine-tuning before a machine finally produces the number of high-quality parts that it is supposed to.

holding cost
the cost of keeping inventory until it is used or sold, including storage, insurance, taxes, obsolescence, and opportunity costs

Holding cost, also known as carrying or storage cost, is the cost of keeping inventory until it is used or sold. Holding costs include the cost of storage facilities, insurance to protect inventory from damage or theft, inventory taxes, the cost of obsolescence (holding inventory that is no longer useful to the company), and the opportunity cost of spending money on inventory that could have been spent elsewhere in the company. For example, it's estimated that at any one time, North American airlines have a total of at least $60 billion worth of airplane parts in stock for maintenance, repair, and overhauling their planes. The holding costs for managing, storing, and purchasing these parts is over $12 billion—almost as much as the parts themselves![41]

Stockout costs are the costs incurred when a company runs out of a product. There are two basic kinds of stockout costs. The first is the transaction costs of overtime work, shipping, etc., that are incurred in trying to quickly replace out-of-stock inventories with new inventories. The second and perhaps most damaging cost is the loss of customers' goodwill when a company cannot deliver the products that it promised. Marc Pritchard, vice president and general manager for Procter & Gamble, said, "Research shows the number-one complaint of mass shoppers is product availability. Twenty-five percent of shoppers walk out of the mass store without a purchase. What's worse is what you'd find in the back of stores and in manufacturers' warehouses—$1.3 billion [U.S.] in inventory, think of that—but we still can't keep the right product in stock."[42]

stockout costs
the costs incurred when a company runs out of a product, including transaction costs to replace inventory and the loss of customers' goodwill

5.4 Managing Inventory

Inventory management has two basic goals. The first is to avoid running out of stock and angering and dissatisfying customers. Consequently, this goal seeks to increase inventory levels to a "safe" level that won't risk stockouts. The second is to efficiently reduce inventory levels and costs as much as possible without impairing daily operations. Thus, this goal seeks a minimum level of inventory. The following inventory management techniques—economic order quantity (EOQ), just-in-time inventory (JIT), and materials requirement planning (MRP)—are different ways of balancing these competing goals.

Economic order quantity (EOQ) is a system of formulas that helps determine how much and how often inventory should be ordered. EOQ takes into account the overall demand (D) for a product while trying to minimize ordering costs (O) and holding costs (H). The formula for EOQ is

$$EOQ = \sqrt{\frac{2DO}{H}}$$

economic order quantity (EOQ)
a system of formulas that minimizes ordering and holding costs and helps determine how much and how often inventory should be ordered

For example, if a factory uses 40 000 litres of paint a year (D), and ordering costs (O) are $75 per order, and holding costs (H) are $4 per litre, then the optimal quantity to order is 1225 litres.

$$EOQ = \sqrt{\frac{2(40\ 000)(75)}{4}} = 1\ 225$$

And, with 40 000 litres of paint being used per year, the factory uses approximately 110 litres per day.

$$EOQ = \frac{40\ 000\ litres}{365\ days} = 110$$

Consequently, the factory would order 1225 new litres of paint approximately every 11 days.

$$EOQ = \frac{1225\ litres}{110\ litres\ per\ day} = 11.1\ days$$

While EOQ formulas try to minimize holding and ordering costs, the just-in-time (JIT) approach to inventory management attempts to eliminate holding costs by reducing inventory levels to near zero. A **just-in-time (JIT) inventory system** is a system in which component parts arrive from suppliers just as they are needed at each stage of production. By having parts arrive "just in time," the manufacturer has little inventory on hand, avoiding the costs associated with holding inventory. For example, thanks to its JIT inventory system, one of Toyota's North American car factories has only 2.8 hours' worth of inventory on hand at any one time. This low level of inventory saves Toyota millions of dollars a year in inventory expenses.[43] When Ford needs more seats at its Taurus plant, it uses an electronic system to give its seat supplier two hours' notice to make its next delivery of seats to the factory.[44]

just-in-time (JIT) inventory system
inventory system in which component parts arrive from suppliers just as they are needed at each stage of production

To have just the right amount of inventory arrive at just the right time requires a tremendous amount of coordination between manufacturing operations and suppliers. One way to promote tight coordination under JIT is close proximity. At the Toyota plant noted above, most parts suppliers are located within 300 kilometres of the plant. Furthermore, parts are picked up from suppliers and delivered to Toyota as often as 16 times a day.[45]

A second way to promote close coordination under JIT is shared information systems. These systems allow manufacturers and their suppliers to know the quantity and kinds of parts inventory the other has in stock. One way to facilitate information sharing is for factories and suppliers to use the same parts numbers and names. Ford's seat supplier accomplishes this by sticking a bar code on each seat. Ford then uses the same bar code in its factories to determine when the seat is needed, which car the seat is installed in, and which workstation on the assembly line will install the seat.

Another way to facilitate close coordination between manufacturing operations and their parts suppliers is the Japanese system of kanban. **Kanban**, which is Japanese for "sign," is a simple ticket-based system that indicates when it is time to reorder inventory. Suppliers attach kanban cards to batches of parts. Then when an assembly line worker uses the first part out of a batch, the kanban card is removed. The cards are then collected, sorted, and quickly returned to the supplier, who begins resupplying the factory with parts that match the order information on the kanban cards. And, because prices and batch sizes are typically agreed to ahead of time, kanban tickets greatly reduce paperwork and ordering costs.[46]

A third method for managing inventory is **materials requirement planning (MRP)**. MRP is a production and inventory system that, from beginning to end, precisely determines the production schedule, production batch sizes, and inventories needed to complete final products. The three key parts of MRP systems are the master production schedule, the bill of materials, and inventory records. The master production schedule is a detailed schedule that indicates the quantity of each item to be produced, the planned delivery dates for those items, and the time by which each step of the production process must be completed in order to meet those delivery dates. Based on the quantity and kind of products set forth in the master production schedule, the bill of materials identifies all the necessary parts and inventory, the quantity or volume of inventory to be ordered, and the order in which the parts and inventory should be assembled. Inventory records indicate the kind, quantity, and location of inventory that is on hand or that has been ordered. When inventory records are combined with the bill of materials, the resulting report indicates what to buy, when to buy it, and what it will cost to order. Today, nearly all MRP systems are available in the form of powerful, flexible computer software.[47]

Which inventory management system should you use? Economic order quantity (EOQ) formulas are intended for use with **independent demand systems**, in which the level of one kind of inventory does not depend on another. For example, because inventory levels for automobile tires are unrelated to the inventory levels of ladies' dresses, Sears could use EOQ formulas to calculate separate optimal order quantities for dresses and tires. By contrast, JIT and MRP are used with **dependent demand systems**, in which the level of inventory depends on the number of finished units to be produced. For example, if Yamaha makes 1000 motorcycles a day, then it will need 1000 seats, 1000 gas tanks, and 2000 wheels and tires each day. So when optimal inventory levels depend on the number of products to be produced, use a JIT or MRP management system.

Review 5
Inventory

There are four kinds of inventory: raw materials, component parts, work-in-process, and finished goods. Because companies incur ordering, setup, holding, and stockout costs when handling inventory, inventory costs can be enormous. To control those costs, com-

---

kanban
a ticked-based system that indicates when to reorder inventory

materials requirement planning (MRP)
a production and inventory system that determines the production schedule, production batch sizes, and inventory needed to complete final products

independent demand systems
inventory system in which the level of one kind of inventory does not depend on another

dependent demand system
inventory system in which the level of inventory depends on the number of finished units to be produced

panies measure and track inventory in three ways: average aggregate inventory, weeks of supply, and turnover. Companies meet the basic goals of inventory management (avoiding stockouts and reducing inventory without hurting daily operations) through economic order quantity (EOQ) formulas, just-in-time (JIT) inventory systems, and materials requirement planning (MRP). EOQ formulas minimize holding and ordering costs by determining how much and how often inventory should be ordered. By having parts arrive just when they are needed at each stage of production, JIT systems attempt to minimize inventory levels and holding costs. JIT systems often depend on proximity, shared information, and the Japanese system of kanban. MRP precisely determines the production schedule, production batch sizes, and the ordering of inventories needed to complete final products. The three key parts of MRP systems are the master production schedule, the bill of materials, and inventory records. Use EOQ formulas when inventory levels are independent, and JIT and MRP when inventory levels are dependent on the number of products to be produced.

What Really Happened?

At the beginning of this chapter, you read about the problems *Newsday* was having trying to cover more late-breaking news and still deliver newspapers to customers when they want them. Solutions to its problems involve managing productivity and quality, services, operations, and inventory. Find out what really happened at *Newsday* by reading the following answers to the opening case.

How can *Newsday* change its writing, editing, production, printing, and delivery processes to include as many late-breaking stories as possible but still deliver newspapers by 5:30 each morning? In other words, how can *Newsday* become more productive during each 24-hour news cycle?

Organizations are production systems that take inputs, such as labour, raw materials, capital, and knowledge, and turn them into outputs in the form of finished products or services. *Newsday* does this by turning facts and events into the news stories, commentary, and photos that make up a daily newspaper. As production systems, organizations become more efficient and productive when they do more (produce more output) with less (fewer inputs). For *Newsday*, being more productive means adding late sports scores (i.e., doing

more) by extending the deadline for sports scores from 11:20 p.m. to 11:55 p.m. and by moving up morning delivery times from 6:00 a.m. to 5:30 a.m. (i.e., with 65 fewer minutes). You'll see below how *Newsday* was able to do this.

Why should *Newsday* or any other company be concerned about productivity? In general, doing more with less results in lower costs, lower prices, higher market share, and higher profits. While it's still too early to determine if these changes will produce the desired results, *Newsday*'s publisher believes that increasing productivity will add "tens of millions of dollars" to its profits.

While productivity is important to companies, quality is what matters to customers. What can *Newsday* do to improve quality for customers while increasing productivity for itself?

Quality means several things. It can mean a product or service free of deficiencies. It can also mean the characteristics of a product or service that satisfy customer needs, such as reliability, serviceability, durability, responsiveness, assurance, and empathy. Of these characteristics, studies clearly show that reliability, the consistent ability to perform a service well, is most important to customers. For *Newsday*, this means delivering papers with complete sports

scores and news by 5:30 each morning. *Newsday* gets just one chance each day. If the paper doesn't arrive on time, or if it arrives without the latest news, customers will be dissatisfied. In short, for *Newsday*'s customers, quality simply means that *Newsday* will consistently do what it promises to do—deliver a fact-filled newspaper by 5:30 a.m. To emphasize the importance of quality to its customers and workers, *Newsday* now offers a money-back guarantee for late papers. Whatever the reason, if your paper is late, it costs you nothing.

However, with the last story filed at 11:55 p.m. and delivery trucks scheduled to leave the loading docks by 3:45 a.m., there's little room for mistakes, breakdowns, or delays. So to make sure that it achieves its 5:30 a.m. guaranteed delivery, *Newsday* needs to make sure that its printing machines and processes are well maintained and reliable. For example, *Newsday* has improved quality by reducing the number of "web breaks," or tears in the two-ton rolls of newsprint on which the paper is printed. Each tear shuts down the line for the ten minutes it takes press workers to pull out the torn sheets and then rethread the press to resume printing. Tears used to occur once every 18 rolls. But by closely monitoring the tension on the rolls of newsprint, tears now occur only once every 30 rolls.

As it makes these changes, what should Newsday's goals be with respect to this production process? Should it focus on speed or flexibility?

When it comes to speed and flexibility, most operation managers believe that you can have one or the other. *Newsday*, however, managed to incorporate both when it completely redesigned its daily production process.

Flexibility is the degree to which manufacturing operations can easily and quickly change the number, kind, and characteristics of products they produce. Flexibility allows companies to respond more quickly to changes in the marketplace and reduce the lead time between ordering and final delivery of products. *Newsday* took away flexibility in some parts of the production process so it could add it in others. Previously, reporters sent stories to copy editors by 6:30 p.m. The editors would make changes in the stories, wait for photos and updates, and then "release" the stories to production at 10:00 p.m. Now, though, editors have moved up the "closing" time, so that some nights as much as 80 percent of the paper is closed before 7:00 p.m. However, *Newsday* added flexibility in other areas by extending the closing time for sports. Now, 22 sports pages close at 11:30 p.m., while another 9 close at 11:50 p.m.

Similar procedures now give *Newsday*'s advertisers more flexibility. Advertisers now have until 7:00 p.m., 19 more hours than before, to change their advertisements. To increase speed and reduce the amount of time it took to write, print, and distribute stories, *Newsday* formed an "End to End Committee" that examined every stage of its daily newspaper production. In addition to moving up the closing time for most of the paper, *Newsday* was able to shorten its press run by 45 minutes. Likewise, it speeded up the distribution of its papers in the following ways. First, instead of loading paper bundles (60 papers held together by plastic or metal wire) one at a time onto trucks, bundles are now placed on wooden pallets and shrink-wrapped in plastic, and then the pallets are loaded onto trucks using forklifts. This process cuts the loading and unloading time by half, shortening the distribution process by 30 minutes. Second, the End to End Committee reduced delivery times by adding more newspaper carriers and reducing the number of papers delivered by each carrier.

Finally, if you think of news stories as unfinished inventory, what techniques for managing inventory might Newsday use to address these problems?

Inventory is the amount and number of raw materials, parts, and finished products that a company has in its possession. So like the steel used to build cars and the silicon used to make computer chips, unfinished news stories are really a form of inventory. However, unlike many kinds of inventory, news stories are perishable, like food. Newspapers must get the latest news into today's newspaper. Tomorrow, it is "old news," and no one will want to read it.

Maintaining an inventory incurs four kinds of costs: ordering, setup, holding, and stockout. The most serious for newspapers are setup and stockout costs. Setup cost is the cost of changing or adjusting a machine or production process to produce a different kind of inventory. Since today's newspaper has completely different stories, pictures, and advertisements than yesterday's, newspapers incur new setup costs every day. Stockout costs are incurred when a company runs out of a product. For newspapers, this means that stockouts occur when papers are not delivered or are delivered late. Stockouts are costly for newspapers because of the additional cost of delivering papers that were not delivered by the normal delivery system, and because of the loss of customers' goodwill.

Given the significant cost of inventory, even for newspapers, what procedures could *Newsday* use to manage its inventory? The first step, which *Newsday* took, is to recognize that it had a dependent demand system, in which the level of inventory depends on the number of finished units (i.e., newspaper pages) produced. Furthermore, in a newspaper, every step of the production process depends on the one before it. Editors edit reporters' stories. Printers position edited stories, along with advertisements, on pages. Completed pages and papers are printed, folded, and then distributed by trucks and individual paper carriers. Each step is dependent on the other.

Given that *Newsday* has a dependent demand system, it had two choices, just-in-time inventory (JIT) or materials resource planning (MRP). In effect, it used a little of both. JIT systems minimize inventory and speed production by having parts arrive just when they are needed at each stage of production. *Newsday* used the basic idea behind JIT when it "closed" 80 percent of its daily pages by 7:00 p.m., but left its sports pages "open" until just before midnight. MRP precisely determines production schedules, batch sizes, and the ordering of inventories needed to complete final products. The goal of MRP is to manage inventory and optimize the entire production process. *Newsday* used the basic ideas behind MRP when its End to End Committee critically reexamined how and when stories were filed, advertisements were approved, printing presses were run, trucks were loaded, and papers were distributed.

Sources: F. Ahrens, "The Washington Post: One Day in the Life," *The Washington Post*, 11 February 1998. G.B. Knecht, "Newsday Changes Playbook to Offer Later Sports Scores," *The Wall Street Journal Interactive Edition*, 12 March 1997.

Key Terms

assemble-to-order operation (449)	inventory turnover (455)	partial productivity (439)
average aggregate inventory (454)	ISO 9000 (443)	productivity (438)
batch production (452)	job shops (452)	project manufacturing (452)
component parts inventories (453)	just-in-time (JIT) inventory (457)	quality (441)
continuous-flow production (451)	kanban (458)	raw material inventories (453)
continuous improvement (444)	line-flow production (451)	service recovery (447)
customer focus (444)	make-to-order operation (449)	setup cost (456)
customer satisfaction (444)	make-to-stock operation (450)	stockout (455)
dependent demand system (458)	manufacturing flexibility (451)	stockout costs (457)
economic order quantity (EOQ) (457)	materials requirement planning (MRP) (458)	teamwork (444)
finished goods inventories (453)		total quality management (TQM) (444)
holding cost (456)	multifactor productivity (440)	variation (444)
independent demand systems (458)	operations management (438)	work-in-process inventories (453)
inventory (453)	ordering cost (456)	

What Would You Do II?

"...Seventeen, eighteen, nineteen, twenty! Thank goodness that's the last pharmaceutical order. I didn't spend all those years in college to get a degree in counting, but you'd never know it if you followed me around."

As head of Pharmacology for Western Canada Hospital, one of your primary responsibilities is overseeing the daily filling of prescriptions. Every night at 10:00 p.m., the scramble begins as Pharmacology receives the fill list containing all of the next day's prescriptions for all the patients in each unit of the hospital (critical care, coronary, orthopedic, newborn, etc.). As one of the largest hospitals in the city, this means that 500 to 600 orders must be filled each night. Typically, it takes four pharmacy technicians eight hours apiece to fill the orders. For each prescription, technicians must retrieve one of 3000 different medications, count the number of pills, mix the medicine (if needed), make sure the dosage is correct, label the order, and then place it in a bin to be delivered to the appropriate nursing station the next day. Then, in the morning, certified pharmacists must check the accuracy of each prescription. With 500 to 600 orders each day, it usually takes each staff pharmacist two to three hours to check all the orders (or, as you call it, making use of your accounting degree).

It's not that you're against making sure that the prescriptions are correct. As head of Pharmacology, that's exactly what you want. But even with all of these precautions, mistakes sometimes occur in the form of miscounts, inappropriate dosages, or wrong medications. However, a more common problem is unexpected reactions to prescribed medications. In fact, a recent article in the *Journal of the American Medical Association* found that reactions to prescriptions and over-the-counter medicines kill 100 000 North Americans a year and seriously injure another 2.1 million. Ironically, if you didn't have to spend so much time checking and counting prescriptions, you and your staff could reduce the number of unexpected reactions to prescription medications by collecting and using information about allergies, reactions to previous medications, and other drugs patients are taking. In other words, preventing problems in one area (making sure patients get their prescribed medications) limits your ability to prevent problems in another (unintended reactions to prescribed medications).

Now the hospital's CEO is pressuring you to cut costs. Because government funding of your hospital has been cut by 10 percent in the last four years, the CEO has told you and the other department heads that costs have to drop by the same amount. Well, the cost savings aren't going to come from layoffs. You're already understaffed and would hire two more technicians and one more pharmacist if you could. And it's not going to come from lower salaries. The hospital is unionized. Cutting salaries is not an option available to you. Maybe the cuts should come from inventories, which have increased substantially in the last few years. But will reducing inventory increase the chance of not having critical drugs on hand when patients need them? Is that a reasonable risk to take just to save costs? And how do you cut costs, reduce inventory, and increase productivity and quality all at the same time?

If you were in charge of the Pharmacology Department at Western Canada Hospital, what would you do?

Sources: L.J. Aron, "Takeout Health Care: New Systems Shorten Supply Chain," *Crain's New York Business*, 26 January 1998, 24. Associated Press, "Drug Side Effects Killing Thousands," MSNBC. [Online] Available www.msnbc.com/news/158473.asp, 15 April 1998. J. Joseph, "Prescription Drugs Save Lives: There's No Question About That," ABCNEWS.com. [Online] Available http://archive. abcnews.com/sections/living/DailyNews/drugreactions980413.html, 14 April 1998.

Continuous Quality Improvement, Yeah, Right!

You've just been promoted as the manager of customer service for a medium-sized general merchandise retailer. Your boss, the former customer service manager, resigned yesterday, when she realized that her department was not going to meet the company's mandate of increasing customer satisfaction by 15 percent for the quarter. You are glad to get the chance to head up the department; however, you realize that your time may also be limited.

Your company has been suffering from low customer satisfaction since you began working there three years ago. Although customer satisfaction has increased during that time period, the company currently holds a 73 percent satisfaction rate, compared to its closest competitor's satisfaction rate of 92 percent. This rate suggests that only 7.3 out of 10 people are satisfied with their shopping experience. The company has tried many tactics to improve satisfaction in the store, ranging from training sales associates to be more customer-friendly, providing bonuses and pay raises for those who receive favourable evaluations from customers, and demoting or terminating sales associates who receive unfavourable evaluations from customers. Despite these programs, the overall customer satisfaction rate has yet to achieve top management's expectations. As the newly appointed customer service manager, what factors might you consider when attempting to solve the current customer satisfaction dilemma?

Source: M. Jordan, "Penney Blends Two Business Cultures," *The Wall Street Journal*, 5 April 2001, www.wsj.com.

Cycle Time and Quality Improvement

In the pursuit of quality improvement, many service organizations attempt to reduce the cycle time of key processes. "Cycle time" refers to the time taken to complete a key step in the delivery of a service or good. For example, cycle time can be the amount of time it takes the purchasing department to approve a purchase request. The cycle time begins when the purchasing department receives the request and ends when the request has been processed and returned to the individual.

Many organizations attempt to improve cycle time by looking at the processes involved in each department and removing any redundant steps or steps that do not create value for the organization. One organization that seems to have a negative image regarding cycle time is the government. At the local motor vehicle department (MVD), it seems that no matter what time of day or what day of the week you visit, you will end up spending a majority of your time standing in line. Likewise, receiving a tax refund or a passport traditionally have not been quick transactions. Wouldn't it be great if governmental agencies took steps to improve quality and decrease the cycle time of the services that they offer!

Another situation in which customers spend time waiting is at the local college, especially during registration. Many colleges tend to send students from one location to another in order for them to complete the registration process. For example, at one school, new students are required to fill out the admissions application and request for transcripts in the registrar's office. Then students must go down the hall to the business office in order to pay their admission fee. Once the fee has been paid, they must return to the registrar's office and show their receipt in order to complete the admission process. Once admitted, they must then go to an advisor's office to set an appointment in order to register for classes. Since they are new students, the advisor typically wants to see a copy of their transcript, which they typically don't have. If a transcript is on file, they have to return to the registrar's office in order to get a copy. Hopefully, with a copy of their transcript in hand, students are now ready to go back to the advisor's office and register for classes. All of these steps take time and confuse and frustrate the customer (in this case the student). If the whole process were inspected and improved, the majority of this confusion and frustration could be prevented.

Your assignment for this management decision is to think back to your last visit to the MVD, registrar, or other place where you had to either wait for a long time or go through several steps before completing the process. Think about ways to decrease the cycle time between steps, improve the overall flow, and increase customer satisfaction with the entire process.

Begin this exercise by describing the situation that you faced. Then list the steps you would take or the changes you would implement to improve the overall quality and outcome of the situation.

Develop Your Management Potential

Take a Factory Tour

Imagine that you're watching the final game of the Stanley Cup final series. As it ends, the camera zooms in on the game's most valuable player. The on-air announcer says to the MVP, "You've just won another championship. What are you going to do next?" And the player responds, "I'm going to Spamtown!" Spamtown? Actually, the winning athlete is supposed to say, "I'm going to Disney World," not Spamtown, the museum that Hormel Corporation established for its best-known product, Spam (www.spam.com).

Well, Spamtown isn't about to displace Disney World, but 60 000 people actually visit Spamtown each year. Thousands more also visit these corporate facilities:

- The BMW Factory Tour (www.bmwusfactory.com) guides viewers through the production process of its top-of-the-line cars.
- Hershey's Chocolate World (www.hersheys.com/chocworld/), Hershey Food Corporation's free visitor's centre with a Disney-like ride through a simulated chocolate factory.
- The Everett Tour Center (www.boeing.com/companyoffices/aboutus/tours/), where Boeing makes its 747, 767, and 777 passenger jets.
- The Vaughn Hockey factory (www.vaughnhockey.com) where hockey goalie equipment is custom made.
- An IBM Chip manufacturing plant (www-3.ibm.com/chips/bluelogic/manufacturing/tour/) Take a video tour of an IBM Microelectronics chip manufacturing clean room.

Your assignment for this Develop Your Management Potential is to take a factory tour. Do a quick Web search on the keywords "factory tour," or just ask around about a good factory tour near you. When on your tour, gather some literature and ask about the following issues.

Questions

1. What steps or procedures does the company take to ensure the quality of its products?
2. How does the company measure productivity and how does its productivity compare to others in the industry?
3. Describe the basic steps used to make the finished products in this factory. As you do this, be sure to describe the raw material inventories, component parts inventories, and work-in-process inventories used to create the finished products.
4. What did you find most impressive about the factory or manufacturing processes? Also, using the material from the chapter, describe one thing that the company could do differently to improve quality, increase productivity, or reduce inventory.

Sources: E. Gehrman, "Factory Facts Show Heart, Soul of America," *Boston Herald*, 29 January 1998. E. Perkins, "Factory Tour Can Be Fun, Not to Mention Real Cheap," *Orlando Sentinel*, 1 February, 1998, L6. L. Singhania (Associated Press), "Breakfast for Battle Creek's New Cereal City," *Grand Rapids Press*, 24 May 1998, F2. C. Quintanilla, "Planning a Vacation? Give Some Thought to Spamtown USA," *The Wall Street Journal*, 30 April 1998, A1.

Discussion Questions

1. Define productivity and provide an everyday example of a measure of productivity that consumers sometimes use in selecting a car to purchase.
2. A rite of passage of many adults is participation, at one time or another, on an elementary, middle, or high school PTA. As a caring aunt or uncle, you have agreed to help out your sister by serving on the PTA for your nephew's school. Welcomed with open arms, you have been asked to use PTA funds to buy $200 worth of basketballs and $500 worth of chairs for one classroom. The only real stipulation suggested to you is that the products purchased are of high quality. In this instance, briefly identify the two possible meanings of the term *quality*.
3. Briefly describe what is meant by TQM.
4. Once a year, the college where you are studying offers a trip to a high-technology manufacturing facility. You are fortunate enough to go to school on the West Island of Montreal which is also home to a number of pharmaceutical operations. Your professor confirms to you and your classmates that indeed, tomorrow you will be touring a drug manufacturing facility. In preparation for the visit, she asks you to explain what the term "manufacturing flexibility" means and list the five types of manufacturing operations. Prepare a brief response for your professor.
5. The next day, during the visit, you notice that inventory in this facility consists of small piles of flour-like additives that occupy very little physical space. This strikes your curiosity and that of your professor. As an assignment, she asks you to hand in a one-page assignment in which you briefly identify the different methods of inventory management, and specify the circumstances under which each should be used. What does your response look like?

Close your book and write a list of the key concepts in this chapter. Or create flashcards for key concepts (concept on one side, explanation and example on the other). Flashcards are great portable study aids that you can use over and over, in a group, with a partner, or on your own.

CHAPTER 15

Chapter Outline

Learning Objectives

After reading this chapter, you should be able to

1. explain the basics of motivation.
2. use equity theory to explain how employees' perceptions of fairness affect motivation.
3. use expectancy theory to describe how workers' expectations about rewards, effort, and the link between rewards and performance influence motivation.
4. explain what leadership is.
5. describe who leaders are and what effective leaders do.
6. explain Fiedler's contingency theory.
7. discuss Hersey & Blanchard's situational theory.
8. explain how visionary leadership (i.e., charismatic and transformational leadership) helps leaders achieve strategic leadership.

CP (Patrick Sison)

fifteen

Motivation and Leadership

What Would You Do?

With clear skies, bright sunshine, and temperatures predicted to reach the mid-20s by afternoon, it's a beautiful Tuesday in September. In New York City, millions of people are streaming into Manhattan by car, subway, trams, or ferries, including your 170 co-workers who are heading to the Sandler O'Neill offices on the 104th floor of Tower Two of the World Trade Center. Sandler O'Neill is a successful, full-service investment-banking firm that helps small and mid-sized companies and banks with strategic planning, interest rate management, mergers and acquisitions, and nearly any other kind of bonds, stocks, or financial transactions. With 1000 clients and $150 million in annual revenues, Sandler O'Neill has become one of the most successful small firms on Wall Street in its 13 years of existence, and you are one of its three leading partners.

Unlike your co-workers, you're enjoying a rare day off, playing golf at the Bedford Golf and Tennis Club in Westchester, New York, in an attempt to qualify for the U.S. Mid-Amateur Golf Championship tournament. You are on the sixth hole when the call comes, informing you that two planes have flown into Towers One and Two of the World Trade Center. You make it back to the clubhouse just in time to see both build-

ings collapse on TV. Just in case they forgot where you are, your first call is to your family to let them know that you're okay. You ask yourself who is in the office? Did Chris Quackenbush, head of investment banking and your friend of 25 years, make it out? What about the company founder and your mentor, Herman Sandler? Does anyone know what has happened to him? After spending several hours on the phone trying to find out what happened and trying to begin accounting for the whereabouts of Sandler O'Neill's 170 employees, you grab a train and get back to New York as quickly as you can.

At the Sandler O'Neill offices, on the 104th floor of Tower Two of the World Trade Center, only a few people headed straight to the stairs and the elevators when the first plane crashed into Tower One at 8:46 a.m. Karen Fishman, who helps Sandler O'Neill put together bond offerings for companies, stepped out of her office to hear Chris Quackenbush or Herman Sandler say, "A plane hit the other building." Just then, two other company executives rushed past in the hallway, saying, "We're getting the hell out of here." Fishman went with them. She said, "I don't know why I left. I don't know that it was a conscious decision. It was instinct. So much depended on who you saw right at that moment." Most people, though, didn't panic and stayed at

their desks calling family and friends to reassure them they were okay. Why didn't they leave? Because when terrorists exploded a bomb in the basement parking garage of the World Trade Centers in 1993, people who headed down the stairs were swallowed up in smoke, while people who fled to the roof to be rescued froze outside for hours. The people who stayed at their desks were barely affected. Unlike Fishman, who made her way down the stairs, 83 people from Sandler O'Neill stayed on the 104th floor because of that previous experience. Indeed, after the first plane crashed into Tower One, company founder Herman Sandler said, "I think the safest place to be is right here." Still, he announced, "Whoever wants to leave can leave."

By the time your train reaches Grand Central Station, it is 5 p.m., nearly eight hours after Tower Two collapsed. You literally run toward 48th Street, still in your golf clothes, to a small Sandler O'Neill office where employees have gathered during the day. But as you near 46th Street, you stop running and think, "I can't run in there all crazed. I need to arrive with a sense of calmness. I know people are going to look to me." Other thoughts stream through your mind. "How many people didn't get out? We're getting panicked calls from family members who haven't yet talked to their loved ones. What do we do if they didn't get out of the building? How will we take care of their families? And with our offices gone, how do we keep the business running? We surely can't take care of families if we don't get back in business." No one has heard from Chris Quackenbush and Herman Sandler, your best friend and your mentor. If they didn't get out, that means you're in charge. Do you have what it takes to be in charge? You've always played the tough guy. But that's not what's needed now. Can you change

to provide the right kind of leadership? You just don't know.

If you were the surviving partner of Sandler O'Neill on September 11, 2001, what would you do?

Sources: K. Brooker, "Starting Over," *Fortune,* 21 January 2002, 50. A. Geller, "Firms Decimated in Attacks Work to Rebuild Their Ranks with Alumni; Widespread Layoffs Help by Providing a Supply of High-Quality Applicants," *St. Louis Post Dispatch* (Associated Press), 24 October 2001, C1. "Company Information: Our Approach,"

Sandler O'Neill & Partners, L.P., [Online] Available www.sandleroneill.com/sandler/asp/control.asp?RequestingFrame=MAIN&RequestedAction=Approach, 25 March 2002. "Family Support," Sandler O'Neill & Partners, L.P. [Online] Available http://sandleroneillfamily.com/, 25 March 2002. "Sandler O'Neill Announces Company Open for Business," Sandler O'Neill & Partners, L.P. [Online] Available http://sandleroneillfamily.com/press_releases/press091701.htm, 25 March 2002. R. Smith, "Six Months After: At Sandler, A Client Sees Enormous Strain, Tries to Lend a Hand," *The Wall Street Journal,* 8 March 2002, C11.

Providing for deceased employees' families, struggling to ensure the company's survival with only half of a workforce, and replacing the company's top managers were but some of the major leadership challenges facing Jimmy Dunne at Sandler O'Neill. However, Dunne was not alone. Dozens of other companies that had offices in the World Trade Center faced the same problems. And while they normally don't occur in such dire circumstances, leadership-related issues create severe problems for all kinds of companies each year. Leadership, motivating employees, and working with teams are all key elements of management.

This chapter begins by reviewing the basics of motivation—effort, needs, and intrinsic and extrinsic motivation. We will start with a basic model of motivation and add to it as we progress through each section in the chapter. Next, we will explore how employees' equity perceptions and reward expectations affect their motivation. If you're familiar with the phrase "perception is reality," you're off to a good start in understanding the importance of perceptions and expectations in motivation. We then discuss what leadership is, who leaders are, meaning their traits and characteristics, and what leaders do that makes them different from people who aren't leaders. Next we examine two major contingency theories of leadership that specify which leaders are best suited for which situations or how leaders should change their behaviour to lead different people in different circumstances. The chapter ends by reviewing strategic leadership issues, such as charismatic and transformational leadership, that are concerned with working with others to meet long-term goals and creating a viable future for an organization.

What Is Motivation?

motivation
the set of forces that initiates, directs, and makes people persist in their efforts to accomplish a goal

Motivation is the set of forces that initiates, directs, and makes people persist in their efforts to accomplish a goal.[1] Based on this definition, *initiation of effort* is concerned with the choices that people make about how much effort to put forth in their jobs. ("Gosh, I hate writing performance appraisals, so maybe I'll just add a paragraph to last year's appraisals" rather than "Performance feedback is important. I'm going to schedule an hour to review each file and an hour to write each appraisal.") *Direction of effort* is concerned with the choices that people make in deciding where to put forth effort in their jobs. ("I'm really excited about the new computer system and can't wait to get started" rather than "Yeah, yeah, another new computer system. I'll do what I need to get by with it, but I think my time is better spent working directly with employees and customers.") *Persistence of effort* is concerned with the choices that people make about how long they will put forth effort in their jobs before reducing or eliminating those efforts. ("We're only halfway to our goal with three months to get it done. We'll never make it, so I'm not going to work at this anymore" rather than "We're only halfway to our goal with three months to go, but if we all keep working hard, we can do it.") As shown in Exhibit 15.1, initiation, direction, and persistence are at the heart of motivation.

After reading the next section, you should be able to
1. explain the basics of motivation.

1. Basics of Motivation

Take your right hand and point the palm toward your face. Keep your thumb and pinky finger straight and bend the three middle fingers so the tips are touching your palm. Now rotate your wrist back and forth. If you were in the Regent Square Tavern, that hand signal would tell waitress Marjorie Landale that you wanted a Yuengling beer. However, Marjorie, who isn't deaf, would not have understood that sign a few years ago. But with a school for the deaf nearby, the tavern always had its share of deaf customers, so she decided on her own to take classes to learn how to sign. She said, "It occurred to me that I could learn their language more easily than they could learn mine." At first, deaf customers would signal for a pen and paper to write out their orders. But after Marjorie signalled that she was learning to sign, she said, "Their eyes [would] light up, and they [would] finger-spell their order and [then] we've made a connection." The tavern's regular deaf customers teased her in a friendly way about her poor signing skills, but word quickly spread as the students started bringing in their friends, classmates, teachers, and hearing friends as well. Said Marjorie, "The deaf customers are patient with my amateur signing. They appreciate the effort."[2]

What would motivate an employee like Marjorie to voluntarily learn a new language like sign language? (Sign language is every bit as much a language as French or Spanish.) She wasn't paid to take classes in her free time. She chose to do it on her own. And while she undoubtedly makes more tip money with a full bar than with an empty one, it's highly unlikely that she began her classes with the objective of making more money. Just what is it that motivates employees like Marjorie Landale?

EXHIBIT 15.1

THE COMPONENTS OF MOTIVATION

Let's learn more about motivation by building a basic model of motivation out of these parts: effort and performance, need satisfaction, extrinsic and intrinsic rewards, and motivation with the basics.

1.1 Effort and Performance

When most people think of work motivation, they think that working hard (effort) should lead to doing a good job (performance). Exhibit 15.2 shows a basic model of work motivation and performance, displaying this process.

The first thing to notice about Exhibit 15.2 is that this is a basic model of work motivation and performance. In practice, it's almost impossible to talk about one without mentioning the other. Not surprisingly, managers often confuse the two, saying things such as "Your performance was really terrible last quarter. What's the matter? Aren't you as motivated as you used to be?" In fact, motivation is just one of three primary determinants of job performance. In industrial psychology, job performance is frequently represented by this equation:

$$\text{Job Performance} = \text{Motivation} \times \text{Ability} \times \text{Situational Constraints}$$

In this formula, *job performance* is how well someone performs the requirements of the job. Motivation, as defined above, is effort, the degree to which someone works hard to do the job well. *Ability* is the degree to which workers possess the knowledge, skills, and talent needed to do a job well. And *situational constraints* are factors beyond the control of individual employees, such as tools, policies, and resources that have an effect on job performance. Since job performance is a multiplicative function of motivation times ability times situational constraints, job performance will suffer if any one of these components is weak.

Does this mean that motivation doesn't matter? No, not at all. It just means that all the motivation in the world won't translate into high performance when you have little ability and high situational constraints.

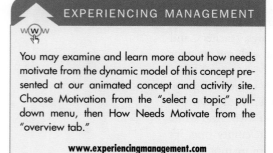

1.2 Need Satisfaction

In Exhibit 15.2, we started with a very basic model of motivation in which effort leads to job performance. However, managers want to know, "What leads to effort?" And they will try almost anything they can to find the answer to this question. For example, a

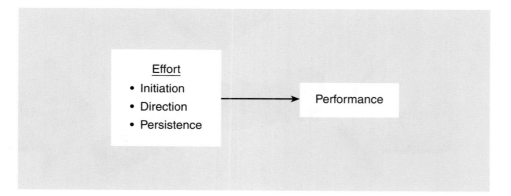

EXHIBIT 15.2

A BASIC MODEL OF WORK MOTIVATION AND PERFORMANCE

Effort
- Initiation
- Direction
- Persistence

→ Performance

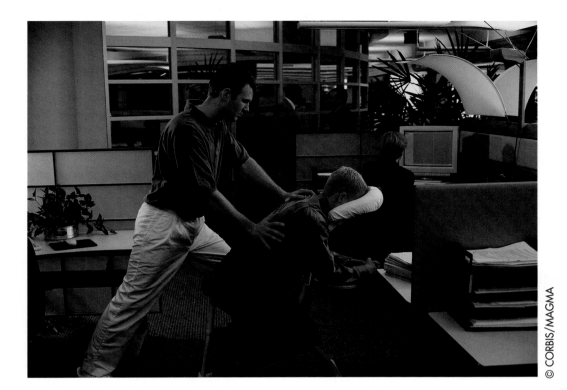

© CORBIS/MAGMA

Vancouver-based mining company, BHP Billiton Diamonds, has a long list of unusual workplace benefits that include foosball, billiards, squash courts and even an indoor driving range and putting green.[3] Employees at Intuit Canada, in Edmonton, can use one of the napping rooms or enjoy the company's big-screen TV or go to the company's gym and get instruction from a personal trainer. Maritime Life, based in Halifax, provides an on-site masseuse and daycare facilities. At Motorola, employees receive $5000 after they have reached 10 years of service.[4] So which of these techniques will motivate employees and lead to increased effort? The answer is all of them and none of them: It depends on employees' needs.

    Needs are the physical or psychological requirements that must be met to ensure survival and well-being.[5] As shown in the left side of Exhibit 15.3, a person's unmet need creates an uncomfortable, internal state of tension that must be resolved. For example, if you normally skip breakfast, but then get stuck working through lunch, chances are you'll be so hungry by late afternoon that the only thing you'll be motivated to do is find

needs
the physical or psychological requirements that must be met to ensure survival and well-being

---

EXHIBIT 15.3

ADDING NEED SATISFACTION TO THE MODEL

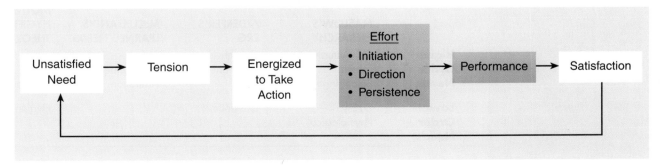

something to eat. So, according to needs theories, people are motivated by unmet needs. But once a need is met, it no longer motivates. When this occurs, people become satisfied, as illustrated on the right side of Exhibit 15.3.

Note: Throughout the chapter, as we build on this basic model, the parts of the model that we've already discussed will appear shaded in colour. For example, since we've already discussed the effort → performance part of the model, those components are shown with a shaded background. However, when we add new parts to the model, those parts will have a white background. For instance, since we're adding need satisfaction to the model at this step, the need-satisfaction components of unsatisfied need, tension, energized to take action, and satisfaction are shown with a white background. This shading convention should make it easier to understand the work motivation model as we add to it in each section of the chapter.

Since people are motivated by unmet needs, managers must learn what those unmet needs are and address them. However, this is not always a straightforward task, since different needs theories suggest different needs categories. Exhibit 15.4 shows needs from four well-known needs theories. Maslow's Hierarchy of Needs suggests that people are motivated by *physiological* (food and water), *safety* (physical and economic), *belongingness* (friendship, love, social interaction), *esteem* (achievement and recognition), and *self-actualization* (realizing your full potential) needs.[6] Alderfer's ERG theory collapses Maslow's five needs into three: *existence* (safety and physiological needs), *relatedness* (belongingness), and *growth* (esteem and self-actualization).[7] McClelland's Learned Needs Theory suggests that people are motivated by the need for *affiliation* (to be liked and accepted), the need for *achievement* (to accomplish challenging goals), or the need for *power* (to influence others).[8] Herzberg's Motivator-Hygiene theory has two basic components. Motivators are gained from doing a job well and receiving rewards such as recognition, advancement, and personal growth. Hygiene factors are associated with the nature of the job and workplace and include job security, working conditions, and supervisory policies.[9]

EXPERIENCING MANAGEMENT

Examine Maslow's Hierarchy of Needs in greater detail at our animated concept and activity site. Choose Motivation from the "select a topic" pull-down menu, then Maslow's Needs Hierarchy from the "overview tab."

www.experiencingmanagement.com

Things become even more complicated when we consider the different predictions made by these theories. According to Maslow, needs are arranged in a hierarchy from low (physiological) to high (self-actualization). Within this hierarchy, people are motivated by their lowest unsatisfied need. And, as needs are met, they work their way up the hierarchy from physiological to self-actualization needs. By contrast, Alderfer says that people can be motivated by more than one need at a time. Furthermore, he suggests that people are just as likely to move down the needs hierarchy as up, particularly when unable to achieve satisfaction at the next-higher need level. McClelland, on the other hand, argues that the degree to which particular needs motivate varies tremendously

EXHIBIT 15.4

NEEDS CLASSIFICATION OF DIFFERENT THEORIES

	MASLOW'S HIERARCHY	ALDERFER'S ERG	McCLELLAND'S LEARNED NEEDS	HERZBERG'S MOTIVATOR-HYGIENE THEORY
Higher-Order Needs	Self-Actualization Esteem Belongingness	Growth Relatedness	Power Achievement Affiliation	Motivators
Lower-Order Needs	Safety Physiological	Existence		Hygiene

from person to person, with some people being motivated primarily by achievement, and others by power or affiliation. Moreover, McClelland says that needs are learned, not innate. For instance, studies show that children whose fathers own a small business or hold a managerial position are much more likely to have a high need for achievement.[10] Herzberg's model differs in that job satisfaction and dissatisfaction are not seen as opposite ends of the same scale but rather as two separate scales. Improving things extrinsic to the job (hygienes) will reduce job dissatisfaction but will not improve motivation. Only through improving motivators will you increase an employee's motivation.

So with three different sets of needs and four very different ideas about how needs motivate, where does this leave managers who want a practical answer to the question "What leads to effort?" Fortunately, the research evidence simplifies things a bit. To start, studies indicate that there are two basic kinds of needs categories.[11] As shown in Exhibit 15.4, *lower-order needs* are concerned with safety and with physiological and existence requirements. However, *higher-order needs* are concerned with relationships (belongingness, recognition, relatedness, and affiliation); challenges and accomplishments (esteem, self-actualization, growth, and achievement); and influence (power). Studies generally show that higher-order needs will not motivate people as long as lower-order needs remain unsatisfied.

So, what leads to effort? In part, needs do. Subsection 1.4 discusses how managers can use what we know from need-satisfaction theories to motivate workers.

1.3 Extrinsic and Intrinsic Rewards

No discussion of motivation would be complete without considering rewards. Let's add two kinds of rewards, extrinsic and intrinsic, to the model, as shown in Exhibit 15.5.[12]

Extrinsic rewards are tangible and visible to others and are given to employees contingent on the performance of specific tasks or behaviours.[13] External agents (managers, for example) determine and control the distribution, frequency, and amount of extrinsic rewards, such as pay, company stock, benefits, and promotions. At Research in Motion, a two-way pager company based in Waterloo, Ontario, stock options are a key extrinsic reward that attracts and keeps people at the company. New employees are awarded options to buy shares at a fixed price. So if the stock was selling for $1, but is now worth $10, employees who exercise their stock options can earn $9 per share. One twenty- something employee was very excited when Research in Motion's shares spiked at over $225. She was worth almost a million dollars on paper. Of course, what can go up can come down as the shares fell to about a tenth of what they used to be.[14]

extrinsic reward
a reward that is tangible, visible to others, and given to employees contingent on the performance of specific tasks or behaviours

EXHIBIT 15.5

ADDING REWARDS TO THE MODEL

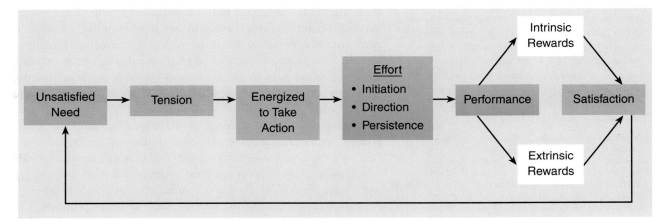

intrinsic reward
a natural reward associated with performing a task or activity for its own sake

Why do companies need extrinsic rewards? To get people to do things they wouldn't otherwise do. Companies use rewards to motivate people to perform three basic behaviours: joining the organization, regularly attending their jobs, and performing their jobs well.[15]

By contrast, **intrinsic rewards** are the natural rewards associated with performing a task or activity for its own sake. For example, aside from the external rewards management offers for doing something well, employees often experience a sense of interest and enjoyment from the activities or tasks they perform. Examples of intrinsic rewards include a sense of accomplishment or achievement, a feeling of responsibility, the chance to learn something new or interact with others, or simply the fun that comes from performing an interesting, challenging, and engaging task.

Which types of rewards are most important to workers in general? A number of surveys suggest that both extrinsic and intrinsic rewards are important. One survey found that the most important rewards were good benefits and health insurance, job security, having a week or more of vacation (all extrinsic rewards) and interesting work, the opportunity to learn new skills, and being able to work independently (all intrinsic rewards). And employee preferences for intrinsic and extrinsic rewards appear to be relatively stable. In 1973, 52 percent of employees listed "important and meaningful work" as very important, while in 1990, 50 percent of employees did. Similarly, in 1973, 19 percent of employees rated high income as very important. By 1990, this had increased only slightly to 24 percent.[16]

1.4 Motivating with the Basics

So, given the basic model of work motivation in Exhibit 15.5, what practical things can managers do to motivate employees to increase their effort?

Start by asking people what their needs are. If managers don't know what workers' needs are, they won't be able to provide them the opportunities and rewards that can satisfy those needs. When trainers begin work at Pegasus Personal Fitness Centers in Dallas, President Kirk Malicki simply asks them to make a list of rewards ranging in value from $35 to $300 that they'd like to receive for reaching weekly and monthly goals. Employees have chosen rock-concert tickets, limousine rentals, and half days off. Malicki said, "They know what motivates them better than I do, so I just ask."[17]

Next, satisfy lower-order needs first. Since higher-order needs will not motivate people as long as lower-order needs remain unsatisfied, companies should satisfy lower-order needs first. In practice, this means providing the equipment, training, and knowledge to create a safe workplace free of physical risks, paying employees well enough to provide financial security, and offering a benefits package that will protect employees and their families through good health and disability insurance. In a Canadian survey, 73 percent of employees said they would not likely work for a company that did not have benefits.[18] A survey based on a representative sample of Americans found that when people choose jobs or organizations, three of the four most important factors—starting pay/salary (62 percent), employee benefits (57 percent), and job security (47 percent)—are lower-order needs.[19]

Expect people's needs to change. As other needs are satisfied, or situations change, managers should expect that employees' needs will change. In other words, what motivated people before may not motivate them again.

Finally, as needs change and lower-order needs are satisfied, satisfy higher-order needs by looking for ways to allow employees to experience intrinsic rewards. Recall that intrinsic rewards, such as accomplishment, achievement, learning something new, and interacting with others, are the natural rewards associated with performing a task or activity for its own sake. And with the exception of influence (power), intrinsic rewards correspond very closely to higher-order needs that are concerned with relationships (belongingness, relatedness, and affiliation) and challenges and accomplishments (esteem, self-actualization, growth, and achievement). Therefore, one way for managers to meet employees' higher-order needs is to create opportunities for employees to experience intrinsic rewards by providing challenging work, encouraging employees to take greater responsibility for their work, and giving employees the freedom to pursue tasks and projects they find naturally interesting. For example, we began this section by asking, "What would motivate an employee like Marjorie Landale to voluntarily learn sign language?" Marjorie wasn't paid to do this. In fact, she even spent her own money and free time to learn how to sign. The reason that Marjorie learned how to sign is that doing so met her higher-order needs. It gave her a sense of accomplishment, and it allowed her to interact with deaf customers with whom she had been previously unable to interact. And Marjorie learned how to sign because her boss was smart enough to realize that there was no downside to giving her the freedom to pursue a task or project that she found naturally interesting.

Review 1
Basics of Motivation

Motivation is the set of forces that initiates, directs, and makes people persist in their efforts over time to accomplish a goal. Managers often confuse motivation and performance. However, since job performance is a multiplicative function of motivation times ability times situational constraints, job performance will suffer if any one of these components is weak. Needs are the physical or psychological requirements that must be met to ensure survival and well-being. When needs are not met, people experience an internal state of tension. But once a particular need is met, it no longer motivates. When this occurs, people become satisfied and are then motivated by other unmet needs. Different motivational theories, such as Maslow's Hierarchy of Needs (physiological, safety, belongingness, esteem, and self-actualization); Alderfer's ERG Theory (existence, relatedness, and growth); McClelland's Learned Needs Theory (affiliation, achievement, and power); and Herzberg's Motivator-Hygiene theory, specify a number of different needs. However, studies generally show that there are only two general kinds of needs, lower-order needs and higher-order needs, and that higher-order needs will not motivate people as long as lower-order needs remain unsatisfied. Both extrinsic and intrinsic rewards motivate people. Extrinsic rewards, which include pay, company stock, benefits, and promotions, are used to motivate people to join organizations and attend and perform their jobs. The basic model of motivation suggests that managers can motivate employees by asking them what their needs are, satisfying lower-order needs first, expecting people's needs to change, and satisfying higher-order needs through intrinsic rewards.

How Perceptions and Expectations Affect Motivation

On January 1, 2002, Europe's new currency, the euro, replaced the currencies of 11 countries (Austria, Belgium, Finland, France, Germany, Ireland, Italy, Luxembourg, Netherlands, Portugal, and Spain). Consumers can now easily compare the prices of goods from one country to those of another without having to make cumbersome currency translations. ("Let's see, 100 deutsche marks are worth 335 French francs, and 100 Spanish pesetas are worth 1,164 Italian lira, so that means it's cheaper if I buy it in....") But consumers won't be the only ones making cross-border euro comparisons. Companies and employees will, too, as they compare salaries and benefits from one country to those of another. For example, salaries tend to be much higher in northern than in southern Europe. In Germany, a sales and marketing director in a medium-sized company would be paid about 160 000 euros ($255 000) a year. But in Spain, the same job pays about 100 000 euros ($160 000). Yet even after taxes, which are higher in Germany, the German sales and marketing director takes home 80 000 euros a year ($128 000), while the Spanish sales and marketing director takes home 55 000 euros ($88 000). The difference is a whopping 45 percent.[20]

Companies are expecting to have to make significant wage adjustments now that much of Europe's workforce is being paid in euros. William Scott, who heads the Paris office of Hewitt Associates, a human resources consulting company, said, "We're doing many more cross-border [pay] comparisons. The need to compete and pay on a European-wide basis is quite significant. There will be a pay extravaganza for some folks." And if companies don't make salary adjustments, they can expect some employees to leave for higher pay in other companies or countries, especially multilingual employees who possess technical skills. Although it is expected that it will take many years for salaries to converge, a recent study by Hay Group, a consulting firm specializing in executive pay, has found that salaries for senior executives have already converged significantly.[21]

After reading the next two sections, you should be able to
2. *use equity theory to explain how employees' perceptions of fairness affect motivation.*
3. *use expectancy theory to describe how workers' expectations about rewards, effort, and the link between rewards and performance influence motivation.*

2. Equity Theory

equity theory
theory states that people will be motivated when they perceive that they are being treated fairly

Equity theory says that people will be motivated when they perceive that they are being treated fairly. In particular, equity theory stresses the importance of perceptions. So, regardless of the actual level of rewards people receive, they must also perceive that, relative to others, they are being treated fairly. For instance, by any objective measure it's hard to make the argument that the best professional athletes, who make upwards of $15 million a year (and no doubt more by the time you read this), are treated unfairly, especially when the average Canadian earns $ 41 600 a year (www.statcan.ca). But, as is explained below, equity theory doesn't focus on objective equity. Instead, equity, like beauty, is in the eye of the beholder. So, according to equity theory, if people truly perceive that they are being treated unfairly, then inequity exists, regardless of the "objective equity." Witness the inclusion of escalator clauses in top athletes' contracts that specify that if another player at the same position receives a larger contract then their contract will automatically be revised to that higher amount. So, despite their already enormous paycheques, top athletes still want to be paid as much as or more than other top athletes.

Let's learn more about equity theory by examining the components of equity theory, people's reaction to perceived inequity, and motivating with equity theory.

2.1 Components of Equity Theory

inputs
in equity theory, the contributions employees make to the organization

outcomes
in equity theory, the rewards employees receive for their contributions to the organization

referents
in equity theory, others with whom people compare themselves to determine if they have been treated fairly

The basic components of equity theory are inputs, outcomes, and referents. **Inputs** are the contributions employees make to the organization. Inputs include education and training, intelligence, experience, effort, number of hours worked, and ability. **Outcomes** are the rewards employees receive in exchange for their contributions to the organization. Outcomes include pay, fringe benefits, status symbols, job titles and assignments, and even the leadership style of their superiors. And since perceptions of equity depend on how you are being treated compared to others, **referents** are others with whom people compare themselves to determine if they have been treated fairly. Usually, people choose to compare themselves to referents who hold the same or similar jobs, or are otherwise similar to themselves in some way, such as in gender, race, age, or tenure.[22]

According to the equity theory process shown in Exhibit 15.6, employees compare inputs, their contributions to the organization, to outcomes, the rewards they received from the organization in exchange for those inputs. This comparison of outcomes to inputs is called the **outcome/input (O/I) ratio**. After an internal comparison in which they compare their outcomes to their inputs, employees then make an external comparison in which they compare their O/I ratio with the O/I ratio of a referent.[23] When people perceive that their O/I ratio is equal to the referent's O/I ratio, they conclude that they are being treated fairly. But when people perceive that their O/I ratio is different from their referent's O/I ratio, they conclude that they have been treated inequitably or unfairly.

There are two kinds of inequity, underreward and overreward. **Underreward** occurs when a referent's O/I ratio is better than your O/I ratio. In other words, the referent you compare yourself to is getting more outcomes relative to his or her inputs than you are. When people perceive that they have been underrewarded, they tend to experience anger or frustration. For example, when a manufacturing company received notice that some important contracts had been cancelled, management cut employees' pay by 15 percent in one plant but not in another. Just as equity theory predicts, theft doubled in the plant that received the pay cut. This was not surprising, as the Retail Council of Canada found that companies that paid 20 percent more than their competition had substantially lower employee theft rates.[24] Also, at the manufacturing plant that cut pay employee turnover increased from 5 percent to 23 percent.[25]

By contrast, **overreward** occurs when a referent's O/I ratio is worse than your O/I ratio. In this case, you are getting more outcomes relative to your inputs than your referent is. In theory, when people perceive that they have been overrewarded, they experience guilt. Not surprisingly, people have a very high tolerance for overreward. It takes a tremendous amount of overpayment before people decide that their pay or benefits are more than they deserve.

2.2 How People React to Perceived Inequity

What happens when people perceive that they have been treated inequitably? Exhibit 15.7 shows that perceived inequity affects satisfaction. In the case of underreward, this usually translates into frustration or anger, while with overreward the reaction is guilt. In turn, these reactions lead to tension and a strong need to take action to restore equity in some way. At first, a slight inequity may not be strong enough to motivate an employee to take immediate action. However, if the inequity continues or there are many inequities, tension may build over time until a point of intolerance is reached, and the person is energized to take action.[26]

There are five ways in which people try to restore equity when they perceive that they have been treated unfairly: reducing inputs, increasing outcomes, rationalizing inputs or outcomes, changing the referent, or simply leaving. These will be discussed in relation to the inequity associated with underreward, which is much more common than the inequity associated with overreward.

People who perceive that they have been underrewarded may try to restore equity by decreasing or withholding their inputs (i.e., effort). Increasing outcomes is another way in which people try to restore equity. This might include asking for a raise or pointing out the inequity to the boss and hoping that she takes care of it. Sometimes, however,

outcome/input (O/I) ratio
in equity theory, an employee's perception of the comparison between the rewards received from an organization and the employee's contributions to that organization

underreward
when the referent you compare yourself to is getting more outcomes relative to inputs than you are

overreward
when you are getting more outcomes relative to your inputs than the referent to whom you compare yourself

EXHIBIT 15.6

OUTCOME/INPUT RATIOS

$$\frac{\text{OUTCOMES}_{\text{SELF}}}{\text{INPUTS}_{\text{SELF}}} = \frac{\text{OUTCOMES}_{\text{REFERENT}}}{\text{INPUTS}_{\text{REFERENT}}}$$

EXHIBIT 15.7

ADDING EQUITY THEORY TO THE MODEL

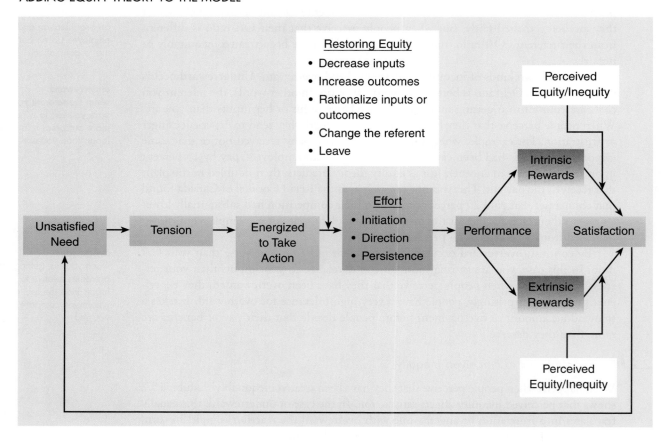

employees may go to external organizations, such as labour unions or provincial labour boards, to get some help in increasing outcomes to restore equity. Joining a union is another way to increase outcomes. Service industries are noted for not paying high wages. As a result, workers in the restaurant industry are increasingly turning to unions. In March 1999, the McDonald's restaurant in Squamish, British Columbia, became the first in North America to be unionized.[27] The Canadian Auto Workers have been successful in unionizing a number of fast food restaurants across British Columbia, including 50 KFC outlets.[28] Low pay is often a key issue in these unionizing drives.

Another method of restoring equity is to rationalize or distort inputs or outcomes. So instead of actually decreasing inputs or increasing outcomes, employees restore equity by making mental or emotional "adjustments" in their O/I ratios or the O/I ratios of their referents. For example, say a company downsizes 10 percent of its workforce. It's likely that the survivors, the people who still have jobs, will be angry or frustrated with company management because of the layoffs. However, if alternative jobs are difficult to find, the employees who are still with the company may rationalize or distort their O/I ratios and conclude, "Well, things could be worse. At least I still have my job." Rationalizing or distorting outcomes may be used when other ways to restore equity aren't available.

Changing the referent is another way of restoring equity. In this case, people compare themselves to someone other than the referent they had been using for previous O/I ratio comparisons. Since people usually choose to compare themselves to others who hold the same or similar jobs or are otherwise similar, they may change referents to restore equity when their personal situations change, such as a decrease in job status or pay.

Finally, when reducing inputs, increasing outcomes, rationalizing inputs or outcomes, or changing referents doesn't restore equity, employees may leave by quitting their jobs, transferring, or increasing absenteeism.[29] For example, Disney Corporation's Internet divisions have had a very difficult time keeping their top talent. Disney is well managed and pays very well but, because it's an established company, it hasn't been able to offer the stock options that Internet start-up companies are able to offer their employees. Both former Disney Online President Richard Wolpert and Winney Wechsler, head of Disney.com, left to take jobs with start-up companies.[30]

2.3 Motivating with Equity Theory

What practical things can managers do to use equity theory to motivate employees?

Start by looking for and correcting major inequities. One of the difficulties that equity theory makes us aware of is that an employee's sense of fairness is based on subjective perceptions. So what one employee considers grossly unfair may not affect another employee's perceptions of equity at all. While this makes it difficult for managers to create conditions that satisfy all employees, it's critical that they do their best to take care of major inequities that can energize employees to take actions, such as decreasing inputs or leaving, that can be extremely disruptive, costly, and harmful. So, whenever possible, managers should look for and correct major inequities.

Reduce employees' inputs. Increasing outcomes is often the first and only strategy that companies use to restore equity. This approach is unfortunate, because reducing employee inputs is just as viable a strategy. In fact, with 50-hour weeks, dual-career couples, and working at work and home being more the norm than the exception, more and more employees are looking for ways to reduce stress and restore a balance between work and family. In this context, it makes sense to ask employees to do less, not more, to have them identify and eliminate the 20 percent of their jobs that doesn't increase productivity or add value for customers, and to have managers eliminate company-imposed requirements that really aren't critical to managers', employees', or companies' performance (i.e., unnecessary meetings, reports, etc.). The SAS Institute, maker of the Statistical Analysis Software used by nearly every major company in North America, has been reducing employees' inputs with success for years. Unlike most software companies that expect employees to work 12- to 14-hour days, SAS offices close at 6 p.m. every evening. Also, employees receive unlimited sick days each year. And, to encourage employees to spend time with their families, there's an on-site daycare facility, the company cafeteria has plenty of highchairs and baby seats, and the company even has a seven-hour workday. The payoff? With an employee turnover of just 3.7 percent a year (compared to 20 percent and up for most software companies), the company saves $100 million a year in unnecessary costs and expenses.[31]

Make sure decision-making processes are fair. Equity theory focuses on **distributive justice**, the degree to which outcomes and rewards are fairly distributed or allocated. However, **procedural justice**, the fairness of the process used to make reward allocation decisions, is just as important.[32] Procedural justice matters because even when employees are unhappy with their outcomes (i.e., low pay), they're much less likely to be unhappy with company management if they believe that the procedures used to allocate outcomes were fair. For example, employees who are laid off tend to be hostile toward their employer when they perceive that the procedures leading to the layoffs were unfair. By contrast, employees who perceive layoff procedures to be fair tend to continue to support and trust their employers.[33] Also, if employees perceive that their outcomes are unfair (i.e., distributive injustice), but that the decisions and procedures leading to those outcomes were fair (i.e., procedural justice), they are much more likely to seek constructive ways of restoring equity, such as discussing these matters with their managers. In

PERSONAL PRODUCTIVITY TIP

Asking for a Raise

Getting a raise can restore equity. What's the best way to ask for one? First, make sure you're worth it. Critically evaluate your contributions and results, not just your efforts. Be ruthlessly honest about this; your boss will be. Drop hints to give your boss time to consider it before officially asking for a raise. Be patient. It usually takes three to six months to get raises approved. Be persistent, but don't issue ultimatums. Bosses sometimes wear down, but not if you make them angry. Is money all you want? Would you take a smaller raise and more vacation time? Be sure before you ask.

Source: C. Goforth, "Fishing for a Raise? Here's How You Can Land One," *San Diego Union-Tribune* (Knight Ridder News Service), 20 August 2001, C1.

distributive justice
the perceived degree to which outcomes and rewards are fairly distributed or allocated

procedural justice
the perceived fairness of the process used to make reward allocation decisions

contrast, if employees perceive both distributive and procedural injustice, they may resort to more destructive tactics, such as withholding effort, absenteeism, tardiness, or even sabotage and theft.[34]

Review 2
Equity Theory

The basic components of equity theory are inputs, outcomes, and referents. After an internal comparison in which employees compare their outcomes to their inputs, they then make an external comparison in which they compare their O/I ratio with the O/I ratio of a referent, a person who works in a similar job or is otherwise similar. When their O/I ratio is equal to the referent's O/I ratio, employees perceive that they are being treated fairly. But when their O/I ratio is different from their referent's O/I ratio, they perceive that they have been treated inequitably or unfairly. There are two kinds of inequity, underreward and overreward. Underreward occurs when a referent's O/I ratio is better than the employee's O/I ratio. Underreward leads to anger or frustration. Overreward occurs when a referent's O/I ratio is worse than the employee's O/I ratio. Overreward can lead to guilt, but only when the level of overreward is extreme. When employees perceive that they have been treated inequitably (i.e., underreward), they may try to restore equity by reducing inputs, increasing outcomes, rationalizing inputs or outcomes, changing the referent, or simply leaving. Managers can use equity theory to motivate workers by looking for and correcting major inequities, reducing employees' inputs, and emphasizing procedural as well as distributive justice.

3. Expectancy Theory

How attractive would you find the following rewards? A company concierge service that sends someone to be at your house when the cable guy or repair person shows up, or picks up your car from the mechanic? A "7 to 7" travel policy that stipulates that no one has to leave home for business travel before 7 a.m. on Mondays and that everyone should return home from their business travels by 7 p.m. on Fridays? The opportunity to telecommute so that you can feed your kids breakfast, pick them up after school, and then tuck them into bed at night? A "circle of excellence" award, in which employees nominate co-workers for outstanding work, and the winners get company-paid trips to Hawaii and the Bahamas? A full-sized basketball court with a real wooden floor? Or a sabbatical program that gives employees the chance to take a paid leave so they can work for local charities?[35]

If you had kids, you might love the chance to telecommute; but if you didn't, you might not be interested. If you didn't travel much on business, you wouldn't be interested in the "7 to 7" travel policy; but if you did, you'd probably love it. One of the hardest things about motivating people is that rewards that are attractive to some employees are unattractive to others. **Expectancy theory** says that people will be motivated to the extent to which they believe that their efforts will lead to good performance, that good performance will be rewarded, and that they are offered attractive rewards.[36]

Let's learn more about expectancy theory by examining the components of expectancy theory and motivation with expectancy theory.

3.1 Components of Expectancy Theory

Expectancy theory holds that people make conscious choices about their motivation. The three factors that affect those choices are valence, expectancy, and instrumentality.

Valence is simply the attractiveness or desirability of various rewards or outcomes. Expectancy theory recognizes that the same reward or outcome—say, a promotion—will be highly attractive to some people, highly disliked by others, and for some may not make much difference one way or the other. Accordingly, when people are deciding how much effort to put forth, expectancy theory says that they will consider the valence of all

expectancy theory
theory that states that people will be motivated to the extent to which they believe that their efforts will lead to good performance, that good performance will be rewarded, and that they will be offered attractive rewards

valence
the attractiveness or desirability of a reward or outcome

possible rewards and outcomes that they can receive from their jobs. The greater the sum of those valences, each of which could be positive, negative, or neutral, the more effort people will choose to put forth on the job.

Expectancy is the perceived relationship between effort and performance. When expectancies are strong, employees believe that their hard work and efforts will result in good performance, so they work harder. By contrast, when expectancies are weak, employees figure that no matter what they do or how hard they work, they won't be able to perform their jobs successfully, so they don't work as hard.

Instrumentality is the perceived relationship between performance and rewards. When instrumentality is strong, employees believe that improved performance will lead to better and more rewards, and they will choose to work harder. When instrumentality is weak, employees don't believe that better performance will result in more or better rewards, so they will choose not to work as hard.

Expectancy theory holds that for people to be highly motivated, all three variables—valence, expectancy, and instrumentality—must be high. Thus, expectancy theory can be represented by the following simple equation:

$$\text{Motivation} = \text{Valence} \times \text{Instrumentality} \times \text{Expectancy}$$

So if any one of these variables (valence, instrumentality, or expectancy) declines, overall motivation will decline, too.

Exhibit 15.8 incorporates the expectancy theory variables into our motivation model. Valence and instrumentality combine to affect employees' willingness to put forth effort (i.e., the degree to which they are energized to take action), while expectancy

expectancy
the perceived relationship between effort and performance

instrumentality
the perceived relationship between performance and rewards

EXHIBIT 15.8

ADDING EXPECTANCY THEORY TO THE MODEL

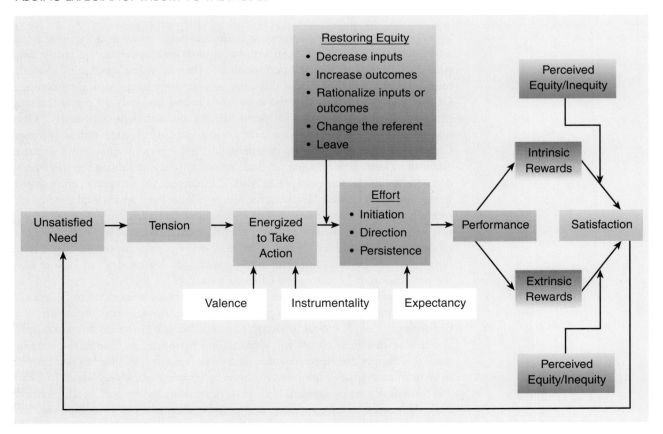

transforms intended effort ("I'm really going to work hard in this job") into actual effort. If you're offered rewards that you desire, and you believe that you will in fact receive these rewards for good performance, you're highly likely to be energized to take action. However, you're not likely to actually exert effort unless you also believe that you can do the job (i.e., that your efforts will lead to successful performance).

3.2 Motivating with Expectancy Theory

What practical things can managers do to use expectancy theory to motivate employees?

Systematically gather information to find out what employees want from their jobs. In addition to individual managers' directly asking employees what they want from their jobs (see "Motivating with Equity Theory"), companies still need to survey their employees regularly to determine their wants, needs, and dissatisfactions. Since people consider the valence of all the possible rewards and outcomes that they can receive from their jobs, regular identification of wants, needs, and dissatisfaction gives companies the chance to turn negatively valent rewards and outcomes into positively valent rewards and outcomes, thus raising overall motivation and effort. For example, even the most successful companies, like Microsoft, need to keep track of what employees want from their jobs. In the last few years, some of Microsoft's most talented managers and employees have begun to leave. After years of 14-hour days, these people, now mostly in their mid-30s and early 40s, want to spend more time with their families and on outside interests. As a result of these and other departures, Microsoft increased its compensation packages and doubled the number of steps in its pay scales, so that employees could receive promotions more frequently. However, since most of the top managers who are leaving are multimillionaires thanks to their Microsoft stock, it's unlikely that they'll find these changes attractive. Therefore, Microsoft is also now encouraging workers to go home earlier, take weekend time off, take the company sabbaticals that they've earned, and, ultimately, spend more time with their families.[37]

Take clear steps to link rewards to individual performance in a way that is clear and understandable to employees. Unfortunately, most employees are extremely dissatisfied with the link between pay and performance in their organizations. One Canadian survey found that that less than half of Canadian workers were happy with their compensation. Of even more concern is that the same study found that only 19 percent of employees surveyed were happy with pay-for-performance systems in their companies.[38] Other than making sure there is a connection between pay and performance in their companies (see Chapter 13 for a discussion of compensation strategies), another way for managers to establish a clearer link between pay and performance is to publicize the way in which pay decisions are made. For example, at Allstate Insurance, the company compensation team wrote a pamphlet called "Tracking the Clues to Your Pay," which explained how Allstate carefully used market value surveys and analyses to determine employee pay. Importantly, this helped counter the widespread belief that employee pay was determined in some random way. When asked "To what extent does the pay system competitively reward you for results?" 27 percent more employees responded "A great deal" or "Quite a bit" after the publication of "Tracking the Clues to Your Pay."[39]

Empower employees to make decisions if you really want them to believe that their hard work and effort will lead to good performance. If valent rewards are linked to good performance, people should be energized to take action. However, this works only if they also believe that their efforts will lead to good performance. One of the ways in which managers destroy the expectancy that hard work and effort will lead to good performance is by restricting what employees can do or by ignoring employees' ideas. In Chapter 11, you learned that empowerment is a feeling of intrinsic motivation, in which workers perceive their work to have meaning and perceive themselves to be competent, having an impact, and capable of self-determination.[40] So if managers want workers to have strong expectancies, they should empower them to make decisions. Doing so will motivate employees to take active rather than passive roles in their work.

Review 3
Expectancy Theory

Expectancy theory holds that three factors affect the conscious choices people make about their motivation: valence, expectancy, and instrumentality. Valence is simply the attractiveness or desirability of various rewards or outcomes. Expectancy is the perceived relationship between effort and performance. Instrumentality is the perceived relationship between performance and rewards. Expectancy theory holds that for people to be highly motivated, all three factors must be high. So if any one of these factors declines, overall motivation will decline, too. Managers can use expectancy theory to motivate workers by systematically gathering information to find out what employees want from their jobs, by linking rewards to individual performance in a way that is clear and understandable to employees, and by empowering employees to make decisions, which will increase their expectancies that hard work and efforts will lead to good performance.

What Is Leadership?

When Cynthia Danaher became general manager of Hewlett-Packard's Medical Products Group, she told her 5300 employees, "I want to do this job, but it's scary and I need your help." And you finally have a boss who "knows how to make coffee." After three years of experience as a leader, she now regrets that choice of words. If she had a chance to hold that meeting again, she says that she would emphasize goals and challenge her people to find ways to meet them. She said, "People say they want a leader to be vulnerable just like them, but deep down they want to believe you have the skill to move and fix things they can't. And while anyone who starts something new is bound to feel some anxiety, you don't need to bare your soul." Moreover, she says that for leaders, setting a direction is more important than making employees feel comfortable.[41]

As H-P's Cynthia Danaher discovered, **leadership** is the process of influencing others to achieve group or organizational goals.

leadership
the process of influencing others to achieve group or organizational goals

After reading the next two sections, you should be able to
4. explain what leadership is.
5. describe who leaders are and what effective leaders do.

4. Leadership

Southwest Airlines, the airline that Westjet has modelled itself on, flies two to three times as many passengers per employee as other U.S. airlines at a cost 25 percent to 40 percent below its competitors.[42] A key part of Southwest's performance is that it empties its planes, refills them with passengers, crews, fuel, and food (peanuts and soft drinks), and has them back on the runway in 20 minutes, compared to an hour for most airlines. This allows Southwest to keep each of its planes filled with paying passengers about three more hours a day. Why is Southwest able to achieve such incredible results? Herb Kelleher, Southwest's CEO and co-founder, answered the question this way: "We pay just as good wages and benefits as other airlines, but our costs are lower because our productivity is higher, which is achieved through the dedicated energy of our people. It's sheer willpower—no mechanical tricks. We've got exactly the same equipment. The difference is, when a plane pulls into a gate, our people run to meet it. Ponce de León was looking for the Fountain of Youth in the wrong place—he should have come to Southwest Airlines." In other words, the people of Southwest Airlines have been successfully influenced to achieve company goals (i.e., leadership).

Let's learn more about leadership by exploring leaders versus managers, and substitutes for leadership.

4.1 Leaders versus Managers

In Chapter 1, we defined *management* as getting work done through others. In other words, managers don't do the work themselves. Managers help others do their jobs better. By contrast, *leadership* is the process of influencing others to achieve group or organizational goals. So what are the key differences between leadership and management?

According to Professor Warren Bennis, the primary difference, as shown in Exhibit 15.9, is that leaders are concerned with doing the right thing, while managers are concerned with doing things right.[43] In other words, leaders will begin with the question "What should we be doing?" while managers start with "How can we do what already we're doing better?" Leaders focus on visions, missions, goals, and objectives, while managers focus solely on productivity and efficiency. Managers see themselves as preservers of the status quo, while leaders see themselves as promoters of change, as challengers of the status quo in that they encourage creativity and risk taking. According to Bill Black, president of Halifax-based Maritime Life Assurance, "At the senior levels it's more important to be a good leader than a good manager. My feeling is that the person who is a good leader is able to identify a long-term direction for the organization..."[44] Carol Bartz, CEO of Autodesk, Inc., a software company, said managers "know how to write business plans, while leaders get companies—and people—to change." She went on to say that "human nature says cling to what you have, whether that's an old coat, a boyfriend, or a way of doing business," but that leaders have to "leave that behind."[45] Managers have a relatively short-term perspective, while leaders take a long-term view. Managers are more concerned with means, how to get things done, while leaders are more concerned with ends, what gets done. Managers are concerned with control and limiting the choices of others, while leaders are more concerned with expanding people's choices and options.[46] Finally, managers solve problems so that others can do their work, while leaders inspire and motivate others to find their own solutions.

While leaders are different from managers, in practice, organizations need them both. Managers are critical to getting out the day-to-day work, and leaders are critical to inspiring employees and setting the organization's long-term direction. The key issue is the extent to which organizations are properly led or properly managed. Warren Bennis

EXHIBIT 15.9

MANAGERS VERSUS LEADERS

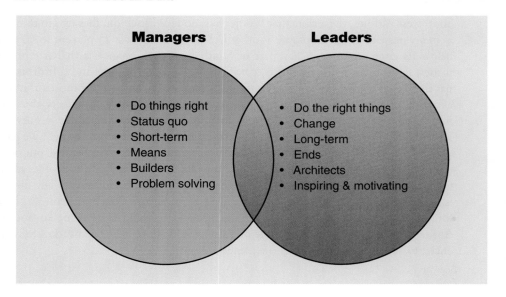

Managers
- Do things right
- Status quo
- Short-term
- Means
- Builders
- Problem solving

Leaders
- Do the right things
- Change
- Long-term
- Ends
- Architects
- Inspiring & motivating

summed up the difference between leaders and managers by noting that "organizations ... are underled and overmanaged. They do not pay enough attention to doing the right thing, while they pay too much attention to doing things right."[47]

4.2 Substitutes for Leadership: Do Leaders Always Matter?

One of the basic assumptions about leadership is that leaders always matter. The thinking goes that without sound leadership, organizations are sure to fail. In fact, when companies struggle, their leaders are almost always blamed for their poor performance.

However, there are situations and circumstances in which leadership isn't necessary, or is unlikely to make much of a difference, or where leaders aren't to blame for poor performance. These are known as leadership substitutes and leadership neutralizers.[48] Exhibit 15.10 lists a number of subordinate, task, or organizational characteristics that can act as leadership substitutes or neutralizers for either task-related or people-related leader behaviours.

EXHIBIT 15.10

LEADERSHIP SUBSTITUTES AND NEUTRALIZERS

CHARACTERISTIC	PEOPLE-RELATED LEADERSHIP BEHAVIOURS	TASK-RELATED LEADERSHIP BEHAVIOURS
SUBORDINATE CHARACTERISTICS		
• Ability, experience, training, knowledge	Neutralize	Substitute, Neutralize
• Need for independence	Neutralize	Neutralize
• Professional orientation	Substitute, Neutralize	Substitute, Neutralize
• Indifference toward organizational rewards	Neutralize	Neutralize
TASK CHARACTERISTICS		
• Unambiguous and routine tasks	No effect	Substitute, Neutralize
• Performance feedback provided by the work itself	No effect	Substitute, Neutralize
• Intrinsically satisfying work	Substitute, Neutralize	Neutralize
ORGANIZATIONAL CHARACTERISTICS		
• Formalization, meaning specific plans, goals, and areas of responsibility	No effect	Neutralize
• Inflexibility, meaning rigid, unbending rules and procedures	No effect	Neutralize
• Highly specified staff functions	No effect	Neutralize
• Cohesive work groups	Substitute, Neutralize	Substitute, Neutralize
• Organizational rewards beyond a leader's control	Neutralize	Neutralize
• Spatial distance between supervisors and subordinates	Neutralize	Neutralize

Source: S. Kerr & J.M. Jermier, "Substitutes for Leadership: Their Meaning and Measurement," *Organizational Behavior and Human Performance* 22 (1978): 375–403.

leadership substitutes
subordinate, task, or organizational characteristics that make leaders redundant or unnecessary

Leadership substitutes are subordinate, task, or organizational characteristics that make leaders redundant or unnecessary. For instance, when leadership substitutes such as ability and performance feedback are present, task-related leader behaviour that specifies goals, task assignments, and how to do the job aren't likely to improve a subordinate's work performance. Think about it. Workers already have the capability to do their jobs. And the job itself provides enough information to let them know how well they're doing their jobs or what they might do to correct performance problems. In situations like this, where leadership substitutes are strong, leaders don't need to tell workers what to do or how to do their jobs.

leadership neutralizers
subordinate, task, or organizational characteristics that can interfere with a leader's actions or make it impossible for a leader to influence followers' performance

Leadership neutralizers are subordinate, task, or organizational characteristics that can interfere with a leader's actions or make it impossible for a leader to influence followers' performance. Unlike substitutes, which simply take the place of leaders, leadership neutralizers create an "influence vacuum." In other words, leadership neutralizers create a need for leadership by ironically preventing leadership from working. For example, when subordinates are indifferent toward organizational rewards, there may be nothing that a leader can do to reward them for good performance. Likewise, union contracts that specify that all employees be paid the same, organizational policies that reward employees by seniority, and salary and raise processes that don't give leaders enough money to substantially reward good performers effectively neutralize the ability of leaders to reward workers. Spatial distance (an organizational characteristic) can also neutralize leadership. *Spatial distance* is a situation in which supervisors and subordinates don't work in the same place, such as with telecommuters or people working thousands of kilometres away in overseas offices. Spatial distance typically means infrequent feedback, little or no face-to-face contact, and being "out of sight and out of mind," all of which make it very difficult for leaders to lead. In fact, some companies find telecommuting to be so disruptive to leadership processes that they require their telecommuters to come into the office at least once or twice a week.

So do leaders *always* matter? Leadership substitutes and neutralizers indicate that sometimes they don't. However, this doesn't mean that leaders don't matter at all. Quite the opposite. Leaders do matter, but they're not superhuman. They can't do it all by themselves. And they can't fix every situation. In short, leadership is very important. But poor leadership isn't the cause of every organizational crisis, and changing leaders isn't the solution to every company problem.

Review 4
Leadership

Leadership is the process of influencing others to achieve group or organizational goals. Leaders are different from managers. The primary difference is that leaders are concerned with doing the right thing, while managers are concerned with doing things right. Furthermore, managers have a short-term focus and are concerned with the status quo, with means rather than ends, and with solving others' problems. By contrast, leaders have a long-term focus and are concerned with change, with ends rather than means, and with inspiring and motivating others to solve their own problems. Organizations need both managers and leaders. But, in general, companies are overmanaged and underled. While leadership is important, leadership substitutes and neutralizers create situations in which leadership isn't necessary or is unlikely to make much of a difference. Leadership substitutes are subordinate, task, or organizational characteristics that make leaders redundant or unnecessary. By contrast, leadership neutralizers are subordinate, task, or organizational characteristics that interfere with a leader's actions or make it impossible for a leader to influence followers' performance.

5. Who Leaders Are and What Leaders Do

Every year, *Fortune* magazine conducts a survey to determine corporate America's "most admired" companies. And, every year, as part of that study, it takes a look at the leaders of those companies. However, the last time it did this, it found that the CEOs of its ten most admired companies were surprisingly different. In fact, *Fortune* wrote that "every conceivable leadership style is represented by these CEOs."[49] General Electric's Jack Welch was described as "combative," as someone who "tilts his head, and thrusts out his chin as if to say, 'Go ahead, take your best shot'—and is never happier than when you do." Southwest Airline's Herb Kelleher was described as "a prankster and a kisser so unabashedly affectionate that his company's ticker symbol is LUV, so hands-on he has loaded baggage and served peanuts to passengers."

So if the CEOs of *Fortune*'s "most admired" corporations are all different, just what makes a good leader? Let's learn more about who leaders are by investigating leadership traits and behaviours.

5.1 Leadership Traits

Trait theory is one way to describe who leaders are. **Trait theory** says that effective leaders possess a similar set of traits or characteristics. **Traits** are relatively stable characteristics, such as abilities, psychological motives, or consistent patterns of behaviour. For example, according to trait theory, leaders were commonly thought to be taller, more confident, and have greater physical stamina (i.e., higher energy levels). Trait theory is also known as the "great person" theory, because early versions of trait theory stated that leaders were born, not made. In other words, you either had the "right stuff" to be a leader, or you didn't. And if you didn't, there was no way to get "it."

Until recently, studies indicated that trait theory was wrong, that there were no consistent trait differences between leaders and nonleaders, or between effective and ineffective leaders. However, more recent evidence shows that "successful leaders are not like other people," that successful leaders are indeed different from the rest of us.[50] More specifically, leaders are different from nonleaders on the following traits: drive, the desire to lead, honesty/integrity, self-confidence, emotional stability, cognitive ability, and knowledge of the business.[51]

Drive refers to high levels of effort and is characterized by achievement, motivation, ambition, energy, tenacity, and initiative. With regard to achievement and ambition, leaders always try to make improvements or achieve success in what they're doing and have strong desires to "get ahead." Leaders typically have more energy, and they have to, given the long hours they put in year after year. Furthermore, leaders don't have the luxury of being "down." Since we tend to take our cues from leaders, we expect them to be positive and "up." Thus, leaders must have physical, mental, and emotional vitality. Leaders are also more tenacious than nonleaders and are better at overcoming obstacles and problems that would deter most of us. Most change takes place slowly, and leaders need to have a "stick-to-it-iveness" to see changes through. Leaders also show more initiative. For example, GE's former CEO Jack Welch said, "Some CEOs think the day they become CEO is the high point of their careers. They ought to feel they're just beginning." Indeed, legendary investor Warren Buffett once said, "Jack [felt] there [had been] more to do at GE than when he started," more than 15 years before.[52] So rather than waiting for others to take action, leaders move forward quickly to promote change or solve problems.

Successful leaders also have a stronger *desire to lead*. They want to be in charge and think about ways to influence or convince others about what should or shouldn't be done. *Honesty/integrity* is also important to leaders. *Honesty*, that is, being truthful with others, is a cornerstone of leadership. Without honesty, leaders won't be trusted. But with it, subordinates are willing to overlook other flaws. For example, one follower said this about the leadership qualities of his manager: "I don't like a lot of the things he does, but he's basically honest. He's a genuine article and you'll forgive a lot of things because of that. That goes a long way in how much I trust him."[53] *Integrity* is the extent to which leaders do what they said they would do. Leaders may be honest and have good intentions, but if they don't consistently deliver on what they promise, they won't be trusted.

trait theory
leadership theory that holds that effective leaders possess a similar set of traits or characteristics

traits
relatively stable characteristics, such as abilities, psychological motives, or consistent patterns of behaviour

---

EXPERIENCING MANAGEMENT

w(w)w

Learn how managerial use of power affects employee behaviour and productivity. Visit our animated concept and activity site. Choose Leadership from the "select a topic" pull-down menu, then Power from the "overview tab."

www.experiencingmanagement.com

WhatReallyWorks

Leadership Traits Do Make a Difference

For decades, researchers assumed that leadership traits, such as drive, emotional stability, cognitive ability, and charisma were not related to effective leadership. However, more recent evidence shows that there are reliable trait differences between leaders and nonleaders. In fact, 54 studies based on more than 6000 people clearly indicate that with regard to leadership traits, "successful leaders are not like other people."

Traits and Perceptions of Leadership Effectiveness

Several leadership models argue that successful leaders will be viewed by their followers as good leaders. (This is completely different from determining whether leaders actually improve organizational performance.) Consequently, one test of trait theory is whether leaders with particular traits are viewed as more or less effective leaders by their followers.

Intelligence. On average, there is a 75 percent chance that intelligent leaders will be seen as better leaders than less intelligent leaders.

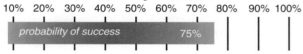

Dominance. On average, there is only a 57 percent chance that leaders with highly dominant personalities will be seen as better leaders than those with less dominant personalities.

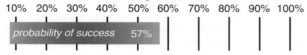

Extroversion. On average, there is a 63 percent chance that extroverts will be seen as better leaders than introverts.

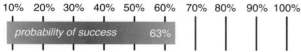

Charisma and Leadership Effectiveness

As discussed at the end of the chapter, charismatic leadership is the set of behavioural tendencies and personal characteristics of leaders that creates an exceptionally strong relationship between leaders and their followers. More specifically, charismatic leaders articulate a clear vision for the future that is based on strongly held values or morals, model those values by acting in a way consistent with the vision, communicate high performance expectations to followers, and display confidence in followers' abilities to achieve the vision.

Performance and Charisma. On average, there is a 72 percent chance that charismatic leaders will have better performing followers and organizations than less charismatic leaders.

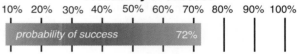

Charisma and Perceived Leader Effectiveness. On average, there is an 89 percent chance that charismatic leaders will be perceived as more effective leaders than less charismatic leaders.

Charisma and Leader Satisfaction. On average, there is a 90 percent chance that the followers of charismatic leaders will be more satisfied with their leaders than the followers of less charismatic leaders.

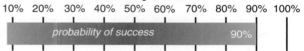

Sources: J.B. Fuller, C.E.P. Patterson, K. Hester, & D. Stringer, "A Quantitative Review of Research on Charismatic Leadership," *Psychological Reports* 78 (1996): 271–287. R.G. Lord, C.L. De Vader, & G.M. Alliger, "A Meta-Analysis of the Relation Between Personality Traits and Leadership Perceptions: An Application of Validity Generalization Procedures," *Journal of Applied Psychology* 71, no. 3 (1986): 402–410.

Self-confidence, believing in one's abilities, also distinguishes leaders from nonleaders. Self-confidence is critical to leadership. Leaders make risky, long-term decisions and must convince others of the correctness of those decisions. Self-confident leaders are more decisive and assertive and more likely to gain others' confidence. Moreover, self-confident leaders will admit mistakes, because they view them as learning opportunities rather than a refutation of their leadership capabilities. This also means that leaders have *emotional stability*. Even when things go wrong, they remain even-tempered and consistent in their outlook and the way in which they treat others. Leaders who can't control their emotions, who anger quickly or attack and blame others for mistakes are unlikely to be trusted. For example, Steve Jobs, CEO and cofounder of Apple Computers, is well known for his temper and for being an extremely demanding boss. When one of his assistants was late installing a high-speed, T-1 Internet connection, Jobs marched out to his cubicle and said, "No T-1. You're fired." The assistant went home, not sure whether Jobs was serious. Jobs apologized the next morning, but the assistant resigned soon after the incident.[54]

Leaders are also smart. Leaders typically have strong cognitive abilities. This doesn't mean that leaders are geniuses—far from it. But it does mean that leaders have the capacity to analyze large amounts of seemingly unrelated, complex information and can see patterns or opportunities or threats where others might not see them. Finally, leaders also "know their stuff," which means they have superior technical knowledge about the businesses they run. Leaders who have a good *knowledge of the business* understand the key technological decisions and concerns facing their companies. More often than not, studies indicate that effective leaders have long, extensive experience in their industries.

5.2 Leadership Behaviours

Thus far, you've read about who leaders are. However, traits alone are not enough to be a successful leader. Traits are a precondition for success. After all, it's hard to imagine a truly successful leader who lacks all these qualities. Leaders who have these traits (or many of them) must then take actions that encourage people to achieve group or organizational goals.[55] Accordingly, we now examine what leaders do, meaning the behaviours they perform or the actions they take to influence others to achieve group or organizational goals.

Research at the University of Michigan, Ohio State University, and the University of Texas examined the specific behaviours that leaders use to improve subordinate satisfaction and performance. Hundreds of studies were conducted and hundreds of leader behaviours were examined. At all three universities, two basic leader behaviours emerged as central to successful leadership: initiating structure (called *job-centred leadership* at the University of Michigan and *concern for production* at the University of Texas) and considerate leader behaviour (called *employee-centred leadership* at the University of Michigan and concern for people at the University of Texas).[56] In fact, these two leader behaviours form the basis for many of the leadership theories discussed in this chapter.

Initiating structure is the degree to which a leader structures the roles of followers by setting goals, giving directions, setting deadlines, and assigning tasks. A leader's ability to initiate structure primarily affects subordinates' job performance. Indeed, in an article entitled "Why CEOs Fail," *Fortune* magazine indicated that CEOs who do initiate structure are likely to succeed, while those who don't are likely to fail and often lose their jobs. *Fortune* wrote, "Watch the likes of [Jack] Welch [GE's CEO] or EDS's [CEO] Richard Brown or [Lawrence] Bossidy [CEO of Allied Signal] or any other proven implementer in a meeting. Near the end he'll grab a pen and start writing: He's noting exactly what is supposed to be done by whom, by when. He'll go over this with everyone before the meeting closes, and he'll probably send each one a reminder afterward." That, in a nutshell, is initiating structure.[57]

Consideration is the extent to which a leader is friendly, approachable, supportive, and shows concern for employees. Consideration primarily affects subordinates' job satisfaction. Specific leader consideration behaviours include listening to employees' problems and concerns, consulting with employees before making decisions, and treating employees as equals.

initiating structure
the degree to which a leader structures the roles of followers by setting goals, giving directions, setting deadlines, and assigning tasks

consideration
the extent to which a leader is friendly, approachable, supportive, and shows concern for employees

While researchers at all three universities generally agreed on the two kinds of basic leader behaviours, initiating structure and consideration, they differed on the interaction and effectiveness of these behaviours. The University of Michigan studies indicated that initiating structure and consideration were mutually exclusive behaviours on opposite ends of the same continuum. In other words, leaders who wanted to be more considerate would have to do less initiating of structure (and vice versa). The University of Michigan studies also indicated that only considerate leader behaviours (i.e., employee-centred) were associated with successful leadership. By contrast, researchers at Ohio State University and the University of Texas found that initiating structure and consideration were independent behaviours, meaning that leaders can be considerate and initiate structure at the same time. Additional evidence confirms this finding.[58] The same researchers also concluded that the most effective leaders were strong on both initiating structure and considerate leader behaviours.

This "high-high" approach can be seen in the upper right corner of the Blake and Mouton Leadership Grid shown in Exhibit 15.11. Blake and Mouton used two leadership behaviours, concern for people (i.e., consideration) and concern for production (i.e., initiating structure), to categorize five different leadership styles. Both behaviours are rated on a 9-point scale, with 1 representing "low" and 9 representing "high." Blake and Mouton suggest that a "high-high" or 9-9 leadership style is the best. They call this style *team management* because leaders who use it display a high concern for people (9) and a high concern for production (9). By contrast, leaders use a 9-1 *authority-compliance* leadership style when they have a high concern for production and a low concern for people. A 1-9 *country club* style occurs when leaders really care about producing a friendly and enjoyable work environment but don't really pay much attention to production or performance. The worst leadership style, according to the grid, is the 1-1 *impoverished* leader, who shows little concern for people or production and does the bare minimum needed to keep his or her job. Finally, the 5-5 *middle-of-the-road* style occurs when leaders show a moderate amount of concern for people and production.

Is the team management style, with a high concern for production and a high concern for people, the "best" leadership style? Logically, it would seem so. Why wouldn't you want to show high concern for both people and production? However, nearly 50 years' worth of research indicates that there isn't one "best" leadership style. The "best" leadership style depends on the situation. In other words, no one leadership behaviour by itself and no one combination of leadership behaviours works well across all situations and employees.

Review 5
Who Leaders Are and What Leaders Do

Trait theory says that effective leaders possess traits or characteristics that differentiate them from nonleaders. Those traits are drive, the desire to lead, honesty/integrity, self-confidence, emotional stability, cognitive ability, and knowledge of the business. However, traits aren't enough for successful leadership. Leaders who have these traits (or many of them) must behave in ways that encourage people to achieve group or organizational goals. Two key leader behaviours are initiating structure, which improves subordinate performance, and consideration, which improves subordinate satisfaction. There is no "best" combination of these behaviours. The "best" leadership style depends on the situation.

Situational Leadership

After leader traits and behaviours, situational leadership is the third major approach to the study of leadership. Two major situational leadership theories—Fiedler's contingency theory and Hersey and Blanchard's situational theory—both assume that the effective-

EXHIBIT 15.11

BLAKE / MOUTON LEADERSHIP GRID

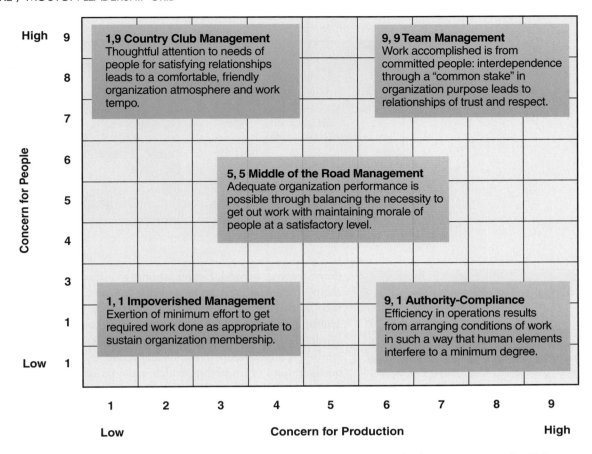

Source: R.R. Blake and A. A. McCanse, "The Leadership Grid," *Leadership Dilemmas—Grid Solutions* (Houston: Gulf Publishing Company), 29. Copyright 1991, by Scientific Methods, Inc.

ness of any leadership style, the way a leader generally behaves toward followers, depends on the situation.[59] Accordingly, there is no one "best" leadership style. However, these theories differ in one significant way. Fiedler's contingency theory assumes that leadership styles are consistent and difficult to change. Therefore, leaders must be placed in or "matched" to a situation that fits their leadership style. However, Hersey and Blanchard's situational theory assumes that leaders are capable of adapting and adjusting their leadership styles to fit the demands of different situations.

After reading the next two sections, you should be able to
6. explain Fiedler's contingency theory.
7. discuss Hersey & Blanchard's situational theory.

6. Putting Leaders in the Right Situation: Fiedler's Contingency Theory

Fiedler's **contingency theory** states that in order to maximize work group performance, leaders must be matched to the right leadership situation.[60] More specifically, as shown in Exhibit 15.12, the first basic assumption of Fiedler's theory is that leaders are effective when the work groups they lead perform well. So instead of judging leader effectiveness by what a leader does (i.e., initiating structure and consideration) or who the leader is (i.e., trait theory), Fiedler assesses leaders by the conduct and performance of the people

contingency theory
leadership theory that states that in order to maximize work group performance, leaders must be matched to the situation that best fits their leadership style

EXHIBIT 15.12

FIEDLER'S CONTINGENCY THEORY

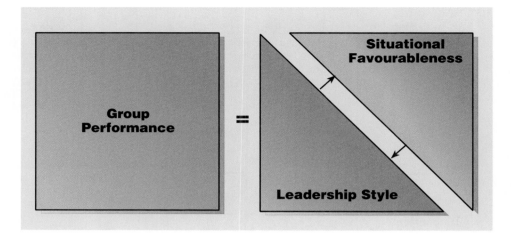

they supervise. Second, Fiedler assumes that leaders are generally unable to change their leadership styles and that leaders will be more effective when their leadership styles are matched to the proper situation. The third assumption is that the favourableness of a situation for a leader depends on the degree to which the situation permits the leader to influence the behaviour of group members. Thus, Fiedler's third assumption is consistent with our definition of leadership, which is the process of influencing others to achieve group or organizational goals.

Let's learn more about Fiedler's contingency theory by examining leadership styles, situational favourableness, and matching leadership styles to situations.

6.1 Leadership Style: Least Preferred Co-worker

When Fiedler uses the term leadership style, he means the way in which a leader generally behaves toward followers. However, Fiedler also assumes that leadership styles are tied to leaders' underlying needs and personality. And since personality and needs are relatively stable, he assumes that leaders are generally incapable of changing their leadership styles. For example, earlier in the chapter you read about the hot temper of Apple CEO Steve Jobs and how he fired one of his assistants when a high-speed Internet connection was installed late. However, stories about Jobs's temper have been around for more than 20 years. In fact, his temper is one of the reasons that he was fired from Apple in the 1980s (before returning in the last few years). In other words, over the last two decades, Jobs's leadership style and personality have been remarkably consistent.[61]

Fiedler uses a questionnaire called the Least Preferred Co-worker scale (LPC) to measure leadership style. When completing the LPC scale, people are instructed to consider all the people with whom they have ever worked and then to choose the one person with whom they "least preferred" to work. Take a second yourself to identify your LPC. It's usually someone you had a big disagreement with, or, for whatever reason, you couldn't get along with or didn't like. After identifying their LPC, people use the LPC scale shown in Exhibit 15.13 to "describe" their LPC.

Complete the LPC yourself. Did you describe your LPC as pleasant, friendly, helpful, supportive, interesting and cheerful? Or did you describe the person as unpleasant, unfriendly, frustrating, hostile, boring, and gloomy? People who describe their LPC in a positive way (scoring 64 and above) have *relationship-oriented* leadership

EXHIBIT 15.13

LEAST PREFERRED CO-WORKER SCALE

Pleasant	8	7	6	5	4	3	2	1	Unpleasant
Friendly	8	7	6	5	4	3	2	1	Unfriendly
Rejecting	1	2	3	4	5	6	7	8	Accepting
Helpful	8	7	6	5	4	3	2	1	Frustrating
Unenthusiastic	1	2	3	4	5	6	7	8	Enthusiastic
Tense	1	2	3	4	5	6	7	8	Relaxed
Distant	1	2	3	4	5	6	7	8	Close
Cold	1	2	3	4	5	6	7	8	Warm
Cooperative	8	7	6	5	4	3	2	1	Uncooperative
Supportive	8	7	6	5	4	3	2	1	Hostile
Boring	1	2	3	4	5	6	7	8	Interesting
Quarrelsome	1	2	3	4	5	6	7	8	Harmonious
Self-assured	8	7	6	5	4	3	2	1	Hesitant
Efficient	8	7	6	5	4	3	2	1	Inefficient
Gloomy	1	2	3	4	5	6	7	8	Cheerful
Open	8	7	6	5	4	3	2	1	Guarded

Source: Least Preferred Co-worker Scale, F.E. Fiedler & M.M. Chemers, *Improving Leadership Effectiveness: The Leader Match Concept,* 2nd Edition (New York: John Wiley and Sons, 1984). Reprinted by permission of the authors.

styles. After all, if they can still be positive about their least preferred co-worker, they must be people-oriented. By contrast, people who describe their LPC in a negative way (scoring 57 or below) have *task-oriented* leadership styles. Given a choice, they'll focus first on getting the job done and second on making sure everyone gets along. Finally, there is a third group with moderate scores (from 58 to 63) who are somewhat more flexible in their leadership style and can be somewhat relationship-oriented or somewhat task-oriented.

situational favourableness
the degree to which a particular situation either permits or denies a leader the chance to influence the behaviour of group members

leader-member relations
the degree to which followers respect, trust, and like their leaders

task structure
the degree to which the requirements of a subordinate's tasks are clearly specified

Fiedler assumes that leaders will be more effective when their leadership styles are matched to the proper situation. More specifically, Fiedler defines **situational favourableness** as the degree to which a particular situation either permits or denies a leader the chance to influence the behaviour of group members.[62] In highly favourable situations, leaders find that their actions influence followers. However, in highly unfavourable situations, leaders have little or no success influencing them.

Three situational factors determine the favourability of a situation: leader-member relations, task structure, and position power. **Leader-member relations**, which is the most important situational factor, is how well followers respect, trust, and like their leaders. When leader-member relations are good, followers trust the leader and there is a friendly work atmosphere. **Task structure** is the degree to which the requirements of a subordinate's tasks are clearly specified. With highly structured tasks, employees have clear job responsibilities, goals, and procedures. Position power is the degree to which leaders are able to hire, fire, reward, and punish workers. The more influence leaders have over hiring, firing, rewards, and punishments, the greater their power.

Exhibit 15.14 shows how leader-member relations, task structure, and position power can be combined into eight different situations that differ in their favourability to leaders. In general, Situation I is the most favourable leader situation. Followers like and trust their leaders and know what to do because their tasks are highly structured. Also, the leader has the formal power to influence workers through hiring, firing, rewarding, and punishing them. Therefore, in Situation I it's relatively easy for a leader to influence followers. By contrast, Situation VIII is the least favourable situation for leaders. Followers don't like or trust their leaders. As well, followers are not sure what they're supposed to be doing, given that their tasks or jobs are highly unstructured. Finally, leaders find it difficult to influence followers since they don't have the ability to hire, fire, reward, or punish the people who work for them. In short, it's very difficult to influence followers given the conditions found in Situation VIII.

6.3 Matching Leadership Styles to Situations

After studying thousands of leaders and followers in hundreds of different situations, Fiedler found that the performance of relationship- and task-oriented leaders followed the pattern displayed in Exhibit 15.15. Relationship-oriented leaders with high LPC scores were better leaders (i.e., their groups performed more effectively) under moderately favourable situations. In moderately favourable situations, the leader may be liked somewhat, tasks may be somewhat structured, and the leader may have some position power. In this situation, a relationship-oriented leader improves leader-member relations, which is the most important of the three situational factors. In turn, morale and performance improve. By contrast, task-oriented leaders with low LPC scores were better leaders in highly favourable and unfavourable situations. Task-oriented leaders do well in

---

EXHIBIT 15.14

SITUATIONAL FAVOURABLENESS

Leader–Member Relations	Good	Good	Good	Good	Poor	Poor	Poor	Poor
Task Structure	High	High	Low	Low	High	High	Low	Low
Position Power	Strong	Weak	Strong	Weak	Strong	Weak	Strong	Weak
Situation	I	II	III	IV	V	VI	VII	VIII
Favourable				**Moderately Favourable**			**Unfavourable**	

EXHIBIT 15.15

MATCHING LEADERSHIP STYLES TO SITUATIONS

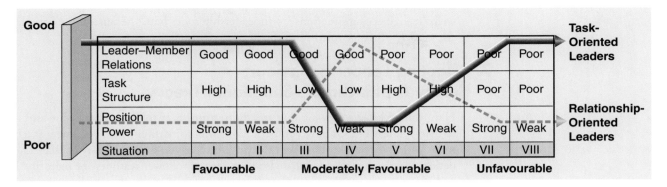

Leader–Member Relations	Good	Good	Good	Good	Poor	Poor	Poor	Poor
Task Structure	High	High	Low	Low	High	High	Poor	Poor
Position Power	Strong	Weak	Strong	Weak	Strong	Weak	Strong	Weak
Situation	I	II	III	IV	V	VI	VII	VIII

Favourable   **Moderately Favourable**   **Unfavourable**

favourable situations where leaders are liked, tasks are structured, and the leader has the power to hire, fire, reward, and punish. In these favourable situations, task-oriented leaders effectively step on the gas of a highly tuned car that's in perfect running condition. Their focus on performance sets the goal for the group, which then charges forward to meet it. But task-oriented leaders also do well in unfavourable situations where leaders are disliked, tasks are unstructured, and the leader doesn't have the power to hire, fire, reward, and punish. In these unfavourable situations, the task-oriented leader sets goals, which focuses attention on performance, and clarifies what needs to be done, thus overcoming low task structure. This is enough to jump-start performance, even if workers don't like or trust the leader.

Recall, however, that Fiedler assumes that leaders are incapable of changing their leadership styles. Accordingly, the key to making Fiedler's contingency theory practical in the workplace is to accurately measure and match leaders to situations or to teach leaders how to change situational favourableness by changing leader-member relations, task structure, or position power. While matching or placing leaders in appropriate situations works particularly well, practising managers have had little luck with "re-engineering situations" to fit their leadership styles. The primary problem, as you've no doubt realized, is the complexity of the theory. In a study designed to teach leaders how to reengineer their situations to fit their leadership styles, Fiedler found that most of the leaders simply did not understand what they were supposed to do to change their leadership situations. Furthermore, if they didn't like their LPC profile (perhaps they felt they were more relationship-oriented than their scores indicated), they arbitrarily changed it to better suit their view of themselves. Of course, the theory won't work as well if leaders are attempting to change situational factors to fit their perceived leadership style rather than their real leadership style.[63]

Review 6
Putting Leaders in the Right Situation: Fiedler's Contingency Theory

Fiedler's theory assumes that leaders are effective when their work groups perform well, that leaders are unable to change their leadership styles, that leadership styles must be matched to the proper situation, and that favourable situations permit leaders to influence group members. According to the Least Preferred Co-worker (LPC) scale, there are two basic leader styles. People who describe their LPC in a positive way have relationship-oriented leadership styles. By contrast, people who describe their LPC in a negative way have task-oriented leadership styles. Situational favourableness occurs when leaders can influence followers and is determined by leader-member relations, task structure, and position power. In general, relationship-oriented leaders with high LPC scores are better leaders under moderately favourable situations, while task-oriented leaders with low LPC scores are better leaders in highly favourable and unfavourable situations. Since Fiedler assumes that leaders are incapable of changing their leadership styles, the key is to accurately measure and match leaders to situations or to teach leaders how to change situational factors. While matching or placing leaders in appropriate situations has worked well, "reengineering situations" to fit leadership styles hasn't because of the complexity of the model, which people find difficult to understand.

7. Adapting Leader Behaviour: Hersey & Blanchard's Situational Theory

Have you ever had a new job that you didn't know how to do and the boss wasn't around to help you learn it? Or have you been in the other situation where you knew exactly how to do your job but your boss kept treating you like you didn't? Hersey & Blanchard's situational leadership theory is based on the idea of follower readiness or maturity. Hersey and Blanchard argue that just like children at different stages of maturity, employees have different levels of readiness for handling different jobs, responsibilities, and work assignments. Accordingly, Hersey & Blanchard's **situational theory** states that leaders need to adjust their leadership styles to match followers' maturity.[64]

Let's learn more about the Hersey & Blanchard situational theory by examining worker maturity and leadership styles.

7.1 Worker Maturity

Worker maturity is the ability and willingness to take responsibility for directing one's behaviour at work. Maturity is made up of two components. *Job maturity* consists of the amount of knowledge, skill, ability, and experience people have to perform their jobs. As you would expect, people with greater skill, ability, and experience do a better job of supervising their own work. *Psychological maturity*, on the other hand, is a feeling of self-confidence or self-respect. Likewise, confident people do a better job of guiding their own work than do insecure people.

The bottom of Hersey & Blanchard's situational theory model shows how job maturity and psychological maturity are combined to produce four different levels of maturity. The lowest level, M1, represents insecure people who are neither willing nor able to take responsibility for guiding their own work. The second level, M2, represents people who are confident and are willing but not able to take responsibility for guiding their own work. The third level, M3, represents people who are insecure and are able but not willing to take responsibility for guiding their own work. And the highest level, M4, represents people who are confident and willing and able to take responsibility for guiding their own work. It's important to note that a follower's maturity is usually task specific. For example, you may be highly confident and capable when it comes to personal computers but know nothing about setting up budgets for planning purposes. Thus, you would be mature (M4) with computers and immature (M1) with budgets.

7.2 Leadership Styles

Similar to Blake and Mouton's managerial grid, situational theory defines leadership styles in terms of task behaviour (i.e., concern for production) and relationship behaviour (i.e., concern for people). Hersey & Blanchard's situational theory model shows that these two behaviours can be combined to form four different leadership styles: telling, selling, participating, and delegating. Leaders choose one of these styles depending on the maturity a follower has for a specific task.

situational theory
leadership theory that states that leaders need to adjust their leadership styles to match followers' maturity

worker maturity
the ability and willingness to take responsibility for directing one's behaviour at work

EXPERIENCING MANAGEMENT

You may learn more about Hersey & Blanchard's Situational Theory by examining the model and completing the activities at our animated concept and activity site. Choose Leadership from the "select a topic" pull-down menu, then Situational Leadership from the "overview tab."

www.experiencingmanagement.com

A *telling* leadership style (high task behaviour and low relationship behaviour) is based on one-way communication, in which followers are told what, how, when, and where to do particular tasks. Telling is used when people are insecure and neither willing nor able to take responsibility for guiding their own work (M1). For instance, someone using a telling leadership style might say, "We're going to start a company newsletter. I want you to contact three printers for cost estimates. Then get together with each manager and get a one-page update with the latest activities from each department. Don't write these yourself. Have the managers write them and we'll edit them as we see fit. Also, call the CEO's assistant to remind her that we need her comments. Finally, have this all assembled in a three-ring notebook for me next Friday."

A *selling* leadership style (high task behaviour and high relationship behaviour) involves two-way communication and psychological support to encourage followers to "own" or "buy into" particular ways of doing things. Selling is used when confident people are willing but not able to take responsibility for guiding their own work (M2). For instance, someone using a selling leadership style might say, "We're going to start a company newsletter. I really think that's a great idea, don't you? We're going to need some cost estimates from printers and some comments from each of the managers. But that's pretty straightforward. Oh, don't forget that we need the CEO's comments, too. She's expecting you to call. I know that you'll do a great job on this. We'll meet next Tuesday to see if you have any questions once you've dug into this. By the way, we need to have this done by next Friday."

A *participating* style (low task behaviour and high relationship behaviour) is based on two-way communication and shared decision-making. Participating is used when insecure people are able but not willing to take responsibility for guiding their own work (M3). Since the problem is with motivation and not ability, someone using a participating leadership style might say, "What do you think about starting a company newsletter? Uh-huh, uh-huh (listening)? Okay, I think so, too. What kind of stuff do you hate in company newsletters? Uh-huh (listening). Okay, I agree. That stuff drives me nuts, too. Well, what do you think we should put in our company newsletter. Uh-huh (listening). Those are great ideas. I'd like to see you implement them. We've got about 10 days to put it together. Why don't you put together a first draft, based on what we talked about here today, and we can meet on Tuesday to review those ideas. Great!"

A *delegating* style (low task behaviour and low relationship behaviour) is a style in which leaders basically let workers "run their own show" and make their own decisions. Delegating is used when people are willing and able to take responsibility for guiding their own work (M4). For instance, someone using a delegating leadership style might say, "We're going to start a company newsletter. You've got 10 days to do it. Run with it. Let me know when you've got it done. I'll e-mail you a couple of ideas, but other than that, do what you think is best. Thanks."

In general, Hersey & Blanchard's situational theory shows that at first, as people become more mature, and thus increasingly willing and capable of guiding their own behaviour, leaders should become less task oriented and more relationship oriented. However, after people mature even more, leaders should become both less task-oriented and less relationship-oriented as people eventually manage their own work with little input from their leaders.

How well does Hersey & Blanchard's situational theory work? Despite its intuitive appeal (managers and consultants tend to prefer it over Fiedler's contingency theory because of its underlying logic and simplicity), most studies don't support situational theory.[65] While managers generally do a good job of judging followers' maturity levels, the theory doesn't seem to work well, except at lower levels, where a telling style is recommended for people who are insecure and neither willing nor able to take responsibility for guiding their own work.[66]

According to situational theory, leaders need to adjust their leadership styles to match follower's maturity, which is the ability (job maturity) and willingness (psychological maturity) to take responsibility for directing one's work. Job maturity and psychological maturity combine to produce four different levels of maturity (M1–M4) in which people vary in their confidence, ability, and willingness to guide their own work. Situational theory combines task and relationship behaviour to create four leadership styles: telling (M1), selling (M2), participating (M3), and delegating (M4), that are used with employees at different maturity levels.

Strategic Leadership

Thus far, you have read about two major leadership ideas: traits and behaviours. Leader traits are relatively stable characteristics, such as abilities or psychological motives. Traits capture who effective leaders are. Leader behaviours are the actions leaders takes to influence others to achieve group or organizational goals. Behaviours capture what effective leaders do (i.e., initiate structure and consideration). This leadership topic of the chapter introduces a third major leadership idea—strategic leadership—and its components: visionary, charismatic, and transformational leadership.

strategic leadership
the ability to anticipate, envision, maintain flexibility, think strategically, and work with others to initiate changes that will create a positive future for an organization

Strategic leadership is the ability to anticipate, envision, maintain flexibility, think strategically, and work with others to initiate changes that will create a positive future for an organization.[67] For example, General Electric's former CEO, Jack Welch, was one of the most successful CEOs ever, having increased GE's stock market value from $18 billion when he took over in 1981 to more than $600 billion 20 years later when he retired. From the start, Welch imparted strategic leadership by making it clear that every GE business (there are more than a dozen) needed to be "#1 or #2 in its industry." For two decades, he has reinforced GE's strategic leadership by holding half-day "classes" with more than 15 000 GE managers and executives at GE's executive centre. Every week, Welch also used surprise visits to GE plants and offices to maintain connections with GE's lower- and middle-level managers. Brian Nailor, a GE marketing manager, said, "We're pebbles in an ocean, but he knows about us."[68]

Thus, strategic leadership captures how leaders inspire their followers to change and to give extraordinary effort to accomplish organizational goals.

After reading this next section, you should be able to
8. *explain how visionary leadership (i.e., charismatic and transformational leadership) helps leaders achieve strategic leadership.*

8. Visionary Leadership

visionary leadership
leadership that creates a positive image of the future that motivates organizational members and provides direction for future planning and goal setting

In Chapter 4, we defined a vision as a statement of a company's purpose or reason for existing. Similarly, **visionary leadership** creates a positive image of the future that motivates organizational members and provides direction for future planning and goal setting.[69]

Two kinds of visionary leadership are charismatic leadership and transformational leadership.

8.1 Charismatic Leadership

Charisma is a Greek word meaning "gift from God." The Greeks saw people with charisma as divinely inspired and capable of incredible accomplishments. German sociologist Max Weber viewed charisma as a special bond between leaders and followers.[70] Weber wrote that the special qualities of charismatic leaders enable them to strongly influence followers. Weber also noted that charismatic leaders tended to emerge in times of crisis and that the radical solutions they propose enhance the admiration that followers feel for them. Indeed, charismatic leaders tend to have incredible influence over their followers, who become zealously inspired by and attracted to their leaders. From this perspective, charismatic leaders are often seen as bigger-than-life or uniquely special.

Charismatic leaders have strong, confident, dynamic personalities that attract followers and enable them to create strong bonds between themselves and their followers. Followers trust charismatic leaders, are loyal to them, and are inspired to work toward the accomplishment of the leader's vision. Because of these qualities, followers become devoted to charismatic leaders and may go to extraordinary lengths to please them. Therefore, we can define **charismatic leadership** as the behavioural tendencies and personal characteristics of leaders that create an exceptionally strong relationship between them and their followers. Charismatic leaders also

charismatic leadership
the behavioural tendencies and personal characteristics of leaders that create an exceptionally strong relationship between them and their followers

- articulate a clear vision for the future that is based on strongly held values or morals,
- model those values by acting in a way consistent with the vision,
- communicate high performance expectations to followers, and
- display confidence in followers' abilities to achieve the vision.[71]

Orit Gadiesh, chairman of Bain & Co., a management consulting firm, is an example of charismatic leadership. Gadiesh led Bain out of serious financial problems, expanded the company from 990 to 1400 employees, and increased revenues by 25 percent a year. Gadiesh dresses with flair and is described as complex, intense, driven, painfully direct, and a lot of fun. Founder Bill Bain recalls interviewing Gadiesh for the job: "The way she listened made my energy level go up. She asked the most thoughtful, original questions. There was nothing boilerplate about her." Bain managing director Tom Tierney says, "Her style comes from this intense passion about being true to herself and the client." Says James Morgan, CEO of Philip Morris USA, one of Bain's clients, "Orit has that talent for making you feel you're the most important person in the room."[72]

British billionaire adventurer Richard Branson dons a Virgin Cola costume and sprays the soft drink during a promotion in Tokyo. Branson's charismatic leadership has catapulted his business undertakings into the limelight and brought great success to his companies.

AP/Wide World Photos

ethical charismatics
charismatic leaders that provide developmental opportunities for followers, are open to positive and negative feedback, recognize others' contributions, share information, and have moral standards that emphasize the larger interests of the group, organization, or society

Does charismatic leadership work? Studies indicate that it often does. In general, the followers of charismatic leaders are more committed and satisfied, are better performers, are more likely to trust their leaders, and simply work harder.[73] However, the risks associated with charismatic leadership are at least as large as its benefits, particularly if ego-driven leaders take advantage of fanatical followers.

In general, there are two kinds of charismatic leaders, ethical charismatics and unethical charismatics.[74] **Ethical charismatics** provide developmental opportunities for followers, are open to positive and negative feedback, recognize others' contributions, share information, and have moral standards that emphasize the larger interests of the group, organization, or society. Ethical charismatics produce stronger commitment, higher satisfaction, more effort, better performance, and greater trust.

By contrast, unethical charismatics pose a tremendous risk for companies. Followers can be just as supportive and committed to unethical charismatics as they are to ethical charismatics. However, unethical charismatics control and manipulate followers, do what is best for themselves instead of their organizations, only want to hear positive feedback, only share information that is beneficial to themselves, and have moral standards that put their interests before everyone else's. John Thompson, a management consultant, said, "Often what begins as a mission becomes an obsession. Leaders can cut corners on values and become driven by self-interest. Then they may abuse anyone who makes a mistake."[75]

Exhibit 15.16 shows the stark differences between ethical and unethical charismatics on several leader behaviours: exercising power, creating the vision, communicating with followers, accepting feedback, stimulating followers intellectually, developing followers, and moral standards. For example, with regard to creating the vision, ethical charismatics include followers' concerns and wishes by having them participate in the development of the company vision. By contrast, unethical charismatics develop the vision by themselves solely to meet their personal agendas. One unethical charismatic said, "The key thing is that it is my idea; and I am going to win with it at all costs."[76]

So what can companies do to reduce the risks associated with unethical charismatics?[77] To start, they need a clearly written code of conduct that is fairly and consistently enforced for all managers. Next, companies should recruit, select, and promote managers with high ethical standards. Also, companies need to train leaders how to value, seek, and use diverse points of view. Leaders and subordinates also need training regarding ethical leader behaviours so abuses can be recognized and corrected. Finally, companies should celebrate and reward people who exhibit ethical behaviours, especially ethical leader behaviours.[78]

8.2 Transformational Leadership

transformational leadership
leadership that generates awareness and acceptance of a group's purpose and mission and gets employees to see beyond their own needs and self-interest for the good of the group

While charismatic leaders are able to articulate a clear vision, model values consistent with that vision, communicate high performance expectations, and establish very strong relationships between themselves and their followers, **transformational leadership** goes further by generating awareness and acceptance of a group's purpose and mission and by getting employees to see beyond their own needs and self-interest for the good of the group.[79] Transformational leaders, like charismatic leaders, are visionary. However, transformational leaders transform their organizations by getting their followers to accomplish more than they intended and even more than they thought possible. Transformational leaders are able to make their followers feel as if they are a vital part of the organization and can help them see how their jobs fit with the organization's vision. By linking individual and organizational interests, transformational leaders encourage followers to make sacrifices for the organization, because they know that they will prosper when the

EXHIBIT 15.16

ETHICAL AND UNETHICAL CHARISMATICS

CHARISMATIC LEADER BEHAVIOURS	ETHICAL CHARISMATICS	UNETHICAL CHARISMATICS
Exercising power	Power is used to serve others.	Power is used to dominate or manipulate others for personal gain.
Creating the vision	Followers help develop the vision.	Vision comes solely from leader and serves his/her personal agenda.
Communicating with followers	Two-way communication: Seek out viewpoints on critical issues.	One-way communication: Not open to input and suggestions from others.
Accepting feedback	Open to feedback. Willing to learn from criticism.	Inflated ego thrives on attention and admiration of yes-men. Avoid or punish candid feedback.
Stimulating followers intellectually	Want followers to think and question status quo as well as leader's views.	Don't want followers to think. Want uncritical, unquestioning acceptance of leader's ideas.
Developing followers	Focus on developing people with whom they interact. Express confidence in them and share recognition with others.	Insensitive and unresponsive to followers' needs and aspirations.
Moral standards	Follow self-guided principles that may go against popular opinion. Have three virtues: courage, a sense of fairness or justice, and integrity.	Follow standards only if they satisfy immediate self-interests. Manipulate impressions so that others think they are "doing the right thing." Use communication skills to manipulate others to support their personal agenda.

Source: J.M. Howell & B.J. Avolio, "The Ethics of Charismatic Leadership: Submission or Liberation?" *Academy of Management Executive 6*, no. 2 (1992): 43–54.

organization prospers. There are four components of transformational leadership: charismatic leadership or idealized influence, inspirational motivation, intellectual stimulation, and individualized consideration.[80]

Charismatic leadership or *idealized influence* means that transformational leaders act as role models for their followers. Because transformational leaders put others' needs ahead of their own and share risks with followers, they are admired, respected, and trusted, and followers want to emulate them. Thus, in contrast to purely charismatic leaders (especially unethical charismatics), transformational leaders can be counted on to do the right thing and maintain high standards for ethical and personal conduct. For example, GE's former CEO, Jack Welch, acted as a role model for his employees (three vice presidents and the heads of GE's 12 businesses) by setting and monitoring specific performance targets for each of them. Each of these top managers also received a detailed, handwritten, two-page performance evaluation from Welch each year. Said Welch, "I do the evaluations on Sunday nights in my library at home. It gives me a chance to reflect on each business." Modelling their behaviour after Welch, these top managers do the same with their direct reports. Thomas E. Dunham of GE's Medical Systems said, "Welch preaches it from the top, and people see it at the bottom."[81] Accordingly, Welch served as a role model for all of GE's managers.

EXPERIENCING MANAGEMENT

Learn why transformational leaders are necessary when organizations face crises by visiting our animated concept and activity site. Choose Leadership from the "select a topic" pull-down menu, then Transformational Leadership from the "overview tab."

www.experiencingmanagement.com

Inspirational motivation means that transformational leaders motivate and inspire followers by providing meaning and challenge to their work. By clearly communicating expectations and demonstrating commitment to goals, transformational leaders help followers envision future states, such as the organizational vision. In turn, this leads to greater enthusiasm and optimism about the future.

Intellectual stimulation means that transformational leaders encourage followers to be creative and innovative, to question assumptions, and to look at problems and situations in new ways, even if they are different from the leader's ideas. For example, at General Electric's Corporate Executive Council sessions, where GE's top 30 managers meet before the end of each financial quarter, CEO Welch pressed top managers by insisting on candid, unfiltered discussions and opinions from everyone. His executives describe these sessions as "food fights" and "free-for-alls." The intent is not to bruise egos or shame poor performers, but to realistically face up to problems that need solving. Welch also brought managers and employees from GE's 12 businesses together each January in Boca Raton, Florida, to communicate ideas and successes so that best practices were shared across all parts of GE. The point, again, is to look for good solutions wherever they can be found.

Individualized consideration means that transformational leaders pay special attention to followers' individual needs by creating learning opportunities, accepting and tolerating individual differences, encouraging two-way communication, and being a good listener. One of the ways in which Jack Welch showed individualized consideration is through the personal, spontaneous handwritten notes that he sent to people throughout GE. When William Woodburn, who managed GE's industrial diamonds business, turned down a promotion because he didn't want to uproot his teenage daughter, Welch wrote to him, saying, "Bill, we like you for a lot of reasons—one of them is that you are a very special person. You proved it again this morning. Good for you and your lucky family. Make Diamonds a great business and keep your priorities straight." Woodburn responded that this gesture "showed me he cared about me not as a manager but as a person," and "that means a lot."[82]

Finally, a distinction needs to be drawn between transformational leadership and transactional leadership. While transformational leaders use visionary and inspirational appeals to influence followers, **transactional leadership** is based on an exchange process, in which followers are rewarded for good performance and punished for poor performance. When leaders administer rewards fairly and offer followers the rewards that they want, followers will often reciprocate with effort. However, transactional leaders often over-rely on discipline or threats to bring performance up to standards. While this may work in the short run, it's much less effective in the long run. Many leaders and organizations have difficulty successfully linking pay practices to individual performance. The result is that studies consistently show that transformational leadership is much more effective on average than transactional leadership. In Canada, the United States, Japan, and India, and at all organizational levels, from first-level supervisors to upper level executives, followers view transformational leaders as much better leaders and are much more satisfied when working for them. Furthermore, companies with transformational leaders have significantly better financial performance.[83]

Review **8**
Strategic Leadership

Strategic leadership requires visionary, charismatic, and transformational leadership. Visionary leadership creates a positive image of the future that motivates organizational members and provides direction for future planning and goal setting. Charismatic leaders have strong, confident, dynamic personalities that attract followers, enable them to create

---

PERSONAL PRODUCTIVITY TIP

Be a Good Follower

David Ogilvy, founder of Olgilvy & Mather, told this story about the importance of being a good follower. He wrote:

On the night before a major battle, the first Duke of Marlborough was reconnoitering the terrain. He and his staff were on horseback. Marlborough dropped his glove. Cadogan, his chief of staff, dismounted, picked up the glove and handed it to Marlborough.... Later that evening, Marlborough issued his final order: "Cadogan, put a battery of guns where I dropped my glove." "I have already done so," replied Cadogan. He had read Marlborough's mind, and anticipated his order. Cadogan was the kind of follower who makes leadership easy.

Source: D. Ogilvy, "Leadership," in *The Book of Business Wisdom*, ed. P. Krass (New York: Wiley, 1997).

---

transactional leadership
leadership based on an exchange process, in which followers are rewarded for good performance and punished for poor performance

---

strong bonds, and inspire followers to accomplish the leader's vision. Followers of ethical charismatic leaders work harder, are more committed and satisfied, are better performers, are more likely to trust their leaders. Followers can be just as supportive and committed to unethical charismatics, but these leaders can pose a tremendous risk for companies. Unethical charismatics control and manipulate followers and do what is best for themselves instead of their organizations. To reduce the risks associated with unethical charismatics, companies need to enforce a clearly written code of conduct; recruit, select, and promote managers with high ethical standards; train leaders how to value, seek, and use diverse points of view; teach everyone in the company to recognize unethical leader behaviours; and celebrate and reward people who exhibit ethical behaviours. Transformational leadership goes beyond charismatic leadership by generating awareness and acceptance of a group's purpose and mission and by getting employees to see beyond their own needs and self-interest for the good of the group. The four components of transformational leadership are charisma or idealized influence, inspirational motivation, intellectual stimulation, and individualized consideration.

What Really Happened?

At the beginning of the chapter, you read how 83 of the 170 people who worked for Sandler O'Neill, a small financial firm located on the 104th floor of World Trade Center Tower Two, died when the towers collapsed after terrorist attacks on September 11, 2001. Jimmy Dunne, the manager portrayed in this case, had taken a day off and was on the golf course when he learned about the disaster. Right after he got to the clubhouse to watch the news on TV, the towers collapsed, taking the lives of his friends and partners, Chris Quackenbush and Herman Sandler, and leaving him in charge of the company. Read the answers to the opening case to see what really happened and to learn how Jimmy Dunne met this extraordinary leadership challenge.

How many people didn't get out? We're getting panicked calls from family members who haven't yet talked to their loved ones. What do we do if they didn't get out of the building? How will we take care of their families?

Leaders generally use two key behaviours to achieve group and organizational goals, consideration and initiating structure, the latter of which will be discussed in the answer to the next question. Consideration is the

extent to which leaders are friendly, approachable, and supportive and show concern for employees. Consideration primarily affects subordinates' job satisfaction. Specific leader consideration behaviours include listening to employees' problems and concerns, consulting with employees before making decisions, and treating employees as equals. Consideration is also very similar to the idea of supportive leadership in path-goal theory. Consideration and supportive leadership can lead to improved performance when it increases employee confidence, lowers employee job stress, or improves relations and trust between employees and leaders.

For Jimmy Dunne and the surviving employees of Sandler O'Neill, there was never any question that the company would take care of the families of the co-workers who were killed on September 11. The company immediately hired grief counsellors for them, organized a centre to help them go about the grisly task of recovering remains, and established a charity fund to which people could contribute to benefit the families. Many companies affected by the tragedy took similar steps. But Dunne and Sandler O'Neill felt they should do more. Within two weeks of the tragedy, the company sent each deceased employee's family a

cheque paying their salary through the end of the year. It also extended their health benefits for the next five years. In addition, Dunne told the families that it would also pay them the sales commissions and year-end bonuses that their loved ones would have collected had they lived. In the end, the company paid families more than 30 percent of its capital.

Why did Dunne and Sandler O'Neill extend so much consideration to deceased co-workers' families? Said Dunne, "Fifteen years from now, my son will meet the son or daughter of one of our people who died that day, and I will be judged on what that kid tells my son about what Sandler O'Neill did for his family."

And with our offices gone, how do we keep the business running? We surely can't take care of families if we don't get back in business.

As mentioned above, leaders use two key behaviours, consideration and initiating structure, to achieve group and organizational goals. Initiating structure is the degree to which a leader structures the roles of followers by setting goals, giving directions, setting deadlines, and assigning tasks. A leader's ability to initiate structure primarily affects subordinates' job performance.

With its primary offices completely destroyed, most of its computerized and paper records vaporized, and with almost half of its workforce dead, Sandler O'Neill's surviving managers and workers faced a tremendous challenge just keeping the company going. But the moment that Jimmy Dunne walked into the company's small office on 48th Street, he declared that the company would not only survive, but would find a way to thrive. Said one employee, "He made us feel like 'I'll show you the path through the trees.'" That first night, Dunne worked till 3 a.m., went home to shower, hug his wife, look in on his sleeping children, and was back at the office in a suit by 5 a.m. to begin rebuilding the company.

Because its survival was at stake, Dunne directed everyone to do everything they could, to call in every favour, to make sure that the company would complete all the major bond issues it was scheduled to complete before September 11. However, with its offices and files completely destroyed, how could they get started, especially in a financial business as complex as theirs? Their first break came in the form of the photographic memory of an office assistant. After answering the company phones for years, she knew the names and phone numbers of key clients from memory. This allowed people to begin working the phones and continue business. The next big break came from competitors, who gave Sandler O'Neill small slices of their business without asking anything in return. For instance, the benevolence of J.P. Morgan resulted in a $23 000 fee. Numerous other competitors were just as generous. And with the company's survival at risk, Dunne encouraged people to put their pride aside and take any such offers. The third major break came from the large number of layoffs that were occurring on Wall Street at that time. After a year of recession, financial firms laid off thousands of employees. Dunne told a friend at another company, "If there's someone good getting cut, let me know.

But only if they're good. I can't waste time on duds." By November, the company had hired bond traders, investment bankers, and researchers, two dozen new employees in all, and its recovery was well under way.

No one has heard from Chris Quackenbush and Herman Sandler, your best friend and your mentor. If they didn't get out, that means you're in charge. Do you have what it takes to be in charge? You've always played the tough guy. But that's not what's needed now. Can you change to provide the right kind of leadership? You just don't know.

Every company seems to have a "good cop, bad cop" combination in its leadership team. Prior to September 11, Herman Sandler was the "good cop" who encouraged people and showed patience when they made mistakes. By contrast, Jimmy Dunne was the "bad cop" who delivered bad news, confronted people when they made expensive mistakes, and fired people when it was time for them to go. Dunne once screamed at a trader, "The next time you do something smart, monkeys'll fly out of my a**." But as the lone remaining member of the leadership team, Jimmy Dunne quickly realized that he couldn't play the "bad cop" any more. Hoping to acquire Herman Sandler's patience and overt friendliness, he began saying, "I need to be more like Herman now." Hoping to acquire Chris Quackenbush's negotiation skills and ability to remain calm, he began saying, "I need to be more like Chris now." However, leadership researchers disagree on whether leaders have the ability to adapt or change their leadership styles. Fiedler's contingency theory assumes that leadership styles are consistent and difficult to change. Therefore, leaders must be placed in or "matched" to a situation that fits their leadership style.

Was Jimmy Dunne able to change and adapt his leadership style? In part, yes, and, in part, no. Dunne became more patient and supportive because of the tender emotional state of his

employees and his extraordinary commitment to providing for deceased employees' families. However, he remained true to himself by maintaining a strong focus on helping the business survive. For example, less than a week after the attacks, he issued this statement: "For the past several days, Sandler O'Neill employees, families, friends, clients, and competitors have joined together in an amazing way to do everything possible to locate our missing colleagues and to share all new information with their families. At the same time, we have also rallied our team to ensure that our business not only survives, but prospers. The best way we can honor our people is not to let terrorism stand in the way of Sandler O'Neill moving forward."

In the end, Jimmy Dunne did a remarkable job of leading Sandler O'Neill's dedicated managers and employees. Just two months after losing their main office, most of the management team, and half of its workforce, the company was again earning a profit. By the end of the year, less than four months after the disaster, the company ended up having a better financial year than the year before, allowing it to pay even larger bonuses and sales commissions to the families of its deceased workers.

Sources: K. Brooker, "Starting Over," *Fortune*, 21 January 2002, 50. A. Geller, "Firms Decimated in Attacks Work to Rebuild Their Ranks with Alumni: Widespread Layoffs Help by Providing a Supply of High-Quality Applicants," *St. Louis Post Dispatch* (Associated Press), 24 October 2001, C1. "Company Information: Our Approach," Sandler O'Neill & Partners, L.P., [Online] Available www.sandleroneill.com/sandler/asp/control.asp?RequestingFrame=MAIN&RequestedAction=Approach, 25 March 2002. "Family Support," Sandler O'Neill & Partners, L.P. [Online] Available www.sandleroneillfamily.com/, 25 March 2002. "Sandler O'Neill Announces Company Open for Business," Sandler O'Neill & Partners, L.P. [Online] Available http://sandleroneillfamily.com/press_releases/press091701.htm, 25 March 2002. R. Smith, "Six Months After: At Sandler, a Client Sees Enormous Strain, Tries to Lend a Hand," *The Wall Street Journal*, 8 March 2002, C11.

Key Terms

charismatic leadership (499)

consideration (489)

contingency theory (491)

distributive justice (479)

equity theory (476)

ethical charismatics (500)

expectancy (481)

expectancy theory (480)

extrinsic reward (473)

initiating structure (489)

inputs (476)

instrumentality (481)

intrinsic reward (474)

leader-member relations (494)

leadership (483)

leadership neutralizers (486)

leadership substitutes (486)

motivation (468)

needs (471)

outcome/input (O/I) ratio (477)

outcomes (476)

overreward (477)

procedural justice (479)

referents (476)

situational favourableness (494)

situational theory (496)

strategic leadership (498)

task structure (494)

trait theory (487)

traits (487)

transactional leadership (502)

transformational leadership (500)

underreward (477)

valence (480)

visionary leadership (498)

worker maturity (496)

What Would You Do II?

Motivation in the Call Centre

As companies begin selling direct to customers, customer service is becoming increasingly critical. You should know—you are the manager of the customer service contact centre for Borders Group, the parent company of Borders Books and Music. You directly supervise approximately 100 customer-service agents, and your employees are, in many cases, the only contact between Borders and the customer. If a customer experiences an unfriendly customer-service encounter, there is a high probability that the customer will break all ties with the company. Therefore, customer-service agents become Borders' primary spokespeople and set the tone for future relationships between the company and the customer.

Contact centres have become a booming industry in recent years. They have also gained a reputation for having a high turnover rate and low employee morale. Having been a customer-service agent for six years, you are one of the first to realize that customer-service agents have a tough job. Every day they answer hundreds of phone calls, facing a wide variety of situations, and never knowing who is on the other end of the line or what the question, comment, concern, or complaint may be. Many times, customer-service agents have to diffuse heated situations and turn disgruntled and often hostile customers into satisfied and happy ones. Additionally, most call-centre agents work in a cubicle-farm, surrounded by other agents who rarely have the opportunity to leave their stations, except at usual break times.

These challenges, coupled with the fact that most call-centre agents receive a starting wage that is slightly above minimum wage, ensure that you have a steady stream of customer-service agent positions to fill at any given time. The average starting salary is $12 an hour and the average turnover rate is 60 percent per year. In addition to low morale and high turnover, the industry also faces a growing absenteeism problem, especially around holidays. Ironically, the weeks before, during, and after holidays—especially Thanksgiving and Christmas—tend to pose the greatest demand for a contact centre's staff.

As December approaches, you are concerned about employee burnout. When an extremely dissatisfied (and maybe somewhat abusive) customer is on the line, are your employees paid enough to care? The job isn't easy, the quarters are a bit cramped, and no one would describe the work as glitzy. What could possibly motivate employees to listen to angry customer complaints—often rudely and condescendingly expressed—all day long, five days a week, year after year?

If you were the manager of the customer-service contact centre at Borders, what would you do to reduce turnover and motivate employees at the holidays and throughout the year?

Sources: J. Bowles, "Motivating the Front Line," *Customer Interface*, March 2001. R. Sanbandam, "Phone Reps. Can Make, Break Overall C.S.," *Marketing News*, 7 May 2001. T. Heath, "Study Reveals British Columbia's Low Call-Center Labor Costs," *Site Selection*, January 2001. Bureau of Labor Statistics website, www.bls.gov. S. Jarvis, "Call Centers Raise Bar on Hiring Criteria," *Marketing News*, 11 September 2000.

Critical Thinking Video Case

Nova Scotian Crystal

In Chapter 1, we defined *management* as getting work done through others. In other words, managers don't do the work themselves. Managers help others do their jobs better. By contrast, *leadership* is the process of influencing others to achieve group or organizational goals. Think back to Chapter 1 and the discussion about Nova Scotian Crystal, the company that makes fine crystal in Halifax. In that video you observed how two seemingly opposites, chairman Denis Ryan and president Rod McCallum, use their distinct skills to guide Nova Scotian Crystal through a series of ups and downs in its quest for growth and sustainability.

Denis Ryan and president Rod McCallum are described as being the "odd couple" because they bring different skills and personalities to the company. Nonetheless, both are important to the continued success of the company. While there has been much debate over the differences between management and leadership, in this chapter we discussed the concept of leadership and the differences between leadership and management. There are different traits and skills associated with each role and both can be important to an organization's success. As you watch the video, consider the following critical thinking questions.

Critical Thinking Questions

1. The two Nova Scotian Crystal executives portrayed in the video play different roles. How would you describe their roles?
2. What traits and behaviours do they exhibit? Which of these traits and behaviours are associated with leaders and which are associated with managers?
3. Do they both exhibit leadership and management behaviours and traits? What are these traits and how might they affect the success of the company?

Management Decisions

Subbing for Leaders

Six months ago when you accepted the job as the president of a small marketing agency, you knew that it would be a tough task. You had no idea, however, that it would be nearly impossible. While interviewing, you conducted some basic research and found that even though the company was profitable, it had a bad reputation of not playing fair in the advertising industry. Many people that you talked to voiced their concerns about the firm, saying that its people were sneaky, backstabbing individuals who would stop at nothing to make a buck. Despite their concerns, you accepted the position, assuming that their perceptions were somewhat biased.

Unfortunately, soon after your arrival, you began to realize that many people's perceptions might not have been far off base. Initially, George, your assistant and the vice president of the company, seemed like a good guy—a little different, possibly even abrasive, but otherwise an okay person. At first his personality didn't pose a problem. Then you began to hear conversations about George's reliance on punishment and manipulation to ensure that the marketing sales force increased their sales revenue each quarter. In fact, the more you listened, the more you heard, and the uneasier you became.

As you began to watch George more closely, you realized that he was definitely an ends-versus-the-means person. His main focus was on increasing advertising dollars for the firm (and eventually for himself), regardless of the tactics used. You also began to notice that during important meetings discussing current customers' marketing strategies, George always did a majority of the talking. Anyone who attempted to interject ideas inconsistent with George's was immediately cut off and publicly scolded. In fact, this morning as you walked past one such meeting, you overheard John, a junior-level marketing agent, propose a new strategy for an important customer. George replied to John in front of the group, saying, "Now you folks see why John is only a junior-level agent after working over 12 years with this firm. Does anyone else have any stupid comments to offer, or can we move on with our meeting?"

As you stood outside the conference room, you realized that something must be done to change the culture, perception, and success of this firm. Clearly things can't continue as is, but George is a valuable employee despite his shortcomings. Maybe you should have a talk with him about what you expect from leaders. Resolving the problem may mean better matching George's leadership style to another work group within the company. Is that even feasible? You really need to change the culture inside the firm and the perception of the firm from outside. If not, the very existence of the firm will be on the line.

Questions

1. What should your expectation be of George as a leader? Is he meeting this expectation?
2. What type of leadership style is George exhibiting? Do you move George out of the leadership role, or do you coach him to change? If you coach him, what leadership style do you try to cultivate in him?
3. Which leadership substitutes could you develop to insulate your company from leadership gaps, such as the one described above?

Management Decisions

Employee of the Month!

As you get back to your desk with your third cup of coffee this morning, your boss stops at your desk in the middle of his morning rounds. He says, "Hey, you've got a degree in management, don't you? Heck, even if you don't, you're probably more up to date on all these new motivational theories and ideas than I am. Here's what I want. We need an employee-of-the-month award for our clerical employees. I want to boost their morale and motivate them to work harder and do their jobs better! So take a couple of weeks and design a basic employee award program, but make sure that it's got an employee-of-the-month award in it. That's the key. Have it on my desk two weeks from Friday." Before you can say yes, he's off to another co-worker's desk, to give her some other assignment that he brainstormed last night. You're not even sure he heard you say, "Sure, Mr. Smith, no problem."

However, what you really wanted to say was, "I don't know, Mr. Smith. I've never seen an employee-of-the-month award

motivate anyone." In fact, no one really seemed to care about being employee-of-the-month in the places you had worked before, even when there was a small amount of cash involved. You think to yourself, "Well, if he wants an employee-of-the-month award, I'll make sure that's in there. But there have got to be better ways to motivate the clerical staff. I'm just going to have to figure out what those are."

Questions

1. What is wrong with many employee-of-the-month award programs? Why wouldn't they be particularly effective at motivating employees?

2. Describe the three most important steps you'd take to motivate the clerical staff in your office. Explain what the steps are, the reasoning behind them, and what they're meant to accomplish. Be specific.

Develop Your Management Potential

Show Me the Noncash Rewards?

"Show me the money! Show me the money!" Lots of managers mistakenly assume that money is the primary motivator for most employees. However, studies regularly show that while money affects people's decisions to take or leave jobs, it is not one of the primary motivators once someone has a job.

New managers also assume that they'll have access to the money they need to "really motivate" their workers. This is wrong in two ways. First, most managers are given a pool of money to allocate among all employees as raises. So if they give one employee a large raise, they have less money for other raises. Second, psychological studies show that pay increases must be at least 15 to 20 percent before employees really feel that they've got a substantial increase in pay. In other words, with most annual pay raises between 2 and 4 percent, most managers

simply aren't given the money they need to create the wow-what-a-great-raise reaction they want from their employees.

As a result of these factors, more and more managers are turning to noncash rewards to motivate their employees.

Questions

1. Develop a list of 10 creative, noncash rewards that would be effective in motivating employees. If you're not sure what would be effective, think of the things that motivate you and your friends. You also might want to ask two or three managers about the noncash rewards they offer their employees.

2. Describe how you would administer each of these rewards. In other words, explain when and why you would give employees these particular rewards. Be specific.

Discussion Questions

1. Think back on the jobs that you have had. What sorts of things did the companies you worked for do to motivate you? Did they work? Why or why not?
2. Have you ever felt underrewarded in a job? Why did you feel underrewarded? What could have been done to address the perceived inequity?
3. What is the difference between a leader and a manager? Provide specific examples.
4. Provide examples of good leaders. What characteristics make them good leaders?

Study Tip

Your professor and TA are the most valuable resources in your course. If you have questions on the fundamental concepts of motivation and leadership, go to them during office hours. Report back to your study partner or group.

16

CHAPTER

Chapter Outline

Learning Objectives

After reading this chapter, you should be able to

1. explain the role that perception plays in communication and communication problems.
2. describe the communication process and the various kinds of communication in organizations.
3. explain how managers can manage effective one-on-one communication.
4. describe how managers can manage effective organization-wide communication.

Managing Communication

What Would You Do?

Buckman Labs is a maker of a variety of specialty chemicals used to treat pulp and paper for recycling and publishing; to keep mechanical equipment corrosion free; to preserve and cure animal hides into fine leather; to slow or prevent fires through the use of fire retardants, dispersants, and defoamers; and to enhance wood products by preventing staining and rotting.

As sales director for Buckman Labs, you spend nearly half of your time helping Buckman's domestic and international sales representatives solve problems for existing customers. For example, when a client, Manistique Papers, was unable to remove the ink from the old magazine paper it was recycling, your local sales representatives called wanting you to put the company in touch with people at Buckman who could solve the problem. Traditionally, the solution has been to hire more Ph.D.-trained chemists and fly them to customers who needed their help and expertise. This worked well when the company was small. But with significant growth and overseas expansion, there just aren't enough company chemists to go around anymore. And, even if there were, with customers in Africa, Europe, the Pacific Rim, and South America, it would take too long to fly technical support to every customer who needed immediate help.

Not surprisingly, sales representatives have been frustrated by how long it takes to get answers to customers' questions. Indeed, since questions were typically routed to you and then out to the appropriate technical experts, it usually took three to five days to begin addressing customer problems—an eternity for sales representatives who are being pressured by customers for solutions. You thought that the corporate e-mail would speed things up and encourage faster, better communication. But it hasn't. While e-mail is great for quickly identifying problems ("Hey, one of my customers is having some problems with rotting wood and we can't figure out why. Here's the situation..."), it still has to be routed to the right people. And, here's the critical part, those people have to be willing to share their expertise with customers and sales representatives. In fact, what surprised you the most was that people in different parts of the company weren't always willing to share their knowledge with others.

Well, with customer satisfaction on the line, you've got to find a way to improve communication within and outside the company. The first thing you need to figure out is why people in different parts of the company are so reluctant to communicate with each other. Is it perception, culture, or simply poor communication techniques? Next, anything's got to be better than having you, the sales manager, as the first point of contact for expert help, but what? How can you match sales representatives with the right technical experts without having to serve as the go-between? There's got to be a reasonable technological solution. But if e-mail wasn't the technological solution, and everybody uses e-mail, what's the answer?

If you were the sales director at Buckman Labs and wanted to improve company communications, what would you do?

Sources: Buckman Laboratories. [Online] Available www. buckman.com/home.html, 5 September 1999. J. Eckhouse, "Get Creative with Knowledge Sharing—In Today's Culture, Businesses Must Rebuild Their Processes to Take Advantage of Their Knowledge Base," *Information Week*, 8 February 1999, ER19. D.J. Knight, "Strategy in Practice: Making It Happen," *Strategy & Leadership* 26, No. 3 (1 July 1998): 29. M.N. Martinez, "The Collective Power of Employee Knowledge," *HR Magazine* 43, No. 2 (1 February 1998): 88. S. Thurm, "What Do You Know? Getting Employees to Share Their Knowledge Isn't as Simple as Installing New Software; Just Ask Buckman Labs," *The Wall Street Journal*, 21 June 1999, R10.

Like Buckman Labs' sales director, it's estimated that managers spend over 80 percent of their day communicating with others.[1] Indeed, much of the basic management process—making things happen, meeting the competition, organizing people, projects, and processes, and leading—cannot be performed without effective communication. If this weren't reason enough to study communication, consider that oral communication, such as listening, following instructions, conversing, and giving feedback, is the most important skill for college graduates who are entering the workforce.[2] Furthermore, across all industries, poor communication skill is the single most important reason that people do not advance in their careers.[3] Finally, communication is especially important for top managers. In a recent study of Canadian CFOs, 64 percent said that the biggest challenge their companies face is a lack of communication with staff.[4] Without a doubt the issue is one all managers should be concerned about.

This chapter begins by examining the role of perception in communication and how perception can make it difficult for managers to achieve effective communication. Next, you'll read about the communication process and the various kinds of communication found in most organizations. In the last half of the chapter, the focus is on improving communication in organizations. You'll learn about the significant barriers to effective one-on-one communication and organization-wide communication. But, more importantly, you'll learn ways to overcome those barriers, too.

Communication

When Grand Metropolitan PLC, a British-based firm, purchased Pillsbury Corporation, which operates primarily in North America, the new management sensed that Pillsbury's top managers had become isolated and that they weren't receiving the information, good or bad, that they needed to run the company well. And, they were right. Pillsbury employees generally ignored the company's highly promoted suggestion box system, refused to call its in-house whistleblower hotline (to report problems), and had little, if any, contact with top management.

To change this situation, Pillsbury hired InTouch, a neutral outside firm that uses voice-mail technology to anonymously record employees' comments, which are then transcribed and forwarded straight to Pillsbury's new CEO. And to encourage employees to call, Pillsbury distributed the InTouch phone number on stickers, wallet cards, and even refrigerator magnets. Karen Gustafson, director of employee communications, said, "We wanted people to call whenever a thought hit them." And, because callers knew the system was completely anonymous (transcripts don't even identify a caller's gender), the calls started flooding in. As a result, management began learning about problems (an inaccurate time clock and slow methods of reimbursing employees for travel expenses) and opportunities (employees identified stores that didn't carry Pillsbury food products) that it wasn't otherwise hearing from its employees.[5]

communication
the process of transmitting information from one person or place to another

Communication is the process of transmitting information from one person or place to another. When Pillsbury's employees began calling InTouch, information was transmitted from them directly to Pillsbury's CEO. Why didn't Pillsbury's employees simply share this information with top management? Why did it take the InTouch phone system to get employees to communicate? Because it was widely perceived that employees would be punished if they came forward with negative information about the company or its managers.

After reading the next two sections, you should be able to
1. *explain the role that perception plays in communication and communication problems.*
2. *describe the communication process and the various kinds of communication in organizations.*

1. Perception and Communication Problems

One study showed that when asked whether their supervisor gives recognition for good work, 13 percent of employees said that their supervisor gives a pat on the back, while 14 percent said that their supervisor gives sincere and thorough praise. But when the supervisors of these employees were asked if they give recognition for good work, 82 percent said they gave pats on the back, while 80 percent said that they give sincere and thorough praise.[6] Given that these managers and employees worked closely together, how could they have had such different perceptions of something as simple as praise?

Let's learn more about perception and communication problems by examining the basic perception process, perception problems, perceptions of others, and self-perception.

1.1 Basic Perception Process

As shown in Exhibit 16.1, **perception** is the process by which individuals attend to, organize, interpret, and retain information from their environments. And since communication is the process of transmitting information from one person or place to another, perception is obviously a key part of communication. However, perception can be a key obstacle to communication, as well.

As people perform their jobs, they are exposed to a wide variety of informational stimuli, such as e-mails, direct conversations with the boss or co-workers, rumours heard over lunch, stories about the company in the press, or a video broadcast of a speech from the CEO to all employees. However, exposure to an informational stimulus is no guarantee that an individual will pay attention or attend to that stimulus. People experience stimuli through their own **perceptual filters**—the personality-, psychology-, or experience-based differences that influence them to ignore or pay attention to particular stimuli. Because of filtering, people exposed to the same information will often disagree about what they saw or heard.

These same perceptual filters also affect the transmitting of information from one person or place to another. As shown in Exhibit 16.1, perceptual filters affect each part of the perception process: attention, organization, interpretation, and retention.

Attention is the process of noticing or becoming aware of particular stimuli. Because of perceptual filters, we attend to some stimuli and not others. *Organization* is the process of incorporating new information (from the stimuli that you notice) into your existing knowledge. Because of perceptual filters, we are more likely to incorporate new knowledge that is consistent with what we already know or believe. *Interpretation* is the process of attaching meaning to new knowledge. Because of perceptual filters, our preferences and beliefs strongly influence the meaning we attach to new information (e.g., "This must mean that top management supports our project"). Finally, *retention* is the process of remembering interpreted information. In other words, retention is what we recall and commit to memory after we have perceived something. Of course, perceptual filters also affect retention, that is, what we're likely to remember in the end.

For instance, imagine that you missed the first ten minutes of a TV show and that you turned on your TV to a scene in which two people were talking to each other in a living room. As they talked, they walked around the room and picked up and then put

perception
the process by which individuals attend to, organize, interpret, and retain information from their environments

perceptual filters
the personality-, psychology-, or experience-based differences that influence people to ignore or pay attention to particular stimuli

EXHIBIT 16.1

BASIC PERCEPTION PROCESS

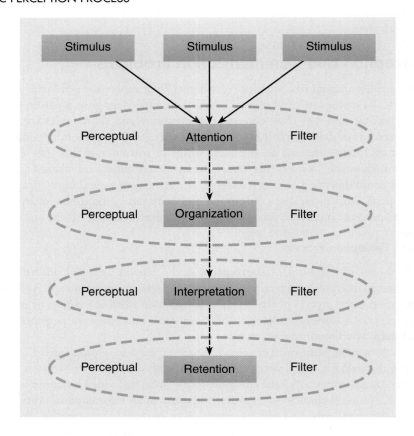

down various items, some of which were valuable, such as a ring, a watch, and a credit card, and some of which appeared to be drug related, such as a water pipe for smoking marijuana. In fact, this situation was depicted on videotape in a well-known study that manipulated people's perceptual filters.[7] One-third of the study participants were told that these people were there to rob the apartment. Another third of the participants were told that police were on their way to conduct a drug raid and that the people in the apartment were getting rid of incriminating evidence. The remaining third of study participants were told that these people were simply waiting for a friend to show up.

After watching the video, participants were asked to list all of the objects from the video that they could remember. Not surprisingly, the different perceptual filters (theft, drug raid, and waiting for a friend) affected what the study participants attended to, how they organized the information, how they interpreted the information, and ultimately what objects they remembered from the video. People who thought a theft was in process were more likely to remember the valuable objects in the video. Those who thought a drug raid was imminent were more likely to remember drug-related objects. There was no discernable pattern to the items remembered by those who thought that the people in the video were simply waiting for a friend.

In short, because of perception and perceptual filters, people are likely to pay attention to different things, organize and interpret what they pay attention to differently, and finally remember things differently. Consequently, even when people are exposed to the same communications (e.g., organizational memos, customers, discussions with managers), they can end up with very different perceptions and understandings. This is why communication can be so difficult and frustrating for managers. Let's review some of the communication problems created by perception and perceptual filters.

1.2 Perception Problems

Perception creates communication problems for organizations because people exposed to the same communication and information can end up with completely different ideas and understandings. Two of the most common perception problems in organizations are selective perception and closure.

At work, we are constantly bombarded with sensory stimuli—the phone ringing, people talking in the background, the sounds of our computers dinging as new e-mail arrives, people calling our names, etc. As limited processors of information, we cannot possibly notice, receive, and interpret all of this information. As a result, we attend to and accept some stimuli but screen out and reject others. However, this isn't a random process. **Selective perception** is the tendency to notice and accept objects and information consistent with our values, beliefs, and expectations, while ignoring or screening out or not accepting inconsistent information.

Once we have initial information about a person, event, or process, **closure** is the tendency to fill in the gaps where information is missing, that is, to assume that what we don't know is consistent with what we already know. If employees are told that budgets must be cut by 10 percent, they may automatically assume that 10 percent of employees will lose their jobs, too, even if that isn't the case. Not surprisingly, when closure occurs, people sometimes "fill in the gaps" with inaccurate information, and this can create problems for organizations.

1.3 Perceptions of Others

Attribution theory says that we all have a basic need to understand and explain the causes of other people's behaviour.[8] In other words, we need to know why people do what they do. And, according to attribution theory, we use two general reasons or attributions to explain people's behaviour: an internal attribution, in which behaviour is thought to be voluntary or under the control of the individual, and an external attribution, in which behaviour is thought to be involuntary and outside the control of the individual.

For example, have you ever seen anyone changing a flat tire on the side of the road and thought to yourself, "What rotten luck—somebody's having a bad day"? If you did, you perceived the person through an external attribution known as the defensive bias. The **defensive bias** is the tendency for people to perceive themselves as personally and situationally similar to someone who is having difficulty or trouble.[9] And when we identify with the person in a situation, we tend to use external attributions (i.e., the situation) to explain the person's behaviour. For instance, since flat tires are fairly common, it's easy to perceive ourselves in that same situation and put the blame on external causes, such as running over a nail.

Now, let's assume a different situation, this time in the workplace:

> *A utility company worker puts a ladder on a utility pole and then climbs up to do his work. As he's doing his work, he falls from the ladder and seriously injures himself.*[10]

Answer this question: Who or what caused the accident? If you thought, "It's not the worker's fault. Anybody could fall from a tall ladder," then you're still operating from a defensive bias in which you see yourself as personally and situationally similar to someone who is having difficulty or trouble. In other words, you made an external attribution and attributed the accident to an external cause, meaning the situation.

However, most accident investigations end up blaming the worker (i.e., an internal attribution) and not the situation (i.e., an external attribution) in which people do their jobs. Typically, 60 percent to 80 percent of workplace accidents that occur each year are blamed on "operator error," that is, the employees themselves. However, more complete

selective perception
the tendency to notice and accept objects and information consistent with our values, beliefs, and expectations, while ignoring or screening out or not accepting inconsistent information

closure
the tendency to fill in gaps of missing information by assuming that what we don't know is consistent with what we already know

attribution theory
theory that states that we all have a basic need to understand and explain the causes of other people's behaviour

defensive bias
the tendency for people to perceive themselves as personally and situationally similar to someone who is having difficulty or trouble

fundamental attribution error
the tendency to ignore external causes of behaviour and to attribute other people's actions to internal causes

investigations usually show that workers are really only responsible for 30 percent to 40 percent of all workplace accidents.[11] Why would accident investigators be so quick to blame workers? Because they are committing the **fundamental attribution error**, which is the tendency to ignore external causes of behaviour and to attribute other people's actions to internal causes.[12] In other words, when investigators examine the possible causes of an accident, they're much more likely to assume that the accident is a function of the person and not the situation.

Which attribution, the defensive bias or the fundamental attribution error, are workers likely to make when something goes wrong? In general, workers are more likely to perceive events and explain behaviour from a defensive bias. Because they do the work themselves, and because they see themselves as similar to others who make mistakes, have accidents, or are otherwise held responsible for things that go wrong at work, workers are likely to attribute problems to external causes, such as failed machinery, poor support, or inadequate training. By contrast, because they are typically observers (who don't do the work themselves), and see themselves as situationally and personally different from workers, managers tend to commit the fundamental attribution error and blame mistakes, accidents, and other things that go wrong on workers (i.e., an internal attribution).

Consequently, in most workplaces, when things go wrong, the natural response is one in which workers and managers can be expected to take completely opposite views. Therefore, together, the defensive bias, which is typically used by workers, and the fundamental attribution error, which is typically made by managers, represent a significant challenge to effective communication and understanding in organizations.

1.4 Self-Perception

A manager at a large oil company decided that he wanted to find a way to help his poor-performing employees improve their performance. So he sat down with each one of them and, in a positive, nonconfrontational way, explained that "I'm here to help you improve." Most of his employees took his offer in the spirit it was meant and accepted his help. However, one employee burst into tears because no one had ever told her that her performance needed improvement. In fact, her hour-long outburst was so emotional that her manager decided that he would never "criticize" her again.[13]

self-serving bias
the tendency to overestimate our value by attributing successes to ourselves (internal causes) and attributing failures to others or the environment (external causes)

The **self-serving bias** is the tendency to overestimate our value by attributing successes to ourselves (internal causes) and attributing failures to others or the environment (external causes).[14] As the example with the upset oil company employee illustrates, the self-serving bias can make it especially difficult for managers to talk to employees about performance problems. In general, people have a need to maintain a positive self-image. This need is so strong that when people seek feedback at work, they typically want verification of their worth (rather than information about performance deficiencies) or assurance that mistakes or problems haven't been their fault.[15] And when managerial communication threatens people's positive self-image, they can become defensive and emotional. In turn, they quit listening, and communication becomes ineffective. In the second half of the chapter, which focuses on improving communication, we'll explain ways in which managers can minimize this self-serving bias and improve effective one-on-one communication with employees.

Review 1
Perception and Communication Problems

Perception is the process by which people attend to, organize, interpret, and retain information from their environments. However, perception is not a straightforward process. Because of perceptual filters, such as selective perception and closure, people exposed to the same information stimuli often end up with very different perceptions and understandings. Perception-based differences can also lead to differences in the attributions (internal or external) that managers and workers make when explaining workplace behaviour. In general, workers are more likely to explain behaviour from a defensive bias, in which they attribute problems to external causes (i.e., the situation). Managers, on the other hand, tend to commit the fundamental attribution error, attributing problems to internal causes (i.e., the worker associated with a mistake or error). Consequently, when things go wrong, it's common for managers to blame workers and for workers to blame the situation or context in which they do their jobs. Finally, this problem is compounded by a self-serving bias that leads people to attribute successes to internal causes and failures to external causes. So when workers receive negative feedback from managers, they can become defensive and emotional and not hear what their managers have to say. In short, perceptions and attributions represent a significant challenge to effective communication and understanding in organizations.

2. Kinds of Communication

In a Toronto manufacturing plant a janitor accidentally mixed chemicals that produced a toxic cloud. As the fumes wafted through the building, workers thought that someone had pulled a stink bomb prank but as the chemical smell intensified, employees' eyes started to water and some had difficulty breathing. The occupational health and safety officer had not been told what the problem was and just recommended that the windows and doors be opened to provide some ventilation. Soon it became clear that the problem was serious and the supervisor had to clear the building, but not before many of the workers had been subjected to enough toxic fumes to be hospitalized. If there had been better communication, the janitor may not have mixed the chemicals that created the problem. If there had been better communication after the accident, no one would likely have been hospitalized.[16]

In this situation, the communication process between senders and receivers broke down at some point. However, this isn't surprising. Miscommunication is possible with every kind of communication, even simple things. For example, Americans travelling in Canada are often confused when asked by a waiter or waitress if they want brown bread with their meal. In the United States, they usually call it whole wheat, often leaving them puzzled over their breakfast toast.[17]

Let's learn more about the different kinds of communication by examining the communication process, formal communication channels, informal communication channels, one-on-one communication, and nonverbal communication.

EXPERIENCING MANAGEMENT

Learn more about the basic communication process at our animated concept and activity site. Choose Communication from the "select a topic" pull-down menu, then Communication Process from the "overview tab."

www.experiencingmanagement.com

2.1 The Communication Process

Earlier in the chapter, we defined communication as the process of transmitting information from one person or place to another. Exhibit 16.2 displays a model of the communication process and its major components: the sender (message to be conveyed, encoding the message, transmitting the message), the receiver (received message, decoded message, and the message that was understood), and noise, which interferes with the communication process.

The communication process begins when a sender thinks of a message he or she wants to convey to another person. This could be what the sender wants someone else to know ("The meeting has been changed to 3:00 p.m."), to do ("Make sure to include last quarter's financial information in the proposal"), or not to do ("Sorry, the budget is tight. You'll have to fly coach rather than business class"). The next step is to encode the message. **Encoding** means putting a message into a written, oral, or symbolic form that can be recognized and understood by the receiver. The sender then transmits the message via *communication channels*, such as the telephone or face-to-face communication, which allow the sender to receive immediate feedback; or e-mail (text messages and file attachments), fax, beepers, voice-mail, memos, and letters, in which senders must wait for receivers to respond.

encoding
putting a message into a written, oral, or symbolic form that can be recognized and understood by the receiver

EXHIBIT 16.2

THE INTERPERSONAL COMMUNICATION PROCESS

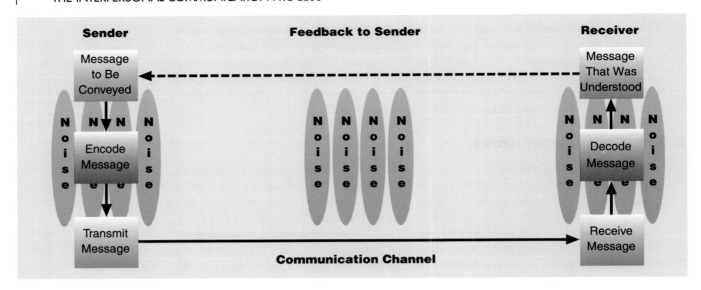

decoding

the process by which the receiver translates the written, oral, or symbolic form of a message into an understood message

If the message is received—and because of technical difficulties (e.g., fax down, dead battery on the mobile phone, inability to read e-mail attachments) or people-based transmission problems (e.g., forgetting to pass on the message), messages often aren't received—the next step is for the receiver to decode the message. **Decoding** is the process by which the receiver translates the written, oral, or symbolic form of the message into an understood message. However, the message, as understood by the receiver, isn't always the same message that was intended by the sender. Because of different experiences or perceptual filters, receivers may attach a completely different meaning to a message than was intended. A North American baby food company tried to market its product in Africa where, due to the relatively high rate of illiteracy, the custom was to place a picture of the product on the label. They put a picture of a baby on the jar, leading the local population to think that the jars contained ground-up babies. Needless to say sales were not great.[18] Something got lost in the decoding.

feedback

in the communication process, a return message to the sender that indicates the receiver's understanding of the message

The last step of the communication process occurs when the receiver gives the sender feedback. **Feedback** is a return message to the sender that indicates the receiver's understanding of the message (of what the receiver was supposed to know, to do, or not to do). Feedback makes senders aware of possible miscommunications and enables them to continue communicating until the receiver understands the intended message.

Unfortunately, feedback doesn't always occur in the communication process. Complacency and overconfidence about the ease and simplicity of communication can lead senders and receivers to simply assume that they share a common understanding of the message and to not use feedback to improve the effectiveness of their communication. This is a serious mistake, especially since messages and feedback are always transmitted with and against a background of noise. **Noise** is anything that interferes with the transmission of the intended message. Noise can occur if

noise

anything that interferes with the transmission of the intended message

1. the sender isn't sure about what message to communicate.

2. the message is not clearly encoded.

3. the wrong communication channel is chosen.

4. the message is not received or decoded properly.

5. the receiver doesn't have the experience or time to understand the message.

When managers wrongly assume that communication is easy, they reduce communication to something called the "conduit metaphor."[19] Strictly speaking, conduit is a pipe or tube that protects electrical wire. The **conduit metaphor** refers to the mistaken assumption that senders can pipe their intended messages directly into the heads of receivers with perfect clarity and without noise or perceptual filters interfering with the receivers' understanding of the message. However, this just isn't possible. Even if managers could telepathically direct their thoughts straight into receivers' heads, there would still be misunderstandings and communication problems because, depending on how they're used, words and symbols typically have several meanings. For example, Exhibit 16.3 shows several meanings of an extremely common word, "fine." Depending on how you use it, "fine" can mean a penalty, a good job, or that something is delicate, small, pure, or flimsy. Many years ago someone received a parking ticket for parking in an area with a sign saying "Fine for Parking." He fought the ticket, arguing that the sign meant that it was a good place to park. The judge did not agree, although one can see the potential ambiguity of the language used on the sign.

In summary, the conduit metaphor causes problems in communication by making managers too complacent and confident in their ability to easily and accurately transfer messages to receivers. Managers who want to be effective communicators need to carefully choose words and symbols that will help receivers derive the intended meaning of a message. Furthermore, they need to be aware of all the steps of the communication process, beginning with the sender (message to be conveyed, encoding the message, transmitting the message) and ending with the receiver (received message, decoded message, understanding the message, and using feedback to communicate what was understood).

2.2 Formal Communication Channels

The **formal communication channel** is the system of official channels that carry organizationally approved messages and information. Organizational objectives, rules, policies, procedures, instructions, commands, and requests for information are all transmitted via the formal communication system or "channel." There are three formal communication channels: downward communication, upward communication, and horizontal communication.[20]

Downward communication flows from higher to lower levels in an organization. Downward communication is used to issue orders down the organizational hierarchy, to give organizational members job-related information, to give managers and workers performance reviews from upper managers, and to make clear organizational objectives and

conduit metaphor
the mistaken assumption that senders can pipe their intended messages directly into the heads of receivers with perfect clarity and without noise or perceptual filters interfering with the receivers' understanding of the message

formal communication channel
the system of official channels that carry organizationally approved messages and information

downward communication
communication that flows from higher to lower levels in an organization

---

EXHIBIT 16.3

MEANINGS OF THE WORD "FINE"

1. If you exceed the 100 km/h speed limit, you may have to pay a fine (meaning a penalty).
2. During the playoffs, Mario Lemieux turned in a fine performance (meaning excellent).
3. The machine has to run at a slow speed, because the tolerance is extremely fine (meaning delicate).
4. It is difficult to put this puzzle together, since many of the pieces are so fine (meaning small).
5. Recently, experiments have been conducted on manufacturing certain drugs in space. It is hoped that these drugs, as compared to those manufactured on Earth, will be extremely fine (meaning pure).
6. Be careful when you handle that antique book. Its pages are extremely fine (meaning flimsy).

goals.[21] When an economic downturn quickly produced a significant drop in sales at Agilent, a technology company, CEO Ned Barnholt pulled together his top managers. Together, they decided that their first strategy would be to freeze hiring, cut expenses, and cut temporary workers. Then, through e-mails, the twice-weekly company newsletter, and a speech played over the public-address system at all Agilent facilities, Barnholt explained why the cuts were necessary, how the cuts would help the company, and then encouraged the troops to cut costs any way they could. Agilent managers reinforced the message at "coffee talks," the regular brainstorming meetings that they hold with their employees. Employees responded by using websites to house data electronically (to avoid printing costs), by staying with friends and family when on company travel (to avoid hotel charges), and by bringing bags of potato chips to company recruiting events (to avoid costly catering charges). Within months, thanks to effective downward communicating, travel expenses dropped by 50 percent, whereas purchases of personal computers had dropped by 70 percent.[22]

upward communication
communication that flows from lower to higher levels in an organization

Upward communication flows from lower levels to higher levels in an organization. Upward communication is used to give higher-level managers feedback about operations, issues, and problems; to help higher-level managers assess organizational performance and effectiveness; to encourage lower-level managers and employees to participate in organizational decision-making; and to give those at lower levels the chance to share their concerns with higher-level authorities. Information can flow from lower levels to higher levels in a number of ways. Upward communication can occur through such methods as grievance procedures, open-door policies, ombudsman, suggestion boxes, and meetings.[23] Sundog Printing, based in Calgary, has become one of the largest privately owned commercial printers in western Canada. Dale Hodson, president, and Ray Remada, vice president, credit Sundog's growth and success to their employees. One key element they identify in their success in dealing with employees is their open-door policy, which both of them support and maintain. "You have to be open ... you have to be approachable" says Remada.[24]

horizontal communication
communication that flows among managers and workers who are at the same organizational level

Horizontal communication flows among managers and workers who are at the same organizational level. For instance, horizontal communication occurs when the day-shift supervisor comes in at 7:30 a.m. for a half-hour discussion with the midnight-shift supervisor who leaves at 8:00 a.m., or when the regional marketing director meets with the regional accounting director to discuss costs and plans for a new marketing campaign. Horizontal communication helps facilitate coordination and cooperation between different parts of a company and allows co-workers to share relevant information. It also helps people at the same level resolve conflicts and solve problems without involving high levels of management. At Oracle Software, Ray Lane implemented a program called "Vision and Values" that structured company rules regarding interpersonal communication. Because the company had grown to more than 20 000 employees, it had to stop employees from taking problems straight to founder and CEO Larry Ellison. This worked well while the company was small, but produced bottlenecks and slow decisions now that it was large. So, according to "Vision and Values," horizontal communication became the first step in problem solving. In fact, employees were not allowed to elevate problems and issues to higher levels unless they communicated first with managers and workers at their organizational level.[25]

EXPERIENCING MANAGEMENT

Test what you have learned about communication channels by visiting our animated concept and activity site. Choose Communication from the "select a topic" pull-down menu, then Channels of Communication from the "overview tab."

www.experiencingmanagement.com

In general, what can managers do to improve formal communication? First, decrease reliance on downward communication. Second, increase chances for upward communication by increasing personal contact with lower-level managers and workers. Third, like at Oracle software, encourage much greater use of horizontal communication.

Gossip is an informal communication channel and is commonly referred to as the grapevine. This form of communication is usually faster than formal communication channels.

2.3 Informal Communication Channels

The **informal communication channel**, sometimes called the "**grapevine**," is the transmission of messages from employee to employee outside of formal communication channels. The grapevine arises out of curiosity, that is, the need to know what is going on in an organization and how it might affect you or others. And to satisfy this curiosity, employees need a consistent supply of relevant, accurate, in-depth information about "who is doing what and what changes are occurring within the organization."[26] For example, when top AT&T managers told Wall Street security analysts that it was planning to eliminate thousands of jobs, the analysts blabbed the news to reporters, and AT&T's employees learned about the job cuts in the newspapers. As a result, work in AT&T offices practically stopped as employees worked the corporate grapevine to find out what was going to happen next. A former AT&T manager said, "No one in top management stepped forward and said the rumours weren't true. Nobody told us anything official at all, in fact. So the grapevine went berserk."[27]

Grapevines arise out of informal communication networks, such as the gossip or cluster chains shown in Exhibit 16.4. In the *gossip chain*, one "highly connected" individual shares information with many other managers and workers. By contrast, in the *cluster chain*, numerous people simply tell a few of their friends. The result in both cases is that information flows freely and quickly through the organization. Some believe that grapevines are a waste of employees' time, that they promote gossip and rumours that fuel political speculation, and that they are sources of highly unreliable, inaccurate information. Yet studies clearly show that grapevines are highly accurate sources of information for a number of reasons.[28] First, because grapevines typically carry "juicy" information that is interesting and timely, information spreads rapidly. Second, since information is typically spread by face-to-face conversation, senders can seek feedback to make sure they understand the message that is being communicated. This reduces misunderstandings and increases accuracy. Third, since most of the information in a company moves along the grapevine, as opposed to formal communication channels, people can usually verify the accuracy of information by "checking it out" with others.

informal communication channel ("grapevine") the transmission of messages from employee to employee outside of formal communication channels

EXHIBIT 16.4

GRAPEVINE COMMUNICATION NETWORKS

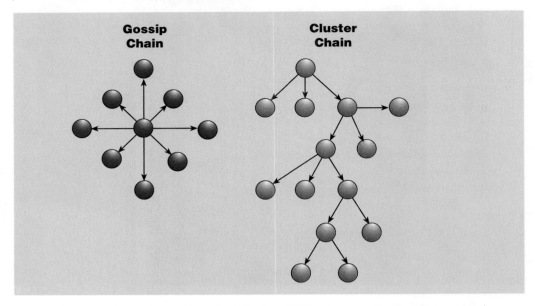

Source: Grapevine Communication Networks, K. Davis and J. W. Newstrom, *Human Behavior at Work: Organizational Behavior*, 8th ed. (New York: McGraw-Hill, 1989), p. 373. Reproduced with permission of the McGraw-Hill Companies.

What can managers do to "manage" organizational grapevines? The very worst thing managers can do is withhold information or try to punish those who share information with others. The grapevine abhors a vacuum, and in the absence of information from company management, rumours and anxiety will flourish. Maureen Shaw, president of Ontario-based Industrial Accident Prevention Association, tries to prevent the grapevine from taking on a life of its own as it did in the AT&T example. She meets regularly with all employees and calls them "water cooler chit-chats." Every three weeks she distributes a "Friday update." It is intended to discuss the most current rumours on the grapevine. "I collect things that I hear before the rumour mill gets started. I let people know what's really happening."[29] Clearly she recognizes the power of the grapevine.

A better strategy is to embrace the grapevine to keep employees informed about possible changes and strategies. Management consultant Arnold Brown said managers should "identify the key people in your company's grapevine and, instead of punishing them, feed them information. When a company issues a press release it knows what newspapers to contact, so why not know your internal media?"[30]

Finally, in addition to using the grapevine to communicate with others, managers should not overlook the fact that the grapevine can be a tremendous source of valuable information and feedback. In fact, information flowing through organizational grapevines is estimated to be 75 percent to 95 percent accurate.[31]

2.4 Coaching and Counselling: One-on-One Communication

In one study CEOs were asked, "If you could go back and change one thing, what would it be?" The answer? "The way we communicated with our employees." CEOs stated that instead of flashy videos, printed materials, or formal meetings, they would make greater use of one-to-one communication, especially with employees' immediate supervisors, and not higher-level executives that employees didn't know.[32]

There are two kinds of one-on-one communication: coaching and counselling. **Coaching** is communicating with someone for the direct purpose of improving the person's on-the-job performance or behaviour.[33] By contrast, **counselling** is communicating with someone about non-job-related issues that may be affecting or interfering with the person's performance. For example, after a top-performing employee was repeatedly late and absent from work, he was asked if he had some personal problems that he needed to discuss. It turned out that he had gone through a divorce and that his teenage son, who was in trouble for truancy and stealing, was now his sole responsibility. Marina London, who counselled this manager, said, "It's very common that the personal problem is coming from somewhere else, that someone is dragging him (the employee) down with them."[34]

While we'll discuss a number of specific steps for effective one-on-one communication later in the chapter, you should know that, in general, openness is one of the most important factors in effective one-on-one communication. Consistent with our discussion of the communication model, *openness in message sending* is the candid disclosure of information. *Openness in message receiving* is encouraging employees to respond with candid, forthright opinions, even when they disagree.[35]

2.5 Nonverbal Communication

When people talk, they send verbal and nonverbal messages. Verbal messages are sent and received through the words we speak. "That was a great presentation." By contrast, nonverbal messages are sent through body language, facial expressions, or tone of voice. For instance, hearing "THAT was a GREAT presentation!" is very different from hearing "ahem (clearing throat), that was, ahem, ahem, a great presentation."

More specifically, **nonverbal communication** is any communication that doesn't involve words. Nonverbal communication and messages almost always accompany verbal communication and may support and reinforce the verbal message or contradict it. The importance of nonverbal communication is well established. Researchers have estimated that as much as 93 percent of any message is transmitted nonverbally, with 55 percent coming from body language and facial expressions and 38 percent coming from tone and pitch of voice.[36] And since many nonverbal cues are unintentional, receivers often consider nonverbal communication to be a more accurate representation of what senders are really thinking and feeling. If you have ever asked someone out on a date and been told "yes," but realized that the real answer was "no," then you understand the importance of paying attention to nonverbal communication.

Kinesics and paralanguage are two kinds of nonverbal communication.[37] **Kinesics** are movements of the body and face.[38] These movements include arm and hand gestures, facial expressions, eye contact, folding arms, crossing legs, and leaning toward or away from another person. For example, people tend to avoid eye contact when they are embarrassed or unsure of the message they are sending. Crossed arms and/or legs usually indicate defensiveness or that the person is not receptive to the message or the sender. Also, people tend to smile frequently when they are seeking someone's approval. Lawyers frequently use body language and facial movements to communicate nonverbal messages to jurors. Attorney and trial consultant Lisa Blue said, "If you want to show that the cross-examination of your witness was ridiculous or boring, you could start looking at your watch."[39]

Paralanguage includes the pitch, rate, tone, volume, and speaking pattern (i.e., use of silences, pauses, or hesitations) of one's voice. For example, when people are unsure what to say, they tend to decrease their communication effectiveness by speaking softly.

By contrast, when people are nervous, they tend to talk faster and louder. These characteristics have a tremendous influence on whether listeners are receptive to what speakers are saying. Again, lawyers have long used the power of their voices to influence whether jurors were receptive to arguments that supported their clients. For instance, tobacco company lawyers complained about the dramatic way in which plaintiffs' attorney Stanley Rosenblatt would read secret company documents aloud to jurors. Rosenblatt, who would vary his voice from a slow whisper to a fast, loud voice that filled the entire courtroom, said that opposing attorneys always complained that "I should read in a very flat monotone."[40]

In short, since nonverbal communication is so informative, especially when it contradicts verbal communication, managers need to learn how to monitor and control their nonverbal behaviour.

Review 2
Kinds of Communication

Organizational communication depends on the communication process, formal and informal communication channels, one-on-one communication, and nonverbal communication. The major components of the communication process are the sender, the receiver, noise, and feedback. The conduit metaphor refers to the mistaken assumption that senders can pipe their intended messages directly into receivers' heads with perfect clarity. However, with noise, perceptual filters, and little feedback, this just isn't possible. Formal communication channels, such as downward, upward, and horizontal communication, carry organizationally approved messages and information. By contrast, the informal communication channel, called the "grapevine," arises out of curiosity and is carried out through gossip or cluster chains. Managers should use the grapevine to keep employees informed and to obtain better, clearer information for themselves. Effective one-on-one communication, such as coaching and counselling, depends on openness in message receiving and message sending. Nonverbal communication, such as kinesics and paralanguage, account for as much as 93 percent of a message's content and understanding. Since nonverbal communication is so informative, managers need to learn how to monitor and control their nonverbal behaviour.

Improving Communication

An employee comes in late every day, takes long lunches, and leaves early. His co-workers resent his tardiness and having to do his share of the work. Another employee makes as many as ten personal phone calls a day on company time. Another employee has seen her job performance drop significantly in the last three months. How do you communicate with these employees to begin solving these problems? On the other hand, if you supervise a division of 50 or 100, or even 1000 people, how can you communicate effectively with everyone in that division? Moreover, how can top managers communicate effectively with everyone in the company when employees work in different offices, provinces, countries, and time zones? Turning that around, how can managers make themselves accessible so that they can hear what employees feel and think throughout the organization?

When it comes to improving communication, managers face two primary tasks, managing one-on-one communication and managing organization-wide communication.

After reading the next two sections, you should be able to
3. explain how managers can manage effective one-on-one communication.
4. describe how managers can manage effective organization-wide communication.

3. Managing One-on-One Communication

In Chapter 1, you learned that, on average, first-line managers spend 57 percent of their time with people, middle managers spend 63 percent of their time directly with people, and top managers spend as much as 78 percent of their time dealing with people.[41] These numbers make it clear that managers spend a great deal of time in one-on-one communication with others.

Learn more about managing one-on-one communication by reading how to improve communication by choosing the right communication medium, listening, giving feedback, and improving cross-cultural communication.

3.1 Choosing the Right Communication Medium

Sometimes messages are poorly communicated simply because they are delivered using the wrong **communication medium**, which is the method used to deliver a message. For example, the wrong communication medium is being used when an employee returns from lunch, picks up the note left on her office chair, and learns she has been fired. Or the wrong communication medium is being used when an employee pops into your office every ten minutes with a simple request.

communication medium
the method used to deliver an oral or written message

There are two general kinds of communication media: oral and written communication. *Oral communication* includes face-to-face and group meetings, as well as telephone calls or other ways, such as videoconferencing, in which spoken messages are sent and received. Studies show that managers generally prefer oral communication, because it provides the opportunity to ask questions about parts of the message that they don't understand. Oral communication is also a rich communication medium because it allows managers to receive and assess the nonverbal communication that accompanies spoken messages (i.e., body language, facial expressions, or the voice characteristics associated with paralanguage). Furthermore, you don't need a personal computer and an Internet connection to conduct oral communication. Simply schedule an appointment, track someone down in the hall, or catch someone on the phone. In fact, management consultant Tom Durel worries that with voice-mail and e-mail, managers are not as willing to engage in meaningful face-to-face, oral communication as they once were. He said, "Why is it that the first thing people do in the morning is turn on their computers and send e-mail to a colleague in the office next door? What's wrong with getting up, walking over there, and actually talking to that person?"[42] However, oral communication should not be used for all communication. In general, when messages are simple, such as a quick request or presentation of straightforward information, memos or e-mail are often the better communication medium.

Written communication includes letters, e-mail, and memos. While most managers like and use oral communication, they are generally less receptive to using written communication. They may avoid written communication for a number of reasons, such as poor writing skills, being a poor typist, or not knowing (or refusing to learn) how to use Internet or corporate e-mail systems. However, written communication is well suited for delivering straightforward messages and information. Furthermore, with e-mail access available at the office, at home, and on the road (by laptop computer or Web-based e-mail), managers can use e-mail to stay in touch from anywhere at almost any time. And, since e-mail and other written communications don't have to be sent and received simultaneously, messages can be sent and stored for reading at any time. This allows managers to send and receive many more messages using e-mail than with oral communication, which requires people to get together in person or by phone or videoconference.

PERSONAL PRODUCTIVITY TIP

Writing Memos

Memos often create misperceptions and send unintended messages. Yet they are sometimes necessary to create a record of decisions or responsibilities. To write good memos: (1) Don't use accusatory or autocratic language, such as "I am appalled by your decision" or "I don't like your attitude." (2) Avoid absolutes, such as "never," "cannot," and "must not." (3) Keep them short and to the point—use bullet points for structure. (4) Never write anything in a memo that you don't want everyone else to see. (5) Always consider whether a phone call or personal conversation would be more effective than a memo.

Source: R. Davidhizar and S. Erdel, "Send Me a Memo on It, or Better Yet, Don't," *Health Care Supervisor* 15 (1997): 42–47. J. Gannon, "Clear Writing Leads to Better Business," *Star-Ledger (Pittsburgh Post-Gazette)*, 30 April 2002. 52.

However, written communication is not well suited to ambiguous or emotionally laden topics, which are better delivered through oral communication. Management consultant Tom Durel said, "Don't assume that you did your part just because you sent out a bunch of memos. If you really want to communicate, you need to take the time to get real-time feedback."[43]

3.2 Listening

Are you a good listener? You probably think so. But, in fact, most people, including managers, are terrible listeners, retaining only about 25 percent of what they hear.[44] You qualify as a poor listener if you frequently interrupt others, jump to conclusions about what people will say before they've said it, hurry the speaker to finish his or her point, are a passive listener (not actively working at your listening), and simply don't pay attention to what people are saying.[45] On this last point, attentiveness, college students were periodically asked to record their thoughts during a psychology course. On average, 20 percent of the students were paying attention (only 12 percent were actively working at being good listeners), 20 percent were thinking about sex, 20 percent were thinking about things they had done before, and the remaining 40 percent thought about a number of things (worries, religion, lunch, daydreaming, etc.), none of which were related to the class.[46]

How important is it to be a good listener? In general, about 45 percent of the total time you spend communicating with others is spent listening. Furthermore, listening is particularly important for managerial success. Neil Kadisha, CEO of HPM, a plastics manufacturer, said, "No one has a thing to fear about coming to me and lodging a complaint or making a suggestion. In all of my companies, janitors to the highest level of management can come to me.... We manage by respect, not by fear. We respect our employees' opinions and suggestions. They have the right to

---

Good listening skills require active, empathetic involvement.

© PhotoDisc, Inc.

get upset and angry, and they have the right to be heard."[47] In fact, managers with better listening skills are rated as better managers by their employees and are much more likely to be promoted.[48]

So what can you do to improve your listening ability? First, understand the difference between hearing and listening. According to *Webster's New World Dictionary*, **hearing** is the "act or process of perceiving sounds," whereas **listening** is "making a conscious effort to hear." In other words, we react to sounds, such as bottles breaking or music being played too loudly, because hearing is an involuntary physiological process. By contrast, listening is a voluntary behaviour. So if you want to be a good listener, you have to choose to be a good listener. Typically, that means choosing to be an active, empathetic listener.[49]

Active listening means assuming half the responsibility for successful communication by actively giving the speaker nonjudgmental feedback that shows you've accurately heard what he or she said. Active listeners make it clear from this behaviour that they are listening carefully to what the speaker has to say. Active listeners put the speaker at ease, maintain eye contact, and show the speaker that they are attentively listening by nodding and making short statements.

Several specific strategies can help you be a better active listener. First, *clarify responses* by asking the speaker to explain confusing or ambiguous statements. Second, when there are natural breaks in the speaker's delivery, use this time to paraphrase or summarize what has been said. *Paraphrasing* is restating what has been said in your own words. *Summarizing* is reviewing the speaker's main points or emotions. Paraphrasing and summarizing give the speaker the chance to correct the message if the active listener has attached the wrong meaning to it. Paraphrasing and summarizing also show the speaker that the active listener is interested in the speaker's message. Exhibit 16.5 lists specific statements that listeners can use to clarify responses, paraphrase, or summarize what has been said.

Active listeners also avoid evaluating the message or being critical until the message is complete. They recognize that their only responsibility during the transmission of a message is to accurately receive it and derive the intended meaning from it. Evaluation and criticism can take place after the message is accurately received. Finally, active listeners also recognize that a large portion of any message is transmitted nonverbally and thus pay very careful attention to the nonverbal cues transmitted by the speaker.

Empathetic listening means understanding the speaker's perspective and personal frame of reference and giving feedback that conveys that understanding to the speaker. Empathetic listening goes beyond active listening, because it depends on our ability to set aside our own attitudes or relationships to be able to see and understand things through someone else's eyes. Empathetic listening is just as important as active listening, especially for managers, because it helps build rapport and trust with others.

The key to being a more empathetic listener is to show your desire to understand and to reflect people's feelings. You can *show your desire to understand* by listening first, that is, by asking people to talk about what's most important to them and then giving them sufficient time to talk before responding or interrupting. Management consultant Neil Grammer said, "One of the best sales meetings I've ever had taught me a valuable lesson about the importance of listening. The meeting was with an investment bank's managing director. The appointment lasted 30 minutes—28 of those minutes were spent by the director telling me everything about his business and personnel. I told him nothing more about my company and its services than I had in our initial phone conversation. As the meeting concluded, he enthusiastically shook my hand and proclaimed how much he was looking forward to working with me—someone who understood his business."[50]

Reflecting feelings is also an important part of empathetic listening, because it demonstrates that you understand the speaker's emotions. But unlike active listening, in which you would restate or summarize the informational content of what had been said, the

hearing
the act or process of perceiving sounds

listening
making a conscious effort to hear

active listening
assuming half the responsibility for successful communication by actively giving the speaker nonjudgmental feedback that shows you've accurately heard what he or she said

empathetic listening
understanding the speaker's perspective and personal frame of reference and giving feedback that conveys that understanding to the speaker

EXHIBIT 16.5

CLARIFYING, PARAPHRASING, AND SUMMARIZING RESPONSES FOR ACTIVE LISTENERS

CLARIFYING RESPONSES

- Could you explain that again?
- I don't understand what you mean.
- I'm confused, would you run though that again?
- I'm not sure how...

PARAPHRASING RESPONSES

- What you're really saying is...
- If I understand you correctly...
- So your perspective is that...
- In other words...
- Tell me if I'm wrong, but what you're saying is...

SUMMARIZING RESPONSES

- Let me summarize...
- Okay, your main concerns are...
- Thus far, you've discussed...
- To recap what you've said...

Source: E. Atwater, *I Hear You*, revised ed. (New York: Walker, 1992).

focus is on the affective part of the message. As an empathetic listener, you can use the following statements to reflect the speaker's emotions:

- So, right now you're feeling...
- You seem as if you're...
- Do you feel a bit...?
- I could be wrong, but I'm sensing that you're feeling...

3.3 Giving Feedback

In Chapter 13, you learned that performance appraisal feedback (i.e., judging) should be separated from developmental feedback (i.e., coaching).[51] At this point, we now focus on the steps needed to communicate feedback one-on-one to employees.

To start, managers need to recognize that feedback can be constructive or destructive. **Destructive feedback** is disapproving without any intention of being helpful and almost always causes a negative or defensive reaction in the recipient. In fact, one study found that 98 percent of employees responded to destructive feedback from their bosses with either verbal aggression (two-thirds) or physical aggression (one-third).[52] By contrast, **constructive feedback** is intended to be helpful, corrective, and/or encouraging. It is aimed at correcting performance deficiencies and motivating employees. However, even when they want to give constructive rather than destructive feedback, managers still get nervous about discussing problems with employees. Joan Hill, president of human resource consulting firm Core Consulting, based in Mississauga, Ontario, said, "After many years in the business, even I don't enjoy them."[53]

In order for feedback to be constructive rather than destructive, it must be immediate, focused on specific behaviours, and problem oriented. Because the mistake or incident can be recalled more accurately and discussed in detail by the manager and the worker, *immediate feedback* is much more effective than delayed feedback. For example, if a worker is rude to a customer and the customer immediately reports the incident to

destructive feedback
feedback that disapproves without any intention of being helpful and almost always causes a negative or defensive reaction in the recipient

constructive feedback
feedback intended to be helpful, corrective, and/or encouraging

management, and the manager, in turn, immediately discusses the issue with the employee, there should be little disagreement over what was said or done. By contrast, if the manager waits several weeks to discuss the incident, it's unlikely that either the manager or the worker will be able to accurately remember the specifics of what occurred. When that happens, it's usually too late to have a meaningful conversation.

Specific feedback focuses on particular acts or incidents that are clearly under the control of the employee. For instance, instead of telling an employee that he or she is "always late for work," it's much more constructive to say, "In the last three weeks, you have been 30 minutes late on four occasions and more than an hour late on two others." Furthermore, specific feedback isn't very helpful unless employees have control over the problems that the feedback addresses. Indeed, giving negative feedback about behaviours beyond someone's control is likely to be seen as unfair. Similarly, giving positive feedback about behaviours beyond someone's control may be viewed as insincere.

Last, *problem-oriented feedback* focuses on the problems or incidents associated with the poor performance rather than on the worker or the worker's personality. Giving feedback does not give managers the right to personally attack workers. While managers may be frustrated by a worker's poor performance, the point of problem-oriented feedback is to draw attention to the problem in a nonjudgmental way, so that the employee has enough information to correct it. So, rather than telling people that they're "idiots," focus on the problem. For instance, a shipping clerk at a restaurant had a bad case of body odour. Rather than telling him "You stink" or "You're doing a lousy job because you stink," the manager explained the specific ways in which his body odour was "getting in the way of doing his job." Because the manager's feedback was specific and problem oriented and didn't attack or blame the employee, the employee didn't get defensive and took steps to take care of his body odour.[54]

3.4 Improving Cross-Cultural Communication

As you know by now, effective communication is very difficult to accomplish. However, **cross-cultural communication**, which involves transmitting information from a person in one country or culture to a person from another country or culture, is much more difficult. But there are a number of things you can do to increase your chances for successful cross-cultural communication: familiarize yourself with that culture's work norms, address terms, and attitudes toward time.[55]

In Chapter 8, you learned that expatriates who receive predeparture language and cross-cultural training make faster adjustments to foreign cultures and perform better on their international assignments.[56] Therefore, *familiarizing yourself with cultural work norms* is the first step for successful cross-cultural communication.

Next, *know the address terms* that people in that culture use to address each other in the workplace. **Address terms** are the cultural norms that establish whether you address businesspeople by their first names, family names, or titles. When meeting for the first time, North Americans and Australians tend to be informal and address each other by first names, even nicknames. However, such immediate informality is not accepted in many cultures. For instance, an American manager working in one of his company's British subsidiaries introduced himself as "Chuck" to his British employees and co-workers. However, even after six months on the job, his British counterparts still referred to him as Charles. And the more he insisted they call him "Chuck," the more they seemed to dig in their heels and call him "Charles."[57] So, to decrease defensiveness, know your address terms before addressing your international business counterparts.

Understanding cultural attitudes toward time is another major consideration for effective one-on-one communication when conducting international business. Four important temporal concepts affect cross-cultural communication: appointment time, schedule time, discussion time, and acquaintance time.[58] **Appointment time** is concerned with how punctual you must be when showing up for scheduled appointments or meetings. In Canada, any amount beyond 5 minutes late is considered "late." However, Swedes

cross-cultural communication
transmitting information from a person in one country or culture to a person from another country or culture

address terms
cultural norms that establish whether you should address businesspeople by their first names, family names, or titles

appointment time
cultural norm for how punctual you must be when showing up for scheduled appointments or meetings

don't even allow 5 minutes, expecting others to arrive by their appointment time. By contrast, in Latin countries, people can arrive 20 to 30 minutes after a scheduled appointment and still not be considered late. Nicholas Benedict, an MBA student from Toronto who took a two-month job in the United Arab Emirates, quickly learned the difference between meeting times in the UAE and Canada. He found that he had to grow "accustomed to setting business and personal meeting times at least a half hour before I planned to arrive."[59]

Schedule time is the time by which scheduled projects or jobs should actually be completed. In North American and other Anglo cultures, a premium is placed on completing things on time. By contrast, more relaxed attitudes toward schedule time can be found throughout Asia and Latin America.

Discussion time concerns how much time should be spent in discussion with others. In North America, we carefully manage discussion time to avoid "wasting" time on nonbusiness topics. In Brazil, though, because of the emphasis on building relationships, as much as two hours of general discussion on nonbusiness topics can be required before moving on to business issues.

Finally, **acquaintance time** is how much time you must spend getting to know someone before the person is prepared to do business with you. Again, in North America, people are quick to get down to business and are willing to strike a deal on the same day if the terms are good and initial impressions are positive. In the Middle East, however, it may take two or three weeks of meetings before reaching this comfort level. The French also have a different attitude toward acquaintance time. Polly Platt, author of *French or Foe*, a book that explains French culture and its people for travellers and businesspeople, says, "Know that things are going to take longer and don't resent it. Realize that the time system is different. Time is not a quantity for them. We save time, we spend time, we waste time; all this comes from money. The French don't. They pass time. It's a totally different concept."[60]

Review 3
Managing One-on-One Communication

One-on-one communication can be managed by choosing the right communication medium, being a good listener, giving effective feedback, and understanding cross-cultural communication. Managers generally prefer oral communication, because it provides the opportunity to ask questions and assess nonverbal communication. Oral communication is best suited to complex, ambiguous, or emotionally laden topics. Written communication is best suited for delivering straightforward messages and information. Listening is important for managerial success, but most people are terrible listeners. To improve your listening skills, choose to be an active listener (clarifying responses, paraphrasing, and summarizing) and an empathetic listener (show your desire to understand, reflect feelings). Feedback can be constructive or destructive. To be constructive, feedback must be immediate, focused on specific behaviours, and problem oriented. Finally, to increase chances for successful cross-cultural communication, familiarize yourself with the culture's work norms, address terms, and attitudes toward time (appointment time, schedule time, discussion time, and acquaintance time).

4. Managing Organization-Wide Communication

While managing one-on-one communication is important, managers must also know how to effectively communicate to a larger number of people throughout an organization. For instance, Barry Salzman, president of DoubleClick International, an Internet advertising firm, spends 75 percent of his time travelling to 14 international offices. And every Monday, no matter where he is, he conducts a conference call with DoubleClick managers in Canada, Europe, and Asia. Says Salzman, "We try to maintain voice contact. We lose that with computers and e-mail."[61] While this is an effective method of managing a small group of geographically dispersed people, managers can't hold a con-

---

schedule time
cultural norm for the time by which scheduled projects or jobs should actually be completed

discussion time
cultural norm for how much time should be spent in discussion with others

acquaintance time
cultural norm for how much time you must spend getting to know someone before the person is prepared to do business with you

ference call with everyone in the company. Thus, managers need additional methods for organization-wide communication and for making themselves accessible, so they can hear what employees throughout their organizations are feeling and thinking.

Learn more about organization-wide communication by reading the following sections about improving transmission, including getting the message out and improving reception.

4.1 Improving Transmission: Getting the Message Out

Several methods of electronic communication—e-mail, online discussion forums, televised/videotaped speeches and conferences, corporate talk shows, and broadcast voice-mail—now make it easier for managers to communicate with people throughout the organization and "get the message out." Although we normally think of *e-mail*, the transmission of messages via computers, as a means of one-on-one communication, it also plays an important role in organization-wide communication. For example:

> *Perot Systems Corporation publishes three online newsletters via e-mail. The internal communication department produces one every week and writes the others on an as-needed basis. Perot Systems chose this "low frills" approach for its simplicity and affordability. The department spends 15 hours a week collecting information. Copy approvals are completed within 24 hours, and the newsletters are distributed to its 2,400 associates (employees). The newsletters are typically no longer than three pages and include briefs about the latest company news.[62]*

Also, with the click of a button, managers can send e-mail to everyone in the company via e-mail distribution lists. Many CEOs now use this capability regularly to keep employees up to date on changes and developments in the company. Also, many CEOs and top executives make their e-mail addresses public and encourage employees to contact them directly. There are of course drawbacks to e-mail. For example, a writer for the *National Post*, Jonathan Kay, received an e-mail that had Bill Gates' Christmas list by mistake. Pushing the wrong button can be hazardous.[63]

Another way to electronically promote organization-wide communication is through discussion forums. **Online discussion forums**, which are the in-house equivalent of Internet newsgroups, are Web- or software-based discussion tools that are available across the company to permit employees to easily ask questions and share knowledge with each other. The point is to share expertise and not duplicate solutions already "discovered" by others in the company. Furthermore, because online discussion forums remain online, they provide a historical database for people who are dealing with particular problems for the first time.

Online discussion forums are typically organized by topic. For example, at Ernst & Young, a major accounting and management-consulting corporation, consultants who have questions about multinational tax analysis can simply log on to the E & Y tax forum (or dozens of other forums, too). They can either post new questions and get help from others who respond with answers, or read previously posted questions and answers to see if the information they need has already been discussed. If either of those options fails, they can at least come away with the names of people in the organization that they can contact for help.[64] British Petroleum Amoco has taken this a step farther by creating "Connect," which is essentially a company Yellow Pages where more than 12 000 managers and workers have entered their contact information and listed their expertise to make it easier for others to find expert help for their problems.[65] Exhibit 16.6 lists the steps companies need to take to establish successful online discussion forums.

PERSONAL PRODUCTIVITY TIP

The Dangers of Corporate E-mail

E-mail is fast and convenient but has serious pitfalls. It can be easily saved, duplicated, forwarded, and printed. The original sender has no control over who sees it. And while senders delete e-mail on their machines, most likely other copies can be found on the company's mail server or backup tapes, which most companies run every night. E-mail also allows disgruntled employees to easily send out sensitive or fraudulent information to competitors or outsiders. Finally, many employees use easily guessed passwords or don't log off their computers, making it easy for outsiders to e-mail while posing as members of your company.

Source: M. Coles, "Warning Note over E-Mail Legal Danger: Firms Face Big Damages for Careless Chat," *Sunday Mail*, 20 August 2000, 41.

online discussion forums the in-house equivalent of Internet newsgroups; Web- or software-based discussion tools available across the company to permit employees to easily ask questions and share knowledge with each other

EXHIBIT 16.6

ESTABLISHING ONLINE DISCUSSION FORUMS

1. *Perform a "Knowledge" Audit*—to pinpoint your company's top intellectual assets; then spread that knowledge throughout the organization.
2. *Create an Online Directory*—detailing the expertise of individual workers, and make it available to all employees.
3. *Set Up Discussion Groups on the Net*—so that managers and workers can collaborate on problem-solving.
4. *Reward Information Sharing*—make sharing knowledge online a key part of performance ratings.

Source: G. McWilliams & M. Stepanek, "Knowledge Management: Taming the Info Monster," *Business Week*, 22 June 1998, 170.

televised/videotaped speeches and meetings
speeches and meetings originally made to a smaller audience that are either simultaneously broadcast to other locations in the company or videotaped for subsequent distribution and viewing

Televised/videotaped speeches and meetings are a third electronic method of organization-wide communication. **Televised/videotaped speeches and meetings** are simply speeches and meetings originally made to a smaller audience that are either simultaneously broadcast to other locations in the company or videotaped for subsequent distribution and viewing.

Corporate talk shows are a variant on televised/videotaped speeches and meetings. But instead of simply watching a televised/videotaped speech or meeting, **corporate talk shows** allow remote audience members, all of whom are typically workers or managers, to pose questions to the show's host and guests. For example, once a month, Emma Carasco, vice president of marketing and communication, and Dan Hunt, president of Caribbean and Latin American operations, host the Virtual Leadership Academy, which is a corporate talk show for Nortel Networks. A typical broadcast is seen live by 2000 employees in 46 countries, who call in with questions about Nortel and its competitors. Why a corporate talk show? Carrasco said, "We're always looking for ways to break down barriers in the company, and people are comfortable with the talk-show format. People watch talk shows in every country in the region, and they've learned that it's okay to say what's on their mind. In fact, it's expected."

corporate talk shows
televised company meetings that allow remote audiences (employees) to pose questions to the show's host and guests

In Chapter 5, you learned that *voice messaging*, or "voice-mail," is a telephone answering system that records audio messages. Eighty-nine percent of respondents believe that voice messaging is critical to business communication, 78 percent believe that it improves productivity, and 58 percent would rather leave a message on a voice messaging system than with a receptionist.[66] However, most people are unfamiliar with the ability to broadcast voice-mail by sending a recorded message to everyone in the company. Broadcast voice-mail gives top managers a quick, convenient way to address their work forces via oral communication.

4.2 Improving Reception: Hearing What Others Feel and Think

When people think of "organization-wide" communication, they think of the CEO and top managers getting their message out to people in the company. However, organization-wide communication also means finding ways to communicate and stay in touch with people throughout the organization. Company hotlines, survey feedback, frequent informal meetings, and surprise visits are ways of accomplishing this.

company hot lines
phone numbers that anyone in the company can anonymously call to leave information for upper management

Company hot lines are phone numbers that anyone in the company can anonymously call to leave information for upper management. For instance, Toyota's employee handbook says, "Don't spend time worrying about something. Speak up!" The Toyota hot line is anonymous and available 24 hours a day, seven days a week. Every message is reviewed and fully investigated by Toyota's top human resources manager. Moreover, if the questions or statements left on the hot line would be of interest to others in the company, they are then posted on company bulletin boards (without sacrificing callers' anonymity).[67]

Survey feedback is information collected by survey from organizational members that is then compiled, disseminated, and used to develop action plans for improvement. Many organizations make use of survey feedback by surveying their managers and employees several times a year. For example, Maritime Life, located in Halifax, surveys employees once or twice a year. Employees are asked about their job satisfaction and they can also anonymously evaluate their boss. The feedback from surveys helps Maritime Life maintain its rating as one of the top 50 companies in Canada to work for.[68]

Frequent, *informal meetings* between top managers and lower-level employees are one of the best ways for top managers to hear what others feel and think. Many people assume that top managers are at the centre of everything that goes on in organizations. However, it's common for top managers to feel isolated from most of the managers and employees in their companies. Consequently, more and more top managers are scheduling frequent, informal meetings with people throughout their companies. Remember Maureen Shaw, president of Ontario-based Industrial Accident Prevention Association? She met regularly with all her employees for her water cooler chats.

Have you ever been around supervisors when they found out that upper management was going to be paying a visit? First, there's shock. Next, there's anxiety. And then there's panic, as everyone is told to drop what he or she is doing to polish, shine, and spruce up the workplace, so it looks perfect for top management's visit. Of course, when visits are conducted under these conditions, top managers don't get a realistic look at what's going on in the company. Consequently, one of the ways to get an accurate picture is to pay *surprise visits* to various parts of the organization. However, surprise visits should not be surprise inspections. Instead, surprise visits should be used as an opportunity to increase the chances for meaningful upward communication from those who normally don't get a chance to work with upper management. Indeed, surprise visits like these are part of the culture at Enterprise Rent-a-Car. Fred Sorino, who manages an Enterprise office in Eatontown, New Jersey, said, "Once I was working at a branch in Cranbury, New Jersey, and a corporate vice president and a regional president showed up for a surprise visit. I was outside washing cars in 20-degree weather, and we were very busy. These two executives offered to help me clean the cars. I felt so awkward that I said I didn't need help, but they did it anyway." Enterprise's CEO, Andy Taylor, tells a similar story, saying, "We were visiting an office in Berkeley and it was mobbed, so I started cleaning cars. As it was happening, I wondered if it was a good use of my time, but the effect on morale was tremendous."[69]

Review 4
Managing Organization-Wide Communication

Managers need methods for organization-wide communication and for making themselves accessible, so they can hear what employees throughout their organizations are feeling and thinking. E-mail, online discussion forums, televised/videotaped speeches and conferences, corporate talk shows, and broadcast voice-mail make it much easier for managers to improve message transmission and "get the message out." By contrast, anonymous company hot lines, survey feedback, frequent informal meetings, and surprise visits help managers improve reception by hearing what others in the organization feel and think.

survey feedback
information collected by survey from organizational members that is then compiled, disseminated, and used to develop action plans for improvement

What Really Happened?

In the opening case, you learned that Buckman Laboratories was having communication problems. As sales director, you were frustrated because sales representatives would contact you looking for answers to their clients' technical questions. In turn, you would send those messages to technical experts in the company, who weren't very fast or reliable about getting back in touch with sales representatives. Any way you looked at it, organizational communication was not very good. Read the answers to the opening case to find out what Buckman Labs did to address these communication issues.

The first thing you need to figure out is why people in different parts of the company are so reluctant to communicate with each other. Is it perception, culture, or simply poor communication techniques?

Perception is the process by which individuals attend to, organize, interpret, and retain information from their environments. As people perform their jobs, they are exposed to a wide variety of informational stimuli, such as e-mails, direct conversations with the boss or co-workers, rumours heard over lunch, stories about the company in the press, or a video broadcast of a speech from the CEO to all employees. However, because of perceptual filters, exposure to an informational stimulus is no guarantee that an individual will pay attention or attend to that stimulus. Indeed, since sales representatives had frequent face-to-face contact with customers and technical experts did not, it's not surprising that sales representatives wanted customer problems to be solved imme-

diately. However, because of their Ph.D. training, technical experts were much more interested in figuring the problem out right than in figuring it out quickly.

Next, anything's got to be better than having you, the sales manager, as the first point of contact for expert help, but what? How can you match sales representatives with the right technical experts without having to serve as the go-between? There's got to be a reasonable technological solution. But if e-mail wasn't the technological solution, and everybody uses e-mail, what's the answer?

One way to promote organization-wide communication is through discussion forums. Online discussion forums, which are the in-house equivalent of Internet newsgroups, are Web- or software-based discussion tools that are available across the company to permit people to easily ask questions and share knowledge with each other. Buckman solved its problems by creating online discussion forums, called K'Netix, for its customers, sales representatives, technical experts, and everyone else in the company. K'Netix allows Buckman's 1300 employees, who work all over the world, to come together to share knowledge via voice or video conferences, text chats, or document sharing. For example, a sales representative in Indonesia needed help in quickly writing a client proposal. He obtained the marketing information he needed from existing information on K'Netix and then was able to obtain answers to detailed technical questions from technical experts who regularly log on to the K'Netix system. In fact, technical answers were obtained from people at

headquarters in six hours, from people in Europe in eight hours, and from six other Buckman people at various places around the globe in forty-eight hours. All of this timely information helped him create a successful sales proposal in just three days, the result of which was a new $9-million contract.

K'Netix was also important as a communication system because it had as much appeal for Buckman's technical experts as it did for Buckman's clients and sales representatives. Buckman's vice president of human resources, Mark Koskiniemi, said, "We have Ph.D.s in our lab who know everything about everything. If they don't share their knowledge, they are not valuable." In contrast to the previous system in which requests were routed through the sales director, the K'Netix network encourages open, unrestricted communication among Buckman's experts and the free exchange of ideas. This helps Buckman to find innovative solutions to customer challenges, as well as to develop products in anticipation of future needs. And it makes the application of innovation easier.

Sources: Buckman Laboratories. [Online] Available www. buckman.com/home.html, 5 September 1999. J. Eckhouse, "Get Creative with Knowledge Sharing—In Today's Culture, Businesses Must Rebuild Their Processes to Take Advantage of Their Knowledge Base," *Information Week*, 8 February 1999, ER19. D.J. Knight, "Strategy in Practice: Making It Happen," *Strategy & Leadership* 26, No. 3 (1 July 1998): 29. M.N. Martinez, "The Collective Power of Employee Knowledge," *HR Magazine* 43, No. 2 (1 February 1998): 88. S. Thurm, "What Do You Know? Getting Employees to Share Their Knowledge Isn't as Simple as Installing New Software; Just Ask Buckman Labs," *The Wall Street Journal*, 21 June 1999, R10.

Key Terms

acquaintance time (520)
active listening (527)
address terms (529)
appointment time (529)
attribution theory (515)
closure (515)
coaching (523)
communication (512)
communication medium (525)
company hot lines (532)
conduit metaphor (519)
constructive feedback (528)
corporate talk shows (532)
counselling (523)
cross-cultural communication (529)

decoding (518)
defensive bias (515)
destructive feedback (528)
discussion time (520)
downward communication (519)
empathetic listening (527)
encoding (517)
feedback (518)
formal communication channel (519)
fundamental attribution error (516)
hearing (527)
horizontal communication (520)
informal communication channel
 (grapevine) (521)
kinesics (523)

listening (527)
noise (518)
nonverbal communication (523)
online discussion forums (531)
paralanguage (523)
perception (513)
perceptual filters (513)
schedule time (530)
selective perception (515)
self-serving bias (516)
survey feedback (533)
televised/videotaped speeches and meetings
 (532)
upward communication (520)

What Would You Do II?

At 9 a.m. each day at a Mercedes-Benz plant, the workers take their first beer break of the day. When they've finished their beers, the workers light up cigarettes and return to the manufacturing line. At 10:00 a.m. each day in a Chrysler plant, the workers take their first coffee break, have cigarettes outside (because smoking isn't permitted inside the plant), and then return to the manufacturing line. Stuttgart, Germany, and Auburn Hills, Michigan. Mercedes-Benz and Chrysler. These two very different places and two very different companies are now one, having merged into the fourth-largest auto company in the world, DaimlerChrysler.

And while, legally, the merger is now final officially—DaimlerChrysler is a German-registered company in management terms—the merger has barely started. To facilitate the merger of two different languages and two different business cultures, the company bought an Airbus A320 jet, which normally seats 150 people. The plane, which now comfortably sleeps 53 people, makes four round-trip flights a week, shuttling Germans and Americans between the Stuttgart and Detroit international airports.

But despite significant efforts to make the merger run smoothly, significant cultural and communication differences keep getting in the way. For instance, there were arguments over whether new automobile plants should be highly automated (the German preference) or streamlined to increase efficiencies and reduce inventories (the American preference). Furthermore, freewheeling Chrysler managers bristled under the strict planning-

oriented approach used by their German counterparts. Steve Harris, formerly Chrysler's chief of communications (now with General Motors), said, "You'd go into a meeting and have to turn to Volume 7, Section 42, page 597 of the planning book." He went on to say that "the Germans pride themselves on analytical research that produces a plan, while the American way is to try for the impossible and keep coming up with new ideas to make it happen."

While some differences were expected—after all, these were both very successful companies with their own ways of doing things—it's obvious that the two sides aren't communicating very well, especially when you consider the silly disagreements they continue to have. For example, just as the new company, DaimlerChrysler, was about to be listed on the New York Stock Exchange, the merger almost fell apart over whether to use American-sized business cards, which are smaller, or the European-sized business cards, which are larger. Tom Stallkamp, Chrysler's president, said, "It got all the way up to me, and I said, What the hell, they're only business cards," so he chose the slightly larger European-sized cards because they were unique. Likewise, the German emphasis on hierarchy and titles became a point of contention, especially when German managers insisted on their customary title of "Doctor" (the way in which Germans address upper management).

The question, of course, is what to do to handle all these cultural and communication difficulties. It certainly won't be easy, especially since Daimler's own research indicates that 70 percent of such mergers fail within the first three years. In the end, it comes down to communication and people. One financial analyst said, "The biggest challenge in a merger like this is on the [production] floor. The chairmen and boards of directors can be all for it, but it eventually comes down to the workforces."

If you were in charge of the DaimlerChrysler merger, what would you do?

Sources: D.A. Blackman, "Autos: A Factory in Alabama Is the Merger in Microcosm," *The Wall Street Journal*, 8 May 1998, B1. F. Gibney, Jr. & J.R. Szczesny, "Worldwide Fender Blender Billed as a Merger of Equals, the Union of Chrysler with Daimler-Benz Has Been Anything But. Yet Amid Crashed Marriages and Careers, a Transglobal Company Is Emerging," *Time*, 24 May 1999, 58. C.J. Williams, "Steering Around Culture Clashes Autos: An Integration Team at Daimler-Chrysler Is Trying to Cope with Cross-Border Differences Everything from Labor-Management Relations to Germany's 9 A.M. Beer Breaks," *Los Angeles Times*, 17 January 1999, C1.

Management Decisions

Selling in Latin America

As you glance at the calendar on your desk, you realize that you have only two weeks left to prepare for your first international assignment. Since your recent promotion to the position of a regional sales manager for a mid-sized, multinational, telecommunications firm, you have spent the majority of your time working out of the home office. What time you did spend travelling was spent visiting customers and offices in and around your sales region. Your new job entails describing your firm's products and services; explaining the benefits, price, and terms; and, once the customer agrees, closing the sale by signing a formal contract containing the necessary information.

During last month's regional managers' meeting, your boss informed you that because of your ability to speak Spanish fluently and your recent success and promotion, you would soon assume part of the Latin American region and would be responsible for meeting and dealing with customers in Mexico and parts of South America, in addition to your current duties. Although you are excited at the prospect of travelling abroad, you are also a little nervous because, other than a week-long, school-sponsored trip to Ciudad Juarez, Mexico, you have never left the country before.

The company's travel office has helped relieve some of your anxiety by performing a majority of the paperwork involved, preparing your passport, making your travel arrangements, and putting you in touch with the former regional manager for Latin America. Even though she has been a tremendous asset by telling you which hotel chains and restaurants are "decent" and which are not, showing you how to avoid some of the customs inspection problems, and giving you an updated potential-customer database, she hasn't provided much information regarding the local culture of the area or your prospective customers' expectations. As a continent, Latin America is less developed in the area of telecommunications than North America, so you are excited about the sales potential of the area. However, you also have some concerns.

One major area of concern is the myriad of cultural differences between North America and Latin America. You believe that one of the reasons that you were so successful in your region is because you really knew and understood your customers and their needs. Given the fact that you will be making cold calls, requesting appointments, making presentations to individuals and groups, and attempting to close on contractual agreements involving thousands of dollars, you feel your concerns are legitimate.

Questions

1. As the manager in question, what could you do to help put an end to your uneasiness?
2. Although you speak Spanish, you know that language is not the only element of cross-cultural fluency. What issues will you be confronting with regards to cross-cultural communication in your new Latin American position? What can you do to overcome the obstacles to cross-cultural communication?

Sources: D. Benton, *Applied Human Relations*, 5th Edition (Prentice Hall, 1995), 533–544. G. Hofstede, "Organizational Dynamic," *AMACOM*, Summer 1980, 375–394.

Management Decisions

Is Upward Communication Worth the Risk?

It's been 18 months now since the new CEO was hired, and what a breath of fresh air he's been. He's exciting and visionary, but also friendly and approachable, and has gone out of his way to meet as many people as possible, holding quarterly town hall meetings and doing lunch with lower-level managers and workers at least once a week. And every time you've heard him speak, he's announced his e-mail address and encouraged anyone who wanted to contact him directly.

In fact, people throughout the organization have been energized by his leadership and the changes he's made to bring about a more open, innovative culture. Of course, not everything can change at once. In fact, things haven't changed much in your division at all. Your division head, Tim Howard, hasn't really embraced the new leadership style. You might even say he's rejected it. Tim is short with subordinates, prone to yelling when things aren't done to his satisfaction, and, in the last year or so, incredibly indecisive. Each week, dozens of big and little decisions that need to be made aren't being made. The whole division just sits there with no direction and no momentum.

And if you come up with an idea that might make the division more competitive and are brave enough to discuss it with Tim, you find out that he's not completely indecisive. Indeed, Tim has a bad case of "not invented here" syndrome, so if it's not his idea, the automatic answer is "no."

It's obvious to you and everyone else that Tim is burned out and that you need a new division head. You're tempted to e-mail the new CEO about the situation—after all, he's open to communication from anyone in the company. However, you worry about going around Tim to top management. And what if the CEO isn't quite as open as he makes himself out to be?

Questions

1. What risks do you incur if you e-mail the CEO about Tim's leadership of your division?
2. If you were going to e-mail the CEO, what would your opening paragraph say?
3. Would you e-mail the CEO about Tim? Yes or no? Explain your decision.

Develop Your Management Potential

I Don't Agree, but I'm Listening

Being a good listener is a critical part of effective communication. Without it, you're unlikely to be a good manager. Therefore, the purpose of this assignment is to help you develop your listening skills. And there's no better way to do that than to talk to someone whose views are quite different from yours.

In the best of situations, being a good listener is difficult. Because of perceptual filters, distractions, or daydreams, you retain only about 25 percent of what you hear. However, it can be almost impossible to be a good listener when you're talking to someone who has very different views and opinions. When you talk to people with different views, it's easy to interrupt, jump to conclusions about what they'll say, and hurry them to finish their points (which you don't want to listen to anyway), so you can "correct" their thinking with your opinions.

To complete this assignment, you'll have to find someone who has different views or opinions on some topic (gun control, abortion, and euthanasia are just some of the topics on which you can always find someone with a different viewpoint). Once you've found someone, conduct a ten-minute listening session, following this simple rule: Before stating your opinion, you must first accurately reflect or paraphrase the statement that your listening partner just made (be sure to reread section 3.2 on listening). So if your listening partner said, "Women shouldn't

have to ask anyone for permission for what they do to their bodies. If they decide they want an abortion, they should go ahead and have it," you would have to accurately paraphrase that statement in your own words before being allowed to make your point or disagree with that of your partner. If you don't paraphrase it correctly, your listening partner will tell you. If you or your partner have difficulty accurately paraphrasing a statement, then ask the other person to repeat the statement, and try again. Also, don't parrot the response by repeating it word for word. Good listening isn't mimicry. It's capturing the essence of what others have said in your own words. And before your listening partner responds, he or she, too, has to accurately paraphrase what you say. Continue this listening-based discussion for ten minutes.

Questions

1. Was this different from the way in which you normally discuss contentious topics with other people? Why or why not?
2. Was it difficult to reflect or paraphrase your listening partner's perspectives? Explain and give an example.
3. What led to more effective listening for you, active listening techniques or empathetic listening techniques? Explain.

Discussion Questions

1. Identify a situation where you have misunderstood what someone was trying to tell you. What was the cause of the misunderstanding (relate it back to the theory in the chapter)?
2. Compare the advantages and disadvantages of e-mail and face-to-face communication. When are they the most appropriate to use?
3. What four skills are essential for managers to use during face-to-face communication? Give examples from your workplace.
4. What is the difference between coaching and counselling? Give examples.

Study Tip

Studying for comprehensive exams doesn't have to be a chore. Form a study group. Photocopy the glossary of the text and cut it into strips, one term per strip. Put all the strips into a large bowl. Divide into teams and draw one strip out at time. Quiz the opposing team and then read the correct answer. You can do the same with the chapter outlines at the beginning of each chapter.

absolute comparisons
a process in which each criterion is compared to a standard or is ranked on its own merits

accommodative strategy
a social responsiveness strategy in which a company chooses to accept responsibility for a problem and to do all that society expects to solve that problem

acquaintance time
cultural norm for how much time you must spend getting to know someone before the person is prepared to do business with you

acquisition
purchase of a company by another company

acquisition cost
the cost of obtaining data that you don't have

action plan
the specific steps, people, and resources needed to accomplish a goal

active listening
assuming half the responsibility for successful communication by actively giving the speaker nonjudgmental feedback that shows you've accurately heard what he or she said

address terms
cultural norms that establish whether you should address businesspeople by their first names, family names, or titles

advocacy groups
groups of concerned citizens who band together to try to influence the business practices of specific industries, businesses, and professions

aggregate product plans
plans developed to manage and monitor all new products

in development at any one time

analyzers
an adaptive strategy that seeks to minimize risk and maximize profits by following or imitating the proven successes of prospectors

anchoring and adjustment bias
unrecognized tendency of decision makers to use an initial value or experience as a basis of comparison throughout the decision process

application sharing
communications system that allows two or more people in different locations to make changes in a document by sharing control of the software application running on one computer

appointment time
cultural norm for how punctual you must be when showing up for scheduled appointments or meetings

Asia-Pacific Economic Cooperation (APEC)
regional trade agreement between Australia, Canada, Chile, China, Hong Kong, Japan, Mexico, New Zealand, Papua New Guinea, Peru, Russia, South Korea, the United States, and all the members of ASEAN, except Cambodia, Laos, and Myanmar

assemble-to-order operation
manufacturing operation that divides manufacturing processes into separate parts or modules that are combined to create semi-customized products

assessment centres
a series of managerial simulations, graded by trained observers, that are used to

determine applicants' capability for managerial work

Association of Southeast Asian Nations (ASEAN)
regional trade agreement between Brunei Darussalam, Cambodia, Indonesia, Laos, Malaysia, Myanmar, the Philippines, Singapore, Thailand, and Vietnam

association or affinity patterns
when two or more database elements tend to occur together in a significant way

attack
a competitive move designed to reduce a rival's market share or profits

attribution theory
theory that states that we all have a basic need to understand and explain the causes of other people's behaviour

a-type conflict (affective conflict)
disagreement that focuses on individual- or personally-oriented issues

authority
the right to give commands, take action, and make decisions to achieve organizational objectives

autonomous work groups
groups that operate without managers and are completely responsible for controlling work group processes, outputs, and behaviour

availability bias
unrecognized tendency of decision makers to give preference to recent information, vivid images that evoke emotions, and specific acts and behaviours that they personally observed

average aggregate inventory
average overall inventory during a particular time period

background checks
procedures used to verify the truthfulness and accuracy of information that applicants provide about themselves and to uncover negative, job-related background information not provided by applicants

balanced scorecard
measurement of organizational performance in four equally important areas: finances, customers, internal operations, and innovation and learning

bar code
a visual pattern that represents numerical data by varying the thickness and pattern of vertical bars

bargaining power of buyers
a measure of the influence that customers have on a firm's prices

bargaining power of suppliers
a measure of the influence that suppliers of parts, materials, and services to firms in an industry have on the prices of these inputs

batch production
manufacturing operation that produces goods in large batches in standard lot sizes

BCG matrix
a portfolio strategy, developed by the Boston Consulting Group, that managers use to categorize the corporation's businesses by growth rate and relative market share, helping them decide how to invest corporate funds

behaviour control
regulation of the behaviours and actions that workers perform on the job

behavioural addition
the process of having managers and employees perform

new behaviours that are central to and symbolic of the new organizational culture that a company wants to create

behavioural formality
workplace atmosphere characterized by routine and regimen, specific rules about how to behave, and interpersonal detachment

behavioural informality
workplace atmosphere characterized by spontaneity, casualness, and interpersonal familiarity

behavioural observation scales (BOS)
rating scales that indicate the frequency with which workers perform specific behaviours that are representative of the job dimensions critical to successful job performance

behavioural substitution
the process of having managers and employees perform new behaviours central to the "new" organizational culture in place of behaviours that were central to the "old" organizational culture

benchmarking
the process of identifying outstanding practices, processes, and standards in other companies and adapting them to your company

biographical data (biodata)
extensive surveys that ask applicants questions about their personal backgrounds and life experiences

boundaryless organization
a speedy, responsive, and flexible organization in which vertical, horizontal, external, and geographic boundaries are removed or minimized

bounded rationality
decision-making process restricted in the real world by limited resources, incomplete and imperfect information, and managers' limited decision-making capabilities

brainstorming
a decision-making method in which group members build on each other's ideas to generate as many alternative solutions as possible

budgeting
quantitative planning through which managers decide how to allocate available money to best accomplish company goals

bureaucratic control
use of hierarchical authority to influence employee behaviour by rewarding or punishing employees for compliance or noncompliance with organizational policies, rules, and procedures

bureaucratic immunity
the ability to make changes without first getting approval from managers or other parts of an organization

business confidence indices
indices that show managers' level of confidence about future business growth

buyer dependence
degree to which a supplier relies on a buyer because of the importance of that buyer to the supplier and the difficulty of selling its products to other buyers

cafeteria benefit plans (flexible benefit plans)
plans that allow employees to choose which benefits they receive, up to a certain dollar value

cash cow
a company with a large share of a slow-growing market

centralization of authority
the location of most authority at the upper levels of the organization

chain of command
the vertical line of authority that clarifies who reports to whom throughout the organization

change agent
the person formally in charge of guiding a change effort

change forces
forces that produce differences in the form, quality, or condition of an organization over time

change intervention
the process used to get workers and managers to change their behaviour and work practices

character of the rivalry
a measure of the intensity of competitive behaviour between companies in an industry

charismatic leadership
the behavioural tendencies and personal characteristics of leaders that create an exceptionally strong relationship between them and their followers

closure
tendency to fill in gaps of missing information by assuming that what we don't know is consistent with what we already know

coaching
communicating with someone for the direct purpose of improving the person's on-the-job performance or behaviour

coercion
using formal power and authority to force others to change

cognitive ability tests
tests that measure the extent to which applicants have abilities in perceptual speed, verbal comprehension, numerical aptitude, general reasoning, and spatial aptitude

cognitive maps
graphic depictions of how managers believe environmental factors relate to possible organizational actions

cohesiveness
the extent to which team members are attracted to a team and motivated to remain in it

commission
a compensation system in which employees earn a percentage of each sale they make

common-enemy mission
company goal of defeating a corporate rival

communication
the process of transmitting information from one person or place to another

communication cost
the cost of transmitting information from one place to another

communication medium
the method used to deliver an oral or written message

company hot lines
phone numbers that anyone in the company can anonymously call to leave information for upper management

company vision
a company's purpose or reason for existing

compensation
the financial and nonfinancial rewards that organizations give employees in exchange for their work

competitive advantage
providing greater value for customers than competitors can

competitive analysis
a process for monitoring competitors that involves identifying competitors, anticipating their moves, and determining their strengths and weaknesses

competitive inertia
a reluctance to change strategies or competitive practices that have been successful in the past

competitors
companies in the same industry that sell similar products or services to customers

complex environment
an environment with many environmental factors

component parts inventories
the basic parts used in manufacturing that are fabricated from raw materials

compression approach to innovation
an approach to innovation that assumes that incremental innovation can be planned using a series of steps, and that compressing those steps can speed innovation

concentration of effect
the total harm or benefit that an act produces on the average person

conceptual skill
the ability to see the organization as a whole, how the different parts affect each other, and how the company fits into or is affected by its environment

concertive control
regulation of workers' behaviour and decisions through work group values and beliefs

concurrent control
a mechanism for gathering information about performance deficiencies as they occur, eliminating or shortening the delay between performance and feedback

conditions of certainty
conditions in which decision makers have complete information and knowledge of all possible outcomes

conditions of risk
conditions in which decision makers face a very real possibility of making the wrong decision

conditions of uncertainty
conditions in which decision makers don't know the odds of winning or losing

conduit metaphor
the mistaken assumption that senders can pipe their intended messages directly into the heads of receivers with perfect clarity and without noise or perceptual filters interfering with the receivers' understanding of the message

conferencing system
communications system that lets two or more users in different locations see and talk to each other as if they were in the same room

consideration
the extent to which a leader is friendly, approachable, supportive, and shows concern for employees

constructive feedback
feedback intended to be helpful, corrective, and/or encouraging

contingency theory
leadership theory that states that in order to maximize work group performance, leaders must be matched to the situation that best fits their leadership style

continuous-flow production
manufacturing operation that produces goods in a continuous, rather than a discrete, rate

continuous improvement
an organization's ongoing commitment to constantly assess and improve the processes and procedures used to create products and services

control
a regulatory process of establishing standards to achieve organizational goals, comparing actual performance against the standards, and taking corrective action, when necessary

control loss
situation in which behaviour and work procedures do not conform to standards

controlling
monitoring progress toward goal achievement and taking corrective action when needed

conventional level of moral development
second level of moral development in which people make decisions that conform to societal expectations

conversations for closure
conversations that end the change process by indicating that the work is done and the change process is complete

conversations for performance
conversations about action plans, in which managers and workers make specific requests and promise specific results

conversations for understanding
conversations that generate a deeper understanding of why change is needed, what problems have been occurring, and what might be done to solve those problems

cooperative contract
an agreement in which a foreign business owner pays a company a fee for the right to conduct that business in his or her country

core capabilities
the internal decision-making routines, problem-solving processes, and organizational cultures that determine how efficiently inputs can be turned into outputs

core firms
the central companies in a strategic group

corporate talk shows
televised company meetings that allow remote audiences (employees) to pose questions to the show's host and guests

corporate-level strategy
the overall organizational strategy that addresses the question "What business or businesses are we in or should we be in?"

cost leadership
the positioning strategy of producing a product or service of acceptable quality at consistently lower production costs than competitors can, so that the firm can offer the product or service at the lowest price in the industry

counselling
communicating with someone about non-job-

related issues that may be affecting or interfering with the person's performance

country of manufacture
country where product is made and assembled

country of origin
the home country for a company, where its headquarters is located

creativity
the production of novel and useful ideas

cross-cultural communication
transmitting information from a person in one country or culture to a person from another country or culture

cross-functional team
team composed of employees from different functional areas of the organization

cross training
training team members how to do all or most of the jobs performed by the other team members

c-type conflict (cognitive conflict)
disagreement that focuses on problem- and issue-related differences of opinion

customer defections
performance assessment in which companies identify which customers are leaving and measure the rate at which they are leaving

customer departmentalization
organizing work and workers into separate units responsible for particular kinds of customers

customer focus
an organizational goal to concentrate on meeting customers' needs at all levels of the organization

customer satisfaction
an organizational goal to provide products or services that meet or exceed customers' expectations

cybernetic feasibility
the extent to which it is possible to implement each step in the control process

data clusters
when three or more database elements occur together (i.e., cluster) in a significant way

data encryption
transforms data into complex, scrambled digital codes that can only be unencrypted by authorized users who possess unique decryption keys

data mining
the process of discovering unknown patterns and relationships in large amounts of data

data warehouse
stores huge amounts of data that have been prepared for data-mining analysis by being cleaned of errors and redundancy

decentralization
the location of a significant amount of authority in the lower levels of the organization

decision criteria
the standards used to guide judgments and decisions

decision-making
the process of choosing a solution from available alternatives

decision rule
set of criteria that alternative solutions must meet to be acceptable to the decision maker

decision support system (DSS)
an information system that helps managers to understand specific kinds of problems and potential solutions and to analyze the impact of different decision options using "what if" scenarios

decoding
the process by which the receiver translates the written, verbal, or symbolic form of a message into an understood message

defenders
an adaptive strategy aimed at defending strategic positions by seeking moderate, steady growth and by offering a limited range of high-quality products and services to a well-defined set of customers

defensive bias
the tendency for people to perceive themselves as personally and situationally similar to someone who is having difficulty or trouble

defensive strategy
a social responsiveness strategy in which a company chooses to admit responsibility for a problem but do the least required to meet societal expectations

de-forming
a reversal of the forming stage, in which team members position themselves to control pieces of the team, avoid each other, and isolate themselves from team leaders

degree of dependence
the extent to which a company needs a particular resource to accomplish its goals

delegation of authority
the assignment of direct authority and responsibility to a subordinate to complete tasks for which the manager is normally responsible

Delphi technique
a decision-making method in which a panel of experts responds to questions and to each other until reaching agreement on an issue

de-norming
a reversal of the norming stage, in which team performance begins to decline as the size, scope, goal, or members of the team change

departmentalization
subdividing work and workers into separate organizational units responsible for completing particular tasks

dependent demand system
inventory system in which the level of inventory depends on the number of finished units to be produced

design competition
competition between old and new technologies to establish a new technological standard or dominant design

design iteration
a cycle of repetition in which a company tests a prototype of a new product or service, improves on that design, and then builds and tests the improved prototype

desktop videoconferencing
communications system that allows two or more people in different locations to use video cameras and computer monitors to see and hear each other and share documents

de-storming
a reversal of the storming phase, in which the team's comfort level decreases, team cohesion weakens, and angry emotions and conflict may flare

destructive feedback
feedback that disapproves without any intention of being helpful and almost always causes a negative or defensive reaction in the recipient

devil's advocacy
a decision-making method in which an individual or a subgroup is assigned the role of a critic

dialectical inquiry
a decision-making method in which decision makers state the assumptions of a proposed solution (a thesis) and generate a solution that is the opposite (antithesis) of that solution

dictionary rule
decision rule that requires decision makers to rank criteria in order of importance and then test alternative solutions against those criteria in rank order, so that alterna-

tives that meet the most important criterion must then meet the second most important criterion, and so on

differentiation
the positioning strategy of providing a product or service that is sufficiently different from competitors' offerings such that customers are willing to pay a premium price for it

direct competition
the rivalry between two companies that offer similar products and services, acknowledge each other as rivals, and act and react to each other's strategic actions

discretionary responsibilities
the expectation that a company will voluntarily serve a social role beyond its economic, legal, and ethical responsibilities

discussion time
cultural norm for how much time should be spent in discussion with others

disseminator role
the informational role managers play when they share information with others in their departments or companies

distal goals
long-term or primary goals

distinctive competence
what a company can make, do, or perform better than its competitors

distributive justice
the perceived degree to which outcomes and rewards are fairly distributed or allocated

disturbance handler role
the decisional role managers play when they respond to severe problems that demand immediate action

diversification
a strategy for reducing risk by buying a variety of items (stocks or, in the case of a corporation, types of businesses), so that the failure of

one stock or one business does not doom the entire portfolio

document conferencing
communications system that allows two or more people in different locations to simultaneously view and make comments about a document

dog
a company with a small share of a slow-growing market

dominant design
a new technological design or process that becomes the accepted market standard

downsizing
the planned elimination of jobs in a company

downward communication
communication that flows from higher to lower levels in an organization

dynamic environment
environment in which the rate of change is fast

dysfunctional turnover
loss of high-performing employees who voluntarily choose to leave a company

early retirement incentive programs (ERIPs)
programs that offer financial benefits to employees to encourage them to retire early

economic order quantity (EOQ)
a system of formulas that minimizes ordering and holding costs and helps determine how much and how often inventory should be ordered

economic responsibility
the expectation that a company will make a profit by producing a valued product or service

economic value added (EVA)
the amount by which company profits (revenues, minus expenses, minus taxes) exceed the cost of capital in a given year

effectiveness
accomplishing tasks that help fulfil organizational objectives

efficiency
getting work done with minimum of effort, expense, or waste

electronic brainstorming
a decision-making method in which group members use computers to build on each other's ideas and generate many alternative solutions

electronic data interchange (EDI)
the direct electronic transmission of purchase and ordering information from one company's computer system to another company's computer system

electronic scanner
an electronic device that converts printed text and pictures into digital images

empathetic listening
understanding the speaker's perspective and personal frame of reference and giving feedback that conveys that understanding to the speaker

employee involvement team
team that provides advice or makes suggestions to management concerning specific issues

employee separation
the voluntary or involuntary loss of an employee

employee stock ownership plans (ESOPs)
a compensation system that awards employees shares of company stock in addition to their regular compensation

employee turnover
loss of employees who voluntarily choose to leave the company

employment benefits
a method of rewarding employees that includes virtually any kind of compensation other than wages or salaries

employment references
sources such as previous employers or co-workers who can provide job-related information about job candidates

empowering workers
permanently passing decision-making authority and responsibility from managers to workers by giving them the information and resources they need to make and carry out good decisions

encoding
putting a message into a written, verbal, or symbolic form that can be recognized and understood by the receiver

entrepreneur role
the decisional role managers play when they adapt themselves, their subordinates, and their units to incremental change

entrepreneurial orientation
the set of processes, practices, and decision-making activities that lead to new entry, characterized by five dimensions: autonomy, innovativeness, risk-taking, proactiveness, and competitive aggressiveness

entrepreneurship
the process of entering new or established markets with new goods or services

environmental change
the rate at which a company's general and specific environments change

environmental complexity
the number of external factors in the environment that affect organizations

environmental munificence
degree to which an organization's external environment has an abundance or scarcity of critical organizational resources

environmental scanning
searching the environment for important events or issues that might affect an organization

equity theory
theory that states that people will be motivated when they perceive that they are being treated fairly

era of ferment
phase of a technology cycle characterized by technological substitution and design competition

escalation of commitment
the tendency for a person who has already made a decision to more strongly support that original decision despite negative information that clearly indicates it was wrong

ethical behaviour
behaviour that conforms to a society's accepted principles of right and wrong

ethical charismatics
charismatic leaders that provide developmental opportunities for followers, are open to positive and negative feedback, recognize others' contributions, share information, and have moral standards that emphasize the larger interests of the group, organization, or society

ethical intensity
the degree of concern people have about an ethical issue

ethical responsibility
the expectation that a company will not violate accepted principles of right and wrong when conducting its business

ethics
the set of moral principles or values that defines right and wrong for a person or group

evaluation apprehension
fear of what others will think of your ideas

executive information system (EIS)
data processing system that uses internal and external data sources to provide the information needed to monitor and analyze organizational performance

expatriate
someone who lives and works outside his or her native country

expectancy
the perceived relationship between effort and performance

expectancy theory
theory states that people will be motivated to the extent to which they believe that their efforts will lead to good performance, that good performance will be rewarded, and that they will be offered attractive rewards

experiential approach to innovation
an approach to innovation that assumes a highly uncertain environment, and uses intuition, flexible options, and hands-on experience to reduce uncertainty and accelerate learning and understanding

expert system
information system that contains the specialized knowledge and decision rules used by experts and experienced decision makers, so that nonexperts can draw on this knowledge base to make decisions

exporting
selling domestically produced products to customers in foreign countries

external environments
all events outside a company that have the potential to influence or affect it

external recruiting
the process of developing a pool of qualified job applicants from outside the company

extranet
allows companies to exchange information and conduct transactions with outsiders by providing them direct, Web-based access to authorized parts of a company's intranet or information system

extrinsic reward
a reward that is tangible, visible to others, and given to employees contingent on the performance of specific tasks or behaviours

feedback
the amount of information the job provides to workers about their work performance

feedback control
a mechanism for gathering information about performance deficiencies after they occur

feedforward control
a mechanism for monitoring performance inputs rather than outputs to prevent or minimize performance deficiencies before they occur

figurehead role
the interpersonal role managers play when they perform ceremonial duties

finished goods inventories
the final outputs of manufacturing operations

firewall
hardware or software device that sits between the computers in an internal organizational network and outside networks, such as the Internet

firm-level strategy
corporate strategy that addresses the question "How should we compete against a particular firm?"

first-line managers
managers who train and supervise performance of nonmanagerial employees and who are directly responsible for producing the company's products or services

first-mover advantage
the strategic advantage that companies earn by being the first to use new information technology to substantially lower costs or to make a product or service different from competitors

flexible benefit plans
See **cafeteria benefit plans**

focus strategy
the positioning strategy of using cost leadership or differentiation to produce a specialized product or service for a limited, specially targeted group of customers in a par-

ticular geographic region or market segment

foreign direct investment (FDI)
a method of investment in which a company builds a new business or buys an existing business in a foreign country

formal communication channel
the system of official channels that carry organizationally approved messages and information

forming
the first stage of team development in which team members meet each other, form initial impressions, and begin to establish team norms

franchise
a collection of networked firms in which the manufacturer or marketer of a product or service, the franchisor, licenses the entire business to another person or organization, the franchisee

Free Trade Area of the Americas (FTAA)
regional trade agreement that, when signed, will create a regional trading zone encompassing 36 countries in North and South America

freeware
computer software that is free to whoever wants it

functional departmentalization
organizing work and workers into separate units responsible for particular business functions or areas of expertise

functional turnover
loss of poor-performing employees who voluntarily choose to leave a company

fundamental attribution error
the tendency to ignore external causes of behaviour and to attribute other people's actions to internal causes

gainsharing
compensation system in which companies share the financial value of performance gains, such as productivity, cost savings, or quality, with their workers

General Agreement on Tariffs and Trade (GATT)
worldwide trade agreement that reduces and eliminates tariffs, limits government subsidies, and protects intellectual property

General Electric Workout
a three-day meeting in which managers and employees from different levels and parts of an organization quickly generate and act on solutions to specific business problems

general environment
the economic, technological, sociocultural, and political trends that indirectly affect all organizations

generational change
change based on incremental improvements to a dominant technological design such that the improved technology is fully backward compatible with the older technology

geographic departmentalization
organizing work and workers into separate units responsible for doing business in particular geographical areas

global business
the buying and selling of goods and services by people from different countries

global new ventures
new companies with sales, employees, and financing in different countries that are founded with an active global strategy

goal commitment
the determination to achieve a goal

grand strategy
a broad corporate-level strategic plan used to achieve strategic goals and guide the strategic alternatives that managers of individual businesses or subunits may use

groupthink
a barrier to good decision-making caused by pressure within the group for members to agree with each other

growth strategy
strategy that focuses on increasing profits, revenues, market share, or the number of places in which the company does business

hearing
the act or process of perceiving sounds

holding cost
the cost of keeping inventory until it is used or sold, including storage, insurance, taxes, obsolescence, and opportunity costs

horizontal communication
communication that flows among managers and workers who are at the same organizational level

hostile work environment
form of sexual harassment in which unwelcome and demeaning sexually related behaviour creates an intimidating and offensive work environment

human resource information systems (HRIS)
computerized systems for gathering, analyzing, storing, and disseminating information related to the HRM process

human resource management
the process of finding, developing, and keeping the right people to form a qualified work force

human resource planning (HRP)
using an organization's goals and strategy to forecast the organization's human resource needs in terms of attracting, developing, and keeping a qualified workforce

human skill
the ability to work well with others

imperfectly imitable resource
a resource that is impossible or extremely costly or difficult for other firms to duplicate

incremental change
the phase of a technology cycle in which companies innovate by lowering costs and improving the func-

tioning and performance of the dominant technological design

independent demand system
inventory system in which the level of one kind of inventory does not depend on another

individualism-collectivism
the degree to which a person believes that people should be self-sufficient and that loyalty to one's self is more important than loyalty to team or company

industry regulation
regulations and rules that govern the business practices and procedures of specific industries, businesses, and professions

industry-level strategy
corporate strategy that addresses the question "How should we compete in this industry?"

informal communication channel ("grapevine")
the transmission of messages from employee to employee outside of formal communication channels

information
useful data that can influence people's choices and behaviour

information overload
situation in which decision makers have too much information to attend to

initiating structure
the degree to which a leader structures the roles of followers by setting goals, giving directions, setting deadlines, and assigning tasks

initiative conversations
conversations that start the change process by discussing what should or needs to be done to bring about change

innovation streams
patterns of innovation over time that can create sustainable competitive advantage

inputs
in equity theory, the contributions employees make to the organization

instrumentality
the perceived relationship between performance and rewards

internal environment
the events and trends inside an organization that affect management, employees, and organizational culture

internal recruiting
the process of developing a pool of qualified job applicants from people who already work in the company

internal-transformation mission
company goal of remaining competitive by making dramatic changes in the company

Internet
a global network of networks that allows users to send and retrieve data from anywhere in the world

interorganizational process
a collection of activities that take place among companies to transform inputs into outputs that customers value

interpersonal skills
skills, such as listening, communicating, questioning, and providing feedback, that enable people to have effective working relationships with others

interviews
selection tool in which company representatives ask job applicants job-related questions to determine whether they are qualified for the job

intranets
private company networks that allow employees to easily access, share, and publish information using Internet software

intraorganizational process
the collection of activities that take place within an organization to transform inputs into outputs that customers value

intrinsic reward
a natural reward associated with performing a task or activity for its own sake

inventory
the amount and number of raw materials, parts, and finished products that a company has in its possession

inventory turnover
the number of times per year that a company sells or "turns over" its average inventory

ISO 9000
a series of five international standards, from ISO 9000 to ISO 9004, for achieving consistency in quality management and quality assurance in companies throughout the world

job analysis
a purposeful, systematic process for collecting information on the important work-related aspects of a job

job description
a written description of the basic tasks, duties, and responsibilities required of an employee holding a particular job

job design
the number, kind, and variety of tasks that individual workers perform in doing their jobs

job enlargement
increasing the number of different tasks that a worker performs within one particular job

job enrichment
increasing the number of tasks in a particular job and giving workers the authority and control to make meaningful decisions about their work

job evaluation
a process that determines the worth of each job in a company by evaluating the market value of the knowledge, skills, and requirements needed to perform it

job rotation
periodically moving workers from one specialized job to another to give them more variety and the opportunity to use different skills

job shops
manufacturing operations that handle custom orders or small batch jobs

job specialization
a job composed of a small part of a larger task or process

job specifications
a written summary of the qualifications needed to successfully perform a particular job

joint venture
a strategic alliance in which two existing companies collaborate to form a third, independent company

just-in-time (JIT) inventory system
inventory system in which component parts arrive from suppliers just as they are needed at each stage of production

kanban
a ticket-based system that indicates when to reorder inventory

kinesics
movements of the body and face

knowledge
the understanding that one gains from information

leader role
the interpersonal role managers play when they motivate and encourage workers to accomplish organizational objectives

leader-member relations
the degree to which followers respect, trust, and like their leaders

leadership
the process of influencing others to achieve group or organizational goals

leadership neutralizers
subordinate, task, or organizational characteristics that can interfere with a leader's actions or make it impossible for a leader to influence followers' performance

leadership substitutes
subordinate, task, or organizational characteristics that make leaders redundant or unnecessary

leading
inspiring and motivating workers to work hard to achieve organizational goals

learning-based planning
learning better ways of achieving goals by continually testing, changing, and improving plans and strategies

legal responsibility
the expectation that a company will obey society's laws and regulations

liaison role
the interpersonal role managers play when they deal with people outside their units

licensing
agreement in which a domestic company, the licensor, receives royalty payments for allowing another company, the licensee, to produce its product, sell its service, or use its brand name in a specified foreign market

line authority
the right to command immediate subordinates in the chain of command

line function
an activity that contributes directly to creating or selling the company's products

line-flow production
manufacturing processes that are pre-established, occur in a serial or linear manner, and are dedicated to making one type of product

listening
making a conscious effort to hear

Maastricht Treaty of Europe
regional trade agreement between most European countries

magnitude of consequences
the total harm or benefit derived from an ethical decision

make-to-order operation
manufacturing operation that does not start processing or assembling products until a customer order is received

make-to-stock operation
manufacturing operation that orders parts and assembles standardized products before receiving customer orders

management
getting work done through others

management by objectives (MBO)
a four-step process in which managers and employees discuss and select goals, develop tactical plans, and meet regularly to review progress toward goal accomplishment

manufacturing flexibility
degree to which manufacturing operations can easily and quickly change the number, kind, and characteristics of products they produce

market commonality
the degree to which two companies have overlapping products, services, or customers in multiple markets

materials requirement planning (MRP)
a production and inventory system that determines the production schedule, production batch sizes, and inventory needed to complete final products

matrix departmentalization
a hybrid organizational structure in which two or more forms of departmentalization, most often product and functional, are used together

maximizing
choosing the best alternative

mechanistic organization
organization characterized by specialized jobs and responsibilities, precisely defined, unchanging roles, and a rigid chain of command based on centralized authority and vertical communication

media advocacy
an advocacy group tactic of framing issues as public issues, exposing questionable, exploitative, or unethical practices, and forcing media coverage by buying media time or creating controversy that is likely to receive extensive news coverage

meta-analysis
a study of studies, a statistical approach that provides the best scientific estimate of how well management theories and practices work

middle managers
managers responsible for setting objectives consistent with top management's goals, and planning and implementing subunit strategies for achieving these objectives

milestones
formal project review points used to assess progress and performance

minimum threshold rule
decision rule that requires alternative solutions to meet all the established minimum decision criteria

mission
statement of a company's overall goal that unifies company-wide efforts toward its vision, stretches and challenges the organization, and possesses a finish line and a timeframe

modular organization
an organization that outsources noncore business activities to outside companies, suppliers, specialists, or consultants

monitor role
the informational role managers play when they scan their environment for information

Moore's law
prediction that every 18 months, the cost of computing will drop by 50 percent as computer-processing power doubles

motivation

the set of forces that initiates, directs, and makes people persist in their efforts to accomplish a goal

motivation to manage

an assessment of how enthusiastic employees are about managing the work of others

multifactor productivity

an overall measure of performance that indicates how much labour, capital, materials, and energy it takes to produce an output

multifunctional teams

work teams composed of people from different departments

multinational corporation

corporation that owns businesses in two or more countries

multivariable testing (MVT)

a systematic approach of experimentation used to analyze and evaluate potential solutions

national culture

the set of shared values and beliefs that affects the perceptions, decisions, and behaviour of the people from a particular country

needs

the physical or psychological requirements that must be met to ensure survival and well-being

needs assessment

the process of identifying and prioritizing the learning needs of employees

negative frame

couching a problem in terms of a loss, thus influencing decision makers toward becoming risk-seeking

negotiator role

the decisional role managers play when they negotiate schedules, projects, goals, outcomes, resources, and employee raises

noise

anything that interferes with the transmission of the intended message

nominal group technique

a decision-making method that begins and ends by having group members quietly write down and evaluate ideas to be shared with the group

nonsubstitutable resource

a resource, without equivalent substitutes or replacements, that produces value or competitive advantage

nontariff barriers

nontax methods of increasing the cost or reducing the volume of imported goods

nonverbal communication

any communication that doesn't involve words

normative control

regulation of workers' behaviour and decisions through widely shared organizational values and beliefs

norming

the third stage of team development, in which team members begin to settle into their roles, group cohesion grows, and positive team norms develop

norms

informally agreed-upon standards that regulate team behaviour

North American Free Trade Agreement (NAFTA)

regional trade agreement between the United States, Canada, and Mexico

objective control

use of observable measures of worker behaviour or outputs to assess performance and influence behaviour

objective performance measures

measures of job performance that are easily and directly counted or quantified

online discussion forums

the in-house equivalent of Internet newsgroups; Web- or software-based discussion tools available across the company to permit employees to easily ask ques-

tions and share knowledge with each other

open office systems

offices in which the physical barriers that separate workers have been removed in order to increase communication and interaction

operational plans

day-to-day plans, developed and implemented by lower-level managers, for producing or delivering the organization's products and services over a 30-day to 6-month period

operations management

managing the daily production of goods and services

opportunistic behaviour

transaction in which one party in the relationship benefits at the expense of the other

optical character recognition

software to convert digitized documents into ASCII text (American Standard Code for Information Interchange) that can be searched, read, and edited by word processing and other kinds of software

options-based planning

maintaining planning flexibility by making small, simultaneous investments in many alternative plans

ordering cost

the costs associated with ordering inventory, including the cost of data entry, phone calls, obtaining bids, correcting mistakes, and determining when and how much inventory to order

organic organization

organization characterized by broadly defined jobs and responsibility, loosely defined, frequently changing roles, and decentralized authority and horizontal communication based on task knowledge

organizational ceremonies

planned activities or events that emphasize culturally

consistent assumptions, decisions, and actions

organizational change

a difference in the form, quality, or condition of an organization over time

organizational culture

the values, beliefs, and attitudes shared by organizational members

organizational decline

a large decrease in organizational performance that occurs when companies don't anticipate, recognize, neutralize, or adapt to the internal or external pressures that threaten their survival

organizational development

a philosophy and collection of planned change interventions designed to improve an organization's long-term health and performance

organizational dialogue

the process by which people in an organization learn to talk effectively and constructively with each other

organizational heroes

people celebrated for their qualities and achievements within an organization

organizational innovation

the successful implementation of creative ideas in organizations

organizational process

the collection of activities that transforms inputs into outputs that customers value

organizational rituals

routine activities that emphasize the organization's culture

organizational stories

stories told by organizational members to make sense of organizational events and changes and to emphasize culturally consistent assumptions, decisions, and actions

organizational structure

the vertical and horizontal configuration of departments, authority, and jobs within a company

organizational symbols
something that represents another thing

organizing
deciding where decisions will be made, who will do what jobs and tasks, who will work for whom

outcome/input (O/I) ratio
in equity theory, an employee's perception of the comparison between the rewards received from an organization and the employee's contributions to that organization

outcomes
in equity theory, the rewards employees receive for their contributions to the organization

outplacement services
employment-counselling services offered to employees who are losing their jobs because of downsizing

output control
regulation of worker results or outputs through rewards and incentives

overreward
when you are getting more outcomes relative to your inputs than the referent to whom you compare yourself

overt integrity test
written test that estimates employee honesty by directly asking job applicants what they think or feel about theft or about punishment of unethical behaviours

paralanguage
the pitch, rate, tone, volume, and speaking pattern (i.e., use of silences, pauses, or hesitations) of one's voice

partial productivity
a measure of performance that indicates how much of a particular kind of input it takes to produce an output

perception
the process by which individuals attend to, organize, interpret, and retain information from their environments

perceptual filters
the personality-, psychology-, or experience-based differences that influence people to ignore or pay attention to particular stimuli

performance appraisal
the process of assessing how well employees are doing their jobs

performing
the fourth and final stage of team development, in which performance improves because the team has matured into an effective, fully functioning team

personal aggression
hostile or aggressive behaviour toward others

personality-based integrity test
written test that indirectly estimates employee honesty by measuring psychological traits, such as dependability and conscientiousness

personality tests
tests that measure the extent to which applicants possess different kinds of job-related personality dimensions

piecework
a compensation system in which employees are paid a set rate for each item they produce

planning (management functions)
determining organizational goals and a means for achieving them

planning
choosing a goal and developing a strategy to achieve that goal

policy
standing plan that indicates the general course of action that should be taken in response to a particular event or situation

policy uncertainty
the risk associated with changes in laws and government policies that directly affect the way foreign companies conduct business

political deviance
using one's influence to harm others in the company

political uncertainty
the risk of major changes in political regimes that can result from war, revolution, death of political leaders, social unrest, or other influential events

pooled interdependence
work completed by having each job or department independently contribute to the whole

portfolio strategy
corporate-level strategy that minimizes risk by diversifying investment among various businesses or product lines

positive frame
couching a problem in terms of a gain, thus influencing decision makers toward becoming risk-averse

post conventional level of moral development
third level of moral development in which people make decisions based on internalized principles

preconventional level of moral development
first level of moral development in which people make decisions based on selfish reasons

predictive patterns
help identify database elements that are different

primary stakeholder
any group on which an organization relies for its long-term survival

principle of distributive justice
ethical principle that holds that you should never take any action that harms the least among us: the poor, the uneducated, the unemployed

principle of government requirements
ethical principle that holds that you should never take any action that violates the law, for the law represents the minimal moral standard

principle of individual rights
ethical principle that holds that you should never take any action that infringes on others' agreed-upon rights

principle of long-term self-interest
ethical principle that holds that you should never take any action that is not in your or your organization's long-term self-interest

principle of personal virtue
ethical principle that holds that you should never do anything that is not honest, open, and truthful, and which you would not be glad to see reported in the newspapers or on TV

principle of religious injunctions
ethical principle that holds that you should never take any action that is not kind and that does not build a sense of community

principle of utilitarian benefits
ethical principle that holds that you should never take any action that does not result in greater good for society

private spaces
spaces used by and open to just one employee

proactive strategy
a social responsiveness strategy in which a company anticipates responsibility for a problem before it occurs and would do more than society expects to address the problem

probability of effect
the chance that something will happen and then harm others

problem
a gap between a desired state and an existing state

procedural justice
the perceived fairness of the process used to make reward allocation decisions

procedure
standing plan that indicates the specific steps that should

be taken in response to a particular event

processing cost
the cost of turning raw data into usable information

processing information
transforming raw data into meaningful information

product boycott
an advocacy group tactic of protesting a company's actions by convincing consumers not to purchase its product or service

product departmentalization
organizing work and workers into separate units responsible for producing particular products or services

product prototype
a full-scale, working model of a final product that is being tested for design, function, and reliability

production blocking
a disadvantage of face-to-face brainstorming in which a group member must wait to share an idea because another member is presenting an idea

production deviance
unethical behaviour that hurts the quality of work produced

productivity
a measure of performance that indicates how many inputs it takes to produce or create an output

profit sharing
a compensation system in which a percentage of company profits is paid to employees in addition to their regular compensation

project manufacturing
manufacturing operations designed to produce large, expensive, specialized products

project team
team created to complete specific, one-time projects or tasks within a limited time

property deviance
unethical behaviour aimed at the organization's property

prospectors
an adaptive strategy that seeks fast growth by searching for new market opportunities, encouraging risk-taking, and being the first to bring innovative new products to market

protecting information
the process of insuring that data are reliably and consistently retrievable in a usable format for authorized users, but no one else

protectionism
a government's use of trade barriers to shield domestic companies and their workers from foreign competition

proximal goals
short-term goals or subgoals

proximity of effect
the social, psychological, cultural, or physical distance between a decision maker and those affected by his or her decisions

public communications
an advocacy group tactic that relies on voluntary participation by the news media and the advertising industry to get an advocacy group's message out

punctuated equilibrium theory
theory that holds that companies go through long, simple periods of stability (equilibrium), followed by short periods of dynamic, fundamental change (revolution), and ending with a return to stability (new equilibrium)

purchasing power
a comparison of the relative cost of a standard set of goods and services in different countries

quality
a product or service free of deficiencies, or the characteristics of a product or service that satisfy customer needs

quasi-control
reducing dependence or restructuring dependence when control is necessary but not possible

question mark
a company with a small share of a fast-growing market

quid pro quo sexual harassment
form of sexual harassment in which employment outcomes, such as hiring, promotion, or simply keeping one's job, depend on whether an individual submits to sexual harassment

quota
limit on the number or volume of imported products

rare resource
a resource that is not controlled or possessed by many competing firms

rater training
training performance appraisal raters in how to avoid rating errors and increase rating accuracy

rational decision-making
a systematic process of defining problems, evaluating alternatives, and choosing optimal solutions

raw data
facts and figures

raw material inventories
the basic inputs in a manufacturing process

reactive strategy
a social responsiveness strategy in which a company chooses to do less than society expects

reactors
an adaptive strategy of not following a consistent strategy, but instead reacting to changes in the external environment after they occur

reciprocal interdependence
work completed by different jobs or groups working together in a back-and-forth manner

recovery
the strategic actions taken after retrenchment to return to a growth strategy

recruiting
the process of developing a pool of qualified job applicants

reducing dependence
abandoning or changing organizational goals to reduce dependence on critical resources

reengineering
fundamental rethinking and radical redesign of business processes to achieve dramatic improvements in critical measures of performance, such as cost, quality, service, and speed

referents
in equity theory, others with whom people compare themselves to determine if they have been treated fairly

refreezing
supporting and reinforcing the new changes so they "stick"

regional trading zones
areas in which tariff and non-tariff barriers on trade between countries are reduced or eliminated

related diversification
creating or acquiring companies that share similar products, manufacturing, marketing, technology, or cultures

relationship behaviour
mutually beneficial, long-term exchanges between buyers and suppliers

relative comparisons
a process in which each decision criterion is compared directly to every other criterion

reliability
the degree to which a measure (test) is free from random error and is consistent

representative bias
unrecognized tendency of decision makers to judge the likelihood of an event's occurrence based on its similarity to previous events

resistance forces
forces that support the existing state of conditions in organizations

resistance to change
opposition to change resulting from self-interest, misunderstanding and distrust, or a general intolerance for change

resource
anything that can be used to fulfil a need or solve a problem

resource allocator role
the decisional role managers play when they decide who gets what resources

resource flow
the extent to which companies have access to critical resources

resource similarity
the extent to which a competitor has similar amounts and kinds of resources

resources
the assets, capabilities, processes, information, and knowledge that an organization uses to improve its effectiveness and efficiency, to create and sustain competitive advantage, and to fulfil a need or solve a problem

response
a competitive countermove, prompted by a rival's attack, to defend or improve a company's market share or profit

restructuring dependence
exchanging dependence on one critical resource for dependence on another

results-driven change
change created quickly by focusing on the measurement and improvement of results

retrenchment strategy
strategy that focuses on turning around very poor company performance by shrinking the size or scope of the business

retrieval cost
the cost of accessing already-stored and processed information

risk propensity
a person's tendency to take or avoid risks

role-model mission
company goal of imitating the characteristics and practices of a successful company

rules and regulations
standing plans that describe how a particular action should be performed, or what must happen or not happen in response to a particular event

satisficing
choosing a "good enough" alternative

scenario planning
the process of developing plans to deal with several possible future events and trends that might affect the business

schedule time
cultural norm for the time by which scheduled projects or jobs should actually be completed

S-curve pattern of innovation
a pattern of technological innovation characterized by slow initial progress, then rapid progress, and then again by slow progress as a technology matures and reaches its limits

secondary firms
the firms in a strategic group that follow related, but somewhat different, strategies than do the core firms

secondary stakeholder
any group that can influence or be influenced by the company and can affect public perceptions about its socially responsible behaviour

selection
the process of gathering information about job applicants to decide who should be offered a job

selective perception
the tendency to notice and accept objects and information consistent with our values, beliefs, and expectations, while ignoring or screening out or not accepting inconsistent information

self-control (self-management)
control system in which managers and workers control their own behaviour by setting their own goals, monitoring their own progress, and rewarding themselves for goal achievement

self-designing team
team that has the characteristics of self-managing teams but that also controls team design, work tasks, and team membership

self-management
See **self-control**

self-managing team
team that manages and controls all the major tasks of producing a product or service

self-serving bias
the tendency to over-estimate our value by attributing successes to ourselves (internal causes) and attributing failures to others or the environment (external causes)

semi-autonomous work group
group that has the authority to make decisions and solve problems related to the major tasks of producing a product or service

sequence patterns
when two or more database elements occur together in a significant pattern, but one of the elements precedes the other

sequential interdependence
work completed in succession, with one group or job's outputs becoming the inputs for the next group or job

service recovery
restoring customer satisfaction to strongly dissatisfied customers

setup cost
the costs of downtime and lost efficiency that occur when changing or adjusting a machine to produce a different kind of inventory

sexual harassment
form of discrimination in which unwelcome sexual advances, requests for sexual favours, or other verbal or physical conduct of a sexual nature occur while performing one's job

shadow-strategy task force
a committee within the company that analyzes the company's own weaknesses to determine how competitors could exploit them for competitive advantage

shared spaces
spaces used by and open to all employees

shareholder model
view of social responsibility which holds that an organization's overriding goal should be profit maximization for the benefit of shareholders

shareware
computer software that you can try before you buy, but if you keep it beyond the trial period, usually 30 days, you must buy it

shrinkage
employee theft of company merchandise

simple environment
an environment with few environmental factors

single-use plans
plans that cover unique, one-time-only events

situational (SWOT) analysis
an assessment of the strengths and weaknesses in an organization's internal environment and the opportunities and threats in its external environment

situational favourableness
the degree to which a particular situation either permits or denies a leader the chance to influence the behaviour of group members

situational theory
leadership theory that states that leaders need to adjust their leadership styles to match followers' maturity

skill-based pay
compensation system that pays employees for learning additional skills or knowledge

S.M.A.R.T. goals
goals that are specific, measurable, attainable, results-oriented, and time-bounded

social consensus
agreement on whether behaviour is bad or good

social loafing
behaviour in which team members withhold their efforts and fail to perform their share of the work

social responsibility
a business's obligation to pursue policies, make decisions, and take actions that benefit society

social responsiveness
the strategy chosen by a company to respond to stakeholders' economic, legal, ethical, or discretionary expectations concerning social responsibility

span of control
the number of people reporting to a specific supervisor

specific ability tests (aptitude tests)
tests that measure the extent to which an applicant possesses the particular kind of ability needed to do a job well

specific environment
the customers, competitors, suppliers, industry regulations, and advocacy groups that are unique to an industry and that directly affect how a company does business

spokesperson role
the informational role managers play when they share information with people outside their departments or companies

stability strategy
strategy that focuses on improving the way in which the company sells the same products or services to the same customers

stable environment
environment in which the rate of change is slow

staff authority
the right to advise, but not command, others who are not subordinates in the chain of command

staff function
an activity that does not contribute directly to creating or selling the company's products, but instead supports line activities

stakeholder model
theory of corporate responsibility which holds that management's most important responsibility, long-term survival, is achieved by satisfying the interests of multiple corporate stakeholders

stakeholders
persons or groups with a "stake" or legitimate interest in a company's actions

standardization
solving problems by consistently applying the same rules, procedures, and processes

standards
a basis of comparison when measuring the extent to which various kinds of organizational performance are satisfactory or unsatisfactory

standing plans
plans used repeatedly to handle frequently recurring events

star
a company with a large share of a fast-growing market

stepladder technique
when group members are added to a group discussion one at a time (i.e., like a stepladder), the existing group members first take the time to listen to each new member's thoughts, ideas, and recommendations, and then the group, in turn, shares the ideas and suggestions that it had already considered, discusses the new and old ideas, and then makes a decision

stock options
a compensation system that gives employees the right to purchase shares of stock at a set price, even if the value of the stock increases above that price

stockout
situation in which a company runs out of finished product

stockout costs
the costs incurred when a company runs out of a product, including transaction costs to replace inventory and the loss of customers' goodwill

storage cost
the cost of physically or electronically archiving information for later use and retrieval

storming
the second stage of development, characterized by conflict and disagreement, in which team members disagree over what the team should do and how it should do it

strategic alliance
agreement in which companies combine key resources, costs, risk, technology, and people

strategic dissonance
a discrepancy between upper management's intended strategy and the strategy actually implemented by lower levels of management

strategic group
a group of companies within an industry that top managers choose to compare, evaluate, and benchmark strategic threats and opportunities

strategic leadership
the ability to anticipate, envision, maintain flexibility, think strategically, and work with others to initiate changes that will create a positive future for an organization

strategic plans
overall company plans that clarify how the company will serve customers and position itself against competitors over the next two to five years

strategic reference points
the strategic targets managers use to measure whether a firm has developed the core competencies it needs to achieve a sustainable competitive advantage

stretch goals
extremely ambitious goals that, initially, employees don't know how to accomplish

structural accommodation
the ability to change organizational structures, policies, and practices in order to meet stretch goals

structured interviews
interviews in which all applicants are asked the same set of standardized questions, usually including situational, behavioural, background, and job-knowledge questions

subjective performance measures
measures of job performance that require someone to judge or assess a worker's performance

suboptimization
performance improvement in one part of an organization but only at the expense of decreased performance in another part

subsidies
government loans, grants, and tax deferments given to domestic companies to protect them from foreign competition

supervised data mining
user tells the data mining software to look and test for specific patterns and relationships in a data set

supplier dependence
degree to which a company relies on a supplier because of the importance of the supplier's product to the company and the difficulty of finding other sources of that product

suppliers
companies that provide material, human, financial, and informational resources to other companies

survey feedback
information collected by surveys from organizational

members that is then compiled, disseminated, and used to develop action plans for improvement

sustainable competitive advantage
a competitive advantage that other companies have tried unsuccessfully to duplicate and have, for the moment, stopped trying to duplicate

tactical plans
plans created and implemented by middle managers that specify how the company will use resources, budgets, and people over the next six months to two years to accomplish specific goals within its mission

targeting
mission stated as a clear, specific company goal

tariff
a direct tax on imported goods

task interdependence
the extent to which collective action is required to complete an entire piece of work

task structure
the degree to which the requirements of a subordinate's tasks are clearly specified

team diversity
the variances or differences in ability, experience, personality, or any other factor on a team

team leaders
managers responsible for facilitating team activities toward goal accomplishment

team level
the average level of ability, experience, personality, or any other factor on a team

teamwork
collaboration between managers and nonmanagers, across business functions, and between companies, customers, and suppliers

technical skills
the ability to apply the specialized procedures, tech-

niques, and knowledge required to get the job done

technological discontinuity
scientific advance or unique combination of existing technologies that creates a significant breakthrough in performance or function

technological substitution
purchase of new technologies to replace older ones

technology
knowledge, tools, and techniques used to transform input into output

technology cycle
cycle that begins with the "birth" of a new technology and ends when that technology reaches its limits and is replaced by a newer, substantially better technology

televised/videotaped speeches and meetings
speeches and meetings originally made to a smaller audience that are either simultaneously broadcast to other locations in the company or videotaped for subsequent distribution and viewing

temporal immediacy
the time between an act and the consequences the act produces

testing
systematic comparison of different product designs or design iterations

threat of new entrants
a measure of the degree to which barriers to entry make it easy or difficult for new companies to get started in an industry

threat of substitute products or services
a measure of the ease with which customers can find substitutes for an industry's products or services

360-degree feedback
a performance appraisal process in which feedback is obtained from the boss, subordinates, peers and

co-workers, and the employees themselves

top managers
executives responsible for the overall direction of the organization

total quality management (TQM)
an integrated, principle-based, organization-wide strategy for improving product and service quality

trade barriers
government-imposed regulations that increase the cost and restrict the number of imported goods

traditional work group
group composed of two or more people who work together to achieve a shared goal

training
developing the skills, experience, and knowledge employees need to perform their jobs or improve their performance

trait rating scales
a rating scale that indicates the extent to which a worker possesses particular traits or characteristics

trait theory
leadership theory that holds that effective leaders possess a similar set of traits or characteristics

traits
relatively stable characteristics, such as abilities, psychological motives, or consistent patterns of behaviour

transactional leadership
leadership based on an exchange process, in which followers are rewarded for good performance and punished for poor performance

transformational leadership
leadership that generates awareness and acceptance of a group's purpose and mission and gets employees to see beyond their own needs and self-interest for the good of the group

transition management team (TMT)
a team of 8 to 12 people whose full-time job is to completely manage and coordinate a company's change process

uncertainty
extent to which managers can understand or predict which environmental changes and trends will affect their businesses

underreward
when the referent you compare yourself to is getting more outcomes relative to their inputs than you are

unfreezing
getting the people affected by change to believe that change is needed

unity of command
a management principle that workers should report to just one boss

unrelated diversification
creating or acquiring companies in completely unrelated businesses

unsupervised data mining
user simply tells the data mining software to uncover whatever patterns and relationships it can find in a data set

upward communication
communication that flows from lower to higher levels in an organization

valence
the attractiveness or desirability of a reward or outcome

validation
the process of determining how well a selection test or procedure predicts future job performance. The better or more accurate the prediction of future job performance, the more valid a test is said to be.

validity
the degree to which a measure (selection technique) is shown to accurately predict

what it is expected measure (job performance)

valuable resource
a resource that allows companies to improve efficiency and effectiveness

value
customer perception that the product quality is excellent for the price offered

variation
a deviation in the form, condition, or appearance of a product from the quality standard for that product

virtual organization
an organization that is part of a network in which many companies share skills, costs, capabilities, markets, and customers to collectively solve customer problems or provide specific products or services

virtual private network
encrypts Internet data at both ends of the transmission process

virtual team
team composed of geographically and/or organizationally dispersed co-workers who use telecommunication and information technologies to accomplish an organizational task

virus
a program or piece of code that attaches itself to other programs on your computer and can trigger anything from a harmless flashing message to the reformatting of your hard drive to the system-wide network shutdown

visible artifacts
visible signs of an organization's culture, such as the office design and layout, company dress code, and company benefits and perks, like stock options, personal parking spaces, or the private company dining room

vision
inspirational statement of an organization's enduring purpose

visionary leadership
leadership that creates a positive image of the future that motivates organizational members and provides direction for future planning and goal setting

voluntary export restraints
voluntarily imposed limits on the number or volume of products exported to a particular country

whistle blowing
reporting others' ethics violations to management or legal authorities

wholly owned affiliates
foreign offices, facilities, and manufacturing plants that are 100 percent owned by the parent company

worker maturity
the ability and willingness to take responsibility for directing one's behaviour at work

workforce forecasting
the process of predicting the number and kind of workers with specific skills and abilities that an organization will need in the future

work-in-process inventories
partially finished goods consisting of assembled component parts

workplace deviance
unethical behaviour that violates organizational norms about right and wrong

work sample tests
tests that require applicants to perform tasks that are actually done on the job

work team
a small number of people wit complementary skills who hold themselves mutually accountable for pursuing a common purpose, achieving performance goals, and improving interdependent work processes

world gross national product
the value of all the goods and services produced annually worldwide

wrongful dismissal
a legal doctrine that requires employers to have a job-related reason to terminate employees

Chapter 1

1. "U.S Dept. of Commerce Industry Sector Analysis: Canada, Mgt. Consulting Services," June 1998. [Online] Available http://strategis.ic. gc.ca/pics/bp/mgt.pdf. Quoted in March 2001, Industry Canada, *Management Consulting Industry,* Service Industries Overview Series.

2. "Management, Scientific and Technical Consulting." Table Four, Annual Survey of Management and *1998 Survey of Service Industries*, Statistics Canada. [Online] Available http://strategis.ic. gc.ca/pics/bp/mgt.pdf. Quoted in March 2001, Industry Canada, *Management Consulting Industry,* Service Industries Overview Series.

3. *Management Consulting Industry.* Services Industry Overview Series, Industry Canada. 2001, March. [Online] Available http://strategis.ic. gc.ca.

4. T. Peters, "The Leadership Alliance" (Pat Carrigan excerpt), *In Search of Excellence* (Northbrook, IL: Video Arts, distributor, 1985), videocassette.

5. R. Stagner, "Corporate Decision Making," *Journal of Applied Psychology* 53 (1969): 1–13.

6. D.W. Bray, R.J. Campbell, & D.L. Grant, *Formative Years in Business: A Long-Term AT&T Study of Managerial Lives* (New York: Wiley, 1993).

7. B. Dumaine, "The New Non-Manager Managers," *Fortune,* 22 February 1993, 80–84.

8. B. Dumaine, "The New Non-Manager Managers," *Fortune,* 22 February 1993, 80–84

9. S.B. Garland, S.Hamm, & M. France. "The Cops Converge on Microsoft," *Business Week,* 18 May 1998, 34–37.

10. Anne Fisher, "Making Change Stick," *Fortune,* 17 April 1995, 121–127.

11. M. Carter, "Back from the Dead (Ford Revitalizes Jaguar Cars)," *The European,* 6 April 1998, 22–23.

12. A. Farnham, "Mary Kay's Lessons in Leadership," *Fortune,* 20 September 1993, 68–77.

13. M. MacDonald, "Legacy of Chrysler Canada Chief: A Revitalized Car Maker," *Canadian Press Newswire,* 16 March 1998.

14. H.S. Jonas, III, R.E. Fry, & S. Srivastva, "The Office of the CEO: Understanding the Executive Experience," *Academy of Management Executive* 4 (1990): 36–47.

15. J. Vardy, "CEO's Post Some Spectacular Departures: Boards Getting More Vigilant Less Tolerant of Mediocrity," *Financial Post,* 7 December 2001, 7.

16. K. Dorrell, "A Tough Act to Follow: The Death of Yves Landry Leaves a Large Void at Chrysler Canada Ltd. and in the Industry," *Plant* 57, no. 6 (1998): 42.

17. H.S. Jonas, III, R.E. Fry, & S. Srivastva, "The Office of the CEO: Understanding the Executive Experience," *Academy of Management Executive* 4 (1990): 36–47.

18. B. Saporito, "David Glass Won't Crack under Fire," *Fortune,* 3 February 1991, 75–80.

19. B.M. Bass, *Stogdill's Handbook of Leadership* (New York: Free Press, 1981).

20. S. Tully, "What Team Leaders Need to Know," *Fortune,* 20 February 1995.

21. K. Hultman, "The 10 Commandments of Team Leadership," *Training & Development,* 1 February 1998, 12–13.

22. S. Tully, "What Team Leaders Need to Know," *Fortune,* 20 February 1995.

23. J.S. Case, "What the Experts Forgot to Mention," *Inc.,* 1 September 1993, 66.

24. H. Mintzberg, *The Nature of Managerial Work* (New York: Harper & Row, 1973).

25. C.P. Hales, "What Do Managers Do? A Critical Review of the Evidence," *Journal of Management Studies* 23, no. 1 (1986): 88–115.

26. C. Vibert, personal correspondence, 17 October 2002.

27. R. Gibson, "McDonald's Makes Changes in Top Management," *The Wall Street Journal,* 1 May 1998, A3.

28. J. Vardy, "CEOs Post Some Spectacular Departures: Boards Getting More Vigilant, Less Tolerant of Mediocrity," *Financial Post,* 1 December 2001, 7.

29. "Latest Boss Eyes Growth Through Acquisition for 'Better Positioned' GEAC," *Canadian Press Newswire,* 5 December 2001.

30. F. Sheikh, "The Turnaround: GEAC Has a New Blueprint for Growth. But Does the Blueprint Come with a New Mindset?" *Silicon Valley North – GTA* 7, no. 2 (January 2001): 5.

31. L.A. Hill, *Becoming a Manager: Mastery of a New Identity* (Boston, MA: Harvard Business School Press, 1992).

32. R.L. Katz, "Skills of an Effective Administrator," *Harvard Business Review,* September–October 1974, 90–102.

33. C.A. Bartlett & S. Ghoshal, "Changing the Role of Top Management: Beyond Systems to People," *Harvard Business Review,* May–June 1995, 132–142.

34. F.L. Schmidt & J.E. Hunter, "Development of a Causal Model of Process Determining Job Performance," *Current Directions in Psychological Science* 1 (1992): 89–92.

35. J.B. Miner, "Sentence Completion Measures in Personnel Research: The Development and Validation of the Miner Sentence Completion Scales," in *Personality Assessment in Organizations,* eds. H. J. Bernardin & D.A. Bownas (New York: Praeger, 1986), 147–146.

36. A. Wahl, M. McClearn, R. Robin, & D. Calleja, "Survivor, MBA Edition," *Canadian Business* 74, no. 21 (December 2001), 58–64.

37. M.W. McCall, Jr. & M.M. Lombardo, "What Makes a Top Executive?" *Psychology Today,* February 1983, 26–31; E. van Velsor & J. Brittain, "Why Executives Derail: Perspectives across Time and Cultures," *Academy of Management Executive,* November 1995, 62–72.

38. M.W. McCall, Jr. & M.M. Lombardo, "What Makes a Top Executive?" *Psychology Today,* February 1983, 26–31.

39. S. Stecklow, "Chief Prerequisite for College President's Job: Stamina," *The Wall Street Journal,* 1 December 1994, B1.

40. M.A. Huselid, "The Impact of Human Resource Management Practices on Turnover, Productivity, and Corporate Financial Performance," *Academy of*

Management Journal 38 (1995): 635–672.

41. D. McDonald & A. Smith, "A Proven Connection: Performance Management and Business Results," *Compensation & Benefits Review* 27, no. 6 (1 January 1995): 59.

42. B. Schneider & D.E. Bowen, "Employee and Customer Perceptions of Service in Banks: Replication and Extension," *Journal of Applied Psychology* 70 (1985): 423–33; B. Schneider, J.J. Parkington, & V.M. Buxton, "Employee and Customer Perceptions of Service in Banks," *Administrative Science Quarterly* 25 (1980): 252–67.

Chapter 2

1. Indepth Backgrounder: Softwood Lumber, [Online] Available http://cbc.ca/news/indepth/background/softwood_lumber.html, 18 August 2003; "Softwood Exports Plunge on 27% U.S. Duty," *Financial Post*, 8 July 2002; "Abitibi Closes Mills, Cuts Jobs; U.S. Softwood Duties 'Left No Alternative,'" *Financial Post*, 26 June 2002.

2. E. Romanelli & M.L. Tushman, "Organizational Transformation as Punctuated Equilibrium: An Empirical Test," *Academy of Management Journal* 37 (1994): 1141–1166.

3. E. G. Fisher & Alex Kondra, "Canada's Airlines: Recent Turbulence and Changing Flight Plans," in *Industrial Relations in Canadian Industry*, Richard P. Chaykowski & Anil Verma, eds. (Toronto: Holt, Rinehart and Winston of Canada Limited, 1992) pp. 358–404; Statistics Canada, *Air Carrier Operations in Canada*, 1977–1994; "West Jet—About Us," [Online] Available http://c2dsp.westjet.com/internet/sky/about/index.jsp, 21 August 2003.

4. G. Morgenson, "Denial in Battle Creek," *Forbes*, 7 October 1996, 44–46.

5. K.A. Dolan, "Help Wanted: Urgent!" *Forbes*, 7 October 1996, 18–20.

6. Jill Vardy, "High-tech Friend Worth $3,000 to Employees: Firm's Incentive," *Financial Post*, 13 January 2001, D1, D7.

7. Statistics Canada, Table Number 3790017.

8. "The Economic Hit: One Year Later," [Online] Available http://cbc.ca/pcgi-bin/templates/sportsView.cgi?/news/2002/09/10/bizsept11_020910, 21 August 2003.

9. "Help-wanted Index Unchanged in June," *Financial Post*, 9 July 1998, 6.

10. R. Norton, "Where Is this Economy Really Heading?" *Fortune*, 7 August 1995, 54–56.

11. T. Grillo, "Trying to Turn Over a New Leaf: With Sales Sagging, Encyclopedia Britannica Looks to Go On Line," *Boston Globe*, 16 June 1995.

12. *Women in Canada: Work Chapter Updates*, Statistics Canada, Cat. No.89F011XIE, 2002.

13. Sonya Felix, "Running on Empty: Tight Money Has Curtailed the Drive to Provide On-site Daycare Centres, but the Long-term Benefits to Employees and Employers Might Outweigh the Costs," *Benefits Canada*, 21, no. 6 (June 1997): 109, 111.

14. R.J. Bies & T.R. Tyler, "The Litigation Mentality in Organizations: A Test of Alternative Psychological Explanations," *Organization Science* 4 (1993): 352–366

15. Vicki Barnett, "Wrongful Dismissal Damages Rise," *Calgary Herald*, 7 August 1999, W1.

16. D. Smart & C. Martin, "Manufacturer Responsiveness to Consumer Correspondence: An Empirical Investigation of Consumer Perceptions," *Journal of Consumer Affairs* 26 (1992): 104.

17. Cotton Incorporated, What's New in Cotton: Lifestyle Monitor. [Online] Available www.cottoninc.com/lifemon2a.htm, 4 October 1996.

18. S.G. Maycumber, "Cotton Inc.'s Lifestyle Monitor Puts Together a Year's Data; Price Looms Large in Apparel Purchases," *Daily News Record*, 4 January 1996, 11.

19. S.A. Zahra & S.S. Chaples, "Blind Spots in Competitive Analysis," *Academy of Management Executive* 7 (1993): 7–28.

20. J.M. Moran, "Getting Closer Together—Videophones Don't Deliver TV Quality Sound, Visuals, But They're Improving," *The Seattle Times*, 15 March 1998.

21. T. Shurley, "Internet Phone System Could Revolutionize Long Distance," *Springfield Business Journal*, 29 May 1995.

22. K.G. Provan, "Embeddedness, Interdependence, and Opportunism in Organizational Supplier-Buyer Networks," *Journal of Management* 19 (1993): 841–856.

23. D. Takahashi, "How the Competition Got Ahead of Intel in Making Cheap Chips," *The Wall Street Journal*, 12 February 1998, A1.

24. F. Shalom, "Clothing Firms Fight Wal-Mart Price Rollbacks," *Montreal Gazette*, 6 July 1995.

25. B.K. Pilling, L.A. Crosby, & D.W. Jackson, "Relational Bonds in Industrial Exchange: An Experimental Test of the Transaction Cost Economic Framework," *Journal of Business Research* 30 (1994): 237–251.

26. M. Hertsgaard, "Are the French Headed for a Meltdown? A Motley Flotilla and Consumer Boycotts Could Give Paris Fits over Nuclear Testing," *Washington Post*, 3 September 1995.

27. N. Wingfield, "UPS Strike Proves a Mixed Bag for Merchants in Cyberspace," *The Wall Street Journal Interactive Edition*, 15 August 1997.

28. D.F. Jennings & J.R. Lumpkin, "Insights Between Environmental Scanning Activities and Porter's Generic Strategies: An Empirical Analysis," *Journal of Management* 4 (1992): 791–803.

29. B. Ettore, "Managing Competitive Intelligence," *Management Review*, October 1995, 15–19.

30. S.E. Jackson & J.E. Dutton, "Discerning Threats and Opportunities," *Administrative Science Quarterly* 33 (1988): 370–387.

31. J.B. Thomas, S.M. Clark, & D.A. Gioia, "Strategic Sensemaking and Organizational Performance: Linkages among Scanning, Interpretation, Action, and Outcomes," *Academy of Management Journal* 36 (1993): 239–270.

32. R. Daft, J. Sormunen, & D. Parks, "Chief Executive Scanning, Environmental Characteristics, and Company Performance: An Empirical Study," *Strategic Management Journal* 9 (1988): 123–139; D. Miller & P.H. Friesen, "Strategy-Making and Environment: The Third Link," *Strategic Management Journal* 4 (1983): 221–235.

33. S. Kraft, "Tradition under Siege/Supermarkets? Sacre Bleu!/A Shopping Revolution Imperils French Merchants," *Los Angeles Times*, 5 May 1996, D10.

34. "High Sales, Low Fat," *Financial Post*, 8 February 1996, 63.

35. L. Hays, "Gerstner Is Struggling as He Tries to Change Ingrained IBM Culture," *The Wall Street Journal*, 13 May 1994, A1.

36. W. Gulger, "Getting and Keeping Good People in the 21st Century," *Hardware*

and Home Centre Magazine 24, no. 1 (January/February 2000): 37–38.

37. P. Elmer-DeWitt, "Mine, All Mine; Bill Gates Wants a Piece of Everybody's Action. But Can He Get It?" *Time,* 5 June 1995.

38. D.M. Boje, "The Storytelling Organization: A Study of Story Performance in an Office-Supply Firm," *Administrative Science Quarterly* 36 (1991): 106–126.

39. M.H. McCormack, *What They Don't Teach You at Harvard Business School* (New York: Bantam, 1984).

40. T.K. McCraw, "Henry Ford and Alfred Sloan," Case 26 in *Management: Past and Present, A Casebook on the History of American Business,* by A.D. Chandler, Jr., T.K. McCraw, & R.S. Tedlow (Cincinnati, OH: South-Western College Publishing, 1996).

41. A.L. Wilkins & N.J. Bristow, "For Successful Organization Culture, Honor Your Past," *Academy of Management Executive* 1 (1987): 221–229.

42. Mark Stevens, "The Store to End All Stores," *Canadian Business Review* 67, no. 5 (May 1994): 20.

43. R.L. Daft, *Organizational Theory and Design* (Cincinnati, OH: South-Western College Publishing, 2001).

44. D.R. Denison & A.K. Mishra, "Toward a Theory of Organizational Culture and Effectiveness," *Organization Science* 6 (1995): 204–223.

45. L. Hays, "Gerstner Is Struggling as He Tries to Change Ingrained IBM Culture," *The Wall Street Journal,* 13 May 1994, A1.

46. A. Deutschman, "How H-P Continues to Grow and Grow," *Fortune,* 2 May 1994, 90–100.

47. T.A. Stewart, "Company Values that Add Value," *Fortune,* 8 July 1996, 145–147.

48. D.Q. Mills, "The Decline and Rise of IBM," *Sloan Management Review* 37 (1 June 1996).

49. S. Albert & D.A. Whetten, "Organizational Identity," *Research in Organizational Behavior* 7 (1985): 263–295; C.M. Fiol, "Managing Culture as a Competitive Resource: An Identity-Based View of Sustainable Competitive Advantage," *Journal of Management* 17 (1991): 191–211.

50. Mary Rother, "The Will to Succeed: Besides a Good Product or Service, What Does It Take to Beat the Volatility of the IT Industry? Three Parables Provide Some Answers,"

Financial Post Magazine, March 1999, 44–50.

51. Claudia Cattaneo, "Petrocan Rids Itself of Pariah Legacy; Once Viewed as a Federal Government Invader, the Firm Is Now Accepted in Its Home Town," *Financial Post,* 17 November 1999, C8; David Olive, "The Brightest Stars in Canada's Oilpatch: This Generation of Executives Has Changed the Face of the Country's Oil Sector," *Financial Post,* 13 June 2000, C8, C9; James Sanford, "Oil Patch's Highest Perch Has a New View: Petro-Canada's Chief Stanford Has the Privatized Company in Fighting Trim and He's Ready to Lead It to New Conquests," *Financial Post,* 7/9 October 1995, 5.

Chapter 3

1. A. Losciale, "Survey Finds More Than 75% of Workers Say They Have Seen Unethical Conduct," *The Salt Lake Tribune,* 27 May 2000, C2.

2. C. Smith, "The Ethical Workplace," *Association Management* 52 (2000): 70–73.

3. E. Petry, A. Mujica, & D. Vickery, "Sources and Consequences of Workplace Pressure: Increasing the Risk of Unethical and Illegal Business Practices," *Business & Society Review* 99 (1998): 25–30.

4. M. Jackson (Associated Press), "Workplace Cheating Rampant, Half of Employees Surveyed Admit They Take Unethical Actions," *Peoria Journal Star,* 5 April 1997.

5. A. Losciale, "Survey Finds More Than 75% of Workers Say They Have Seen Unethical Conduct," *The Salt Lake Tribune,* 27 May 2000, C2.

6. C. Smith, "The Ethical Workplace," *Association Management* 52 (2000): 70–73.

7. G. Stern & J.S. Lublin, "New GM Rules Curb Wining, Dining by Suppliers," *The Wall Street Journal Interactive Edition,* 5 June 1996.

8. M. Maremont, "Blind Ambition: How the Pursuit of Results Got Out of Hand at Bausch & Lomb," *Business Week,* 23 October 1995.

9. M. Bordwin, "Don't Ask Employees to Do Your Dirty Work," *Management Review,* 1 October 1995.

10. L.S. Paine, "Managing for Organizational Integrity," *Harvard Business Review,* March-April 1994, 106–117.

11. K. Gibson, "Excuses, Excuses: Moral Slippage in the Workplace," *Business*

Horizons 43, no. 6 (2000): 65; S.L. Robinson & R.J. Bennett, "A Typology of Deviant Workplace Behaviors: A Multidimensional Scaling Study," *Academy of Management Journal* 38 (1995): 555–572.

12. Peter Brieger, "Office Crime: Many Know, Few Tell: Huge Problem: Survey," *National Post,* 9 August 2002, FP5.

13. K. Gibson, "Excuses, Excuses: Moral Slippage in the Workplace," *Business Horizons* 43, no. 6 (2000): 65; S.L. Robinson & R.J. Bennett, "A Typology of Deviant Workplace Behaviors: A Multidimensional Scaling Study," *Academy of Management Journal* 38 (1995): 555–572.

14. L. Peek & B. Webster, "Sabotage Feared over Airliners' Cut Wires," *The Times of London,* 9 June 2001, 16; S. Gaudin, "Computer Sabotage Case Back in Court," *Network World Fusion,* 19 April 2001, 12.

15. 2001 Canadian Retail Security Report. Retail Council of Canada. [Online] Available www.retailcouncil.org, 21 October 2002.

16. Marina Strauss, "Retailers Put Squeeze on Shrinkage," *Globe and Mail,* 13 July 2001, M1.

17. L. Lorek, "Sticky Fingers," *Interactive Week from ZDWire,* 27 March 2001.

18. David Ray, "Workplace Violence: Strategies for Prevention," *Law Now,* 26, no. 5, April-May 2002.

19. Shelley Boyles, "Workplace Violence: Coping in a Dangerous World," *The Canadian Consulting Engineer* 43, no. 1 (January-February 2002): 51–52.

20. Shelley Boyles, "Workplace Violence: Coping in a Dangerous World," *The Canadian Consulting Engineer* 43, no. 1 (January-February 2002): 51–52.

21. Shelley Boyles, "Workplace Violence: Coping in a Dangerous World," *The Canadian Consulting Engineer* 43, no. 1 (January-February 2002): 51–52.

22. "Work Rage," *BC Business Magazine* 29, no. 1 (January 2001): 23.

23. M.P. Coco, Jr., "The New War Zone: The Workplace," *SAM Advanced Management Journal* 63, no. 1 (1998): 15; M.G. Harvey & R.A. Cosier, "Homicides in the Workplace: Crisis or False Alarm?" *Business Horizons* 38, no. 10 (1995): 11.

24. L.A. Hays, "A Matter of Time: Widow Sues IBM over Death Benefits," *The Wall Street Journal,* 6 July 1995.

25. T.M. Jones, "Ethical Decision Making by Individuals in Organizations: An

Issue-Contingent Model," *Academy of Management Review* 16 (1991): 366–395.

26. B. Mook, "Group Gets Tough on 'Software Piracy,'" *Denver Business Journal,* 6 March 1998, 19A.

27. L. Kohlberg, "Stage and Sequence: The Cognitive-Developmental Approach to Socialization," in *Handbook of Socialization Theory and Research,* ed. D.A. Goslin (Chicago: Rand McNally, 1969); L. Trevino, "Moral Reasoning and Business Ethics: Implications for Research, Education, and Management," *Journal of Business Ethics* 11 (1992): 445–459.

28. L.T. Hosmer, "Trust: The Connecting Link Between Organizational Theory and Philosophical Ethics," *Academy of Management Review* 20 (1995): 379–403.

29. M.R. Cunningham, D.T. Wong, & A.P. Barbee, "Self-Presentation Dynamics on Overt Integrity Tests: Experimental Studies of the Reid Report," *Journal of Applied Psychology* 79 (1994): 643–658.

30. H.J. Bernardin, "Validity of an Honesty Test in Predicting Theft among Convenience Store Employees," *Academy of Management Journal* 36 (1993): 1097–1108.

31. J.M. Collins & F.L. Schmidt, "Personality, Integrity, and White Collar Crime: A Construct Validity Study," *Personnel Psychology* (1993): 295–311.

32. W.C. Borman, M.A. Hanson, & J.W. Hedge, "Personnel Selection," *Annual Review of Psychology* 48 (1997).

33. Shell Canada Statement of General Business Principles and Corporate Ethics. [Online] Available www.shellcanada.com. With Permission Obtained: October 22, 2002.

34. P.E. Murphy, "Corporate Ethics Statements: Current Status and Future Prospects," *Journal of Business Ethics* 14 (1995): 727–740.

35. S.J. Harrington, "What Corporate America Is Teaching about Ethics," *Academy of Management Executive* 5 (1991): 21–30.

36. R. McGarver, "Doing the Right Thing," *Training* 30 (1993): 35–38.

37. Canada Statement of General Business Principles and Corporate Ethics. [Online] Available www.shellcanada.com. With Permission Obtained: October 22, 2002.

38. Diane Francis, "Livent: A Bean Counter Scandal: A Tale of Woes Raises Interesting Questions," *Financial Post,* 10 May 2001, 3.

39. M. Schwartz, "Business Ethics: Time to Blow the Whistle?" *Globe and Mail,* 5 March 1998, B2.

40. M.P. Miceli & J.P Near, "Whistleblowing: Reaping the Benefits," *Academy of Management Executive* 8 (1994): 65–72.

41. H.R. Bower, *Social Responsibilities of the Businessman* (New York: Harper & Row, 1953).

42. B. Carton, "Animal Instincts: Gillette Faces Wrath of Children in Testing on Rats and Rabbits," *The Wall Street Journal,* 5 September 1995.

43. M. Zetlin, "Companies Find Profit in Corporate Giving," *Management Review* 79 (1990): 10–15.

44. S.L. Wartick & P.L. Cochran, "The Evolution of the Corporate Social Performance Model," *Academy of Management Review* 10 (1985): 758–769.

45. T. Donaldson & L.E. Preston, "The Stakeholder Theory of the Corporation: Concepts, Evidence, and Implications," *Academy of Management Review* 20 (1995): 65–91.

46. Donalee Moulton, "Irving Gets Auto Makers Choice Designation for Its Fuels," *Financial Post-National Post,* 19 November 1999, E15.

47. Michael MacDonald, "Automakers Encourage Clean Fuel Use," *Canadian Press Newswire,* 14 October 1999.

48. M. Silver, "Doing Your Bit to Save the Earth," *U.S. News & World Report,* 2 April 1990, 61–62.

49. E.W. Orts, "Beyond Shareholders: Interpreting Corporate Constituency Statutes," *The George Washington Law Review* 61 (1992): 14–135.

50. A.B. Carroll, "A Three-Dimensional Conceptual Model of Corporate Performance," *Academy of Management Review* 4 (1979): 497–505.

51. J. Lublin & M. Murray, "CEOs Leave Faster Than Ever Before as Boards, Investors Lose Patience," *The Wall Street Journal Interactive,* 27 October 2000.

52. Google.ca key word search (Mastercard, Affinity). Available www.google.ca. Retrieved, 24 October 2002.

53. www.scouts.ca.

54. "T. Bryant, "Judge Rejects New Trial in Case of Woman Paralyzed in Suzuki Samurai Accident," *St. Louis Post-Dispatch,* 2 February 1998, C4; "Inclined to Roll, Suzuki Samurai Car Gets Unfavorable Rating Because of Tipping Tendency," *Time,* 13 June 1988, 51.

55. S. Power & N. Shirouzu, "Bridgestone Position Angers Lawmakers—Firm Balks at Wider Recall of Tires, Setting Stage for House Showdown," *The Wall Street Journal,* 5 September 2000, A3.

56. R. Silverman & K. Dunham, "Tire Recall: The Road Gets Rough—Consultants Split on Bridgestone's Crisis Management," *The Wall Street Journal,* 11 August 2000, A6.

57. K. Kranhold & E. White, "The Perils and Potential Rewards of Crisis Managing for Firestone," *The Wall Street Journal,* 8 September 2000, B1.

58. Toby Heaps, "Actions Speak Louder Than Words," Corporate Knights. [Online] Available www.corporateknights.ca. June 2001.

59. N. Templin, "Nissan Recalls and Destroys Some Minivans," *The Wall Street Journal,* 9 December 1993, B1.

60. Paul Fengler and Toby Heaps, "Aqua Purus," Corporate Knights. [Online] Available www.corporateknights.ca. June 2002.

61. Socially Responsible Mutual Funds. Social Investment Organization. [Online] Available www.socialinvestment.ca. 17 October 2002.

62. Pablo Fuchs, "Real Assets Aims to Prove You Don't Have to Lose Money to Be Socially Responsible," *Canadian Business* 74, no. 13 (2001): 142–146.

63. Canadian Social Investment Review 2000. Social Investment Organization. [Online] Available www.socialinvestment.ca.

64. Pablo Fuchs, "Real Assets Aims to Prove You Don't Have to Lose Money to Be Socially Responsible," *Canadian Business* 74, no. 13 (2001): 142–146.

65. H. Haines, "Noah Joins Ranks of Socially Responsible Funds," *Dow Jones News Service,* 13 October 1995.

66. M.B. Meznar, D. Nigh, & C.Y. Kwok, "Effect of Announcements of Withdrawal from South Africa on Stockholder Wealth," *Academy of Management Journal* 37 (1994): 1633–1648.

67. Paul Fengler & Toby Heaps, "Aqua Purus," Corporate Knights. [Online] Available www.corporateknights.ca. June 2002.

68. Paul Fengler & Toby Heaps, "Aqua Purus," Corporate Knights. [Online] Available www.corporateknights.ca. June 2002.

69. D. Kadlec & B. Van Voorst, "The New World of Giving: Companies Are

Doing More Good, and Demanding More Back," *Time*, 5 May 1997.

70. P. Carlin, "Will Rapid Growth Stunt Corporate Do-Gooders?" *Business and Society Review*, Spring 1995, 36–43.

71. Katherine Macklem, "Canada's Top 100 Employers," *Maclean's*, 28 October 2002, 26–34.

72. Katherine Macklem, "Canada's Top 100 Employers," *Maclean's*, 28 October 2002, 28.

Chapter 4

1. Hollie Shaw, "Forzani Earnings Soar 64%," *National Post*, 23 March 2002, FP3.

2. Norma Ramage, "Forzani Sticks to Offence: How Canada's Top Sporting Goods Retailer Regained Lost Yardage, and Then Some," *Marketing Magazine* 105, no. 40 (9 October 2000), 23.

3. E.A. Locke & G.P. Latham, *A Theory of Goal Setting and Task Performance* (Englewood Cliffs, NJ: Prentice Hall, 1990).

4. M.E. Tubbs, "Goal-Setting: A Meta-Analytic Examination of the Empirical Evidence," *Journal of Applied Psychology* 71 (1986): 474–83.

5. Michael Clarkson, "Weir Sets Major Goals: Canadian Golfer Hopes to Build on 2000 Success," *The Ottawa Citizen*, 11 January 2001, D5; Joe Scanlon, "Road to Success Filled with Bumps," *Calgary Herald*, 28 April 2003, C4.

6. J. Bavelas & E.S. Lee, "Effect of Goal Level on Performance: A Trade-Off of Quantity and Quality," *Canadian Journal of Psychology* 32 (1978): 219–240.

7. A. Farnham, "Mary Kay's Lessons in Leadership," *Fortune*, 20 September 1993. "Company Information: Products and Sales," Mary Kay Cosmetics. [Online] Available, www.marykay.com/Home/Community/Headquarters/Company/Products.asp, 29 June 2001.

8. Mark Evans, "Telus Plans to Slash $300M in Operating Costs, 10% of Workforce May Go," *National Post*, 7 June 2002, FP1; Mark Evans, "Telus to Slash 6000 Jobs," *National Post*, 12 July 2002, FP1; Mark Evans, "Telus Chief Juggles Growth Strategy, Fiscal Responsibility," *National Post*, 14 November 2002, FP1.

9. C.C. Miller, "Strategic Planning and Firm Performance: A Synthesis of More Than Two Decades of Research," *Academy of Management Performance* 37 (1994): 1649–1665.

10. H. Mintzberg, "Rethinking Strategic Planning," Part I: Pitfalls and Fallacies, *Long Range Planning* 27 (1994): 12–21; Part II: New Roles for Planners: 22–30. H. Mintzberg, "The Pitfalls of Strategic Planning," *California Management Review* 36 (1993): 32–47.

11. K. Pope, "International: Runaway Growth at Phone Giant Nokia Humbles Newcomer after Early Success," *The Wall Street Journal*, 12 March 1996.

12. K. Capell, W. Echikson, & P. Elstrom, "Surprise! Nokia Doesn't Walk on Water: Its About-Face on Growth Will Hurt Credibility," *Business Week*, 25 June 2001, 30.

13. H. Mintzberg, "The Pitfalls of Strategic Planning," *California Management Review* 36 (1993): 32–47.

14. P. Tam, "Will Quantity Hurt Pixar's Quality?—Computer-Animation Studio Bets It Can Boost Output to One Feature a Year," *The Wall Street Journal*, 15 February 2001, B1.

15. E.A. Locke & G.P. Latham, *A Theory of Goal Setting and Task Performance* (Englewood Cliffs, NJ: Prentice Hall, 1990).

16. G.A. Bricker, "Performance Agreements: The Key to Increasing Motivation," *Sales and Marketing Management* (February 1992), 69; A. King, B. Oliver, B. Sloop, & K. Vaverek, *Planning and Goal Setting for Improved Performance, Participant's Guide* (Cincinnati, OH: Thomson Executive Press, 1995).

17. E.A. Locke & G.P. Latham, *A Theory of Goal Setting and Task Performance* (Englewood Cliffs, NJ: Prentice Hall, 1990).

18. J.R. Hollenbeck, C.R. Williams, & H.J. Klein, "An Empirical Examination of the Antecedents of Commitment to Difficult Goals," *Journal of Applied Psychology* 74 (1989): 18–23.

19. G. Lucier & S. Seshadri, "GE Takes Six Sigma Beyond the Bottom Line," *Strategic Finance* 82, no. 11 (2001): 40–46.

20. S. Creedy, "USAir Flies New Route to Financial Survival," *Pittsburgh Post-Gazette*, 7 January 1996.

21. Mark Evans, "Telus Plans to Slash $300M in Operating Costs, 10% of Workforce May Go," *National Post*, 7 June 2002, FP1.

22. A. Bandura & D.H. Schunk, "Cultivating Competence, Self-Efficacy, and Intrinsic Interest through Proximal Self-Motivation," *Journal of Personality and Social Psychology* 41 (1981): 586–598.

23. E. Walker, "CEO of Office Depot Works to Help Firm Reach Goals," *The Miami Herald*, 12 May 2001, 1C.

24. E.A. Locke & G.P. Latham, *A Theory of Goal Setting and Task Performance* (Englewood Cliffs, NJ: Prentice Hall, 1990).

25. L. McCauley, "Relaunch!: Unit of One," *Fast Company*, 1 July 2000, 97.

26. E.H. Bowman & D. Hurry, "Strategy through the Option Lens: An Integrated View of Resource Investments and the Incremental-Choice Process," *Academy of Management Review* 18 (1993): 760–782.

27. D. Takahashi, "Deals and Deal Makers: Intel Rolls Dice on Tech Upstarts—And Hits Jackpot," *The Wall Street Journal*, 8 February 2000, C1.

28. N.A. Wishart, J.J. Elam, & D. Robey, "Redrawing the Portrait of a Learning Organization: Inside Knight-Ridder, Inc.," *Academy of Management Executive* 10 (1996): 7–20.

29. N.A. Wishart, J.J. Elam, & D. Robey, "Redrawing the Portrait of a Learning Organization: Inside Knight-Ridder, Inc.," *Academy of Management Executive* 10 (1996): 7–20.

30. J. Samuelson, "The Geeky Garbageman," *Forbes*, 8 April 1996.

31. J.C. Collins & J.I. Porras, "Organizational Vision and Visionary Organizations," *California Management Review*, Fall 1991, 30–52.

32. Ken MacQueen, "The Anti-Retailer: Vancouver's Mountain Equipment Co-op Succeeds in Spite of Itself," *Maclean's*, 29 April 2002, 30.

33. Ken MacQueen, "The Anti-Retailer: Vancouver's Mountain Equipment Co-op Succeeds in Spite of Itself," *Maclean's*, 29 April 2002, 30.

34. J.C. Collins & J.I. Porras, "Organizational Vision and Visionary Organizations," *California Management Review*, Fall 1991, 30–52.

35. J.C. Collins & J.I. Porras, "Organizational Vision and Visionary Organizations," *California Management Review*, Fall 1991, 30–52.

36. J.C. Collins & J.I. Porras, "Organizational Vision and Visionary Organizations," *California Management Review*, Fall 1991, 30–52.

37. W. George, "Building a Mission-Driven, Values-Centered Organization," Speech given at the Premier CEO's Conference in Aspen Colorado

17 September 1998. [Online] Available www.medtronic.com/newsroom/mgmtspeech_sept17.html, 1 July 2001.

38. W. George, "Building a Mission-Driven, Values-Centered Organization," Speech given at the Premier CEO's Conference in Aspen Colorado 17 September 1998. [Online] Available www.medtronic.com/newsroom/mgmtspeech_sept17.html, 1 July 2001.

39. Peter Morton, "Southwest Blazes Trail," *Financial Post*, 17 December 1999, C1, C9.

40. J.A. Pearce & F. David, "Corporate Mission Statements: The Bottom Line," *Academy of Management Executive* 1 (1987): 109–116.

41. S. Kraft, "Disney Magic Is Finally Starting to Work at French Theme Park," *Los Angeles Times*, 4 February 1996, Business p. 1.

42. P. Prada, "Euro Disney's Net Income Climbs 64%," *The Wall Street Journal*, 17 November 2000, A17; P. Prada, "Ja, Ja, Americana's Fabulosa—In Europe, Theme Parks Draw Crowds with Thrill Rides, Burgers and Bugs Bunny," *The Wall Street Journal*, 21 June 2001, B1.

43. L. Iococca, with W. Novak, *Iococca* (New York: Bantam, 1984).

44. E. Marlow & R. Schilhavy, "Expectation Issues in Management by Objectives Programs," *Industrial Management* 33, no. 4 (1991): 29.

45. "WebMBO Teams with Deloitte & Touche to Deliver Innovative Web-Based 'Management-By-Objectives and Performance Management' Solutions," *PRNewswire*, 19 June 2001.

46. Peter Fitzpatrick, "CP Split to Unlock Value: Five New Divisions," *National Post*, 14 February 2001, C1; James Stevenson, "CP Spinoff Called an 'Unqualified Success'," *Financial Post*, 2 October, 2002, FP 9.

47. CIBC, "Career Quest," [Online] Available www2.cibc.com/inside/careers/template/job_postings.html, 8 November 2002.

48. Canadian Human Rights Commission, "About the Canadian Human Rights Commission." [Online] Available www. chrc-ccdp.ca/AboutCHRC_AproposCCDP/about.asp, 8 November 2002.

49. N. Humphrey, "References a Tricky Issue for Both Sides," *Nashville Business Journal* 11 (8 May 1995): 1A.

50. M. Seminerio, "Nielsen: Penthouse Website Popular with PC Companies," *PC Week Online*, 2 April 1996.

51. M. Savage, "Keeping Watch—It's Not 1984, But Tools for Monitoring Employee Web Activity Are Catching On, Solution Providers Say," *Computer Reseller News*, 2 October 2000, 32.

52. M. Savage, "Keeping Watch—It's Not 1984, But Tools for Monitoring Employee Web Activity Are Catching On, Solution Providers Say," *Computer Reseller News*, 2 October 2000, 32.

53. S. Sherman, "Stretch Goals: The Dark Side of Asking for Miracles," *Fortune*, 13 November 1995, 231.

54. S. Sherman, "Stretch Goals: The Dark Side of Asking for Miracles," *Fortune*, 13 November 1995, 231.

55. "No Guts, No Glory: When Richmond Savings Took on the Humungous Bank(s) in a Cheeky Ad Campaign, the Big Six Were Not Amused," *B.C. Business Magazine*, September 1996, 30–34; "Richmond Savings Wins Ad Battle," *Marketing Magazine* , 2 October 2000, 1; Timothy Renshaw, "Credit Union Puts People First," *National Post*, 18 December 2002, SR3.

56. C. O'Dell, "Out-of-the-Box Benchmarking," *Management Review* 83 (1 January 1994): 63.

57. R. Vartabedian, "Chrysler Board Cuts Bonuses of Top Execs, Cites Lag in Quality," *Los Angeles Times*, 29 March 1996, D-1.

58. B. Wysocki, Jr., "Power Grid: Soft Landing or Hard? Firm Tests Strategy on 3 Views of Future—Most Likely, Duke Energy Decides, Is a Growth Era of 'Flawed Competition'—Retailing Gas on the Internet," *The Wall Street Journal*, 7 July 2000, A1.

59. G. Robbins, "Scenario Planning," *Public Management*, 1 March 1995, 4.

60. P.J. Schoemaker, "Scenario Planning: A Tool for Strategic Thinking," *Sloan Management Review* 36 (1995): 25.

61. M. Stepanke, "How Fast Is Net Fast? On the Internet, Companies Have to Be Ready to Change Goals or Strategy Virtually Overnight," *Business Week*, 1 November 1999, EB52.

62. F. Keenan, "Opening the Spigot: Faucet Maker Moen Uses the Web to Stream-line Design. Rivals Are Eating Dust," *Business Week*, 4 June 2001, EB16.

63. S.C. Wheelwright & K.B. Clark, "Creating Project Plans to Focus Product Development," *Harvard Business Review*, March-April 1992, 70.

64. D. Dimancescu & K. Dwenger, "Smoothing the Product Development Plan," *Management Review* 85, no. 6 (1996): 36.

65. S.L. Brown, "Product Development: Past Research, Present Findings, and Future Directions," *Academy of Management Review* 20 (1995): 343–378.

66. L. Ohr, "Delivering Taste and Convenience," *Prepared Foods*, February 2001, 28.

67. L. Ohr, "Delivering Taste and Convenience," *Prepared Foods*, February 2001, 28.

68. J. Martin, "Ignore Your Customer," *Fortune*, 1 May 1995, 121.

69. M. Iansiti, "Shooting the Rapids: Managing Product Development in Turbulent Environments," *California Management Review* 38 (1995): 36–58.

70. F. Warner, "Lear Won't Take a Back Seat: For Decades, Lear Corp. Made Car Seats. Today, with the Help of Virtual Reality and Other Digital Technologies, Lear Makes a Whole Lot More—And Makes It a Whole Lot Faster. Along the Way, The Company Learned How to Get Real about What Technology Can and Cannot Do," *Fast Company*, 1 June 2000, 178.

71. F. Warner, "Lear Won't Take a Back Seat: For Decades, Lear Corp. Made Car Seats. Today, with the Help of Virtual Reality and Other Digital Technologies, Lear Makes a Whole Lot More—And Makes It a Whole Lot Faster. Along the Way, The Company Learned How to Get Real about What Technology Can and Cannot Do," *Fast Company*, 1 June 2000, 178.

Chapter 5

1. R. Lenzner, "The Reluctant Entrepreneur," *Forbes*, 11 September 1995, 162–166.

2. M. Rich, "Dear CEO: Are You Tracking Your Cubicles?" *The Wall Street Journal*, 19 April 2001, B8.

3. M. Rich, "Dear CEO: Are You Tracking Your Cubicles?" *The Wall Street Journal*, 19 April 2001, B8.

4. Cable Modem Market Stats & Projections. Cable Datacom News. Kinetics Strategies Inc. [Online] Available www.cabledatanews.com, 9 September 2002.

5. Canada and Broadband Internet Access. CNEWS Tech News. [Online] Available www.canoe.ca, 1 May 2002.

6. R.D. Buzzell & B.T. Gale, *The PIMS Principles: Linking Strategy to Performance* (New York: Free Press, 1987); M. Lambkin, "Order of Entry and Performance in New Markets,"

Strategic Management Journal 9 (1988): 127–40.

7. N. Deogun, "Banks Introduce New ATMs That Deliver Host of Services," *The Wall Street Journal Interactive Edition*, 5 June 1996.

8. G.L. Urban, T. Carter, S. Gaskin, & Z. Mucha, "Market Share Rewards to Pioneering Brands: An Empirical Analysis and Strategic Implications," *Management Science* 32 (1986): 645–659.

9. G. Hamel, "Smart Mover, Dumb Mover: Think the First Mover Advantage Is a Myth? You're Wrong: Most Pioneering Dot Coms Failed Not Because They Were First but Because They Were Dumb," *Fortune*, 3 September 2001, 191.

10. E. Nelson, "Retailing: Why Wal-Mart Sings, 'Yes, We Have Bananas!'" *The Wall Street Journal*, 6 October 1998, B1.

11. U. Tosi, "Commercial Aircraft Are Fast Becoming Flying Computer Systems: Their Downlinked Bitstreams Can Be Critical to High Profits and Happy Landings," *Forbes ASAP*, 4 December 1995, 100–102.

12. U. Tosi, "Commercial Aircraft Are Fast Becoming Flying Computer Systems: Their Downlinked Bitstreams Can Be Critical to High Profits and Happy Landings," *Forbes ASAP*, 4 December 1995, 100–102.

13. U. Tosi, "Commercial Aircraft Are Fast Becoming Flying Computer Systems: Their Downlinked Bitstreams Can Be Critical to High Profits and Happy Landings," *Forbes ASAP*, 4 December 1995, 100–102.

14. U. Tosi, "Commercial Aircraft Are Fast Becoming Flying Computer Systems: Their Downlinked Bitstreams Can Be Critical to High Profits and Happy Landings," *Forbes ASAP*, 4 December 1995, 100–102.

15. J. Novack, "The Data Miners," *Forbes*, 12 February 1996.

16. M. Halper, "Setting Up Is Hard to Do: Data Warehouses Do Not Grow on Trees," *Forbes ASAP*, 8 April 1996, 50–51.

17. J. Novack, "The Data Miners," *Forbes*, 12 February 1996.

18. N. Hutheesing, "Get the Bugs Out," *Forbes*, 8 April 1996.

19. T. Mack & T. Ewing, "In the Real World, Meanwhile . . . ." *Forbes*, 18 December 1995, 284.

20. Steven D. Lubar, *Infoculture* (Boston: Houghton Mifflin, 1993).

21. L. Finnegan, "WinWedge 32 May Be Too Good; Easy-To-Use Software Collects Data So Well It's Overloading Federal Systems," *Government Computer News* 15 (15 April 1996): 35.

22. Steven D. Lubar, *Infoculture* (Boston: Houghton Mifflin, 1993).

23. N. Rubenking, "Hidden Messages," *PC Magazine*, 22 May 2001, 86.

24. "Data Mining: Advanced Scout," *IBM Research Website*. [Online] Available www.research.ibm.com/xw-scout, 31 December 1995.

25. "Data Mining: Advanced Scout," *IBM Research Website*. [Online] Available www.research.ibm.com/xw-scout, 31 December 1995.

26. N. Rubenking, "Hidden Messages," *PC Magazine*, 22 May 2001, 86.

27. F.J. Derfler, Jr., "Secure Your Network," *PC Magazine*, 27 June 2000, 183–200.

28. "Virus Attack: Protect your PC," *Cnet.com Website*. [Online] Available http://home.cnet.com/software/0-3746.html, 1 October 2000.

29. N. Wingfield, "A Stolen Laptop Spells Trouble for Qualcomm Chief Jacobs," *The Wall Street Journal Interactive Edition*, 19 September 2000.

30. A. Laplante, "Invitation to Customers: Come into Our Database," *Forbes ASAP*, 28 August 1995, 124–130.

31. C. Ey, "E-Mail Saves Companies Time, Money and Effort," *Dallas Business Journal*, 17 November 1995, C13–14.

32. M.A. Verespej, "The E-Mail Monster: Can One Manager Handle 250 E-Mail Messages a Day, Plus 15 Voicemails an Hour?" *Industry Week*, 19 June 1995, 52–53.

33. M. Campanelli & N. Friedman, "Welcome to Voice Mail Hell: The New Technology Has Become a Barrier Between Salespeople and Customers. Here's How Smart Sellers Are Breaking Through," *Sales & Marketing Management* 147 (May 1995): 98–101.

34. T. Andrews, "E-Mail Empowers, Voice-Mail Enslaves," *PC Week*, 10 April 1995, E11.

35. P. Hise, "Life after Voice-Mail Hell. Winguth, Donahue and Co., Los Altos, CA Executive Search Firm, Brings Back Human Receptionist Due to Customer Dissatisfaction with Voice Mail Service," *Inc.*, August 1994, 101.

36. C. O'Malley, "Document Conferencing," *Computer Shopper Online*. [Online] Available www.zdnet.com/cshopper/content/9604/feature3/sub1.html, 23 June 1996. Originally published in the April 1996 issue of *Computer Shopper*.

37. J. Young, "The Transcontinental Blackboard," *Forbes*, 23 October 1995, 322–323.

38. J. van den Hoven, "Executive Support Systems & Decision Making," *Journal of Systems Management* 47, no. 8 (March-April 1996): 48.

39. M. Stevenson, "He Sees All He Knows All," *Canadian Business* 67, no. 5 (Spring 1994): 30.

40. "Intranet," Webopoedia [Online] Available www.webopedia.com/TERM/i/intranet.html, 26 August 2001.

41. B. Richards, "Intranet Offers Rewards for Firms Big and Small," *The Wall Street Journal Interactive Edition*, 17 June 1996.

42. J. Barlow, "Intranet Replaces Office Grapevine," *Houston Chronicle*, 7 May 2000, Business 1.

43. S. Hamm, D. Welch, W. Zellner, F. Keenan, & P. Engardio, "Down but Hardly Out: Downturn Be Damned. Companies Are Still Anxious to Expand Online Because the Net Is a Way to Boost Sales and Shrink Costs," *Business Week*, 26 March 2001, 126.

44. J. Barlow, "Intranet Replaces Office Grapevine," *Houston Chronicle*, 7 May 2000, Business 1.

45. V.S. Pasher, "Employee Benefits Info within a Few Clicks," *National Underwriter Life & Health—Financial Services Edition*, 14 April 1997, S4.

46. R. Ayre, "Intranet How-To: Setting Up Shop," *PC Magazine*, 23 April 1996, 151–158.

47. F.J. Derfler, "The Intranet Platform: A Universal Client?" *PC Magazine*, 23 April 1996, 105–113.

48. R.C. Kennedy, "Intranets in Action," *PC/Computing*, June 1996, 150.

49. D. Zimmerman, "Report on EDI Tracks Labor Savings," *Supermarket News*, 16 January 1995, S2.

50. D. Tobey, "Paperless Purchasing," *Hotel & Motel Management* 2, no. 3 (6 November 1995): 104.

51. "Extranet," Webopoedia [Online] Available www.webopedia.com/TERM/E/extranet.html, 26 August 2001.

52. S. Hamm, D. Welch, W. Zellner, F. Keenan, & P. Engardio, "Down but Hardly Out: Downturn Be Damned. Companies Are Still Anxious to Expand Online Because the Net Is a Way to Boost Sales and Shrink Costs," *Business Week*, 26 March 2001, 126.

53. M. McDonald, "SWA: Ticket Less Travel Saved Us Millions in Agent Pay," *Travel Weekly* 2 (20 November 1995): 1.

54. S. Hamm, D. Welch, W. Zellner, F. Keenan, & P. Engardio, "Down but Hardly out Downturn Be Damned. Companies Are Still Anxious to Expand Online Because the Net Is a Way to Boost Sales and Shrink Costs," *Business Week*, 26 March 2001, 126.

55. K.C. Laudon & J.P. Laudon, *Management Information Systems: Organization and Technology* (Upper Saddle River, NJ: Prentice Hall, 1996).

56. T. Chea, "Apache Shareholders Approve Sale of Assets," *Washington Post*, 14 June 2001, E5.

57. S. Oliver, "What Are My Chances, Doc?" *Forbes*, 31 July 1995, 136–137.

58. M. France, "Smart Contracts," *Forbes ASAP* 2 (29 August 1994): 117.

Chapter 6

1. L.A. Hill, *Becoming a Manager: Mastery of a New Identity* (Boston: Harvard Business School Press, 1992).

2. K.R. MacCrimmon, R.N. Taylor, & E.A. Locke, "Decision Making and Problem Solving" in *Handbook of Industrial and Organizational Psychology*, ed. M.D. Dunnette (Chicago: Rand McNally, 1976), 1397–1453.

3. N. Wingfield, "Amazon Gives Upbeat Earnings Outlook, Plans to Start Selling PCs at Its E-store," *The Wall Street Journal*, 6 June 2001, B2.

4. K.R. MacCrimmon, R.N. Taylor, & E.A. Locke, "Decision Making and Problem Solving" in *Handbook of Industrial and Organizational Psychology*, ed. M.D. Dunnette (Chicago: Rand McNally, 1976), 1397–1453.

5. G. Kress, "The Role of Interpretation in the Decision Process," *Industrial Management* 37 (1995): 10–14.

6. S. Hansell, "Listen Up! It's Time for a Profit," *New York Times*, 20 May 2001, 1.

7. Nick Wingfield, "Leading the News: Amazon Boosts Forecasts as Sales Soar," *The Wall Street Journal*, 24 January 2003, A3.

8. J. Delaney, "Buying Guide: Desktops," *PC Magazine*, 20 June 2001. [Online] Available www.pcmag.com/article/ 0,2997,s%253D1564%2526a% 253D5587,00.asp, 4 July 2001.

9. J. Koblenz, "How a Car Earns a Best Buy," *Consumers Digest*, 1 January 1993, 54.

10. P. Djang, "Selecting Personal Computers," *Journal of Research on Computing in Education*, 25 (1993): 327.

11. J.G. March, *A Primer on Decision Making: How Decisions Happen* (New York: Free Press, 1994).

12. R. Johnson, "Surviving a Slowdown— Strategies for the Storm: How Some Managers Are Hoping to Weather the Economic Slump," *The Wall Street Journal*, 14 May 2001, R6.

13. J. Orbell, "Hamlet and the Psychology of Rational Choice under Uncertainty," *Rationality and Society* 5 (1993): 127–140.

14. J. Nocera, "Bill Gross Blew Through $800 Million in 8 Months (and He's Got Nothing to Show for It). Why Is He Still Smiling?," *Fortune*, 5 March 2001, 70.

15. M.H. Bazerman, *Judgment in Managerial Decision Making* (New York: John Wiley & Sons, 1994).

16. B. Silverman, "Unconventional Wisdom: Twelve Remarkable Innovators Tell How Intuition Can Revolutionize Decision Making," *Sales & Marketing Management* 146 (1994): 106–107.

17. P.J. Hoffman, P. Slovic, & L.G. Rorer, "An Analysis-of-Variance Model for Assessment of Configural Cue Utilization in Clinical Judgment," *Psychological Bulletin* 69 (1968): 338–349.

18. L. Gutierrez & J. Fussell, "In a Culture of Mistrust, Fear Is Part of Parenting. Statistics Are Reassuring, But Parents Remain Wary," *The Kansas City Star*, 25 March 2001, A1.

19. K.C. Cole, "Brain's Use of Shortcuts Can Be a Route to Bias," *Los Angeles Times*, 1 May 1995, A1.

20. P.J. Schoemaker & J.E. Russo, "A Pyramid of Decision Approaches," *California Management Review*, Fall 1993, 9–33.

21. I. Graham, I. Stiell, A. Laupacis, L. McAuley, M. Howell, M. Clancy, P. Durieux, N. Simon, J. Emparanza, J. Aginaga, Jr., A. O'Connor, & G. Wells, "Awareness and Use of the Ottawa Ankle and Knee Rules in 5 Countries: Can Publication Alone Be Enough to Change Practice?" *Annals of Emergency Medicine* 37, no. 3 (2001): 259–66.

22. G. Bell, "'I Want My MVT' Drive Marketing Results with Multivariable Testing Techniques," *Direct Marketing* 60, no. 8 (December 1997): 346.

23. R. Koselka, "The New Mantra: MVT," *Forbes*, 11 March 1996, 114–118.

24. G. Bell, "'I Want My MVT' Drive Marketing Results with Multivariable Testing Techniques," *Direct Marketing* 60, no. 8 (December 1997): 346.

25. G. Bell, "'I Want My MVT' Drive Marketing Results with Multivariable Testing Techniques," *Direct Marketing*, 60 no. 8 (December 1997): 346.

26. W. Mossberg, "In Time for Elections: Software to Help You Make Up Your Mind," *The Wall Street Journal*, 8 February 1996.

27. K. Yakai, "To Do or Not To Do: Two Business-Oriented Decision Makers," *PC Magazine*, 23 January 1996.

28. B.M. Staw. "Knee-Deep in the Big Muddy: A Study of Escalating Commitment to a Chosen Course of Action," *Organizational Behavior and Human Performance* 16 (1976): 27–44.

29. A. Curry, "The First Couldn't Last," *U.S. News & World Report*, 8 January 2001, 37; J. McCormick, "You Snooze, You Lose," *Newsweek*, 21 July 1997, 50.

30. Paul Kedrosky, "BC's Fast Ferry Fiasco a Voyage into Dark Sea of Government Bungling," *Financial Post*, 30 January 1999, D5.

31. Daphne Bramham, "Fast Ferries— They'll Stick Around to Make Taxpayers Seasick," *The Vancouver Sun*, 29 March 2003, B1; "A Chronology of BC Ferries' Problem-Plagued Fast Ferry Project," *Canadian Press Newswire*, 13 March 2000; John Schreiner, "A Really Fast Boat to Nowhere," *Financial Post*, 26 February 1999, C9.

32. J. McCormick, "You Snooze, You Lose," *Newsweek*, 21 July 1997, 50.

33. D. Ghosh, "De-Escalation Strategies: Some Experimental Evidence," *Behavioral Research in Accounting* 9 (1997): 88–112.

34. D. Ghosh, "De-Escalation Strategies: Some Experimental Evidence," *Behavioral Research in Accounting* 9 (1997): 88–112.

35. Derek DeCloet, "Scuttle the Fleet! Why Cancelling the Second and Third Fast Ferries Might Be the Only True Course," *British Columbia Report*, 22 March 1999, 22.

36. J. Ross & B.M. Staw, "Organizational Escalation and Exit: Lessons from the Shoreham Nuclear Power Plant," *Academy of Management Journal* 36 (1993): 701–732.

37. J. Angwin, "Can These Dot-Coms Be Saved?—Profit Eludes Priceline as Expansion Takes Its Toll," *The Wall Street Journal*, 25 January 2001, B1.

38. Press Releases, "WebHouse Club Announces 90-Day Wind-Down of Name-Your-Price Grocery and Gasoline Internet Service," Priceline.com [Online], Available www.corporate-ir.net/ireye/ir_site.zhtml?ticker=pcln&script=410&layout=-6&item_id=121342, October 5, 2000.

39. Ray Dyck & Norman Halpern, "Team-Based Organizations Redesign at Celestica," *The Journal for Quality and Participation* , 22, no. 5 (Sept./Oct. 1999): 36–40.

40. L. Pelled, K. Eisenhardt, & K. Xin, "Exploring the Black Box: An Analysis of Work Group Diversity, Conflict, and Performance," *Administrative Science Quarterly* 44, no. 1 (March 1, 1999): 1.

41. T. Gutner, "Do Top Women Execs = Stronger IPOs? A Study Finds That the More of Them a Startup Has, The Better It Does," *Business Week*, 5 February 2001, 122.

42. "How to Form Hiring Teams," *Personnel Journal* 73, no. 3 (August 1994): S14.

43. I.L. Janis, *Groupthink* (Boston: Houghton Mifflin, 1983).

44. C.P. Neck & C.C. Manz, "From Groupthink to Teamthink: Toward the Creation of Constructive Thought Patterns in Self-Managing Work Teams," *Human Relations* 47 (1994): 929–952.

45. G. Moorhead, R. Ference, & C.P. Neck, "Group Decision Fiascoes Continue: Space Shuttle Challenger and a Revised Framework," *Human Relations* 44 (1991): 539–550.

46. A. Mason, W.A. Hochwarter, & K.R. Thompson, "Conflict: An Important Dimension in Successful Management Teams," *Organizational Dynamics* 24 (1995): 20.

47. C. Olofson, "So Many Decisions, So Little Time: What's Your Problem?" *Fast Company*, 1 October 1999, 62.

48. C. Olofson, "So Many Decisions, So Little Time: What's Your Problem?" *Fast Company*, 1 October 1999, 62.

49. R. Cosier & C.R. Schwenk, "Agreement and Thinking Alike: Ingredients for Poor Decisions," *Academy of Management Executive* 4 (1990): 69–74.

50. R. Cosier & C.R. Schwenk, "Agreement and Thinking Alike: Ingredients for Poor Decisions," *Academy of Management Executive* 4 (1990): 69–74.

51. K. Jenn & E. Mannix, "The Dynamic Nature of Conflict: A Longitudinal Study of Intragroup Conflict and Group Performance," *Academy of Management Journal* 44, no. 2 (2001): 238–251; R.L. Priem, D.A. Harrison, & N.K. Muir, "Structured Conflict and Consensus Outcomes in Group Decision Making," *Journal of Management* 21 (1995): 691–710.

52. A. Van De Ven & A.L. Delbecq, "Nominal Versus Interacting Group Processes for Committee Decision Making Effectiveness," *Academy of Management Journal* 14 (1971): 203–212.

53. A.R. Dennis & J.S. Valicich, "Group, Sub-Group, and Nominal Group Idea Generation: New Rules for a New Media?" *Journal of Management* 20 (1994): 723–736.

54. S.G. Robelberg, J.L. Barnes-Farrell, & C.A. Lowe, "The Stepladder Technique: An Alternative Group Structure Facilitating Effective Group Decision Making," *Journal of Applied Psychology* 77 (1992): 730–737; S.G. Rogelberg & M.S. O'Connor, "Extending the Stepladder Technique: An Examination of the Self-Paced Stepladder Groups," *Group Dynamics: Theory, Research, and Practice* 2 (1998): 82–91.

55. R.B. Gallupe, W.H. Cooper, M.L. Grise, & L.M. Bastianutti, "Blocking Electronic Brainstorms," *Journal of Applied Psychology* 79 (1994): 77–86.

56. Greg Crone, "Electrifying Brainstorms: Strategic-Planning Sessions Can Easily Collapse under the Weight of Rancorous Debate and Filibustering. But a High-Tech Approach Developed at Queen's University Lets Everyone Have Their Say, Without Recrimination," *National Post*, 3 July 1999, D11.

57. R.B. Gallupe & W.H. Cooper, "Brainstorming Electronically," *Sloan Management Review*, Fall 1993, 27–36.

58. R.B. Gallupe & W.H. Cooper, "Brainstorming Electronically," *Sloan Management Review*, Fall 1993, 27–36.

59. G. Kay, "Effective Meetings through Electronic Brainstorming," *Management Quarterly* 35 (1995): 15.

60. A. LaPlante, "90s Style Brainstorming," *Forbes ASAP*, 25 October 1993, 44.

Chapter 7

1. R. Leifer & P.K. Mills, "An Information Processing Approach for Deciding upon Control Strategies and Reducing Control Loss in Emerging Organizations," *Journal of Management* 22 (1996): 113–137.

2. "Say Baa-Baa to Bad Driving," *London Times*, 28 July 1996.

3. D. Machan, "Polishing the Golden Arches," *Forbes*, 15 June 1998, 42.

4. Kelly Shermach, "The Battle for the Canadian Market," *Credit Card Management* 12, no. 1 (April 1999): 42–46.

5. J. Martin & J.E. Davis, "Are You as Good as You Think You Are? There's Only One Way to Know for Sure," *Fortune*, 30 September 1996, 142.

6. P. Scott, "Selling Civility: Secret Shoppers," *The Wall Street Journal*, 29 June 2001, W17.

7. "Service Intelligence, Inc. — Press Room," [Online] Available www.serviceintelligence.com/intheNews.html, 21 August 2003.

8. R. Simons, "Control in an Age of Empowerment," *Harvard Business Review*, March-April 1995, 80–98.

9. H. Koontz & R.W. Bradspies, "Managing Through Feedforward Control: A Future-Directed View," *Business Horizons*, June 1972, 25–36.

10. D. Clark, "Marketing, Performance Earn Windows NT Place in the Sun," *The Wall Street Journal Interactive Edition*, 29 July 1996.

11. R. Leifer & P.K. Mills, "An Information Processing Approach for Deciding upon Control Strategies and Reducing Control Loss in Emerging Organizations," *Journal of Management* 22 (1996): 113–137.

12. C.A. Jaffe, "Magellan's Billion-Dollar 'Oops' Was a Simple Slip of the Hand," *Fort-Worth Star-Telegram*, 11 December 1994, D3.

13. S.G. Green & M.A. Welsh, "Cybernetics and Dependence: Reframing the Control Concept," *Academy of Management Review* 13 (1988): 287–301.

14. Joshua Avram, "Hey, Wanna Score Some Fridge Coolant?," *British Columbia Report* 9, no. 5 (29 September 1997): 26.

15. "Blue Bottle Refrigerant Recovery and Reclamation" [Online] Available www.oceta.on.ca/profiles/halozone/bottle.html, 24 October 2002.

16. J. Stossel, "Protect Us from Legal Vultures," *The Wall Street Journal*, 2 January 1996.

17. S. Joyce, "Tort Wars: Curb Frivolous Lawsuits, Unjust Awards," *San Diego Union-Tribune*, 19 November 1995.

18. M. Brannigan & E. de Lisser, "Ground Control: Cost Cutting at Delta Raises the Stock Price but Lowers the Service,"

The Wall Street Journal, 20 June 1996, A1.

19. N. Deogun, "Pepsi Has Had Its Fill of Pizza, Tacos, Chicken," *The Wall Street Journal*, 24 January 1997, B1.

20. S. Carey, "Frustrated Firms Buy Planes to Streamline Travel Plans," *The Wall Street Journal Interactive Edition*, 11 October 1996.

21. P. Davis, "Outrageous Perks: Coffee Breaks Are Becoming Coffee Escapes," *The Wall Street Journal Interactive Edition*, 8 August 1996.

22. D. Biers, M. Rose, M. Schumann, & N. Cho, "Labor Complaints Could Prompt International Strife for Korea," *The Wall Street Journal Interactive Edition*, 18 July 1996.

23. M. Weber, *The Protestant Ethic and the Spirit of Capitalism* (New York: Scribner's, 1958).

24. A.C. Greenberg, "Memos from the Chairman," *Fortune*, 29 April 1996, 173–175.

25. Mark Jaffe, "No Bonus for CEO at Precision Drilling: 'Pretty Fair' Formula," *National Post*, 11 April 2003, FP 8.

26. Ken MacQueen, "The Anti-Retailer: Vancouver's Mountain Equipment Co-op Succeeds in Spite of Itself," *Maclean's*, 29 April 2002, 30.

27. J.R. Barker, "Tightening the Iron Cage: Concertive Control in Self-Managing Teams," *Administrative Science Quarterly* 38 (1993): 408–437.

28. J.R. Barker, "Tightening the Iron Cage: Concertive Control in Self-Managing Teams," *Administrative Science Quarterly* 38 (1993): 408–437.

29. J.R. Barker, "Tightening the Iron Cage: Concertive Control in Self-Managing Teams," *Administrative Science Quarterly* 38 (1993): 408–437.

30. C. Manz & H. Sims, "Leading Workers to Lead Themselves: The External Leadership of Self-Managed Work Teams," *Administrative Science Quarterly* 32 (1987): 106–128.

31. J. Slocum & H.A. Sims, "Typology for Integrating Technology, Organization and Job Design," *Human Relations* 33 (1980): 193–212.

32. C.C. Manz & H.P. Sims, Jr., "Self-Management as a Substitute for Leadership: A Social Learning Perspective," *Academy of Management Review* 5 (1980): 361–367.

33. S. Levy, "Strip Mining the Corporate Life," *Newsweek*, 12 August 1996, 54–55.

34. B. McWilliams, "The Measure of Success," *Across the Board*, 1 February 1996, 16.

35. R.S. Kaplan & D.P. Norton, "Using the Balanced Scorecard as a Strategic Management System," *Harvard Business Review*, January-February 1996, 75–85; R.S. Kaplan & D.P. Norton, "The Balanced Scorecard: Measures That Drive Performance," *Harvard Business Review*, January-February 1992, 71–79.

36. R.S. Kaplan & D.P. Norton, "Using the Balanced Scorecard as a Strategic Management System," *Harvard Business Review*, January-February 1996, 75–85; R.S. Kaplan & D.P. Norton, "The Balanced Scorecard: Measures that Drive Performance," *Harvard Business Review*, January-February 1992, 71–79.

37. S.L. Fawcett, "Fear of Accounts: Improving Managers' Competence and Confidence Through Simulation Exercises," *Journal of European Industrial Training*, February 1996, 17.

38. M.H. Stocks & A. Harrell, "The Impact of an Increase in Accounting Information Level on the Judgment Quality of Individuals and Groups," *Accounting, Organizations and Society*, October-November 1995, 685–700.

39. B. Morris, "Roberto Goizueta and Jack Welch: The Wealth Builders," *Fortune*, 11 December 1995, 80–94.

40. B. Morris, "Roberto Goizueta and Jack Welch: The Wealth Builders," *Fortune*, 11 December 1995, 80–94.

41. Kevin Lawrence, "How to Profit from Customer Complaints," *The Canadian Manager*, Fall 2000, 25, 29.

42. M. Hepworth, "Connecting Customer Loyalty to the Bottom Line," *Canadian Business Review*, 1 January 1994, 40.

43. C.B. Furlong, "12 Rules for Customer Retention," *Bank Marketing* 5 (January 1993): 14.

44. M. Hepworth, "Connecting Customer Loyalty to the Bottom Line," *Canadian Business Review*, 1 January 1994, 40.

45. T.K. Gilliam, "Closing the Customer Retention Gap," *Bank Marketing* 3 (December 1994): 51.

46. C.A. Reeves & D.A. Bednar, "Defining Quality: Alternatives and Implications," *Academy of Management Review* 19 (1994): 419–445.

47. "Readers' Choice Poll 1997: International Airline Rankings," *Conde Nast Traveler*. [Online] Available http://travel. epicurious.com/travel/ g_cnt/05_poll97/air/inter_intro.html, 26 June 1998.

48. "Airline Way Above Rest in Rankings," *South China Morning Post*, 9 August 1996.

49. D.R. May & B.L. Flannery, "Cutting Waste with Employee Involvement Teams," *Business Horizons*, September-October 1995, 28–38.

50. M.A. Verespej, "Trash to Cash: The Bottom Line, The Environment, and Companies Can Profit from Waste Reduction," *Industry Week*, 5 December 1995, 53–55.

51. M.A. Verespej, "Trash to Cash: The Bottom Line, The Environment, and Companies Can Profit from Waste Reduction," *Industry Week*, 5 December 1995, 53–55.

52. J.C. Ruthenburg, "Waste Minimization Pays Big Dividends at Red Spot Painting Co.," *American Paint & Coatings Journal* 4 (31 May 1993): 42.

53. J. Szekely & G. Trapaga, "From Villain to Hero (Materials Industry's Waste Recovery Efforts)," *Technology Review*, 1 January 1995.

54. M. Keller, "Many in Dark about Disposal of Fluorescents," *Minneapolis-St. Paul City Business*, 14 January 1994, 11.

55. C.A. Reeves & D.A. Bednar, "Defining Quality: Alternatives and Implications," *Academy of Management Review* 19 (1994): 419–445.

Chapter 8

1. Micro-Economic Policy Analysis Branch of Industry Canada, "Trends in Canada's Inward FDI." [Online] Available http://strategis.ic.gc.ca. Retrieved 10 April 2003.

2. Micro-Economic Policy Analysis Branch of Industry Canada, "Trends in Canada's Inward FDI." [Online] Available http://strategis.ic.gc.ca. Retrieved 10 April 2003.

3. Department of Commerce, National Trade Data Bank.

4. B. Emmott, "Multinational: Back in Fashion," *The Economist*, 27 March 1993, 58.

5. "Japan: Annual Fresh Deciduous Fruit Report," *U.S. Department of Agriculture Reports*, 17 September 1997.

6. "At Loggerheads: The Canada-U.S. Softwood Lumber Dispute." [Online] Available www.archives.CBC.ca. Accessed 8 March 2003.

7. M. du Bois, "EC Car Sales Plunged 11% in September," *The Wall Street Journal*, 8 October 1993, B4B.

8. World Trade Organization, "The Agreements: Anti-Dumping, Subsidies,

Safeguards, Contingencies, etc." [Online] Available www.wto.orgabout/ agmnts7.htm#subsidies, 24 January 1999.

9. Associated Press, "U.S. Takes Aim at Chinese Beetle in Trade Battle," *The Plain Dealer,* 12 September 1998, 2c.

10. C. Goldsmith, "After Trailing Boeing for Years, Airbus Aims for 50% of the Market," *The Wall Street Journal,* 16 March 1998, A1.

11. A. Tanzer, "Here's One Asian Industry That Isn't Declining: Software Piracy. It Is Costing American Companies Billions of Dollars in Lost Revenues," *Forbes,* 7 September 1998, 162.

12. Links to National Parliaments' websites, www.europarl.eu.int/natparl/en/ Linkspem.htm.

13. G. Smith & E. Malkin, "Mexico's Makeover," *Business Week,* 21 December 1998, 28; D. Blount, "Canada Favors Life after NAFTA," *Denver Post,* 22 November 1998, A10.

14. P. Behr, "NAFTAmath: A Texas-Sized Surge in Trade; Six Months after Treaty's Enactment, Booming Sales to Mexico Overshadow U.S. Job Losses," *Washington Post,* 21 August 1994, H1.

15. Declaration of Principles, Summit of the Americas, "Free Trade Area of the Americas." [Online] Available www. ftaa-alca.org/EnglishVersion/ miami_e.htm, 27 January 1999.

16. P. Dwyler, P. Engardio, Z. Schiller, & S. Reed, "Tearing Up Today's Organization Chart," *Business Week,* 18 November 1994, 80–83.

17. "Canada's Tilano Fresco Cracks U.S. Market," *CanadExport* 21, no. 6 (1 April 2003): 1–2.

18. A. Sundaram & J.S. Black, "The Environment and Internal-Organization of Multinational Enterprises," *Academy of Management Review* 17 (1992): 729–757.

19. H.S. James, Jr., & M. Weidenbaum, *When Businesses Cross International Borders: Strategic Alliances and Their Alternatives* (Westport, CT: Praeger Publishers, 1993).

20. "Canadian Wine in Sweden, Finland and Norway," *CanadExport* 21, no. 6 (1 April 2003): 1–6.

21. P. Fuhrman & M. Schuman, "Now We Are Our Own Masters," *Forbes,* 23 May 1994, 128–138.

22. L. Luxner, "Getting a Slice of the Onion Market," *The Atlanta Journal Constitution,* 30 December 1994, C1.

23. McDonald's Corporation, "McDonald's Reports Global Results (Part 2 of 2)." [Online] Available www.mcdonalds. com/whatsnew/pressrelease/ Press_Release15880642.html, 17 April 1998; B. McDowall, "The Global Market Challenge," *Restaurants & Institutions,* 1 November 1994, 52.

24. "Company Profile," Fuji Xerox. [Online] Available www.fujixerox.co.jp/ eng/company/profile.html, 14 September 2001.

25. A. Choi, "International: GM Seeds Grow Nicely in Eastern Europe, Strategy of Starting Small and Expanding Pays Off," *The Wall Street Journal,* 3 May 1995, A11.

26. B.R. Schlender, "How Toshiba Makes Alliances Work," *Fortune,* 4 October 1993, 116–120.

27. B.A. Walters, S. Peters, & G.G. Dess, "Strategic Alliances and Joint Ventures: Making Them Work," *Business Horizons,* July–August 1994, 5–10.

28. W. Beaver, "Volkswagen's American Assembly Plant: Fahrvernugen Was Not Enough," *Business Horizons,* 11 November 1992, 19.

29. M.W. Hordes, J.A. Clancy, & J. Baddaley, "A Primer for Global Start-Ups," *Academy of Management Executive,* May 1995, 7–11.

30. B.M. Oviatt & P. P. McDougall, "Toward a Theory of International New Ventures," *Journal of International Business Studies,* Spring 1994, 45–64.

31. L. Brokaw, "Foreign Affairs: Start-Ups Such as National Gyp-Chipper Are Proving That, When You Move from Doing Business Next Door to Doing Business Around the World, the Same Basic Rules Still Apply," *Inc.,* 1 November 1990, 92.

32. *Local Authority.* Beverage World, 15 October 2000, 58–60.

33. B. Ortega, "Foreign Forays: Penney Pushes Abroad in Unusually Big Way as It Pursues Growth," *The Wall Street Journal,* 1 February 1994, A1.

34. A. Snyder, "European Expansion: How to Shop Around," *Management Review,* 1 November 1993, 16.

35. K.D. Miller, "A Framework for Integrated Risk Management in International Business," *Journal of International Business Studies,* 2nd Quarter 1992, 311.

36. M. Farley, "Foreign Investors in China Feel Cold Slap of Reality," *Los Angeles Times,* 27 December 1994, A-1.

37. G. Anping, "Old Contract Laws Need Repair to Fit into New Reality," *China Daily,* 7 May 1994, 4-1.

38. F. Bleakley, "High School Seniors Mind Their Business and Even Profit by It: Teens Learn by Their Goofs in Import-Export World; Racy Towels Go Too Far," *The Wall Street Journal,* 20 June 1995, A1.

39. G. Hofstede, "The Cultural Relativity of the Quality of Life Concept," *Academy of Management Review* 9 (1984): 389–398; G. Hofstede, "The Cultural Relativity of Organizational Practices and Theories," *Journal of International Business Studies,* Fall 1983, 75–89; G. Hofstede, "The Interaction Between National and Organizational Value Systems," *Journal of Management Studies,* July 1985, 347–357.

40. R. Hodgetts, "A Conversation with Geert Hofstede," *Organizational Dynamics,* Spring 1993, 53–61.

41. M. Janssens, J.M. Brett, F.J. Smith, "Confirmatory Cross-Cultural Research: Testing the Viability of a Corporation-Wide Safety Policy," *Academy of Management Journal* 38 (1995): 364–382.

42. R.G. Linowes, "The Japanese Manager's Traumatic Entry into the United States: Understanding the American-Japanese Cultural Divide," *Academy of Management Executive* 7 (1993): 21–40.

43. J.S. Black, M. Mendenhall, & G. Oddou, "Toward a Comprehensive Model of International Adjustment: An Integration of Multiple Theoretical Perspectives," *Academy of Management Journal* 16 (1991): 291–317; R.L. Tung, "American Expatriates Abroad: From Neophytes to Cosmopolitans," *Columbia Journal of World Business,* 22 June 1998, 125.

44. L. Copeland & L. Griggs, *Going International* (New York: Random House, 1985).

45. R.A. Swaak, "Expatriate Failures: Too Many, Too Much Cost, Too Little Planning," *Compensation and Benefits Review* 27, no. 6 (21 November 1995): 47.

46. J.S. Black & M. Mendenhall, "Cross-Cultural Training Effectiveness: A Review and Theoretical Framework for Future Research," *Academy of Management Review* 15 (1990): 113–136.

47. W. Arthur, Jr., & W. Bennett, Jr., "The International Assignee: The Relative Importance of Factors Perceived to

Contribute to Success," *Personnel Psychology* 48 (1995): 99–114.

48. R. Donkin, "Recruitment: Overseas Gravy Train May Be Running Out of Steam—Preparing Expatriate Packages Is Challenging the Expertise of Human Resource Management," *The Financial Times,* 30 November 1994, 10.

Chapter 9

1. J. Barney, "Firm Resources and Sustained Competitive Advantage," *Journal of Management* 17 (1991): 99–120; J. Barney, "Looking Inside for Competitive Advantage," *Academy of Management Executive* 9 (1995): 49–61.

2. S. Hart & C. Banbury, "How Strategy-Making Processes Can Make a Difference," *Strategic Management Journal* 15 (1994): 251–269.

3. R.A. Burgelman, "Fading Memories: A Process Theory of Strategic Business Exit in Dynamic Environments," *Administrative Science Quarterly,* 39 (1994): 24–56; R.A. Burgelman & A.S. Grove, "Strategic Dissonance," *California Management Review* 38 (1996): 8–28.

4. M. Robichaux, "The Pizza-Pan-Size Dishes Fly Off the Shelves; Prices Plunge," *The Wall Street Journal Interactive Edition,* 7 November 1996.

5. A. Fiegenbaum, S. Hart, & D. Schendel, "Strategic Reference Point Theory," *Strategic Management Journal* 17 (1996): 219–235.

6. S. Alsop, "Apple's Next Move Misses the Mark," *Fortune,* 3 February 1997.

7. D.J. Collis, "Research Note: How Valuable Are Organizational Capabilities?" *Strategic Management Journal* 15 (1994): 143–152.

8. A. Fiegenbaum & H. Thomas, "Strategic Groups as Reference Groups: Theory, Modeling and Empirical Examination of Industry and Competitive Strategy," *Strategic Management Journal* 16 (1995): 461–476.

9. R.K. Reger & A.S. Huff, "Strategic Groups: A Cognitive Perspective," *Strategic Management Journal* 14 (1993): 103–124.

10. W.B. Werther, Jr. & J.L. Kerr, "The Shifting Sands of Competitive Advantage," *Business Horizons,* May-June 1995, 11–17.

11. W.B. Werther, Jr. & J.L. Kerr, "The Shifting Sands of Competitive Advantage," *Business Horizons,* May-June 1995, 11–17.

12. M. Lubatkin, "Value-Creating Mergers: Fact or Folklore?" *Academy of Management Executive,* 2 (1988): 295–302; M. Lubatkin & S. Chatterjee, "Extending Modern Portfolio Theory into the Domain of Corporate Diversification: Does It Apply?" *Academy of Management Journal,* 37 (1994): 109–136; M.H. Lubatkin & P.J. Lane, "Psst . . . The Merger Mavens Still Have It Wrong!" *Academy of Management Executive* 10 (1996): 21–39.

13. J.A. Pearce, II, "Selecting Among Alternative Grand Strategies," *California Management Review,* Spring 1982, 23–31.

14. J. Hayes, "Acquisition Is Fine, but Organic Growth Is Better," *Forbes,* 30 December 1996, 52–55.

15. P. Damas, "Danzas Refines 'Core Carriers' Policy," *American Shipper,* August 1996, 39–40.

16. J.A. Pearce, II, "Retrenchment Remains the Foundation of Business Turnaround," *Strategic Management Journal* 15 (1994): 407–417.

17. S. Silcoff, "Moore CEO's Exit 'Shocks' Market: Shares Fall 11%: Robert Burton Says 'Objectives Have Been Realized,' *Financial Post,* 10 December 2002, FP5.

18. "Business Forms Maker Moore Corp. Reports Big Q2 Earning Turnaround," *Financial Post,* 24 July 2002.

19. "Moore Swings Back to Profit in Third Quarter," *Financial Post,* 24 October 2002, FP2.

20. Autobytel website, "Customer Endorsements." [Online] Available www.autobytel.com, 8 March 1997.

21. S. Kichen, "Cruising the Internet (Car-Shopping on the Internet)," *Forbes,* 24 March 1997, 198.

22. S. Muto, "Firms Battle for On-Line Car Buyers," *The Wall Street Journal,* 25 February 1998, A1.

23. E. Tanouye & R. Langreth, "Top Firms Must Prepare for Onslaught of Generics," *The Wall Street Journal Interactive Edition,* 12 August 1997.

24. R.E. Miles & C.C. Snow, *Organizational Strategy, Structure, and Process* (New York: McGraw-Hill, 1978); S. Zahra & J.A. Pearce, "Research Evidence on the Miles-Snow Typology," *Journal of Management* 16 (1990): 751–768; W.L. James & K.J. Hatten, "Further Evidence on the Validity of the Self Typing Paragraph Approach: Miles and Snow Strategic Archetypes in Banking," *Strategic Management Journal* 16 (1995): 161–168.

25. G.G. Knecht, "Small Book Publisher Turns Controversies into Best Sellers," *The Wall Street Journal Interactive Edition,* 6 March 1997.

26. E. Ramstad, "Using a Personal Approach, Many Tiny PC Firms Thrive," *The Wall Street Journal Interactive Edition,* 8 January 1997.

27. R. Gibson & C.Y. Coleman, "How Burger King Emerged as a Threat to McDonald's," *The Wall Street Journal Interactive Edition,* 27 February 1997.

28. R. Gibson & C.Y. Coleman, "How Burger King Emerged as a Threat to McDonald's," *The Wall Street Journal Interactive Edition,* 27 February 1997.

29. M. Chen, "Competitor Analysis and Interfirm Rivalry: Toward a Theoretical Integration," *Academy of Management Review* 21 (1996): 100–134; J.C. Baum & H.J. Korn, "Competitive Dynamics of Interfirm Rivalry," *Academy of Management Journal* 39 (1996): 255–291.

30. M. Chen, "Competitor Analysis and Interfirm Rivalry: Toward a Theoretical Integration," *Academy of Management Review* 21 (1996): 100–134.

31. M. Stopa, "Wendy's New Fashioned Growth: Buy Hardee's," *Crain's Detroit Business,* 21 October 1996.

32. N. Shirouzu, "Though Japan Nears Saturation, Burger King Turns Up the Heat," *The Wall Street Journal Interactive Edition,* 31 January 1997.

33. R. Narisetti, "P&G Diaper-Patent Trial Expected to Begin Monday," *The Wall Street Journal Interactive Edition,* 3 February 1997.

34. R. Narisetti, "P&G Diaper-Patent Trial Expected to Begin Monday," *The Wall Street Journal Interactive Edition,* 3 February 1997.

35. J.C. Baum & H.J. Korn, "Competitive Dynamics of Interfirm Rivalry," *Academy of Management Journal* 39 (1996): 255–291.

36. L. Gomes, "Apple May Sell Key Units to Further Reduce Costs," *The Wall Street Journal Interactive Edition,* 3 February 1997.

37. G.T. Lumpkin & G.G. Dess, "Clarifying the Entrepreneurial Orientation Construct and Linking It to Performance," *Academy of Management Review* 21 (1996): 135–172.

38. R.B. Lieber, "Beating the Odds," *Fortune,* 31 March 1997, 82–90.

39. D. Miller & P. Friesen, "Archetypes of Strategy Formulation," *Management Science* 24 (1978): 921–933.

40. N. Venkatraman, "Strategic Orientation of Business Enterprises: The Construct, Dimensionality, and Measurement," *Management Science,* 35 (1989): 942–962.

41. Z. Moukheiber, "Cybercops," *Forbes,* 10 March 1997, 170–172.

Chapter 10

1. B. Richards, "Ad Business for Blimps Rises Because of One Bright Idea," *The Wall Street Journal Interactive,* 14 October 1997.

2. T.M. Amabile, R. Conti, H. Coon, J. Lazenby, & M. Herron, "Assessing the Work Environment for Creativity," *Academy of Management Journal* 39 (1996): 1154–1184.

3. Canada's Innovation Strategy. National Summit on Innovation and Learning. Government of Canada. [Online] Available www.innovationstrategy.gc.ca. Retrieved 9 April 2003.

4. P. Anderson & M.L. Tushman, "Managing Through Cycles of Technological Change," *Research/Technology Management,* May/June 1991, 26–31.

5. R.N. Foster, *Innovation: The Attacker's Advantage* (New York: Summit, 1986).

6. iComp Index 2.0. Intel Corporation website. [Online] Available www.intel.com/procs/performance/icomp/index.htm, 5 December 1997.

7. J. Burke, *The Day the Universe Changed* (Boston: Little, Brown, and Company, 1985).

8. W. Gibson, "The Thin Web Line," *Canadian Business* 75, no. 19 (2003): 85–86.

9. M.L. Tushman, P.C. Anderson, & C. O'Reilly, "Technology Cycles, Innovation Streams, and Ambidextrous Organizations: Organization Renewal Through Innovation Streams and Strategic Change," in *Managing Strategic Innovation and Change,* eds. M.L. Tushman & P. Anderson (1997), 3–23.

10. "Pony Express," Encyclopedia Britannica Online. [Online] Available www.eb.com:180/bol/topic?eu= 62367&sctn=1, 6 March 1999.

11. J.R. Aldern, "The Victorian Internet: The Remarkable Story of the Telegraph and the Nineteenth Century's On-Line Pioneers (Review)," *Smithsonian,* 1 January 1999.

12. E. Schlossberg, *Interactive Excellence: Defining and Developing New Standards for the Twenty-First Century* (New York: Ballantine, 1998).

13. W. Abernathy & J. Utterback, "Patterns of Industrial Innovation," *Technology Review,* 2 (1978): 40–47.

14. K.M. Eisenhardt, "Accelerating Adaptive Processes: Product Innovation in the Global Computer Industry," *Administrative Science Quarterly* 40 (1995): 84–110.

15. K.M. Eisenhardt, "Accelerating Adaptive Processes: Product Innovation in the Global Computer Industry," *Administrative Science Quarterly* 40 (1995): 84–110.

16. R. Gibson, "Starbucks Plans to Test a Paper Cup that Insulates Hands from Hot Coffee," *The Interactive Wall Street Journal,* 22 February 1999; S. Kravetz, "These People Search for a Cup that Suits the Coffee It Holds," *The Wall Street Journal,* 24 March 1998, A1.

17. F. Yanor, "No Friend of Mines," *Canadian Business* 75, no. 19 (14 October 2003): 89–90.

18. R. Winslow, "Atomic Speed: Utility Cuts Red Tape, Builds Nuclear Plant Almost on Schedule," *The Wall Street Journal,* 22 February 1984.

19. L. Kraar, "25 Who Help the U.S. Win: Innovators Everywhere Are Generating Ideas to Make America a Stronger Competitor. They Range from a Boss Who Demands the Impossible to a Mathematician with a Mop," *Fortune,* 22 March 1991.

20. M.W. Lawless & P.C. Anderson, "Generational Technological Change: Effects of Innovation and Local Rivalry on Performance," *Academy of Management Journal* 39 (1996): 1185–1217.

21. S. Anderson & M. Uzumeri, "Managing Product Families: The Case of the Sony Walkman," *Research Policy* 24 (1995): 761–782.

22. P. Ponticel, "Integrated Product Process Development," *Automotive Engineering,* 1 October 1996.

23. T. Parker, "Avon's Retooling to Include Fewer Products, Retail Stores," *The Wall Street Journal,* 27 October 1997.

24. P. Strebel, "Choosing the Right Change Path," *California Management Review,* Winter 1994, 29–51.

25. K. Lewin, *Field Theory in Social Science: Selected Theoretical Papers* (New York: Harper & Brothers, 1951).

26. W. Weitzel & E. Jonsson, "Reversing the Downward Spiral: Lessons from W.T. Grant and Sears Roebuck," *Academy of Management Executive* 5 (1991): 7–22.

27. W. Weitzel & E. Jonsson, "Reversing the Downward Spiral: Lessons from W.T. Grant and Sears Roebuck," *Academy of Management Executive* 5 (1991): 7–22.

28. Tom McFeat & John McHutchion, "The Nortel Headache (or the Pain of Watching $397 Billion Disappear)," CBC News Online [Online] Available www.cbc.ca, accessed 27 September 2002.

29. Tom McFeat, "Nortel – The Rise and Fall of Canada's Most Watched Stock," CBC News In Depth Backgrounder [Online] Available www.cbc.ca, accessed 16 September 2002.

30. Douglas Hunter, "Nortel's Slide Toward Penny-Stock Status," *The Financial Post,* 15 October 2002, FP1, FP6.

31. K. Lewin, *Field Theory in Social Science: Selected Theoretical Papers* (New York: Harper & Brothers, 1951).

32. J. Bolt, "The Acadia Advantage," in *Ubiquitous Computing,* ed. D.G. Brown. (Bolton, MA: Anker Publishing Company, 2003), 117–127.

33. R.H. Schaffer & H.A. Thomson, J.D., "Successful Change Programs Begin with Results," *Harvard Business Review on Change* (Boston: Harvard Business School Publishing, 1998), 189–213.

34. H.A. Thomson. Personal phone conversation, 9 April 2003.

35. R.N. Ashkenas & T.D. Jick, "From Dialogue to Action in GE Work-Out: Developmental Learning in a Change Process," in *Research in Organizational Change and Development,* Vol. 6, eds. W.A. Pasmore & R.W. Woodman (Greenwhich, CT: JAI Press, 1992), 267–287.

36. T. Stewart, "GE Keeps Those Ideas Coming," *Fortune,* 12 August 1991, 40.

37. J.D. Duck, "Managing Change: The Art of Balancing," *Harvard Business Review on Change* (Boston: Harvard Business School Publishing, 1998), 55–81.

38. L. Landro, "Viacom Names Team to Consolidate Assets of Paramount and Blockbuster," *The Wall Street Journal,* 16 March 1994, B4.

39. W.J. Rothwell, R. Sullivan, & G.M. McLean, *Practicing Organizational Development: A Guide for Consultants* (San Diego, CA: Pfeiffer & Company, 1995).

40. W.J. Rothwell, R. Sullivan, & G.M. McLean, *Practicing Organizational Development: A Guide for Consultants* (San Diego, CA: Pfeiffer & Company, 1995).

41. R.N. Ashkenas & T.D. Jick, "From Dialogue to Action in GE Work-Out: Developmental Learning in a Change Process," in *Research in Organizational Change and Development,* Vol. 6, eds. W.A. Pasmore & R.W. Woodman (Greenwich, CT: JAI Press, 1992), 267–287.

42. J. Ford & L.W. Ford, "The Role of Conversations in Producing Intentional Change in Organizations," *Academy of Management Review* 20 (1995): 541–570.

43. J.P. Kotter, "Leading Change: Why Transformation Efforts Fail," *Harvard Business Review* 73, no. 2 (March-April 1995): 59.

44. M. Hammer & S.A. Stanton, "The Pioneering Consultants Who Touched Off the Reengineering Movement Are Urging a New Imperative: Getting Top Managers to Stop and Reassess Where Their Companies Are Headed," *Fortune,* 24 November 1997, 291–296.

Chapter 11

1. "Reynolds Metals Announces Organizational and Management Changes," Reynolds Metals Press Release. [Online] Available www.rmc.com/pressrel/reorg0397.html, 27 March 1997.

2. J.G. March & H.A. Simon, *Organizations* (New York: John Wiley & Sons, 1958).

3. "Outline of Principal Operations," Sony Corporation. [Online] Available www.sony.com/SCA/outline.html, 4 November 2001.

4. "Business Segments," Bayer Group. [Online] Available www.bayer.com/en/unternehmen/arbeitsgebiete/index.html, 4 November 2001.

5. H. Mintzberg, *Structure in Fives: Designing Effective Organizations.* New York: Prentice Hall, 1992.

6. General Electric's Annual Report. [Online] Available www.ge.com/annual00/financial/images/GEannual00_financials.pdf, November 3, 2001.

7. L.R. Burns, "Adoption and Abandonment of Matrix Management Programs: Effects of Organizational Characteristics and Interorganizational Networks," *Academy of Management Journal* 36 (1993): 106–138.

8. H. Fayol, *General and Industrial Management, translated by Constance Storrs* (London: Pitman Publishing, 1949).

9. M. Weber, *The Theory of Social and Economic Organization,* translated and edited by A.M. Henderson & T. Parsons (New York: The Free Press, 1947).

10. H. Fayol, *General and Industrial Management,* translated by Constance Storrs (London: Pitman Publishing, 1949).

11. E.E. Lawler, S.A. Mohrman, & G.E. Ledford, *Creating High Performance Organizations: Practices and Results of Employee Involvement and Quality Management in Fortune 1000 Companies* (San Francisco: Jossey-Bass, 1995).

12. C. Quintanilla, "Food: Come and Get It! Drive-Throughs Upgrade Services," *The Wall Street Journal,* 5 May 1994.

13. R.W. Griffin, *Task Design* (Glenview, IL: Scott, Foresman, 1982).

14. F. Herzberg, *Work and the Nature of Man* (Cleveland, OH: World Press, 1966).

15. T. Burns & G.M. Stalker, *The Management of Innovation* (London: Tavistock, 1961).

16. M. Hammer & J. Champy, *Reengineering the Corporation: A Manifesto for Business Revolution* (New York: HarperBusiness, 1993).

17. M. Hammer & J. Champy, *Reengineering the Corporation: A Manifesto for Business Revolution* (New York: HarperBusiness, 1993).

18. J.D. Thompson, *Organizations in Action* (New York: McGraw-Hill, 1967).

19. J.B. White, "'Next Big Thing': Re-Engineering Gurus Take Steps to Remodel Their Stalling Vehicles," *The Wall Street Journal Interactive Edition,* 26 November 1996.

20. G.M. Spreitzer, "Individual Empowerment in the Workplace: Dimensions, Measurement, and Validation," *Academy of Management Journal* 38 (1995): 1442–1465.

21. D.A. Morand, "The Role of Behavioral Formality and Informality in the Enactment of Bureaucratic Versus Organic Organizations," *Academy of Management Journal,* 20 (1995): 831–872.

22. K.A. Edelman, "Take Down the Walls!" *Across the Board* 34 (1 March 1997).

23. "Designing the Ever-Changing Workplace," *Architectural Record,* September 1995, 32–37.

24. R. Nilson, "Virtual Corporations: From the Rolling Stones to IBM to Start-ups, 'Outsourcing' Is the Way to Go," *Sunday Telegram,* 30 July 1995.

25. G.G. Dess, A.M.A. Rasheed, K.J. McLaughlin, & R.L. Priem, "The New Corporate Architecture," *Academy of Management Executive* 9 (1995): 7–18.

26. "Building the CEO: Robert Eaton Has Parlayed Teamwork and Technology to Turn a Troubled Auto," *Industry Week,* 16 September 1996, 10–14.

27. H. Voss, "Virtual Organizations: The Future Is Now," *Strategy & Leadership,* 17 July 1996.

28. C.C. Snow, R.E. Miles, & H.J. Coleman, Jr., "Managing 21st Century Network Organizations," *Organizational Dynamics,* Winter 1992, 5–20.

29. J.H. Sheridan, "The Agile Web: A Model for the Future?" *Industry Week,* 4 March 1996.

30. D. Ulrich & S. Kerr, "Creating the Boundaryless Organization: The Radical Reconstruction of Organization Capabilities," *Planning Review,* September-October 1995, 41–45.

31. R. Ashkenas, D. Ulrich, T. Jick, & S. Kerr, *The Boundaryless Organization: Breaking the Chains of Organizational Structure* (San Francisco: Jossey-Bass, 1995).

32. G.G. Dess, A.M.A. Rasheed, K.J. McLaughlin, & R.L. Priem, "The New Corporate Architecture," *Academy of Management Executive* 9 (1995): 7–18.

Chapter 12

1. J.R. Katzenback & D.K. Smith, *The Wisdom of Teams* (Boston: Harvard Business School Press, 1993).

2. "Born-Again Basket Case," *Canadian Business* 66, no. 5 (May 1993): 38–44.

3. S.E. Gross, *Compensation for Teams* (New York: American Management Association, 1995). B.L. Kirkman & B. Rosen, "Beyond Self-Management: Antecedents and Consequences of Team Empowerment," *Academy of Management Journal* 42 (1999): 58–74; G. Stock & T.M. Hout, *Competing Against Time* (New York: Free Press, 1990); S.C. Wheelwright & K.B. Clark, *Revolutionizing New Product Development* (New York: Free Press, 1992).

4. M. Selz, "Testing Self-Managed Teams, Entrepreneur Hopes to Lose Job," *The Wall Street Journal,* 11 January 1994, B1.

5. R.D. Banker, J.M. Field, R.G. Schroeder, & K.K. Sinha, "Impact of Work Teams on Manufacturing Performance: A Longitudinal Field Study," *Academy of Management Journal* 39 (1996): 867–890.

6. R.S. Wellins, W.C. Byham, & G.R. Dixon, *Inside Teams* (San Francisco: Jossey-Bass Publishers, 1994).

7. C. Fishman, "Whole Foods Is All Teams," *Fast Company,* April 1996, 103.

8. "Beating the Joneses (Learning What the Competition Is Doing)," *Industry Week* 1 (7 December 1998): 27.

9. G. Stalk & T.M. Hout, *Competing Against Time: How Time-Based Competition Is Reshaping Global Markets* (New York: The Free Press, 1990).

10. H.K. Bowen, K.B. Clark, C.A. Holloway, & S.C. Wheelwright, *The Perpetual Enterprise Machine* (New York: Oxford Press, 1994).

11. J.L. Cordery, W.S. Mueller, & L.M. Smith, "Attitudinal and Behavioral Effects of Autonomous Group Working: A Longitudinal Field Study," *Academy of Management Journal* 34 (1991): 464–476; T.D. Wall, N.J. Kemp, P.R. Jackson, & C.W. Clegg, "Outcomes of Autonomous Workgroups: A Longterm Field Experiment," *Academy of Management Journal* 29 (1986): 280–304.

12. J. Cooper, "The Friendly Factor," *Canadian Grocer* 111, no. 7 (September 1997): 14–17.

13. R.S. Wellins, W.C. Byham, & G.R. Dixon, *Inside Teams* (San Francisco: Jossey-Bass Publishers, 1994).

14. J. Hoerr, "The Payoff from Teamwork— The Gains in Quality Are Substantial— So Why Isn't It Spreading Faster?" *Business Week,* 10 July 1989, 56.

15. J. George, "Extrinsic and Intrinsic Origins of Perceived Social Loafing in Organizations," *Academy of Management Journal* 35 (1992): 191–202.

16. T.T. Baldwin, M.D. Bedell, & J.L. Johnson, "The Social Fabric of a Team-Based M.B.A. Program: Network Effects on Student Satisfaction and Performance," *Academy of Management Journal* 40 (1997): 1369–1397.

17. C. Joinson, "Teams at Work," *HRMagazine,* 1 May 1999, 30.

18. R. Wageman, "Critical Success Factors for Creating Superb Self-Managing Teams," *Organizational Dynamics* 26, no. 1 (1997): 49–61.

19. M.A. Cusumano, "How Microsoft Makes Large Teams Work Like Small Teams," *Sloan Management Review* 39, no. 1 (Fall 1997): 9–20.

20. R.T. King, Jr., "Jeans Therapy: Levi's Factory Workers Are Assigned to Teams, and Morale Takes a Hit— Infighting Rises, Productivity Falls as Employees Miss the Piecework System— 'It's Not the Same Company,'" *The Wall Street Journal,* 20 May 1998, A1.

21. R.T. King, Jr., "Jeans Therapy: Levi's Factory Workers Are Assigned to Teams, and Morale Takes a Hit— Infighting Rises, Productivity Falls as Employees Miss the Piecework System— 'It's Not the Same Company,'" *The Wall Street Journal,* 20 May 1998, A1.

22. M. Curtius, "There Is No 'I' in 'Team'—And Maybe No Point, Either: The Trend Continues but Doesn't Always Succeed. Finding the Proper Structure, Motivating Employees and Getting Managers Out of the Way Can Sometimes Help," *Los Angeles Times,* 24 February 1997, D25.

23. R.T. King, Jr., "Jeans Therapy: Levi's Factory Workers Are Assigned to Teams, and Morale Takes a Hit— Infighting Rises, Productivity Falls as Employees Miss the Piecework System— 'It's Not the Same Company,'" *The Wall Street Journal,* 20 May 1998, A1.

24. B.L. Kirkman & B. Rosen, "Beyond Self-Management: Antecedents and Consequences of Team Empowerment," *Academy of Management Journal* 42 (1999): 58–74.

25. M. Curtius, "There Is No 'I' in 'Team'—And Maybe No Point, Either: The Trend Continues but Doesn't Always Succeed. Finding the Proper Structure, Motivating Employees and Getting Managers Out of the Way Can Sometimes Help," *Los Angeles Times,* 24 February 1997, D25.

26. "Now Everyone Can Be a Boss," *Canadian Business* 65, no. 5 (May 1994): 48–50; J. Terrett, "Honeywell Wins NQI's Quality Trophy," *Plant* 59, no. 17 (27 November 2000).

27. B.L. Kirkman & B. Rosen, "Beyond Self-Management: Antecedents and Consequences of Team Empowerment," *Academy of Management Journal* 42 (1999): 58–74.

28. K. Kelly, "Managing Workers Is Tough Enough in Theory. When Human Nature Enters the Picture, It's Worse," *Business Week,* 21 October 1996, 32.

29. S. Easton & G. Porter, "Selecting the Right Team Structure to Work in Your Organization," in *Handbook of Best Practices for Teams,* Volume 1, ed. Glenn M. Parker (Amherst, MA: Irwin, 1996).

30. D. Stafford, "Hotel Lets Its Workers 'Own' Their Duties: Ritz-Carlton, Kansas City, Tries a Program That Emphasizes Teamwork, Self-Direction," *The Kansas City Star,* 6 February 1996, D1.

31. M. Maynard, "Saturn Workers May Dump Unique Contract," *USA Today,* 17 February 1998, 03B.

32. R.J. Recardo, D. Wade, C.A. Mention, & J. Jolly, *Teams* (Houston: Gulf Publishing Company, 1996).

33. D.R. Denison, S.L. Hart, & J.A. Kahn, "From Chimneys to Cross-Functional Teams: Developing and Validating a Diagnostic Model," *Academy of Management Journal* 39, no. 4 (1996): 1005–1023.

34. A.M. Townsend, S.M. DeMarie, & A.R. Hendrickson, "Virtual Teams: Technology and the Workplace of the Future," *Academy of Management Executive* 13, no. 3 (1998): 17–29.

35. A.M. Townsend, S.M. DeMarie, & A.R. Hendrickson, "Are You Ready for Virtual Teams?" *HRMagazine* 41, no. 9 (1996): 122–126.

36. Selah School District website, "The Boeing 777." [Online] Available www.selah.wednet.edu, 9 September 1998.

37. R.S. Wellins, W.C. Byham, & G.R. Dixon, *Inside Teams* (San Francisco: Jossey-Bass Publishers, 1994).

38. A.M. Townsend, S.M. DeMarie, & A.R. Hendrickson, "Virtual Teams: Technology and the Workplace of the Future," *Academy of Management Executive* 13, no. 3 (1998): 17–29.

39. R. Katz, "The Effects of Group Longevity on Project Communication and Performance," *Administrative Science Quarterly* 27 (1982): 245–282.

40. D. Mankin, S.G. Cohen, & T.K. Bikson, T*eams and Technology: Fulfilling the Promise of the New Organization* (Boston: Harvard Business School Press, 1996).

41. L. Holpp & H.P. Phillips, "When Is a Team Its Own Worst Enemy?" *Training,* 1 September 1995, 71.

42. S. Asche, "Opinions and Social Pressure," *Scientific America* 193 (1995): 31–35.

43. S.G. Cohen, G.E. Ledford, & G.M. Spreitzer, "A Predictive Model of Self-Managing Work Team Effectiveness," *Human Relations* 49, no. 5 (1996): 643–676.

44. L. Clarke, "Changing Work Systems, Changing Social Relations," *Relations Industrielles* 52, no. 4 (1997): 839–862.

45. K. Bettenhausen & J.K. Murnighan, "The Emergence of Norms in Competitive Decision-Making Groups," *Administrative Science Quarterly* 30 (1985): 350–372.

46. M.E. Shaw, *Group Dynamics* (New York: McGraw-Hill, 1981).

47. S.E. Jackson, "The Consequences of Diversity in Multidisciplinary Work Teams," in *Handbook of Work Group Psychology*, ed. Michael A. West (Chichester, England: Wiley, 1996).

48. A.M. Isen & R.A. Baron, "Positive Affect as a Factor in Organizational Behavior," in *Research in Organizational Behavior* 13, eds. L.L. Cummings & B.M. Staw (Greenwich, CT: JAI Press, 1991), 1–53.

49. C.R. Evans & K.L. Dion, "Group Cohesion and Performance: A Meta Analysis," *Small Group Research* 22, no. 2 (1991): 175–186.

50. R. Stankiewicsz, "The Effectiveness of Research Groups in Six Countries," in *Scientific Productivity*, ed. F.M. Andrews (Cambridge: Cambridge University Press, 1979), 191–221.

51. F. Rees, *Teamwork from Start to Finish* (San Francisco: Jossey-Bass, 1997).

52. S.M. Gully, D.S. Devine, & D.J. Whitney, "A Meta-Analysis of Cohesion and Performance: Effects of Level of Analysis and Task Interdependence," *Small Group Research* 26, no. 4 (1995): 497–520.

53. E. Matson, "Four Rules for Fast Teams," *Fast Company*, August 1996, 87.

54. F. Tschan & M.V. Cranach, "Group Task Structure, Processes and Outcomes," in *Handbook of Work Group Psychology*, ed. Michael A. West (Chichester, England: Wiley, 1996).

55. D.E. Yeatts & C. Hyten, *High Performance Self Managed Teams* (Thousand Oaks, CA: Sage Publications, 1998).

56. D.E. Yeatts & C. Hyten, *High Performance Self Managed Teams* (Thousand Oaks, CA: Sage Publications, 1998).

57. D.S. Kezsbom, "Re-Opening Pandora's Box: Sources of Project Team Conflict in the '90s," *Industrial Engineering* 24, no. 5 (1992): 54–59.

58. A.C. Amason, W.A. Hochwarter, & K.R. Thompson, "Conflict: An Important Dimension in Successful Management Teams," *Organizational Dynamics* 24 (1995): 20.

59. A.C. Amason, "Distinguishing the Effects of Functional and Dysfunctional Conflict on Strategic Decision Making: Resolving a Paradox for Top Management Teams," *Academy of Management Journal* 39, no. 1 (1996): 123–148.

60. K.M. Eisenhardt, J.L. Kahwajy, & L.J. Bourgeois, "How Management Teams Can Have a Good Fight," *Harvard Business Review*, July-August 1997, 77–85.

61. K.M. Eisenhardt, J.L. Kahwajy, & L.J. Bourgeois, "How Management Teams Can Have a Good Fight," *Harvard Business Review*, July-August 1997, 77–85.

62. C. Nemeth & P. Owens, "Making Work Groups More Effective: The Value of Minority Dissent," in *Handbook of Work Group Psychology*, ed. Michael A. West (Chichester, England: Wiley, 1996).

63. J.M. Levin & R.L. Moreland, "Progress in Small Group Research," *Annual Review of Psychology* 9 (1990): 72–78; S.E. Jackson, "Team Composition in Organizational Settings: Issues in Managing a Diverse Work Force," in *Group Processes and Productivity*, eds. S. Worchel, W. Wood, & J. Simpson (Beverly Hills, CA: Sage, 1992).

64. K.M. Eisenhardt, J.L. Kahwajy, & L. Bourgeois, III, "How Management Teams Can Have a Good Fight," *Harvard Business Review* 75, no. 4 (July-August 1997): 77–87.

65. B.W. Tuckman, "Development Sequence in Small Groups," *Psychological Bulletin* 63, no. 6 (1965): 384–399.

66. S.E. Gross, *Compensation for Teams* (New York: American Management Association, 1995).

67. J.F. McGrew, J.G. Bilotta, & J.M. Deeney, "Software Team Formation and Decay: Extending the Standard Model for Small Groups," *Small Group Research* 30, no. 2 (1999): 209–234.

68. J.F. McGrew, J.G. Bilotta, & J.M. Deeney, "Software Team Formation and Decay: Extending the Standard Model for Small Groups," *Small Group Research* 30, no. 2 (1999): 209–234.

69. J. Case, "What the Experts Forgot to Mention: Management Teams Create New Difficulties, But Succeed for Xel Communication," *Inc.*, 1 September 1993, 66.

70. J.R. Hackman, "The Psychology of Self-Management in Organizations," in *Psychology and Work: Productivity, Change, and Employment*, eds. M.S. Pallak, & R. Perloff (Washington DC: American Psychological Association, 85–136).

71. O. Leary-Kelly, J.J. Martocchio, & D.D. Frink, "A Review of the Influence of Group Goals on Group Performance," *Academy of Management Journal* 37, no. 5 (1994): 1285–1301.

72. Nucor Homepage, "The Nucor Story." [Online] Available www.nucor.com/story.htm, 10 May 1999.

73. A. Zander, "The Origins and Consequences of Group Goals," in *Retrospections on Social Psychology*, ed. L. Festinger (New York: Oxford University Press, 1980), 205–235.

74. M. Erez & A. Somech, "Is Group Productivity Loss the Rule or the Exception? Effects of Culture and Group-Based Motivation," *Academy of Management Journal* 39, no. 6 (1996): 1513–1537.

75. S. Sherman, "Stretch Goals: The Dark Side of Asking for Miracles," *Fortune*, 13 November 1995.

76. S. Tully, "So, Mr. Bossidy, We Know You Can Cut. Now Show Us How to Grow," *Fortune*, 21 August 1995, 70.

77. K.R. Thompson, W.A. Hochwarter, & N.J. Mathys, "Stretch Targets: What Makes Them Effective?" *Academy of Management Executive* 11, no. 3 (1997): 48–60.

78. S. Sherman, "Stretch Goals: The Dark Side of Asking for Miracles," *Fortune*, 13 November 1995.

79. S. Shellenbarger, "Are Saner Workloads the Unexpected Key to More Productivity?" *The Wall Street Journal*, 10 March 1999, B1.

80. C. Ashton, "KI Pembroke Succeeds Through Teamwork, Empowerment and Rewards," *Human Resource Management International Digest* 8, no. 7.

81. B. Dumaine, "The Trouble with Teams," *Fortune*, 5 September 1994, 86–92.

82. G.A. Neuman, S.H. Wagner, & N.D. Christiansen, "The Relationship Between Work-Team Personality Composition and the Job Performance of Teams," *Group & Organization Management* 24, no. 1 (1999): 28–45.

83. M.A. Campion, G.J. Medsker, & A.C. Higgs, "Relations Between Work Group Characteristics and Effectiveness: Implications for Designing Effective Work Groups," *Personnel Psychology* 46, no. 4 (1993): 823–850.

84. B.L. Kirkman & D.L. Shapiro, "The Impact of Cultural Values on Employee

Resistance to Teams: Toward a Model of Globalized Self-Managing Work Team Effectiveness," *Academy of Management Review* 22, no. 3 (1997): 730–757.

85. M.A. Campion, G.J. Medsker, & A.C. Higgs, "Relations Between Work Group Characteristics and Effectiveness: Implications for Designing Effective Work Groups," *Personnel Psychology* 46, no. 4 (1993): 823–850.

86. S. Caudron, "Team Staffing Requires New HR Role," *Personnel Journal* 73, no. 5 (1994): 88.

87. L. Clarke, "Changing Work Systems, Changing Social Relations," *Relations Industrielles* 52, no. 4 (1997): 839–862.

88. M.A. Verespej, "Super Sack," *Industry Week,* 16 October 1995, 53.

89. R.S. Wellins, W.C. Byham, & G.R. Dixon, *Inside Teams* (San Francisco: Jossey-Bass Publishers, 1994).

90. C. Joinson, "Teams at Work," *HRMagazine,* 1 May 1999, 30.

91. C. Joinson, "Teams at Work," *HRMagazine,* 1 May 1999, 30.

92. R.S. Wellins, W.C. Byham, & G.R. Dixon, *Inside Teams* (San Francisco: Jossey-Bass Publishers, 1994).

93. S. Caudron, "Tie Individual Pay to Team Success," *Personnel Journal* 73, no. 10 (October 1994): 40.

94. S. Caudron, "Tie Individual Pay to Team Success," *Personnel Journal* 73, no. 10 (October 1994): 40.

95. S.E. Gross, *Compensation for Teams* (New York: American Management Association, 1995).

96. R.S. Wellins, W.C. Byham, & G.R. Dixon, *Inside Teams* (San Francisco: Jossey-Bass Publishers, 1994).

97. J.R. Schuster & P.K. Zingheim, *The New Pay: Linking Employee and Organizational Performance* (New York: Lexington Books, 1992).

98. R.E. Yates, "Molding a New Future for Manufacturer, Keys Are Planning, People—and Plastics," *Chicago Tribune,* 2 January 1994.

99. S.G. Cohen & D.E. Bailey, "What Makes Teams Work: Group Effectiveness Research from the Shop Floor to the Executive Suite," *Journal of Management* 23, no. 3 (1997): 239–290.

100. "How NCR Uses Compensation to Support Teams," *ACA Journal* 5, no. 4 (Winter 1996): 74–75.

101. J.H. Sheridan, "'Yes' to Team Incentives," *Industry Week,* 4 March 1996, 63.

Chapter 13

1. M. Barrier, "Hiring the Right People," *Nation's Business* 84, no. 6 (June 1996): 18.

2. Jill Vardy, "High-Tech Friend Worth $3,000 to Employees: Firm's Incentive," *Financial Post,* 13 January 2001, D1, D7.

3. G.A. Poole, "Silicon Valley Serves Up Worker Perks: Fine Dining, Fitness Rooms, Concerts Are Used to Keep Top Talent," *Houston Chronicle,* 14 February 1999, 8.

4. Geoffrey Downey, "Skills Shortage, Part Two, Imminent," *Computing Canada* 28, no. 11 (24 May 2002): 19.

5. B. Schneider & N. Schmitt, *Staffing Organizations,* 2d ed. (Glenview, IL: Scott, Foresman and Company, 1986).

6. M. Jones, "Four Trends to Reckon With," *HR Focus* 73 (1996): 22–24.

7. C. Joinson, "Moving at the Speed of Dell," *HRMagazine* 44, no. 4 (1 April 1999): 50.

8. D.M. Atwater, "Workforce Forecasting," *Human Resource Planning* 18, no. 4 (1995): 50.

9. Mark Evans, "Telus Offers Departure Packages to 11,000 Staff: Part of $300 Million in Cuts," *Financial Post,* 8 June 2002, FP1, FP8.

10. Mark Evans, "3,500 Jobs Go as Nortel Lowers Bar on Sales," *Financial Post,* 30 May 2002, FP1, FP10.

11. D.M. Atwater, "Workforce Forecasting," *Human Resource Planning* 18, no. 4 (1995): 50; D. Ward, "Workforce Demand Forecasting Techniques," *Human Resource Planning* 19, no. 1 (1996): 54.

12. C. Joinson, "Moving at the Speed of Dell," *HRMagazine* 44, no. 4 (1 April 1999): 50.

13. A.J. Walker, "The Analytical Element Is Important to an HRIS," *Personnel Administrator* 28 (1983): 33–35, 85.

14. L. Asinof, "Click & Shift: Workers Control Their Benefits On-Line," *The Wall Street Journal,* 21 November 1997, C1.

15. Robert Colman, "Flip the Switch," *CMA Management* 76, no. 6 (September 2002): 34–37.

16. L. Asinof, "Click & Shift: Workers Control Their Benefits On-Line," *The Wall Street Journal,* 21 November 1997, C1.

17. T. Jolls, "Technology Continues to Redefine HR's Role," *Personnel Journal* 76, no. 7 (July 1997): 46.

18. T. Jolls, "Technology Continues to Redefine HR's Role," *Personnel Journal* 76, no. 7 (July 1997): 46.

19. T. Jolls, "Technology Continues to Redefine HR's Role," *Personnel Journal* 76, no. 7 (July 1997): 46.

20. Alex Kondra & Richard Sparkman, "Modeling U.S. and Canadian Equality Programs," *Journal of Individual Employment Rights* (forthcoming).

21. Alex Kondra and Richard Sparkman, "Modeling U.S. and Canadian Equality Programs," *Journal of Individual Employment Rights* (forthcoming).

22. E. Peirce, C.A. Smolinski, & B. Rosen, "Why Sexual Harassment Complaints Fall on Deaf Ears," *Academy of Management Executive* 12, no. 3 (1998): 41–54.

23. A. Levin, "Prudential Hit with 10 Discrimination Suits," *National Underwriter* 103, no. 4 (1999): 2.

24. W. Peirce, C.A. Smolinski, & B. Rosen, "Why Sexual Harassment Complaints Fall on Deaf Ears," *Academy of Management Executive* 12, no. 3 (1998): 41–54.

25. U.S. Equal Employment Opportunity Commission, "Facts about Sexual Harassment." [Online] Available www. eeoc.gov/facts/fs-sex.html, 23 May 1999.

26. Cheryl Cornacchia, "Female Boss Accused," *The Montreal Gazette,* 14 September 1998, F1; Howard Levitt, "Sexual Harassment Is Not Just Between Men and Women," *National Post,* 12 July 1999, D9.

27. Rick Ouston, "Customer's Conduct Ruled as Harassment," *Vancouver Sun,* 4 November 1996, B2.

28. W. Peirce, C.A. Smolinski, & B. Rosen, "Why Sexual Harassment Complaints Fall on Deaf Ears," *Academy of Management Executive* 12, no. 3 (1998): 41–54.

29. John Geddes & Stephanie Nolen, "Answering the Call," *Maclean's,* 8 June 1998, 28–31.

30. James Stevenson, "Shell Canada Warns of Higher Costs for Oilsands Project in Northern Alberta," *Canadian Press Newswire,* 24 October 2001.

31. "In Oil-Rich Fort McMurray, Service Industry Jobs Go Begging," *Financial Post,* 1 June 2000, C6.

32. P. Nakache, "Cisco's Recruiting Edge Find 'Em, Lure 'Em, Keep 'Em Happy: Devising New Ways to Steal Top Talent from Competitors Has Given This Silicon Valley Standout an Important Advantage," *Fortune,* 29 September 1997, 275.

33. R.D. Gatewood & H.S. Field, *Human Resource Selection* (Fort Worth, TX: Dryden Press, 1998).

34. R.D. Gatewood & H.S. Field, *Human Resource Selection* (Fort Worth, TX: Dryden Press, 1998).

35. *The Worklife Report* 14, no. 2 (2002): 13.

36. J.A. Breaugh, *Recruitment: Science and Practice* (Boston: PWS-Kent, 1992).

37. A. Campbell, "Baxter Healthcare Gets to the Root of the Issue," *HR Focus* 75, no. 8 (1998): S9.

38. P.R. Chowdhury, "Human Resources: Beyond Downsizing, Growing the TCM Manager," *Business Today*, 7 January 1999, 172.

39. P. Nakache, "Cisco's Recruiting Edge Find 'Em, Lure 'Em, Keep 'Em Happy: Devising New Ways to Steal Top Talent from Competitors Has Given This Silicon Valley Standout an Important Advantage," *Fortune*, 29 September 1997, 275.

40. "Life on the Web for Matters of Life, Liberty, and the Pursuit of a Nicer Job, There's Help on the Internet," *Fortune*, Special Issue, Technology Buyer's Guide (Winter 1999).

41. L.J.S. Vohra, "Online Recruiting Fills Positions," *Denver Business Journal*, 9 August 1996, 27A.

42. J. King, "Who's in the Online Pool?" *Computerworld*, 10 February 1997, 24; L.J.S. Vohra, "Online Recruiting Fills Positions," *Denver Business Journal*, 9 August 1996, 27A.

43. D. Fenn, "Hiring: Searching for the Chosen Few," *Inc.*, March 1996, 96.

44. J.S. Pouliot, "Topics to Avoid with Applicants," *Nation's Business* 80, no. 7 (1992): 57.

45. R.D. Broussard & D.E. Brannen, "Credential Distortions: Personnel Practitioners Give Their Views," *Personnel Administrator* 31 (1986): 129–146; K.A. Edelman, "Fiction 101: Resume Writing," *Across the Board*, February 1997, 62.

46. M. Mandell, "The High Cost of Hiring Fakers," *World Trade* 11, no. 3 (1998): 56.

47. S. Adler, "Verifying a Job Candidate's Background: The State of Practice in a Vital Human Resources Activity," *Review of Business* 15, no. 2 (1993/1994): 3–8.

48. Jonathan Finer, "A Resumé Full of Lies," *Far Eastern Economic Review* 165, no. 20 (23 May 2002): 55; Robin Raizel, "He Likes to Watch: Applying for a Job?", *Canadian Business* 74, no. 16 (3 September 2002): 38–41.

49. J. Hunter, "Cognitive Ability, Cognitive Aptitudes, Job Knowledge, and Job Performance," *Journal of Vocational Behavior* 29 (1986): 340–362.

50. Victor M. Catano, Steven F. Cronshaw, Willi H. Wiesner, Rick D. Hackett, & Laura L. Methot, *Recruitment and Selection in Canada* (Toronto: ITP Nelson, 1997).

51. J.R. Glennon, L.E. Albright, & W.A. Owens, *A Catalog of Life History Items* (Greensboro, NC: The Richardson Foundation, 1966).

52. Victor M. Catano, Steven F. Cronshaw, Willi H. Wiesner, Rick D. Hackett, & Laura L. Methot, *Recruitment and Selection in Canada* (Toronto: ITP Nelson, 1997); R.D. Gatewood & H.S. Field, *Human Resource Selection* (Fort Worth, TX: Dryden Press, 1998).

53. J.M. Digman, "Personality Structure: Emergence of the Five-Factor Model," *Annual Review of Psychology* 41 (1990): 417–440; M.R. Barrick & M.K. Mount, "The Big Five Personality Dimensions and Job Performance: A Meta-Analysis," *Personnel Psychology* 44 (1991): 1–26.

54. M.S. Taylor & J.A. Sniezek, "The College Recruitment Interview: Topical Content and Applicant Reactions," *Journal of Occupational Psychology* 57 (1984): 157–168.

55. M.A. Campion, D.K. Palmer, & J.E. Campion, "A Review of Structure in the Selection Interview," *Personnel Psychology* 50, no. 3 (1997): 655–702.

56. D. Stafford, "Workers Train, Companies Gain: Harmon Industries, Sprint, Others Make a Big Commitment," *Kansas City Star*, 16 February 1999, D1.

57. D. Stafford, "Workers Train, Companies Gain: Harmon Industries, Sprint, Others Make a Big Commitment," *Kansas City Star*, 16 February 1999, D1.

58. S. Livingston, T.W. Gerdel, M. Hill, B. Yerak, C. Melvin, & B. Lubinger, "Ohio's Strongest Companies All Agree That Training Is Vital to Their Success," *Plain Dealer*, 21 May 1997, 30S; Harvey Schachter, "Leading-Edge Learning," *Canadian Banker* 107, no. 2 (Second Quarter 2002): 16–27.

59. T.D. Schellhardt, "Management: Behind the Scenes at One CEO's Performance Review," *The Wall Street Journal*, 27 April 1998, B1.

60. Asha Tomlinson, "T&D Spending up in the U.S. as Canada Lags Behind," *Canadian HR Reporter* 15, no. 6 (25 March 2002): 1, 18.

61. J.D. Moore & R.L. Gehrig, "Rehearsing for a Robbery," *Security Management* 35, no. 8 (1991): 51.

62. D.L. Kirkpatrick, "Four Steps to Measuring Training Effectiveness," *Personnel Administrator* 28 (1983): 19–25.

63. J. Stack, "The Curse of the Annual Performance Review," *Inc.*, 1 March 1997, 39.

64. T.D. Schellhardt, "Annual Agony: It's Time to Evaluate Your Work, and All Involved Are Groaning—Employees Dislike Reviews, Even If Favorable; Bosses Wonder How to Do Them, Some Prefer Frequent Talks," *The Wall Street Journal*, 19 November 1996, A1.

65. Ian Gray, "Fear and Loathing Behind Closed Doors," *Financial Post* 91, no. 15 (12/14 April 1997): 26.

66. J. Yankovic, "Are the Reviews In?" *Pittsburgh Business Times* 16 (28 October 1996): 7.

67. T.D. Schellhardt, "Annual Agony: It's Time to Evaluate Your Work, and All Involved Are Groaning—Employees Dislike Reviews, Even If Favorable; Bosses Wonder How to Do Them, Some Prefer Frequent Talks," *The Wall Street Journal*, 19 November 1996, A1.

68. U.J. Wiersma & G.P. Latham, "The Practicality of Behavioral Observation Scales, Behavioral Expectation Scales, and Trait Scales," *Personnel Psychology* 39 (1986): 619–628; U.J. Wiersma, P.T. Van Den Berg, & G.P. Latham, "Dutch Reactions to Behavioral Observation, Behavioral Expectation, and Trait Scales," *Group & Organization Management* 20 (1995): 297–309.

69. D.J. Woehr & A.I. Huffcutt, "Rater Training for Performance Appraisal: A Quantitative Review," *Journal of Occupational and Organizational Psychology* 67, no. 3 (1994): 189–205.

70. J. Stack, "The Curse of the Annual Performance Review," *Inc.*, 1 March 1997, 39.

71. B. O'Reilly, "360-Degree Feedback Can Change Your Life," *Fortune*, 17 October 1994, 93.

72. D.A. Waldman, L.E. Atwater, & D. Antonioni, "Has 360 Feedback Gone Amok?" *Academy of Management Executive* 12, no. 2 (1998): 86–94.

73. Stephane Brutus & Mehrdad Derayeh, "Multisource Assessment Programs in Organizations: An Insider's Perspective," *Human Resource*

Development Quarterly 13, no. 2 (Summer 2002): 187–202.

74. H.H. Meyer, "A Solution to the Performance Appraisal Feedback Enigma," *Academy of Management Executive* 5, no. 1 (1991): 68–76.

75. T.D. Schellhardt, "Annual Agony: It's Time to Evaluate Your Work, and All Involved Are Groaning—Employees Dislike Reviews, Even If Favorable; Bosses Wonder How to Do Them, Some Prefer Frequent Talks," *The Wall Street Journal*, 19 November 1996, A1.

76. G.C. Thornton, "Psychometric Properties of Self-Appraisals of Job Performance," *Personnel Psychology* 33 (1980): 263–271.

77. H.H. Meyer, "A Solution to the Performance Appraisal Feedback Enigma," *Academy of Management Executive* 5, no. 1 (1991): 68–76.

78. Geoffrey Scotton, "Calgary Faces Jobs Squeeze," *Calgary Herald*, 5 October 2000, D1.

79. G.T. Milkovich & J.M. Newman, *Compensation*, 4th ed. (Homewood, IL: Irwin, 1993).

80. M.L. Williams & G.F. Dreher, "Compensation System Attributes and Applicant Pool Characteristics," *Academy of Management Journal* 35, no. 3 (1992): 571–595.

81. Kathryn May, "Federal Auditors Vow to Make Businesses Pay unless Wage Fight Settled: Government Salaries Far below Those in the Private Sector," *Ottawa Citizen*, 30 April 1998, C4.

82. "Sun, Hangovers Keep Teenagers from Summer Jobs," *Daily Commercial News*, 28 September 1998, B8.

83. Coleman, "Operating Profit at DaimlerChrysler Jumped 29% in '98 on 12% Sales Rise," *The Wall Street Journal*, 26 February 1999, A4.

84. Perry Phillips, "ES|OPs Offer IT Staff a Piece of the Ownership Pie," *Computing Canada* 24, no. 6 (16 March 1998): 34.

85. M. Bloom, "The Performance Effects of Pay Dispersion on Individuals and Organizations," *Academy of Management Journal* 42, no. 1 (1999): 25–40.

86. W. Grossman & R.E. Hoskisson, "CEO Pay at the Crossroads of Wall Street and Main: Toward the Strategic Design of Executive Compensation," *Academy of Management Executive* 12, no. 1 (1998): 43–57.

87. M. Bloom, "The Performance Effects of Pay Dispersion on Individuals and Organizations," *Academy of*

Management Journal 42, no. 1 (1999): 25–40.

88. J.S. Rosenbloom, "The Environment of Employee Benefit Plans," in *The Handbook of Employee Benefits*, ed. J.S. Rosenbloom (Chicago: Irwin, 1996), 3–13.

89. KPMG, *Employee Benefit Costs in Canada* (Toronto: KMPG, 1991, 1996).

90. A.E. Barber, R.B. Dunham, & R.A. Formisano, "The Impact of Flexible Benefits on Employee Satisfaction: A Field Study," *Personnel Psychology* 45 (1992): 55–75; B. Heshizer, "The Impact of Flexible Benefits on Job Satisfaction and Turnover Intentions," *Benefits Quarterly* 4 (1994): 84–90; D.M. Cable & T.A. Judge, "Pay Preferences and Job Search Decisions: A Person-Organization Fit Perspective," *Personnel Psychology* 47 (1994): 317–348.

91. B.T. Beam & J.J. McFadden, *Employee Benefits* (Chicago: Dearborn Financial Publishing, 1996).

92. K. Labich & E.M. Davies, "How to Fire People and Still Sleep at Night. Shedding Employees Is Something Almost Every Manager Dreads. But If You Don't Think Hard about the Process, You and Your Company Could Be Headed Straight for a World of Woes," *Fortune*, 10 June 1996, 64.

93. K. Labich & E.M. Davies, "How to Fire People and Still Sleep at Night. Shedding Employees Is Something Almost Every Manager Dreads. But If You Don't Think Hard about the Process, You and Your Company Could Be Headed Straight for a World of Woes," *Fortune*, 10 June 1996, 64.

94. P. Michal-Johnson, *Saying Good-Bye: A Manager's Guide to Employee Dismissal* (Glenview, IL: Scott, Foresman and Company, 1985).

95. M. Bordwin, "Employment Law: Beware of Time Bombs and Shark-Infested Waters," *HR Focus*, 1 April 1995, 19.

96. S. Gruner, "Hot Tip," *Inc.*, December 1996, 121.

97. J.R. Morris, W.F. Cascio, & C.E. Young, "Downsizing after All These Years: Questions and Answers about Who Did It, How Many Did It, and Who Benefited from It," *Organizational Dynamics* 27, no. 3 (1999): 78–87.

98. "Los Angeles Times. Layoffs Rise as Firms Find It's Profitable; 523,000 Are Fired as of Oct., 200,000 More than in

1997; Pink Slips in Golden Times; Study Shows Strategy May Ultimately Lower Earnings, Stock Prices," *Baltimore Sun*, 30 November 1998, 5C.

99. J.R. Morris, W.F. Cascio, & C.E. Young, "Down-sizing after All These Years: Questions and Answers about Who Did It, How Many Did It, and Who Benefited from It," *Organizational Dynamics* 27, no. 3 (1999): 78–87.

100. Rick Maurer, "Stop! Downsizing Doesn't Work," *The Canadian Manager* 24, no. 1 (Spring 1999): 11–13.

101. K.E. Mishra, G.M. Spreitzer, & A.K. Mishra, "Preserving Employee Morale during Downsizing," *Sloan Management Review* 39, no. 2 (1998): 83–95.

102. David Brown, "Take My Workers Please," *Canadian HR Reporter* 15, no. 3 (11 February 2002): 3.

103. R. Mullins, "Early Retirement Programs Can End Up Being Costly," *Business Journal-Milwaukee*, 20 January 1996, Section 1, p. 25.

104. D.R. Dalton, W.D. Todor, & D.M. Krackhardt, "Turnover Overstated: The Functional Taxonomy," *Academy of Management Review* 7 (1982): 117–123.

105. J.R. Hollenbeck & C.R. Williams, "Turnover Functionality versus Turnover Frequency: A Note on Work Attitudes and Organizational Effectiveness," *Journal of Applied Psychology* 71 (1986): 606–611.

106. C.R. Williams, "Reward Contingency, Unemployment, and Functional Turnover," *Human Resource Management Review* 9, no. 4 (Winter 1999): 549–576.

Chapter 14

1. T. Petzinger, Jr., "How a Ski Maker Recovered from a Potential Fatal Spill," *The Wall Street Journal Interactive Edition*, 3 October 1997.

2. W.M. Cox & R. Alm, *The Myths of Rich & Poor* (New York: Basic Books, 1999); R.L. Bartley, "The Seven Fat Years," *The Wall Street Journal*, 30 April 1992; S. Nasar & L. Smith, "Do We Live as Well as We Used To?" *Fortune*, 14 September 1987.

3. O. Suris, "Chrysler Leads Big Three in Efficiency of Car Factories, But All Trail Japanese," *The Wall Street Journal*, 30 May 1996.

4. J.B. White, "Wide Gap Exists Between GM, Rivals in Labor Productivity," *The Wall Street Journal*, 16 July 1998, A4.

5. Bureau of Labor Statistics, "Multifactor Productivity: Frequently Asked Questions." [Online] Available http://stats.bls.gov/mprfaq.htm, 7 March 1998.

6. "Multifactor Productivity," *The Daily*. Statistics Canada. 10 July 2003. [Online] Available www.statcan.ca/daily/english/030710/.

7. E. Peters, "Dawn of the Trouble-Free Automobile?" *Consumers' Research Magazine,* 1 January 1998.

8. American Society for Quality, "ASQ Glossary of Terms Search." [Online] Available www.asq.org/abtquality/glossary.cgi, 24 March 1998.

9. R.E. Markland, S.K. Vickery, & R.A. Davis, "Managing Quality" (Chapter 7), *Operations Management: Concepts in Manufacturing and Services* (Cincinnati, OH: South-Western College Publishing, 1998).

10. B. Weber, "Quicker Fixes: Big 3 Innovations Make 1997 Cars Easier to Repair," *Chicago Tribune,* 3 November 1996.

11. Lightsource.com. [Online] Available www.light-source.com/incandescent.html, 28 March 1998.

12. L.L. Berry & A. Parasuraman, *Marketing Services* (New York: Free Press, 1991).

13. S. McCartney, "A Service-Minded Manager Is Improving Newark Airport," *The Wall Street Journal Interactive Edition,* 9 June 1997.

14. S. McCartney, "A Service-Minded Manager Is Improving Newark Airport," *The Wall Street Journal Interactive Edition,* 9 June 1997.

15. American Society for Quality, "ANSI ASC Z-1 Committee on Quality Assurance Answers the Most Frequently Asked Questions about the ISO 9000 (ANSI/ASQ Q9000) Series." [Online] Available www.asq.org/standcert/iso.html, 29 March 1998.

16. R. Henkoff, "The Not New Seal of Quality (ISO 9000 Standard of Quality Management)," *Fortune,* 28 June 1993.

17. R. Henkoff, "The Not New Seal of Quality (ISO 9000 Standard of Quality Management)," *Fortune,* 28 June 1993.

18. National Quality Institute. *Canada Awards for Excellence.* [Online] Available, www.nqi.ca.

19. J.W. Dean, Jr & D.E. Bowen, "Management Theory and Total Quality: Improving Research and Practice through Theory Development," *Academy of Management Review* 19 (1994): 392–418.

20. G. Baum, "The Dynamic 100 Cisco's CEO John Chambers: If You Can't Beat 'Em, Buy 'Em," *Forbes ASAP,* 23 February 1998.

21. R.L. Rose, "Kentucky Plant Workers Are Cranking Out Good Ideas," *The Wall Street Journal,* 13 August 1996.

22. R. Hallowell, L.A. Schlesinger, & J. Zornitsky, "Internal Service Quality, Customer and Job Satisfaction: Linkages and Implications for Management," *Human Resource Planning* 19 (1996): 20–31; J.L. Heskett, T.O. Jones, G.W. Loveman, W.E. Sasser, Jr., & L.A. Schlesinger, "Putting the Service-Profit Chain to Work," *Harvard Business Review,* March-April 1994, 164–174.

23. G. Brewer, "The Ultimate Guide to Winning Customers: The Customer Stops Here," *Sales & Marketing Management* 150 (March 1998): 30.

24. T. Levitt, "Production-Line Approach to Service," *Harvard Business Review,* September-October 1972, 41–52; T. Levitt, "Industrialization of Service," *Harvard Business Review,* September-October 1976, 63–74.

25. L.L. Berry & A. Parasuraman, "Listening to the Customer—The Concept of a Service-Quality Information System," *Sloan Management Review* 38, no. 3 (Spring 1997): 65; C.W.L. Hart, J.L. Heskett, & W.E. Sasser, Jr., "The Profitable Art of Service Recovery," *Harvard Business Review,* July-August 1990, 148–156.

26. B. Gladstone, "Trusting in the Power of People," *The Globe and Mail,* 21 October 1997.

27. D.E. Bowen & E.E. Lawler, III, "The Empowerment of Service Workers: What, Why, How, and When," *Sloan Management Review* 33 (Spring 1992): 31–39; D.E. Bowen & E.E. Lawler, III, "Empowering Service Employees," *Sloan Management Review* 36 (Summer 1995): 73–84.

28. D.E. Bowen & E.E. Lawler, III, "The Empowerment of Service Workers: What, Why, How, and When," *Sloan Management Review* 33 (Spring 1992): 31–39.

29. R. Henkoff, "Finding Training and Keeping the Best Service Workers," *Fortune,* 3 October 1994.

30. A. Serwer, L. Smith, & P. de Llosa, "Michael Dell Rocks," *Fortune,* 11 May 1998, 58.

31. J. Leib, "Wilkerson's Breath of Fresh Air: Pneumatics Firm Re-Engineers Its Production Ways," *Denver Post,* 9 June 1997, E1.

32. G.V. Frazier & M.T. Spiggs, "Achieving Competitive Advantage through Group Technology," *Business Horizons* 39 (1996): 83–88.

33. "Bottling Line Catapults Beermaker Beyond Microbrewing," *Packaging Digest,* 1 September 1995, 8.

34. J. Kunerth, "Manufacturing Finds Foothold: Companies Praise the Area's Diverse Labor Pool, But Some Smaller Firms Say Finding Financing Can Be Difficult," *Orlando Sentinel,* 23 September 1996, 14.

35. "Ford to Close Plant for 2 Weeks, Adjust Levels of Its Inventory," *The Wall Street Journal Interactive Edition,* 20 February 1998.

36. C. Marshall, "Linerboard: Market Recovery Will Continue; Price Hikes Predicted for 1998," *Pulp & Paper,* 1 January 1998, 13.

37. Alpert, "3Com Says Inventory Glut, Asian Slump Depress Profits," *Barrons,* 8 December 1997, 5.

38. G. Taninecz, "Best Practices & Performances, Part 2," *Industry Week,* 1 December 1997, 28.

39. F. Zappa, "The End of Paperwork? Electronic Commerce Promises to Save Billions of Dollars and Millions of Hours," *Nation's Restaurant News,* 3 November 1997, S10.

40. J.R. Henry, "Minimized Setup Will Make Your Packaging Line S.M.I.L.E.," *Packaging Technology & Engineering,* 1 February 1998, 24.

41. D.W. Nelms, "The Path Best Taken; As the Airline Industry Refines the Purchasing Process, the Question Becomes Which Direction Will Produce Optimum Results," *Air Transport World,* 1 November 1996, 81.

42. F. Brookman, "Managing Inventory (EDI)," *Women's Wear,* 19 September 1997, 20.

43. T. Minahan, "JIT: A Process with Many Faces," *Purchasing,* 4 September 1997, 42.

44. "Fully Automated System Achieves True JIT," *Modern Materials Handling,* 1 April 1998, DPI22.

45. T. Minahan, "JIT: A Process with Many Faces," *Purchasing,* 4 September 1997, 42.

46. T. Minahan, "JIT: A Process with Many Faces," *Purchasing,* 4 September 1997, 42.

47. C. Crowell, "Seeing the Big Picture through Software (Manufacturing Resource Planning Computer Programs)," *American Metal Market*, 22 July 1997, 12.

Chapter 15

1. J.P. Campbell & R.D. Pritchard, "Motivation Theory in Industrial and Organizational Psychology," *Handbook of Industrial and Organizational Psychology*, ed. M.D. Dunnette (Chicago: Rand McNally, 1976).

2. P. Thomas, "Waitress Makes the Difference in Bringing Deaf to Pittsburgh," *The Wall Street Journal Interactive Edition*, 2 March 1999.

3. Katherine Macklem, "Canada's Top 100 Employers," *Maclean's*, 28 October 2002, 26–34.

4. K.A. Dolan, "When Money Isn't Enough," *Forbes*, 18 November 1996, 164–170.

5. E.A. Locke, "The Nature and Causes of Job Satisfaction," *Handbook of Industrial and Organizational Psychology*, ed. M.D. Dunnette (Chicago: Rand McNally, 1976).

6. A.H. Maslow, "A Theory of Human Motivation," *Psychological Review* 50 (1943): 370–396.

7. C.P. Alderfer, *Existence, Relatedness, and Growth: Human Needs in Organizational Settings* (New York: Free Press, 1972).

8. D.C. McClelland, "Toward a Theory of Motive Acquisition," *American Psychologist* 20 (1965): 321–333; D.C. McClelland & D.H. Burnham, "Power Is the Great Motivator," *Harvard Business Review* 54, no. 2 (1976): 100–110.

9. F. Herzberg, B. Mausner & B.B. Snyderman, *The Motivation to Work* (New York: Wiley, 1959). H.M. Weiss & R. Cropanzano, "Affective Events Theory: A Theoretical Discussion of the Structure, Causes and Consequences of Affective Experiences at Work," *Research in Organizational Behavior* 18 (1996): 1–74.

10. J.H. Turner, "Entrepreneurial Environments and the Emergence of Achievement Motivation in Adolescent Males," *Sociometry* 33 (1970): 147–165.

11. L.W. Porter, E.E. Lawler, III, & J.R. Hackman, *Behavior in Organizations* (New York: McGraw-Hill, 1975).

12. E.E. Lawler, III & L.W. Porter, "The Effect of Performance on Job Satisfaction," *Industrial Relations* 7 (1967): 20–28.

13. L.W. Porter, E.E. Lawler, III, & J.R. Hackman, *Behavior in Organizations* (New York: McGraw-Hill, 1975).

14. P. Kuitenbrouywer, "Daddy, I'm Almost a Millionaire," *Financial Post*, 21 April 2000, C1, C3.

15. L.W. Porter, E.E. Lawler, III, & J.R. Hackman, *Behavior in Organizations* (New York: McGraw-Hill, 1975).

16. C. Caggiano, "What Do Workers Want?" *Inc.*, November 1992, 101–104.

17. "Tailor-Made Rewards," *Inc.*, February 1991, 76.

18. John Tompkins & Sarah Beech, "Do Benefits Attract and Retain Talent?", *Benefits Canada* 26, no. 10 (October 2002): 49–54.

19. Aon Consulting, "America@ Work: A Focus on Benefits and Compensation." [Online] Available www.aon.com/pdf/america/awork2.pdf, 12 June 1999.

20. D. Woodruff, "Salary Spread in Euroland May Force Firms to Compete More for Top Workers," *The Wall Street Journal*, 20 January 1999, B9B.

21. "Europe Company: How the Euro Is Affecting Executive Pay," *Country ViewsWire*, 8 April 2003.

22. C.T. Kulik & M.L. Ambrose, "Personal and Situational Determinants of Referent Choice," *Academy of Management Review* 17 (1992): 212–237.

23. J.S. Adams, "Toward an Understanding of Inequity," *Journal of Abnormal Social Psychology* 67 (1963): 422–436.

24. Zena Olijnyk, "Workers Steal Less when Paid More," *Financial Post Daily*, 15 April 1997, 25.

25. J. Greenberg, "Employee Theft as a Reaction to Underpayment Inequity: The Hidden Costs of Pay Cuts," *Journal of Applied Psychology* 75 (1990): 561–568.

26. R.A. Cosier & D.R. Dalton, "Equity Theory and Time: A Reformulation," *Academy of Management Review* 8 (1983): 311–319; M.R. Carrell & J.E. Dittrich, "Equity Theory: The Recent Literature, Methodological Considerations, and New Directions," *Academy of Management Review* 3 (1978): 202–209.

27. Drew Hasselback, "BC Chapters Employees Await Word on Union Request," *Financial Post*, 7 July 1999, C4.

28. Jack Keating, "Unhappy Kids Ripe for Union Cards," *The Province*, 21 August 1998, A2.

29. K. Aquino, R.W. Griffeth, D.G. Allen, & P.W. Hom, "Integrating Justice Constructs into the Turnover Process: A Test of a Referent Cognitions Model," *Academy of Management Journal* 40, no. 5 (1997): 1208–1227.

30. B. Orwall & K. Swisher, "Of Mouse and Men: As Web Riches Beckon, Disney Ranks Become a Poacher's Paradise—Media Giant Can't Compete in Giving Stock Options, and Isn't 'Freewheeling'—Eisner Flames the Techies," *The Wall Street Journal*, 9 June 1999, A1.

31. C. Fishman, "Sanity, Inc.," *Fast Company*, January 1999, 85–96.

32. R. Folger & M.A. Konovsky, "Effects of Procedural and Distributive Justice on Reactions to Pay Raise Decisions," *Academy of Management Journal* 32 (1989): 115–130.

33. E. Barret-Howard & T.R. Tyler, "Procedural Justice as a Criterion in Allocation Decisions," *Journal of Personality and Social Psychology* 50 (1986): 296–305; R. Folger & M.A. Konovsky, "Effect of Procedural and Distributive Justice on Reactions to Pay Raise Decisions," *Academy of Management Journal* 32 (1989): 115–130.

34. R. Folger & J. Greenberg, "Procedural Justice: An Interpretive Analysis of Personnel Systems," in *Research in Personnel and Human Resources Management*, Volume 3, eds. K. Rowland & G. Ferris (Greenwich, CT: JAI Press, 1985); R. Folger, D. Rosenfield, J. Grove, & L. Corkran, "Effects of 'Voice' and Peer Opinions on Responses to Inequity," *Journal of Personality and Social Psychology* 37 (1979): 2253–2261; E.A. Lind & T.R. Tyler, *The Social Psychology of Procedural Justice* (New York: Plenum Press, 1988).

35. K.A. Dolan, "When Money Isn't Enough," *Forbes*, 18 November 1996, 164–170.

36. V.H. Vroom, *Work and Motivation* (New York: John Wiley & Sons, 1964); L.W. Porter & E.E. Lawler, III, *Managerial Attitudes and Performance* (Homewood, IL: Dorsey Press & Richard D. Irwin, 1968).

37. D. Bank, "As Microsoft Matures, Some Top Talent Is Opting to Leave, at Least Temporarily," *The Wall Street Journal Interactive Edition*, 16 June 1999.

38. Owen Parker & Liz Wright, "The Missing Link: Pay and Employee

Commitment," *Ivey Business Journal* 65, no. 3 (January/February 2001): 70–73.

39. S. Scholl, "Allstate Pay for Performance Methodology Rewards Excellence," *ACANEWS* 41, no. 8 (1998): 24.

40. K.W. Thomas & B.A. Velthouse, "Cognitive Elements of Empowerment," *Academy of Management Review* 15 (1990): 666–681.

41. C. Hymowitz, "In the Lead: How Cynthia Danaher Learned to Stop Sharing and Start Leading," *The Wall Street Journal*, 16 March 1999, B1.

42. G. Colvin, "The Changing Art of Becoming Unbeatable," *Fortune*, 24 November 1997, 299–300. Katherine Macklem, "Then There Were Three," *Maclean's*, 21 May 2001, 72–73.

43. W. Bennis, "Why Leaders Can't Lead," *Training & Development Journal* 43, no. 4 (1989).

44. "CEOs Talk," *Canadian HR Reporter* 15, no. 17 (7 October 2002): 18, 20.

45. C. Hymowitz, "In the Lead: Some Managers Are More than Bosses— They're Leaders, Too," *The Wall Street Journal*, 8 December 1998, B1.

46. A. Zaleznik, "Managers and Leaders: Are They Different?" *Harvard Business Review* 55 (1977): 76–78; A. Zaleznik, "The Leadership Gap," *The Washington Quarterly* 6 (1983): 32–39.

47. W. Bennis, "Why Leaders Can't Lead," *Training & Development Journal* 43, no. 4 (1989): 35–39.

48. J.P. Howell, D.E. Bowen, P.W. Dorfman, S. Kerr, & P.M. Podsakoff, "Substitutes for Leadership: Effective Alternatives to Ineffective Leadership," *Organizational Dynamics*, 22 June 1990, 20; S. Kerr & J.M. Jermier, "Substitutes for Leadership: Their Meaning and Measurement," *Organizational Behavior and Human Performance* 22 (1978): 375–403.

49. T.A. Stewart, A. Harrington, & M.G. Solovar, "America's Most Admired Companies: Why Leadership Matters," *Fortune*, 2 March 1998, 70.

50. S.A. Kirkpatrick & E.A. Locke, "Leadership: Do Traits Matter?" *Academy of Management Executive* 5, no. 2 (1991): 48–60.

51. S.A. Kirkpatrick & E.A. Locke, "Leadership: Do Traits Matter?" *Academy of Management Executive* 5, no. 2 (1991): 48–60.

52. T.A. Stewart, A. Harrington, & M.G. Solovar, "America's Most Admired Companies: Why Leadership Matters," *Fortune*, 2 March 1998, 70.

53. J.J. Gabarro, *The Dynamics of Taking Charge* (Boston: Harvard Business School Press, 1987).

54. J. Carlton, "Thinking Different: At Apple, a Fiery Jobs Often Makes Headway and Sometimes a Mess—He Knows How to Market but Clashes with Cloners and Belittles His Foes— Skewered on the Gil-O-Meter," *The Wall Street Journal*, 14 April 1998, A1.

55. S.A. Kirkpatrick & E.A. Locke, "Leadership: Do Traits Matter?" *Academy of Management Executive* 5, no. 2 (1991): 48–60.

56. E.A. Fleishman, "The Description of Supervisory Behavior," *Personnel Psychology* 37 (1953): 1–6; L.R. Katz, *New Patterns of Management* (New York: McGraw-Hill, 1961).

57. R. Charan & G. Colvin, "Why CEOs Fail," *Fortune*, 21 June 1999, 69–78.

58. P. Weissenberg & M.H. Kavanagh, "The Independence of Initiating Structure and Consideration: A Review of the Evidence," *Personnel Psychology* 25 (1972): 119–130.

59. R.J. House & T.R. Mitchell, "Path-Goal Theory of Leadership," *Journal of Contemporary Business* 3 (1974): 81–97; F.E. Fiedler, "A Contingency Model of Leadership Effectiveness," in ed. L. Berkowitz, *Advances in Experimental Social Psychology* (New York: Academic Press, 1964); V.H. Vroom & P.W. Yetton, *Leadership and Decision Making* (Pittsburgh: University of Pittsburgh Press, 1973); P. Hersey & K.H. Blanchard, *The Management of Organizational Behavior*, 4th ed. (Englewood Cliffs, NJ: Prentice-Hall, 1984); S. Kerr & J.M. Jermier, "Substitutes for Leadership: Their Meaning and Measurement," *Organizational Behavior and Human Performance* 22 (1978): 375–403.

60. F.E. Fiedler & M.M. Chemers, *Leadership and Effective Management* (Glenview, IL: Scott, Foresman, 1974).

61. J. Carlton, "Thinking Different: At Apple, a Fiery Jobs Often Makes Headway and Sometimes a Mess—He Knows How to Market but Clashes with Cloners and Belittles His Foes— Skewered on the Gil-O-Meter," *The Wall Street Journal*, 14 April 1998, A1.

62. F.E. Fiedler, "The Effects of Leadership Training and Experience: A Contingency Model Interpretation," *Administrative Science Quarterly* 17, no. 4 (1972): 455; F.E. Fiedler, *A Theory of Leadership Effectiveness* (New York: McGraw-Hill, 1967).

63. L.S. Csoka & F.E. Fiedler, "The Effect of Military Leadership Training: A Test of the Contingency Model," *Organizational Behavior and Human Performance* 8 (1972): 395–407.

64. P. Hersey & K. Blanchard, *Management of Organizational Behavior: Utilizing Human Resources,* 4th ed. (Englewood Cliffs, NJ: Prentice Hall, 1982).

65. W. Blank, J.R. Weitzel, & S.G. Green, "A Test of the Situational Leadership Theory," *Personnel Psychology* 43, no. 3 (1990): 579–597; W.R. Norris & R.P. Vecchio, "Situational Leadership Theory: A Replication," *Group & Organization Management* 17, no. 3 (1992): 331–342.

66. W. Blank, J.R. Weitzel, & S.G. Green, "A Test of the Situational Leadership Theory," *Personnel Psychology* 43, no. 3 (1990): 579–597; W.R. Norris & R.P. Vecchio, "Situational Leadership Theory: A Replication," *Group & Organization Management* 17, no. 3 (1992): 331–342.

67. R.D. Ireland & M.A. Hitt, "Achieving and Maintaining Strategic Competitiveness in the 21st Century: The Role of Strategic Leadership," *Academy of Management Executive* 13, no. 1 (1999): 43–57.

68. J.A. Byrne, "A Close-up Look at How America's #1 Manager Runs GE," *Business Week*, 8 June 1998, 90.

69. P. Thoms & D.B. Greenberger, "Training Business Leaders to Create Positive Organizational Visions of the Future: Is It Successful?" *Academy of Management Journal* [Best Papers & Proceedings], 1995, 212–216.

70. M. Weber, *The Theory of Social and Economic Organizations*, translated by R.A. Henderson & T. Parsons (New York: Free Press, 1947).

71. D.A. Waldman & F.J. Yammarino, "CEO Charismatic Leadership: Levels-of-Management and Levels-of-Analysis Effects," *Academy of Management Review* 24, no. 2 (1999): 266–285.

72. P. Sellers, "What Exactly Is Charisma?" *Fortune*, 15 January 1996, 68.

73. K.B. Lowe, K.G. Kroeck, & N. Sivasubramaniam, "Effectiveness Correlates of Transformational and Transactional Leadership: A Meta-analytic Review of the MLQ Literature," *Leadership Quarterly* 7 (1996): 385–425.

74. J.M. Howell & B.J. Avolio, "The Ethics of Charismatic Leadership: Submission or Liberation?" *Academy of Management Executive* 6, no. 2 (1992): 43–54.

75. P. Sellers, "What Exactly Is Charisma?" *Fortune*, 15 January 1996, 68.

76. J.M. Howell & B.J. Avolio, "The Ethics of Charismatic Leadership: Submission or Liberation?" *Academy of Management Executive* 6, no. 2 (1992): 43–54.

77. J.M. Howell & B.J. Avolio, "The Ethics of Charismatic Leadership: Submission or Liberation?" *Academy of Management Executive* 6, no. 2 (1992): 43–54.

78. J.M. Burns, *Leadership* (New York: Harper & Row, 1978). B.M. Bass, "From Transactional to Transformational Leadership: Learning to Share the Vision," *Organizational Dynamics* 18 (1990): 19–36.

79. B.M. Bass, "From Transactional to Transformational Leadership: Learning to Share the Vision," *Organizational Dynamics* 18 (1990): 19–36.

80. B.M. Bass, *A New Paradigm of Leadership: An Inquiry into Transformational Leadership* (Alexandra, VA: U.S. Army Research Institute for the Behavioral and Social Sciences, 1996).

81. J.A. Byrne, "A Close-up Look at How America's #1 Manager Runs GE," *Business Week*, 8 June 1998, 90.

82. J.A. Byrne, "A Close-up Look at How America's #1 Manager Runs GE," *Business Week*, 8 June 1998, 90.

83. B.M. Bass, "From Transactional to Transformational Leadership: Learning to Share the Vision," *Organizational Dynamics* 18 (1990): 19–36.

Chapter 16

1. E.E. Lawler, III, L.W. Porter, & A. Tannenbaum, "Manager's Attitudes toward Interaction Episodes," *Journal of Applied Psychology* 52 (1968): 423–439; H. Mintzberg, *The Nature of Managerial Work* (New York: Harper & Row, Publishers, 1973).

2. J.D. Maes, T.G. Weldy, & M.L. Icenogle, "A Managerial Perspective: Oral Communication Competency Is Most Important for Business Students in the Workplace," *Journal of Business Communication* 34 (1997): 67–80.

3. R. Lepsinger & A.D. Lucia, *The Art and Science of 360 Degree Feedback* (San Francisco: Pfeiffer, 1997).

4. "We Need to Talk: CFO Survey Reveals Poor Communication Is Most Common Management Mistake," *Canadian Manager* 25, no. 1 (Spring 2000): 1.

5. T. Petzinger, Jr., "Two Executives Cook Up Ways to Make Pillsbury Listen," *The Wall Street Journal*, 27 September 1996, B1.

6. E.E. Jones & K.E. Davis, "From Acts to Dispositions: The Attribution Process in Person Perception," in *Advances in Experimental and Social Psychology*, Volume 2, ed. L. Berkowitz (New York: Academic Press, 1965), 219–266; R.G. Lord & J.E. Smith, "Theoretical, Information-Processing, and Situational Factors Affecting Attribution Theory Models of Organizational Behavior," *Academy of Management Review* 8 (1983): 50–60.

7. E.E. Jones & K.E. Davis, "From Acts to Dispositions: The Attribution Process in Person Perception," in *Advances in Experimental and Social Psychology*, Volume 2, ed. L. Berkowitz (New York: Academic Press, 1965), 219–266; R.G. Lord & J.E. Smith, "Theoretical, Information-Processing, and Situational Factors Affecting Attribution Theory Models of Organizational Behavior," *Academy of Management Review* 8 (1983): 50–60.

8. H.H. Kelly, *Attribution in Social Interaction* (Morristown, NJ: General Learning Press, 1971).

9. J.M. Burger, "Motivational Biases in the Attribution of Responsibility for an Accident: A Meta-Analysis of the Defensive-Attribution Hypothesis," *Psychological Bulletin* 90 (1981): 496–512.

10. D.A. Hofmann & A. Stetzer, "The Role of Safety Climate and Communication in Accident Interpretation: Implications for Learning from Negative Events," *Academy of Management Journal* 41, no. 6 (1998): 644–657.

11. C. Perrow, *Normal Accidents: Living with High-Risk Technologies* (New York: Basic Books, 1984).

12. A.G. Miller & T. Lawson, "The Effect of an Informational Opinion on the Fundamental Attribution Error," *Journal of Personality and Social Psychology* 47 (1989): 873–896; J.M. Burger, "Changes in Attribution Errors over Time: The Ephemeral Fundamental Attribution Error," *Social Cognition* 9 (1991): 182–193.

13. E. Bernstein, "The Stagnant, Uncriticized Employee—But Those Open to Feedback Seen as Approachable, Primed for Success," *San Antonio Express-News*, 20 February 1997, 1F.

14. F. Heider, *The Psychology of Interpersonal Relations* (New York: Wiley, 1958); D.T. Miller & M. Ross, "Self-Serving Biases in Attribution of Causality: Fact or Fiction?" *Psychological Bulletin* 82 (1975): 213–225.

15. J.R. Larson, Jr., "The Dynamic Interplay between Employees' Feedback-Seeking Strategies and Supervisors' Delivery of Performance Feedback," *Academy of Management Review* 14, no. 3 (1989): 408–422.

16. "Crisis in Communications: Are You Prepared to Communicate Clearly and Effectively During an Emergency?", *Occupational Health and Safety* 1, no. 2 (April/May 1996): 48–50.

17. "What Is Zee True International Language?" *Canadian Press Newswire*, May 12, 1995.

18. David A. Ricks, *Big Business Blunders* (Homewood, IL: Dow Irwin Jones, 1983).

19. M. Reddy, "The Conduit Metaphor— A Case of Frame Conflict in Our Language about Our Language," in *Metaphor and Thought*, ed. A. Ortony (Cambridge, England: Cambridge University Press, 1979), 284–324.

20. G.L. Kreps, *Organizational Communication: Theory and Practice* (New York: Longman, 1990).

21. G.L. Kreps, *Organizational Communication: Theory and Practice* (New York: Longman, 1990).

22. D. Roth, "How to Cut Pay, Lay Off 8,000 People, And Still Have Workers Who Love You," *Fortune*, 4 February 2002, 62.

23. David M. Saunders & Joanne D. Leck, "Formal Upward Communication Procedures: Organizational and Employee Perspectives," *Canadian Journal of Administrative Sciences* 10, no. 3 (September 1993): 255–268.

24. "A Rising Star in the West: With Sales of $13.5m and Growing, Sundog Printing Has Staked Its Claim as One of Calgary's Top Printers," *Canadian Printer* 101, no. 9 (November 1993): 20–21; Ian McKinnon, "DBF Acquires Sundog Printing," *Financial Post*, 2 April 1999, C6.

25. J. Martin & A. Kover, "Meet Six Hot Young Managers Who Have What It Takes to Lead in the 21st Century," *Fortune*, 26 June 1996, 76.

26. G.L. Kreps, *Organizational Communication: Theory and Practice* (New York: Longman, 1990).

27. A.B. Fisher, "The Downside of Downsizing," *Fortune*, 23 May 1988, 42.

28. W. Davis & J.R. O'Connor, "Serial Transmission of Information: A Study of the Grapevine," *Journal of Applied*

Communication Research 5 (1977): 61–72.

29. "CEOs Talk," *Canadian HR Reporter* 15, no. 5 (11 March 2002): 17–19.

30. C. Hymowitz, "Managing: Spread the Word, Gossip Is Good," *The Wall Street Journal*, 4 October 1988.

31. W. Davis & J.R. O'Connor, "Serial Transmission of Information: A Study of the Grapevine," *Journal of Applied Communication Research* 5 (1977): 61–72; C. Hymowitz, "Managing: Spread the Word, Gossip Is Good," *The Wall Street Journal*, 4 October 1988.

32. W.C. Redding, *Communication within the Organization: An Interpretive View of Theory and Research* (New York: Industrial Communication Council, 1972).

33. D.T. Hall, K.L. Otazo, & G.P. Hollenbeck, "Behind Closed Doors: What Really Happens in Executive Coaching," *Organizational Dynamics* 27, no. 3 (1999): 39–53.

34. "Surviving a Work-Life Crisis: Troubles at Home Can Make It Hard for Workers to Do Their Best Job," *Buffalo News*, 24 August 1999, D1.

35. M. McWhorter, "Energen CEO Believes Open Communication Is the Key to Successful Management," *Business First—Birmingham*, Volume 6, Section 1 (1992): 8.

36. A. Mehrabian, "Communication without Words," *Psychology Today* 3 (1968): 53; A. Mehrabian, *Silent Messages* (Belmont, CA: Wadsworth, 1971); R. Harrison, *Beyond Words: An Introduction to Nonverbal Communication* (1974); A. Mehrabian, Non-Verbal Communication (Chicago, IL: Aldine, 1972).

37. M.L. Knapp, *Nonverbal Communication in Human Interaction*, 2nd ed. (New York: Holt, Reinhart & Winston, 1978).

38. H.M. Rosenfeld, "Instrumental Affiliative Functions of Facial and Gestural Expressions," *Journal of Personality and Social Psychology* 24 (1966): 65–72; P. Ekman, "Differential Communication of Affect by Head and Body Cues," *Journal of Personality and Social Psychology* 2 (1965): 726–735; A. Mehrabian, "Significance of Posture and Position in the Communication of Attitude and Status Relationships," *Psychological Bulletin* 71 (1969): 359–372.

39. R.B. Schmitt, "Judges Try Curbing Lawyers' Body-Language Antics," *The Wall Street Journal*, 9 September 1997, B1.

40. R.B. Schmitt, "Judges Try Curbing Lawyers' Body-Language Antics," *The Wall Street Journal*, 9 September 1997, B1.

41. C.A. Bartlett & S. Ghoshal, "Changing the Role of Top Management: Beyond Systems to People," *Harvard Business Review*, May-June 1995, 132–142.

42. P. Roberts, "Homestyle Talkshows," *Fast Company*, October 1999, 162.

43. P. Roberts, "Homestyle Talkshows," *Fast Company*, October 1999, 162.

44. R.G. Nichols, "Do We Know How to Listen? Practical Helps in a Modern Age," in *Communication Concepts and Processes*, ed. J. DeVitor (Englewood Cliffs, NJ: Prentice Hall, 1971); P.V. Lewis, *Organizational Communication: The Essence of Effective Management* (Columbus, OH: Grid Publishing Company, 1975).

45. E. Atwater, *I Hear You*, revised ed. (New York: Walker, 1992).

46. R. Adler & N. Towne, *Looking Out/Looking In* (San Francisco: Rinehart Press, 1975).

47. T.D. Zweifel, "Be Still and Hear: The Art and Science of Listening Is Good Business," *Christian Science Monitor*, 22 September 1998, 11.

48. B.D. Seyber, R.N. Bostrom, & J.H. Seibert, "Listening, Communication Abilities, and Success at Work," *Journal of Business Communication* 26 (1989): 293–303.

49. E. Atwater, *I Hear You*, revised ed. (New York: Walker, 1992).

50. N. Grammer, "The Art—and Importance—of Listening," *The Globe and Mail*, 25 June 1999, B11.

51. H.H. Meyer, "A Solution to the Performance Appraisal Feedback Enigma," *Academy of Management Executive* 5, no. 1 (1991): 68–76.

52. T.D. Schellhardt, "Annual Agony: It's Time to Evaluate Your Work, and All Involved Are Groaning—Employees Dislike Reviews, Even if Favorable; Bosses Wonder How to Do Them—Some Prefer Frequent Talks," *The Wall Street Journal*, 19 November 1996, A1.

53. "Make Your Next Performance Review Count," *Financial Post*, 11 April 1998, R14.

54. L. Reibstein, "What to Do When an Employee Is Talented and a Pain in the Neck," *The Wall Street Journal*, 8 August 1986.

55. R. Mead, *Cross-Cultural Management* (New York: Wiley, 1990).

56. J.S. Black & M. Mendenhall, "Cross-Cultural Training Effectiveness: A Review and Theoretical Framework for Future Research," *Academy of Management Review* 15 (1990): 113–136.

57. R. Mead, *Cross-Cultural Management* (New York: Wiley, 1990).

58. E.T. Hall & W.F. Whyte, "Intercultural Communication: A Guide to Men of Action," *Human Organization* 19, no. 1 (1961): 5–12.

59. Nicholas Benedict, "Sojourn in the Gulf," *Maclean's*, 18 November 2002, 96.

60. N. Libman, "French Tip: Just Walk the Walk and Talk the Talk, but Not Too Loud," *Chicago Tribune*, 17 March 1996.

61. H. Lancaster, "Global Managers Need Boundless Sensitivity, Rugged Constitutions," *The Wall Street Journal*, 13 October 1998, B1.

62. R. Miller, "Going Inside with the Internet," *IABC Communication World*, November 1995.

63. Jonathan Kay, "Someone Will Watch over Me," *National Post Business*, January 2001, 59–64.

64. H. Lancaster, "Contributors to Pools of Company Know-How Are Valued Employees," *The Wall Street Journal*, 9 December 1997, B1.

65. T.A. Stewart, "Telling Tales at BP Amoco: Knowledge Management at Work," *Fortune*, 7 June 1999, 220.

66. M. Campanelli & N. Friedman, "Welcome to Voice Mail Hell: The New Technology Has Become a Barrier Between Salespeople and Customers. Here's How Smart Sellers Are Breaking Through," *Sales & Marketing Management* 147 (May 1995): 98–101.

67. Toyota Motor Manufacturing, USA, *Team Member Handbook*, February 1988, 52–53; G. Dessler, "How to Earn Your Employees' Commitment," *Academy of Management Review* 13, no. 2 (1999): 58–67.

68. Uyen Vu, "Top Firms See Advantage in Employee Satisfaction," *Canadian HR Reporter*, 27 January 2003, 1–2.

69. B. O'Reilly, "Forget Hertz and Avis: Enterprise's Quiet Invasion of Small-Town America—Along with Quirky Hiring Practices and a Generous Supply of Doughnuts—Has Made It the Nation's Biggest Rental Car," *Fortune*, 28 October 1996, 125.

Quinn, Tim, 204
Qwiz, Inc., 397

Radford, Toby, 229
Raffio, Tom, 380
Rainforest Relief and Wetlands
    Rainforest Action Group,
    79
Rank Xerox, 241
Rathbun, David, 16
Raymer, Carol, 206
Raymond, Lee, 189
Red Hat Software, 101
Red Spot Paint and Varnish
    Company, 219
Reese, John, 397
Regent Square Tavern, 469
Regnery Publishing, 279
Remada, Ray, 520
Research in Motion, 473–74
Respect, Inc., 426
Retail Council of Canada, 66,
    477
Reuters, 275
Reynolds, R.J., 148
Reynolds Metals, 328
Richmond Savings, 112–13
Ricks, David, 238, 249
Ritz-Carlton, 368–69
Robinson, Peter, 208
Rocketinfo, 15
Rogan Corporation, 383
Rolling Stones, 346–47
Rollnick, William, 80
Rosenblatt, Stanley, 524
Roth, John, 16, 307
Royal Bank of Canada, 288, 320
R.R. Donnelley & Sons, 135
Rudenstine, Neil, 21
Ryan, Denis, 28

Safeway Canada, 261
Sagawa, Paul, 307
Salzman, Barry, 530
Samsung Corporation, 271
Sandler, Herman, 467, 504
Sandler O'Neill, 467, 503–4
Sara Lee, 116
SAS Institute, 479
SaskTel, 12
Saturn, 369
Savastano, Paul, 129
Schlage Lock Company, 105
Schlossberg, Edwin, 298
Schrader, Bob, 369
Scott, William, 476
Scouts Canada, 80–81
Sears Roebuck, 8, 293, 402
Sejen Electronics TV, 206–7
Sellers, Patricia, 224
Sematec, 143
Service Intelligence Inc., 200

Shartzer, Sandi, 368–69
Shaw, Maureen, 522, 533
Sheehan, Jeremiah, 328
Shell Oil, 44, 72, 73, 75, 189,
    320, 391
Shift Central, 3, 26
Shoppers Drug Mart, 66, 76
Silicon Graphics Incorporated,
    116–17, 300
Singapore International Airlines,
    215
Sobey, J.W., 261
Sobeys Inc., 261–62, 264, 275,
    286
Society of Competitive
    Intelligence Professionals, 3
Software & Information Industry
    Association, 223
Software Publisher's Association,
    69
Sokolof, Phillip, 44
Solutia, 115
Sony, 303, 329
Sorino, Fred, 533
Southwest Airlines, 53, 93–94,
    483, 487
Spamtown, 463
Spar Handels AG, 252
Sport Chek, 94
Sport Experts, 94
Sprint, 414
Stalker, G.M., 341
Stallkamp, Tom, 535
Staples, 100, 155
Star Choice, 130, 266
Starbucks Coffee, 301
Statistics Canada, 167
Staw, Barry, 179
StayWell Health Management
    Systems, 222
Steelcase, 346
Stelco, 42
Stevenson, Mark, 327, 352
Stone, Michael, 123
Streetprices.com, 155
Stronach, Frank, 49
Stybel, Laurence, 425
Subway, 41, 281–82
Sumitomo Corporation, 238
Sun Media, 267
Sun Microsystems, 143
Sunbeam Corporation, 409
Sundog Printing, 520
Super Sack, 380–81
Superstore, 203
Surrey Metro Savings, 113
Suzuki Corporation, 81
Svoboda, Jeff, 115
Swartout, Hank, 208
Swenson, Winn, 62
Swissair, 54
Sympatico, 140

Taco Bell, 116, 215
Tandem Computer, 57
Taylor, Andy, 533
Teamsters Union, 45
Telus, 12, 96, 395
Texas Instruments, 363
Theriault, Mario, 3, 26
3Com, 455
3M, 270, 274, 456
Tickets.com, 172
Tierney, Tom, 499
Tilano Fresco, 238
Tim Hortons, 41, 281, 344
Time Warner Enterprises, 173
Timex, 230
Toronto Dominion Bank, 414
Torstar Corporation, 267
Toshiba, 241
Toyota, 293, 439–40, 457–58,
    532–33
Tracy, John A., 213
TransCanada Pipelines Ltd., 311
Treybig, Jimmy, 57
Trimmer, Tiberio, 407
Tsang, Daniel, 122
Tupperware, 39, 120
Tyco, 63

Unilever, 3, 84
United Airlines, 133, 134, 148
United Auto Workers, 16
United Cigar Stores, 146
United Parcel Service, 5, 45, 283
United Waste Systems, 103–4
University of Michigan, 224,
    489–90
University of Southern
    California Center for
    Effective Organizations,
    366, 382
University of Texas, 489–90
University of Toronto and
    Hospital for Sick Children,
    87
UPS, 5, 45, 283
Urban, Andrew, 282
Urban, Tammy, 373
U.S. Consumer Product Safety
    Commission, 441
U.S. Federal Aviation
    Administration, 133–34
U.S. National Highway Traffic
    Safety Administration, 81
U.S. Postal Service, 45
U.S. Steel, 293
USAir, 100

Vadasz, Leslie, 101
Vasquez, Jamie, 229
Vaughn Hockey, 463
Village Food Markets, 363
Vineland, 239

Virgin Atlantic Airways, 34
Virtual Leadership Academy, 532
Vision, Kera, 414
Volant, Inc., 438
Volkswagen, 242

Wal-Mart, 12, 35, 42, 47, 49,
    50, 63, 131–32, 139, 147,
    229, 252–53, 283, 293,
    301, 449
Walker, Jay, 179
Walt Disney Company, 105,
    107, 235, 300, 373, 479
Walton, Sam, 229
Wardair, 35
Waste Management
    International, 103–4
Watson, Thomas J., 49, 51
Weber, Max, 207, 498
WebHouse Club, 179
Webopedia, 129
Wechselberg, Irene, 121
Wechsler, Winney, 479
Weir, Mike, 95
Welbourne, Theresa, 181
Welch, Jack, 49–50, 349, 487,
    489, 498, 501, 502
Wendy's, 281, 283
Wertkauf GmbH, 252
Western Oil Sands, 391
WestJet Airlines, 35, 93–94, 107,
    119, 134
Whole Foods, 363
Wilkerson Corporation, 450–51
Wilson, Andy, 12
Wilson Sporting Goods, 381
Winguth, Dohahue & Co., 144
Winguth, Ed, 144
Wolpert, Richard, 479
Woodburn, William, 502
Woodhouse, Kathleen, 396
Wooten, Claren, 101
World Trade Organization
    (WTO), 34, 234, 235
Woznick, Charles, 129
Wright, Barry, 19
Wu, Fay, 423

XEL Communications Inc., 13,
    377, 382
Xerox, 111, 241

Yates, John, 443

Zellers, 5, 47, 230, 445
Zenon Environmental Inc., 82,
    84
Zillig, Jeff, 169

American Express example, 332
Customer focus, 444
Customer monitoring
    proactive, 41
    reactive, 41
Customer satisfaction, teams and, 362–63
Customer satisfaction, 444
Customers, cultivate your most demanding, 300
Customs classification, 234
Cybernetic control process, 201
Cybernetic feasibility, 204
Cycle time, 462

Data
    raw, 129
    security threats to, 141
    See also Information
Data, market-basket, 131–32
Data clusters, 139
Data encryption, 142
Data mining, 137–40
    supervised, 139
    unsupervised, 139
Data warehouse, 139
Decentralization, 337
Decision criteria, 165
    identifying, 165
    weighing, 165–67
Decision-making, 162
    BP Amoco case, 161, 189–90
    common mistakes, 172–74
    ethical. *See* Ethical decision-making
    group, 180–88
    improving individual, 175–80
    paralysis by analysis, 172
    rational. *See* Rational decision-making
    recognitional, 194
Decision rules, 175–76
Decision software, 177–78
Decision support systems (DSS), 149, 397
Decline, organization, 306–8
Decoding, 518
Defenders, 279
Defensive bias, 515–16
Defensive strategy toward social responsibility, 81
De-forming stage of team development, 377
Degree of dependence, 203
Delegating leadership style, 496–97
Delegation of authority, 337–38
    how to be more effective, 338
Dell Computers case, 127, 151
Delphi technique, 183
Denial-of-service attacks, 141

De-norming stage of team development, 377
Departmentalization, 329
    customer, 331–33
    functional, 329
    geographical, 333–34
    matrix, 334–35
    product, 329–30
Dependence
    buyer, 42
    degree of, 203
    reducing, 204
    restructuring, 204
    supplier, 42
Dependent demand system, 458
Derailers, 19–21
Design
    dominant, 299–300
    job, 339–41
Design competition, 298
Design iteration, 301
Desire to lead, 487
Desktop videoconferencing, 144, 146
De-storming stage of team development, 377
Destructive feedback, 528
Deviance
    political, 66
    production, 65–66
    property, 65–66
    workplace, 64–67, 72
Devil's advocacy, 182, 184
Dialectical inquiry, 183, 184
Dictionary rule, 175
Differentiation, 278
Direct competition, 271, 280–84
Direct foreign investment, 230–32
Direct management input forecasting, 395
Direction of effort, 468
Discontinuity, technological, 298
Discontinuous change, 305–6
    managing innovation during, 301–3
Discretionary responsibility, 80–81
Discrimination, employment, 399, 400–1
Discussion forums, online, 531–32
Discussion time, 530
Dismissal, wrongful, 426
Disseminator role, 16
Dissolution stage of organization decline, 308
Distal goals, 100
Distinctive competence, 266
Distributive justice, 70–71, 479
Disturbance handler role, 16

Diversification, 270
    related, 273, 274
    risk and, 270
    strategies for, 270–74
    unrelated, 271
Diversity, team, 379–80
Document conferencing, 144
Documentary training, 251
Dog, 272, 273
Dominant design, 299–300
Downsizing, 427
Downtime, 456
Downward communication, 519–20
Drive, 487
DSS, 149, 397
Dual-career issues in global assignments, 251
Durability, 441–42
DVDs, 138
Dynamic environment, 34
Dysfunctional turnover, 427

Early retirement incentive programs (ERIPs), 427
EasyJet case, 33–34, 53–54
Economic order quantity (EOQ), 457
Economic performance, social responsibility and, 83–84
Economic responsibility, 80
Economic value added (EVA), 213–14
Economy, 38
EDI, 147–48
Effectiveness, 5
Efficiency, 5
    lost, 456
    teams and, 363
Effort
    direction of, 468
    initiation of, 468
    performance and, 470
    persistence of, 468–69
EIS, 146–47
Electronic brainstorming, 186–88
Electronic communication, 531–32
Electronic data interchange (EDI), 147–48
Electronic resumés, 405
Electronic scanners, 137
E-mail, 143
    corporate, 531
    filtering, 171
    risks of, 88
    snooping, 141
Emotional stability, 410
Empathetic listening, 527–28
Employee benefits, 424
Employee health costs, 222

Employee involvement, 51
Employee involvement teams, 368
Employee satisfaction, 446–47
Employee selection. *See* Selection
Employee separations, 425–28
    downsizing, 427
    involuntary, 426
    outplacement services, 426–27
    retirement, 427
    terminations, 425–26
    turnover, 427–28
    voluntary, 425
Employee stock ownership (ESOPs), 423
Employee turnover, 427–28
Employees, hiring ethical, 71–72
Employment discrimination, 399, 400–1
Employment legislation, 398–403
    and application forms, 407
    Employment Equity Act, 43
    federal, 398–403
    sexual harassment, 401–2
Employment references, 409
Employment tests, computerized, 397
Empowering workers, 344, 447–49
Empowerment, 344
Encoding, 517
Encryption
    data, 142
    public key, 143
Enlargement, job, 340–41
Enrichment, job, 341
Entrants, threat of new, 277
Entrepreneur orientation, 284
Entrepreneur role, 16
Entrepreneurship, 284–85
Environmental change, 34–35
Environmental complexity, 35
Environmental factors, interpreting, 45–46
Environmental munificence, 36
Environmental scanning, 45
Environments
    changing, 34–37, 45–48
    complex, 35
    creative work, 304
    dynamic, 34
    external, 34–48
    general, 37–38
    hostile work, 402
    internal, 48–52
    simple, 35
    specific, 38
    stable, 34
EOQ, 457
Equilibrium theory, punctuated, 34–35
    Canadian airline industry example, 35